Kohlhammer

International Exegetical Commentary on the Old Testament (IECOT)

Edited by:

Walter Dietrich, David M. Carr,

Adele Berlin, Erhard Blum, Irmtraud Fischer, Shimon Gesundheit, Walter Groß, Gary Knoppers, Bernard M. Levinson, Ed Noort, Helmut Utzschneider and Beate Ego (Apocrypha/Deuterocanonical books)

Cover:
Top: Panel from a four-part relief on the "Black Obelisk of Shalmaneser III" (859–824 BCE) depicting the Israelite king Jehu (845–817 BCE; 2 Kings 9f) paying obeisance to the Assyrian "King of Kings." The vassal has thrown himself to the ground in front of his overlord. Royal servants are standing behind the Assyrian king whereas Assyrian officers are standing behind Jehu. The remaining picture panels portray thirteen Israelite tribute bearers carrying heavy and precious gifts.
Photo © Z.Radovan/BibleLandPictures.com

Bottom left: One of ten reliefs on the bronze doors that constitute the eastern portal (the so-called "Gates of Paradise") of the Baptistery of St. John of Florence, created 1424–1452 by Lorenzo Ghiberti (c. 1378–1455). Detail from the picture "Adam and Eve"; in the center is the creation of Eve: "And the rib that the Lord God had taken from the man he made into a woman and brought her to the man." (Gen 2:22)
Photograph by George Reader

Bottom right: Detail of the Menorah in front of the Knesset in Jerusalem, created by Benno Elkan (1877–1960): Ezra reads the Law of Moses to the assembled nation (Neh 8). The bronze Menorah was created in London in 1956 and in the same year was given by the British as a gift to the State of Israel. A total of 29 reliefs portray scenes from the Hebrew bible and the history of the Jewish people.

Steven L. McKenzie

1 Kings 16 – 2 Kings 16

W. Kohlhammer

1. Edition 2019

Production: W. Kohlhammer GmbH, Stuttgart

Print:
ISBN 978-3-17-034040-4

E-Book-Formats:
pdf: 978-3-17-034041-1
epub: 978-3-17-034042-8
mobi: 978-3-17-034043-5

In memory of my mother, Germaine “Lynn” McKenzie, and of my daughter, Bonnie Lynn McKenzie.

Content

Editors' Foreword

The International Exegetical Commentary on the Old Testament (IECOT) offers a multi-perspectival interpretation of the books of the Old Testament to a broad, international audience of scholars, laypeople and pastors. Biblical commentaries too often reflect the fragmented character of contemporary biblical scholarship, where different geographical or methodological sub-groups of scholars pursue specific methodologies and/or theories with little engagement of alternative approaches. This series, published in English and German editions, brings together editors and authors from North America, Europe, and Israel with multiple exegetical perspectives.

From the outset the goal has been to publish a series that was "international, ecumenical and contemporary." The international character is reflected in the composition of an editorial board with members from six countries and commentators representing a yet broader diversity of scholarly contexts.

The ecumenical dimension is reflected in at least two ways. First, both the editorial board and the list of authors includes scholars with a variety of religious perspectives, both Christian and Jewish. Second, the commentary series not only includes volumes on books in the Jewish Tanach/Protestant Old Testament, but also other books recognized as canonical parts of the Old Testament by diverse Christian confessions (thus including the Deuterocanonical Old Testament books).

When it comes to "contemporary," one central distinguishing feature of this series is its attempt to bring together two broad families of perspectives in analysis of biblical books, perspectives often described as "synchronic" and "diachronic" and all too often understood as incompatible with each other. Historically, diachronic studies arose in Europe, while some of the better known early synchronic studies originated in North America and Israel. Nevertheless, historical studies have continued to be pursued around the world, and focused synchronic work has been done in an ever greater variety of settings. Building on these developments, we aim in this series to bring synchronic and diachronic methods into closer alignment, allowing these approaches to work in a complementary and mutually-informative rather than antagonistic manner.

Since these terms are used in varying ways within biblical studies, it makes sense to specify how they are understood in this series. Within IECOT we understand "synchronic" to embrace a variety of types of study of a biblical text *in one given stage of its development*, particularly its final stage(s) of development in existing manuscripts. "Synchronic" studies embrace non-historical narratological, reader-response and other approaches along with historically-informed exegesis of a particular stage of a biblical text. In contrast, we understand "diachronic" to embrace the full variety of modes of study of a biblical text *over time*.

This diachronic analysis may include use of manuscript evidence (where available) to identify documented pre-stages of a biblical text, judicious use of clues within the biblical text to reconstruct its formation over time, and also an examination of the ways in which a biblical text may be in dialogue with earlier biblical (and non-biblical) motifs, traditions, themes, etc. In other words, diachronic study focuses on what might be termed a "depth dimension" of a given text – how a text (and its parts) has journeyed over time up to its present form, making the text part of a broader history of traditions, motifs and/or prior compositions. Synchronic analysis focuses on a particular moment (or moments) of that journey, with a particular focus on the final, canonized form (or forms) of the text. Together they represent, in our view, complementary ways of building a textual interpretation.

Of course, each biblical book is different, and each author or team of authors has different ideas of how to incorporate these perspectives into the commentary. The authors will present their ideas in the introduction to each volume. In addition, each author or team of authors will highlight specific contemporary methodological and hermeneutical perspectives – e.g. gender-critical, liberation-theological, reception-historical, social-historical – appropriate to their own strengths and to the biblical book being interpreted. The result, we hope and expect, will be a series of volumes that display a range of ways that various methodologies and discourses can be integrated into the interpretation of the diverse books of the Old Testament.

Fall 2012 The Editors

Acknowledgements

I gratefully recognize the contributions of the following individuals and groups to this commentary. In the spring semester of 2011, 2012, and 2013 I taught a course entitled "Stories about Prophets" focused on the prophetic stories in 1–2 Kings at Rhodes College. I am indebted to the students in those courses for their comments and observations about the material in Kings and my own developing analytical work. One of those students, Elizabeth Hollingsworth, worked during the summer of 2012 reading through *Old Testament Abstracts* to help me to isolate articles that might be useful resources.

The travel and research for this commentary were underwritten by my position as Spence L. Wilson Senior Research Fellow at Rhodes, and I am constantly indebted to Spence and Becky Wilson for ther support.

I participated in seminars on the text of Kings at the Universidad Complutense in Madrid in 2012 with Jan Joosten, Jean Koulagna, Andrés Piquer, Julio Trebolle, and Pablo Torijano; in 2013 with Jan Joosten, Andrés Piquer, Matthieu Richelle, Julio Trebolle, and Pablo Torijano; and in 2016 with Jan Joosten, Andrés Piquer, Julio Trebolle, and Pablo Torijano. My debt to the participants, especially to Julio Trebolle, is evident throughout the commentary.

Portions of the commentary were presented in draft form at various professional meetings, including the Divinity in Ancient Israel continuing seminar at the Catholic Biblical Association in 2011 (1 Kings 19) and 2016 (2 Kings 5) and the Biblical Colloquium in 2013 (2 Kgs 6:24–7:20). I am grateful to Christoph Levin for the invitation to read a paper on the Elijah stories as one of the main lectures at the 2013 IOSOT meeting in Munich and to Sara Milstein for organizing a session at the 2014 SBL meeting in which I read on Jezebel. An earlier draft of the latter had been given at the CBA meeting in Providence, RI, in the summer of 2014. My treatment of the chronological problems in 2 Kings 15 was presented in a conference on "The Last Days of Israel" organized by Shuichi Hasegawa in Munich in March, 2016.

I am indebted to my colleagues, John Kaltner, for help with Arabic at several points and Rhiannon Graybill, for reading and commenting on drafts of numerous chapters; to Ralph Klein for consulting with me about text-critical matters; and to Mark Smith for consultation about Ugaritic parallels.

Per series protocol, works cited only in the treatment of one lemma appear in full the first time in the footnotes; those that are used for more than one lemma are cited in full in the bibliography and in abbreviated form in footnotes. I am grateful to many other scholars whose writings inform my thought and approach but who are not cited directly in the commentary.

My sincere thanks to Walter Dietrich, the series editor, for saving me from many embarrassing errors and for trying to save me from others that may remain. David Carr, the series co-editor, made several suggestions that improved the manuscript at different points. Linda Maloney corrected the prose and made me a better writer. Finally, I am grateful to Florian Specker of Kohlhammer Press for his oversight of the project and for his sensitivity in allowing me to include the dedication to my mother and my daughter, whose lives came to an end during the time I was working on this commentary.

Introduction

1. Content and Structure

The book of Kings falls into three sections: the reign of Solomon (1 Kgs 1–11), the divided monarchy (1 Kgs 12–2 Kgs 17), and the kingdom of Judah alone (2 Kgs 18–25). The contents of the second section, the bulk of which is the subject of this present volume, are represented in the following table.

The contents of 1 Kings 12 – 2 Kings 17 in the Masoretic Text

	Texts	Kings of Israel	Kings of Judah	Prophets
	1 Kgs 12–14		Rehoboam	Shemaiah, unnamed older and younger prophets
House of Jeroboam	12:16–14:20	**Jeroboam**		
	15:1-8		Abijam	
	15:9-24		Asa	
	15:25-32	Nadab		
House of Baasha	15:33–16:7	**Baasha**		Jehu ben Hanani
	16:8-14	Elah		
	16:15-20	Zimri		
	16:21-22	Tibni (interregnum)		
House of Omri	16:23-28	**Omri**		
	16:29–22:39	Ahab		Elijah (17–19; 21) nameless (ch. 20) Micaiah (ch. 22)
	22:40, 51–2 Kgs 1:18	Ahaziah		
	1 Kgs 22:41-50		Jehoshaphat	
	2 Kgs 2			Elijah and Elisha
	3:1–8:26	Jehoram		Elisha (3:1–8:15)
	8:16-24		Joram	
	8:25–9:29		Ahaziah	Elisha and a disciple
House of Jehu	10	**Jehu**		
	11		Athaliah	
	12		Joash	
	13:1-9	Jehoahaz		
	13:10–14:16	Jehoash		
	13:14-25			Elisha

Texts	Kings of Israel	Kings of Judah	Prophets
14:1-22		Amaziah	
14:23-29	Jeroboam II		
15:1-7		Azariah/Uzziah	
15:8-12	Zechariah		
15:13-16	Shallum		
15:17-22	Menahem		
15:23-26	Pekahiah		
15:27-31	Pekah		
15:32-38		Jotham	
16		Ahaz	

The stories of the two kingdoms of Israel and Judah are recounted simultaneously. They are interwoven in dentate fashion, with the kings of each kingdom being dated over against those of the other. This system of cross-dating forms the backbone of this section of Kings. Driver aptly described the overall pattern:[1]

In the arrangement of the reigns of the two series of kings a definite principle is followed by the compiler. When the narrative of a reign (in either series) has once begun, it is continued to its close—even the contemporary incidents of a prophet's career, which stand in no immediate relation to public events, being included in it; when it is ended, the reign or reigns of the other series, which are synchronized with it, are dealt with; the reign overlapping it at the end having been completed, the compiler resumes his narrative of the first series with the reign next following, and so on.

Regnal formulae

The discrete account of a king's reign typically consists of three parts: opening formulae, materials set during the reign, and closing formulae.

Opening formulae

The elements of the opening formulae are:[2]

1. synchronism of the accession year with the regnal year of the king from the other country;
2. king's age at accession (lacking for kings of Israel);
3. length of reign;
4. name of Queen Mother (lacking for kings of Israel);
5. theological evaluation.

Closing formulae

The elements of the closing formulae, all of which rarely occur together, include:

1. source notice;
2. brief supplemental details about the reign, if any;
3. death and burial notices;
4. succession notice.

---

1 S. R. Driver, *An Introduction to the Literature of the Old Testament* (Gloucester, MA: Peter Smith, 1972), 189.

2 The list is adapted from Shenkel, *Chronology and Recensional Development*, 24–25.

The observation of this pattern is significant for reconstructing the composition of the books of Kings. When a king's account or his formulae vary from these patterns, an explanation is required. For instance, when an anecdote is not incorporated within the regnal formulae for any king, it may be an indication that the anecdote has come into that location secondarily either as a displacement or as an addition. Synchronically, such a situation directs the reader's attention to some particular feature or connection in the narrative.

Like a backbone, the frame formed by the interlocking regnal accounts is flexible enough to allow for other structural features.[3] There are opportunities to draw comparisons and analogies between kings, especially with the earlier, more idealized figures of David and Solomon. The repeated evaluation of the kings along religious lines gives rise to patterns of apostasy and reform.[4] The foregoing table shows that the central section of Kings is dominated by prophetic stories, especially those of Elijah and Elisha, in 1 Kings 17–2 Kings 13. Hence prophecy and fulfillment comprise another very important component to the book that is at once structural and thematic.

Pattern in the arrangement of Israelite kings

A pattern that has often been overlooked but may be highly significant for the book is perceptible in the list of the kings of Israel.[5] The sixth king following Jeroboam I is Ahab (Nadab, Baasha, Elah, Zimri, Omri, Ahab), who is portrayed as Israel's worst king. The sixth king after Ahab is Jeroboam II (Ahaziah, Jehoram, Jehu, Jehoahaz, Jehoash, Jeroboam II). The sixth after Jeroboam II is Hoshea (Zechariah, Shallum, Menahem, Pekahiah, Pekah, Hoshea), in whose reign the kingdom comes to an end. The story of the kingdom of Israel, all of whose kings are evaluated as having done what YHWH considered evil, thus forms a pattern of six-six-six in its narrative recounting and assessment. As one short of seven, six is the quintessential number of imperfection.

2. *Text*

A distinctive feature of this commentary is its focus on textual criticism. The reason is the importance of textual criticism in the history of critical scholarship on the book of Kings on the one hand and, on the other, the tendency of commentaries on Kings to ignore the topic for the most part.

Dead Sea Scrolls

The discovery, beginning in 1947, of the "Dead Sea Scrolls" has revolutionized our understanding of the text of the HB and its development. Not that the Qumran caves yielded significant quantities of materials related directly to Kings. On the contrary, there were only fragments, most quite small, of three manuscripts, each from a different cave, and of these only a handful contain passages covered in this volume.[6] But the Qumran

---

3 The following examples are drawn from the observations of Nelson, *Kings*, 98–100.
4 Hoffmann, *Reform und Reformen.*
5 Leithart, *Kings*, 245.
6 The full list is 1 Kgs 1:1, 16-17, 27-37 from 5QKgs; 1 Kgs 7:20-21, 25-27, 29-42, 51 from 4QKgs; and 1 Kgs 3:12-14; 12:28-31; 22:28-31; 2 Kgs 5:26; 6:32; 7:8-10, 20; 8:1-5; 9:1-2; 10:19-21 from 6QpapKgs. Cf. Ulrich, *Biblical Qumran Scrolls.*

finds demonstrate the value of the Greek texts, particularly Codex Vaticanus (G^B) and the Lucianic manuscripts (G^L), as independent witnesses to an early Greek translation ("Old Greek" = OG) of a pre-Masoretic Hebrew text. It has long been recognized that these Greek texts betray stages of recension toward the developing Masoretic Text (MT).[7] In Kings, the OG is preserved in G^B only in 1 Kgs 2:12–21:29. Otherwise G^B reflects an early recension known as *kaige* after its idiosyncratic translation of the Hebrew גם. In the rest of Kings, G^L is the closest witness to the OG.[8] In addition, the "Old Latin" (OL), the collective of extant Latin manuscripts translated from Greek before the Vulgate in the fourth century CE, frequently safeguards OG readings. Old Greek

The value of the OG through its various attestations as a witness to both the content of the text of Kings and the process by which it was composed has been richly explored by Julio Trebolle in a series of publications beginning in the 1980s. While Trebolle's insights have achieved high regard among his peers in biblical studies and textual criticism, much of his earlier work has been overlooked and underutilized because it was written in Spanish. It is hoped that the obvious influence of his ideas on this commentary will lead to greater appreciation and consideration of them in the interpretation of Kings. Nevertheless, there are two important types of textual differences between the MT and OG where I differ with Trebolle's prioritization of the OG. These relate to chronology and to extended "supplements" in the Greek witnesses. Julio Trebolle

2.1 The MT and OG Chronologies

Since the regnal formulae with their interlocking chronological references are the backbone for the book of Kings, the frequent differences in chronological data are disconcerting.

In his 1968 monograph Shenkel sought to counter previous explanations for these chronological differences that resorted rather arbitrarily to postulations of coregencies and separate and alternating systems of reckoning; instead, Shenkel offered a text-critical explanation.[9] He pointed out that the MT and OG operate under two different chronological systems, and he argued that the OG's chronology was more primitive and the MT's a secondary development.[10] Though not without its critics,[11] Shenkel's explanation has been very influential over the past five decades. Shenkel's argument for the priority of the Greek chronology

7 For a more thorough discussion see Shenkel, *Chronology*, 5–21.

8 The history of the Lucianic text is complex and debated. It is generally recognized as consisting of two strata, the older of which ("proto-Lucianic") was very similar to the OG and has even been considered OG by some scholars, notably Barthélemy. Shenkel, *Chronology*, 5–21.

9 Shenkel, *Chronology*. Much of Shenkel's work was aimed at Thiele's explanations in *Mysterious Numbers*.

10 J. M. Miller's unpublished 1964 Emory dissertation ("The Omride Dynasty in the Light of Recent Literary and Archaeological Research") anticipated Shenkel's results in arguing for the primacy of the OG chronology. See his "Elisha Cycle" and "Another Look."

11 See the early review of Shenkel's book by D. W. Gooding in *JTS* 21 (1970): 118–31. Also Galil, *Chronology*, 138–43.

Hendel on 1 Kings 16:21

Hendel has recently criticized Shenkel for basing his conclusions on redactional and historical considerations and proffered his own argument on text-critical grounds.[12] He shows how the MT and OG construe the starting point of Omri's reign differently. The difference becomes clear in 1 Kgs 16:29, where MT dates Ahab's accession to the 38th year of Asa of Judah, while the OG dates it to the second year of Asa's son, Jehoshaphat, a difference of five years. The reason for this difference is that the MT construes the beginning of Omri's twelve-year reign from the point in v. 21 when half of the people followed Omri and half Tibni or, more accurately, from v. 16 when *all Israel* made Omri king. This was, according to v. 15, the 27th year of Asa of Judah. The OG, on the other hand, dates Omri's reign from the 31st year of Asa, after Tibni had died. Its phrase *after Tibni* at the end of v. 22 makes its dating clear. Hendel argues that from a text-critical standpoint the MT's construal of v. 23, which is idiosyncratic and therefore a kind of *lectio difficilior*, is more likely to have been altered by the OG's more "literal" construal than the other way around.[13] That "literal" interpretation in turn led to (hyper)correction of the chronology in the OG in a manner typical of Second-Temple hermeneutics. Contrary to Shenkel's assessment, therefore, the MT chronology is primitive and the OG revisionist.

2 Kings 8:16

Additional text-critical evidence for the primacy of the MT chronology is found in 2 Kgs 8:16.[14] The OG is not extant here, but based on its previous numbers it had Jehoram of Judah taking the throne in the second year of Ahaziah of Israel and reigning eleven years.[15] Since Ahaziah's reign spans the end of Jehoshaphat's and the beginning of Jehoram's in the OG, the proper place for the account of Jehoram's reign according to the OG chronology would have been immediately before the beginning of Joram of Israel's reign, i.e., between 2 Kgs 1:17 and 1:18. Not coincidentally, this is where the single instance of OG chronology in the MT is found, what Shenkel calls "a precious witness to the OG chronology in a Hebrew text"[16] However, there is no evidence in the Greek tradition for the account of Jehoram ever having been present here.[17] The OG account of Jehoram was always in 2 Kings 8, where the MT has it, as shown by the occurrence of two historical presents—distinguishing features of the OG—in 8:22, 24, as Shenkel points out. This means that the OG placement and the OG numbers are at odds. The OG account of the reign of Jehoram is in the wrong place according to the "rules" of the composition of Kings. The only way this could have happened is if the MT chronology was in fact the older one. The OG introduced its revised figures into the MT's placement.

---

12 Hendel, "Two Editions."

13 The use of אז + imperfect indicates that the events of vv. 21-22 are set at an earlier time, i.e., with those of v. 16 (Rabinowitz, "'ĀZ Followed by Imperfect"). The OG's construal of the verse, therefore, is actually a misunderstanding of this feature and another indication of MT's primacy. See the commentary on this passage.

14 See S. L. McKenzie, "The Priority of the MT Chronology in Kings," in *Biblical and Ancient Near Eastern Studies in Honor of P. Kyle McCarter, Jr.* (ed. C. Rollston *et al.*, forthcoming).

15 As per Shenkel's reconstruction in *Chronology*, 37–38, 68–82.

16 Shenkel, *Chronology*, 74.

17 The notice in G^L at 1:17b in agreement with MT is hexaplaric and therefore the result of secondary adjustment.

Yet another indication of the MT's primacy comes from the story in 2 Kings 3, though the evidence here is mainly literary rather than text-critical. Shenkel argued that the king of Judah in the story was originally anonymous. The reason for Elisha's response to the kings' appeal for help (v. 14) was part of DtrH's polemic against Israel: YHWH had regard for Judah because of the promise to David but was opposed to Israel because of the sin of Jeroboam. MT's identification of the king of Judah as Jehoshaphat was based on similarities with 1 Kings 22 and led to a shift in the entire chronology of the period, while the OG's identification with Ahaziah preserved the older chronology and may have retained the tradition about the identity of the king of Judah in the original story.[18] If, however, this story is a post-DtrH addition that drew from the start on 1 Kings 22, as I contend, then it was righteous Jehoshaphat for whom YHWH had regard (v. 14), and the identification of Ahaziah undermines the point of the story and must be secondary—part of the OG's programmatic revision of the chronology. 2 Kings 3

2.2 OG "Supplements"

Overlapping with the matter of the OG's different chronology is that of its "supplements" or "miscellanies." These are multi-verse pluses attached at the following locations in the OG: 1 Kgs 2:35; 2:46; 5:14; 6:1; 8:53; 10:22; 12:24; 16:28; 2 Kgs 1:18; 10:36. Some of them are doublets of material in the MT. Thus 1 Kgs 16:28+ contains the account of the reign of Jehoshaphat found in the MT at 1 Kgs 22:41-51. Like the minor plus *after Tibni* at the end of 1 Kgs 16:22, 1 Kgs 16:28+ reflects a chronological variance. The OG dates Jehoshaphat's accession to Omri's eleventh year (1 Kgs 16:28a G^L) in contrast to the MT's date of his accession to Ahab's fourth year (22:41). Similarly, 2 Kgs 1:18+ effectively duplicates 2 Kgs 3:1-3 MT. Another kind of plus is represented by 2 Kgs 10:36+ (a more extensive example is 1 Kgs 12:24+). It consists of materials mostly found in the MT but dispersed there rather than gathered as in the OG plus.

The debate that has raged among critical scholars concerns the origin of these "supplements" in relation to the MT and their value for textual criticism.[19] There is general recognition that these passages are not Greek inventions but are derived

---

18 Shenkel, *Chronology*, 104–108.

19 See the following items and the bibliographies cited in them. On 1 Kgs 2:35+ and 2:46+: R. P. Pennoyer, "Solomonic Apologetic: Text and Redaction in the Succession Narrative with Special Attention to the So-called 'Miscellanies' in 3 Reigns 2," PhD diss., Johns Hopkins University, 1992; Z. Talshir, "The Miscellanies in 2 Reigns 2:35a-o, 46a-l and the Composition of the Book of Kings/Reigns," in *XIV Congress of the International Organization for Septuagint and Cognate Studies. Helsinki 2010* (ed. M. K. H. Peters; SBLSCS 59; Atlanta: SBL, 2013), 155–74; and E. Tov, "The Septuagint Additions ('Miscellanies') in 1 Kings 2 (3 Reigns 2)," in *The Greek and Hebrew Bible: Collected Essays on the Septuagint*, (VTSup 72; Leiden: Brill, 1999), 549–70. On 1 Kgs 12:24a-z: P. S. F. van Keulen, *Two Versions of the Solomon Narrative: An Inquiry into the Relationship between MT 1 Kgs 2-11 and LXX 3 Reg. 2-11* (VTSup 104; Leiden: Brill, 2004); McKenzie, *Trouble with Kings*, 21–40; Trebolle, *Salomón y Jeroboán*; Z. Talshir, *The Alternative Story of the Division of the Kingdom: 3 Kingdoms 12:24a-z* (Jerusalem: Simor, 1993). On 2 Kgs 10:31+ see Trebolle, *Jehú y Joás*.

from Hebrew *Vorlagen*. Each of the pluses within the scope of this commentary is treated at the appropriate location. It is already clear, though, that the pluses are part of the same process of Second-Temple scribal revision as the OG chronology. In 1 Kgs 16:28+ there is a causal relationship. The chronological adjustment in the OG placed Jehoshaphat's accession in the reign of Omri, leading in turn to the transfer of the account of Jehoshaphat's reign to an earlier point in the narrative. The movement of Joram of Israel's opening formulae to 2 Kgs 1:18+ accommodated the stories in ch. 2, enclosing them within the reign of Joram of Israel rather than between the reigns of Ahaziah and Joram, where they had been interpolated into the text represented by the MT. As for 2 Kgs 10:36+, close reading shows that the material collected in it cannot stand on its own but can only be understood in light of the MT account in 2 Kings 8–9.

2.3 Textual Reconstruction

These indications of revision in the OG do not necessarily compromise its value for textual criticism where individual readings are concerned. Each case must be considered on its own merits, and it often comes down to a judgment call, particularly where the MT is difficult. Is the easier or more fitting reading in such a case the OG's retention of the more primitive text that has suffered corruption in the MT? Or is the OG reading due to second-hand smoothing of the troublesome MT? There are no hard and fast rules. General principles are only rough guidelines that are not applicable in every instance. Preference for the shorter reading should be invoked when no other explanation for the variants is evident. One must weigh the dictum *lectio difficilior praeferenda est* ("the more difficult reading is to be preferred") against making sense of the text. One must also consider such matters as the degree of certainty in the Hebrew reconstruction from the Greek text. My judgment that there are many instances where the Greek reading is superior is based on the premise that there is usually (though not always!) less at stake than for an issue like chronology and therefore less motive to make detailed alterations.[20]

The text that is reconstructed for each pericope treated in this commentary is an eclectic one, the "earliest inferable text," based on my assessment of the MT and the witnesses to the OG just described. The approach and its theoretical underpinning are well articulated by Troxel in describing his work with Isaiah 1–39:

> My sole affirmation is that the eclectic text of Isaiah 1–39 I propose will comprise those readings with the best claim to priority, based on my evaluation of evidence from the witnesses and the literary contexts in which they stand. There is no escaping the subjectivity of these judgments, for there is no Archimedean point from which to

---

20 Chronicles provides additional evidence for textual reconstruction where it is extant. The Chronicler's text of Kings was the same type as that of the MT. See S. L. McKenzie, *The Chronicler's Use of the Deuteronomistic History* (HSM 33; Atlanta: Scholars Press, 1984), 119–58. Agreements of Chr with Kgs OG against Kgs MT are rare and usually due to corruption in the latter. Chronicles also seems to preserve some primitive readings on its own.

assay them. And yet, the evident genetic relationship between many variants compels such an assessment.[21]

While it may not always come across in the course of an argument, all text-critical decisions in this commentary are made with humility and trepidation. Many have been changed more than once. It is a matter of considerable comfort to find a text-critical judgment by Trebolle or by one of the eminent figures of the past, such as Burney, Klostermann, or Stade, with which I agree or to whom I can appeal. There is certainly room for disagreement. My main hope is that the spotlight on the text in this volume influences future commentators to incorporate textual criticism more fully into the interpretive process.

Because this is a commentary and not a critical edition of the text, the space devoted to textual notes is limited.[22] The focus is on textual differences that have significance for content or meaning, recognizing that even small differences can fall into this category. The Textual Notes will generally ignore the following variants unless there is some other reason for comment: stylistic differences, such as G's supplying of personal names for clarity, where MT has pronouns; the absence or presence of the conjunction except when it alters meaning; minor pluses, such as titles (e.g., "king of Israel," the repetition of patronymics, the presence/absence of the definite object, and the word "all"); the absence/presence of the indirect object ("to him/them") after verbs like "said," "spoke"; the different order of words/phrases where order seems unimportant; different prepositions where there is little difference in meaning (e.g., εν/επι vs. ב/על). The copy-text that breaks the tie, so to speak, between equivalent variants in the MT and OG and which is followed in most matters of spelling and other "accidentals," is the MT represented in Codex Leningradensis.[23]

Ignored variants

MT as copy text

3. *Composition*

On more than one occasion in considering the process of composition behind 1 Kings 16–2 Kings 16 I thought of Festus's words to Paul in Acts 26:24: "You are out of your mind, Paul! Too much learning is driving you insane!" (NRSV). It is

---

21 The quotation is from the first draft of R. L. Troxel, "What is a Text?" *VT* 66 (2016): 603–26. Unfortunately, this quotation did not survive the editing process to the final form of the article. It is used here by permission of the author. See also R. Hendel, "The Oxford Hebrew Bible: Prologue to a New Critical Edition," *VT* 58 (2008): 324–51. The phrase "earliest inferable text" is adapted from p. 329 of this article, where Hendel cites E. J. Kenney, "Textual Criticism," *Encyclopaedia Britannica* 17, 192. The term "original (text)," as Hendel explains on pp. 333-34, is understood as an ideal goal that is indeterminable. See also R. Hendel, "The Oxford Hebrew Bible: Its Aims and a Response to Criticisms," *HBAI* 2 (2013): 63–99.

22 The reader will find more detailed notes in *The Hebrew Bible: A Critical Edition*—1 Kings edited by J. Joosten, 2 Kings by A. Piquer Otero and P. Torijano Morales. Fuller textual notes will be available in the *Biblia Hebraica Quinta* and the Hebrew University Bible Project, both currently in preparation.

23 On the idea and function of a copy-text see Hendel, "Prologue," 343–46 and "Response," 70–75.

not the great learning portion of these words that struck a chord in me but being driven to the edge of madness by the complicated and sometimes contradictory indications regarding how the material in Kings came about. Walter Dietrich, the editor of this series and a man of great learning, writes about 1 Kgs 16:7 that it *hat viel Kopfzerbrechung gemacht.*[24] The same could be said about the book of Kings as a whole, or at least of 1 Kings 16–2 Kings 16.[25] What makes my obsession with this issue bearable, aside from knowing I am in good company, is the hope that the model I propose goes some distance toward solving the most bedeviling compositional problems in this section of Kings. This model finds two principal levels of composition in Kings: a primary Deuteronomistic one and a secondary prophetic one. Each was the work of a distinct author/editor who each made use of different kinds of sources. Each also received later glosses and additions. These different levels of composition are signaled in the translation by the use of different fonts:

Compositional model

`DtrH's sources, including regnal formulae`
DtrH
 Glosses and additions (other than PN) to DtrH
 Glosses and additions to secondary material

Prophetic and battle stories used by PN. (For different sources within the same lemma, normal, *italic* and **bold** text is used.)
Prophetic Narrative/Narrator (PN)
 Glosses and additions to PN
 Glosses and additions to secondary material

3.1 Pre-DtrH Sources

3.1.1 Regnal Formulae

A constant refrain in the closing regnal formulae is the statement that more information about the individual king is available in the book or scroll of the chronicles of the kings of Israel or Judah. There are reasons for taking this "source notice" seriously as pointing to a real document. These include the existence of annals and similar official records from other ancient Near Eastern countries, the presence of historically accurate information (e.g., names, approximate time frame, and the like) within the biblical accounts in Kings, and differences in the information proffered for the kings of Israel and those of Judah, i.e., the king's age at accession and the name of the Queen Mother in the formulae for kings of Judah but not for those of Israel.[26] The exact nature of the "chronicles" remains elusive. The usual assumption that they were annals is based mainly on Assyrian and Babylonian parallels and is far from certain. They are probably more accu-

24 Dietrich, *Prophetie und Geschichte*, 10n.

25 P. Welten ("Naboths Weinberg," *EvTh* 33 [1973] 20) notes that the variety of material and genres within 1 Kgs 17 – 2 Kgs 13 makes their analysis extraordinarily difficult.

26 L. Grabbe, *1 & 2 Kings: History and Story in Ancient Israel* (London: T & T Clark, 2017), 21–22.

rately designated king lists.[27] The differences in the information they contain indicate that there were separate lists for Israel and Judah. Indeed, since Israel and Judah were separate countries, there was no reason for the kings in one to date themselves over against those in the other.[28] The synchronistic or integrated list reflected in Kings, therefore, was a compilation rather than a primary source.[29] Noth built his theory in Kings around his view that the compiler was DtrH himself. However, there are reasons to think it more likely that the compilation was done before DtrH and served as a source for him.[30] One such reason is the distinction between the data about accession and succession, which would have belonged to the integrated king list, and the religious evaluations of the kings, which come from DtrH.[31] Another reason relates to Israel and Judah as separate kingdoms. Very recent scholarship has stressed their distinctiveness historically, socially, and politically and the artificiality as a whole of their treatment as a single, albeit divided, entity in Samuel–Kings.[32] One must then ask why DtrH, clearly writing from a Southern perspective and advocating YHWH's choice of David and Judah, bothers to treat Israel at all—especially since his treatment is entirely negative. The two monarchies must already have been linked, and the integrated king list provided the closest such link.

An integrated king list

By way of delineating more precisely the content of the information found in the integrated king list, we should say that it probably did not include most of the items in the closing formulae (see the list provided above).[33] That is, it would not have included the source notice referring to itself. It may have contained supplemental details, but these are not always supplied as a distinct element in the formulae. The death and burial notices are likely DtrH's invention, since they are used to express approval/disapproval of the kings. The succession notice reiterates information in the opening formulae. Hence the integrated king list probably contained only the material in the opening formulae, absent the theological evaluation, and occasional supplemental details. For kings of Israel this means

---

27 J. Van Seters, *In Search of History: Historiography in the Ancient World and the Origins of Biblical History* (New Haven: Yale, 1983), 291–301.

28 An observation made long ago by F. Rühl, "Chronologie der Könige von Israel und Juda," *DZGW* 12 (1895), 44.

29 What C. Levin ("The Synchronistic Excerpt from the Annals of the Kings of Israel and Judah," in *Re-reading the Scriptures: Essays on the Literary History of the Old Testament* [FAT 87; Tübingen: Mohr Siebeck, 2013] calls an "excerpt."

30 Levin, "Excerpt," 186–89. Also Grabbe, *1 & 2 Kings*, 22–23 and idem, "Mighty Oaks from (Genetically Manipulated?) Acorns Grow: *The Chronicles of the Kings of Judah* as a Source of the Deuteronomistic History," in R. Rezetko, T. H. Lim, and W. B. Aucker (eds.), *Reflection and Refraction: Studies in Biblical Historiography in Honour of A. Graeme Auld* (Leiden: Brill, 2007): 155–73. K. Weingart ("2Ki 15–18") reaches a similar conclusion.

31 Levin, "Excerpt," 191–92. The former may reflect a political agenda—probably from the reign of Josiah—in the form of a claim of Judah to be the heir to Israel by virtue of their joint history.

32 See especially D. E. Fleming, *The Legacy of Israel in Judah's Bible: History, Politics, and the Reinscribing of Tradition* (Cambridge: Cambridge University Press, 2012), esp. 91–113.

33 Grabbe, *1 & 2 Kings*, 26.

that the information regularly available from this source was limited to the synchronistic accession notice and length of reign.[34]

3.1.2 Narratives

Aside from the supplemental details in the integrated king list, DtrH may have derived some brief notices—such as those about Zimri, Tibni, and Omri's purchase of Samaria in 1 Kings 16—from inscriptions or oral traditions. However, he evidently had access to virtually no narrative material about Israel for his account in 1 Kings 16–2 Kings 16. The one exception is the account of Jehu's *putsch* in 2 Kings 9–10*. Even here, though, the story has received significant elaboration, some of it by DtrH. The nature and origin of the underlying narrative are not known. It appears to be of Northern provenance. Surprisingly, there is also not much for Judah. The story of Athaliah's overthrow in 2 Kings 11* is exceptional. While it attests DtrH's interest in the survival of the Davidic dynasty, its language is not typically Deuteronomistic. Its origin is uncertain.

3.2 DtrH

The history of research on the Deuteronomistic History is too voluminous to be rehearsed here. Fortunately, it is also well known, at least in its broad contours.[35] The questions that surround its composition are complex, and many remain open (or have been reopened). I confine myself here to laying out the position reflected in this commentary.

By DtrH(istory/istorian) I mean the author/editor of the fundamental Deuteronomistic work behind 1 Kings 16–2 Kings 16 and presumably the rest of the book of Kings. This is essentially Noth's Dtr. I assume that this same author/editor was responsible for the fundamental Dtr level of the other books in the Former Prophets as well. I find no compelling evidence of subsequent Dtr editors in this central section of Kings. Whether such evidence exists in the "bookends" sections (1 Kgs 1–15; 2 Kgs 17–25), I leave to the commentator(s) on those chapters. This will affect the date of DtrH, about which I am ambivalent—whether to place it at the time of Josiah or of the exile. I lean toward the latter in part because of the integrated king list, which precedes DtrH and seems to come from the time of

---

34 Variations in the regnal formulae have been seen as evidence of redactional changes. See especially H. Weippert, "Die 'deuteronomistischen' Beurteilungen der Könige von Israel und Juda und das Problem der Redaktion der Königsbücher," *Bib* 53 (1972): 301–39, and B. Halpern and D. S. Vanderhooft, "The Editions of Kings in the 7th–6th Centuries B.C.E.," *HUCA* 62 (1991): 179–244. Also Provan, *Hezekiah and the Books of Kings*. The matter is not addressed in detail here because the redactional changes are seen as taking place with the account of Hezekiah and beyond. It is worth observing, though, that the separation of the religious evaluation from the integrated king list causes problems for this approach, as does the interpretation of the burial notice as referring not to manner of death but to dynastic succession (Suriano, *Politics of Dead Kings*).

35 For a recent and broad overview see T. Römer, "Deuteronomistic History," *EBR* 6:648–53. For more detail see his *So-called Deuteronomistic History*.

Josiah.[36] I use the abbreviation DtrH because of its familiarity to scholars and to distinguish this Dtr from potential later ones. The use of "DtrH" is also prompted by the prophetic stories, some of which attest diametrically different theological viewpoints. To call them "post-Dtr" is not entirely accurate, because they are included in the Deuteronomistic History to the extent that it is identified with the Former Prophets and because they often make use of classically Dtr terminology. Above all, the inclusion of the H is intended to avoid the pitfall of a term that is used with vastly differing understandings of what it connotes.[37]

Content of DtrH

The content of 1 Kings 16–2 Kings 16 at the DtrH level was significantly less without the prophetic stories that presently dominate this section. DtrH consisted of 1 Kgs 15:33–16:6, 8-30; [probably a version of the Naboth story replaced by 21:1-16]; 21:17, 20bβ-22, 24, 27-29; 22:39-54; 2 Kgs 1:1-2, 5-8, 17-18; 3:1-3; 8:16-29bα; 9:17-28*; 10:1-14*, 17, 31b-36*; 11–12*; 13:1-6a, 22, 24-25a; 14–16*. DtrH worked the integrated king list into a theological explanation (etiology) of the history of Israel and Judah that was particularly interested, especially in 1 Kings 16–2 Kings 16, in accounting for Israel's fall and Judah's survival. This was accomplished by means of two sets of related themes.

3.2.1 *The Sin of Jeroboam and the Dynastic Promise to David*

The sin of Jeroboam

As Cross showed, these two themes work together in Kings to explain the contrasting fates of Israel and Judah.[38] The two are closely entwined. The theme of Jeroboam's sin presupposes the promise to David, though it harks back to Deuteronomy's covenant theology with its doctrine that apostasy leads to destruction. Ahijah's oracle (1 Kgs 11:31-39) explains that Yhwh is about to tear the kingdom from Solomon because of his apostasies and to hand it over to Jeroboam. If Jeroboam exhibits the same faithfulness as David, he will also receive a "sure house" (בית נאמן) like David's. But as the theme unfolds, Jeroboam is a signal

36 Levin, "Excerpt."

37 Deuteronomism is characterized by some, especially in the so-called "Smend" or "Göttingen" school, as a stream of tradition that continued even into the New Testament. To refer to texts in Kings as "post-Dtr" is meaningless by this understanding. On the other hand, the tendency toward "Pan-Deuteronomism" makes the term "Deuteronomistic" itself essentially meaningless. See L. S. Schearing and S. L. McKenzie, *Those Elusive Deuteronomists: The Phenomenon of Pan-Deuteronomism* (JSOTSup 268; Sheffield: Sheffield Academic Press, 1999), especially the article by R. R. Wilson, "Who Was the Deuteronomist? (Who Was Not the Deuteronomist?): Reflections on Pan-Deuteronomism," pp. 67–82. The prophetic stories in 1 Kgs 16–2 Kgs 16 well illustrate this phenomenon. The problem is inherent in the texts; Jeremiah is much more Deuteronomistic than the Elijah stories. Römer's leading synthesis addressed the matter by conceiving of a Dtr scribal school with a Dtr library while also acknowledging post-Dtr editing of the materials in the Former Prophets. I am uncomfortable with some of the items he includes in the library, such as the editions of some Latter Prophets (*So-called*, 153; see R. A. Kugler, "The Deuteronomists and the Latter Prophets," in *Elusive Deuteronomists*, 127–44). Römer faults Van Seters and me for failing to locate secondary (post-DtrH) materials or relate them to other canonical sections (*So-called*, 32). I hope to remedy both of these shortcomings for the prophetic stories in 1 Kgs 16–2 Kgs 16, which Römer and I agree are post-DtrH.

38 Cross, *Canaanite Myth*, 278–85.

The shrines at Dan and Bethel

failure. He quickly commits apostasy as egregious as Solomon's by building the shrines with their golden calves at Dan and Bethel (1 Kgs 12:26-33). "This thing became a sin" (12:30)—the sin that would bring about Israel's fall as an independent kingdom. That was because all the kings of Israel would follow suit and perpetuate the same sin. From a historical perspective this is perfectly reasonable, since Jeroboam's shrines were the official royal shrines of the Northern Kingdom. They were probably not newly founded—certainly not in the case of Bethel, whose antiquity as the location of a shrine is betrayed by its very name ("temple of El"). This explains, furthermore, why Jeroboam chose to locate the national shrines where he did rather than next to the king's residence in Tirzah. As they were the official shrines of the kingdom, all of Israel's monarchs would have maintained them—would have felt constrained to do so, in fact, for their domain's well-being.

Anachronism

The notion that these shrines were sinful was a patent anachronism in DtrH., which considers them acts of apostasy on two grounds. First, they violated the principle of centralization, the idea that YHWH could only be properly worshiped in the temple in Jerusalem. This principle, however, was conceived under Josiah in the late seventh century, long after Jeroboam had built the shrines, indeed after the kingdom of Israel had ceased to exist. The same is true for DtrH's second and more serious concern—that the shrines were idolatrous because of the golden calves. The repudiation of images for YHWH was also a late development in Israel's history and may likewise have originated in the seventh century.[39] Besides, the calves or young bulls may not have been representations of YHWH at all but rather a pedestal upon which he was thought to be standing or enthroned.[40] In any case the shrines were certainly used for YHWH rather than some other god as implied in 1 Kgs 12:28. It is clear, after all, from the names of the Israelite kings that they were worshipers of YHWH. Ironically, their maintenance of the shrines at Dan and Bethel illustrated as much.

DtrH found in the continued presence of the shrines at Dan and Bethel a sin that permeated that monarchy and eventually caused its downfall. Hence every king of Israel, including Zimri who reigned only a week, "walked in the sin of Jeroboam."[41] By doing so they "made Israel sin," and their failure to depart from this sin brought about their destruction as a kingdom (2 Kgs 17:21-23). The "sin of Jeroboam," then, is key to understanding DtrH's view of the Northern Kingdom. It was representative for him of Israel's disobedience. It illustrated the devastating impact that wicked leadership could have for its nation. As initially committed by Jeroboam it might be thought of as sealing Israel's fate from the start. However, every king of Israel participated in the sin. When that is taken into consideration, the fact that Israel lasted through five royal houses (including Menahem's) and four additional kings (including Zimri) could be seen as demonstrating YHWH's patience and mercy.

The promise to David

The theme of the Davidic promise begins with Nathan's oracle awarding David a dynasty in 2 Samuel 7. It is intimately connected with the temple, since David's re-

---

39 On the lateness of the prohibition of images see J. C. H. Laughlin, "Idolatry," *NIDB* 3:11–14; T. J. Lewis, "Divine Images and Aniconism in Ancient Israel," *JAOS* 118 (1998): 36–53; and T. Mettinger, *No Graven Image? Israelite Aniconism in Its Ancient Near Eastern Context* (ConBOT 42; Stockholm: Almqvist & Wiksell, 1995).

40 Cross, *Canaanite Myth*, 73n.

41 A statement to this effect is actually missing for Shallum (2 Kgs 15:13), probably due to accident.

quest to build a temple occasioned YHWH's response through Nathan, and with Jerusalem, as the site of David's domain. The tie with Jerusalem again draws on Deuteronomy and its motif of the place YHWH would choose to set his name (Deut 12:5, 11, 14, 18, 21, 26; 14:23-25; 15:20; 16:2, 6-7, 11, 15-16; 16:8, 10; 18:6; 26:2; 31:11). It is because of YHWH's promise and David's faithfulness that the Davidic line retains a kingdom in Judah despite Solomon's apostasy (1 Kgs 11:12-13). In the narrative about the divided monarchy (1 Kings 12–2 Kings 17), which covers more kings of Israel than kings of Judah, the theme of the Davidic promise has a more subtle role than the sin of Jeroboam. Nevertheless, it is present in several forms. First, at two strategic points YHWH's promise to David is recalled as the reason that Judah and the Davidic dynasty continued despite some wicked kings. The first of these is with Abijam, the son and successor of Rehoboam and contemporary of Jeroboam. The mention of the promise to David (1 Kgs 15:4-5) follows shortly after Ahijah's oracle forecasting the downfall of Jeroboam's house (14:7-10). Between them is the end of Jeroboam's reign (14:19-20) and the account of Rehoboam's (14:21-31). Both of them did evil; so did Abijam. The mention of the promise to David in 15:4-5 explains why David's house continues to rule while Jeroboam's is doomed to destruction.

1 Kings 15:4-5

The other explicit reminder of the Davidic promise comes with the introduction of Jehoram, son of Jehoshaphat, of Judah (2 Kgs 8:19). The account of Jehoram's reign is brief, encompassing only nine verses (8:16-24), but it makes clear that he has close ties with the Omrids through his wife, who is Ahab's daughter. These ties were initiated by Jehoram's father, Jehoshaphat; the difference is that Jehoram is not basically righteous like his father but "walked in the way of the kings of Israel, as the house of Ahab had done" (v. 18). His contemporary in Israel is Joram, the last of the Omrids. Judah has come under Israel's evil influence on the eve of the destruction of the most wicked northern dynasty. The mention of the Davidic promise reminds the reader why Judah will continue under Davidid reign, even in its sinful state, while the Omrids will fall. It may also provide reassurance that the Davidic line will continue on the other side of Athaliah's proximate rule.

2 Kings 8:19

In addition to these two explicit references to the Davidic promise, David is often the standard against which his heirs are measured. The kings of Judah do not, of course, maintain the Northern shrines and are not therefore automatically judged apostate for participating in the sin of Jeroboam. Hence the assessments of them vary; some were righteous and others were wicked. Abijam's heart was not true to YHWH as was David's (1 Kgs 15:3). Asa, on the other hand, did what was right, as David had done (15:11), and Jehoshaphat walked in Asa's way (16:28b[G] = 22:43). Amaziah, like his father Joash, did right, but not as David had done (2 Kgs 14:3). Ahaz did not do right as David had done (2 Kgs 16:2). Then, after Israel's demise, Hezekiah and Josiah were especially faithful, doing right according to *all* that David had done (18:3), walking in *all* his way (22:2). These references show that David is the yardstick, at least in name, against which the kings of Judah are assessed.[42]

David as the standard

42 A. Joseph (*Portrait of the Kings: The Davidic Prototype in Deuteronomistic Poetics* [Minneapolis: Fortress, 2015]; idem, "Who Is Like David? Was David Like David? Good Kings in the Book of Kings," *CBQ* 77 [2015] 20–41) treats the distinction between the promissory David in Samuel and the prototypical David in Kings as a literary strategy of DtrH, the latter built more on the model of Josiah than of David.

Burial notices A third, more subtle way in which the Davidic promise surfaces in the story of the divided monarchy is in the burial notices for the kings of Judah. The standard notice states that the deceased king "was buried with his fathers in the city of David." Such is the case for Rehoboam (1 Kgs 14:31), Asa (15:24), Jehoshaphat (22:50), J(eh)oram (2 Kgs 8:24), Amaziah (14:20), Jotham (15:38), and Ahaz (16:20). The same notice occurs with slight variations in wording for Abijam (1 Kgs 15:8), Ahaziah (2 Kgs 9:28), Joash (12:21), and Azariah (15:7). Thus every king of Judah up to Hezekiah is said to have been buried in the city of David, but the same is not reported for any king from Hezekiah on. This phenomenon has been observed by others, and it has been taken as a change either in royal burial practice or in DtrH's official sources.[43] It may be, though, that the notice was intended as a reminder of the fiefdom promised to David and his heirs in Jerusalem in contrast to Israel's inability to install a lasting dynasty because of its kings' persistence in the sin of Jeroboam. The contrast disappeared with the fall of the North, which occurred during Hezekiah's reign, so that there was no need for the notice of burial in the city of David for Hezekiah or any king of Judah after him.

Athaliah and Joash Yet a fourth way in which the theme of the Davidic promise appears in DtrH's divided kingdom narrative—and it may be the most important of the four—is in the accounts of Athaliah and Joash (2 Kings 11–12). Athaliah is presented as an interloper who threatens to derail the Davidic promise (and may have succeeded). There are no regnal formulae for her because DtrH does not consider her a legitimate monarch. There is nothing said about her seven years of rule (perhaps a round number) other than her seizure of power and her overthrow. DtrH focuses on the latter. Despite her best effort she does not kill all the royal heirs; the loyalists save one, Joash, and place him on the throne at the age of seven, which they must have considered their earliest realistic opportunity. The account shows Yhwh's faithfulness to his promise, all the more since it was priests who rescued and reared the boy, engineered the coup that crowned him, and no doubt guided his early decisions. Athaliah's reign is a brief pause in the fulfillment of the Davidic promise but not a break. However, it might also be considered a warning about the freedom of Yhwh to allow such a pause—maybe even a much longer one—while still keeping the promise alive.

3.2.2 The Oracles against the Northern Royal Houses

The oracles of Nathan in 2 Samuel 7 and of Ahijah in 1 Kings 11 show DtrH's use of prophecy and fulfillment for conveying the themes of the sin of Jeroboam and the promise to David. A further series of oracles against the ruling houses of Israel (1 Kgs 14:7-11; 16:1-4; 21:20-24) serves as a structural device for working out the sin of Jeroboam.[44] These are directed at the head of the current ruling house rather than the head of the dynasty, as the instance of Ahab (rather than Omri) shows, but they are anti-dynastic to the extent that they prophesy the annilation of all the male kin and supporters of the ruling house. All three oracles are

---

43 S. Bin-Nun, "Formulas from Royal Records of Israel and of Judah," *VT* 18 (1968): 414–32, at 430–31.

44 Additional iterations of this oracle or portions thereof are found in OG 2 Kgs 1:6+ and 2 Kgs 9:8-9, which I regard as post-DtrH.

matched by fulfillment notices (1 Kgs 15:27-30; 16:11-13; 2 Kgs 10:10, 17) in conjunction with accounts of *coups de état*. Together these prophecy-fulfillment pairs function etiologically to explain not only the ultimate demise of Israel but its series of royal houses in contrast to the single dynasty of David in Judah. This etiological function is apparent in 2 Kgs 10:30, 31b with its explanation for Jehu's house lasting through five kings over four generations. The sin-of-Jeroboam theme continues into 2 Kings 17, where it has its climax as the principal reason for Israel's fall (vv. 21-23). There is one more father-son royal house—Menahem overthrows Shallum only a month after Shallum has overthrown Zechariah, the last Jehuid king, and Menahem is succeeded by his son Pekah. There was no need, though, to reiterate the anti-dynastic oracle for Menahem because the point had been made; the contrast with Judah was clear. Jehu's house was the longest-lasting in Israel as a special reward for his obliteration of the Omrids/Ahabids. Etiological

The three oracles share the form of a judgment oracle. They all begin with an indictment introduced by יען (14:7aβ; 16:2) or יען אשר (21:20bβ) and move to a pronouncement of sentence introduced by הנני (16:3; 21:21) or לכן הנני (14:10). The observation is important because there is a fourth oracle, 2 Kgs 9:6b-10a, that is different. It lacks both the indictment and the sentence and is not a judgment oracle. Its genre is determined by the order to strike down the house of Ahab (9:7a) and might best be designated a commission. The form-critical difference is one of several reasons for considering this oracle imitative that will be explained in the commentary.

1 Kgs 14:7aγ-11a	1 Kgs 16:2-4	1 Kgs 21:20bβ-22, 24
יַעַן אֲשֶׁר הֲרִימֹתִיךָ מִתּוֹךְ הָעָם וָאֶתֶּנְךָ נָגִיד עַל עַמִּי יִשְׂרָאֵל׃	2 יַעַן אֲשֶׁר הֲרִימֹתִיךָ מִן־הֶעָפָר וָאֶתֶּנְךָ נָגִיד עַל עַמִּי יִשְׂרָאֵל	יַעַן הִתְמַכֶּרְךָ לַעֲשׂוֹת הָרַע בְּעֵינֵי יְהוָה׃
8 וָאֶקְרַע אֶת־הַמַּמְלָכָה מִבֵּית דָּוִד וָאֶתְּנֶהָ לָךְ וְלֹא־הָיִיתָ כְּעַבְדִּי דָוִד אֲשֶׁר שָׁמַר מִצְוֹתַי וַאֲשֶׁר־הָלַךְ אַחֲרַי בְּכָל־לְבָבוֹ לַעֲשׂוֹת רַק הַיָּשָׁר בְּעֵינָי׃		
9 וַתָּרַע לַעֲשׂוֹת מִכֹּל אֲשֶׁר־הָיוּ לְפָנֶיךָ וַתֵּלֶךְ וַתַּעֲשֶׂה־לְּךָ אֱלֹהִים אֲחֵרִים וּמַסֵּכוֹת לְהַכְעִיסֵנִי וְאֹתִי הִשְׁלַכְתָּ אַחֲרֵי גַוֶּךָ׃ ס	| וַתֵּלֶךְ בְּדֶרֶךְ יָרָבְעָם וַתַּחֲטִא אֶת־עַמִּי יִשְׂרָאֵל לְהַכְעִיסֵנִי בְּחַטֹּאתָם׃	
10 לָכֵן הִנְנִי מֵבִיא רָעָה אֶל־בֵּית יָרָבְעָם וְהִכְרַתִּי לְיָרָבְעָם מַשְׁתִּין בְּקִיר עָצוּר וְעָזוּב בְּיִשְׂרָאֵל וּבִעַרְתִּי אַחֲרֵי בֵית־יָרָבְעָם כַּאֲשֶׁר יְבַעֵר הַגָּלָל עַד־תֻּמּוֹ׃	3 הִנְנִי מַבְעִיר אַחֲרֵי בַעְשָׁא וְאַחֲרֵי בֵיתוֹ וְנָתַתִּי אֶת־בֵּיתְךָ כְּבֵית יָרָבְעָם בֶּן־נְבָט׃	21 הִנְנִי (מֵבִי) [מֵבִיא] אֵלֶיךָ רָעָה וּבִעַרְתִּי אַחֲרֶיךָ וְהִכְרַתִּי לְאַחְאָב מַשְׁתִּין בְּקִיר וְעָצוּר וְעָזוּב בְּיִשְׂרָאֵל׃
		22 וְנָתַתִּי אֶת־בֵּיתְךָ כְּבֵית יָרָבְעָם בֶּן־נְבָט וּכְבֵית בַּעְשָׁא בֶן־אֲחִיָּה אֶל־הַכַּעַס אֲשֶׁר הִכְעַסְתָּ וַתַּחֲטִא אֶת־יִשְׂרָאֵל׃
11 הַמֵּת לְיָרָבְעָם בָּעִיר יֹאכְלוּ הַכְּלָבִים וְהַמֵּת בַּשָּׂדֶה יֹאכְלוּ עוֹף הַשָּׁמָיִם	4 הַמֵּת לְבַעְשָׁא בָּעִיר יֹאכְלוּ הַכְּלָבִים וְהַמֵּת לוֹ בַּשָּׂדֶה יֹאכְלוּ עוֹף הַשָּׁמָיִם׃	24 הַמֵּת לְאַחְאָב בָּעִיר יֹאכְלוּ הַכְּלָבִים וְהַמֵּת בַּשָּׂדֶה יֹאכְלוּ עוֹף הַשָּׁמָיִם׃

In addition to those already mentioned, there are several terms and expressions that are important in these oracles. The only term that all three have in common is כעס (*Hipʿîl*) "to provoke" (14:9; 16:2; 21:22). Thus, while the oracles are obviously similar and related to each other, they also evince flexibility in addressing different settings. כעס also occurs in the fulfillment notices in 15:30 and 16:13, as does "cause Israel to sin" (16:3; 21:22). The latter, along with the expression "make like the house of Jeroboam" is related to the DtrH theme of the sin of Jeroboam. כעס is a favorite term of DtrH. The same is true of נגיד in the expression "I raised you up and made you *ruler* over my people Israel" (14:7; 16:2). To "do evil (in YHWH's eyes)" (14:9; 21:20bβ) is reminiscent of the DtrH evaluations in the regnal formulae. These terms and expressions show that the oracles against the Northern ruling houses were a creation or adaptation by DtrH. Other expressions shared by the oracles that are less commonly recognized as DtrH are "bring (*Hipʿîl* of בוא) evil upon" (14:10; 21:21) and "burn, consume" בער אחר (16:3; 21:21). Despite this litany of DtrH terminology, these oracles are really built around three peculiar expressions that merit further analysis. These three are משתין בקיר, commonly translated "one who urinates on a/the wall," which is found in all but the oracle against Baasha's house (16:2-4) but does occur in the fulfillment notice for it in 16:11; the accompanying phrase עצור [ו] עזוב, often rendered "bond or free," which also occurs in all but the oracle against Baasha and is replaced in its fulfillment notice with וגאליו ורעהו; and the sentence "the one belonging to X who dies in the city the dogs will eat, and the one [of his] who dies in the country the birds of the air will eat" (14:11; 16:4; 21:24).

3.2.2.1 משתין בקיר

Outside of the oracles against the Northern ruling houses, משתין בקיר occurs only twice in the Hebrew Bible, both in the Abigail story in 1 Sam 25:22, 34. All six occurrences are in contexts threatening the annihilation of a royal household. While Nabal is not a king *per se*, he is a figure of Saul and is cast as a king. Hence all six passages concern the slaughter of the ruling line. It is usually rendered *one who urinates on a wall* and understood as a figure of speech for males.[45] The first word, משתין, is clear enough. It is a rare Gt (i.e., *Qal* with infixed -t-) participle

---

45 1 Sam 25 reinforces the use of the expression for males, as Abigail, by virtue of being female, is the only one able to approach David and to dissuade him from carrying out his oath to wipe out all of the males in Nabal's household. For different views of the kind of figure of speech here see D. E. Smith ("'Pisser against a Wall': An Echo of Divination in Biblical Hebrew," *CBQ* 72 [2010] 699–700), who suggests that the expression was shorthand drawn from dream omens for a person who hopes for progeny. B. Birch ("The First and Second Books of Samuel," *NIB* 2:1168) and G. J. Park ("El's Member in *KTU* 1.23," *UF* 39 [2008]: 617–27) take it as a euphemism, though the context of slaughter suggests that the opposite—a dysphemism—is more likely. J. Schwartz ("Dogs, 'Water' and Wall," *SJOT* 14 [2000]: 101–16) revives an alternate idiomatic interpretation that understands it to refer not to humans but to guard dogs that would fail to protect the royal house and also be killed and eaten. He does not explain the reason for the use of the expression rather than the common word for dog (כלב). A bigger problem is that his interpretation misses the main point of the oracles in the context of hereditary monarchs.

from the root שין, "urinate."[46] The meaning of קיר is less certain.[47] Talmon and Fields relate it to עלית המקרה in Judg 3:20, deriving both from √קרה, and see it as referring to an upstairs bathroom reserved for the upper echelon of society.[48] A משתין בקיר, therefore, was a class designation for a member of royalty who had the privilege of access to such a facility. This explanation is attractive for the way it relates to the social level of the males to whom it refers, which in turn accounts for why this expression is used rather than a more mundane term for male (איש or זכר).[49]

Talmon and Fields

3.2.2.2 עצור ועזוב

Well characterized by Noth as an *uns nicht mehr sicher verständliche stereotype Redewendung* (a stereotypical expression whose meaning is no longer comprehensible to us), this is another expression that is virtually limited to the oracles against the northern ruling houses.[50] It occurs once more in Deut 32:36 (preceded by אפס), and 2 Kgs 14:26 attests ואפס עצור ואפס עזוב. It obviously qualifies משתין בקיר in some way, but the two expressions are also independent of one another. The qualifier בישראל is an additional factor in adjudicating between the different proposals for עצור ועזוב; it is part of the expression used in the oracles but is absent from Deut 32:36 and 2 Kgs 14:26, suggesting that it was not original to the *topos*.[51]

The basic meanings of the two principal roots seem clear at first glance. Both appear to be passive participles. עצר has the basic sense of "restrain," while עזב means "leave, abandon." Hence the common rendering, "bond or free." Even so, the precise nuance and *Sitz im Leben* of the expression are debated. Its two main

---

46 This is the one clear Gt form in the Hebrew Bible (*HALOT* 1479; WO, 424n.), although there may be others (see J. Blau, "Über die t-Form des Hif'il im Bibelhebräisch," *VT* 7 [1957], 387). In addition to the Hebrew *Hitpa'ēl*, other infixed –t- forms are attested in cognate languages to express a middle or indirect reflexive sense (Joüon §53a, p. 157). A Gt form occurs in the Mesha stela (l. 11) with the verb *lḥm*, which usually occurs in *Nip'al* in the HB (Dray, *Translation and Interpretation*, 142–43).

47 S. Iwry ("The Curse of Contamination of Water in Israel and the Ancient East," *Beth Mikra* 28 [1982–83]: 322–35) argued for emending בקיר to בקור and understanding the latter, which is not otherwise attested in the HB, by analogy with Ugaritic *qr*, to mean "spring, well." The reference then is to one who pollutes a well by urinating into it. This meaning does not fit well with the biblical contexts in which the expression is used. Iwry acknowledged as much by arguing that the expression was adopted in these contexts after its original meaning was lost.

48 Talmon and Fields, "Collocation," esp. 92–101. See B. Halpern's discussion of מקרה in Judges 3 in *The First Historians: The Hebrew Bible and History* (San Francisco: Harper & Row, 1988), 45–46.

49 The other alternative that strikes me as a good possibility is that the expression is a dysphemistic synecdoche, that is, a disparaging reference to a person using a slang or vulgar term for the male sexual and scatological organ, like calling a man a "dick" or "prick" today. This kind of objectifying language fits the context of wholesale slaughter that these passages have in common. It does not, however, reflect the social and political context as well as the Talmon-Fields proposal, nor does it work as well in conjunction with עצור ועזוב.

50 Noth, *Überlieferungsgeschichtliche Studien*, 75n.

51 *Pace* E. Kutsch, "Die Wurzel עצר im Hebräischen," *VT* 2 (1952) 61.

Interpretations as opposites

elements have been treated both as opposites and as synonyms.[52] As opposites the two terms are typically taken as a merism and have been interpreted as categories within various facets of life—social (slaves or serfs vs. freemen[53] or those under the protection of a tribe/clan vs. unprotected strangers[54]), military (those deterred at home vs. those released for war, i.e., civilians vs. military,[55] or the opposite—conscripts vs. those released from duty, i.e., military vs. civilians[56]), and cultic (based on Jer 36:5, those under taboo vs. the ritually pure[57]). None of these interpretations is well suited to the royal heirs who are the targets of the oracles since they would not include serfs or be concerned about military conscription; there are also fixed terms for ritual purity/impurity that one would expect to find here if such were the issue.[58] Hence Kutsch's proposal that the two terms highlight a man's coming of age when he is no longer "restrained" under parental control but "released," having come of age = minors and adults, is attractive.[59] Its one possible drawback is that it does not relate at all to the social status of the royal heirs.

Interpretations as synonyms

An entirely different approach is to consider עצור and עזוב not as opposites but as equivalents. Saydon has been the leading advocate of this view, arguing that the two terms together ("derelict" and "helpless") refer to the most destitute of the population and are a way of denoting the universality of the event, from which not even the most miserable could escape.[60] Cogan and Tadmor opt for a similar strategy with their translation "the restricted and the abandoned," as does Hobbs with "those locked up and forsaken."[61] Nonetheless, it is hard to see how a reference to the most destitute, incapacitated, or forgotten could apply to the ruling house. It is also somewhat counterintuitive in that the lowest element of the population is not the class who typically escape such fates as the wholesale slaughter described in these oracles. Talmon and Fields also advocate the synonymous meaning of עצור and עזוב, which they take as a nominal hendiadys referring to a ruler-deliverer, largely because of the parallel expression *his kinsmen and friends* (גאליו ורעהו) in 1 Kgs 16:11.[62] Thus, like משתין בקיר, this is also a technical

---

52 The alliteration of the expression may have been as much the point as its exact meaning and a further obstacle to discerning the latter.

53 W. Gesenius, *Thesaurus Philologicus Criticus Linguae Hebraeae et Chaldaeae Veteris Testamenti* (Leipzig, 1839, 1008a; E. König, *Hebräisches und aramäisches Wörterbuch zum Alten Testament* (Leipzig: Dietrich, 1910), 344a.

54 A. S. Yahuda, "Ueber עָצוּר וְעָזוּב und עֵר וְצֹנֶה im Alten Testament," *ZA* 16 (1902): 240–61.

55 J. Levy, *Neuhebräisches und chaldäisches Wörterbuch über die Talmudim und Midraschim* (Leipzig, 1876–1884), vol. 3, 680.

56 H. Seebass, "Tradition und Interpretation," 182–83.

57 C. Brockelmann, *Hebräische Syntax* (Neukirchen: Buchhandlung des Erziehungsvereins, 1956), 14; F. Schwally, *Semitische Kriegsaltertümer.* Vol. 1. *Der heilige Krieg im alten Israel* (Leipzig: T. Weicher, 1901), 59–60.

58 See the critiques of E. Kutsch, "Die Wurzel עצר im Hebräischen," *VT* 2 (1952), 61–62.

59 Kutsch, "Wurzel," 63–65.

60 P. P. Saydon, "The Meaning of the Expression עָצוּר וְעָזוּב," *VT* 2 (1952): 371–74.

61 Cogan and Tadmor, *II Kings*, 107; Hobbs, *2 Kings*, 115.

62 They contend that both words should be taken as actives and derive from lesser known roots that refer to leading and saving.

expression for a "specific social stratum ... designating ranking members of the royal houses in Israel."[63]

3.2.2.3 The Curse of Dogs and Birds

The refrain about being consumed by dogs and birds has to do with non-burial (cf. 2 Kgs 9:10a). Its likely origin as a treaty curse is suggested by Deut 28:16, 26 and in vassal treaties from the ancient Near East.[64] It was pressed into new service by DtrH in the anti-dynastic oracles. Thus the male descendants of the royal house, in addition to being murdered, were to have their corpses strewn about to rot and be fed upon by animals both domestic and wild. The threat here is twofold. First, they would not be memorialized in a marked tomb and thus the implication was that every memory of their existence would be lost—all the more since their line of descendants was obliterated. Ironically, the account in Kings would prove to be the only record of them. Second, the destruction of one's line had implications for the afterlife. The king or the dynastic head was responsible to his ancestors for the continuation of their heritage. Non-burial and non-memorialization meant that any sustenance he and they might otherwise have anticipated in funerary rites or ancestor cults would be cut off. They would fade in the underworld.[65] The curse of non-burial plays out especially in DtrH's account of the end of the house of Omri/Ahab, where Jehoram is slain in the country (2 Kgs 9:17-24*) and the rest of Ahab's heirs die in the city (2 Kgs 10:1-9*).

3.3 Prophetic *Legenda*

An important step for understanding the development of prophetic stories in Kings was Rofé's identification of their genre as *legenda*.[66] He borrowed the term ("things to be read") from stories about early Christian saints that were read on designated occasions and were popular for their miraculous content.[67] Rofé distinguished the basic or simple *legenda* from the elaborated variety. Alexander Rofé

The former is a brief story of two to seven verses with a simple plot in which there is typically a crisis requiring supernatural intervention that leads to a plea to the man of god for help, which induces him to perform a miracle that resolves Simple *legenda*

---

63 Talmon and Fields, "Collocation," 112.

64 H. N. Wallace, "The Oracles Against the Israelite Dynasties in 1 and 2 Kings," *Bib* 67 (1986) 34–35. Cf. D. R. Hillers, *Treaty Curses and the Old Testament Prophets*, BibOr 15 (Rome: Biblical Institute, 1964) 68–69.

65 See E. Bloch-Smith, *Judahite Burial Practices and Beliefs about the Dead*, JSOTSup 123 (Sheffield: Sheffield Academic Press, 1992); T. J. Lewis, *Cults of the Dead in Ancient Israel and Ugarit*, HSM 39 (Atlanta: Scholars Press. 1989); B. Schmidt, *Israel's Beneficent Dead: Ancestor Cult and Necromancy in Ancient Israelite Religion and Tradition* (Winona Lake, IN: Eisenbrauns, 1996).

66 A. Rofé, *The Prophetical Stories* (Jerusalem: Magness, 1988). See also his "Classes in the Prophetical Stories: Didactic Legenda and Parable," in *Studies in Prophecy*, VTSup 26 (Leiden: Brill, 1974): 143–64, and "The Classification of the Prophetical Stories," *JBL* 89 (1970): 427–40.

67 Cf. R. M. Hals, "Legend: A Case Study in OT Form-Critical Terminology," *CBQ* 34 (1972): 166–76.

the crisis. The story contains a single miracle and is independent, with no effort made to link it with its surroundings. The characters are ordinary people who are anonymous and whose significance lies in the roles they play. The story lacks any real moral value and might even be considered immoral from a modern standpoint. It illustrates fear and respect for the holy man on the part of the characters in the story and perhaps seeks to inculcate these feelings in the hearers or readers of the tale. The miracle is performed by the holy man alone, using sympathetic magic and without explicit resort to the deity.[68]

Elaborated *legenda*

Elaborated *legenda*, as the name suggests, are stories that have undergone literary elaboration. They are longer and may recount more than one miracle. Their characters are more fully developed and may be named. They are of a more ideological bent and may address theological, ethical, or political issues. The prime examples are the Shunammite tale (2 Kgs 4:8-37), the Naaman story (ch. 5), and Elisha's defeat of the Aramaean raiders (6:8-23).

Elaborated by PN

I accept Rofé's characterization of the *legenda* with two provisos. First, I would ascribe much of the elaboration of the *legenda* to the Prophetic Narrator (see below). This is not to deny the distinction between basic and elaborated *legenda* as PN's sources. The basic *legenda*, however, often attest light elaboration primarily shifting the credit for the miracle to Yhwh or his word rather than the man of god and his magic, though without denying the role of the latter (2 Kgs 2:20-22; 4:1-7, 42-44). Elaborated *legenda* have their miracles further enhanced by PN or are supplemented by him with new characters and new episodes with additional moral lessons.

Originally about Elisha

The second proviso is that I regard the *legenda* as the property of Elisha. It is possible that the man of god was originally nameless in some of the *legenda*, but this is impossible to prove because as they now stand Elisha's name and the title "man of god" are used interchangeably.[69] There are *legenda* about Elijah. However, in two cases (1 Kgs 17:10-16; 17-24) they are revisions of Elisha *legenda* in 2 Kings 4. Other *legenda* about Elijah give evidence of having been originally about Elisha or borrowed from stories about him (2 Kgs 1:9-15; 2:1-18). This suggests that the Elisha *legenda* had been gathered into a collection from which the Elijah stories were adapted. The existence of such a collection is also indicated by the stories about Elisha's succession to Elijah in 1 Kgs 19:19-21; 2 Kgs 2:1-18*, which anticipate Elisha's career.

Collections of Elisha tales?

It is common to posit different older collections of Elisha stories based on theme or content, such as those dealing with Elisha's succession to Elijah (1 Kgs

---

68 The assumption that divine power lies behind the holy man's deeds is implicit. Ritual magic is the means of accessing that power. The dichotomy sometimes drawn between religion and magic in antiquity is false. See Cranz, "Naaman's Healing." Also R. Albertz, "Magie II," *TRE* 21:692–93S; S. Dolansky, *Now You See It, Now You Don't: Biblical Perspectives on the Relationship between Magic and Religion* (Winona Lake, IN: Eisenbrauns, 2008); and R. Schmitt, *Magie im Alten Testament*, (AOAT 313; Münster: Ugarit-Verlag, 2004).

69 Schmitt (*Elisa*, 37–38, 138) argued for a man-of-god redaction. Trebolle (*Centena*, 174) showed that the name and title are used together and do not correspond to editorial layers. The nameless man of god in 1 Kgs 20:28 is editorial and based on the Elisha *legenda*, raising further doubt about the claim that the *legenda* were originally about one or more nameless "men of god."

19:15-18, 19-21; 2 Kgs 2:1-18), the "sons of the prophets" (2 Kgs 4:1-7, 38-41, 42-44; 6:1-7; 13:20-21), Elisha as an itinerant holy man (2 Kgs 2:19-22, 23-24; 4:8-37; 8:1-7), and with Israel's wars, especially with the Aramaeans (3:4-27; 5:1-27; 6:8-23; 6:24-7:20; 13:14-19).[70] Such divisions, however, are problematized upon scrutiny; 1 Kgs 19:15-18 assumes the complete Elisha collection and is not an old tradition; the war in 2 Kgs 3:4-27 is with Moab, not Aram, and Elisha is not original to the story; Elisha is also secondary in 2 Kgs 6:24–7:20; the "sons of the prophets" are not named in 2 Kgs 4:42-44 or 13:20-21, and they have been added in other texts (1 Kgs 20:35; 2 Kgs 5:22; 9:1). Add to these considerations the fact that Elisha seems in different stories to reside in Abel Meholah, Gilgal, Mount Carmel, Samaria, and Dothan. If there were separate collections of *legenda*, therefore—and there may well have been—scholars have not yet successfully identified them. The *legenda* are also virtually impossible to date. Some may have originated as oral tales in the ninth century during or shortly after the life of the prophet, assuming there was such a figure; others probably developed much later.[71]

The reason for the present arrangement of the *legenda* in Kings is unknown, though different explanations have been offered, at least for specific texts. De Vaux, for instance, suggested that 4:38–7:20, which begins and concludes with a famine, was inserted between 4:37 and 8:1-6 in order to represent the seven-year famine mentioned in 8:1.[72] But this does not account for the arrangement of the other Elisha materials. To that end Long observes that, beginning with 2 Kgs 3:1, the Elisha stories alternate between those dealing with his activities on the international stage and those about his local deeds.[73] The explanation is not fully satisfying, though, as Long sometimes has to lump separate stories together (e.g., 2 Kgs 4) in order to make it work. He also does not include the stories about Elisha in 2 Kings 2 or 13.

3.4 The Prophetic Narrator

The theory of a distinct level of prophetic writing in Kings is not new. Walter Dietrich's dissertation postulated a prophetic Deuteronomist (DtrP) who followed DtrH by about a decade.[74] But Dietrich did not deal in any detail with the Elijah-

70 See the comments of Sauerwein (*Elischa*, 4–5) with the bibliography. The division goes back at least to Šanda (*Könige* II, 79–89), who further distinguished stories about Elisha's wonders among the "sons of prophets" (2 Kgs 2:1-18, 19-22, 23-24; 4:38-41, 42-44; 6:1-7; 13:14-21) from those about him as an individual miracle worker apart from the prophetic guild (2 Kgs 4:8-37; 8:1-6). Sauerwein notes that there are "grey zones" in such categorizations.

71 Some of the *legenda*, notably in 2 Kings 4, contain what have been taken to be Northern forms that indicate their age and provenance, though this conclusion has been questioned, and there are other explanations.

72 De Vaux, *Rois*, 149.

73 Long, *1 & 2 Kings*, 347. The order is: the Moabite campaign (2 Kgs 3), miracles in Israel (2 Kgs 4), the Naaman story (2 Kgs 5), the floating axehead (6:1-7), the Aramaean siege (6:8–7:20), the Shunammite's property (8:1-6), the "anointing" of Hazael (8:7-15), the anointing of Jehu (9:1-10).

74 Dietrich, *Prophetie und Geschichte* (1972).

Elisha materials. Schmitt's influential study of the Elisha stories, which appeared the same year, distanced these materials from deuteronomism and postulated a series of independent collections (Jehu's revolt, Aramaean wars, wonder stories, other battle stories, Elijah-Elisha succession) that experienced different apologetic and theological redactions and were brought into the book of Kings in stages.[75] The process covered some 400 years, from the late ninth to the fifth centuries. Campbell advanced a more coherent process, arguing for a ninth-century "Prophetic Record" that covered the period from the beginning of the monarchy to Jehu's extermination of the Baal cult in Israel.[76] He included most of the Elijah stories but very little of the Elisha materials, except to suggest that the PR had arisen in circles associated with the latter.[77]

Differences from Dietrich, Schmitt, and Campbell

The "Prophetic Narrative" that I reconstruct in this commentary has elements in common, as well as differences, with each of these foregoing proposals. Like Dietrich and Campbell, but unlike Schmitt, I see PN as a distinct layer in Kings by a single author/editor. Unlike Campbell, I do not regard PN as a source for DtrH but as a post-DtrH addition. But I would not, *pace* Dietrich, label PN a Deuteronomist.

3.4.1 The Elijah and Elisha Stories

Post-DtrH

Prophetic stories dominate the Kings narrative from 1 Kings 17 to 2 Kings 13. These fall into three blocks according to their main prophetic character: stories about Elijah (1 Kings 17–19; 21; 2 Kings 1; 2:1-11); stories about Elisha (2 Kings 2–8; 9:1-12; 13:14-21), and stories about other prophets (1 Kings 20; 22). The issue of their place in Kings has focused on the Elijah materials in 1 Kings 17–19. The idea that these stories were added to Kings at a secondary, post-DtrH editorial stage was suppressed by the popularity of Noth's theory of the Deuteronomistic History in his *Überlieferungsgeschichtliche Studien* of 1943.[78]. Noth agreed with his predecessors about the non-deuteronomistic nature of the Elijah stories. But instead of taking them as secondary to the DtrH, as he did for other extensive materials (e.g., the tribal lists in Joshua 13–21 and the Samson stories in Judges 13–16), Noth

---

75 Schmitt, *Elisa*, esp. 137–38.

76 A. F. Campbell, *Of Prophets and Kings: A Late Ninth-Century Document (1 Samuel, 1-2 Kings 10)* (CBQMS 17; Washington, DC: CBA, 1986). See also Campbell and M. A. O'Brien, *Unfolding the Deuteronomistic History: Origins, Upgrades, Present Text* (Minneapolis: Fortress, 2000). P. K. McCarter (*I Samuel; II Samuel*), following B. C. Birch (*The Rise of the Israelite Monarchy: The Growth and Development of 1 Samuel 7-15* [SBLDS 27; Missoula, MT: Scholars Press, 1976]) had already hypothesized an eighth-century Prophetic History behind Samuel.

77 Campbell, *Of Prophets*, 115. A lynchpin of Campbell's case is his view of 1 Kgs 16:1-4, which he takes to be a DtrH imitation of the anti-dynastic oracles. The absence of a PR oracle against the house of Baasha is a serious problem for the existence of such a running prophetic source. The problem is exacerbated by the separation of Elijah's oracle (21:20-24*) from the Naboth story (21:1-16).

78 C. Steuernagel, *Lehrbuch der Einleitung in das Alte Testament* (Tübingen: Mohr [Siebeck], 1912), 348–49, 369. Similar positions were taken by Hölscher ("Das Buch der Könige," 158–213), who assigned these chapters to his pre-dtr Elohist, and R. Pfeiffer (*Introduction to the Old Testament* [New York: Harper, 1941], 396–409).

instead viewed the Elijah tales as a source that had been compiled into a collection before the composition of the DtrH and then incorporated *verbatim* (*in ihrem überlieferten Wortlaut*) by DtrH.[79] His Deuteronomistic History thesis was so influential that most scholars have assumed ever since that the Elijah (and Elisha) stories are part of it.[80]

Fohrer's criteria

The evidence for DtrH editing of the Elijah stories, though, is weak. The only systematic argument for it was put forward in 1957 by Fohrer, who built his case on six expressions that he took to be characteristic of DtrH.[81] Yet Fohrer himself showed that these expressions are attested in late prophetic literature in general, especially Jeremiah and Ezekiel, and in some cases in P and Chronicles; none is exclusively or distinctly DtrH.[82] Thus while the Elijah stories are riddled with late expressions, there is a notable absence of distinctly DtrH language in them.

Differences with Dtr's prophets

Conversely, there are several reasons for regarding 1 Kings 17–19 as a post-DtrH addition. First, Elijah appears unexpectedly in the narrative in 1 Kgs 17:1, and the stories about him interrupt the account of Ahab's reign. Elijah receives no introduction apart from his title, "the Tishbite," and there is nothing in the preceding introduction of Ahab to prepare for Elijah's advent. There is also a change in style from the foregoing series of succinct accounts of kings' reigns bracketed by introductory and concluding regnal formulae to tales about Elijah and the prophets. In one instance (2 Kgs 2), the story even lies outside of the DtrH structural framework of the book of Kings furnished by the regnal formu-

---

79 With only a few DtrH additions, most notably "Horeb" in 1 Kgs 19:8 and the oracle in 21:21-26*. Noth, *Überlieferungsgeschichtliche Studien*, 82–83.

80 E. Nielsen (*Oral Tradition: A Modern Problem in Old Testament Introduction* [SBT 11; Chicago: Alec R. Allenson, 1954], 70), even stated that the Elijah stories had been "subjected to a thoroughly artistic and tendentious revision" by DtrH to such an extent that it was no longer possible to trace the original prophetic legends. W. Thiel ("Deuteronomistische Redaktionsarbeit in den Elia Erzählungen," in *Congress Volume. Leuven 1989* [ed. J. A. Emerton; VTSup 43; Leiden: Brill, 1991], 154) pointed out the paucity of Dtr terminology in these prophetic narratives but then concluded, essentially in agreement with Noth, that DtrH's editing was so light because the Deuteronomists had found so many examples of their ideas already in their sources. C. Alcaina Canosa ("Panorama crítico del ciclo de Eliseo," *EstBíb* 23 [1964]: 217–34) and Miller ("Elisha Cycle," 441–54) each suggested in the 1960s that the Elijah-Elisha materials were post-DtrH. More recent advocates of this position include Stipp, *Elischa - Propheten - Gottesmänner*, esp. 477–80; McKenzie, *Trouble with Kings*, 81–100; Otto, *Jehu, Elia und Elisa*, esp. 151–57; and Römer, *So-Called Deuteronomistic History*, 98n, 153–54.

81 G. Fohrer, *Elia*, 53–57. The six expressions are: *before whom I stand*, *the word of* Yhwh *came*, *to bring to remembrance*, *to know that you are god*, Elijah as *the servant of* Yhwh, and *the hand of* Yhwh *came upon*.

82 Thiel ("Deuteronomistische Redaktionsarbeit," 150–51) points out that Fohrer's Dtr interventions lack any kind of overall scheme or order. N. J. Tromp ("Water and Fire on Mount Carmel: A Conciliatory Suggestion," *Bib* 56 [1975], 501) put it this way: "Fohrer looked for traces of a deuteronomistic revision in our text and indicated some elements as such. The result is hardly impressive." Saint-Laurent ("Light from Ras Shamra,"127), who holds that the Elijah cycle was included in the DtrH because "the man of god meets the most fundamental criterion of Deuteronomistic theology" also acknowledges that "the stories betray none of the characteristic Deuteronomic (*sic*) language."

lae.[83] Second, these stories are very different from those about prophets encountered previously in Kings. They do not mention the sin of Jeroboam, which is the principal concern of those earlier prophetic interventions. Rather, the stories of Elijah in 1 Kings 17–19, and even more so those of Elisha in 2 Kings, are legendary tales about the miraculous exploits of their heroes. They tend to be of two kinds—personal anecdotes involving the miraculous deeds of the men of god interacting with ordinary people, and political tales, including war stories, involving interactions with kings of Israel and other nations. Thus while the rest of 1 Kings is essentially set during Ahab's reign, he here plays a minor role for the most part, giving way to Elijah. He is mentioned in 1 Kings 17, for instance, only in v. 1. The other facet of this difference concerns the view of prophecy. Elijah in 1 Kings 17–19 (and Elisha even more so) is a miracle-working man of god rather than a messenger with a divine word like Ahijah (1 Kgs 14:7-11) or Jehu ben Hanani (1 Kgs 16:2-4). This points to a third difference: There are striking tensions in these stories with DtrH theology. Elijah's construction of an altar on Mount Carmel is a flagrant violation of the DtrH doctrine of cultic centralization. Elijah also complains about the people having torn down YHWH's altars (1 Kgs 19:10, 14).[84] These considerations suggest that the stories about Elijah and Elisha were basically added to Kings at a post-DtrH level. There are two exceptions—the DtrH anti-dynastic oracle in 1 Kgs 21:20-24* and Elijah's prophecy of Ahaziah's death in 2 Kgs 1:2-8*.

3.4.2 1 Kings 20; 22:1-38

Linked accounts

Textual, literary, and historical considerations tie 1 Kings 20 and 22 together. The Old Greek places them together with its order (*vis-à-vis* MT) 21, 20, 22. The statement in 22:1 that there was a three-year hiatus without war between Aram and Israel continues the narrative of the Aramaean-Israelite wars from ch. 20. The apparent reason for the change of order in MT was to link Elijah's denunciation of Ahab in ch. 21 more closely to the story of his death in ch. 22. Literarily, the stories 1 Kgs 20; 22:1-38 contain are not related to either Elijah or Elisha but come in the period of transition between them, as the replacement of Elijah is heralded at the end of 1 Kings 19 but is not completed until 2 Kings 2.

Distinct from Elijah and Elisha

83 Otto (*Jehu, Elia und Elisa,* 155–57), who responds to general arguments advanced by Smend, Dietrich, and Thiel, also points (pp. 151–54) to various inconsistencies between 1 Kgs 17–19 and the surrounding DtrH narrative, among them: (1) While the people decide in 18:39-40 to follow YHWH and kill the prophets of Baal, DtrH attests no interruption or setback in the worship of Baal and describes Ahaziah's apostasy as a matter of continuity with his father's (1 Kgs 22:53). (2) DtrH says nothing about any kind of cultic reform following the Mount Carmel events despite elsewhere reporting much less decisive reforming acts (2 Kgs 3:2). (3) The relationship between Ahab and Elijah in chs. 17–19 is more complex than the pure animus depicted by DtrH. Other tensions that Otto perceives are addressed in the course of the commentary.

84 Similarly, Elisha in 2 Kgs 2:23-24 "fails to condemn the cult of the calf of Bethel" (Saint-Laurent, "Light from Ras Shamra," 127).

Historically, 1 Kgs 20; 22:1-38 belong in the reign of one of the kings of the later Jehu dynasty rather than with Ahab.[85] Inscriptional and archaeological evidence contradicts the portrait in these two chapters of Ahab as a weakling dominated by the Aramaeans, with whom he is constantly at war; elsewhere the reigns of Omri and Ahab appear as a time of military strength for Israel when it also enjoyed significant international ties and a prosperous and ambitious building program. Of particular importance is the Kurkh Monolith Inscription of Shalmaneser III, which describes his battle with a coalition of Syro-Palestinian kings in 853 BCE at Qarqar on the Orontes. Ahab is named as a key member of the coalition, contributing the largest contingent of chariotry (2000) plus 10,000 troops.[86] The Mesha stela also indicates Israel's strength under Ahab when it dominated Moab.[87] Further corroboration is found in certain summative biblical texts (1 Kgs 16:24, 31; 22:39; 2 Kgs 3:4) and in archaeological evidence indicating energetic and prosperous construction activity in ninth-century Israel.[88] These separate pieces of evidence combine to form a picture of the reigns of Omri and Ahab as the apex of the kingdom of Israel in terms of military, political, and administrative prowess. This picture contrasts with 1 Kings 20; 22:1-38, where Israel can field only a pitifully small army (20:15) that is vastly outnumbered by the Aramaeans (20:27) and must have virtually no chariotry, since the Aramaeans expect an easy victory on the plain (20:23-25).[89] First Kings 20:34 is all the more untenable in implying that Ahab's father Omri was also weak and dominated by Aram. The Monolith's mention of Ahab's participation in the coalition of 853 shows that Israel under Ahab was not the constant enemy of Aram depicted in 1 Kings 20; 22:1-38. The premise of 22:1-38, that Ramoth-Gilead was held by Aram and needed to be restored to Israel (vv. 3-4) is contradicted in 2 Kgs 8:28-29; 9:1-14, where Jehu is "on guard" (שמר) at Ramoth and launches his *coup d'etat* from there. The fact that Yhwh begins *to cut off parts of Israel* in Gilead during the reign of Jehu (2 Kgs 10:32-33) hints at the original setting of the stories in 1 Kgs 20; 22:1-38 in the Jehu dynasty.

Pertaining to Jehu dynasty

Kurkh monolith

Mesha stela

Ramoth-Gilead

---

85 Jepsen, "Israel und Damaskus," 153–72; Whitley, "Deuteronomic Presentation;" Miller, "The Elisha Cycle and the Accounts of the Omride Wars;" "The Fall of the House of Ahab;" "The Rest of the Acts of Jehoahaz (I Kings 20. 22,1-38)," *ZAW* 80 (1968): 337–42. Pitard, *Ancient Damascus*, 114–25; "Ben-Hadad," *ABD* 1:663–65; Stipp, *Elisha - Propheten - Gottesmänner*, 198–99; McKenzie, *Trouble with Kings*, 88–93; Miller and Hayes, *History*, 284–326.

86 K. A. Grayson, *Assyrian Rulers of the Early First Millennium BC. Vol. II (858–745 BC)* (RIMA 3; Toronto: University of Toronto, 1996), 11–24. Cf. also *ANET* 276–81; *COS* 2.113A. The figure may be exaggerated (see the bibliography in *COS* 2, 263n), but Ahab is still portrayed as the second-most-powerful member of the coalition, so that the tensions with 1 Kgs 20 remain.

87 Miller ("Moabite Stone as Memorial Stela") argues that this was a memorial rather than a victory stela, such that it locates the starting point of the change in Moab's relationship with Israel at Mesha's accession rather than his revolt. Historically, Mesha probably acceded to his father's throne about halfway through Ahab's reign but did not revolt against Israel until after Ahab's death.

88 For a concise summary see Miller and Hayes, *History*, 295; also Frevel, *Geschichte Israels*, 194-202.

89 Pitard, *Ancient Damascus*, 115–16.

Additional indications that 1 Kgs 20; 22:1-38 originally pertained to a later king of Israel and not to Ahab are manifold in the texts themselves. For one thing, Ahab's name is rather rare in these stories—occurring in the MT only three times in ch. 20 (vv. 2, 13, 14) and only once in 22:1-38 (v. 20); most of the time the king is designated by title, *the king of Israel*. The Greek witnesses add to this evidence by their variation from the MT in the placement of the name,[90] giving the impression that the identification of the king of Israel with Ahab in these chapters is tentative and secondary.[91]

The perspective of these chapters and the issues they deal with are radically different from those of the Elijah stories and much closer to those in the Elisha collection. For instance, 20:35 contains the first reference to the "sons of the prophets" who are mentioned often in the Elisha stories. The animosity between the prophets of YHWH and Ahab that existed in the Elijah tales is ameliorated here; the prophets are often on good terms with the king and even serve as his advisors against the Aramaeans. The king is not a worshiper of Baal but a Yahwist. In ch. 22 the conflict between YHWH and Baal and their prophets is replaced by conflict among Yahwistic prophets, and the hitherto unknown Micaiah steps into a role previously played by Elijah.[92] While the stories in 1 Kgs 20; 22:1-38 fit poorly with Ahab, they are quite appropriate to the reigns of Jehu's son Joahaz and grandson Joash, whose reigns overlap with the career of Elisha. The key text here is 2 Kings 13. The Israelites under Joahaz in particular have a paltry army (13:7) and are dominated by Aram (13:3-4). Furthermore, an oracle by the dying Elisha (13:14-19) predicts a threefold victory for Joash over Aram that is said to be fulfilled and to include the recovery of cities (13:25).[93] The similarity of this text to the three battles in 1 Kgs 20; 22:1-38 and the mention of the recovery of cities in 20:34 led Jepsen and Whitley to identify the king in 1 Kgs 20; 22:1-38 as Joash.[94] Miller argued for Joash's father Joahaz.[95] For the present the point is that he was a member of the later Jehu dynasty and not an Omrid at all; the identification with Ahab is secondary; the stories 1 Kgs 20; 22:1-38 are out of place historically.

---

90 The OG, attested in G^B, has the name four times in ch. 20 (vv. 2, 14 [twice], 15), but only twice overlapping with the MT occurrences. G^L agrees with G^B but then has the name once more in v. 34. In ch. 22, G^B agrees with MT in reading the name only in v. 34, while the Lucianic witnesses have it four more times in vv. 2, 5, 10, 37.

91 An additional argument is that the statement in 22:40 that Ahab *lay with his forebears* is used elsewhere only for kings who died in peace and therefore contradicts the account in 22:34-38, which must pertain to a later king. However, Suriano (*Politics of Dead Kings*) has shown that the formula "lie with one's forebears" refers not to manner of death but to dynastic succession. Ahab was succeeded by his son, so the formula in 22:40 is appropriate. Still, the king in 22:34-38 was only secondarily identified with Ahab, who evidently died peacefully.

92 Pitard, *Ancient Damascus*, 118.

93 Robker (*Jehu Revolution*, 107) places 1 Kings 20 between 2 Kgs 13:24 and 25. He observes (p. 108) that the verb "to strike" (נכה) occurs three times in 1 Kgs 20 (vv. 20, 21, 29), which corresponds to the threefold striking of Aram by Joash in 2 Kgs 13:25.

94 Jepsen, "Israel und Damaskus," 157; Whitley, "Deuteronomic Presentation," 144–45.

95 Miler, "The Elisha Cycle and the Accounts of the Omride Wars," 442–43.

Cogan's counterarguments

The commentaries by Cogan and Sweeney offer counterarguments in favor of the placement of 1 Kgs 20; 22:1-38 and the identification of these stories with Ahab. Cogan asserts that the identification of Jehoshaphat as the king of Judah in 1 Kings 22 necessitates the identification of Ahab as the king of Israel and that the denunciation in 20:35-43 would be inappropriate for Joash if he was remembered for his victories over Aram as indicated in 2 Kgs 13:25.[96] The first point ignores the complications surrounding the presence of the king of Judah in 1 Kings 22 and his identification as Jehoshaphat.[97] The second carries no weight since, however he is identified, the king of Israel in these stories is credited with defeating Aram and is punished for leniency toward its king. The problem is addressed on the compositional level by recognizing 20:35-42 as an addition. Moreover, anonymity of the king of Israel in these stories and the complications surrounding 2 Kgs 13:14-19 indicate that there was confusion in the memory of just which king was responsible for the victories over Aram. In his further effort to accommodate 1 Kgs 20; 22:1-38 within Ahab's reign Cogan's defense is faulty on at least two scores. First, he goes on to argue that ch. 20 reflects an earlier point of military weakness in Ahab's reign, undercutting his view that the chapter must be associated with the Omrids because of the identification of the king of Judah as Jehoshaphat, who is only mentioned in 22:1-38. He overlooks the references to Ramoth-Gilead (2 Kgs 8:28-29; 9:1, 4, 14) indicating that it was held by Israel until the end of Jehu's reign (2 Kgs 10:32-33) and did not need to be "restored" (1 Kgs 22:3). Cogan also discounts the indications of Omri's strength when he claims that Israel under Ahab "emerged from its underdog position vis-à-vis Damascus."[98] It is hardly conceivable that the Aramaeans penetrated all the way to Samaria to besiege it during Ahab's reign as per 20:1.

Sweeney's counterarguments

Sweeney claims that Aram's oppression of Israel under Ahab as portrayed in 1 Kgs 20; 22:1-38 is historically viable because the border between the two countries was a frequent "flashpoint of conflict."[99] While this may hold for Ramoth, the penetration to Samaria is much more than a border conflict. Sweeney adds two other arguments. First, the Aramaean king in 1 Kgs 20; 22:1-38 can no longer be identified with Ben-Hadad son of Hazael, who is mentioned in the Elisha stories. This argument is founded on Pitard's identification of Bir-Hadad in the Melqart inscription as a non-Damascene unrelated to Ben-Hadad in the biblical stories.[100] But Sweeney misses Pitard's larger point. Pitard believes the stories in 1 Kgs 20; 22:1-38 to be from the reign of Joash in the Jehu dynasty, and he identifies the Ben-Hadad in them as the son of Hazael.[101] But since this Ben-Hadad did not overlap with the Omri dynasty, the king of Israel here must be a member of Jehu's house rather than Ahab's. Sweeney's second argument is that the conflict between Israel and Aram depicted in 1 Kgs 20; 22:1-38 would not necessarily obviate their alliance against Shalmaneser III. Sweeney proposes that Aram compelled Israel to join the coalition against Shalmaneser III to keep Ahab from allying with Assyria. Then Ahab capitalized on his defeat of Aram (1 Kgs 20) with treaty terms that favored Israel and used Aram as a buffer against Assyria. Ahab's loss in his substantial contribution to the coalition shifted the power balance between the two states back in Aram's favor. This scenario, though, raises more questions than it solves. For

96 Cogan, *I Kings*, 471–74.
97 In addition to the treatment in this commentary, see Miller, "Elisha Cycle," and Miller and Hayes, *History*, 288–90.
98 Cogan, *I Kings*, 474.
99 Sweeney, *Kings*, 239–40.
100 Pitard, *Ancient Damascus*, 138–44; "Identity of the Bir-Hadad," 3–21.
101 W. T. Pitard, "Ben-Hadad," *ABD* 1:663–65.

> instance, why would Ahab not have sought an alliance with Assyria when Samaria was besieged or when he faced the overwhelming numbers of Aramaeans? And why would he have contributed so heavily to the coalition if he was just using Aram as a buffer?

The failed attempts of Cogan and Sweeney to uphold the historicity of 1 Kgs 20; 22:1-38 vis-à-vis Ahab serve rather to reinforce the arguments for their being out of place and about a different king of Israel.

3.4.3 PN's Editorial Activity and Coherence

It is often assumed that the blocks of prophetic stories—those about Elijah, those about Elisha, and 1 Kgs 20; 22:1-38—or even their constituent parts (1 Kgs 17–18; 19; 21:1-16; the subcategories of Elisha stories) entered Kings separately. Certainly these materials evince a good deal of diversity and even tension among themselves, which is attributable at least in part to their different origins. The possibility that they were the work of a single editorial hand, which is suggested here, is sparked by the observations of Blum[102] and is based on my perception of similarities in editorial technique and the coherence of an overarching ideological agenda. As a whole these prophetic stories provide a paradigm in Elijah for judgment prophecy. They add precedents to DtrH's mention of prophets sent by YHWH to warn Israel in 2 Kgs 17:13, 23. The graphically recounted deaths of Ahab (1 Kgs 22:34-38) and Jezebel (2 Kgs 9:30-37) show the working out of Elijah's judgments on them (1 Kgs 21:20-26). The Elisha *legenda* as elaborated by PN attest the power of YHWH's word through the prophet to control the forces of nature even to life and death.

PN began with the Elisha *legenda*, which he elaborated especially by attributing many of the wonders in them explicitly to the word and power of YHWH. He composed the Elijah stories in 1 Kings as an introduction to the Elisha *legenda* and as the model of a judgment prophet.[103] He made use of sources—including some stories about Elijah, but above all the Elisha *legenda* themselves—to fashion his account of Elijah. It helped that those *legenda* already related Elisha's succession to Elijah. He made frequent use of *Wiederaufnahme* as an editorial device for interpolating prophetic material. He also used the order-compliance motif. He used the stories in 1 Kings 17–19 in particular as a forum for presenting the prophetic word as a source of divine power and revelation. He built much of the subsequent account around the DtrH oracle in 1 Kgs 21:20*-22, 24. PN shifted three stories of Israel's victories over Aram from the end of 2 Kings 13 to 1 Kgs 20; 22:1-38 in order to provide retribution upon Ahab so that he did not personally escape judgment as he had in DtrH. PN also added the Naboth story in 1 Kgs 21:1-16, perhaps replacing a previous version of the story (2 Kgs 9:25-26a). He

---

102 Blum, "Der Prophet und das Verderben Israels," and "Die Nabotüberlieferungen."

103 On the technique of revision by introduction see S. Milstein, *Tracking the Master Scribe: Revision through Introduction in Biblical and Mesopotamian Literature* (New York: Oxford University Press, 2016). Blum ("Der prophet und das Verderbnis Israels," esp. 278–81) calls 1 Kgs 17–19 *apologia* for judgment prophecy. To speculate, PN's work may have been intended as a prelude to an incipient collection of writing prophets, perhaps to compensate for DtrH's lack of mention of the writing prophets, on which see C. Begg, "The Non-mention of Amos, Hosea and Micah in the Deuteronomistic History," *BN* 32 (1986): 41–53.

portrayed Jezebel as the main culprit and inserted v. 23 into Elijah's oracle, so that her grisly end in 2 Kgs 9:30-37 was also a fulfillment of YHWH's word of judgment. PN is probably best dated to the Persian period, as indicated by certain expressions and terms, not least in the Naboth story (1 Kgs 21:1-16), and he had access to the books of Jeremiah and Ezekiel. His theological outlook as evinced especially in 1 Kings 18 and 2 Kings 5 is close to that of 2 Isaiah as pragmatic, if not fully ontological monotheism.

4. *History and Chronology*

Historical issues

The foregoing discussion of composition shows that the book of Kings is not history writing in a modern sense. As is evident from the themes discussed above, DtrH's interests are primarily etiological and theological; PN's are theological and sociological in promoting prophets over kings and other classes.[104] Kings reflects the use of historical data such as the integrated king list, as well as stories and traditions from the past, and it purports to pass on historical information and to offer explanations about why things happened as they did. However, DtrH's evaluations of kings and PN's displacement of 1 Kgs 20; 22:1-38 make clear that historical accuracy was not the paramount concern. The setting of 1 Kgs 20; 22:1-38 is one of several historical problems presented in Kings, often as a result of tensions with other biblical passages and/or data and documents from elsewhere in the ancient Near East. Such problems include the number and identities of the Ben-Hadad(s), whether the Ahaziahs who ruled Israel and Judah at roughly the same time were in fact a single individual, and similarly whether the two J(eh)orams were one and the same, whether it was Jehu or the Aramaean king (Hazael?) who assassinated the kings of Israel and Judah, and issues surrounding the reign of Joash of Judah, such as whether he truly was a Davidid and whether his regnal years incorporated the rule of Athaliah. These and other historical issues will be discussed in the context of the biblical passages for which they are most pertinent.

Chronological issues

The question of the overlap of Athaliah's and Joash's reigns raises the general historical problem of chronology. There are chronological disagreements throughout the book of Kings. The problem is most acute in the final three chapters covered by this commentary, 2 Kings 14–16. There are discrepancies within the regnal formulae about the accession years for some kings, and the totals for the kings of Judah and kings of Israel during the same period are not even close. The OG chronology is not extant here, and we have seen that it is derivative anyway. These problems and others, as well as the proposals advanced to address them, will be probed in the analyses of these chapters. However, some of the problems are not resolvable, and the precise chronology of the period cannot be reconstructed in more detail than the broad parameters established by Assyrian evidence. For this reason I do not try to reconstruct the absolute chronology (i.e., dates) of the period covered in this commentary. The chronological chart that follows is for heuristic purposes only. That is, it is intended to give the reader a basic chronological structure rather than to establish definitive dates for the

104 Grabbe, *1 & 2 Kings*, 6–14.

kings. The dates are those of Galil.[105] The places where his reconstructions are open to question are discussed in the contexts of the relevant chapters in Kings.

Israel		Judah	
Jeroboam I	931/30–909	N Rehoboam	931/30–914
		Abijah	914–911
Nadab	909–908	Asa	911–870
Baasha	908–885		
Elah	885–884		
[Tibni	884–880]		
Omri	884–873	Jehoshaphat	870–845
Ahab	873–852		
Ahaziah	852–851		
Joram	851–842/1	Jehoram	851–843/2
		Ahaziah	843/2–842/1
Jehu	842/1–815/4	[Athaliah	842/1–835]
Jehoahaz	819–804/3	Joash	841/1–802/1
Jehoash	805–790	Amaziah	805/4–776/5
Jeroboam II	790–750/49	Azariah (Uzziah)	788/7–736/5
Zechariah	750/49	Jotham	758/7–742/1
Shallum	749		
Menahem	749–38	Ahaz	742/1–726
Pekahiah	738–736		
Pekah	750?-732/1		
Hoshea	732/1–722	Hezekiah	726–697/6

5. *Format*

The present commentary follows a five-part format, according to series protocol, in the discussion of each lemma: Translation, Textual Notes, Synchronic Analysis, Diachronic Analysis, and Synthesis.

The *Translation* aims to present a coherent rendering of the reconstructed text that is at once fluid and relatively idiomatic while being accurate and consistent in its conversion of vocabulary and expressions. The reconstructed text reflects both text-critical judgments and literary-(source-)critical ones. The latter are conveyed by the different fonts, as explained earlier.

105 Galil, *Chronology*, 147.

The *Textual Notes* explain the reasons for text-critical decisions as well as the meanings of and translations adopted for various terms and expressions. They also discuss technical points of grammar and syntax, the etymologies of personal and place names, and matters of topography and geography, including the locations of sites mentioned in the text.

The *Synchronic Analysis* treats the finished product of the MT and seeks to understand it as a coherent whole along with its interpretational possibilities for ancient and modern readers. The focus on the MT in its final form is intentional; it is the usual object of synchronic study. It would be possible theoretically to conduct a synchronic analysis of another text (e.g., the LXX) or even a stage in the text's development, such as DtrH. However, the MT is an agreed-upon stage rather than a reconstruction, and it is the typical object of a commentary. Moreover, adherence to the MT compels one (me) to wrestle with the text as it is rather than resorting too readily to textual variants or compositional theories, and this is often a useful discipline for perceiving the sophistication and artistry of the narrative. Thus phenomena such as gaps and tensions in the narrative can be valuable clues for discerning aesthetics as well as ideology behind a text. Synchronic analysis pays attention to the narrative's structure and its use of literary devices. The present commentary makes use of relatively recent approaches in biblical scholarship such as narrative criticism, reader response, rhetorical criticism, intertextuality, and ideological approaches (e.g., feminist and ecological readings) in synchronic analysis.

The *Diachronic Analysis*, by contrast, focuses on more traditional (in biblical studies) concerns and approaches in order to study the development of the text and its contents over time. It attempts to determine the historical basis, if any, behind biblical accounts and/or how they have been shaped by other literary, social, and historical influences in the ancient Near East. It is interested in the archaeology of the earth as well as the archaeology of the text. Its other leading tools include textual criticism, literary (source) criticism, form criticism, tradition-historical and redaction criticism, comparative studies, and sociological analysis. It attempts to trace how the text took shape over time, to identify the authors and editors who composed it as well as its transmission through processes of copying, translation, and recension to produce different versions and witnesses. An important consequence of these facets of study is that the line between composition and transmission has become increasingly blurred. The results of diachronic analysis often agree with those of synchronic analysis, but sometimes they contrast sharply and in interesting and instructive ways. Thus, the reader should expect to find such disagreements reflected between the Synchronic and Diachronic Analysis sections on given lemmas in this commentary.

The *Synthesis* is the most uneven of the sections. I have chosen to use it to articulate the "take-away" of analysis for each lemma. Sometimes this is a genuine synthesis or reiteration of the main results. Such syntheses may focus more on either the synchronic or diachronic results. Sometimes it is more along the lines of a reflection on the possible enduring significance of the lemma for modern readers. At times it also raises questions about the relevance or usefulness of the lemma for today. The main purpose in all cases is the same—to leave the reader with something further to ponder about the fascinating data and marvelous stories that comprise the book of Kings.

The Reign of Baasha (1 Kings 15:33–16:7)

Text

[DtrH's sources; DtrH; Additions to DtrH; Additions to additions]
33 In the third year of Asa king of Judah, Baasha son of Ahijah
became king over Israel in Tirzah, reigning for twenty-four
years. 34 He did what YHWH considered evil, following Jeroboam and his sin
which he made Israel commit. 16:1 YHWH's word came to Jehu son of Hanani
against Baasha, 2 "Because I raised you up from the dust and made you king
designate over my people Israel but you have followed Jeroboam, causing my
people Israel to sin, provoking me with their idols, 3 I am going to incinerate
Baasha and his house, leaving his house like the house of Jeroboam son of Ne-
bat; 4 anyone belonging to Baasha who dies in the city the dogs will eat, and
anyone of his who dies in the country the birds of the sky will eat." 5 The rest
of Baasha's affairs, including what he accomplished and his power, are of
course written on the scroll of the chronicles of the kings of Israel. 6 Baasha lay
down with his forebears and was buried in Tirzah, and his son Elah reigned in
his stead. 7 Moreover, YHWH's word came through Jehu son of Hanani against
Baasha and his house because of all the evil which he had done in YHWH's
view, provoking him with the work of his hands, to become like Jeroboam's
house, and because he had destroyed it.

Textual Notes

15:33 **Baasha**: An abbreviated form (hypocoristicon) of a theophoric personal name with Baal as the first element. The second element is uncertain; the longer form of the name may have meant "Baal hears" (בעל שמע) or "Baal acts" (בעל עשה). The name appears in Neo-Punic and might be of Phoenician origin.[1] "Baal," meaning "lord, master," could also be used as an epithet of YHWH, so the name does not necessarily mean that Baasha was not a Yahwist.

Israel: So G^{BL}. MT: *all Israel.*

Tirzah: Identified with Tell el-Far'ah, north (vs. Tell el-Far'ah, south, in the Negeb), Tirzah was an attractive site for a capital because of its scenery (the name means "beauty, pleasure," Song 6:4) and its strategic location.[2] It sat eleven km

---

1 *HALOT* I:147; Harris, *Grammar of the Phoenician Language*, 91; Noth, *Personennamen*, 40.

2 On the identification of Tell el- Far'ah, north with Tirzah see R. de Vaux, "The Excavations at Tell el-Far'ah and the Site of Ancient Tirzah," *PEQ* 88 (1956): 125–40, and his entry in *NEAEHL* 2:433. On the archaeology of the site see the series of reports by de Vaux and Stève in *RB* 54–69 (1947–62) and the other entries under "Tell el-Far'ah (north)," *NEAEHL* 2:432–40.

north of Shechem, between it and Beth Shan on a major route from the central hill country to the Jordan Valley. It was, therefore, more or less centrally located on a north-south axis and represented a good site from which to rule the Northern kingdom. "Foundations of unfinished structures built over a level with burned debris have been interpreted to mean that Omri started to rebuild the city after its destruction but then aborted the plan, presumably when he turned attention to Samaria."[3] It is listed as one of the cities whose king was killed by Joshua and the invading Israelites (Josh 12:24) and as one of the clans referred to as the daughters of Zelophehad in the territory of Manasseh (Josh 17:3-13; cf. Num 26:33; 27:1; 36:11). The mention of Tirzah in 1 Kgs 14:17 suggests that it served as Jeroboam's capital in lieu of or in addition to Shechem (1 Kgs 12:25). Baasha, though, is the first king explicitly stated to have reigned in Tirzah.

34 **sin**: So MT. G, Syr: *sins*. With Stade[4] I take the singular as more primitive, referring to a specific sin of Jeroboam, and reconstruct it throughout Kings.

which he made Israel commit: אשר refers to Jeroboam's sin, not to Jeroboam. See Joüon 139a, 158i.

16:1 **to**: So MT (אל), G^L (πρὸς); G^B: ἐν χειρὶ = ביד, *by the hand of*. Either is possible, though ביד may reflect harmonization with v. 7. OL lacks the reference to Jehu ben Hanani as the result of haplography in its *Vorlage* (אל...א[ע]ל).

Jehu: A sentence name meaning "Yhwh is he," i.e., "Yhwh (alone) is god."[5] Jehu ben Hanani is mentioned elsewhere only in 2 Chr 19:2-3; 2 Chr 20:34.

Hanani: An abbreviated form of Hananiah, "Yhwh is gracious."

against: MT (על); G^{BL}: *to* (πρὸς = אל). While the two prepositions are often interchangeable, the change to אל here might have come about as a result of the second-person address in v. 2.

Baasha: So MT, which continues with לאמר, which introduces a quotation and need not be translated. G^B lacks it, perhaps for Greek style. G^L + *king of Israel.*

2 **king designate**: The term *nāgîd* is an old passive form referring to someone who is singled out for a particular office. It may refer to one who has been designated but has not yet assumed the office or to an incumbent who holds the office, though the use of the term in the latter sense for kings is rare in the HB.[6]

with their idols: So G: ἐν τοῖς ματαίοις αὐτῶν = בהבליהם, as in vv. 13, 26; MT: *with their sins* (בחטאתם), under the influence of the use of ותחטא. הבל "vanity" in the sense of something empty or useless is used for idols in Deut 32:21 and Jeremiah (8:19; 10:8; 14:22). It occurs in this sense in the expression הבלי־שוא "false idols" in Ps 31:7 and Jonah 2:9. Outside of the present chapter it occurs in Kings only in 2 Kgs 17:15, where it refers to the ways of the surrounding nations. In 1 Kings 16, though, it is used three times (vv. 2, 13, 26) in reference to the calves at Dan and Bethel.

3 **incinerate**: Reading מבער vocalized as a *Pi'el* participle with some Hebrew mss (cf. *BHS*). For the idiom with אחרי ("after") see 1 Kgs 21:21. G^{BL}: ἐξεγείρω ("I will raise up") probably = מעיר reflecting the loss of ב. Cogan defines the verb as "light, kindle, burn, consume completely" and points out that it is commonly used in the

---

3 Miller and Hayes, *History*, 302–303.

4 Stade, *Kings*, 143 *et passim*.

5 Kittel, *Könige*, 228; Noth, *Personennamen*, 143; Fowler, *Theophoric Personal Names*, 129, 155. The abbreviation of the divine name would originally have been *yô* (cf the Assyrian *Ya'ûa*), but became *yē* by dissimilation.

6 McCarter, *I Samuel*, 178–79.

Pi'el in Deuteronomy (13:6; 17:7, 12; 19:13, 19; 21:21, 22, 24; 24:7) for eliminating evil(doers) from Israel, hence the nuance "stamp/root/sweep out."[7]

his house: So G^{BL}, OL, Syr. MT: *your house* influenced by the previous verse.

5 **are of course written**: Based on Joüon's rendering of the rhetorical question (161c): "they are written, as is well known." The formula consistently appears in a variant form in G as οὐκ ἰδοὺ ταῦτα γεγραμμένα [B]/γέγραπται [L], with "behold" (הלא הנם כתובים).

6 **Elah**: The noun means "terebinth." But as a name it is most likely a theophoric with the divine element El.[8] In 1 Kgs 4:18 it occurs uniquely with final א. It is not certain, though, that the two names have the same etymology, since they are shortened at the predicate.

in his stead: G^{BL}, OL, Syr + *in the 20th year of King Asa*. See on v. 8.

7 This verse is found at different places in G^{B} (= OG) and MT, i.e., after and before the opening line of Asa's regnal formula in v. 8. See the Diachronic Analysis.

Yhwh's word came: So MT (דבר יהוה היה). G^{BL}: ἐλάλησεν κύριος = דבר יהוה. The verb היה was lost by haplography following the divine name and then דבר was read as a verb.

Jehu son of Hanani: MT + *the prophet*. G^{B} lacks *son of* due to Greek haplography (Εἰοὺ – υἱοῦ).

against Baasha and his house: So G^{BL} (ἐπὶ ... καὶ ἐπὶ = על ... ועל). MT: ואל ... אל = *to*. MT's reading is less likely, since Jehu could not have spoken directly to all of Baasha's house.

destroyed it: G^{L} + ἐν τῷ Ασα βασιλεῖ Ιουδα, a remnant of the opening of v. 8 that was disrupted by the interpolation of v. 7. See on 16:8.

Synchronic Analysis

Length of the account

After eleven chapters covering Solomon's reign and three for those of Jeroboam and Rehoboam, the narrative pace quickens to treat seven kings (or eight, depending on Tibni's status) in the space of two chapters (15–16). This accelerated coverage is due in part to the brevity of the reigns of some of these kings—Nadab and Elah reign only two years each and Zimri a mere seven days. But Baasha's twenty-four-year reign (compare Jeroboam's 22 years) shows that there is not necessarily a correspondence between the length of a king's reign and the length of the account devoted to him. Also, the total number of years covered in chs. 15–16 is more than the number covered in chs. 1–14. It is the significance of events and characters to the narrator that determines the quantity of coverage devoted to them. Baasha, therefore, is not presented as a particularly important king despite the length of his reign and the allusion to his power and accomplishments (16:5). The only event recorded for his reign, apart from his regnal formulae (15:33-34; 16:5-6) is the denunciation of him and his house by Jehu (16:1-4). This relative neglect may reflect an effort to discredit Baasha. But then there is a great amount of space devoted to Ahab, indicating that the narrative employs different techniques for disparaging wicked kings.

---

7 Cogan, *I Kings*, 379.

8 *Noth, Personennamen*, 90.

Pace of the narrative

The quickened pace and the narrative's "staccato" treatment of kings one after another can give a sense of incoherence.[9] This sense is countered by the regnal formulae, which remind the reader that the kings are not the final word in determining or evaluating Israel's history.[10] For all their importance the kings are only part of a much larger whole. For all their power they are not ultimately in control. The staccato is also countered by two themes that play a major role in Kings: prophecy-fulfillment and the sin of Jeroboam.[11]

Baasha's sin

The sin contrasts with the theme of the promise to David in the accounts of the kings of Judah. Both are under the umbrella of prophecy and fulfilment. The two themes work together, stretching back to 2 Samuel 7 and even to Deuteronomy and its covenant theology of destruction as an inevitable consequence of apostasy. In the wake of Solomon's apostasy Jeroboam had the chance to receive a "sure house" (בית נאמן) like David's (1 Kgs 11:38), but his construction of the shrines at Dan and Bethel with their golden calves "became a sin" (12:30) to which every king of Israel would adhere. The offer of a sure house is not explicit for Baasha, but the prophecy against his house implies that it was understood. He has a chance to reverse Jeroboam's course, but instead he continues in it.

16:1-4: The oracle of Jehu ben Hanani

Although he is not called a prophet until v. 7, Jehu son of Hanani is recognized as such by the *Wortereignisformel* ("word event formula," in Heb: *the word of* YHWH *came*) in v. 1. Jehu's oracle has two parts: indictment (v. 2) and judgment (vv. 3-4). These are customarily connected with לכן (*therefore*), which is lacking here. The indictment falls into two parts describing what YHWH did for Baasha in v. 2a and Baasha's crimes against YHWH in v. 2b.[12] It begins with a causal clause, *because I raised you up*, pointing out YHWH's elevation of Baasha to kingship. This beginning recalls Ahijah's oracle to Jeroboam in 14:7-11 and suggests that Jehu is prophesying the destruction of Baasha's line as Ahijah did Jeroboam's.

16:2: "I raised you up from the dust"

The expression "raise from the dust" occurs in 1 Sam 2:8 (the "Song of Hannah") and Ps 113:7, both with the root קום (*Hip'îl*) instead of רום as here, both in poetic contexts, and both referring to the elevation of the poor (דל) and needy (אביון) to royalty.[13] Jeroboam is said to have been exalted *from the people* (14:7), suggesting that Baasha's origins were lowlier, so that his debt to YHWH is greater. The implication of the statement that YHWH made Baasha *nāgîd* is that YHWH raised Baasha to replace Jeroboam in the hope that Baasha would reverse course. But Baasha has proven to be a profound disappointment. YHWH indicts Baasha for walking in the way of Jeroboam, that is, continuing the same behavior for which Jeroboam had been replaced—this despite what happened to Jeroboam and despite what YHWH had hoped for Baasha. Such is the irony of Baasha's reign.[14]

The irony of Baasha's reign

9 Walsh, *1 Kings*, 206.
10 M. Leuchter, "Sociolinguistic and Rhetorical Implications," 131–32.
11 Cross, *Canaanite Myth*, 278–85.
12 Dietrich, *Prophetie und Geschichte*, 9–10.
13 W. Brueggemann ("From Dust to Kingship," *ZAW* 84 [1972]: 1–16) suggested that the expression is part of an enthronement formula, which he then used to interpret the creation of *'adam* from dust in Genesis 2–3. However, the expression is not found for any other king in the book of Kings.
14 Hens-Piazza, *Kings*, 155.

The sin of Jeroboam

The *sin of Jeroboam* is worship of idols at the shrines of Dan and Bethel as described in 12:26-33. Built as national sanctuaries, they were where the people of Israel, or at least its kings, went to worship. They competed with and essentially replaced Jerusalem, which had been designated by YHWH as the only place where he could be worshiped legitimately. Moreover, the calves at Dan and Bethel were idolatrous and thus sinful. By perpetuating the worship there Baasha, like Jeroboam before him, was leading the people to sin. Thus the punishment for Baasha is the same as for Jeroboam. His "house," i.e., his line will be obliterated. The metaphor is that of utter consumption by fire (מבעיר, v. 3). The pronoun is first person; it is YHWH himself who will do the burning and clear away Baasha's legacy like so much refuse. The reality involves the slaughter of Baasha's heirs and supporters, whose corpses will be left unburied for scavengers (v. 4).

16:5-6: Baasha's closing formulae

The closing regnal formulae (vv. 5-6) have implications for understanding the nature of the intended audience of Kings.[15] The source citations indicate that the book's main audience is literate or expected to be so and aware of the genre of royal chronicles. This is not the population at large but elites associated with royal and cultic institutions. The narrator seeks the assent of these readers, as is indicated by the use of a rhetorical question in the source citation: "they are written ... are they not?" The question does double duty as a citation and a referral. The invitation to check out the source is really an invitation to acknowledge the validity of the information presented in the narrative and its judgments.

The reiteration in v. 7

Verse 7 follows Baasha's closing regnal formulae in vv. 5-6 as a postscript to the account of his reign. It reiterates Jehu's denunciation in vv. 1-4, reaffirming its message and reinforcing the certainty of its threat against Baasha. Given the fast pace of the narrative, this pause for reiteration is significant. Its location between the reigns of Baasha and Elah highlights the relevance of Jehu's oracle to the whole house of Baasha.[16] It offers some new and different information beyond what is in vv. 1-4. The designation of Jehu as a prophet confirms what the reader deduces from the *Wortereignisformel* in v. 1. The reference to all the evil that Baasha did raises the suspicion that he went beyond the *sin of Jeroboam* and was worse in some ways than his predecessor. The phrase *to become like Jeroboam's house* is ambivalent. In the first instance it indicates that Baasha did not learn from Jeroboam's mistake, despite being his replacement and the instrument of his removal, but imitated Jeroboam in the commission of sin. Appropriately, therefore, it also means that Baasha's house will become like Jeroboam's in being removed from power and obliterated.

Verse 7b

And because he had destroyed it in v. 7b offers a new rationale for the condemnation of Baasha's house—namely, the violence that he perpetrated against Jeroboam's house. This seems contradictory to the implication in vv. 1-4 that as *nāgîd* he was designated by YHWH to destroy Jeroboam's line and to replace them on the throne. How can he be condemned for doing what YHWH chose him to do? The condemnation of Baasha for the blood of his revolt brings to mind Jehu ben-Nimshi, whose violence in overthrowing the Omri dynasty is denounced by Hosea (1:4-5). The Jehu alluded to by v. 7b complements the Jehu of v. 1, bookending the

---

15 Again, see Leuchter, "Sociolinguistic and Rhetorical Implications," esp. 122–24.
16 Walsh, *1 Kings*, 214.

larger account of Baasha's reign. At the same time the allusion to Jehu ben-Nimshi invites comparison of the revolt he led with that of Baasha, and the indictment in v. 7b hints at a significant contrast between the two kings. Unlike Jehu (2 Kgs 9:1-10), there is no mention of Baasha receiving a prophetic commission to lead his *coup d'etat.* His initiative and motives in demolishing Jeroboam's line are open to the criticism that v. 7b articulates. The fact that he failed to alter Jeroboam's sinful course makes the charge of unnecessary violence all the more pressing. His murderous overthrow of Jeroboam's dynasty was all for naught because he did not alter the religious occasion for it. Baasha's continuation in Jeroboam's sin shows that his motive in leading the revolt was selfish rather than righteous, so he must bear the guilt for his bloodshed. Jehu ben-Hanani informs him that his own family will be the subject of bloody slaughter of the sort that he perpetrated upon Jeroboam's house.

Diachronic Analysis

Possible sources

The account of Baasha's reign is basically a DtrH product. The information derived from the integrated king list amounts to 15:33: the name and patronymic of Baasha, his synchronism with Asa of Judah, the location of his capital at Tirzah, and the length of his reign. The information about Baasha's death and burial in Tirzah and the name of his son and successor, Elah, in 16:6 may also derive from sources, although these data were discernible from the king list, since the expression "to lie with one's forebears" refers to dynastic succession.[17] A treaty curse of non-burial probably lies behind 16:4 and its parallel in the other oracles against the northern ruling houses, but the source cannot be reconstructed. While Jehu ben Hanani's name may have been known from some previous tradition, it is also possible that DtrH simply adopted the name for his prophet based on its meaning, "YHWH is he" (= YHWH is god). There is no indication of an older story or oracle behind DtrH in 16:1-4, and the absence of any independent reference to this Jehu in the Bible recommends skepticism about his derivation from source material.[18] Thus, in contrast to 1 Kings 14, where DtrH used a previous story about the consultation of the prophet Ahijah concerning Jeroboam's sick son for the setting of the anti-dynastic oracle, no such story was evidently available for Baasha, so DtrH conveyed a version of the anti-dynastic oracle by itself.

The basis of the indictment here and in the other anti-dynastic oracles is what YHWH did for the accused, raising him up from obscurity to become king of Israel. The indictments differ slightly because circumstances differed for each

---

17 Suriano, *Politics of Dead Kings.*

18 The references to Jehu in 2 Chr 19:2-3; 20:34 are dependent on 1 Kgs 16:1-7. 2 Chr 20:34 attributes a written source of some kind to him. But the existence of an independent document written by Jehu is doubtful; the Chronicler has almost certainly taken the reference to the prophet from Kings, as suggested by his statement that Jehu's words were "taken up" (העלה) on the scroll of the kings of Israel. Cf. Wilson, *Prophecy and Society*, 191–92.

king. Thus there is no need to mention tearing the kingdom from David in the indictment against Baasha as there was for Jeroboam (14:8). Nor is the comparison of Baasha with David germane as it is for Jeroboam. It is sufficient to point out that Baasha followed in the footsteps of Jeroboam. YHWH is thus seen as directing the rise and fall of Israel's rulers (*I made you king designate*, ואתנך נגיד). This is a fundamental principle in the book of Kings and the DtrH.

Cultic centralization

YHWH's deeds on behalf of these kings bring with them the responsibility to behave according to standards articulated in Deuteronomic *tôrāh*. The imposition of these standards is anachronistic, because neither Deuteronomy nor the principle of cultic centralization existed at the time of Jeroboam or Baasha; they arose no earlier than the late seventh century. Hence, not surprisingly, both are found in violation. The purpose is etiological—to explain Israel's demise and Judah's survival beyond it. Historically, the shrines at Dan and Bethel were installations for Israel's royal cult, dedicated to the worship of the national god, YHWH. The allegation that they were illegitimate because YHWH could only be worshiped in Jerusalem betrays DtrH's southern roots. Nor were they idolatrous. DtrH calls them "vanities, useless things" (הבלים). But this is a caricature. The calves were not representations of YHWH but parts of a pedestal upon which YHWH was thought to stand or sit, even if the two were not always cleanly distinguished.[19] Ironically, then, DtrH indicts the Israelite kings for showing piety and devotion to YHWH by maintaining those shrines. He casts loyalty to the shrines on the part of Israelite kings as provocation (√כעס), a characteristic term for him (14:90; 15:30; 16:13; 21:22). DtrH ties this cultic behavior to the sequence of royal houses by assassination and overthrow in Israel in contrast to the single Davidic dynasty in Judah, and uses this as a theological explanation for the eventual destruction of the kingdom. Israel's larger fate was sealed from the start. The more its kings sought to appease YHWH through cultic service at the royal shrines, the more they provoked YHWH's anger expressed in the form of expulsion and exile.[20]

The usual announcement about YHWH cutting off every "royal member" (משתין בקיר) in the royal house (e.g., 14:10a) has no correspondence in the oracle against Baasha.[21] Still, it is clear by comparison with the other oracles that those who are threatened are the males in Baasha's family, especially those in his direct line. It was common practice in a *coup d'état* to kill the male heirs, who might seek revenge and try to restore the fallen dynasty.

The curse of non-burial

Not only will Baasha's heirs be assassinated, but their corpses will be left as food for scavenging animals. Dogs in ancient Israel were not pets but feral creatures that survived around humans by scavenging.[22] This would also have important implications for the afterlife according to Israelite conception. Without heirs to remember him or to sustain him with funerary offerings an unburied individual would fade in the underworld, as would his ancestors.

---

19 Cross, *Canaanite* Myth, 73n.

20 See D. E. Grant, *Divine Anger in the Hebrew Bible* (CBQMS 52; Washington, DC: CBA, 2014), 30–32.

21 On the meaning of משתין בקיר see the Introduction and Talmon and Fields, "Collocation."

22 O. Borowski, "Dog," *NIDB* 1 (2007), 155–56; E. Firmage, "Zoology," *ABD* 6 (1992), 1143–44.

The account of Baasha's reign closes with the standard set of DtrH regnal formulae (vv. 5-6). Included in them is the referral to a source that furnished some of the information in the account and that may be consulted for further details. The phrase ספר דברי הימים means "the scroll of the daily affairs." This is probably the integrated king list used by DtrH, which may also have incorporated some information from inscriptions and the like.[23] There is no reason to deny that DtrH had access to valid historical information, albeit mostly in secondary form. At the same time the source citations have a rhetorical function—legitimating the claims of the account—and for that reason are assigned to DtrH. 16:5-6

The main diachronic problem of the passage is v. 16:7.[24] The text-critical evidence has typically been ignored but points rather decisively to its being secondary: it is found at different places in the OG and MT, and in both cases it is intrusive; in the OG it interrupts the accession formulae of Elah; in the MT it stands between the closing formulae for Baasha and the opening formulae for Elah and thus falls "in the crack" between the regnal formulae that mark the discrete accounts of two different kings. It is effectively a doublet of vv. 1-4 in that it reiterates an indictment against Baasha. Its identification of Jehu as a prophet is a deduction based on the *Wortereignisformel* in v. 1 and the tenor of Jehu's message in vv. 1-4. Its use of the verb כעס (*Hipʿîl*) does not necessarily signal DtrH authorship but could be imitative. It is unlikely, then, that the verse is an earlier or independent version of the oracle.[25] Its language and phrasing point to a different, less skillful hand than the one responsible for vv. 1-4. It begins with וגם, as is typical of additions. The MT is awkward in its statement that Jehu spoke to (אל) Baasha and his house, that being impossible; in the OG the awkwardness is evident in the reflection of על three times in a row but in two different senses ("*about* Baasha and *about* his house *because* of all the evil").[26] The awkwardness comes from the author of v. 7 under the influence of v. 3, including Baasha's house in the audience of Jehu's oracle. The problem of 16:7

Verse 7 was added in stages. The motive for the initial addition in v. 7a may have been to clarify vv. 1-4. The idiom *work of his hands* is used with the verb כעס for idol worship in v. 7 instead of "vanities" as in v. 2 (Deut 31:29; 2 Kgs 22:17; Jer 25:6-7; 32:30.; cf. 2 Kgs 19:18; 2 Chr 32:19; Ps 115:4; 135:15; Isa 2:8; 37:19; Jer 10:9; Hos 14:4; Mic 5:12). As suggested in the Synchronic Analysis, v. 7 may offer a broadening of the indictment against Baasha to include *all the evil that he did* and the suggestion that Baasha's house would become like Jeroboam's. *To become like Jeroboam's house* is ambiguous. Does it refer to sin, i.e., Baasha's provocations of YHWH resembling Jeroboam's, or to destruction of his house because of such provocations? The other oracles against the Northern dynasties, which announce that YHWH will make a given ruling house *like the house of Jeroboam*, suggest the latter.

---

23 See the Introduction and the bibliography cited there.

24 This is where Dietrich (*Prophetie und Geschichte*, 10n), surveying the major explanations, remarks that the verse has caused a lot of headaches.

25 *Pace* H. Seebass, "Tradition und Interpretation," 190; Stade, *Kings*, 144; and Sweeney, *Kings*, 199.

26 So G^L; G^B does not reflect the third ועל, perhaps because of the awkwardness, and yields a nonsensical reading.

In the final phrase of the verse (*and because he had destroyed it*) the object pronoun אתו could refer to Jeroboam ("him") or his house ("it"). If Jeroboam, he is viewed as the personification of his house, so that the meaning is essentially the same. In either case the clause is in tension with vv. 1-4: Why should Baasha be condemned for striking Jeroboam's house if he was carrying out YHWH's threat (14:7-11)? The tension has led to the proposal that ועל be understood as adversative or concessive rather than causative: "even though/despite the fact that he smote it."[27] Seebass rightly objects to this interpretation on the grounds that it takes two identical constructions differently: "*because of* all the evil he had done ... *even though* he had smitten it."[28] If, however, the previous phrase about becoming like Jeroboam's house refers not to Baasha's sin but to the demise of his house, then the ועל cannot be concessive but is, rather, a gloss, a *Nachtrag zum Nachtrag*, as Noth put it.[29]

Synthesis

Baasha's failure

The account of Baasha's reign well illustrates DtrH's view of history as the arena of YHWH's activity. The transitions of royal houses were determined by the kings' disobedience to YHWH rather than political, social, and military factors. Moreover, they were announced beforehand by YHWH's messengers the prophets. Hence Baasha owed his royal position to YHWH's elevation of him. As king he was vested with weighty responsibility and there were severe consequences for his failure to correct Jeroboam's apostasy. Overall, his reign is a sad irony. He could have been the remedy to the sin instituted by Jeroboam; instead, he continued in that sin, adding the charge of murder to that of the sin of Jeroboam. Despite the length of his reign, which exceeds that of Jeroboam, DtrH spends less time with Baasha, offering a brief glance at what might have been, and then a sketch of the reality.

The anachronism of cultic centralization

The historical Baasha, however, would not have seen the shrines at Dan and Bethel as apostasy. Like any ancient Near Eastern king he would have regarded the maintenance of his kingdom's national shrines as piety. Failure to maintain such shrines would have been seen by people and king alike as jeopardizing the nation by inviting divine wrath upon them. The notion of centralization and the sole legitimacy of the Jerusalem temple had not yet been conceived at the time of Baasha, even in Judah. It could not really have originated before the end of the Northern Kingdom. The anachronism was irrelevant to DtrH, if he was even aware of it. It was the explanation that suggested itself to him from his observation of history

---

27 E.g., Gray, *Kings*, 361; Montgomery, *Kings*, 282, 289.

28 Seebass, "Tradition und Interpretation," 175–76. Seebass holds that the verse is not saying that the oracle comes against him even though he destroyed Jeroboam's house but that Baasha followed Jeroboam's bad example despite having destroyed his house. However, Seebass's own rendering of the final clause, "despite the fact that he had smitten it," in reference not to the reason for the judgment against Baasha but to his failure to alter Jeroboam's policies, is open to his own criticism.

29 Noth, *I Könige 1–16*, 346.

and his belief that it was directed by YHWH, as well as his subscription to the law in Deuteronomy. In spite of the brevity of the account about him, Baasha's reign is an important one in Kings because it affirms the trajectory begun by Jeroboam that will end in tragedy for Israel.

The Reigns of Elah, Zimri, and Omri (1 Kings 16:8-28)

Text

[DtrH's sources; DtrH]

16:8 In the twenty-sixth year of Asa king of Judah, Elah son of Baasha became king over Israel and reigned in Tirzah two years. 9 Zimri, commander of half of his chariotry, conspired against him while he was in Tirzah drinking himself drunk in the house of Arza who was over the house in Tirzah. 10 Zimri came in and struck him down, killing him in the twenty-seventh year of Asa king of Judah, and then reigned in his stead. 11 When he began to reign, as soon as he sat on his throne, he killed all of Baasha's house, not leaving him any royal member, including his kinsmen and friends. 12 So Zimri exterminated all of Baasha's house, according to the word that YHWH had spoken against Baasha through Jehu the prophet 13 because of all the sins of Baasha and Elah his son which they committed and made Israel commit, provoking YHWH with their idols. 14 The rest of Elah's affairs, including all that he accomplished, are of course written on the scroll of the chronicles of the kings of Israel. 15 In the twenty-seventh year of Asa king of Judah, Zimri reigned seven days in Tirzah. While the army was besieging Gibbethon, which belonged to the Philistines, 16 the troops in the camp heard it said, "Zimri has led a conspiracy and has also killed the king." So the troops made Omri, commander of the army, king over Israel on that day in the camp. 17 Then Omri and all Israel went up from Gibbethon and laid siege to Tirzah. 18 When Zimri saw that the city had been captured he came to the citadel of the king's house and burned the king's house on himself so that he died 19 because of his sin that he committed, doing what YHWH considered evil, walking in the path of Jeroboam and in his sin which he made Israel commit. 20 The rest of Zimri's affairs, including the conspiracy that he led, are of course written on the scroll of the chronicles of the kings of Israel. 21 It was then that the army became divided; half following Tibni son of Ginath intending to make him king, and half following Omri. 22 The troops following Omri defeated the troops following Tibni son of Ginath with the result that Tibni died—and Joram his brother—at that time, so that Omri became king. 23 In the thirty-first year of King Asa, Omri began to reign over Israel twelve years, six of which he reigned in Tirzah. 24 He purchased the hill of Samaria from Shemer for two talents of silver and built up the hill, naming the city he had built Samaria after Shemer, the hill's former owner. 25 Omri did what YHWH considered evil; he did more evil than all who preceded him. 26 He walked in all the way of Jeroboam the son of Nebat and in his sin which he made Israel commit, provoking Yhwh with their idols. 27 The rest of Omri's affairs, including what he accomplished and his power, are of course written on the scroll of the chronicles of the kings of Israel. 28 Omri lay down with his forebears and was buried in Samaria, and Ahab his son reigned in his stead.

Textual Notes

8 **In the twenty-sixth year of Asa king of Judah**: So MT. At the end of v. 6 G^{BL}, OL, and Syr have *in the twentieth year of King Asa*, which betrays the beginning of Elah's accession formula. The formula has been disrupted by the secondary insertion of v. 7. It is continued in v. 8 G^{BL}, but the use of the aorist ἐβασίλευσεν indicates that it is not OG. In the MT the intrusiveness of v. 7 is evinced by the placement of Jehu's judgment against Baasha after the notice of the accession of his son Elah. The Hebrew idiom with the repetition of "year" (בשנת X שנה ל) as here in the MT, is predominant, occurring this way in the MT for all Israelite kings whose synchronisms begin with בשנת except Baasha and Hoshea. On the construction, see GKC §134o; Joüon §142o. The G^{B} rendering repeats "year" only in 2 Kgs 13:1, 10 (Jehoahaz and Jehoash). The different accession year in the Greek text may also be a corruption resulting from the insertion of v. 7. It does not affect the subsequent chronology.

in Tirzah two years: So MT, according to the order with place first that is the norm for Israelite kings where both data are included (Baasha, Elah, Ahab, Jehoahaz, Jehoash, Jeroboam II, Zechariah, Pekahiah, Pekah). G^{BL} have *two years in Tirzah*. On Tirzah as the capital see on 15:33.

9 **Zimri**: So G^{BL}. MT: *his servant Zimri*. The name is comparable to that of Zimri-Lim of Mari and is probably an abbreviated or hypocoristic form with the root *ḏmr, "protection."[1] It means "Yhwh has protected." A Hebrew seal attests the full form *zmryhw*,[2] and Samaria ostracon 12 has the similar *b'lzmr*, "Baal protects."[3] G^{BL} have Ζαμβρει and Josephus Ζαμβριας reflecting the common confusion of the labials *m* and *b* and vocalization with *a* in the first syllable. The latter is probably original, MT's vocalization reflecting assimilation.

Arza: Noth regards this as an example of a Semitic animal name meaning "woodworm."[4] But a hypocoristic employing the root רצה ("to be pleased, favorably disposed toward") seems more likely.[5]

10 **in the twenty-seventh year of Asa king of Judah**: So MT. The phrase is omitted in G^{BL} in accord with its different figure for Zimri's accession in v. 15.

11 **as soon as he sat on his throne**: On the sense *as soon as* see Joüon §166l.

he killed: Reading with G^{B}: καὶ ἐπάταξεν = ויך, which is better Hebrew style than MT's perfect הכה.

---

1 F. M. Cross, Jr. and D. N. Freedman, *Early Hebrew Orthography* (New Haven: American Oriental Society, 1952), 243n; H. B. Huffmon, *Amorite Personal Names in the Mari Texts: A Structural and Lexical Study* (Baltimore: Johns Hopkins University Press, 1965), 187–88; Noth, *Personennamen*, 176; Olyan, "2 Kings 9:21—Jehu as Zimri," 203; Fowler, *Theophoric Personal Names*, 163, 343.

2 Diringer, *Le iscrizioni*, 210–12 (seal 54).

3 Diringer, *Le iscrizioni*, 25.

4 Noth, *Personennamen*, 230.

5 Cf. Gray, *I & II Kings*, 328.

not leaving ...: G^{BL} lack the rest of the verse as part of a haplography that continues into v. 12 and was occasioned by the repetition of the phrase *all of Baasha's house.*

royal member: On this rendering of משתין בקיר see the Introduction.

including his kinsmen and friends: The final word (ורעהו) appears to be singular in the MT, though it may be an instance of a plural with the *yod* omitted (GKC 91k; cf. 1 Sam 30:26; Job 42:10); in any case I read it as plural with OL, Syr, Tar and *ad sensum.* The word appears to be a title for a royal official in 2 Sam 15:37; 16:16, perhaps "best man,"[6] and that may be its sense here as well. The first *waw* in the phrase is epexegetical, "connecting an exhaustive category to a previous more general statement."[7]

12 **So Zimri exterminated the whole house of Baasha**: Lacking in G as part of the haplography in the previous verse.

against ... through: See the Note on 16:1.

Baasha: So MT. G^{BL}: *house of Baasha,* probably an expansion, although haplography occasioned by the repetition of ב is also possible.

Jehu the prophet: G^{L} + Jehu's patronymic.

13 **because of**: Reading על with G^{BL} (περὶ) for sense in preference to MT's אל.

and Elah: So G. MT: *and the sins of Elah.*

which they committed and made Israel commit: So MT: אשר חטאו ואשר החטיאו את־ישראל. G^{BL} lack חטאו ואשר because of haplography. They also reflect the singular החטיא.

provoking Yhwh: This reading is suggested by the OL, which reflects the name *Yhwh* alone but lacks the infinitive *provoking.* G^{L} has *provoking him*, but there is quite a distance between the suffix and the last occurrence of Yhwh's name. MT and G^{B} have *provoking Yhwh the god of Israel,* which seems expansionistic. On the nuance of the infinitive here, *viz., in such a way as to provoke,* cf. Joüon §124l.

with their idols: See the Note on 16:2.

14 **The rest of Elah's affairs including all that he accomplished**: So G^{B} (καὶ τὰ λοιπὰ τῶν λόγων Ηλα ἃ ἐποίησεν = ויתר דברי אלה וכל־אשר עשה) the short form of the formula, as in 2 Kgs 1:18; 14:15; 16:19; 21:25 (all MT). OL inexplicably has *Baasha* for *Elah.*

are of course written: See the Note on 16:5.

15 **In the twenty-seventh year of Asa king of Judah**: So MT. G^{B} lacks the phrase. G^{L} (= OG) has *twenty-second.* The reason for the difference is unclear, but it does not affect the subsequent chronology.

seven days: G^{B}: *seven years*, an error.

While the army was besieging: So MT, OL (*exercitus castra posuit*): והעם חנים; G^{BL}: καὶ ἡ παρεμβολὴ Ισραηλ = ומחנה ישראל = *and the camp of Israel.* Burney suggests that the G *Vorlage* came about as the result of the loss of ע, leading to המחנה, to which *Israel* was added for explanatory reasons.[8] For עם in the sense of *army* cf. 20:15; 2 Kgs 8:21; 13:7.

Gibbethon: G^{B}: *Gibeon.* See the Diachronic Analysis.

16 **the troops in the camp**: So G^{BL} (ὁ λαὸς ἐν τῇ παρεμβολῇ = העם במחנה); the repetition of העם החנים in MT is suspicious.

heard it said: Burney explains the construction here as follows: "The use of לאמר with a subj. different from that of the preceding clause is idiomatic after the verb שמע. ... The new subj. is really the *implied obj.* of the preceding וישמע, e.g., את־השמע 'the report.'"[9] He cites Gen 31:1; 1 Sam 24:10; 2 Kgs 5:6.

the king: G^{L} + *Elah.*

---

6 McCarter, *II Samuel*, 372.

7 Burney, *Notes*, 201. Similarly Talmon and Fields ("Collocation," 94–95), who call it "an inner-textual explanatory expansion" specifying the sense of משתין בקיר.

8 Burney, *Notes*, 201.

9 Burney, *Notes*, 201–202.

the troops (2): Lit.: "the people." So G^{L} (ὁ λαὸς = העם). MT: *all Israel*; G^{B}: *in Israel*, both of which make less sense and may have come in under the influence of *Israel* later in the verse.

made ... king: MT, G^{B} have the plural while G^{L}, OL reflect the singular; either is possible given the collective nature of *ʿam/Israel*.

Omri: G^{AB} inexplicably reflect *Zimri* for Omri's name here and through the rest of the chapter. The name *Omri* is unique in the Bible, and its etymology uncertain. Three main explanations have been offered:[10] (1) from √*ʿmr* not elsewhere attested in Hebrew but found in Arabic *ʿamara* "to live," and in the name Omar; Noth took it as a foreign, i.e., Arab name, but Gray posited a hypocoristic of *ʿomriyāhû* meaning "the life that Yahweh (has given);"[11] (2) from the Amorite *ḫamr-* attested in the names *Ḫamrurapi*, *Ḫamru*, *Ḫumranu* referring to pilgrim status, hence meaning "pilgrim (to the temple) of Yahweh;"[12] (3) related to Hebrew *ʿomer* "sheaf" and meaning in a derisory sense "man of the sheaf" as a complement to Tibni, "man of straw."[13] To these must be added the possibility that the name is Phoenician, based on the occurrence of the root *ʿmr* in Phoenician/Punic names.[14] The occurrence of the name in Neo-Assyrian sources in the phrase "house of Omri" (*bit Humri*) makes the third possibility unlikely. The possible foreign origin of the name has led to considerable speculation about Omri's ethnic origins (see the Diachronic Analysis).

commander of the army: without the article in Hebrew (שר צבא), perhaps indicating an official title.[15]

17 **all Israel**: MT, G: + *with him* (עמו); omit with OL.

went up: OL reflects a plural, while MT, G have the singular; either is possible.

from: So MT, G^{L}. G^{B}: εν = ב, which is nonsensical in view of the siege of Tirzah that follows.

18 **he came**: So MT, G^{L}, OL. G^{B}: *they came*.

citadel: Here and in 2 Kgs 15:25 the term ארמון refers to a specific fortified section of the palace, perhaps the king's living quarters, since elsewhere, especially in the Latter Prophets, it is used for the fortified and luxurious dwellings of kings and other elites (cf. Isa 23:13; 32:14; Jer 6:5; 9:20; 17:27; 30:18; 49:27; Hos 8:14).[16]

on himself: So G^{B}. MT, G^{L} + *with fire*.

19 **his sin**: So MT (*ketiv*). G^{B}: *his sins*. G^{L}: *the sins*. The sin is specified as the sin of Jeroboam, hence singular. G^{L}'s reading may have arisen from a dittography of the initial ח, which was then taken as the article (ה), leading to the loss of the suffix.

in his sin: So MT. G^{BL}, OL have the plural, and OL and some Greek miniscules precede with *all*.

---

10 Cf. *HALOT*, 850.

11 Noth, Personennamen, 63, 222n; Gray, *Kings*, 365. The Arabic root can have the secondary meaning of "believe," which is apparently where Šanda (*Könige* I, 401) gets the proposal "YHWH is my veneration."

12 G. Buccellati, *The Amorites of the Ur III Period* (Naples: Instituto Orientale di Napoli, 1966), 148; Huffmon, *Amorite Personal Names*, 198–99.

13 Gray, *Kings*, 365.

14 Benz, *Personal Names in the Phoenician and Punic Inscriptions*, 380; J. K. Kuan, "Was Omri a Phoenician?" in M. P. Graham, W. P. Brown, and J. K. Kuan (eds.), *History and Interpretation: Essays in Honour of John H. Hayes* (JSOTSup 173; Sheffield: Sheffield Academic Press, 1993), 234–35.

15 Joüon §137r; WO, 240.

16 Rendsburg (*Israelian Hebrew*, 44–45) argues that the word is of Northern provenance because of its predominant occurrence in Northern contexts. Compare Schniedewind and Sivan, "Test Case," esp. 303–14.

which he made Israel commit: Reading the *Hip'îl* perfect (החטיא) as reflected in G^{BL}. MT: עשה להחטיא, with which OL agrees, though it reads *the people* for *Israel* at the end.

20 **the conspiracy**: Lit. *his conspiracy*. So MT, G^{B}. G^{L}: plural.

are of course written: See the Note on 16:5.

21 **It was then that**: The particle אז with the imperfect denotes approximate time or circumstances in the past rather than signaling sequence as does אז with the perfect. It is also frequently a device for the interpolation of an independent anecdote into a standing narrative.[17]

the army: MT reads העם ישראל. The construction is ungrammatical and probably conflates two variants.

became divided: Omitting לחצי, which is not reflected in the other witnesses and is likely a dittography.

Tibni: Ostensibly "man of straw," that is, the noun תבן with a *nisbe* ending. Perhaps associated with the Phoenician name *tbnt*.[18] However, its application remains uncertain. Suggestions include a name given to a frail child, a nickname, and a short form of a longer name no longer preserved.[19]

Ginath: Apparently originally a place name meaning "enclosure," from the root גנן, that was secondarily adopted as a personal name.[20] If Cogan's identification with Beth-haggan is correct,[21] Tibni may have been from Manasseh (2 Kgs 9:27).

and half following Omri: So MT. G^{BL} repeat τοῦ λαοῦ γίνεται (*of the people was*) from earlier in the verse, but SyrH marks them as Hexaplaric. G^{L} + *to make him king*.

22 **the troops ... the troops**: So MT, G^{L}. G^{B} reflects a haplography occasioned by repetition of *the troops following* (העם אשר אחרי).

defeated: So MT (ויחזק), G^{L} (ὑπερεκράτησε); lost from G^{B} after the haplography just described when it no longer made sense. This is the only place in the HB where חזק occurs with the direct object marker את, leading to the suggestion that the latter be emended to מן or על.[22] However, the verb does occur with the objective suffix in Jer 20:7; 2 Chr 28:20, so there is no need to emend.

and Joram his brother at that time: Reading ויורם אחיו בעת ההיא based on G^{BL}. "The genuineness of this text is favoured by the fact that the additional words supply a detail unessential to the narrative, and thus not to be explained as a later invention."[23]

became king: So MT. G^{BL} + *after Tibni*. The plus shows that the OG dated Omri's accession from this point, i.e., the death of Tibni in Asa's thirty-first year (v. 23). MT dates Omri's accession from Zimri's death in Asa's twenty-seventh year (vv. 15-16). The discrepancy shows up in v. 29, where the MT dates the start of Ahab's reign to Asa's thirty-eighth year (of 41), while the OG dates Ahab's start to the second year of Asa's successor Jehoshaphat. The same discrepancy is then leveled through the witnesses such that the MT and OG contain distinct chronologies for the period from Omri to Jehu, when the deaths of the kings of Israel and Judah at essentially the same time place the chronologies on even ground again.

---

17 Rabinowitz, "'ĀZ Followed by Imperfect," 54–56. Rabinowitz's conclusions were anticipated to a large extent by J. Dus, "Gibeon—Eine Kultstätte des ŠMŠ und die Stadt des Benjaminischen Schicksals," *VT* 10 (1960): 353–74.

18 Noth, *Personennamen*, 232.

19 *HALOT*, 1686.

20 *HALOT*, 190.

21 Cogan, *I Kings*, 416.

22 *BHS*; Burney, *Notes*, 203.

23 Burney, *Notes*, 203.

23 **of King Asa**: So G^{B} (τοῦ βασιλέως Ασα = המלך אסא). MT, G^{L}: *of Asa king of Judah.* The longer reading appears to be shared also by a Hexaplaric text and by an OL text, indicating that it is a Hexaplaric reading derived from MT.[24]

six of which he reigned in Tirzah: OL has *and* before this final clause suggesting an additional six years of reign for Omri as assumed by Josephus (*Ant* 8.312).[25]

24 **the hill of Samaria**: Lit: *the hill Samaria* (את־ההר שמרון), may be appositional[26] or reflect a dittography (cf. Amos 4:1; 6:1). The modern site is Sebastiyeh, ca. seven miles NW of Shechem. Visited by repeated archaeological expeditions, the site has yielded evidence of impressive fortifications and foundations of monumental buildings with dressed masonry as well as ivory inlays and the furnishings that held them—all discoveries that correlate well with various descriptions in the Bible of Omrid Samaria as a prosperous venue, at least for elites (1 Kgs 22:39; Amos 3:15; 4:1; 6:4). The Hebrew vocalization *šōmrôn* attests the *-on* ending common on place-, especially mountain, names (Hermon, Lebanon, Zion). The rendering in other languages—Aramaic (*shamrin*), Assyrian (*samerina*), Greek (*samareia*)—attests a variant place ending (*-ain/-ên/-în*). More intriguing is the vocalization of the first syllable. The short *a* reflected in other languages indicates an original *i* in the first syllable, and there is ample evidence of clan names with this vocalization (*shimrî, shimrôn, shimrāt, shemer*).[27] *šōmrôn* would not have derived from such a name but only from a name with *ā* in the first syllable. It seems likely, therefore, that the hill was originally named after the clan that possessed it (probably Issacharite, see below). The name *šōmrôn* was either an ancient alternate (Judg 10:1 has *šāmîr* perhaps in reference to the same place) or a later development introducing the designation "hill of watching," i.e., observation point.[28] The hill of Samaria, though isolated, is "not distinguished by its elevation"[29] and does not stand as high as some of the other nearby hills. Nor is there evidence that it was strongly fortified before the time of Omri, as one would expect for a site known as a "guardian" (*šōmēr*). Another possibility is that the first *ō* may be assimilation to the second one.

from Shemer: So MT (מאת שמר). G^{BL}, SyrH (sub ÷) + *the owner of the hill.* The name *Shemer* is likely an etiological explanation of the name Samaria, perhaps influenced by the name Shimrîn/Shimron of an Issacharite clan in the vicinity (Gen 46:13; Num 26:24; 1 Chr 7:1). See the Diachronic Analysis.

for two talents: This is an example of the *beth pretii* used to express exchange or purchase.[30] The vocalization of בככרים is what Joüon (§91b) calls a *lectio mixta*—written as a dual but vocalized as a construct form (*kikk^{e}rayim* < *kikk^{e}rê*) instead of *kikkārayim*;[31] in the latter case *silver* would be in apposition or an accusative. A talent was equal to 3000 shekels, in the neighborhood of 34 kg or approximately seventy-five pounds.

naming ... built: G^{B} has plurals.

the city: So MT (העיר). G: *the hill* = ההר, perhaps under the influence of the three other occurrences of the word in this verse.

26 **in his sin**: So MT (*qere'*). G, MT (*ketiv*): *in his sins.* OL: + *which he sinned against the Lord.* See the Notes on 15:34; 16:19.

---

24 Hendel ("Two Editions," n. 10), citing P. Torijano.

25 The system of references used for citing Josephus in this commentary is that of the Loeb Classical Library (LCL).

26 Cogan, *I Kings*, 417.

27 Stade, *Kings*, 166–67.

28 Galling, *BRL*, 437; Würthwein, *1. Könige 1–16*, 199.

29 Miller and Hayes, *History*, 303.

30 GKC §119p; Joüon §132c; WO, 197.

31 Joüon §91b.

which he made Israel commit: See the Note on 15:34.

Yahweh: So OL. MT, G^{L} + *god of Israel*. G^{B} lacks the reference to YHWH, leaving the infinitive *provoke* without an object.

their idols: G^{L} reflects a singular suffix: *his idols*. On the term הבלים as a reference to idols, see the Note on 16:2.

27 **including what he accomplished and his power**: Reading ואשר עשה וגבורתו. The *waw* before אשר matches 16:5. MT lacks *all*, which is an expansion in G^{BL}. G^{L} and OL have plurals for *power*, apparently referring to acts of power. MT repeats אשר עשה after וגבורתו, a dittography that is to be omitted with G^{BL}.

are of course written: See the Notes on 16:5, 14.

28 **Ahab**: See the Note on 16:29.

At the end of 16:28 G^{BL} have a lengthy plus that is equivalent to MT 22:41-51, where it is treated.

Synchronic Analysis

The rapid pace of the narrative

The quickened pace of the narrative in this chapter is especially evident in the present pericope where four kings are treated in addition to a lengthy civil war. The kings receive roughly the same depth of treatment, relegating them to the same level of importance. Thus while Zimri and Omri are opposites in overall significance in the book of Kings, the same number of verses is devoted to each of them. The pace leaves the impression that the narrative is in a hurry to get somewhere with the story and that Israel is in an uncontrolled downward spiral. Ahab will halt the spiral but not its downward direction.

16:8-14: Elah's ineptness and overthrow

The account of Elah (vv. 8-14) lacks the usual evaluation in his opening regnal formulae. The account is cut short, as is his reign, by Zimri. The glimpse of Elah in v. 9 is of an ineffective king with no redeeming personal qualities. Elah reigns just long enough for his subjects to see what kind of king he will be and to prove his incompetence. His two years invite comparison with Nadab's similar tenure (15:25). Elah's ineptness is suggested by his army besieging (still? again?) the city where his father Baasha led the *coup* that brought him to power (15:27). Instead of leading the attack Elah stays behind and proceeds to drink himself drunk (v. 9). He is out of touch not only with his military but also with his staff; his chief steward is the one getting him drunk and is evidently involved in, perhaps even the architect of, the assassination. Elah's drinking is like Ben-Hadad's in 20:12, 16 and similarly leads to his defeat. Elah makes himself an easy target for assassination—by his own chariot commander, Zimri. The description of the conspiracy and assassination is similar to that of Baasha's conspiracy against Nadab in 15:27-28: "What goes around comes around." The reader is not drawn to either individual. Elah is an inept fool, Zimri an opportunistic assassin. The resulting impression is one of chaos and instability.

The narrative's primary concern is the fulfillment of prophecy. Zimri's first act as king is to exterminate Baasha's line (v. 11) in fulfillment of Jehu's oracle (vv. 1-4). The sin of Jeroboam is not mentioned but is implied by the similarity of language between vv. 2 and 13, particularly *causing Israel to sin* and *provoking* YHWH *with idols*. The same terminology, except for *idols*, occurs in the explanation of Baasha's annihilation of Jeroboam's house (15:30). This and the other parallels with Jeroboam's house highlight the efficacy of the message of YHWH's prophets as exhibited in fulfillments.[32] The fate of Baasha's house is the same as that of Jeroboam's and is also brought about by adherence to Jeroboam's sin.

Elah's similarity to Nadab

As with the evaluation formula and in parallel to Nadab (15:31), the usual notices about death, burial, and successor are missing from Elah's closing regnal formulae in 16:13-14. Not only is this a sign of disrespect, it is also in line with the oracle against Baasha's house. Elah, and the other male members of that house, like Nadab of Jeroboam's line, were not buried because their corpses were left to be eaten by dogs and birds according to prophetic prediction.

16:15-16: Zimri's reign

It is indicative of Zimri's poor character and reputation that when word of the overthrow reaches the troops besieging Gibbethon they declare their own commander, Omri, king rather than following Zimri (v. 16). This further suggests the futility of Zimri's revolt and the accompanying bloodshed. Zimri's kingship was never undisputed; he was never king over "all Israel." Indeed, *all Israel* made Omri king, so that he emerged as the final victor. He is the first king since Jeroboam to have popular support and the first king of Israel to found a real dynasty beyond the probationary first years of his successor.[33]

16:17-20: Zimri's end

With the army at his command, Omri marches on Tirzah and besieges it (vv. 17-19). The brevity of Zimri's seven-day reign means that the city falls almost immediately. His support is minimal. Isolated and without hope of escape, he holes up in the king's residence and sets it on fire. Even his means of suicide is self-centered—if he can't have the palace, no one will. The real cause of his death, though, is the *sin of Jeroboam* (v. 19). This is formulaic, yet the charge of sin is real. Zimri's week was enough to see that he would stay on the idolatrous path begun by Jeroboam. In only seven days and without any real following, Zimri still succeeded in causing Israel to sin. The absence of a burial notice in Zimri's closing regnal formulae (v. 20) is fitting for a man whose tribal affiliation, father's name, and the like are undisclosed. He is a blip on the screen of Israel's story. His only legacy is treason, for which his name becomes synonymous (2 Kgs 9:31).

16:21-22: The Tibni interlude

Mystery also surrounds Tibni's appearance and role. It is not clear whether his rivalry with Omri took place before or after Zimri's reign. The position of vv. 21-22 suggest that they were after, but the insistence that *all Israel* made Omri king (v. 16) and the use of אז with the imperfect may mean that he defeated Tibni before Zimri claimed power.[34] Nothing is known of Tibni beyond his patronymic—not where he came from, what position he held, or even his manner of death. Nor is it clear whether he actually became king. The statement in v. 21 that half of the people followed him *to make him king* is ambiguous. Does it express intent and imply failure: they wanted to make him king (but failed to do so)? Even if they succeeded, it was still only half of the people, and the weaker half at that. There are no regnal formulae for Tibni. For all the success that half of the people implies, Tibni does not attain even Zimri's position of being king unambiguously. His name, "man of straw," alludes to failure.

32 DeVries, (*1 Kings*, 197) notes that the narrative "accentuate[s] the parallelism between Jeroboam-Nadab and Baasha-Elah."

33 Walsh, *1 Kings*, 216.

34 Rabinowitz, "'ĀZ Followed by Imperfect," 54–56.

16:23-28: Omri's reign

The lack of clarity about whether Tibni was considered king contrasts with Omri, who achieves kingship two or three times in the narrative. He is made king by the army and *all Israel* in v. 16, and his accession formula is given in v. 23. In v. 21 the other half of the people who do not support Tibni favor Omri. Omri's success is unambiguous. In answer to the question raised by v. 23b about where Omri's capital was after Tirzah (and especially Zimri's burning of the palace),[35] v. 24 describes his move to Samaria. For a reader familiar with geography and the trade routes the shift in capital to Samaria signals increased intercourse with the Phoenicians and forebodes Jezebel's advent.[36] This may explain another non-formulaic element of Omri's account—the notice that he did more evil than his predecessors (v. 25b). The reasons for this notice are otherwise unstated. The offenses named in v. 26, committing *the sin of Jeroboam* and *provoking* Yhwh *with idols*, are identical to those of Baasha and Elah (15:33; 16:2b, 13), so it is not clear what Omri did that was worse. Perhaps the treaty with Phoenicia, which led to Ahab's marriage to Jezebel, was Omri's doing, though the text does not say this, and Ahab is blamed in v. 31. Maybe it is just that Omri was Ahab's father and the founder of Israel's most important dynasty. There is a grudging admission of his greatness as king in the mention of his *power* in v. 27.[37] Since all the kings of Israel were evil, and Omri was the founder of the most prominent dynasty and father of the worst king, he must have been worse than his predecessors.

Diachronic Analysis

This passage is DtrH's composition based on sources and traditions available to him. The recognition of source material in v. 8 shows it to have been an integrated list, perhaps with other details, of the kings of Israel and Judah. That is, the kings of one kingdom are already dated by the reigns of their counterparts in the other kingdom.

16:8: Absence of evaluation

There may already have been some discontent with Baasha's policies, and when Elah showed his intent to follow in his father's footsteps discontent led to conspiracy.[38] The usual negative evaluation that one expects to find after v. 8 is lacking for Elah—not because he is judged righteous; it is clear from v. 13 that he was considered an evildoer like his father and every other king of Israel—but

35 Walsh, *1 Kings*, 217.

36 Tirzah was slightly farther east and more oriented toward the Transjordan, while Samaria was oriented more toward the Mediterranean and Phoenicia.

37 Walsh (*1 Kings*, 217) points to the credit Omri receives for reigning during the war with Tibni and to the absence of any mention of violent deaths during his reign—Omri's own or anyone else's—as indications of stability. The fact that he has leisure and resources to build Samaria is another grudging recognition of his regnal success.

38 The actual length of Elah's reign could theoretically have been less than a calendar year if antedating was being practiced and he received credit for a full year for the time before his first New Year. Since Zechariah is said to have reigned 6 months (2 Kgs 15:8) it is a fair assumption that Elah occupied the throne longer, presumably at least one full calendar year.

perhaps as a way of implying Elah's overall insignificance: he is so incidental that he does not merit a word of evaluation. Still, Zimri, who reigns only seven days, has a full evaluation. DtrH may be suggesting that Elah was merely an extension of his father and did not require an independent evaluation. The absence of an evaluation could also be due to oversight or accidental loss.

16:9-10: Zimri's conspiracy

The account of Zimri's *coup d'état* in vv. 9-10 follows a pattern used to report such episodes, consisting of (1) a notice of conspiracy (קשר) identifying the conspirator (v. 9); (2) a statement that the conspirator struck down (נכה) and killed (מות) the king (v. 10a); and (3) the statement that the conspirator reigned in the former king's place (v. 10b). There is variation especially in the first element (15:27-28; 2 Kgs 15:14, 25, 30). The motive for Zimri's conspiracy is not explained. It may have been driven by Elah's (and Baasha's?) military ineffectiveness against the Philistines and against Judah.[39] Elah's army was besieging the Philistine city of Gibbethon (v. 15), where his father assassinated Nadab (15:27), implying that Israel had lost ground under Elah. Of course, one should not discount Zimri's personal ambition. The conspiracy seems to have been a relatively limited affair. No one besides Zimri is mentioned as having a part in it, although Arza, in whose home Elah was killed, is suspect. The exact nature of Arza's position (*who was over the house*) remains elusive, in part because of the ambiguity of the term "house." The duties might have been limited to the palace or included all the royal estates in Tirzah and perhaps beyond. In either case the position is best considered that of a "chief steward."[40] Zimri may have taken leave of his post in Gibbethon to return to Tirzah, or his part of the chariot force may have been stationed near Tirzah.[41] Taking advantage of the absence of the rest of the army, he used his military position to gain access to the king,[42] who was vulnerable due to inebriation, and murdered him. What role Arza may have played is not spelled out.

16:11-13: Zimri's coup

Using the soldiers under his command in Tirzah, Zimri exterminates Baasha's line as his first royal act—at least according to DtrH's presentation (vv. 11-13). The phrase *when he sat on his throne* in v. 11 has sometimes been seen as a gloss on the grounds that it is superfluous, especially in comparison with 15:29, where *when he began to reign* (במלכו) stands alone.[43] On the other hand, the stress on the immediacy of Zimri's deed makes sense here. Yhwh's word through Jehu in vv. 1-4 was fulfilled even in Zimri's very brief reign, in accord with DtrH's themes of prophecy-fulfillment and punishment for the *sin of Jeroboam*. Obliteration of the previous royal house solidified the usurper's hold on the throne. In this case, though, ideological theme supersedes historical fact, since Zimri was otherwise occupied and did not have the time or resources to track down and dispatch each and every one of Elah's *kinsmen and friends*.[44] This collocation is unique among

39 Cogan, *I Kings*, 410; Jones, *Kings*, 292; Sweeney, *Kings*, 200.

40 See Fox, *In the Service of the* King, 81–96; Eph'al-Jaruzelska, "Officialdom and Society." The title occurs elsewhere in 1 Kgs 4:5; 18:3; 2 Kgs 10:5; 15:5; 18:18, 37; 19:2. Cf. also Gen 39:4-5; 44:1, 4; *COS* 2.54.

41 Wiseman (*Kings*, 171) suggests that half of the chariot force was in Megiddo and half near Tirzah, based on the identification of Megiddo as a chariot city.

42 Würthwein, *1. Könige 1–16*, 195.

43 Benzinger, *Könige*, 102; Noth, *I. Könige 1–16*, 348.

44 Walsh *1 Kings*, 216n.

the anti-dynastic oracles and fulfillments. Those assassinated were the males in the royal household who were threats as potential rulers and avengers of the assassinated king. While the focus was on the direct heirs of the king who might succeed him, other family members and supporters who could pose a threat to the usurper were no doubt executed as well. This is especially true of the "kinsman" or "redeemer" (*gō'ēl*) whose duty it was to avenge the deaths of family members.[45] Thus *kinsmen and friends* may be equivalent to עצור ועזוב, the more common expression in the anti-dynastic oracles (1 Kgs 14:10; 21:21; 2 Kgs 9:8; cf. 14:26), which probably refers to leaders.[46] *Kinsmen and friends* expresses inclusiveness in relation to the royal household—i.e., both those affiliated by blood and those who were dignitaries and supporters. What was a standard political expediency for securing power is, in DtrH's presentation, the prophetic word of Yhwh coming to fruition. It was part of a larger tragic pattern in Israel effected by one man whose sin led his people astray and was reiterated until it brought the nation to an end. Jeroboam's name is not present, but the terminology and the repeated prophecy-fulfillment scheme keep the finger pointed at him.

Zimri's isolation from the army as a whole is apparent from their reaction to the news that he has initiated a *putsch* (v. 16). They do not rally to his support but instead declare their own commander, Omri, king. This could reflect a division between the chariotry, the smaller and more elite segment of the military consisting of professional soldiers, and the larger, non-professional עם. It is the first of three references to Omri being made king (vv. 22, 23). The repetition results from the unusual historical circumstances that brought Omri to power through a protracted civil war.

"All Israel" in 16:16-17

Commentators have puzzled over the statement in v. 16 MT that "all Israel" made Omri king. While text-critical analysis suggests that "all Israel" is not the best reading here, the phrase occurs in v. 17. A variety of explanations have been offered: it is a term for Israel's fighting force;[47] it means the tribal assembly as in ch. 12;[48] it portends Omri as the first king since Jeroboam to have popular support and the first to found a real dynasty;[49] it refers to the unanimity of the force in Gibbethon in contrast to the division in Israel as a whole (v. 21).[50] There is something of value in all of these explanations. "All Israel" does refer to the unanimity of the fighting force under Omri's command, also known as the עם, "people." It is the term for the popular "army" or "troops," in contrast to the professional soldiers in the chariotry commanded in part by Zimri. The עם probably consisted of landowning citizens with a military obligation and political entitlement.[51] In that sense it constituted the popular assembly and represented the nation as a whole. In refusing to recognize Zimri as king and rallying instead behind their own general, Omri, the "people" may have been drawing on a tradition asserting their

---

45 Cogan, *I Kings*, 412.

46 Talmon and Fields, "Collocation, 94."

47 Cogan, *I Kings*, 413.

48 Provan, *Kings*, 129.

49 Walsh, *1 Kings*, 216.

50 Würthwein, *1. Könige 1–16*, 197.

51 Buis, *Rois*, 135; Würthwein *1. Könige 1–16*, 196.

right to choose the king (2 Sam 2:4; 5:3; 1 Kings 12). In any case, Zimri's reign was recognized only in Tirzah, and apparently tepidly there.

Gibbethon (v. 17) is usually identified with Tell el-Melat, ca. three miles west of Gezer on the boundary between Israelite and Philistine territory. Baasha probably defeated the Philistines at the beginning of his reign (1 Kgs 15:27), and they then revolted when he died, forcing Elah to repeat the siege.[52] Nothing is said about Omri's origins except that he was "commander of the army" at Gibbethon. The possible foreign origin of the name (see the Note on v. 16) has fostered speculation about his ethnicity. Gray and Würthwein raise the possibility that Omri was a foreign mercenary, though both admit that it would have been irregular for the army to choose a non-Israelite as king.[53] Würthwein suggests that Omri's ethnicity was an issue behind the war with Tibni and that Omri overcame this liability by virtue of his forceful personality. Gray posits that Omri's family was Canaanite and had been absorbed within Israel. He also suggests that the family came from Jezreel, thus accounting for Ahab's interest in that city.[54] Kuan posits a Phoenician origin.[55] These conjectures, though, make too much of Omri's name. If, as Gray proposes, Omri is an abbreviated Yahwistic name he may not have been foreign at all. First Chronicles 7:1-3, which refers to Shimron as one of the main clans of Issachar, and 1 Chr 27:18, which mentions an Omri from Issachar, might indicate that King Omri was from this tribe,[56] and this in turn could account for the Omrid interest in both Samaria and Jezreel.[57]

Omri's origins

Zimri's seven days as king mean that he had virtually no military support within Tirzah, which was captured almost immediately (v. 18). He fled to the citadel, the best fortified portion of the city and probably the place where the king's residence was. It is possible that the citadel was burned in the course of the assault on the city. The narrative attributes the fire to Zimri, but his isolation suggests there were no eyewitnesses. It is unlikely that this is seen as a heroic end.[58] Zimri is hardly treated as a hero. He was probably motivated by the desire to avoid capture and torture ahead of execution.

16:18: Zimri's death

52 It is highly unlikely that the siege launched by Baasha had continued for the 24 years of his reign. *Pace* Sweeney, *Kings*, 202. DtrH may have reused the name of Gibbethon because he had no concrete information about where Elah's army was camped (Fritz, *Kings*, 176.).

53 Gray, *Kings*, 364; Würthwein, *1. Könige 1–16*, 197.

54 Cf. also Buis, *Rois*, 135.

55 Kuan, "Was Omri a Phoenician?"

56 The Issacharite origin of Omri was posited by Šanda (*Könige* I, 402–403) based on the connection with Jezreel. See also B. Mazar, "The House of Omri," *EI* 20 (1989) 215–19 (Hebrew), followed by Cogan, *I Kings*, 416. Caution is in order here, though, in view of the striking similarity between the list of the sons of Issachar in Gen 46:13; Num 26:23-24; 1 Chr 7:1 and the notice about Tola in Judg 10:1. The genealogy may have been created from the wording in Judg 10:1 or that verse might have been phrased so as to pun on the names in the genealogy. See Klein, *1 Chronicles*, 218; S. L. McKenzie, *1-2 Chronicles* (AOTC; Nashville: Abingdon, 2004), 97.

57 See L. E. Stager, "Shemer's Estate," *BASOR* 277–78 (1990), 103–104.

58 *Pace* Cogan (*I Kings*, 413), citing the legend of Sin-shar-ishkun, the last king of Assyria, who perished in the fire of Nineveh rather than fall into the hands of invaders.

16:19: Zimri's guilt in DtrH's scheme

The explanation that Zimri died because of his sins and the sin of Jeroboam (v. 19) has been thought peculiar because of the brevity of his reign. It is not an evaluation of his overall life since it occurs as part of the formulae evaluating his reign.[59] It is seen as a later addition by some scholars.[60] However, there is no real reason to deny it to DtrH, as it fits with his theme. From a strictly historical perspective Zimri's seven-day rule was insufficient time for him to do a great deal of evil. But we have already seen how DtrH overrides historical considerations for his theological program and his prophecy-fulfillment scheme (vv. 11-12). *L'automatisme des formules l'emporte sur la vraisemblance historique!*[61] The shrines at Dan and Bethel continued to operate during Zimri's reign, so that he is considered as guilty of following Jeroboam's lead as every other king of Israel.

16:20: Missing burial notice

The absence of a burial notice does double duty in the account of Zimri's reign. The fire left no remains to be buried, and this fits nicely with the curse of non-burial leveled against each of the royal houses, even though there is no prophecy specifically against Zimri's house because of the brevity of his reign. The absence of a burial notice also showed disrespect. There was no memorial for Zimri or tomb to bring his name to remembrance. In this way he resembled Nadab and Elah. The story that disparages them is, ironically, the only thing that keeps their memory alive.

16:21-22: The Tibni interregnum

Verses 21-22 form a distinct unit, as indicated by their introduction with *'az* plus imperfect, their framing with *pĕtûḥôt*, and their location between the regnal formulae of Zimri (v. 20) and Omri (v. 23).[62] This last feature means that they lie outside the DtrH structural framework, yet the discrepancy between the twenty-seventh and thirty-first year of Asa in vv. 15 and 23 shows that DtrH was aware of the gap caused by Tibni's insurgence and must have incorporated the anecdote about him. Thus DtrH presents Tibni's insurgence as a true interregnum, one that led to different interpretations of the chronology for the Omri dynasty.[63] There is no background information for Tibni aside from his patronymic, nor are the details about his death supplied. There is more information about Zimri's seven-day reign than about Tibni's five-year struggle for power. This paucity of information has occasioned a good bit of speculation about the circumstances of these events. Some have guessed that Tibni was an ally or supporter of Zimri.[64] Aside from the depiction of Tibni as having more support than Zimri, this proposal may be ruled out by the אז-plus-imperfect construction in v. 21, which indicates that Tibni's war with Omri took place before Zimri's rise.[65] The most influential theory sees Tibni as the last king chosen by popular assembly, while Omri was supported by the professional army and mercenaries, a watershed moment in Israel's socio-

---

59 *Pace* House, *Kings*, 201.

60 From a later Dtr redactor (Jones, *1 Kings 1–16:34*, 294) or imitator (Noth, *I. Könige 1–16*, 349–50).

61 Buis, *Rois*, 135. "The automatic nature of the formula prevails over historical probability."

62 Rabinowitz, "'*ĀZ* Followed by Imperfect," 54–56; Trebolle, "Division Markers," esp. 208.

63 Hendel, "Two Editions." See the discussion of Chronology in the Introduction.

64 Benzinger, *Könige*, 103; Sweeney, *Kings*, 202.

65 Rabinowitz, "'*ĀZ* Followed by Imperfect," 54–56.

political history.[66] However, vv. 21-22 are not clear about the exact makeup of the constituencies of Omri and Tibni or the means by which the latter was chosen. The עם, probably the non-professional army, is divided. More serious, the ascription of professional troops to Omri and the popular militia to Tibni reverses what appears to be the situation in v. 16, where Omri receives the support of the עם over against Zimri and the chariotry. It is just as possible that the division between Omri and Tibni arose from tribal disputes, personal rivalry, or the like.[67] The absence of regnal formulae for Tibni suggests that DtrH did not regard him as a king but as an interloper who ultimately failed. Yet the five-year gap between vv. 15 and 23 leaves the question of Tibni's status open. The Greek chronology, which does treat Tibni as a king (*after Tibni*, v. 22) reflects an attempt to correct and clarify.[68]

Omri's historical significance

Omri was arguably the most important king in Israel's history. His significance is indicated by archaeological evidence of extensive building activity on large public structures especially in Samaria, Jezreel, Megiddo, and Hazor.[69] It is further attested by references to Omri and his dynasty in contemporary ancient Near Eastern texts. Israel comes to be known as the "house of Omri" in Neo-Assyrian inscriptions until the end of its existence as a kingdom.[70] Additionally, according to the Mesha stela Omri subjugated Moab (*ANET* 320–21; *COS* 2.23). He or Ahab

---

66 J. A. Soggin, *Königtum in Israel: Ursprünge, Spannungen, Entwicklung* (BZAW 104; Berlin/New York: de Gruyter, 1967), esp. 98–99; idem, "Tibni, King of Israel in the First Half of the 9th Century B.C.," in *Old Testament and Oriental Studies* (BibOr 29; Rome: Biblical Institute Press, 1975), 50–55. Soggin ("Tibni," 52) suspected that there had been a systematic effort to suppress information about Tibni because of the paucity of details in MT and the OG's mention of Tibni's brother Joram without further specifics. The likelihood of the two men dying of natural causes at the same time in the midst of a *putsch* seems negligible. Josephus (*Ant* 8.311) believed they were assassinated. But since DtrH readily reports assassination as part of his own agenda and since he has no interest in protecting Omri, it is unlikely that he would have suppressed any information about the assassination of Tibni that came to him. Miller's proposal ("So Tibni Died" [1 Kings xvi.22]," *VT* 18 [1968] 392–94) that Tibni's "death" refers to the loss of royal authority suffers not only from the criticism that the Hittite parallels he cites are from an earlier period and not the identical expression but also from a consideration of the fact that assassination was the typical practice in such power struggles. See Würthwein, *1. Könige 1-16*, 198.

67 See G. Buccellati, *Cities and Nations of Ancient Syria: An Essay on Political Institutions with Special Reference to the Israelite Kingdom* (Studi Semitici 26; Rome: Instituto di studi del vicino oriente, 1967), 232; Cogan, *I Kings*, 418.

68 DtrH's handling of the event is unusual, though contextually plausible, as Hendel ("Two Editions," 104) observed. On vv. 21-23 and the MT and OG chronologies, see the Introduction.

69 See Miller and Hayes, *History*, 295 and their bibliography on p. 326.

70 For a general discussion see Miller and Hayes (*History*, 291–94, 303–11) and Frevel (*Geschichte Israels*, 194-202). R. E. Tappy (*The Archaeology of Israelite Samaria. Vol. 2. The Eighth Century BCE* [HSS 50; Winona Lake, IN: Eisenbrauns, 2001], 601–11) provides a comprehensive list of Neo-Assyrian references, samples of which are translated in *ANET* 280–81, 284–85 and *COS* 2.113F.

also appears to have made a vassal of Judah.[71] They also took back territory previously lost to Aram Damascus[72] before joining Aram in opposition to the Assyrians. His reign, together with Ahab's, marked the zenith of the kingdom of Israel.[73]

16:23-28: Omri's reign

Given his historical importance, the account of Omri's reign is remarkably brief. The six verses devoted to it (vv. 23-28) consist of regnal formulae with two exceptions—the notice of his purchase and construction of Samaria (v. 24) and the extension of his evaluation to state that he did more evil than all his predecessors (v. 25b). The reason for the condemnation of Omri as worse than his predecessors (v. 25b) is unclear, since the named offenses (v. 26) are identical to those of Baasha and Elah (15:33; 16:2b, 13). Perhaps it was driven by Omri's identity as the founder of the dynasty that included Ahab. Since Ahab was the worst king of Israel, Omri, who founded the dynasty, must have been nearly as bad. There is a backhanded compliment here. Omri and Ahab set the high mark for Israel's international status and power; there must be something bad about Israelite kings with so many links to other nations. The evaluation also betrays a political agenda. Denouncing the wealth, power, and international prestige of the most important Northern kings through a religious assessment makes the smaller, weaker Judah appear more on a par with Israel.[74]

16:24: The placement of the notice about Samaria

The notice about Samaria in v. 24 interrupts the usual arrangement of the regnal formulae in which the evaluation of a king immediately follows his chronological data. Additional information normally follows the end of the opening regnal formulae (v. 26). However, the burial notice in v. 28 presupposes Omri's acquisition of Samaria, precluding the possibility that v. 24 is post-Dtr. The Deuteronomist evidently viewed v. 24 as a continuation of the matter of the location of Omri's capital raised in v. 23 and so did not consider it new information *per se* but an extension of the notice concerning where Omri reigned.

Alt's theory of personal union

Omri's purchase of Samaria (v. 24) has been of pivotal significance in the discussion of state formation in Israel and in the interpretation of the archaeology of the site of Samaria. Alt proposed that, like David's Jerusalem, Samaria was the property of the crown, unaffiliated with any tribe and politically neutral.[75] This was part of a larger agenda involving Alt's view of state formation in Syria-Palestine. He believed that Omri, following David's model, acquired Samaria as his personal property in order to set up a dynastic monarchy in contrast to the charis-

71 So Miller and Hayes (*History*, 304), based on the following considerations: (1) Jehoshaphat placed his army at Ahab's disposal (1 Kgs 22:4); (2) Jehoshaphat's peace treaty (1 Kgs 16:28c; 22:45) with Israel could be a way of expressing submission; (3) Akkadian sources do not mention Judah as a separate kingdom until Tiglath-Pileser III, suggesting that Israel controlled diplomacy for Judah. Similarly Frevel, *Geschichte Israels*, 193.

72 Miller and Hayes, *History*, 306, based on a comparison of 1 Kgs 15:20 and the Tel Dan inscription, the former mentioning the capture of Israelite lands by Ben-Hadad I, the latter referring to renewed Israelite activity in these areas, indicating that Israel had recaptured them in the meantime.

73 Miller and Hayes, *History*, 300. Frevel (*Geschichte Israels*, 193) describes the Omrid period as the actual origin of Israel as a nation-state.

74 So G. N. Knoppers, personal communication.

75 A. Alt, "Die Stadtstaat Samaria," in *Kleine Schriften zur Geschichte des Volkes Israel* (Vol. 3; Munich: Beck, 1959), 258–302.

matic tradition that had existed in Israel before him. He then held the city-state of Samaria and the kingdom of Israel together by "personal union" as David had done with Jerusalem, Judah, and Israel previously. Alt's views were rebuffed by Buccellati, who pointed *inter alia* to evidence in the biblical account for the principle of dynastic succession being assumed before Omri.[76] Still, recent commentaries continue to assert that Omri acquired Samaria as personal property that was politically neutral.[77] But without the theoretical underpinning in the notion that Israel's monarchy was not dynastic there is no reason to view Samaria as anything other than the capital of the kingdom.

Advantages of Samaria

The choice of Samaria as a capital was a good one for reasons of both political and military strategy. Centrally located and eminently defensible by virtue of its isolation from the surrounding terrain,[78] it was relatively close to the Mediterranean coast and the main commercial route between Egypt and Phoenicia. It sat upon both the best east-west route between the Mediterranean and the interior and the best north-south route connecting Shechem with the Jezreel Valley and access to the Transjordan, Damascus, and beyond. The move to Samaria from Tirzah represented a shift in orientation for Omri and his dynasty. The trade advantages offered by Samaria and its greater orientation toward the Mediterranean and Phoenicia were exploited by Omri and Ahab and helped to account for the prosperity of their reigns. Phoenician influence is apparent in the archaeological discoveries at Samaria, especially the style of the dressed ashlar blocks and the motifs on ivory plaques.

Omri's purchase of Samaria

Major excavations were conducted at Samaria in 1908–1910 and again in the early 1930s. On the basis particularly of the latter expedition Kenyon concluded that there was an occupational gap between the Early Bronze Age and its Iron Age II settlement under Omri.[79] She thus understood 16:24 to mean that the site purchased by Omri was previously uninhabited. The evidence has recently been reinterpreted, however, as indicating the presence of a significant oilery from the Iron I period that must have belonged to an extended family or clan.[80] The value of the site is reflected in the high price that Omri paid for it.[81] An alternate and probably older form of the name Samaria probably derives from a clan known as "Shimrîn" or the like (see the Note). Hence there may be something to v. 24's account of how Omri acquired the hill of "Samaria," although the name Shemer is a secondary etiology. Since Omri bought the site and did not originate from there, his ancestors would not have been buried there, making clear that *lay down with his forebears* (v. 28) was not a euphemism for burial.

---

76 Buccellati, *Cities and Nations*, esp. 200–208; cf. also Ishida, *Royal Dynasties*, esp. 171–82.

77 E.g., Brueggemann, *Kings*, 200–201; Sweeney, *Kings*, 204; Walsh, *1 Kings*, 217–18.

78 Long (*Kings*, 199) points out that Samaria successfully resisted sieges according to 1 Kgs 20; 2 Kgs 6:24–7:20 until its walls were breached by the Assyrians, after a three-year assault, in 721 BCE.

79 K. M. Kenyon, *The Royal Cities of the Old Testament* (London: Barrie & Jenkins, 1971), 71–73.

80 Stager, "Shemer's Estate;" R. E. Tappy, *The Archaeology of Israelite Samaria*. Vol. 1. *Early Iron Age through the Ninth Century BCE* (HSS 44; Atlanta: Scholars Press, 1992); "Samaria," *NIDB* 5 (2009), 63.

81 Stager, "Shemer's Estate," 103 and n. 7.

Synthesis

DtrH's ideological presentation of history

There may be no better example of the ideological nature of Kings' presentation of history than the present passage. Despite the great difference between them in historical significance, Zimri and Omri receive about the same narrative space (six verses), with more details actually provided for Zimri. Their respective evaluations are also much the same: both made Israel sin by walking in the way of Jeroboam. From DtrH's standpoint both were kings of Israel and hence were wicked by virtue of their perpetuation of the Northern royal shrines. Yet Zimri barely had time to sit on the throne, much less to commit grave offenses. Omri's impact on Israel's history and monarchy, which was so great that it can hardly be overstated, is largely ignored. The only recognition he receives is for founding the capital of Samaria and being assessed, on theological grounds, as the worst of the Israelite kings so far. DtrH's theological program and his prophecy-fulfillment scheme outweigh historical reality.

DtrH's cursory account of Omri's reign

The episode that stands out in the narrative is that of the civil war between Tibni and Omri (vv. 21-22). Unfortunately, the paucity of information about Tibni and the lack of detail about this war raise more questions than answers when it comes to historical reconstruction. The civil war undercuts any claim of divine designation for the Omrid dynasty as far as DtrH is concerned, all the more since there is no oracle against the house of Zimri that Omri might be seen as fulfilling. All in all, the DtrH account of Omri is cursory. This may be due to the lack of information, although that seems unusual for a king of Omri's historical significance. More likely it is for theological reasons, i.e., speeding toward Ahab (and Jezebel), who will shortly snatch the title of worst king (in DtrH's view) from Omri.

The Beginning of Ahab's Reign (1 Kgs 16:29-34)

Text

[DtrH's sources; DtrH; *PN*; *Additions to PN*]
29 Ahab the son of Omri became king in the thirty-eighth year
of Asa the king of Judah, reigning over Israel in Samaria
twenty-two years. 30 Ahab did what YHWH considered evil; he did more
evil than all who preceded him. 31 *It was not enough for him to walk in the sins*
of Jeroboam the son of Nebat—he took as wife Jezebel the daughter of Ethbaal
king of the Sidonians and then proceeded to serve Baal and worship him, 32 *erect-*
ing an altar to Baal in the temple of his offenses that he built in Samaria.
33 *Ahab made the asherah, and Ahab provoked YHWH further to destroy him, do-*
ing more evil than all the kings of Israel who preceded him. 34 *Hiel of Bethel re-*
built Jericho; at the cost of Abiram his firstborn he founded it, and at the cost of
Segub his youngest he set up its doors, according to the word of YHWH that he
spoke through Joshua son of Nun.

Textual Notes

29 **Ahab the son of Omri became king in the thirty-eighth year of Asa the king of Judah**: So MT. G^{BL}: *In the second year of Jehoshaphat* [L: *the king of Judah*] *Ahab the son of Omri* [B: *Zimri*] *became king.* The original vocalization of the name Ahab was *Ahiab* as preserved in the spelling Αχιαβ (Jer 36[29]:21) and Αχιαβος (Josephus *Ant* 15.250).[1] The name is theophoric and means "the father (god) is my brother."

reigning: Lit: *and he reigned.* So G^{L}. G^{B} lacks the *and* before the verb. MT + *Ahab the son of Omri.*

30 **Ahab**: So G^{BL}. MT + *the son of Omri.*

he did more evil: So G^{BL} as in 16:25. MT lacks the verb וירע (*he did evil*).

31 **It was not enough for him**: Reading ויהי הנקל לו based on G^{BL} (καὶ οὐκ ἦν αὐτῷ ἱκανὸν). הנקל is construed as *hannāqēl*, the definite article plus *Nip'al* participle, meaning "the smallest thing, insignificant, insufficient." This is a frequently adopted repointing.[2] The MT reading—interrogative plus *Nip'al* perfect (*hănāqēl*) as a rhetorical question—"Was his walking in the way of Jeroboam a light thing?"—is possible and is adopted by many commentators mainly because of its use in Ezek 8:17.[3] It might even be considered the *lectio difficilior.* However, the weight of the OG and the present context, which unlike Ezek 8:17 is not direct address, support the emendation. MT has lost לו by haplography.

---

1 See the discussions of the names Ab(i)ner, Ab(i)shalom, and Am(i)non in 1 Sam 2:8; 3:3; 13:20 by McCarter, *II Samuel*, 82, 101, 319.

2 Cf. BHS; GKC §150d

3 Burney, *Notes*, 206; Cogan, *I Kings*, 420; Gray, *Kings*, 367–68; Sweeney, *Kings*, 205n.

the sins of Jeroboam: In DtrH's ideology it is the sin (singular) of Jeroboam that plagues Israel and is the cause of its ultimate demise.[4] Here, though, the witnesses are unanimous in reading the plural, and vv. 31-33, as an interpolation, are imitative (see Diachronic Analysis).

Jezebel: The original form of the name was *ʾî-zěbûl*, meaning, "where is (the) Prince?"[5] in reference to Baal as attested in the Ugaritic Baal Cycle (*KTU* 1.6.4.16). It is analogous to the name *Ichabod* ("where is [the] glory?") in 1 Sam 4:21. The vocalization was changed to the Hebrew word *zebel* "dung" in denigration of the god Baal and the character of Jezebel and as befitting her end in 2 Kings 9.[6]

Ethbaal: Josephus, citing Menander of Ephesus, refers to Ithobal (Ἰθόβαλος) as a priest of Astarte who usurped the throne of Tyre in the ninth century (*Contra Apion* 1.123). He later spells the same name Ἰθωβαλος (1.156) This indicates that the original form of the name was *ʾIttobaʿl*, as attested on the tenth century sarcophagus of Ahiram.[7] The name means "Baal is with him," and is analogous to the Hebrew name *ʿImmānûʾēl*, "god is with us/him" (Isa 7:14). The later Tabnit inscription (fifth century) similarly refers to Tabnit and Eshmunʿazar as kings of Sidon and priests of Astarte.[8] Ethbaal's status as priest could explain Jezebel's devotion to her native deity, although there is reason to question the missionary fervor ascribed to her in the biblical account.

proceeded to serve Baal: The verb *hālak* has the sense of "proceed" and does not mean that Ahab traveled to Tyre to worship Baal.[9] The deity referred to is usually understood as Melqart, the chief god of Tyre, though Baal Shamem may be a better possibility, based on 1 Kings 18.[10]

worship him: Lit. "prostrate himself to him," a causative reflexive (*-št-* infix) of חוה. See Joüon §79t.

32 **in the temple of his offenses**: So G^{BL}: ἐν οἴκῳ τῶν προσοχθισμάτων αὐτοῦ = בית שקוציו. MT: בית הבעל. Timm argued that the original text underlying the reading G^{BL} was בית אלהים,[11] and Niehr in his reconstruction of the religious history of Israel and Judah contended that Ahab built an altar to Baal in the temple of Yhwh in Samaria.[12] The argument for the emendation is twofold: (1) The MT, which states that Ahab erected an altar to Baal in the temple of Baal that he built in Samaria, is tautological and

---

4 See on 15:34. See also Stade, *Kings*, 143.

5 Or possibly *yēš* or *ʾîš zěbûl*, "Prince exists;" so N. Avigad, "The Seal of Jezebel," *IEJ* 14 (1964): 274–76; Cogan, *I Kings*, 420.

6 Avigad ("Seal") argued that the name occurs on a Phoenician seal with the spelling יזבל for איזבל. Also Avigad and Sass, *Stamp Seals*, 275 (#740). Avigad stopped short of identifying Jezebel on the seal with the biblical character. The identification was recently advanced by M. Korpel, "Seals of Jezebel and Other Women in Authority," *Journal for Semitics* 15 (2006): 358–62; "Queen Jezebel's Seal," *UF* 38 (2006): 379–98; and "Fit for a Queen: Jezebel's Royal Seal," *BAR* 34 (2008): 32–37, 80. It was criticized on paleographical grounds by C. Rollston, "Prosopography and the יזבל Seal," *IEJ* 59 (2009) 86–91.

7 *ANET* 661; *COS* 2:55.

8 *ANET* 662; *COS* 2:56.

9 Cogan, *I Kings*, 421. *Pace* Šanda, *Könige* I, 41.

10 See on 18:21. Cogan *I Kings*, 421; J. Day, "Baal (Deity)," *ABD* 1:548. Cf. also the Zakkur inscription *ANET* 655–56; *COS* 2:35. On Melqart, "king of the city (of Tyre)," see S. Ribichini, "Melqart," *DDD* 563–65.

11 Timm, *Die Dynastie Omri*, 32–36.

12 H. Niehr, "The Rise of Yhwh in Judahite and Israelite Religion: Methodological and Religio-Historical Aspects," in *The Triumph of Elohim: From Yahwisms to Judaisms* (ed. D. Edelman; Kampen: Kok Pharos, 1995), 56.

nonsensical, since a temple by definition houses an altar to the god to whom it is devoted; it only makes sense to refer separately to the erection of an altar or other cult object if it is to a god other than the one whose temple it is; (2) The Greek word προσόχθισμα ("offense, provocation") is used elsewhere, especially in 1 Kgs 11:33, to translate אלהים, which in this verse was later replaced by הבעל under the influence of its previous two occurrences. Emerton responded in defense of the MT.[13] He pointed out that the phrase בית יהוה, the equivalent of the proposed reading בית אלהים, occurs in Kings only in reference to the temple in Jerusalem but never for a temple in the North. Moreover, since the Greek reflects the suffix, אלהיו would likely mean "his gods" rather than "his god" (i.e., YHWH), especially where Ahab is concerned. Emerton observed further that while προσοχθισμάτων in 16:32 could render אלהים there is no consistent correspondence between the two words; it could just as easily render הבעל, though the latter is usually translated ὁ Βααλ. While both Timm and Emerton note that προσόχθισμα is sometimes used for שקוץ (1 Kgs 11:5-7; 2 Kgs 23:13, 24), neither of them considers the possibility that שקוציו was the older reading in 16:32, despite Emerton's stating twice that the point of discussion must be the present text. Reading שקוציו resolves the tautology of the MT, which Emerton downplays,[14] and accounts for G's use of προσοχθισμάτων. It may be, as Emerton implies, that because שקוציו is a pejorative it is more likely to have replaced הבעל than the reverse. But on strictly textual grounds the use of Baal's name twice previously in vv. 31-32 as well as the reference to the temple of Baal in 2 Kgs 10:21-27 could have led to the introduction of the name here as well. There is no such factor that could have influenced the replacement of the name with שקוציו.

33 **the asherah**: An *asherah* was a cult object in the shape of an upright tree or pole representing the goddess Asherah, who was considered YHWH's consort.[15] The inscriptions from Kuntillet 'Ajrud and Khirbet el-Qom have made clear that *asherot* were regarded as a legitimate part of the worship of YHWH in both Israel and Judah before the DtrH polemic against them. Hence the *asherah* referred to in the present verse stood in YHWH's temple, not Baal's, which accounts for its mention separately from that of the temple of Baal in the previous verse. It occurs with the article as elsewhere in Kings, referring to the specific cultic objects in both Samaria and Jerusalem (1 Kgs 18:19; 2 Kgs 13:6; 18:4; 21:7; 23:6).

and Ahab provoked YHWH further to destroy him, doing more evil: Reading ויוסף אחאב להכעיס את־יהוה את־נפשו להשחית ויעש הרע. There are three issues. The first con-

---

13 J. A. Emerton, "The House of Baal in 1 Kings XVI 32," *VT* 47 (1997): 293–300.

14 Emerton cites Gen 24:16 and Judg 11:34 as examples of similar redundancy in the HB. Each of these verses gives a term ("virgin," "only daughter"), which is then further defined for absolute clarity. In Judg 11:34 the further definition is required to make clear that Jephthah had no son as well as no other daughter. This is different from 1 Kgs 16:32, which does not define a term. A more comparable "tautology" would be the statement that Ahab built a temple of Baal in which was an altar to Baal. But Timm and Niehr are right that the statement that he erected an altar of Baal in the temple of Baal is nonsensical.

15 In some cases it may have been a grove, as suggested by the Greek ἄλσος, which may also refer to the sacred area. In some cases also it probably bore the likeness in wood of its namesake. See McCarter, "Aspects of the Religion of the Israelite Monarchy," 137–55, and S. Ackerman, *Under Every Green Tree: Popular Religion in Sixth-Century Judah* (HSM 46; Atlanta: Scholars Press, 1992), 62–66, as well as Olyan, *Asherah and the Cult of Yahweh in Israel*. The exhaustive treatment of the topic is Frevel, *Aschera*.

cerns להכעיס את־ יהוה *to provoke* Yhwh. The OL juxtaposes two alternatives:[16] (1) *ut faceret exacerbationem* = τοῦ ποιῆσαι παροργίσματα G^{BL} (= לעשות כעסים), which is partially preserved in the MT's לעשות, and (2) *ut exacerbaret deum* = להכעיס את־יהוה/אלהים, which is likewise partially represented in G^{B}'s infinitive τοῦ παροργίσαι but is preserved and expanded in MT's להכעיס את־יהוה אלהי ישראל. The two readings are variants. The second issue is the G^{BL} plus that follows: (καὶ) τὴν ψυχὴν αὐτοῦ (τοῦ) ἐξολεθρευθῆναι (*to destroy his life*), which is shared by the OL, *et animam suam disperderet*. It is lacking in the MT but probably reflects להכרית את־נפשו, a clause that was evidently lost from MT as a result of the other disturbances in the verse. This expression is a *hapax legomenon* in the HB, but it is drawn from the formulation הנפש [ההיא] יכרת, *[that] person shall be cut off*, which is a sentence of death or exile in P (and H) texts (Gen 17:14; Exod 12:15, 19; 30:33; 31:14; Lev 7:20, 21, 27; 17:4; 19:8; 22:3; Num 9:13; 15:30; 19:13, 20; similarly Exod 30:33, 38; Lev 7:25; 17:9, 14; 18:29; 20:18; 23:29). The third issue is the Greek reading (L: ἀνθ' ὧν) ἐκακοποίησεν, "he did evil," also reflected in the OL (*et*) *malignum fecit*. Though lacking in MT, the corresponding clause, ויעש הרע, seems required by the comparative מכל מלכי ישראל, *more than all the kings of Israel*.

34 This verse is absent from G^{L} and is widely regarded as a late addition. See Diachronic Analysis.

Hiel of Bethel: Lit: *Hiel the Bethelite*. Preceded in MT by *in his days* (בימיו), a gloss designed to accommodate this verse to the preceding narrative. *Hiel* is a shortened form of *Ahiel*, which is reflected in G^{B}'s Αχειηλ. The name means "El (god) is my brother" and is thus very similar to *Ahab* (16:29).

at the cost of Abiram: MT: באבירם On the *beth pretii* see GKC §119p; Joüon §132c; WO, 197. *Abiram* means "my father is exalted," identical to Abram/Abraham. It occurs for one other person in the HB—the Reubenite son of Eliab who was swallowed by the earth for revolting against Moses (Num 16; Deut 11:6; Ps 106:17).

Segub: So MT *qere'* (cf. 1 Chr 2:21) and G^{B} (Ζεγουβ). The *ketiv* has *Segib* (שגיב), perhaps under the influence of the next word, צעירו. It is an abbreviation of a longer name meaning "El/Yhwh is exalted."

doors: G^{B} has the singular. Read with MT for sense.

Synchronic Analysis

16:29-30: Ahab as Israel's nadir

With Ahab the account in ch. 16 reaches its goal. It is a watershed moment, as hinted by the subject first construction in v. 29. Ahab reigns nearly twice as long as Omri, but the account of his reign takes as many chapters (17–22) as Omri received verses (16:23-28). The difference is not due to historical importance but to the theological significance of the involvement of Elijah and Jezebel. The narrative focuses so much attention on Ahab because Israel reaches a new nadir during his reign (v. 30). He is its worst king. The language is nearly identical to v. 25. Omri was the worst king of Israel until his son surpassed him. Ahab's longer reign afforded him time to do more evil. Jeroboam was also said to be worse than his predecessors (14:9), so Ahab's evaluation places him in rather exclusive company: Jeroboam, Omri, and, as the last of the three, Ahab is the worst of all.

16 So Trebolle, *Centena*, 136–38.

16:31-33: Ahab's sins

In distinction from the evaluation of Omri, there is a clear explanation given for Ahab's evil. The next three verses specify his sins, and v. 34 suggests yet another. By one reading Ahab is accused of five specific sins: the sins of Jeroboam, marriage to Jezebel, worship of Baal, building a temple to Baal, and erecting an *asherah.*[17] Alternatively, the last three of these fall under the umbrella of the marriage to Jezebel. This marriage sets Ahab apart as the worst king. All the kings of Israel are guilty of the sin(s) of Jeroboam. The phrase occurs with both the singular and plural because it was a composite sin, one that eventually brought about the destruction of the kingdom of Israel. Yet the marriage to Jezebel makes the sin(s) of Jeroboam seem trivial.[18] Her very name, with its *zebel* ("dung") element, expresses the narrative's disgust for her. Her fervor for Baal is further suggested by the name of her father, Ethbaal, king of Sidon. This bare description sets off alarms about the impact she will have on Israel. She is female, foreign, and, as the daughter and wife of kings, formidable. Her effect on Ahab is considerable. In statements reminiscent of the account of Solomon (11:1-7), vv. 31-33 indirectly blame Jezebel for leading Ahab to worship Baal and to adopt extraneous cultic practices.[19] Jezebel induced Ahab to build a temple to Baal in Samaria and to install an altar to Baal in it (v. 32 MT). The redundance of both altar and temple compounds Ahab's offense. The repeated references to Baal—his altar and his temple—drive home the sense of outrage in the narrative. As if the worship of Baal were not enough, Ahab also introduced an *asherah*. The two names together anticipate the participation of the prophets of Baal and Asherah in the contest in ch. 18. It is never asserted that Ahab abandoned the worship of YHWH. He gave his sons Yahwistic names after the national god. But he supplemented the worship of YHWH with the worship of Baal. The text also implies that he perverted the worship of YHWH by erecting the *asherah*.

16:34: The deaths of Hiel's sons

The anecdote in v. 34 at first seems unrelated to Ahab, but there are points of contact.[20] Both Ahab and Hiel are engaged in construction activities that are contrary to YHWH's will. The verb בנה ("to build") is used for both of them. Each has an additional pair of verbs—"erect" and "make" for Ahab and "found" and "set up" for Hiel—to form two triads devoted to his construction activities. The deaths of Hiel's two sons point forward to the deaths of Ahab's sons Ahaziah (2 Kgs 2) and Joram (2 Kgs 9). The deaths are also linked as having occurred *according to YHWH's word* (1 Kgs 16:34; 2 Kgs 1:17; 9:26). The reference to the word of YHWH ties 16:34 with the advent of Elijah and the divine word to his announcing the drought and then sending him into hiding (17:1-2). The references to Bethel and Jericho in conjunction with Hiel in 16:34 connect with those cities in the stories of Elijah and Elisha, especially in 2 Kings 2, when the two prophets pass through on their way to the Jordan, where Elijah is taken into heaven. Since rebuilding

17 Walsh, *Ahab*, 21–22.

18 Walsh (*Ahab*, 22) observes that the construction ויהי הנקל "subtly invites our assent" to this proposition.

19 Brewer-Boydston, *Good Queen Mothers, Bad Queen Mothers*, 103.

20 See C. Conroy, "Hiel Between Ahab and Elijah-Elisha: 1 Kgs 16,34 in its Immediate Literary Context," *Bib* 77 (1996): 210–18. Cf. also H. Dharamraj, *A Prophet Like Moses? A Narrative-Theological Reading of the Elijah Stories* (Milton Keynes, U.K.: Paternoster, 2011), 8; Hens-Piazza, *Kings*, 159; Provan, *Kings*, 131; Walsh *1 Kings*, 219.

Jericho would be beyond the resources of a single individual, Hiel must be some sort of official, and the project would require royal endorsement and support. Hence the rebuilding of Jericho and its consequences lie at Ahab's doorstep. The disregard that the project shows for Joshua's curse attests Ahab's disrespect of sacral traditions from the past, and the deaths of Hiel's sons serve as an evil omen for Ahab's regime. Hiel's origin from Bethel is a reminder that this city, which houses one of Jeroboam's shrines, is impious and under threat. The effectiveness of Joshua's curse fits well with the prophecy-fulfillment scheme that is a major structural motif in the book of Kings and places Ahab's reign under the shadow of death. The anecdote also foreshadows themes of Elijah's ministry.[21] The rebuilding of Jericho represents the threat of re-Canaanization of the land, and the city becomes, in turn, the home of Elijah and his band of prophets who work to counter this threat. Just as Joshua's curse proved true, so can the reader trust that the word borne by Elijah will come to pass.

Diachronic Analysis

16:30: DtrH's assessment of Ahab

Wiederaufnahme in 16:31-33

To the chronological data for Ahab's reign (v. 29), presumably taken from an integrated king list, DtrH added the assessment in v. 30. As with Omri (16:25), DtrH evaluated Ahab as worse than his predecessors. His reasons for this assessment were evidently displaced by PN's interpolation by *Wiederaufnahme* in vv. 31-33. The case for interpolation is reinforced by the phrase *to destroy him* (v. 33), which is adapted from P (see the Note). The purpose of the interpolation was to introduce Jezebel as the main cause of Ahab's apostasies. Ahab combined the sins (plural!) of Jeroboam, of which all Israelite kings were guilty, with additional apostasies inspired by his Phoenician wife. DtrH's evaluation of Ahab was terse, as it had been for his father: each was the worst so far (16:25). At the same time it must have mentioned the sin of Jeroboam as in Omri's case (16:26). The statement that Ahab walked in the way of Jeroboam was replaced in the interpolation with the remark that the sin of Jeroboam was a small thing compared with the worship of Baal into which Jezebel led him. Jezebel is not mentioned in the DtrH level of Kings, which blames Ahab alone for his faults and for the fall of the Omrid dynasty (21:20-24*).

Historical veracity?

The historical validity of v. 31-33 is generally assumed, and some details make historical sense. The marriage would have sealed a treaty between Israel and the Phoenicians that would have been of mutual interest for its trade benefits.[22] But there are reasons

---

21 M. A Sweeney, "On the Literary Function of the Notice Concerning Hiel's Re-Establishment of Jericho in 1 Kings 16:34," in *Seeing Signals, Reading Signs. The Art of Exegesis. Studies in Honour of Antony F. Campbell, SJ for his Seventieth Birthday* (ed. M. A. O'Brien and H. N. Wallace; JSOTSup 415; London/New York: T & T Clark, 2004): 104–15.

22 For an attempt to reconstruct Ethbaal's/Ittobaal's reign, see H. J. Katzenstein, *The History of Tyre: From the Beginning of the Second Millennium B.C.E. until the Fall of the Neo-Babylonian Empire in 538 B.C.E.* (Jerusalem: The Schocken Institute for Jewish Research, 1973) 129-66.

for doubt. The existence of this Ethbaal is suspect. His identity with the Ittobaal mentioned in the Ahiram inscription is usually assumed, but it is something of a stretch to makes the dates work.[23] Otherwise, the Ethbaal of 1 Kgs 16:31 is documented outside of the Bible only in Josephus (see the notes), who claims to be quoting Menander's account of the Tyrian king list, and is thus a third-hand witness at best. There is a second Ittobaal mentioned in the 8th century Assyrian inscription, known as the Iran inscription, by the name Tuba'lu (*ANET* 287-88; *COS* 2:287) and a third Ittobaal in the 6th century (Josephus, *Ant* 10. 228; *Ag Ap* 1.156). The latter would help to account for the title "king of the Sidonians," which is well attested in the Babylonian and Persian periods but curious earlier.[24] It would also fit well with my dating of PN, who might have been attracted to the Hebrew rendition of the name for its ostensible meaning, "with Baal."

The exaggeration of Jezebel's proselytizing

Ahab's devotion to Baal and Jezebel's efforts at proselytizing have been overblown because of the exaggerated way they are presented in PN's accretions. The temple Ahab is accused of building in Samaria amounted at most to a shrine he had built for Jezebel to practice her native religion, comparable to what Solomon is said to have done for his foreign wives (1 Kgs 11:7-8).[25] The historical Ahab was an adherent of Yhwh. Each god was understood to have his distinct territory and people, and vice-versa (cf. 2 Kgs 5:17-18). Israel was Yhwh's people and land, meaning that Yhwh was Israel's god, who should be worshiped in Israel. If there was a historical Jezebel, she would have assumed as much. The children of Ahab and Jezebel mentioned in the Bible all possess Yahwistic names. While names are not a foolproof indicator of religious affiliation, this suggests that Ahab and Jezebel were not as fanatic about importing the worship of Baal as Kings implies. The *asherah* in v. 33 was not a foreign import but a component of the cult of Yhwh. Ironically, the accusation that Ahab sought to replace the worship of Yhwh with the worship of Baal is contradicted by the accusation that he was complicit in the sin of Jeroboam. His maintenance of the national sanctuaries at Dan and Bethel indicates that he worshiped Yhwh, the national god, as one would expect the king to do.[26]

The final verse of the chapter raises more questions than it supplies information. Verse 34 is unrelated to the context and concerned directly with neither Ahab nor Elijah. It interrupts the connection between the negative evaluation of Ahab and the

23 Ahiram's dating ca. 1000 BCE would put his son and successor, Ittobaal, too early to overlap with Ahab in the mid-9th century. Thus, McCarter avoids identifying the Ittobaal of the Ahiram inscription with Jezebel's father, stating, "'Ittoba'l was also the name of the mid-ninth century king of Tyre whose daughter, Jezebel, was the queen of King Ahab of Israel" (*COS* 2:181, n. 1).

24 See Philip J. Boyles, "'The King of the Sidonians': Phoenician Ideologies and the Myth of the Kingdom of Tyre-Sidon," *BASOR* 365 (2012): 33-44.

25 W. M. Schniedewind ("History and Interpretation: The Religion of Ahab and Manasseh in the Book of Kings," *CBQ* 55 [1993]: 649–61, at 650) highlights 2 Kgs 10:18: *Ahab served Baal a little.*

26 See M. Köckert, "Yhwh in the Northern and Southern Kingdom," in *One God – One Cult – One Nation: Archaeological and Biblical Perspectives* (ed. R. G. Kratz and H. Spieckermann; Berlin: de Gruyter, 2010): 357–94. For an attempt at a more balanced presentation of Ahab see M. A. Cohen, "In All Fairness to Ahab: A Socio-Political Consideration of the Ahab-Elijah Controversy," *EI* 12 (1975): 87–94.

punishment for it in the drought announced by Elijah and is widely recognized as an addition drawn from Josh 6:26, which is well integrated in its context. The phrase *in his days* (בימיו) is a gloss added to ease the transition from vv. 31-33 to v. 34. Our verse also misconstrues the genre of Josh 6:26, taking a curse as prophecy.[27] The curse in Josh 6:26 employs rhetorical language and merism (oldest and youngest) in order to leave the city a perpetual ruin in conformity with the prescription of Deut 13:17. First Kings 16:34 takes the curse as a prophecy and provides a fulfillment for it. Exactly what *rebuilt Jericho* in v. 34 means is not clear. The reference to the city precludes the notion that Hiel built just a single residence. It implies, rather, the construction of large public structure(s) or the refortification of the site by a new city wall. Then the question becomes when the anecdote may have arisen. The most significant Iron Age construction on the site took place in the seventh century, long after Ahab's reign and after the end of the kingdom of Israel. There is evidence of continuous occupation of the site throughout the monarchic period.[28] It may be that Hiel was commissioned to fortify Jericho in response to Moab's revolt against Israel (2 Kgs 3:5).[29] Laying the foundations and setting the doors, whether of the city wall or of public buildings, represented the beginning and end, respectively, of the building process.[30]

The deaths of Hiel's sons

As for what lies behind the statement that Hiel's project came *at the cost* of his oldest and youngest sons, two basic interpretations have been offered. Either the deaths of the sons, however they came about, are explained etiologically as the result of the curse hanging over the site from the time of Joshua or the sons perished as human sacrifices made to ensure the city's continued well-being. While the question of child sacrifice in ancient Israel is complex and ranges beyond this passage, the interpretation of this verse has had a small but significant role in the discussion of the matter. Archaeological evidence of child sacrifice is abundant in Punic remains, but

---

27 See L. Mazor, "The Origin and Evolution of the Curse upon the Rebuilder of Jericho: A Contribution of Textual Criticism to Biblical Historiography," *Textus* 14 (1988), 23–25; Brueggemann, *Kings*, 204. For the opposite view—that Josh 6:26 derives from 1 Kgs 16:34—see Dietrich, *Prophetie und Geschichte*, 110–12; Noort, "Child Sacrifice in Ancient Israel: The Status Quaestionis," 111–12. Josh 6:26 may have been glossed to enhance the connection with 1 Kgs 16:34. The phrases את־יריחו and *before* YHWH in Josh 6:26 are additions. Both are unnecessary; Josh 6:26 is so well ensconced in its context that it is clear that the city Joshua curses is Jericho without the explicit naming. Cf. Mazor, "Origin and Evolution," 23–25.

28 See H. Weippert and M. Weippert, "Jericho in der Eisenzeit," *ZDPV* 92 (1976): 105–48. Cf. also T. A. Holland and E. Netzer, "Jericho," *ABD* 3:723–40.

29 So Šanda, *Könige* I, 411; Gray, *Kings*, 335; and Weippert and Weippert, "Jericho," 148. Benzinger (*Könige*, 105) suggests that Jericho was in the territory of Judah in the ninth century rather than of Israel. Located on the border between Israel and Judah and between Ephraim and Benjamin, it changed hands periodically. Joshua 18:21 locates it in the tribal territory of Benjamin, though the date of this list is uncertain. Assuming Israel was the more powerful partner in the treaty with Judah and Jehoshaphat, it may have had access to and control of Jericho in the ninth century. It is also quite possible that this anecdote dates from a later period.

30 Würthwein, *1. Könige 1–16*, 204.

sparse and ambiguous elsewhere in the ancient Near East.[31] Scholars debate whether child sacrifice in Israel involved actual immolation or was a ceremonial dedication of some kind. They also debate whether such sacrifices were offered to a Canaanite god named Molech or whether the term *mulch* was used for a type of sacrifice. These matters are discussed in greater detail in the treatments of 2 Kings 3 and 2 Kings 16. They are, however, largely irrelevant for the present verse, which does not mention Molech and is different from child sacrifice as described elsewhere in the Bible. Neither does the present verse represent a case of exigency like those of Isaac (Gen 22) Jephthah's daughter (Judg 11:30-40), and Mesha (2 Kgs 3:27). Rather, the practice presumed to lie behind this verse—that of foundation sacrifices for the ongoing benefit of the city (or building) and its occupants—is of questionable attestation in Mesopotamia. The alleged instances of it in Syria-Palestine have been extrapolated from this verse.[32] It is possible that the author of the verse meant to defame Hiel by accusing him of child sacrifice, but the cryptic nature of the notice makes that unlikely. The vagueness of the accusation could foster the insinuation of child sacrifice on Hiel's part, which the author probably would not mind. Hence, while the possibility that Hiel's sons were sacrificial victims cannot be ruled out conclusively, it must be considered unlikely. The better understanding of the notice is that Hiel's sons died in the course of the construction and that their deaths, which normally would have been regarded as routine, considering the high rate of infant mortality, received special notice because of the curse attributed to Joshua.[33]

Synthesis

The diachronic shape of the introduction to Ahab

For the third time, the second in a row, a king of Israel is said to have done more evil than his predecessors. Ahab combines the deeds of the two "worsts" before

31 See Green, *The Role of Human Sacrifice*; Heider, *The Cult of Molek: A Reassessment*, 195–222; Noort, "Status Quaestionis;" L. E. Stager, "The Rite of Child Sacrifice at Carthage" in *New Light on Ancient Carthage* (ed. J. G. Pedley; Ann Arbor: University of Michigan, 1980): 1–11; "Carthage: A View from the Tophet" in *Phönizer im Westen* (ed. H. G. Niemeyer; Madrider Beiträge 8; Mainz am Rhein: Philipp von Zabern, 1982): 155–63; and L. E. Stager and S. R. Wolff, "Child Sacrifice at Carthage: Religious Rite or Population Control?" *BAR* 10 (1984): 30–51. Most recently, Heath Dewrell (*Child Sacrifice in Ancient Israel* [Winona Lake, IN: Eisenbrauns, 2017]) examines the existence and diversity of viewpoints about child sacrifice within the HB.

32 See Green, *The Role of Human Sacrifice*, 152–56, 169.

33 Würthwein, *1. Könige 1-16*, 204, suggests further that the idea that ruined places possessed spiritual powers may lie behind the curse in Josh 6:26 as well as 1 Kgs 16:34. I. M. Blake's idea ("Jericho [Ain Es-Sultan]: Joshua's Curse and Elisha's Miracle—One Possible Explanation," *PEQ* 97 [1967]: 86–97) that the curse reflected radioactive contamination of the spring in Jericho, the temporary nature of which was attributed to Elisha's cleansing in 2 Kgs 2:19-22, misconstrues the nature of both stories. B. Gosse ("La reconstruction de Jericho en 1 Rois 16,34 dans le cadre de la rédaction des livres historiques," *SJOT* 7 [1993]: 152–55) explains the curse redactionally as a symbol of the threatened end of Yahwism in Israel to which Elijah's advent in ch. 17 is a response.

him, Jeroboam and Omri, and sinks Israel to a new low. He not only practices the *sin of Jeroboam* but makes it appear as "the slightest thing" by all the other evil he does. Above all, he marries the foreign princess, Jezebel, and inculcates her religious belief and practice into Israel. His apostasy is exacerbated by comparison with the righteous Jehoshaphat of Judah. Such at least is the perspective on Ahab presented by these verses as they stand. The diachronic reality appears to be rather different both literarily and historically. DtrH is responsible only for Ahab's introductory formulae in vv. 29-30, the chronological details of which (v. 29) he inherited from an integrated king list. Hence DtrH's work in the case of Ahab was limited to providing the theological evaluation in v. 30. PN elaborated on Ahab's wickedness by inserting vv. 31-33, where the cause of Ahab's wickedness is attributed to his Phoenician wife. This later level of composition, which introduced Jezebel, altered the book of Kings considerably going forward and changed its portrait of Ahab's reign and of Israel's history.

The historical reality of Ahab's reign and religion

Historically, Ahab was a powerful king whose reign, along with that of his father, represented the high point of Israel's power and international prestige. The two brought stability and prosperity to their kingdom. In contrast to his depiction in Kings he was a worshiper of YHWH. His maintenance of the royal shrines at Dan and Bethel and the names of his children attest as much. His construction of a temple or altar to Baal may have represented an accommodation for his wife but did not signal a change in his own religious stance or practice. Other accoutrements, such as the *asherah*, were not innovations and would have been accepted at the time as appropriate features in the worship of YHWH. But for the post-DtrH interpolator these activities were provocations that further distanced Israel from YHWH and would eventually lead to its demise.

16:34

The final verse is unrelated in any direct way to its surrounding context and is intrusive. It is an even later addition. Its content, though elusive, probably had nothing to do with child sacrifice. It is best understood as an etiology accounting for the deaths of two sons of Hiel, a builder in Jericho, as the fulfillment of a curse issued by Joshua. It misconstrues Joshua's curse as prophecy. Despite these inconcinnities, the verse does correspond roughly to the theme of prophecy-fulfillment in Kings and points forward to the careers of Elijah and Elisha. It indirectly attests, at least in memory, the power and influence of the Omrid dynasty in its assumed control of Jericho and highlights the spirit of disdain for past traditions that the book of Kings sees as endemic in Ahab's reign.

Elijah and the Drought (1 Kings 17)

Text

[Prophetic sources; *PN*]
1 Elijah the Tishbite said to Ahab, "By the life of YHWH, in whose service I stand,
there will be no dew or rain during these years except at my command." 2 YHWH's
word came to him: 3 "Go east from here and hide in the Wadi Cherith near the
Jordan. 4 You can drink from the wadi, and I have ordained the ravens to provi-
sion you there." 5 He went *according to YHWH's word* and stayed in the Wadi Cher-
ith near the Jordan. 6 The ravens brought him bread in the morning and meat
in the evening, and he drank from the wadi. *7 After some time when the wadi*
dried up because there was no rain in the land, 8 YHWH's word came to him,
9 "Get up, go to Zarephath of Sidon where I have ordained a widow, to provision
you." 10 He got up and went to Zarephath, to the city entrance, where he found a
widow gathering sticks. He called to her and said, "Please bring me some water in
a cup so that I may drink." 11 As she went to fetch it, he called after her and said,
"Please bring me a morsel of bread in your hand." 12 She replied, "By the life of
YHWH your god, I have nothing except a handful of flour in the jar and a little oil
in the flask, and I am gathering a couple of sticks so that I can go and prepare
them for my children and me to eat before we die." 13 Elijah said to her, "Don't be
afraid. Go, do as you have said. Only first make me a small loaf from what you
have there and bring it to me. Then after that prepare food for yourself and your
children. 14 For thus says YHWH, 'The flour in the jar will not run out nor will the
flask lack oil' until the day when YHWH sends rain upon the earth." 15 So she went
and gave it to him. Then she ate—she and he and her children; 16 the flour in the
jar did not run out nor did the flask lack oil, according to YHWH's word which he
spoke through Elijah. 17 Afterwards, the son of the woman, the mistress of the
house, became ill. His illness was very serious to the point that he stopped breath-
ing. 18 She said to Elijah, "What do you have against me, man of god, in coming
to me to call attention to my iniquity and cause my son's death?" 19 He replied,
"Give me your son." Then he took him from her arms and brought him up to the
upper room where he was staying and laid him on his bed. 20 Elijah cried out and
said, "Alas, YHWH, have you brought disaster even upon the widow with whom I
am staying by killing her son?" 21 He breathed on the boy three times and cried
out to YHWH and said, "Oh YHWH my god, let the life of this boy come back to
him." 22 YHWH listened to Elijah so that the boy's life returned to him and he lived.
23 Elijah took the boy, brought him down from the upper room into the house,
and gave him back to his mother, saying "See, your son is alive." 24 The woman re-
plied to Elijah, "Now indeed I know that you are a man of god and that YHWH's
word is truly in your mouth."

Textual Notes

1 **Elijah**: Meaning “my god is Yhwh,” this name is highly appropriate for the character of Elijah in the subsequent stories, especially ch. 18, where he is the defender of Yhwh against the incursion of Baalism. G^{B} + *the prophet.*

the Tishbite: MT, G^{BL} + מתשבי גלעד, a gloss distinguishing Elijah’s hometown from Tishbe in upper Galilee (Tob 1:2). The MT vocalization, מִתֹּשָׁבֵי (“from the sojourners [of Gilead]”) is problematic: the *o*-vowel is written defectively rather than with the *waw mater* as expected and as is the case with all other occurrences of the word in the Hebrew Bible; the *a*-vowel under שׁ is not reduced;[1] and it is counterintuitive that Elijah the prophet of Yhwh would be a resident alien. Hence the vocalization indicated by G^{BL} is preferable: ἐκ Θεσβων = מִתִּשְׁבֵי, “from Tishbe [of Gilead].”[2] The location of Elijah’s *Tishbe* is unknown, The identification with el-Istib on Jebel Ajlun, 13 km north of the Jabbok in present-day Jordan, stems from the Byzantine period when the chapel to Mar Elias (“Saint Elijah”) was built.[3]

By the life of Yhwh: So G^{L}, OL. MT, G^{B} + *the god of Israel.* G^{B} precedes with ὁ θεὸς τῶν δυνάμεων (= אלהי צבאות)—a further expansion. The noun חי is used in oath formulas to swear by the *life* of a deity as was common in the ancient Near East.[4]

in whose service I stand: Lit: “before whom I stand,” an idiom for being at someone’s service or waiting on someone as in 1 Kgs 10:8. It also occurs in 18:15; 2 Kgs 3:14; 5:16.

no dew or rain: The conjunction is used in the sense usually conveyed by או to express alternatives (Joüon §175a). Hebrew has several words for rain. The one here (מטר) denotes rainfall in general, as opposed to more specialized terms, יורה for the early [autumn] rains, גשם for the heavy winter rain, and מלקוש for the late (spring) rains. *Dew* (טל) occurs year round, though it is especially welcome during the dry season, May–September.[5]

during these years: An “accusative of temporal determination;” see Joüon §126i.

3 **Wadi Cherith**: The name probably derives from כרה “to give a feast,” which occurs in the HB only in the Elisha story (2 Kgs 6:23).[6]

near the Jordan: על־פני here does not mean “east of” but “nearby, in the vicinity of.”[7]

4 **You can drink from the wadi**: So MT. G^{BL} + *water* after the verb.

ravens: Some advocate reading עֲרָבִים “Arabs”[8] or interpreting עֹרְבִים *ravens* as a nickname for a tribe of Arabs living in the region[9] or in the sense of “merchants.”[10] See Diachronic Analysis.

---

1 GKC §93pp list comparable examples.

2 This rendering takes the final *yod* as a marker of the plural construct rather than a part of the proper name. Jan Joosten (private communication) has suggested that the name may have been *Tišbim* on analogy with other masculine plural names (e.g., Shittim, Bahurim). While no other masculine plural place names are attested in the construct, Joosten points to the occurrence of feminine construct names (e.g., גבעת בנימין) as analogues.

3 B. C. Jones, “Tishbe,” *NIDB* 5 (2009): 607.

4 Greenberg, “The Hebrew Oath Particle *ḤAY/ḤĒ*,” *JBL* 73 (1957): 34–39. Also B. Conklin, *Oath Formulas in Biblical Hebrew* (Winona Lake, IN: Eisenbrauns, 2011), 25–26.

5 King and Stager, *Life in Biblical Israel*, 86–87.

6 R. A. Carlson (“Élie à l’Horeb,” *VT* 19 [1969], 421) cites as analogues בְּכִית “weeping” < בכה and שְׁבִית “captivity” < שׁבה.

7 J. F. Drinkard, Jr., “*ʿAl-pĕnê* as ‘east of,’” *JBL* 98 (1979): 285–88; Cogan, *I Kings*, 426.

8 E.g., Gray, *Kings*, 378.

9 M. S. Seale, “The Black Arabs of the Jordan Valley,” *ExpT* 68 (1956–57), 28; J. W. Wenham, “The Black Arabs of the Jordan Valley,” *ExpT* 68 (1956–57), 121

10 So Qimḥi, *Kings I*, 178.

ordained: Lit: "commanded." The same verb is used in v. 9, where there is no indication that the widow received a direct command from YHWH. It is better understood in an indirect causative sense.

5 **He went according to YHWH's word and stayed**: The clause ויעש כדבר יהוה וילך was interpolated by *Wiederaufnahme*.[11] The text-critical evidence supports this explanation: the respective readings of G^{B} (καὶ ἐποίησεν Ηλιου) and G^{L} (καὶ ἐπορεύθη Ηλιας) suggest that וילך and ויעש are variants that were conflated in the MT. The reading behind the OG and probably the most primitive text was apparently כדבר יהוה וילך.[12] The motive for the addition was the concern for the theme of the word of Yahweh, which is a running motif in 1 Kings 17-18.

near the Jordan: See the Note on v. 3; preceded in MT, G^{L} by *which is*.

6 **brought**: On the use of the participle to express frequentative action in the past ("would bring") as determined by context, see Joüon §121f.

bread in the morning and meat in the evening: So G^{BL}. MT, Syriac read *bread and meat in the morning and bread and meat in the evening*. Turkanik accepts the MT, contending that the OG translator was influenced by Exod 16:8, 12 or by Middle-Eastern custom.[13] The same considerations are used to argue the opposite way for the OG reading.[14] I adopt the shorter reading.[15]

he drank: So MT; G^{BL} + *water* (cf. v. 4).

7 **After some time**: ימים here refers to an indefinite period of time (cf. Gen 4:3; 2 Sam 14:26).

rain: Hebrew גשם. See on v. 1. This word refers to the heavy winter rains that were the main source of precipitation. As a result it can also be used for rain in general, and this is probably its sense here.

9 **Get up, go**: So MT. G^{BL} connect the two verbs with *and*. The imperative קום is an interjection like the English, "Come on," that can be left untranslated as in the NRSV. I have translated it here because it emphasizes the order-compliance motif found here and in the next verse.

Zarephath: The final consonant on the Hebrew name צרפתה is the locative ה. It is paragogic and does not typically alter the vocalization of the name to which it is attached, indicating that the name of this site according to the MT was "Ṣarphath" (GKC §90i; Joüon §93c). It appears in Greek here and in Luke 4:26 as Sarepta (Σαρεπτα) and in Akkadian as *Ṣariptu*. It derives from a root (צרף) meaning "to smelt, refine" or more likely "to dye red" (only the former occurs in Hebrew while both occur in Assyrian—*CAD* 16:102-105). It was located on the Phoenician coast ca. 14 miles (22.5 km) north of Tyre and 8 miles (13 km) south of Sidon at the site of Ras Sarafand, which preserves the ancient name. It is mentioned in the thirteenth-century Papyrus Anastasi I as a port city (*ANET* 477a; *COS* 3.2 (p. 12) and in Sennacherib's annals as one of the cities that surrendered to him in 701 BCE (*ANET* 287b; *COS* 2.119B). Excavations conducted at the tell near the modern village of Sarafand uncovered evidence of an Iron

---

11 Dietrich, *Prophetie und Geschichte*, 123–24.

12 Trebolle, *Centena*, 138–39.

13 Turkanik, *Of Kings and Reigns*, 76–77; similarly, Carlson, "Élie à l'Horeb," 421.

14 Stade, *Kings*, 150; Šanda, *Könige* I, 420.

15 See also P. Hugo, *Les deux visages*, 195–98.

Age commercial center where the manufacture of pottery and the production of red-purple dye were prominent.[16]

of Sidon: MT + *and stay there*, perhaps under the influence of the Elisha story in 2 Kings 4.[17] There is no evidence for Turkanik's claim that the OG translator sought to avoid saying that Elijah lived in Sidonian territory so as not to jeopardize his prophetic calling and role.[18] Not only do Ezekiel, Jeremiah, and Jonah provide counterexamples, as Turkanik acknowledges, but the present story makes clear that Elijah stayed with the widow for an extended period of time.

ordained: See on v. 4.

a widow: Lit: "a woman, a widow," an apposition genus followed by species (Joüon §131b).

10 **Zarephath**: So MT, G^B. G^L + *of Sidon*.

to the city entrance: MT precedes with ויבא *and when he came*.

a widow: See on v. 9.

gathering sticks: A denominative verb (*Polel* participle) from the noun קש, "stubble, chaff." Its object, עצים ("wood"), should be understood loosely as "twigs, straw," essentially anything that would burn.

He called to her and said: So MT. G^{BL}: *Elijah called after her and [L: Elijah] said to her.* The construction *called after* is relatively rare (1 Sam 20:37-38; 24:8), so that it is unusual to find it here and again in v. 11. The instance here is probably influenced by v. 11, where it makes more sense.

Please bring me: So MT, G^L, Syriac, *et al.* G^B lacks *to me.* The particle נא makes clear that Elijah's words are a request rather than a demand, as appears to be the case in some English translations.

in a cup: Lit: *in the cup.* The reason for the definite article is not clear.

11 **he called after her and said**: See on v. 10. Here the Greek reading *after* makes sense, since the woman has gone to fetch water for him.

Please bring me a morsel of bread in your hand: So MT. The imperative form לקחי is unique. It may be an alternate for קחי by analogy with לקח as the masculine singular imperative (Exod 29:1; Ezek 37:16; Prov 20:16) alongside קח. It may also be a mistake for קחי לה.[19] At the end of the verse G^L and most Greek witnesses expand with *so that I may eat* (φάγομαι), harmonizing with v. 10.

12 **By the life of Yhwh your god**: See on v. 1.

---

16 J. B. Pritchard, *Recovering Sarepta, A Phoenician City* (Princeton, NJ: Princeton University Press, 1978), esp. 111–30. Additional details are available in Pritchard, *Sarepta: A Preliminary Report on the Iron Age* (Philadelphia: University Museum, University of Pennsylvania, 1975) and *Sarepta IV: The Objects from Area II,X* (Beirut: Département des Publications de l'Université Libanaise, 1988). See also W. P. Anderson, *Sarepta I: The Late Bronze and Iron Age Strata of Area II,Y* (Beirut: Département des Publications de l'Université Libanaise, 1988); I. A. Khalifeh, *Sarepta II: The Late Bronze and Iron Age Periods of Area II,X* (Beirut: Département des Publications de l'Université Libanaise, 1988); and R. B. Koehl, *Sarepta III: The Imported Bronze and Iron Age Wares from Area II,X* (Beirut: Libraire Orientale, 1985). On the history of references to the site see Pritchard, "Sarepta in History and Tradition," in *Understanding the Sacred Text: Essays in Honor of Morton S. Enslin on the Hebrew Bible and Christian Beginnings* (ed. John Reumann; Valley Forge, PA: Judson, 1972): 99–114.

17 So Hugo, *Les deux visages*, 173–74.

18 Turkanik, *Of Kings and Reigns*, 119–20.

19 Cf. GKC §66g. Rendsburg, *Israelian Hebrew*, 46–48, takes it as Northern form, but see Schniedewind and Sivan, "Test Case," 322.

nothing: Reading אם יש לי מאומה based on the Syriac and Targum. The MT reading מעוג is dubious; it occurs only one other time in the Hebrew Bible (Ps 35:16) where it is almost certainly an error. It presumably refers to a kind of round loaf of bread baked on stone or in ashes rather than in an oven. At least that is the meaning of עגה (<עוג) (from a Semitic root referring to a round or curved shape), which occurs in 17:13 (cf. also 19:6). The alternative, "anything" (מאומה) fits better with the following qualifier—*except a handful of flour.* Following the oath, *by the life of* Yhwh, אם ("if") has negative force, just as in English "I'll be damned if," is a strong denial. As the rest of the widow's speech demonstrates, her response to Elijah's request is not that she has nothing prepared but that she has virtually nothing to give because she is destitute.

the jar: The כד was a medium size, multi-purpose storage jar. In Genesis 24 it is born by Rebekah upon her shoulders to carry water, and in Judg 7:16-20 it is used by each of Gideon's men to hide their torches. The latter story suggests its abundance and affordability. Both stories indicate that it had a wide mouth, from which handfuls of flour could also be withdrawn, but which could be covered by a lid for storage.[20]

the flask: The צפחת was a small, two-handled juglet—the so-called "pilgrim flask"—that typically served as a canteen (1 Sam 26:11-12). Its use here for oil may result from the widow's desperate circumstances[21] or be of a slightly different variety.[22]

a couple of sticks: On the use of *two* in the sense of *a couple, a few,* as in English, see Joüon §142c (e.g., 2 Kgs 9:32).

my children: Reading the plural with the Greek witnesses; MT has *my son.* The interpretation of בני as singular was influenced by the story that follows, which has in turn been influenced by the story of the Shunammite woman and her one son in 2 Kgs 4:8-37. The woman in the story in 2 Kgs 4:1-7, from which this one in 1 Kgs 17:1-7 is drawn (see below), also has sons or children.

eat: Lit: *we will eat.* MT has the masculine singular suffix: "we will eat it." Omit with G^{BL}.

13 **Don't be afraid**: The expression appears in a variety of contexts in the HB but is best known for its occurrences in 2 Isaiah (40:9; 41:10, 13-14; 43:1, 5; 44:2; 54:4).

small loaf: See the Note on *nothing* in v. 12.

your children: See on v. 12.

14 **Yhwh** (1): So G^{BL}. MT, Syr + *the god of Israel.*

flour in the jar will not run out nor will the flask lack oil: For the *Qal* imperfect of a III- ה verb we expect the vocalization *yikleh*; תִּכְלָה subscribes to the vowel pattern of a III- א verb (GKC §75rr), perhaps for reasons of assonance with the next verb (תֶּחְסָר).[23]

sends: Reading the infinitive construct תת (from נתן "to give") with the *qere'* rather than the *ketiv* תתן.

15 **So she went and gave it to him**: Reading ותלך ותתן לו based on Pablo Torijano's reconstruction of the OG (καὶ ἐπορεύθη ἡ γυνὴ καὶ ἔδωκεν αὐτῷ (private communication). *She did according to the word of Elijah* is an augmentation of the word of Yhwh motif

20 See A. M. Honeyman, "The Pottery Vessels of the Old Testament," *PEQ* 71 (1939): 76–90; J. L. Kelso, *The Ceramic Vocabulary of the Old Testament* (BASORSup; New Haven: ASOR, 1948), 19; King and Stager, *Life in Biblical Israel*, 142–45. The word may be Northern in origin, adding to the local color of this story. See Rendsburg, *Israelian Hebrew*, 48–49; Schniedewind and Sivan, "Test Case," 328.

21 So Honeyman, "Vessels," 89.

22 So Kelso, *Ceramic Vocabulary*, 30–31.

23 So Joüon §79l; Šanda, *Könige* I, 421.

that has been added to the original legend at several points.[24] A reference to the widow giving food to Elijah seems required, and καὶ ἔδωκεν αὐτῷ is widely attested among the Greek witnesses, though absent from G^BL^.

and her children: So G^BL^ as twice previously (vv. 12-13). Hugo reasons that the MT has suppressed the plural "children" throughout this passage for dramatic effect and coherence with the story in vv. 17-24.[25] But this does not explain why the MT here has *house* instead of the singular *son* as elsewhere in vv. 9-16. *House* reflects influence from 2 Kgs 4:1-7 where the story originated. MT's *for many days* (ימים) is a gloss, indicated by its absence from G^BL^.

16 **the flour in the jar did not run out nor did the flask lack oil**: See on v. 14. The verb *lack* (חסר) is masculine rather than feminine as expected for צפחת, the *nomen regens* of the construct chain. Although it is not unprecedented for a verb to agree with the *nomen rectum* or genitive in a construct chain (GKC §146a; Joüon 150n), it is curious that such is the case here, while just two verses earlier (v. 14) the same verb was feminine in agreement with the *nomen regens.*

17 **the mistress of the house**: Klostermann reads בעלית הבית *in the upper room of the house* for בעלת הבית and regards it as a misplaced gloss on שם in v. 19.[26] There is no text-critical evidence supporting this proposal. Rather, בעלת הבית is one of several indications that this story owes its origin to 2 Kgs 4:8-37.

became ill: So MT (חלה). G^BL^ reflect the consecutive preterit ויחל. The two constructions (i.e., perfect and consecutive preterit following ויהי + temporal clause) are variants with no discernible difference in meaning.[27]

he stopped breathing: Lit: *there was no breath left in him* (לא־נותרה־בו נשמה). G^B^ renders this as οὐχ ὑπελείφθη ἐν αὐτῷ πνεῦμα. G^L^ agrees, except that instead of πνεῦμα it has πνοὴ ζωῆς, *breath of life*, reflecting an expansion: נשמת חיים perhaps under the influence of Gen 2:7.

18 **What do you have against me?**: Lit: *What to me and to you?* i.e., *What do we have in common?* Here and in other uses (Judg 11:12; 2 Sam 16:10; 19:23; 2 Chr 35:21) this expression has the sense, *What [issue, problem] do we have between us [that you want to do me harm]?*[28] The woman is saying that Elijah's presence has drawn divine attention to her and her sin, which has in turn occasioned her son's death as punishment.

in coming: One expects either the particle כי or the interrogative marker ה before verb באת: *What do you have against me ...that you have come ...?* or *What do you have against me ...? Have you come ...?* There is no compelling textual evidence for either (though a few Hebrew manuscripts and the Targum have כי) and no apparent mechanism that might explain the loss of either. The text is simply elliptical.

to call attention to: On this translation of the *Hip'il* of זכר see Cogan.[29]

my inquity: So MT (את־עוני). G^BL^: *my iniquities* (τὰς ἀδικίας μου). Either is possible.

19 **He replied**: Lit: *He said to her* (so MT). G^BL^: *Elijah said to the woman.*

his bed: So MT, G^B^. G^L^: *the bed.* Either is possible.

20 **Elijah cried out**: So G^BL^ = ויקרא אליהו. MT: ויקרא אל־יהוה, *he cried out to* Yhwh. They are identical except for the final *heh* on the divine name. Either is possible. However, MT may be influenced by the wording of v. 21.

24 Hugo, *Les deux visages*, 178–88.
25 Hugo, *Les deux visages*, 178–88.
26 Klostermann, *Könige*, 364.
27 See Joosten, *Verbal System*, 43–44.
28 McCarter, *II Samuel*, 374.
29 Cogan, *I Kings*, 428–29.

Alas Yhwh: So G^{BL}: οἴμμοι κύριε = אהה יהוה.[30] MT: *Oh Yhwh my god* (יהוה אלהי).

even upon the widow: So MT (הגם על־האלמנה). The Greek reading, *the witness of the widow* (ὁ μάρτυς τῆς χήρας) may reflect corruption of a variant (ה)עוד על־האלמנה).[31]

21 **He breathed on the boy**: So G^{BL}: καὶ ἐνεφύσησεν = ויפח. MT: *he stretched himself* = ויתמדד, which is based Elijah's actions in 2 Kgs 4:34.[32]

back to him: Reading אל־קרבו for MT's על־קרבו, as suggested by G^{BL} εἰς αὐτόν.

22 **Yhwh listened to Elijah so that the boy's life returned to him and he lived**: So MT. G^{B} (*it happened thus and the boy cried out*) is the result of haplography occasioned by the repetition of על־קרבו from the end of v. 21. The loss left ויחי standing alone, leading to ויהי כן (καὶ ἐγένετο οὕτως = *it happened thus*) The reading *cried out* is an inner Greek corruption or change of ἀνεβίωσεν, which may have been introduced as a correction.[33] G^{L} conflates the two readings, attesting καὶ ἐγένετο οὕτως in agreement with the OG and ἐπιστράφη ἡ ψυχὴ τοῦ παιδαρίου εἰς αὐτόν in accord with MT.

23 **Elijah took the boy**: So MT. Absent from G^{BL} owing to haplography (הילד ... הילד).

24 **Now I indeed know**: So MT (עתה זה ידעתי). G^{BL}: *Behold I know* (ἰδοὺ ἔγνωκα = הנה ידעתי). While both readings are possible, the MT is more idiomatic and fits the context better in its use of עתה. That is, it is *now*—with the revival of her son—that the woman becomes more fully aware of Elijah's status and power. Compare 2 Kgs 5:22.

Synchronic Analysis

The three stories in the chapter and their shared themes

Chapter 17 contains three stories following the introduction in v. 1 (vv. 2-7, 8-16, 17-24). Each has its own literary integrity; each begins with a crisis and builds tension until the crisis is resolved.[34] At the same time, the stories are related to one another. In them Elijah moves from a passive figure whom Yhwh cares for (vv. 2-7), to one who aids the widow designated to take care of him (vv. 8-16), to an active character who takes responsibility for the widow's dead son and prays insistently to Yhwh for his revivification (vv. 17-24). The three stories participate in the themes of the drought announced in v. 1 and of the word of Yhwh. The chapter is bracketed by references to Elijah's word and mouth (v. 1) and Yhwh's word in Elijah's mouth (v. 24), thereby equating them and confirming the

---

30 For the retroversion see Hugo, *Les deux visages*, 131–32.

31 For a very different solution see Hugo (*Les deux visages*, 148–51), who defends the reading *witness of the widow*, arguing that Yhwh is portrayed as the widow's defender as well as the source of her misery, resulting in "*un profond paradoxe*" in the narrative. This is part of Hugo's contention that the MT and G represent two different versions of the story of Elijah's raising of the widow son in 17:17-24, especially in vv. 20-23.

32 Hugo (*Les deux visages*, 127–75) contends that the MT suppressed the older reading out of concern to have Yhwh alone be the one who can impart the breath of life (Gen 2:7; Ezek 37:9-10). A. R. Davis ("Rereading 1 Kings 17:21 in Light of Ancient Medical Texts," *JBL* 135 [2016]: 465–81) proposes a derivation of ויתמדד from מיד "to shake," suggesting that Elijah's actions served as a diagnostic tool for the boy in a coma.

33 Thiel, *Könige (1Kön 17)*, 65; Šanda, *Könige* I, 423; Montgomery, *Kings*, 298. Jan Joosten and Andrés Piquer point out (private communication) that this use of ἀναβιόω is unique in the LXX and the appropriate verb is ζάω.

34 Hens-Piazza, *Kings*, 162.

prophet's authority and credentials as YHWH's representative and spokesman. Together with the "order-compliance" motif, in which one character issues a command or request and another fulfills it in exact detail (vv. 3-5, 9-10, 10-15, 21-22), the theme of YHWH's word permeates vv. 1-16.[35] Thus v. 1 mentions Elijah's word as an oath sworn by YHWH. Verse 2 introduces YHWH's word, and vv. 3-4 relate it, with vv. 5-6 describing its fulfillment. Verse 7 shows fulfillment of Elijah's word about the drought in v. 1. Verse 8 introduces the new word from YHWH in v. 9. Verse 10 is its fulfillment. In vv. 11-15 there is a complex instance of order-compliance involving Elijah and the widow and incorporating a word of YHWH (v. 14). Verse 16 contains a fulfillment notice of the word of YHWH in v. 14. The theme is less conspicuous in vv. 17-24, though vv. 21-22 MT boast a complex instance of order-compliance leading to the widow's confession that the word of YHWH is truly with Elijah in v. 24, such that the powerful conclusion in v. 24 makes the presence of the theme one of quality rather than quantity.

The theme of YHWH's word

17:1: The character of Elijah

The stories about Elijah begin suddenly without any anticipation or announcement (v. 1). This is true to the character of the prophet. He appears and disappears without notice or warning (18:10-12). Like the character, the story is also intrusive. We have just been introduced to Ahab when Elijah steps in and the narrative takes a right turn to become all about the prophet. Verse 1 is an "anchor point for several bands of narrative tension" across the Elijah materials, including the punishment of Ahab, Elijah's relationship to YHWH, the drought, and Elijah's source of authority.[36] Elijah is introduced simply as "the Tishbite," a designation that is repeated five more times in Kings (1 Kgs 17:1; 21:17, 28; 2 Kgs 1:3, 8; 9:36). It is fitting for its bearer that the meaning of the epithet is not entirely certain. Tishbe is probably a place, but its location is unknown. It might also be a clan designation. Nothing about Elijah is crystal clear—not his background, title, occupation, or his credentials. Even his name could be symbolic for his role as a champion of YHWH. The lack of precise information characterizes him as a man possessed of divine mystery. Still, 17:1 tells the reader all s/he needs to know. It is clear from the name "YHWH is my god" what Elijah stands for. His style is confrontational and defiant. He addresses Ahab without any titles or acknowledgement of his status as king. He portrays himself as a servant of YHWH ("before whom I stand"). The statement is more than one of affiliation or profession. It invests his message with YHWH's authority. He is YHWH's representative. His oath by YHWH's life preempts any prospect for negotiating the matter he announces. It alludes to a contrast between YHWH, whose life is constant, and Baal, the dying and rising god. YHWH withholds the rain in order to bring Ahab and Israel back to him, as ch. 18 will show. It is by YHWH's power that there will be no more rain until further notice, and it is by the word of YHWH's representative, Elijah, that rain will next be granted.

The drought as judgment on Ahab

Elijah's elusive background and his status as YHWH's representative carry a powerful socio-economic message. The nobody from nowhere is elevated in status above the king by virtue of being YHWH's representative. Elijah passes judgment

35 See R. Smend, "Das Wort Jahwes an Elia: Erwägungen zur Komposition von 1 Reg. xvii–xix," *VT* 25 (1975): 525–43, esp. 528–29.

36 Walsh, *1 Kings*, 225.

on the king, judgment of the sort that renders the king impotent and essentially irrelevant. "No dew or rain" means drought. It is a direct challenge to the idea that Baal controls fertility and thus to the faith of Jezebel and Ahab. How long the drought will last is not revealed. We find out only at the end of the next chapter when rain finally returns after Baal has been decisively defeated in the contest on Mount Carmel. For the time being, we are told the drought will last *years*. It is a long and serious drought with devastating consequences for agriculture, livestock, and the economy of the country. The drought is Ahab's fault, punishment for his many sins. He is powerless to do anything about it. The power is vested in Elijah. In this way 17:1 sets up Ahab's search for Elijah at the beginning of ch. 18. The brusque glimpse in 17:1, therefore, is a powerful and revealing snapshot of the prophet and man of god despite the absence of those titles from the verse itself.

17:2-3: Elijah hides in the Wadi Cherith

The *Wortereignisformel* announcing YHWH's word to Elijah in v. 2 further confirms his status as YHWH's servant and representative. It is a standard formula for prophetic revelation and thus confirms the prophetic identity that v. 1 hints for Elijah. YHWH commands Elijah to go to the Wadi Cherith (v. 3). If "Cherith" derives from the verb meaning "to make a feast" (see the Note), it prepares for Elijah's sustaining by ravens (vv. 4, 6). The name also resembles the verb *hakrît* used in 18:4 for Jezebel's "cutting off" of YHWH's prophets and again in 18:5 expressing Ahab's hope that they will not have to "cut off" the animals. Elijah hides in Cherith and thereby avoids being "cut off" by Jezebel. He is sustained by animals (ravens), and his call for rain at the end of ch. 18 will prevent "cutting off" other animals because of the drought. The anecdote at once reveals YHWH's concern for and control over his creation.

The location of Wadi Cherith is unknown other than its being in the vicinity of the Jordan. Since Elijah is told to go east, a location east of the Jordan is probably envisioned here. This would place Elijah outside the immediate jurisdiction of Ahab and fit well with YHWH's order to him to hide there. But why is Elijah hiding? The allusion to 18:4 suggests that he flees to the wadi for protection from Jezebel and perhaps from Ahab, who blame him for the drought.[37] Another possibility is suggested by Ahab's search for Elijah in ch. 18. Perhaps Elijah flees not for personal protection but to make himself inaccessible as the drought worsens. This is also in line with Elijah's elusiveness as a character.

17:4-6: Elijah and the ravens

Both Elijah and the ravens comply with YHWH's commands. Elijah goes to the Wadi Cherith, where the ravens care for him. The sequence exhibits a sophisticated set of order-compliance examples within the word-of-YHWH theme. The subject-first construction and use of the perfect (צויתי) in v. 4 effects a chiastic complex of order and compliances:

YHWH commanded the ravens to care for Elijah
    YHWH commands Elijah to go to Wadi Cherith
    Elijah goes to Wadi Cherith
The ravens provide for Elijah

37 Cf. Hens-Piazza, *Kings*, 165.

Elijah receives meat twice a day (v. 6), more than what the Israelites in the wilderness (Exod 16; Num 11) received. This is one of many implicit parallels between Elijah and Moses in these stories.[38] The tale thus drives home the theological point of YHWH's control of the forces of nature and his ability to sustain the life of his people—even extravagantly—in the midst of drought and despair.

17:7: The link between the first two stories

Elijah remains in Wadi Cherith until it, too, dries up from lack of rain (v. 7). "Rain" (*geshem*) here refers to the heavy winter rains, usually the most voluminous in the annual cycle, or to rain in general. In either case the desiccation of the Wadi in the absence of these rains showcases the severity of the drought. The Masoretes regarded v. 7 as the conclusion of the first story and marked it as such with the *setumah* (ס) after the verse. This division has been contested by some modern scholars who prefer to consider v. 7 as the beginning of the next story.[39] In favor of the Masoretic division is the fact that v. 8 is identical to v. 2.[40] The *Wortereignisformel* thus serves as a structural device. As v. 2 initiates Elijah's move to the Wadi Cherith and the first story, so v. 8 initiates his move to Phoenicia for the second story. At the same time v. 7 has a dual role as both the conclusion to vv. 2-7 and the introduction to vv. 8-16. It links the two stories in that the lack of water in the Wadi provides the occasion for Elijah to leave there and move elsewhere. This linking function is signaled in the Translation by rendering v. 7 as a temporal clause.

17:8-16: The widow of Zarephath

As in the first story, so in the second, YHWH initiates the action with a command to Elijah to go somewhere: *Get up, go to Zarephath*. Elijah obeys to the letter (*he got up and went to Zarephath*, v. 10), in accord with the order-compliance motif. Although the text does not say so explicitly, the reader is led to believe that the drought has reached Phoenicia and is the reason why the widow and her son are about to die. The presence of the drought in Phoenicia illustrates YHWH's control outside the borders of Israel. Since the chief god of Phoenicia is Baal, the drought there displays his powerlessness in comparison to YHWH's control of storm and fertility, a point that will be demonstrated decisively in ch. 18. Phoenicia, and Sidon in particular, is Jezebel's home (16:31), making Elijah's deeds there and the stories about them a direct challenge to her belief system and her authority to impose it upon Israel. The widow is the righteous counterpart to Jezebel: Both are Phoenician, but the widow befriends Elijah, giving him water and bread, while Jezebel's efforts to kill the prophets of YHWH lead to them being fed water and bread in hiding (18:4, 13). More important, the widow's act is one of faith in Elijah and in YHWH, while Jezebel is faithless and an active enemy of YHWH and his representative, Elijah.[41]

The story in 17:8-16 shows that YHWH through his prophet acts not only on a "macro" level, sending the drought, but also on a "micro" level, providing daily sustenance to a poor widow. YHWH's word to Elijah that a widow would feed him

---

38 Walsh (*1 Kings*, 285) finds another, subtler allusion to Moses in the word for "flask" (צפחת, *sappaḥat*) in v. 12, which resembles the description of mannah as "wafers" (צפיחת *ṣĕpiḥît*) in Exod 16:31.

39 See Cogan, *I Kings*, 431n for a list of scholars who take this view.

40 Cogan, *I Kings*, 431n.

41 Cf. Blum ("Der Prophet und das Verderben Israels," 283) as well as Buis (*Rois*, 140) and White (*Elijah Legends*, 28), who calls the widow Jezebel's "literary foil."

(v. 9) proves to be ironic on more than one level, since she is preparing to eat her last meal.[42] By feeding Elijah she ensures food for herself and her son and saves them both from starvation. This is good news for the reader, whom the narrative inclines toward sympathy for the widow. It accomplishes this through its subtle characterization of her in such features as the absence of bitterness on her part despite her extreme poverty and her oath by YHWH *your god* in deference to the prophet, even though there is no reason for her to recognize him as such at this point. She also complies with his request to bring him food first, ahead of herself and her son (vv. 13, 15); it is unclear whether she acts out of hopeful trust in his words or resignation to her fate. Hence the reader does not think ill of her when she initially hesitates to carry out Elijah's request (v. 12).[43] Neither does Elijah, who responds with a word of reassurance (v. 13) and then a promissory oracle (v. 14). The widow and her son will not have to starve, because her food supply, meager as it may be, will be inexhaustible for the duration of the drought.

Order-compliance in the story

The story thus exhibits a complex network of order-compliances relating especially to the word of YHWH. YHWH's command to Elijah to go to Zarephath contains the notice that he has commanded a widow there to take care of the prophet (v. 9). Elijah goes to Zarephath and finds the widow. He asks her to bring him water and food. She complies, but not before explaining that she is about to prepare a last, meager meal for herself and her son before they starve to death. Elijah reiterates the command, adding that YHWH has ordered the flour and oil not to run out as long as the drought lasts. The widow follows Elijah's instructions and brings him food. The flour jar and oil flask also comply with YHWH's command and are not exhausted until the drought ends.[44] Implicit in this part of the story is the assumption that the word spoken by YHWH or Elijah is not passive but carries power to transform reality. The fulfillment notice in v. 16 mentions YHWH's word through Elijah and thus links back to the *Wortereignisformel* with which the story began forming an *inclusio*.

17:17-24: The third story

The third story (vv. 17-24) begins not with the messenger formula but with the transitional phrase *after these things*. The same set of characters shows it to be a continuation of the second tale. *The woman* is the widow of vv. 8-16. She is further identified as *the mistress of the house*, a curious descriptor in view of her extreme poverty in the previous story. Either the drought was so severe that it left a once-prosperous woman whose house is the only remnant of her prosperity at the brink of starvation,[45] or vv. 17-24 report an incident that took place considerably later, after the drought, when the woman had grown prosperous enough to own a house and Elijah was once again in the vicinity.

---

42 See R. Gregory, "Irony and the Unmasking of Elijah," in A. J. Hauser and R. Gregory, *From Carmel to Horeb: Elijah in Crisis* (Sheffield: Almond, 1990): 93–118. Also Fritz, *Kings*, 183.

43 Cf. Walsh, *1 Kings*, 227.

44 The Hebrew employs synecdoches as the subjects of both verbs in v. 14: *the jar of flour will not run out or the flask of oil be lacking*. It is clearly the substances in these vessels, not the vessels themselves, that are of interest.

45 Nelson, *Kings*, 110. One might imagine that the drought was so severe that there was no buyer for the house.

Chiastic structure

Several scholars have discerned a chiastic structure in vv. 18-24:[46]

A. speech by the widow (v. 18)
  B. speech by Elijah (v. 19a)
    C. Elijah takes the boy from his mother (v. 19b)
      D. Elijah brings him up to his own room
        E. Elijah puts him on the bed
          F. Elijah raises the child (vv. 20-22)
        E.′ Elijah picks up the child (v. 23a)
      D.′ Elijah brings him down from the room
    C.′ Elijah returns him to his mother (v. 23a)
  B.′ speech by Elijah (v. 23b)
A.′ speech by the widow (v. 24)

The structure graphically illustrates the revival of the boy (vv. 20-22) as the centerpiece of the story. The same is suggested by the plot in which Elijah ascends to and then descends from the upper room.

The woman addresses Elijah as *man of god* (v. 18). The title also occurs for him in 2 Kgs 1:9-16 but is especially common for Elisha to emphasize his wonder-working abilities. Hence the woman's address is ironic. She recognizes Elijah's power but concludes that it is to her detriment. Her *iniquity* probably does not refer to any specific sin but to the general human condition. Her fear is that Elijah's connection with YHWH has served as a lightning rod, bringing divine scrutiny and consequently punishment to her in the form of her son's death.

Raising the dead boy

Elijah takes the dead boy to his room (v. 18). The reason is unexplained, but a couple of possibilities suggest themselves. First, Elijah may wish to take advantage of his intimate relationship with YHWH to cry out to him in private. His move upstairs, therefore, points to the seriousness of the situation and the intensity with which he will make appeal. Second, one of the grounds for his appeal is that the widow has been hospitable to him in allowing him to stay with her (v. 20). Taking the boy to the room that the widow has set apart for him is a tangible reminder to YHWH of the woman's generosity toward his representative. The presence of Elijah and the boy alone in the room also highlights the role of the omniscient narrator who is privy to the intimate details about what Elijah said and did there.

Elijah makes two appeals to YHWH. The first (v. 20) reminds him of the good the woman has done and essentially accuses YHWH of bringing evil upon her in exchange for her good deeds. It thus appeals to YHWH's sense of justice and concern for his spokesman. The second (v. 21) calls on YHWH to restore the boy's life. Between appeals Elijah stretches out on top of the boy three times. His entreaty is not just verbal but ritual as well. He seeks by word and action to solicit YHWH's attention to the boy's condition and to motivate him to act on the boy's behalf. Elijah's role here, in other words, is that of an intercessor or petitioner to YHWH. As such, this portrait prepares for the intercession that Elijah

---

46 Walsh, *1 Kings*, 230–31. Compare R. L. Cohn, "The Literary Logic of 1 Kings 17–19," *JBL* 101 (1982), 336, and Keinänen, *Traditions in Collision*, 32–33.

will undertake in the next chapter and provides another parallel with Moses. The story then makes clear that it is YHWH who restores the boy (v. 22)—in response to Elijah's petitions. The woman's confession at the end of the story says as much. She has learned that Elijah is a man of god and YHWH's spokesman, and this means that Elijah is the conduit to and from YHWH, who is the ultimate source of blessing. The image of the prophet and the woman's confession prepare for Elijah's confrontation as YHWH's spokesman with the prophets of Baal in the next chapter. The outcome of the competition of deities on that occasion is already determined by the present story, which shows that YHWH controls fertility and sterility even in Baal's own land and robs death (Mot), who bettered Baal, as a bonus.

Diachronic Analysis

The Prophetic Narrator

The abrupt appearance of Elijah and the start of a long section of mostly prophetic stories signals a change of writers from DtrH. With the exceptions of 1 Kgs 21:20-22, 24 and 2 Kgs 1:2, 5-8, 17-18*, the prophetic stories from now through 2 Kings 13 are post-DtrH additions. As proposed in the Introduction, the Elijah stories in 17–19* were composed as an introduction to the Elisha stories by means of an apologia for judgment prophecy, paradigmatically illustrated against the house of Ahab. The author/editor responsible for this introduction and for editing the Elisha stories will be designated the Prophetic Narrator (PN). The change actually began with the interpolation in 16:31-33, which indicts Ahab and Jezebel and sets them up as the principal targets of the judgment prophecy of Elijah. They are the reason for the drought that Elijah announces. In chs. 17–18 PN subsumed several independent tales and prophetic *legenda* under the umbrella theme of the drought, even though only one of them (18:1-16*) originally assumed a drought.

17:1: Elijah's announcement

Elijah's announcement of drought in 17:1 is editorial (PN). The verse stresses Elijah's word as what begins the drought and what will end it. This stands out in the context of chs. 17–18, where the word of YHWH is a major theme and has been taken as indicating an independent *legenda* in which the man of god declared the drought on his own.[47] However, as explained in the Synchronic Analysis, a major purpose of these chapters is to identify YHWH's word with Elijah's (17:24) so that Elijah's declaration in v. 1 is appropriate. *Before whom I stand* (v. 1) is the property

---

47 Thiel, *Könige*, 24. Würthwein (*1. Könige 17-2. Könige 25*, 210–11; similarly Fohrer, *Elia*, 34–38, 44; Steck, *Überlieferung und Zeitgeschichte*, 9–10) postulated a pre-DtrH drought composition beginning with something like "once there was a drought" that was subsequently replaced by 17:1. Jepsen ("Elia und das Gottesurteil," 297–98) saw 17:1 as the beginning of an original "Tishbite layer" that continued the drought theme through ch. 18 (vv. 1-2a, 17-18a, 41-46). Thiel (*Könige*, 31) reconstructs a rationale (*Begründung*) to accompany Elijah's announcement (*Ankündigung*), but the reconstruction is speculative. For other views of the "drought composition" see Keinänen, *Traditions in Collision*, 13n.

of the Elijah-Elisha stories, which are alone in using it as the authentication element in the oath formulae found here (18:15; 2 Kgs 3:14; 5:16).[48] Elijah uses general terms for *dew* and *rain* to refer not to Palestine's two seasons but to the cessation of all precipitation.[49] The word pair and Elijah's curse are paralleled in the Ugaritic Aqhat epic (*KTU* 1.19.1.42-45):

šbʿ.šnt yṣrk.bʿl.	Seven years Baal went missing,
ṯmn.rkb ʿrpt.	Eight the Rider on the Clouds.
bl.ṭl.bl rbb	No dew, no drizzle.

The drought—borrowed from the story in 18:1-16*—becomes the theme that arcs over chs. 17–18 and highlights YHWH's control of the rain and fertility.

17:2-4: The order to go to the Wadi Cherith

The continued instructions in vv. 2-4 for Elijah to take refuge in the Wadi Cherith, where he can find drink, are also editorial. The *Wortereignisformel* in v. 2 fits PN's stress on YHWH's word. It should not be labeled "Deuteronomistic;"[50] it may be prophetic in origin, since it occurs in several passages relating to the early monarchy.[51] It becomes widely used in later prophetic texts, especially Jeremiah and Ezekiel, and is not exclusive or distinctive Dtr terminology.[52] The word of YHWH sets in motion the anecdote in vv. 2-7, which is couched in terms of commands and fulfillments. The argument that "from here" (מזה) in v. 3 points to an older story with some specific location that has been lost[53] reads too much into the word. The lack of specificity may suggest that the location is generic. YHWH's order to hide in the Wadi Cherith connects the drought announcement in 17:1 with 18:1-16, where Elijah reveals himself to Ahab, who has been searching in vain for the prophet to bring an end to the drought.

17:5-6: The Wadi Cherith legend

Elijah's sojourn in the Wadi in vv. 5-6 (minus the editorial elaboration *according to YHWH's word*) is an older *legenda* that the PN has used. The fact that Elijah's actions in v. 5 (*he went and stayed*) do not exactly match YHWH's order in v. 3 (*Go ... hide*) confirms this judgment. If related to the verb for "give a feast" the name Cherith (v. 4) may have been coined for this story (v. 5). Carved by rushing rainwater, wadis can be very large (e.g., the Wadi Mujib in Jordan) and quite rugged, making for good hiding places. Sites on both sides of the Jordan have been pro-

48 White, *Elijah Legends*, 16.

49 *Pace* Fretheim, *Kings*, 96. The expression *dew or rain* (טל ומטר) in 17:1 does not occur again in chs. 17–18. מטר occurs alone in 18:1. In 18:41 the word is גשם, suggesting a different origin from 17:1; 18:1.

50 So also Thiel, *Könige*, 43.

51 W. H. Schmidt ("דבר," *TDOT* 3:112–14), though, observes that the antiquity of these passages is questionable.

52 *Pace* Dietrich, *Prophetie und Geschichte*, 71–72. Keinänen (*Traditions in Collision*, 5), who follows Dietrich (*Prophetie und Geschichte*, 122–24) in ascribing 17:2-6* to DtrP, points out that the passage does not fit the pattern Dietrich associates with Dtr, namely *Wortereignisformel, Begründung, Ankündung/Weissagung, Erfüllungsvermerk*. There is no *Begründung*, and the tone of the passage is not condemnatory.

53 Burney, *Notes*, 210 and Thiel, *Könige*, 24.

posed—principally Wadi Qelt on the west and Wadi Yubis (Jabesh) on the east, the latter going back to Eusebius.[54] Wadi Qelt is problematic because it was not particularly isolated.[55] But the argument that Wadi Yubis is intended because Elijah was from Gilead is baseless if the reference to Gilead in v. 1 is a gloss.[56] The point of the *legenda* behind vv. 5-6 may have been the depiction of the holy man's existence as a hermit, alone in the wilderness, fed by animals. The use of animals to sustain divinely favored humans is a folkloric motif.[57] Animals appear elsewhere in the Bible as servants and messengers of god (e.g., Num 22; Matt 3:16). The notion that *ravens* refers to Arabs is driven by the desire to rationalize the miracle and runs counter to the point of the *legenda.*[58] The wonder is all the more impressive considering that ravens are typically aggressive scavengers. As such they are ritually unclean (Lev 11:15; Deut 14:14). This does not necessarily mean that the story predates the legal traditions, since Elijah does not eat the ravens but only the food they bring him. Meat was not typically a part of the daily diet but was limited to special occasions such as feast days. Thus Elijah's consumption of meat every evening (v. 6 OG) is a *topos* for luxurious fare and provides an allusion to Mosaic traditions about Israel's sustenance in the wilderness (Exod 16; Num 11). PN closes this episode and sets the stage for vv. 8-16 by explaining how Elijah was forced to move after the wadi dried up (v. 7).

17:8-16: A revision of 2 Kgs 4:1-7

The *Wortereignisformel* in v. 8 marks the beginning of a new episode and attests PN's word-of-Yhwh theme. The order-compliance relating to Elijah's journey to Zarephath in vv. 9-10aα also signals PN's hand. The *legenda* behind the rest of vv. 8-16 is a recasting of the Elisha *legenda* in 2 Kgs 4:1-7. In both cases there is a widow in dire straits. In both cases the prophet intervenes to rescue her and her children by means of a miracle, using the small quantity of oil she possesses. Scholars have tended to regard the two stories as sister versions from a common ancestor. However, recognizing that the present story is a revision of the Elisha *legenda* answers a number of questions raised by the Elijah version: How does Elijah recognize the widow? Why do the two of them—supposedly strangers to one another—speak to each other on such familiar terms? How does the widow know that Elijah is an adherent of Yhwh? Why does she, not knowing him, follow his instructions, even to the point of giving him the last meal that she and her

---

54 Eusebius of Caesarea, *The Onomasticon* (trans. G. S. P. Freeman-Grenville; Jerusalem: Carta, 2003) 97.

55 R. Younker, "Cherith, Wadi," *NIDB* 1:586.

56 Thiel, *Könige*, 45–47.

57 H. Gunkel, *Elias, Jahwe und Baal* (Religionsgeschichtliche Volksbücher II. 8; Tübingen: Mohr [Siebeck], 1906), 12. More generally on the sustaining role of creation in the Elijah stories see M. A. Sweeney, "Prophets and Priests in the Deuteronomistic History: Elijah and Elisha," in *Israelite Prophecy and the Deuteronomistic History* (ed. M. R. Jacobs and R. F. Person, Jr.; SBLAIL 14; Atlanta: SBL, 2013), 46–48.

58 Gray (*Kings*, 379–80), who adopts this approach by appeal to congruity with the next episode in which Elijah is fed by the Phoenician widow, acknowledges that the feeding of a hero by animals is a theme in folktales—and therefore one to be expected in prophetic *legenda*.

children will eat?[59] Such questions are answered by recognizing 2 Kgs 4:1-7 as the *Vorlage* of the present story so that the two characters are already known to each other.

The *Vorlage* took place in Israel, since its widow was affiliated with the prophetic guild (4:1). PN moved it to the Phoenician city of Zarephath (v. 9) in line with Elijah's hiding and to demonstrate YHWH's control of precipitation and fertility in Baal's and Jezebel's domain. The Elisha *legenda* did not presuppose a drought, but the woman's extreme poverty as a widow fit well under that umbrella theme. The word לכלכלך as in v. 4 signals the same hand and strengthens the tie with PN's story in vv. 1-7. Ironically, Elijah ends up taking care of the widow who is supposed to care for him.[60] Verses 10-16* are built around the order-compliance motif. Elijah complies (v. 10) with YHWH's order to go to Zarephath. His request of the widow and her immediate response (v. 11) presume their familiarity, as in 2 Kgs 4:1-7. The abruptness of the encounter is mitigated slightly by his initial request for water (vv. 10bβ-11bβ), which recalls encounters such as those of Jacob and Rebekah (Gen 29) and Moses and Zipporah (Exod 2:15-16; cf. John 4:7). PN incorporated the request by *Wiederaufnahme* (*he called to/after her, "Please bring me*)[61]—a technique that can be used by authors as well as editors—as an accommodation to the drought theme. He thus revised the Elisha *legenda* to suit his purpose in the Elijah story, including the incorporation of the request for water. PN changed the widow's crisis from debt slavery to starvation because of the drought. In 2 Kgs 4:1-7 the oil was dispensed from a single vessel and sold to pay the debt; in 1 Kgs 17:8-16 there is a more immediate need—to avoid starvation—so there are different containers for oil and flour, the ingredients of bread.

Elijah's request for food provides the entrée into the announcement and realization of the miracle. The widow swears by YHWH *your* god (v. 12) because she is Phoenician. Elijah's use of the prophetic expression "Don't be afraid" (v. 13) assures the woman that he is god's representative and spokesman, who is about to act on her behalf.[62] Verse 14a specifies the reasons for reassurance by predicting the wonder that is about to transpire. This prediction brings in the word of YHWH by using the messenger formula, "Thus says YHWH," and thus betrays PN's hand. The formula also identifies Elijah as YHWH's spokesman. Its use here is different

---

59 Scholars have tended to propose answers by creating or assuming details not explicitly mentioned in the text. For instance: Elijah recognized the widow as such by her dress (Fritz, *Kings*, 182; Würthwein, *1. Könige 17–2. Könige 25*, 212) or because she gave him water and swore by YHWH (Buis, *Rois*, 140); she recognized him as Israelite by his dress and speech (Šanda, *Könige* I, 421); her compliant responses were acts of faith (Buis, *Rois*, 140–41; Hens-Piazza, *Kings*, 167; Würthwein, *1. Könige 17–2. Könige 25*, 213).

60 Fritz, *Kings*, 183.

61 H. Schmoldt, "Zwei 'Wiederaufnahmen' in I Reg 17," *ZAW* 97 (1985), 425–26.

62 See M. Nissinen ("Fear Not: A Study on an Ancient Near Eastern Phrase," in *The Changing Face of Form Criticism for the Twenty-First Century* [ed. M. A. Sweeney and E. Ben-Zvi; Grand Rapids: Eerdmans, 2003]: 122–61), who reviews the history of the study of this expression and demonstrates its roots as an institutionalized formula in kingship and prophecy. The expression occurs twice more in the Elijah/Elisha stories: 2 Kgs 1:15, where a messenger from YHWH speaks to Elijah, and 2 Kgs 6:16, where Elisha addresses his servant.

from elsewhere in the Elijah stories (2 Kgs 1:4, 6, 16) but identical to its "eschatological" use in a group of Elisha stories (2 Kgs 2:21; 3:16-17; 4:43; 7:1), where it deals with the miraculous provision of basic needs like food and water.[63] Verse 14b also spotlights two of PN's interests —the drought, and YHWH as the one who ultimately brings rain (18:1). The widow complies with Elijah's order (v. 15) and is rewarded with the continuing supply of oil and flour as promised *according to YHWH's word* (v. 16).[64]

17:17-24: A revision of 2 Kgs 4:8-37

The story in vv. 17-24 is not an interpolation, as commonly proposed,[65] but is also a rewritten version of an Elisha *legenda*—2 Kgs 4:8-37.[66] *Afterwards* in v. 17 denotes the beginning of a new episode, albeit one involving the same characters and setting. There is no *Wortereignisformel* because Elijah is not sent elsewhere as he was in vv. 2 and 8. Instead, what initiates the story is a crisis—the death of the woman's son. *The woman* is the Phoenician widow (v. 20). Her character is melded with the Shunammite of the Elisha *legenda*, albeit without complete success. Several features from the Elisha version are held over even though they are not entirely appropriate for the circumstances of the Elijah tale. The title *mistress of the house* (v. 17) is ill-suited to the widow's impoverished condition, but is at home in the Elisha story, where the Shunammite is well off. Similarly, the furnished upper room is out of place in 17:19, 23 but integral to the Elisha tale, where the room is built for the man of god. Elijah's transport of the boy to the upper room serves no clear purpose and becomes a blind motif.[67]

---

63 W. Reiser, "Eschatologische Gottesprüche in den Elisa-Legenden," *TZ* 9 (1953): 321–38.

64 Again, Gray's rationalistic explanation (*Kings*, 381), "The factual basis may be that the generosity of the widow touched the conscience of her better-provided neighbours," misses the point of the story. Curiously, he also notes that unfailing food supply is a folklore motif and an indication of the story's legendary nature.

65 *Pace* Otto, *Jehu, Elia und Elisa*, 179–83 (and see the list of scholars who hold this view on p. 181n); as well as Keinänen, *Traditions in Collision*, 25–36; Thiel, *Könige*, 23–24, 31; and Timm, *Die Dynastie Omri*, 59. Notable exceptions include M. Ottosson, "The Prophet Elijah's Visit to Zarephath," in *In the Shelter of Elyon: Essays on Ancient Palestinian Life and Literature in Honor of G. W. Ahlström* (ed. W. B. Barrick and J. R. Spencer; JSOTSup 31; Sheffield: Sheffield Academic Press, 1984), 191 and Blum, "Der Prophet und das Verderben Israels," 281–86. The main arguments for this view are: (1) the lack of reference to drought in vv. 17-24; (2) the use of the title "man of god" for Elijah in these verses and the description of his activities as the use of prayers and magic rather than the proclamation of the divine word; (3) the portrait of the woman in vv. 17-24, which differs from that of the widow in the previous story; (4) the absence of the word-of-YHWH theme, including the lack of the *Wortereignisformel* present in the previous two tales (vv. 2, 8) as well as the lack of any proclamations or fulfillments of YHWH's word.

66 Contrast Kilian ("Die Totenerweckung"), who argues that both Elijah and Elisha boasted traditions about raising a boy from the dead. The Elijah tradition intruded into the Elisha version at an oral stage and suppressed the tradition of Gehazi and Elisha's staff, which was the magical means originally used in the Elisha story to raise the boy. Kilian's case is based mainly on the Shunammite's anticipation of her son's reanimation. He does not deal with most of the evidence presented here.

67 Gray, *Kings*, 382, attributes the move to Elijah's concern for hygiene in dealing with a dead body, but this hardly makes sense if he is planning to revive him. Besides, where did the upper room come from?

The woman's son is the boy mentioned in vv. 8-16 (MT) or better, one of her children (OG). Her relationship with Elijah is established in the previous story. Hence she goes to him when her son dies and accuses him of having brought trouble upon her by coming to stay with her (v. 18). The widow's question in v. 18 and the pain it reflects draw on 2 Kgs 4:28. She in effect accuses Elijah of causing her son's death, as does the Shunammite. The title *man of god* is common in the Elisha stories and is used throughout 2 Kings 4, but occurs for Elijah only in 17:18, 24 and 2 Kgs 1:9-13. It is therefore the original property of the Elisha traditions and only secondarily applied to Elijah. The widow assumes that she is being punished for past sin. Her question anticipates Obadiah's in 18:9.

The son's death and Elijah's revival of him

The absence of an outright statement that the boy died has spawned a good deal of discussion among commentators about the ancient Israelite understanding of death. The issue is moot as far as the present passage is concerned, since the context clearly assumes that the boy died. In addition to v. 17, which states that he ceased breathing,[68] and the widow's accusation that Elijah caused her son's death (v. 18), in v. 22 the boy's נפש ("life, soul") returns to him (v. 22). There is also no doubt about the boy's death in the Elisha *legenda* (2 Kgs 4:20), which is the template for the present story. What is more, an important theological point driving the present story is YHWH's power (through the man of god) over death.

Elijah's transport of the boy to the upper room (v. 19) is left over from 2 Kings 4, as noted. Once there, his breathing on the boy three times (OG) makes better sense than stretching out on him three times as the MT has it (v. 21b).[69] This is a *précis* of Elisha's magic act in 2 Kgs 4:34-35.[70] However, the ritual has become essentially another blind motif because it is prayer moving YHWH to act that leads to the boy's revival. Elijah is only the petitioner. Only YHWH can bring him back to life. Elijah's use of גם, *even* or *also*, is an allusion to the drought, suggesting that the woman—the Phoenician widow—who has aided him is the victim of extra disaster. Her confession at the return of her son (v. 24) acknowledges YHWH's word

---

68 Job 34:14-15 and Dan 10:17 are sometimes cited as equating breath with life; one might also mention Gen 2:7 in this regard. The counterexample of the Queen of Sheba in 1 Kgs 10:5 uses רוח instead of נשמה and describes her astonishment; it has nothing to do with death.

69 The *Wiederaufnahme* detected by Schmoldt ("Zwei 'Wiederaufnahmen,'" 424–25) incorporating vv. 20bβ-21abα is not present in the G reading.

70 Dolansky (*Now You See It, Now You Don't*, 14) provides a useful working definition of magic, especially in the Elijah-Elisha stories: "an act performed by a person (as opposed to theophany or direct acts of God), with or without attribution to God, that has no apparent physical causal connection to the (expected or actual) result." R. Albertz ("Magie II," *TRE* 21:692–93) helpfully describes two kinds of magic in the Bible: sympathetic (*Ähnlichkeitsmagie*) exemplified in 2 Kgs 2:19-22; 4:40-41; 6:6; and contactual (1 Kgs 17:19-23; 2 Kgs 2:8, 14; 4:29-32, 33-37). Dolansky (pp. 68–71) further observes that Elijah and Elisha contrast with other figures in the Bible such as Moses and Aaron in that many of their magic deeds are not attributed to god and that even when they call on god they are typically the initiators of the miracles and do not need explicit instructions from YHWH. As Kings now stands, their acts of magic are understood as testifying to YHWH's power, as stated in 1 Kgs 17:24; 2 Kgs 5:8, 15. But this is a result of PN's elaboration of the original *legenda* where that power resided in the man of god, as is most evident in 2 Kgs 13:21, where contact with Elisha's bones effects a miracle.

as the source of life and truth. It is PN's climax to the word-of-YHWH theme in this chapter.

Synthesis

Composition by revision

This chapter affords a rare glimpse into the compositional activity of a biblical author because we possess the sources PN used for two of his stories. His process of composition turns out to be closer to the model of *Redaktionsgeschichte* used in the study of the New Testament Gospels than to the approach of the same name used for the HB. That is, he revised and rewrote Elisha *legenda* to suit his interests (word of YHWH) and the setting in which he placed them (drought). He broke into the DtrH account of Ahab's reign to insert his composition. The suddenness of Elijah's appearance was appropriate for his character as a mysterious and independent man of god. At the same time PN robbed Elijah of some of the force of the character by turning him into a petitioner and intermediary, a conveyor of the word of YHWH rather than a holy man who acted on his own volition.

YHWH in control

This transformation of Elijah was done *ad maiorem gloriam YHWH*. This is PN's primary theological interest in writing. He especially praised YHWH as superior to Baal. The advent of the drought illustrated YHWH's control of the elements even in Phoenicia, Baal's home turf. If the implication were not clear, the continuous supply of oil and flour for the widow showed that fertility and sterility are also under YHWH's direction, as are life and death themselves; witness the widow's son. This set the stage for the decisive contest between YHWH and Baal in the next chapter. It also answered Ahab's accusation of Elijah leading up to that competition (18:17-18), which blamed the prophet for troubling Israel with the drought. YHWH's positive response to Elijah's petition proved that the ultimate fault for the trouble upon Israel lay not with YHWH but with Ahab and company. By extension, Israel's sufferings are not YHWH's fault or the fault of the messengers he sends to announce and warn; they are caused by faithless leaders. While there is no mention of Jezebel in ch. 17, the widow of Zarephath is a fairly transparent foil for her.

Elijah on Mount Carmel (1 Kings 18)

Text

[Prophetic sources (normal, *italic*, **bold** = different sources); *PN; Additions to PN; Even later glosses]*
1 *After some time the word of YHWH came to Elijah in the third year, "Go show yourself*
to Ahab so that I may send rain on the earth." 2 *So Elijah went to show himself to*
Ahab. When the famine grew severe in Samaria, 3 Ahab summoned Obadiah, who
was over the house. *Obadiah greatly revered YHWH;* 4 *when Jezebel killed the prophets*
of YHWH, Obadiah took 100 prophets and hid them by fifties in a cave, provisioning
them with bread and water. 5 Ahab said to Obadiah, "Come, let us pass through the
land to the springs of water and the wadis; perhaps we will find grass so that we can
keep the horses and mules alive and none of our animals will perish. 6 So they di-
vided the land between them to traverse it; Ahab went one way, and Obadiah went
the other way alone. 7 As Obadiah was on his way, there was Elijah to meet him. He
hurriedly prostrated himself, saying "Is this you, my lord Elijah?" 8 He answered
him, "It is I. Go tell your master, 'Elijah is here.'" 9 *He responded, "How have I sinned*
that you would hand your servant over to Ahab to kill me? 10 *By YHWH your god, there*
has been no people or kingdom where my master has not sent to seek you. And when
they said, "He is not here," he would adjure the kingdom or people that it had not
found you. 11 *Now you say, 'Go tell your master, "Elijah is here."'* 12 *But as soon as I go*
from you [the spirit of] YHWH will carry you to some place I do not know while I go tell
Ahab and he will kill me. Yet your servant has revered YHWH from my youth. 13 *You*
have been told, haven't you, my lord, what I did when Jezebel killed the prophets of
YHWH —how I hid 100 of the prophets of YHWH by fifties in a cave, provisioning them
with food and water? 14 *Now you say, 'Go tell your master, "Elijah is here,"' but he will*
kill me." 15 *Elijah replied, "By the life of YHWH of hosts in whose service I stand, I will*
show myself to him today." 16 So Obadiah went to meet Ahab and when he told him,
Ahab ran to meet Elijah. 17 *When Ahab saw Elijah, Ahab said to him, "Here you are, O*
troubler of Israel." 18 *He replied, "I have not troubled Israel, but rather you and your fa-*
ther's house by abandoning YHWH and going after the Baals. 19 *Now send and gather*
all Israel to me at Mount Carmel as well as the 450 prophets of Baal and the 400 pro-
phets of Asherah who eat at Jezebel's table. 20 *So Ahab sent and gathered all Israel to*
Mount Carmel. 21 *Elijah approached all the people and said, "How long will you limp upon*
two crutches? If YHWH is god go after him, but if Baal [is god] go after him." But the people
did not answer a word. 22 *Elijah said to the people, "I am left alone as a prophet of YHWH,*
while there are 450 prophets of Baal. 23 *Let two bulls be given to us, and let them*
choose one for themselves. Let them cut it in pieces and place it on the wood without
setting fire to it. I will prepare the other bull and set it on the wood without setting fire
to it. 24 *Then call on the name of your god, and I will call on the name of YHWH, and the god*

who answers with fire is truly god." And all the people responded, "This is a good idea." 25 So Elijah said to the prophets of Baal, "Choose one bull for yourselves and prepare it first. Then call on your god, but don't set fire to it." 26 *So they took the bull and prepared it. Then they called on the name of Baal, saying "O Baal, answer us." But there was no voice, no one answering.* 27 *Elijah ridiculed them, saying "Cry out louder; perhaps he is indisposed, or perhaps he is asleep and must be awakened."* 28 *So they cried out louder and cut themselves according to their custom with knives and lances until blood flowed upon them.* 29 *They kept raving as midday passed. Then at the time of the offering when there was still no voice,* Elijah said to the prophets of Baal, "Step aside now and I will prepare my sacrifice." So they stepped aside out of the way. 30 *Elijah said to the people, "Come close to me," and all the people came close to him.* 31 Elijah took twelve stones according to the number of the tribes of Israel, to whom YHWH had said, "Israel will be your name," 32 and he built the stones *and he repaired the altar of YHWH that had been torn down.* Then he made a trench with the capacity of two seahs of seed around the altar. 33 *He arranged the wood upon the altar and dismembered the bull, placing it on the wood.* 34 *He said, "Fill four jars with water and pour it on the offering and on the wood." Then he said, "Do it again," so they did it again. He said, "Do it a third time," so they did it a third time.* 35 *The water ran down around the altar;* he also filled the trench with water. 36 *Then Elijah cried out toward heaven and said, "YHWH* god of Abraham, Isaac, and Israel, Answer *me, YHWH, answer me today with fire,* so that this people may know that (for) *you, YHWH, are god in Israel,* and I am your servant who has done these things through you, 37 *and you turned their hearts back."* 38 *Then the fire of YHWH fell, consuming the offering and the wood and licking up the water that was upon them and the water that was in the trench.* 39 *Then all the people fell on their faces, saying "It is YHWH who is god; he is god."* 40 Elijah said to them, "Seize the prophets of Baal; don't let any of them escape." So they seized them and Elijah brought them down to the Wadi Qishon, where he slaughtered them. 41 Elijah said to Ahab, "Go up. Eat and drink. For I hear the sound of heavy rain." 42 So Ahab went up to eat and drink. **As for *Elijah*, he went up to Carmel and bent down to the ground, placing his face between his knees. 43 He said to his servant, "Go up. Look toward the west." So he looked and reported, "There is nothing." [Elijah] said, "Go back and look seven times." 44 So the servant went back seven times. On the seventh time there was a small cloud like a man's palm coming up from the west.** *[Elijah] told him, "Go up, say to Ahab, 'Harness [your chariot] and go down before the rain stops you.'"* 45 **Momentarily the sky darkened with clouds and wind, and there was a great rain,** *and Ahab mounted his chariot and rode to Jezreel.* 46 *But YHWH's hand was on Elijah so that he girded his loins and ran ahead of Ahab to Jezreel.*

Textual Notes

1 **After some time**: Reading ויהי מימים רבים as found in some Hebrew manuscripts and presupposed by G^{BL} (καὶ ἐγένετο μεθ' ἡμέρας πολλὰς). ויהי מימים also occurs in Josh 23:1; Judg 11:4; 15:1. MT has ויהי ימים רבים, which constitutes a singular verb with a plural subject (but cf. 1 Kgs 11:3).

3 **Obadiah**: Meaning "servant of Yhwh." The root *'bd* in personal names is a confession of allegiance to Yhwh, especially in the postexilic period. It is used for eleven characters in the HB, all in Chronicles-Ezra-Nehemiah except for the prophet behind the book of Obadiah and Elijah's interlocutor.[1]

who was over the house: See on 16:9.

4 **killed**: So G[BL], τύπτειν, which typically translates נכה, *Hip'îl*, this being the only instance in the Hebrew Bible where it stands for כרת. MT was likely influenced by the same verb in the next verse.[2] The link that the verb כרת provides with Wadi Cherith in ch. 17 may have been another influence.

by fifties: Reading חמשים חמשים as in v. 13 and with the versions.[3] MT (חמשים איש) has lost the repetition of the number by haplography and expanded with איש, which is lacking in G[BL]. The older reading is preserved in the paraphrase of the Elijah stories in the "Apocryphon of Elijah" (4Q382, fragment 1, line 2), which attests one occurrence of חמשים and the remains of another. Repetition of the number conveys the distributive sense.

in a cave: So MT with the definite article in the sense of "the object that was the one known and recognized."[4] The distributive (see previous note) indicates that two caves are involved, each housing a group of 50. This interpretation is borne out by other G witnesses that have *in two caves.*[5]

provisioning them: Reading the consecutive preterit, ויכלכלם, in place of the perfect (וכלכלם) in the MT, based on the rehearsal of Obadiah's deed in v. 13, which employs the consecutive preterit. Both forms can be used to express repeated activity.[6]

with bread and water: On the use of two accusatives for the verb כול (*Pilpel*), see Joüon §125u.

5 **Come, let us pass**: So G[BL]: δεῦρο καὶ διέλθωμεν. MT has לך בארץ. The OG, like Classical Greek, uses δεῦρο/δεῦτε for the imperative of הלך in the hortatory sense of "come, come on" and forms of πορευω for the imperative "go."[7] In this instance, therefore, the G indicates that לך was followed by the cohortative, ונעברה, which makes more sense than the MT in view of the first person plural נמצא later in the verse and the infinitive לעבר in v. 6. The primitive reading here was probably לכה (ו)נעברה.[8] This would also furnish the mechanism for the loss of the cohortative by haplography.

and none of our animals will perish: Lit.: *and the animals will not be cut off from us.* Reading tentatively with G[L]: καὶ οὐκ ἐξολοθρευθήσονται ἀφ' ἡμῶν κτήνη = ולא תכרת ממנו בהמה. MT: ולוא נכרית מהבהמה, *so that we will not [have to] kill some of the animals.* Both G[L] and G[B] (καὶ οὐκ ἐξολοθρευθήσονται ἀπὸ τῶν σκηνῶν [an inner-Greek corruption of κτηνῶν]) indicate a passive, which makes more sense than the

---

1 Noth, *Personennamen,* 137; Thiel, *Könige*, 113.

2 Hugo, *Les deux visages*, 252.

3 Burney, *Notes*, 220.

4 Cogan, *I Kings*, 370.

5 Montgomery (*Kings*, 298) suggests that מערה is generic and refers to an area full of caves.

6 Joosten, *Verbal System*, 369–70.

7 H. Avalos, "ΔΕΥΡΟ/ΔΕΥΤΕ and the Imperatives of הלך: New Criteria for the *Kaige* Recension of Reigns," *EstBib* 47 (1989): 165–76; E. Eynikel and J. Lust, "The Use of ΔΕΥΡΟ and ΔΕΥΤΕ in the G," *ETL* 67 (1991): 57–68.

8 So H. M. Orlinsky, "On the Commonly Proposed *lēk wᵉnaʿᵃbōr* of 1 Kings 18:5," *JBL* 59 (1940): 515–17. See also Avalos, "ΔΕΥΡΟ/ΔΕΥΤΕ," 172n.

MT, since the pasturage will prevent the animals from starving rather than being killed by humans. תכרת is reconstructed as a *Nip'al* as reflected by G^{L}'s ἐξολοθρευθήσονται. A second problem is the partitive מן. Ahab's hope is that he will not have to kill any of the animals, not that he will be able to avoid killing *some* of them.[9] Again G^{L} is more appropriate.

6 **the land**: So MT (הארץ). G^{BL} have *the way* (τὴν ὁδὸν). Either reading is possible. Conversely, either reading could have come in through scribal error under the influence of the context, בארץ occurring in the previous verse and דרך twice more in v. 7.[10]

Ahab went one way: So G^{BL}. MT + *alone* (לבדו) by influence of the word later in the verse.

7 **on his way**: So MT. G^{BL} + *alone* (μόνος).

there was Elijah: So MT, G^{L}: והנה אליהו = καὶ ἰδοὺ Ἠλιου, as in vv. 8, 11. G^{B} *Elijah came* (καὶ ἦλθεν Ηλιου).

he hurriedly prostrated himself: Based on G^{B}: καὶ Ἀβδιου ἔσπευσεν, G^{L}: καὶ ἔσπευσεν Ἀβδειου. MT has ויכרהו, *he recognized him*. The verb ἔσπευσεν = וימהר, *he hastened [to prostrate himself]* makes better sense (compare 1 Sam 28:20) and avoids the contradiction in the MT between Obadiah's recognition of Elijah and his question as to his identity.[11]

9 **that you would hand**: On the unreal quality of the participle here, see Joosten, *Verbal System*, 279.

10 **By Yhwh your god**: See on 17:1.

he would adjure the kingdom or people: So MT: והשביע את־הממלכה ואת־הגוי. G^{BL}: *he would burn the kingdom and its land* reflects an inner-Greek corruption of ἐνέπλησεν (<ἐμπίπλημι, "to fill, satisfy," rendering Hebrew השביע) to ἐνέπρησεν (<ἐμπίπρημι "to burn, ignite").[12] This corruption probably influenced the change from "people" to "land." On the use of the imperfect to express repeated action in the past see GKC §107e.

11 **Elijah is here**: So MT. Lacking in G^{BL} because of haplography (הנה ... והיה). It is repeated in the *Wiederaufnahme* in v. 14a.

12 **But as soon as I go from you, the spirit of Yhwh will carry you**: On the syntax here involving two instantaneous actions see Joüon §166i. רוח may be a gloss to build in separation from the deity; it is typically feminine, but the verb ישא is masculine.[13] However, there are other instances of רוח as masculine,[14] and the textual witnesses are unanimous in retaining it.

my youth: So MT. G^{BL} have *his youth* in keeping with the third person. Either is possible.

13 **You have been told, haven't you, my lord**: So MT, which actually lacks the second person reference *to you* found in G^{BL}. The second person best conveys the sense in English.

---

9 Burney (*Notes*, 221) calls the latter reading "impossible." WO's rendering (213–14) "We shall cut off not one of the cattle" is forced by the meaning required of the statement in context rather than by grammatical or syntactical considerations.

10 Turkanik's explanation of G as a deliberate change motivated by "perceived court etiquette" is a reach (Turkanik, *Of Kings and Reigns*, 201–202).

11 Hugo (*Les deux visages*, 259–61) retroverts ἔσπευσεν as ויבהל because of Obadiah's implied fear, but וימהר would lend itself more easily to corruption to ויכרהו.

12 Klostermann, *Könige*, 366.

13 Stade, *Kings*, 153.

14 *HALOT* 1197. These are explained away by K. Albrecht ("Das Geschlecht der hebräischen Hauptwörter," *ZAW* 16 [1896], 42–44), who nonetheless concludes that the noun is common in gender, if predominantly feminine.

I hid 100 of the prophets of Yhwh: So MT (ואחבא מנביאי יהוה מאה איש), G^{B}. G^{L} and the majority of Greek witnesses have two verbs: *I took 100 of the prophets of Yhwh and hid them*, in agreement with v. 4.

by fifties: That is, חמשים חמשים indicating distribution. MT + איש. See on v. 4.

in a cave: See on v. 4.

15 **By the life of:** See on 17:1.

in whose service I stand: See on 17:1. Here and in 2 Kgs 3:14; 5:16 the idiom may also allude to the prophet having stood in the presence of the divine council as in 1 Kgs 22:19; Jer 23:18, 22.[15]

16 **Ahab ran:** MT: *Ahab went* (וילך אחאב); G^{BL}: καὶ ἐξέδραμεν Ἀχααβ καὶ ἐπορεύθη = וירץ אחאב וילך. The better reading is וירץ. It has been replaced in MT and conflated in G with the more pedestrian וילך, under the influence of the beginning of the verse.

17 **Here you are:** On the exclamatory nuance of the interrogative particle see Joüon §161b.

18 **Yhwh:** MT has *the commandments of Yhwh* (compare 19:10; 2 Kgs 17:16; 2 Chr 7:19; Ezra 9:10). G^{BL}: *Yhwh your god.*

going after: Reading the infinitive absolute הלוך as suggested by G^{L}. MT, G^{B} have the second person singular ותלך, which is in tension with the suffix on בעזבכם. Other witnesses (Syriac, Vulgate, Targum) have the second plural, but this does not account for the G^{L} reading.[16]

19 **Mount Carmel:** A triangular ridge running ca. 15 miles south-southeast from the modern city of Haifa to the western entrance to the Jezreel Valley and separating the coastal plain of Acco from that of Dor. The name probably means "vineyard-like," i.e., "fruitful, lush," alluding to its rich vegetation.[17] It probably marked the boundary between Israel and Phoenicia.[18] "Mount Carmel" (Jebel Kurmul) typically refers to the promontory on the Mediterranean at Haifa. As another name for it—Jebel Mar Elias (Saint Elijah)—suggests, this is the traditional location of the contest described in the present chapter. El-Muhraka ("the burning") on a southwestern peak of the ridge, where there is a Carmelite monastery erected in 1883, commemorates the site. The promontory has a long history of recognition as a sacred site. Among the probable references to it in Egyptian and Neo-Assyrian inscriptions is the "Antelope's Nose" mentioned by an official of the Sixth Dynasty pharaoh Pepi I (*ANET* 228b).[19] Then Thutmose III mentions *Rosh Qadesh*, "Holy Head" (*ANET* 243a), and Shalmaneser III names it *Ba'li-ra'si*, "Baal of the Promontory."[20] Subsequent references in Greek and Roman sources to the sacredness of Carmel continue this venerable tradition. These include Pseudo-Scylax (5th-4th century BCE), Tacitus and

15 Cf. Chavel, "The Face of God and the Etiquette of Eye Contact," 1–55.

16 Pablo Torijano and Andrés Piquer reconstruct the G^{L} reading here as the OG (oral communication).

17 J. M. Sprinkle, "Carmel," *DOTHB*, 150–53.

18 Y. Aharoni, "Mount Carmel as Border," in *Archäologie und Altes Testament. Festschrift für Kurt Galling.* (ed. A. Kuschke and E. Kutsch; Tübingen: Mohr, 1970), 1–7; M. C. Astour, "Carmel, Mount," *IDBS*, 141.

19 For details see Sprinkle, "Carmel," and H. O. Thompson, "Carmel, Mount," *ABD* 1:874–75.

20 So Aharoni, "Mount Carmel," 6–7 and Astour, "Carmel." Also S. Ahituv, *Canaanite Toponyms in Ancient Egyptian Documents* (Jerusalem/Leiden: Magnes/Brill, 1984), 163–64. But see also Cogan and Tadmor (*II Kings*, 121 n. 11), who argue from the further descriptor "facing Tyre" in another edition of Shalmaneser's annals that *Ba'li-ra'si* designates Rosh Haniqra farther north.

Suetonius (both referring to Emperor Vespatian ca 69 CE), and Iamblichus (ca 300 CE).[21] A 2nd-3rd century CE dedicatory inscription found at the site associates Carmel with Heliopolitan Zeus, the god of Baalbek.[22]

prophets of Baal: So MT (נביאי הבעל). G^{BL} reflect the disparaging substitution for Baal: τοὺς προφήτας τῆς αἰσχύνης = נביאי הבשת.

Asherah: So MT. G^{BL} have the plural. Hugo, following Schenker, argues that the MT harmonizes with 1 Kgs 16:33; 2 Kgs 13:6 in referring to the asherah in Samaria.[23] But the asherah in 16:33 is a cult object rather than a deity as here.

20 **So Ahab sent and gathered all Israel to Mount Carmel**: Following White's reconstruction: וישלח אחאב ויקבץ את־כל־ישראל אל־הר הכרמל.[24] MT has Ahab send through all Israel (בכל־בני ישראל) to summon the prophets of Baal, who are already present (v. 22) and are headquartered in Jezreel (v. 19).

21 **how long will you limp upon two crutches?**: So MT (עד־מתי אתם פסחים על־שתי הסעפים). G^{BL} have ἕως πότε ὑμεῖς χωλανεῖτε ἐπ᾽ ἀμφοτέραις ταῖς ἰγνύαις = *How long will you limp upon both* [G^{L}, OL: *your*] *knees*?" The exact meaning of the question is uncertain because of the ambiguity of the verb and the noun translated "opinions." פסח is used in the Bible in two senses that have been traced to originally distinct roots (compare BDB 820 and *HALOT* 947): (1) to "jump over, pass by," the origin of or a pun on the name of Passover (Exod 12:13, 23, 27) and hence, "spare, protect" (Isa 31:5); (2) a denominative from the noun for "lame," פסח (cf. 2 Sam 4:4, *Nip'al*) with the meaning "limp" (1 Kgs 18:26, *Pi'el*).[25] In the latter verse the verb describes or parodies the ritual dance of the prophets of Baal. It remains unclear whether the verb in v. 21 has the sense of "hop" or "limp." The other main part of the question, the noun סעפים is a *hapax legomenon.* It comes from a root with the sense of "cleave, divide" and thus might refer to divided crags, roads, opinions, or branches and hence crutches. The image, then, could be that of a bird or animal hopping between branches or clefts, a person hobbling on crutches, or someone alternating between roadways. Or, it could be an idiom for changing one's mind or opinion. The translation here tentatively follows Thiel, who argues that the key to understanding the expression is the number "two."[26] Thus, while walking with a single crutch was common, trying to walk with two of them instead of legs eventuated in stumbling and falling. Hence, *limping upon two crutches* was a metaphor for instability.

did not answer: So G^{BL}. MT + *him.*

22 **450 prophets of Baal**: So MT. G^{BL} + *and 400 prophets of Asherah*, drawn from v. 19.

---

21 Psuedo Scylax, *Periplus* 104; Tacitus, *Historiae* 2.78.3; Suetonius, *Vesp* 5.6; Iamblichus, *De vita Pythagorica* 3.15 (Dillon and Hershbell 1991, 42–43). See M. J. Mulder, "Carmel," *TDOT* 7:331–33 and Sprinkle, "Carmel," 152.

22 ΔΙΙ ΗΛΙΟΠΟΛΕΙΤΗ ΚΑΡΜΗΛΩ. M. Avi-Yonah, "Mount Carmel and the God of Baalbek," *IEJ* 2 (1952): 118–24.

23 Hugo, *Les deux visages*, 270–76; Schenker, *Älteste Textgeschichte*, 32–33.

24 White (*Elijah Legends*, 26–27), who suggests that the corruption in MT was influenced by 2 Kgs 10:18-21.

25 G. Gerleman ("Was heisst פָּסַח?" *ZAW* 88 [1976]: 409–13) argued for a meaning of "strike" or "rebound" for all occurrences of this verb in the HB. This meaning is forced and particularly out of place in Isa 31:5.

26 Thiel, *Könige*, 144-48. A critique of Thiel's interpretation might be that the saying appears to be a popular aphorism, yet he observes that the first attested use of two crutches is in the Middle Ages. Still, the use of something like a crutch was probably significantly older.

23 **one**: So G^{BL}: (τὸν ἕνα). MT: *one bull.*

the other bull: So G^{BL}: τὸν βοῦν τὸν ἄλλον = הפר האחר. MT has הפר האחד, by graphic confusion. It also adds *and set it on the wood*, an expansion based on Elijah's previous instructions.

24 **on the name of Yhwh**: So MT. G^{BL} + *my god*. OL omits the divine name and reads *my god*, suggesting that *Yhwh* and *my god* are ancient variants.

the god who answers: So MT, G^{B}. G^{L}, OL + *today* (σήμερον).

truly god: So MT with the article (האלהים הוא).

This is a good idea: Lit.: "the word is good." So MT: טוב הדבר. G^{BL} + *which you have spoken.*

25 **Baal**: So MT. G^{BL}: *the abomination* (τῆς αἰσχύνης = הבשת).

Choose one bull for yourselves and prepare it first: The clause *for you are the ones who are most numerous* (WO, 248) is attested in different locations, G^{L} and OL reading it after *yourselves*, while MT and G^{B} have it after *first*, suggesting that it is a gloss stressing the number of Elijah's opponents.

26–29 OL, preserving the OG, retains a more pristine text than MT in these verses.[27] In particular, the OL does not divide the action into two movements, before and after noon, as does MT, but describes a single sweep of time from the beginning of the contest, at an unspecified time, until the time of the evening offering.

26 **they took the bull**: So G^{BL}, OL. MT + *which one had given to them.*

they called on the name of Baal: So G^{L}, OL. MT, G^{B} + *from the morning until noon* in anticipation of the reference to noon in v. 29.

O Baal, answer us: So MT. G^{BL}, OL: *Answer us, O Baal, answer us.*

no one answering: MT, G^{B} + *then they limped around the altar which they had made.* Lacking in the OL and inappropriate for other reasons.[28] The verb פסח appears here with a different sense than in v. 21. There it refers to vacillating between Yhwh and Baal, while here it describes the cultic dance of the prophets of Baal. Also, the singular verb עשׂה, which matches the נתן of the gloss or expansion earlier in the verse, makes little sense here, where it refers most naturally to Elijah. The G witnesses and MT *Sebir* resolve the problem by reading the plural עשו, but the sentence is most likely a late elaboration punning on פסח and adding color to the depiction of the Baal prophets. Elijah's mocking in the next verse refers to their crying out to Baal without response but does not acknowledge their limping around the altar.

27 **Elijah ridiculed them**: Preceded in MT, G^{BL} by *at midday.* This notice, which divides the narrative in MT into two sections, before and after noon, is absent from the OL and is part of an elaboration attested in the MT and then by recension in the Greek witnesses.[29] The OG expands Elijah's title, reading *the Tishbite* (so G^{BL}, OL). The verb ויהתל is a secondary formation from √תלל (BDB 251; *HALOT* 257) conveying a sense of deceit, i.e., that Elijah deluded the Baal prophets into thinking he was serious about Baal being god.[30]

saying: So MT, G^{B} (ויאמר = καὶ εἶπεν). G^{L}, OL: καὶ προσέθετο λέγων = ויסף לאמר = *saying again.*

Cry out louder: On this translation as a comparative see WO, 264; Joüon §102g.

perhaps he is indisposed, or perhaps is asleep and must be awakened: Reading: אולי שׂיג הוא אולי ישן הוא ויקץ. This is the *Vorlage* of the OG reading reconstructed by Trebolle on the basis of the OL.[31] He suggests that MT attests a variant to this reading in its

27 J. Trebolle, "Textcritical Value."
28 Trebolle, "Textcritical Value," 327–29.
29 It was not part of the OG. See Trebolle, "Textcritical Value," 327–28.
30 Cogan, *I Kings*, 440.
31 Trebolle, "Textcritical Value," 318–19.

כי־אלהים הוא כי שיח לו and that its present text represents a fusion of these two variants. I would reconstruct the process behind MT somewhat differently. As Trebolle notes, the phrase וכי־דרך לו found in MT but not the Greek witnesses is secondary. The same is probably true of כי־אלהים הוא found in MT and G^B but not G^L. The word שיח is a gloss on שיג, which is a *hapax legomenon.* The gloss was made first in MT, followed by the two additions. The etymology of שיג points to the meaning "go away, go to the side" or "expulsion, defecation" (*HALOT* 1319). שיח also can refer to defecation or urination,[32] and this is the meaning that the gloss sought to clarify. It is possible that שיח was originally intended to refer to Baal meditating or musing, as many modern commentators and most English translations have it (cf. 2 Kgs 9:11). However, the reference to bodily functions accords with Elijah's mocking of his opponents and their god. This understanding goes back at least as far as Targum Jonathan, which employs its own euphemism, and which may have influenced Rashi.[33]

28 **according to their custom**: So MT, G^L. Lacking in G^B, perhaps due to haplography occasioned by the similarity of כ and ב.

29 **They kept raving as midday passed**: Reading ויתנבאו עד אשר עבר הצהרים with G^L: καὶ ἐπροφήτευσαν ἕως οὗ παρῆλθε τὸ μεσημβρινόν. MT agrees with the timing of events (as does OL) but has the reverse order of clauses: ויהי כעבר הצהרים ויתנבאו. G^B essentially agrees with G^L except for reflecting *evening* (הערב) in place of *midday* (הצהרים), perhaps the result of a miswriting of ערב for צהרים under the influence of עבר.

Then at the time of the offering when there was still no voice, Elijah said to the prophets of Baal, "Step aside now and I will prepare my sacrifice." So they stepped aside out of the way: MT suffered a long haplography occasioned by the repetition of *Elijah said* here and at the beginning of v. 30. The haplography led to a subsequent shift in the wording of the MT and its expansion at the end with ואין־ענה ואין קשב.[34] See further on vv. 30-32 below.

30 **to the people**: So G^{BL}. MT: *to all the people.*

came close to him: MT + *and he repaired the altar of* Yhwh *that had been torn down.* See on v. 32.

31 **number of the tribes**: So MT, G^B. G^L: *number of the twelve tribes.*

of Israel: So G^{BL}. MT: *of the sons of Jacob.*

Yhwh had said: So G^{BL}: ἐλάλησεν κύριος; MT: *the word of* Yhwh *came* (היה דבר יהוה).

32 **he built the stones**: So G^L, OL. MT and G^B, respectively, read *he built the stones into an altar in the name of* Yhwh[35] and *he built the stones in the name of* Yhwh. All three readings accommodate the interpolation in vv. 31-32a (discussed below). I adopt the shortest reading. For another example of בנה used with an object of material only see 1 Kgs 15:22 = 2 Chr 16:6. The longer form ויבנה (instead of ויבן) occurs often in Kings and seems to be preferred before a guttural (10:29; 16:25; 2 Kgs 3:2; 13:11).[36]

---

32 G. A. Rendsburg, "Hebrew *św/yḥ* and Arabic *šḫḫ*," in *Fucus: A Semitic/Afrasian Gathering in Remembrance of Albert Ehrman* (ed. Y. L. Arbeitman; Amsterdam, 1988): 419-30; "The Mock of Baal in 1 Kings 18:27," *CBQ* 50 (1988): 414–17; and "*lāśûaḥ* in Genesis XXIV 63," *VT* 45 (1995): 558–60.

33 See Dray, *Translation and Interpretation*, 150–51.

34 Hugo (*Les deux visages*, 222–28) overlooks the haplography and explains MT's variation as an effort to distinguish Elijah's altar completely from that of the prophets of Baal.

35 On the use of בנה with a double accusative see GKC §118ii, 118kk; WO, 175, 222; Joüon §125w.

36 Joüon §79; Cogan, *I Kings*, 322. See also H.-J. Stipp, "Narrativ-Langformen 2. und 3. Person von zweiradikaligen Basen nach qalY im biblischen Hebräisch," *JNSL* 13 (1987): 109–49.

He repaired the altar of YHWH that had been torn down: MT has this reading at the end of v. 30, while G^{BL} have it here after v. 32a. G^{B} lacks the phrase *of YHWH*, for stylistic reasons, since the divine name already occurred in v. 32a.[37] The different locations are the result of the insertion of vv. 31-32a, which MT has after the sentence and G^{BL} before it. The insertion has Elijah building a new altar in obvious contradiction to the statement that he repaired an existing one.[38] On the use of רפא "to heal" for repairing an inanimate object see Jer 19:11. Neh 3:34 also refers to reviving (√חיה) stones, probably of an altar.

trench: So MT (תעלה) here and in vv. 35, 38, where it is transliterated in G^{L} (θααλα). G^{B} has forms of θαλασσα ("sea") in all three instances.

33 **He arranged the wood upon the altar and dismembered the bull, placing it on the wood**: Reading ויערך את־העצים על המזבח וינתח את־הפר וישם על־העצים. This is the MT reading plus the phrase *upon the altar*. G^{BL} have a longer reading: *he arranged the wood upon the altar which he had made and dismembered the holocaust placing [it] upon the wood and arranging [it] upon the altar.* The MT appears defective in not mentioning the altar. G's *which he had made* appears expansive, and the final clause (*arranging [it] upon the altar*) is repetitive and out of place. Once these features are corrected, the only significant difference between the readings is *bull/holocaust*, which may be ancient variants.

34 **Fill**: So MT. G^{BL}: *Bring to me* (λάβετέ μοι = קחו לי).

four jars: So MT, G^{B}. G^{L}: *two jars*, probably under the influence of "second" later in the verse. On the nature of the כד, see on 17:12.

on the offering and on the wood: So MT. G^{L} precedes with *on the altar*; G^{B} follows with *they did so.*

35 **he also filled the trench**: So MT, G^{L}. G^{B} has a plural verb influenced by the plurals in the previous verse.

36 **Then Elijah cried out toward heaven**: So G^{BL}. MT has a very different reading: *at the time of the offering, Elijah the prophet approached.* The latter is full of difficulties that suggest it is a misplaced gloss: the time of the offering has already been mentioned and has passed (v. 29); the title *prophet* does not occur elsewhere for Elijah in these narratives (but see 19:16); and the verb *approached* seems out of place; whom or what did he approach?

36-37 **Answer me, YHWH, answer me today with fire, so that this people may know that you, YHWH, are god in Israel, and I am your servant who has done these things through you, and you turned their hearts back**: So G^{L} and OL:[39] ἐπάκουσόν μου κύριε ἐπάκουσόν μου σήμερον ἐν πυρί καὶ γνώτω πᾶς ὁ λαὸς οὗτος ὅτι σὺ εἶ μόνος κύριος ὁ θεὸς Ισραηλ καὶ ἐγὼ δοῦλός σὸς καὶ διὰ σὲ πεποίηκα ταῦτα πάντα καὶ σὺ ἔστρεψας τὴν καρδίαν τοῦ λαοῦ τούτου ὀπίσω σου and *exaudi me, domine, exaudi me hodie in igne ut sciant omnis populous hic quoniam tu es dominus deus Israel et ego servis tuus et propter te feci haec opera et tu versasti cor populi huius retro.* MT attests the reverse order of the two main clauses in v. 36-37: *let it be known that you are god in Israel and I am your servant and by your word I have done all these things. Answer me, YHWH, answer me so that this people may know that you, YHWH, are god and have turned their hearts back.* G^{B} is longer because in v. 37 it reflects a reproduction of the MT: *Answer me, YHWH, answer me today by fire so that all this people may know that you, YHWH, are the god of Israel and I am your servant and through you I have done these things. Answer me, YHWH, answer me so that this people may know that you,*

---

37 Trebolle, Centena, 141.

38 The rationale that Hugo (*Les deux visages*, 228–37) offers for the MT fits better as an explanation for the insertion of vv. 31-32a than for the differences between MT and G.

39 Trebolle, "Textcritical Value," 322–26.

YHWH, are god and you have turned the heart of this people back. MT's reading indicates minor expansions in the OG witnesses in two places: *this people* as opposed to *all this people* and *their heart* rather than *the heart of this people.* On the other hand, MT and G^{L} expand slightly in reading *all these things.* The textual difficulties in this verse stem in part from the clause *and I am your servant who has done these things through you*, which is a later gloss.

38 **fire of YHWH:** So MT. G^{BL} + *from heaven.*

consuming the offering and the wood and licking up the water that was upon them and the water that was in the trench: ותאכל את־העלה ואת־העצים ואת־המים אשר עליהם והמים אשר־בתעלה לחכה. MT: *consuming the offering and the wood and the stones and the dust, and licking up the water that was in the trench.* G^{BL}: *consuming the offering and the wood and the water that [L: was on them and the water that] was in the trench and the stones, and the fire licked up the stones and the dust.* The different placements of *the stones and the dust* suggest that these words are an expansion.[40] MT interprets the stones and dust in the string of objects of תאכל, while the G^{B} construes them as objects of the later verb *licked.*[41] In addition, G^{L} suggests haplography of the phrase עליהם והמים אשר.

39 **Then all the people fell on their faces:** So G^{BL}. MT: *When all the people saw, they fell on their faces.*

It is YHWH who is god, he is god: All major witnesses appear to expand. MT: *YHWH is god, YHWH is god.* G^{BL}: *Truly, YHWH is god, he is god.* If the G reading were influenced by Deut 7:9, as is sometimes asserted, one would expect the suffix: "YHWH is *our* god, he is god."

40 **Elijah said to them:** So MT. G^{BL}: *Elijah said to the people.* Either reading is possible.

Wadi Qishon: The Nahr al-Muqaṭṭa, essentially the watercourse of the same name today that runs along the northeastern edge of Carmel and empties into the Mediterranean east of Haifa, referred to in the Deborah story (Judg 4:7, 13; 5:21) and in Ps 83:10.[42]

41 **I hear:** For this translation of קול + genitive see Joüon, §162e.

heavy rain: Lit. "the roar of rain," so MT (המון הגשם). G^{BL}: τῶν ποδῶν τοῦ ὑετοῦ, *the approaching* (lit. "feet") *of rain.*

42 **to Carmel:** So G^{BL}. MT: *to the top of Carmel.*

bent down: The verb גהר occurs three times in the HB, here and in 2 Kgs 4:34-35 in the context of Elisha's revival of the Shunammite's son. The word has traditionally been understood to mean "bend" or "crouch." Smith proposed a new interpretation of it based on its presumed presence in a Ugaritic incantation (*KTU* 1.178.11).[43] Assuming

---

40 So also Montgomery, *Kings*, 311.

41 Hugo (*Les deux visages*, 243–44) takes the plus as a late addition. Turkanik (*Of Kings and Reigns*, 38) argues that G reflects a deliberate change of the translators because dust and stones are not flammable.

42 D. M. Stith, "Kishon," *NIDB* 3:535.

43 M. S. Smith, "Recent Study of Israelite Religion in Light of the Ugaritic Texts," in *Ugarit at Seventy-*Five (ed. K. L. Younger, Jr.; Winona Lake: Eisenbrauns, 2007), 12–13. P. Bordreuil and D. Pardee, "Une incantation," in *Études ougaritiques*. I. *Travaux 1985–1995* (ed. M. Yon and D. Arnaud; RSOu 14; Paris: Éditions Recherche sur les Civilisations, 2004), 387–92; D. Pardee, *Ritual and Cult at Ugarit* (SBLWAW 10; Atlanta: SBL, 2002), 159; *COS* 1.100. The reading may not be secure. *KTU* has *gġrt* rather than *ghrt*. While the drawing supplied by Bordreuil and Pardee shows a *h*, the photo in G. del Olmo Lete (*Photographic Archive: Incantations and Anti-Witchcraft Texts from Ugarit* [SANER 4; Boston/Berlin: de Gruyter, 2014]) is obscure, the first readable sign being *r*.

the word to mean “sound forth” or “be loud (of voice),” he suggested that Elijah is imitating the sound of the approaching rainstorm. The idea is intriguing but leaves the next clause unexplained. Elijah’s putting his head between his knees must be imitative as well. It seems to define גהר and perhaps to represent a cloud. If so, one would expect the sound of rain to follow the cloud formation, not precede it. See on 2 Kgs 4:34-35.

his knees: MT *ketiv*: *his knee.*

43-44 **“Go back and look seven times.” So the servant went back seven times**: So G^{L}. G^{B} reflects dittography: *And you go back seven times; and go back seven times. So the servant went back seven times.* MT is haplographic: *Go back seven times.*

44 **there was a small cloud**: So G^{BL}. MT: *he said, “There is a small cloud ...”*

coming up from the west: So MT: עלה מים. G^{BL}: ἀνάγουσα ὕδωρ = מעלה מים, *bringing up water*; OL, which reflects “bringing up water from the sea” (מעלה מים מים) is dittographic. MT is preferable because it is clear to Elijah alone that the cloud will bring rain.

Harness [your chariot]: So MT: אסר. G^{BL}: ζεῦξον τὸ ἅρμα σου = אסר רכבך. Cf. 2 Kgs 9:21.

before the rain stops you: The verb is inexplicably vocalized יַעַצָרְכָה in Codex Leningradensis rather than the יַעֲצָרְכָה, as in other mss. The longer suffix in *–kh* rather than *–k* is relatively rare in the MT (cf. Gen 10:19; 27:7) but typical of late second-temple-period orthography.[44]

45 **Momentarily**: עד־כה occurs in Exod 7:16; Josh 17:14, where it means “until now, hitherto.” The repetition adds a sense of immediacy, i.e., “between one moment and the next” or “just at that moment.”[45]

Ahab mounted his chariot and rode to Jezreel: So MT: וירכב אחאב וילך יזרעאלה. G^{L}: καὶ ἔκλαιε καὶ ἐπορεύετο Αχααβ εἰς Ιεζραελ = *Ahab wept and went to Jezreel.* G^{B}’s ἔκλαεν is an error for ἔκλαιεν = ויבך,[46] which is itself an error for וירכב.[47] The verb רכב refers to the act of mounting and to the symbol of being mounted on a royal animal or conveyance.[48] Thus the presence of the chariot is implicit in the verb.

46 **he girded**: The verb שנס used here in the *Pi'el* is a *hapax legomenon* in the HB. However, it occurs in Ugaritic (*KTU* 1.3.2.11-13) in the depiction of Anat the warrior:

ʿtkt rišt lbmth	She fixes heads to her torso;
šnst kpt bḥšh	She cinches hands to her belt.

It has the same function in combination with מתנים “loins” as חגר (2 Kgs 4:29; 9:1). The expression probably originated from the act of cinching an outer garment around one’s waist or loins in order to free the legs for vigorous physical activity;[49] it is used especially in military contexts. Elijah is preparing to run.

44 Cogan, *I Kings*, 445.

45 Walsh, *1 Kings*, 257

46 So also Turkanik, *Of Kings and Reigns*, 181.

47 D. W. Gooding, “Ahab According to the Septuagint,” *ZAW* 76 (1964), 272. Hugo (*Les deux visages*, 287–97) defends the G reading as part of a motif of Ahab’s repentance that was suppressed in the MT.

48 W. L. Moran, “Some Remarks on the Song of Moses,” *Bib* 43 (1962): 317–27; W. B. Barrick, “The Meaning and Usage of RKB in Biblical Hebrew,” *JBL* 101 (1982): 481–503.

49 Cogan, *I Kings*, 445.

to Jezreel: So G[B] (εἰς Ισραηλ) = יזרעאלה.[50] G[L]: ἕως Ιεζραελ. MT is expansive: עד־באכה יזרעאלה.

Synchronic Analysis

The continuning drought

The *Wortereignisformel* in 18:1 marks the beginning of a new episode that is, nonetheless, a literary continuation of ch. 17. This is reinforced by the *after some time* (ויהי ימים רבים), which led to the inverted form (subject first) of the *Wortereignisformel*. The drought that Elijah announced in 17:1 has continued for "many days" amounting to "three years." The double time reference gives the sense that it has dragged on and tested the endurance of those who suffer under it. The narrative only describes events at the beginning (ch. 17) and end (ch. 18) of the drought, which is thus the umbrella theme that unites the two chapters. Its center post is 18:1; YHWH's announcement that he will send rain means that the drought is coming to an end. The word for rain—מטר—is the same as in 17:1. As in 17:2-7, YHWH is in control of creation. He wields it to instruct and discipline Israel, who under the aegis of Ahab and Jezebel has put its trust in a powerless deity, Baal. The drought demonstrates this. Its dramatic conclusion will make the point doubly clear. The announcement in 18:1 comes by the word of YHWH, which continues as a theme from ch. 17. Its content—namely, that the time has come when YHWH will give rain again—reaffirms the message in the last chapter that Elijah's word (17:1) is YHWH's word. The order-compliance motif also continues, as YHWH tells Elijah to show himself to Ahab, and the prophet immediately goes to do so (v. 2). Elijah's hiding from 17:3 ends as he returns to Israel to seek out Ahab, who has been seeking him.

18:1-2: Elijah comes out of hiding

The three episodes in ch. 18—finding Ahab (vv. 1-18), the decisive defeat of Baal (vv. 17-40), and the end of the drought (vv. 41-46)—are not as clearly distinguished from one another as those in ch. 17 with markers like the *Wortereignisformel*. Rather, they flow one into the next. 18:1 leads into the first episode as Elijah sets out to "be seen" (להראות) by Ahab. The encounter with Obadiah (vv. 2b-16) informs the reader just how desperately Ahab has been seeking him and becomes the means for their reunion. The notice that the famine was severe in Samaria (v. 2b) explains Ahab's anxiety. The results of the drought have hit home in the capital. Elijah, though, does not appear before Ahab as his subject. Their roles are reversed. It is Ahab who seeks an audience with Elijah, and it is YHWH who sets the timetable. As YHWH's representative, Elijah is Ahab's superior. He allows the king to see him because YHWH commands it.

18:3-4: Obadiah

As the steward "over the house" Obadiah had duties that included administration of the royal estates, so his involvement at this point is logical (v. 3). The initial impression of him is mixed. His name implies that he is a "servant of YHWH," yet he is summoned by Ahab. How can he be a servant of both? His character thus foreshadows Israel's vacillation between two religions (v. 21). The narrative moves to assure the reader that Obadiah greatly reveres YHWH. He cared

50 Hugo, *Les deux visages*, 285–86.

for prophets of YHWH whom Jezebel was trying to kill (v. 4). This meant risking his position and his life. So Obadiah is a man of courage. Provisioning 100 prophets without getting caught would also require great caution, and this caution makes Obadiah skittish about announcing Elijah's return to Ahab (vv. 9-15). Obadiah's provisioning of the prophets is another touchstone to the stories in ch. 17—the raven's provisioning Elijah (17:4) and the widow of Zarephath doing the same (17:9)—all three using the same verb (כול, *Pilpel*). "The cave" where Obadiah hid the prophets anticipates Elijah taking refuge in "the cave" in 19:9.

18:5-6: Searching for pasture

Scarcity of food for humans means no food for animals, which would be the first casualties of the drought unless some pasture can be found for them (v. 5). The animals in question are horses and mules. These were royal mounts but also probably animals trained for military purposes. Losing them would mean a weakening of defense. The fact that the king and his steward personally scour the land for viable pasturage (v. 6) shows the seriousness of the crisis. The description of two characters departing in opposite directions is fairly rare in the HB (cf. Gen 13:9-11). It confirms spatially that Ahab and Obadiah are on opposite sides and heading in different theological directions.[51]

Three meetings

The meeting of Ahab and Obadiah sets the stage for the encounters that follow between Obadiah and Elijah (vv. 7-15) and Elijah and Ahab (vv. 17-18). The arrangement of three encounters between different pairs of three characters may reflect an ancient literary convention of including only two characters in a scene at a time.[52] It moves the narrative forward through dialogue and thus develops the reader's interest in them as individuals. The key meeting is the final one, between Ahab and Elijah, which leads into the next episode in vv. 19-40.

18:7-8: "Is it really you, Elijah?"

Obadiah's scene with Elijah (vv. 7-15) is the longest of the three encounters. The language describing Elijah's appearance to Obadiah (והנה אליהו) suggests that he materialized essentially "out of thin air," much as in his entrance into the book of Kings (17:1). Obadiah prostrates himself, showing proper respect for the prophet. It is not clear whether he knows Elijah personally or recognizes him from his description or clothing (2 Kgs 1:8).[53] His humility and obeisance are rare for a high official (cf. 2 Kgs 1:13) and represent another point in his favor. The people will also prostrate themselves before YHWH in 18:39, so the two occurrences of the verb enclose the stories of Elijah's reappearance and the Carmel contest. The fact that Obadiah lies prostrate suggests that his question (האתה זה) is rhetorical. On the other hand, the question reflects some incredulity resulting from Elijah's lengthy absence and sudden reappearance. One might render it "Is this *really* you?" Ahab will ask the same question when he sees Elijah (v. 17). Elijah responds with the single word אני, "It is I" (v. 8). The terse response suggests that he does not trust someone who is tied so closely to Ahab. Perhaps for that reason he offers no explanation about where he has been. His reply has the flavor of a rebuke in its correction of Obadiah's polite address: "Go tell your *real* lord Elijah is here." The last two words are the same as in v. 7 (הנה אליהו), forming an *inclusio* surrounding Elijah's advent. He speaks of himself in the third person to maintain

---

51 I owe this observation to John Kaltner.

52 Nelson, *Kings*, 115.

53 Thiel (*Kings*, 117) argues for the latter.

distance from Obadiah. The clause means both "Elijah is here" and "Look, YHWH is my god." He leaves no doubt about whose side he is on. Again he seems to question Obadiah's allegiance.

18:9: First impressions

Obadiah's question about how he has sinned (v. 9) is reminiscent of the widow's in 17:18. Both ask what they have done to deserve the harm, befallen or anticipated, brought upon them by Elijah. It is not immediately clear how Elijah's order to inform Ahab that he has returned might put Obadiah in danger. For the moment he appears to Elijah as a man who fears Ahab more than YHWH. The reader knows that this impression is incorrect, because Obadiah risked his life to save the prophets of YHWH (v. 4). Obadiah's oath by YHWH *your god* reminds one of the Phoenician widow in 17:12. Obadiah stresses Elijah's closeness to YHWH, but Elijah may take it to mean that Obadiah is a worshiper of Baal.

18:10-15: Obadiah's reticence

Obadiah launches into a lengthy explanation by observing that Ahab has sought Elijah in all the surrounding countries, even extracting oaths from them that they were unable to find him (v. 10), such has been his desperation to find Elijah. Obadiah is afraid that YHWH's spirit will snatch Elijah away, making him unavailable to meet Ahab. This will anger Ahab, who will blame Obadiah and have him killed (vv. 11-12). The explanation attests Elijah's reputation for appearing and disappearing without warning (17:1). In Obadiah's understanding this trait is not willful on Elijah's part but a result of his affinity with YHWH. The concept of YHWH's spirit that is articulated here differs from that found in Judges (6:34; 11:29; 14:6, 19; cf. 1 Sam 10:6), in which the spirit took possession of a person inwardly and moved that person to action. In the present text the spirit is a force outside of Elijah that transports him.[54] It is a notion found elsewhere in Kings only in 2 Kgs 2:16 and outside of Kings only in Ezekiel (2:2; 3:12, 24; 8:3; 11:1; 43:5). Obadiah reinforces his protest by rehearsing for Elijah what the narrator has already told the reader, that he reveres YHWH and that he saved prophets whom Jezebel was trying to kill (vv. 12b-13). He adds that he has revered YHWH from his youth, suggesting that it is a part of his basic identity, like his name. In view of his righteousness it is unjust of Elijah to put him in a situation where he is likely to lose his life (v. 14). Elijah reassures him with an oath by YHWH that he will show himself to Ahab that very day (v. 15). He employs the same form of oath that he used in 17:1 and that the widow used in 17:12, pairing it with the expression "before whom I stand," harking back to 17:1 and looking forward to 2 Kgs 3:14; 5:16. The prophet swears by the god to whom he devotes his life in service. It is this oath that finally persuades Obadiah to go to Ahab. Its substance—that Elijah will "be seen" (ראה, *Nip'al*) by Ahab recalls YHWH's command at the beginning of the story (18:1-2) and informs the reader that the anticipated encounter between Ahab and Elijah is imminent.

YHWH's transporting spirit.

18:17-18: Elijah and Ahab

The climax of this series of encounters is the final one in vv. 17-18. Obadiah disappears from the narrative and is not heard from again. Despite the partial development of his character in vv. 2b-4, he is still a role player. He has facilitated the meeting of Elijah and Ahab and highlighted the mysterious and powerful character of Elijah. He also foreshadowed Israel's ambivalence toward YHWH and Baal. The meeting of Ahab and Elijah is far from cordial (v. 17), a confrontation

54 Šanda, *Könige* I, 429.

really, anticipating the confrontation of YHWH and Baal in the next section of the chapter.[55] Ahab calls Elijah the *troubler of Israel*. The moniker refers to someone whose behavior brings misfortune upon others especially in the form of supernatural retribution (cf. Josh 6:18; 7:25; Judg 11:35; 1 Sam 14:29). Ahab blames Elijah for the drought. The charge is a tacit admission that YHWH controls fertility in Israel. Elijah turns the accusation back upon Ahab (v. 18) in accord with the idea common in the ancient Near East that kings were responsible for ensuring the well-being of their subjects and domains. The real cause of the disaster, he asserts, is Ahab and his family, who have brought trouble by abandoning YHWH's commandments in favor of the Baals. Israel's real trouble, in other words, is not the drought but the worship of other gods that Ahab and the Omrids have led them into.[56] This statement prompts the contest about who is the real god. Thus vv. 17-18 are both the climax of the encounter between Elijah and Ahab in vv. 1-18 and the transition into the story of the contest on Mount Carmel. They are a hinge, or part of one, between the episodes of the search for Elijah and the contest on Carmel.[57] The contest will prove both Ahab and Elijah right in a way: The drought came upon Israel at the behest of Elijah because YHWH is the one who controls the weather. But it did not come because of Elijah; it was sent by YHWH to discipline Ahab and Israel and to show them YHWH's superiority over their adopted gods.

18:19-20: Hinge to the contest story

The second major segment of the chapter is the contest on Mount Carmel. Elijah determines to prove once for all that the god Ahab has rejected is more powerful than the one he has chosen. If vv. 17-18 function as one doorplate of a hinge, vv. 19-20 are the other. The former close the first episode and the latter open the second. Elijah orders Ahab to gather all Israel as well as the prophets of Baal and Asherah to Carmel (v. 19), and Ahab complies (v. 20). Prophecy commands monarchy. The reference to the prophets of Baal and Asherah apart from the people of Israel shows that the former are not Israelites but Jezebel's Phoenician prophets. She provides for them at significant cost in tax revenue from Israelites! They contrast with the prophets of YHWH who are forced because of her to subsist on bread and water (vv. 4, 13), if they are not killed outright. Although the verb כול is not used, the contrast with the ravens and the widow of Zarephath who provided for Elijah is implicit. The king's table is a place of honor (1 Sam 20:29; 2 Sam 9:7-13; 19:28; 1 Kgs 2:7; cf. 2 Kgs 25:29). Jezebel has usurped it. She wears the pants in the royal family. Ahab is only the convener of the prophets who belong to Jezebel. She is the real threat and the real royal power, the one who is ultimately responsible for Ahab's apostasy and Israel's vacillation. It is no coincidence, therefore, that Ahab disappears from the narrative at this point. He has served his purpose in assembling the prophets of Baal according to Elijah's order. He is not mentioned again in the account of the contest but only resurfaces when Elijah warns him of the impending rain (v. 41). Whether he was present for the contest is unclear. It is also immaterial. Ahab is a pawn to his wife. The contest is really

55 D. Nocquet, *Le "livret noir de Baal": La polémique contre le dieu Baal dans la Bible Hébraïque et l'ancien Israël* (Actes et recherches; Geneva: Labor et Fides, 2003), 98.

56 Nocquet, *"Livret noir,"* 112.

57 Thiel, *Könige*, 112.

with her. The prophets of Baal are hers, and she is the one who has been killing YHWH's prophets. She is Elijah's true adversary.

Setting on Mount Carmel

Mount Carmel initially seems an odd choice as the setting for the contest, since it is not centrally located in Israel and thus does not facilitate Elijah's didactic exhibition for all the people. This drawback is outweighed by its relative proximity to Tyre, its fertility, and its history as a sacred site. YHWH's victory lays solid claim to the mountain range as Israel's. Carmel's many caves align nicely with 18:4, 13 and, as a *Leitmotif*, with 19:9, 13. Setting the story here also paves the way for the tales about Elisha, whose sometime home is in Carmel.

18:21-40: Time to choose

Like vv. 3-16, the contest narrative in vv. 21-40 has three scenes, each involving two of the three sets of characters: Elijah and the people (vv. 21-24), Elijah and the prophets of Baal (vv. 25-29), and Elijah and the people again (vv. 30-40).[58] Elijah approaches (נגש) the people (v. 21), who will later approach him (v. 30), before he approaches to cry out to YHWH (v. 36). His opening question: "How long?" registers a complaint against the people that initiates the contest.[59] The question makes use of what appears to have been a popular saying or aphorism whose precise meaning is lost (see the Note). If the translation "limp upon two crutches" is correct, the saying is a metaphor for instability. Whatever its exact origin, Elijah is clearly accusing the people of indecisiveness. They cannot "have it both ways" by trying to serve both Baal and YHWH. They must make a choice. It is also a choice between the prophet and the king. As if to illustrate their indecision, the people *do not answer a word*, highlighting the theme of answering that plays an increasingly significant role in the contest culminating in the answer summoned by Elijah.

18:22-24: Elijah's proposal of a contest

Elijah proposes a contest (vv. 22-24) to move the people to decision. He is in charge; his authority is not questioned by the people, the prophets of Baal, or Ahab. He begins the proposal with a statement that he is alone as a prophet of YHWH (v. 22) over against the 450 prophets of Baal. The statement agrees with vv. 4, 13, since the other Yahwistic prophets have been killed or driven into hiding by Jezebel. He is aware of the 100 prophets hidden by Obadiah (vv. 4, 13), but they are unavailable. His claim to be alone protects them from Jezebel.[60] It is also part of his rhetorical strategy for the challenge he is about to issue. The title "prophet" is rare for Elijah (18:36; 19:16) and sets him in opposition to the 450 prophets of Baal—not to mention the 400 prophets of Asherah. The odds are stacked against him. The prophets of Baal can hardly decline to participate, especially with all the people of Israel looking on. His being so clearly at a disadvantage will make Elijah's ultimate success all the more spectacular.[61] Ultimately, though, this numbers game is a ruse because the real contest is between two gods.

---

58 Thiel, *Könige*, 151.

59 Thiel (*Könige*, 144) observes that עד־מתי registers a complaint about a situation that the speaker finds intolerable (Jer 4:21; 12:4; Ps 6:4; 74:10; 80:5; 90:13; 94:3; Zech 1:12). It typically leads into an appeal, charge, or grievance of a controversy (Ps 82:2; 94:3; Jer 4:14), according to DeVries (*1 Kings*, 228). The difference is that in these other passages the complaint is directed toward YHWH, while Elijah addresses the people of Israel.

60 Walsh's (*1 Kings*, 259) interpretation that Elijah holds the other prophets of YHWH in disdain goes against the narrative's efforts to establish Obadiah and the 100 prophets in his care as true Yahwists.

61 Provan, *Kings*, 141.

18:23-24: The terms of the contest

Elijah's terms call for each party to prepare a bull for sacrifice, taking all the steps except setting it on fire (v. 23). Each is then to call upon its god, and the god who *answers with fire* will thereby prove himself genuine (האלהים, "the god"). Elijah ostensibly affords every advantage to his opponents, allowing them to go first. If the verb ויתנו ("let them give") is taken as referring to the prophets of Baal, Elijah even allows them to choose the two bulls.[62] By his own design Elijah is the underdog. There is a certain practicality to this plan, as it will take him longer to prepare since he is working alone.[63] It also indicates his confidence that the Baalists will fail.[64] From a narrative standpoint having the prophets of Baal go first creates suspense and prolongs the story's climax. It elevates frustration with the Baal prophets and highlights the contrast between their failure and Elijah's success. In v. 24 Elijah changes back from the jussive to the second plural (וקראתם). The people have been his addressees since v. 21 and continue as such. The jussives in v. 23 prescribe what the prophets of Baal are to do for their part in the contest. Thus in v. 24 Elijah includes the people as participants to the extent that they are to call on Baal along with the prophets. Their inclusion with his opponents further stacks the deck against him. As his addressees, the people approve the "rules" of the contest in v. 24b. Elijah nowhere refers to Baal by name, but simply calls him *your god*. His use of YHWH's name, in contrast, affirms that Baal is unreal.

18:25: The prophets of Baal prepare their sacrifice

The contest proper begins in v. 25 as Elijah instructs the prophets of Baal to choose their bull and prepare it for sacrifice. They follow his instructions (v. 26). The subject of the verb נתן in v. 26 is not Elijah, since v. 23 indicated that the bulls were supplied by someone else. In that verse the question was whether the prophets of Baal were the suppliers. That is not a possibility here since they are the recipients. Hence in both verses the verb should be taken as impersonal. Verse 26 then details the efforts of the prophets of Baal to summon a response. They prepare their bull as instructed by Elijah and begin calling on Baal. They continue calling all morning. Despite their pleas—*Oh Baal answer us*, there is *no voice, no answerer*. The latter statement does not use Baal's name but is in the abstract or impersonal and implies that there is no one to answer. The "voice" is the signature sound of the storm god, i.e., thunder (e.g., Exod 19:19; Deut 4:36; 2 Sam 22:14//Ps 18:14; Job 37:1-5; 38:34; 40:9; Ps 29:3-9; 68:34; Isa 30:30-31; Jer 10:13; 51:16), which is associated with lightning, the "fire" (e.g., Exod 9:23-24; Deut 4:36; 5:22-26; Ps 29:7; 97:3-4) that constitutes an answer from the god.[65] The complete absence of the "voice" and the "fire" calls into question the essence of the religion of Baal and the god's very existence. There is no response because Baal is unreal, nonexistent, a nonentity.

18:26: Cultic dance

The prophets of Baal begin to "hop" or "limp" around their altar in a ritual dance. There is a pun on the same verb in v. 21. Here in v. 26 it may be parody. To be sure, dance is attested as a cultic activity in ancient Israel (2 Sam 6:14; Ps

62 So Walsh, *1 Kings*, 246. But see below on v. 26.

63 Walsh, *1 Kings*, 247.

64 Würthwein, *1. Könige 17-2. Könige 25*, 217–18.

65 See further M. S. Smith, *Ugaritic Baal Cycle*, Vol. 1 (VTSup 40; Leiden: Brill, 1994), 347–48; M. L. Barré, "Lightning," *DDD*, 519–20; J. L. Lawlor, "Thunder and Lightning," *NIDB* 5:590–91.

149:3; 150:4; Jer 31:13) and in other cultures.[66] It may be a sign of prophetic ecstasy or a means to achieve it but is not necessarily incantational or designed to bring rain.[67] Its primary function here is narratival. Following the statement that there was *no voice and no answerer*, the hopping/leaping is an act of desperation, like the self-laceration in v. 28.[68] The verb פסח suggests an awkwardness or ungainliness to the activity that accords with the polemic against Baal.[69] Elijah's own mocking in the next verse (v. 27) enhances the likelihood that the narrative is joining its hero in ridiculing his opponents. The awkwardness of the dance and the curiosity of the spectacle enhance readers' interest and create sympathy for Elijah that invites readers to share in the mocking.

18:27: Elijah's mocking

As observed in the Note, there are connotations of deception in the root התל. Elijah's ostensibly helpful suggestions about the activities that may be distracting Baal are sarcasm. The scenarios he poses attest the creation of a god in the image of humans. They are found in myth and are eminently mundane human activities.[70] He urges his opponents to cry louder to Baal, *for he is a god*. Elijah does not believe that Baal is god, and he is reveling in their frustration. He ridicules the notion that divine life is analogous with human,[71] even to the point of suggesting that Baal must relieve himself. In reality Baal is no god. His failure to respond is not because he is otherwise engaged but because he does not exist.

No response

If the Baal prophets recognize Elijah's sarcasm as such, they ignore it. Still, they take his advice to increase the volume of their cries (v. 28), thereby conceding that Baal is inattentive. They lacerate themselves and go into prophetic trances (ויתנבאו, v. 29) in their effort to attract Baal's attention. The response, however, remains the same: *no voice, no answerer.* They continue their ecstatic frenzy until the time of the evening oblation—after 3:00 PM.[72] YHWH's liturgical schedule thus sets the time frame for the contest.[73] They have had more than their fair chance.

18:30: Elijah's turn

The day is nearly gone. If Elijah is to have his turn he must take it now. He dismisses the prophets of Baal. They have failed. He summons the people to draw

---

66 See the ancient parallels adduced by de Vaux, *Bible and the Ancient Near East* (trans. D. McHugh; Garden City, NY: Doubleday, 1971), 241n. To these, scholars often add references to the more recent Whirling Dervishes and the practice of circumambulation of the Kaaba during the Hajj in Mecca. Cf. Harris, *Grammar of the Phoenician Language*, 88, 147.

67 *Pace* Fritz, *Kings*, 191; Cogan, *I Kings*, 440; and R. Patai, "The 'Control of Rain'" in Ancient Palestine: A Study in Comparative Religion," *HUCA* 14 (1939), 254–55.

68 DeVries, *1 Kings*, 229.

69 Cf. Hauser, "Yahweh Versus Death—The Real Struggle in 1 Kings 17–19," in *From Carmel*, 42; Walsh *1 Kings*, 248.

70 L. Bronner, *The Stories of Elijah and Elisha as Polemics against Baal Worship* (Leiden: Brill, 1968), 134–38; Saint-Laurent, "Light from Ras Shamra," 132–33. Cf. also J. R. Battenfield, "YHWH's Refutation of the Baal Myth through the Actions of Elijah and Elisha," in *Israel's Apostasy and Restoration: Essays in Honor of Roland K. Harrison* (ed. A. Gileadi; Grand Rapids: Baker, 1988), 19–37.

71 Fritz, *Kings*, 191.

72 I.e., the ninth hour; so Josephus (*Ant* 14.65-66) and the Mishnah (*Pesahim* 5.1).

73 Nelson, *Kings*, 118.

near to him.[74] Their proximity affords them a clear view of all that Elijah does so as to quell any allegations of deception.[75] The account of his preparations in vv. 30b-35 followed by his prayer in vv. 36-37 slows the narrative and builds suspense before the climax in v. 38.

18:31-33: Building and readying the altar

Elijah begins by repairing an altar to YHWH that had been torn down (v. 32b). Exactly when this older altar was destroyed is not clear, but its presence indicates that Mount Carmel once pertained to YHWH and the Israelites; the Phoenician Baalists are encroaching. Elijah's repair entails rebuilding the altar. He uses twelve stones corresponding to the sons of Jacob and the tribes of Israel (v. 31), recalling similar altars built by Moses (Exod 24:4) and Joshua (Josh 4:20). This symbolizes the unity of Israel as YHWH's people. The clause *Israel will be your name*, quoted from Gen 35:10, shows that it was YHWH who chose Jacob/Israel as his people. Their defection to Baal is foolish.

18:33b-45: Water everywhere

The significance of the water is confirmed by the way in which the entire episode is narrated around it (vv. 32b-35). Each step is detailed with a repeated order-compliance: *Elijah said, 'Do it again,' so they did it again. He said, 'Do it a third time,' so they did it a third time*. Then the narrative notes how the water flowed around the altar and filled the surrounding trench (v. 35). The fact that drenching takes place in the midst of a drought and on a remote mountainside highlights its significance even more. The extended description prolongs the suspense as the tale teeters on the brink of its climax. Preoccupation with the water enhances the miracle. The fire will consume the thoroughly wet sacrifice as well as the water in the trench (not to mention the wood and stones!). It is fire from god, not from humans.[76]

18:36-37: Elijah's prayer

The narrative reminds the reader that it is the time of the evening offering (v. 36). Elijah's appeal to YHWH will be simpler and take less time than the theatrics of the prophets of Baal. It will also be effective. Elijah appeals to YHWH to act for his divine glory. The basis of the appeal is the longstanding relationship YHWH has with his people going back to their ancestors. The identification of YHWH as the god of Abraham, Isaac, and Israel is reminiscent of Moses (Exod 3:6, 13, 15-16; 4:5) and stresses Elijah's continuity with them as YHWH's servants. Elijah affords himself no credit for his great deeds but admits that they are all accomplished through YHWH. The appeal concludes in v. 37 with the expression of hope that YHWH's "answer" will lead Israel to "know" YHWH, i.e., to reestablish their relationship with him.

---

74 De Vries (*1 Kings*, 228) points out that נגש often signals the opening of a controversy or the demand for a decision (Gen 18:23; 27:21; 45:4; Josh 14:6; 21:1; 1 Sam 14:38; Isa 41:1; 50:8; Joel 4:9) or the prelude to delivering or receiving an oracle (1 Kgs 20:22, 28; 2 Kgs 2:5; Jer 42:1).

75 Cogan, *I Kings*, 442.

76 "Das reichliche Vergießen des Wassers über den Opferstücken und vor allem über dem aufgeschichteten Holz macht deutlich daß es kein normales, von Menschenhand entzündetes Feuer ist, dass das Opfer in Brand setzt, sondern ein überirdisches Feuer, kurz: das Feuer Jahwes" = "The plentiful pouring of water over the pieces of the victims and especially over the stacked wood makes clear that it is no normal fire kindled by human hands that sets the sacrifice ablaze but an unearthly fire, in short, the fire of Yhwh" (Thiel, *Könige*, 179).

Elijah's final statement in v. 37 *and you have turned their hearts back* has been understood in two diametrically opposed ways. Is he saying that Yhwh restored Israel to himself or that Yhwh is the one responsible for turning them away in the first place? The answer, surprisingly, appears to be the latter.[77] The expression סבב (*Hip'îl*) + לב occurs elsewhere in the Bible only in Ezra 6:22. It has the meaning "incline the favor of." The adverb אחרנית, "back," implies movement in the wrong or uncustomary direction. If the sense were that of restoration the verb would most likely be a form of שוב. The emphatic use of the pronoun אתה and of the divine name (each three times in Elijah's prayer in vv. 36-37) suggests that the contrast is between Yhwh and Baal. It must have been Yhwh who attracted Israel to backslide, since Baal's ineffectiveness has been proven. The idea that Yhwh could be responsible for his people's regression is not unique to this prayer (cf. 1 Kgs 12:15, which uses the noun סבה, and Isa 63:17). It also provides another similarity with the Moses story in the latter's account of the hardening of Pharaoh's heart. It is paired with the idea that Yhwh effects his people's return, to his greater glory.

18:38-39: Fire from heaven

The "answer" in the form of fire from heaven finally comes, and with it the climax of the contest (vv. 38-39). Its arrival is all the more dramatic at dusk when the brightness of the lightning and light from the fire contrast with the enveloping darkness. The fire signals divine acceptance and sanctification of an altar (Lev 9:24; 1 Chr 21:26; 2 Chr 7:1). It also consumes the stones, destroying the altar and answering Elijah's prayer while also removing what would otherwise violate the principle of cultic centralization. Fire from heaven is lightning, especially where a storm god is involved, and as such is a symbol of Yhwh's presence (Exod 19:18; 24:17) as well as a demonstration of his power over the storm. It may be a harbinger of coming rain[78] that Elijah will summon at the end of the story. (vv. 42-45). Above all, the fire harks back to v. 24, where Elijah said and the people agreed that *the god who answers with fire is truly god.* The people therefore confess "*Yhwh is truly god*" (v. 39), a contrast to their silence in v. 21.[79] They no longer vacillate between two opinions as before the contest (v. 21). In view of the emphasis on the divine name and the nature of the contest, I have translated this confession *It is Yhwh [as opposed to Baal] who is god.* This is also the meaning of Elijah's name. The narrative at this point becomes a "conversion story," a feature it shares with the end of ch. 17. Like the widow, the people become convinced that Yhwh is god and Elijah is his prophet. The confession does not explicitly deny the existence of other gods as do Deut 4:35, 39. The question of Baal's ontological existence is moot. He has been shown to be inattentive, ineffective, and impotent. Rendering him service or worship is futile.

18:40: Elijah slaughters the prophets of Baal

After humiliating the prophets of Baal, Elijah slaughters them at Wadi Qishon (v. 40). The verse brings together the three constituencies of the contest story—Elijah, the prophets of Baal, and the people.[80] The fate of the Baal prophets, though appalling from a modern perspective, is appropriate in ancient Israel. They

---

77 Cogan, *I Kings*, 443; Montgomery, *Kings*, 305; Walsh *1 Kings*, 263.

78 Šanda, *Könige* I, 440.

79 E. Würthwein, "Die Erzählung vom Gottesurteil auf dem Karmel," *ZTK* 59 (1962): 131–44.

80 Thiel, *Könige*, 107–108.

are representatives of Baal, who has been proven to be powerless and whose very existence is doubtful. They are encroaching on the worship of YHWH within his own territory. Like Baal himself, they must be gotten rid of. Nevertheless, their slaughter betrays some anxiety about the attractiveness of Baalism to the people of Israel—an anxiety that is justified by the resurgence that requires another purge a few years later under Jehu.[81] The reason for transferring to the Wadi Qishon is to avoid desecrating the now holy site on Carmel and to remove the blood of the prophets from the land in the direction of Phoenicia. It was also remembered as the site of Deborah's defeat of Sisera (Judg 4:7; 5:21), which Elijah's deed recalls. Psalm 83:9 calls on YHWH to do to his enemies what was done to Jabin and Sisera at Wadi Qishon. The wholesale slaughter of the prophets of Baal might also be conceived of as an offering (*ḥerem*) to YHWH in line with the commands in Deut 13:1-11.[82] It rids the land of those who have encroached on a god's territory. It is also a fitting response to Jezebel's killing of YHWH's prophets (vv. 4, 13). Finally, it anticipates and prepares for Jehu's bloody revolt. They are seized (תפש) and slaughtered (שחט) according to Elijah's word (order-compliance), just as the Judahite princes will be seized and slaughtered according to Jehu's command (2 Kgs 10:14).[83] Elijah and Jehu exemplify zeal for YHWH that is lauded by their respective stories.

18:41-46: Elijah brings rains

Ahab resurfaces

The final section of the chapter (vv. 41-46) begins with Elijah addressing Ahab. The king has not been mentioned since v. 20 when he assembled the prophets of Baal on Mount Carmel. Presumably he witnessed the contest but was not mentioned because he was not a participant. Alternatively, he went to the Wadi Qishon and waited for Elijah there.[84] He does not object to Elijah's slaughter of the Baal prophets or try to stop him. Perhaps he is even convinced of YHWH's supremacy and Baal's inefficacy. That would explain why he and Elijah seem to be on good terms with one another in this final episode.

The verb "go up" (עלה) is a key word in vv. 41-44. In v. 41 it is probably better understood as an interjection ("Go on") rather than a command for Ahab to ascend the mountain from the wadi. It is followed by two other imperatives ordering Ahab to eat and drink. They presuppose that Ahab has been fasting in an effort to break the drought.[85] The narrative presents a two-step process in which Elijah first announces the coming of rain, telling Ahab to break his fast (v. 41), and then warns him to go to Jezreel to avoid the rain (v. 44).[86] His announcement of rain completes the arc begun with 17:1, where it was said that rain would come again only by Elijah's word. The reason for ending the drought is the people's return to YHWH.[87]

After Ahab leaves in compliance with Elijah's order (v. 42a), the latter goes up to the top of Carmel where he crouches on the ground with his head between his

---

81 I am grateful to Rhiannon Graybill for the observation about the anxiety of Yahwism that is implicit here.

82 Hauser, *From Carmel*, 53; House, *Kings*, 220; Walsh *1 Kings*, 254;

83 Otto, *Jehu, Elia und Elisa*, 176.

84 So Walsh, *Ahab*, 30.

85 Würthwein, *1. Könige 17–2. Könige 25*, 213.

86 For Hauser (*From Carmel*, 58) the delay is a narrative strategy that builds tension.

87 Buis, *Rois*, 149.

knees. There is no mention of prayer or even of YHWH's name.[88] This is, rather, an act of ritual magic, as indicated by the verb גהר, "crouch," which occurs elsewhere only in the description of a magic rite in 2 Kgs 4:34-35 (see the Note). A common interpretation is that Elijah draws himself up to symbolize a cloud.[89] The sudden appearance of a servant is surprising. Narratively, he attenuates the drama, measuring Elijah's progress with the ritual. The sevenfold repetition of his ascent fits with the magic element of the ritual.[90] On the seventh time the servant sees a small cloud, the size of one's palm—presumably one that can be blocked from vision by a hand extended at arm's length, though possibly an idiom for smallness.[91] Elijah then tells the servant to "go up" again—this time to warn Ahab to leave the mountain before the rain comes (v. 44b). This seems to be an act of courtesy; the rain would make the roads impassable.[92] The warning of imminent rain is again based on Elijah's prescience since the cloud is still a trifle. The episode as a whole brings to mind Danel's plea for rain and searching of the sky in the Aqhat Epic (*KTU* 1.19.1.28-49), which uses "seven" in the pair seven/eight for the number of years of drought caused by Baal's absence.

Ritual magic

The sky darkens and the winds pick up quickly—while Elijah is speaking and while Ahab is making ready (or dawdling). When the rain comes, it is a downpour, a testimony to Elijah's prowess and YHWH's power. The impression is that Ahab is barely able to get away. The mud on the road may have slowed his progress, but the main reason that Elijah beats him back to Jezreel is that YHWH's "hand," i.e., "strength" or "power," was upon him (v. 46). Elijah's run is a superhuman feat.

Diachronic Analysis

Tensions among the three parts of this chapter (vv. 1-16, 17-40, 41-46) betray their different origins, yet there is also evidence of substantial continuity, suggesting that the chapter as it stands is the work of a single author/editor.

18:1-16: The prophetic *legenda*

The episode in vv. 1-16* is the only one in chs. 17–18 in which the drought is inherent. It is the subject of the nominal clause in v. 2b that marks the beginning of the underlying story. That story included Ahab's summoning of Obadiah (v. 3a) and the foray of the two of them throughout the land on which Obadiah encountered Elijah (vv. 5-8). The notion of the king personally scouring the countryside for viable pasturage (vv. 5-6) was already denigrating. Elijah's sudden appearance (v. 7) resembles 2 Kgs 2:16-18, which may be its origin (cf. 17:1).

---

88 So Otto, *Jehu, Elia und Elisa*, 171–72; Würthwein, *1. Könige 17–2. Könige 25*, 214; *pace* Buis, *Rois*, 149; Fritz, *Kings*, 188–89.

89 D. R. Ap-Thomas, "Elijah on Mount Carmel," *PEQ* 92 (1960): 154.

90 It is possible to construe the total as eight (the first ascent + 7 more), but seven is more likely since the number seven is known for its presumed magical qualities. See M. E. Boring, "Numbers, Numbering," *NIDB* 4:294–99; Würthwein, *1. Könige 17–2. Könige 25*, 214.

91 Walsh, *1 Kings*, 257.

92 Nelson, *Kings*, 120.

True to character, Elijah offers no explanation about where he has been, but he tells Obadiah to inform Ahab of his presence (v. 8). In the initial story Obadiah did just that (v. 16), which led to Ahab's going to meet Elijah (v. 16). That story then continued with Elijah's announcement that Ahab could give up his fast because the end of the drought was imminent (vv. 41-42a). The source of this story is unknown. It may derive from the Elisha materials, where there are several references to famine (2 Kgs 4:38; 6:25; 7:4; 8:1),[93] in which case the king would not have been Ahab.

PN's revision

The older story was revised and enlarged by PN. Verses 1-2a are his doing; they use the *Wortereignisformel* (inverted) that began the stories in 17:2 and 8 and thus refer to the word of YHWH as well as the hiddenness of Elijah, both motifs from ch. 17. They also employ order-compliance in YHWH's instruction to Elijah to show himself to Ahab. Of the two time references in v. 1, "after many days" and "in the third year," the latter is a gloss, since a copyist would be more inclined to add a more specific time rather than a more general one—all the more so since three years is a round number for a moderate period of time elsewhere in 1 Kings (2:9; 10:22; 22:11).[94] Elijah's compliance (וילך אליהו להראות, v. 2) with YHWH's order (לך הראה, v. 1) is a sign of PN's authorship in common with ch. 17. The account of Obadiah's protection of the 100 prophets of YHWH in vv. 3b-4 is PN's addition. These verses are intrusive, disturbing the continuity between vv. 3a and 5. They name Jezebel as the source of Ahab's and Israel's apostasy and the opponent of YHWH's prophets, especially Elijah, in agreement with the defamation of her in 16:31-33, and as the evil counterpart to the widow of Zarephath. They also cast Obadiah as Ahab's righteous counterpart. Jezebel's treatment of YHWH's prophets justifies Elijah's slaughter of the prophets of Baal in v. 40.

18:9-15: The encounter of Elijah and Obadiah as PN's work

The interview between Elijah and Obadiah in vv. 9-15 is another PN addition. It is reminiscent of Elijah's sojourn with the widow (17:8-16).[95] Verse 9 recalls the widow's question about her past sins in 17:18. Verses 10-12a elaborate on the themes of Elijah's hiddenness and sudden disappearances and reappearances in ch. 17. Verse 12a stresses Elijah's propensity to disappear (v. 12a), leading Obadiah to fear retribution from Ahab.[96] Obadiah's claim that Ahab required

---

93 The famine in Samaria in 2 Kgs 6:25; 7:4 is due to siege, though some think the famine preceded the siege. Thiel (*Könige*, 100–101) concludes that the bulk of the story was drawn from prophetic circles surrounding Elisha. However, he includes 18:9-16 in the older story and thus finds commonalities in material that I assign to PN.

94 Josephus (*Ant.* 8.324), citing Menander, has the drought last a year. Luke 4:25 and James 5:17 ascribe a length of three and one-half years to it—a stereotypical figure (1/2 X 7) for a period of distress in apocalyptic literature. Cf. J. A. Fitzmyer, S. J., *The Gospel According to Luke (I-IX)* (AB 28; Garden City, NY: Doubleday, 1979), 537–38, who cites Dan 7:25; 12:7; Rev 11:2; 12:6, 14.

95 Blum ("Der Prophet und das Verderben Israels," 283).

96 Würthwein (*1. Könige 17–2. Könige 25*, 221–22) takes v. 12a as an interpolation and interprets v. 10 on its own as the reason for the accusation: After the exhaustive search Ahab has conducted, if Obadiah now claims that Elijah is there, a frustrated Ahab may think he has been lying and sheltering Elijah. This is similar to what Walsh (*1 Kings*, 240–41) calls Obadiah's first argument. However, Elijah's assurance in v. 15 is a response to the concern in v. 12a.

oaths of all peoples and kingdoms is hyperbolic. Still, clauses requiring the extradition of fugitives were a common stipulation of suzerain treaties,[97] so that the claim suggests Ahab's international status. The notion of the divine spirit as a force that transports an individual rather than one that inspires draws from Ezekiel (see Synchronic Analysis) and suggests an exilic (or later) date for PN. Verses 12b-14 are a reiteration of vv. 3b-4 and again name Jezebel as the real adversary.

Würthwein (*1. Könige 17–2. Könige 25*, 207, 221–22) believed that the original story went from v. 8 to v. 16, but saw vv. 9-11 + 15, 12b-14, 12a as a series of separate augmentations. Trebolle (*Centena*, 139–40) corrected Würthwein's reconstruction, arguing that vv. 12b-14a were first introduced by *Wiederaufnahme* ("and now you say, 'Go tell your master Elijah is here,' but he will kill me") and then a second interpolation in v. 12a separated והרגני ("but he will kill me") from its original place at the end of v. 11, so that v. 11 was followed directly by v. 14b. (ולא מצאך in v. 12a is an explicative gloss in MT that is absent from OG.) The main problem with both reconstructions is v. 15. Elisha's assurance that he will appear to Ahab *today* answers Obadiah's fear in v. 12a that he might disappear in the meantime. Trebolle's view that v. 12a is an interpolation leaves Obadiah's fear vague and unaddressed. Würthwein perceived the problem and assigned v. 15 to the same hand as vv. 9-11. But v. 15 lies outside of the *Wiederaufnahme* (הנה אליהו) that Würthwein thinks was used to add vv. 9-11. The repetitions in these cases represent PN's use of *Wiederaufnahme* as an authorial technique.

Obadiah provides for (כלכל) the prophets of YHWH as the widow (17:9) and the ravens (17:4) did for Elijah. Elijah's oath in v. 15, assuring Obadiah that he will show himself to Ahab that day, is similar to the one he takes in 17:1 ("by the life of YHWH before whom I stand") and that the widow swears in 17:12. Elijah swears by *YHWH of hosts*, a martial title imaging YHWH as divine warrior.[98] The heavenly army is significant in the Elisha stories (2 Kgs 2:12; 6:17; 13:14). In PN's edition it is the oath that convinces Obadiah to take the news to Ahab. The inconsistency between YHWH's command to Elijah to show himself to Ahab (vv. 1-2a) and Ahab's running to Elijah (v. 16 G) results from PN's addition of v. 1.[99] It fits with the presentation of Elijah as superior. PN replaced the verb "go" as in YHWH's order in v. 1 with "run" in anticipation of v. 46, where Elijah runs to Jezreel. Ahab's eagerness to find Elijah shows his awareness that the drought is Elijah's and YHWH's doing, which in a way makes the contest unnecessary.

18:17-40: PN's contest story

With these verses, which include the contest story, PN separates Ahab's finding of Elijah from Elijah's notice to Ahab that rain is on its way (vv. 41-42a). There are two parts to vv. 17-40: the "hinge" in vv. 17-20 and the contest proper in vv. 21-40. The former were written by PN, except for v. 18bβ (ותלך אחרי הבעלים) and

---

97 See Cogan (*I Kings*, 438) for examples.

98 The title occurs elsewhere in Kings in 2 Kgs 3:14; 19:31 with the variant "YHWH god of hosts" in 1 Kgs 19:10, 14. But it is used more widely—in Samuel, Chronicles, Psalms, and the Latter Prophets, Isaiah, Jeremiah, Amos, Micah, Nahum, Habakkuk Zephaniah, Haggai, Zechariah, and Malachi. See H. Niehr, "Host of Heaven," *DDD* 428–30.

99 Keinänen (*Traditions in Collision*, 54–60) and Thiel (*Könige*, 96).

the reference to the prophets of Asherah in v. 19, which are glosses.[100] PN was influenced in his composition of the hinge by the Jehu account.[101] Ahab's question to Elijah (1 Kgs 18:17) and Elijah's accusation (1 Kgs 18:18) are matched by Jehu's accusatory response to Joram (2 Kgs 9:22). Both passages mention the king sending through all Israel and assembling (קבץ) the prophets of Baal (1 Kgs 18:19-20; 2 Kgs 10:18-19, 21). The contest on Mount Carmel (1 Kgs 18:21-40), which was inserted by PN, matches Jehu's demolition of the Baal cult (2 Kgs 10:18-28). The model of the Jehu story also accounts for the conclusion in 1 Kgs 18:40 where Elijah slaughters all 450 prophets of Baal.

The players in the story

The drought lies behind the debate between Elijah and Ahab in vv. 17-18 about who is the *troubler of Israel* but then disappears from the contest narrative, as do Ahab and Obadiah. Ahab's role in vv. 17-20 is transitional, preparing for the contest. The tension between the mutual animosity of Elijah and Ahab in vv. 17-18 and their cooperation in vv. 19-20 is also part of the transition.[102] Ahab's name calling and Elijah's retort (v. 18) reflect PN's animosity toward Ahab and his house. Their apostasy (*abandoning* YHWH) is the main offense and the reason for the contest to determine the true god. The summons of *all Israel* makes the contest story a public demonstration. It is most likely hyperbolic, although it is possible that popular representation of some sort is envisioned. The prophets of Baal are also summoned. They are Jezebel's. As in previous PN texts, she is the one culpable for Israel's apostasy. The confusion in v. 20, which has Ahab send through all Israel to gather just the prophets, is resolved text-critically (see the Note). The existence of such prophets is attested in the Zakkur inscription, which refers to seers (*ḥzyn*) and diviners (*ʿddn*) of Baal Shemem (*COS* 2.35; *KAI* 2:202). However, cultic activities are typically performed by priests, not prophets, and 2 Kgs 10:19; 11:18 mention priests of Baal, making clear that their functions were differentiated. In 1 Kings 18 the priests and prophets, borrowed from 2 Kings 10, are collapsed by PN into a single group in order to place Elijah's competitors on the same level as he and to show that the divine response was not because of the profession of the supplicants.

---

100 The gloss in v. 18bβ is indicated by its use of the plural *Baals*, which is unique in Kings, and by the change of number from plural (בעזבכם) to singular (ותלך). Alternatively, all of v. 18aβb (after ואתה) is secondary (Frevel, *Aschera*, 45–48), but this leaves the abrupt shift from בעזבכם to ותלך unexplained. The plural occurs elsewhere especially, but not exclusively, in DtrH contexts (Judg 2:11; 3:7; 8:33; 10:6; 10:10; 1 Sam 7:4; 12:10; Jer 2:23; 9:13; Hos 2:15, 19; 2 Chr 34:4); see Thiel, *Könige*, 104, 130. It probably referred to local manifestations of Baal or local cults of non-Israelite deities; cf. McCarter, *I Samuel*, 143. The 400 prophets of Asherah (v. 19bβ) is a long-recognized gloss, since they play no role in the story and are mentioned again only in a Greek expansion (v. 22). The reference to the prophets of Asherah also lacks the definite object marker את. Cf. Frevel, *Aschera*, 28–31. Also Wellhausen, *Composition des Hexateuchs*, 279n; Olyan, *Asherah*, 8n.

101 White, *Elijah Legends*, 24–63.

102 ועתה in v. 19 is dependent on v. 18, highlighting the literary shift (Keinänen, *Traditions in Collision*, 68).

The Baal in the story

The identity of the Baal named here has been the topic of considerable discussion. Proposals include a local deity—the Baal of Carmel,[103] Baal Shamem,[104] the Aramaean Baal Hadad or Hadad Rimmon,[105] and the Tyrian Melqart.[106] The question is to some extent moot, since the title "baal," "lord, master," and the name Baal could be used for any of these deities, and the author probably lumped them together as foreign and counter to Yhwh (compare "Baals" in the addition in v. 18bβ). The identity of the Baal may also have changed in the process of revising the original tradition.[107] The narrative does not identify Baal's national affiliation but implies that he was Phoenician, especially in light of 16:31-33. By at least the first millennium Baal and Hadad were distinct deities of the Phoenicians/Canaanites and Aramaeans respectively,[108] so that it is not Hadad who is intended here. Nor is the identification with Melqart likely, considering that (1) Baal is not attested as an epithet for Melqart until the second century BCE, (2) the storm-god attributes of Baal do not suit Melqart, and (3) Melqart was later equated with Heracles rather than Zeus.[109] The Baal of 1 Kings 18, therefore, is most likely the storm god of the mythological texts from Ugarit and of the Phoenicians,[110] yet in a sense he represents all foreign deities, which the author considers powerless if not nonexistent.

18:21-24: The beginning of the original contest story

The contest story was initially independent and told of a showdown between Elijah and the people over which god, Yhwh or Baal, was genuine.[111] It began with Elijah raising the issue of the people's indecisiveness with an aphorism (v. 21). To "go after" refers to cultic veneration. It is common, but not exclusive, to Deuteronomistic material and is pre-exilic in origin.[112] While its exact meaning is uncertain, its sense is clear: The people are divided between Yhwh and Baal, and it is time to choose between them. Hence in the underlying story some of the people were fervent Baalists and others were observers, who were perhaps inclined toward

---

103 A. Alt, "Das Gottesurteil auf dem Karmel," in *Festschrift Georg Beer zum 70. Geburtstag* [Stuttgart: Kohlhammer, 1935]: 1–18 = *Kleine Schriften zur Geschichte des Volkes Israel* II [Munich: Beck, 1953]: 135-49. As Alt (p. 139n) observes, בעל כרמל is genitival, but the misunderstanding of it as appositional probably lies behind Tacitus's reference to Carmel as the name of the mountain as well as the deity (*Historiae* 2.78.3).

104 Cogan, *I Kings*, 421, 439; O. Eissfeldt, "Baʿalšamēm und Jahwe," *ZAW* 57 (1939): 1–31, esp. 19–20.

105 Avi-Yonah, "Mount Carmel and the God of Baalbek," 122–24; Cogan, *I Kings*, 439.

106 de Vaux, *Bible and the Ancient Near East*, 239–40.

107 Cf. Thiel, *Könige*, 134–35.

108 W. Hermann, "Baal בעל," *DDD* 132.

109 J. Day, "Baal (Deity)," *ABD* 1:548; S. Ribichini, "Melqart," *DDD*, 563–65.

110 Cf. M. S. Smith, *God in Translation: Deities in Cross-Cultural Discourse in the Biblical World* (FAT 57; Tübingen: Mohr Siebeck, 2008), 122–24.

111 Alt ("Gottesurteil") theorized that it was a *hieros logos* for a reclaimed Yahwistic cult site on Carmel. But the legitimation of an altar by heavenly fire (v. 38) is used elsewhere for new altars, not a rebuilt one (Lev 9:24; 1 Chr 21:26; 2 Chr 7:3). Besides, the reason for the fire here is not to legitimate the altar but to demonstrate Yhwh's genuineness as god. It resembles the use of the motif in 2 Kgs 1. Frevel's reconstruction (*Aschera und der Ausschließlichkeitsanspruch Yhwhs*, 92–123) is closer to the mark, and I have followed it with some exceptions.

112 Frevel, *Aschera*, 106–107.

YHWH but needed reinforcement. In addition to not involving Ahab or drought, the older story did not take place on Mount Carmel[113] or involve the prophets of Baal. Elijah addressed the people (v. 22aα). His claim to be alone in the rest of v. 22 is PN's addition in accord with vv. 3b-4, 12b-14, which show that the other prophets of YHWH are either dead or in hiding. Verse 23aβb assumes PN's revised scenario of opposition between Elijah and the prophets of Baal with the people as audience.[114] Calling on a deity's name (v. 24) has dual meaning as both a cultic activity and an expression of religious adherence.[115] The sacrifices in this exhibition had no meaning on their own but only as a means for calling forth a divine response (i.e., fire) as a proof of genuine divinity (האלהים).[116]

18:25-26: Baal's impotence

Verse 25, identifying the prophets of Baal as the first to prepare their sacrifice is from PN, but the failure of the Baalists in vv. 26-29abα* goes back to the older story. The depiction of the Baal prophets limping around[117] the altar (v. 26b), is an addition in the MT (see the Note). The most important part of v. 26 is the statement that there was *no voice, no answerer* (ואין קול ואין ענה), which is reminiscent of the Aqhat passage cited earlier: *bl ṭbn.ql.b'l*, "No welcome voice of Baal."[118] Baal's disappearance into the underworld and its disastrous consequences for nature and humans are described in the Ugaritic Baal Cycle. The older story may have played on that tradition and contrasted it with the belief in YHWH's permanence and availability. PN's edited version, though, presents him as impotent and even nonexistent; this is similar to the perspective on idols in 2 Isaiah (40:19-20; 41:6-7; 44:9-20; 46:5-8).[119]

18:27: Elijah's mocking

Contrary to MT (v. 27), Elijah does not wait until afternoon to mock his opponents but begins to do so as soon as their outcries fail to evoke a response. His mocking was part of the original story. The interpretation of Elijah's words offered here assumes (1) that התל, a *hapax legomenon*, has connotations of deceit and mockery, such that Elijah proposes scenarios based on myths about the Canaanite gods that would explain Baal's inattentiveness and lack of response, and (2) the text-critical determination of only two activities for Baal where MT has four. The four are: שיח, usually understood as contemplation, שיג, typically taken as withdrawal or being detained, דרך, a journey, and ישן, sleeping. The reference to a journey, found only in MT, is secondary, and שיח is a gloss on שיג (see the Note) that refers not to contemplation or withdrawal but to the bodily functions of defecation/

---

113 Jepsen (*Elia und das Gottesurteil*, 304–305) suggests that the story was originally set in the vicinity of Samaria. PN probably took the location from the *legenda* behind vv. 41-46.

114 Frevel, *Aschera*, 67–68.

115 Thiel (*Könige*, 155–56). In cultic contexts it is especially associated with altar building and the foundation of holy sites (Gen 12:8; 13:4; 26:25; cf 21:33; Isa 12:4; Ps 105:1; 1 Chr 16:8; Ps 80:19; 116:4, 13, 17). It is used to designate people who are adherents of YHWH in Zeph 3:9 (cf. Isa 41:25; 43:7; Zech 13:9) with a nuance similar in meaning to קרא אל in 1 Kgs 8:52. It occurs in 2 Kgs 5:11 in the description of a healing ritual that Naaman expected Elisha to perform.

116 Thiel, *Könige*, 153.

117 Or "before" or "beside." See Thiel, *Könige*, 159.

118 *KTU* 1.19.1.45-46. The translation is that of Parker, *Ugaritic Narrative Poetry*, 69.

119 Otto, *Jehu, Elia, und Elisa*, 175; Würthwein, *1. Könige 17–2. Könige 25*, 220.

urination. Such activities are described of the gods at Ugarit,[120] and in the HB Yhwh sleeps (Isa 51:9; Ps 44:24; 59:5; 78:65). The use of sleep as a metaphor for death (Dan 12:2) adds nuance to Elijah's suggestion. It is in the nexus of myth and eminently human activities that Elijah's duplicity has its roots; he mockingly proposes what the Baal priests might regard as real activities of deities.

18:28-29: The activities of the Baal prophets

Self-laceration (v. 28) as cultic practice is mentioned in an Akkadian text from Ugarit as typical among ecstatic prophets: "My brothers are drenched in their own blood like ecstatics."[121] It is also well attested in contexts of ritual mourning in and outside of the Bible, including lamentation for Baal's disappearance into the underworld in the Baal epic, and that is probably its intent here.[122] The worshipers of Baal are not cultic personnel enacting a ritual but are mourning his disappearance and perhaps hoping to effect his return.[123] Similarly, ecstatic behavior, "raving" (*Hitpa'ēl* of נבא), in v. 29, though attested elsewhere in the Bible (Num 11:25-27; 1 Sam 10:5-13; 18:10; Jer 29:26) among prophets, is not limited to them (1 Sam 19:20-24) and can even be used to describe irrational behavior (1 Sam 18:10).[124]

18:29: The time and nature of the evening offering

The evening offering (עלות המנחה) took place "between the evenings" (Exod 29:39; Num 28:4), i.e., between twilight and full dark.[125] The late hour would not afford time for the events in the subsequent verses, but the older contest story did not include vv. 40-46. Elijah takes his turn as the sun begins to set. The offering of a burnt animal sacrifice (עלה) in the morning and a grain offering (מנחה) in the evening was standard in the monarchic period (cf. 2 Kgs 16:15), while a burnt offering twice a day, morning and evening, was late and Priestly (Exod 29:38-42;

---

120 *KTU* 1.114.20-21 describes El as collapsing from inebriation in his own feces and urine. See M. Pope, "A Divine Banquet at Ugarit," in *The Use of the Old Testament in the New and Other Essays: Studies in Honor of William Franklin Stinespring* (ed. J. M. Efird; Durham, NC: Duke University Press, 1972): 170–203, esp. 195–97. On the *marzeaḥ* see J. L. McLaughlin, *The* Marzēah *in the Prophetic Literature: References and Allusions in Light of the Extra-Biblical Literature* (VTSup 86; Leiden: Brill, 2001).

121 *aḫu-ú-a ki-ma maḫ-ḫe-e [d]a-mi-šu-nu ra-am-ku* in *Ugaritica V* 162:11 and cited in *CAD* M/1, p. 90a. See J. J. M. Roberts, "A New Parallel to I Kings 18:28-29," *JBL* 89 [1970] 76–77. My thanks to Mark Smith for pointing out this reference.

122 Deut 14:1; Lev 19:28; 21:5; Hos 7:14; Mic 4:14; Jer 16:6; 41:5; 47:5. El and Anat both cut themselves after learning of Baal's death (*KTU* 1.5.6.17-22 and 1.6.1.2-5; Saint-Laurent, "Light from Ras Shamra," 134). Cf. Also KTU 1.19.4.9-11. Again, Lucian (*De Dea Syria* 50) describes a similar rite. Once more, de Vaux (*Bible and the Ancient Near East*, 242–43) lists references to similar practices mostly in Classical and later sources. See the discussion of Frevel, *Aschera*, 111–15.

123 Their acts are not imitative magic intended to prompt the sending of rain. *Pace* Gray, *Kings*, 399.

124 See also Wen-Amun (*ANET* 26b). The pejorative understanding of נבא is confirmed by Targum Jonathan, which uses שטא, "to act foolishly" here and in 1 Sam 18:10 (Dray, *Targum*, 115). Prophetic ecstasy is attested outside of the Bible in Lucian's *De Dea Syria* 36. Cf. also de Vaux, *Bible and Ancient Near East*, 240–43.

125 Šanda (*Könige* I, 436) thinks vv. 40-46 require the earlier hour (3:00 PM) indicated by Josephus (*Ant* 14.65) and the Mishnah (*Pesaḥim* 5.1) for the evening sacrifice. But these later sources probably reflect retrofitting of post-70 CE practice into the Israelite period (DeVries, *1 Kings*, 229.).

Num 28:2-8).[126] The change took place during the exilic or early post-exilic period.[127] However, the term מנחה can also mean "offering" in general without specifying a grain offering.[128] In 2 Kgs 3:20 מנחה occurs for the morning offering. It is possible, then, for מנחה to include the burnt offering. That would make Elijah's sacrifice of a bull at this time especially appropriate. It is equally possible that in both 1 Kgs 18:29 and 2 Kgs 3:20 the references to offerings are simply time references with no significance for the content of the sacrifice.[129] In short, the evening offering in v. 29 presents no conclusive evidence for the date of the composition of 1 Kings 18.

18:30: The altar of YHWH

Verse 30 initiates the third and final scene in the contest story, with Elijah calling the people to himself. The worshipers of Baal have failed; it is Elijah's turn. In PN's version the Baal prophets, who have been contestants, now become spectators. Verse 30b, where Elijah repairs an older altar to YHWH, contradicts vv. 31-32a, where he builds a new one. Some have argued that the "repair" version was a correction in accord with the Deuteronomic principle of cultic centralization, producing a story in which Elijah did not build a new altar but repaired an older one for temporary use.[130] Others take the "repair" version as original, suggesting that vv. 31-32a represent a correction of the idea of the existence of an altar outside of Jerusalem, such that Elijah builds a new altar that is almost immediately destroyed (v. 38).[131] The text-critical evidence shows that vv. 31-32a were interpolated (see the Note) and proves the validity of the latter position. The older text and the older story had Elijah repairing an altar of YHWH rather than building a new one.[132] Its presence does not support the reconstruction of an older *ieros logos*, since there is no stress in the story on its location. Rather, it illustrates the derelict state of the worship of YHWH. The absence of any mention of the older altar before this and the assumption of a standing altar to Baal (v. 26) make it unlikely that the altar was destroyed during the rites of the prophets of Baal;[133] this occurred earlier.[134] The recognition of a legitimate altar to YHWH outside of Jerusalem is a strong

---

126 Rendtorff, *Studien zur Geschichte des Opfers*, 74–76, 196; Levine, *Numbers 21-36*, 48, 395–98.

127 Levine, *Numbers 21-36*, 48 states, "as of the destruction of the First Temple of Jerusalem we have no evidence of a two-phased *tāmîd*" and "it is in overtly postexilic literature that we find references to the two-phased *tāmîd*." Rendtorff shows that there are traces in P texts (Lev 9:17; Num 28:3) of an earlier practice of a single morning *tāmîd*, and both he and Levine point to Ezek 46:13-15 as also presupposing a single burnt offering in the morning.

128 G. A. Anderson, *Sacrifices and Offerings in Ancient Israel: Studies in Their Social and Political Importance*. (HSM 41; Atlanta: Scholars Press, 1987), 29; "Sacrifice and Sacrificial Offerings," *ABD* 5:874.

129 Rendtorff, *Studien zur Geschichte des Opfers*, 195–96.

130 DeVries, *1 Kings*, 229; Timm, *Die Dynastie Omri*, 78n.

131 Fohrer, *Elia*, 17n. Würthwein (*1. Könige 17–2. Könige 25*, 216) thinks that the original story did not mention an altar.

132 DeVries (*1 Kings*, 226) and Montgomery (*Kings*, 304) object that there is neither traditional nor archaeological support for a Yahwistic sanctuary on Mount Carmel. This supports the likelihood that this story was initially not associated with Mount Carmel but was set elsewhere.

133 *Pace* House, *Kings*, 220.

134 Sweeney, *Kings*, 229.

indication of the pre-DtrH origin of the older story. Also, PN does not qualify it. If the reconstruction of v. 38 is correct, the rebuilt altar is not destroyed by the heavenly fire. Even in its edited version, therefore, the story reflects no concern for cultic centralization or for sacerdotal regulations concerning cultic propriety. It betrays a prophetic orientation. Its interest and focus are on the man of god and his demonstration of YHWH's superiority to other gods, if not his exclusivity.

The additions in 18:31-32a, 35b

The twelve stones in the interpolation in vv. 31-32a representing the twelve tribes recall altars built by Moses (Exod 24:4) and Joshua (Josh 4:20) and symbolize the unity of Israel as YHWH's people, but they are ill suited to a story set in the Northern (divided) kingdom. The reference to YHWH changing Jacob's name to Israel (v. 31b) draws on Gen 35:10 (P).[135] This collection of parallels evinces a Priestly-oriented concern for the sanctity of a rebuilt altar (cf. 1 Macc 4:44-47), which is affirmed by the fire from heaven (Lev 9:24; 1 Chr 21:26; 2 Chr 7:3). The trench in v. 32b also betrays a Priestly concern. It has a capacity of two seahs of seed (v. 32b). If this is the capacity of the trench *per se* it held only 10 to 30 liters (= 2.5 to 8 gallons) of water.[136] A better possibility, therefore, is that it refers to the area that could be planted by two seahs of seed as a sacred precinct around the altar.[137] According to the Talmud (*Erub* 23b) this was the size of the area of the tabernacle, 100 x 50 cubits. The concern for the demarcation of a sacred precinct also reflects Priestly interests and suggests that v. 32b is an addition. Verse 35b, which is suspect because of its beginning with וגם, appears to be an even later interpretation of the trench as holding the runoff water.[138]

The purpose of the water

The purpose of the water is debated. At least five distinct proposals have been floated: (1) a guarantee against trickery on Elijah's part;[139] (2) enhancement of the miracle;[140] (3) ritual washing of the sacrifice (Lev 1:9, 13);[141] (4) libation;[142] and (5) ritual magic for summoning rain.[143] The third option may be dismissed. Elijah's order to "pour" (יצק) water differs from the instruction in Leviticus to "wash"

---

135 A similar late gloss is 2 Kgs 17:34.

136 King and Stager, *Life in Biblical Israel*, 200, estimate that a seah contained about five liters; *HALOT*'s estimate is 15 liters (p. 737).

137 Jones, *Kings*, 322; Sweeney, *Kings*, 229.

138 Thiel (*Könige*, 175–77) suggests that the resemblance to the tabernacle precinct legitimates Elijah's altar by its parallel with Moses. Sweeney (*Kings*, 229) proposes that the trench was to convey sacrificial blood into the ground in accordance with prohibitions against eating it (Deut 12:16, 23-24; 15:23; Lev 17:12-13; 1 Sam 14:31-35). But this does not fully explain why the trench went around (סביב) the altar or why its capacity is given.

139 Buis *Rois*, 147.

140 Hauser and Gregory, *From Carmel*, 48–49; Walsh, *1 Kings*, 252.

141 Buis, *Rois*, 147.

142 Walsh, *1 Kings*, 259.

143 Buis, *Rois*, 147; Jones, *Kings*, 322; Patai, "Control of Rain," 254–58; N. J. Tromp, "Water and Fire on Mount Carmel: A Conciliatory Suggestion," *Bib* 56 (1975): 480–502, esp. 495–97. We can ignore, except for the purpose of amusement, the theory of G. H. F. Hitzig (*Geschichte des Volkes Israel*, vol. 1 [Leipzig: S. Hirzel, 1869], 176), elaborated by R. H. Kennett (*Old Testament Essays* [Cambridge: Cambridge University Press, 1928], 103–104), that what Elijah poured was not water but naphtha, an accelerant, which he ignited with the use of some kind of reflector. Montgomery's response (*Kings*, 307) is apposite: "Such rationalizing would preserve the historicity of the story at the cost of its morality."

(רחץ). Besides, in Leviticus it is not the entire sacrifice that is washed, and not on the altar, but only the entrails and legs, which are not placed on the altar. In addition, there would be no need to perform the deed three times. The total number of jars of water (4 x 3 = 12) matches the number of stones used for the altar and might support the libation interpretation[144] but it does not account for the text's preoccupation with the water or for its being poured on top of the sacrifice. Option five is attractive in view of the focus of the prophetic stories on acts of ritual magic and helps pinpoint the genre of the older contest story as prophetic *legenda*. PN may not have understood the nature of the water ritual and in any case added vv. 41-46* in which Elijah summons rain separately. PN interpreted Elijah's dousing of the sacrifice along the lines of the first two options, which can be combined: the water shows that Elijah "has nothing up his sleeve," that the sacrifice is not ignited by accident, and that the fire that falls and absorbs even the water is not of human origin. Elijah's generous use of water and its ready availability show that the older story did not presuppose the drought; summoning rain would also bring thunder and lightning.

18:36-37: PN's version of Elijah's petition

Elijah's cry in the original story (*Yhwh answer me today with fire, for you Yhwh are god in Israel*) stressed Yhwh's aegis in the land of Israel, which was the point of the contest.[145] In PN's revision the prayer remains simple (vv. 36-37) in contrast to the elaborate activities of the adherents of Baal. The reference to Abraham, Isaac, and Israel in v. 36 is part of an interpolation by *Wiederaufnahme* (the divine name). The epithet *god of Abraham, Isaac, and Israel*, as opposed to the more common "Abraham, Isaac, and Jacob," is a late formulation (1 Chr 29:18; 2 Chr 30:6; cf. Exod 32:13). The *Erkenntnisformel* occurs in DtrH, but also in Ezekiel, 2 Isaiah, and P; it is PN's addition.[146] The passive version in v. 36 MT (יִוָּדַע, "let it be known," cf. Deut 4:39) is later than the active "that this people may know that you are god" in OG and v. 37 MT.[147] The first-person reference to Elijah as Yhwh's servant who did *all these things* by Yhwh's word interrupts the second-person sequence (*you are god and you turned*) and is an addition that identifies Elijah's words and actions with Yhwh's.[148] The cryptic comment at the close of Elijah's petition that the people would recognize that it was Yhwh who "turned their hearts back"

144 Walsh, *1 Kings*, 251. On the nature of the כד see the note on 17:12.

145 Trebolle ("Textcritical Value") highlights the difference between *you are god* (האלהים) and MT's *you are god* (אלהים) *in Israel*, arguing that the former is preferred here and the latter belongs to a polemical genre concerning the consultation of an Israelite prophet by a foreigner (2 Kgs 5, esp. v. 15) or the consultation of a foreign god by an Israelite (2 Kgs 1:3, 6, 16). But the main witnesses are unanimous in referring to Israel. The *legenda* in 18:21-40* *is* polemical; the monotheistic interpretation is in the later redaction. Cf. Frevel, *Aschera*, 118–19.

146 Cf. E. Würthwein ("Zur Opferprobe Elias I Reg 18,21-39," in *Prophet und Prophetenbuch: Festschrift für Otto Kaiser zum 65. Geburtstag* [ed. V. Fritz, K.-F. Pohlmann, and H.-C. Schmitt; BZAW 185; Berlin/New York: de Gruyter, 1989], 282–83), who considers this a late dtr composition because of this formula. But his observation about the formula's distribution supports the view that this text is post-DtrH in origin. See further on 20:13.

147 Thiel, *Könige*, 106.

148 It may have been added to justify Elijah's cultic activities—his building of an altar outside of Jerusalem and his sacrificing upon it. So Turkanik, *Of Kings and Reigns*, 121.

appears to mean that it was YHWH who led Israel to backslide in order to provide the opportunity to show his power and decisively defeat Baal (see the Synchronic Analysis).

18:38-40: Fire from heaven

Elijah's prayer receives an immediate answer. Fire (lightning) falls from the sky (v. 38). While the motif elsewhere signals divine acceptance and sanctification of an altar (Lev 9:24; 1 Chr 21:26; 2 Chr 7:1), here it substantiates Elijah's claim that YHWH is true god. YHWH's use of lightning, the weapon of the storm god, shows that he and not Baal controls the storm and fertility. It is typically the precursor of rain[149] and affords the perfect opportunity for resolution of the drought, yet that resolution does not come until Elijah's ritual on Carmel (vv. 41-46), and the sky is cloudless between the two events. This is because the older story did not assume the drought and because PN has Elijah undertake a distinct ritual to bring rain. The fire burns the wood and sacrifice at once and licks up the water around and on top of it as well. The people respond by prostrating themselves before YHWH and Elijah and confessing that YHWH is god (האלהים). The repetition matches Elijah's repeated cry for an answer in PN's edition. In the original story the confession excludes Baal, but PN lends it a monotheistic interpretation. Victorious, Elijah orders the people to seize all the Baal prophets (v. 40). He takes them to the Wadi Qishon and slaughters them all. This is PN's addition; it assumes Jezebel's treatment of YHWH's prophets in vv. 3b-4, 12b-14 and anticipates Jehu's slaughter of the Baalists in 2 Kgs 10:18-28 on which it is based. Elijah's order resembles that of Jehu (2 Kgs 10:24).

18:41-46: Elijah brings rain

The final episode of the chapter is based on a prophetic *legenda* distinct from the *Vorlagen* of the previous two units. Preserved in vv. 42b-44a, 45a, it described an act of symbolic magic in which the holy man crouched with his head between his knees representing a cloud in order to summon rain. His servant checked repeatedly for signs of weather, and on his seventh trip spotted a small cloud that soon became a torrential rainstorm. As is typical of basic prophetic *legenda*, there is no reference to prayer or an act of YHWH. It shares affinities with the Elisha materials and may have been among them: Elisha is regularly accompanied by a servant, while Elijah is alone except for here and 19:3; the prescience that Elijah exhibits is characteristic of Elisha (2 Kgs 5:26; 6:12, 32); the verb גהר occurs elsewhere in the HB only in the Elisha *legenda* in 2 Kgs 4:34-35; the servant's seven ascents to look for clouds are matched by the seven sneezes of the boy whom Elisha restores to life and Naaman's sevenfold dip in the Jordan (2 Kgs 5:10, 14); Mount Carmel is a home base for Elisha (2 Kgs 2:25; 4:25).

The *legenda* and PN's revision

PN prefaced this *legenda* with the conclusion of the drought story in vv. 41-42a, which he used as the fulfillment of Elijah's announcement of rain in 17:1. This explains the use of different words for rain— מטר in 17:1, גשם in 18:41—in the two texts. Elijah's advice to Ahab to *go up* (v. 41) gives the impression that he was at the Wadi Qishon and witnessed the slaughter of the prophets of Baal without objecting. The order to *eat and drink* assumes that he has been fasting during the drought.[150] Elijah's warning about the impending rain shows his prescience but

149 *Pace* Šanda, *Könige* II, 440.

150 K. L. Roberts's proposal ("God, Prophet, and King: Eating and Drinking on the Mountain in First Kings 18:41," *CBQ* 62 [2000] 632–44) that Ahab is celebrating covenant renewal in parallel with Exod 24 does not fit the context or the literary-critical evidence as well.

creates tensions with the *legenda* in vv. 42b-44a, 45a: Elijah hears the sound of rain (v. 41) before the ritual to bring it (vv. 42b-44a); Ahab goes up to eat and drink, breaking his fast (v. 42a) before there is any sign of rain (vv. 43-44); and Elijah announces the coming of rain twice (vv. 41, 44b). Other tensions with the contest story include Ahab's return, Elijah's cordial treatment of him, and the presence of an unfamiliar servant. There was also a shift in time from twilight in the contest story to full daylight here.

18:44-46: PN's conclusion

PN added vv. 44b, 45b-46 in order to move Elijah to Jezreel where Jezebel is (21:1-16, 23; 2 Kgs 9:30-37), as a link to 19:1-3.[151] This creates a final wonder in which Elijah outruns Ahab's chariot the thirty-five kilometers or twenty-one miles from Mount Carmel to Jezreel because YHWH's hand was upon him. The expression occurs only here in the Elijah stories. It is found in 2 Kgs 3:15 in reference to the advent of prophetic ecstasy upon Elisha. Its use in the present passage, though, is closer to the idea and expression repeated in Ezekiel (1:3; 3:22; 33:22; 37:1; 40:1) describing "extraordinary sensory experiences."[152] The order to Ahab to harness his chariot and go down in v. 44b is unnecessary after the warning to him in v. 42a. It also breaks the continuity between the report of the cloud in v. 44a and the rain in v. 45a.

Synthesis

PN's editorial unit based on different sources

The chapter is a well-crafted editorial unit. Internal tensions result from different sources that the PN has fused together. The drought continues from ch. 17 as the overriding theme. It may have been borrowed from the story of Ahab's and Obadiah's search for pasturage in vv. 1-16*, since that is the only story in which drought is inherent to the plot. Elijah's announcement of rain to Ahab in v. 41 concludes the drought theme as anticipated in 17:1. The *legenda* about Elijah's magic summons of rain (vv. 41-46*) extends the conclusion in dramatic fashion.

PNs revision of the *legenda* behind the contest story

The highlight of the drought cycle is a *legenda* from the monarchic period[153] about a contest between the followers of YHWH and those of Baal to determine which of them was god in Israel. Because of the means chosen to determine the contest—fire from heaven—PN incorporated it under the drought theme. His transition to the story established the cause of the drought as the unfaithfulness of Ahab and his house to YHWH. He introduced the prophets of Baal, rather than the people, as Elijah's opponents, moving the contestants into more official circles dominated by Jezebel and anticipating Jehu's rivalry. The people's exuberant confession at the climactic moment when fire falls encapsulates the theological high point of the chapter and the drought cycle: "YHWH, he is (the) god; he is (the) god." Syncretism—the amalgamation of YHWH and Baal in theology and practice—

---

151 *Pace* Stipp (*Elischa - Propheten - Gottesmänner*, 432–35) and Otto (*Jehu, Elia und Elisa*, 159) who tie Jezreel here to 21:1 and the G order of chapters—21, 20, 22—taking ch. 19 as a later addition.

152 Greenberg, *Ezekiel*, 41–42; cf. Würthwein, *1. Könige 17–2. Könige 25*, 214.

153 Frevel (Aschera, 120–21) dates it to the 8th–7th century.

may have been the target of the initial tale,[154] but PN presents Yhwh and Baal as distinct alternatives. The people's confession (v. 39) of Yhwh in the older tale was not monotheistic, but a declaration of Yhwh's dominion in Israel (v. 36). It was also not a question of metaphysical existence but of effectiveness: Baal does not answer, *ergo* for all practical purposes he is not real; Yhwh is genuine because he acts. Hence Yhwh is the one who truly controls the elements and the fertility that springs from them. For PN the issue is more ideological. Elijah's derisive comments in the original story drawn from the mythic and ritual traditions associated with Baal imply that Baal is created in the image of man and unsuited for the quality of "god."[155] The older tale may be on the threshold of monotheism;[156] PN's edition is fully inside. Baal and—by implication—other deities do not respond because they do not exist. For PN יהוה הוא האלהים means Yhwh alone is god.

Practical monotheism

---

154 Hens-Piazza, *Kings*, 181; Nelson, *Kings*, 120. The main basis for this assumption is the people's silence in v. 21 as though the need for a decision that Elijah presents makes no sense to them.

155 Jepsen, "Elia und das Gottesurteil," 301: "Das bedeutet aber doch, dass hier die Frage nach dem wirklichen Gott, d.h. dem wirkend eingreifenden Gott gestellt ist. Es geht nicht allein darum, dass für Israel nur Jahwe Gott is; sondern es ist dem Baal die Qualität "Gott" überhaupt abgesprochen ... Das heisst aber, dass nur Jahwe das Attribut "Gott" für sich in Anspruch nehmen kann ..." = "But that means that the question of the real God, i.e., the actively involved God is raised. It is not just that for Israel only Yahweh is God; but Baal is completely denied the quality 'God' ... But that means that only Yahweh can claim the attribute 'God' for himself ..."

156 Frevel, *Aschera*, 120, quoting G. Braulik.

Elijah on Mount Horeb (1 Kings 19)

Text

[Prophetic source; *PN; Additions to PN]*

1 *When Ahab told Jezebel his wife all that Elijah had done and how he had killed the prophets with the sword,* 2 *Jezebel sent to Elijah and said, "If you are Elijah then I am Jezebel; so will the gods do to me and so will they add—by this time tomorrow I will make your life like one of theirs."* 3 *Fearful, he arose and fled for his life. Arriving at Beersheba, which belonged to Judah, he left his servant there.* 4 *He himself went a day's journey into the wilderness and sat under a broom tree, where he asked to die, "Enough now! Take my life, because I am no better than my forefathers."* 5 *He lay down and slept. Someone touched him and said to him, "Get up. Eat."* 6 *He noticed at his head a loaf baked on coals and a flask of water. He got up, ate and drank, and then lay down again.* 7 *The angel of YHWH returned again and touched him, saying "Get up. Eat. For the road ahead of you is long."* 8 *So he got up, ate and drank, and then went on in the strength of that meal for forty days and nights to Mount Horeb.* 9 *Coming to a certain cave there, he lodged there, and the word of YHWH came to him and said to him, "What are you doing here, Elijah?"* 10 *He said, "I have been most zealous for YHWH of hosts, because the Israelites have abandoned you, torn down your altars, and killed your prophets with the sword so that I alone am left, and they are seeking to take my life."* 11 *[YHWH] said, "Go out and stand on the mountain before YHWH." As YHWH passed by, a mighty wind preceded YHWH (YHWH was not in the wind), and after the wind a powerful earthquake that tore apart mountains and shattered crags (YHWH was not in the earthquake),* 12 *and after the earthquake fire (YHWH was not in the fire), and after the fire a delicate whisper.* 13 *When Elijah heard [it] he wrapped his face in his mantle, and he went out and stood at the opening of the cave where a voice came to him saying, "What are you doing here, Elijah?"* 14 *He responded, "I have been most zealous for YHWH of hosts. For the Israelites have abandoned you, torn down your altars, and killed your prophets with the sword to the point that I alone am left and they are seeking to take my life."* 15 *YHWH said to him, "Go back the way you came through the wilderness to Damascus, and go anoint Hazael as king of Aram.* 16 *Also Jehu son of Nimshi you shall anoint as king over Israel, and Elisha son of Shaphat from Abel Meholah you shall anoint as prophet in your place.* 17 *Whoever escapes from the sword of Hazael, Jehu will kill, and whoever escapes from the sword of Jehu, Elisha will kill.* 18 *I will leave in Israel 7000 who do not bow the knee to Baal or kiss him with their mouths."* 19 Departing from there [Elijah] found there Elisha son of Shaphat who was plowing with twelve parcels in front of him, he being in the twelfth. When [Elijah] went over to him and cast his mantle on him, 20 [Elisha] left the oxen and ran after Elijah. "Let me kiss my father," he said, "so that I may follow you." [Elijah] said, "Go back, for what have I done to you?" 21 So [Elisha] went back and taking the yoke of oxen, he slaughtered them and boiled them with the oxen's yoke apparatus, and he gave [the meat] to the people, who ate [it]. Then [Elisha] got up and followed Elijah *as his attendant.*

Textual Notes

1 **his wife**: So G^{B}. Absent from MT, G^{L} because of haplography.[1]

and how: Reading וכאשר as indicated by G^{BL}: καὶ ὡς. MT: ואת כל־אשר as previously in the verse.

the prophets: So G^{BL} (τοὺς προφήτας). MT + *all.*

2 **sent**: MT + *a messenger.*

and said, "If you are Elijah then I am Jezebel: So OL: *Et dixit si tu es Helias et ego sum Iezabel, Et dixit* = לאמר אם אתה אליהו ואני איזבל לאמר and partially in G^{BL} (καὶ εἶπεν εἰ σὺ εἶ Ηλιου καὶ ἐγὼ [G^{L}: εἰμι]. Lost by haplography (לאמר ... לאמר).[2]

so will the gods do to me and so will they add: So G^{BL}, OL. MT lacks *to me* because of haplography.[3] G^{B} and OL read singular verbs, but Jezebel presumably swears by her gods.[4]

3 **Fearful**: So G^{BL}: καὶ ἐφοβήθη = וַיִּרָא. MT vocalizes as וַיַּרְא = *When he saw.* But Elijah responds to the threat he has heard from Jezebel, not to something he has seen. MT also lacks an object. It may be a case of *tiqqun soferim* designed to guard the character of Elijah.[5]

for his life: On this translation of the preposition אל, see WO, 194

4 **a broom tree**: Reading the *Qere'* אחד here and in v. 5. On the indefinite use of the numeral "one" see Joüon §137u. The broom tree (*Retama raetam*) is a bush native to desert, hill, and rocky regions that grows up to twelve feet high and can provide the only available shade.[6] רתם, transliterated in the G^{B} as ῥαθμέν (G^{L} ῥαθαμείν) = ῥαθμ ἕν, occurs elsewhere in the HB only in Job 30:4; Ps 120:4.

where he asked to die: For other examples of an accusative + infinitive in place of an objective clause see GKC §157bN2.

Enough now: So G^{BL} (ἱκανούσθω νῦν). MT + *Yhwh.*

Take my life: So MT. Some mss; G^{BL}: + *from me* (B + *Yhwh*). Joosten (132n) suggests that the imperative without נא expresses Elijah's despair.

5 **and slept**: MT + *under a broom tree.* G^{BL} + *under a bush* (φυτόν = שיח). The use of a different word than in v. 4 in G (ῥαθμ) indicates that the plus is a gloss rather than

---

1 Occasioned by the repetition of א in אשתו and את. See Burney, *Notes,* 228.

2 O. Eissfeldt, "'Bist Du Elia, so bin Ich Isebel' (I Kön. xix 2)," *Hebräische Wortforschung: Festschrift zum 80. Geburtstag von Walter Baumgartner* (VTSup 16; Leiden: Brill, 1967), 65–70 and his "Nachträge zu 'Adrammelek und Damarus' und zu 'Bist Du Elias, so bin Ich Isebel,'' *Bibliotheca orientalis* 26 (1969): 182–84. See also Schenker, *Älteste Textgeschichte der Königsbücher,* 134–35.

3 אלי before אלהים. 1 Sam 14:44 is also haplographic, *pace* Driver, *Notes on the Hebrew Text of Samuel,* 90.

4 On the nature and occurrences of the oath and the possibility that it may have been accompanied by a symbolic act see Driver (*Notes,* 36); McCarter (*I Samuel,* 99); and the discussion by Muraoka in Joüon §165aN.

5 Barthélemy, *Critique textuelle,* 371; P. Hugo, "Text and Literary History: The Case of 1 Kings 19 (MT and LXX)," in *Soundings in Kings: Perspectives and Methods in Contemporary Scholarship* (ed. M. Leuchter and K.-P. Adam; Minneapolis: Fortress, 2010), 24–25; C. McCarthy, *The Tiqqune Sopherim and Other Theological Corrections in the Masoretic Text of the Old Testament* (OBO 36; Fribourg/Göttingen: Éditions Universitaires/Vandenhoeck & Ruprecht, 1981), 234. A similar *Tendenz* is evident in R. B. Allen's defense of the MT ("Elijah the Broken Prophet," *JETS* 22 [1979]: 193–202).

6 I. Jacob and W. Jacob, "Flora," *ABD* 2:805; D. Lipovitch, "Broom," *NIDB* 1:505.

Wiederaufnahme.[7] This is suggested also by the change in gender of רתם from v. 4 to v. 5 in MT and by the absence of the definite article in the instance in v. 5, which would be expected for a narrative resumption.

someone: So G^{BL} (τις = איש, cf. Judg 4:20; 1 Sam 10:12; 24:20; 2 Sam 19:23). MT's *behold an angel [touches him]* (והנה־זה מלאך) is a gloss from v. 7.

6bβ-8a From וישב in v. 6 through וישתה in v. 8 is absent from G^{L}, Syr as a result of haplography.[8] This emphasizes the arduousness of Elijah's journey by having him eat twice and also identified the "man" in v. 5 (cf. Judg 13:10-11) as an angel.[9]

6 **a loaf baked on coals**: Lit. *a cake of coals*; cf. GKC §129g, WO, 153. The word *coal* (רצף) occurs only here as a masculine plural, and as a feminine singular (רצפה) in Isa 6:6.

He got up, ate, and drank: So G^{B}. G^{L} also has all three verbs. MT lacks *he got up*. Its absence is probably accidental in view of the occurrence of the same sequence of verbs in the repetition in v. 8a.

8 **Mount Horeb**: So G^{BL}. MT: *the mountain of god, Horeb*.

9 **a certain cave**: For this translation of the definite article see Joüon §137n.

What are you doing here: מה־לך פה, lit., *what do you have here?* i.e., *what is your business here?*

10 **zealous**: Zeal or "fervor" = קנא + ל (Num 11:29; 25:11,13; 2 Sam 21:2; 2 Kgs 10:16; Ps 69).[10]

for Yhwh of hosts: See the Note on 19:14.

have abandoned you: So G^{BL}. MT: *have abandoned your covenant*. Cf. 18:18.

11 **Go out**: G^{BL}, Josephus, *Ant* 8.351 + *tomorrow* (מחר). A misplaced dittography of בהר.[11]

On the mountain before Yhwh: So MT. G^{BL} have the reverse order of the two clauses.

As Yhwh passed by: WO (678) translate as part of the quote ("because Yhwh is about to pass by," similarly NRSV). But Elijah does not exit the cave until after Yhwh has passed (v. 13).

A mighty wind preceded Yhwh (Yhwh was not in the wind), and after the wind a powerful earthquake that tore apart mountains and shattered crags (Yhwh was not in the earthquake):

Following Jepsen's proposal in *BHS* that חזק מפרק הרים ומשבר סלעים originally described the earthquake rather than the wind and has been misplaced. This would explain why חזק, a masculine adjective, modifies the typically feminine רוח, which is modified first by גדולה.[12] The destruction of mountains and crags is also more appropriate as the result of earthquake than of wind.[13]

12 **a delicate whisper**: קול דממה דקה is unique to the HB. It is either a construct formation ("sound of silence") or a nominal hendiadys (voice/sound, silence = "a silent

---

7 *Pace* Trebolle, *Centena*, 142–43. For explanations, see the authors Trebolle cites. Also Hugo, "Text and Literary History," 22–23.

8 So De Vries, *1 Kings*, 233, and Hugo, "Text and Literary History," 23–24. Trebolle (*Centena*, 143–44) argued for an interpolation by *Wiederaufnahme*.

9 Compare Trebolle, *Centena*, 143–44.

10 E. Reuter, "קנא," *TDOT* 13:53; G. Sauer, "קִנְאָה," *TLOT* 3:1145–47.

11 DeVries, *1 Kings*, 233.

12 Other instances cited by grammars (GKC §132d, Joüon §148a, n. 1, WO, 258n) of two adjectives following a feminine noun where only the first is feminine (1 Sam 15:9; Jer 20:9; Ps 63:2) are likewise textually suspect.

13 Instead of "Yhwh was not in the wind" G^{B} reads ἐν τῷ πνεύματι κύριου, an inner-Greek error resulting from the euphonic similarity of οὐκ after κύριου (so Law, *Origenes Orientalis*, 333). Hugo, ("*Text and Literary* History," 18–19) takes the negative in Hebrew as secondary.

sound") followed by an adjective modifying דממה. The latter may be more likely in view of Job 4:16 (דממה וקול אשמע), where the two words occur in reverse order and דממה is not in construct. The sense of the expression depends largely on the meaning of דממה, which occurs elsewhere in the HB only in Ps 107:29 and Job 4:16. Levine showed that there are two דמם roots in Biblical Hebrew, one connoting the absence of movement and sound and the other referring to moaning, sighing, and mourning.[14] He argued that דממה came from the second root and took the expression here to mean "a soft murmuring sound" (*NJPS*). Reymond has since countered that it is unnecessary to posit the דמם II root for דממה, which derives from דמם I and means "silence."[15] An important part of Reymond's case is the contention that a word associated with silence may modify one associated with speech or sound and is not an oxymoron. He provides examples from Hebrew and Aramaic where the sense is that of a quiet sound/speech rather than complete silence. His article points the way forward for translating קול דממה as "a quiet/hushed voice" or "whisper." Exactly what דקה ("thin, fine"), means in terms of sound remains enigmatic (low? slight? faint?). Reymond's word "gentle" implies an emotional content that is not inherent to the word. "Delicate" conveys what Walsh calls the tactile nature of דק.[16]

Special translation note on קול דממה דקה: This expression has been understood in many different ways.[17] The context helps to determine its meaning. Given the identification of it with (the word of) Yhwh that speaks to Elijah in v. 13, it is hardly a "gentle little breeze."[18] The rendering "sound of sheer silence" is also misleading in the context where the קול speaks and Elijah hears it.[19] In Job 4:16, as well, the דממה וקול is audible. Nonetheless, "a hardly audible murmur" is inadequate to the extent that it implies incoherence,[20] since Elijah comprehends the words of the voice. The expression was used at Qumran for angelic songs without words sung for internal illumination, but this meaning does not fit the sense in Kings, where Elijah comprehends what the voice says.[21] The translation *a delicate whisper* satisfies the linguistic requirements of דממה as well as the context of 19:12.[22]

13 **mantle**: The *mantle* (אדרת) was a rectangular cape or wrapper.[23] It could be a marker The אדרת
of wealth or social prominence (Josh 7:21, 24; Jon 3:6). Elijah's hairy mantle (of fur or wool?) became his trademark (1 Kgs 1:8) and by extension that of prophets in general (Zech 13:4). It was a symbol of the office and power of the man of god

---

14 B. A. Levine, "Silence, Sound and the Phenomenology of Mourning in Biblical Israel," *JANES* 22 (1993): 89–106, esp. 102.

15 E. D. Reymond, "The Hebrew word דממה and the Root *d-m-m* I ("To Be Silent")," *Bib* 90 (2009): 374–88.

16 Walsh, *1 Kings*, 276.

17 See the review of translations presented by M. Masson, "L'expérience mystique du prophète Elie: *Qol demama daqqa*," *RHR* 208 (1991), 245–55.

18 J. J. Stamm, "Elia am Horeb," *Studia biblica et semitica Theodoro Christiano Vriezen* (Wageningen: Veenman & Sons, 1966): 327–34, esp. 329, followed by DeVries, *1 Kings*, 236.

19 So Cogan, *I Kings*, 452; Walsh, *1 Kings*, 276; NRSV.

20 Fritz, *Kings*, 198.

21 *Pace* Buis, *Rois*, 153. For the occurrence of the expression at Qumran see J. Strugnell, "The Angelic Liturgy at Qumrân – 4Q Serek Šîrôt ʿôlat Haššabbāt," in *Congress Volume: Oxford, 1959* (VTSup 7; Leiden: Brill, 1960): 318–45. See also Reymond ("דממה," 381–87), who points out that the Qumran references to דממה interpret 1 Kgs 19:12

22 For an entirely different understanding of the phrase as "a roaring thunderous sound" see J. Lust, "A Gentle Breeze or a Roaring Thunderous Sound? *VT* 25 (1975): 110–15.

23 King and Stager, *Life in Biblical Israel*, 271

(19:19) and functioned much like Moses' staff (2 Kgs 2:8, 13-14).[24] The word also means "splendor, majesty," and its associated verb is used in the description of YHWH's theophany (Exod 15:11).[25] The majesty of the divine presence is in the prophetic office. Moses, too, experienced the divine majesty. It made his face glow so that he had to don a veil to quell the fear of the people (Exod 34:29-35). Elijah's אדרת resembles both the cause and the remedy of Moses' brightness.

at the opening: So MT: פתח. G^{B}: ὑπὸ = תחת, a corruption of פתח. G^{L}: παρά = מאת?

What are you doing here: See the Note on v. 9.

14 **for YHWH of hosts**: So G^{B} (τῷ κυρίῳ παντοκράτορι). MT, G^{L}: *YHWH god of hosts.* The longer epithet is unusual in Samuel–Kings and occurs outside of 19:10, 14 only in 2 Sam 5:10, while the designation "YHWH of hosts" is much more common (13x) and is variously translated in G.[26]

have abandoned you: So G^{BL}. See v. 10. G^{B} also reads *your covenant* after *children of Israel*. The different placements confirm its secondary nature.

15 **through the wilderness to Damascus**: G^{BL} reflect the verb ובאת before this phrase rather than after it as in MT. The different locations suggest that the phrase is a gloss.[27] Its meaning is unclear.

anoint: משח refers to smearing or pouring olive oil on a person's head as a ritual sign of appointment to an office or position.[28] Typically associated with kingship (Judg 9:8, 15; 1 Sam 9:16; 10:1; 16:1-13; etc.), anointing is also used to designate Aaron and his successors as priests (Exod 29:7; Lev 6:22; etc.). The verb need not always connote physical anointing but may be used figuratively for "appoint," as shown by the reference to Cyrus as YHWH's anointed in Isa 45:1. This is its sense here for Hazael. Elisha's anointing is comparable to the appointment of a prophetic figure in Isa 61:1.

Hazael: The king of Aram-Damascus ca. 843–800 BCE, during the reigns of Joram, Jehu, and Jehoahaz of Israel, whose reign represented the zenith of its power. Hazael was remembered as a brutal oppressor of Israel (2 Kgs 8:7-15). Allusions to his wars with and oppression of Israel run through 2 Kings 9–13.

16 **Elisha son of Shaphat**: This is the first mention of Elisha, whose name was probably originally vocalized *Elyāšāʿ*, meaning "El/god is salvation/deliverance/victory." It is attested in several seals and inscriptions from the 8th–6th centuries.[29] His father's

---

24 R. B. Coote, "Yahweh Recalls Elijah" in *Traditions in Transformation: Turning Points in Biblical Faith* (ed. B. Halpern and J. D. Levenson; Winona Lake, IN: Eisenbrauns, 1981), 119.

25 G. W. Ahlström, "אדר," *VT* 17 (1967): 1–7; "אַדֶּרֶת, אַדִּיר," *TDOT* I:73–74.

26 So also Hugo, "Text and Literary History," 20–21. Cf. Z. Talshir, "The Representation of the Divine Epithet *ṣb'wt* in the Septuagint and the Accepted Division of the Books of Kingdoms," *JQR* 78 (1987): 57–75.

27 Stade (*Kings*, 157) suggests that מדברה glossed דרך and then *Damascus* entered because of Hazael's name.

28 See also the Diachronic Analysis on 2 Kgs 9:1-13. Anointing oil may well have been a specially prepared blend of oil and spices as argued by W. Dietrich (*Samuel* [BKAT 8.1; Neukirchen-Vluyn: Neukirchener, 2011], 367–68), based on the comparative work of Schottroff and Ebeling.

29 On an 8th–7th century ostracon from Nimrud: J. B. Segal, "An Aramaic Ostracon from Nimrud," *Iraq* 19 (1957), 142 (l. 1 reverse) and W. F. Albright, "An Ostracon from Calah and the North-Israelite Diaspora," *BASOR* 149 (1958), 34 (n. 10 on l. 7). Among the Samaria ostraca: Diringer, *Le inscrizioni*, 42. And on a 7th–6th century seal from Babylon: Diringer, *Le inscrizioni*, 200. Avigad and Sass (*Corpus*, 334–35) list two unprovenienced seals.

name, Shaphat, is an abbreviated form without the theophoric element—"GN judges/is judge"—making it the same as Jehoshaphat.

18 **I will leave**: So MT, G^{L}. G^{B}, Rom 11:4 have the second person under the influence of v. 16. If taken as a reference to the past, the subject must be Yhwh, since Elijah believes himself to be the lone adherent of Yhwh (v. 10); if as a reference to the future it must also refer to Yhwh, since Elijah will have been replaced by Elisha. The twofold occurrence of ימית in the previous verse indicates that והשארתי here is best understood as a converted perfect with future meaning.

7000: So MT; G^{BL} + *men.*

who do not bow the knee to Baal: So MT, lit. *7000—all the knees that have not bowed to Baal.* The following reference to mouths shows that *knees* refers to 7000 people, not 7000 knees = 3500 people.

or kiss him with their mouths: So MT; lit., *and every mouth that has not kissed him.* G: *worshiped.*[30]

19 **found there**: So G^{L}. *There* is superfluous so soon after משם, but may furnish a clue to the editing of this text.[31]

who was plowing: So MT: והוא חרש. G^{BL} + *among the oxen.*

with twelve parcels: So MT, G^{B}: שנים־עשר צמדים לפניו = δώδεκα ζεύγη ἐνώπιον αὐτοῦ. G^{L}: δώδεκα ζεύγη βοῶν ἦν ἐνώπιον αὐτου. צמד can refer to a pair of yoked oxen or to a measure of land—what a pair of oxen can plow in a day (BDB 855). See the Diachronic Analysis.

in the twelfth: On the use of cardinals for ordinals above ten, see GKC §134o; Joüon 142o.

When [Elijah] went over to him: So G^{B} (καὶ ἐπῆλθεν ἐπ' αὐτὸν). MT supplies Elijah's name. G^{L} has both his name and Elisha's.

20 **my father**: So G^{B}. MT, G^{L} + *and my mother.*

[Elijah] said: Reading ויאמר alone. The witnesses expand, G^{BL} with Elijah's name, MT + *to him.*

Go back: So G^{BL} (ἀνάστρεφε = שוב). MT: *Go, return* (לך שוב).

21 **he slaughtered them**: So MT: ויזבחהו. G^{BL} (καὶ ἔθυσε[ν]) lacks the object, which nonetheless seems required for sense in Hebrew.[32]

and boiled them with the oxen's yoke apparatus, and he gave [the meat] to the people: So G^{BL}: καὶ ἥψησεν αὐτὰ ἐν τοῖς σκεύεσι τῶν βοῶν καὶ ἔδωκεν τῷ λαῷ = ויבשלם בכלי הבקר ויתן לעם. MT: ובכלי הבקר בשלם הבשר ויתן לעם, is corrupt due in part to the insertion of הבשר, a misplaced gloss (cf. GKC §131m).

Synchronic Analysis

This chapter has five sections: Jezebel's threat against Elijah (vv. 1-3), Elijah's journey to Horeb (vv. 4-8), the theophany on Horeb (vv. 9-14), the commissioning of Elijah's

19:1-2: Jezebel's threat

---

30 Perhaps a *double entendre* in Greek if προσκυνέω came to mean worship from blowing a kiss (κυνέω = "to kiss") to the god (LSJ 1518).

31 In Trebolle's words it is the *lectio difficilior* (*Centena*, 145).

32 G evidently understands Elisha to be making a sacrifice, while the Hebrew is more ambiguous, the context indicating secular slaughter. Dray (*Translation and Interpretation*, 109) argues that other witnesses, such as the Targums, avoided verbs with sacrificial connotations in accordance with *halakah.*

subsequent mission (vv. 15-18), and the investiture of Elisha as Elijah's servant (vv. 19-21). It begins with Ahab's report to Jezebel about the fate of her prophets. The "sword" mentioned here does not occur in 18:40. It is a recurring motif in ch. 19 (vv. 10, 14, 17), and its occurrences here and in v. 17 form an *inclusio* for 19:1-18. As in ch. 18 Jezebel is the one in charge, while Ahab is a weakling. He goes running back to her like a schoolboy tattletale to tell her *all* that Elijah had done and *all* about how he had killed *all* her prophets (v. 1). In terms of the chapter's Moses imagery Jezebel is Pharaoh, her prophets the magicians. Like Pharaoh, she ignores the miracle in ch. 18, fixating on the slaughter of her prophets. The reference to her here is balanced by the commission of Jehu (vv. 16-17), who will destroy her. She sends Elijah a threat against his life (v. 2). This contrasts with YHWH's messenger in v. 5, who brings food to sustain Elijah's life.[33] The threat is a "promissory oath" swearing to do to Elijah as he had done to the Baal prophets.[34] It is one-upsmanship: what he has done in killing her prophets she will do better—by killing *him*![35] *Tomorrow* may be a conventional ingredient in threats;[36] it recalls Moses' threats of individual plagues "tomorrow" (Exod 9:5, 18; 10:4). The tables are turned as the queen threatens the prophet. Of course, it makes no sense for her to warn him if she really wants to kill him. Perhaps she is reluctant to move against the hero of the moment and only wants to drive him away.

19:3-4: Into the wilderness

The account accelerates with the report that Elijah saw (וירא MT), i.e., perceived the threat against him (v. 3). Since there is no mention of a messenger from Jezebel reaching him, he may have become aware of the threat by prescience. With two verbs he moves from Jezreel all the way to Beersheba in southern Judah. He is about to leave traditional Israel and go into the wilderness. His wilderness journey (vv. 4-8) calls to mind both his departure to Wadi Cherith (17:2-4) and the flight of Moses into the wilderness (Exod 2:11-15) along with Israel's experience there (Num 11). It is a liminal space, away from everyday life. Time spent there is formative. Elijah's physical journey is replicated by a psychological one as he leaves his servant behind and continues alone. His wilderness is the sterility of isolation emphasized by the lone broom tree under which he stops a day in (v. 4). The tree brings to mind Moses' encounter with god at the burning bush (Exod 3). Elijah asks to die. The word נפש occurs twice here, the fourth and fifth times in three verses, highlighting Elijah's life as a central concern of the narrative and the reason for his journey. He is depressed by the feeling that ultimately he has been no more successful than his "fathers," i.e., the prophets who preceded him.[37] He has given up and wants god to end it all.[38] Such profound discouragement, especially after the success on Mount Carmel, seems unwarranted and leads one to question Elijah's psychological state.

19:5-7: Encounters with an angel

Exhausted from his journey and his depression, Elijah falls into sleep (v. 5), a symbol of the death he has requested. Awakened by an angel and told to eat, he finds food and water at his head. The scene is reminiscent of 17:5-6, where he was sustained by ravens. The word צפחת for the water jug also recalls the widow's provision in 17:10-16. After more sleep the angel wakes him again with the invita-

---

33 Thiel, *Könige*, 242.
34 Westbrook, "Law in Kings," 459–60.
35 Cf. Thiel, *Könige*, 242.
36 De Vries, *1 Kings*, 235.
37 Thiel, *Könige*, 252–54.
38 Thiel, *Könige*, 249.

tion to eat and drink, adding that the journey ahead will be too great for him otherwise (v. 7). The word *great* (רב) is the same as that translated *enough* in v. 4. The frustration Elijah felt there had become too much for him. His present journey would be his undoing were it not for divine sustenance. The chain of miraculous provisionings directs him toward the upcoming encounter with YHWH

19:8-9: Forty days and nights to Horeb

Refreshed, Elijah presses on. After forty more days and nights of travel without eating he comes to Mount Horeb (v. 8b). This is an obvious allusion to Moses' fast before he received the tablets of the law (Exod 24:18; 34:28; Deut 9:9, 11, 18, 25; 10:10) on the same Horeb. The cave where Elijah lodges (v. 9) is easily associated with the hole or crevice in the rock (נקרת הצור) where Moses stood while god passed by (Exod 33:22). The entire scene resembles Exodus 32–33, where Moses complains about having to bear the burden of leading the people alone—even asking YHWH to take his life (Exod 32:32)—and YHWH responds with a theophany.[39] It also recalls the caves in which Obadiah hid Elijah's fellow prophets (1 Kgs 18:4, 13). He is now in the same situation as they were, and both because of Jezebel.

19:10: Elijah's complaint

Elijah has sought an audience with god, so now YHWH asks him what he is doing there. Elijah's complaint that the people have abandoned the covenant with YHWH (MT), torn down his altars, and killed his prophets (19:10) is unrealistic. In ch. 18 it was Ahab and the Omrids who abandoned YHWH's commandments (18:18), Jezebel who killed YHWH's prophets (18:4, 13) and has threatened him (19:2), and unnamed persons who tore down YHWH's altar (18:30). Also, the people there fell prostrate, acknowledging YHWH as god (18:39). The claims that bookend Elijah's complaints about the people show that he is driven by self-pity. His lament that he is the only prophet left overlooks the hundred prophets rescued by Obadiah (18:4, 13). The Israelites (בני ישראל), he claims, not just Jezebel, are seeking to kill him (19:10). His self-pity leads him to exaggerate and may even affect his grasp on reality.

19:11-12: Theophany

YHWH responds to Elijah with the theophany in vv. 11-12. By affording Elijah the same sort of revelation as Moses received on Horeb, YHWH legitimates Elijah's career as a prophet and as YHWH's representative, despite his complaints. YHWH is pleased with Elijah's work and, far from seeing him as a failure, regards him as a leader on a par with Moses. Equally, the theophany legitimates Elijah and the prophetic vocation by the changes it makes to the Mosaic theophany. YHWH is not in any of the usual theophanic manifestations—wind, earthquake, or fire—but in the *delicate whisper.* YHWH controls the storm, as he showed in the Carmel contest, but his real presence, like the simple prayer of Elijah in that story, is in the soft-spoken word to the prophet. The Moses episode is comparable rather than contrastive. Moses experienced the theophany. But the durative significance of the event was in the commandments he received on the mountain rather than in the manifestations of power. The prophet communes intimately with god, as did Moses, who was also a prophet. Prophecy is elevated to the status of *Torah* received on stormy Horeb. It is in the word of Moses and the prophets that YHWH is to be found. Fittingly, Elijah wraps his face in his mantle. This is another Moses-like feature. In Exod 3:5 Moses covered his face before YHWH at the burning bush and in Exod 33:22 YHWH covered Moses' face while passing him in the cleft in the rock (Exod 33:22). Elijah covers his face before the word of YHWH.

---

39 Walsh, *1 Kings*, 271. Similarly, in Num 11:15 Moses complains about the burden of the people and asks god to take his life.

19:13-17: A new commission

Hearing the voice and the cessation of theophanic activities, Elijah goes out and stands at the cave's entrance (v. 13) in obedience to YHWH's command (v. 11). The question is put to him again, *What are you doing here, Elijah?* This time the speaker is not identified as YHWH but as "a voice" (קול), suggesting that this is the *delicate whisper* (קול דממה דקה) of the previous verse. Since it is the same question as in v. 9 the voice is to be identified as the word of YHWH, confirming that the *delicate whisper* is YHWH's revealed word. Elijah responds as before (v. 14). The theophany has changed nothing as far as he is concerned. His stubbornness is perhaps the downside of his strength of character. He still sees himself as persecuted by the people and wants to call it quits. YHWH accepts his resignation, but not effective immediately. YHWH gives him a new set of commissions, culminating in the designation of his successor (vv. 15-17). Returning by the way he came, he is to proceed to the environs of Damascus and anoint Hazael as king of Aram. His return from there to Israel is assumed, since he is then to anoint Jehu as king of Israel (v. 16a). Finally, he is to anoint Elisha as his replacement (v. 16b). He does not personally anoint any of these men in subsequent stories. Neither does Elisha. Elijah does cast his mantle over Elisha, designating him as his servant and successor; Elisha tells Hazael that he will be Aram's next king and thereby motivates him to murder his master and seize the throne (2 Kgs 8:7-15); Elisha also sends a trainee of his to anoint Jehu (2 Kgs 9:1-10). One may deduce, therefore, that *anoint* in 19:15-16 is figurative for "appoint" or install" and that Elijah fulfills his commission through Elisha. Verse 17 implies that the reason for this series of anointings is to bring judgment upon Israel. Hazael is known for his brutal defeat and oppression of Israel (2 Kgs 8:12; 10:32-33; 13:3, 7), which is here envisioned as YHWH's judgment. Jehu's bloody purge of Baalism (2 Kgs 9–10) makes plain that the reason for the judgment is Israel's apostasy. As the one who installs both Hazael and Jehu it is Elisha who ultimately wields the sword of YHWH's judgment. The sword of the prophetic word of YHWH is sharper than those of kings like Hazael and Jehu.

19:18: 7000 who do not bow the knee to Baal

YHWH assures Elijah that after executing judgment against Israel and its Baal worshipers he will leave 7000 faithful (v. 18). This is a round number for a large group. The punishment of Israel and the purge of its Baalists will not wipe out the population. There will remain a substantial number of people who are loyal to YHWH. Elijah is not, as he claimed, the only Israelite who is faithful to YHWH. *Knee* and *mouth* here are both synecdoches for persons, specifically those who show homage to Baal by bowing before or kissing his statue.

19:19-20: The investment of Elisha

Several words in the Horeb encounter are used in the next episode: pass by (עבר), mantle (אדרת), kiss (נשק), and return (שוב). There is also continuity of theme as Elijah goes to find Elisha, whom he recognizes as the key to the completion of his mandate. Elisha's hometown of Abel-Meholah (v. 16) is conceivably on the way to Damascus.[40] Elisha's patronymic (Shaphat = "judge") points to his role as the one to mete out YHWH's justice. While Elijah and Elisha have a good deal in common, Elisha is no carbon copy of his mentor. They are separate individuals with different backgrounds. Elisha is prosperous.[41] He owns the twelve parcels of land (or 12 yokes of oxen) that

---

40 Probably to be identified with Tell Abu Sus on the west bank of the Jordan about 10 miles south of Beth Shan. See D. V. Edelman, "Abel-Meholah," *ABD* I:11–12; H.-J. Zobel "Abel Mehola," *ZDPV* 82 (1966) 83–108.

41 There is no indication, *pace* Buis, *Rois*, 155, that he was royalty.

he is working when Elijah comes upon him. The number twelve is symbolic for the twelve tribes of Israel that Elisha is about to lead (cf. 18:31). The mantle that Elijah casts on Elisha is symbolic of the prophetic office held by Elijah (2 Kgs 2, esp. 13). Elijah's act is a literal investment of Elisha as his successor. Elisha understands the symbolism, for he immediately leaves the oxen and runs after Elijah (v. 20). The running shows his eagerness for the opportunity that is offered him. He begs leave only to bid his parents goodbye. He thus has family ties where Elijah has none, so that he is less of a loner or hermit than his mentor. This may be the result of the age difference between them and the different stages in their respective careers. Elisha is just starting out and still has family ties. His request to bid his parents goodbye is not a delaying tactic to give him time to make a decision.[42] He is severing family ties and embarking on a new life as an itinerant holy man in YHWH's service. Elijah's response (*Go, return, for what have I done to you?*) is opaque but obviously permissive (v. 21). The כי can be read as adversative: "Go but (remember) what I've done to you"[43] or the שׁב as Elijah's command for Elisha to return to him rather than to his parents: "Go (but) return, for (consider) what I have done to you."

19:21: Elisha's farewell

In addition to taking leave of his parents Elisha slaughters his yoke of oxen and uses the meat for a celebratory party. The statement that he boiled the oxen with the ploughing implements means that he used the implements for the fire (1 Sam 6:14; 2 Sam 24:22). It is a complete break with his former life—both family and livelihood. In his new role as Elijah's attendant (משרת) he assists the prophet and attends to his needs. He is also Elijah's disciple and his designated successor.

Diachronic Analysis

The transitional role of 19:1-3

This chapter at once presupposes and is in tension with the previous chapters. Ahab's report to Jezebel (v. 1) obviously assumes the story in ch. 18, especially Elijah's slaughter of the Baal prophets (18:40). Jezebel's oath to have him killed (v. 2) presumes her relationship to those prophets (18:19) and fits with her persecution of YHWH's prophets (18:4, 13). It also provides a glimpse of her character that fits well with her confrontational nature elsewhere (e.g., 1 Kgs 21:1-16; 2 Kgs 9:30-36) and shows the narrator's familiarity with those later stories.[44] While Jezebel's notification of Elijah makes no sense if she really wants to kill him, it is effective for providing narrative transition to Elijah's journey in vv. 4-18. Elijah's fearfulness (reading וַיִּרָא in v. 3) is part of the transition; it is inconsistent with the portrait of the bold prophet in ch. 18 who summoned fire from heaven, but it initiates Elijah's journey toward his eventual encounter on Mount Horeb.[45] The transition (vv. 1-3) is not secondary to vv. 4-18 because without vv. 1-3 there is no explanation for Elijah's journey. The transitional function of vv. 1-3 means that we are dealing with the same PN who composed chs. 17–18. The notice in

42 Pace DeVries (*1 Kings*, 239), since Elisha has shown his eagerness to follow Elijah.

43 Gray, *Kings*, 413.

44 Cf. Eissfeldt, " Komposition von I Reg 16,29–II Reg 13,25."

45 The repointing of the verb in the MT to state that Elijah "saw" rather than "feared" may reflect an effort to address this tension (see the Note).

v. 3a that Beersheba belonged to Judah makes clear that Elijah is now far outside of Jezebel's immediate jurisdiction. It need not, therefore, be seen as a gloss.[46] Nor is it a chronological peg dating the story before the fall of the Northern Kingdom in 721 BCE. Its mention may come from the Hagar story, which provided the plot outline for vv. 4-18 (cf. Gen 21:14). The servant whom Elijah leaves at Beersheba (v. 3) is drawn from 18:42-43. Leaving him behind fits with Elijah's feelings of abandonment in the wilderness.[47]

19:4-14: Themes and continuity

The continuity persists in vv. 4-14, again despite the inconcinnity of Elijah's discouragement with his victory on Carmel. His frustration that the Israelites have abandoned YHWH, torn down his altars, and killed his prophets (19:10, 14) articulates the very issues dealt with in ch. 18.[48] There are also thematic continuities with chs. 17–18. The order-compliance scheme, for instance, continues in ch. 19 in the twofold order of the angel to get up and eat (vv. 5-6, 7-8) and in the voice's order to go outside the cave and stand (vv. 11, 13). Even more significantly, the word-of-YHWH theme occurs in 19:9, 13 in a very powerful way as it is identified with the quiet voice that displaces theophanic exhibitions as YHWH's preferred means of revelation. The climax in 19:9, 13 of this theme, which has been prominent in the previous two chapters, again indicates that 19:4-14 are the work of PN as they stand. Their basic outline is strikingly similar to the Hagar story in Gen 21:14-19, which may have served as a template.[49]

---

46 *Pace* Thenius, *Die Bücher der Könige*, 227–28.

47 Würthwein (*1. Könige 17–2. Könige 25*, 224, 227) assigns v. 3b to the same level as the *legenda* in 18:42b-44a because of the mention of the servant. But leaving the servant behind is part of the transitional function of 19:1-3 in preparing for the motif of Elijah's isolation in the wilderness and at Horeb in vv. 4-14.

48 The people are not explicitly blamed for any of these three offenses in ch. 18. While the Baal adherents have clearly abandoned YHWH, the accusation is leveled at Ahab and his house (18:18); unnamed persons tore down YHWH's altar (18:30) and Jezebel killed YHWH's prophets (18:4, 13). Even more striking, Elijah's complaint in 19:10, 14 ignores the people's confession of YHWH in 18:39. These issues are best solved on the synchronic level. In addition to the possibility that Elijah is exaggerating, the writer probably treats people and rulers as a unit and sees their profession of loyalty to YHWH as temporary. See Blum, "Der Prophet und das Verderben Israels," 289–90. PN is more interested in theology than in logical consistency. Some scholars (Buis, *Rois*, 151; E. von Nordheim, "Ein Prophet kündigt sein Amt auf," *Bib* 59 [1978]: 153–73) have addressed these problems by positing that the wilderness journey was once set *before* the Carmel victory.

49 Both stories take place in the wilderness around Beersheba. Hagar leaves her son under a bush שיח (Gen 21:15) because she cannot bear to watch him die; Elijah stops in the shade of a solitary broom tree and asks to die before falling asleep under a bush. An angel appears to Hagar and tells her to get up, that YHWH has heard the boy's voice, and shows her the well (באר) where she can draw water (Gen 21:17-18). An angel also appears to Elijah, showing him water and food to sustain him in the further journey. In both stories there is ambiguity about the being that appears (cf. Gen 16:13). God asks Hagar what is the matter (מה־לך הגר, 21:17) as YHWH asks Elijah what he is doing on Horeb (מה־לך פה אליהו, 19:9, 13). The angel tells Hagar to "fear not" (21:17), and it is fear that drives Elijah into the wilderness (19:3). Finally, in the variant account in Genesis 16 Hagar is sent back to Sarah (16:9) just as Elijah is sent back by the way he came (19:15aα). Cf. Thiel, *Könige*, 230.

Elijah's first request to die and his sleep in vv. 4b-5a are bounded in MT by the repetition of the phrase *under a broom tree* (תחת רתם אחד), which might suggest PN's revision of an earlier tale. However, the Greek witnesses presuppose a different word in v. 5 (שיח), indicating that the repetition is the result not of interpolation but of glossing (see the Note). A second alleged interpolation is MT vv. 6bβ-8a.[50] These verses create two appearances of the angel and two instances of the order-compliance motif in place of one. They also introduce the idea of a lengthy trek in the wilderness and work with the references to forty days and nights and Mount Horeb in v. 8b to portray Elijah in the image of Moses. Without these verses, though, the "man" in v. 5 is not identified as an angel, a point that is crucial for the passage.[51] Hence the absence of these verses in G^L is due to haplography (*he ate and drank*) and does not point to an interpolation.[52]

19:4b-5a, 6bβ-8a: Possible interpolations

Elijah's pause under the broom tree a day into his journey (vv. 4b-5a) highlights his despondency and anticipates the request he will make at Horeb. He sees himself as a failure like his prophetic antecedents and asks to join them. YHWH's response on the mountain will legitimate not only his career but those of all prophets of judgment.[53] The *man* in v. 5b who rouses Elijah to get him to eat is an angel (vv. 6bβ-8a). The עגת in v. 6a, like the מעוג of 17:12, was some kind of bread or cake cooked over live coals in the open rather than in an oven (Ezek 4:12).[54] Its use here along with צפחת for the water jug recalls the miraculous provisioning of Elijah in 17:1-7, 8-16. There is also a reminder of the manna in the wilderness under Moses (Exod 16:31-35; Num 11:6-9; Deut 8:3, 16), especially in view of the mention of the 40-day-and-night trek to Horeb in v. 8 (e.g., Deut 8:2; 9:9, 25). The location of *Horeb*/Sinai is unknown; while at least a dozen candidates have been nominated, the two leading possibilities are in western Saudi Arabia (ancient Midian) and the Sinai Peninsula, both of which fit the meaning of the name—"desert, wasteland." While it was once commonly asserted that Elijah's journey was a pilgrimage to the source of Israel's covenant for the purpose of renewing his commitment as a prophet, this view has been challenged by scholars observing that Elijah goes to Horeb to renounce his calling as a prophet.[55] Horeb was chosen for its connection with Moses and Elijah's likeness to him. The definite article on *cave* and the repetition of the word *there*[56] in v. 9 further highlight the Moses imagery, identify-

Elijah's despondency

50 Trebolle, *Centena*, 143–44.

51 Trebolle rightly cites Judg 13:10-11 as a parallel, but in 13:4, 11 the man is identified as an angel by the narrator.

52 De Vries, *1 Kings*, 233, and Hugo, "Text and Literary History," 23–24.

53 Cf. Blum, "Der Prophet und das Verderben Israels."

54 Borowski, *Life in Biblical Times*, 66; King and Stager, *Life in Biblical Israel*, 66. Also Greenberg, *Ezekiel 1–20*, 107.

55 Cf. Walsh, *1 Kings*, 265 and the scholars he cites. See especially von Nordheim, "Ein Prophet kündigt sein Amt auf." The pilgrimage idea seems to have had its origin with M. Noth ("Der Wallfahrtsweg zum Sinai," *PJ* 36 [1940]: 5–28). Würthwein (*1. Könige 17–2. Könige 25*, 226–27) argues that a fragmentary pilgrimage legend underlies the account of Elijah's journey to Horeb and that it was overwritten successively by DtrP and DtrN. However, there is no real evidence that Sinai was a pilgrimage site in the HB (so G. I. Davies, "Sinai, Mount," *ABD* 6:49). The uncertainty about Sinai/Horeb's location buttresses Davies's conclusion.

56 The first שם refers to the mountain where Elijah arrives, the second to the cave where he lodges.

ing this place with the “cleft of the rock” (נקרת הצור) where Moses stood while god passed by (Exod 33:22).

19:9-10: Elijah’s zeal

YHWH’s question in v. 9, *What are you doing here?* is neither rhetorical nor a rebuke[57] but an inquiry about the nature of an issue or grievance between parties (see on 17:18). Its sense is along the lines of “What issue or problem has brought you here?” Elijah’s statement of zeal (קנא ל) for YHWH (v. 10) expresses exclusive devotion[58] and contentiousness against YHWH’s opponents (Num 25:13). Elijah’s actions on Mount Carmel and his slaughter of the Baal prophets (18:40) illustrate zeal and anticipate Jehu, who boasts of his zeal for YHWH (2 Kgs 10:16). Elijah’s complaint draws from other particulars of the Carmel contest—torn down altars (18:30), slain prophets (18:4, 13), and Elijah’s isolation (18:22). The mention of altars (plural) of YHWH flies in the face of the doctrine of cultic centralization and indicates the non-DtrH composition of this passage.

19:11-14: The theophany

Elijah’s complaint is addressed by the theophany in vv. 11-14, which has been incorporated by means of the repetition of Elijah’s confession of his zeal for YHWH in response to YHWH’s question about why he is there (vv. 9b-10, 13bβ-14). However, since Elijah’s complaint in vv. 10, 14 assumes the three main issues dealt with in PN’s edition of ch. 18, the theophany scene is not PN’s interpolation into an earlier document but his use of *Wiederaufnahme* as an authorial, envelope device. The description of the theophany details a sort of procession in which YHWH is preceded by wind, earthquake, and fire serving as his vanguard.[59] There is an explicit denial of YHWH’s presence in each of these elements, followed by the advent of the קול דממה דקה. Though the text, at least of MT, does not say so directly, YHWH is to be identified with this קול, as indicated by the contrast between the force of the wind, earthquake, and fire in which YHWH’s presence is explicitly denied, and the tranquility of the voice.[60] It is also indicated by the absence of a denial of YHWH’s presence in the קול after three straight denials. Furthermore, Elijah wraps his face in his mantle upon hearing the קול דממה דקה—an act of deference in recognition of the divine presence. The question *What are you doing here, Elijah?* is repeated (v. 13), this time by *a voice* (קול) rather than *the word of YHWH* (v. 9), thus identifying the *voice* as the *word of YHWH* and further confirming the identity of the קול דממה as YHWH.

Prophetic revelation

The *delicate whisper* contrasts the powerful elements of storm theophany with quiet prophetic revelation. The contrast is especially meaningful on the heels of Elijah’s victory at Carmel. The polemic against Baal is pointed. More, it is a repudiation of storm-god theophany as a form of revelation.[61] The religion of Jezebel, the worship of Baal, is defunct. Even the method of revelation associated with it is obsolete. At the same time it is an affirmation of prophecy as YHWH’s preferred means of revelation to humans: equivalent, if not superior, to *Torah*. See the Synchronic Analysis.

---

57 *Pace* Cogan (*I Kings*, 452) and Montgomery (*Kings*, 317).

58 Gray, *Kings*, 409.

59 Fretheim, *Kings*, 109.

60 Most G witnesses, but not G^{BL}, add “YHWH was there” (κἀκεῖ [= καὶ ἐκεῖ] κύριος).

61 Cross, *Canaanite Myth and Hebrew Epic*, 190–94.

19:15-18: Commissions to anoint

Yhwh's instructions in vv. 15-18 presuppose the materials about Elijah, Hazael, and Jehu in 2 Kings and thus are clearly editorial.[62] The naming of the three figures anticipates the punishment against Israel for apostasy under Ahab and Jezebel led by Hazael and Jehu and directed in some way by Elisha. The interest in judgment prophecy, especially leveled at the Ahabids, is PN's, and the commission in these verses represents the range of his editorial activity all the way through the Elisha stories. But there are problems. Elijah does not anoint any of these three figures nor does he kill anyone with a sword (v. 15). Alt postulated that a redactor had cut off the end of the Elijah stories in order to accommodate them to the Elisha stories such that the account of Elijah's fulfillment of his commission was left on the cutting-room floor.[63] But this assumes the one-time existence of an independent set of traditions according to which Elijah personally anointed Elisha, Jehu, and Hazael. Such is highly unlikely considering the strength of traditions connecting Hazael and Jehu with Elisha. Rather, "anoint" here is figurative.[64] The commission in vv. 15-16 presupposes the stories of the succession of Elijah by Elisha and the coups of Hazael and Jehu after Elijah is long gone. Elisha does not anoint either Hazael or Jehu, but he does foretell (and motivate?) Hazael's accession (2 Kgs 8:13) and send the prophet who personally anoints Jehu (2 Kgs 9:1-10). The use of *anoint* for all three characters creates symmetry and places the three under the aegis of Elijah. Elijah's commission of Elisha is parallel to Moses' commission of Joshua and provides another point of resemblance between Moses and Elijah.[65] This metaphorical interpretation is further suggested by the statement about Elisha killing in v. 17. Just as he does not anoint, so he carries out no executions personally. Again there is symmetry with Hazael and Jehu. Elisha is the one through whom the swords of Hazael and Jehu are empowered and activated.[66] Then v. 18 is not a rebuke or correction of the perspective of Elijah's sense of isolation, as often claimed, or a reflection of the (post)exilic hope in a righteous remnant,[67] but an *ex eventu* prophecy about the remains of Jehu's purge. The 7000 are symbolic of a large group of Israelites who will be left alive after Jehu's execution of the apostate royal household and their adherents. These faithful will not bow to Baal or kiss him. The expression *bow the knee* uses a synecdoche to express a person's submission; the usual posture in the ANE involved bowing on both knees and/or prostration.[68] Kissing a god's statue was also an act of worship alluded to in Hos 13:2.

19:19-21: Elijah claims Elisha as his servant

As has been generally recognized since Alt, vv. 19-21 belonged originally to the Elisha materials and were secondarily affixed to the stories about Elijah by

62 Cf. Sauerwein, *Elischa*, 13–14.
63 A. Alt, "Die literarische Herkunft von 1 Reg 19,19-21," *ZAW* 32 (1912):123–25.
64 See the Synchronic Analysis. It is clearly figurative in Isa 61:1, the only other instance of the anointing of a prophetic figure in the HB.
65 White, *The Elijah Legends*, 8.
66 R. A. Carlson, "Élie à l'Horeb," 438–39.
67 Würthwein, *1. Könige 17–2. Könige 25*, 231.
68 See for instance the figures on the relief of the fall of Lachish from Nimrud or that of Jehu on the Black Obelisk. A counterexample is the relief at Naqsh-e Rustam of Philip the Arab kneeling on one knee before the Persian emperor Shapur I.

means of the first two words of v. 19 (וילך משם).[69] G^L's שם (*there*) after the verb *found*, which is nonsensical so soon after משם, is an additional text-critical trace of the suture. The Elisha story evidently named the place (Abel-Meholah?) where Elijah found Elisha, but it was cut off when the anecdote was joined to the Elijah stories. Elijah finds Elisha at home plowing (vv. 19-21). He either has twelve yokes of oxen before him (driven by other workers, perhaps "the people" of v. 21) or twelve parcels of land to work. Either way he hails from a prosperous family. Elijah's casting of his mantle lays claim to Elisha as his servant (Ezek 16:8; Ruth 3:9).

The symbolism of the mantle

Elijah does not surrender his mantle (אדרת) to Elisha permanently here, so this anecdote was not a doublet to 2 Kings 2 but shared the mantle motif with it. The nature of the mantle as a symbol of Elijah's identity and power (2 Kgs 1:8; 2:8, 13, 15) alluded to Elisha's succession to Elijah, which came to fruition in 2 Kings 2. PN exploits the allusion in the commission in vv. 15-18 by naming Elisha as Elijah's successor (v. 16) and drawing on the similarity with Moses and Joshua (Exod 24:13; Num 11:28; Josh 1:1). The use of the verb שלך (*Hipʿîl*) in the plague stories (Exod 4:3; 7:9-10; 15:25) and the Elisha stories (2 Kgs 2:21; 4:41; 6:6) for acts of magic hinted at Elisha as the benefactor of some kind of transfer of power or status.[70] PN's addition of וישרתהו at the end of the verse further emphasizes the continuity with Moses (Exod 24:13; Num 11:28; Josh 1:1) and ties nicely with the Moses theme in vv. 4-14. Like Joshua, Elisha here becomes Elijah's servant as a prelude to assuming his mentor's office.

Elisha is eager to accept the role with which Elijah has invested him. He only begs leave to *kiss*, i.e., bid farewell to, his father (v. 20).[71] Elijah's response is cryptic and has been variously interpreted:

- as a disclaimer: "Do as you wish since I have done nothing to you;"[72] or "If you don't want to follow me, I have not compelled you;"[73] or "Go, return to kiss him, for what have I done to you that you may not do this?"[74]
- as a rebuke: "You want to return, but do you think I've done nothing to you?"[75]
- as an affirmation that the significance of what Elijah has done should lead Elisha to bid his family goodbye;[76]
- as permission with a warning to contemplate what Elijah is doing in taking Elisha as his servant;[77]

---

69 Alt, "Literarische Herkunft," esp. 125; Sauerwein, *Elischa*, 15. Also K. Seybold, "Elia am Gottesberg: Vorstellungen prophetischen Wirkens nach 1 Kön 19*," *EvTh* 33 (1973): 3–18. Alt, however, argued that 19:19-21 displaced the original conclusion of chs. 17–19.

70 Thiel, *Könige*, 306.

71 The mention of the mother is an expansion. See the Note.

72 Favored by Buis, *Rois*, 155; Kittel, *Könige*, 155.

73 Ewald quoted by Šanda, *Könige*, 454.

74 This is Šanda's own preference.

75 Buis, *Rois*, 156.

76 Sweeney, *Kings*, 233.

77 Gray, *Kings*, 413; Würthwein *1. Könige 17–2. Könige 25*, 233. Similarly Stade, *Kings*, 158: "Go, but return, for remember what I have done for you (casting my mantle upon you and making you my successor)."

- as a literal question: "What does investiture mean?" since Elisha thinks Elijah is calling him as his successor when in reality he is to be a servant.[78]

Since Elisha goes home to say his good-byes, Elijah's question is best interpreted as affirmation or permission. The command *return* (שוב) is ambiguous and might grant Elisha permission to return home or command him to return to Elijah after going home. The slaughter of the oxen and distribution of their meat (v. 21) point to celebration. A disclaimer, a warning, and a literal question about investiture are all ill-suited to such a setting. Elijah, then, allows Elisha to tell his father goodbye because he is embarking on a new life as Elijah's assistant and eventually as his replacement. This passage marks the beginning of the Elisha stories and the beginning of the end for Elijah.

Synthesis

A transitional chapter and an apology for prophecy

This chapter is transitional. Elijah's flight to Horeb and encounter with YHWH on the mountain extend and resolve matters begun on Carmel. Then the new commission Elijah receives and his investment of Elisha provide an entrée into the Elisha tales and anticipate the rise of Hazael and Jehu and the judgments they will execute on Israel and the Ahabids. The chapter's centerpiece is the theophany on Horeb, which constitutes YHWH's response to Elijah's complaint and request to depart this life. YHWH's advent in the delicate whisper of prophetic revelation repudiates storm theophany in the wake of the defeat of Baal on Carmel. It is also a kind of apology for prophecy.[79] It puts forward a different possible outcome of prophecy to the "happy ending" of chs. 17–18 in which the people listen and repent.[80] The reader knows that the repentance on Carmel will not last. Going back to Moses, the HB traces a history of apostasy often shortly after great miracles by YHWH on Israel's behalf. The realistic outcome of ch. 19 foreshadows Israel's and Judah's futures. Even in this contrast, continuity between the chapters is implicit. Prophecy is a conduit of divine power and revelation. It is by the word of YHWH that Elijah is directed (17:2, 5, 8; 18:1; 19:9, 15), and it is through YHWH's word delivered by the prophet that power and truth are conveyed (17:14, 16, 24; 18:37-38). The prophet is YHWH's special servant and representative (17:1, 24; 18:1, 36). He is the messenger who brings salvation as well as judgment, but he is not the cause of Israel's troubles, which are in fact brought on by disloyalty to YHWH (18:17-18). Prophetic revelation is the counterpart to *Torah*. It comes from YHWH himself, and he is present in it, eclipsing or corroborating other forms of revelation (19:11-12). For Elijah as for Moses, who was also a prophet (19:8-9), the enduring entity from the mountain of god is the word of god. YHWH's answer to Elijah

78 Walsh, *1 Kings*, 279.

79 Blum, "Der Prophet und das Verderben Israels," 286.

80 Blum, "Der Prophet und das Verderben Israels," esp. pp. 289–90. Blum argues that there is a wider horizon in view than just the time of Elijah, that "Israel" here really refers to Israel throughout the monarchic period, at least from the 8th century on, when judgment prophecy originated.

is to commission him to designate his replacement and thereby set in motion the disciplining and refining activities of Hazael and Jehu. Prophecy speaks softly but wields a sharp sword.

Nameless Prophets (1 Kings 20 MT; 21 G)

Text

[Battle story; *PN]*
1 Ben-Hadad assembled all his army and came up and laid siege to Samaria *with thirty-two kings and horses and chariots they came up and laid siege to Samaria* and fought against it. 2 He sent to Ahab king of Israel 3 and said to him, "Thus says Ben-Hadad, 'Your silver and gold belong to me; your wives and your children are mine also.'" 4 The king of Israel answered, "As you say, my lord king, I and all that I have are yours." 5 The messengers returned and said, "Thus says Ben-Hadad, 'I sent saying, "You must give me your silver and gold, and your wives and children," 6 about this time tomorrow I will certainly send my servants to you, and they will search your house and the houses of your servants and whatever is valuable to you they will seize and take away.'" 7 So the king of Israel summoned all the elders and said, "Be aware how this fellow is trying to stir up trouble; for he sent to me for my wives and children, my silver and gold, and I did not withhold [anything] from him." 8 The elders and all the people responded to him, "Don't obey. You shall not consent!" 9 So he said to Ben-Hadad's messengers, "Tell your master, 'All that you sent to your servant previously I will do. But this thing I cannot do.'" And the men conveyed his response. 10 Then Ben-Hadad sent to him and said, "So will the gods do to me and so will they add if enough dust of Samaria is left to fill the hands of all those who follow me." 11 The king of Israel responded, "Enough! Let him who girds on not boast like him who looses.'" 12 When Ben-Hadad heard *(he was drinking—he and the kings—in the booths),* he told his servants, "Lay siege." So they laid siege to the city." 13 *Then a prophet approached the king of Israel and said, "Thus says* Yhwh, *'Do you see this great multitude? I will place it in your control today so that you will know that I am* Yhwh.'" 14 *[Ahab] asked, "By whom?" [The prophet] answered, "Thus says* Yhwh, *'By the young men of the district commanders.'" [Ahab] said, "Who should initiate the battle?" [The prophet] answered, "You."* 15 Then [the king of Israel] mustered the young men of the district commanders (they were 230) and after them he mustered the army, every warrior, 7000 strong. 16 When they marched out *at noon—now Ben-Hadad was drinking himself drunk in the booths—he and the thirty-two kings who had come to his aid—* 17 and when the young men of the district commanders *marched out* first, they sent and told the king of Aram, "Men are marching out from Samaria." 18 He replied, "If they have marched out for peace, seize them alive, and if for war seize them alive." 19 But these having marched out from the city—the young men of the district commanders and the army that was behind them— 20 each of them killed his opponent and did so a second time so that Aram fled and Israel pursued them. Ben Hadad, king of Aram, escaped upon a cavalry horse. 21 The king of Israel went out and captured the horses and chariotry and effected a great slaughter against Aram. 22 *The prophet approached the king of Israel and said, "Strengthen yourself and carefully con-*

sider what you should do, because next year the king of Aram will come up against you." [23] *The servants of the king of Aram said, "Their god is a mountain god. That is why they defeated us. But let us fight them on the plain and we will surely defeat them.* [24] *So do this: Remove each of the kings from his position and replace them with officials.* [25] *Substitute an army for yourself like the army that fell—horse for horse and chariot for chariot. Then let us fight them on the plain, and we will surely defeat them." So he listened to them and did so.* [26] *A year later* Ben-Hadad mustered Aram and came up to Aphek for war against Israel. [27] The Israelites were mustered and went to meet him. Israel camped opposite them like a couple of flocks of goats, while Aram filled the land. [28] *The man of god approached and said to the king of Israel, "Thus says Yhwh, 'Because Aram has said, "Yhwh is the god of the mountains but he is not the god of the valleys," I will give this great multitude into your control so that you may know that I am Yhwh.'"* [29] They camped opposite one another for seven days. Then on the seventh day when the battle was joined, Israel killed 100,000 Aramaean foot soldiers in one day. [30] The rest fled to the city of Aphek where the wall fell on 27,000 men who were left. As for Ben-Hadad, he had fled into an innermost chamber of a particular house. [31] His servants said to him, "We have heard that the kings of Israel are merciful. So let us put sackcloth on our waists and cords on our heads and go out to the king of Israel in hopes that he will spare your life." [32] So they girded sackcloth on their waists and [put] cords on their heads and said to the king of Israel, "Your servant Ben-Hadad says, 'Please spare my life.' [The king of Israel] said, "Is he still alive? He is my brother." [33] The men were looking for an omen, so they quickly seized on what he said, and they replied, "Your brother Ben-Hadad." Then [the king of Israel] said, "Go, bring him." And when Ben-Hadad came out [the king of Israel] invited him up into the chariot. [34] [Ben-Hadad] said to him, "The cities that my father took from your father I will return and you can build bazaars for yourself in Damascus such as those my father built in Samaria." [The king of Israel] said, "I will send you away with [this] agreement." So he made a treaty with him and sent him away from his house, and he went *from him.* [35] *But a member of the prophetic guild said to his friend by the word of Yhwh, "Strike me." But the man refused to strike him.* [36] *So he said to him, "Because you disobeyed Yhwh, when you go from me a lion will kill you." And when he went from him a lion encountered him and killed him.* [37] *He found another man and said, "Strike me," and the man struck him, wounding him with the blow.* [38] *Then the prophet went and waited for the king beside the road, disguising himself with a bandage over his eyes.* [39] *As the king was passing, the prophet appealed to the king and said, "Your servant went out in the midst of the battle, where someone brought me a man, telling me, 'Guard this man; if he should go missing your life will substitute for his or you will have to pay a talent of silver.'* [40] *But as your servant was looking around here and there, he disappeared." The king said to him, "This is your judgment; you yourself have decided it."* [41] *Then [the prophet] hurriedly removed his bandage from his eyes so that the king of Israel recognized that he was one of the prophets.* [42] *He said to him, "Thus says Yhwh, 'Because you released the man destined for destruction from your control, your life will substitute for his life and your army for his army.'"* [43] Then the king of Israel went away *in a resentful rage* and came to Samaria.

Textual Notes

1 **Ben-Hadad assembled**: Reading ובן־הדד קבץ. Omitting the epithet *king of Aram*, which is lacking in G^{B}. G regularly reflects *Hadar* instead of *Hadad* as the king's name, the result of graphic confusion between *resh* and *dalet*. As the name of the Aramaean deity, *Hadad* is correct.

and came up and laid siege to Samaria, with thirty-two kings and horses and chariots they came up and laid siege to Samaria and fought against it: Following G^{BL} except for their reading of *all* before *horses and chariots*. The reading shows the interpolation by *Wiederaufnahme* that led to the present verse.[1]

2 **He sent**: So G^{B}. MT, G^{L} + *messengers*

king of Israel: So G^{L}, Syr. MT, G^{B} + *in the city*.

3 **your wives and your children**: So G^{B}. MT, G^{L} + הטובים.

5 **I sent**: So G^{BL} (ἐγὼ ἀπέσταλκα = אנכי שלחתי). MT's כי is a remnant of the first person pronoun. MT, G^{L} + *to you*.

your wives and children: So MT. G^{BL} lack *and children* due to haplography; cf. v. 7.[2]

6 **certainly**: כי אם is emphatic; cf. Joüon §173c.[3]

your house: So MT, G^{B}; G^{L}: *your houses* influenced by the plural in the following clause.

whatever is valuable to you: Reading: מחמד עיניך. This is MT's reading except for כל, which is expansive. G^{BL}: *whatever they desire* (τὰ ἐπιθυμήματα [L: τῶν] ὀφθαλμῶν αὐτῶν = מחמד עיניהם). But מחמד especially in construct with *eyes* refers to a person's own property, not someone else's.[4]

they will seize: Lit: *place in their hand*: So MT (ישימו בידם). G^{BL}: ἐφ' ἃ ἂν ἐπιβάλωσι τὰς χεῖρας αὐτῶν = אשר ישימו ידיהם עליו = *whatever they lay their hands on*, which accords with the understanding that the Aramaean envoys will take whatever they find desirable.

7 **all the elders**: So G^{B}. MT + *of the land*, which G^{L} further expands with *of Israel*.

for my wives and children, my silver and gold, and I did not withhold [anything] from him: So MT. G^{BL} reflect a slightly different reading: περὶ τῶν γυναικῶν μου καὶ περὶ τῶν υἱῶν [L: τέκνων] μου [B: καὶ περὶ τῶν θυγατέρων μου] τὸ ἀργύριόν μου καὶ τὸ χρυσίον μου οὐκ ἀπεκώλυσα [L: ἐκώλυσα] ἀπ' αὐτοῦ. G^{B}'s inclusion of daughters is an expansion. Otherwise, the Greek witnesses reflect the preposition על where MT has ל, and they limit the items that the king did not withhold to his silver and gold, but not family members. MT's *waw* before the negative particle will not permit this interpretation.

8 **The elders**: So G^{BL}; MT: *all the elders*.

9 **your master**: So G^{BL}; MT: *my lord the king* as in v. 4.

All that you sent: So MT, G^{B}; G^{L}: *According to all*, a dittography (ככל for כל).

the men: So G^{BL}; MT: *the messengers* as earlier in the verse.

10 **So will the gods do to me and so will they add**: G^{BL} have the singular, *god*, and singular verbs. Presumably, though, Ben-Hadad would have sworn by his gods. On the oath formula, see on 19:2.

to fill the hands: So MT (לשעלים, *handfuls*), G^{L} (δραξὶ); misunderstood in G^{B} as לשועלים, *foxes*.[5]

---

1 Trebolle, *Centena*, 145–46.

2 Cf. Law, *Origenes Orientalis*, 334.

3 Also Walsh, *1 Kings*, 296.

4 Ehrlich, *Randglossen* 267–68. See also T. J. Meek, "I Kings 20 1-10," *JBL* 78 (1959), 74.

5 Klostermann (*Die Bücher Samuelis und der Könige*, 375) accepts the LXX^{B} reading as referring to jackals that entered the Aramaean camp at night to scavenge.

who follow me: Lit. *who are at my feet*, an idiom.[6]

11 **Enough**: So G^{B} (ἱκανούσθω = רב or רב די[7]), expanded in G^{L} with ὑμῖν = לכם, and corrupted in MT to the superfluous דברו.

Let him who girds on not boast like him who looses: So MT. G^{BL} inexplicably read "Let the hunchback not boast like the righteous" (μὴ καυχάσθω ὁ κυρτὸς ὡς ὁ ὀρθός [L: ὄρθιος]).

12 **When Ben-Hadad heard**: So MT: Lit. *When he heard this word* (ויהי כשמע את־הדבר הזה), construing Ben-Hadad as the subject. G^{BL} have *When he answered him this word* (καὶ ἐγένετο ὅτε ἀπεκρίθη αὐτῷ τὸν λόγον τοῦτον = ויהי כענותו את־הדבר הזה), taking Ahab as the subject. כשמע and כענותו appear to be variants.

he was drinking—he and the kings—in the booths: See v. 16.

Lay siege. So they laid siege: Reading with MT שימו וישימו. The verb שים, "place, set," is used in a technical sense.[8] This is probably the reason behind G^{BL} οἰκοδομήσατε χάρακα καὶ ἔθεντο χάρακα (*build a trench and they set a trench*).

13 **a prophet**: On the indeterminate use of אחד see the Note on 19:4.

the king of Israel: So G^{BL}; preceded in MT by Ahab's name.

Do you see: Taking the ה before the verb as the interrogative particle, which may have an exclamatory nuance (Joüon §161b).

this great multitude: So G^{BL}. MT + *all*.

14 **[Ahab] asked**: Reading ויאמר. Though attested in the major witnesses, Ahab's name is marked with the obelus in the Syr.[9]

15 **the young men of the district commanders**: So MT as in v. 14. G^{B}: *the commanders, the young men of the districts*; G^{L}: *the commanders and the young men of the districts*.

230: So G^{B}. MT, G^{L}: 232, which has been influenced by the number of kings (32) helping Ben-Hadad (v. 16). In fact, G^{L} continues with καὶ ὁ βασιλεὺς ἑζὲρ μετ' αὐτοῦ, a misplacement of the description of Ben-Hadad's allies at the end of v. 16.

the army: So G^{BL}. MT: *all the army*.

every warrior: So G^{BL} (πᾶν υἱὸν δυνάμεως = כל־בן־חיל). MT has *all the children of Israel*. Both are possible, but the G reading is more distinctive.

7000 strong: So MT. G^{B} has 60, which is too small. Most G witnesses add the word *thousand*, but 60,000 is too large in the light of vv. 27, 29. 7000 is an idealized number (cf. 1 Kgs 19:18).

16 **When they marched out**: So MT (ויצאו). G^{B} has the singular in line with the previous verbs. G^{L} seems to combine the two readings with *they marched out, the king with them*. That MT is the better reading is indicated by the same verb in v. 17, which marks the resumption of the narrative (*Wiederaufnahme*) following the interpolation of essentially all of v. 16.

in the booths: So MT, as in v. 12. G^{BL}: *in Succoth*. Yadin argues for the latter in both verses.[10] He locates the Aramaean base camp at Succoth from which the messengers and the Aramaean chariotry were sent to Samaria. Homan points out, however, that the distance between Samaria and Succoth (Tell Deir ʿAlla, east of the Jordan near the mouth of the Jabbok)—some sixty kilometers or forty miles—is a long way to travel in a day to search the palace (v. 6).[11] It also makes vv. 17-20 all but incomprehensible:

---

6 See Burney (*Notes*, 233) for a list of parallels.

7 So DeVries, *1 Kings*, 242.

8 Stade, *Kings*, 159.

9 T. M. Law, *Origenes Orientalis: The Preservation of Origen's Hexapla in the Syrohexapla of 3 Kingdoms* (DSI 2; Göttingen: Vandenhoeck & Ruprecht, 2011), 173–74.

10 Y. Yadin, "Some Aspects of the Strategy of Ahab and David (I Kings 20; II Sam. 11)," *Bib* 36 (1955): 332–51.

11 M. M. Homan, "Booths or Succoth? A Response to Yigael Yadin," *JBL* 118 (1999): 691–97.

by the time the Aramaean soldiers report to Ben-Hadad and then receive his order to capture the Israelites coming out of the city, the entire Israelite army would have emerged and the battle would be well underway if not over.

17 **and when the young men of the district commanders**: So MT (נערי שרי המדינות), G^{L} as in v. 14. G^{B}: *the commanders, the young men of the districts* (ἄρχοντες παιδάρια τῶν χωρῶν). G^{L} reflects a double writing of שרי: οἱ ἄρχοντες καὶ τὰ παιδάρια ἀρχόντων τῶν χωρῶν.

They sent and told the king of Aram: So G^{BL}: καὶ ἀποστέλλουσι[ν] καὶ ἀπαγγέλλουσι[ν] τῷ βασιλεῖ Συρίας λέγοντες = וישלחו ויגדו למלך ארם לאמר. MT is corrupt: וישלח בן־הדד ויגידו לו לאמר = *Ben-Hadad sent and they told him saying.*

18 **he replied**: So MT. G^{B} + *to them*; G^{L} + *to the king of Aram.*

If they have marched out for peace: So MT. G^{B}: εἰς εἰρήνην οὗτοι οὐ γὰρ ἐκπορεύονται. The Greek has lost the conditional particle by haplography and added the negative particle by dittography.

and if for war: So G^{B}. MT, G^{L} repeat the verb.

19 **These having marched out**: So MT, G^{L}. G^{B} has καὶ μὴ ἐξελθάτωσαν = ואל יצאו, *do not let them march out.*

the young men of the district commanders: As consistently in MT; so also G^{L}. See on v. 14. G^{B} has ἄρχοντα τὰ παιδάρια ἄρχοντα τῶν χωρῶν, *commander—the young men—the commander of the provinces.*

and the army that was behind them: Jepsen (BHS) suggests transposing this phrase to after v. 20aα and v. 20b to after v. 21. The resulting text would read [20]*each of them killed his opponent so that Aram and the army that was after them fled.* [21]*The king of Israel went out and captured the horses and chariotry and effected a great slaughter against Aram. Israel pursued them, but Ben Hadad, king of Aram, escaped upon a cavalry horse.* The improvement in order effected by the conjecture is minimal and unwarranted in view of the lack of textual evidence for it.

20 **and did so a second time**: That is, ויכו שנית איש אישו based on G^{BL}: ἐπάταξεν ἕκαστος τὸν παρ' αὐτοῦ καὶ ἐδευτέρωσεν ἕκαστος τὸν παρ' αὐτοῦ. MT lost the sentence by haplography.

Aram fled: MT has the plural (וינסו), while G^{B} reflects the singular (καὶ ἔφυγεν). G^{L} agrees with MT in reading the plural and has οἱ σύροι as the subject, construing ארם as a collective.

upon a cavalry horse: So G^{BL}: ἐφ' ἵππου [L: ἵππῳ] ἱππέως = על סוס פרש, *upon the horse of a rider/ horseman.* MT has: על־סוס ופרשים *upon a horse and horsemen*, which is senseless. Mowinckel argued that the MT phrase was idiomatic and referred to a span of chariot horses as part of his thesis that in pre-exilic military contexts horses were almost always for chariots.[12] While horses were usually associated with chariotry rather than cavalry during the Israelite monarchy, mounted cavalry appeared in Egypt in the tenth century and in Mesopotamia in the 9th century.[13] Horseback riders may also have been used as messengers. MT's reference to פרשים seems to distinguish the horse on which Ben-Hadad escaped from chariot horses, though the possibility that פרש was an alternate term for a chariot driver cannot be ruled out[14] and would make better sense in this context where chariots are plentiful.

12 S. Mowinckel, "Drive and/or Ride in OT," *VT* 12 (1962): 278–99, esp. 292–93. It is unclear how Mowinckel envisioned Ben-Hadad escaping on a span of chariot horses without the chariot.

13 King and Stager, *Life in Biblical Israel*, 116; Cantrell, *Horsemen of Israel*, esp. 136–41.

14 See Richelle, *Le testament d'Élisée*, 41.

21 **captured**: So G^{BL}: ἔλαβεν = ויקח. MT's ויך makes less sense with *chariotry* as an object. It came into the text under the influence of the two subsequent instances of נכה in this verse.[15]

22 **and said**: So G^{B}. MT + *to him*. G^{L} + *saying*.

strengthen yourself: So G^{BL}. MT precedes with *Go* (לך).

the king of Aram: So MT; G^{BL} expand with Ben-Hadad's name.

23 **said**: So G^{L}. MT + *to him* (אליו); G^{B} precedes with *and*.

Their god is a mountain god: So MT; G^{BL}: *the god of Israel is a god of the mountains and not of the valleys*, anticipating v. 28.

they defeated: So MT, G^{L} (ἐκράτησαν); G^{B} reads the singular (ἐκραταίωσεν) with Israel as subject.

surely: i.e., אם־לא, an oath formula or asseveration otherwise attested in Josh 14:9; 2 Kgs 9:26; Isa 5:9; 14:24; Jer 15:11; Job 1:11; 22:20; Ps 131:2.

24 **So do this**: So MT (ואת־הדבר הזה עשה), G^{B} (καὶ τὸ ῥῆμα τοῦτο ποίησον). G^{L} reflects a slightly different reading: ποίησον κατὰ τὸ ῥῆμα τοῦτο = עשה כדבר הזה.

from his position: So MT (ממקמו); G^{B}: εἰς τὸν τόπον αὐτῶν = למקומם; G^{L}: εἰς τὸν τόπον αὐτοῦ = למקומו. The verb סור in the *Hip'îl* regularly occurs with the preposition מן.

25 **Substitute**: Reading החלף, the *Hip'îl* imperative of חלף, "to change, exchange." The root is suggested by Jepsen (BHS), who tentatively reads the first person plural with G^{B} (ἀλλάξομέν). However, G^{L} (ἄλλαξόν) has the imperative, which is supported by the statement at the end of the verse that Ben-Hadad acted. MT: ואתה תמנה (*You count!*).

that fell: So G^{BL}. MT + *from you*.[16]

he listened to them: So MT, G^{L}; G^{B}: *he listened to him*.

27 **were mustered**: MT has two verbs, התפקדו וכלכלו, which are variants. Only the first is reflected in G^{BL}. התפקדו is unusual—a *hotpā'al*. It occurs three other times in the HB—Num 1:47; 2:33; 26:62—and is interpreted as either a passivized form of the *hitpa'el* or a reflexive of the *qal* (GKC §54l; Joüon §53g). It appears to be a frozen form with a technical meaning: "to be passed in review."

to meet him: So G^{B}. MT: *to meet them*. The antecedent in v. 26 is Ben-Hadad.

Israel camped: So G^{BL}. MT: *the children of Israel camped*.

flocks: The meaning and etymology of the *hapax* חשפי are uncertain. The translation *flocks* is based on the versions. The root חשף means "strip, expose," such that its passive חשיף might mean "exposed, segregated (flock)"[17] or "a piece of land exposed [by goats]."[18]

28 **and said to the king of Israel**: So G^{BL}; MT has a second ויאמר following *king of Israel*.

---

15 Cogan (*I Kings*, 465), following Montgomery (*Kings*, 328) adopts a suggestion of Orlinsky's that ἔλαβεν is an error for ἔβαλεν ("he cast down"). However, the latter occurs only once (Hos 14:6) in the LXX for נכה and would thus be a very unusual translation here.

16 On the use of מאותך for מאתך, see Burney, *Notes*, 237–38 and Rendsburg, *Israelian Hebrew*, 61–65, who considers this an example of Northern Hebrew

17 Cogan, *I Kings*, 466.

18 A. Baruchi-Unna, "Two Clearings of Goats (1 Kings 20:27): An Interpretation Supported by an Akkadian Parallel," *JBL* 133 (2014): 247–49. Šanda (*Könige* I, 481) cites an Arabic root, *hasafa* "to lead a flock" as supporting the usual rendering, but a search of leading Arabic dictionaries failed to find such a root with this meaning. The same is true of G. R. Driver's ("Studies in the Vocabulary of the Old Testament II," *JTS* 32 [1931], 255–56) claim that an Arabic root *ḥašafa* means "to give birth prematurely" yielding the meaning "helpless as two kids prematurely born."

this great multitude: So G^{BL}: MT + *all.*

so that you may know: So G^{BL}; MT has the plural. All three agree in reading the singular in v. 13.

29 **Israel killed**: So G^{BL}. MT: *the children of Israel killed.*

100,000: So MT, G^{B}; G^{L}: 120,000.

30 **of a particular house**: So G^{BL} (εἰς τὸν οἶκον); MT: *of the city.*

31 **His servants said to him, “We have heard**: So MT (ויאמרו אליו עבדיו הנה־נא שמענו). G^{BL}: *He said to his servants, “I know ...”* (καὶ εἶπε[ν] τοῖς παισὶν αὐτοῦ οἶδα). In v. 32 the servants are described, distinct from the king, as the ones who are dressed in sackcloth.

kings of Israel: So G^{BL}. MT: *kings of the house of Israel.*

are merciful: So G^{BL}. Prefaced in MT with כי.

to the king of Israel: Prefaced in G^{B} with ἔτι = עוד. Perhaps influenced by the occurrence of this particle near the end of v. 32.

your life: So MT. G^{BL}: *our lives* in accord with the G reading that Ben-Hadad is the speaker.

32 **and [put] cords on their heads**: So MT, which is elliptical in its lack of a verb and induced G^{BL} to supply different verbs—ἔθεσαν and ἔδησαν respectively.

and said to the king of Israel: So G^{BL}, themselves now elliptical. MT: *they came to the king of Israel and said.*

my life: So MT. G^{BL}: *our lives.* Ben-Hadad’s survival is the topic of the subsequent verses.

33 **were looking for an omen**: The imperfect signals durative or iterative action in the past.[19]

they quickly seized: A verbal hendiadys: וימהרו ויחלטו (MT). ויחלטו is a *hapax.* It is probably *Hip‘il* (GKC 53n), but *Qal* is also possible. It may be an Aramaism.[20] The meaning attributed to it here—“snatch, sieze” (BDB)—is based on its rendering in the versions.[21]

on what he said: Following the consonantal text of MT (הממני), but taking the ה as the suffixed object of the previous verb rather than the interrogative with BHS. Hence, lit.: *they seized it from him.* G^{BL}: “the word from his mouth” (τὸν λόγον [L: αὐτοῦ] ἐκ τοῦ στόματος αὐτοῦ) is interpretive.

invited him up into the chariot: So MT (ויעלהו על־המרכבה). G^{BL} + *to him* at different locations indicating the phrase’s secondary nature.

34 **[Ben-Hadad] said to him**: So MT, G^{B}. G^{L}: *the king of Syria said to Ahab.*

I will return: So MT; G^{BL} + *to you*

[The king of Israel] said: Reading ויאמר (so Jepsen BHS) as required by sense.

from his house, and he went away from him: So G^{L} (ἐκ τῆς οἰκίας αὐτοῦ καὶ ἀπῆλθεν ἀπ’ αὐτοῦ = מביתו וילך ממנו). The reading is supported by the *Wiederaufnahme* formed by וילך here and in v. 43.[22]

37 **wounding him with the blow**: On the use of the two infinitives expressing simultaneous action see Joüon §123m; WO, 590.

38 **waited**: This is the meaning of the idiom עמד ל, found also in 2 Kgs 5:9; Qoh 2:9.

for the king: So MT; G^{BL} + *of Israel.*

---

19 *Pace* Joosten, *Verbal System*, 287, who sees it as an exceptional use of the imperfect with preterit, non-modal meaning.

20 Schniedewind and Sivan, “Test Case,” 325.

21 Cf. F. E. Greenspahn, *Hapax Legomena in Biblical Hebrew: A Study of the Phenomenon and Its Treatment Since Antiquity with Special Reference to Verbal Forms* (SBLDS 74; Chico, CA: SBL, 1984), 115.

22 Trebolle, *Centena*, 147.

disguising himself: So MT (ויתחפש). G^{BL} κατεδήσατο = ויתחבש (*he bound himself*). While the Greek reading makes sense, the verb חבש does not occur elsewhere in the HB in the *Hitpāʿēl*.

with a bandage: Reading באפר, which is the MT consonantal text. A *hapax legomenon* in the HB, אפר is apparently cognate to Akkadian *apāru*, "to place a headdress on" (*CAD* A/2, 166-68; AHw, 57). Context suggests that in this instance the headdress was a bandage or wrapping, as per G^{BL} [L: ἐν] τελαμῶνι "bandage" (LSJ, 1769), since it was placed over his eyes.

39 **appealed to**: The idiomatic meaning of צעק אל, lit., *cried out to* (cf. 2 Kgs 8:3).[23]

in the midst of the battle: So MT (בקרב־המלחמה). G^{BL}: ἐπὶ τὴν στρατιὰν τοῦ πολέμου = בצבא המלחמה, *with the army into battle*. Either reading is possible.

where someone brought me a man: So G^{BL} (καὶ ἰδοὺ ἀνὴρ εἰσήγαγεν πρός με ἄνδρα = והנה־איש הביא אלי איש), which is the *lectio brevior* over against MT (והנה־איש סר ויבא אלי איש).[24]

if he should go missing: G^{L} reflects a reading prefaced with ויהי. On the use of the infinitive here, which may be important for meaning, see Joüon §51b, §123g; WO, 587 and Synchronic Analysis.

40 **But as your servant was looking around**: So G^{B}: καὶ ἐγενήθη περιεβλέψατο ὁ δοῦλός σου, G^{L}: καὶ ἐγένετο ὡς ὁ δοῦλός σου περιεβλέψατο, reflecting the verb שעה where MT has עשה.

This is your judgment; you yourself have decided it: So MT (כן משפטך אתה חרצת). G^{B} appears corrupt: ἰδοὺ καὶ τὰ ἔνεδρα παρ' ἐμοὶ ἐφόνευσας = *you have destroyed traps set for me* (?). Similarly G^{L} (ἰδοὺ.. δικαστὴς σὺ παρ' ἐμοὶ ἐφόνευσας). Both reflect רצחת instead of חרצת.

41 **from**: So MT *qere'* (מעל) in lieu of the *ketiv* (מעלי).

42 **the man destined for destruction from your control**: So G^{BL}: ἄνδρα ὀλέθριον ἐκ χειρός σου = את־איש־חרם מידך. MT's את־איש־חרמי מיד = *the man of my destruction from control*.

your life will substitute: So MT (והיתה נפשך), G^{B} (καὶ ἔσται ἡ ψυχή σου). G^{L} has ἰδοὺ in place of καὶ ἔσται, reflecting הנה instead of והיתה.

43 **went away**: So G^{BL}. MT + על־ביתו.

Synchronic Analysis

Outline of the chapter

This chapter recounts two military victories of Israel over the Aramaeans (vv. 1-21, 26-34) with a description between them of the change in Aramaean strategy (vv. 22-25). The victories are directed by prophets (vv. 13-15, 22, 28). Yhwh gives Israel victory in order to show the king of Israel who Yhwh is (v. 13) and to show the Aramaeans (v. 28) that they are wrong to think Yhwh's power is limited to mountainous regions (v. 28). The second victory is extended with an anecdote recounting prophetic denunciation of the Israelite king, Ahab, for releasing the Aramaean king, Ben-Hadad (vv. 35-43).

---

23 Cogan, *I Kings*, 470.

24 Robker's (*Jehu Revolution*, 104) reconstruction (*and behold! A man* [sic] *a man came to me* =והנה־איש בא אלי) is not attested by any witness. It also lacks any mention of the prisoner.

20:1-8: Ben-Hadad's bullying sparks resistance

The abruptness of the notice of Ben-Hadad's (v. 1) siege is the first in a series of narrative displays signaling his unwarranted aggression. Thus negotiations (vv. 2-6) follow rather than precede the assault. The verb שלח, "to send" occurs six times in vv. 1-10, all with Ben-Hadad as subject. He sends message after message to Ahab with demands. When the verb occurs in v. 42 (*Pi'ēl*) with Ahab as the subject it is to dismiss Ben-Hadad, who is now his vassal.[25] Ben-Hadad's demands escalate. He starts by laying claim to Ahab's wealth and family (v. 3)—perhaps the exaction of an admission of fealty, with which Ahab complies.[26] But then in v. 5 he demands that Ahab actually turn over these items. Finally, in v. 6 he demands that his servants be allowed to pillage the palace. It is bullying in order to humiliate Ahab. Ironically, it drives Ahab to resist, since his fate will be no worse if he fights and loses than if he submits (v. 7). He calls on the elders, who serve as his advisors, to recognize (*know* and *see*) how Ben-Hadad is trying to stir up trouble (lit. "seeking evil").[27] This might mean that Ben-Hadad is picking a fight or that he is seeking Israel's ruin—or both. In any case Ahab has the unanimous support (v. 8) of the elders and the people alike. They concur that the demands of the Aramaean are outrageous, and they encourage Ahab in his resistance. Their encouragement is not hollow since in siding with their king they are putting their own property and lives at risk.

20:9-11: Ben-Hadad's threats, Ahab's defiance.

Ahab's message to Ben-Hadad (v. 9) continues to express deference. He refers to the Aramaean king as *my master*.[28] He also tells Ben-Hadad that he is unable to comply (*I cannot*) with the king's demand rather than refusing outright ("I will not").[29] This is the occasion Ben-Hadad has been pushing toward, as the narrative implies. He responds to Ahab with a threat (v. 10) in the form of an oath that is reminiscent of Jezebel's threatening oath in 19:2. He will, he says, more than pulverize Samaria. He will obliterate it so that there will not remain even handfuls of the former city for everyone in his army. This is hyperbole, and Ahab understands it as such. He seems emboldened by the threat, or perhaps it is mere bravado that leads him to reply aphoristically (v. 11): *the one who girds on should not boast like the one who looses* (אל־יתהלל חגר כמפתח). The meaning is roughly equivalent to "Don't count your chickens before they hatch." The verb forms חגר and מפתח have a distinctly military nuance in this context (e.g., 1 Sam 17:39; Isa 45:1). The message to Ben-Hadad is that he has not yet defeated Israel and that this may prove more difficult than he anticipates. The succinctness of this response contrasts with Ben-Hadad's exaggerated threat and lends the reader optimism about Israel's chance for victory.

20:12: The drunken king orders the siege

Ben-Hadad is with the thirty-two kings who are his allies *in the booths*, i.e., their army tents, where he has been all morning (v. 16) drinking himself drunk. The repetition of this notice (vv. 12, 16) hints at its importance to the plot of the

25 Walsh, *1 Kings*, 295.
26 Walsh, *1 Kings*, 295.
27 The lack of explanation as to how Ahab was able to gather the elders from all Israel within the 24-hour time frame outlined by Ben-Hadad (v. 6) is a "narrative flaw" according to Walsh (*1 Kings*, 296).
28 *My master* may be construed as the opening of the message: "He told Ben-Hadad's messengers, 'Say: "To my lord the king ..."'" So Cogan, *I Kings*, 464.
29 So Walsh, *1 Kings*, 297–98.

story. This behavior indicates Ben-Hadad's overconfidence about the impending battle. In the larger narrative the drunkenness is YHWH's doing (at least the timing of it); it is the mechanism by which YHWH brings victory to Israel. Upon receipt of Ahab's response Ben-Hadad immediately orders his men to lay siege to the city. It is not clear exactly how this order (שימו, see the Note) relates to v. 1. The latter may be anticipatory. But Ben-Hadad is drunk. His slurred order may show his confusion about where they are in the siege process.

20:13: A nameless prophet

As abrupt as the siege is the appearance of the prophet in v. 13. We have no details about him or where he approaches (נגש) Ahab. He is not identified as Elijah but his style accords with Elijah's ability to appear and disappear.[30] The prophet begins his oracle with the messenger formula, *Thus says YHWH*, and he then speaks in the first person for YHWH. He is a welcome change from the messengers that Ben-Hadad has been sending with demands and threats. His message is positive: YHWH will give him control over the Aramaean army that is in front of him. The oracle is something of a surprise, given that this is Ahab, the worst king of Israel. But the prophet explains that the victory is not because Ahab is deserving but so that *you may know that I am YHWH*. The verb "know" is singular, so that YHWH's self-authentication is specifically for Ahab's benefit. To know that YHWH is god is to recognize his right to exclusive worship. Ahab is targeted because of his apostasy under Jezebel's influence.

20:14: The young men of Ahab's army

Ahab believes the prophet and asks only about strategy (v. 14): At whose hands will the victory be won and who should initiate the battle? He is told that the *young men of the district commanders* will win the battle and that he should initiate it.[31] The presence of the *Erkenntnisformel* means that a miracle pointing to YHWH's power is performed here, and that miracle relates to the identity of the young men of the district commanders. The *young men* (נערים) may be "servants" who are not trained as fighters.[32] The miracle would then be that untrained youthful servants defeat a seasoned army. Alternatively, *young men* can be a military designation (e.g., 2 Sam 2:14),[33] so that the reference here could be to some kind of elite force consisting of young men who were unmarried and thus could serve professionally.[34] In that case the miracle consists of victory over superior numbers.

---

30 Compare Nelson, *Kings*, 130.

31 There are two interpretations of the question מי־יאסר המלחמה (v. 14). While it has commonly been understood to mean "who will initiate the battle," some have recently taken it to ask precisely the opposite: "who will conclude/ clinch the battle" (Nelson, *Kings*, 133; Provan, *Kings*, 155; Walsh, *1 Kings*, 300). The latter is based on the meaning of the root אסר as "bind, tie." But the expression "tie up," meaning "conclude" is an English idiom, not a Hebrew one (Cogan, *I Kings*, 465), and the comparable Akkadian idiom *tāḫaza kaṣāru* has the meaning "prepare for battle" (*CAD* 8 [K], 260). In addition, the expression occurs in 2 Chr 13:3 where it refers to Abijah enjoining the war with Jeroboam that is about to be recounted (*Pace* Provan, *Kings*, 155).

32 So Cogan, *I Kings*, 465; Provan, *Kings*, 151.

33 McCarter, *II Samuel*, 96–97; cf. W. F. Albright, "Mitannian *maryannu* "Chariot-Warrior" and the Canaanite and Egyptian Equivalents," *AO* 6 (1930-31): 217–21; Y. Sukenik (Yadin), "'Let the Young Men, I Pray Thee, Arise and Play before Us,'" *JPOS* 21 (1948), 114; Fox, *In the Service of the King*, 185n.

34 See Brueggeman, *Kings*, 248; Buis, *Rois*, 161; DeVries, *1 Kings*, 249; Gray, *Kings*, 424; Würthwein *1. Könige 17–2. Könige 25*, 239.

The נערים number only 232. There is also the Israelite army of 7000 (v. 15)—the same number as those who do not bow the knee to Baal (19:18). But the Aramaean army is a great *multitude* (v. 13) that dwarfs the Israelite force (v. 27).

20:15-21: Victory!

Following the prophet's instructions, Ahab musters his forces, sending the נערים at their head (v. 15). The pace of the narrative accelerates as the narrator switches back and forth between Israel and Aram. They begin to march out of the city in the heat of midday (vv. 15-16a). The move catches Ben-Hadad's force by surprise. The *young men* are at the head (v. 17a). The Aramaeans quickly send a report to Ben-Hadad (v. 17b). They seem to believe that the emerging force of *young men* is a small, expeditionary one and not the advance guard of the entire Israelite army. This may be another factor, in addition to intoxication (v. 16b), behind Ben-Hadad's lapse in judgment. He does not grasp the gravity of the situation. He issues a foolish order for his men to capture the Israelites alive (v. 18), which seriously impedes his troops because the Israelite soldiers are free to kill them. The result is a rout. The Aramaeans flee; Ben-Hadad himself escapes on horseback (v. 20). Verse 21 then summarizes and concludes this first battle account with the notice that the king of Israel effected a *great slaughter* of Aram. Its reference to the capture (G) of the Aramaean horses and chariotry furnishes a nice *inclusio* with the mention of horses and chariotry in v. 1. With YHWH's help and prophetic direction Ahab defeats Ben-Hadad and his sizeable Aramaean army.

20:22: A warning about the next assault

Verses 22-25 bridge the two battle accounts in this chapter with two scenes that are effectively simultaneous planning sessions from opposite sides about the same anticipated event—the revenge attack of the Aramaeans in the coming year.[35] The prophet who appears in v. 22 is designated with the definite article, indicating that he is the same prophet as in v. 13, and this is confirmed by the mutual resemblance of the introductions to their oracles: והנה נביא אחד נגש אל־אחאב מלך־ישראל ויאמר (v. 13) and ויגש הנביא אל־מלך ישראל ויאמר (v. 22). The prophet again offers Ahab intelligence about the forthcoming assault. As in v. 13, he uses the verb "to see" (ראה). This time, though, he does not offer a word from YHWH but admonishes Ahab to *see and know*—a verbal hendiadys with the nuance "carefully consider."[36] Ahab needs to figure out how he can strengthen himself in preparation for the Aramaeans' return in a year.

20:23-25: The Aramaean plans

In the second scene the Aramaeans reason that the Israelites won the first battle on the uneven terrain near Samaria because YHWH is a god of the highlands, and that they will defeat Israel on flat land (v. 23). Their thinking is no doubt influenced by the location of Damascus on a plain. They also propose that Ben-Hadad depose the kings who were with him and replace them with *officials* (פחות). This suggests a demotion of what were formerly independent vassal states into districts or provinces within Ben-Hadad's kingdom. The point seems to be to make them more directly responsible to him in hopes of creating greater cohesion within the army. Hence the vassal kings become the scapegoats for Aram's defeat. This is also suggested by the language of v. 25, which begins with the emphatic pronoun: *You yourself muster an*

---

35 לתשובת השנה lit., "at the turn of the year," does not mean "Spring," though it was typically in the spring or summer when kings went to war. See McCarter, *I Samuel*, 284–85.

36 Cogan, *I Kings*, 466.

army. The next level of blame, then, falls on the Aramaean army, which was slain or deserted—the verb "fall" (נפל) can mean both.[37] This time, with Ben-Hadad firmly in command, success is assured! Ben-Hadad succumbs to the flattery and follows their advice (v. 25). Still, the words *horse* and *chariot*, both repeated in v. 25, recall the *inclusio* around the story of the defeat in vv. 1 and 21, so that the astute reader has misgivings about this assurance of victory for Aram.

20:26-28: The Aramaeans encroach again

As predicted, a year after the first battle the Aramaeans return for war, this time in Aphek (v. 26). The exact location is uncertain, though we can reasonably conclude that it was a flat location somewhere between Damascus and Samaria. It is presumably the same Aphek as in 2 Kgs 13:17 and thus had a reputation as a battleground between the two countries. The connection with 2 Kings 13 bolsters the reputation of the nameless prophet as an Elisha-like figure. The Israelites, apparently on the lookout because of the prophet's warning, hear of the advance of the Aramaeans and rally their own army to meet them (v. 27). As the two armies encamp opposite one another it is clear that the Israelites are vastly outnumbered. In the midst of this military posturing a prophet approaches Ahab for the third time (v. 28). He is called *the man of god*, but his approach (ויגש) and use of the messenger formula and *Erkenntnisformel* all identify him as the same prophet of vv. 13 and 22. "Man of god" characterizes him as an Elijah/Elisha-like figure and further enhances his reputation. This is important not only because he is otherwise unknown but also because his message is positive rather than one of judgment as might be expected for Ahab. Yhwh will again give Israel victory, not because Ahab deserves it but for Yhwh's own reputation—to disprove the Aramaean claim that his power is limited to the highlands. Thus the audience for this demonstration is not just Ahab (*you may know* is plural) but the Israelites and the Aramaeans as well.

20:29-30a: Jericho reversed

Several elements in the account of the battle in vv. 29-30a are reminiscent of the story of the defeat of Jericho under Joshua (Josh 6). These include the seven-day hiatus before the onset of the battle, the notice of the battle without details, and especially the collapse of the city wall. There is no liturgical activity beforehand and no express attribution of the wall's collapse to Yhwh, so it may be that the wall was undermined by the Israelites. Still, the *Erkenntnisformel* inclines one to see the collapse as Yhwh's handiwork.

20:30b-32: A desperate plea and a foolish acquiescence

In the melee Ben-Hadad hides out in an innermost room somewhere in the city (v. 30b)[38] where his servants advise him on his next move. Their advice is premised on their understanding that the kings of Israel are מלכי חסד. This might mean that the Israelite kings are loyal to treaties.[39] However, any treaty Israel had as Aram's vassal would be void now that their relative circumstances are reversed, particularly considering Ben-Hadad's behavior. Also, the immediate concern of Ben-Hadad and his servants is survival rather than a future treaty. A better interpretation may be that Israelite kings observed international conventions whereby surrendering kings were

---

37 On the meaning "desert" for this verb see Cogan and Tadmor, *II Kings*, 82.

38 Walsh (*Kings*, 306) interprets חדר בחדר to mean "room by room." But this interpretation does not work for the parallel in 2 Kgs 9:2, where the expression must refer to the innermost chamber.

39 S. J. DeVries ("A Reply to G. Gerleman on *malkê ḥesed* in 1 Kings XX 31," *VT* 29 [1979], 361) interprets as "kings who will recognize and respect agreements" based on the semantic range of חסד.

spared by their overlords.[40] For conciseness I have retained the translation *merciful.* The servants volunteer to approach the king of Israel dressed in clothes of mourning and lamentation (שקים) with cords on their heads. The latter are either additional symbols of mourning or represent submission, perhaps the cords by which they are to be led away as captives (v. 31).[41] They speak only of their king's fate, appealing to his self-interest but also aware that their fate is bound up with his. Intriguingly, Ben-Hadad does not speak, perhaps indicating his reticence about their plan after the defeat in which he followed their advice.[42] On the other hand, his only alternative is to wait until the Israelites find him, in which case they may be less merciful. Willing submission to the king of Israel at this point may save his life. And indeed, the plan works. The request to Ahab and his response are two halves of a chiasm (v. 32): *Your servant Ben-Hadad says, 'Please spare my life.' "Is he still alive? He is my brother."*[43] The correspondence shows that they are "on the same page." Ahab's question complements Ben-Hadad's order in v. 18 to take the Israelites *alive.* His change of *servant* to *brother* acknowledges Ben-Hadad as a peer and may allude to their treaty relationship.[44] If so, it is remarkable that despite the treatment he received from Ben-Hadad Ahab now regards him not as a vassal but as a partner. *My brother* is also an acknowledgment of social equality, and this may be the grounds of Ben-Hadad's appeal and of Ahab's acquiescence. Either way, Ahab is a fool. He is so unaccustomed to being in the position of the victor that he does not know how to behave. Letting Ben-Hadad go will only bring Israel trouble down the road. Instead of consulting YHWH, he places his trust in a human treaty.[45]

20:33: Pouncing on Ahab's words

The next two verses show just how offensive Ahab's actions are. Ben-Hadad's envoys were divining (ינחשו). The statement is odd in this context, and the meaning is debated. It is typically taken to mean that the men were looking for any kind of signal that they might exploit in Ben-Hadad's favor (cf. BDB, 638). Whatever the nuance, the root refers to an activity that is expressly forbidden in the law (Lev 19:26; Deut 18:10). Of course, since the Aramaeans are the ones divining, the remark does not disparage Ahab *per se.* They fixate on his use of the term *brother.* The Hebrew text expresses their incredulity: ויחלטו הממנו, which means *They seized (it).Was it (really) from him?* They repeat the word back to him, as if to confirm that Ahab has actually said it: *(Yes,) your brother, Ben-Hadad.* Ahab's act of bringing Ben-Hadad up (ויעלהו) into his chariot (cf. 2 Kgs 10:15) reminds the reader that Ben-Hadad "came up" (ויעל) against Samaria to attack it in the first place (20:1). Ahab spurns YHWH's gift of victory with a pact that will enhance his own international prestige. This alliance with the Aramaeans recalls the one with the Phoenicians that brought Jezebel to Israel.

20:34: Putting Ben-Hadad back in charge

Verse 34 suggests that Ahab's other motive for the treaty was wealth. The promise to allow bazaars in Damascus *such as those my father built in Samaria* makes clear that the speaker is Ben-Hadad. He continues as the speaker for the last two sentences of the verse. It is he who sets the terms of the treaty and dismisses Ahab. Ahab goes so

40 Würthwein, *1. Könige 17–2. Könige 25*, 241.
41 Gray, *Kings*, 429; Provan *Kings*, 153; Šanda, *Könige* I, 482.
42 Walsh (*1 Kings*, 306–307) suggests that the servants' own reticence in approaching their king after the loss is indicated here by the double occurrence of the particle נא.
43 Walsh, *1 Kings*, 308.
44 Brueggemann, *Kings*, 250–51; Long, *1 Kings*, 215.
45 Hens-Piazza, *Kings*, 200.

far in trying to placate the foreign king that he puts Ben-Hadad back in charge and reverts to the subject status he had at the beginning of the narrative. He shows no appreciation for the power YHWH has displayed or for the gifts he has been given.

20:35: Another prophet

The subject-first clause in v. 35 signals a new episode. We are not surprised at the advent of a prophet because the ending of the previous episode prepared us for a rebuke of Ahab. This character is introduced with אחד, one, functioning as an indefinite article, indicating that he is not the prophet who appeared previously. He is one of the *sons of the prophets* (בני הנביאים), an expression that occurs here for the first time in Kings. It is especially common in the Elisha stories where these individuals often seem to be trainees. This prophet, therefore, is probably a young man who has been in training for just such a moment. He is a counterpart to the נערים in the previous story. His dress or tonsure may indicate affiliation with the guild.

20:35-38: Waiting for Ahab

The first part of this anecdote (vv. 35-37) has affinities with the story of the young prophet and old prophet in 1 Kings 13. The expression *by the word of YHWH* in v. 35 is a repeated motif in that chapter (vv. 1, 2, 5, 9, 17, 18, 32); it occurs only four other times in the HB (1 Sam 3:21; Jer 8:9; Ps 33:62; 2 Chr 30:12). It refers to a discreet command from YHWH. This raises the question whether the companion whom the prophet orders to strike him is aware that the command emanates from YHWH. The harsh punishment the companion receives suggests that בדבר יהוה does double duty, that the prophet receives the command from YHWH and passes it along to his companion as such. Obedience to the divine word prophetically mediated is an absolute requirement that tolerates no refusal. Non-compliance is disobedience to YHWH himself. For that reason the companion loses his life (v. 36). The use of a lion as an agent of divine punishment is another obvious similarity with 1 Kings 13 (13:24; 20:36). The prophet finds another man to strike and wound him (v. 37), so that he stands waiting for Ahab with a bandage over his eyes. While the wound adds realism, it is technically unnecessary for the prophet's disguise; all that is needed is the bandage. Its purpose in the story is to convey the lesson about obedience to prophetic command. The harsh judgment on the companion for refusing to comply with the divine will sets the tone for the prophet's encounter with Ahab and bodes ill for him.

20:39: A legal case

The rest of the anecdote is narrated in vivid fashion such that the appeal signaled by the prophet's outcry in v. 39aα does not come until v. 41. In between is the case laid out for judgment. It is a sort of parable, like those in 2 Samuel 12 and 14, intended to solicit a self-judgment from the king. The construction הפקד יפקד in v. 39 may indicate an improbable contingency (see the Note), thereby suggesting that the petitioner (= Ahab) was especially careless in allowing the prisoner to escape. The patently fictional nature of the case undercuts much of the speculation about the nature of the relationship between the putative soldier, his captive, and the captor.[46] It is not clear, therefore, whether substituting for the life of the prisoner means death or slavery for the

46 Thenius (*Könige*, 242) says that the price exacted for the loss of the prisoner suggests that he was an important person. Slotki (*Kings*, 149) adds that the man who brought the prisoner must be envisioned as a superior officer. Westbrook ("Law in Kings," 458–59) contends that the agreement assumed here has features of a "contract for deposit of safekeeping" (Exod 22:6-8), which would have required a formal agreement in the form of a solemn oath between the parties. He further argues that the fine of a talent of silver is so high because the real punishment is death.

petitioner,[47] though for Ahab it is obviously the former. There is the possibility of redemption, but the price—a talent of silver—is outrageously high and far beyond the ability of a commoner to pay.[48] From the perspective of the "parable" and its function in the story these punishments make clear the seriousness of Ahab's offense. The outrageous price of redemption invites Ahab to be as magnanimous to one of his own soldiers as he was to the foreign king and to pardon the debt. His refusal to do so reveals his hypocrisy.

20:40-43: Ahab judges himself

Ahab judges that the petitioner's fate is sealed by the circumstances of the case: his prisoner escaped, so he is culpable. His statement *you yourself have decided it* pronounces judgment also on himself. At this the prophet removes his bandage and proceeds to apply the sentence to Ahab. Ahab's immediate recognition of the man as one of the prophets suggests that he bore a mark peculiar to that guild, since the story gives no reason to believe that the two men were previously acquainted. The prophet's judgment is sharp: Ahab must compensate YHWH for freeing YHWH's enemy and prisoner. This is an invocation of holy war ideology: It was YHWH's war, and he gave the victory; hence the spoils belong to him and are to be "devoted" through ritual slaughter or immolation. Ahab freed the devoted Ben-Hadad and now must substitute his own life. Ahab receives his sentence with resentment and rage. The words סר וזעף convey stubbornness and anger rather than depression.[49] Ahab is incapable of introspection. The resulting expectation of an account of Ahab's death will be met in 22:34-38.

Diachronic Analysis

Relationship of this chapter to 1 Kgs 21; 22; 2 Kgs 13

This chapter contains two battle accounts (vv. 1-21* and 26-43*) that once directly preceded the one in 22:1-38. The Greek witnesses preserve this order and are followed here. The three battle stories pertained to one of the kings of the Jehu dynasty and were located at the end of 2 Kings 13 as the fulfillment of Elisha's prediction of three victories over Aram in 13:19. The name of the king is not preserved. PN revised them and moved them to Ahab's reign in order to "correct" DtrH's account, which left Ahab personally unpunished despite being Israel's worst king, and thus to provide partial fulfillment of the PN oracle in 1 Kings 21. The later positioning of the Naboth story after ch. 20 in MT (= ch. 21) sought to bring Ahab's punishment closer to his crime.

20:1-2: The first step of the siege

The aggression of the king of Aram in vv. 1-21 is a surprise in part because the story is out of its original context with the Aramaean-Israelite wars during the Jehu dynasty. His siege of Samaria (v. 1) is the first step in the process of assaulting a city.[50] First the city is surrounded to prevent escape. Only when negotiations fail are siege works put in place (v. 12). The reference to the thirty-two kings accompanying Ben-

---

47 Provan (*Kings*, 156) argues that it was death; Walsh (*1 Kings*, 311) argues for slavery.

48 A talent equaled ca. 3000 shekels or 100 times the value of a slave according to Exod 21:32.

49 The two words form an adjectival hendiadys. סר (< סרר) refers to obstinacy, even rebellion, while זעף expresses anger and vexation.

50 Würthwein, *1. Könige 17–2. Könige 25*, 237; Yadin, "Some Aspects," 333–34.

Hadad in vv. 1aβbα is the first of three PN additions about them (vv. 12aβ, 16) that stress the size of Ben-Hadad's force; it was added by *Wiederaufnahme* (see the Note) as G^{BL} show.

Identification of Ben-Hadad

The identification of Ben-Hadad here is a long-standing problem caused in large measure by the mention on the Melqart stela of a Bir-Hadad who was assumed to be one of the rulers of Damascus. Pitard's re-reading of Bir-Hadad's patronymic on the stela indicated that he was not one of that city-state's kings. (See the excursus on 2 Kgs 6:24.) There is no indication of a Bir-Hadad who ruled Damascus during the Omri dynasty. The Aramaean king in 1 Kings 20 is to be identified with the son of Hazael, who ruled Damascus in the first quarter of the eighth century during the Jehu dynasty. Thus 1 Kings 20 and its sequel in 22:1-38 are historically out of place. While the references to thirty-two kings in vv. 1, 12, and 16 are editorial, the Zakkur inscription does refer to seventeen kings being allied with this Bir-Hadad. Several of these may have been tribal chieftains who were bound to Bir-Hadad by treaty.[51]

20:3-6: Ben-Hadad crosses a line

Ben-Hadad's claim to the Israelite king's treasury and family (v. 3) may be intended to elicit a confession of loyalty to him as suzerain in a treaty relationship. The king of Israel seems to take it as a formality and acknowledges his subordination, calling the Aramaean *my lord* (v. 4). But Ben-Hadad crosses a line with his subsequent demands that the king of Israel turn over these items (v. 5) and allow the Aramaeans to enter and plunder the houses of the king and his elites (v. 6). Such a demand goes beyond the treaty stipulations for suzerain and vassal, especially since the Israelite king has not revolted. The intent is to humiliate the king of Israel.[52] That is especially true in the MT reading in v. 6, "what you consider valuable" (contrast G "what they consider valuable"), which suggests that the Aramaeans will spitefully seize what is precious to the Israelite king rather than what they themselves may desire.

20:7-8: Prelude to war

Despite his relative weakness the king of Israel cannot acquiesce to this latest demand. He gathers the elders to seek their approval for his decision (v. 7), since it will affect their property as well. Following G^{B} the text reads *elders* rather than *elders of the land* (MT) or *elders of Israel* (G^{L}). The meaning, therefore, is ambiguous. Does it refer to the elders of all Israel or only to those of Samaria? The latter is more appropriate considering that the city is surrounded. Also the king would not have time within the twenty-four hours allotted to him to summon and consult elders from all Israel. Alternatively, there may have been a group of senior royal officials who served as advisors to the king and were therefore present at court.[53] The king explains how he has complied with Ben-Hadad's demands to this point, thereby upholding treaty protocol. But the Aramaean remains unsatisfied because his real intent is to *seek evil*,

---

51 *COS* 2:.35. The precise number is uncertain. The "17" in line 5 is broken and might be read as "16." Only 7 kings, including Bir-Hadad, are listed before a break in the text. Aside from Bir-Hadad these are all from northern Syria and Anatolia. The "7" in line 8, which is also broken, has been construed as another "17" and as a summary reference to 7 minor vassal kings (Pitard, "Identity of the Bir-Hadad," 171). On the likelihood that these were chieftains see Cogan, *I Kings*, 462; De Vries, *1 Kings*, 248; Sweeney, *Kings*, 241; Walsh, *1 Kings*, 295.

52 So J. M. Robker, "Satire and the King of Aram," *VT* 61 (2011), 651–52, who contends that the portrait of Ben-Hadad is satirical.

53 So Fox, *In the Service of the King*, 63–72. Robker (*Jehu Revolution*, 648) argues that vv. 7-8 are secondary because the elders disappear from the story thereafter.

i.e., to find a cause for war against Israel, as is transparent in his latest demand to allow his servants to ransack the Israelite palace.[54] The elders and people (= army) agree with the king's sentiment that enough is enough. They are willing to go to war (v. 8).

20:9-11: The Israelite king resists

In his return message (v. 9) the king of Israel no longer expresses subservience. Following G[BL], he refers to Ben-Hadad as *your master*, addressing the messengers, not *my master* (so MT) as before. His message is pointed. He cannot comply with the latest demand.[55] Ben-Hadad's reply is a boastful threat (v. 10) in the form of an oath (cf. 19:2). He swears that he will obliterate Samaria, leaving too little of it for his army to take up two handfuls each. It is a vivid image, but the king of Israel is not cowed. He has been pushed to the point of resistance by Ben-Hadad's escalating demands and bullying. The content of his return message appears to be an aphorism (v. 11). The verbs for girding and loosing are not limited to armament but can refer to putting on and taking off any kind of clothing (e.g., v. 32; Isa 20:2). The saying might mean "let the person who dresses not boast like the one who undresses," with the Qohelet-like sense that one should not celebrate the day until one has successfully faced its challenges.

20:12-14: PN adds a prophet

Hearing the king of Israel's now-defiant response, Ben-Hadad issues the order to *set in place* the siege works against the city (שימו), although the order is made somewhat enigmatic by the lack of a direct object (v. 12). PN's note that Ben-Hadad and his allies are drinking in v. 12aβ is parenthetical and separates the temporal clause (*when he heard*) from its continuation (*he said*). It offers an explanation for Ben-Hadad's foolish order in v. 18. PN then added vv. 13-14, which also break into the older battle narrative with a subject-first sentence. They introduce a nameless prophet who predicts Yhwh's victory over Aram and provides strategy. Yhwh's motive is expressed with the *Erkenntnisformel—that you will know that I am Yhwh.*[56] It occurs in contexts in which

---

54 C. Begg ("'This I Cannot Do' (1 Kgs 20,9)," *SJOT* 2 (1989): 23–27) proposes on the basis of analogy with the eighth-century victory stela of King Piye that Ben-Hadad suspects Ahab of holding out on his payment of tribute and wishes to search his palace for untallied valuables. Ahab takes offense and refuses to comply.

55 Walsh (*1 Kings*, 297–98) regards the king's statement that he "cannot" (לא אוכל) comply (as opposed to the imperfect "I will not") as the retention of polite subservience.

56 Foundational studies of the *Erkenntnisformel* assumed that the instances here and in v. 28 were among the earliest in the HB. Thus W. Zimmerli, *I Am Yahweh* (ed. W. Brueggemann; trans. D. W. Stott; Atlanta: John Knox, 1982), 101) stated, "Thus the archaic stereotyped formulation of the divine oracle in 1 Kings 20 unquestionably leads us back into an early stage of prophetic speech." Cf. R. Rendtorff, "The Concept of Revelation in Ancient Israel," in *Revelation as History* (ed. W. Pannenberg; trans. D. Granskou; New York: Macmillan, 1968), 25–53. However, since they are interpolations this is not necessarily so. Rather, the formula emanates from DtrH theology (Deut 4:35, 39; 7:9; Josh 2:11) as a call to recognize Yhwh's right to exclusive worship. It is especially common in Ezekiel (Ezek 5:13; 6:7, 10, 13, 14; etc.; see also Isa 49:23, 26), where it is aphoristic. The use of the formula in the interpolations in 1 Kgs 20 is dependent on Deuteronomy and DtrH as well as Ezekiel. This does not mean that PN was Deuteronomistic but only that he was familiar with Deuteronomy and Ezekiel. A similar point pertains to the formula about giving enemies into one's "hand" or control in 20:13. This is a DtrH expression that is especially common in Joshua (2:24; 6:2; 8:1, 18; 10:8, 19; cf. Judg 1:2; 1 Sam 23:4, 2 Sam 5:19).

Yhwh's deeds authenticate him and his power against other deities. It thus anticipates a miracle. There was no miracle in the older battle story, although the defeat of much larger and superior force could be so interpreted.

20:15-21: PN's revision of a battle story

The *young men* (נערים) mentioned in v. 15 may be a military designation for an elite force of professional soldiers.[57] It was this group that led the counterassault that defeated the Aramaeans. There is no need to see them as untrained so as to posit a miracle, because the *Erkenntnisformel* that requires the miracle is a part of the interpolation, not of the older battle story. The second mention of Ben-Hadad drinking and of the thirty-two kings in v. 16 is another PN interpolation, here by the repetition of the verb *they marched out* (ויצאו) at the beginning of vv. 16 and 17. The sally of the young men was reported to Ben-Hadad, who issued an order to take the Israelite soldiers alive (v. 18). The reason for his order is unclear, but it was probably not due to mercy. He may have intended to torture them as entertainment. Nonetheless, the order put his troops at a disadvantage that led to their defeat (vv. 19-20). According to v. 20 (G^{BL}) the Israelite soldiers not only kill their counterparts but double that number, routing the Aramaeans. Ben-Hadad himself barely escapes (v. 20). The full frontal assault of the entire Israelite army evidently caught the Aramaeans off guard. Ben-Hadad may have expected the advance נערים to be a small party from the king of Israel suing for peace, as the first part of v. 18 suggests. The defeated Aramaeans left behind a sizeable chariotry force (v. 21), which they found ineffective in the highlands around Samaria. This battle account, then, was straightforward and realistic: Israel's defeat of a superior force resulted from a tactical error by the Aramaeans and the ineffectiveness of their chariotry in hilly terrain. It remains intact, supplemented by a few PN additions.

20:22-26aα: The prophetic anecdote linking the two battle stories

PN added a second prophetic anecdote in vv. 22-26aα. It links the two battle accounts with a prophetic warning about the return of the Aramaeans and their new strategy. This anecdote presupposes the one in vv. 13-14 by referring to *the* prophet (v. 22) and to the first defeat (v. 23). The Aramaean servants offer their king two pieces of advice. The first is to fight on level ground where they think Yhwh will be ineffective because his *forté* is the hill country. This explains the Israelites' capture of Aramaean horses and chariots in the first battle (v. 21 G^{BL})—which the Aramaean king needs to replace before the second battle (v. 25)—and the shift in location from Samaria to Aphek. The term *plain* (מישור) is used in v. 25. It refers elsewhere to the transjordanian plateau north of the Arnon (Mujib) that was disputed among Israel, Moab, and Ammon (Deut 3:10; 4:43; Josh 13:9, 16-17, 21; 20:8; Jer 48:8, 21). But since the Aphek of our passage does not appear to have been located in this area, מישור here is best understood as a generic reference to tableland rather than to a specific geographical region. The other piece of advice from Ben-Hadad's servants is to depose the kings who were with him the first time and replace them with *officials* (v. 24). The term פחה is a loanword from Akkadian *pāḫatum/pīḫatum* ("duty," *bēl pā/īḫatum* = "deputy"), so that the idea expressed here would emulate the Assyrian (or Babylonian or Persian) provincial system by turning the kings' vassal states into districts within Aram's empire.

57 Cf. 2 Sam 2:14; see McCarter, *II Samuel*, 96–97 and the other sources cited in the Synchronic Analysis.

It is also possible, though, that the term is used in a broader general sense of "administrator," since their primary function in this context is military.[58]

The second battle story originally began with the notice in v. 26 that Ben-Hadad mustered the Aramaeans. The clause *a year later* concurs with v. 22 in dating the second battle a year after the first and is part of PN's addition beginning in v. 22. Aphek ("stream") was a relatively common name. There are different Apheks mentioned in the Bible: Aphek of Lebanon (Josh 13:4, demarcating the northern boundary of Canaan), probably Afqa northeast of Beirut; Aphek of Asher (Josh 19:30; Judg 1:31), identified with Tell Kurdana or Tell Kabri; and Aphek of Sharon (Josh 12:18; 1 Sam 4:1), identified with Ras el-'Ain on the coastal plain.[59] Some commentators have sought to identify the Aphek of 1 Kings 20 with one of these three, despite the fact that none of them fits very well with the details of the story.[60] We should expect a site somewhere between Samaria and Damascus. The Aphek in 1 Kings 20, therefore, is most likely a fourth one, for which three sites have been posited: (1) on the Golan plateau (מישור), either at the site of modern Fiq[61] or at nearby Tell Soreq;[62] (2) En-Gev on the eastern shore of the Sea of Galilee;[63] and (3) an unidentified site in the Jezreel Valley in the vicinity of Mount Gilboa whose name may be preserved in its alternate name, Jebel Faqqu'a.[64] Of these, the first identification, though common, is problematic, since Fiq attests Middle Bronze and Hellenistic remains with nothing in between.[65] Soreq has also been disqualified because of its small size.[66] However, the size consideration is partly based on the reference to the wall collapsing and killing 27,000 people (v. 30), which is probably a motif borrowed from the Jericho story. The other two candidates for Aphek remain possibilities, and the third fits well with the reference to Aphek in 1 Sam 29:1 as the campsite of the Philistines, in fighting against whom Saul is killed in battle.[67] Another passage to be considered is 2 Kgs 13:14-19, where Elisha on his deathbed foresees three victories of Israel over Aram in Aphek. In 13:17 Elisha tells King Joash to shoot an arrow eastward, presumably toward Aphek, from the window

20:26: Aphek

58 Even so, פחה occurs elsewhere in the HB predominantly in exilic and postexilic texts (Jer 51:23, 28, 57; Ezek 8:36; 23:6, 12, 23; Hag 1:1, 14; 2:2, 21; Mal 1:8; Neh 2:7, 9; 5:14; Est 3:12, 8:9, 9:3) and is a pointer to PN's late date. Cf. Benzinger, *Könige*, 120; Schmitt, *Elisa*, 70–71.

59 R. Frankel, "Aphek," *ABD* 1:275–77; J. M. Miller and G. M. Tucker, *The Book of Joshua* (CBC; Cambridge: Cambridge University Press, 1974), 190.

60 Provan (*Kings*, 156) identifies the Aphek of 1 Kings 20 with Aphek of Asher Hens-Piazza (*Kings*, 199) identifies it with Aphek of Sharon.

61 So Buis (*Rois*, 161); Gray (*Kings*, 428); Würthwein (*1. Könige 17–2. Könige 25*, 240).

62 Fritz, *Kings*, 206.

63 Aharoni, 335; Cogan *I Kings*, 466; Sweeney, *Kings*, 243.

64 Miller and Hayes, *History*, 346; Miller and Tucker, *Joshua*, 190; Thenius, *Könige*, 238.

65 Fritz, *Kings*, 206; Frankel, "Aphek," 276. But see Aharoni (*Land of the Bible*, 335 and n. 45) who points out the proximity of En-Gev to Fiq and suggests that they may have represented upper and lower Aphek. En-Gev attests remains from the 10th–8th centuries BCE.

66 Cogan (*I Kings*, 466) states that it was too small to have been an Aramaean stronghold. Cf. Frankel, "Aphek," 276.

67 Miller and Hayes (*History*, 130–32) also identify this site as the Aphek of the "Ark Narrative" (1 Sam 4:1), which they consider a garbled memory of the story of Saul's death.

of his (Elisha's) house. The eastward orientation makes it unlikely that the Aphek in question is the one in Asher or the one in Sharon. Unfortunately, the location of Elisha's house is not clear. If it is assumed to be on Mount Carmel as it is in others of the Elisha tales the other three proposed sites for Aphek would all be possible.

20:27-28: Victory from YHWH

The contrast between the Aramaean and Israelite camps is remarkable (v. 27). The Aramaeans cover the countryside while the Israelites resemble a couple of flocks of goats. Even if the exact meaning of the word *flocks* in v. 27 is unknown, the point of the comparison is clear. The discrepancy sets the stage for the victory that follows, implying that it is from YHWH's hand. This is spelled out by PN's addition in v. 28, which interrupts the description of the two camps in vv. 27 and 29. It assumes the Aramaeans' rationale behind their second attack (v. 23) and uses it to account theologically for Israel's second victory as a gift from YHWH. The Aramaeans insult YHWH by failing to perceive that he is not limited by topography. Hence YHWH will act for the sake of his own reputation, so that once more *you may know that I am YHWH*. The singular *you* (G^{BL}) is probably impersonal and the expression aphoristic as in Ezekiel. It forges a link with v. 13 and establishes the main theological point of the chapter.

20:29-30: A stylized account of victory

The account of the battle in v. 29 consists of stylized elements that suggest its legendary nature—a seven-day hiatus, a recap of the battle without details, and an extraordinarily high number of casualties.[68] The seven days and the collapse of the city wall (v. 30) are reminiscent of the fall of Jericho and again imply that the victory was YHWH's doing. They may be enhancements lifted from the Jericho story but they are difficult to delimit literarily.[69] Absent the prophetic additions, there is no explicit mention of divine intervention in the older battle story.

20:31-34: Turning victory into parity

Ben-Hadad hides out in the city of Aphek and takes council with his servants about their next move. Deciding that their best option is to appeal to the king of Israel's *ḥesed*, the servants volunteer to approach him in sackcloth with cords of submission on their heads. There is uncertainty among the witnesses about whether Ben-Hadad speaks in vv. 31-32 and whether his servants are focused on saving his life or plead for their own lives as well, but with the response of the king of Israel in v. 32b the focus is clearly on Ben-Hadad. The Israelite king invites solicitation by referring to him as *my brother*, thereby acknowledging the Aramaean king as a social equal and a treaty partner rather than a vassal. The Aramaean envoys seize on the word as a favorable sign (v. 33). Since the text does not make any point about them engaging in divinatory activity, the verb נחש ("seek an omen") may simply mean that the men were looking for any sign of mercy that they might manipulate (cf. BDB, 638). This is certainly what they do with the affirmation that their master is the king of Israel's brother. The invitation to Ben-Hadad to come up into the chariot is a further courtesy extended to a social and political equal. In the older battle story the strategy employed by the king of Israel is effective. Ben-Hadad, relieved to be alive and well treated,

---

68 DeVries *1 Kings*, 250; Würthwein, *1. Könige 17–2. Könige 25*, 240.

69 Würthwein, *1. Könige 17–2. Könige 25*, 240 takes the reference to the collapse of the wall in v. 30aβ as a later addition, but he adduces no literary evidence. F. Schwally ("Zur Quellenkritik der historischen Bücher," *ZAW* 12 [1892], 159] argued that ותפל החומה על־עשרים ושבעה אלף איש הנותרים ובן־הדד נס in v. 30 is secondary on the grounds that there is no notice of the Israelites entering the city after the collapse of the walls. Rather, they conduct the negotiations with Ben-Hadad outside the city. However, this is not clear from the text.

pledges to allow the Israelite king to place *bazaars* in Damascus. These were streets or squares where similar wares were sold (cf. Jer 37:21; Zeph 1:10; Neh 12:39; 13:16), comparable to the different sections (spice market, gold market, etc.) of the *suqs* in Middle Eastern cities today. Since Damascus was an important stop on the trade routes north and east this was a significant marketing opportunity for Israel. The reference to the cities taken by Ben-Hadad's father is an important clue to the original setting of this story. It cannot refer to the time of Omri, who suffered no losses at the hands of the Aramaeans; it is remarkably similar to the mention in 2 Kgs 13:25 of cities recovered by Joash, indicating that the king of Israel in 1 Kings 20 was initially one of Jehu's heirs rather than Ahab. The text does not indicate a change of speaker for the last sentence in v. 34a, making Ben-Hadad the one who sets the terms of the treaty and dismisses the king of Israel. The Israelite victory, however, requires that the king of Israel be the subject, releasing Ben-Hadad when the latter agreed to satisfactory treaty provisions. Reconstruction of the verb ויאמר (*and he said*) between בשמרון (*in Samaria*) and ואני (*and I*), effecting a change of person, is necessary (see the Note).

20:35-42: PN revises the ending

The battle story did not end with the dismissal of Ben-Hadad in v. 34 but continued in v. 43 with the notice that the king of Israel departed and returned to Samaria: וילך מלך־ישראל ויבא שמרונה.[70] PN added the final encounter with a nameless prophet in vv. 35-42, actually beginning with the last word of v. 34—ממנו, reflected in G^{BL}. The *setumah* after v. 34 in Codex Leningradensis and the subject-first clause at the start of v. 35 are further marks of a distinct unit.

PN's prophetic anecdote

The anecdote in these verses consists of two parts dealing with (dis)obedience to the prophetically mediated divine word (vv. 35-37) and the obligation to devote the enemy to destruction (*ḥerem*) (vv. 38-42). Both of these themes are new vis-à-vis vv. 1-34. The two parts are so distinct that they might stand alone as separate anecdotes. That is, vv. 38-42 could be understood following v. 34 as another encounter with *the prophet* of vv. 13-14, 22-26aα = the *man of god* of v. 28. The bandage worn by the prophet would be pure disguise. There is no need for him to suffer real wounds. The account of his wounding in vv. 35-37 draws on 1 Kings 13.[71] Its purpose is to illustrate the importance of obedience to the prophetically mediated divine word and the consequences of disobedience. This is a different theme from *ḥerem*.[72] Verses 35-37, therefore, could be an even later interpolation after the addition of vv. 38-42. However, the two parts together bear a striking thematic resemblance to the story in 1 Samuel 15,

70 Würthwein, *1. Könige 17–2. Könige 25*, 236, 242. Trebolle (*Centena*, 147) buttressed Würthwein's observation by pointing out the *Wiederaufnahme* here. See the Note on v. 34.

71 Verse 35 is the first reference in Kings to the *sons of the prophets*. Apart from it the expression occurs exclusively in the Elisha tales (but cf. 1 Sam 10:10; 19:20; Amos 7:14). The exact nature of this group can only be deduced from the stories about them. They appear to have lived together in structured brotherhoods of some kind in northern Israelite cities. "Son" is used in the sense of the member of a guild or company (BDB 121). The "sons of the prophets," then, were guilds or social groups consisting of prophets. If their leader was known by the title *father*, as suggested by 1 Sam 10:12, Elisha may have been their overall leader (2:12; 6:21; 13:14). See Wilson, *Prophecy and Society*, 140–41 and J. G. Williams, "A Brief Explanation of the Term 'Sons of the Prophets.'" *JBL* 85 (1966): 344–48.

72 As Würthwein (*1. Könige 17–2. Könige 25*, 243) notes, the reference to *ḥerem* turns a war about political and economic matters into holy war.

where Saul disobeys YHWH's command through Samuel to execute *ḥerem* against the Amalekites by keeping their king, Agag, alive. Saul's intentions, like those of the prophet's companion in 1 Kings 20, are good, but he is disobedient. Hence all of vv. 35-42 was probably composed together on the model of 1 Samuel 15, combining the themes of obedience and holy war. As a whole the anecdote represents a continuation of PN's theme of divine recognition presented in the earlier prophetic anecdotes. YHWH's miraculous deeds gave Israel victory so that those involved would come to know YHWH's power. In vv. 35-42 the theological gain from those victories is undercut by the king of Israel's unwarranted release of Ben-Hadad. In doing this the king of Israel usurps YHWH's prerogative and effectively takes credit for the victory. The anecdote ends, therefore, appropriately with a denunciation of the king of Israel that prophesies his death as recompense for the condemned prisoner he released. The prophecy looks forward to Ahab's death in 22:37-38.

20:43: The resentful king

After the prophet's condemnation the king returns to Samaria (v. 43). The description of him as *resentful and enraged* is an addition that assumes the prophetic encounter in vv. 35-42.[73] As a description of the king's reaction to the denunciation in vv. 35-42 it originates from PN. The reference to Samaria links ch. 20 with its sequel in ch. 22, which will begin in Samaria. The king's resentfulness also prepares for the story in ch. 22, where he is reluctant to summon the prophet of YHWH who never prophesies anything good about him.

Synthesis

PNs handiwork

In this chapter PN combined two battle accounts originally set during the Jehu dynasty and connected with 2 Kings 13. He supplemented them with materials that made prophets the leading characters who directed the actions of the king of Israel (now Ahab) and disciplined him for his failure to carry out YHWH's implicit command. The main theme of these prophetic additions was the *Erkenntnisformel*—the statement that people would recognize YHWH's power and status as Israel's god or as *the* god as a result of observing his miraculous deeds. This theme was also central to the contest story in ch. 18. PN built the present chapter around the theme. Israel's legendary victories against superior Aramaean forces became miraculous gifts from YHWH predicted by his prophets in order to display and bring acknowledgement of his power.

Condemning Ahab

In vv. 35-42 PN drew on 1 Samuel 15 and 1 Kings 13 to build a story condemning the king. Ahab acts as though the victory were his own doing by releasing the enemy king, thereby undermining YHWH's purpose. For this reason he is condemned to die in place of his former prisoner. The chapter thus moves toward the goal of condemning Ahab and forecasting his downfall. He is a weak and faithless character who is more concerned with his personal status and reputation than with his standing before YHWH (v. 34). Hence the reader already approaches

73 The phrase על־ביתו that precedes them is a gloss in the MT (see the Note). Besides, the king's house is in Samaria, not in Aphek. On the use of the same expression in 21:4 see the Note on that verse.

the sequel in 22:1-38 with a sense of anticipation about the end of Israel's worst king and with a conviction that YHWH is in charge and communicates his will and judgment through the vehicle of prophecy.

Naboth's Vineyard (1 Kings 21 MT; 20 G)

Text

[DtrH; *PN; Additions and glosses to PN]*
1 *There was a vineyard belonging to Naboth the Jezreelite beside the palace of Ahab*
king of Samaria. 2 *Ahab said to Naboth, "Give me your vineyard so I can turn it into a*
vegetable garden, since it is close to my house, and let me give you a better vineyard
in its place, or if you prefer let me pay you the value of your vineyard in silver so that I
can turn it into a vegetable garden." 3 *But Naboth said to Ahab, "I'll be damned if I'll*
give you my ancestral inheritance." 4 *So Ahab became resentful and lay on his bed cov-*
ering his face and refusing to eat anything. 5 *Jezebel his wife came and spoke to him,*
"Why are you resentful and not eating?" 6 *Ahab replied to her, "Because I spoke to Na-*
both the Jezreelite, 'Give me your vineyard for money or if you wish I'll give you an-
other vineyard in its place,' but he said, 'I will not give you my ancestral heritage.'"
7 *Jezebel his wife responded to him, "Is this how you reign over Israel? Get up; eat*
some food; be happy. I will get the vineyard of Naboth the Jezreelite for you." 8 *So she*
wrote a letter in Ahab's name and sealed [it] with his seal. She sent the letter to the
elders and nobles who lived with Naboth. 9 *In the letter was written, "Call a fast and*
seat Naboth at the head of the people. 10 *Then seat two men, scoundrels, opposite*
him so they can testify against him, 'He cursed god and the king.' Then take him out
and execute him by stoning." 11 *So the men of the city, the elders and nobles who*
lived in his city, did as was written in the letter Jezebel sent to them. 12 *They called a*
fast and set Naboth at the head of the people. 13 *Then two men, scoundrels, came for-*
ward and sitting opposite him, they testified against him, "He cursed god and king."
Then they took him outside the city and executed him by stoning him with stones.
14 *Then they sent to Jezebel, "Naboth has been executed by stoning."* 15 *When Jezebel*
heard, she said to Ahab, "Get up; take possession of the vineyard of Naboth the Jez-
reelite which he refused to sell you, because Naboth is not alive but is dead." 16 *When*
Ahab heard that Naboth was dead, he tore his garments and put on sackcloth. After-
wards, Ahab arose to go down to the vineyard of Naboth the Jezreelite to take posses-
sion of it. 17 YHWH's word came to Elijah the Tishbite, 18 *"Arise; go down to meet*
Ahab the king of Israel who is in Samaria; he is in Naboth's vineyard where he has
gone down to take possession of it. 19 *Speak to him, 'Thus says YHWH, "You have killed*
and dispossessed, haven't you?" Thus says YHWH, "In the place where the dogs licked
the blood of Naboth the dogs will lick your blood and the prostitutes will wash them-
selves in your blood."'" 20 *Ahab said to Elijah, "You have found me, haven't you, my en-*
emy?" He replied, "I have found you. Because you sold yourself in vain to do what
YHWH considers evil, 21 I am going to bring disaster upon you and consume you ut-
terly, annihilating from Ahab every high class royal member in Israel. 22 I will make
your house like the house of Jeroboam son of Nebat and like the house of Baasha

son of Ahijah because of the anger you have provoked causing Israel to sin. 23 *Also*
with reference to Jezebel Yhwh had spoken, 'The dogs will eat her within the rampart
of Jezreel.' 24 The one belonging to Ahab who dies in the city the dogs will eat, and
the one who dies in the open field the birds of the sky will eat." 25 *Only there was*
no one who sold himself to do what Yhwh considered evil like Ahab whom Jezebel his
wife incited. 26 *He committed serious abominations by following idols according to all*
the practices of the Amorites whom Yhwh dispossessed in favor of the Israelites.
27 When Ahab heard these words, he tore his clothes, put on sackcloth, fasted, and
went around weeping. 28 Yhwh's word came to Elijah, 29 "Have you seen how Ahab
has humbled himself before me? I will not bring the disaster in his days; (rather) in
the days of his son I will bring the disaster."

Textual Notes

1 Following G's order of chapters: 21, 20, 22 vis-à-vis MT. The stories in chs. 20 and 22 go together. MT's numbering is retained to avoid confusion. This order is confirmed by 21:4 where an interpolation linking it with 20:43 is found in MT but not in G. See ch. 20.

There was a vineyard belonging to Naboth the Jezreelite: So G^{B} (καὶ ἀμπελὼν εἷς ἦν τῷ Ναβουθαι τῷ Ιεζραηλίτῃ). MT's *after these things* (also G^{L}) and *which was in Jezreel* are glosses. G^{L} lacks *the Jezreelite*. Naboth means "child, offspring."[1] G: Ναβουθαι = "my offspring." Jezreel is Tel Jizreel/Zerin, ca. 15 km east of Megiddo at the entrance to the Jezreel Valley. Excavations in the 1990s uncovered fortifications but no palace.[2] The impressiveness of Jezreel's construction, its location, and its abandonment suggest that Omri built the site not primarily for defensive purposes but for internal control after the civil war that launched his kingship.[3]

palace: So MT (היכל). G^{B}: *threshing floor* (= גרן), perhaps an inner-Greek error (ΑΛΩ for ΝΑΩ).[4] G^{L} has *house* (οἴκῳ = בית) under the influence of v. 2.

2 **close to**: Reading קרוב אל for MT's קרוב אצל with G^{BL} (ἐγγίων οὗτος τῷ οἴκῳ μου). MT was influenced by אצל in v. 1.

a better vineyard: So MT (כרם טוב ממנו). G^{L} attests a variant: ἀμπελῶνα ἄλλον = כרם אחר. G^{B} conflates: ἀμπελῶνα ἄλλον ἀγαθὸν ὑπὲρ αὐτόν.[5]

the value of your vineyard in silver so that I can turn it into a vegetable garden: Based on the plus in G^{BL}. The word זה at the end of the verse in MT is a place marker for the lost material.[6]

---

1 Noth, *Personennamen*, 221.

2 D. Ussishkin and J. Woodhead, "Excavations at Tel Jezreel 1990-1991, Preliminary Report," *Tel Aviv.* 19 (1992): 3–56; "Excavations at Tel Jezreel 1992-1993, Second Preliminary Report," *Levant* 26 (1994): 1–48; "Excavations at Tel Jezreel 1994-1996: Third Preliminary Report," *Tel Aviv.* 24 (1997): 6–72.

3 So H. G. M. Williamson, "Jezreel in the Biblical Texts," *Tel Aviv* 18 (1991): 72–92; "Tel Jezreel and the Dynasty of Omri," *PEQ* 128 (1996): 41–51. See also N. Na'aman, "Historical and Literary Notes on the Excavation of Tel Jezreel," *Tel Aviv* 24 (1997): 122–28.

4 Thenius, *Könige*, XIV.

5 Trebolle, *Centena*, 148–49.

6 Trebolle, *Centena*, 147–48.

3 **I'll be damned**: חלילה לי מיהוה. G^{BL}: μή μοι γένοιτο παρὰ [L + κυρίου] θεου μου is an oath and an expression of outrage by Naboth.[7]

4 **So Ahab became resentful**: So G^{B}: καὶ ἐγένετο τὸ πνεῦμα Αχααβ τεταραγμένον = ותהי רוח אחאב סרה. MT's longer reading is an addition by *Wiederaufnahme* (את־נחלת אבתי).[8] G^{L} is conflate. The first part of the MT plus (ויבא אחאב אל־ביתו סר וזעף) gathers elements from 20:43 in order to consolidate the two chapters according to the MT's order. The remainder in v. 4a is overfull and repetitive of v. 3 and impedes the fluidity between v. 4 and Jezebel's response in v. 5.

covering his face: G^{BL}: "covering his face" (καὶ συνεκάλυψε[v] = ויכס). MT's ויסב את־פניו is paralleled in 1 Kgs 8:14; Judg 18:23, where it means "turn around." But this is less appropriate for someone lying in bed. The change resulted from graphic confusion and metathesis of כ and ס.

6 **wish**: G^{L} precedes the verb with the negative, *if you do not wish* [to sell your vineyard].

another vineyard: So MT, G^{L}: כרם תחתיו. G^{B}: ἀμπελῶνα ἄλλον ἀντ' αὐτου = כרם אחר תחתיו. See v. 2.

my ancestral heritage: So G^{BL}: κληρονομίαν πατέρων μου = את־נחלת אבתי corresponding to Naboth's response at the end of v. 3. MT: *my vineyard* influenced by *vineyard* twice previously in the verse.

7 **Is this how you reign**: So G^{BL} (σὺ νῦν οὕτως ποιεῖς βασιλέα = אתה עתה כה תעשה מלוכה). MT lost כה by haplography.

be happy: So MT (ויטב לבך), lit., *let your heart be glad*. G^{BL}: καὶ ἑαυτοῦ γενοῦ, "be your own master"? has an uncertain *Vorlage*.

8 **a letter**: So G^{BL}. MT: *letters* in agreement with the mention of elders and nobles.

the letter: So G^{BL} (τὸ βιβλίον). MT again has the plural.

who lived with Naboth: So G^{BL}. MT precedes with *who were in his city*, an effort to clarify the ambiguity in PN by locating the vineyard in Samaria, away from Naboth's home in Jezreel.[9]

9 **In the letter**: So G^{L} (ἐν τῷ βιβλίῳ) as in v. 8. MT, G^{B} have the plural, *letters*.

was written: Reading the Qal passive וכתוב with G^{B} (καὶ ἐγέγραπτο). MT repeats the verb in v. 8.

10-13 **scoundrels ... scoundrels**: Lost from G^{B} by haplography.[10]

10 **He cursed**: Lit. *blessed*, a euphemism to avoid writing "cursed god." So G^{BL}. MT's second person was influenced by the accusers' position opposite Naboth.

take him out and execute him by stoning: So MT, G^{L}. G^{B} reflects third person verbs (καὶ ἐξαγαγέτωσαν αὐτὸν καὶ λιθοβολησάτωσαν αὐτόν) either referring to the two scoundrels or as impersonals.

11 **the city**: So G^{L}. MT: "his city," influenced by *his city* later in the verse.

---

7 See Y. Ziegler, *Promises to Keep: The Oath in Biblical Narrative* (Leiden: Brill, 2008), 123–47.

8 See Trebolle, *Centena*, 149–50; also Timm, *Die Dynastie Omri*, 112.

9 B. D. Napier, "The Omrides of Jezreel," *VT* 9 (1959): 367–68. The reading obviates translation of ישב את as "preside in council with" or the like. *Pace* R. Bohlen, *Der Fall Nabot. Form, Hintergrund und Werdegang einer alttestamentlichen Erzählung (1 Kön 21)* (TTS 35; Trier: Paulinus, 1978), 61–62.

10 The word בליעל that forms part of the expression for "scoundrel" probably derives from the negative בלי + יעל as "profit, worth," hence "worthless men," or as a form of עלה, thus "that which/the place from which one does not go up," i.e., from the underworld. See B. Otzen, בְּלִיַּעַל, *TDOT* 2:131–36.

as was written in the letter Jezebel sent to them: Based on MT but with the singular *letter.* G^{L} (*as Jezebel sent to them*) reflects haplography (כאשר ... אשר).

12 **and set**: Reading ויושבו, *Hip'il* consecutive preterit. MT's והשיבו is syntactically awkward. It is formally identical to the imperative in v. 9 and was probably influenced by it.

13 **they testified against him**: So G^{BL} (καὶ κατεμαρτύρησαν αὐτοῦ = ויעדהו); cf. v. 10. MT is expansive: *and the scoundrels testified against him, against Naboth before the people.*

He cursed: Lit. *blessed*, a euphemism as in v. 10. Also as there read the third person, here attested by MT, though expanded with Naboth's name. G^{BL} have the second person.

15 **When Jezebel heard**: So G^{B}. MT, G^{L} + *that Naboth had been executed by stoning.*

which he refused to sell: So MT (אשר מאן לתת). G^{BL}: ὃς οὐκ ἔδωκέν, perhaps reading אין for מאן.

16 **Naboth** (1): So MT, G^{L}. G^{B} + *the Jezreelite.*

he tore his garments and put on sackcloth. Afterwards: So G^{BL}. Lost from MT by haplography (ויקרע ... ויקם).[11] *Sackcloth* (v. 16), a transliteration of Hebrew שק, was some kind of garment or cloth, perhaps made of goat's hair, worn loosely on the body as a symbol of mourning or contrition.

17 **Yhwh's word came**: So MT (ויהי דבר־יהוה). G^{BL}: καὶ εἶπε[ν] κύριος = וידבר יהוה.

19 **Thus says Yhwh, "In the place**: So MT, G^{L}. G^{B}: *in every place.* Before this G^{BL} and MT appear expansive. G^{BL} precede with *therefore*; MT repeats *you shall say to him* (ודברת אליו לאמר). Syriac lacks both. All of these witnesses follow with *thus says Yhwh.*

where the dogs licked: So MT. G^{BL}: *where the pigs and the dogs licked.* G^{A} and other witnesses place *the pigs* after the dogs. The different placements suggest that *pigs* is a disparaging expansion.

of Naboth: So MT. G^{BL} + *there.*

the dogs will lick your blood and the prostitutes will wash themselves in your blood: So G^{BL}. Lost by haplography from MT; the loss is reflected in the unusual emphatic גם־אתה (compare 2 Sam 17:5).

20 **in vain**: So G^{BL} (μάτην = לשוא). Lost from MT by haplography before לעשות, its original position as reflected in G^{L}.

what Yhwh considers evil: So MT (lit. *the evil in YHWH's eyes*). G^{BL} + *to provoke him* ([τοῦ] παροργίσαι αὐτόν = להכעיסו), an expansion from other instances of the anti-dynastic oracle absent any mechanism for haplography in MT.

21 **I am going to bring**: So *Qere* מביא in preference to *ketiv* מבי.

high class royal member: On the expressions משתין בקיר and עצור ועזוב see the Introduction.

22 **because of the anger**: על־הכעס *ad sensum.* MT: אל־הכעס. G^{BL}: [L = *all*] *the provocations.*

23 **within the rampart**: Following Cronauer, who identified a wide, flat area between the outer wall and the inner ramparts area as the חל.[12] Williamson proposed that the חלק of Jezreel "ought to be the area between the gate and the residence, which on current understanding would be within the royal enclosure."[13] Accepting the usual emendation of חל to חלק, he asserted that "Jehu's horses could not trample Jezebel underfoot if her body were lying on the rampart."[14] But חל might mean the

11 Compare Schenker, *Älteste Textgeschichte*, 97–98; Hugo, *Les deux visages*, 336–38.

12 Cronauer, *Stories about Naboth*, 81n. Ussishkin and Woodhead, "Excavations at Tel Jezreel 1992-1993," 1–48, esp. 46–47; D. Oredsson, "Jezreel—Its Contribution to Iron Age Chronology," *SJOT* 12 (1998): 86–101, esp. 91–92.

13 Williamson, "Jezreel in the Biblical Texts," 82.

14 Williamson, "Jezreel in the Biblical Texts," 87.

entire rampart complex, including both inner and outer walls (so HALOT, 312 for Middle Hebrew; BDB, 298 for biblical). G^{BL} (ἐν τῷ προτειχίσματι) reflect חל. The emendation to חלק is based on 2 Kgs 9:10, 36-37, where חלק refers to the "town land" in the immediate vicinity of a city (BDB 324). While Rendsburg has argued that the חל/חלק variation is an artistic device by the Israelite "wordsmith," it is hard to believe that the prophecy in 1 Kgs 21:23 and the fulfillment in 2 Kgs 9:36 did not originally match. But the usual emendation has it backwards if חל is the preferred reading in 1 Kgs 21:23. The change to חלק in 2 Kgs 9:10, 36, 37 probably occurred under the influence of the reference to Naboth's חלקה in 2 Kgs 9:21, 25.[15]

24 **and the one who dies**: So MT. G^{BL} + *of his* (αὐτοῦ = לו). Elsewhere in both forms (14:11; 16:4).

25: Only there was no one who sold himself to do what Yhwh considered evil like Ahab: So MT. G^{B} is corrupt: πλὴν ματαίως Αχααβ ὡς ἐπράθη ποιῆσαι τὸ πονηρὸν ἐνώπιον κυρίου.[16]

incited: Vocalizing as הֵסַתָּה. Joüon (§80m) explains MT as a misconstrual of the form as a 2nd person.

27: When Ahab heard these words: So MT. G^{BL}: καὶ (L: ἀλλ') ὑπὲρ τοῦ λόγου ὡς κατενύγη Αχααβ ἀπὸ προσώπου (B: τοῦ) κυρίου = על הדבר כי נכנע אחאב מלפני יהוה). The latter is based on v. 29, which it cites nearly verbatim.[17]

and went around weeping: The reading is uncertain but is based on G^{BL}'s καὶ ἐπορεύετο κλαίων, which, however, precedes the tearing of clothes, donning sackcloth and fasting. MT's ויהלך אט at the end of this list may be a corruption of the reading. It is unattested elsewhere, though ההלכים לאט in Isa 8:6 is similar. The *Pi'el* of הלך is attested mostly in poetry (Ezek 18:9; Hab 3:11; Job 24:10; 30:28; Pss 38:7; 55:15; 81:14; 86:11; 89:16; 104:3; 115:7; 131:1; 142:4; Prov 6:11, 28; 8:20; Qoh 4:15; 11:9; Lam 5:18). At the end of the verse G^{BL} have the following plus: καὶ περιεβάλετο σάκκον ἐν τῇ ἡμέρᾳ ᾗ ἐπάταξεν (L: Ιεζαβελ) Ναβουθαι τὸν Ιεζραηλίτην (L: + καὶ τὸν υἱὸν αὐτοῦ = *he also put on sackcloth when he* (L: *Jezebel*) *killed Naboth the Jezreelite* (L: *and his son*). The plus is a gloss intended to explain that Ahab repented not just of the sins of apostasy detailed in vv. 25-26 but also of the murder of Naboth. G^{L} reflects further elaboration of the gloss in attributing the murder to Jezebel and including Naboth's son as a victim in agreement with 2 Kgs 9:26.[18]

21:28 **Yhwh's word came to Elijah**: So MT, minus *the Tishbite*, which is absent from G^{BL}. They in turn expand: [L: καὶ] ἐγένετο ῥῆμα κυρίου ἐν χειρὶ [L: τοῦ] δούλου αὐτοῦ Ηλιου περὶ Αχααβ καὶ εἶπεν κύριος.

21:29 **Have you seen how Ahab has humbled himself before me?**: So G^{BL}. MT + *Because he has humbled himself before me.* While haplography in OG is possible, this is more likely a double reading in the MT, since G^{BL} presume מפני rather than מלפני.[19]

I will bring: So MT *qere'* (אביא). *Ketiv* = אבי.

---

15 Similarly Eissfeldt, "Die Komposition von I Reg 16,29–II Reg 13,25," 57.

16 See Stade's explanation, *Kings*, 166.

17 Cf. Gooding ("Ahab according to the Septuagint," 274–75), who nonetheless errs in contending that the plus here took place in the Greek text rather than the Hebrew.

18 *Pace* Schenker (*Älteste Textgeschichte*, 98–99), who argues for the authenticity of the plus. He emphasizes the uniqueness of the reference to Naboth's son (singular) in L but ignores its mention of Jezebel. The variation between son and sons is best explained as confusion between בנו and בניו, indicating that the gloss arose in the OG *Vorlage*.

19 Trebolle, *Centena*, 150–51.

the disaster (2): So G^{BL}. MT + *upon his house*. The phrase is superfluous, since the disaster is the fall of the dynasty. The difference between the MT and G^{B} is not as great as has been supposed.[20]

Synchronic Analysis

The story of Naboth (vv. 1-16) and Elijah's oracle (vv. 17-29) comprise the two sections of this chapter. The Naboth story consists of six scenes in a chiastic pattern.[21]

The structure of the chapter

21:1 Introduction
21:2-3 Ahab and Naboth
21:4-7 Ahab and Jezebel in their bedroom
21:8-10 Jezebel writes letters
21:11-14 Jezebel's written orders are carried out
21:15 Jezebel reports Naboth's death to Ahab
21:16 Ahab goes to take possession of the vineyard

The second section falls into two parts—Elijah's oracle (vv. 17-24) and reactions to it (vv. 25-29) from a narrative voice (vv. 25-26) and from Ahab (vv. 27-29).

21:1-3: Ahab's offer

The chapter is loosely tied with ch. 20 by the phrase *after these things* in v. 1. The absence of other chronological details creates a timelessness for the story that is evinced in the next clause, *There once was a vineyard belonging to Naboth the Jezreelite.*[22] The narrative shares Ahab's perspective that what is important about Naboth is his vineyard in Jezreel, since it provides few other details about him. Despite being king, Ahab cannot get the vineyard (vv. 2-3). Its location next to his palace is ideal for a vegetable garden and is the reason he wants it. The mention of vegetables (ירק) recalls the land of Egypt before the exodus (Deut 11:10-17), casting Ahab as oppressive Pharaoh. Vineyards take years to cultivate with constant tending, while a vegetable garden is more fleeting; Naboth's connection with the land is deep-seated while Ahab's desire is frivolous. The vineyard is Naboth's

---

20 *Pace* D. W. Gooding, "Ahab According to the Septuagint," 277; Hugo, *Les deux visages*, 236.

21 Compare J. T. Walsh, "Methods and Meanings: Multiple Studies of 1 Kings 21," *JBL* 111 (1992), 194–95.

22 Rofé (*Prophetical Stories*, 90) points to this sentence as highlighting the story's novelistic flavor. Similarly K. Baltzer, "Naboths Weinberg (1. Kön. 21). Der Konflikt zwischen israelitischem und kanaanäischem Bodenrecht," *WuD* n.s. 8 (1965): 77; Miller, "The Fall of the House of Ahab," 311–12; and Welten, "Naboths Weinberg (1. Könige 21)," *EvT* 33 (1973): 27. See also M. Oeming, "Naboth, der Jesreeliter. Untersuchungen zu den theologischen Motiven der Überlieferungsgeschichte von I Reg 21," *ZAW* 98 (1986): 379–80, who sketches the stereotypical nature of the characters in 21:1-16, which he sees as a Wisdom tale. As fiction the story has "features of authentic ancient Near Eastern political intrigue," for which see A. M. Kitz, "Naboth's Vineyard after Mari and Amarna," *JBL* 134 (1015): 529–45, at 545.

family identity and stake in Israel.[23] No exchange or amount of money can compensate for it. That is why Israelite law (Lev 25:23-25; Num 36:7-9) forbids the sale of family land in perpetuity (v. 3). Ahab's offer ignores the law.

21:4-5: Ahab's reaction to Naboth's refusal

Ahab is resentful and angry at his powerlessness against Naboth's sense of values (v. 4). It is the same way he felt after his prophetic rebuke at the end of ch. 20 (v. 43). He is not accustomed to being refused. Like a spoiled child, he takes to his bed, turning away and refusing to eat. His refusal to eat contrasts with Elijah's consumption of bread provided by ravens (19:1-7) and an angel (19:5-6), and his own provision of bread for the widow (17:8-16). Eating and fasting are themes in the present chapter:[24] the elders and nobles proclaim a fast to accuse Naboth (v. 12) in accord with Jezebel's instructions (v. 9); Ahab fasts in repentance (v. 27); Jezebel urges Ahab to eat (v. 7) and is herself to be eaten by dogs (v. 23).

21:6-7: Ahab's report to Jezebel

Ahab's account to Jezebel of the exchange with Naboth reverses the elements of his offer (v. 6), placing silver before a trade. He does not mention that he offered a more valuable vineyard or say why he wants the vineyard in the first place. Nor does he explain that Naboth refused because it was his family's ancestral heritage guarded by Israelite law. These differences cast Naboth as unreasonable, especially to Jezebel, "an imperious queen whose attitudes toward royal prerogative are quite different from those envisaged in Israelite law and tradition."[25] This attitude informs her remark: אתה עתה תעשה מלוכה על־ישראל (v. 7a). The sentence is halting Hebrew and somewhat obscure in meaning, a reminder that she is foreign.[26] She also has trouble understanding Israelite royal ideology. Her question may be rhetorical, expressing surprise and a rebuke: "You are king of Israel, aren't you?" As a statement these sentiments are stronger and verge on outrage: "You are king of Israel!" The emphatic *you* is ironic, since it is Jezebel, not Ahab, who will abuse royal power to get the vineyard. Her follow-up statement in v. 7b uses a contrasting pronoun ("*I* will give you Naboth's vineyard") that signals her usurpation of power. She refers to the property as a vineyard; the concept of ancestral heritage in Israel means nothing to her. Her command to Ahab to get up and eat shows that she is running the show. She organizes and oversees the conspiracy against Naboth, as the conspirators recognize (v. 14). Ahab is uninvolved in the machinations against Naboth. His name does not appear after v. 4 until v. 15, when Jezebel notifies him that Naboth is dead. It is not the first time that Ahab is weak and Jezebel the one who wields power and makes decisions (18:4, 13; 19:1-2). He may be manipulative rather than weak.[27] This would explain the differences between the conversation with Naboth (vv. 2-3) and Ahab's report of it (v. 6): He casts Naboth's refusal to sell as insolence rather than piety so as to provoke a response from Jezebel. It would also explain how Jezebel got his seal (v. 8) and why Elijah condemns Ahab rather than Jezebel (vv. 18-29). Thus while the story blames Jezebel for the dirty work it leaves open the possibility that Ahab manipulated her.

---

23 Hens-Piazza, *Kings*, 206.
24 Hens-Piazza, *Kings*, 205.
25 Walsh, *1 Kings*, 320.
26 Williamson, "Jezreel in the Biblical Texts," 86.
27 Hens-Piazza, *Kings*, 207; D. N. Freedman in his addendum to n. 3 in Cogan, *I Kings*, 485. For others who hold Ahab responsible see Cronauer, *Stories about Naboth*, 131.

21:8-9: Jezebel hatches her plot

Jezebel's sense of royal privilege is not policy in Israel, so she acts surreptitiously. She writes secret letters in Ahab's name and bearing his seal (v. 8). Is she creating a trail back to the manipulator? How secret can letters be, after all? Her written Hebrew is better than her spoken (v. 7), though not good enough to mask her real identity (v. 14). She is even careful to employ a euphemism (v. 13) so as not to offend religious sensibilities with a linguistic *faux pas*. Letters portend disaster in the HB, especially in Samuel–Kings,[28] and Jezebel's letters lay out the plot against Naboth's life. They are addressed to the officials—elders and nobles—of Naboth's city (vv. 8, 11). The two groups are not mentioned together elsewhere in the HB. Ironically, in Deut 19:11-12; 21:1-9, 18-21; 22:13-21; 25:5-10 the local elders are the administrators of justice as moral leaders of their communities.[29] Naboth's neighbors are evidently corrupt or too cowed by Jezebel to stand up to her. Her scheme calls for them to proclaim a fast in the city (v. 9). Fasting is an act of penitence and signals a crisis for the community. The people are led to believe that the danger is from Naboth. He is literally set up for a fall—seated at their head, typically a place of honor or leadership.[30] His conspicuousness will enhance popular indignation at his alleged crimes.

21:10-11: Jezebel's manipulation of Israelite law

Jezebel herself recognizes the nefariousness of her plot, referring to the two false witnesses as "scoundrels" (בני־בליעל, v. 10). She understands Israelite law and tradition well enough to manipulate them. Her instructions adhere to the legal prescriptions in the HB requiring (a) a minimum of two witnesses for conviction of a capital offense (Deut 17:6; 19:15), (b) execution by stoning for the crime of cursing god (Lev 24:15-16), cursing the king also considered criminal (Exod 22:27), and (c) stoning to take place outside of a city (Lev 24:14). The success of her plan depends, ironically, on the people's observance of the law and their loyalty to YHWH, whom Naboth is accused of cursing.

21:12-14: The execution of the plan

There is no substantive difference between Jezebel's orders and the execution of them by the elders and nobles. In v. 12 the verb *they set* (והשיבו) is formally identical to the imperative in v. 9 and signals the exact correspondence between Jezebel's orders and their execution. This correspondence is helpful for determining the subject of the verbs *they brought him out* and *they stoned him* in v. 13. Just as the instructions regarding the testimony of the two *scoundrels* are incorporated into Jezebel's orders in v. 10, so v. 13 relates their entry and testimony within the larger sequence of compliance, which is taken up again by the verbs *they brought him out* and *they stoned him*. The subject of the latter two verbs, in other words, is

---

28 David's letter to Joab (2 Sam 11:15) gives the death order for an unsuspecting Uriah. The king of Israel who receives the letter from the king of Aram in 2 Kgs 5:5-7 is convinced that the latter is seeking an occasion for war. Jehu's letters to the leaders of Samaria and Jezreel (2 Kgs 10:2, 6-7) mean death for Ahab's sons. The letter Hezekiah receives from Sennacherib contains threats that lead him to agonized prayer (2 Kgs 19:14//Isa 37:14).

29 Cf. T. M. Willis, *The Elders of the City: A Study of the Elders-Laws in Deuteronomy* (SBLMS 55; Atlanta: SBL, 2001) and "Elder in the OT," *NIDB* 2:233–34.

30 *Head of the people* occurs elsewhere only in Deut 20:9 in reference to army commanders. The word *head* commonly refers to positions of leadership and honor: Num 1:4; 25:15; 31:26; Josh 22:14; 1 Sam 15:17; 2 Sam 23:8, 18 // 1 Chr 11:11, 20; 1 Chr 5:15; 1 Chr 11:42; 12:19; 27:5; Neh 11:17; 12:46; Ezek 38:2, 3; 39:1.

not the two *scoundrels* alone but all the people.[31] The elders and nobles then notify Jezebel that Naboth is dead (v. 14).

21:15-16: Taking possession

Jezebel's command to Ahab (קום רש) echoes her order to him in v. 7 and confirms that she orchestrated events. She does not mention Ahab's offer to exchange the vineyard for another but only his offer to buy it. The issue as she sees it is Naboth's refusal (מאן) of the king. She blames Naboth for his own death, which she sees as justified for what she considers rebellion. Without any sign of remorse or interest in how Naboth died, Ahab obeys (v. 16). His possession (ירש) of the vineyard is a reversal of Israel's possession of Canaan, to the extent that doing right and obeying the law are requirements for conquering it (Deut 4:1; 6:18; 8:1)—all the more so if Ahab is trying to usurp YHWH's role of controlling fertility as suggested by his plan for a vegetable garden in light of Deut 11:10-17.

21:17-24: Elijah's oracle

With v. 17 the tale shifts from recounting the crime to detailing YHWH's response through Elijah. YHWH's command to Elijah in v. 18 (קום רד) resembles Jezebel's orders to Ahab in vv. 7, 15, especially קום רש in the latter. The threefold repetition of *arise* ties the story together. Elijah's going down to meet Ahab, who has come to possess, signals confrontation. Elijah speaks first, beginning with a rhetorical question: *You've killed and taken possession, haven't you?* He announces a measure-for-measure punishment: the dogs will lick Ahab's blood in the very place where they licked the blood of Naboth (v. 19). The denunciation makes Elijah Ahab's enemy. Ahab is held responsible for the crime, supporting the interpretation that he manipulated Jezebel. Ahab has his own rhetorical question: *You've found me, haven't you, my enemy?* It is a reversal of 18:10, where Ahab sought Elijah. Elijah's acknowledgment, *I have found you*, implies "I have found you out, am aware of what you have done." This is the foundation for the anti-dynastic oracle in vv. 20-24, which, like those against Jeroboam (1 Kgs 14:7-11) and Baasha (1 Kgs 16:2-4), condemns Ahab for selling himself (מכר *Hitpāʿēl*) to do what YHWH considered evil. The expression "do evil in YHWH's sight" is typically used in Deuteronomy and the Deuteronomistic History for worshiping other gods.[32] Ahab's crimes go beyond his culpability in Naboth's death. Even if he was only an accessory in that episode he had already perverted his reign and his dynasty and had sealed the fate of both by his apostasy. So, like the houses of Jeroboam and Baasha, Ahab's house will be obliterated: every male in Ahab's line will be killed and their corpses left unburied (v. 24). Jezebel is directly and uniquely threatened (v. 23). No other queen mother receives such a condemnation. She has usurped the male role and is therefore to be treated as one of the males of Ahab's house. The verse looks forward to her assassination (2 Kgs 9:30-37).

21:25-26: No evildoer like Ahab

The narrative voice in the parenthetical note of vv. 25-26 highlights Ahab's uniqueness in evildoing in a reiteration or interpretation of 16:31-33. Ahab was worse than all his predecessors and, by implication, his successors. The blame falls on Jezebel, who *urged* Ahab *on* or *incited* him, though this does not render Ahab innocent. The verb *sell oneself* as primarily a reference to idol worship is confirmed in v. 26, where the nature of Ahab's evil is spelled out. He followed idols like the peoples whom YHWH dispossessed before Israel. His reign, therefore, was a giant step backwards to the days of the Canaanites, before Israel entered

---

31 *Pace* Bohlen (*Der Fall Nabot*, 67), with Cronauer (*Stories about Naboth*, 151).

32 Cronauer, *Stories about Naboth*, 83n.

the land. The parenthesis affirms the narrative's disgust for Ahab in anticipation of the mercy to be extended to him in vv. 27-29, and in so doing it registers a subtle complaint that the mercy is not entirely just.

21:27-29: Postponement of Ahab's punishment

Despite his evildoing, Ahab's punishment is postponed (vv. 27-29). He is moved by Elijah's oracle in vv. 20-24 (*these words*) to acts of penitence—tearing his clothes, putting on sackcloth, and fasting—which YHWH notices and rewards. The parenthetical note in vv. 25-26, however, raises doubt about the appropriateness of the postponement, reminding us that Ahab had *sold himself* to apostasy (v. 20) and in so doing had taken Israel back to the days of the Amorites whom YHWH dispossessed. Even more disturbing is the comparison between Ahab and David that the postponement invites. Both commit crimes of murder and theft; both repent when denounced by prophets; and both have their guilt transferred to their heirs (2 Sam 12:13-14). Thus there does not seem to be much difference between the best and worst kings of Israel either in their crimes or in the judgments they receive.

Diachronic Analysis

A PN story added to a DtrH oracle

The distinct concerns of the two parts of the chapter—the crime against Naboth with Jezebel as its perpetrator in vv. 1-16 vs. the condemnation of Ahab for apostasy in vv. 17-29—are due to PN's use of the DtrH oracle of Elijah centered in vv. 20bβ-22, 24.[33] The Naboth story in vv. 1-16 was written by PN to set the DtrH oracle in a new context, one that cast the primary blame for the crime on Jezebel. It was composed on the model of the David and Bathsheba story in 2 Samuel 11–12 and replaced an older ver-

33 This reconstruction draws on Cronauer, *Stories about Naboth*, who elaborated Rofé, "The Vineyard of Naboth." Steck (*Überlieferung und Zeitgeschichte*, 40–44) had previously advocated the secondary status of vv. 11-16 vis-à-vis vv. 17-29. The weakness of Cronauer's analysis is his assumption that 21:17-19a, 20abα were an old, free-floating fragment in which the elements of the story in vv. 1-16* were implicit. See his discussion and chart on pp. 106–109. The same criticism applies to Bohlen (*Der Fall Nabot*, 172–95), who sees vv. 17-19a, 20abα (up to יען) as such a fragment, which he dates as the oldest part of the chapter (p. 302). The notion that a loose fragment would have been preserved independent of the situation it once addressed seems unlikely, as does the idea that the tale in vv. 1-16* once existed as an independent story without the resolution provided by an oracle. So also Würthwein, *1. Könige 17–2. Könige 25*, 245–51. For other scholars who take this view see Blum ("Die Nabotüberlieferungen," 115–16), who objects to it, noting the need for punishment that is inherent in the tale. As R. Albertz ("Macht und Recht—der Kampf Nabots gegen den König 1. Könige 21," in *Der Mensch als Hüter seiner Welt* [Stuttgart: Calwer, 1990], 26), puts it, Ahab's unjust acquisition in vv. 1-16 "cries out to heaven." The solution to this conundrum is to recognize that the Naboth story in vv. 1-16, along with 1 Kgs 17–19; 20; 22, are later insertions (though 21:1-16 probably replaced an older version of the Naboth story). Cf. Otto (*Jehu, Elia und Elisa*, 133), who acknowledges the secondary nature of 1 Kgs 17–19; 20; 22 but does not see that the Naboth story in 21:1-16 is also later.

sion of the story that remains only in traces in 2 Kgs 9:25-26a.[34] Thus the description of Naboth's property as a vineyard in 1 Kings 21 differs from that of 2 Kgs 9:21-27 (plot of land) as an accommodation to the notion of beauty and desirability that is integral to the Bathsheba story. The Bathsheba template accounts for several features of the present story that are at odds with the account in 2 Kings 9, including the location of Naboth's property, Jezebel's letter, the conspiratorial nature of the crime, and Elijah's role in denouncing Ahab. The story's novelistic and fictional nature is established by its beginning, *Naboth the Jezreelite had a vineyard* (v. 1), which resembles the once-upon-a-time start of a fairy tale.

21:1: The location of Naboth's property

In addition to the identification of the property as a vineyard, its location next to Ahab's palace derives from the proximity of Bathsheba's house to David's palace in 2 Samuel 11 (contrast 2 Kgs 9:11 where it is located some distance from Jezreel). But was the property in Jezreel where Naboth resided, or in Samaria where Ahab reigned? The question is resolved by recognizing that *which was in Jezreel* in v. 1 is a gloss in MT and that the references to Samaria here and in v. 18 are part of PN's preparation for the account of Ahab's death in ch. 22.[35] Some scholars contend that the original version of the Naboth story was set in Samaria rather than Jezreel, citing excavations in the 1990s that failed to turn up a palace in Jezreel, and arguing that Jezreel's location on a plain would be less conducive to the cultivation of vines than the hill country around Samaria.[36] The Bathsheba template aside, there are elements of the story that favor its location in Jezreel. It is hard to see how Naboth's property could have been located in Samaria, which had recently been purchased by Omri (16:24) and could not therefore have remained part of Naboth's ancestral inheritance. Also, since Naboth is consistently referred to as a Jezreelite, his ancestral heritage would have to be located in Jezreel. The description of Jezebel sending letters to the elders and nobles in Naboth's city (v. 8) is more appropriate if Jezebel is somewhere other than *in his city*, i.e., Jezreel, but this phrase is textually dubious.[37] To judge from 2 Kings 9:21, 25-26a, Naboth's property was a plot of land (חלקה), not a vineyard, somewhere in the vicinity of Jezreel though outside its city walls.[38]

21:2-3: The reason for Naboth's refusal

The *Wiederaufnahme* in v. 2aβb (*vineyard* [1] ... *vineyard* [3] with OG, see the Note) imparts the same information as v. 6 and is another instance of the use of this technique by PN as an author. Ahab's request can be construed as a demand highlighting the abuse of royal power. Still, the verb *give* could have the sense of sell or exchange (Deut 2:28, 14:25; 1 Chron 21:22). Such is Ahab's claim to Jezebel

---

34 Cf. White, *Elijah Legends*, 17–24 and "Naboth's Vineyard and Jehu's Coup: The Legitimation of a Dynastic Extermination," *VT* 44 (1994) 66–76. See also Cronauer, *Stories about Naboth*, 107–109, 191–93.

35 The mention of Samaria in 20:43 is a link to ch. 22, which was its original sequel as preserved in the G order and is meaningless for the setting of 21:1-16.

36 See esp. Williamson, "Jezreel in the Biblical Texts," 88–89; also Timm, *Die Dynastie Omri*, 118–21. The point about Jezreel's greater conduciveness to a vineyard is made by Fritz, *Kings*, 211.

37 See the Note. White (*Elijah Legends*, 21) argues, anyway, that the phrase is a result of the contrived scene of Jezebel's letter-writing campaign in parallel with the David story. The same holds for v. 11.

38 Cf. N. Na'aman, "Naboth's Vineyard and the Foundation of Jezreel," *JSOT* 33 (2008): 197–218.

in v. 6. While he may be lying to her, the story indicates that the issue for Naboth is not price but the nature of the land. In his response (v. 3) he uses the expression *heritage of my ancestors* (נחלת אבתי). He does not try to negotiate or complain about compensation but is scandalized at the idea of giving up his family property. Ahab is candid with Jezebel on this point: Naboth refuses to give him his נחלה (v. 6, OG). As Israel was an endogamous society, maintaining real estate within the family, clan, tribe, and nation was an important tradition. The ancestral inheritance was a vital bond with one's family, the land, and YHWH. In the case of a vineyard it reflected the work of generations whose continuity was represented by their burial on the property.[39] Naboth's refusal is also grounded in Israelite law (Lev 25:23-25; Num 36:7-9), which forbids the sale or transfer of Israelite land in perpetuity.[40] It does so on the basis of the ideology that the land belongs to YHWH, who apportioned it among the Israelites, so that each family, clan, and tribe has its own sacrosanct heritage in perpetuity. Given Jezebel's familiarity with laws later in the story, Naboth's refusal here also presupposes the law, i.e., the biblical *Torah*, whatever the legal situation in ninth-century Israel may have been.

21:4-7: The bedroom conversation of Ahab and Jezebel

The conversation between Ahab and Jezebel in vv. 4-7 takes place in the royal bedroom. The report of a private conversation shows the fictional nature of the narrative. Ahab is sullen. He lies on his bed with his face covered (G^{B-}), refusing to eat. When Jezebel questions him about his behavior (v. 5), he reports his conversation with Naboth (v. 6) with several changes vis-à-vis v. 3. He could be filling in details, but he seems to be elaborating or even lying outright in order to portray himself as generous and Naboth as obstinate. He claims that he offered Naboth money or an exchange for the vineyard and that Naboth refused. He quotes Naboth as referring to his ancestral heritage (G^{BL}) but does not mention Naboth's near oath in v. 3. Jezebel's opaque response in MT (*You now exercise kingship over Israel*) is clarified by G^{BL}, which presupposes כה, *thus.* It is a rhetorical question expressing disdain at the lack of royal privilege in Israel.[41] Feeling no such restric-

39 See T. J. Lewis, "The Ancestral Estate in 2 Sam 14:16," *JBL* 110 (1999), esp. 608–609.

40 *Pace* Westbrook ("Law in Kings," 453), who objects that "the idea that King Ahab could have proposed an illegal transaction for the transfer of inalienable land is illogical" since "it would not have given him good title." But if the story is modeled on 2 Sam 11–12 what is driving it is not legal propriety but narrative template. Naboth's land was off limits to him just as another man's wife was off limits to David. H. Seebass ("Der Fall Nabot in I Reg. XXI," *VT* 24 [1974]: 474–88, following F. Horst "Das Eigentum nach dem Alten Testament," *Gottesrecht: Gesammelte Studien zum Recht im Alten Testament* [Munich: Kaiser, 1961 [orig. 1949], 203–21; similarly Bohlen, *Der Fall Nabot*, 320–50), suggests that the debate over the legal status of Naboth's property results from the ambiguity of נחלה, which could refer to tribal land that was not to be sold in perpetuity but also to privately owned tracts acquired secondarily that were not under that restriction. He indicates that Naboth's land was in the latter category and that he refused to sell it because of the tradition of retaining it within his family but without legal restriction.

41 Blum ("Die Nabotüberlieferungen," 115) takes it as a statement rather than a question, reflecting satirical logic; Jezebel tells Ahab that he exercises kingship, which then qualifies her to engineer Naboth's murder and the seizure of his property. Blum does not consider the G^{BL} reading. He is right that this could be rendered as a statement, but it must be an expression of incredulity or sarcasm: "This is the way you exercise kingship in Israel!"

tions, she offers to undertake the acquisition of the vineyard, and her offer, assuming Ahab's acquiescence, leads into the account of the plot against Naboth.

21:8: Jezebel's letter

Jezebel is one of two women in the Bible—the other being Esther (Est 9:29)—who are said to write (v. 8). Judging from written accounts and images of scribes, only males were typically trained to do so. As a king's daughter Jezebel may have been exceptional.[42] PN may intend this as another instance of Jezebel usurping a male role in the story (see the Synchronic Analysis). However, Jezebel's letter (singular with G^{BL}) owes its origin here above all to modeling on the Bathsheba story (2 Sam 11–12) and David's letter there; the elders and nobles stand in the place of Joab, so that the model also accounts for the conspiratorial nature of the murder. Jezebel's letter is written in Ahab's name and bears his seal. The process involved writing a letter on leather or papyrus, rolling it, wrapping a string around it, and securing the string with a lump of damp clay into which was pressed the king's signet.[43] How she acquired the signet is unexplained.[44] It has fostered the allegation that Ahab was complicit in the plot, indeed that he was really the one behind it, manipulating Jezebel (see the Synchronic Analysis). What ultimately lies behind this proposal is the failure to recognize the oracle against Ahab in vv. 20-24* as distinct from and earlier than the story in vv. 1-16.

Jezebel's lackies

The root חתם "seal" occurs predominantly in the HB in texts that are typically dated to the exilic period or later.[45] The letter is addressed to the *elders and nobles* who live with Naboth.[46] The two groups are not mentioned together anywhere outside of this passage (vv. 8, 11). "Nobles" (חרים) is a term found outside of vv. 8 and 11 only in late texts, especially in Nehemiah (Isa 34:12; Jer 27:20; 39:6; Neh 2:16; 4:8, 13; 5:7; 6:17; 7:5; 13:17; Qoh 10:17). It is a loan word from Aramaic and refers to individuals who were "free from compulsory labour to the Persian king."[47] The nobles are envisioned,

---

42 Like Enheduanna, the daughter of Sargon of Akkad, who was a High Priestess and a prolific poet. Leuchter ("Sociolinguistic and Rhetorical Implications," 121) observes that literacy is central to the story, in contrast to what seems to be the originally oral nature of the Elisha traditions.

43 See C. A. Rollston, "Seals and Scarabs," *NIDB* 5:141–46.

44 F. I. Andersen ("The Socio-Juridical Background of the Naboth Incident," *JBL* 85 [1966]: 46–57) argued from Ugaritic parallels that the seal mentioned here was not the king's personal seal but the state or dynastic seal used to endorse legal documents (Hebrew ספר can be "letter" or "document") and that it was such documents, rather than letters, that Jezebel sent. The documents provided (forged) evidence that Naboth had promised to sell his land to Ahab and thus laid the legal groundwork for Ahab's claim to the property after Naboth's death. The interpretation founders on the evidence for the patterning of this story after the David-Bathsheba tale and vv. 9-10, which quote Jezebel's written message in the form of a letter rather than a decree or legal texts.

45 Lev 15:3; Deut 32:34; Neh 10:1-2; Est 3:12; 8:8, 10; Job 9:7; 14:17; 24:16; 33:16; 37:7; SoS 4:12; Isa 8:16; 29:11; Jer 32:10, 11, 14, 44; Ezek 28:12; Dan 9:24; 12:4, 9.

46 The reference to the elders and nobles living (הישבים) with Naboth has sometimes been taken to mean that Naboth sat on some kind of town council with the elders and nobles, though this possibility is weakened by the recognition of the phrase *who were in his city* is secondary. See the Note; Cronauer, *Stories about Naboth*, 134–35.

47 Rofé, *Prophetical Stories*, 98–99. Na'aman ("Naboth's Vineyard and the Foundation of Jezreel," 200–203) attempts, unsuccessfully in my view, to refute Rofé's linguistic evidence.

along with the elders, as exercising a leadership role that entails the authority to call a fast (v. 9). The fast is a solemn occasion of penitence designed to avert punishment for some guilt brought upon the corporate body though its actions or those of an individual. Placing Naboth *at the head* of the people may refer to a position of leadership or honor, though there is no indication in the context that this is the case. Rather, the point seems to be accessibility. Jezebel orders Naboth's *Mitbürger* literally to set him up for a kangaroo trial.

21:9-10: The scheme detailed

Spelling out the details of her scheme in writing would leave incriminating evidence, but it is another feature that this story has in common with the one in 2 Samuel 11. The details evince a thorough acquaintance with Israelite law. Two witnesses are required for a capital offense (Deut 17:6; 19:15) in order to avoid abetting personal vendettas. Cursing god was a capital offense (Lev 24:14-16) punishable by stoning (Lev 24:14). Cursing the king was also criminal (Exod 22:27). Both the accusations and the process are contrived in such a way as to ensure Naboth's execution. Jezebel is thus depicted as knowing Israelite law well enough to manipulate it for nefarious purposes. Since the laws in Leviticus are P or H(oliness Code), this means that PN knows the Torah in its more-or-less final form. Rofé further points out that the verb עוד (*Hip'îl*) means "testify" only from the fifth century on.[48] These data confirm the late dating of the story in vv. 1-16.

21:11-14: Naboth executed

The elders and nobles carry out Jezebel's instructions as ordered. The two phrases *the men of his city* (אנשי עירו) and *who were the ones who lived in his city* (אשר הישבים בעירו) are disruptive, as is widely recognized, and are part of the same effort as in v. 8 (see the note) to clarify PN's ambiguity about the location of Naboth's property. The differences between the accounts of Jezebel's written orders in vv. 9-10 and their execution in vv. 12-13 are minimal and insignificant. They call a fast and set Naboth at the head of the people (v. 12) as ordered (v. 9b). The command to seat two scoundrels opposite Naboth (v. 10) is fulfilled by the statement that they came and sat opposite him (v. 13). After they testify as instructed, Naboth is taken outside the city and stoned to death *per* Jezebel's mandate (v. 13b). The report in v. 14 confirms that her plan was carried out without recounting details. Ironically, the execution that is supposed to prevent further guilt from accruing to the community in fact makes the community guilty of innocent blood.

21:15

When Jezebel reports the news to Ahab (v. 15) she leaves out the details about the manner of Naboth's death, such that he is not an accomplice or an accessory.[49] She acknowledges Ahab's offer to buy the property. As in v. 7, she still refers to it as a vineyard rather than ancestral heritage. Her description of the vineyard as *which [Naboth] refused to sell you* is telling. The verb מאן, *refuse*, shows that she considers Naboth obstinate and hence responsible for his own death for refusing

---

48 Rofé, "Vineyard of Naboth," 99–100.

49 Westbook ("Law in Kings," 456–57) argues that Jezebel's words are a legalism using the expression "shall not live" as an order of summary execution (2 Kgs 10:19; Gen 31:32) and thereby making Ahab aware of the conspiracy. But there is no reason for Jezebel to use legal code in a private conversation with her husband. Jezebel does not even mention that Naboth was executed by stoning. Her point is simply that Ahab can now claim the vineyard because Naboth is dead. He may suspect foul play but he does not know enough to be complicit.

the king. Ahab's ritual mourning before he takes possession (v. 16) resembles the mourning period Bathsheba observes before David marries her (2 Sam 11:26-27). It also suggests Ahab's cynicism; his torn clothes and donning of sackcloth are hardly sincere, considering that he has what he wanted all along—all the more since he complies with Jezebel's order in v. 15, arising (ויקם) and descending (לרדת) to claim the vineyard (לרשתו).

The basis of Ahab's claim

The story does not explain the grounds on which Ahab laid claim to Naboth's vineyard. The gap is especially prominent after its concern to show Jezebel following legal prescriptions in her plot against Naboth. Scholars have surmised that the text assumes a law or custom whereby the king could confiscate the property of an executed criminal.[50] The Bible, though, mentions no such procedure. This is another feature resulting from the dependence of the Naboth story on 2 Samuel 11. Naboth's death clears the way for Ahab to take the vineyard as Uriah's death made it possible for David to take Bathsheba.

21:17 Connecting story and oracle

Ahab's possession of the vineyard rounds out the story but leaves it unresolved; Jezebel gets away with murder and Ahab gets his garden—hardly a gratifying ending. This shows that vv. 1-16 as they now stand were never an independent unit[51] but were written to foreground Elijah's anti-dynastic oracle beginning in v. 17. That oracle's beginning is signaled by the *Wortereignisformel* in v. 17, which goes back to DtrH. On the epithet *the Tishbite* see 17:1. DtrH brought in Elijah, as Jehu ben Hanani was introduced in 16:1, to deliver the anti-dynastic oracle. Both appear out of nowhere, as it were, to prophesy the demise of the ruling house. DtrH apparently adopted an older version of the Naboth story (cf. 2 Kgs 9:25-26a) as the occasion for Elijah's oracle. Still, Ahab's crimes were idolatry and maintenance of the Northern royal shrines ("walking in the way of Jeroboam") rather than the murder of Naboth, which DtrH returns to in the fulfillment in 2 Kings 9.

21:18-20abα : PN's further connections

For PN, Elijah's role as denouncer reflects that of Nathan in 2 Samuel 12. He added vv. 18-19, which presuppose vv. 1-16*, to accommodate the story to the oracle. They, along with the phrase *king of Samaria* in v. 1, reflect the effort to locate the event in Samaria, despite Naboth's association with Jezreel (2 Kgs 9:21), in order to connect it with Ahab's death in 22:37-38.[52] The repetition of *thus says* Yhwh in v. 19b does not signal a different hand but a felt need to separate the judgment beginning there from the indictment in v. 19a. In v. 20abα Ahab's greeting Elijah as *my enemy* assumes a relationship of enmity with Elijah that reflects acquaintance with 1 Kings 18, confirming PN's hand.[53]

---

50 Provan, *Kings*, 160; Westbrook, "Law in Kings," 455; Würthwein, *1. Könige 17–2. Könige 25*, 250. For a more nuanced presentation of this idea drawing on comparative anthropological evidence about the hierarchy of landed estates see S. C. Russell, "The Hierarchy of Estates in Land and Naboth's Vineyard," *JSOT* 38 (2014): 453–469. In 2 Kgs 8:4 the Shunammite appeals to the king for the restoration of land she has lost in her absence, but it is unclear who has taken possession of it.

51 *Pace* Würthwein, *1. Könige 17–2. Könige 25*, 245–51.

52 Napier, "The Omrides of Jezreel," 367–68; White, *Elijah Legends*, 20–22.

53 E. Blum, "Die Nabotüberlieferungen und die Kompositionsgeschichte der Vorderen Propheten," in *Schriftauslegung in der Schrift. Festschrift für Odil Hannes Steck zu seinem 65. Geburtstag* (ed. R. G. Kratz, T. Krüger, K. Schmid; BZAW 300; Berlin: de Gruyter, 2000), 120–21.

21:20bβ: The start of the oracle

DtrH's anti-dynastic oracle proper begins in v. 20bβ with the יען clause. It is similar to the oracles against the houses of Jeroboam and Baasha, though not identical, because each has been tailored to its setting with a particular dynasty.[54] The indictment in 21:20bβ is shorter than the other two. The language about raising him from obscurity is inappropriate for Ahab, who was a king's son. DtrH may have identified the dynasty as the "house of Ahab" instead of the "house of Omri" because Ahab came to eclipse Omri in Israel's collective memory, especially where tolerance of Baal worship was concerned.[55] But the influence of 2 Kings 9–10* may also have been a factor; there it is Ahab's sons who are slaughtered by Jehu just as it was Jeroboam's and Baasha's heirs whose slaughter marked the end of their houses. The oracle is still anti-dynastic, because the house of Ahab is synonymous with the house of Omri.

21:21-22, 24

The judgment in 21:21-22, 24 threatens evil from Yhwh for the evil done by Ahab (measure for measure), as against Jeroboam (14:10), as well as "consuming" (√בער + אחר), as against Baasha. It contains the same threats as the other two oracles—obliteration of every male or royal member (משתין בקיר) of the line, including kinsmen and non-related supporters, and their non-burial (cf. on 16:11). The aiming of the judgment at Ahab individually (v. 21) could be a retouching by PN. However, the individual reference is not unique, since 16:3 pronounces judgment on Baasha as an individual as well as on his house.[56] The rest of the verse with its mention of every *royal member* shows that the threat is still against the royal line. *In Israel* at the end of the verse excludes Southern relatives of Ahab; the judgment is against the Northern dynasty, as is made explicit in v. 22. Ahab's name in the curse shared by all three passages (v. 24) is synecdochal for his house.

21:23: PN's anti-Jezebel prophecy

The word against Jezebel in v. 23 in the middle of the anti-dynastic oracle is PN's addition. It is widely recognized as secondary.[57] It is introduced with וגם and interrupts the continuity between the threat of annihilation in vv. 21-22 and the curse of non-burial in v. 24 as in the previous anti-dynastic oracles (14:10-11; 16:3-4). Its interest in someone other than the male heirs of the ruling dynasty diverges from the main concern of these oracles.

21:25-26: There was none like Ahab for PN

The most striking inconsistency in this half of the chapter is between vv. 25-26 on the one hand and vv. 27-29 on the other. Verses 25-26 are PN's doing. They are secondary, as is widely recognized.[58] They interrupt the continuity between Elijah's denunciation of Ahab and Ahab's repentance at *these words* (v. 27). In so doing they change abruptly from the direct address of vv. 20-22, 24 to the third person, adopting PN's voice rather than Elijah's. The accusation that Ahab *sold himself* (borrowed from v. 20b) to do evil by worshiping idols like the Amorites is reminiscent of 16:31-33 in at least three ways. First, they show awareness of Jezebel and lay the blame for Ahab's apostasy at her feet. Second, they interpret 16:31-33 in the light of Deuteronomy 13, using the verb סות ("entice, incite") to explain how she led him astray. Third, they stress the incomparability of Ahab in doing evil precisely because of Jezebel. The reason for the addition of vv. 25-26 was to

54 See the chart in the Introduction and Blum, "Die Nabotüberlieferungen," 127–28.
55 Cf. Ishida, "House of Ahab." Cf. Timm, *Die Dynastie Omri*, 136; Buis, *Rois*, 168.
56 Contrast Stipp, *Elischa - Propheten - Gottesmänner*, 483–84.
57 Otto's (*Jehu, Elia und Elisa*, 129–32) position to the contrary notwithstanding.
58 See especially Otto, *Jehu, Elia und Elisa*, 135–36.

mitigate a situation that was intolerable for PN: In DtrH's account Israel's worst king escaped without punishment. He even received a natural death and burial. PN was compelled to add vv. 25-26, which reiterated and reinforced the portrait of Ahab's extreme wickedness from 16:31-33 and distinguished Ahab's individual sin and fate from those of the dynasty in preparation for his death in ch. 22. PN was thus aware of the account of Ahab's death in 22:1-38 and sought to make the point that Ahab would get what he deserved. As we will see in the next chapters, this was a larger project on PN's part that entailed shifting the stories in chs. 20; 22:1-38 from their original location at the end of 2 Kings 13 and revising them to fit his purpose.

21:27-29: DtrH's etiology

Verses 27-29 are the continuation of DtrH's account of Ahab, as indicated by *these words* in v. 27, referring back to Elijah's oracle.[59] The oracle moved Ahab to repentance, which in turn moved YHWH to defer *the disaster* (הרעה) prophesied against his house (vv. 27-29). The deferral is surprising. The falls of the previous two dynasties (Jeroboam and Baasha) did not occur during the lifetimes of their founders who were the recipients of the anti-dynastic oracles but in the days of their sons. So why the special notice for Ahab? The answer is that these verses are etiological and explain both the length of the Omri dynasty overall and its destruction not with Ahab's immediate successor, Ahaziah, but with his second son and successor Joram. Ahab's repentance in v. 27 resembles the account of Josiah's finding of the law (2 Kgs 22:11, 19) in the use of ויהי כשמע, in the reference to Ahab tearing his clothes, and in the use of כנע *Nip'al* (v. 29). The *evil* or *disaster* in v. 29 (cf. v. 21) alludes to the bloody revolt of Jehu (2 Kgs 9–10).

Synthesis

The abuse of power and manipulation of law

PN created the episode in this chapter by supplementing the DtrH anti-dynastic oracle against Ahab that was ascribed to Elijah. The two stories highlight the constant danger and temptation, endemic to human beings, to abuse power and privilege for personal gain. The Naboth story shows that even the law can easily be manipulated by the powerful and elite. Judgment prophets—those in antiquity like Nathan and Elijah and those with us today—who warn against such abuses have an important role as the conscience of society, especially among the privileged.

---

59 So also H.-J. Stipp, "Ahabs Buße und die Komposition des deuteronomistischen Geschichtswerkes," *Bib* 76 (1995): 471–97; who is followed by M. Beck, *Elia und die Monolatrie: Ein Beitrag zur religionsgeschichtlichen Rückfrage nach dem vorschriftprophetischen Jahwe-Glauben* (BZAW 281; Berlin/New York, 1999), 59–61; Otto, *Jehu, Elia und Elisa*, 127–29; and Pruin, *Geschichten und Geschichte*, 245–46. Of special importance is Stipp's counter (p. 480) of A. Jepsen's claim ("Ahabs Buße. Ein kleiner Beitrag zur Methode literarhistorischer Einordnung," in *Archäologie und Altes Testament. Festschrift für Kurt Galling* [ed. A. Kuschke and E. Kutsch; Tübingen: Mohr Siebeck, 1970], 145–55) about the late date of 21:27-29 based on its use of כנע *Nip'al*. Stipp observed that the principle of individual responsibility here has its precedent in Deut 24:16; cf. 2 Kgs 14:6.

The caricature of Jezebel

At the same time it is well to keep in mind that Jezebel, the main villain in the story, is a caricature. She is foreign, female, and formidable. As a Phoenician royal she gladly sacrifices justice for royal privilege and even whim, ignoring Israelite tradition and law except where she can manipulate it to her ends. Her character may also represent a salvo fired in the controversy over marriages to "foreign" women at the time of Ezra and Nehemiah.[60] While marriage *per se* is not a focus of the story it is implicit throughout in the scenes between Ahab and Jezebel, especially in vv. 3-7. She usurps her husband's insignia and authority to engineer her crime, ostensibly on his behalf. She leads her husband and Israel astray religiously (16:31-33) and threatens to undermine the very fabric of Israelite society and life on the land given to it as an inheritance from YHWH. The stereotypes she embodies work to reinforce the xenophobic and male-dominated society of ancient Israel in which property is passed to male heirs in order to maintain tribal and national boundaries.

60 Cronauer, *Stories about Naboth*, 193–98, 203–204; also Blum" Die Nabotüberlieferungen," 119. The idea was anticipated in a way by G. Fohrer, *Elia*, 42, who in regard to the Naboth story wrote, "Statt der Vorwürfe des Götzendienstes oder der Verfolgung spricht sich darin der einfache und blanke Hass gegen sie aus." ("This is an expression not of condemnation of idol worship or persecution, but of simple and sheer hatred against her [Jezebel].

The Prophet Micaiah and the Death of Ahab (1 Kings 22:1-40)

Text

[DtrH; Prophetic story/battle account; *PN*]
1 *[The king of Israel] stayed home for three years while there was no war between Aram and Israel.* 2 *In the third year Jehoshaphat king of Judah went down to the king of Israel.* 3 The king of Israel said to his servants, "You know, don't you, that Ramah of Gilead belongs to us? Yet we do nothing about taking it from the king of Aram?" 4 *He said to Jehoshaphat, "You will go up with me to Ramah of Gilead, won't you?" Jehoshaphat replied, "I am like you, and my army is like your army."* 5 *Jehoshaphat said to the king of Israel, "Please inquire first of YHWH."* 6 The king of Israel gathered the prophets—*400 men*—and asked them, "Should I go against Ramah of Gilead for war or not?" They answered, "Go up, for YHWH will surely place [it] under the king's control." 7 *But Jehoshaphat said, "Isn't there a prophet of YHWH here through whom we can make inquiry?"* 8 *The king of Israel said to Jehoshaphat, "There is one man through whom we may inquire, but I hate him because he does not prophesy good concerning me but only disaster—Micaiah son of Imlah." Jehoshaphat replied, "Let the king not say such a thing."* 9 So the king of Israel called an official and said, "Bring Micaiah son of Imlah here quickly." 10 *The king of Israel and Jehoshaphat king of Judah were sitting on their respective thrones dressed in their robes at the gateway of Samaria while all the prophets were prophesying before them.* 11 *Zedekiah son of Canaanah made horns of iron for himself and said, "Thus says YHWH, 'With these you will gore Aram until you finish them off.'"* 12 *And all the prophets prophesied this way saying, "Go up to Ramah of Gilead; YHWH will give you success and will deliver the king of Aram into your control."* 13 *The messenger who went to summon Micaiah spoke to him, "Look, the prophets have spoken univocally favorably concerning the king, so let your message be as one of theirs and speak favorably."* 14 *But Micaiah said, "By YHWH's life, what YHWH says to me, that I will speak."* 15 When he came to the king, the king said to him, "Micaiah, should I go to Ramah of Gilead to war or not?" [Micaiah] replied, "Go up! YHWH will give you success and will deliver [it] into the king's control." 16 The king said to him, "How many times must I adjure you to tell me the truth in YHWH's name?" 17 [Micaiah] said, "I saw Israel scattered on the hills like sheep without a shepherd, and YHWH said, 'These have no master. Let them each return to his house in peace.'" 18 *The king of Israel said to Jehoshaphat, "Did I not tell you he would not prophesy good about me but only bad?"* 19 *[Micaiah] said "Therefore, hear YHWH's word: I saw YHWH sitting on his throne with all the heavenly army standing at his service on his right and his left.* 20 *And he said, 'Who will entice Ahab into going up to Ramah of Gilead that he may fall there?' And each one said something different. [YHWH] said, 'You will not be effective.* 21 *Then a*

certain spirit came out and stood before YHWH and said, 'I will entice him.' YHWH asked him 'By whom?' [The spirit] said, 'By you.'" [22] *[The spirit] said, 'I will go out and become a spirit of falsehood in the mouths of all his prophets, and I will entice him.' [YHWH] said, "You will succeed. Go. Do it."* [23] *Now YHWH has placed a spirit of falsehood in the mouths of these prophets of yours, because YHWH himself has decreed disaster for you."* [24] *Then Zedekiah son of Canaanah approached and struck Micaiah on the jaw, saying, "Which way did YHWH's spirit pass from me to speak by you?"* [25] *Micaiah responded, "You will see when you go into an inner room to hide yourself."* [26] *The king of Israel said, "Take Micaiah and return him to Amon the city mayor. And to Joash the king's son* [27] *say, "Put this [fellow] in jail on subsistence rations of food and water until I return in peace."* [28] *Micaiah said, "If you return in peace, YHWH has not spoken through me."* [29] So the king of Israel *and Jehoshaphat king of Judah* went up to Ramah of Gilead. [30] The king of Israel said *to Jehoshaphat,* "Let me disguise myself and go into battle *while you dress in your royal robes."* So the king of Israel disguised himself and went into battle. [31] Meanwhile, the king of Aram had commanded the captains of his chariotry, "Don't fight with anyone small or great except the king of Israel alone." [32] *So when the captains of the chariotry saw Jehoshaphat they thought, "That is the king of Israel" and they surrounded him to fight. When he cried out, YHWH helped him.* [33] *When the captains of the chariotry realized that he was not the king of Israel, they turned from pursuing him.* [34] A certain man drew the bow unawares and shot the king of Israel between the attachments and the body armor, and he told his driver, "Turn around and take me out of the battle because I am wounded." [35] As the battle grew more intense on that day the king was propped up in the chariot facing Aram until he died *in the evening and the blood from the wound flowed into the recesses of the chariot.* [36] *At sunset the herald stood announcing, "Everyone to his city and to his inheritance."* [37] *So the king died,* and they went to Samaria and buried the king in Samaria. [38] *When the chariot was rinsed at the pool of Samaria, the dogs licked his blood and the prostitutes washed themselves in it according to the word of YHWH.* [39] The rest of Ahab's affairs including all that he did, the ivory house that he built, and all the cities that he built, are of course written on the scroll of the chronicles of the kings of Israel. [40] Ahab lay down with his forebears and Ahaziah his son reigned in his place.

Textual Notes

1 **[The king of Israel] stayed home**: So G^{BL}: καὶ ἐκάθισε[ν] = וישב in reference to the king of Israel at the end of ch. 20. MT has the plural.[1]

2 **to the king of Israel**: So MT, G^{B}. G^{L}: *to Ahab king of Israel.*

---

1 MT seems to take *three years* as the subject, but ישב never occurs elsewhere with a time reference as subject. Cogan (*I Kings*, 489) takes the subject as the kings of Israel and Aram in 20:34 and construes ישב to mean "stay home." But since the battle story ended with 20:43 it is more likely that the subject here is the king of Israel.

3 **Ramah**: So 1 Kgs 8:29 MT and suggested by G^{BL} Ρεμμαθ. MT: *Ramoth* (= plural construct). The site is identified as Tell er-Ramith, ca. seven km south of Ramtha near the border between modern Syria and Jordan and ca. sixty km north of Amman.

4 **go up**: So G^{BL} ([εἶ] ἀναβήσῃ = התעל) as in vv. 12, 15, 20, 29. MT: התלך.

to Ramah of Gilead: So 2 Chr 18:3. MT, G^{BL} precede or follow with *for war to Ramah of Gilead*. The different locations of the phrase are further indication that the phrase is secondary.

I am like you and my army is like your army: So 2 Chr 18:4 (כמוני כמוך וכעמך עמי) in a neat chiasm. MT, G^{B} (כמוני כמוך כעמי כעמך) attest a different order of suffixes and continue with a reference to horses (כסוסי כסוסיך). Chronicles has its own expansion: in ועמך במלחמה (ועמך is a dittography, and במלחמה was added to accommodate it). G^{L} agrees with Chronicles' order of suffixes but also has the plus about horses.

5 **Please inquire first:** So MT, 2 Chr 18:4. G^{B} has the plural *inquire*; G^{L}: *Let us inquire.*

of Yhwh: So G^{L}. The other witnesses attest the circumlocution *of the word of Yhwh.*

6 **400 men**: So 2 Chr 18:5. Preceded by *about* in the Kings witnesses.

against Ramah of Gilead: So MT: על. G^{BL} reflect אל. Cf. Joüon §133b.

for Yhwh will surely place: So G^{L}. MT and G^{B} both have the conjunction in lieu of כי (ὅτι). MT reads a purpose clause, *so that the Lord may give* (ויתן אדני). G^{BL} understand this as a prediction: διδοὺς δώσει κύριος (= יהוה נתון יתן) *Yhwh will surely give.* The idiomatic Hebrew has the ring of authenticity. The infinitive was lost from MT by haplography. The divine name may have been replaced to avoid its utterance by prophets of Baal; 2 Chr 18:5 has האלהים.

7 **Jehoshaphat said**: So MT. G^{BL} + *to the king of Israel.*

a prophet of Yhwh: So G^{BL}. MT + *still* (עוד).

through whom we can make inquiry: Reading מֵאִתּוֹ for MT's מֵאֹתוֹ. G^{BL} read *of Yhwh.*

8 **one man**: So G^{B}. MT + עוד. G^{L} + ὧδε = פה.

through whom: Again read מֵאִתּוֹ and מֵאֹתוֹ as in v 7.

he does not prophesy: So MT. G^{BL}: *he does not speak.*

Micaiah son of Imlah: So MT, G^{BL}. Micaiah means "Who is like Yhwh?"[2] Imlah's etymology is uncertain, but it may come from √מלא (cf. 2 Chr 18) and mean "May god/ Yhwh fulfill." מלא is stative in the *Qal*, though, so another possibility is that the name derives from מלך or מלט.[3]

9 **an official**: The term סריס, from Akkadian *ša rēši* "the one at the head," designates a royal official, especially an attendant for the royal family. Such officials, especially those in charge of the harem, were often eunuchs, so the term takes on that meaning too. Hence the G translation εὐνοῦχον.[4]

10 **dressed in their royal robes**: So MT (מלבשים בגדים). G^{BL}: ἔνοπλοι, *armed*, perhaps "uniformed."[5]

at the gateway of Samaria: Reading בדרך שער שמרון based on G^{L} (= OG): ἐν ὁδῷ πύλαις Σαμαρείας and the OL: *ad viam portae Samariae*.[6] MT's בגרן פתח שער שמרון is corrupt: בגרן, *on the threshing floor*, is absent from 2 Chr 18:9 and is probably a corruption of בגדים;[7] פתח and שער are variants.

---

2 Noth, *Personennamen*, 144.

3 Noth, *Personennamen*, 246.

4 See I. Eph'al-Jaruzelska, "Officialdom and Society," 483–84 and Fox, *In the Service of the King*, 196–203. Also J. S. Everhart, "Jezebel: Framed by Eunuchs?" *CBQ* 72 (2010): 688–98.

5 Šanda, *Könige* I, 493.

6 Cf. 1 Sam 17:52; 2 Sam 15:2; 2 Kgs 11:19; 25:4. See Trebolle, "Practice of Textual Criticism."

7 In the Aqhat myth (*KTU* 1.17.5.6-7) *grn* occurs in reference to the public space at the opening of a gate. Hence it would be appropriate here architecturally. But it is still text-critically suspect.

11 **With these**: So MT, 2 Chr 18:10. G^{BL} + *horns*.

12 **Yhwh will give you success**: So G^{L} (καὶ εὐοδώσει σε κύριος), OL (*Et diriget te bona via*). G^{B} (καὶ εὐοδώσει) has lost σε by haplography.[8] It also has the divine name following the next verb. MT reads the imperative והצלח as a dependent clause (cf. GKC §110f).

and will deliver the king of Aram into your control: So OG: καὶ δώσει κύριος εἰς χεῖράς σου τὸν βασιλέα Συρίας as the sequel of the previous reading.[9] MT, 2 Chr 18:11: ונתן יהוה ביד המלך, *Yhwh will place [it] in the king's control*.

13 **the prophets have spoken**: So G^{BL} (B: λαλοῦσιν πάντες οἱ προφῆται; L: πάντες οἱ προφῆται λαλοῦσιν = כל־הנביאים דברו) except for *all*. MT's *good* is suspicious, since it does not match the plural *words*.[10]

concerning the king: So G^{BL}: κατὰ τοῦ βασιλέως (על־המלך); MT: *to the king* (אל־המלך).

your message: Lit. *your word*. So MT (*Qere'*) and most of the versions, as well as 2 Chr 18:12. The singular matches the verb יהי. MT (*ketiv*), G^{BL} have the plural *your words*.

14 **that I will speak**: So MT, 2 Chr 18:13 (אתו אדבר). G^{BL}: *those things* (ταῦτα) *I will speak*.

15 **should I go to Ramah of Gilead to war or not**: So G^{BL}: εἰ ἀναβῶ εἰς Ρεμμαθ Γαλααδ εἰς πόλεμον ἢ ἐπίσχω. MT has plural verbs: *should we go ... or should we refrain*. 2 Chr 18:14 has the plural for the first verb but the singular for the second, though it then has plural imperatives עלו והצליחו. The singular accords with the narrative's focus on Micaiah's response to the king of Israel; the plural seeks to include the king of Judah.

Yhwh will give you success: See v. 12.

and will deliver [it] into the king's control: So MT. The absence of this verb in G^{BL} is due to inner-Greek haplography (εὐοδώσει ... δώσει) (cf. v. 12).

16 **The king said to him**: So MT, G^{B}. G^{L} + *again*.

to tell me the truth: So G^{BL}: ὅπως λαλήσῃς πρός με ἀλήθειαν, as the shorter reading. MT employs a double negative: אשר לא־תדבר אלי רק־אמת, *that you tell me nothing but the truth*.

17 **I saw**: So MT. G^{BL} precede with οὐχ οὕτως, a *kaige* translation of לכן.[11]

Israel: Omitting *all* with certain mss and the Syriac (BHS).

on the hills: Reading על־ההרים, which is attested in some manuscripts and versions as well as in 2 Chr 18:16. MT has אל, and G^{BL} reflect ב.

without: So 2 Chr 18:16 (אשר אין־להן), with the feminine suffix corresponding to *sheep* where MT has the masculine suffix.

These have no master: So MT. G^{B} (οὐ κύριος τούτοις θεὸς) and G^{L} (εἰ κυρίως αὐτοὶ πρὸς θεόν) seem to reflect dittography: לא־אדנים לאלה אל and לא־אדנים אכה לאל, respectively.

18 **he would not prophesy**: So MT. G^{BL} + οὗτός *this [fellow]*.

about me: So MT (עלי) in preference to "to me" (אלי) as reflected in G^{BL}.

19 **Therefore**: On οὐχ οὕτως in G^{BL} see on v. 17. οὐκ ἐγώ, not reflected in the OL, is hexaplaric.[12]

---

8 The reconstruction is Trebolle's, "Practice of Textual Criticism after Qumran."

9 Minus the καὶ before τὸν βασιλέα in G^{BL}, which is absent in the rest of the manuscript tradition. Trebolle, "Practice of Textual Criticism after Qumran."

10 DeVries, *1 Kings*, 261; cf. Klostermann, *Könige*, 387.

11 J. Trebolle, "Redaction, Recension, and Midrash in the Books of Kings," *BIOSCS* 15 (1982), 28–30. As *kaige* it cannot be part of an OG reading indicating a double *Wiederaufnahme* in vv. 17aα and 19bα (*therefore I saw ... therefore hear Yhwh's message, "Therefore I saw"*). *Pace* Trebolle, *Centena*, 151–52.

12 Trebolle, "Practice of Textual Criticism after Qumran."

I saw Yhwh: So MT. G^{L} + *the god of Israel*; G^{B}: *the god of Israel* without the divine name.

20 **And he said**: So G^{L}. MT and G^{B} supply the divine name.

entice: The verb (פתה) means "to be simple, inexpert, gullible" (HALOT). The *Pi'el* has the sense of persuading someone to do something—usually something that brings negative consequences—out of ignorance, foolishness, or naiveté.

Ahab: So MT. G^{BL}, 2 Chr 18:19 + *the king of Israel.*

And each one said something different: So G^{BL} καὶ εἶπεν οὗτος οὕτως καὶ οὗτος οὕτως = ויאמר זה ככה וזה ככה. MT: ויאמר זה בכה וזה אמר בכה; אמר is superfluous, and בכה stems from graphic confusion of ב and כ (cf. 2 Chr 18:19).

[Yhwh] said, 'You will not be effective: Based on G^{L} (καὶ εἶπεν οὐ δυνήσῃ = ויאמר לא תוכל). The expected plural (תוכלו) was probably replaced by the singular in G^{L} under the influence of the singular in v. 22. The remainder of G^{L}'s plus here (καὶ εἶπεν ἐν σοί) belongs at the end of v. 21 (see below).

21 **By whom?**: So G^{BL} (ἐν τίνι = במי) in preference to MT's *How?* (במה). The question finds a parallel in 20:14 and inquires about the agent through whom an oracle will be fulfilled.[13]

[The spirit] said, "By you": This is the proper location of the GL plus at the end of v. 20. It addresses Yhwh's question, which is unanswered in MT.[14]

22 **"and I will entice him." [Yhwh] said, "You will succeed"**: So G^{L}: καὶ εἶπεν ἀπατήσω αὐτόν καὶ εἶπεν δυνήσει in line with the G^{L} readings in vv. 20-21. MT, G^{B}: ויאמר תפתה וגם תוכל.

23 **these prophets**: So 2 Chr 18:22; the witnesses in Kings have *all.*

24 **"Which way did Yhwh's spirit pass from me to speak by you?"**: So G^{L}: ποῖον πνεῦμα κυρίου ἀπέστη ἀπ' ἐμοῦ τοῦ λαλῆσαι ἐν σοί = אי־זה עבר רוח יהוה מאתי לדבר בך. MT is anomalous in its use of אי־זה with a verb, and that verb (עבר) does not match its subject (רוח, usually feminine) in gender. 2 Chr 18:23 (אי־זה הדרך עבר רוח יהוה מאתי לדבר אתך) is similar. The preposition ב at the end in place of את accords with Yhwh's question in v. 21. G^{B} (ποῖον πνεῦμα κυρίου τὸ λαλῆσαν ἐν σοί) reflects the loss of ἀπέστη ἀπ' ἐμοῦ by homoioteleuton, κυρίου ... ἐμοῦ).

25 **to hide yourself**: So 2 Chr 18:24 (להחבא), the more correct spelling of MT's להחבה.

26 **Take Micaiah**: So MT in contrast to the plural imperative in G^{BL}, 2 Chr 18:25, as indicated by אמרת in v. 27 (see below).

and return him: Again, singular with MT where G^{BL} and 2 Chr 18:25 have the plural.

city mayor: Lit. *the ruler of the city* (שר־העיר).

And to Joash: If charge of political prisoners was a duty of the mayor, then he alone would be the recipient of Micaiah and v. 26b begins a separate order (see Diachronic Analysis).

27 **say**: Reading אמרת as required by the indirect object at the end of v. 26. This means that Ahab's orders in v. 26a were to an individual. MT + *thus says the king.*

Put: The order to imprison Micaiah is given to Joash alone rather than to both Amon and Joash (שימו) as in MT.

subsistence rations of food and water: Reading *Hip'îl* imperative single (*feed him*) in accord with the foregoing series of verbs; jussive (*let him eat*) is also possible. On the construction *bread and water of oppression*, the "attributive accusative of limitation," see Joüon §127b; also GKC §131c; WO, 230.

return: So G^{BL}, 2 Chr 18:26 (שובי), and the next verse. MT: *come* (באי).

---

13 Trebolle, "Practice of Textual Criticism after Qumran."

14 I am grateful to Jan Joosten for this insight.

28 At the end of the verse MT adds, *He said, "Hear, all you peoples"* a plus from Mic 1:2.[15]

29 **king of Judah**: So MT. G^{BL} + *with him.*

30 **Jehoshaphat**: So MT. G^{BL}, 6QpapKgs5[16] + *king of Judah.*

Let me disguise myself and go: So MT and 2 Chr 18:29 with infinitives absolute (WO, 594). G^{BL} have the first person form but may be interpretive rather than reflecting a different text.

in your royal robes: So MT, 6QpapKgs5, 2 Chr 18:29. G^{BL} read the first-person suffix *my robes.* It seems more likely in view of the subsequent story that the original *your* was changed to *my* than the other way around.

31 **Meanwhile, the king of Aram had commanded**: So MT (ומלך ארם צוה). 6QKgs: ויצו מלך ארם.

32 **That is the king of Israel**: So 2 Chr 18:31. MT + אך. G^{BL}: φαίνεται, *it appears* is interpretive or reflects the preposition כ before מלך.

they surrounded him: So G^{BL}, 2 Chr 18:31 (καὶ ἐκύκλωσαν αὐτὸν = ויסבו עליו); compare Job 16:13. MT: ויסרו עליו, *they turned aside against him.*

Yhwh helped him: So G^{L}, OL. The plus is also reflected in 2 Chr 18:31 with expansion: ויהוה עזרו ויסיתם אלהים ממנו, *Yhwh helped him and god enticed them away from him.* MT, G^{B} reflect its loss by haplography (ויהוה...ויהי).

34 **the bow**: So MT, G^{B}. G^{L}, OL: *his bow.* Either is possible.

unawares: The word תם ("integrity, completeness") in the expression לתמו has the sense "in his integrity," i.e., "innocently, naïvely," as indicated by its one other occurrence in the HB in 2 Sam 15:11. Here it may mean that the soldier drew his bow without aiming or that he was unaware he was aiming at the king of Israel (see Diachronic Analysis). The Greek witnesses have εὐστόχως "aiming well" (G^{B}) and ἀφελῶς, "simply" (G^{L}). Both attempt to render the MT reading.

attachments: Used elsewhere only in Isa 41:7 to mean "soldering, joining," דבק here refers to "the jointed attachment or appendage to the rigid breast-armour, which covered the abdomen" (BDB, 180). The location of the arrow strike *between the attachments and the body armor* might be rendered "between the attachments *of* the body armor."[17] "Body armor" (שרין) is a loanword referring to the cuirass covering the breast if not the entire torso.[18] This would have been a leather garment covered by metal scales or plates.[19] "Attachments" (הדבקים) could refer to the scales, the soldering (Isa 41:7) joining the chest portion to that covering the abdomen, or the clasps that buckle the armor to the body.[20] Yet another possibility illustrated in a relief of Thutmose IV is that the joint in question was between the sleeve and the body armor proper.[21]

out of the battle: So G^{BL} (מן־המלחמה). MT: *out of the camp* (מן־המחנה). Weippert defends the MT, arguing that this was an early-morning test shot of a new bowstring.[22] She thus assumes that the shooter was Israelite not Aramaean. But why would an

---

15 See E. Ball, "A Note on I Kings XXII.28," *JTS* 28 (1977): 90–94, though Ball does not think this is a gloss.

16 Judging from space considerations; see Ulrich, *Biblical Qumran Scrolls*, 328.

17 Cogan, *I Kings*, 494; Y. Yadin (Sukenik), *The Art of Warfare in Biblical Lands in the Light of Archaeological Discovery* (London: Weidenfeld and Nicolson, 1963), 196.

18 E. A. Speiser, "On Some Articles of Armor and their Names," *JAOS* 70 (1950): 47–48.

19 As indicated by 1 Sam 17:5, "a plated cuirass," where שרין seems to refer to the armor alone covered by scales. See McCarter, *I Samuel*, 292.

20 Sweeney, *Kings*, 261.

21 Yadin, *The Art of Warfare in Biblical Lands*, 192–93, 196; *ANEP* 314.

22 H. Weippert, "Ahab el Campeador? Redaktionsgeschichtliche Untersuchungen zu 1 Könige 22," *Bib* 69 (1988), 460–61.

Israelite bowman take a practice shot toward his own camp, especially toward the king's tent?

35 **grew more intense**: So 2 Chr 18:34 (ותעל). MT has the longer form ותעלה, lit. *went up, increased*. G^{BL}: καὶ ἐτροπώθη, *was turned, raged*.

until he died in the evening and the blood from the wound flowed into the recesses of the chariot: So MT. G^{L}: *from morning till evening and the blood from the wound flowed into the recesses of the chariot until the king died in the evening*. The root of the problem here was the interpolation by *Wiederaufnahme* (repetition of וימת) in vv. 35bβ-37aα. The OG (= G^{L}) corrected the awkward placement of the reference to the blood by putting it before the mention of the king dying. G^{B} conflates the two with references to the blood both before and after the notice of the king's death.

36 **the herald stood**: So G^{BL}: καὶ ἔστη ὁ στρατοκῆρυξ = ויעמד הרנן, as opposed to MT's use of a masculine verb (ויעבר) with a feminine subject, הרנה. MT also expands with *in the camp*.

and to his inheritance: Reading נחלתו with G^{L} for MT's more pedestrian ארצו.

37 **they went**: So G^{BL}. MT: *he went*.

38 **When the chariot was rinsed out**: So MT. Lit. *when one rinsed out* (Joüon §155e). G^{BL}: *when they rinsed out*. G^{B} reads *blood* (αἷμα) for *chariot* (ἅρμα), an inner-Greek corruption. G^{L} conflates: *the blood from the chariot*.

the dogs: So MT, G^{L}. G^{B}: *the pigs and the dogs*, as in 21:19.

his blood: So MT. G^{BL}: *the blood*. Either is possible.

according to the word of Yhwh: So G^{L}. MT, G^{B} + *which he had spoken*.

39 **built** (2): So MT. G^{BL}: *made*.

are of course written: See the note on 16:5.

Synchronic Analysis

Segments of the chapter

The passage divides into four sections:

vv. 1-4 – background to the battle story that follows, explaining the reason for Ahab's aggression;

vv. 5-28 – consultation with prophets, especially Micaiah;

vv. 29-38 – battle with Aram and death of Ahab;

vv. 39-40 – closing regnal formulae for Ahab.

22:1-3: Links with preceding chapters

The opening verses of the chapter link it with ch. 20, dating the present narrative three years after the last war with Aram. It becomes clear that the location is Samaria, going back to 20:43 (cf. 22:10). The Naboth story in ch. 21 takes place in the three-year interval and shows that Ahab's external policies will not ultimately succeed because his kingdom is corrupt from the inside out. He spurned the victories given him by Yhwh by releasing Ben-Hadad (ch. 20). Little wonder that the Aramaean has failed to keep his promise to return Ramoth Gilead (20:34). He no doubt considers Ahab weak. Ahab's call for action (v. 3) is misguided. He speaks of *us* and *we*, apparently buoyed by his previous victories but failing to recognize that they were gifts from Yhwh. The action he proposes is doomed to fail because Yhwh, whom he has offended, will not help him this time. Yhwh will use the occasion to bring about Ahab's downfall (20:20), as anticipated in chs. 20 and 21.

22:4-9: Contrasts—Ahab with Jehoshaphat, Micaiah with the prophets

Jehoshaphat is Ahab's opposite. His statement, "I am like you" (v. 4), is ironic, because the two are nothing alike.[23] Jehoshaphat is righteous and has YHWH's favor. This may be why Ahab proposes the assault on Ramoth during Jehoshaphat's visit. He is aware of the threat hanging over his head because he antagonized YHWH (20:42). But if he teams with Jehoshaphat, YHWH may grant success to the enterprise. The strategy fails as YHWH shows his adeptness at saving Jehoshaphat while getting rid of Ahab. As it turns out, the strategy is not Ahab's to begin with, for it is YHWH who induces him to launch the assault (v. 20). The contrast between Ahab and Jehoshaphat is implicit in the latter's immediate impulse to inquire of YHWH (v. 5) and in the number of prophets Ahab summons—400. The association with the 400 prophets of Asherah (18:19) not killed by Elijah in 18:40 is inescapable. The term אדני (v. 6) suggests that their religious allegiance is unclear; the narrator cannot countenance the divine name on their lips. They are court prophets, sustained by the king, as those in 18:19 were sustained by Jezebel. They are sycophants who will speak what they think Ahab wants to hear. Thus their approval of his plan is unanimous. Still, their message to him is ambiguous: *Go up, so that the Lord may give into the king's hand.* The king who will receive the gift is unnamed, as is the Lord who gives it. The ambiguity resembles the famous oracle to Croesus that if he marched against the Persians he would destroy a great empire.[24] Perhaps for that reason Jehoshaphat is suspicious (v. 7); the unanimity of the prophets, their indebtedness to the king, their sycophantic attitude and appearance, their apparent affiliation with other gods and their failure to preface their message with the oracular formula "Thus says YHWH" are other potential reasons for skepticism. He asks if there is *yet a prophet of YHWH* present at court. Micaiah (v. 8) is similar to Elijah as the single true and trustworthy prophet of YHWH who is vastly outnumbered. His name— "Who is like YHWH?" i.e., "YHWH is incomparable"—like Elijah's, is suited to his role. Ahab's hatred[25] for him because he only speaks ill of the king also signals his reliability. He is not a sycophant and has to be brought in from the outside, showing that he is not sustained by the court. He is a prophet of woe who stands with such figures as Amos, Hosea, Micah, and Jeremiah (cf. Jer 28). He is sent for at Jehoshaphat's insistence (v. 9).

22:10-12: At the threshing floor

Micaiah's arrival in v. 15 is delayed by two scenes (vv. 10-12, 13-14), each introduced with a subject-first sentence. These further prepare for but also prolong suspense regarding what Micaiah will say. In vv. 10-12 the two kings sit enthroned in their royal robes presiding over the prophets at the city gate of Samaria. The prophets do not necessarily all speak at once, but they do voice the same message: Ahab should proceed with his plans to attack Ramoth because YHWH will give it to the king (v. 12). The ambiguity of v. 6 is not diminished by the addition of the imperative והצלח, usually rendered "be successful," since it could be interpreted as a wish, as in "be well" or, as a *Hip'îl* in the causative sense, "bring success" with an unspecified object. One of the prophets, Zedekiah son of Canaanah, surfaces not necessarily as their leader but as their answer to the

23 Doubly ironic in light of the later battle, where Ahab disguises himself while having Jehoshaphat look "like" the king of Israel to the Aramaeans (Walsh, *1 Kings*, 343).

24 Herodotus, *Histories*, 1.53.

25 Walsh (*1 Kings*, 346) prefers "spurns" or "rejects."

request for a prophet of YHWH because of his Yahwistic name. He reinforces the salvific message with a symbolic act (v. 11) reminiscent of the yoke in Jeremiah 28. Zedekiah makes horns—a symbol of strength, all the more when made of iron—that he says Ahab will use to gore Aram. Despite his use of the messenger formula, the reader is wary of Zedekiah's message because of its positive nature and because his patronymic reflects the name "Canaan."

22:13-14: Micaiah and the messenger

The second scene (vv. 13-14) is a conversation between Micaiah and the messenger sent to retrieve him, presumably the official of v. 9. The change in terminology emphasizes the role of messenger that Micaiah has as YHWH's prophet—all the more since the conversation occurs while the court prophets are prophesying and Micaiah is *en route* to court where he will counter their message. This change also adds irony to the messenger's admonition that Micaiah say what the king wants to hear. He would not dare betray his own office or his king by falsifying what he has been charged with, as he is encouraging Micaiah to do with a divine message. His admonition reveals a cynical view of prophecy that confirms the suspicion that the 400 are yes-men for Ahab. Micaiah sets the messenger straight on the nature of true prophecy: He will speak only what YHWH tells him. A similar principle is articulated by Balaam in Num 23:12, 26. The imperfect יאמר shows that Micaiah does not yet know what YHWH will tell him to say.[26]

22:15: Micaiah's initial response

This makes Micaiah's agreement with the prophets in v. 15 jarring, even more so when one discovers that Micaiah does not speak the truth. The tension between vv. 14 and 15 is part of a series of contrasts between truth and lies: Micaiah swears to tell the truth (v. 14), but then lies (v. 15); only the lie is truly a word from YHWH, who has put a *spirit of falsehood* in the mouths of the court prophets (vv. 19-23). It is not a "lying spirit," as it is sometimes translated, because its message to the king is not exactly a lie; it is just misleading. Israel does win the battle at Ramoth-Gilead. Hence the only prophet who really lies is Micaiah. Ahab recognizes his lie and demands the truth. He suspects the other prophets of lying, though their message is what he wants to hear.[27] Something about Micaiah's response in v. 15 tells Ahab that he is not speaking YHWH's truth (v. 16). He may be contrasting *truth* with the ambiguity he has heard from the other prophets and now hears from Micaiah. But there may be other reasons for his reaction. Micaiah could be mimicking them. Or maybe it is because he does not preface his words with "Thus says YHWH." Perhaps it is simply that his words are positive toward Ahab—which immediately raises the suspicions of both the king and the reader. Indeed, it calls Ahab's credibility into question because of his claim that Micaiah spoke only ill of him. This raises the question of the king's motive in sending for Micaiah in the first place. Was he trying to placate Jehoshaphat or was he really interested in getting YHWH's response?

22:16-23: Micaiah's visions

At Ahab's adjuration (v. 16) Micaiah details his vision (v. 17). Its meaning is that Israel will end up victorious but leaderless if they go to war at Ramoth. That they are scattered and shepherdless means the king will die (cf. 2 Sam 5:2), but the fact that they are allowed to return home *in peace* indicates that they will win

---

26 Šanda, *Könige* I, 494.
27 Cf. Nelson, *Kings*, 146.

the battle.[28] For Ahab the vision is confirmation that Micaiah speaks only ill of him (v. 18). Micaiah follows up with another vision explaining how Ahab was misled into going to war (vv. 19-23). He saw the heavenly host (צבא השמים) or "divine council" (cf. Isa 6 and Job 1–2), a mirror of his own context in the presence of King Ahab with the members of the court standing in attendance. This vision distinguishes Micaiah from the "prophets of Samaria" who have prophesied by Baal and threaten to lead Israel astray because they have not stood in the council (סוד) of YHWH (Jer 23:13, 18, 22). The expectation that YHWH will employ his heavenly force to fight on behalf of Israel is reversed as YHWH instead convenes the host to determine how to get rid of Ahab. He asks for a volunteer to "entice" (פתה) Ahab into going to Ramoth. Jeremiah and Ezekiel speak of YHWH enticing prophets. Jeremiah himself is enticed by YHWH into speaking the truth, which causes him to be ostracized and ridiculed (Jer 20:7), leading his enemies to seek a way to entice him in order to do him physical harm (Jer 20:10). In Ezekiel 14:9 YHWH takes credit for enticing, and the implication is that the prophet who is so enticed speaks falsehood. Likewise, in 1 Kgs 22:20-23 the Israelite prophets are led by the *spirit of falsehood* from YHWH into speaking in support of Ahab's plan. The prophets are not the object of the verb; it is rather Ahab who is enticed by the *spirit of falsehood* through the prophets. Still, the implication is that they are enticed into speaking falsehood in order to induce Ahab to destruction. The spirit (הרוח) that volunteers (v. 21) is the *spirit of falsehood* (רוח שקר) of vv. 22-23 and the spirit of YHWH in v. 24. It is the same spirit of YHWH that inspires other characters to prophesy (e.g., Num 11:25-29; 1 Sam 10:10) and thus can inspire false prophecy as well as true. The king's prophets are not false in the sense that they say what they know to be lies. On the contrary, they speak what they have received by revelation from YHWH's spirit.[29] Moreover, what they say is not technically false if Israel wins the battle at Ramoth. Their message is false because that spirit is a spirit of falsehood sent by YHWH to (mis)lead Ahab to his doom. The irony and play on meaning is rich. Lest one be tempted to feel sorry for the prophets it should be recalled that they are sycophants of the king—Ahab's prophets (vv. 22-23)—rather than spokesmen for YHWH.

22:24-28: True and false prophecy

Incensed at Micaiah's revelation, Zedekiah strikes him and mockingly asks how the *spirit of falsehood* passed from him to Micaiah (v. 24). He is claiming, in other words, that what Micaiah has just said is false. He thereby raises the question of how to distinguish true prophecy from false. Micaiah's response (v. 25) looks toward the future fulfillment of his words in accord with Deut 18:22: the prophet whose words do not come true is not from YHWH. False prophecy in this instance comes from YHWH but is misleading. Micaiah's use of the verb *see* evokes their mutual profession as prophets or "seers." He says that Zedekiah will flee to an innermost room to hide himself out of fear for his life. Exactly what disaster Micaiah foresees is not clear. It is probably not Jehu's revolt or the fall of Sama-

---

28 There is no indication that the vision is an anticipation of the fall of Samaria (*pace* Brueggemann, *Kings*, 270–71).

29 The *spirit of falsehood* is not a "non-YHWH spirit," *pace* E. Hamori ("The Spirit of Falsehood," *CBQ* 72 [2010] 16), but a hypostasis of YHWH, especially if my reading of 22:21 is correct. See the Note and Diachronic Analysis.

ria.[30] Perhaps he is envisioning Zedekiah's fear of execution when he and the other court prophets are held accountable for Ahab's death after their optimistic message about Ramoth proves untrue. Micaiah does not sway Ahab, who orders him held in prison on subsistence rations until he returns (vv. 26-27). Again there is rich irony: by ignoring the word of YHWH's true prophet, Ahab accomplishes YHWH's will. But Micaiah's true words bring him suffering, for the king will not return *in peace* (v. 28). One would like to think that Micaiah received accolades after events verified his prediction, but the story, though not precluding the possibility, tenders no hope in that direction either.

22:29-33: Ahab's disguise

Ahab believes Micaiah's prediction just enough to disguise himself and make Jehoshaphat the more conspicuous target in the battle (vv. 29-30).[31] Ironically, Ahab's anonymity makes it impossible for him to exit the battle and receive attention after he has been wounded, so that he bleeds to death.[32] Ahab's precaution is effective in countering the order of the Aramaean king to his commanders to focus on the king of Israel (v. 31). His thinking may be that the Israelites will panic and flee without their king. The order recalls YHWH's express objective for this battle to bring about Ahab's fall (v. 20), against which his precaution proves fruitless. The Aramaeans target Jehoshaphat but become aware that he is not the king of Israel when he cries out (v. 32). The force of כראות in v. 33 is not "when they saw" but "when they recognized." Something Jehoshaphat says or the way he says it makes the Aramaeans aware that he is not the king of Israel, and they withdraw from him. Exactly what that telltale feature was remains unclear, leading to proposals that include his war cry, his call to the men of Judah, and his accent.[33]

22:34: Ahab is wounded

The climactic moment of the story comes with the wounding of the king, signaled by the subject-first sentence in v. 34. The unnamed subject is presumably an Aramaean, though "friendly fire" is a possibility.[34] The key word of the verse is לתמו. The root תמם has the basic meaning "completeness, perfection." It has been understood as a reference to the bow being drawn "to its completeness." This understanding is unlikely, since a soldier would normally draw his bow to its full extent in warfare, so there would be no reason to take special note of it. Also, the noun typically has a moral quality in the HB, expressing guilelessness and innocence.[35] It does not necessarily mean that the man did not aim[36] or that his act was random or accidental. Rather, he did not know that his target was the king of Israel because of the latter's disguise. The use of the term further emphasizes YHWH's role in the event. Ahab's wounding was in fulfillment of Micaiah's prophecy. Whatever the significance of the word for "attachments" (see the Note),

The placement of the arrow

---

30 *Pace*, respectively, Šanda, *Könige* I, 46 and Würthwein, *1. Könige 17–2. Könige 25*, 260.

31 Würthwein, *1. Könige 17–2. Könige 25*, 257. Šanda (*Könige* I, 497–98) offers the opposite interpretation—Ahab sought to protect Jehoshaphat by putting him behind the line of combat. But that does not account for Ahab's disguise.

32 Klostermann, *Kings*, 390.

33 Gray, *Kings*, 454. 2 Chr 18:31-32 interprets it as a cry for help to YHWH, who then diverts the Aramaeans.

34 Buis, *Rois*, 175.

35 *HALOT*, 1742–43.

36 Cogan, *I Kings*, 494.

it refers to a small space of vulnerability, again hinting that the arrow's success was due to divine guidance.

22:35-38: Ahab's death

The wound from the arrow is serious but not immediately fatal. Ahab orders the driver to "turn your hand," i.e., to tug or pull on the reins in order to turn the horses in a particular direction (2 Kgs 9:23). But it evidently proves impossible for the chariot to exit the battle because of the intensity of the fighting (v. 35aα), and since Ahab is in disguise he does not receive special clearance as king. He is propped up in the chariot until evening, when he dies from loss of blood. The account is similar to the assassination of Joram in 2 Kgs 9:22-24: both men are shot by an arrow while riding in a chariot in connection with the fulfillment of a prophecy of Elijah. However, Ahab is wounded and lingers while Joram dies instantly. Joram also drives his own chariot and is the direct target of assassination while Ahab is a casualty of war and is thwarted by his own plan to disguise himself. The cry to return home at sunset with the death of the king (v. 36) is not a call for retreat but suggests that Israel is victorious. The narrative is less interested in the victory than in Ahab's death and the fulfillment of Elijah's oracle (21:19; 22:38). The reference to prostitutes, who are not featured in the oracle, further disparages Ahab by associating him with the lowest rung on the social ladder. It brings to mind the apostasy of Ahab, since whoredom is a metaphor for apostasy in the Bible. The bloody nature of Ahab's death anticipates Jezebel's end as well. Her blood spatters the wall (9:33) as his leaks onto the chariot floor, and her flesh is consumed by dogs (9:35) as his blood is lapped up by them. She is also guilty of her own whoredoms (2 Kgs 9:22).

22:39-40: Ahab's closing formulae

The epitaph in Ahab's closing regnal formula recalls the positives—the prosperity of his reign evinced by his ivory house, probably in Samaria, and his construction projects in different cities (v. 39). It also notes that Ahab was succeeded by his son, thus continuing the dynastic line of which he was a part. This also is a fulfillment. Ahab dies, but the overthrow of his house is deferred to the time of his son, as Elijah prophesied (21:28-29).

Diachronic Analysis

Redactional reconstructions

The general consensus that 22:1-38 is a unit changed in 1967 with Würthwein's argument for an original battle account (vv. 1-4, 29-37*) into which the prophetic story in vv. 5-28 was interpolated in stages.[37] Since then the redactional model has dominated, sometimes with complex reconstructions.[38] The greatest problem

37 E. Würthwein, "Zur Komposition von I Reg 22,1-38," in *Das ferne und nahe Wort* (Fs. L. Rost; Berlin: Töpelman, 1967). See also his *1. Könige 17–2. Könige 25*, 255–57. Cf. Long, *1 Kings*, 261.

38 See H. Schweizer, "Literarkritischer Versuch zur Erzählung von Micha ben Jimla (1 Kön 22)," *BZ* 23 (1979): 1–19; Stipp, *Elischa - Propheten - Gottesmänner*, 176–229; and Weippert, "Ahab el Campeador?". DeVries (*1 Kings*, 25–32; *Prophet Against Prophet: The Role of the Micaiah Narrative [I Kings 22] in the Development of the Early Prophetic Tradition* [Grand Rapids: Eerdmans, 1978]) takes the present narrative as a composite of two independent sources.

with Würthwein's conclusion, pointed out by later studies, was his assumption that the king of Judah was part of the older account. In fact, that account is recoverable to a large degree by excising the references to Jehoshaphat, who is part of PN's supplement.

22:1-2: Jehoshaphat's visit to Ahab

PN sets the beginning of this story on the occasion of a visit from Jehoshaphat (vv. 1-2). The mention of the king of Israel not warring with Aram (v. 1) connects to ch. 20, as does the mention of a three-year interval. This may be conventional for a relatively short period of time,[39] but it is more than enough for the king of Aram to keep his promise to return cities to Israel (20:34). In keeping with convention, Jehoshaphat is described as descending from Jerusalem. He serves as a contrast to Ahab (v. 20) and plays two specific roles in the narrative—calling for a prophet of YHWH and assisting with the scheme of disguise. The reason for his visit is not stated. It has been construed as the annual visit of a vassal.[40]

22:3-8: The king of Israel decides to retake Ramah of Gilead

The older account began with v. 3. The king of Israel's reason for launching the campaign (v. 3) was unrelated to the battles in ch. 20 and was simply because he wished to (re)take the disputed site of Ramah for Israel. His question to his servants is not a request for approval but is rhetorical and expresses his intent to attack. It is, therefore, a unilateral decision. Jehoshaphat is not among the servants and is not consulted. The verb translated *do nothing* (חשה) literally means "be silent" but is used also for physical inaction (e.g., Judg 18:9). Ramah is listed in 1 Kgs 4:13 as the capital of Solomon's district of Gilead. It was an important regional center in territory that was often disputed between Israel and Aram. The need to retake Ramah presupposes a setting much later than the Omrid dynasty when Israel had control of Ramah and was on guard there against Aramaean incursion (2 Kgs 9:14). Having decided for war, the king takes the next logical step—to consult with his prophets, who unanimously approve (v. 6*). He speaks and is addressed in the singular; Jehoshaphat is not present. In PN's revision Ahab does this only at Jehoshaphat's request (v. 5). The number 400 is PN's addition, drawn from 18:19, and invites comparison with Jezebel's 400 Asherah prophets. The implication is that the court prophets are not true prophets of YHWH and thus are not trustworthy. This is confirmed by the preferred reading of Jehoshaphat's request for a prophet of YHWH in v. 7 (without MT's עוד, "still, yet"). PN draws on ch. 18 in portraying the court prophets as unanimously affirming Ahab's plan. This unanimity is another sign of their unreliability, especially since they support the wicked king. Their positive outlook also brands them as false prophets according to Jeremiah (esp. chs. 23 and 27–28), which is another of PN's sources for this

---

39 So Cogan, *I Kings*, 489; DeVries, *1 Kings*, 266.

40 Würthwein, *1. Könige 17–2. Könige 25*, 255. In support of this construal one might point to the marriage of Jehoshaphat's son and successor, Jehoram, to Ahab's daughter, Athaliah (2 Kgs 8:18), which suggests a treaty between them, and the regnal summary for Jehoshaphat, which implies that he submitted to Israel (see on 22:44). PN may have assumed Jehoshaphat's subservience based on DtrH. Thus Jehoshaphat goes to the king of Israel; the latter's *servants* (v. 3), might include Jehoshaphat (v. 4); Jehoshaphat and his army may be *like* their counterparts in Israel because they are bound by treaty (v. 4); he refers to Ahab as "king" (v. 8); he follows Ahab's instructions that place his life in jeopardy (vv. 30-33). However, since Jehoshaphat's presence is supplementary, caution about historical matters is warranted.

narrative. Hence Ahab's response that Micaiah never prophesies anything positive about him (v. 8) is a recommendation of Micaiah as a genuine prophet.

The prophetic tale behind 22:9-17 and its PN revision

In the original tale the unanimity of the court prophets and the ambiguity of their oracle (see Synchronic Analysis) set off alarms even for the king of Israel, who sent for Micaiah (v. 9). PN set the event at the entrance to Samaria (v. 10) in order to provide an open area large enough for the 400 prophets to be engaged in the ecstatic activity that is probably part of their prophesying (1 Sam 10:5-13; 19:20-24). The verse (10) interrupts the narrative sequence of converted verb forms and is an aside while Micaiah is fetched. The scene is again reminiscent of the gathering of the Baal prophets on Mount Carmel (18:26-29). PN adapted Zedekiah's symbolic act with horns of iron in vv. 11-12 from Jeremiah 27–28.[41] His name is the same as the king's (Jer 27:1, 3, 12; 28:1); the encounter occurs at the city gate rather than the temple (Jer 28:1); Zedekiah's iron horns resemble Jeremiah's iron (first wooden) yoke. PN's version of the optimistic oracle of the prophets (v. 12) is specific in declaring victory for the king of Israel over Aram (contrast v. 6). He uses the singular, referring to Ahab alone (also in vv. 11, 13) in response to v. 6. In v. 13 the *official* (סריס) from the older story (v. 9) becomes a *messenger* (מלאך). The conversation between him and Micaiah (vv. 13-14) also has roots in Jeremiah: Implicit in the messenger's plea to Micaiah is the understanding that the 400 court prophets control the content of their oracles and tailor it to please their hearers. Micaiah's response resembles Jeremiah's confession (Jer 20:8-9) that YHWH's word is like a fire inside him that he cannot contain but must proclaim.

The original story picks up again in vv. 15-17, where Micaiah, summoned in v. 9, arrives. The king asks him the same question as he did the court prophets: *Should I go to Ramah to war?* He speaks again in the singular, and Micaiah responds in kind because Jehoshaphat is not in the story. Micaiah's answer is essentially the same as the court prophets':

v. 15: עלה והצלח ונתן יהוה ביד המלך
v. 12: עלה רמת גלעד והצלח ונתן יהוה ביד המלך

The answer is jarring after his promise to speak only what YHWH says to him (v. 14) and is an indication of the different authors of the two verses. Still, in the original story there is something in what Micaiah says or the way he says it that makes the king suspect he is not getting the real story, and he places Micaiah under oath, compelling him to speak "only truth" (רק־אמת), that is, "the truth, the whole truth, and nothing but the truth" in YHWH's name (v. 16). With that Micaiah reveals his vision of the Israelite army without a king (= *shepherd*, v. 17; cf. 2 Sam 5:2; 7:7; Isa 44:28; Ezek 37:24). Once more there is no indication of Jehoshaphat's presence. The soldiers are scattered because they are in battle. This is why YHWH says that each should return home (from fighting). The vision means that the king will be killed if he goes to war. YHWH's instruction to go home *in peace* implies that they have won the battle. The death of a king in a battle that is won is unusual and may be part of the reason that the king of Israel made the decision to go ahead with his campaign.

41 For the interpretation of this act as one of symbolic magic based on his interpretation of iconographic images see Keel, *Wirkmächtige Siegeszeichen*, 125–34.

22:18-28: PN's addition

In PN's revision (vv. 18-28) Ahab takes Micaiah's warning as proof of Micaiah's grudge against him (vv. 8, 18). The animosity escalates in Micaiah's second vision (vv. 19-23), where it proves to be YHWH who is against Ahab rather than Micaiah. The vision borrows from Jeremiah's distinction between the judgment prophet who has stood in YHWH's council and the more popular prophets of optimism who have not (Jer 23). It shows how YHWH is using the court prophets to lure (פתה used only here in Kings) Ahab to his death. Micaiah sees YHWH surrounded by the "host of heaven" (צבא השמים). This expression is typically used in Dtr literature for celestial bodies worshiped by non-Israelites (Deut 4:19; 17:3; 2 Kgs 17:16; 21:5; 23:4; Jer 8:2; 19:13; 33:22). Here, however, it refers to a deliberative body, the "divine council," like that described in Isaiah 6 and Job 1–2.[42] As in Isaiah 6, YHWH seeks a volunteer to carry out a mission, that of inducing Ahab to go to war at Ramah so that he will *fall*, i.e., be killed. After various council members make proposals that YHWH rejects as ineffective, a particular spirit volunteers. YHWH's question to this spirit, following G^L, is not "how?" but *by whom?* (v. 21). It is a question of personal agency as in 20:14. The spirit's answer is *by you*, i.e., by YHWH himself. That is, the *spirit of falsehood* from YHWH will inspire the king's prophets to mislead him into thinking he will be successful (vv. 21, 23). And this tactic, YHWH says, will work (v. 22). The warning about lying prophets leading a king to his death is again adapted from Jeremiah 27 (vv. 9-10, 14). It differs in making YHWH the ultimate source of the deception for the purpose of destroying Ahab (contrast Jer 27:15).

1 Kgs 22:24-28: Micaiah pays the price

Micaiah's forthrightness costs him. First, Zedekiah resorts to violence in his retort, striking Micaiah on the jaw and calling him a liar, in effect, by asking rhetorically (and sarcastically) how the *spirit of falsehood* transferred from him (Zedekiah) to Micaiah for the latter to relate his vision (v. 24). Micaiah responds that Zedekiah will finally *see* the truth when the disaster he (Micaiah) has foreseen transpires and Zedekiah is held responsible (v. 25). The mention of hiding in an inner room reminds one of Ben-Hadad in 20:30. Then Ahab takes Micaiah's freedom, ordering him imprisoned on subsistence rations *until I come in peace.* He is returned to Amon, the שר־העיר or highest municipal authority (*mayor*), whose duties included the incarceration of political prisoners.[43] The verb *return* suggests that Micaiah was already in Amon's custody, though he was not mentioned before (v. 9). The present order to imprison Micaiah is given specifically to Joash the *king's son.* While there has been some contention that the latter title designated an administrative office, the evidence favors the interpretation that it indicates royal descent.[44] The other instances of the expression "son(s)/daugh-

---

42 For comparisons, especially form-critical, of 1 Kgs 22 and Isa 6 see R. Knierim, "The Vocation of Isaiah," *VT* 18 (1968): 47–68, and M. Tsevat, "The Throne Vision of Isaiah," in *The Meaning of the Book of Job and Other Biblical Studies: Essays on the Literature and Religion of the Hebrew Bible* (New York/Dallas: Ktav/Institute for Jewish Studies, 1980): 155–76. The latter (p. 175) points out the commissioning scene that the two texts share in common (1 Kgs 22:20-22; Isa 6:8-9): YHWH's search for an agent, an individual who volunteers, and confirmation of the volunteer as the agent.

43 Fox, *In the Service of the King*, 150–58.

44 See the review of Fox, *In the Service of the King*, 43–53, and especially her discussion on p. 45.

ter(s) of the king" in Samuel–Kings (2 Sam 9:11; 13:4, 18, 23-36; 18:12, 20; 1 Kgs 1:9-25; 2 Kgs 9:34; 10:6-13; 11:2, 4, 12; 15:5) are to be taken literally, and there is no text in the HB where any bearer of this title can be shown not to be in the royal line. This passage, along with a handful of others, suggests that the king's son could be allocated a judicial role. The only reason for taking the present instance as an exception is the assumption that Joash would have to be Ahab's son. But we have seen that the identification of this story with Ahab is secondary. Joash's name fits with the theory that the story originally concerned a king in the Jehu dynasty. It does not fit with the end of 2 Kings 13 exactly, however, since there the king is Joash rather than his father. It is not a remnant of the original story but the result of PN's adaptation of Joash's name from the story's original setting for his own creative purpose, just as he did with Zedekiah's name. Micaiah's parting words (v. 28) articulate a principal criterion for discerning true prophecy—whether it comes true. As with so much of this story, this criterion accords with an idea laid out in Jeremiah (28:9; cf. Deut 18:22). Micaiah's willingness to endure imprisonment and suffering for his message might be seen as a further attestation to its veracity.

22:29-38: The prophetic tale of the king's death

In vv. 29-31 we rejoin the older story. The king of Israel proceeds to Ramah but disguises himself before entering battle in order to avoid Micaiah's prediction. Thus v. 30 presupposes v. 17.[45] PN added Jehoshaphat to these verses. Note the singular ויעל in v. 29 and the focus of the king of Aram on the king of Israel in v. 31 with no mention of the king of Judah. While the use of a body double is attested among Neo-Assyrian kings, the use of another king like Jehoshaphat for such a purpose is not, and nothing like the ritual associated with the Assyrian practice is mentioned in 1 Kings 22.[46] It is also not clear that Ahab is using Jehoshaphat as a substitute, as he simply tells Jehoshaphat to dress in his own royal robes. The G^{BL} reading, which has Jehoshaphat dress in Ahab's robes rather than his own, supports the substitution theory but is a secondary change (see the Note). The disguise proves successful to the extent that the Aramaeans are unable to target the Israelite king as they have been ordered to do (v. 31). In the older story this was the point of לתמו in v. 34. Without specifically targeting the king as such—hence in violation of his orders—an Aramaean archer wounded him, so that his disguise did not in the end save him. The lack of awareness or intent or aim on the part of the archer in v. 34 and the placement of the arrow in a rare spot unprotected by armor show that its success comes from divine manipulation. The king ordered his driver to take him out of the battle, but the driver was unable to comply because the king was in disguise and the battle intense (v. 35). He remained in the chariot propped up and losing blood until he died. He was then taken to Samaria and buried there (v. 37aβ).

---

45 *Pace* Schweizer ("Literarkritischer Versuch"), whose reconstructed *Grundtext* does not include v. 17. Without it, though, there is nothing in the text to suggest that the king is singled out for death while his army thrives.

46 See S. Parpola, *Letters from Assyrian Scholars to the Kings Esarhaddon and Assurbanipal* (AOAT 5/2; Neukirchen-Vluyn: Neukirchener Verlag, 1982), xxii–xxxii, who observes that the substitute was a person regarded as unimportant or condemned to die, that the real king stayed close to the palace during the substitution period, and that the substitute was executed afterwards. None of these practices is paralleled in 1 Kgs 22.

Similarities of the prophetic tale to 2 Kgs 8:28–9:28

The king's wounding in this older story is similar to the story of Joram of Israel's death in 2 Kgs 8:28–9:28, especially 9:15, 23-24.[47] They share the setting in Ramah in battle with the Aramaeans and the wounding of the king of Israel by arrow(s) while he is in his chariot. Both 1 Kgs 22:35 and 2 Kgs 9:23-24 describe the death of the king of Israel on his chariot; both contain similar descriptions of where he was wounded (between pieces of armor/shoulder blades); both use the expression "turn the hand(s)" for altering the course of the chariot. The similarities are general and may simply reflect shared battle motifs. The older story in 22:1-38 was a prophetic one. It supplied Israel's third victory predicted by Elisha and showed the futility of the king's attempt to escape his fate as foreseen by the prophet.[48]

PN's revised version

In PN's version the Aramaeans turn their attack on Jehoshaphat, mistaking him for the king of Israel (v. 32). It is only when he cries out that they recognize that he is not the king of Israel (v. 33). Exactly how his cry signals his identity remains a mystery and is due to divine intervention according to the reading adopted for v. 32bβ (see the Note). Nowhere is the contrast between Ahab and Jehoshaphat greater; Yhwh steps in to help Jehoshaphat but is out to kill Ahab. Ahab can elude humans but not Yhwh. PN interpolated vv. 35bβ (from בערב on) through 37aα by *Wiederaufnahme* to match v. 17 (the king is dead, the people go home in peace) and added v. 38 making explicit the fulfillment of Elijah's oracle in 21:19, indicating clearly that Ahab did not escape retribution for his sins. He inserted the entire story, along with ch. 20, into DtrH's account between Ahab's repentance (21:27-29) following the anti-dynastic oracle (21:20-22, 24) and his closing regnal formulae (22:39-40).

22:29-30: DtrH's closing formulae for Ahab

In DtrH's regnal formulae Ahab was remembered for his building projects and his ivory house. Both notes receive affirmation from archaeology, which has found evidence of extensive building during the ninth century at the Israelite cities of Samaria, Dan, Hazor, Megiddo, and Tirzah.[49] The "ivory house" probably refers to Ahab's palace in Samaria, which was richly decorated with ivory plaques and furniture inlaid with ivory. This, at least, is a reasonable interpretation of the 500 or so ivory objects found in Samaria, mostly in the royal precinct.[50] The motifs on these ivories suggest manufacture in northern Syria and Phoenicia and indicate cultural connections between Ahab and these areas.[51]

The notice in v. 40 that Ahab lay down with his forebears has been taken since 1923 as assuming a peaceful death.[52] If this interpretation is correct it is a

---

47 Cf. Miller, "The Elisha Cycle and the Accounts of the Omride Wars," 445–46 and Whitley, "Deuteronomic Presentation," 148–49.

48 I agree with Schweizer's *Grundtext* ("Literarkritischer Versuch") up to v. 17, which he sees as secondary, instead of Micaiah's report in vv. 19-28. The latter, however, identify the king as Ahab and assume strong animosity between him and Micaiah, both of which must stem from PN's revision.

49 See Miller and Hayes, *History*, 300–14; A. Mazar, *Archaeology of the Land of the Bible, 10,000–586 B.C.E.* (New York: Doubleday, 1990), 406–15.

50 J. W. Crowfoot and G. M. Crowfoot, *Early Ivories from Samaria, 1938* (London: Palestine Exploration Fund, 1938); B. B. Schmidt, "Ivory," *NIDB* 3:165–66.

51 See R. D. Barnett, *Ancient Ivories in the Middle East and Adjacent Countries* (Qedem 14; Jerusalem: Institute of Archaeology, 1982).

52 Hölscher, "Das Buch der Könige," 185; also B. Alfrink, "L'expression שכב עם אבותיו," *OTS* 2 (1943): 109–10.

strong indication that DtrH was unaware of the story of Ahab's death in battle in 22:1-38 and that therefore the story was a later insertion. However, Suriano has challenged this interpretation, arguing that it signifies undisrupted dynastic succession. His view has much to recommend it, including explaining how the expression fits in its broader social and cultural environment.[53] This means that the occurrence of the expression here in 22:40 cannot be used as an argument for the post-DtrH insertion of the story of "Ahab's" death in battle; that case must be and has been made on other grounds.

Synthesis

Judgment prophecy

Like 1 Kings 17–19; 21; and 20, 1 Kgs 22:1-38 is about judgment prophecy. It was composed and inserted into the DtrH framework immediately before the concluding formulae for Ahab in 22:39-40 in order to link Ahab's death with Elijah's prophecy in 21:19 as its fulfillment.

The original prophetic story

The older stage of the story was about a king of Israel in the Jehu dynasty who failed to heed a prophet's warning that an attack he planned to launch against Aram would cost him his life. The king sought to avoid the forecast by the ruse of disguise, but it did not work. YHWH reveals the future to his prophets and his will is inescapable; it cannot be fooled. There is no indication in the story at this level that the king was wicked or that he had anything against the prophet, or vice-versa. He was just self-deluded and perhaps overconfident. No king's will or plan supersedes YHWH's. Nor is the story about incontrovertible Fate, as Josephus (*Ant.* 8.409, 413) has it. The king has choices and makes his own decisions. He decides to go to war *incognito*. To that extent he is responsible for his own fate.[54]

The PN version

The Prophetic Narrator turned this story into a vindictive fulfillment of Elijah's oracle in 21:19 so that Ahab would not go unpunished for his sins despite the postponement of the judgment against his house in DtrH. At the same time the story that emerged has a great deal to say about the nature of true versus false prophecy. YHWH and his council determine what happens to humans on earth, and he reveals it through his servants the prophets. Yet both true and false prophecy can emanate from YHWH. Not every prophet who claims a word from YHWH speaks truth, because YHWH can endow prophets with false oracles. True prophets, in fact, are the distinct minority. So how does one distinguish true

53 Suriano, *The Politics of Dead Kings*, esp. 71–97. His view accounts for the use of the expression for Amaziah, who was assassinated (2 Kgs 14:22), and of its cognate, "gathered to his forebears in peace," for Josiah, who was killed (2 Kgs 22:20). In addition, this interpretation makes clear that the differences in usage of the expression for Northern and Southern kings are unrelated to scribal or burial practices differing in the two countries but rather stem from the fact that dynastic succession was the norm in Judah, while overthrow and dynastic change occurred with some regularity in Israel.

54 See J. M. Hamilton, "Caught in the Nets of Prophecy? The Death of King Ahab and the Character of God," *CBQ* 56 (1994), 651–53.

prophecy from false? The interplay in 1 Kings 22 between truth and falsehood is complex because answering this question is not easy. The court prophets do not lie outright, especially if Israel is victorious. But their message, which is misleading, emanates from YHWH's own spirit, so they themselves have been misled. Micaiah is the only prophet who tells what he knows to be a baldfaced lie (v. 15), even if he does so in mocking imitation of his counterparts.

Criteria for determining true and false prophecy

Our story offers several criteria for distinguishing true and false prophecy based especially on Jeremiah 27–28. First and most obvious, the oracles of true prophets come to pass. This consideration underlies the Jeremiah chapters, and Micaiah articulates as much when he says that if the king of Israel returns in peace YHWH has not spoken through him (v. 28). The final proof of Micaiah's veracity is Ahab's death despite his best efforts to evade it by disguise. The arrow that finds him does so not from human aim or intention but at YHWH's direction. A second criterion is that the true prophet is solitary. We have seen this quality already with Elijah, who was a loner. Like Jeremiah, who stands over against King Zedekiah's prophets as well as his diviners, dreamers, soothsayers, and sorcerers (27:9), Micaiah is alone in his message. He stands against the tide of the court prophets and can only speak what YHWH has given him, whether it accords with the majority or not (vv. 13-14), at least when he speaks in YHWH's name (v. 15). However, Jeremiah and Micaiah have the tradition of judgment prophecy from antiquity on their side (Jer 27:8). Micaiah is meant to be one of Jeremiah's earliest predecessors. This leads to the third and fourth criteria, which go together. The true prophet is usually at odds with the king and typically prophesies doom. Although there are counterexamples especially in the Elisha tales, these two criteria are well illustrated elsewhere in the Former and Latter Prophets. Beginning with Samuel (1 Sam 13; 15) a major function of prophets is to monitor and condemn kings for their abuses of power and violations of religious principles and practices. It is certainly a feature of the Latter Prophets, beginning with their eighth-century representatives (Hosea, Amos, Micah, Isaiah), to forecast destruction. Jeremiah 26 cites a specific example from Micah, Micaiah's namesake. The destruction of Israel and Judah in Kings was verification of their prophecies (cf. 2 Kgs 17:13) in accord with the first criterion.[55] It could have been avoided by listening to the prophets (Jer 26:19-20). Thus the true prophet, Micaiah, predicts the demise of the king of Israel while the court prophets tout his military success. A fifth criterion is related to these two and is hinted at in v. 27, where the king orders Micaiah imprisoned. True prophets are often persecuted because they speak truth to power and go against the majority optimism. Jeremiah 26:20-23 cites an example in Uriah son of Shemaiah, and Jeremiah himself well illustrates the principle (e.g., Jer 37–38). The final criterion is the most important but the hardest to verify. The true prophet has stood in the divine council to receive his commission as the messenger of the heavenly king and court. Micaiah embodies the principle articulated by Jeremiah (23:18, 22) and exemplified also by Isaiah (ch. 6) and Ezekiel (ch. 1).[56]

---

55 "Israel's disastrous history is the yardstick of prophecy" (Fritz, *Kings*, 220).

56 On the significance of this scene for verification in its broad ideological context see Chavel, "The Face of God and the Etiquette of Eye Contact," esp. 35–36.

The characters of YHWH and Ahab

In the course of its lessons about prophecy this story gives glimpses into the characters of the two main, non-prophetic characters, YHWH and Ahab. YHWH reacts to and interacts with the human characters. YHWH's will is irresistible, but he does not always play fair; he employs deceit (שקר) to lure Ahab to his death. As for Ahab, he sustains his image as Israel's most villainous king. He refuses to trust the word of YHWH's true prophet despite knowing deep down that Micaiah speaks the truth, as suggested both by the king's statement in 22:16 and his donning a disguise. He punishes the messenger by putting Micaiah in prison for telling him an inconvenient truth. To the extent that he placed Jehoshaphat at risk in his attempt to avoid that truth he is a coward. His disguise suggests that he is suspicious of his own prophets. If he had accepted the reliability of the prophetic word and repented he might have induced YHWH to change his mind again (21:29). The threats of biblical prophecy are conditioned on the response of its audience,[57] something Hezekiah's response to Micah (Jer 26:18-19) again illustrates. In this respect Ahab typifies Israel and Judah: He refuses to give full heed to YHWH's prophets; his repentance is minimal. His wickedness exhausts YHWH's patience. His doom is sealed.

57 Tsevat ("Throne Vision," 173) makes the point that Micaiah's revelation of his vision in vv. 19-22 keeps open the possibility of salvation for repentance.

The Reign of Jehoshaphat (1 Kings 22:41-51)

Text

[DtrH's sources; DtrH]

41 Jehoshaphat son of Asa began to reign over Judah in the fourth year of Ahab king of Israel. 42 He was thirty-five years old when he became king, and he reigned twenty-five years in Jerusalem. His mother's name was Azubah daughter of Shilhi. 43 He walked in the way of Asa his father, not turning from it, doing what Yhwh considered right, 44 except that the cultic installations were not removed; the people were still slaughtering animals and burning food offerings at the cultic installations. 45 Jehoshaphat sued the king of Israel for peace. 47 He removed the remainder of the cultic functionaries who had been left in the land in the time of Asa his father. 48 There was no king in Edom; a prefect was king. 49 Jehoshaphat made Tarshish-style ships to sail to Ophir for gold, but they did not go because the ships were wrecked at Ezion-Geber. 50 Then Ahaziah Ahab's son said to Jehoshaphat, "Let them send my servants with your servants in ships." But Jehoshaphat refused. 46 The rest of Jehoshaphat's affairs, including his power which he demonstrated, are of course written on the scroll of the chronicles of the kings of Judah. 51 Jehoshaphat lay down with his forebears and was buried with his forebears in the city of David. Then his son Jehoram reigned in his place.

Textual Notes

G^{BL} relate the account of Jehoshaphat's reign in 16:28a-h as part of OG's adjustment of the MT chronology, which has Jehoshaphat accede to the throne of Judah before Omri died.

41 **Jehoshaphat son of Asa began to reign over Judah in the fourth year of Ahab king of Israel**: So MT. G^{BL} have a year-first format and date the beginning of Jehoshaphat's reign to the eleventh year of Omri (Zimri in G^{B}). Jehoshaphat means "Yhwh has judged." The phrase *over Judah* is lacking in G^{B} due to haplography (ἐπὶ ... ἔτει).

42 **he was thirty-five years old**: MT and G^{L} (16:28a) attest Jehoshaphat's name in different places, suggesting it was added.

Azubah: So MT (עזובה). G^{BL} (16:28a): Γαβουζα, a metathesis. The meaning "abandoned"[1] would be appropriate for a person who was orphaned or sold as a child but odd for a Queen Mother, though it might indicate that she was a concubine.

---

1 Noth, *Personennamen*, 173.

Another proposal is "sweet," based on Arabic *'adab*.[2] It might also derive from *'db*, "prepare, arrange," found in Ugaritic (*KTU* 1.4.5.14, 30, 37; 1.12.2.26) and in Neh 3:8. Nothing more is known about Shilhi.[3]

43 **in the way**: So G^{BL} (16:28b), 2 Chr 20:32. MT + *all*, which occurs in some instances of the formula (16:26; 2 Kgs 22:2) but not others (1 Kgs 15:26, 34; 16:2, 19; 22:53; 2 Kgs 8:18, 27; 16:3).

44 **except that the cultic installations were not removed**: So MT as in 2 Kgs 12:4; 14:4; 15:4, 35a. 2 Chr 20:33: אך הבמות לא־סרו. OG typically reflects the *Hip'il* singular הסיר (so G^L 16:28b). G^B has the plural under the influence of the following two plural verbs.[4]

the people were still slaughtering animals and burning food offerings: The verbs מזבחים and מקטרים are used for a single sacrificial act. קטר is denominative and does not refer to burning incense as often assumed but to making food offerings smoke.[5] The expression with the two participles (2 Kgs 14:4; 15:4, 35) outlines the entire rite of animal sacrifice performed on the *bāmôt*.

cultic installations: The usual translation of *bāmôt* as *high places* is misleading, since the conception of these as hilltop shrines is wrong.[6] So is the competing idea that they were open-air platforms or podiums. The basic meaning of במה is anatomical (upper torso). It becomes a technical term for cultic installations mostly in urban centers that were entered for the purpose of ritual slaughter and sacrifice.

45-46 **Jehoshaphat ... Jehoshaphat's affairs**: So MT, G^L (16:28c). G^B (16:28c) reflects haplography occasioned by the repetition of Jehoshaphat's name, after which the relative (ἃ) was added in order to make sense of the remaining text.[7]

47-50 These verses in both their MT and OG locations (16:28d-f) are out of place, since they interrupt Jehoshaphat's closing regnal formulae.[8] They must have preceded the beginning of the formulae in 22:46 in DtrH. The translation restores them to their presumed original location immediately before Jehoshaphat's closing formula (22:46). They were probably lost from this place by haplography occasioned by the repetition of ויתר (*the rest of*) at the beginning of 22:47, 46 and subsequently put back into the text in the wrong location.

47 **cultic functionaries**: Lit. *holy* or *devoted one*, a collective, referring to individuals involved in some sort of ritual activity to Yhwh or other deities. The rendering *cult prostitutes* referring to persons of both sexes "who were 'set apart' for the immoral rites of the Canaanites carried on within the precincts of their sanctuaries"[9] should

---

2 Šanda (*Könige* I, 502). Montgomery (*Kings*, 347) points to *'dbt* as a South Arabic clan name.

3 Patronymics are supplied for Queen Mothers in the Judahite regnal formulae from Jotham on but are present in those of earlier kings only in cases of famous mothers: Maacah (1 Kgs 15:2, 10) and Athaliah (2 Kgs 8:26).

4 Shenkel, *Chronology*, 55–56. The other exception to the usual OG rendering is 2 Kgs 12:4.

5 D. V. Edelman, "The Meaning of *qiṭṭēr*," *VT* 35 (1985): 395–405.

6 Barrick, "The Word BMH in the Old Testament;" "What Do We Really Know about "High Places?" 50–57; and "The Funerary Character of 'High Places' in Ancient Palestine: A Reassessment," *VT* 25 (1975), 565. See also Vaughn, *Meaning of "bama" in the Old Testament*.

7 Contrast Turkanik, *Of Kings and Reigns*, 174, who explains the omission as deliberate.

8 Vv. 47-50 are absent from the G^B of ch. 22 perhaps because the *kaige* recension in this chapter was focused only on the regnal formulae and/or because the notice about there being no king in Edom at the time was in conflict with MT's chronology. See Shenkel, *Chronology*, 58–59, 102–104.

9 Burney, *Notes*, 193.

be abandoned absent evidence of ritualized prostitution in the Bible and ancient Near East.[10] See the Diachronic Analysis.

48 **Edom**: So MT (22:48). G^B (16:28e): Συρια = ארם, reflecting ר/ד confusion in OG's *Vorlage.*

prefect: Reading נציב based on OG and OL, νασειβ and *nasibus* in lieu of MT's *Nip'al* participle נצב.

49 **made**: So MT *Qere* (עשה) and other witnesses. MT *Ketib*: עשר, *ten.*

Tarshish-style ships: Vessels of the style and size used for the Phoenicians' travel to their colony at Tartessus in southern Spain. Their substantial cargo space maximized profit over long-distance journeys.

Ophir: G^B (16:28f): Σωφείρ. The location of Ophir is uncertain. The chief candidates include locations in Arabia, Africa, and India. Some have even suggested that it was not a location but a kind of gold.

the ships: So G^{BL} (16:28f). In MT the article was misconstrued as the feminine ending on נשבר.

Ezion-Geber: Identification uncertain. Clearly in the vicinity of Aqaba and Elat; additional candidates (besides these two modern cities) include Tell el-Kheleifeh and the island of Jezirat Faraun.

50 **Ahaziah, Ahab's son**: So MT (22:50; cf. 2 Chr 20:35-37). G^{BL}: *king of Israel*, motivated by the chronological revision in the OG.

Let them send: So MT, an impersonal. G^{BL} 16:28g: *Let me send.* Either reading is possible.

my servants with your servants: So MT, G^L. G^B (16:28g): *your servants and my servants.*

46 **his power**: So MT, G^B 22:46. G^{BL} OL 16:28c: *all his power.*

which he demonstrated: G^B 16:28c, MT 22:46 + *and which he fought.* The plus is absent from G^B 22:46 and may be a hexaplaric addition.[11]

of the chronicles of the kings of Judah: G^B 22:46 has λόγων Ιωσαφατ, *[the book of the] deeds of Jehoshaphat*, as opposed to the more usual λόγων τῶν ἡμερῶν τῶν βασιλέων Ιουδα = דברי הימים למלכי יהודה. It may have resulted from a vertical dittography of דברי יהושפט.

51 **Jehoshaphat**: Lacking in the *kaige* recension (G^B 22:51), which resumes at this point.

and was buried with his forebears: Lost from the OG (G^B) in 16:28h by haplography triggered by the repetition of *with his forebears.*

David: So G^{BL}. MT (22:51): + *his father.*

Jehoram: The name, meaning "YHWH is exalted" is the same as its short form *Joram.* The short form is used for Jehoram of Judah only in 2 Kgs 8:21, 23, although it was probably the older and predominated in pre-exilic times, with the longer form being adopted later for its more official or sacral ring.[12] For the sake of convenience *Joram* will be used for the king of Israel and *Jehoram* for the king of Judah except in the Translation, which will reflect the version used in Hebrew.

---

10 P. A. Bird, "The End of the Male Cult Prostitute: A Literary-Historical and Sociological Analysis of Hebrew *QĀDĒŠ-QĔDĒŠÎM*," in *Congress Volume. Cambridge 1995* (ed. J. A. Emerton; VTSup 66; Leiden: Brill, 1997), 37–80; T. Frymer-Kensky, *In the Wake of the Goddesses: Women, Culture, and the Biblical Transformation of Pagan Myth* (New York: The Free Press, 1992), 199–202; J. H. Tigay, *Deuteronomy* (JPS Torah Commentary; Philadelphia/ Jerusalem: JPS, 1996), 480–81.

11 Shenkel, *Chronology*, 56.

12 See S. Norin, "Jô-Namen und J^{e}hô-Namen," *VT* 29 (1979): 87–97.

Synchronic Analysis

An ambivalent impression

Despite his righteousness—and he is painted as one of the best kings of Judah—the account of Jehoshaphat's reign is relatively brief. His name, "YHWH has judged," stresses the divine judgment that has just fallen on Ahab. The account of his reign provides welcome relief from the seemingly unrelenting sequence of evil Israelite kings, etching the contrast between Israel and Judah in clear relief. Nevertheless, the primary impression left on the reader who examines the Jehoshaphat account closely is one of ambivalence. This impression begins with the evaluation in his opening regnal formulae (v. 43). He was righteous, following the example of his father Asa, who followed the example of David (15:11). This is in contrast to the kings of Israel who followed the example of Jeroboam, who *made Israel sin.* Jehoshaphat has a substantial reign, if not quite as substantial as his father's (25 years vs. 41 years). At the same time, he does not remove the non-centralized cultic installations (במות) as one might expect a truly righteous king to do, but allows illicit cultic activity at those sanctuaries to continue. Jehoshaphat is not unique in this respect. Asa did not remove them either (15:14), but the text adds that his heart was true to YHWH. The same is not said for Jehoshaphat, leaving the reader to wonder whether he fell short of his father's example. On the other hand he did exterminate the cultic functionaries (קדש) whom his father had left in Judah, so perhaps he excelled Asa in some respects. The thorn of the *bāmôt* is a motif that runs throughout the book of Kings beginning with Solomon (1 Kgs 3:2). Jehoshaphat is one of a series of Judahite kings—in addition to Asa, Jehoash (2 Kgs 12:3), Amaziah (2 Kgs 14:4), Azariah (2 Kgs 15:4), and Jotham (2 Kgs 15:35)—who are assessed as basically righteous except for their failure to remove the *bāmôt*. He is, therefore, a second-tier king. He is one of the best of that class, along with his father, but he is a step below Hezekiah and Josiah, who did remove or defile the במות (2 Kgs 18:4, 22; 23:8, 13, 19).

Ambivalence in the details

The ambivalence about Jehoshaphat continues in the details about his reign. According to 22:45 Jehoshaphat sued for peace with the king of Israel. The namelessness of the king of Israel suggests that they are all the same, i.e., evil, as far as the narrative is concerned. The root (שלם), with its connotations of peace and reminiscence of Solomon, at first seems to cast a favorable light on Jehoshaphat. He is mending the history of frayed relations between Israel and Judah dating back to their division into two kingdoms (14:30; 15:6, 7, 16, 32). But the form of the verb used here often indicates submission. His regnal formulae (22:46) mention his *power*, and in 22:50 he refuses King Ahaziah's proposal for a joint maritime venture. Still, the verb at least hints at submission on Jehoshaphat's part. It can even be read as a continuation of the reservation about Jehoshaphat's righteousness expressed in the foregoing verse, paraphrasing: "Jehoshaphat did what was right except he did not remove the high places and he sued the king of Israel for peace (by giving in to him)." So rendered, such a statement amounts to an accusation that by suing for peace Jehoshaphat was acknowledging the legitimacy of Israel's apostate cultic practices. This marks another contrast with Asa, who constantly warred with Baasha (15:16, 32).

Jehoshaphat and his predecessors

Verses 46-50 invite comparison between Jehoshaphat and his predecessors. As mentioned, he improves on Asa's administration by doing away with the *cultic functionaries* (22:47). The dominance over Edom that is implied by Jehoshaphat's control of the Red Sea port (22:48-50) recalls the administrations of both David (2 Sam 8:13-14) and Solomon (1 Kgs 11:14-22). The attempted journey to Ophir to fetch gold reminds one of Solomon's expeditions for the same purpose (1 Kgs 9:26-28; 10:22). The entire venture with the ships at Ezion-Geber is made possible because, like David and Solomon, Jehoshaphat dominated Edom. But if Jehoshaphat's effort to recapture some of Solomon's glory is commendable,[13] the mission's failure highlights how far he is from attaining it. The precise reason for the failure is unclear. However, the force of *then* at the beginning of v. 50 indicates that the offer from the king of Israel was in response to the shipwreck.[14] This in turn suggests that the cause of the shipwreck was the lack of maritime expertise on the part of Jehoshaphat's servants and Jehoshaphat's own failure to acquire individuals with such expertise, as Solomon did.[15] Again there is ambivalence. The invitation to compare Jehoshaphat with David and Solomon is a compliment, but Jehoshaphat falls short. At least he has the strength and the good sense to decline the proposal of the king of Israel. Even here, though, there is ambivalence. Given the implication that his venture failed because of lack of expertise, his refusal of help that might bring wealth could be viewed as foolish and stubborn, calling his competence into question. This would seem to be the case all the more if he was motivated by greed and did not want to share a lucrative opportunity, since without ships the opportunity was worthless. On the other hand, if his decision was grounded in religious considerations he was right to avoid dealings with his wicked Northern neighbor. But that must then be weighed against the treaty he made linking the two kingdoms together. Furthermore, on two occasions Jehoshaphat does go on joint ventures with the king of Israel, even placing his army at the disposal of his peer (1 Kgs 22:4; 2 Kgs 3:7). Granted, in 1 Kings 22 Jehoshaphat is the one who presses for an inquiry through a prophet of YHWH, and in 2 Kgs 3:14 Jehoshaphat is the only reason why YHWH responds to the king of Israel. So Jehoshaphat is faithful to YHWH, but his cooperation with Israel is suspect. Ambivalence.

Diachronic Analysis

22:41-42: Jehoshaphat in the integrated king list

The Jehoshaphat account is from DtrH, who drew on the integrated king list for the chronological information in vv. 41-42. That DtrH used sources is apparent from the differences in regnal formulae for the kings of Judah as opposed to those for the kings of Israel. Two such differences are evident in the opening formulae

---

13 House, *Kings*, 242.

14 Walsh (*1 Kings*, 366) asserts that אז here does not necessarily imply subsequent action (i.e., that it was after the shipwreck when the king of Israel made his proposal), but only indicates approximate time. This is the case with אז plus imperfect used for past action, but not for אז plus perfect, which "always marks a consecution in an uninterrupted narration of past actions or events" (Rabinowitz, "*'az* Followed by Imperfect," 54).

15 Würthwein, *1.Könige 1–16*, 264.

of Jehoshaphat after the series of opening formulae for Northern kings in this chapter. These are the king's age at accession and the name of the king's mother (v. 42).[16] Except for the evaluation in v. 43 the rest of the information about Jehoshaphat could go back to a source like an elaborated king list. Even so, it was reconfigured by DtrH.

The *bāmôt*, which constitute DtrH's single reservation about Jehoshaphat (vv. 43-44) in his otherwise positive evaluation, were temples or shrines to YHWH outside of Jerusalem. They may have enjoyed royal sponsorship and shared priestly personnel with the national shrines such as those at Bethel and Jerusalem. DtrH seems to have distinguished between the *bāmôt* sanctioned by kings of Judah and those erected and maintained by the kings of Israel as part of the "sin of Jeroboam" (1 Kgs 12:31-32). The ones in Judah conflicted with the principle of cultic centralization and should have been removed by its kings. The ones in Israel constituted a much more serious offense; the *bāmôt* at Dan and Bethel were idolatrous as well as a violation of cultic centralization, according to DtrH.[17] The royal houses of Israel are annihilated for their shrines, while Jehoshaphat and others like him in Judah can still be judged righteous despite the *bāmôt*.

22:43-44: The *bāmôt*

Jehoshaphat made peace with the king of Israel (v. 45), who was evidently not identified in DtrH's source. The lack of specificity facilitated the displacement of the Jehoshaphat account in the OG. The *Hip'îl* of שלם in similar contexts in the HB often has the sense of surrender or submit (Deut 20:12; 1 Chr 19:19 [also with עם], Josh 10:1; 2 Sam 10:19 [with את], Josh 11:19 [with אל]. Hence the NJPS translates "submitted to." This rendering probably reflects the historical situation accurately. Israel was at its zenith in military power, international prestige, and building activity under Omri and Ahab, and Jehoshaphat was quite likely a vassal or client king.[18] Even the post-DtrH materials in 1 Kgs 22:1-38 and 2 Kings 3 may retain something of Jehoshaphat's obligation to accompany the king of Israel to war. The end of the conflict between Israel and Judah, therefore, may have cost Jehoshaphat a degree of independence. His power (22:46) was probably due largely to his sailing in the wake of his Northern neighbor.

22:45: Jehoshaphat's subjection to Israel

DtrH's account suggests that Jehoshaphat's treaty with Israel came at even greater cost to Judah's future. International treaties were often sealed by a marriage, in this case probably the one reported in 2 Kgs 8:18 of Jehoshaphat's son

---

16 The order of elements in the accession formula is also different. MT begins with the king's name rather than the synchronism as was the case with the previous kings in this chapter. OG begins with the synchronism just as in those previous cases. Shenkel (Chronology, 47–50) has shown that the synchronism-first formula is more common overall but that for kings of Judah from Jehoshaphat to Ahaziah there is a significant divergence of practice between MT and OG that shows that the latter was dependent on a different Hebrew *Vorlage*.

17 Provan, *Hezekiah and the Books of Kings*, 63–65.

18 See Frevel, *Geschichte Israels*, esp. 230-31. Cf. also O. Sergi, "Judah's Expansion in Historical Context," *TA* 40 (2013): 226-46 and "The Omride Dynasty and the Reshaping of the Judahite Historical Memory," Bib 97 (2016): 503-25. More broadly, Frevel holds that after Jehoshaphat, Judah was ruled by Israel (Joram, Ahaziah, and Joash were single kings over both states) and only returned to independent, albeit client, status after the Jehu dynasty, under Jotham.

Jehoram to Ahab's daughter, presumably Athaliah. DtrH depicts her as the counterpart of Jezebel in Judah. She would threaten the Davidic house and may have succeeded in bringing it to an end (2 Kgs 11). In that sense Jehoshaphat could be seen as a member by marriage of the Omrid dynasty.

22:47-50: A misplacement

While supplemental remarks sometimes intervene between the source and death notices, they are quite brief (1 Kgs 14:30; 15:7b; 15:23b; 2 Kgs 15:37) except when they detail the king's manner of death. Even then they are only slightly longer (2 Kgs 12:20-21a; 14:19; 23:29-30a). Also, most if not all of these supplemental notices are secondary. The supplemental information about Jehoshaphat in vv. 47-50 is clearly anomalous in this respect, being much longer than others and having nothing to do with Jehoshaphat's death. These verses interrupt the usual continuity between the source notice in v. 46 and the death notice in v. 51 and are therefore out of place. The question is whether they are an addition or a misplacement. The latter is more likely in view of the relatively simple explanation for how they came to their present location (see the Note). Another reason for including these verses in the DtrH level is that the *cultic functionaries* mentioned in v. 47 are an interest of his in the accounts of other kings of Judah beginning with Rehoboam (14:24; 15:12; 2 Kgs 23:7; cf. Deut 23:18). Their disappearance from Kings until the reign of Josiah probably reflects the casting of Jehoshaphat in Josiah's image.

The cultic functionaries

The role of these cultic functionaries has received a good deal of scholarly attention. The long-held notion that they were cult prostitutes involved in fertility rituals has been shown to be based more on imagination than on historical evidence.[19] Exactly what they did has yet to be understood. That it involved sexual activity of some kind is suggested by texts outside of Kings in which the feminine terms *qĕdēšāh/ qĕdēšôt* occur in context with *zônah/zônôt*, "prostitute(s)" (Gen 38:21-22 [cf. v. 15]; Deut 23:18-19; Hos 4:14). But the exact nature of the sexual activity is unknown, and different proposals have been offered. One is that the masculine and feminine terms referred to two separate classes, non-Yahwistic priests and prostitutes, respectively;[20] another posits that the term refers to prostitution whose income profited the temple but was unconnected with fertility rites.[21] It is also not entirely certain, especially in Genesis 38 and Hosea 4, that *qĕdēšāh* must carry a sexual connotation. In Gen 38:21 Hirah uses *qĕdēšāh* instead of *zônah* in conversation with the men near Timnah for reasons that are unclear; in Hosea 4 *qĕdēšāh* may allude to apostasy, for which harlotry is a metaphor.

22:48: The king of Edom

The statement that there was no king in Edom at the beginning of v. 48 raises the question of the beginning of the Edomite state, which has long been a source of debate.[22] Part of the reason for the debate is conflicting evidence within the Bible and the book of Kings. The picture of Edom's development has changed and

---

19 See the bibliography cited in the Note.

20 E. A. Goodfriend, "Prostitution (OT)," *ABD* 5:507–509.

21 K. van der Toorn, "Prostitution, Cultic," *ABD* 5:510–13.

22 On the history and archaeology of Edom see J. R. Bartlett, *Edom and the Edomites* (JSOTSup 77; Sheffield: Sheffield Academic Press, 1989); "Edom in History," *ABD* 2 (1992): 287–95; K. G. Hoglund, "Edomites," in *Peoples of the Old Testament World* (ed. A. J. Hoerth, G. L. Mattingly, and E. M. Yamauchi; Grand Rapids: Baker, 1994), 335–47; B. MacDonald, "Edom, Archaeology of," *ADB* 2 (1992): 295–301.

been clarified with continuing archaeological work, but it is still incomplete. There is little archaeological evidence for extensive population of Edom, much less the existence of a state there, during the Middle and Late Bronze periods. Texts such as the Edomite king list in Gen 36:31-39 and the account in Num 20:14-21 about the king of Edom's refusal to allow the Israelites after the exodus to enter his land are later compositions in the service of Israelite tradition and cannot be used for historical reconstruction. Edomite national consciousness probably developed in the Iron I period under the influence of the Israelite monarchy, but it was held in check by Israel's subjugation of the region. The kingdom of Edom appears to have been founded only in the Iron II period during the reign of Joram of Judah as 2 Kgs 8:20-22 claims. The story in 2 Kings 3 in which the king of Edom plays a role was probably written at a much later period and is anachronistic; the references to the king of Edom in it may even be later additions. Hence the statement in 20:47 that there was no king in Edom at the time of Jehoshaphat is historically accurate. The words that follow, נצב מלך, confuse the matter. They might be rendered as a substantive—*a prefect was king* (see the Note) or as a verb—*a king was appointed*. Either way the use of the word *king* immediately after the statement that Edom had no king is confusing. Jehoiakim (2 Kgs 23:34) and Zedekiah (2 Kgs 24:17) were appointed as kings of Judah by Necho and Nebuchadrezzar, respectively, thus indicating that kings could be appointed over secondary (vassal) states by their overlords. However, the verb נצב is not used in either of these cases, nor is it used as a title for a king anywhere else. Also, monarchy was already in place in Judah, and Jehoiakim and Zedekiah were both members of the royal family. But monarchy had yet to be established for Edom, according to 2 Kgs 8:20 The statement may be a gloss intended to account for the mention of an Edomite king in 2 Kgs 3:9, 10 before the establishment of the Edomite kingdom (2 Kgs 8:20).[23]

22:49-50: The failed Ophir expedition

The anecdote about Jehoshaphat's failed venture in v. 49 is significant for what it reveals about the king's economic and military strength. It assumes that Jehoshaphat, perhaps through a prefect, controlled the port at Eilat/Aqaba because Judah dominated Edom, which had yet to crown a king of its own. Control of this port was extremely important for the access to international trade that it afforded. It was a recurring point of contention between Edom and Judah (cf. 2 Kgs 14:22; 16:6). Jehoshaphat's control of it was a significant boon to Judah's economy and suggests that Judah prospered under his reign. The loss of his fleet was no doubt a serious blow economically, but it would not have been crippling. The ships were built for a mission that would bring further wealth to Judah. Their destruction did not mean a loss of the revenue already accruing to Judah since it still controlled the port. The value of that trade makes it all the more remarkable that Jehoshaphat was able to refuse the proposal of the king of Israel (Ahaziah) for a joint venture (v. 50). This proposal was not an offer to help but a scheme to get in on the revenue generated by the trade at Eilat. Jehoshaphat resisted because he did not want to share that revenue.[24] Better to give up the prospect of retriev-

23 C. Levin, "Aram und/oder Edom in den Büchern Samuel in Könige," *Textus* 24 (2009), 744. Levin posits further that it is part of a redactional effort that used Edom as a gauge of Judahite kings' piety.

24 Bartlett, *Edom and the Edomites*, 116.

ing gold than to have to share the income he could already count on. The king of Israel's decision not to press the matter was also probably an economic one. The cost of maintaining the port at a distance if Judah was hostile would have been greater than the income it produced.

22:46, 51: Jehoshaphat's closing formulae

The two remaining verses together constitute Jehoshaphat's closing regnal formulae—the source report (v. 46), the death and burial, and succession notices (v. 51). Elsewhere these notices are joined. Their separation here indicates that vv. 47-50, which interrupt them, are out of place.

Synthesis

Jehoshaphat's contrast with Ahab and Omri

Jehoshaphat's account, coming after that of Ahab, temporarily halts the literary freefall of religious decline in the sinful kings of Israel in 1 Kings 16, culminating in the two worst, Omri and Ahab. In the midst of this history of apostasy in Israel, Jehoshaphat provides hope in the kingdom of Judah and its intermittent righteous kings. The Old Greek changed this placement because of its chronological revision, sandwiching Jehoshaphat's account between those of Omri and Ahab.

The ambivalent portrait of Jehoshaphat

Despite these differences of location and chronology, the MT and OG agree in casting Jehoshaphat with ambivalence. He is righteous like his father, Asa, who was like David. He even follows Asa in getting rid of the cultic functionaries, destroying those who still remained following his father's purge (15:12). Yet he tolerates the illicit sanctuaries (*bāmôt*). He is remembered for his military power and for standing up to the king of Israel on at least one occasion. Yet the verb form used in the notification that he made peace with Israel implies that he did so by submitting, and this possibility is reinforced by the historically well-attested prowess of Omri and Ahab. The peace Jehoshaphat negotiated with the house of Omri may have meant the loss of some of Judah's independence. The marriage that sealed the treaty also brought Athaliah to power and threatened to end the Davidic line. In narrative structure and content, as in historical reality, therefore, Jehoshaphat submits to Israel. He maintains his integrity as a good king over against the Israelite kings but the reader is left to wonder whether he did enough to distinguish himself from them.

The Reign of Ahaziah (1 Kings 22:52–2 Kings 1:18)

Text

[DtrH's sources; DtrH; Prophetic *legenda; PN; Additions and glosses to PN]*

22:52 Ahaziah son of Ahab became king over Israel in Samaria in the seventeenth year of Jehoshaphat king of Judah and reigned over Israel two years. 53 He did what YHWH considered evil, walking in the way of his father *and of Jezebel his mother*, and in the sin of Jeroboam son of Nebat, which he made Israel commit. 54 He served Baal, prostrating himself before him, and provoked YHWH the god of Israel to anger just as his father did. 1:1 Moab rebelled against Israel after Ahab's death. 2 Ahaziah climbed up the latticework of his upper chamber which was in Samaria and was injured when he fell through; he sent messengers telling them, "Go, divine of Baal-Zebub god of Ekron whether I will survive this injury of mine." So they went to divine. 3 *YHWH's angel/messenger told Elijah the Tishbite, "Arise, go up to meet the messengers of the king of Samaria and say to them, 'Is it because there is no god in Israel that you are going to divine of Baal-Zebub god of Ekron? 4 Therefore thus says YHWH, "You will not descend from the bed on which you have gone up, because you will certainly die."'" And Elijah went away and spoke to them.* 5 The messengers returned to him, and he said to them, "How is it that you have returned?" 6 They said to him, "A man came up to meet us and said to us, 'Go back to the king who sent you and tell him, "Thus says YHWH, 'Is it because there is no god in Israel that you are sending to divine of Baal Zebub god of Ekron? Therefore, you will not descend from the bed on which you have gone up, because you will certainly die.'"'" 7 He said to them, "What is the description of the man who came up to meet you and told you these things?" 8 They said, "He was a hairy man with a leather waistcloth." He thought, "It was Elijah the Tishbite." 9 *So he sent* a captain of fifty with his fifty [men] to [Elijah]. When they came to him (*he was sitting on the top of the mountain*) he said, "Man of god, the king orders [you], 'Come down.'" 10 Elijah answered the captain of fifty, "If I am a man of god, let fire come down from heaven and consume you and your fifty [men]." Then fire came down from heaven and consumed him and his fifty [men]. 11 [The king] sent another captain of fifty with his fifty [men] who told [Elijah], "Man of god, the king orders you to come down at once." 12 Elijah answered him, "If I am a man of god, let fire come down from heaven and consume you and your fifty [men]." Then fire came down and consumed him and his fifty [men]. 13 [The king] sent another captain of fifty with his fifty [men]. When the third captain of fifty came [to where Elijah was], he got down on his knees opposite Elijah and sought his

favor, saying to him, "Man of god, please consider my life and the lives of these your
servants valuable. 14 *Fire came down from heaven and consumed the first two cap-
tains of fifty and their fifties, so now please consider your servants' lives valuable."*
15 *YHWH's angel/messenger told Elijah, "Go down with him; don't be afraid of them."*
So [Elijah] arose and went down with him to the king. 16 *He told him, "Thus says
YHWH, 'Because you sent to divine of Baal Zebub god of Ekron, therefore you will not
descend from the bed on which you have gone up, because you will certainly die.'"*
17 So he died according to YHWH's word which Elijah had spoken.
18 As for the rest of the affairs of Ahaziah which he accomplished, they are of
course recorded on the scroll of the chronicles of the kings of Israel.

Textual Notes

22:52 **Ahaziah son of Ahab became king over Israel in Samaria in the seventeenth year of Jehoshaphat king of Judah and reigned over Israel two years:** So MT, G^{B}. G^{L}: *In the twenty-fourth year of Jehoshaphat king of Judah, Ahaziah son of Ahab became king over Israel for two years.*[1]

53 **his father**: So MT. G^{L}: *Ahab*. The two are conflated in G^{B}.

and of Jezebel his mother: So G^{L} as the shortest reading. MT: *and in the way of his mother*; G^{B}: *and in the way of Jezebel his mother.*

and in the sin of Jeroboam: Based on G^{L}, which reads *sins*. MT: *and in the way of Jeroboam*. G^{B}: *and in the sin of the house of Jeroboam.*

54 **He served Baal, prostrating himself before him**: So MT. G^{BL} have plurals *the Baals ... them*. Cf. 16:31; 2 Kgs 17:16; 21:3-4.

provoked YHWH the god of Israel to anger: So MT, G^{B}. G^{L} lacks the reference to YHWH, reading just the verb *provoking to anger.*

just as his father did: So MT (ככל אשר עשה אביו). G^{BL} reflect *more than all who preceded him*, perhaps influenced by 1 Kgs 16:33.

1:1 **Moab rebelled against Israel after Ahab's death**: Repeated in G^{B} at the end of 1 Kings and beginning of 2 Kings as a device to link the two books. G^{L} repeats this verse and the next sentence. Similar repetitions occur in G^{B} at the divisions of 1–2 Samuel (1–2 Reigns), 2 Samuel and 1 Kings (2–3 Reigns), and 1–2 Chronicles. The same phenomenon on a larger scale is apparent at the end of 2 Chronicles and the beginning of Ezra. Ahaziah's account overlapping 1 Kings and 2 Kings shows the artificiality of the division, which was inherited from G and does not appear in extant Hebrew manuscripts until the Rabbinic Bible of Daniel Bomberg in 1516–1517.

2 **Ahaziah climbed up the latticework of his upper chamber which was in Samaria and was injured when he fell through**: So G^{L}, OL. MT, G^{B} are less complete: *Ahaziah fell through the latticework of his upper chamber which was in Samaria and was injured.*

whether: On the use of אם to introduce indirect question see Jouon 161f.[2]

this injury of mine: So G^{BL} (ἐκ τῆς ἀρρωστίας μου ταύτης = מחליי זה). The construction חלי זה is rare in biblical Hebrew, while the demonstrative without the

---

1 Shenkel, *Chronology*, 64–68. G^{L} = OG; G^{B} = *kaige*.

2 Rofé (*The Prophetical Stories*, 36) argues that its use in lieu of the interrogative particle is Second Temple Hebrew.

article following a suffixed noun is common.[3] At the end of the verse G^{BL} have the plus *so they went to divine* (L + *of him*). Since there is no good trigger for haplography from MT, it is probably best considered an expansion.

3 **Yhwh's messenger**: So MT, G^{B}. G^{L}: *god's messenger* is equally possible.

told: So MT, G^{L}: דבר אל (ἐλάλησε). G^{B}: ἐκάλησεν, an error for ἐλάλησεν.

go up: So MT. G^{BL}: *go* (= לך).

the king of Samaria: So MT. G^{B}: *Ahaziah king of Samaria;* G^{L}: *Ahaziah king of Israel in Samaria.*

no god: So MT, G^{B}. G^{L} has *no prophet* and in v. 6 *no god or prophet*. The two words may be variants, both appropriate to the story. On the use of the double negative (המבלי אין) see Joüon 160p and GKC 152y. The latter suggest that it makes the negation more emphatic (cf. Exod 14:11).

god of Ekron: So MT, G^{B}. Preceded in G^{L} with προσόχθισμα = שקוץ, *detestable thing.*

4 **you will certainly die**: So MT, G^{B}. G^{L} + *on it* (ἐν αὐτῇ).

and spoke to them: So G^{BL} (καὶ εἶπεν πρὸς αὐτούς = וידבר אליהם), lost by haplography from MT (אליהו ... אליהם).

5 **How is it that you have returned**: On the use of the enclitic זה with no perceptible change in meaning see Joüon 143g.

6 **no god**: So MT, G^{B}. G^{L}: *no god or prophet*. See on v. 3.

you are sending: So MT. G^{BL} *you are going*, but the king is not among the messengers.

god of Ekron: Again preceded, as in v. 3, in G^{L} with προσόχθισμα = שקוץ, detestable thing.

you will certainly die: G^{L} + *Because you did evil before me to provoke me, I will bring evil on Ahab's house and will consume him, cutting off from Ahab every high class royal member in Israel.* The use of ἐνώπιον instead of ἐν ὀφθαλμοῖς to translate לפני shows this plus to be OG.[4] It is similar to the DtrH oracles against the ruling houses in 1 Kgs 14:9-10; 16:2-4; 21:21, 24. It would be another in the series of prophetic oracles used by Dtr to organize the book of Kings if it is original to the Dtr level. However, it is probably secondary since it is easier to explain why it would be added to the OG than why it would be deleted from the MT. See the Diachronic Analysis.

8 **a hairy man**: So G^{BL}: ἀνὴρ δασὺς, reflecting איש שער. MT: איש בעל שער, a double reading. The testimony of the Greek witnesses along with the proximity of בעל and the contrast it provides with Baal-Zebub suggest that איש is the more primitive reading.

9 **When they came to him (he was sitting on the top of the mountain)**: Following Trebolle,[5] who reconstructs the first clause with G^{L}: καὶ ἐπορεύθησαν πρὸς αὐτόν. This is the first of a double reading in G^{L}, the second being καὶ ἀνέβη ὁ ἡγούμενος καὶ οἱ πεντήκοντα αὐτοῦ καὶ ἦλθον ἕως τοῦ ἀνθρωπου τοῦ θεοῦ = *When the captain and his fifty went up and came to the man of god*. The subject (*the captain and his fifty*) and the reference to the man of god are supplied in Greek for syntactical reasons. The main variation between them, therefore, is in the verbs *came* and *went up*. Both are reflected in G^{A}, while MT and G^{B} have *went up*, which reflects the parenthesis locating Elijah on a mountaintop. That this is a gloss is indicated by its placement in G^{L} between the two variants as well as by its introduction with הנה in MT. The association of Elijah with Mount Carmel influenced the portrait of the prophet on

---

3 Burney, *Notes*, 261–62. GKC 126y also note that the omission of the article from the demonstrative occurs especially when the noun is made definite by a suffix.

4 Shenkel, *Chronology*, 13–17; Trebolle, *Centena*, 155–56.

5 Trebolle, *Centena*, 157–59.

a mountain in this verse and the story at large (see the Notes on vv. 11, 13). In the DtrH story in vv. 3, 6 Elijah actually "goes up" to meet the first envoy (vv. 3, 6). The language in vv. 7-16 was initially consistent about Elijah "coming down" to Samaria rather than about the soldiers "going up" to the prophet.

the king orders [you], 'Come down': So MT (המלך דבר רדה). G^B adds the object: *the king orders you*. G^L: *Thus says the king.*

11 **who told [Elijah]**: Reading וידבר אליו. All major witnesses expand: MT precedes with ויען. G^B supplies *the captain of fifty* (ὁ πεντηκόνταρχος) as subject; it also attests *and said* before the quote. G^L agrees with G^B in supplying the subject; it also reads *came up* (= ויעל) instead of ויען, on which see above on v. 9. Finally, instead of the pronoun *to him*, G^L reads *to the man of god.*

at once: So MT, G^B: מהרה = ταχέως. Lost from the G^L *Vorlage* by haplography preceding רדה. It should be vocalized as a *Pi'el* imperative (מַהֲרָה) instead of the adverb as in MT.

12 **Elijah answered him***:* So G^L: καὶ ἀπεκρίθη Ηλιας καὶ εἶπεν πρὸς αὐτὸν. MT: ויען אליה וידבר אליהם. G^B is conflate: καὶ ἀπεκρίθη Ηλιου καὶ ἐλάλησεν πρὸς αὐτὸν καὶ εἶπεν.

Then fire came down: So G^{BL}. MT: *Then the fire of god came down.*

13 **[The king] sent another captain of fifty**: As in v. 11, G^{BL} supply *the king*. MT has *a third* (שלשי), properly without the final ם following *the captain of fifty.*[6]

came: So G^{BL}. MT expands with *came up* (ויעל). See on v. 9 above.

and the lives of these your servants: So G^B (καὶ ἡ ψυχὴ τῶν δούλων σου τούτων). MT, G^L: + *fifty.*

14 **and their fifties**: So MT, G^L. Lost by haplography from G^B.

have regard for your servants' lives: So G^{BL} (ἐντιμωθήτω δὴ ἡ ψυχή τῶν δούλων σου). MT has *my life*, which is evidently a deliberate change disparaging the third captain to make clear that he was motivated by fear not by piety (see below).

15 **YHWH's messenger**: So MT, G^B. G^L: *god's messenger.* Either reading is possible.

told Elijah: So MT. G^{BL} + לאמר.

with him ... with him: So with some Hebrew manuscripts and the versions: אתו, *with him*, in lieu of MT's direct object marker (אותו). Before the second occurrence of the word G^L reflects an additional verb – καὶ ἐπορεύθη–so that it reads *he arose, went down and went with him.*

don't be afraid of them: So G^{BL}. MT has *don't be afraid of him* by attraction to *with him.*

16 **you sent**: So G^B. MT, G^L + *messengers.*

god of Ekron: As in vv. 3, 6 preceded in G^L with προσόχθισμα = שקוץ, "detestable thing." MT + *Is it because there is no god in Israel of whom you might divine?* is secondarily adapted from v. 6.

17 **which Elijah had spoken**: So G^B. MT + *Jehoram reigned in his place in the second year of Jehoram son of Jehoshaphat king of Judah because he had no son.* G^L has a similar plus, but it is hexaplaric.[7] The MT plus is out of place because it describes the beginning of Jehoram's reign before the closing formulae for his predecessor. It constitutes the late insertion of an OG fragment.[8]

18 **which he accomplished**: So MT, G^B. G^L: + *all.*

18+ The long plus in G^{BL} that parallels 3:1-3 is treated with the rest of ch. 3.

---

6 Another possible reading advocated by Thenius (*Könige*, 263) is שלשית, "a third time," the ת having been replaced by ם from attraction to the plural ending of the previous word.

7 Shenkel, *Chronology and Recensional Development*, 73–74.

8 So Shenkel, *Chronology*, 74; also Hendel, "Two Editions," 107.

Synchronic Analysis

Ahaziah's reign lies astride the artificial division between 1 and 2 Kings. His counterpart in Judah is Jehoshaphat. The contrast between the two is stark.[9] Jehoshaphat reigns much longer than Ahaziah. Jehoshaphat does what is right while Ahaziah does what is evil. Jehoshaphat follows the example of David, the best king of Israel, while Ahaziah walks not only in way of Jeroboam but also of his own parents, Ahab and Jezebel (22:54). Jehoshaphat ruled over Edom, while Ahaziah lost Moab (2 Kgs 1:1). Like his predecessors, Ahaziah provoked (כעס *Hip'îl*) YHWH by worshiping other gods, specifically Baal (22:54).

The contrast between Ahaziah and Jehoshaphat

Moab's revolt (2 Kgs 1:1) sounds an ominous note. No response by Ahaziah is recorded. This suggests military weakness and signals the beginning of the dynasty's decline. It points ahead to the story in ch. 3 about the war with Moab, where the notice of revolt is repeated (3:5) and Ahaziah's brother and successor is left to deal with it. Ahaziah, then, is apostate like his father and grandfather but without the virtue of military strength or resolve; he is a weakling.

1:1: Moab revolts

The account of Ahaziah's reign is mostly about Elijah; Ahaziah is only important for his encounter with him. Otherwise he is remembered for being unfaithful to YHWH. His regnal formulae enclose the Elijah story but do not contain it. Elijah transcends the boundaries of kings' reigns in both time and significance. The story about Elijah in 2 Kings 1 effectively stands in the transition between Elijah and Elisha. It provides a kind of summary of Elijah's personality and character traits while looking forward to the career of Elisha and Jehu's anti-Baal campaign.[10] While the story shares features with the Elijah tales, above all his victory on Mount Carmel (1 Kgs 18), it is more like the Elisha stories in other particulars, especially its use of the title *man of god* and the destruction of innocents (cf. 2 Kgs 2:23-24).

The transitional nature of the story

The story unfolds in two parts: Elijah's interception of Ahaziah's inquiry (1:2-8) and Elijah's dealings with the envoys sent to arrest him (1:9-16). Given Ahaziah's weakness it is no surprise that he is injured or "weak" (חלה) from a fall. The text leaves open the question whether it was an accident or YHWH's doing.[11] The injuries are serious. Ever apostate, Ahaziah sends to a Baal figure to inquire about his prospects for recovery. Presumably Baal-Zebub was renowned for his healing prowess and that is why Ahaziah sends all the way to Ekron. The reference to Baal recalls Ahab's affinity for his wife's deity and Elijah's defeat of the Baal prophets in 1 Kings 18. The very act of inquiry bodes ill for him because the other two cases in which a king inquires about an illness yield bad news (1 Kgs 14:1-18; 2 Kgs 8:7-10).[12] Sending and messengers are linked themes in this story. The story

Ahaziah's illness and inquiry

9 Cf. Nelson, *Kings*, 154.

10 Cohn, *2 Kings*, 4.

11 Scholars typically assume it was accidental, but Sweeney (*Kings*, 269) asserts that it was YHWH's doing.

12 2 Kgs 20:1-11 is somewhat different. It is not stated that Hezekiah sent to Isaiah to inquire whether he would recover. Still, Isaiah initially gives him bad news. The news is changed after Hezekiah's intense prayer and because of his righteousness. Such is decidedly not the case for Ahaziah.

revolves around messages—from the king to Baal-Zebub, from YHWH to his messenger (angel), from Elijah to the king's messengers, from the messengers to Elijah, and from Elijah directly to the king. The contrast—or perhaps rivalry—between the king's messengers and YHWH's messenger or "angel" embodies the contrast and rivalry between their respective senders. Elijah is the recipient of both and must decide whom to obey. As a prophet he is, by definition, also a messenger of YHWH, so his decision is never really in doubt. In v. 3 he becomes the sender as he intercepts Ahaziah's messengers and sends them back with an answer to the king's inquiry. Elijah, YHWH's messenger, commissioned by another of YHWH's messengers, thwarts the errand of Ahaziah's messengers.

1:3: A god in Israel

The question in v. 3 occurs twice more in the story (vv. 6, 16) and constitutes a major theme. It functions in each case as the indictment for the prophetic judgment oracle of which it is a part. It is rhetorical and sarcastic. It asserts that there is a god in Israel—YHWH—whom Ahaziah has spurned by sending to Baal-Zebub. Elijah addresses his words to the messengers (אתם הלכים), denoting their complicity.[13] Still, the punishment will fall squarely on Ahaziah (v. 4). He will not recover but will die. This is the judgment segment of the oracle, typically introduced by *therefore* (לכן). The verbs "go up" and "come down" are a *Leitmotif* for the chapter; Elijah is in the superior position on the mountain and counters the efforts of the king's envoys to bring him down to Samaria.[14] The title "king of Samaria" (v. 3) is rare (1 Kgs 21:1) and reminds the reader of Ahaziah's heritage in the line of Omri, who bought Samaria and established his capital there.

1:4-8: The manner of Elijah

There is an obvious ellipse between v. 4 and v. 5, as v. 4 details what Elijah is to say to the king's messengers and v. 5 reports the return of the messengers without any account of the actual encounter with Elijah. The ellipse lends chiastic efficiency to the interchange, as the angel addresses Elijah in the singular, while he speaks to the king's envoys in the second person plural and gives them the message for Ahaziah in the second singular. The ellipse also heightens the drama and air of mystery around Elijah, who never meets with the envoys in the narrative.[15] The messengers' perception of Elijah is artfully delayed until vv. 6, 8 where they respond to the king's question about why they returned so quickly (v. 5). Their rapid return is implicit acknowledgment of Elijah's authority even though they know him only as *a man* (איש). The bold spirit of his oracle with its condemnation of the king endows him with such authority. They do not know his name because he has avoided Samaria and Jezreel after Jezebel's threat (1 Kgs 19:2-3). But when the king asks about the man's משפט ("manner, characteristics," v. 7), the messengers answer with a description that Ahaziah recognizes immediately (v. 8). Elijah is a *lord of hair* (בעל שער) in contrast to the *lord of flies* (בעל זבוב).[16] Whether a description of his clothes or his person—it has been interpreted both ways—it characterizes him as a wild man who subsists on the fringes of the royal domain, an outsider who critiques society and protests against it, especially against the elite.

---

13 Würthwein, *1. Könige 17–2. Könige 25*, 269

14 C. T. Begg, "Unifying Factors in 2 Kings 1:2-17a," *JSOT* 32 (1985), 81–82.

15 Cogan and Tadmor, *II Kings*, 26; Nelson, *Kings*, 155.

16 Nelson, *Kings*, 155.

1:9-16: Three captains and squads of fifty

The anecdote in vv. 9-16 delays the story's conclusion and builds anticipation of the confrontation between Elijah/YHWH and Ahaziah. The story uses the motif of a threefold event with the decisive change the third time around. The first two encounters between Elijah and the squads of fifty follow the same pattern: a description of the squad and the captain's words to Elijah (vv. 9, 11), Elijah's response (vv. 12a, 15a), and the climax of the encounter.[17] These two encounters have the same content: the captain orders Elijah, the *man of god*, to come down from atop the hill. Elijah bids fire come down from heaven instead to consume the captain and his squad, which it does. In the third encounter the captain's attitude toward Elijah changes radically. He begs Elijah to spare him and his men (vv. 13-14). As a result, at the behest of YHWH's messenger, Elijah accompanies the third captain to the king, where he personally delivers the same oracle as in vv. 3 and 6.

1:9-10: The first captain and his fifty

The power dynamics of these three encounters are stressed by means of the language. The king's purpose in sending the three embassies is a display of power and authority that is turned back on him. The final episode shows that he wishes to have Elijah arrested and brought to him. Fifty men—soldiers at that, since their leader is a commander (שר)— seems to be overkill for such a simple mission. But they are not enough. The first captain speaks with the king's authority and commands Elijah to come down (v. 9). He utters the title *man of god* derisively, without an appreciation of its significance.[18] He uses the verb *dibber* to articulate the king's official order. Elijah is above the soldiers in every sense. Instead of coming down he draws on his identity as a *man* (*'îš*) *of god* to bid god's *fire* (*'ēš*) *come down* (v. 10), demonstrating his intimate fellowship with YHWH, as on Mount Carmel (1 Kgs 18). *Man of god* signals a special connection that allows the individual to wield divine power. The scene has nothing to do with self-protection but is about Elijah's exhibition of power as a man of god. The alliteration in the repetition of *aleph* is striking: אם־איש אלהים אני תרד אש מן־השמים ותא כל אתך ואת־חמשיך ותרד אש מן־השמים ות אכל אתו ואת־חמשיו.

1:11-12: The second captain and his fifty

Ahaziah shows no concern about the fate of the first envoys, yet the awareness of the third captain (v. 13) means that he must have known what happened to them. Concerned only for himself, he callously dispatches another unit with the same mission. The second captain is equally arrogant and foolish, filled with hubris and false bravado. He haughtily repeats the order to Elijah, even adding the word *quickly* (מהרה). Like the first captain, he treats Elijah dismissively as a subordinate (v. 11). And like the first captain he receives the same response—fire from heaven consuming him and his squad (v. 12).

1:13-16: The third captain; Elijah goes to Ahaziah

The third captain, though, has learned the lesson (vv. 13-14). He kneels before the man of god, acknowledging his superiority. He issues no order but pleads for for mercy. However, v 14 makes clear that he is not really much better than his predecessors. He obviously knows of their fate and is motivated by fear rather than piety. He is also not concerned for the lives of his men as much as he is for his own life. Elijah's response to the third captain is not detailed. He moves at the behest of YHWH's messenger (v. 15). Although this captain has not requested it,

17 Nelson, *Kings*, 155.
18 Hens-Piazza, *Kings*, 228; Šanda, *Könige* II, 5.

Elijah follows the messenger's instruction to *go down* with the captain. He thus follows the orders of YHWH's messenger(s) but not those of the king's messenger(s). The messenger's instruction not to fear is ironic in view of the power Elijah has demonstrated; it recalls Elijah's fear of Jezebel after his victory on Carmel (19:1-3). Elijah now delivers directly to Ahaziah (v. 16) the oracle he gave to his messengers (v. 16); the king will die. The lack of detail about their meeting places the focus on the three encounters rather than on Ahaziah's death.

1:17-18: Ahaziah's death and closing formulae

Ahaziah dies shortly thereafter in fulfillment of Elijah's oracle (v. 17aα), and the usual closing source citation (v. 18) follows. The absence of further details about Ahaziah's death and burial suggests a lack of respect for him. The intervening material in v. 17aβb reports Jehoram's accession, which serves a double purpose. First, it further sullies Ahaziah's reputation with its notice that he had no son. This also may be viewed as YHWH's doing in punishment for Ahaziah's sinfulness. His death marks the end of his branch of the royal house. Hence, and secondly, his untimely death is the first step in the fulfillment of Elijah's oracle against the house of Ahab in 1 Kgs 21:21-22, 24 and thus is a clue that the end of the dynasty is imminent. That end will come in full with the bloodbath that will terminate the reign of his brother, also a son of Ahab, and end the life of the influential and despised Jezebel. Ahaziah's brief reign is a slight delay in the movement of the larger narrative toward the obliteration of the house of Ahab; Jehoram's accession signals the beginning of the end.

Diachronic Analysis

A layered account

The question of this passage's unity is a topic of longstanding debate, with the negative position typically arguing that vv. 9-16 were interpolated.[19] This position can be refined with input from the other prophetic texts we have treated and from textual criticism. The source citation closing Ahaziah's account in 1:18 is DtrH's. The notice of Moab's revolt in 1:1 should also be attributed to DtrH. It illustrates his *modus operandi*. Although the revolt occurred after Ahab's death, DtrH placed the notice about it within Ahaziah's regnal formulae, in accord with his organizational scheme.

1 Kings 22:52-54: Ahaziah's evaluation

Ahaziah's two-year reign (22:52) was probably less than two full years—a full year and some months by antedating, if that was the system of calculation used. Perhaps more important, Nadab (1 Kgs 15:25) and Elah (1 Kgs 16:8) each reigned two years, placing Ahaziah in their company as short-lived successors. DtrH's evaluation of Ahaziah (22:53-54) condemned him both for following his father's bad example and for continuing the sin of Jeroboam. Ahaziah is condemned, in other words, not only for maintaining the Northern Yahwistic shrines that DtrH considered illegitimate but also for worshiping other gods. The latter involved not only tolerating the Baal cult as his father had done but personally bowing down to Baal (22:54). The verse mentions Ahaziah's father alone as the one whom he

19 Long (*2 Kings*, 11–12) summarizes the positions. The lists of scholars he gives on either side of the debate could be updated, but the positions remain essentially the same.

emulated. DtrH does not regularly use the queen mother in evaluations; the reference to Jezebel (G^{BL}) is PN's doing.

2 Kings 1:1: Moab's revolt

Moab's rebellion is consistent with ancient Near Eastern practice; revolting after a king's death was a typical strategy of vassals as it was an opportune time to test the new ruler's strength. The Mesha inscription claims that its namesake revolted against Israel after it had possessed the land of Medeba (Madaba) during the days of Omri "and half the days of his son, 40 years" (*COS* 2.23). These details do not match those in the Bible, but the discrepancy is explained if the Mesha stela is interpreted as a memorial that anachronistically cast the starting point of the change in Moab's relationship with Israel as Mesha's accession rather than his successful revolt.[20] The setting of Moab's revolt in both Ahaziah's reign and Joram's (3:5) may be attributable to the brevity of Ahaziah's reign.

1:2: The emissary to Baal-Zebub

In vv. 2, 5-8 DtrH included a story illustrating Ahaziah's proclivity toward Baal. It may be based on a prophetic *legenda* representing the genre about a king's consultation concerning illness as in 1 Kgs 14:1-6, 12, 17-18a.[21] The king may have initially been nameless (vv. 3, 5, 6). If so, DtrH identified him as Ahaziah (v. 2). The prophet was already identified as Elijah (vv. 7-8).[22] The king injured himself by falling through the latticework of an upper story in his house. The latticework may have been a kind of trellis or a screen over a window or around a rooftop. Most scholars opt for the last, invoking the design of the Syrian-style palace or *bit hilani* ("house of windows"). These possessed a flat-roofed second story that could be closed off with latticework to afford privacy while still permitting the passage of air. However, the preferred reading in v. 2 indicates that the king fell while climbing, whether on the latticework itself or on a ladder is not clear. The text does not explain the nature of the injury, though one assumes that it was to the king's head and/or internal organs. Instead of inquiring of YHWH, the king sent messengers to a god called Baal Zebub (v. 2). The verb דרש is a technical term for inquiry or divination through an oracle. There are two main explanations for the name of the deity.[23] One is that it refers to a deity apotropaic to, i.e., for warding off, flies. Examples of such deities are cited by several scholars.[24] But

Baal Zebub

20 Miller, "Moabite Stone as Memorial Stela," 9–18.

21 The consultation is for purposes of prognosis, as in 1 Kgs 14, rather than treatment as in 2 Kgs 5. Consultations for prognosis are well attested in the ANE. See Zucconi, "Aramean Skin Care," 170. R. C. Culley ("Punishment Stories in the Legends of the Prophets," in *Orientation by Disorientation: Studies in Literary Criticism and Biblical Literary Criticism Presented in Honor of William A. Beardslee* [ed. R. A. Spencer; Pittsburgh, PA: Pickwick, 1980], 167–81) designates 2 Kgs 1:2-17 a "punishment story" along with 1 Kgs 13:7-20; 20:33-43; 21; 2 Kgs 2:23-25; and 5:20-27. The focus on the outcome is appropriate, but only 2 Kgs 5:20-27 of the stories Culley cites involves the consultation of a prophet about illness/injury.

22 Pace Trebolle (*Centena*, 155–56), who argues that vv. 7-16 were interpolated by *Wiederaufnahme*. But this would leave a story in vv. 2-6 + 17 that is incomplete because the king never discovers the identity of the mysterious "man" who sends the emissary back. The problem is exacerbated if vv. 3-4 are secondary, as Würthwein (*1. Könige 17–2. Könige 25*, 266, 269) recognized.

23 For other explanations that have failed to find a following see W. Herrmann, "Baal Zebub בעל זבוב," *DDD* 154–56.

24 E.g., Herrmann, "Baal Zebub," 154; Montgomery, *Kings*, 349; Šanda, *Könige* II, 3.

since the king's circumstance is one of injury, not of disease contracted from flies, the apotropaic explanation is unlikely and is usually rejected in favor of the second explanation[25]—that the name is a pejorative adaptation of the title "Baal Zebul," Prince Baal. This interpretation is supported by the frequent reference in the Ugaritic mythological tablets to the god Baal as *zbl*, "prince," and by the NT references to Beelzebul (Matt 10:25; 12:24; Mark 3:22; Luke 11:15).[26] Exactly why this god is approached remains an open question; presumably he was renowned for healing powers.

Ekron

Ekron is securely identified as Tel Miqne/Khirbet al-Muqanna', based on the dedicatory inscription of King Ikausa, "ruler of Ekron," found there in 1997.[27] The northernmost in the Philistine pentapolis on the border between Philistia and Judah, it thrived throughout the period of the Israelite and Judahite monarchies, particularly during the eighth-seventh centuries when it was a center for oil production.[28] It was destroyed by the Babylonians ca. 603 BCE. This suggests that the story behind vv 2, 5-8, 17 originated in the pre-exilic period. However, occupation of some sort either continued there or reemerged, since it is mentioned as Akkaron in the second century BCE as a possession of the Hasmonean ruler Jonathan (1 Macc 10:89). Again, it is not clear why the king would have chosen such a distant sanctuary, except that Baal Zebul was well known for healing.

1:3-4: PN's addition

PN added the mission from YHWH to intercept the king's envoy in vv. 3-4. This is indicated by several features of these verses. The first is the mention in v. 3 of the angel, which surfaces in the Elijah materials only in PN additions (1 Kgs 19:6-8). The title *king of Samaria* is used elsewhere in Kings only in PN's Naboth story (1 Kgs 21:1). The question in v. 3 is reminiscent of the *Erkenntnisformel* in 1 Kgs 18:36 and Elisha's similar concern in the Na'aman story (2 Kgs 5:8) to show that there is a prophet in Israel. In the present text v. 3 functions as an indictment. Then v. 4 does double duty as both the oracle responding to the king's inquiry and the judgment following that indictment. The gap between v. 4 and v. 5 in MT is the result of haplography at the end of v. 4, as is apparent from the G^{BL} reading, which reports Elijah's completion of YHWH's command (see the Note). The envoy turns around and returns to the king, who is surprised to see them back so soon and inquires as to the reason.

1:5-8: The king's interview with his emissary in DtrH

DtrH's version of the story went from the commission of the emissaries in v. 2 to their nearly immediate return in v. 5. They report their encounter with the unknown *man* and the unfavorable oracle he delivered (v. 6). The OG plus in v. 6

---

25 A. Tångberg ("A Note on Ba'al-Zebub in 2 Kgs 1:2, 3, 6, 16," *SJOT* 6:293–96) and Sweeney (*Kings*, 269) are in the minority in favoring the interpretation of Baal Zebub as an apotropaic god, though Cogan and Tadmor (*II Kings*, 25) seem open to this possibility. Würthwein's comment is apropos (*1. Könige 17-2. Könige 25*, 267): "Das wäre zwar nicht ohne Analogie, ist aber nicht wahrscheinlich." [This would not be without analogy, but it is improbable.]

26 M. Dietrich and O. Loretz, "Die Ba'al-Titel *b'l arṣ* und *aliy qrdm*," *UF* 12 (1980): 392.

27 S. Gitin, T. Dothan, and J. Naveh, "A Royal Dedicatory Inscription from Ekron," *IEJ* 47 (1997): 1–16.

28 On the archaeological history of the site see T. Dothan and S. Gitin, "Ekron," *ABD* 2: 415–22; C. S. Ehrlich, "Ekron," *NIDB* 2:227–28; and B. P. Irwin, "Ekron," *DOTHB* 246–48 and the works cited in these articles.

contains another instance of the oracle against the ruling houses. While it may go back to DtrH it is unusual in that it is directed at Ahaziah, who was the head neither of the dynasty (Omri) nor of the ruling house (Ahab). As indicated in the Note, it is also difficult to account for the oracle's absence from the MT. It was probably added to the OG in conformity with the oracles in 1 Kgs 14:9-10; 16:2-4, which came before the king in whose reign the prophecy was fulfilled.[29]

The description of Elijah

The king's inquiry about the nature (משפט) of the man who spoke to them (v. 7) evokes the description of Elijah in v. 8. The phrase איש שער could characterize person or clothing. In favor of the former is the parallel in Gen 27:11 and the contrast with the bald-headed Elisha (2 Kgs 2:23). The clothing interpretation is supported by the mention of his leather belt and by texts that identify this manner of dress with the prophetic office (Zech 13:4; Matt 3:4; 11:8-11).[30] The story cast Elijah as the embodiment and originator of that tradition. The point of the story required that his appearance be unusual in order for Ahaziah to identify him. Beyond that, however, Elijah becomes the quintessential judgment prophet, who is recognizable by his dress and demeanor but also by his opposition to the king.

1:17-18: The end of the DtrH account of Ahaziah

From v. 8 the DtrH account moved to v. 17 and the conclusion of the prophetic story with the notice of the king's death as a fulfillment. DtrH then included the closing formulae for Ahaziah in v. 18. The usual mention of him lying with his forebears was not included because he failed to place a son on the throne.[31]

1:9-16: PN's further revision

In addition to vv. 3-4, PN added a second prophetic story in vv. 9-15 that moves from the issue of the king's apostasy to that of Elijah's power and authority. The story has much in common with the Elisha *legenda*, including the depiction of the prophet as a miracle-working man of god and the slaughter of innocents. Like 2:23-24 it emphasizes the need for proper respect and treatment of the man of god. Whether PN borrowed it from the Elisha collection and changed the hero to Elijah or it became associated with Elijah before PN is impossible to determine. The *legenda* began with the statement that a captain and squad of fifty came (ויבא) to the man of god (v. 9) or the like. PN changed the verb to *he sent* to link to the foregoing story."[32] The man of god was not explicitly on a mountain as the current

---

29 Trebolle (*Centena*, 155–56) refers to the plus as a collection of stereotypical formulas from previous contexts. The judgment (*I will bring evil* ...) is identical to 1 Kgs 21:21 except for the change from second- to third-person pronoun (*upon him*) and is probably lifted from that verse. It is anomalous, however, among the anti-dynastic oracles in its indictment of an individual (*because you did evil*) followed by the judgment against the royal house of which he is a part but which does not bear his name.

30 Brueggemann, *Kings*, 285; Würthwein, *1. Könige 17-2. Könige 25*, 268. Also J. Lindblom, *Prophecy in Ancient Israel* (Philadelphia: Fortress, 1962), 66–67. The "prophetic wardrobe" has also been interpreted as a symbol of repentance on the people's behalf and of mourning for their coming punishment (Thenius, *Könige*, 262, citing Keil).

31 The MT plus in v. 17 that Jehoram became king "in [Ahaziah's] place" (תחתיו) stipulates succession by a legitimate ruler within the dynasty but not necessarily a son. Cf. Suriano, *Politics of Dead Kings*, 132–34.

32 The sending of messengers (vv. 2, 6, 9, 11, 13, 16) is a primary argument adduced by Begg ("Unifying Factors") for the unity of the passage. PN's use of *sent* in v. 9 contributes to this theme, which the two *legenda* have in common.

story has it (see the Note on v. 9), but was an itinerant. The “up-and-down” language in vv. 9, 11, and 13 plays on the status conferred by the writer on the man of god and on the motif of calling fire down from heaven. As in 1 Kings 18 that fire is lightning and the background is storm-god theophany. The man of god uses it to assert his power and command respect. It was only after the third captain showed him proper respect (v. 13) that the man of god accompanied him (v. 15b).

The explanation in 1:14

Verse 14 is PN’s explicative addition to the *legenda*. It rehearses what has happened and is not strictly necessary to the narrative. It also concludes with a *Wiederaufnahme* (בעיניך), and it uses הנה and עתה, each of which can signal a secondary addition.[33] It alters the characterization of the third captain. Absent the verse it is not clear whether he was aware of what had happened to the first two squads of fifty. His attitude of deference to the man of god could stem from piety and humility rather than raw fear and contrasts more markedly with that of the first two captains. With the verse it is clear that fear is the motivation. In PN’s edition he is no better than his precursors.

The angel/messenger motif in 1:15

YHWH’s order via angel in v. 15a telling Elijah to accompany the third captain without fear is like the report of Elijah’s fear of Jezebel in 1 Kgs 19:3 and is also PN’s addition. The mentions of the angel in vv. 3 and 15a link the present story to 1 Kings 19 (vv. 6-8). They are the only places in the Elijah materials where an angel is involved.[34] They enhance the messenger motif in the chapter, since the same Hebrew word means angel and messenger (vv. 2, 3, 5, 15, 16). Elijah receives orders from YHWH’s messenger; he himself is also YHWH’s messenger. He is in competition with the king’s messengers. By implication, YHWH and the king are rivals. Elijah follows YHWH’s orders, which the story makes clear are superior to those of the king. Elijah also destroys the king’s messengers, implying that not only YHWH but also YHWH’s prophet is above the king.

Synthesis

A weaker version of his father

Ahaziah’s reign is characterized as more of the same, only weaker. He should have anticipated Moab’s revolt after Ahab’s death, yet he is entirely unprepared for it. While the text gives no details about the revolt, the implication is that it was successful. Israel’s prestige is fading fast. The fact that the story of Ahaziah’s intercepted emissary to Baal-Zebub follows immediately after the notice of Moab’s revolt suggests that part of the reason for the loss of Moab was Ahaziah’s unfaithfulness to YHWH. He continued the apostasies of his father (and mother) on top of those of Jeroboam. Things might have been different with Moab if Ahaziah had been an exclusive Yahwist.

---

33 See Trebolle, *Centena*, 159–60.

34 K. Koch (*The Growth of the Biblical Tradition: The Form-Critical Method* [New York: Charles Scribner’s Sons, 1969], 187), among others, take them as glosses. According to Buis (*Rois*, 179), this is the only case before Zechariah in which a prophet receives his/her message from an intermediary rather than directly from god.

A contest of power

It is not just defeat that Ahaziah suffers for his faithlessness, but also death. Elijah's announcement to the king through his envoy both assumes and demonstrates Elijah's ability as YHWH's prophet to foretell the future—the reason for the envoy to begin with—as well as YHWH's power over life and death. YHWH's displeasure at being passed over by a leader of his own people for consultation of a non-Israelite deity is palpable. The point is stressed in the *legenda* behind vv. 9-16, which has to do with treating YHWH's prophet respectfully. The first two captains who demean the man of god and try to order him about lose their lives and their men. The third squad survives because their captain shows the proper deference. This is a story about power dynamics. The king's effort to display his power and authority by sending the three emissaries is turned back on him. YHWH's prophet trumps the king.

The quintessential judgment prophet

The two prophetic stories in the chapter both contrast and collaborate. In the first, Elijah is YHWH's spokesman who delivers the divine word of judgment on the king. He is the paradigmatic prophet in that he wears the garb that comes to be associated with the office. The second story resonates with other prophetic *legenda* in its portrait of the prophet as having divine power at his disposal. Above all it is quite similar to the account of Elijah's encounter with the prophets of Baal on Mt. Carmel (1 Kings 18). Here Ahaziah, son of Ahab and Jezebel, leads Israel astray by placing his trust in other gods, specifically Baal. YHWH's presence and power in Israel are demonstrated in the fire from heaven that consumes Ahaziah's envoys and confirms Elijah as YHWH's prophet, superior to earthly authorities. Together the two stories present Elijah as the quintessential prophet of judgment.

Elijah's Ascension, Elisha's Succession (2 Kings 2:1-25)

Text

[Prophetic legenda; *PN]*
1 *When* YHWH *took Elijah to heaven in the tempest,* Elijah and Elisha departed from Gilgal. 2 *Elijah said, "Stay here, because* YHWH *has sent me to Bethel." But Elisha replied, "By* YHWH*'s life and by your life, I will not leave you." When they came to Bethel* 3 *the members of the prophetic guild who were in Bethel came out to meet them and said to Elisha, "Do you know that today* YHWH *is taking your master from above you?" He replied, "Yes, I know. Say no more."* 4 *Elijah said to Elisha, "Stay here, because* YHWH *has sent me to Jericho." But he replied, "By* YHWH*'s life and by your life, I will not leave you." When they came to Jericho,* 5 *the members of the prophetic guild who were in Jericho approached Elisha and asked him, "Do you know that* YHWH *is taking your master from above you today?" He replied, "Yes, I know. Say no more."* 6 *Elijah said to him, "Stay here, because* YHWH *has sent me to the Jordan." But he said, "By* YHWH*'s life and by your life, I will not leave you." So the two of them walked on—* 7 *meanwhile, fifty men from the members of the prophetic guild went and stood at a distance*—and the two of them came to stand beside the Jordan. 8 Elijah took his mantle, rolled it up, and struck the water so that it divided in two and the two of them crossed on dry ground. 9 After they had crossed, Elijah said to Elisha, "Ask what you want me to do for you before I am taken from you." Elisha responded, "Let me receive a double portion of your spirit." 10 [Elijah] said, "You have made a difficult request. If you see me taken from you, it will be yours; but if you do not see, it will not be." 11 As they continued walking and talking, a chariot of fire and horses of fire appeared and separated the two of them so that Elijah was taken up to heaven in the tempest. 12 As Elijah watched, he kept crying out, "My father, my father, Israel's charioteer and horseman!" When he no longer saw him, he took hold of his clothes and tore them in two. 13 Then rolling up Elijah's mantle, which had fallen from him, *he returned and stood on the bank of the Jordan.* 14 *Taking Elijah's mantle which had fallen from him,* he struck the water. When it did not divide, he said, "Where is Elijah's god?" Then Elisha struck the water a second time, and the water divided so that he crossed over on dry ground. 15 *When the members of the prophetic guild who were in Jericho at a distance saw his return, they said, "The spirit of Elijah has come to rest on Elisha." They came to meet him and prostrated themselves on the ground in front of him.* 16 *They said to him, "There are fifty strong men with your servants. Let them go and search for your master, in case* YHWH*'s spirit has carried him away and thrown him on one of the mountains or one of the valleys." He told them not to send.* 17 *But when they pressed him until he was embarrassed, he acquiesced, "Send them." So they sent*

the fifty men who searched for three days without finding him.
18 *When they re-
turned to him (he was still in Jericho), he said, "I told you not to go, didn't I?"*
19 The people of the city said to Elijah, "The city is a pleasant place to live, as
my lord can see, but the water is bad and causes miscarriage."
20 [Elisha] re-
sponded, "Bring me a new bowl and put salt in it." When they brought it to
him,
21 he went out to the spring of water where he threw the salt, saying,
"Thus says *Yhwh,* 'I hereby heal these waters; no more death or miscarriage will
result from them.'"
22 The water has remained wholesome until today *according
to the message that Elisha had spoken.*
23 *When he went up from there to Bethel,*
as he was ascending on the road some small children came out from the city
and proceeded to pelt him with stones and make fun of him, saying, "Go away,
Baldy. Go away, Baldy."
24 Turning around and seeing them, he cursed them *in
Yhwh's name.* Two bears came out of the woods and tore to pieces forty-two of
the children.
25 *He continued on from there to Mount Carmel before returning to
Samaria.*

Textual Notes

1 **from Gilgal**: So MT, G^{L}. G^{B*}: *from Jericho*, under the influence of the references to Jericho in the stories that follow.

2 **Stay here**: So MT, G^{L}: שב־נא פה. G^{B}: ἰδοὺ δὴ ἐνταῦθα κάθου, a minor expansion with הנה.

Yhwh (1): So MT, G^{L}. G^{B}: *god*.

when they came to Bethel: So G^{L}: καὶ ἔρχονται εἷς Βαιθηλ with the historical present that preserves the OG and renders ויבאו as in v. 4. G^{B} has the aorist singular ἦλθεν. MT *they descended to Bethel* (וירדו בית־אל) is anomalous as the only instance in the HB of descending to Bethel. See the Diachronic Analysis.

3 **members of the prophetic guild**: See the Note on 1 Kgs 20:35.

who were in Bethel: Place names compounded with בית do not need a preposition when in the accusative of place (2 Sam 2:32). See Burney, *Notes*, 264.

to meet them and said to Elisha: So G^{L}: εἰς συνάντησιν αὐτῶν καὶ εἶπον πρὸς Ελισσαιε = לקראתם ויאמרו אל־אלישע. MT, G^{B}: *to Elisha and said to him* (אל־אלישע ויאמרו אליו). While either reading is possible, G^{L} specifies Elijah's presence.

your master: The plural of rank is applied to Elijah (BDB, 10–11).

Say no more: Lit. *be quiet*. Reading הֶחֱשׁוּ, *Hip'il* imperative of חשה on analogy with the perfect form.[1]

4 **Elijah said to Elisha**: So G^{BL}. MT: ויאמר לו אליהו אלישע.

7 **went and stood**: So MT, G^{L}. G^{B} lacks *went*.

at a distance: מנגד מרחוק occurs nowhere else in the HB and probably results from מרחוק as a gloss on מנגד. For the meaning of מנגד as *at a distance* see BDB 617 and v. 15.

8 **mantle**: See the Note on 1 Kgs 19:13.

---

1 For other instances with first guttural verbs see Burney, *Notes*, 264.

rolled it up: The verb גלם occurs only here in the HB but is found in Rabbinic Hebrew, and the related noun is attested in Ezek 27:24. An alternate possibility based on Arabic is "cut."[2]

struck the water: So MT, G^{B}. G^{L} + *with it* (ἐν αὐτῇ).

9 **Ask what you want me to do for you**: So MT, G^{L} (שאל מה אעשה־לך). G^{B*} lacks שאל, which is retained in the rest of the Greek tradition.

10 **taken**: Though listed in older grammars (GKC 52s) as a *pu'al* participle lacking the מ preformative, this form is now recognized as a *qal* passive (Joüon 58b; WO, 375n).

it will be yours: So MT, G^{L} (יהי־לך כן). G^{B} καὶ ἔσται οὕτως reflects ויהי־כן, which is reminiscent of the formula in Genesis 1 (e.g., 1:7) and probably drawn from there.

but if you do not see, it will not be: So G^{L}: ἐὰν δὲ μή ἴδῃς οὐ μὴ γένηται = ואם לא תראה לא יהיה. MT, G^{B} (ואם־אין לא יהיה) is shorter but lacks the balance with the first part of the condition that is present in G^{L}.

11 **as they continued walking and talking**: For other examples of this construction cf. Joüon 123m.

horses of fire ... separated: So MT, G^{L}. G^{B}: *horse* with singular verb, perhaps a collective.

was taken up: So G^{BL} (καὶ ἀνελήμφθη = וַיִּקַּח) matching Elijah's word in v. 10 and one of the themes of this story. MT: ויעל.

12 **Israel's charioteer and horseman**: Reading רכב ישראל ופרשו with the two nouns vocalized either as *Qal* participles or as *qattāl* forms designating professions as indicated by G^{BL} and OL. The translation and interpretation follow a proposal by Richelle that both nouns refer to chariot driving and together form a hendiadys constituting a military title.[3]

13 **rolling up**: So G^{L}: καὶ ἀνείλατο as in v. 8. MT, G^{B}: וירם = καὶ ὕψωσεν, *picked up*. The change in verbs was occasioned partly by the subsequent interpolation in vv. 13b-14αα with its repetition of the statement that the garment had fallen from Elijah.

Elijah's mantle, which had fallen from him: So MT. G^{L} glosses Elijah's name with Elisha's. G^{B} has *Elijah's mantle which had fallen from Elisha.*

14 **he struck the water. When it did not divide, he said, "Where is Elijah's god?" Then Elisha struck the water a second time, and the water divided so that he crossed over on dry ground**: Based on G^{L}: καὶ ἐπάταξε τὰ ὕδατα καὶ οὐ διῃρέθη. καὶ εἶπεν Ελισσαιε ποῦ δὴ ἐστὶν ὁ θεὸς Ηλιου αφφω καὶ οὕτως ἐπάταξε τὰ ὕδατα καὶ διῃρέθη καὶ ἐπάταξεν Ελισσαιε τὰ ὕδατα ἐκ δευτέρου καὶ διῃρέθη τὰ ὕδατα καὶ διῆλθε διὰ ξηρᾶς. This is a double reading.[4] The underlined section is *kaige* and corresponds with the MT (אף־הוא ויכה את־המים ויחצו). The remainder of the MT reading (הנה והנה ויעבר אלישע) is drawn from v. 8. The part of G^{L} that is not underlined represents the OG reading. Most G witnesses (G^{B} is an exception) agree with G^{L} in describing Elisha's first

---

2 J. Kaltner, "What Did Elijah Do to His Mantle? The Hebrew Root *GLM*," in *Inspired Speech. Prophecy in the Ancient Near East. Essays in Honour of Herbert B. Huffmon* (ed. J. Kaltner and L. Stulman; London: T & T Clark, 2004): 225–30. While this sense would fit with the dividing of the Jordan and the double portion requested by Elisha, it also raises questions: With what did Elijah cut the mantle, and why did he cut it when Elisha tears his (v. 12)? Also, Elisha's torn clothes contrast with Elijah's mantle, which seems to remain intact (vv. 13-14).

3 Richelle, *Le testament d'Élisée*, 38–42. See also his "Elie et Élisée, auriges en Israël. Une métaphor militaire oubliée en 2 R 2, 12 et 13, 14," *RB* 117 (2010): 321–36 and "Revisiting 2 Kings 13:14-21," 65.

4 Trebolle, *Centena*, 162.

attempt as a failure. MT assumes as much in Elisha's outcry about the location of Elijah's god.

15 **When the members of the prophetic guild who were in Jericho at a distance saw his return**: So G^{L}: καὶ εἶδον οἱ υἱοὶ τῶν προφητῶν οἱ ἐν Ιεριχω ἐξ ἐναντίας ἀναστρέφοντα αὐτὸν = ויראו בני־הנביאים אשר־ביריחו מנגד את־שובו in preference to MT (ויראהו בני־הנביאים אשר־ביריחו מנגד). On מנגד in the sense of *at a distance* see v. 7.

16 **strong men**: בני־חיל is ambiguous in meaning, as חיל can refer to valor, strength, wealth, integrity, etc.

Yhwh's spirit: Though usually feminine, רוח here takes a masculine verb because of its association with Yhwh.[5]

valleys: So MT (*qere'*): הגאיות. G^{L} reflects הגבעות. The two words are aural variants; either is possible. G^{B} is expansive: *in the Jordan or on one of the mountains or one of the hills.*

18 **When they returned to him**: So MT, G^{L}. G^{B} lacks it due to haplography (αὐτὸν ... αὐτὸν).

19 **The city**: So MT, G^{B}. G^{L}: *this city.*

as my lord can see: So MT, G^{B}. G^{L} has *as you, my lord, can see.*

and causes miscarriage: So G^{L} (καὶ ἀτεκνοῦντα = ומשכלים) modifying מים. MT, G^{B}: *and the land causes miscarriage* (והארץ משכלת). The shorter reading also fits the story's focus on the Jericho spring.[6]

20 **bowl**: The exact nature of צלחית, a *hapax*, is unknown. Obviously related to צלחת, *dish* (21:13; Prov 19:24; 26:15) and צלחות, *cooking pots, dishes* (2 Chr 35:13), it has been taken as a jar or flask.[7]

21 **I hereby heal**: רפאתי is a III א verb vocalized as III ה.[8] On the present-tense translation see Ehrlich, *Randglossen*, 282.

no more death or miscarriage will result from them: So MT (לא־יהיה משם עוד מות ומשכלת). G^{B} (οὐκ ἔσται ἔτι ἐκεῖθεν θάνατος καὶ ἀτεκνουμένη) is identical except for the reversal of משם and עוד. G^{L} (καὶ οὐκ ἔσται ἔτι ἐκεῖθεν ἀποθνήσκων καὶ ἀτεκνουμένη δι' αὐτά) agrees with the G^{B} word order but reflects *and* at the beginning and *because of them* at the end of the lemma. The word משכלת is a *pi'el* participle, feminine singular, "one who miscarries." An abstract noun ("miscarriage") better fits the parallel with מות and needs to be vocalized differently, as מַשְׁכֶּלֶת or מַשְׁכֹּלֶת.

22 **according to the message that Elisha had spoken**: So G^{L}: κατὰ τὸ ῥῆμα ὃ ἐλάλησεν Ελισσαιε. MT, G^{B}: כדבר אלישע אשר דבר = *according to the word of Elisha which he spoke.*

23 **and proceeded to pelt him with stones and make fun of him**: So G^{L}: καὶ ἐλίθαζον αὐτὸν καὶ κατέπαιζον αὐτου) = ויסקלוהו ויתקלסו בו. MT and G^{B} lack ויסקלוהו because of haplography. Pelting with stones was a way of displaying contempt and driving out an unwanted person (2 Sam 15:5-8).

Go away, Baldy. Go away, Baldy: So MT, G^{L}. G^{B} uniquely lacks the repetition.[9]

24 **Two bears came out**: So MT, G^{L}. G^{B} precedes with *behold.* דב, a feminine noun, is treated elsewhere as masculine (Hos 13:8) and appears to be a case in which one noun, regardless of gender, is used for an entire species (Joüon 134c).

---

5 WO, 104n.

6 Šanda (*Könige* II, 14) proposes that the original ומשכלים was changed to the feminine singular in view of v. 21 and then *earth* was added as its subject.

7 Cogan and Tadmor, *II Kings*, 36. But see also Rendsburg, *Israelian Hebrew*, 82–83.

8 Cf. Burney, *Notes*, 267; GKC 75oo; Joüon 78g.

9 On עלה as *go away* see Cogan and Tadmor, *II Kings*, 38 and Num 16:27; 1 Kgs 15:19; 2 Kgs 12:19; Jer 21:2; 37:5.

Synchronic Analysis

A time of transition

This chapter stands between the closing formulae for Ahaziah of Israel and the opening formulae for Jehoram of Judah and therefore outside of the structural skeleton of Kings. This placement affords it a liminal setting in accord with the content of the stories it contains. It is the time of transition between Elijah and Elisha. Spatially, Elijah's mortal existence culminates between earth and heaven. He does not die like a human, but neither is he divine. His translation places him in the exalted company of Enoch, who *walked with god and was not because god took him* (Gen 5:24) and Moses, whose burial place no one knows (Deut 34:6). His successor, Elisha, is in the process of finding his own prophetic legs as he first fails, then succeeds at replicating Elijah's division of the Jordan. Elisha's healing of the spring at Jericho shows that he has the same power as his mentor. But his encounter with the children at Bethel suggests that some doubts linger because of his contrasts with Elijah—even if he dispels them with his curse. In the end the two stories in vv. 19-22 and 23-24 serve to confirm and illustrate the power and authority Elisha has inherited as Elijah's heir and successor.

Connections with surrounding material

The three stories share motifs with surrounding material. The fiery chariot and horses recall the fire Elijah summoned from heaven (1 Kgs 18); Elisha's journey to Carmel at the end of the story (v. 25) recalls that same episode; the fifty "sons of the prophets" in vv. 7, 16-17 bring to mind the three captains of fifty in the previous chapter; Elijah's mantle retrieved by Elisha and used by both to divide the Jordan reminds the reader of Elijah's designation of Elisha in 1 Kgs 19:19. The links to the subsequent Elisha tales are even more integral. The title *Israel's charioteer and horseman* occurs elsewhere for him (2 Kgs 13:14) and fits with his involvement in politics and warfare (2 Kgs 6:17). The stories about Elisha are also more focused on his role as a wonder-worker, so that an explanation of how he came into such power is especially appropriate as a prelude to them.

Structure of the chapter

The chapter evinces a concentric structure that has been noticed in previous scholarly treatments:[10]

Elijah and Elisha leave Gilgal (v. 1-2a)
  Journey to Bethel, encounter with sons of prophets (vv. 2b-4a)
    Journey to Jericho, encounter with sons of prophets (vv. 4b-6)
      Fifty sons of prophets watch, v. 7
        Elijah divides the Jordan, he and Elisha cross (v. 8)
          Elisha requests double portion of Elijah's spirit vv. 9-10)
            Elijah taken into heaven (vv. 11-12)
        Elisha picks up Elijah's mantle (v. 13)
       Elisha divides and recrosses the Jordan (v. 14)
      Fifty sons of prophets search for Elijah, vv. 15-18
    Healing of spring in Jericho (vv. 19-22)
  Elisha journeys to Bethel, encounter with jeering children (vv. 23-24)
Elisha goes from Bethel to Samaria via Mount Carmel (v. 25)

10 Compare J. S. Burnett, "'Going Down' to Bethel,' Elijah and Elisha in the Theological Geography of the Deuteronomistic History," *JBL* 129 (2010), 288–89, and Cohn, *2 Kings*, 11.

The chapter and the story in vv. 1-18 especially are built around geographic locations with Elijah and Elisha at the center. The members of the prophetic guild ("sons of the prophets") are on the periphery.[11] The moment of Elijah's translation is central as the point at which the transition from Elijah to Elisha occurs. The mantle of Elijah that Elisha retrieves and uses to split the Jordan is a symbol of the power transferred to Elisha, but it is the spirit that is the source of the power, not the mantle. This power is the foundation of Elisha's career.

2:1-6: The journey of Elijah and Elisha

The focal point of Elijah's translation is evident in the anticipatory summary with which the chapter begins: *when YHWH took Elijah up to heaven in the tempest* (v. 1a). The first six verses recount the trek by Elijah and Elisha to Gilgal, Bethel, Jericho, and the Jordan (vv. 1-6). The reason for their journey is not clear except that it is under YHWH's direction, as Elijah repeatedly tells Elisha. Gilgal, Bethel, and Jericho are all settings for stories mentioning the "sons of the prophets," so this may be Elijah's "farewell tour." The three sites also retrace Israel's itinerary in the Promised Land under Joshua. The itinerary is a touchstone for the transition from Elijah to Elisha and resembles that from Moses to Joshua. The journey is a test of Elisha's perseverance, proving that he is a worthy successor.[12] Elijah's repeated order to Elisha to stay behind tests the disciple's persistence. Narratively the journey is a constant anticipation of Elijah's imminent departure. In each city the "sons of the prophets" inform Elisha of what he already knows—that YHWH will take Elijah from him *today.*

Repeated conversations

The conversations in Gilgal and Bethel (vv. 2-6) are repetitive, with vv 2, 4, and 6 being nearly identical and v. 3 closely paralleling v. 5. These repetitions function for different but related purposes.[13] Elijah tells Elisha to stay behind because YHWH has sent him on to the next location. Elisha in turn invokes YHWH in an oath, swearing that he will not leave his master, so that the two of them go on together. Elisha's staying power points to him as a fitting successor. The reason for his adherence becomes clear in the encounters with the "sons of the prophets;" Elijah is to be taken from him. Their words *taken* and *from above your head* allude to his manner of departure. Elisha is aware of YHWH's plans and instructs the prophets to keep silence.[14] At the same time, the word "taken" is ambiguous. The narrator and readers already familiar with the story understand its full implications. The verb is used for Enoch's translation (Gen 5:24), though without particulars about the process. But the sons of the prophets and perhaps Elisha himself, as well as readers who do not know the story, believe this statement to mean that Elijah will die and thus no longer be available as Elisha's mentor. The idea that someone would be bodily taken up into heaven is unexpected, the (rare) precedent of Enoch notwithstanding. The surprising nature of Elijah's disappearance[15] is what motivates the search for him in vv. 16-18.

---

11 A. Schmitt, *Entrückung-Aufnahme-Himmelfahrt. Untersuchungen zu einem Vorstellungsbereich im AT* (FB 10; Stuttgart: Katholisches Bibelwerk, 1976^{2}), 76.

12 Hens-Piazza, *Kings*, 234; Sweeney, *Kings*, 272.

13 R. A. Carlson, "Élisée le successeur d'Élie," *VT* 20 (1970), esp. 386–87. Also J. R. Lundbom, "Elijah's Chariot Ride," *JJS* 24 (1973), 45, who notes that the repetitions give the stories their rhythm while the narrative moves forward through variations.

14 The force of גם in Elisha's repeated response, גם־אני ידעתי, is assurance: "Yes, I know this as well as you."

15 Or the suspicion of murder? A suggestion by Walter Dietrich (personal communication).

2:7: Fifty men The journey that Elijah and Elisha take together transforms their relationship. Verses 6 and 7 speak of *the two of them*. The social gap between them has diminished; they have become partners.[16] They cross the Jordan, just the two of them, together. The mention of the fifty men from the prophets in v. 7 prepares for the search undertaken in vv. 16-18. It also provides witnesses to Elijah's dividing of the Jordan parallel to those in v. 15 who witness the same feat at Elisha's hands. It thus clarifies how those in v. 15 can know that Elijah's spirit has come to rest on Elisha—because both performed the same wonder.

2:8: Elijah divides the Jordan Having come to the Jordan, Elisha stands by as Elijah removes his mantle, a symbol of his prophetic authority (v. 8), and after rolling it up, strikes the water with it, dividing it so that the two of them walk across on dry land. The parallelism with Moses and Joshua that was hinted at in the itinerary in vv. 2-6 is more pronounced here.[17] Elijah's mantle replaces Moses' rod that he extends to divide the sea of reeds (Exod 14:16) and with which he performs other wonders. Like the people of Israel, Elijah and Elisha cross over the water on dry land. As Moses died east of the Jordan, so Elijah's earthly walk ends on the east side of the Jordan. This is where Elisha's career, like his mentor's (1 Kgs 17), begins. In succeeding verses (esp. vv. 13-15) Elisha is presented as Joshua to Elijah's Moses.[18]

2:9: Elisha's request Elijah asks his protégé, who has now made the final crossing with him, what he can do for him before he is *taken* (v. 9). It is the key moment in their relationship. Now more than partners, they are linked in succession. Elisha alone has crossed with Elijah; he is worthy to be heir.[19] Elisha's request is not for double Elijah's spirit, nor for two-thirds of it.[20] Rather, he seeks the right of the firstborn who receives a double portion of his deceased father's property (Deut 21:17). Elisha thus claims Elijah as his "father" and asks for the share coming to the principal heir. At the same time, as the heir he is the "double" of Elijah in the sense of being a kind of "copy" or a second version of his mentor. The spirit for which Elisha lobbies emanates from YHWH and brings the gift of prophecy (1 Sam 10:5-10; 19:18-24). The פִּי־שְׁנַיִם is "double mouth." Elisha is the spokesman for YHWH just as Elijah was. Elijah's mantle is not magic in and of itself; Elisha's prophetic power and authority are endowed by YHWH.

2:10: Seeing and perceiving The spirit can be apportioned (Num 11:24-30), but it is YHWH who does the apportioning. Elisha's request is difficult to grant (v. 10) because only YHWH can grant it. Elisha is assured of receiving it if he sees Elijah taken. This is more than a simple condition. The verb *see* entails comprehension, perception. Prophets are *seers* (1 Sam 9:9; Isa 30:10), who have the gift of seeing things invisible to others (cf. Num 22:22-35; 2 Kgs 6:16-17; Dan 10:7). If, therefore, Elisha sees or perceives

---

16 C. Schäfer-Lichtenberger, "'Josua' und 'Elischa' – eine biblische Argumentation zur Begründung der Autorität und Legitimität des Nachfolgers," *ZAW* 101 (1989), 215.

17 See R. P. Carroll, "The Elijah-Elisha Sagas: Some Remarks on Prophetic Succession in Ancient Israel," *VT* 19 (1969), esp. 411–14.

18 See Schäfer-Lichtenberger, "Josua und Elischa," 198–222, who develops this theme using Weberian categories, although she attributes the theme, erroneously in my view, to DtrH.

19 Schäfer-Lichtenberger, "Josua und Elischa," 215.

20 *Pace* Joüon 101b. In Zech 13:8, which Joüon cites in support, פִּי־שְׁנַיִם has the sense of two-thirds only because it occurs with הַשְּׁלִשִׁית, *one-third* (Burney, *Notes*, 265).

Elijah being taken into heaven, then he will have been endowed with the prophetic spirit of his mentor. Without such a gift he will not comprehend the disappearance. Thus the description of Elijah's translation that follows confirms Elisha's endowment.

2:11: The fiery chariot

As they continue walking and talking, a fiery chariot and horses of fire appear and come between the two of them. The fire is reminiscent of the scenes on Carmel (1 Kgs 18) and in the previous chapter (2 Kgs 1) where it signaled divine presence and approval of the prophet. More generally in the Hebrew Bible fire is an element of theophany, especially on Sinai (Exod 3:2; 13:21; 19:18; 24:17; Deut 33:2; Isa 30:27; Ezek 1:4; 8:2; Hab 3:3-5). The image partakes of the myth of the divine warrior, which also depicts YHWH as a chariot rider (Deut 33:26; 2 Sam 22:11//Ps 18:11; Isa 19:1; Hab 3:8; Ps 68:5, 34), like Baʿal, the "rider on the clouds" in Ugaritic texts. Closer to home, the image here is like 2 Kgs 6:17, where Elisha's servant sees the divine warrior's entire force of fiery chariots and horses supporting Israel.

Elijah's assumption

Contrary to popular rehearsal of this scene in painting and song, Elijah is not transported in a chariot.[21] He is taken up in the storm or tempest (סערה). He disappears as suddenly as he appeared (1 Kgs 17:1).[22] The סערה reminds one of the theophany on Horeb in 1 Kings 19. Despite the apparent repudiation of storm theophany in that passage, the סערה is a common theophanic element (Job 38:1; 40:6; Isa 29:6; Ezek 1:4; Zech 9:14). Because of its association with the divine warrior it is especially common in contexts describing divine wrath and punishment (Jer 23:19; 30:23; Ezek 13:11, 13; Ps 83:16). In Elijah's translation it conveys a sense of the numinous and powerful but also of YHWH's judgment for which Elijah has stood and that he has invoked. It is this tradition that Elisha will continue and further. The moment is transformative for him; it is his encounter with the divine for which the journey with Elijah and the questions of the members of the prophetic guild have prepared him.[23]

2:12: Elisha's transformation

The vividness of the scene in v. 12 is conveyed by the use of participles. While Elisha is watching Elijah's departure, he keeps crying out "*My father, my father, Israel's charioteer and horseman.*" The expression occurs in 2 Kgs 13:14 in the context of Elisha's own death scene. It is a lament, as suggested by the repetition of *my father* and King Joash's weeping as he says these words.[24] The designation of Elijah as *father* recognizes his leadership role and his close relationship with his disciple.[25] When he can no longer see his mentor Elisha, overcome with emotion, seizes his garments and tears them in two, further confirmation that the cry is one of lament, since tearing clothes is a well-known sign of grief (Gen 37:34; 2 Sam 1:11; 13:31; Job 1:20). It is also a symbolic act, as the parallel with 1 Kgs 11:30 shows.[26] Tearing his clothes in two fits with the two lead characters in the context. It is an acknowledgment that he has received the double portion of Elijah's spirit

---

21 The interpretation is ancient, appearing in Sir 48:9.

22 Schmitt, *Entrückung-Aufnahme-Himmelfahrt*, 111.

23 Schäfer-Lichtenberger, "Josua und Elischa," 217.

24 K. Galling, " Der Ehrenname Elisas und die Entrückung Elias," *ZTK* 53 (1956), 130–31.

25 Carlson ("Élisée," 387) notes that the cry of *my father* in 2:12 especially exudes respect, affection, and pain.

26 Schmitt, *Entrückung-Aufnahme-Himmelfahrt*, 118–19.

as requested. His own garment is unusable; from now on he will wear Elijah's mantle, a literal investment with the master's spirit and power. In the stories that follow Elisha exhibits a distinct lack of emotion, an "asceticism of character" brought upon him by the spirit he has received.[27] He becomes a person of greater *gravitas* and self-confidence than he was as Elijah's disciple.

2:13-14: Elisha at the Jordan

Retrieving Elijah's mantle, Elisha returns to the Jordan, where he stands poised on the bank ready to cross, this time alone (v. 13). Taking the mantle, which is evidently still rolled up, he performs the same wonder as Elijah, dividing the water and crossing over the river. The repetitions noting the fallen mantle and Elisha's use of it to divide the water stress his place as Elijah's successor.[28] The clause from v. 8aα, ויקח אליהו את־אדרתו, is repeated nearly *verbatim* in v. 14aα, ויקח את־אדרת אליהו, and it sets the two prophets in parallel. The divided water corresponds to Elisha's now divided garment. Still, there are differences. Elisha strikes the water twice, where Elijah did so only once. Elisha also calls upon Yhwh, asking about the whereabouts of *the god of Elijah.* What is more, the description of Elisha's deed does not mention that he crossed on dry ground as in v. 8 but only that Elisha crossed over. The overall impression is that Elisha is not yet fully at ease with the power he wields. He falters slightly in this, his first miracle. He is not quite to the level of his master. He possesses, in other words, not all of Elijah's power but two portions of it. The description of the water dividing (ויחצו הנה והנה) is identical to v. 8, so Elisha eventually accomplishes the same thing, albeit without the same facility as Elijah. The use of the passive (*Nip'al*), *the waters were divided*, suggests that they were acted upon by an outside force. The description of them as "here and here" would be fitting for an oral presentation of the story.[29]

Elisha takes on a new role

Elisha's crossing calls to mind Israel's crossing of the Jordan under Joshua (Josh 3). He is Joshua as Elijah was Moses. Elisha ministered to Elijah as Joshua did to Moses (שרת, Exod 33:11; 34:13; Num 11:28; 1 Kgs 19:22), and both of their masters divided water for passage on dry ground. Both Joshua and Elisha crossed the Jordan from east to west, into the Promised Land to begin a new mission and a new leadership role. Yhwh's word to Joshua also holds for Elisha: "This day I will begin to exalt you in the sight of all Israel, so that they may know that I will be with you as I was with Moses [Elijah]" (Josh 3:7). Their names even have the same meaning: "Yhwh /god gives victory."

2:15 The prophetic guild members recognize Elisha

Having known beforehand that Elijah would be taken, the members of the prophetic guild in Jericho see Elisha divide and cross the Jordan alone using Elijah's mantle and recognize that Elijah's spirit has come to rest upon him. They acknowledge his authority by bowing before him (v. 15). This means that v. 15 is further confirmation of Elisha's request in v. 9. It thereby initiates the stories about Elisha that will dominate 2 Kings until his death in chapter 13. That said, vv. 15-18 are ambiguous about how much the sons of the prophets actually witnessed. Verse 15 implies that they saw Elisha divide the Jordan. But does that mean that they also saw Elijah's ascension? Verse 10 suggests that this was the

27 Long, *2 Kings*, 29.
28 Carlson, "Élisée," 387.
29 I owe this observation to my student, Wes Parker.

special property of Elisha, so they must not have witnessed what Elisha *saw*. This explains their use of the word *spirit* in two different senses in vv. 15-16, first as a metaphor for prophetic power and authority and then as a hypostasis of YHWH, which they think may have transported Elijah's body elsewhere.

2:16-18: The search for Elijah

Verses 16-18 indicate that the prophets know that Elijah was *taken* by YHWH's spirit while also suggesting that they were unaware of the exact manner of the event, for they go searching for him in the terrain east of the Jordan. They see his disappearance as just another of the sort for which he is famous, so their request reminds one of Obadiah's fear that YHWH's spirit would carry him away (1 Kgs 18:12).[30] The fact that Elisha gives in to their request suggests that he has not fully matured in his new role or does not have the full spirit of Elijah. Still, the failure of the search party to find any trace of Elijah further confirms Elisha's authority. The futile search is another parallel with Moses, who was buried by YHWH in a place only he knows (Deut 34:6). The expedition confirms what Elisha already knows—that Elijah is nowhere to be found because he was translated out of "sight" of the members of the prophetic guild.

2:19-22: Cleansing the Jericho spring

The two anecdotes that follow in vv. 19-22 and 23-25 continue to illustrate Elisha's newfound power resulting from his inheritance of Elijah's spirit. They show Elisha becoming comfortable in his new role as he exhibits the power to give life and take it. The first anecdote concerns the spring at Jericho and how it came to produce such good water. The story resembles Exod 15:23-25a in its transformation of defective water by adding some common item to it, and Elisha now appears in the role of Moses. The story relates that the water of Jericho's famous spring was once bad and caused miscarriages. How it was known that the water was the culprit is not explained. The reader may recall Hiel's loss of his two sons as a consequence of his rebuilding of Jericho (1 Kgs 16:34). Is the trouble experienced by the prophets a continuation of the curse uttered against the city by Joshua (6:26)? The text does not draw this correlation, but it is appropriate that Elisha, the new Joshua, is the one who heals the spring, and perhaps undoes the curse. Salt is used elsewhere to effect ritual purification (Lev 2:13; Ezek 43:24) and symbolizes cleansing here. The newness of the vessel connotes purity and ensures that the salt remains ritually clean. Tossing the salt into the spring, Elisha pronounces its water wholesome (v. 21). This is no magic trick, for it is YHWH who pronounces the healing formula. Elisha, as YHWH's spokesman, quotes him (v. 22). These two verses remind the reader of the ultimate source of Elijah's power and spirit, which now rest upon Elisha.

2:23-24: The derisive children of Bethel

The final anecdote of the chapter in vv. 23-24 is one of the most disturbing stories in the HB. Though simple on the surface, it presents a number of interpretive challenges, including the location of Bethel, the identity of the נערים, and the nature and motive for their derision of Elisha by calling him *baldy*. The story takes place as Elisha approaches Bethel. Infamous as the site of one of the royal shrines erected by Jeroboam (1 Kgs 12:26-33; 13), it thus possesses a reputation that stands in the background despite the absence of any explicit link in the present tale. The mention of Bethel further disparages the site as the home of such impudent children even if it does not furnish a motive for their ridicule of the prophet.

30 G. del Olmo Lete, "La vocación de Eliseo," *EstBib* 26 (1967): 287–93.

The meaning of םינטק םירענ

Burnett links the נערים קטנים to the cult site at Bethel, arguing that they are not small children but young adult males associated with the royal and priestly establishment at the shrine.[31] He points to David (1 Sam 16:11; 17:14), Solomon (1 Kgs 3:7), and Hadad the Edomite (1 Kgs 11:17) as others called נערים קטנים and to Rehoboam's peers as ילדים, the other term used for Elisha's mockers (2 Kgs 2:24). But while both נער and ילד/ילדים can refer to young adults, the case for נערים קטנים/נער having that sense here fades upon examination. While David is referred to as a נער and as הקטן *the youngest* among his brothers, he is never called a נער קטן. Solomon uses the expression metaphorically referring to his lack of experience. It does not, therefore, refer to his age or status at the time of his prayer. Indeed, for the metaphor to work it must refer to a child who lacks wisdom and experience because of its young age. The reference to Hadad as a נער קטן concerns an earlier time of his life when he fled to Egypt and not the point at which YHWH raised him up as an adversary (*śatan*) to Solomon. The text does not give his age at the time of flight but implies that he was very young, since the flight occurred during David's reign and this notice about YHWH raising Hadad against Solomon is set near the end of the latter's reign. The fact that Hadad fled with a group of Edomites also suggests that he was a minor.

Respect for the holy man

There is every reason, then, to think that the נערים קטנים in 2 Kgs 2:23 were young children, not young adults. This in turn suggests that the tale is less a polemic against Bethel than a cautionary tale about showing proper respect for the man of god if not for prophets in general. The children's cry of עלה is not a call for the prophet to commit apostasy by worshiping at Bethel but an order to *go away*.[32] They mock him with the nickname "Baldy" (קרח), which is sometimes taken to refer to Elisha's tonsure as a holy man. Sweeney, for instance, notes that head shaving was associated with ritual activities such as mourning for the dead (Lev 21:5; Deut 14:1; Isa 15:2; Jer 16:6; Ezek 7:18; 27:31; Amos 8:10; Mic 1:16) and that the Levitical name Korah means "bald."[33] Buis even proposes that baldness was the characteristic that the nameless prophet in 1 Kgs 20:38 disguised and that allowed the king of Israel to recognize who he was (v. 41).[34] If Elisha's baldness is a mark of his status, then the children are mocking not just him but his profession. However, no priestly function is claimed for Elisha, and he would not be in mourning because Elijah did not die. Also, passages like Lev 19:27 speak of certain kinds of tonsure but not of baldness, and these legal texts prohibit ritual haircutting rather than allowing it. The link with 1 Kgs 20:38, 41 is weak, since that story explicitly has the prophet covering his eyes. Moreover, it was long hair rather than baldness that was associated with asceticism, as in the case of the Nazirite (Num 6:1-21). Elisha's baldness, then, seems to be natural and the ridicule of the children personal. That said, it is interesting that Elijah, in just the previous chapter, was designated a hairy man (איש בעל שער). The contrast between the two men is marked, and the mocking *Baldy* inevitably calls to mind that contrast. Thus the children's derision raises Elisha's self-doubts about his suitability as Elijah's successor. His response may also be compelled by codes of honor and shame, lest

---

31 Burnett, "'Going Down' to Bethel."
32 *Pace* Olley, *Kings*, 221. See the Note.
33 Sweeney, *Kings*, 275.
34 Buis, *Rois*, 189.

he damage his status and that of the prophetic community.[35] He curses the children in Yhwh's name. The actualization of the curse in the form of the two attacking bears confirms Elisha's legitimacy as Elijah's successor as Yhwh's personal representative and his control in that position of divine power.

2:25: To Samaria via Mount Carmel

The notice of Elisha's return first to Mount Carmel and then to Samaria in v. 25 prepares for the next mention of him in 3:11, where he is with the Israelite army that has marched out from Samaria to campaign in Edom. Elisha comes to bridge the prophetic (Mount Carmel) and the royal (Samaria) worlds much better than his mentor did, as the following chapters will illustrate.

Diachronic Analysis

Outside of the DtrH structure

The secondary nature of the present chapter vis-à-vis DtrH is evident because of its location between the closing formulae for Ahaziah at the end of ch. 1 and the opening formulae for Joram at the start of ch. 3, thus outside the structural framework of Kings in MT.[36]

2:1: The beginning of the first *legenda* and PN's introduction to it

The three stories in the chapter were originally independent *legenda* about Elisha. The first in vv. 1-18 consisted of vv. 1b, 7b-13a, 14aβb (ויכה .. אלישע).[37] It had its origin in the Elisha *legenda* and sought to show how Elisha inherited Elijah's spirit and succeeded his mentor as a man of god.[38] The rest of the story (vv. 1a, 2-6, 7a, 13b-14aα, 15-18) is PN's supplementation. Verses 1a, 2-6 anticipate Elijah's translation and stress the foreknowledge of it by Elisha and the members of the prophetic guild. The opening clause, v. 1a, is anticipatory. The *legenda* proper began with Elijah's and Elisha's departure together from Gilgal (v. 1b) The prophetic guild (v. 2) is almost the exclusive property of the Elisha materials (1 Kgs 20:35; 2 Kgs 2:3, 5, 7, 15; 4:1, 38; 5:22; 6:1; 9:1). PN adapted it for the present tale. As he presents it in vv. 2-6, there were different branches of the guild in different cities. In other tales they seem to be marginalized and to have lived on the periphery of Israelite society. They may have followed different leaders or "fathers" (2:12; 6:21; 13:14; 1 Sam 10:12), but the series of visits here suggests that Elijah

---

35 D. Neufeld, "Mocking Boys, Baldness, and Bears: Elisha's Deadly Honour (2 Kgs 2.23-24)," *Not Sparing the Child: Human Sacrifice in the Ancient World and Beyond. Studies in Honor of Professor Paul G. Mosca* (ed. V. D. Arbel, *et al.*; London: Bloomsbury T&T Clark, 2015): 114–30. Some caution is in order, however, since Neufeld's evidence for such codes is drawn from the Greco-Roman world rather than the ancient Near East.

36 See the Note on 3:1 regarding the OG arrangement.

37 Similarly Würthwein (*1. Könige 17–2. Könige 25*, 274), though he overlooks the *Wiederaufnahme* in vv. 13b-14aα.

38 See the Diachronic Analysis on 1 Kgs 19:19-21 for discussion of its relationship to 2 Kgs 2. Schäfer-Lichtenberger ("Josua und Elischa," 213) sees the two as so closely related that they can be viewed as two parts of the same composition. By contrast, Eissfeldt ("Die Komposition von I Reg 16,29–II Reg 13,25," 50–51, 54–55) saw them as doublets. Sauerwein (*Elischa*, 27) observes that Elijah's ascension explains why he disappears from the narrative henceforth as well as the origins and source of Elisha's miraculous powers.

and Elisha oversaw them all. In vv. 3 and 5 the prophets speak to Elisha of *your* master, who is above or over *your* head, suggesting that he had a special relationship with Elijah and that the two of them were in a separate class from the others. As prophets, they advise Elisha of Elijah's imminent departure. But he is a prophet too, so he already knows. His instruction for them to keep silent is not necessarily a rebuke but just an affirmation that he is aware of the situation and not in need of their counsel. It is not clear how much they really know. They say that YHWH will take Elijah from above or over his head, but do they understand this literally (transported to heaven) or metaphorically (death)?

2:2-7a: The geographical problem

Verse 2 presents problems of geography and itinerary. It is the only instance in the HB of someone going down to Bethel. G^L avoids this problem and is preferable. Even so, Joshua's Gilgal, Khirbet el-Mafjar, which is the site of the Umayyad Hisham's Palace, is close to Jericho, so that Elijah and Elisha would have to backtrack from there to Bethel and then return to Jericho. The distance—ca. 65 km[39]—is too great for a single day's journey. Thenius, observing these problems long ago, proposed that this was a different Gilgal, namely modern Jiljulia, ca. 11 km north of Bethel.[40] This proposal is accepted by many scholars. It is within a day's walking distance and more direct than the better-known Gilgal. The parallel with Moses and Joshua is retained in the name Gilgal even if the location is different.[41]

2:7b-13a, 14aβ b: The rest of the *legenda*

Elisha goes with Elijah all the way to the Jordan despite Elijah's repeated attempts to get him to stay behind. In this way he shows his worthiness to be Elijah's successor. At this point (v. 7b) the older *legenda* resumed, picking up from v. 1b, but not before PN introduces the fifty men who will later be commissioned to search for Elijah's body (v. 7a). Standing on the shore of the Jordan, Elijah uses his rolled-up mantle to divide the water for the two of them to cross on dry ground (v. 8). They keep walking and talking for some time (V 11aα), which is the source of the ambiguity in the *legenda* about the distance of the site of Elijah's

---

39 Würthwein, *1. Könige 17–2. Könige 25*, 274.

40 Thenius, *Könige*, 265. There are several different Gilgals in the Bible (W. R. Kotter, "Gilgal," *ABD* 2 [1992]: 1022–24; J. Muilenburg, "Gilgal," *IDB* 2 [1962]: 398–99. This is not surprising since the name, "stone circle," refers to a simple sanctuary. Jiljuliah is mentioned by Eusebius (*Onomasticon* 66) as the "other Gilgal very close to Bethel."

41 Burnett's argument ("'Going Down' to Bethel") that the descent to Bethel disparages the site for its cultic affiliations faces several problems. First, he assumes MT without taking stock of G^L's evidence for a less problematic reading. Second, he sees the descent to Bethel as originating with Elijah's descent from the mountain in the previous chapter, a datum that is textually suspect. Third, he locates the source of the negative perspective on Bethel in DtrH ideology, yet the Elijah-Elisha stories do not share DtrH's concern for cultic centralization (e.g., 1 Kgs 18) and are mostly post-DtrH additions as revised by PN. Finally, 2 Kgs 2:23 has Elisha ascending to Bethel in conformity to the norm. Burnett argues (1) that there is no danger of assuming a cultic purpose on Elisha's part in this instance because he does not enter the city, (2) that the expression *go up from there* is never used for worship, and (3) that Elisha's cursing of the נערים shows disapproval of the sanctuary there. The third point is dubious, as noted. The other two do not explain why the author misses this opportunity to disparage Bethel by speaking of descent to it if this was what was intended in v. 2. The result is that going down to Bethel in v. 2 remains anomalous and continues to defy explanation if one adopts the MT reading.

assumption from the Jordan. In the conversation Elisha makes his request for the double portion of Elijah's spirit (vv. 9-10). The rest of the *legenda* shows how Elisha fulfills the stipulation of seeing Elijah taken and thus receives the promised double portion (vv. 11-12), by which he is able to divide the Jordan and cross just as Elijah had done (vv. 13-14*). Elijah does not just vanish before Elisha's eyes; Elisha sees the translation in all senses of the verb (cf. the Synchronic Analysis) so that his request is granted. The garments he tears in lament (v. 12) mark the end of his former life, and the mantle he retrieves is the vestment for his new role. He strikes the water of the Jordan with it in an effort to duplicate Elijah's miracle (vv. 13a + 14aβ). The initial attempt is ineffective (see the Note), so he cries out for Elijah's god and then strikes the water again, this time with success. He crosses the Jordan, which he has divided, entering into his new life as Elijah's successor with the heir's portion of his spirit. With that the older *legenda* ended.

The role of the chariot and horses of fire

Since Elijah was taken up in a tempest, the actual role and purpose of the fiery chariot and horses are not immediately evident.[42] Some have pointed to 2 Kgs 23:11 as suggesting a mythic origin for them as symbols of the sun.[43] However, both the image and the title (*my father, Israel's charioteer and horseman*) are features that are intimately connected with Elisha's interventions in Israelite wars (6:17; 13:14) and are secondarily applied here to Elijah, for whom no such interventions are recorded.[44] The title derives its significance from 6:17, which envisions Elisha as the commander of YHWH's heavenly army (6:17).[45] Joash's lament using the title in 13:14 expresses the fear that the loss of Elisha will mean the loss of the heavenly armies from defending Israel. Similarly, in 2:12 Elisha laments Elijah's loss for himself and for Israel. Beyond Elisha's use of the title, the heavenly chariot and horses clarify Elijah's fate. He is not born away in a windstorm but is transported into the realm of the divine.

The function of PN's additions

The *legenda* left some ambiguity as to where Elijah's ascension took place and whether it was witnessed by the other prophets. PN's additions were intended in part to clarify this ambiguity.[46] He interpolated vv. 13b-14aα by *Wiederaufnahme* (את־אדרת אליהו אשר נפלה מעליו) in order to accommodate vv. 15-18. The interpolation brings Elisha back to the Jordan. While the two prophets continue to walk and talk after crossing to the east side, Elijah's mantle is recovered by Elisha on the

42 Würthwein (*1. Könige 17–2. Könige 25*, 277) even argues that they are additional.

43 C. Alcaina-Canosa, "Eliseo sucede a Elías (2 Re 2:1-18)," *EstBib* 31 (1972): 323; Kittel, *Könige*, 188–89; Montgomery, *Kings*, 353.

44 Schmitt (*Entrückung-Aufnahme-Himmelfahrt*, 126–31) adds the following: the oath in 2:2, 4, 6 occurs elsewhere only in 4:30; הנה והנה in v. 8 is found only in 4:35; the inquiry *what can I do for you* in 2:9 is found also in 4:2, 13; and the fiery chariot and horsemen in 2:11 are like those in 6:17. See also H. N. Rösel, "2 Kön 2,1-18 als Elija- oder Elischa-Geschichte?" *BN* 59 (1991) 33–36, in response to J. Conrad, "2.Kön 2,1-18 als Elija-Geschichte," in *Wünschet Jerusalem Frieden* (ed. M. Augustin and K.-D. Schunck, BEATAJ 13; Frankfurt: Peter Lang, 1988), 263–71. See most recently K. Weingart, "'My Father, My Father! Chariot of Israel and Its Horses!' (2 Kings 2:12 // 13:14): Elisha's or Elijah's Title?" *JBL* 137 (2018): 257-70.

45 Khalid ibn al-Walid, buried in Hama, Syria, and known as the "sword of Allah," is an analog. Gray, *Kings*, 476.

46 Trebolle, *Centena*, 160–61.

river's bank (vv. 13a, 14aβb). Verses 15-18 remove any doubt about the nature of Elijah's ascension since they assume that it took place at some distance from the Jordan, where the fifty prophets conduct their search, anticipated by PN's interpolation in v. 7a.[47] The guild members do not fully understand what happened to Elijah despite their foreknowledge that he would be *taken* from his position over Elisha. They evidently believe him dead. Their fruitless search confirms that he was *taken* alive, bodily, into god's presence at some place beyond the Jordan to the east and that Elisha alone witnessed the event. The location and corporality of Elijah's translation were also important to PN for highlighting Elijah's likeness to Moses, who was buried by YHWH personally in an unknown location east of the Jordan.

2:19-24: The *legenda* and its revision

The remaining two tales in vv. 19-24 were independent *legenda* that described wonders performed by the man of god on his own. PN revised them, ascribing the miracles to YHWH, and used them to show Elisha coming into his own as Elijah's heir and successor. The first one (vv. 19-22a minus *thus says YHWH* in v. 21) may have doubled as an etiology for the sweet water of the Jericho spring, although Jericho is not presently mentioned.[48] It began as a straightforward *legenda* about Elisha healing the spring by an act of ritual magic (vv. 20-21a) that entailed the use of salt, an agent of ritual purification, from a new (hence, ritually clean) bowl, and the pronunciation of a ritual formula: *I hereby heal this water* (v. 21b). The act may have been understood as an exorcism, driving out the harmful spirits of the water with the aid of the purifying agent.[49] PN modified it into a story about the efficacy of the prophetic word by the addition of the *Wortereignisformel* in v. 21bα (כה־אמר יהוה) and the fulfillment in v. 22b (כדבר אלישע אשר דבר).[50] This recasting of a magic act by a holy man into a miracle of YHWH executed by prophetic speech was a move very similar to the development of 1 Kgs 17:17-24.

2:23-24: *Legenda* and PN

The other independent basic *legenda* preserved in vv. 23b-24* was a cautionary tale about the power of holy men and the need to treat them respectfully that was associated with the itinerant Elisha.[51] The location of the encounter is not given, as the focus is on the event and the person of the man of god; "the city" or "a certain city" in v. 23 is nameless. PN identified it with Bethel, not as a polemic against Northern shrines but in order to tie the three stories in the chapter together. The journey of Elijah and Elisha began in Gilgal and progressed to Bethel, Jericho, and the Jordan. In v. 23 Elisha is on his way back; having

---

47 Structural considerations lend additional support to the view that vv. 15-18 are secondary. The chiastic outline of the chapter in the Synchronic Analysis reveals not only the centrality of Elijah's translation but also the disruptive nature of vv. 7a, 15-18. While they are correctly placed in terms of the order of elements in the structure, the difference in their respective sizes creates imbalance. Vv. 15-18 also disturb the progression of the narrative by stalling it in Jericho. Long (*2 Kings*, 24) gives a partial list of those who have argued for the secondary nature of vv. 16-18.

48 Thus there is no indication that the *legenda* related in any way to Joshua's curse on the city of Jericho or its fulfillment in Hiel's sons (1 Kgs 16:34), though the texts can be related intertextually as in the Synchronic Analysis.

49 J. Heller, "Drei Wundertaten Elias," *Communio Viatorum* 2 (1959), 83–84.

50 So also Würthwein, *1. Könige 17–2. Könige 25*, 277–78.

51 Again, so also Würthwein, *1. Könige 17–2. Könige 25*, 278.

come from the Jordan through Jericho, he now passes through Bethel. The *legenda* contained no mention of YHWH; the curse was efficacious because it was spoken by the man of god. PN added *in YHWH's name* at the end of v. 24a to lend divine approbation to Elisha's curse and to attribute the wonder ultimately to YHWH rather than Elisha.[52] The number of mauled children—forty-two—was part of the old *legenda*; it is a conventional number for ill fortune and those who encounter it in and outside of the Bible.[53]

2:25: PN's conclusion

Finally, in conjunction with his ordering of the stories and his relating them to one another through geographical references PN added v. 25 with its mentions of Mount Carmel and Samaria. These references tied the three stories in this chapter with upcoming tales about Elisha in which he has a home on Mount Carmel (4:25) and is found with the Israelite army that emerged from Samaria (3:11).[54] Though editorial, it provides a fitting end to the chapter as Elisha returns to the site of the greatest victory of his mentor, whom he now replaces.

Synthesis

The transitions from Elijah to Elisha

In PN's hand the three distinct *legenda* that comprise this chapter make the transition from Elijah to Elisha and open the door for the collection of stories about the latter. They function together to initiate and legitimate Elisha's full and independent career. PN's presentation of the first *legenda* in vv. 1-18 cooperates with and furthers the related story in 1 Kgs 19:19-21 to explain how Elisha came to succeed Elijah. The mantle Elijah cast upon Elisha in 1 Kgs 19:19-21 claimed ownership of him as attendant (משרת), but the transfer of the mantle was not permanent as it is in 2 Kings 2, where Elisha takes over his mentor's office. The succession, therefore, is presented in stages, much like Joshua's succession to Moses. The story elevates prophecy through Elijah as the paradigmatic prophet. He is a leader, a pioneer, a founding father like Moses. Also as in the case of Moses there is no commemorative gravesite for him. That is because Elijah did not die; he was assumed bodily into heaven. Elisha is the successor and heir of the quintessential prophet and man of god. He receives the gift of second sight and it marks his succession and heritage from Elijah. Elisha will die; he is not equal to his master but he does receive a double portion of his mentor's spirit. By extension all true prophets are also heirs of Elijah, though only Elisha can claim primogeniture. The other two *legenda* show Elisha coming into his own in his new role as Elijah's

---

52 See H. A. Brongers, "Die Wendung *běšēm jhwh* im Alten Testament," *ZAW* 77 (1965): 1–20.

53 It is the number of Jehu's victims (2 Kgs 10:14) and the number of days that the nations trample Jerusalem (Rev. 11:2) and that the beast rules (Rev. 13:5). Cf. also Judg 12:6; Ezra 2:24//Neh 7:28. There are also 42 judges in the underworld according to the Egyptian book of the dead, ch. 125. Cf. J. Herrmann, "Die Zahl zweiundvierzig im AT," *OLZ* 13 (1910): 150–52; Levin, *Sturz*, 87n; Würthwein, *1. Könige 17–2. Könige 25*, 278n.

54 Sauerwein's (*Elischa*, 32) suggestion of two levels, v. 25a preparing for ch. 4 and v. 25b linking to ch. 3, is unnecessary. It implies that ch. 3 is later, which is unwarranted, and it leaves 4:1-7 unexplained, since they can hardly be set on Mt Carmel.

successor. PN makes clear, as he did for Elijah in 1 Kings 17, that the wonders he performs are not from himself but emanate from YHWH and from his office as YHWH's prophet. This understanding was already implicit in the older *legenda*, but PN removes any ambiguity. Thus the spring at Jericho is healed at YHWH's word (vv. 21-22). The curse on the children in v. 24, much to the discomfort of modern readers, also is effected at YHWH's word. The word of YHWH is an affirmation of the prophetic role.

War with Moab
(2 Kings 3)

Text

[DtrH; Battle account; *PN*]
1 Jehoram son of Ahab became king over Israel in Samaria in the 18th year of
Jehoshaphat king of Judah, and he reigned 12 years. 2 He did what YHWH con-
sidered evil, though not like his father *and his mother*: he removed the pillar of
Baal that his father had made. 3 Still, he clung to the sin of Jeroboam son of
Nebat which he made Israel commit, without turning from it. 4 Mesha king of
Moab was a stockman who used to pay the king of Israel tribute of 100,000
lambs and 100,000 rams laden with wool. 5 When Ahab died, the king of Moab re-
belled against Israel. 6 So the king of Israel went out on that day from Samaria
and mustered Israel. 7 *Then he sent to Jehoshaphat king of Judah, "The king of*
Moab has rebelled against me. Will you go with me against Moab for war?" [Je-
hoshaphat] replied, "I will go; I am like you, my army like your army, my horses
like your horses." 8 *He asked, "By what way shall we go up?" He answered, "By*
way of the wilderness of Edom." 9 *The king of Israel, the king of Judah, and the*
king of Edom marched on a circuitous route of seven days; they ran out of water
for the camp and for the animals following them. 10 *The king of Israel remarked,*
"Alas, YHWH has summoned these three kings to turn us over to Moab's dominion."
11 *Jehoshaphat said, "Is there not a prophet of YHWH here that we may inquire of*
YHWH by him?" One of the servants of the king of Israel replied, "Elisha son of
Shaphat is here, he who poured water on Elijah's hands." 12 *Jehoshaphat re-*
sponded, "The word of YHWH is with him." So the king of Israel and Jehoshaphat
and the king of Edom went down to him. 13 *Elisha said to the king of Israel,*
"What do you and I have in common? Go to your father's prophets and to your
mother's prophets." But the king of Israel said to him, "No, because YHWH has sum-
moned these three kings to turn us over to Moab's dominion." 14 *Elisha said, "As*
YHWH of hosts, in whose service I stand, lives, if I did not have regard for Jehosha-
phat the king of Judah I would pay you neither attention nor notice. 15 *But now*
bring me a minstrel." So they brought [a minstrel] to him, and while the minstrel
played, the power of YHWH came upon him 16 *such that he said, "Thus says YHWH,*
'This wadi will be made full of cisterns.' 17 *For thus says YHWH, 'You will see neither*
wind nor rain, yet that wadi will be filled with water, and you will drink, you, your
camps, and your animals. 18 *This is an easy thing in the eyes of YHWH, who will*
turn Moab over to your dominion. 19 *You will destroy every fortified city; every via-*
ble tree you will fell; every spring of water you will stop up; and every good plot
of land you will ruin with stones." 20 *In the morning when the offering went up,*
water came from the direction of Edom so that the land was filled with water.
21 *Now all Moab had heard that the kings had come up against them for war, so*

that all of those old enough to gird on armor and above had been called out and had stationed themselves on the border. 22 *When they woke up early in the morning and the sun rose over the water the Moabites observed the water at a distance to be red like blood.* 23 *They said, "This is blood. The kings must have quarreled among themselves and destroyed one another. So now to the spoil, Moab!"* 24 *When they came to the camp of Israel,* Israel arose and defeated Moab, *so that they fled from before them.* 25 *They tore down the cities; each cast his stone on every good plot of land until they had filled it; they stopped up every spring of water; and they felled every good tree. They defeated Moab* until only Qir Hareseth remained. Then the slingers surrounded and attacked it. 26 When the king of Moab saw that the battle was going against him, he took 700 swordsmen with him and tried to break through to the king of Aram, but they were unable to do so. 27 Then he took his firstborn son who would have reigned after him and sacrificed him as a whole burnt offering on the wall, so that a great wrath came against Israel and they withdrew from him and returned to their land.

Textual Notes

1 **Jehoram son of Ahab became king over Israel in Samaria in the eighteenth year of Jehoshaphat king of Judah**: So MT. The OG chronology is preserved in the G^{BL} plus at 1:18a.[1] This is because the OG corrected the anomalous placement of ch. 2 MT after the closing formulae for Ahaziah of Israel at the end of 2 Kings 1 (v. 18) but before the opening formulae for Joram in 3:1, i.e., outside of the structural framework for the book of Kings. The (mis)placement was PN's doing. The OG *Vorlage* shifts Joram's regnal formulae to 1:18a-d, thereby enclosing the materials in ch. 2. The OG dates Joram of Israel's accession to the second year of Jehoshaphat's son Jehoram in accord with its revised chronology. This led to a change in the identification of the king of Judah from Jehoshaphat to Ahaziah in 3:4-27 OG.

2 **like his father**: So MT; G^{BL} 1:18c: *like his brothers*, a miswriting of אחיו for אביו.

pillar: So MT. G^{BL} have the plural both in 3:2 and in 1:18c. The singular also occurs in 10:27.

had made: So MT 3:2. G^{BL} 1:18c + *and destroyed them* (καὶ συνέτριψεν αὐτάς) in conformity with such texts as Exod 23:24.

3 **sin of Jeroboam**: So G^{B} 3:3. The other witnesses in 3:3 and in 1:18c (including G^{B}) have *sins*. The singular is confirmed by ממנה at the end of the verse. G^{BL} 1:18c: *sins of the house of Jeroboam.*

without turning from it: So MT, G^{B}. G^{BL} 1:18d + *so that* YHWH *was angry with the house of Ahab* (B)/*with him and with the house of Ahab* (L).

4 **Mesha**: A participial form (*Hip'îl*) from the root ישע without its divine complement, the name means "GN saves, gives victory." The god was Chemosh, whom the Mesha inscription credits as having saved Mesha (a pun on the name) from enemy kings (l. 4). G's Μωσα indicates מושע instead of מישע, a variant spelling attested with other names from first ו/י roots, e.g., מודד/מידד (Num 11:27).

---

1 G^{BL} in 3:1-3 are *kaige*. Key indicators of the OG are the historical present (1:18a) and ἐνώπιον (1:18b) instead of ἐν ὀφθαλμοῖς. The plus in MT 1:17 also agrees with OG. See Shenkel, *Chronology*, 70–71, 82–83.

stockman: *nōqēd* is found elsewhere in the HB only in Amos 1:1 (plural), though it occurs in Akkadian (*nāqidu*) and Ugaritic (*KTU* 1.6.6.56-57) for some kind of official (*rb nqdm*). It refers to a breeder or stockman of sheep or cattle and coordinates with the tribute Mesha is charged with delivering to Israel.[2]

who used to pay the king of Israel: So MT: והשיב למלך־ישראל. G^{L} (καὶ ἦν φέρων φόρον καὶ ἐπεστρέφων τῷ βασιλεῖ Ισραηλ) conflates OG (καὶ ἦν φέρων φόρον) and *kaige* (καὶ ἐπεστρέφων) readings.[3] The perfect והשיב is frequentative.[4] G^{B} + ἐν τῇ ἐπαναστάσει evidently means *in* [i.e., *because of*] *the uprising.*[5] Its antecedent is uncertain (בפשע? cf. Amos 1:3, 6, 9, 11, 13; Prov 28:2). It seems to go against the transparent meaning of the verse that Moab was Israel's vassal and paid annual tribute (cf. 2 Kgs 17:3).

laden with wool: So MT (צמר), G^{L} (ἐπιπόκον).[6]

5 **against Israel**: So G^{L}. MT, G^{B}: *against the king of Israel.*

6 **the king of Israel**: MT, G^{B}: *King Jehoram*; G^{L}: *Jehoram king of Israel.* The different readings suggest that Joram's name was secondary.

mustered Israel: So G^{BL}. MT: *mustered all Israel.*

7 **Then he sent**: Reading וישלח. MT, G^{B}: וילך וישלח. G^{L}: καὶ ἐξαπέστειλεν Ιωραμ. וילך in MT, G^{B} is an expansion.

Jehoshaphat: So MT, G^{B}. G^{L} (= OG): *Ahaziah*, a secondary change in conformity to the OG's revised chronology. See the Note on 3:1 and the discussion of the text in the Introduction. The king of Judah was not nameless, as has been supposed,[7] but was identified from the start as Jehoshaphat, as will be shown in the Diachronic Analysis.

against Moab: So G^{L}: ἐπὶ Μωαβ. MT, G^{L}: אל־מואב.

I will go: So G^{L}: πορεύσομαι = אלך using the verb in Joram's question. MT, G^{B}: אעלה.

I am like you, my army like your army, my horses like your horses: So MT, G^{B}. G^{L}'s ὡς ἂν σύ καὶ ἐγὼ ὅμοιός σοι ὅμοιός μοι is a double translation of כמוני כמוך. Also, in this comparison and the next two G^{L} attests the reverse order, with the second person preceding the first.[8]

8 **shall we go up**: So MT, G^{L}. The other G witnesses read the singular, "shall I go up."

9 **the king of Israel, the king of Judah**: So MT, G^{B}. G^{L} and OL have the names Joram and Ahaziah, respectively, reflecting the OG chronology.

following them: Lit. *at their feet*, an idiom for followers. See 1 Kgs 20:10.[9]

10 **these three kings**: G^{B} lacks האלה, reading παρερχομένους (= הלכים?), possibly a dittography.

---

2 S. Paul, *Amos* (Hermeneia; Minneapolis: Fortress, 1991), 34–35; R. C. Steiner, *Stockmen from Tekoa, Sycamores from Sheba* (CBQMS 36; Washington, DC: CBA, 2003), 70–87. Steiner counters the claim of I. Engnell (*Studies in Divine Kingship in the Ancient Near East* [Uppsala: Almqvist & Wiksell, 1943] 87–89) that *nōqēd* was a cultic term.

3 Trebolle ("Pre-Lucianic Readings of III–IV Regnorum in Marginal Notes of the Syro-Hexaplaric Version and in the Syriac Text of Jacob of Edessa," forthcoming, 6–7) on the basis of the OL.

4 Burney, *Notes*, 268; Joüon 111e, 119v; WO, 534.

5 *GELS*, 259.

6 Trebolle ("Pre-Lucianic Readings," 3) shows that ἐπιπόκον is an OG reading *contra* J. K. Aitken, *No Stone Unturned. Greek Inscriptions and Septuagint Vocabulary* (Winona Lake, IN: Eisenbrauns, 2014), 59.

7 Miller, "Another Look," 276–88; Shenkel, *Chronology*, 98–108.

8 For an attempt to unravel the relationship between the witnesses here and in the 1 Kgs 22:4 parallel see S. J. De Vries, "The Three Comparisons in 1 Kings XXII 4B and its Parallel and 2 Kings III 7B," *VT* 39 (1989) 283–306.

9 Burney (*Notes*, 233) provides a list of parallels.

us: So G^L. MT, G^B have *them*, which may be due to graphic confusion of אותנו and אותם but probably also reflects influence from the third-person reference.

11 **Jehoshaphat said**: So MT, G^B. G^L reads *the king of Judah* in accord with its identification of the king of Judah with Ahaziah. It also has the plus *to him* after the verb.

Is there not a prophet of Yhwh here: So MT, G^B as in 1 Kgs 22:7. G^L frames the question positively: *Is there a prophet of Yhwh here?*

by him: Reading מאתו with the versions and for sense in preference to MT's מאותו.

Shaphat: So MT, G^L. G^B: Ιωσαφατ influenced by the king's name elsewhere in this context.

12 **Jehoshaphat**: So MT, G^B. G^L: *the king of Judah* in accord with its revised chronology.

the word of Yhwh: So MT, G^L. G^B: *word* without the divine name.

with him: Reading אתו for MT's אותו. G^L: ἐν αὐτῷ. G^B: αὐτῷ.

So the king of Israel and Jehoshaphat and the king of Edom went down to him: So MT. G^L: *the king of Judah* as part of the OG chronological adjustment. G^B conflates the name and title. The Greek witnesses also have the singular verb while MT has the plural.

13 **What do you and I have in common**: מה־לי ולך. See the Note on 1 Kgs 17:18 (cf. 2 Sam 16:10; 19:23). Here, the question is elliptical and seems to stress the difference between the two men. In essence, "We have nothing to do with each other."

and to your mother's prophets: So MT, G^L. G^B uniquely lacks this phrase perhaps due to haplography. Joüon (129b) explains the construction as an example of a *nomen regens* used with more than one genitive, such that the reference here is to the same prophets rather than two distinct groups.

No: For אל in an absolute sense see Gen 19:18; Judg 19:23; 2 Sam 13:16; 2 Kgs 4:16; Ruth 1:13.

these three kings: See on 3:10. G^B lacks "these" as the result of inner-Greek haplography (τούτους τοῦ).

turn us over: As in 3:10 G^L. See the Note on that verse.

14 **Yhwh of hosts**: A military title. See on 1 Kgs 18:15.

in whose service I stand: See the Note on 1 Kgs 17:1.

Jehoshaphat the king of Judah: MT, G^B. G^L omits Jehoshaphat's name.

15 **bring me a minstrel**: Reading the plural verb with MT, G^L. G^B has the singular.

So they brought [a minstrel] to him, and while the musician played: So G^L. Lost from MT by haplography.

16 **will be made**: So MT: עשה, an infinitive absolute. G^{BL}: ποιήσατε = עשו (imperative). The infinitive may be a surrogate for the imperative.[10] Since the subject of the command is unclear (the kings and armies? the heavenly host?) and may be impersonal, it functions essentially as a passive.[11]

full of cisterns: The noun גב occurs only once more in the HB (Jer 14:3), again in the plural.[12] It seems to refer to an agricultural installation for the catchment and retention of water. The repetition of the noun is for emphasis (WO 119) or hyperbole (GKC 123e).

17 **your camps**: So G^L, a metonymy for the armies (v. 9). MT, G^B: ומקניכם, *your cattle*, which is a variant of ובהמתכם.

18 **This is an easy thing**: The mismatch of subject and verb in gender (ונקל זאת) has precedent, especially where the feminine subject can be considered a collective denot-

10 Joüon 123u; WO, 594. Schniedewind and Silvan ("Test Case," 332) take it as a Northernism.

11 Similarly, Cogan and Tadmor, *II Kings*, 42, 45, who translate it as "will produce."

12 In Jer 39:10 ויגבים is often emended to וגבים.

ing males (GKC 145e). Here the antecedent of זאת is YHWH's compound wonder described in the previous two verses.

in the eyes of YHWH: G^L + *to do it* (ποιῆσαι αὐτό).

who will turn Moab over: So MT: ונתן את־מואב. G^B has the first person, "I will give."

to your dominion: G^L + *today.*

19 **You will destroy every fortified city**: So G^B. G^L + *in Moab.* MT + וכל־עיר מבחור = *and every choice city,* a double reading.

you will ruin: Reading תאבדו (*Hip'îl*).[13] MT's תכאבו *cause pain* (*Hip'îl*) is inappropriate or possibly metaphorical.[14]

20 **when the offering went up**: See on 1 Kgs 18:29.

from the direction of Edom: So MT, G^B (מדרך אדום). G^L: ἐξ ὁδοῦ Εδωμ τῆς ἐρήμου Σουδ ἐξ Εδωμ. Σουδ may be a corruption of שעיר.

21 **the kings**: So MT, G^B. G^L: *these kings.*

all of those old enough to gird on armor and above had been called out: So MT (ויצעקו מכל חגר חגרה ומעלה). G^B: καὶ ἀνεβόησαν ἐκ παντὸς περιεζωσμένοι ζώνην καὶ εἰπὸν Ω. The last phrase is a corruption of καὶ ἐπάνω. Hence the only real difference between G^B and MT is that the former takes ויצעקו as active (*Qal*) rather than passive (*Nip'al*). The latter is preferred as the less common reading and for sense. G^L (καὶ παρήγγειλαν παντὶ περιζώννυμένῳ παραζώνην καὶ παρατείνοντι καὶ ἐβόησαν ἐκ παντὸς παραζώννυμένου παραζώνην καὶ ἐπάνω) attests a double reading. The precise meaning of חגר חגרה (lit. *one who wears a belt*") is uncertain. Hobbs suggests that it refers to the wearing of belts rather than the loose-fitting clothing of boys as a distinction of males old enough to serve in the military.[15] If so, the expression has nothing to do with armor *per se* but describes a difference in style of dress for adolescents and above.

22 **like blood**: So MT, G^B. Absent from G^L as a result of haplography (אדם כדם).

23 **This is blood. The kings must have quarreled among themselves and destroyed one another**: So MT. G^B (αἷμα τοῦτο τῆς ῥομφαίας ἐμαχέσαντο οἱ βασιλεῖς καὶ ἐπάταξαν ἀνὴρ τὸν πλησίον αὐτου) is the same, though it construes החרב as *the sword.* G^L (αἷμα τοῦτο ῥομφαίας ἐρίσσαντες γὰρ ἤρισαν οἱ τρεῖς βασιλεῖς καὶ ἐμαχέσαντο καὶ ἐπάταξαν ἕκαστος τὸν πλησίον αὐτου) is overfull and appears to conflate the G^B translation with ἐρίσσαντες γὰρ ἤρισαν (*for they quarreled*). The construction החרב נחרבו is a rare instance, outside of *Qal*, of the use an infinitive absolute of one stem (*Hop'al*) with a finite verb of a different stem (*Nip'al*) (Joüon 123p; WO 582). The construction is rare enough to call the vocalization of החרב as *Hop'al* into question and to emend it to *Nip'al* (so BHS).

24 **and defeated Moab so that they fled from before them**: Verse 24b, including the *ketiv/qere'*, is a corrupt repetition of the earlier clause *they defeated Moab* (ויכו את־מואב).

25 **each cast his stone**: So MT, G^B: ישליכו. G^L's singular matches the distributive איש/ἀνὴρ.

They defeated Moab: So G^L: καὶ ἐξέσεισαν τὸν Μωαβν.[16] Its presence is necessitated by the עד ("until") in the next clause which indicates that something in missing in the MT.[17]

until only Qir Hareseth remained: Reading עד־נשאר לבדה קיר חרשת. All witnesses are corrupt: MT has עד־השאיר אבניה בקיר חרשת *until he left its stones in Qir Hareseth*; G^B: ἕως τοῦ καταλιπεῖν τοὺς λίθους τοῦ τοίχου καθηρημένους = *until they left the stones of the torn down wall*; G^L: ἕως τοῦ καταλιπεῖν λίθον ἐν τοίχῳ τεκτονικῆς = *until they left a*

---

13 Klostermann, *Könige*, 399.
14 *HALOT* 454; Stade, *Kings*, 187.
15 Hobbs, *2 Kings*, 37.
16 Apparently a variant of the *qere'* in v. 24; so Montgomery, *Kings*, 366.
17 Trebolle, *Centena*, 163–64.

stone in a builder's wall. The reading here follows the conjecture of BHS. BHS's *Hip'îl* is unlikely given that the previous verbs are all plurals. Qir Hareseth (instead of Haresheth, as some mss have it) is mentioned in Isa 16:7, in Isa 16:11; Jer 48:31, 36 as Qir Heres, and in Isa 15:1 as Qir Moab. It is usually identified with Kerak between Wadis Zered (Hesa) and Arnon (Mujib). However, Jones has shown the weakness of this identification and proposed a location north of the Arnon.[18] He points out that Qir Hareseth "city of shards" may be a taunt name.

26 **that the battle was going against him**: Reading חזקה in place of MT's חזק to match the gender of the subject, המלחמה.

with him: Reading אתו for MT's אותו based on G^{BL} μεθ' ἑαυτοῦ.

king of Aram: So OL. Aram would be a more likely source of aid for the king of Moab than Edom, especially if there is no king there yet.[19]

27 **to their land**: Lit. *to the land* (MT, G^{B}). G^{L} supplies the suffix that is implicit in the other witnesses.

Synchronic Analysis

3:1-2: A slight improvement

Ahaziah's successor is his brother. Despite being another son of Ahab, he is not as bad as his parents or his brother. He removes the cultic pillar that had been set up for Baal by Ahab in Samaria. Joram thus seems at first to be true to his name, which is the same as his counterpart in Judah, in exalting Yhwh rather than Baal. Yet his good deed raises doubts about the genuineness and depth of his devotion to Yhwh. There is no previous mention of a pillar (מצבה) of Baal erected by Ahab, and it was apparently restored or replaced before Jehu's reform since it is torn down in 10:26-27. Hence Joram's single reform act was not very far-reaching. He may have removed the pillar but kept it intact so that it was restored at some point.[20] Or perhaps he removed only one pillar of several.[21] Nothing is said of the temple or the altar built by Ahab (1 Kgs 16:32) or any other appurtenance of the Baal cult, so that Joram evidently tolerated the worship of Baal even if he did not participate in it.[22] The narrator dutifully reports Joram's

---

18 B. C. Jones, "In Search of Kir Hareseth: A Case Study in Site Identification," *JSOT* 52 (1991): 3–24. He (pp. 20–24) suggests an identification with Kiriathaim, perhaps al-Qureiya, on the Madaba plateau. Similarly E. Gass, "Topographical Considerations and Redaction Criticism in 2 Kings 3," *JBL* 128 (2009), 65–69. Timm (*Die Dynastie Omri*, 168–69) identifies it with Qarhoh, mentioned in the Mesha inscription, and somewhere near Dibon, as do K. A. D. Smelik, *Converting the Past*, 85–89, and Hayes and Miller (*History*, 323).

19 Cf. Gray, *Kings*, 484; Montgomery, *Kings*, 363; Robinson, *Second Kings*, 36–37. So also Barthélemy, *Critique textuelle*, 384, and N. Na'aman, "Royal Inscription vs. Prophetic Story: Mesha's Rebellion according to Biblical and Moabite Historiography," in *Ahab Agonistes: The Rise and Fall of the Omri Dynasty* (L. L. Grabbe, ed.; LHBOTS 421; London/New York: T & T Clark, 2007), 161, though the latter incorrectly ascribes the reading *Aram* to G.

20 So Nelson (*Kings*, 165), who refers to Joram's reform as halfhearted.

21 Cogan and Tadmor, *II Kings*, 43.

22 Provan, Kings, 181.

act but then dismisses the significance of any improvement he represented. Thus the qualification in 3:2 (רק) is immediately qualified again in the next verse, which begins with another רק. Even if Joram truly reformed the cultic aberrations of his parents he did not veer at all from the sinful path down which Jeroboam had set the nation. The overall impression of Joram's reign is that he was a slight improvement over his parents and brother but not enough to stop the looming obliteration of the house of Ahab. He is too little too late.

A complicated story

The story that follows initiates a section (3:3–8:6) focused on Elisha's miracles.[23] This story is complex, with twists and turns. Israel sets out to confront Moab yet marches around it. Elisha would have nothing to do with King Joram of Israel yet is found with his army. Elisha detests Joram yet helps him out of a predicament and forecasts victory for him. His prophecy is technically accurate yet proves to be misleading. Israel defeats Moab yet loses it as a vassal. The narrative is sophisticated, replete with puns, complex character interaction, and double entendre. Its sophistication has been unpacked by Long and Sneed, who perceive a chiastic structure to the story with Elisha's oracle at its center:

Structure

A. Mesha rebels (vv. 4-5)
  B. Joram asks Jehoshaphat to fight with him against Moab (vv. 6-8)
    C. There is no water, and the kings go to Elisha (vv. 9-12)
      X. Elisha's oracle (vv. 13-19)
    C'. Water flows, the Moabites come against Israel (vv. 20-23)
  B'. Israel fights Moab (vv. 24-25)
A'. Mesha sacrifices, Israel withdraws (vv. 26-27)[24]

Dialogue drives the story

The story is built around four kings and Elisha. Only two of the kings, those of Israel and Judah, plus Elisha, have speaking roles. Lines are also assigned to a nameless servant of Joram (v. 11) and to the Moabite defenders (v. 23). The plot of the story is largely driven by dialogue—between Joram and Jehoshaphat (vv. 7-8), the two kings, with a response from the servant (vv. 10-12), Elisha and Joram (vv. 13-14), Elisha to the kings (vv. 15-19), and then the Moabites (v. 23). Only the final two scenes (vv. 24-25, 26-27) lack dialogue. The similarities and allusions to 1 Kings 22 signal it as the lens through which the present story is to be read. So read, the story presents Elisha as a reliable prophet of Yhwh who succeeds in deluding Joram and enticing him to failure against Moab. Joram is not killed in this battle as the parallel with 1 Kings 22 might lead the reader to expect, because

---

23 J. T. Walsh, "The Organization of 2 Kings 3–11," *CBQ* 72 (2010), 240–41. I am less persuaded by Walsh's redactional explanation of the asymmetry in the current arrangement of stories in 3:3–8:6 (pp. 241–46).

24 J. C. Long, Jr., and M. Sneed, "'Yahweh Has Given These Three Kings into the Hand of Moab': A Socio-Literary Reading of 2 Kings 3," *Inspired Speech. Prophecy in the Ancient Near East. Essays in Honour of Herbert B. Huffmon* (ed. J. Kaltner and L. Stulman; London/New York: T & T Clark, 2004): 253–75. See also J. C. Long, Jr., "Unfulfilled Prophecy or Divine Deception? A Literary Reading of 2 Kings 3," *SCJ* 7 (2004): 101–17; "Elisha's Deceptive Prophecy in 2 Kings 3: A Response to Raymond Westbook," *JBL* 126 (2007): 168–71.

he is somewhat better than his parents (3:2). His ultimate end and that of the dynasty are deferred.

Jehoshaphat and Elisha

The story again elevates Jehoshaphat as a righteous king while further denigrating the Omrids for their wickedness. It presents Elisha as a worthy successor to Elijah. Elijah's shadow still falls over Elisha (v. 11), but it is dimming as Elisha develops more of his own character. He is more typically prophetic in some ways than his master. He addresses the inquiry brought to him with the aid of a musician, entering into a prophetic trance. His prophecy is accurate but duplicitous. The story also illustrates Elisha's deep involvement in international politics, which was not the case for Elijah. Thus this story arouses anticipation—and maybe apprehension—about Elisha.

3:4-6: Joram goes to recover Moab

The story's location following 3:1-3 sets it in the reigns of Joram of Israel and Jehoshaphat of Judah. It often refers to the kings by title rather than by name. Thus Mesha is identified by name in v. 4 but called *the king of Moab* in the remainder of the story. Mesha is also identified in v. 4 as a stockman. The seemingly distinct occupations of king and stockman are related to each other by the tribute he delivered to Israel. The annual requirement of tribute payment *per* ancient Near Eastern practice is implied by the iterative perfect (*used to pay*). The verb further implies that Mesha no longer pays and that his act of withholding payment constituted rebellion, again *per* ancient Near Eastern practice. The revolt occurred, typically, upon the death of the preceding overlord, when the transition presented a chance to test the strength and resolve of the successor. Thus Joram's march from Samaria (v. 6) was a campaign to compel Moab to continued vassalage. This is the only verse in the story (MT) that identifies Joram as the king of Israel. His immediate response contrasts with his brother's lack of action in 1:1. His naming reinforces the contrast (Joram as opposed to Ahaziah); the sons of Ahab are not the same.

3:7-8: Jehoshaphat again joins the campaign

Joram asks King Jehoshaphat of Judah to join the campaign (v. 7). Jehoshaphat reprises his role from 1 Kings 22. Both Joram's request and Jehoshaphat's response are essentially the same as in 1 Kgs 22:4. Here, as there, Jehoshaphat places his army at the disposal of the king of Israel. While Joram's evil reputation might lead one to question Jehoshaphat's willingness to go along, the outcome in 1 Kings 22 does not support such reservations. Ahab was killed in the earlier story but Jehoshaphat and the armies of Israel and Judah evidently escaped unscathed and even victorious. The present narrative shows its favor toward Jehoshaphat by consistently naming him (vv. 7, 11, 12 [2x], 14) in contrast to its preference for titles for Mesha and Joram. Verse 8 even leaves ambiguous which king is the superior in the relationship by not identifying the king who decides the route they will take. If it is Jehoshaphat, this might explain the southern trek through Edom, which also required travel through Judah. The inclusion of the king of Edom without further comment (v. 9) suggests that Edom was subject to either Judah or Israel, in accord with 1 Kgs 22:48, which states that a prefect appointed by the king of Judah was Edom's ruler.[25]

3:9-11: Running out of water

The account of the journey proceeds quickly, covering seven days in a single verse (v. 9). This seems like a short time for such a crucial resource as water to

25 Later on Edom would crown a king of its own (2 Kgs 8:20-22).

disappear completely with any modicum of advance planning. It suggests the narrative's haste to get to the heart of the story. Joram blames YHWH and panics (v. 10). The journey in the wilderness, the lack of water, and complaining and blaming YHWH are all reminiscent of the murmuring narratives such as Exodus 16 and Numbers 20.[26] Only here it is not the people of Israel who complain but their king, highlighting Joram's faithlessness. Jehoshaphat retains his composure and faith. He asks about the presence of a prophet of YHWH through whom they might inquire as to their course of action. It is the same question he raised in 1 Kgs 22:7. This time it is not the king of Israel who responds but one of his servants (v. 11). Perhaps he merely answers before the king has a chance. On the other hand, the lack of response from the king implies ignorance on his part of Elisha's whereabouts. The servant, in contrast, knows not only Elisha's name, occupation, and current location, but also his patronym and his history as Elijah's servant, assuming this is the sense of *pour water on the hands.* The expression is otherwise unattested in the HB, but it is usually assumed to refer to a task performed by a servant for washing or refreshment. It may have some further connotation of not just a servant but a protégé or successor. It is especially appropriate to the present context, as the kings and armies are in desperate need of precisely what Elisha used to pour on his master.

3:12-18: Elisha's oracle

Jehoshaphat's familiarity with Elisha as a reliable prophet of YHWH (v. 12) suggests that his fame had already begun to spread beyond Israel's borders, as the subsequent stories in 2 Kings illustrate. The language of descent is ironic since the three kings go to Elisha rather than summoning him; he is their superior. His greeting of Joram displays outright animus (v. 13) and a familiarity that is surprising for someone who, until fairly recently, was a farmer. Evidently Elijah has instructed him well "off stage." The mention of his father's and mother's prophets alludes to Mount Carmel (1 Kgs 18) and to Ahab's sycophants (1 Kgs 22). Joram counters by holding YHWH responsible for the predicament in which he and his colleagues find themselves. Elisha vows that he would have no truck with Joram at all were it not for the presence of Jehoshaphat (v. 14). His oath invokes the life of *YHWH of hosts*, a military epithet appropriate for a warfare setting. In it Elisha also reaffirms his service of YHWH (*before whom I stand*) over against the other prophets. He agrees to help the kings out of regard for Jehoshaphat. He calls for a "strummer" (v. 15) in accord with the use of music to induce an ecstatic state for prophesying (1 Sam 10:5-6). He speaks in the first person as YHWH's messenger (vv. 16-17), but the uncertain meaning of his oracle reflects his state of ecstasy. Is he commanding the kings to dig *pits* for collecting water or announcing that YHWH will create *pools* filled with water? The prediction that water will appear without the signs of storm and the pronouncement of the event as an *easy thing* (v. 18) imply a miracle, favoring the second interpretation.

3:19: Elisha's prediction

The easy thing (*nāqal*) is a pun on the word *wadi* (*nāhāl*) that resonates with Elisha's cursing (קלל) of the children in 2:24, with their mocking (קלס) in 2:23, and

26 See J. R. Bartlett, "The 'United' Campaign Against Moab in 2 Kings 3:4-27," in *Midian, Moab and Edom: The History and Archaeology of Late Bronze and Iron Age Jordan and North-West Arabia* (ed. J. F. A. Sawyer and D. J. A. Clines; JSOTSup 24; Sheffield: Sheffield Academic Press, 1983), 138, and Sweeney, *Kings*, 282.

with the slingers (קלעים) in 3:25; it may also be a *double entendre*, carrying the sense of "be cursed" as a hint of Joram's failure, such that one might render the sentence "This will be cursed in YHWH's eyes—when he delivers Moab into your hands."[27] The change to the third person in v. 18 indicates that the defeat of Moab is Elisha's prediction rather than part of the oracle from YHWH. This explains why the prediction is somewhat misleading. It may even reflect deceit on Elisha's part.[28] There is tension between the total domination envisioned in v. 19 and the ending of the story in vv. 26-27, when Israel withdraws from Qir Hareseth and from Moab. On the one hand Elisha accurately describes what Israel does to Moab in v. 25—including attacking (נכה) Qir-Hareseth; he does not lie. On the other hand Moab gains its independence. The misleading prophecy and the loss of Moab fit with Elisha's animosity toward Joram and the Omrids. The consequences of the measures Elisha foresees for the earth—felling all the trees, stopping up the springs, and *ruining* the land with stones—are poignantly expressed by the verb תכאבו (*cause pain*) in v. 19.

3:20-24: Defeating the Moabite militia

The water comes suddenly on the surface of the ground rather than from seepage (v. 20), beginning shortly after dawn.[29] It flows into the wadi from the direction of Edom, i.e., from the south. There is plenty for the armies and their animals. But the narrative has already moved on to the war with Moab. The function of the water changes from the resolution of the problem faced by invading armies to a weapon of sorts wielded by YHWH to bring them victory. The narrative backtracks in v. 21, using a nominal clause to relate the presence of the Moabite militia marshaled at their southern border. The reference to all those of minimum age and older means that these are not professional warriors but common people inexperienced in war. The geographical setting is germane at this point. The mention of the border, presumably between Moab and Edom, suggests the Wadi Hesa. This *wadi* and the area farther south are known for their red sandstone, accounting for the red color of the water (אדמים), which also puns on the name Edom (v. 22). Seeing the sun reflected off the reddish water in the early morning, the Moabite militia jump to the conclusion that it is blood. They are evidently looking into the sun and have therefore been outflanked by the Israelite army.[30] Their assumption about the nature of the water leads to another leap—that the supposed blood is that of the allied kings and armies who have fought among themselves, leaving their camp open to plundering (v. 23). As a result the

---

27 Long and Sneed, "Yahweh Has Given," 260.

28 Cf. Kissling, *Reliable Characters*, 181–87. Also R. Westbrook ("Elisha's True Prophecy in 2 Kings 3," *JBL* 124 [2005]: 530–32), who agrees that Elisha is cast as a deceptive prophet. The prophecy in v. 19 is fulfilled to the letter: Qir Hareseth is "struck" (נכה) as Elisha predicted (v. 25). Joram should have inferred from the order of elements in the prophecy that attacking the cities was a tactic rather than the culmination of the campaign. Instead, he misinterpreted the meaning of נכה Elisha's oracle and assumed that Qir Hareseth would be destroyed.

29 The morning offering corresponds to the evening offering at twilight. See on 1 Kgs 18:29.

30 Hobbs, *2 Kings*, 37. Having the sun at one's back in the early morning would be a useful military strategy for the difficulty it could cause the enemy's vision, quite apart from possible hallucinations.

Moabites carelessly enter the Israelite camp where they are easy prey (v. 24). They are thus depicted not only as inexpert at war but also as stupid.

3:25: Decimating Moab

As the Moabites flee northward from the Israelite camp, the pursuing Israelites (presumably along with the Judahites and Edomites, though the latter are not mentioned) carry out the measures predicted by Elisha. The order and terminology are somewhat different from v. 19. In v. 25 the Israelites *tear down* (יהרסו) the Moabite cities rather than *destroying* them (והכיתם) as in v. 25. The narrative plays with the meanings of נכה. Qir Hareseth is *attacked* (ויכוה) by slingers but not torn down (v. 25b) and hence not destroyed. The other measures are in reverse order vis-à-vis v. 19. The good plots of land are filled with stones carted in by each soldier, showing what the *pain* (√כאב) mentioned in v. 19 entailed. All the springs are stopped up and all the trees felled. This devastation of Moab's infrastructure and natural resources is self-defeating for Israel to the extent that they make payment of tribute more difficult.

3:26-27: An act of desperation

The slingers (קלעים) pick up on the *double entendre* of נקל in v. 18 and signal this as a crucial moment. Up to this point the invasion has been *easy* for Israel, but vv. 26-27 tell of a "curse" (√קלל) of sorts that will alter the course of the future of Israel and Moab. Finding himself surrounded and hard pressed by the assault, Mesha first tries to break through the siege line to reach the king of Edom, perhaps hoping that he will be a more sympathetic conqueror than the kings of Israel and Judah (v. 26). His failure leads him to perform the desperate act of sacrificing his son on the city wall (v. 27). Surprisingly, this brings "great wrath" (קצף־גדול) upon Israel such that they withdraw and return home. This verse is one of the great *cruxes* of biblical interpretation.[31] Its difficulty revolves around the meaning of *wrath* (קצף). The word's basic sense is "anger." It can refer to human anger (Qoh 5:16; Est 1:18), but usually denotes a response emanating from the divine. In some instances the wrath is explicitly designated as YHWH's (Isa 34:2; Zech 1:2, 15; 2 Chr 19:2; 29:8; 32:26). In others it stands alone as an independent entity (Num 1:53; 18:5; Josh 9:20; 22:20; 1 Chr 27:24; 2 Chr 24:18). Even so, YHWH is the ultimate source of the wrath, which comes as retribution for some kind of offense. In 2 Kgs 3:27 no specific act of offense on Israel's part against YHWH is mentioned. Joram's aspersions against YHWH and Elisha's distaste for him and his family (vv. 10-14) are in the background, but they precede Israel's success to this point. For this reason קצף is often taken to mean something broader than *wrath* such as "disgust,"[32] "sorrow,"[33] "dread, panic,"[34] "fury,"[35] "horror,"[36] and

31 For a review of the interpretations offered for this verse relating to prophecy see R. B. Chisholm, Jr., "Israel's Retreat and the Failure of Prophecy in 2 Kings 3," *Bib* 92 (2011): 70–80.

32 Fritz, *Kings*, 245.

33 Gray, *Kings*, 491, after G. R. Driver, "Studies in the Vocabulary of the Old Testament. VIII," *JTS* 36 (1935), 293.

34 Montgomery, *Kings*, 365.

35 Provan, *Kings*, 186, sees קצף as superhuman rage that drove the Israelites to victory over Moab, but he does not explain the absence of a claim of victory and he ignores the statement that the Israelites withdrew.

36 Würthwein, *1. Könige 17–2. Könige 25*, 284.

"plague."[37] The ambiguity of the term raises the possibility that the wrath might emanate from Chemosh.[38] However, the larger context of the story and its outcome indicate that this is YHWH's doing. The three kings are saved from catastrophe and even given victory over Moab because of righteous Jehoshaphat. At the same time Joram, who is clearly a wicked Omrid as Elisha intimates, suffers the loss of his vassal. This is accomplished by an "act of god" that forces Israel to abandon the field and its otherwise successful quest. The righteous king prospers; the evil one suffers, and it is all *easy* for YHWH to do.

Diachronic Analysis

3:1-3: DtrH's introductory formulae for Joram

The introduction to Joram's reign in vv. 1-3 is DtrH, except for the phrase *and his mother* in v. 2, which is a PN addition like the one in 1 Kgs 22:53. The location of ch. 2 outside of the DtrH framework (see the Note on v. 1) is strong evidence that the chapter—and by extension most of the other prophetic tales in 1 Kings 17–2 Kings 13—was added at a post-DtrH level. The variant location of the formulae in the OG in 1:18a-d was a "correction" to MT precisely because it left ch. 2 outside of the structural frame of Kings. Aside from chronology, the major problem presented by Joram's introductory formulae is the reference in v. 2 to his removal of the pillar (מצבה) or pillars (G^{BL}). This was probably not an image of Baal but a dedicatory stela.[39] Elsewhere in Kings, DtrH portrays מצבות as cultic paraphernalia accompanying the temples (10:26-27) and *bāmôt* (1 Kgs 14:23; 2 Kgs 17:10; 18:4; 23:14), according to the prohibition against them in Deuteronomy (7:5; 12:3) even for the worship of YHWH (Deut 16:21-22). The difficulty is twofold. On the one hand there is no previous mention in Kings of a pillar or pillars erected by Ahab. On the other, 2 Kgs 10:26-27 describes the destruction of the pillar(s) of Baal under Jehu without any note about when they were built or any mention of Joram removing them previously. It could be that מצבה is a corruption of מזבח, "altar," referring to the altar erected by Ahab in 1 Kgs 16:32,[40] but no textual witness attests such a reading. Another possibility is that a minor "reform" of Joram's came to be credited to Jehu.[41]

3:4-27: Compositional history

The nominal clause in v. 4 signals the beginning of a new, independent story. It is fundamentally a battle story in which Elisha appears as a prophet rather

37 Liver ("Wars of Mesha," 30) equates the divine wrath to a plague that broke out in the Israelite army. So also S. Morschauser ("A 'Diagnostic' Note on the 'Great Wrath upon Israel' in 2 Kings 3:27," *JBL* 129 [2010]: 299–302), who overlooks Liver. 1 Chr 27:24 does equate the *wrath* to the plague described in 1 Chr 21. In general, though, *wrath* refers to an intangible entity and the form it takes is not defined.

38 Nelson, *Kings*, 169–70.

39 A. Lemaire ("A Forgotten Cultic Reform: 2 Kings 3:2b," in *Sacred History, Sacred Literature: Essays on Ancient Israel, the Bible, and Religion in Honor of R. E. Friedman on His Sixtieth Birthday* [ed. S. Dolansky; Winona Lake, IN: Eisenbrauns, 2008]): 43–49 suggests it was a votive or commemorative stela dedicated to Baal by Ahab. See Cogan and Tadmor, *II Kings*, 43 and Gray, *Kings*, 482 for further comments on its possible nature.

40 So Hobbs, *2 Kings*, 34.

41 So A. Lemaire, "A Forgotten Cultic Reform?: 2 Kings 3:2b."

than a wonderworker.[42] The king is treated more negatively in the story than the evaluation of Joram in v. 2 would indicate, suggesting the presence of different hands.[43] It has typically been viewed as a unit[44] but there are internal tensions, principally Elisha's sudden appearance and limited involvement in vv. 11-19, the different functions of the water as the means of salvation from thirst in v. 17 but as the trigger of defeat of the Moabites in vv. 22-24, and Elisha's prediction of victory (v. 18), in apparent contradiction to Israel's withdrawal from the siege of the Moabite capital and return home in v. 27.[45] At the same time there is substantial coherence, and it is possible to read the story as a unit.[46]

A clue about composition that has been overlooked is the intrusiveness of v. 7. The invitation to Jehoshaphat should precede the mustering of the army (v. 7) as it does in 1 Kgs 22:4. This clue accords with another—the variation regarding the number of kings/countries opposing Moab. Israel is mentioned alone in vv. 4-6, while in vv. 7-23 Jehoshaphat (vv. 7, 11, 12, 14), Jehoshaphat and the king of Edom (vv. 9, 12), and the (three) kings (vv. 10, 13, 21, 23) appear. Then, beginning with ויקמו in v. 24, Jehoshaphat and the king of Edom disappear from consideration and Israel is again alone as Moab's enemy. This suggests that an older story about war between Israel and Moab in vv. 4-6 + 24aβ-27* underlies the present narrative. The *Wiederaufnahme* in the repetition of *they defeated Moab* in vv. 24-25 (see the Note) suggests that after the notice of Israel's defeat of Moab in v. 24aβ (*Israel arose and defeated Moab*), that story picked up with *until only Qir Hareseth remained* in v. 25. The original battle story, therefore, is in vv. 4-6, 24aβ (*Israel arose and defeated Moab*) + 25aβ (*until only Qir Hareseth remained*)-27. It told of Israel's failure

---

42 Sauerwein (*Elischa*, 32) calls him as a court prophet.

43 Sauerwein, *Elischa*, 36.

44 See B. O. Long, "2 Kings III and Genres of Prophetic Narrative," *VT* 23 (1973), 339, and the commentaries he cites.

45 Gass ("Topographical Considerations," 65–69) provides a more extensive list. See also J. Asurmendi, "Elisée et la guerre. 2 R 3:4-27," *BI* 13 (2005): 1–12. Würthwein (*1. Könige 17–2. Könige 25*, 281) posits three layers of composition: (1) a legendary report of a campaign of Israel and Judah (the reference to the king of Edom being an addition) against Moab in which a hallucination brings Israel success but not complete victory (vv. 4-9a*, 20-27*); (2) a prophetic story about Elisha's rescue of the army on campaign from a lack of water (vv. 9b-17*); (3) Elisha's prediction of Israel's success in vv. 18-19, which anticipates vv. 24-25. Sauerwein (*Elischa*, 41–45) refined Würthwein's view into a theory of four levels: (1) the campaign of Israel and Judah (vv. 5-9aα, 20-24a) picked up on the notice of Moab's revolt in 1:1 as its beginning point, was dependent on 1 Kings 22, did not identify Jehoshaphat as the king of Judah, but was dependent on 1 Kings 22; (2) the prophetic story (vv. 9aβb-13aα, 15-17), also without Jehoshaphat's name) betrayed a theological interest in its introduction of Elisha and the miracles he wrought; (3) a redactor with a special interest in Judah added vv. 13aβb-14 and inserted Jehoshaphat's name into vv. 7, 11, and 12; (4) the final level (vv. 4, 18-19, 24b-27) included Elisha's prediction and fulfillment but also identified the Moabite king with Mesha and changed Israel's victory over Moab to defeat as punishment for its felling of fruit trees in violation of Deut 20:19-20.

46 For instance, A. Wénin ("La cohérence narrative de 2 Rois 3. Un réponse à Jesús Asurmendi," *BI* 14 [2006]: 444–55), who includes vv. 1-3 and sees Joram's failure to destroy Qir-Hareseth as disobedience corresponding to his apostasy in the sin of Jeroboam.

to take the Moabite capital despite having conquered the land of Moab.[47] The rest of the chapter is PN's work, although the different functions of water indicate that he made use of two different motifs or traditions.

3:4-6: Mesha's revolt

The name *Mesha* in v. 4 may be secondary, since he is called *the king of Moab* elsewhere in the story. But this could also be a way of disparaging him. Only Jehoshaphat is regularly called by name. Mesha's other title, נקד, refers to someone on the upper end of the socioeconomic scale, a *stockman*.[48] Mesha was a king who owned a large number of livestock. It was by failure to send the annual tribute that a vassal typically rebelled, and that is what Mesha does. The high numbers of animals claimed as his tribute (200,000 total) do not compromise the requirement that it be made annually.[49] The figures may be exaggerated but the Assyrians claimed to have imposed similarly exorbitant amounts of tribute on vassals. The dating in v. 5 conflicts with the Mesha inscription, which describes a forty-year subjugation of Moab during all of Omri's reign and "half the days of his son" (*COS* 2.23). The conflict is resolved if the Mesha stela is a memorial rather than a victory stela.[50] It is likely that Mesha did revolt shortly after Ahab's death. While the king of Israel was nameless in the older story he must be Joram, given the brevity and weakness of Ahaziah's reign as well as the memory that Ahaziah died during Elijah's lifetime.[51] He responds by mustering his army and preparing to march against Moab, which he does in v. 24aβ, where the older battle story continues. After v. 6, though, PN's account in vv. 7-24aα intrudes.

3:7-9: The route through Edom

Jehoshaphat's response to Joram's invitation (v. 7), especially considering that it is out of place, draws on 1 Kgs 22:4. This means that the king of Judah was never nameless but was identified as Jehoshaphat from the start. His righteous reputation, as in 1 Kings 22, is key to the story (v. 14). G^{L}'s identification of the king of Judah with Ahaziah, who is not righteous, completely undermines the plot of the story and must be secondary.[52] Jehoshaphat's agreement is followed immediately by consultation between the kings (v. 8); PN ignores the length of time it would take for Jehoshaphat to muster his army and march to join Joram. The speakers in v. 8 are not identified, so it is unclear who decides to go by the wilderness of Edom. This route—around the Dead Sea to the south—is improbable for its length and the challenges posed by the terrain.[53] If

---

47 It may have been a counter to the Moabite version of the event, borrowing the suggestion of A. Kunz-Lübcke, "Auf dem Stein und zwischen den Zeilen. Überlegungen zu einer kontrafaktischen Geschichte Israels am Beispiel von 2 Kön 3 und der Mescha-Inschrift," *BZ* 51 (2007): 1–22. However, aside from noting that the battle report is interwoven with a prophetic legend (p. 2), he does not take stock of the levels in the text. Some of the correspondences he finds between the Mesha stela and 2 Kgs 3 are also somewhat farfetched.

48 Steiner, *Stockmen from Tekoa*, 70–87.

49 *Pace* Buis, *Rois*, 189.

50 See Miller, "Moabite Stone as Memorial Stela" and the Diachronic Analysis of 1:1.

51 Miller and Hayes, *History*, 322; Shenkel, *Chronology*, 99.

52 *Pace* Shenkel, *Chronology*, 106–107.

53 N. Glueck ("The Boundaries of Edom," *HUCA* 11 [1936], 150n) thought the route was intended to avoid Moabite fortifications. But see J. M. Miller, "Moab and the Moabites," in *Studies in the Mesha Inscription and in Moab* (ed. J. A. Dearman; Atlanta: Scholars Press, 1989) 36n.

Qir-Hareseth was located north of the Arnon/Mujib, as is likely, the roundabout route is even farther out of the way.[54] However, it is useful for the story in two respects. First, it requires travel through Judah and Edom so that the cooperation of both kings is required. This provides the rationale for Jehoshaphat's participation. The Edomite king is assumed to be an appointee of the king of Judah (1 Kgs 22:48) and thus has no independent role. Hence both kings are integrated into the story at the same level.[55] Second, the longer route is also hotter and dryer, bringing on the crisis of running out of water (v. 9), which sets the stage for what follows.

3:10-14: The contrast of Jehoshaphat and Joram

Verses 10-14 draw on other texts to contrast the king of Israel with Jehoshaphat. The king's complaint recalls that of the Israelites: that YHWH brought them out of Egypt in the wilderness just to kill them (Num 20). It also resembles 2 Kgs 6:31, 33 where the king blames first Elisha and then YHWH for his predicament. The complaint provides the opportunity for the miracle that follows, which shows that YHWH acts on behalf of the righteous (Jehoshaphat) while eschewing the wicked (Joram). There is no previous mention of YHWH having summoned (קרא) the kings to military action against Moab. This does not mean that something has been lost.[56] It is a figure of speech used to assert YHWH's responsibility and thereby provide a segue from Jehoshaphat's question in v. 11, which is adapted from 1 Kgs 22:7. The direction of borrowing is indicated by the suitability of the question to 1 Kgs 22:7 as opposed to 2 Kgs 3:11. In the former the king of Judah seeks an oracle about the advisability of launching an expedition against Ramath Gilead. In 2 Kgs 3:11, though, the expedition is underway. The question of whether to undertake it is no longer viable. What the king of Judah really needs is not an oracle but a miracle to provide water. The question therefore is used as the entrée to the miracle story rather than as a call for an oracle to seek direction.

Elisha's presence

Elisha's presence with the Israelite army is unexpected and also results from borrowing 1 Kgs 22:7. The expression *pour water on the hands of* is otherwise unknown. It alludes to Elisha's role as Elijah's משרת in 1 Kgs 19:19-21 and successor in 2 Kings 2. It is also curious that Jehoshaphat is familiar with Elisha and acknowledges him as a genuine prophet of YHWH (v. 12) even though Elisha is at the beginning of his career and spends it entirely in Israel. This element derives from PN's acquaintance with the Elisha stories and is part of the contrast he builds between Joram and Jehoshaphat. The latter is more appreciative of Elisha than Elisha's own sovereign. The statement in v. 12 that the kings *went down* (וירדו) to Elisha is peculiar in the context of the army encampment and may be drawn from some other setting in which Elisha is approached at his residence in Samaria (cf. 2 Kgs 6:33).[57] The fact that the kings go to him shows their inferiority.

54 Jones, "In Search of Kir-Hareseth," 22.

55 Excising the Edomite king (Würthwein, *1. Könige 17–2. Könige 25*, 282n) also requires attributing the mentions of the three kings in vv. 10b, 13 to a later hand, as Würthwein does. In my reconstruction this is unnecessary. The Edomite king fits PN's work as an interpretation of the Dtr passages in 1 Kgs 22:48, where the king of Edom was a Judahite appointment, and 2 Kgs 8:20-22a, where Edom revolts and establishes its own king.

56 *Pace* Long, *1 & 2 Kings*, 302.

57 Reading *the king* (המלך) in 6:33 in preference to *the messenger* (המלאך); see the Note. See also Buis, *Rois*, 191.

Elisha's animosity toward Joram

Verse 13 articulates Elisha's animosity toward the king of Israel. He begins with a rhetorical question: *What to me and to you?* i.e., *what is there between us* or *what do we have in common*? It is identical to the widow's words to Elijah in 1 Kgs 17:18. Elisha refers the king of Israel to his parents' prophets. These are the prophets of Baal and Asherah in 1 Kings 18 and the court prophets in 1 Kings 22. They cannot serve, though, because it is YHWH, the king avers, who has placed them in this predicament. The accusation that YHWH has called the kings out to turn them over to Moab by causing them to run out of water ties together the two parts of the subsequent story, vv. 18-19 and vv. 24-25, where the advent of water saves the combined armies from thirst and brings them victory.

3:15-17: Elisha's ambiguous prophecy

Elisha wants nothing to do with the king of Israel (v. 14). The only reason for his further involvement is the presence of Jehoshaphat. This is an interpretation of 1 Kings 22, where the only reason for Micaiah's involvement is Jehoshaphat. His presence and his righteousness are even more crucial to the present story than to 1 Kings 22. Without him there is no story. Because he is there, Elisha calls for a musician (v. 15).[58] As the music plays he delivers an oracle in YHWH's name (vv. 16-17). The phrasing of the oracle with the infinitive absolute renders it ambiguous and open to different interpretations. Würthwein takes v. 16 as a command to the kings and their armies to dig pits in the wadi floor that then fill up with water (v. 17), so that the miracle lies in the knowledge that there is water just beneath the surface of the ground.[59] But this interpretation rationalizes the miracle and misconstrues the sense of the verb עשה. There is no mention of the armies digging pits. Elisha's statement that they will see neither wind nor rain indicates that the water will come by unknown, mysterious means and excludes digging pits as the means by which it is collected. Besides, the water does not seep into the pits from underground but flows from the direction of Edom (v. 20). The story resembles that of 6:24–7:20, specifically 7:1-7, in that Elisha delivers an oracle in YHWH's name predicting the seemingly impossible, and the prediction is then fulfilled overnight by some unusual phenomenon.[60] The designation of this as an *easy thing* (נקל, v. 18) signals the same writer as in 1 Kgs 16:31.

3:18-25: Israel's victory and reprisals

In v. 18 Elisha speaks of YHWH in the third person, no longer delivering an oracle but speaking for himself. The focus of his message changes from the rescue of the kings to the defeat of Moab. He foresees the reprisals Israel will enact against Moab (v. 19) in anticipation of v. 25. The change is mirrored in the dual role of the water in vv. 20-24. In v. 20 it is the fulfillment of Elisha's oracle (vv. 16-17).[61] Then in vv. 21-24

---

58 Würthwein (*1. Könige 17–2. Könige 25*, 281) regards v. 15b as a gloss, holding that it explains an older practice no longer familiar to readers, but he does not consider the evidence of G^L. The putative gloss does not so much explain the practice as assume it, and without v. 15b the transition between v. 15a and v. 16 is quite abrupt.

59 Würthwein, *1. Könige 17–2. Könige 25*, 286.

60 The event is often attributed to a natural phenomenon known as *sayl*. E.g., Liver ("Wars of Mesha," 28): "water torrents are known to appear suddenly and fill the parched ravines in this vicinity in the wake of rains which fall in more remote areas." However, it is presented in the story as a miracle rather than an etiology.

61 On the meaning of the morning offering in v. 20 (כעלות המנחה), which Würthwein (*1. Könige 17–2. Könige 25*, 280) unnecessarily takes as a gloss, see the commentary on 1 Kgs 18:29.

its misinterpretation by the enemy militia leads to their being routed and plundered. It is partly their lack of military training, perhaps, that causes them to reason and act so foolishly, though one should not underestimate the lampooning in these verses. They are no match for the Israelite army. Most of all their reaction, like that of the Aramaeans in 7:6-7, is YHWH's doing. The different roles of the water are complementary and need not be assigned to different composers. As anticipated in v. 13, Elisha both solves the crisis caused by lack of water and predicts Israel's devastation of Moab.

3:19: Ruining the land with stones

The first two measures mentioned in v. 19 were common in ancient Near Eastern warfare. Trees were felled both to build siege works and to halt the cultivation of fruit and wood. Springs were stopped to decrease water supply and make resettlement difficult. There is no parallel, though, for the practice of ruining land with stones. Large stones in great numbers such as could be brought in by an army would discourage cultivation by making it labor-intensive to prepare the land. It is sometimes alleged that the felling of all trees is in violation of Deut 20:19-20, where fruit trees are to be left standing. However, Deut 20:15-16 signals a distinction between warfare against distant cities and warfare against those in the promised land, and the prohibition in vv. 19-20 is in the latter category. Since Moab was outside of the land this prohibition did not apply.

Elijah's deceptiveness

Verses 18-19 perform one other important function in the story. In anticipation of the conclusion to the story in vv. 24-27 they highlight the subversiveness of Elisha as a prophet. This is partly related to the change of person in v. 18, where Elisha begins to speak for himself. It is also an interpretation of 1 Kings 22, where prophets and prophecy are used by YHWH as a tool for deceiving Ahab. The word of YHWH spoken by Elisha predicting the abundance of water (vv. 16-17) proves accurate. Elisha's own prophecy about the defeat of Moab (vv. 18-19) is also true—technically (v. 24aβ). The different use of the water in vv. 21-24 indicates a motif distinct from that which comes to a conclusion in v. 20, but there is no indication of an older document. PN has combined the two motifs into a single story.

3:24aβ-27: An unexpected ending

With v. 24aβ the original battle story resumes.[62] This was Israel's response to Moab's revolt following on the mustering of the army (v. 6). The Israelites devastate Moab all the way to Qir-Hareseth (v. 25), which was probably north of the Arnon/Mujib (see the Note)—quite a distance from the Wadi Hesa (Zered)! This fulfills Elisha's prediction in v. 19. YHWH thus delivers Moab into Israel's hands. The Israelites also surround Qir-Hareseth and set slingers to attack (נכה) it (v. 25b).[63] At this point, though, the old battle story took a strange turn. Seeing himself hemmed in and in desperate straits, the Moabite king first tries to break through the Israelite siege line to seek help from Aram (v. 26, see the Note). When that proves unsuccessful he offers his firstborn son as a sacrifice on the city wall (v. 27). This measure is effective in arousing *great wrath* that forces Israel to withdraw. As noted in the Synchronic Analy-

---

62 The reference to the *camp of Israel* without mention of Judah or Edom in v. 24aα is an accommodation to v. 24aβ where Israel alone attacks. It may also be a generalization, since Israel is Moab's primary foe in the story.

63 The significance of slings in the assault on a city is illustrated by the famous reliefs of the siege of Lachish, where a division of the Assyrian army consisted of slingers, and from the flint sling stones found at the site (King and Stager, *Life in Biblical Israel*, 228–29).

sis, this is a notorious interpretive *crux*. There are three principal understandings of the great wrath—that it is Chemosh's wrath, YHWH's wrath, or a numinous power of unclear origin.[64] The main argument for understanding it as YHWH's wrath was presented in the Synchronic Analysis, namely, that the term קצף elewhere in the HB always has YHWH as its source, as retribution for an offense of some sort. Nevertheless, some scholars have argued forcefully for the source of the wrath here as Chemosh.[65] Diachronic considerations suggest that there is validity to all three understandings. That is, in the older battle account the *great wrath* most likely was understood as emanating from Chemosh, whose ownership of the land north of the Arnon is recognized in Judg 11:24.[66] Israelite tradition, however, shied away from ascribing power to a foreign deity and used the ambiguous designation *great wrath* without identifying the source. The story at this stage explained how Israel lost Moab through no fault of its own. *Great wrath* of divine origin kept them from conquering Qir-Hareseth and forced them to return home, leaving Moab independent of Israel's yoke. Moab's successful revolt was something of a fluke—an unexplained "act of god" that handed Israel a loss it should not be ashamed of and Moab independence it did not deserve. In PN's revised version the implication is that YHWH was behind Israel's failure to conquer Qir-Hareseth and its loss of Moab as punishment for Joram's and the Omrids' unfaithfulness. YHWH uses prophecy to deceive Joram as he did Ahab. Elisha's prediction, evidently of his own volition rather than a word from YHWH, still proves to be technically true, even if it is misleading in that Israel lost Moab.

Synthesis

Overview of PN's work in 3:4-27

The opening formulae for Joram (vv. 1-3) overshadow the story that follows. Despite the improvement that Joram represented over his father and brother it was not enough to assuage YHWH's anger at both him and the house of Ahab. Not only

---

64 R. G. Kratz, "Chemosh's Wrath and Yahweh's No. Ideas of Divine Wrath in Moab and Israel," in *Divine Wrath and Divine Mercy in the World of Antiquity* (ed. R. G. Kratz and H. Spieckermann; FAT 33; Tübingen: Mohr Siebeck, 2008), 106. The interpretation of B. Margalit ("Why King Mesha of Moab Sacrificed His Oldest Son," *BAR* 12/6 [1986], 62–63, 76) that the story reflects a ritual prescribed at Ugarit for a sacrifice during siege has been rather roundly rejected (see the article by Burns cited in the next footnote).

65 J. B. Burns, "Why Did the Besieging Army Withdraw?" *ZAW* 102 (1990): 187–94; Westbrook ("Law in Kings," 464–66). Westbrook argues that Mesha's sacrifice sought to appease Chemosh for the violation of his (Mesha's) oath by Chemosh to keep his vassal treaty with Israel. Israel's proper response would have been to accept the payment of tribute. Its continued siege on Qir Hareseth incurred Chemosh's wrath. However, neither an offer of tribute from Mesha nor a rejection of it by Israel is mentioned in the text.

66 See especially the article by Burns in the previous footnote. Schweizer (*Elischa in den Kriegen*, 148–69) argues that the term קצץ occurs in the HB only in late exilic/postexilic contexts. However, his identification of Josh 9:20; 22:20 as Priestly intrusions is debatable. Even if he is correct it does not necessarily mean that the battle story behind 2 Kgs 3 cannot have been older, as Kratz ("Chemosh's Wrath," 106–107) observes.

were his reform efforts meager but he also continued in the sin of Jeroboam. The story in vv. 4-27 is PN's work based on an older report of war between Israel and Moab as the setting for his prophetic tale. He seems to have used two distinct motifs relating to the miraculous appearance of water—one to slake the thirst of a desperate army, the other to cause a hallucination that leads to the defeat of an enemy. PN combined these so that the stories in which these motifs originated cannot be reconstructed. PN also made use of previous canonical materials, especially 1 Kings 22. Indeed, the present story is very similar to 1 Kings 22 in its depiction of YHWH's use of prophecy to subvert a wicked Omrid king and to turn a victory into a loss. At least three major themes can be isolated in the story as it stands.

YHWH's international control. YHWH controls the forces of "nature" in Edom (3:20). He is also in control of events in Moab, where he effects Moab's defeat but then the rescue of Qir-Hareseth (3:27). While the older story may have presented YHWH and Chemosh as gods of separate nations, for PN YHWH is not confined to the land of Israel but is sovereign over all nations and peoples. The *great wrath*, whatever its origin, is from YHWH as far as PN is concerned. For the modern reader concerned with the environment this *wrath* is a reaction not to Joram or at least not to Joram alone but to Israel's mistreatment of creation, even if it is in the land of Moab. Major themes

Characterization of Elisha. Elisha is Elijah's former attendant and successor *who poured water on Elijah's hands.* He is still known as Elijah's attendant rather than as a prophet in his own right. The story suggests some other subtle differences between the two. Elisha does not perform the miracle of the water on his own as Elijah would have done, but merely announces it (vv. 16-18a). He also requires a musician to induce the ecstasy that allows him to access the oracle (3:15). He has the freedom to articulate his own opinions about the king of Israel (vv. 13-14) and to forecast his own vision of the future (vv. 18b-19), which proves to be misleading; the domination of Moab does not come off quite as thoroughly as he implies. The incomplete fulfillment might be chalked up to Elisha's relative newness in the role of Elijah's replacement. On the other hand, the prediction is technically accurate as far as it goes. It is truth, just not the whole truth. Its deceptiveness could be deliberate—on Elisha's part or YHWH's.

Prophecy. This story is about prophecy, its mystery, and its manipulation by YHWH to accomplish his purposes. YHWH's word is reliable, as shown by the actualization of Elisha's pronouncement of it predicting the advent of water (vv. 16-17, 20). But prophecy is a tool for YHWH to employ as he wills. It is not a device for kings to use to further their political aims.[67] In YHWH's control prophecy can be used to deceive kings and undermine their agendas. So it was in 1 Kings 22 and so it is here as well. In 1 Kings 22 YHWH wields prophecy through a member of the divine council; here YHWH's agent is Elisha, who is also privy to the inner workings of the divine as the eyewitness to Elijah's translation. As with the scene about the negotiations of the divine council in 1 Kgs 22:19-23 there is a sense of unsettledness at the end of 2 Kings 3. YHWH again makes use of heavenly forces beyond human ken to foil the plans of his human adversaries.

67 Cf. Bartlett, "Campaign Against Moab," 138.

Elisha's Wonders (2 Kings 4:1-44)

Text

[Prophetic legenda; *PN]*
1 One of the women from the prophetic guild cried out to Elisha, "Your servant,
my husband, is dead, *and you know that he revered YHWH.* Now the creditor has
come to take my two children as slaves." 2 Elisha said to her, "What should I do
for you? Tell me, what do you have in the house?" She answered, "Your servant
has nothing at all except an anointing measure of oil." 3 He said to her, "Go, beg
vessels outside from all of your neighbors—empty vessels, and don't stop at just
a few. 4 Then return and, closing the door behind you and your children, start
pouring oil into these vessels, setting aside each as it is filled." 5 So the woman
went from him and did accordingly. She shut herself and her children in while
they brought vessels to her and she poured oil into them. 6 When the vessels
were full she told her son to bring her another vessel, and he replied, "There
are no more vessels." Then the oil stopped. 7 She came and told the man of god,
who said, "Go, sell the oil and pay your debt, and you and your children live on
the remainder."
8 One day Elisha passed through Shunem where there was a wealthy woman
who prevailed on him to eat, so that as often as he passed through there he
would turn aside and eat there. 9 She told her husband, "I know that this man
who regularly passes our way is a holy man of god. 10 Let's build a small, walled
upper room and put a bed, a table, a chair, and a lamp there, and when he
comes to us he can stay there." 11 One day when he came there he stopped by
the upper room and slept there. 12 *He told Gehazi his servant, "Call this Shunam-*
mite woman." He called her, and when she stood *before him* 13 *he said, "Say to*
her, 'You have gone to all this trouble for us. What should we do for you? Is there
some matter about which you would like us to speak to the king or to the com-
mander of the army for you?'" She replied, "No, I am happy living among my peo-
ple." 14 *He said, "What can be done for her?" Gehazi replied, "Well, she has no son*
and her husband is old." 15 *He said, "Call her." So he called her. When she stood* at
the entrance, 16 he said, "At this time next year you will embrace a son." She re-
sponded, "No, my lord, man of god, do not make sport of your servant." 17 The
woman conceived and bore a son at the same time the following year as Elisha
had told her. 18 The boy grew up and one harvest day went out to his father to
the reapers. 19 He said to his father, "My head, my head." [His father] told the
servant, "Carry him to his mother." 20 So he brought him to his mother, where
he lay on her lap until noon when he died. 21 She took him up and laid him on
the bed of the man of god. Then closing the door behind him, she left. 22 She
called to her husband and said, "Send me one of the servants and one of the

donkeys so that I can run to the man of god and return.” 23 He responded, “Why are you going to him today since it’s neither New Moon nor Sabbath?” She replied, “It’s fine.” 24 Saddling the donkey, she told her servant, “Drive on. Don’t slow down for me unless I tell you to.” 25 She traveled and came to the man of god at the mountain *Carmel. When the man of god saw her from a distance, he told Gehazi his servant, “This is the Shunammite woman.* 26 *Now run to meet her and say to her, ‘Are you all right? Is your husband all right? Is the boy all right?’” So he ran to meet her and said to her, “Are you all right? Is your husband all right? Is the boy all right? She answered, “Fine.”* 27 *But when she came to the man of god on the mountain* she seized his feet. *Gehazi stepped up to push her away, but the man of god said, “Leave her alone, for her spirit is bitter, and* Yhwh *has concealed it from me and not told me.”* 28 *She said, “I did not ask for a son, did I? It was you who did it, wasn’t it? I said, ‘Don’t make sport of me’ didn’t I?”* 29 *[Elisha] said to Gehazi, “Gird your loins. Take my staff in your hand and go. If you meet someone, don’t greet him; if he greets you, don’t answer him. Place my staff on the boy’s face.”* 30 *But the boy’s mother said, “By* Yhwh*’s life and by your life, I’m not going to leave you.”* So he got up and followed her. 31 *Gehazi had gone ahead of them and had placed the staff on the boy’s face, but there was no sound or attentiveness. So he went back to meet [Elisha] and told him, “The boy did not awaken.”* 32 When [Elisha] came to *the house, he found the boy dead, laid out on his bed.* 33 *He went in,* closing the door behind the two of them, *and prayed to* Yhwh. 34 He went up and lay down on the boy, placing his face on [the boy’s] face, his eyes on his eyes, his mouth on his mouth, his palms on his palms. He crouched upon him *until the boy’s flesh grew warm.* 35 *Then he came back and walked once to and fro in the house. He climbed up and crouched upon him* and breathed upon him seven times. Then the boy stirred and opened his eyes. 36 [Elisha] called *Gehazi and said, “Call the Shunammite to me.” When he called* her she came to him, and he told her, “Take your son.” 37 Dropping at his feet she prostrated herself on the ground. Then she picked up her son and left.

38 *After Elisha had returned to Gilgal* there was a famine in the land. The members of the prophetic guild were sitting before him and he told his servant, “Set up the pot and boil some pottage for the members of the prophetic guild.” 39 Then he went out to gather herbs and finding a wild vine he picked wild gourds from it, filling his garment. Then he sliced them into the pot of porridge without knowing what they were. 40 He poured some out for the men to eat, but as they ate the porridge, they cried out, “There is death in the pot, man of god,” and they were unable to eat. 41 He said, “Fetch some meal,” so they fetched some meal, and he threw it into the pot. Then he said, “Pour it out for the people so that they may eat.” And there was nothing bad in the pot.

42 A man from the citizens of Shalishah came bringing the first fruits to the man of god—twenty barley loaves, fresh fruit, and ears of grain. [The man of god] said, “Give it to the people so they may eat.” 43 *But his attendant said, “How can I set this before a hundred men?” But he said, “Give it to the people so*

they may eat, for *thus says Yhwh,* 'They will eat and have some left over.'" 44 So he set it before them and they ate and had some left over *according to Yhwh's word.*

Textual Notes

1 **from the prophetic guild**: Lit. from the sons of the prophets; so G^{BL}. MT: from the wives of the sons of the prophets.

that he revered Yhwh: Reading כי ירא יהוה. MT: כי עבדך היה ירא את־יהוה. G^{B}: ὅτι δοῦλος ἦν φοβούμενος τὸν κύριον. G^{L}: כי עבד יהוה. ירא and עבד are variants that are conflated in MT and G^{B}.

children: Or sons. At least one was a boy (v. 6).

2 **to her**: So MT, G^{L}. G^{B} reflects the loss of אליה by haplography.

what do you have in the house: לכי (*ketiv*) is the first of several cases (vv. 3, 7, 16, 23) of variant forms of pronominal suffixes or personal pronouns that probably reflect or parrot Northern dialect.[1]

nothing at all: So G^{BL}. MT + *in the house.*

an anointing measure of oil: אסוך is a hapax that is understood in some ancient versions (Peshitta, Targum) as a container. G^{B} apparently takes it as a first-person verb (√סוך), ὃ ἀλείψομαι ἔλαιον, oil with which I will anoint myself. G^{L} conflates: ἀγγεῖον ἐλαίου ἐν τῷ οἴκῳ ὃ ἀλείψομαι. The reconstruction here follows a suggestion by Thenius elaborated by Burney.[2]

3 **to her**: So G^{BL}. Lost by haplography from MT.

your neighbors: So MT *ketiv.* (שְׁכֵנָכִי). See on v. 2. G^{B}: *the neighbors.*

4 **into these vessels**: So G^{BL}. MT + *all.* Also read אל for MT's על, based on G^{BL} (εἰς) and on sense.

setting aside each as it is filled: Preceded in G^{L} with καὶ αὐτὸ οὐκ ἀποστήσεται = *but it [the oil] will not run out.* The two readings may be variants.[3]

5 **So the woman went from him and did accordingly**: So G^{L}. MT, G^{B} (*she went from him*) is shorter, but one expects a notice of her compliance.

she poured oil into them: Lit. she poured continuously. Reading מיצקת (Pi'el participle) rather than the MT *Qere* (והיא מוצקת, *Hip'îl*).[4] G^{L} supplies the object *the oil.*

6 **When the vessels were full**: So MT: ויהי כמלאת הכלים. G^{L} + *all.* G^{B} begins with ἕως = עד in continuation of v. 5.

her son: So MT. G^{BL}: her sons/children.

7 **you and your children live**: So G^{BL} (καὶ σὺ καὶ οἱ υἱοί σου ζήσεσθε). MT has ואת בניכי [ובניך] תחיי בנותר which conflates two variants: *you and your children may live* and *keep your children alive.*

on the remainder: G^{L} + *of the oil.*

8 **Shunem**: A town in Issachar (Josh 19:18) identified with the modern village of Solem ca. three miles north of Jezreel at the foot of the hill of Moreh. The birthplace of

---

1 Joüon §94h, i; Schniedewind and Silvan, "Test Case," 331–32. N. Pat-El's critique ("Israelian Hebrew: A Re-Evaluation," *VT* 67 [2017]: 227–63) fittingly cautions against ready appeals to the Northern dialect.

2 Thenius, *Könige*, 279; Burney, *Notes*, 273, who also cites Driver, *Tenses*, §194 on the appositional construction. The anointing in question would not be designation for an office but for cleansing or cosmetic purposes.

3 So Pablo Torijano and Julio Trebolle, personal communication.

4 As proposed by Stade (*Kings*, 190) and others based on sense.

Abishag "the Shunnamite" (1 Kgs 1:3) and the staging place of the Philistines before the battle with Saul on Mount Gilboa (1 Sam 28:4).

and eat there: So MT, G^{L}: שמה לאכל־לחם = ἐκεῖ φαγεῖν ἄρτον. G^{B} lacks *bread*, a haplography in Greek.

10 **walled upper room**: עלית־קיר may refer to "an upper room by a wall," i.e., accessed by a ladder leaned against an outside wall or (2) "an upper room with a wall," as opposed to a hut erected on a rooftop.[5] In either case, the furnishings make clear that this was a permanent structure.

12 **Gehazi**: The ostensible meaning "valley of vision" is inappropriate for a personal name. Gray's assertion that it derives from a root meaning "avaricious" would fit the character, but the Arabic root *jaḥida* that Gray cites is not found in standard Arabic dictionaries.[6] The same is true of Bauer's proposal that it means "googly-eyed."[7] Noth suggests derivation (as a nisbe) from an unknown place name.[8]

13 **No**: So G^{L} (οὐκ ἔστιν = אין) responding to Elisha's question that begins with היש.

14 **Gehazi**: So MT. G^{LB} + his servant" (B), the servant (L).

15 **He said, "Call her"**: G^{B} lacks this sentence, a haplography.

at the entrance: So MT, G^{B}. G^{L} + of the house.

16 **At this time**: So MT, G^{B} (למועד הזה = εἰς τὸν καιρὸν τοῦτον). G^{L} (εἰς τὸ μαρτύριον τοῦτον κατὰ τὸν καιρὸν τοῦτον) attests a double reading and understands מועד as from the root עוד for witnessing.

next year you will embrace a son: So MT (כעת חיה אתי חבקת בן). For the *ketiv* אתי see on v. 2. The meaning of כעת חיה is debated. It occurs elsewhere only in v. 17 and Gen 18:10, 14. Akkadian *ana balaṭ* (*AHw* 99a; *CAD* B 51b) indicates a meaning of next year.[9]

man of god: So MT, G^{L}. The title was systematically removed or replaced in G^{B} in chs. 4–8.[10]

do not make sport of: Reading אל־תצחק/תשחק based on G^{L}: μὴ ἐκγελάσῃ. The verb plays on the Isaac story in Genesis, since the Shunammite's situation resembles Sarah's. MT's אל־תכזב בשפחתך is strange in its use of ב: Do not lie (i.e., deceive) with or by (Ezek 13:9; Ps 78:36). See on v. 28.

17 **as Elisha had told her**: Reading כאשר based on G^{BL} ὡς in lieu of MT's אשר.

18 **and one harvest day went out**: Based on G^{L}: καὶ ἐγένετο ἡμέρα θερισμοῦ καὶ ἐξῆλθε τὸ παιδάριον = ויהי יום קציר ויצא הילד, which supplies information pertinent to the subsequent story. MT: היום ויצא. G^{B}: καὶ ἐγένετο ἡνίκα ἐξῆλθεν τὸ παιδάριον = ויהי כצאת הילד.

19 **My head, my head**: So MT, G^{B}. G^{L}: τὴν κεφαλήν μου ἀλγῶ = ראשי כאב, *my head hurts*. Either is possible.

20 **So he brought him to his mother**: Lost from G^{B} by haplography.

he lay: So G^{B} (καὶ ἐκοιμήθη = וישכב). MT (וישב) has lost the כ. G^{L} (*his mother sat him* = καὶ ἐκάθισεν αὐτὸν ἡ μήτηρ αὐτοῦ) anticipates ותשכבהו in v. 21.

---

5 Montgomery (*Kings*, 371) following Klostermann (*Könige*, 402) emends קיר to קור and equates it with the "cool roof chamber" (עלית המקרה) of Judg 3:20. But the meaning of the expression in Judges is uncertain, as an upper room would hardly be cool.

6 Gray, *Kings*, 495. My thanks to John Kaltner for his help in checking for the root here and in the next note.

7 H. Bauer, "Die hebräischen Eigennamen als sprachliche Erkenntnisquelle," *ZAW* 48 (1930): 73–80.

8 Noth, *Personennamen*, 240.

9 O. Loretz, "*k't ḥyh* - „*wie jetzt ums Jahr*" Gen 18,10," *Bib* 43 (1962): 75–78; R. Yaron, "*Ka'eth ḥayyah* and *koh leḥay*," *VT* 12 (1962): 500–501.

10 Barthélemy, *Critique textuelle de l'Ancien Testament*, 384–85.

21 **closing the door**: G^L supplies the object, which is understood in the idiomatic reading of MT, G^B.

23 **Why are you going**: On the *ketivs* אתי and הלכתי see v. 2.[11]

25 **She traveled and came to the man of god at the mountain Carmel**: So MT. G^B construes the verbs as second masculine singulars rather than third feminines. G^L conflates.

This is the Shunammite woman: The relatively rare demonstrative הלז appears uniquely here as a feminine. As a masculine it is found in 23:17; Judg 6:20; 1 Sam 14:1; 17:26; Zech 2:8.

when the man of god saw her: So MT, G^L. G^B replaces *man of god* with Elisha's name; see v. 16.

26 **So he ran to meet her and said to her, "Are you all right? Is your husband all right? Is the boy all right?**: So G^L. Lost from MT, G^B by haplography.

27 **to the man of god**: So MT, G^L. G^B: to Elisha. See on v. 16.

but the man of god said: So MT. G^B again has Elisha's name in lieu of the title. G^L: *to him*.

from me: So MT, G^L. G^B + *and from you*.

28 **It was you who did it, wasn't it?**: So G^L: οὐχί σὺ πεποίηκας = הלא אתה עשית. Lost from MT, G^B by haplography.

Don't make sport of me: Reading אל־תצחק/תשחק as in v. 16. The woman purports to quote what she said to Elisha in v. 16, but her words are not close to what is in MT in that verse. The use of לא instead of אל is surprising.[12] The *Hip'îl* of שלה occurs only here in the HB, and the sense of "mislead, give false hope" is a guess based on context. The root's basic meaning is to "be quiet, at rest."

29 **Gird your loins**: See on 1 Kgs 18:46.

31 **Gehazi had gone**: On the pluperfect sense of עבר here see Joüon 118d.

ahead of them: So MT. G^B: ahead of her (ἔμπροσθεν αὐτῆς); G^L: ahead of him (ἔμπροσθεν αὐτοῦ). There is no clear basis for deciding between the three.

and told him: G^L (καὶ εἶπεν αὐτῷ καὶ ἀπήγγειλεν αὐτῷ) contains a double reading.

The boy did not awaken: G^L precedes with ὅτι = כי, as an indirect quote.

33 **He went in**: So MT. G^L: *Elisha went in*. G^B reflects further expansion: *Elisha went into the house* as at the beginning of v. 32.

34 **his face on [the boy's] face, his eyes on his eyes, his mouth on his mouth**: So G^L, which follows a logical, top-to-bottom order. MT, G^B: *his mouth on [the boy's] mouth, his eyes on his eyes. His face* (פניו) may have been lost due to its resemblance to *his mouth* (פיו).

on his palms: Reading the plural with MT Qere and the versions.

he crouched upon him: So MT (ויגהר עליו), G^B (καὶ διέκαμψεν ἐπ' αὐτόν). G^L attests a double reading: καὶ συνέκαμψεν ἐπ' αὐτόν καὶ ιγλααδ ἐπ' αὐτόν, with ιγλααδ a mistaken transliteration of יגהר.

35 **and crouched upon him and breathed upon him seven times. Then the boy stirred and opened his eyes**: Textual problems have accumulated around the interpolation marked by the *Wiederaufnahme* of ויגהר עליו in vv. 34b-35a.[13]

---

11 Schniedewind and Silvan ("Test Case," 332) consider them possible Northernisms.

12 Cf. Joosten (*Verbal System*, 270n): "While the volative nuance is clear from the context, the syntax is inexplicable."

13 Trebolle, *Centena*, 167–68. I am also aided significantly by a paper by Pablo Torijano on G ms 460 that dealt with 2 Kgs 4:34-35, presented at the 2015 SBL Annual Meeting in Atlanta. I thank him for sharing the paper with me. The interpolation makes Smith's proposal of "sound forth, be loud of voice" for גהר (see on 18:42) less likely. The clause ויגהר עליו is summative and means the same thing in this context as וישכב.

MT	G^B	G^L
ויגהר עליו	καὶ συνέκαμψεν ἐπὶ τὸ παιδάριον	καὶ συνέκαμψεν ἐπὶ τὸ παιδάριον καὶ ἐνέπνευσεν ἐπ' αὐτόν καὶ ἠνδρίσατο ἐπὶ τὸ παιδάριον ἑπτάκις
ויזורר הנער		
עד־שבע פעמים		καὶ διεκινήθη τὸ παιδάριον
	ἕως ἑπτάκις	
ויפקח הנער את־עיניו	καὶ ἤνοιξεν τὸ παιδάριον τοὺς ὀφθαλμοὺς αὐτοῦ	καὶ διήνοιξε τοὺς ὀφθαλμοὺς αὐτοῦ

συνέκαμψεν and ἠνδρίσατο in G^L are variant translations of ויגהר, constituting a double reading.[14] The OG included the clause "he breathed upon him" (καὶ ἐνέπνευσεν ἐπ' αὐτόν), which is also attested in the OL (*inspirauit in eum*). It makes better sense than MT's reading "the boy sneezed until seven times," and the breathing of the man of god upon the boy is attested in 1 Kgs 17:21 G, which has been adapted from this Elisha *legenda*. MT's ויזורר is suspicious as a hapax not reflected in G^B. G^L's καὶ διεκινήθη (*he stirred, moved*) suggests that it may be a corruption or variant of ויעור (*arouse oneself, awaken*). G^L also indicates that this verb followed the reference to seven rather than preceded it as in MT, such that it is breathing on the boy that Elisha repeats seven times.

36 **to me**: So G^L (= אלי). Lost from MT, G^B by haplography.

37 **Dropping at his feet**: So MT: ותבא ותפל. G^{BL} + *the woman* after the first verb. G^L + *upon her knees* at the end of the sentence.

she prostrated herself: See the Note on 16:31.

38 **Gilgal**: To the considerations in favor of locating Gilgal near Jericho, perhaps Khirbet el-Mafjar, adduced in the Diachronic Analysis of 2 Kgs 2:1, Rehm adds that the wild vine (*citrullus colcynthus*) only grows in the southern Jordan Valley and Dead Sea region.[15]

a famine: So G^L. MT, G^B: *the famine*.

sitting before: The expression ישב לפני is ambiguous. The verb may mean "sit," "stay" or "live, dwell." The preposition might mean "in front of" or "under the supervision of." The "sons of the prophets," as Elisha's disciples, are living under his direction and perhaps actually sitting under his tutelage.

the pot: So G^B. MT, G^L: *the large pot*.

39 **Then he went out to gather herbs**: Reading ויצא ללקט ארת based on OL, which lacks the phrase *into the field*. OL also supplies Gehazi's name as the subject. MT renders the subject as indefinite (אחד). G^{BL} provide no subject for καὶ ἐξῆλθεν, though εἷς (one) may have been lost by haplography preceding εἰς τὸν ἀγρὸν. The noun ארת (sing. אורה) occurs only once more in the HB (Isa 26:19) but is known from Ugaritic (*KTU* 1.19.2.17.24) and post-biblical Hebrew.[16] It refers to some kind of wild sprouts or herbs. See the Diachronic Analysis.

---

14 ἠνδρίσατοis from ἀνδρίζω, middle-passive = "to play the part of a man, take a man's sexual position."

15 Rehm, *Das zweite Buch der Könige*, 57.

16 Rendsburg (*Israelian Hebrew*, 92–93) contends that the word is Northern.

a wild vine: Lit. *a vine of the field*, so MT, G^{L} (גפן שדה = ἄμπελον ἀγρίαν). G^{B}: ἄμπελον ἐν τῷ ἀγρῷ). Compare Exod 22:30 on the use of field to designate wild.

he picked wild gourds from it: So MT, with the plural gourds as befits the mention of filling the garment. G^{BL}: τολύπην (singular). MT's ממנו construes גפן as masculine although it is usually feminine.

Then he sliced them: So MT (ויפלח). G^{BL}: וישלח. MT, G^{L} precede with ויבא. Omit with G^{B}.

without knowing what they were: So G^{L} with the singular verb: ὅτι οὐκ ᾔδει. MT, G^{B} have the plural. BHS suggests reading the final waw on ידעו as the masculine singular suffix matching ממנו, but again גפן is feminine. The waw is a dittography of the conjunction at the beginning of v. 40.

40 **He poured**: So G^{BL}. MT has the plural. The singular is confirmed by the imperative צק in v. 41.

they cried out: So MT, G^{L}: והמה צעק. G^{B} reflects והנה instead of the pronoun. On the use of subject + qāṭal to express simultaneity with the preceding clause see Joosten, *Verbal System*, 139–40.

41 **"Fetch some meal," so they fetched some meal, and he threw it into the pot**: The notice of compliance (*so they fetched some meal*) was probably lost by haplography. The major witnesses suggest disruption. MT reads וקחו־קמח וישלך אל־הסיר. G^{B} reflects two plural imperatives: *Fetch meal and throw it into the pot*. G^{L}, which shares G^{B}'s reading, continues with καὶ ἐνέβαλον (*and they threw [it]*), reflecting a felt need for a compliance notice. But one expects Elisha to be the one who throws meal into the pot.

And there was nothing bad in the pot: So MT (ולא היה דבר רע בסיר). G^{BL}: καὶ οὐκ ἐγενήθη (L: ἐγένετο) (B: ἔτι ἐκεῖ) ῥῆμα πονηρὸν (L: ἔτι) ἐν τῷ λέβητι. The different placements of ἔτι (still, yet) indicate it is secondary.

42 **from the citizens of Shalishah**: Reading מבעלי שלשה *from the lords of Shalishah*.[17] The בית/בעל variation in the G^{B} reading (G^{B}: Βαιθσαρεισα) is attested with other place names (Baal/Beth-Peor, Baal/Beth Maon) and may reflect an attempt to remove the offensive "Baal" element. The G^{L} reading Bethlehem is unexplained, but can hardly be primitive. Shalishah is mentioned in Saul's search for his father's lost donkeys (1 Sam 9:4) and was in southeast Ephraim or northeast Benjamin not far from Gilgal, and perhaps to be identified with Khirbet el-Marjame. The common identification with Kefr Tilt north of Lydda in the vicinity of Shechem is based on the similarity of Shalishah and Tilt (both from the root for "three") with little else to recommend it.[18]

the first fruits: So G^{B}, which lacks the first לחם of MT.

ears of grain: Reading בצקלם. The word is not reflected in G^{BL}. Its meaning is clear because of its occurrence in the Ugaritic texts where it is identified with *šblt*.[19] The

---

17 Following a suggestion by McCarter, *II Samuel*, 174.

18 McCarter, *II Samuel*, 174; Cogan and Tadmor, *II Kings*, 59; B. Mazar, "The Early Israelite Settlement in the Hill Country," *BASOR* 241 (1981), 81; A. Mazar, "Khirbet Marjame ('Ain Sâmiya)," *IEJ* 26 (1976), 138–39. G. A. Herion ("Baal-Shalishah," *ABD* 1 [1992]: 553) objects to the identification with Marjame because its limited rainfall would not lend itself to abundant harvests. But twenty barley loaves and some fresh stalks of grain do not necessarily indicate an abundance, especially if the gift is a collective one. The point, after all, is the miraculous multiplication of foodstuffs. J. A. Wagenaar ("'Someone Came from Baal-Shalisha ...?' The Significance of the Topography in 2Kgs 4.42-44," *BN* 135 {2007]: 35–42) argues that the tale reflects an earlier harvest season in Shalisha.

19 *KTU* 1.19.2.13-16, 20-23. U. Cassuto, *Biblical and Oriental Studies* (trans. Israel Abrahams; Jerusalem: Magnes, 1975), 2.197; H. R. (Chaim) Cohen, *Biblical Hapax Legomena in the Light of Akkadian and Ugaritic* (SBLDS 37; Missoula, MT: SBL, 1978), 112–13.

plural adopted here follows a suggestion of Rendsburg and fits well with the previous two phrases also including a singular noun in construct with a masculine plural.[20]

43 They will eat and have some left over: That is, אכל והותר, infinitives absolute, construed with G^{BL} as surrogates for plural imperfects or jussives: *let them eat ...* (GKC §113ee; Joüon §123w, 155i; WO 594). See the Note on 3:16.

44 So he set it before them: So MT: ויתן לפניהם. Lacking in G^{BL}, but the compliance of the attendant with the command in v. 42 (and repeated in v. 43) is expected.

Synchronic Analysis

Content and structure of the chapter

The four tales in this chapter further illustrate Elisha's power as Elijah's successor. Three of the stories are brief anecdotes, told in bare-bones narrative style with few details, but the third and fourth are integrally connected in such a way that they might be considered together as one story. Combined, they are about the same length as the first one (seven verses). Hence the arrangement of the stories in the chapter is balanced, with the second one highlighted as the centerpiece. It is the longest of them and the only one that is not concerned in some way with food. In it Elisha duplicates the greatest wonder of his mentor (except for his transfer to heaven) and shows himself his near equal. The stories are also tied together thematically. The first two involve women in need. The second and third deal with death and the third and fourth with food, perhaps during famine. Elisha is presented as a liminal figure, removed from the usual rhythms of life. He is a wonder-working "man of god" in all four stories, and all four use this title. His career is not a sequence of activities but an assortment of demonstrations of supernatural power.

4:1-7

The setting of the first story

The first story introduces the basic structure shared by the other three: a crisis occurs; the person(s) in crisis appeals to Elisha for help; Elisha performs a miracle resolving the crisis. The nameless woman at the center of this story is the widow of a member of the prophetic guild. The focus on the miraculous resolution causes the narrative to be stingy with details. There is no location given; the reader may deduce that it takes place in Gilgal, given the reference to that place as the starting point for Elijah and Elisha in 2:1 and the statement in 4:42 that Elisha returned there, though Samaria is also a candidate based on 2:25, as is Mount Carmel, judging from 4:25. There is nothing said about when the woman's husband died. It was evidently recently since the woman appears to be dealing with a new set of circumstances forced upon her.[21] The woman pleads, i.e., "cries out" (צעק) for help from Elisha. The basis of her appeal is that her husband revered (ירא) YHWH. She does not just rely on Elisha's compassion but marshals evidence to show that

20 Rendsburg, *Israelian Hebrew*, 94–95.

21 Jewish tradition identifies the man with Obadiah of 1 Kgs 18:3-7, whose name means "servant of YHWH" and who was also a fearer of YHWH (18:3). See Josephus, *Ant.* 9.47-48, and the Targum on 2 Kgs 4:1.

it is merited.[22] Her main witness is Elisha himself, who *knows* that her husband was loyal to YHWH. Elisha thus has some affiliation with the prophetic guild and is well acquainted with its members.

Thwarting the creditor

The woman is destitute. The "sons of the prophets" live meager lives anyway, and this woman has been left with two children and no means of support. The direct crisis that causes the woman to cry out for help is posed by a creditor. Since the creditor is fully within his rights the woman does not seek legal redress but assistance on a different level.[23] Exactly what her expectations may be the text does not make clear. Perhaps she anticipates a miracle; the reader familiar with this kind of story certainly does. Elisha's question, "What can I do for you?" is rhetorical or "thinking out loud" (v. 2). He has no preconceived plan. Seeking a starting point in terms of what he has to work with, he asks the woman what she has in her house. Just why she has a house if she is destitute is not clear, but one can imagine that she does not own it or that its value is not enough to cover the debt or that there is insufficient time to sell before the debt is due. The only item left to the widow in the house is a small amount of oil—just enough for anointing (see the Note). It is enough for Elisha to use as a starting point. He tells her to borrow all the empty vessels she can from her neighbors (v. 3). The specification *from all your neighbors* is intriguing. The woman's rescue depends in a sense on the generosity of her neighbors in lending these containers. The nameless "minor" characters are crucial for the story's outcome; the neighbors (שכנים) counter the threat of the creditor (שנה).[24] The second part of Elisha's instruction is that the woman shut herself and her children in her house and start pouring the oil she has into the empty containers (v. 4). The closed doors keep curious neighbors from interfering in the woman's execution of Elisha's instructions and in readers' experience of the event (v. 5). This further highlights the neighbors' generosity, as they are willing to lend their vessels without knowing the details of how they will be used. The actual miracle also occurs away from Elisha's presence. He is no illusionist who needs to be present to effect the wonder. Nor is he a magician who speaks magic formulas or carries out special rituals. The reference to YHWH in v. 1 indicates that he is the ultimate source of the wonder. Elisha is the channel for divine power.

The qualities of the widow

The woman is also to be given credit for her own role in her salvation. She is as intriguing and admirable a character in this story as Elisha himself. Her adherence to Elisha's orders leads to a quick resolution of her problem. She does not request any explanation or clarification but goes straightaway to do as he has told her. After the oil has stopped flowing (v. 6) she returns for further instructions. She must have sus-

---

22 Hens-Piazza, *Kings*, 250.

23 Rehm, *Das zweite Buch der Könige*, 50.

24 G. Hens-Piazza, "Cameo Appearances in II Kings 4.1-7: Artifacts of Scenery or Agents of Change," 2016 CBA meeting, Santa Clara University. She argues further that the vessels here would have been large storage jars used for oil, typically one per household, such that lending them would have been a mark of real generosity. The argument is enticing, though it is impossible to substantiate from the text, which uses the generic term כלי. An additional point for consideration is the likelihood that those doing the lending were probably women, though again the masculine form שכנים leaves the point unsubstantiated textually.

pected what Elisha would tell her, but her return points to her obedience and integrity. Destitute as she is, she does not want to make use of the oil for her own benefit without the leave of the man of god. The story does not need to report, therefore, that she sold the oil as commanded (v. 7). The reader knows that this was the case and that she was able to pay her debt and support herself and her children. The absence of an explicit compliance notice places the focus on Elisha and his wonder. The use of the title "man of god" for the first time in v. 7 suggests a slight change of perspective on Elisha on the part of the narrator if not of the woman. It is similar to the confession of the widow in 1 Kgs 17:24. Elisha's true status as a man of god is recognizable through his deeds. The woman has implicitly recognized this all along, as shown by her unquestioning obedience to his orders.

4:8-37

The structure of the story

The second story (vv. 8-37) is significantly longer than the other three and much more intricate and detailed in its plot. It has three parts of uneven lengths, each introduced with the loose time designation "one day" (vv. 8, 11, 18b). The three build on one another, each moving the story to its next stage. The third section (vv. 18b-37) is the longest and is the focus of the story. It deals with the woman's confrontation of the man of god and his response to her crisis. The three-part structure of the other stories in the chapter—crisis, appeal to the man of god, and miracle by the man of god resolving the crisis—occurs in the third section. The story moves forward primarily by means of dialogue interspersed with description. The dialogue occurs between two people except for vv. 13-15 where there are three.[25]

The story's sophistication

The story spends a great deal of time building the background to the characters and the miracle (vv. 8-17). Even more time is devoted to describing the woman's journey to Elisha, her complaint, their return, and Gehazi's failed attempt in the meantime to revive the boy (vv. 18-31). All of this buildup creates enormous interest and anticipation on the part of the reader. When Elisha reaches the house there is still a brief delay effected by the description of his entry into the room (vv. 32-33) before the actual miracle (vv. 34-35). The narration of the miracle is brief but, even so, its progress is paced by details about the way Elisha positions himself upon the boy and paces about between repetitions of this act. The story does not end there but only with a postlude concerning the return of the boy to his mother. It is an extraordinarily well-written story with complex characterization, vivid detail, and a moving plot.

4:8: Characterizing the Shunammite

The woman who is the central character is a study in contrasts to the woman in the first story. She is wealthy (v. 8), literally "a great woman" or "woman of substance."[26] The expression also hints at her social status and respectability as

---

25 A. Schmitt, "Die Totenerweckung in 2 Kön. 4, 8-37. Eine literaturwissenschaftliche Untersuchung," *BZ* 19 (1975): 1–25, at 15.

26 The word "great" might also be translated "old," the translation favored here by J. Tropper ("Elischa und die „grosse" Frau aus Schunem (2Kön 4,8-37)," *KUSATU* 3 (2002): 71–80. As Sauerwein (*Elischa*, 49) observes, this translation would fit the story very well as an explanation for the woman's childlessness and an enhancement of the miracle of her son's birth. Still, the description in v. 10 makes clear that the immediate interest is in her wealth.

well as her character, which is revealed in the story. She has a husband and plenty of resources. She requests nothing from Elisha. She also has no children. The story has a specific setting—Shunem in the Jezreel Valley, where Elisha and the woman met when he passed through *one day* and she *prevailed upon him* to eat with her. The verb, which typically has the sense of "seize, grasp" in *Hip'îl*, presages its use in v. 27. While she will seize hold of Elisha in pleading at that point, at their initial meeting she does so in order to offer him hospitality. The initial encounter becomes a habitual practice, as Elisha begins to stop by for a meal whenever he is in the vicinity (v. 8b). The woman's hospitality, which increases incrementally in the next verse, attests her "greatness" of means and also of spirit; she is a person of high social standing and of high quality—generous, hospitable, and respectable. Part of the basis of the developing relationship between the woman and Elisha may be their shared status as members of the nobility.[27] The woman speaks and behaves with dignity in every situation. She is truly an admirable character.[28] Nevertheless, both text and prophet resist equality for her by treating her as subservient, patronizing her, and not naming her, though both name the servant, Gehazi.[29]

4:9-10: A room for the man of god

The woman makes a proposal to her husband (vv. 9-10). She foregrounds it with the observation that Elisha is a holy man of god. As a term usually reserved for cultic matters, the reference to the prophet Elisha as *holy* is unique. "Holiness" was an entity that had to be handled cautiously in the ancient world. It brought opportunity for both blessing and danger. So in the case of a man of god he might draw divine attention to sin, as feared by the Sidonian widow (1 Kgs 17:18). Also, offending the man of god could have dire consequences (2 Kgs 2:23-24). On the other hand, his presence and power promised great blessing for proper treatment. The woman's proposal to build a room separate from the house *per se* may be an attempt to maintain some distance from the man of god and thus to reap the benefits of his holiness while minimizing the potential danger from it. Still, the characterization of the woman and her husband suggest that she presents the potential for blessing in order to induce him to agree to her proposal and that her own motive is unselfish: she wishes to provide comfortable accommodation for Elisha because she admires him and enjoys his company. The husband's lack of emotional involvement even raises the question whether the woman seeks Elisha as a replacement for her husband, at least in terms of companionship and emotional and psychological engagement. The furnishings make clear that this was a permanent structure to be available whenever Elisha wished to take advantage of it. By modern standards they are rudimentary, but in ancient Israel, where most people sat and slept on the ground, they were luxurious. Their mention is another indication of the wealth and noble status of the woman and her husband as well as her generosity toward Elisha.

---

27 Rehm, *Das zweite Buch der Könige*, 54.

28 See the list in Nelson, *Kings*, 172. Her hospitality is one of the characteristics she shares with Abraham, highlighted by the use of this passage as the *haftorah* portion read in conjunction with the Akedah (Gen 22). For further exposition see A. Deem, "The Great Woman of Shunem," in *Proceedings of the Eighth World Congress of Jewish Studies; A: The Period of the Bible* (Jerusalem: World Union of Jewish Studies, 1982), 21–24 (Hebrew).

29 Shields, "Subverting a Man of God."

4:11-13: What to give the woman who has everything?

There is no reference to the husband's acquiescence or account of the building project. With *one day* in v. 11 the story proceeds to its second phase, which assumes that the upper room has been built. Elisha stops by and remains there for what may be his initial stay. His servant Gehazi is introduced for the first time. He is Elisha's interlocutor who allows the reader access to Elisha's deliberations about what he can do for the woman (esp. v. 14). As Elisha's messenger and spokesman in vv. 12-13, 15 he builds distance between Elisha and the woman that becomes more pronounced when she seeks his help. Elisha's question in v. 13 (מה לעשות לך) is very similar in phrasing to that of v. 2 (מה אעשה־לך). There, however, Elisha was seeking a way to help the woman who had virtually nothing for him to work with; here, in contrast, he faces the problem of what to give to the woman who "has it all." She has given him a valuable and thoughtful gift and he wishes to reciprocate. He offers to speak to the king or commander on her behalf. The offer indicates the extent of the influence Elisha wields and the elite circles to which he is privy, as reflected in other stories about him in chs. 5–8; 13 and especially in 8:1-6, where this woman does require intercession with the king and receives it indirectly from Elisha and Gehazi. Elisha's question is perhaps an offer to solicit a reduction of the civil or military obligations incurred by nobles in ancient Israel. The woman declines the offer by stating that she lives at home among her people. Her point seems to be that her family is well placed and that she requires no patronage beyond the clan or tribal authorities among whom she is well regarded and cared for.

4:14-16: The promise of a son

When Elisha turns again to Gehazi (v. 14), the servant responds that the woman has no son and her husband is old. This is not new information to Elisha but a polite way of suggesting something in the way of a gift for her. Having a son meant financial security. This was not a concern for the woman and her husband, since they were wealthy. However, a son also meant survival of the family name so that not having children—and especially a male—was a social stigma, particularly for women, tantamount to a lack of personal fulfillment in life. For these reasons the promise of a son as a reward for faithfulness is a repeated motif in the HB, beginning with Abraham and Sarah (Gen 17:15-22) and including such figures as Samson (Judg 13) and Samuel (1 Sam 1:1-20). Gehazi's reminder reflects awareness of and participates in that motif. Elisha functions in the role of the angel or messenger (the prophet is a messenger) who typically delivers the promise of a son.[30] The Shunammite, unlike Sarah and Hannah, is not said to be barren. But her husband, like Abraham, is old, the implication being that the couple's childlessness is his fault. Elisha's promise that the woman will embrace a son within the year is met with skepticism by the woman (v. 16), as is typical of such annunciation scenes. The promise has revived in her a hope that was moribund. She begs not to be misled by the hope ultimately proving false. Her plea raises the question of Elisha's reliability. The question is particularly poignant in view of the phrasing of Elisha's promise in v. 16, lit. "at the time of life you will embrace a son," which may be an allusion to v. 20, where the woman holds the boy on her lap as his life passes. The allusion would not be noticed by a first-time reader of the story but only by someone already aware of what will happen to the boy. For the time being, therefore, with the fulfillment of his promise (v. 17) Elisha appears to be trustworthy.

---

30 Long, *2 Kings*, 56.

A modern feminist reading

The dynamics between Elisha and the woman in vv. 12-17 are profoundly disturbing.[31] Elisha does not speak directly to her but asks Gehazi in her presence what she wants. He decides unilaterally, without consulting either the woman or YHWH, to give her a son and ignores the first word from her mouth in response: "No." There is no record of joy or anticipation on her part or her husband's over the next nine months or even at the boy's birth. This account can leave the reader with the sense that the "gift" from Elisha is an unwanted burden, yet the further narrative certainly portrays her as a dutiful and devoted mother. The depiction of the woman's husband throughout the story suggests itself as a means of reconciling these two impressions. He is old and impotent. He is uninvolved in the boy's birth and emotionally detached when the boy becomes ill (v. 19). She does not engage him in seeking a remedy (vv. 22-23) but goes straight to Elisha and presents the matter as his responsibility (vv. 26-28). It is not much of a stretch in this reading to suppose that the boy is Elisha's son.[32]

4:17-20: The boy's death

Verses 17-18a accelerate the pace of the narrative, covering a period of several years in as many sentences. The boy is now able to walk and talk (v. 19) but small enough to sit in his mother's lap (v. 20b). The third "one day" in v. 18bα introduces the main segment of the tale. While visiting his father and the reapers in the field, the boy suddenly suffers a severe headache.[33] The father orders a servant to carry the boy to his mother (v. 19b). The father does not go himself, once more demonstrating his emotional detachment. There is nothing the mother can do except hold her son in her lap until he dies a short time later (v. 20). Thus in the space of three short verses the healthy, growing boy of v. 18 is dead (v. 20).

4:21-24: Going to Elisha

The quick pace continues in the verses that follow (vv. 21-25a). There is no time to waste. The woman's subsequent actions (v. 21) attest her trust in Elisha. She lays her son's corpse on Elisha's bed and sets out to find him. It is not clear what she expects. Perhaps she anticipates a miracle. Or she may reason that Elisha is simply her only hope. Her use of the title "man of god" recalls the miraculous power he wields and the fact that the boy owes his existence to that power. She closes the door as she leaves in order to keep his death a secret and prevent his burial until she can talk to Elisha.[34] She does not tell her husband of the boy's death and hides her emotions from him (v. 22-23). He is obtuse, his flaws accentu-

---

31 Mary E. Shields, "Subverting a Man of God in 2 Kings 4," *JSOT* 58 (1993): 59–69.

32 Shields, "Subverting a Man of God," esp. 59–65; G. Hepner, "Three's a crowd in Shunem: Elisha's misconduct with the Shunamite reflects a polemic against prophetism," ZAW 122 (2010): 387–400. C. Uehlinger ("Totenerweckungen—zwischen volkstümlicher Bettgeschichte und theologischer Bekenntnisliteratur," in *Auferstehung Hat Einen Namen. Biblische Anstöße zum Christsein Heute* [FS H.-J. Venetz; ed. S. Bieberstein and D. Kosch; Lucern, 1998], esp. 21–25) demonstrated the sexual innuendo present in such features as the Shunammite's use of the double negative (v. 15) found elsewhere in the HB in rape scenes (Judg 19:23; 2 Sam 13:12), her use of כזב, which can imply sexual deceit, and her grasping his "feet" while making clear that Elisha is responsible for her son's birth (vv. 27-28).

33 Diagnosed at least since Thenius (*Könige*, 281) as sunstroke.

34 Rehm, *Das zweite Buch der Könige*, 55. Würthwein (*1. Könige 17-2. Könige 25,* 293) argues that here and in v. 31 the concern to close the door is due to a superstition in the original *legenda* that the boy's soul might leave the room.

ated by his wife's virtues.[35] He fails to deduce that her request to visit the man of god is connected with the boy's illness, curious only as to why she wishes to visit on a regular workday (Am 8:5; Hos 2:11; Isa 1:13; 1 Sam 20:5). His question suggests that his only concern is the loss of the labor from a servant and a beast for a day. She reassures him that everything is fine (שלום). Yet he might have noticed that she used the verb *run*, hinting at her haste and distress. The servant she takes is for driving the donkey as quickly as possible (v. 24) and for protection for a woman traveling alone. It is she who saddles the donkey and makes the necessary preparations. She tells the servant not to slow down for her unless she explicitly requests it, and there is no reason to believe that she does.

4:25-27: Reaching Mount Carmel

She rushes as quickly as possible straight to the man of god at his Mount Carmel residence (v. 25). An indication of how fast she travels is the required time frame. An afternoon departure would normally mean arrival at Mount Carmel after dark. Yet Elisha sees her approaching from a distance and recognizes her in what must still be daylight. She has indeed run. Sensing that something is amiss, Elisha sends Gehazi to meet her with questions about the welfare of herself, her husband, and her son (v. 26). She replies with the single word שלום, which doubles as a greeting. It is a clever way of dismissing Gehazi's question, motivated by her desire to talk to Elisha himself. When she comes to him she falls to the ground and seizes his feet. The gesture is one of submission and entreaty (Est 8:3). It is reminiscent of her "seizing" Elisha at the beginning of their relationship to compel him to eat with her (v. 8). Later, in v. 37, she will again fall at Elisha's feet in a posture of gratitude for his having responded to her entreaty. After suppressing her emotions before her husband, her servant, and Gehazi, she now breaks down. Elisha does not allow Gehazi to force her to release him. He perceives that she is deeply upset, but he does not know the cause because Yhwh, for reasons that are unclear, has revealed nothing about it to him. The statement is important for indicating the source of Elisha's prescience and miraculous power.

4:28: The question of Elisha's reliability

The woman asks Elisha two rhetorical questions, anticipating "no" and "yes" responses respectively (v. 28). She reminds him that she did not ask for a son and that when he promised her one she asked him not to deceive her. She alludes to her words in v. 16 but does not quote them. In fact, all three words are different from what she said there: אל־תכזב בשפחתך *Don't lie to your servant* (v. 16) vs. לא תשלה אתי *Do not mislead me* (v. 28). The change is significant for promoting the woman's case. She initially asked Elisha not to lie to her because she did not want to have false hope. He did not lie, since she did have a son. But the boy has died, so that "the hopes that she had not wanted raised have now been dashed."[36] She accuses Elisha of misleading her with hopes and expectations that her son would grow to adulthood and have a full life. His promise in v. 16 was duplicitous. The boy's death calls Elisha's reliability—as well as the reliability and graciousness of Yhwh—into question and resonates especially strongly with the story in chapter 3. Was Elisha only deceptive to the king of Israel because of the latter's wickedness, or is he equally unreliable for the faithful?

4:29: Gehazi with Elisha's staff

The woman's actions and demeanor convince Elisha that the situation is urgent. He orders Gehazi to proceed immediately to her house with his (Elisha's)

35 Nelson, *Kings*, 172.
36 Olley, *Kings*, 231.

staff and to lay it upon the boy's face (v. 29). This shows Elisha's responsiveness and prolongs the suspense of the narrative. The ultimate failure of Gehazi's mission (v. 31) provides a foil to Elisha's ultimate success.[37] The fact that Gehazi is not to greet others or respond to those who greet him indicates the urgency of his mission (cf. Luke 10:4). Gehazi is presumably younger and in any case is alone and can therefore travel faster than Elisha and the woman together. Still, it is not clear whether Elisha is aware that the boy is actually dead, since *YHWH has hidden* it from him (v. 27) and the woman has not explicitly told him that this is the case; he may think the boy is seriously ill and that his staff has sufficient power on its own to heal.[38] This might explain why he sends his servant, although the impression on the reader is that he cannot be bothered to go himself. It is only at the insistence of the woman that he accompanies her (v. 30). Even then he goes after her (אחריה) rather than with her. Like the widow in vv. 1-7, the Shunammite is significantly responsible for her own rescue. Her insistence attests her astuteness in recognizing the necessity of Elisha's personal presence. This contrasts with the story in vv. 1-7 where Elisha did not need to be present. Perhaps restoring life to the dead is more difficult than multiplying oil.

4:30-32: The ineffectiveness of Gehazi and the staff

In v. 30 the oath of the Shunammite (here poignantly called the *mother of the boy*) is the same as Elisha's when Elijah was taken to heaven (2 Kgs 2:2, 4, 6). Hence Elisha recognizes her resolve and goes with her. The oath exhibits her trust in both YHWH and the prophet. Meanwhile Gehazi has gone ahead to Shunem and placed Elisha's staff on the boy's face, but without result (v. 31). The woman travels more slowly on her return to Shunem with Elisha in tow. Gehazi has time to go to Shunem, attempt to revitalize the boy, and then head back, meeting Elisha and the woman on their way. The subject-first construction indicates simultaneous action. That is, Gehazi does this while the woman and Elisha are negotiating and then setting off toward Shunem. Gehazi's ineffectiveness (ואין קול ואין קשב) is reported in much the same language as the ineffectiveness of the prophets of Baal in 1 Kgs 18:29 (ואין־קול ואין־ענה ואין קשב). He returns with a report that the boy did not awaken. The complete lack of response is telling; both Gehazi and Elisha now know that the boy is dead. Verse 32b further assuages ambiguity about the boy's condition: he is not just lying (שכב) on the bed but laid out (משכב), a corpse.

4:33-37: The dramatic conclusion with prayer and ritual

Elisha closes the door for the sake of privacy and concentration. Perhaps it is because his actions take place behind closed doors that the description of them is somewhat obscure. They are of two kinds: prayer and ritual. After praying to YHWH, or perhaps while doing so (v. 33), Elisha crouches upon the boy's body, their parts corresponding, until the body grows warm (v. 34). Then he walks back and forth in the room before repeating this act, upon which the boy sneezes seven times and revives, opening his eyes (v. 35). Elisha has Gehazi summon the woman and for the second time gives her a child (v. 36). His success vindicates her insistence on remaining with him and compelling him to go to Shunem. His extraordi-

---

37 Nelson, *Kings*, 174.

38 By analogy with Moses' and Aaron's staffs, which are depicted as possessing power to perform wonders (Exod 4:17; 7:19; 8:1, 12; 9:23; 10:13; 14:16), Šanda (*Könige* II, 32) argues that the point of placing Elisha's staff on the boy is to prevent his burial until the prophet's arrival the following morning. But there is no indication that the woman's household is aware that the boy is dead.

nary deed is motivated by her extraordinary trust in and regard for him.[39] At the same time it puts her that much more in debt to and subordinate to him.[40] She falls at his feet again, this time in obeisance and with utter gratitude (v. 37), before she takes her son downstairs and home.

4:38-41

In Gilgal with the prophetic community

The chapter's third story is set in Gilgal, from which Elijah and Elisha left on the journey that took Elijah to heaven (2:1). Elisha may have a semi-permanent home there in addition to his residence on Mount Carmel (v. 25), especially if he came from a wealthy family. Or it may be that he has gone there to teach or counsel the members of the prophetic guild, who can be pictured as seated at his feet in the posture of students (v. 38). In either case the prophetic community is under his direction, at least temporarily. Being in charge, he orders his servant to put a large pot on the fire and prepare a pottage. The servant is presumably Gehazi, although he is not named.

Healing the foraged stew

The famine means that food options are limited to what can be foraged. If this is the same famine as in 8:1 it is of long duration and more widespread than just the region around Gilgal. This explains why it is called *the* famine. The prophets do the foraging and one of them gathers wild gourds for the meal, unaware of what the plant is (v. 39). This information sounds an ominous note, as the nature of the preceding stories leads one to expect a crisis to arise. The narrative does not disappoint. However, it is not clear exactly what it is about the stew that leads the prophets to sound the alarm (v. 40). Perhaps they begin to be ill. The reference to *death* implies this, but then why does Elisha not heal those who have partaken? Another possibility is that something about the taste alarms them so that *they were unable to eat*. *Death* would then be hyperbole, although it links this story with the previous one. As in 2:21, Elisha calls for a commonplace substance in order to purge the food of its threat. This time it is meal (v. 41)—no small sacrifice in time of famine. There is no notice of compliance; it is understood since Elisha throws the meal into the pot. The quantity is not specified. Assuming analogy with 2:20, a handful suffices. As with the spring in that story, the stew becomes harmless and edible. To use the language of the earlier passage, Elisha heals it.

4:42-44

4:42: A gift for Elisha

The fourth story also deals with food and the lack of it in sufficient quantity. Following v. 38, this story presumes and is set in Gilgal during *the famine*, although it is not mentioned within vv. 42-44. As such the gift of first fruits to Elisha takes on added significance. It may be a petition, though no request from Baal-shalishah is forthcoming, or it may be payment for prophetic inquiry.[41] The gift of first

39 Würthwein *1. Könige 17–2. Könige 25*, 294

40 D. Jobling, "A Bettered Woman: Elisha and the Shunammite in the Deuteronomic Work," in *The Labour of Reading: Desire, Alienation, and Biblical Interpretation* (ed. F. Black, R. Boer, and E. Runions; Atlanta: SBL, 1999), 181.

41 So Rehm (*Das zweite Buch der Könige*, 58); 1 Sam 9:7-8; 1 Kgs 14:3; 2 Kgs 5:15; 8:8 contain precedents.

fruits might also indicate that the famine has ended in part of the land of Israel and that Elisha had something to do with its end, for which the people of Baal-shalishah in Ephraim/Benjamin express their gratitude.

4:43-44: The gift shared and multiplied

Elisha shares his gift with those around him, i.e., the members of the prophetic guild. The addressee of his order to *give* is not named in v. 42, but the response in v. 43 identifies him as Elisha's *attendant* (משרת), who is nameless. One could identify him as Gehazi except that the different title—*attendant* rather than *servant* (נער)—suggests a separate person. Elisha was Elijah's attendant (1 Kgs 19:21), recalling his origins and training as a prophet. Perhaps this is the reason behind his generosity. The attendant objects that there are too many people for such a small amount of food to satisfy. The question exhibits more naïveté than we might imagine for Gehazi after the resurrection of the boy in vv. 8-37. On the other hand it emphasizes how the man of god acts in unanticipated ways and at unanticipated times. The attendant gives one hundred as the number of people to whom the food is to be offered. This is the number of prophets saved by Obadiah in 1 Kings 18 and of soldiers killed by fire from heaven at Elijah's behest in 2 Kings 2. The number thus alludes to the man of god's ability to save life and to take it. Elisha does not dignify the attendant's question with an answer but simply repeats the order. This time he adds a word from YHWH to the effect that they will all eat to satisfaction and even have some left over. The story ends in v. 44, as is typical of such tales, with the notices of compliance and fulfillment. When the attendant follows Elisha's command the people do eat until they are satisfied, and there are leftovers *according to YHWH's word*. It is one more example of the efficaciousness of the divine word along the lines of the transformation of the widow in 1 Kgs 17:14-16.

Diachronic Analysis

Four *legenda*

The four tales in this chapter (1-7, 8-37, 38-41, 42-44) were originally independent prophetic *legenda*. They were set in different places, which were typically not named, and each had its own introduction and conclusion. They are united by their common theme relating to the miracle working of Elisha and by a common *legenda* form consisting of a crisis, an appeal to the man of god, and a miraculous deed that resolves the crisis. Elisha is designated both by name and by the title *man of god*, but the different designations do not represent different redactional levels.[42] The title occurs indiscriminately along with Elisha's name throughout the stories about him as an honorific highlighting Elisha's miraculous powers (v. 40). All four probably began as oral traditions; this might explain some of the presumed Northern forms in the first *legenda*. However, there is no compelling reason to think that Elisha was not identified as the wonderworker from the outset. All four have also undergone literary revision. Three of them (vv. 1-7, 38-41, 42-44) are basic or simple *legenda* with only light editing, mostly crediting YHWH for their

42 *Pace* Schmitt, *Elisa*, 93–99, 207–209.

miracles.[43] The second *legenda* (vv. 8-37) is an example of the elaborated variety with a more extensive and intricate plot, greater detail and character development. It also received significant editorial revision and supplementation. The editorial techniques—collecting prophetic *legenda*, arranging them paratactically sometimes with loose geographical references, crediting YHWH with the miracles, linking with other Elijah/Elisha stories, and the like—are of the same kind we have witnessed previously and should be assigned to the same hand, that of PN.

4:1-7: The basic *legenda*

This basic *legenda* was altered only by the addition of the reference to the woman's deceased husband as a worshiper of YHWH at the end of v. 1a (*and you know that your servant feared YHWH*).[44] The comment is superfluous, since the man was one of the prophetic guild and therefore by definition a Yahwist. This *legenda* served as the basis for the Elijah story in 1 Kgs 17:8-16 as explained in the discussion of that passage. The prophet's widow and Elisha are already acquainted. She is also not destitute, unlike the widow of Sarepta, but in debt, so there is no tension with her ownership of a house, especially considering the implication that her husband died recently. The threat is against her children. Debt slavery was practiced in ancient Israel and included the selling of family members, who served as a kind of collateral (Exod 21:1-9; Deut 15:12-18; Lev 25:39; Amos 2:9; 8:6; Isa 50:1; Nehemiah 5).[45] The miracle is Elisha's doing without any intervention from YHWH, and the *legenda* reads quite effectively as a unit, as seen in the Synchronic Analysis.

4:1a: PN's addition

PN's addition in v. 1a effects a subtle change in the story by shifting the focus from Elisha to the dead prophet and his widow. The basic *legenda* was about Elisha and his wonder-working ability. The form of the *legenda*—crisis, appeal, and miraculous response—illustrates Elisha's power. The additional clause stresses the dead prophet's merit. He *deserves* Elisha's aid, giving the *legenda* a religious hue and making Elisha's deed an act of service to YHWH on behalf of a faithful Yahwist who is rewarded for his piety.

4:8-37: Overview of the second *legenda*

The second *legenda* is closely tied to 2 Kgs 8:1-6 and was probably bound with it at one time. They may have been separated in order to fill the seven-year interval between them (8:1) with other stories. The famine mentioned in 4:38 and assumed in 4:42-44 may be identified with the one in 8:1, and the collection of stories in chapter 4 would fit the bill for the king's request to hear the "great things" done by Elisha (8:4). The *legenda* was borrowed and adapted into the Elijah

---

43 A. Rofé, "The Classification of the Prophetical Stories," *JBL* 89 [1970], 430–33) points out that orality is indicated by 2 Kgs 8:1-6.

44 Würthwein, *1. Könige 17–2. Könige 25*, 288. Following Schmitt (*Elisa*, 99), Würthwein also considers the title *man of god* in v. 7 to be a secondary replacement of Elisha's name designed to link this story with the next one.

45 For background and overview see G. C. Chirichigno, *Debt-Slavery in Israel and the Ancient Near East* (JSOTSup 141; Sheffield: JSOT, 1993), who suggests (pp. 123, 355) that the social stratification condemned by prophets like Amos hints that debt slavery was on the rise during the Omri dynasty and reached its highest levels during the Jehu dynasty. J. Berman ("The Legal Blend in Biblical Narrative [Joshua 20:1-9, Judges 6:25-31, 1 Samuel 15:2, 28:3-25, 2 Kings 4:1-7, Jeremiah 34:12-17, Nehemiah 5:1-12]," *JBL* 134 [2015], 122–23) argues that the sons were protected from seizure as collateral inside the house (Deut 24:10-11) and that this is why the woman closes her door (v. 5).

story in 1 Kgs 17:17-24, as explained in the treatment of that passage. This was done before the revision of the Elisha *legenda* into the present story. Unlike the Elijah version, in this story the depiction of the woman and her house, including the room she builds for the man of god, are quite appropriate to a character of her wealth and social standing. The *legenda* as it stands has been thoroughly revised through extensive supplementation, especially the introduction of Gehazi as a foil to prolong the suspense and highlight Elisha's power and effectiveness.

4:8-11: The start of the elaborated *legenda*

At the beginning of the *legenda* (v. 8) Elisha is alone and passing through the village of Shunem in the Galilee. Where he is traveling from is not explained, nor are the exact circumstances of his meeting the woman. They establish a relationship such that he is a frequent visitor to her house. She becomes convinced that he is a man of god (v. 9). How she discerns this is also unexplained, but it is the rationale for the proposal she makes to her husband to build a furnished upper room for Elisha (v. 10). The distance from Shunem to Mount Carmel, assuming the latter as Elisha's place of residence, is about a day's journey by foot, so that her house would be a good stopping point for Elisha coming or going.

4:12-15: PN's introduction of Gehazi

The primary evidence of editorial revision is the passages dealing with Gehazi.[46] The scene involving him in vv. 12-15 has long been suspected as an addition because Elisha has the woman summoned and then proceeds to tell Gehazi what to say to her (v. 13), even though she is standing in front of him (v. 12). Then Elisha and Gehazi hold a conversation in front of the woman as if she were not there (v. 14), and Elisha has Gehazi call her again when she is already present (v. 15). Elisha's statement that the woman has gone to a lot of trouble "for us" (v. 13) is at odds with his aloneness to this point and is also a sign of revision. The *Wiederaufnahme* in vv. 12b and 15b (ויקרא־לה ותעמד) delineates the limits of the interpolation and indicates that v. 12a was added as well. The older *legenda* included only the clause *he called her and she stood* in v. 12bα + *in the doorway* (בפתח) at the end of v. 15.[47] Initially Elisha called the woman himself rather than going through Gehazi. She came and politely stood *at the entrance* of the upper chamber, not wishing to intrude on his privacy even though it was on her property. Her politeness is part of her "greatness." The additions in vv. 12-15 make explicit what is only implicit in the older *legenda*—that the woman has no children. Furthermore, the prospect of children is low because her husband is old. The offer to speak to the king on her behalf in v. 13 prepares for 8:1-6, where that is essentially what Elisha does, albeit *in absentia*. The added material also brings the present story into the company of those about Elisha in chapters 5–8 and 13 where he deals closely with the king(s) of Israel.

4:16-25a: The continuation of the *legenda*

The prediction of a son and its fulfillment (vv. 16-17) were in the *legenda*, as was the rest of vv. 18-25a (minus the name *Carmel*). A few years later the boy experiences a severe headache while he is in the field with his father (vv. 18-19) and dies shortly thereafter (v. 20). His age is undisclosed, but he is young enough

46 Würthwein, *1. Könige 17–2. Könige 25*, 289–94. Sauerwein's reconstruction (*Elischa*, 48–53) is very similar to Würthwein's. Both require modest adjustment based in part on text-critical evidence.

47 Trebolle, *Centena*, 165–66. Würthwein (*1. Könige 17–2. Könige 25*, 290) and Sauerwein (*Elischa*, 48–49) acknowledge the *Wiederaufnahme* but then include all of v. 12 in the addition.

for his mother to carry him to the upper room (v. 21)—perhaps about five or six years old. It is not clear whether she anticipates a miracle, but she knows that only the man of god can help.[48] The woman's husband asks why she is going to visit the man of god when it is not New Moon or Sabbath (v. 23b). The New Moon was the first day of the lunar calendar. It was a day of rest (Amos 8:5), feasting (1 Sam 20:5, 18-24), and cultic celebration (Isa 1:13; 66:23; Ps 81:4) entailing special sacrifices (Num 28:11-15; Ezek 46:6; Ezra 4:5) that could be extended for additional days (1 Sam 20:27). Its pairing with Sabbath here and elsewhere (Isa 1:13; 66:23; Ezek 46:1; Amos 8:5) suggests that the Sabbath was initially celebrated in the middle of the month rather than weekly.[49] The man's question may harbor the suspicion that her sudden visit is related to the boy's affliction, in which case her reassurance that everything is all right (v. 23b) is appropriate. The woman saddles her donkey and sets out at full speed with instructions to the servant not to slow down or stop for rest without explicit instructions (v. 24).

New Moon and Sabbath

A second interpolation in vv. 25aβ-27aβ is signaled by *Wiederaufnahme* (ותבא אל־איש האלהים אל־הר). Again this evidence both confirms and sharpens suspicions about an addition in these verses.[50] Since the name of the mountain, Carmel, comes at the point where the *legenda* breaks off in v. 25a, it is part of the interpolation. The *legenda* resumes briefly after the second mention of the mountain with the statement in v. 27aβ that the woman seized Eisha's feet. Verse 27b with its mention of Gehazi is added. This is signaled also by the tension between Gehazi's presence with the woman (v. 26) and his presence back with Elisha (v. 27) without any note of transition. It introduces Yhwh into the story that is otherwise about deeds performed by the man of god on his own and explains Elisha's lack of prescience.

PN's interpolation in 4:25aβ-27aβ

The mountain where Elisha resides was not named in the *legenda*. The interpolation identifies it as Carmel, as in 1 Kings 18; 2 Kgs 2:25. Geographical considerations add support to the text-critical evidence for the name being secondary. The distance from Shunem to Carmel is about twenty miles, depending on where in the mountain range

Mount Carmel

48 *Pace* Kilian, "Die Totenerweckung," esp. 47–51, who takes this as evidence that this story is secondary to the Elijah one in 1 Kgs 17:17-24. The countercase was argued in my treatment of 1 Kings 17. The Shunammite's perceived anticipation of a miracle results from elaboration of the genre, specifically the appeal of a person in crisis to the man of god. She must travel to where he is in order to make her appeal, which she does by seizing Elisha's feet (v. 27). In the Elijah story (1 Kgs 17:18) the widow's accusing questions without a gesture of appeal distort the *legenda* form.

49 So M. Greenberg, "In the Bible" segment of "Sabbath," *EncJud* 14:562. For other discussions of the background of Sabbath see W. W. Hallo, "New Moons and Sabbaths: A Case Study in the Contrastive Approach," *HUCA* 48 (1977): 1–18; M. Tsevat, "The Basic Meaning of the Biblical Sabbath," *ZAW* 84 (1972): 447–59; de Vaux, *Ancient Israel* 475–83. T. Veijola, "Die Propheten und das Alter des Sabbatgebots," in *Prophet und Prophetenbuch. Festschrift für Otto Kaiser zum 65. Geburtstag* (ed. V. Fritz, K.-F. Pohlmann and H.-C. Schmitt; BZAW 185; Berlin: de Gruyter, 1989): 246–64.

50 Trebolle, *Centena*, 166–67. Benzinger (*Könige*, 136) recognized the *Wiederaufnahme*, attributing it to a second version of the tale. As before, Würthwein (*1. Könige 17–2. Könige 25*, 289–90) acknowledges the *Wiederaufnahme* but ignores its specific limits, taking v. 25 after ותלך, all of v. 26, and v. 27b as secondary but v. 27a as original. Sauerwein (*Elischa*, 50, 278) considers vv. 25b-27 as the interpolation.

Elisha lived. An afternoon departure (v. 20) would mean arrival at twilight or after dark so that visibility from a distance (v. 25) would be impossible.[51] The *legenda* lacked the difficulty not only because it did not name the mountain but also because it did not have Elisha recognize her from a distance. The interpolation adds to the portrait of the woman's desperation by showing that she feels the need to deal exclusively with Elisha, deflecting Gehazi's solicitous inquiries. It identifies Elisha's prescience and power as emanating from YHWH and thus ultimately credits him with the miracle that follows. Gehazi was not present in the *legenda*, so there she came straight to Elisha (v. 25a minus *Carmel* + 27aα) and seized hold of his feet in a gesture of appeal that accords with the elements of the genre of the *legenda*.

4:27b-31: Separating the *legenda* from PN

Several scholars distinguish two levels based on the term used for the boy, the older level being identified by its use of ילד while the secondary material prefers נער.[52] This reconstruction is already rendered questionable by v. 26, which is part of an interpolation (so also Würthwein!) yet uses the term ילד. It is further undercut by the text-critical evidence (see below), which indicates that the two terms are variants in this passage, mainly for distinguishing the woman's son from her servant but without source-critical significance.[53] There are, however, additional criteria that are useful for distinguishing the *legenda* from its revision. The woman's complaint in v. 28 is part of PN's addition, as suggested by the change in verbs from v. 16 to which it alludes. Initially her appeal consisted of her gesture alone, which sufficed to convince Elisha to accompany her (v. 30b). The implication in the *legenda* was that he knew the boy was dead. The lack of explicit statement to this effect occasioned the addition of the explanation about Elisha's lack of prescience at the end of v. 27 as well as Gehazi's mission in vv. 29, 31. If the boy is only ill, the prophet's staff might be enough to heal him. Its failure highlights the woman's persistence and well-placed trust in Elisha as well as the importance of Elisha's personal presence. Her oath (v. 30) names YHWH and is thus suspect.[54] Her resolve not to leave Elisha only makes sense in response to Elisha's sending his servant to try to heal the boy with his staff in v. 29 and is therefore part of the revision. The language expressing Gehazi's failure, *there was no sound or attentiveness*, resembles 1 Kgs 18:29 and indicates a relationship between the two; both are products of PN's hand. The term קשב, *attentiveness* suggests that some kind of spoken formula or incantation accompanied the laying on of the staff.[55] Gehazi returns to report his failure to Elisha (v. 31b), setting the stage for the latter's arrival at the house (v. 32a). The timetable is further indication that v. 31 is secondary, as Gehazi's attempt would be unnecessary with his master and the woman right behind.

4:32-37: The raising of the boy in the *legenda* and PN's revision of it

The initial verbs of vv. 32 and 33 (ויבא) constitute a *Wiederaufnahme*, indicating that v. 32 in effect is an interpolation.[56] As the story now has it, Elisha enters the house twice. Also, the information provided in vv. 32-33 is out of logical sequence in that the description of the boy on the bed occurs (v. 32) before the notice that

---

51 The story ignores the nighttime return journey altogether. Cf. Schmitt, "Totenerweckung in 2 Kön. 4, 8-37," 17.

52 Esp. Schmitt, *Elisa*, 93–101; Würthwein, *1. Könige 17–2. Könige 25*, 290.

53 So also Stipp, *Elischa – Propheten – Gottesmänner*, 284–94.

54 So Sauerwein (*Elischa*, 51) *pace* Würthwein (*1. Könige 17–2. Könige 25*, 291, 293), who retains it in the older level.

55 Cogan and Tadmor, *II* Kings, 58.

56 Technically ויבא in v. 32 pertains to the *legenda* and ויבא in v. 33 to the revision.

Elisha closed the door (v. 33).[57] It is worth noting that the interpolation in v. 32 uses נער, while the one in vv. 34b-35a (see below) uses ילד. The reference to Elisha's prayer in v. 33b is an addition comparable to the one at the end of v. 27 enhancing YHWH's involvement.[58] In the *legenda* Elisha performed this wonder on his own through sympathetic magic. In vv. 34b-35a there is another interpolation by *Wiederaufnahme* (the repetition of ויגהר עליו).[59] The interpolation enhances Elisha's ritual activity, making it a more gradual and elaborate process such that Elisha walks about between his sessions on top of the boy, who warms slowly. Elisha breathes upon the boy seven times (see the Note). This is another act of ritual magic transferring breath to the boy. Following G^L, the boy's revival is accomplished when he stirs under his own power and opens his eyes. Verses 34a and 35b were part of the *legenda*. The ritual described in v. 34a involved lying on top of the boy in such a way that facial features and hands corresponded in order to transfer life from the living organs and appendages into the dead ones and reanimate the body.[60] Since Elisha was taller than the boy it was necessary for him to draw up his limbs into a crouch (גהר) in order to match the boy's body parts.[61] The same verb occurs in 1 Kgs 18:42, providing another link between the two chapters from PN. The *legenda* then continued with Elisha summoning the Shunammite in v. 36 and returning her son to her. Here again there is an addition by *Wiederaufnahme* (ויקרא אל־גיחזי ויאמר קרא אל־השנמית הזאת ויקרא) in the order to Gehazi to summon the woman. The *legenda* ended in v. 37 with Elisha delivering the boy back to his mother, who again bows at his feet, this time in gratitude, and then leaves with her living son in her arms.

4:38-41: The third legenda and its PN revision

The basic *legenda* in these verses remains except for the addition of Elisha's return to Gilgal in v. 38aα, which is editorial and locates the last two stories in that city. It also links back to 2:1 as the place from which Elijah and Elisha set out when Elijah was taken up to heaven. The *legenda* was originally independent of vv. 8-37. It was set in time of famine, which was not the case for vv. 8-37.[62] The *legenda* did not mention YHWH at all. Elisha's deed was undertaken purely on his own initiative using his own powers. The *legenda* assumed that Elisha was living with a community of the prophetic guild in an unspecified location in a leadership or teaching capacity (v. 38). Elisha's servant (v. 39) was nameless, though the implication following vv. 8-37 is that he was Gehazi. Elisha commanded him to put on the large cooking pot for a communal meal that consisted of what the

57 Trebolle (*Centena*, 167) shows how the G pluses further help to delimit the interpolation.

58 Schmitt, *Elisa*, 93; Würthwein, *1. Könige 17–2. Könige 25*, 290, 294; Sauerwein, *Elischa*, 51.

59 Trebolle, *Centena*, 167–68. Again the textual evidence both confirms previous suspicions of an addition and delimits it precisely. Cf. Würthwein, *1. Könige 17–2. Könige 25*, 290, 294; Sauerwein, *Elischa*, 50, 280.

60 Cf. S. Daiches, "Zu II Kön. IV, 34 (Elisas Handlung durch babylonische Beschwörungstextstellen erklärt)," *OLZ* 11 (1908): 492–93; A. Jeffers (*Magic and Divination in Ancient Palestine and Syria* (SHCANE 8; Leiden: Brill, 1996), 88n, 234. Albertz ("Magie II," *TRE* 21:692–93) calls it "contactual" magic.

61 Cf. Burney, *Notes*, 276.

62 The story about the Shunammite in 8:1-6 does presuppose a famine, but it is set seven years later.

members of the prophetic guild foraged. The servant (following G) was unfamiliar with the local vegetation and picked some gourds from a wild vine; these he sliced and threw into the stew. While the narrative does not further define the vine, commentators are virtually unanimous in identifying it as *citrullus colcynthus* or the "bitter apple" plant. It produces a yellow fruit the size of an apple that is a strong purgative and can be fatal if ingested in sufficient quantities. The cry of *death in the pot* (v. 40) while they ate suggests that the bitter taste of the stew was the immediate source of concern rather than illness. These factors suggest that the mention of death was something of an exaggeration, though it links this story nicely with the previous one. The crisis, nevertheless, was a real one; the food was ruined, and this was no small matter in a famine. The outcry (צעק) also fit the typical plot of the *legenda*: crisis, appeal, and miraculous resolution. The ready availability of meal in time of famine was a slight inconsistency but not an outright contradiction. The tension is negligible in a *legenda* whose focus is the wondrous deed of the prophet. Besides, only a small quantity was required. The theory that the meal improved the taste of the stew by absorbing its oil and coating the stomach is a rationalization that misses the point of the *legenda*:[63] Elisha's act of magic "healed" the pot of food as he "healed" Jericho's spring (2:19-22).

4:42-44: The last *legenda* and PN revision

The location of the final *legenda* invites construal as taking place during the same famine and in the same place as the previous story. However, the gift of first fruits from nearby Shalishah (see the Note) indicates plenty from a good harvest. This plus the use of the term משרת instead of נער shows this *legenda*'s independence. In PN's revised edition both terms can be taken as titles for Gehazi. The command of the man of god to give the food to the people gives rise to the protest of the *attendant* that there is not enough for so large a group (v. 43). The issue is resolved, as usual, by a wonder performed by the man of god (v. 44). The absence of Elisha's name might suggest that the hero of this *legenda* was nameless and secondarily became identified as Elisha. On the other hand, the similarity to the other Elisha *legenda* and its embeddedness among them are just as strong an argument for seeing him as the original hero. *First fruits* (בכורים) are designated for the priests in other texts (Lev 2:14; 23:17-20; Num 18:13), suggesting that *man of god* here functions in a priestly role or at least that he is considered, like priests, a proper recipient of gifts designated for representatives of the divine. Elisha does not appear in the role of a priest anywhere else in Kings. It may be that a not-too-subtle point is being made about the authority of the prophet to override priestly regulations.[64] The repetition of the clause *he said, Give it to the people so they may eat* from v. 42b in v. 43bα suggests interpolation. The *legenda* that remains is about Elisha receiving a gift of some food and sharing it with *the people*. This presumes a relatively large group, perhaps the prophetic guild. The vagueness of the reference called forth the editorial augmentation in v. 43a that specified one hundred men. The multiplication was originally Elisha's doing alone and did not mention Yhwh. The prediction and fulfillment notices in vv. 43-44 are also additions.[65] They transform the simple *legenda* into a theological lesson about the

---

63 *Pace* Sweeney, *Kings*, 292.

64 Cf. Heller, "Drei Wundertaten Elisas," 84.

65 So Würthwein, *1. Könige 17–2. Könige 25*, 296.

efficaciousness of the divine word like that in 1 Kgs 17:14-16 and identify YHWH as the source of Elisha's power and authority.

Synthesis

Four revised *legenda*

The four stories in this chapter are revised prophetic *legenda* about Elisha. Three of them are basic *legenda* in which he performs an act of magic in order to address an appeal from a person or persons in crisis. The Shunammite story is an elaborated *legenda*; it has the same basic form of crisis, appeal, miracle but is enhanced with significant background details, character development, and the like. All four received editorial revision by PN, whose handiwork is apparent in the crediting of YHWH for the wonders performed by Elisha. His skill as an author/editor is especially evident in the Shunammite story, where his additions prolong the drama and enhance the miracle mainly through the character Gehazi.

The popularity of *legenda*

While the veneer of attribution to YHWH may make explicit what is already implicit, i.e., that YHWH is the power behind them all, much of the enduring appeal of these stories is present in them before YHWH becomes involved. The fourth story, for instance, reappears in the "Feeding of the 5000," uniquely shared by all four NT Gospels (Matt 14:13-21; Mark 6:31-44; Luke 9:10-17; John 6:5-15) as well as the "Feeding of the 4000" in Matt 15:32–16:10; Mark 8:1-9, without any explicit reference to the hand of god. Like the Elisha version of the story these are all about a wonder performed by the holy man. Then again, it is no accident that the Gospels raise the question of Jesus' identity in the context of this and other miracles. The holy man is the man of *god*. The point of the stories is to attest to divine power working in the human sphere. Even if the man of god uses magic he is still somehow able to gain access to the divine for use on earth. The absence of precise time references and dates emphasizes the liminal nature of this kind of figure, the paradigm for which is Elijah.

The humanity of the stories

Another facet of these stories that lends them popular appeal is the divine compassion for human beings they exhibit.[66] Elisha does not perform miracles for entertainment or to attract attention to himself but to help someone in need. All four stories follow a pattern of response to a crisis and an appeal for help. The beneficiaries in three of the stories appear to be poor, explicitly so in the first story, and Elisha's miracles supply them with the basic staple of food. Also, Elisha does not just give, he also empowers.[67] He has the widow gather vessels from her neighbors and the prophets gather herbs and plants for a stew. Moreover, the focus is not just on the poor and socially disadvantaged. The Shunammite is the model of empowerment and initiative, and Elisha does not discourage her (v. 27). Here he meets another need, filling a void in her life and then healing her broken heart by restoring her son to life. None of the beneficiaries is named. They are not famous or important people but everyday folk. They are, nonetheless, deserv-

66 Cf. E. Haller, "Märchen und Zeugnis: Auslegung der Erzählung 2 Könige 4.1-7," in *Probleme Biblischer Theologie*. (Fs. G. Von Rad; ed. H. W. Wolff; Munich: Kaiser, 1971): 108–15.

67 Hens-Piazza, *Kings*, 255–56.

ing people. The women in the first two stories are remarkable characters. They are opposites in some respects. The first is widowed, destitute, and has two sons, while the second is wealthy, married, and childless. Both are strong characters, who take matters into their own hands when necessary and seek tenaciously for what they and their loved ones need. Neither is afraid to ask the man of god for help. Both exhibit admiration for him. The widow trusts completely in what he tells her to do. The Shunammite trusts Elisha but does not hesitate to make demands of him when necessary—albeit with deference. In this respect she is another foil to Jezebel.[68] Yet her constant deference is disturbing for modern readers because of the gender dynamics in the story. The Shunammite is never named despite her elevated character and in contrast to the servant Gehazi. She is of the same social class as Elisha yet is consistently patronized by him. He controls her reproductive sexuality by "awarding" her a son she has not requested and it is not clear she wants. The idea of a son comes from Gehazi. Her husband's age and lack of engagement throughout the narrative identify the boy as Elisha's, certainly in terms of responsibility for him if not biologically.

The collaboration of different methods

Methodologically this chapter, and the story of the Shunammite especially, are fertile territory. The text-critical evidence reinforces and refines preceding source-critical judgments and allows for a more complete picture of the development of the chapter, especially the Shunammite story. Rather than dealing with independent layers, we have a prophetic *legenda* that has been rewritten primarily by supplementation through interpolation by narrative resumption (*Wiederaufnahme*). Form criticism is important for discerning that the Shunammite *legenda*, though elaborated, contains the same scheme of crisis, appeal, and resolution through sympathetic magic as the three basic *legenda* in the chapter. Text- and source-critical analyses are formative for character assessment as they reveal the courtesy of the Shunammite in the *legenda* in waiting at Elisha's open door, before this was obscured by the additions in vv. 12-15. Beyond historical-critical considerations a close feminist reading of the Shunammite story shows the extent to which she is ignored and denied participation in events that shape her life. Since the Bible is a collection of literature that has shaped and continues to shape modern life and thought, especially in the Western world, acknowledgment of such phenomena as the text's treatment of the Shunammite is essential for recognizing and undoing the injustices of sexism and misogyny.

68 Cf. Jobling, "Bettered Woman," 190.

The Healing of Naaman (2 Kings 5:1-27)

Text

[Prophetic legenda; *PN; Additions and glosses to PN]*
1 Naaman, the commander of the king of Aram, was a great man before his mas-
ter and highly favored *because by him YHWH had given victory to Aram*. But the
man had a skin disease. 2 Aram used to go out on raiding parties, and they cap-
tured a young girl from the land of Israel who served Naaman's wife. 3 She told
her mistress, "I wish my master were before the prophet who is in Samaria;
then he could cure him of his skin disease." 4 Then she went and told her hus-
band, "The servant girl from the land of Israel said thus and so." 5 *When [Naa-*
man] told the king, the king of Aram said, "Go on, and I'll write a letter to the
king of Israel." So he went, taking ten talents of silver, six thousand shekels of
gold, and ten changes of clothes. 6 *He brought the letter to the king of Israel; it*
said, "Now when this letter reaches you, know that I have sent Naaman my ser-
vant to you so that you will cure him of his skin disease." 7 *But when the king of*
Israel read the letter he tore his clothes, saying, "I am not a god, am I—to take
away and bestow life, since this guy is sending to me to cure a man of his skin
disease? Only consider and recognize that he is trying to stir up trouble against
me." 8 *When the man of god heard that the king had torn his clothes, he sent to*
the king, "Why did you tear your clothes? Let him come to me so that he will
learn that there is a prophet in Israel." 9 Naaman came with horse and chariot
and waited for Elisha at the door of the house. 10 Elisha sent a messenger to
him, telling him, "Go and wash seven times in the Jordan so that your skin may
be restored and you may become clean." 11 *Naaman became angry and left, say-*
ing, "I thought he would certainly come out and call on the name of YHWH his
god and would wave his hand over the place and cure it of its skin disease.
12 *The Abana and the Pharpar, the rivers of Damascus, are better than all the wa-*
ters of Israel, aren't they? I could wash in them and be clean, couldn't I?" So he
turned around and left angry. 13 *But his servants approached him and spoke to*
him, "If it had been some great deed that the prophet told you to do, you would
have done it, wouldn't you? How much more when he has told you, 'Wash and be-
come clean!'" 14 So he went down and washed seven times in the Jordan as the
man of god had told him; his flesh was restored like the flesh of a small child
and he became clean. 15 *Then he returned—he and his entourage—to the man of*
god. Upon arrival he stood before him and said, "I know that there is no god in
all the earth except in Israel. So now please accept a gift from your servant." 16 *[El-*
isha] replied, "By the life of YHWH in whose service I stand, I won't accept any-
thing." [Naaman] urged him to accept it, but [Elisha] refused. 17 *Naaman said, "If*
not, may your servant please be given two mule loads of dirt because your ser-

vant will no longer worship and sacrifice to other gods but only to YHWH. 18 *Concerning this matter, may YHWH pardon your servant when my master goes to the temple of Rimmon to prostrate himself, for he leans on my arm, and when he prostrates himself in the temple of Rimmon I will prostrate myself with him in the temple of Rimmon—and may YHWH pardon your servant in this matter.* 19 *[Elisha] told him, "Go in peace." When he had gone a certain distance from him,* 20 *Gehazi, the servant of Elisha the man of god, thought, "My master spared Naaman the Aramaean by not accepting what he brought. By YHWH's life, I will certainly run after him in order to get something from him."* 21 *So Gehazi chased after Naaman. When Naaman saw him running after him, he got down from the chariot to meet him and asked if everything was all right.* 22 *[Gehazi] said, "Everything is fine. My master sent me with a message: 'Two young men from the prophetic guild in the highlands of Ephraim have come to me. Please give them a talent of silver and two changes of clothes.'"* 23 *Naaman answered, "Please take two talents." Urging him, he wrapped two talents of silver in two bags with two changes of clothes and gave them to two of his servants who carried them ahead of [Gehazi].* 24 *When they came to the acropolis he took the items from them, stored them in the house, and dismissed the men, who departed.* 25 *When he went in to attend to his master, Elisha said to him, "Where have you come from, Gehazi?" He responded, "Your servant hasn't gone anywhere."* 26 *[Elisha] said to him, "I walked along mentally as Naaman got down from his chariot to meet you, didn't I? Now that you have acquired the silver, will you acquire with it gardens, olive groves, vineyards, sheep, cattle, male and female servants?* 27 *Naaman's skin disease will adhere to you and to your descendants from now on." [Gehazi] left his presence diseased as snow.*

Textual Notes

1 **Naaman**: A well attested name in Aramaic and Ugaritic as well as in the Bible, where it is usually tribal (Gen 46:21; Num 26:40; 1 Chr 8:4, 7), it means "pleasant, gracious, favored," and is probably an abbreviated sentence name referring to a deity's beneficence toward humans ("GN is lovely, delightful").[1]

commander of the king of Aram: So G^L, which makes clear the antecedent of *his master*. G^B: *commander of the army of Aram*. MT conflates.

highly favored: Lit. *one whose face is lifted up* (*Qal* passive participle). The expression refers to a person of privilege, particularly one who is in high standing with the king (Isa 3:3; 9:14; Job 22:8; cf. also Gen 40:13, 20).[2] Naaman is one to whom deference should be shown and who was a favorite of the king.

had a skin disease: So G^L. MT, G^B preceded by *was a great warrior*, but this is superfluous following the designation of Naaman as the army commander and may be a misplaced variant of it. The symptoms of this disease as described in the Bible,

---

1 Noth (*Personennamen*, 166) takes it as a single word expressing the bearer's pleasantness to parents, *et al.*

2 M. I. Gruber ("The Many Faces of Hebrew נשא פנים >lift up the face<," *ZAW* 95 [1983]: 252–60) takes its basic meaning as a smiling face.

especially its infection of fabrics and buildings (Lev 13–14), do not fit leprosy (Hansen's disease).[3] It may be an umbrella term for a variety of disorders of the skin.

2 **Aram used to go out**: So MT, G^B. G^L: *from Aram used to go out.*

3 **I wish my master were before the prophet**: So MT, G^L. G^B + *of god*. The particle אחלי, *would that* occurs elsewhere in the HB only in Ps 119:5 but also twice in Ugaritic (*KTU* 1.19.2.15).[4]

in Samaria: G^L + *and could entreat him.*

he could cure him: The verb אסף usually means *gather* or *remove*. It may have the sense here of removing Naaman from his disease. Another possibility is that the verb is cognate to the Akkadian noun *āšipu*, "exorcist," one associated with ritual healing (*CAD* A 2.431-35).

4 **Then she went and told her husband**: So G^{BL} (καὶ εἰσῆλθε[ν] καὶ ἀπήγγειλε[ν] τῷ κυρίῳ [ἑ]αυτῆς). MT (*Then he went and told his master*) does not explain how Naaman learned the girl's words.

5 **When [Naaman] told the king**: So G^L (καὶ ἀνηγγέλη τῷ βασιλεῖ), which gives a complete chain of communication, while MT and G^B have different gaps.

The king of Aram said: So MT, G^L. G^B + *to Naaman.*

So he went: So MT, G^B. G^L: *So Naaman went to the king of Israel.*

six thousand shekels of gold: So MT, G^B. G^L has *six talents of gold*, an exceedingly high quantity which may have resulted from the miswriting of *talents* for *thousands*. A talent could be either 3000 or 3600 shekels. The shekel was approximately 11.4 grams, making ten talents about 410 kg or 905 pounds of silver and 6000 shekels about 68 grams or 150 pounds of gold. At the end of the verse the witnesses agree in reading *and ten changes of clothes.* However, the references to the changes of clothes in this story have been added secondarily, as indicated by the textual evidence in v. 26 where *garments* (בגדים) is a corruption of בו גנים and by v. 23 where the mention of the garments is an afterthought.

7 **Only consider and recognize**: So G^L. The particles כי and נא are not reflected in G^L.

8 **the man of god**: So G^L. G^B has *Elisha*. See on 4:16.

the king (1): So G^L. MT, G^B + *of Israel.*

the king (2): So MT, G^L. G^B + *of Israel.*

9 **with horse and chariot**: So G^B. MT: *with his horse* [*Qere: horses*] *and his chariot.* G^L: *with his chariots and his horses.*

waited: The nuance of עמד plus ל.[5]

11 **he would certainly come out**: So G^{BL}. MT + *and would stand.*

on the name of Yhwh his god: So. MT, G^L. G^B lacks the divine name, an inner-Greek haplography.

over the place and cure it of its skin disease: Reading והניף ידו על־המקום ואספו מצרעתו. As in vv. 3, 6, and 7 the noun for skin disease is צרעת as opposed to the participle מצרע, which is used for the diseased person (v. 1). The person is the object of אסף in those previous verses and the disease is marked with מן.

---

3 On the unfortunate consequences of this translation see S. G. Browne, *Leprosy in the Bible* (2nd ed.; London: Christian Medical Fellowship, 1986) and "Leprosy in the Bible," in *Medicine & the Bible* (ed. B. Palmer; Carlisle, U.K.: Paternoster, 1986), 101–27. Also E. V. Hulse, "The Nature of Biblical 'Leprosy' and the Use of Alternative Medical Terms in Modern Translations of the Bible," *PEQ* 107 (1975): 87–105. See also See J. F. A. Sawyer, "A Note on the Etymology of ṢĀRAʿAT," *VT* 26 (1976): 241–45.

4 Rendsburg (*Israelian Hebrew*, 96) contends that it is a Northernism despite recognizing Ps 119 as postexilic. More likely it is stylistic, as Schniedewind and Sivan ("Test Case," 320) suggest.

5 1 Kgs 20:39. Cf. Cogan and Tadmor, *II Kings*, 64.

12 **Abana**: Reading with the *ketiv* and the G witnesses. The *qere'* “Amana” is dialectal and may be influenced by Mount Amana, a name for the Ante-Lebanon ridge where the river has its beginnings (*ANET* 277–80; Song 4:8) and perhaps by the root אמן, “constant.” It was later called the Chrysorrhas (“gold”) and is known today as the Barada; it flows through the city of Damascus.

Pharpar: Probably the ʻAwaj, which flows from Mount Hermon to Lake Hijaneh ca. ten miles south of Damascus. The name Pharphar is preserved in the name Wadi Barbar, one of the tributaries of the ʻAwaj.

than all the waters of Israel: So MT, G^{B}. G^{L}: *than the Jordan and than all the waters of Israel.*

I could wash: So MT. G^{BL}: *I could go and wash.*

13 **and spoke to him**: So G^{B} (καὶ ἐλάλησαν πρὸς αὐτόν). G^{L}: *and said to him* (καὶ εἶπεν πρὸς αὐτόν). MT: *and spoke to him and said* (וידברו אליו ויאמרו), a double reading.[6]

If: Reading אם based on G^{L} (πάτερ εἰ) and sense.[7] MT's *my father* (אבי) is corrupt. G^{L} conflates the two. G^{B} has neither, but the conditional particle seems required. This textual solution is preferable to the effort to construe אבי as a deliberative particle (GKC §159cc; Joüon §105f) despite Job 34:36.

14 **the man of god**: So MT, G^{L}. G^{B} has Elisha's name. See the note on 4:16.

his skin was restored: So MT, G^{B}. G^{L} + *upon him.*

like the flesh of a small child: So MT, G^{B}. G^{L} has *like a small child*, an inexact comparison resulting from haplography.

15 **he and his entourage**: So G^{L}. MT, G^{B} + *all.*

to the man of god: So MT, G^{L}. G^{B}: *to Elisha.* See the note on 4:16.

he stood before him: So MT, G^{L}. *Before him* is absent from G^{B}. But the use of ἐνώπιον is typical of OG.

a gift: So MT, G^{L}. G^{B}: *the gift.*

from your servant: So MT, G^{B}: מאת עבדך. G^{L}: *from the hand of your servant* = מיד עבדך. There is no basis for choosing between the variants.

16 **but [Elisha] refused**: So MT, G^{B} (וימאן = καὶ ἠπείθησεν). G^{L}: (καὶ οὐκ ἠθέλησε λαβεῖν = ולא אבה לקחת), a circumlocution.

17 **If not**: So MT, G^{BL} (καὶ εἰ μή). Cf. 2 Sam 13:26.[8]

of dirt: So MT, G^{L}. Absent from G^{B} but required for sense.

only to Yhwh: So MT, G^{B}. G^{L} + *alone.*

18 The reading for this verse is basically that of G^{L} except for its phrase *I to Yhwh my god*, which stands in the place of the third reference to *the temple of Rimmon* and which reflects theological elaboration. This is the only reference in the HB to the god Rimmon by name. It means “pomegranate” and is a deliberate corruption of Rammān, “thunderer,” an epithet of the Aramaean god Hadad.[9] On the unusual verb “prostrate” (-*št*- of חוה) see the note on 1 Kgs 16:31. Joüon (§79t) observes that the infinitive בְּהִשְׁתַּחֲוָיָתִי is vocalized in Aramaic fashion and should properly be בְּהִשְׁתַּחֲווֹתִי.

19 **a certain distance**: The word כברה occurs elsewhere only in Gen 35:16; 48:7 in construct as here with (ה)ארץ. Based on these references it refers to an unspecified or indeterminate distance.[10]

20 **Elisha the man of god**: So MT, G^{L}. G^{B} lacks *man of god.* See the Note on 4:16.

---

6 Wevers, “Double Readings in the Books of Kings,” 309.

7 Burney, *Notes*, 280.

8 GKC §159dd; McCarter, *II Samuel*, 333. Less likely, ולא may be construed as *wālū'* (“would that”). J. C. Matthes, “Miscellen,” *ZAW* 23 (1903), 122–23.

9 See J. C. Greenfield, “The Aramean God Rammān/Rimmōn,” *IEJ* 26 (1976): 195–98.

10 See Burney, *Notes*, 280–81 for a discussion of the word's possible background.

I will certainly run: The perfect is used after כי אם as part of the oath formula: *By Yhwh's life, I can do nothing except run.* Cf. GKC §163d; Joüon §164c.

21 **saw him**: So G^B. MT has lost the suffix. G^L conflates the object pronoun and Gehazi's name.

he got down from the chariot: So MT. G^L: *he got down from his chariot.* G^B has a different verb: *he turned around.* On the use of נפל for descending from a chariot, compare Gen 24:64.[11]

22 **have come to me**: MT precedes with הנה עתה זה, all of which appears expansive.

23 **take two talents:** So MT. G^L + *of silver.* G^B reflects haplography occasioned by the repetition of *two talents* (*of silver*). The verb *took* (καὶ ἔλαβεν = ויקח) was supplied to make sense of what remained.

Urging him: Lit. *he urged him* (ויפצר בו) as in 2:17; 5:16. MT has ויפרץ־בו, which reflects metathesis of ר and צ, since פרץ means "break through." The same metathesis occurs in 1 Sam 28:23; 2 Sam 13:25, 27.

he wrapped: So MT (ויצר) in preference to G^L's more pedestrian *he gave to him* (καὶ ἔδωκεν αὐτῷ).

two talents of silver: כִּכְּרַיִם is a mixed form that combines the construct (כִּכְּרֵי) with the dual absolute (כִּכָּרַיִם). *Silver* is used appositionally or accusatively.

24 **When they came**: So G^BL. MT has the singular in conformity to the following verbs in the verse.

to the acropolis: So MT (אל־העפל) based on sense. G^BL: εἰς τὸ σκοτεινὸν = אל האפל, *to the darkness*, an aural error. *'ophel* was "an urban architectural term denoting the outstanding site of the citadel or acropolis."[12]

from them: Lit. *from their hand*; so MT (מידם). G^B: *from their hands.* G^L *from the hand of the servants.*

who departed: So MT, G^L as in 6:23. Lacking in G^B due to haplography in the Greek text.

25 **Where have you come from**: So G^BL (πόθεν), MT *Qere'* (מאין). MT *ketiv*, מאן was probably occasioned by the use of the particle אן later in the verse.[13]

26 **I walked along mentally ... didn't I?**: So MT (lit. *Didn't my heart walk*). G^B + *with you.* G^L similarly has *Wasn't my heart with you.* Stade unnecessarily restores the interrogative particle before לא.[14]

as Naaman got down from his chariot: So G^L (ὅτε κατεπήδησε Νεεμαν ἀπὸ τοῦ ἅρματος αὐτοῦ), reflecting ירד in place of הפך. MT's הפך־איש מעל is awkward with the lack of the definite article on איש and the reference to turning from the chariot without any mention of his descent from it. Cf. v. 21.

Now that you have acquired the silver, will you acquire with it gardens, olive groves, vineyards, sheep, cattle, male and female servants?: Reading ועתה לקחת את הכסף התקח בו גנים וזיתים וכרמים וצאן ובקר ועבדים ושפחות. The reading is based on G^BL (καὶ νῦν ἔλαβες τὸ ἀργύριον καὶ [B: νῦν ἔλαβες] τὰ ἱμάτια καὶ λήμψη [L: λήψη] ἐν αὐτῷ κήπους καὶ ἐλαιῶνας καὶ ἀμπελῶνας καὶ πρόβατα [L: ποίμνια] καὶ βόας [L: βουκόλια]

---

11 Cf. M. Delcor, "Quelques cas de survivances du vocabulaire nomade en hébreu biblique," *VT* 25 (1975), 313–14.

12 Y. Shiloh, *Excavations at the City of David, vol 1, 1978–1982: Interim Report of the First Five Seasons* (*Qedem* 19; Jerusalem: Institute of Archaeology, Hebrew University, 1984), 27. Also Cogan and Tadmor (*II Kings*, 66), who cite the references to the *'ophel* in Jerusalem and the one in Dibon.

13 Schniedewind and Silvan ("Test Case," 333–34) suggest that the contracted form is a Northernism.

14 Stade, *Kings*, 203.

καὶ παῖδας καὶ παιδίσκας [L: δούλους ὑμῶν καὶ τὰς δούλας]. Comparison of the two indicates that καὶ τὰ ἱμάτια (= ובגדים) is a corruption of בו גנים. The corruption has been secondarily added to G^L. This accounts for the addition of the references to the changes of clothes in vv. 22-23.[15] The reading is best construed as a rhetorical question as in MT and 6QpapKgs6-7.[16] However, they (העת לקחת את־הכסף ולקחת בגדים וזיתים וכרמים וצאן ובקר ועבדים ושפחות) misconstrue עתה as עת and the second person verbs as infinitives and thus turn Elisha's question about the futility of Gehazi's greed into one about the inappropriateness of accepting gifts at the present time.[17]

Synchronic Analysis

Characters and content

The narrative in this chapter is unusual for its complex plot, changes of scenes, and the number of characters. There are ten characters or groups of characters: Naaman, his wife, the Israelite slave girl, the Aramaean king, the Israelite king (identified as Joram by the placement of the story but never named), Elisha, Gehazi, Naaman's servants in v. 13 (= "his camp" in v. 15), and the two servants in v. 23. The characters are not only numerous but are often portrayed with depth and vividness.[18] The chapter is typically divided into three segments (vv. 1-14, 15-19a, 19b-27), each with its focal character—Elisha, Naaman, and Gehazi. Each segment has its own main interest. The first focuses on the healing of Naaman. The second is concerned with the theological implications of that healing—the nature of YHWH and the reach of his power outside of Israel—as well as the proper response of those who revere him when they are outside the borders of Israel and find themselves in compromising religious situations. The third episode has to do with the perils of trying to use divine power for selfish advantage. In addition, a theme running throughout the chapter relates to social classes. The pride of the elite can impede their judgment, as seen especially in the first part of the story; on the other hand, greed can imperil the servant class, as is clear in the third episode. In the larger collection of Elisha stories the one about Naaman fits with those in 6:8–7:20; 8:7-15; 13:14-19 relating to the Aramaean wars, in contrast to those in 2 Kgs 4; 6:1-7 about Elisha's exploits among the prophetic guild.

5:1: The positive character of Naaman

Naaman is the commander of the Aramaean army (v. 1), but he does not come across as a stereotypical military man. True to his name, he is generally a pleasant individual. He is also a fortunate man who owes his success to YHWH, who gave Aram victory through him. The king of Aram esteems him highly, and that will play a role in the story. The expression *great man* is rich in possible nuances. It may refer to his fiscal prosperity, social status, or generosity and thoughtfulness. All three attributes are appropriate at different points in the story. In this respect

15 Šanda, *Könige* II, 45.

16 Ulrich, *Biblical Qumran Scrolls*, 328.

17 There are two fragments of this verse from Qumran Cave 6 (*DJD* 3:108 and Plate 20:6, 7) that appear to agree with MT, though it is difficult to judge from the published photos. If Baillet is correct that traces of the ה in העת are preserved, then it differs from the G reading.

18 Hens-Piazza, *Kings*, 257.

Naaman is like the *great woman* of 4:8, and his story in this location resonates well with hers. An especially unusual attribute Naaman possesses is his willingness to listen to subordinates. This also plays a crucial role in the story. It is not clear against whom YHWH gave Naaman victory. The context indicates that it was Israel, but not necessarily Israel alone. This is an unusual statement in the Hebrew Bible. It is not unusual for YHWH to give victory to a foreign army over his own people if he is angry with them. Here, however, the implication is that he gives Naaman victory because of the Aramaean's personal qualities. The statement is all the more striking in view of Elisha's name, which means "my god is victory."

The function and nature of skin disease

The final descriptor of Naaman is that he had a skin disease. By listing this as the last and only negative attribute the narrative calls attention to it. Initially this seems to detract from the otherwise highly positive portrait of him—but perhaps not. Such disease was normally conceived of as a curse from god, but everything about Naaman is positive. Its function here, therefore, is narrative, as it sets up the story of Naaman's healing. The illness may also be part of the reason for Naaman's greatness. Maybe it mellowed him and made him more generous and attentive to those around him. In any case the reference to skin disease articulates the immediate problem around which the story revolves. The nature of Naaman's skin disease constitutes a major interpretive difficulty. It was not true leprosy. The symptoms in the Bible's (especially legal texts') descriptions do not accord with the disfiguring and debilitating Hansen's disease but seem closer to psoriasis, eczema, or fungus infections with patches of red, scaly, or irritated skin and/or flaking. The attitudes about the disease in the story are perplexing. On the one hand Naaman is not socially or cultically ostracized. He has full interactions with family members, the king of Aram, the king of Israel, Elisha, and his servants. The disease may be localized (v. 11). Naaman is not quarantined as demanded by Israelite law (Lev 13:45-46). Of course, he is not Israelite. Still, by these measures his disease seems to be minor or only in an incipient, benign stage. On the other hand, some references assume that this disease is life-threatening. First there is the knowledge of the Israelite servant girl and her wish that her master might meet Elisha (vv. 2-3). Here Naaman's condition seems to be widely known and a source of deep concern rather than a minor disorder. The reaction of the king of Israel confirms this diagnosis since he likens the ability to cure it to having divine power over life and death (v. 7). Naaman's journey to Israel reflects his desperation to be healed, which again seems out of place for a minor skin condition. His desperation and the ritual he expects (v. 11) suggest that he has been to plenty of purported healers. The disease that passes to Gehazi affects his full body and is congenital. Thus the skin disease has an inconsistent role in the narrative. If it is not socially ostracizing or life-threatening, why is Naaman so desperate to be rid of it? The reason is unclear. However, the uncertainties about the disease make it ideal for this story from a narrative point of view. The variety of disorders described by the term (Lev 13–14) allows Naaman flexibility to maintain his position over the army and to travel while afflicted with it. He can continue to talk and communicate despite the disease and to have social interaction whatever the form and seriousness of the disease or perhaps because he is Aramaean and not subject to Israelite law. At the same time the very mention of the disease strikes fear in the hearts of ancient readers, who would anticipate Naaman's intense desire to be healed.

5:2: The Israelite servant girl

The raiding parties from Aram and the Israelite servant girl in v. 2 along with the attitude of the king of Israel in v. 7 presuppose Israel's subservience to Aram and confirm that Israel was one of those against whom YHWH gave Naaman victory (v. 1). Such holds true even if the raiders were not military but Bedouin or seminomadic Aramaean tribesmen, since Aram's dominance would facilitate raids by such groups.[19] The Israelite servant girl is not named; she is a role player who is nonetheless crucial to the story.[20] It is she who turns Naaman to Israel in the first place (v. 3). In the same way that she is *before* (לפני) her mistress (v. 2) she wishes that her master could be *before* the prophet in Samaria (v. 3). To the extent that being *before* someone implies subordination Naaman has no intention of being before Elisha.[21] In one sense it does not matter, because Naaman is not healed *before* Elisha, but his attitude of social superiority almost thwarts healing.

5:3-5: Naaman goes to Israel

The girl mentions neither Naaman nor Elisha by name, perhaps out of respect. Her concern suggests that Naaman is a kind master and this is the first instance of the attentiveness to subordinates that enables his healing. The story assumes Elisha's residence in Samaria (v. 3) and links with the reference to Elisha going there in 2:25. Naaman's wife obviously conveys the girl's message to her husband, for in the next scene he meets with the Aramaean king (v. 4). The reader supplies the missing link. The Aramaean king is happy to lend his support to Naaman's quest by writing a letter to the king of Israel (v. 5a). The large sum Naaman expects to pay for his healing (v. 5b) hints at the elaborateness of the reception and ritual he expects to receive (vv. 11-12) and anticipates the story of Gehazi's greed (vv. 19b-27).

5:6: The letter from the Aramaean king

The specifics of the communication process are ignored. Is the letter in Aramaic or Hebrew? Does Naaman speak Hebrew? Did he learn it from his wife's servant girl? Does he bring a translator? Such details do not slow the narrative. The purpose of the letter is not clear. Is it a letter of introduction of Naaman, presenting his *bona fides*? Is it a courtesy to avoid offending the king of Israel by encroaching on his territory?[22] Is it designed to protect Naaman, who has defeated Israel in the past? Does it veil a threat that the king of Israel had better see to Naaman's healing or face military action?[23] The letter's lack of formalities and its command (*you will cure him of his skin disease*) support the last possibility.[24] This is the way the king of Israel sees it (v. 7). Narratively, the letter and the reaction of the king of Israel in vv. 6-8 counter the sense of urgency in vv. 3-5 and build suspense by posing obstacles to and thus delaying the story's resolution.[25] Post-

---

19 Fricke, *Das zweite Buch von den Königen*, 70; Gray, *Kings*, 504. T. Römer, "An Illustration – II Kings 5:1-14," in *Aram and Israel* (ed. A. Berlejung and A. Maier), forthcoming. W. Brueggemann ("A Brief Moment for a One-Person Remnant [2 Kings 5:2-3])," *BTB* 31 [2001]: 53–59) refers to her as a "remnant."

20 J. K. Kim, "Reading and retelling Naaman's story (2 Kings 5)," *JSOT* 30 (2005): 49–61.

21 A point made nicely by Römer, "II Kings 5:1-14."

22 Cf. Fricke, *Das zweite Buch von den Königen*, 71.

23 Šanda (*Könige* II, 40) suggests that Naaman's real mission is to spy out Israel's preparedness for war.

24 Provan (*Kings*, 191), followed by Long (*1 & 2 Kings*, 321) thinks that the absence of any mention of Elisha in the letter supports the suspicion of the king of Israel.

25 Long, *2 Kings*, 70.

poning the revelation of the letter's content to this point enhances that suspense. It also places the focus on the king of Israel (Joram) as a man with little familiarity with or faith in Elisha.

5:7: The reaction of the Israelite king

Perhaps the Aramaean king has misunderstood and assumes that the Israelite king himself has the power to heal.[26] Alternatively he may think that Elisha is a court prophet under the control of the Israelite king. The latter is also confounded, as the text notes with a pun: he tears (קרע) his clothes as he reads (קרא) the letter. Rightly or wrongly he thinks that the Aramaean king is seeking a fight (v. 7). He speaks contemptuously of the Aramaean, referring to him as *this so and so* (זה). The picture is darkly humorous as both heads of state are ill-informed and on the verge of bungling the affair into full-scale war. The king of Israel voices his frustration to his courtiers (note the plural imperatives דעו and ראו in v. 7). His observation that only god can give or take life articulates a main theme of the story—the power of YHWH over life and death, illness and health.[27] The same idea is expressed in Deut 32:39 and 1 Sam 2:6. The king's question also brings to mind Elisha's revival of the Shunammite's son in the previous chapter (4:8-37). These connections and the question itself imply that Naaman's disease was terminal and not just a minor skin disorder that does not even merit quarantine. The same is implied by the fact that Naaman has taken the trouble to travel to Israel to seek healing.

5:8: Elisha intervenes

How Elisha hears of the king's quandary we are not told, but it may be an instance of his ability to know from a distance what others are thinking or doing (v. 26; 6:12). His message to the king (v. 8) skips formalities and implies disdain. *Why have you torn your clothes?* is a rebuke. The king's anxiety is unwarranted and shows a lack of faith. He employs a formula (*that he may learn that there is a prophet in Israel*) that is comparable to Ezek 2:5; 33:33 (*that you may learn that a prophet has been in your midst*). Ezekiel's contemporaries will recognize him as a prophet when his threats come to pass, while Elisha's prophetic identity is revealed through the miracles he performs. His presence attests YHWH's engagement.

5:9-12: Elisha's instructions vs. Naaman's expectations

The narrative leaves it to the reader to deduce that the king sent Naaman on to Elisha. Naaman arrives as a VIP with chariot and horses. The prophet evidently lives alone rather than in a community of prophets, and near the royal quarter.[28] Elisha is not impressed. He keeps Naaman waiting (see the Note) and then does not appear in person but sends a messenger with instructions (v. 10). Naaman is not used to such disregard. He does not deign to descend from the chariot (contrast v. 21).[29] Elisha's instructions are the last straw. Naaman leaves feeling angry and disrespected (v. 11). Elisha's instructions are simple but also ambiguous. "Wash seven times in the Jordan and you will be clean." Of course he will be clean—after washing seven times. The number seven is common in the Hebrew Bible and represents completeness. It is used several times in the instructions in Lev 14:1-9 about cleansing from skin disease, including a sevenfold sprinkling of the subject with the blood of a clean bird and a seven-day quarantine outside his tent before

26 Buis, *Rois*, 199.
27 Nelson, *Kings*, 178.
28 Gray, *Kings*, 506
29 Würthwein, *1. Könige 17–2. Könige 25*, 300.

shaving all the hair of his head and washing his clothes on the seventh day. But the expression "be clean" is idiomatic and may not be understood by the Aramaean. Elisha seems to be prodding Naaman's ego, first by his delay, then by not appearing personally, and now by sending ambiguous directions that may be intended to confuse him.[30] Naaman explodes with anger. The sevenfold dip in the Jordan is not elaborate enough for him; he anticipated an ostentatious ritual with the prophet calling on YHWH and waving his hand to effect healing. The phrase *at the place* (אל־המקום) seems to refer to the diseased location, indicating that it is confined to one area of his body. מקום could be a sanctuary, but then the reason for waving is unclear.[31] Naaman concludes his tirade with a bit of chauvinism, asserting that the rivers of Damascus are better than the Jordan, better than all the waters of Israel (v. 12). Here he speaks of becoming clean (v. 12) rather than of being cured (v. 11), suggesting that he does not understand the idiom. He can bathe more effectively, he avers, in Aramaean waters. The contrast between Elisha's instructions and Naaman's expectations is key. Elisha does not claim intrinsic healing powers for the Jordan. Nor does his directive involve ritual, as Naaman is at pains to point out and as Elisha's distance from the Jordan makes clear. Rather, the healing power comes through following Elisha's instructions.

5:13-14: Listening and being healed

Naaman storms off in a rage, and the story is about to have an untimely ending when his servants intervene. They address him affectionately as "my father," asking in effect "What do you have to lose?" (v. 13). They point out that if Elisha had commanded him to accomplish some great deed Naaman would have attempted it. The unusual order of their words stresses *great deed*—the kind Naaman anticipated. So he ought to undertake the much simpler task of washing in the Jordan. Like the Israelite slave girl, they make a suggestion that is crucial to the story and to Naaman's healing. Both speak out of affection for him and the wish to see him healed. Their words of reason counter Naaman's highly emotional and irrational state. To his credit he listens despite their social inferiority and is healed as a result. The point is reinforced by v. 14. Naaman goes and dips seven times in the Jordan. As promised, he *becomes clean*, i.e., his flesh is restored like that of a young boy (נער קטן). The expression forms an *inclusio* with the mention of the *young girl* (נערה קטנה) in v. 2, and the two terms together contrast with the references to the *great man* Naaman (v. 1) and the *great thing* that Elisha might have asked Naaman to do (v. 13). The contrast highlights the point that Naaman's healing is due to the intervention of "little people," minor characters who are nameless and hold no significant rank in society. Part of Naaman's greatness is his willingness to listen to such people. What is more, the *great man* is humbled and submits to the prophet.

5:15a: Returning to Elisha

The next segment turns to the theological implications of Naaman's healing. Disease-free, he returns to Elisha's house. *Return* is an important subtheme.[32] Naaman's flesh returned from its disease as promised (vv. 10, 14) and now he returns to stand before Elisha. His confession of faith in YHWH in v. 15a is a kind of return or at least turning to YHWH in conversion. It is the high point of the story. His

---

30 Römer ("II Kings 5:1-14") observes that ego and nationalism are obstacles to Naaman's healing.

31 A summons of the god to effect healing (Kittel, *Könige*, 205) seems unnecessary after calling on his name.

32 R. L. Cohn, "Form and Perspective in 2 Kings V," *VT* 33 (1983), 177–78; *2 Kings*, 38–39.

healing at a distance from Elisha, which he once protested so vociferously, has proven to him that YHWH was responsible. His exclamation that there is no other god outside of Israel assumes that he has sought help from deities in Aram and elsewhere. His return also enhances his characterization as an honorable man.

5:15b-16: A gift proffered and refused

Naaman's offer of a gift (lit. *blessing*, a polite term, cf. Judg 1:15; 1 Sam 30:26) in v. 15b is tendered to Elisha as a reward for the healing. It also introduces the subtheme of "taking" (קח־נא) that is central to the third segment of the story (vv. 19b-27). In v. 15b Naaman refers to himself as Elisha's servant, a motif that runs through vv. 15-18 and is a sign of Naaman's conversion. The tables have turned; the man who formerly became enraged at the prophet's lack of deference now recognizes the superior status of the man of god and defers to him. Elisha refuses Naaman's offer, even swearing by YHWH that he will not accept it despite Naaman's urging. The reason is not spelled out, but the context implies that acceptance would compromise the lesson of Naaman's confession that healing came from YHWH rather than from Elisha.[33] The refusal also reflects a certain disdain for the Aramaean and his gifts.

5:17-19a: Naaman's requests

Naaman then makes an additional request for two mule loads of Israelite soil (v. 17). The request introduces the motif of duality picked up in vv. 22-23, where there are two visitors, two talents of silver, two changes of clothes, two servants, and two bags. The reason for the request is that Naaman wants to build an altar to YHWH and worship him on Israelite soil. The request mirrors his confession that there is no god except in Israel (v. 15). It is ironic in view of his earlier disparagement of the waters of Israel (v. 12). It also reflects the idea common among pilgrims who bring back rocks or flasks of water from the "Holy Land." Such items have special, even sacred, significance because they hail from places that have witnessed divine activity. Naaman solicits a special dispensation from YHWH for when he is required to accompany the king into the temple of his god (v. 18). His assumption is that his actions on such occasions are devoid of meaning because the Aramaean deity does not really exist. His request for pardon in advance (√סלח) recalls Solomon's prayer at the dedication of the temple in 1 Kings 8. The verse in MT forms a chiasm:[34]

A For this thing
  B May YHWH pardon your servant
    C when my lord comes to the temple of Rimmon to worship there
      X and he leans on my hand,
    C′ and I worship in the temple of Rimmon
  B′ may YHWH pardon your servant
A′ in this thing

The crux referring to the king leaning on Naaman's arm (יד) anticipates Gehazi's statement in v. 20 that Elisha refused to accept anything from Naaman's hand (יד) and contrasts Naaman's faithfulness with Gehazi's treachery. The crux further highlights Naaman's bowing under compulsion as a servant of the king rather

33 Rehm, *Das zweite Buch der Könige*, 64.
34 Cohn ("Form and Perspective," 179; *2 Kings*, 39–40) observed the chiasm and its contrast with v. 20.

than as a believer in Rimmon. Elisha's response—*Go in peace*—is vaguely positive. He does not offer any assurance of YHWH's pardon, but other occurrences of the expression (Exod 4:18; Judg 18:6; 1 Sam 20:42) indicate tacit approval. Judges 18:6 especially points to a positive meaning since the order to go in peace there is followed by the assurance that the journey is under god's eye.[35]

5:19b-21: Gehazi's pursuit

Soon after Naaman's departure from Elisha (v. 19b) Gehazi decides to go after him and acquire some of the payment Elisha refused (v. 20). In addition to greed, he may be motivated by a certain distaste for *this Aramaean.* Naaman, he believes, has gotten off easy, and Gehazi resolves to remedy the situation by securing something for himself. His oath by YHWH contrasts with Elisha's oath in refusal (v. 16) and shows his actions to be diametrically opposed to the prophet's pious resolve not to detract from the credit due YHWH for the healing. Naaman is traveling at a leisurely pace and has gone only a short distance, enabling Gehazi to catch up to him on foot. Naaman sees him coming and gets down from his chariot to meet him (v. 21). In contrast to v. 9, where he waited in his chariot for Elisha to come to him, Naaman now treats Elisha's servant with respect, meeting him on the same level. He is solicitous and asks if everything is all right (השלום). Naaman departed *in peace* (v. 19a) with Elisha's approval, but Gehazi's interference disturbs that peace, and Naaman recognizes it. Here, as in 4:26, the question signals that something is very wrong. Gehazi responds that everything is fine, but it is a lie, as is the rest of his speech in v. 22. The fact that he feels compelled to deceive Naaman with a made-up story is a clue that things are not *shalom*.

5:22-23: Gehazi's deception

Since Elisha was adamant in refusing compensation, Gehazi must invent some pretext for his request. In Elisha's name he asks for a talent of silver to give as a present to two prophets from the Ephraimite highlands who have arrived unexpectedly. It is an artful lie. The Ephraimite origin of the guests means that they would have come to Samaria from essentially the opposite direction toward which Naaman is departing, so that he would not have seen them. It might have struck him as odd that the two men arrived so soon after his departure but he is still celebrating his healing and is not inclined to scrutiny. The limit to a single talent of silver and no gold further allays his suspicions. Gehazi also asks for two changes of clothes, one for each of the visitors. Naaman shows no sign of suspicion but is only too happy to make some payment for the gift, *urging* that Gehazi take twice the silver (v. 23). Elisha steadfastly resisted such urging (v. 16). Naaman even dispatches two servants to carry the bags of loot to Samaria.

5:24-27: Elisha confronts Gehazi

Gehazi returns to Elisha's house and quickly secretes away his treasures (v. 24).[36] He cannot hide anything from Elisha, of course, but perhaps he is hoping

---

35 Wiseman (*Kings*, 324) calls the expression "a statement of confirmed agreement rather than a polite dismissal." J. J. Stamm (*Erlösen und Vergeben im Alten Testament. Eine Begriffsgeschichitliche Untersuchung* [Bern: Francke, 1940], 48–49) states, "Jedenfalls sichert Elisa seinem fremdländischen Gast keine wirkliche Vergebung zu, er läßt ihn eher auf eine gewisse Nachsicht Jahwes hoffen." [In any case Elisha does not assure his foreign guest of genuine forgiveness; rather, he allows him to hope for a certain forbearance from YHWH.] For another option entirely see S. Lasine, "'Go in peace' or 'Go to hell'?: Elisha, Naaman and the meaning of monotheism in 2 Kings 5," *SJOT* 25 (2011): 3–28.

36 "Five brusque consecutive verbs without objects describe his cover up" (Nelson, *Kings*, 180).

that the prophet will once more have a blind spot, as in 4:27. He tries to act as though nothing has happened (v. 25), but the language betrays a change in Gehazi's relationship with Elisha. The usual idiom עמד על for standing in service or attending is altered to עמד אל, implying a confrontational posture.[37] The confrontation is on when Elisha asks Gehazi where he has been and then announces that he accompanied him in mind (*heart*). His description is so vivid that he even supplies a detail not included by the narrator, namely how *a man* (he does not mention Naaman by name) turned around from being in his chariot to meet Gehazi on approach (v. 26). He goes on to list eight items, asking Gehazi whether it is the appropriate time to acquire such things. The question is rhetorical, the list sarcastic, ridiculing Gehazi's greed and endless lust for possessions. The story then ends where it began with reference to Naaman's skin disease, which will henceforth cling to Gehazi (v. 27). He has traded places with Naaman, a fitting swap considering the contrast of Gehazi's disloyalty to Naaman's faithfulness. Gehazi has a more serious case of the disease than Naaman did. It turns him *like snow*, a comparison evoked by the whiteness and flakiness of his skin that recalls Mosaic tradition (Exod 4:6-7; also Num 12). It not only covers his body but is also hereditary, afflicting Gehazi's heirs forever.

Diachronic Analysis

The original *legenda* and PN's revision—an overview

Since the classic work of Schmitt in 1972 the three parts of the chapter have been identified with three compositional levels:[38] (1) the original anecdote in vv. 1-14* that showed there was a prophet in Israel and ridiculed Aramaean religion; (2) a first expansion that added vv. 15a, 17*-19a, which deal with issues concerning non-Israelite converts to Yahwism and are strongly monotheistic; and (3) another expansion in vv. 19b-27, as well as vv. 5b, 15b-16, that turned the story into a didactic tale against using prophecy for personal gain.[39] Stipp criticized the source-critical arguments on which this reconstruction was founded and concluded that the chapter is a unit.[40] Trebolle also disputed the tripartite division, arguing that the gift for paying a prophet was an integral element of the genre of the consultation of a prophet (1 Sam 9:6-8; 1 Kgs 14:3 [G 12:24h]; 2 Kgs 8:8), such that not only v. 5b but vv. 15aαb-16 and the whole Gehazi episode in vv. 19b-

37 Cohn, *2 Kings*, 36 and earlier his "Form and Perspective," 182.

38 Schmitt, *Elisa*, 78–80; Jones, *Kings*, 413. Würthwein (*1. Könige 17–2. Könige 25*, 298–303) included the first three words of v. 17 with the third level so that Naaman's request for earth followed directly on v. 15a. In addition to v. 5b, v. 1aβ (כי־בו נתן־יהוה תשועה לארם) and the references to the man of god and his word in vv. 8, 14 are viewed as secondary.

39 The literary arguments for this reconstruction are (1) the use of Elisha's name in vv. 1-14, 19b-27 but *man of god* in vv. 15-19a and (2) the mention of Gehazi only in vv. 19b-27. *Man of god* occurs in vv. 1-14 (vv. 8, 14) as well as in vv. 19b-27 (v. 20), although advocates of this argument regard these instances of the epithet as secondary.

40 Stipp, *Elischa – Propheten – Gottesmänner*, 315–19.

27 were part of the original story.[41] More recently Sauerwein has reaffirmed much of the source-critical reconstruction.[42] The original anecdote as she perceives it is only a portion of vv. 1-14 (vv. 1aαb-3, 9-10, 14); the remainder of those verses she ascribes to a redactor with a theological interest. Her position can be strengthened by including v. 4 G^{BL} with the original anecdote. The link to the king of Aram in MT (v. 4) results from the editorial revision. Otherwise Sauerwein has succeeded in isolating the original *legenda*: Naaman the commander of the Aramaean army (v. 1*) learns from a captured servant girl about Elisha (vv. 2-4) and goes to his house (v. 9). Without even seeing him Elisha gives instructions (v. 10), which Naaman follows and is healed (v. 14). The remainder of the passage is the work of PN, who supplemented the *legenda* and transformed it into the present story except for a handful of glosses, the most important of which is v. 18.

5:1: The beginning of the legenda and PN's addition

The naming of Naaman is a feature of an elaborated *legenda* since basic *legenda* focus on the man of god and rarely name kings, much less foreign commanders.[43] His name, "pleasant," fits with his theological insight and attentiveness to the counsel of subordinates. His description in v. 1 is overfull due partly to the MT plus, *a powerful warrior*, a misplaced variant of איש גדול that can refer to Naaman's military prowess as well as his wealth, both of which are appropriate to the story. The reference to Yhwh giving Naaman victory at the end of v. 1a (כי־בו נתן־יהוה תשועה לארם) is PN's addition. It implies that Israel was being punished for unfaithfulness. It also assumes Yhwh's power and control of events beyond the borders of Israel in accord with Naaman's confession in vv. 15, 17. It casts Naaman as a person favored by Yhwh despite being the Aramaean commander and makes clear at the outset that Naaman's healing is Yhwh's doing, albeit through his prophet. PN's revisions account for the lack of clarity about Naaman's disease; in the *legenda* it was assumed to be debilitating and ultimately fatal. But Naaman's social interactions with the king of Aram, Elisha, and his servants in PN's additions compromised this understanding.

5:2-7: Naaman's search for healing in Israel

The capture of the Israelite slave girl assumes Aram's oppression of Israel and points to a setting in the Jehu dynasty (8:12; 13:3). The girl is called a נערה קטנה in contrast to the איש גדול who is her master. Her age is not clear, but she is old enough to know of Elisha by reputation if not by name (v. 3). Her suggestion and the subsequent story assume that Elisha's permanent residence is in Samaria in contrast to other Elisha *legenda* that place his home on Mount Carmel (4:25) or in Gilgal (2:1; 4:38). Alternatively the man of god of Samaria in the *legenda* was nameless and secondarily identified by PN with Elisha (but cf. vv. 9-10). The girl's wish that Naaman could be before Elisha to receive healing betrays empathy and perhaps affection for him. It was reported to Naaman (v. 4 G), who went directly to

41 J. Trebolle Barrera, *Salomón y Jeroboán. Historia de la recensión y redacción de 1 Reyes 2–12, 14* (Bibliotheca Salmanticensis; Diss. 3; Salamanca: Universidad Pontificia/Instititut o español bíblico y arqueológico, 1980), 159–60; *Centena*, 170. Mahri Leonard-Fleckman notes (personal communication) that the gift element does not occur in the consultation story in 2 Kgs 1, and in 1 Kgs 14 and 2 Kgs 8 there is no followup explaining the delivery of the gift to the prophet.

42 Sauerwein, *Elischa*, 55–64.

43 Early Jewish tradition identifies Naaman as the archer who killed Ahab in 1 Kings 22. See Josephus *Ant.* 8.15.5.414 and the Targum on 2 Chr 18:33.

Elisha's house (v. 9) in the *legenda*. PN's addition in vv. 5-8 has Naaman report to the king of Aram, who sends him loaded with treasure and a letter of support to the king of Israel. The treasure is to compensate the prophet (1 Sam 9:7-8). Its mention here anticipates vv. 15-16, 19b-27. The changes of clothes here as well as in vv. 22 and 23 are glosses that have entered as the result of textual corruption in v. 26 (see the Note). Royal letters offering and soliciting assistance in medical matters are well attested in the ancient Near East.[44] The full letter is not reproduced; the greeting and other formalities are omitted. ועתה marks the transition from the greeting to the body as is typical for Aramaic and Hebrew letters, so that only the main point of this letter is reproduced (v. 6).[45] As a result it is presented as an order from the Aramaean king. He does not expect the king of Israel personally to heal Naaman but is following protocol, instructing the Israelite king to turn the case over to his court prophet,[46] mistakenly assuming that Elisha is under the king's control. The king of Israel is something of a buffoon, unaware of the power of YHWH or Elisha. He does not know Naaman except possibly by reputation. He makes the observation, important for PN, that only god (i.e., the true god) can save life (v. 7), which abets his leap to the conclusion that the king of Aram is trying to stir up conflict (v. 7). While not out of the realm of possibility historically, the narrative source of his consternation is 1 Kgs 20:7. His command to his servants to *consider and recognize* (דעו־נא וראו) how the king of Aram is trying to cause trouble is identical to the remark in 1 Kgs 20:7. The matter is not pursued; it is a blind motif borrowed to evoke Elisha's involvement (v. 8).

5:8-14: The healing of Naaman

Elisha's message attests the same kind of tension with the king as in the other prophetic stories. The prophet steps in to help, but not without disdain and rebuke. It is not the hostility of Elijah toward the Omrids but the frictional collaboration of Elisha with the Jehuids. His rhetorical question, *Why have you torn your clothes?* and the formula *that he may learn that there is a prophet in Israel* (v. 8) articulate PN's objective—to show by miraculous deed that YHWH the god of Israel is the true god and that Elisha is YHWH's true prophet. The adapted *Erkenntnisformel* resembles 1 Kgs 17:24; 18:36. The invitation to Naaman thus anticipates his confession in v. 15a that there is no god except in Israel and his request for Israelite soil in v. 17. There is actually no need for Naaman to go to Elisha, especially since he does not see him. Elisha could have sent instructions to wash in the Jordan. But the visit sets up vv. 9-13, which describe Naaman's arrival with pomp and his resentment at Elisha's dismissive instructions, followed by his servants' intervention. In the *legenda* Naaman's visit was unannounced (v. 9), but PN's Elisha is expecting him. Still, Elisha does not go out to meet him but sends a prescription. It is a magic ritual that takes advantage of the special properties of the Jordan River as the boundary of the land of Israel, the territory of YHWH.[47] In the *legenda* Naaman carried out the ritual and was healed (v. 14), end of story. But PN is concerned less with Naaman's healing *per se* than with its meaning for

44 *ANET* 29–31; Montgomery, *Kings*, 374; Wiseman, *Kings*, esp. 17

45 See also 2 Kgs 10:2. On the form of Aramaic and Hebrew letters see J. A. Fitzmyer, "Some Notes on Aramaic Epistolography," *JBL* 93 (1974): 201–25, and D. Pardee, "An Overview of Ancient Hebrew Epistolography," *JBL* 97 (1978): 321–46.

46 Fricke, *Das zweite Buch von den Königen*, 71. *Pace* Schmitt, *Elisa*, 78.

47 Cranz, "Naaman's Healing."

signaling the presence and significance of a prophet. The contrast between the elaborate ritual expected by Naaman and the simple but effective order of Elisha brings to mind the contrasting activities of Elijah and the prophets of Baal on Carmel (1 Kgs 18). Naaman leaves indignant (v. 12). Only the sensible counsel of his servants convinces him to give the simple measure a try. He would have complied with more intricate instructions; what could it hurt to complete the easy course specified by the prophet? There is little to lose and potentially much to gain (v. 13). To his credit Naaman accedes. He goes and dips seven times in the Jordan and his disease is removed, his skin restored (v. 14). The process bears some resemblance to the Priestly laws about purification from skin disease in Leviticus 14, especially the washing and repetition of *seven* in Lev 14:8-9. As in 2 Kgs 4:42-44, there may be a subtle assertion of prophetic authority over priestly regulation.[48] With Naaman's healing, YHWH's power has been demonstrated and the miracle portion of the story taken from the underlying *legenda* concludes.

5:15-17: The theological implications of Naaman's healing

The second half of the chapter draws out theological implications of the healing. Naaman returns to pay the man of god (v. 15b) as *per* custom. The gift motif in vv. 15-17 is anticipated by PN in v. 5b. Elisha adamantly refuses despite Naaman's urging (v. 16). His epithet, *in whose service I stand* (1 Kgs 17:1; 18:15; 2 Kgs 3:14, all PN), emphasizes his role as YHWH's prophet, which Elisha wants Naaman to recognize (v. 8). This is the reason for his refusal of compensation. He accepts nothing because it was not he who healed but YHWH. Naaman's confession (v. 15a) and request for soil on which to worship YHWH (v. 17) show that he gets the point. He prefaces his offer of a gift with the confession *there is no god in all the earth except in Israel* (v. 15aβ). The confession is unique in the HB. It resembles certain DtrH texts (Deut 4:35; 2 Sam 7:22//1 Chr 17:20; 2 Kgs 19:15//Isa 37:16; cf. 1 Sam 2:2) but is closest to the monotheistic claims of 2 Isaiah (43:11; 44:6, 8; 45:5, 6, 21; 47:8, 10). The phrase *in Israel* is not necessarily a reference to the Northern kingdom, as it continued to be used for the descendants of Israel and Judah long after those kingdoms were destroyed.[49] Naaman's request for Israelite soil assumes the sacredness of YHWH's land, which includes the Jordan (v. 10), and disproves his previous claim about the superiority of the rivers of Damascus (v. 12). It also betrays the idea that each god has her/his own land and people and each people and land their own god. Thus his claim in v. 15 may not be an ontological one. His point, rather, is much like that of 1 Kings 18, where Baal is ineffective. Whether other gods—like Naaman's native Hadad—actually exist is irrelevant. Only YHWH shows his presence through his deeds (Ps 86:8-10), and that was the reason for Elisha's involvement in the first place (v. 8).

5:18-19a: Monotheisms

Verse 18 is an addition. It is marked as such by its similar beginning and end referring to "this matter" and by its literal interpretation of נשען על־יד, a title for the king's "right-hand man" and confidant (7:2, 27).[50] It extends Naaman's request with a plea for forgiveness that exemplifies a sophisticated monotheism in its idea that bowing to other gods is meaningless because they do not exist. Naaman's

48 Cf. Heller, "Drei Wundertaten," 84.

49 E.g., Matt 2:20, 21; 8:10; 9:33; *et passim*.

50 Trebolle (*Centena*, 168–70) argues that *he leans on my arm* is gloss. But the sentence supplies the rationale for Naaman's petition–he has to bow down in the temple of Rimmon because the king is leaning on his arm.

assumption is that his action is devoid of meaning since he recognizes YHWH's uniqueness and does not believe in Hadad's existence. Further contributing to this disparagement of the Aramaean deity is the change of Hadad's epithet from the august Rammān, *thunderer*, to the harmless Rimmon ("pomegranate"). $\mathfrak{G}^{L}$ even has Naaman say that he will be clandestinely prostrating to YHWH—in Hadad's temple! This is different from the theology behind Naaman's request for Israelite soil, which understands YHWH as the only effective god. The verse seems to address the question of how proselytes, especially in the service of foreign courts, were to worship YHWH outside of Yehud and still perform their duties.[51] Naaman's request for dirt was initially followed in PN's account by Elisha's wish that he *Go in peace* (v. 19) with its tacit approval of the request.

5:19b-23: Gehazi's greed

The episode about Gehazi's greed in vv. 19b-27 presupposes vv. 1-19a and was never independent of them. Naaman has barely left when Gehazi decides to pursue him and claim some of the treasure Elisha declined. He rationalizes his actions (v. 20) with nationalism: Naaman is Aramaean and has gotten away without paying for his valuable healing. But the fact that Gehazi hides the gifts where he alone can recover them shows that greed is his real incentive. Elisha's list in v. 26 also implies that Gehazi plans to use the silver for personal acquisitions. After overtaking Naaman and assuring him that everything is all right (v. 21) Gehazi propounds the fiction he has contrived (v. 22). He requests a talent, only a tenth of the amount Naaman brought but an immense treasure to Gehazi. Again, the two changes of clothes in v. 22 and in v. 23 are glosses. This is especially clear in v. 23 where the phrase appears as an afterthought. The clause *urging him* (ויפרץ־בם) in v. 23 is probably also a gloss to create a match with v. 16; no urging is necessary for Gehazi.[52] Omri bought the entire hill of Samaria for two talents of silver (1 Kgs 16:24), the amount Gehazi eventually receives from Naaman (v. 23). Gehazi does not explain why Elisha feels compelled to give such a valuable gift to guests passing through, and Naaman is not in the mood to inquire. The two *bags* in which Naaman wraps the silver are luxury items in themselves, to judge from the word's occurrence in the list of women's finery in Isa 3:22. The weight of the metal—some 181 pounds—is more than Gehazi can carry, and Naaman dispatches two servants to carry it for him. It would be easier and quicker to turn the chariot around and return to Elisha's house to deposit the silver. That way Naaman would also not have to wait for his servants to return. There are other peculiarities: A servant accompanied by two foreign slaves carrying a large amount of precious metal would be likely to attract unwanted attention. One might also question how Gehazi would be able to sequester such a quantity of silver in Elisha's house without his knowledge. But these curiosities are ignored for the point of the story. That point is the obverse of the gift motif. Elisha refuses Naaman's gift to show that the source of the healing is YHWH. Gehazi's deception undercuts Elisha's refusal by profiting from the healing and assuming credit for it in Elisha's name. The two parts of the motif denounce the use of prophecy for personal gain.[53]

---

51 So Würthwein, *1. Könige 17–2. Könige 25*, 301–302.

52 So Würthwein (*1. Könige 17–2. Könige 25*, 298n).

53 See 8:1-6 for a discussion of the tension between Gehazi's reappearance there and his contraction of Naaman's skin disease in the present passage.

5:24: Elisha's house

The *house* in question (v. 24) may not be Elisha's. At least three other possibilities arise: Gehazi's house, a group house of the prophetic guild, or the temple. It is unlikely that Gehazi, a servant, would own a house. While there are references to communities of the *bĕnê hannĕbî'îm* in different locations, none exists for Samaria, and there is no mention of any communal residence for the prophets in any of the places where they are located. A temple could well be a place of deposit for safekeeping, and the fact that the house is located in the *citadel* is a point in favor of this interpretation. However, there is no clear reference to a temple of Yhwh in Samaria.[54] One may have existed, but it is unlikely that it would be referred to here as *the house* without an antecedent. Since the next verse (v. 25) has Gehazi back with Elisha, presumably in the latter's house, it is probably the place in question, especially as the chapter has indicated previously that Elisha has a house in the city.

5:25-27: The cost of Gehazi's greed

Elisha asks where Gehazi has been and then exposes the hollowness of his lie by describing in detail how Naaman got down from his chariot to meet him (v. 26). Following G^L, Elisha also calls Naaman by name for the only time in the narrative, showing the detail of his knowledge as well as a new intimacy with Naaman, who has shown himself more honorable than Gehazi. The detail of Elisha's description is due to his "heart" (= mind or consciousness) accompanying Gehazi. It is further evidence that there is a prophet in Israel (v. 8). The list of items Elisha asks if Gehazi will acquire with his ill-gotten silver (following G) is reminiscent of 1 Sam 8:13-17, but there is no reason to suspect dependence of one text upon the other; both list items illustrative of wealth and acquisition.[55] Elisha's announcement of punishment reverts to the understanding of Naaman's disease as disfiguring, isolating, and fatal that underlies the *legenda* (v. 27). Gehazi will not be able to enjoy his acquisitions because of the disease, which will adhere to him. Gehazi appears to have a much worse case than Naaman, since it turns him *like snow.*[56] Moreover, it is genetic, for it is passed on to Gehazi's heirs in perpetuity.

Synthesis

The extraordinary character of Naaman

The lessons of this story revolve around its characters. The kings are effectively irrelevant. The king of Israel is faithless and oblivious to the presence of the man of god and Yhwh's power within his borders. The king of Aram is also insignificant.

---

54 1 Kgs 13:32 comes closest in its reference to temples of the high places in the cities of Samaria. 1 Kgs 16:32 mentions a temple in Samaria, but it is a temple of Baal.

55 D. P. O'Brien ("'Is This the Time to Accept ...?' [2 Kings v. 26]: Simply moralizing [G] or an Ominous Foreboding of Yahweh's Rejection of Israel [MT]?" *VT* 46 [1996]: 448–57) understands Elisha's refusal of the gift and the extended list in v. 26 as portending Yhwh's rejection of security and prosperity for Israel because of destruction of the kingdom of Israel and exile. His interpretation depends on his rejection of the G reading in favor of the MT and the assumption of DtrH editing of the story.

56 According to Fritz (*Kings*, 259), the comparison adds to evidence that the disease was a form of eczema. Fricke (*Das zweite Buch von den Königen*, 70) likens it (commenting on v. 1) to vitiligo. Hulse ("Nature of Biblical 'Leprosy,'" 95–96) limits his diagnosis of vitiligo to *bōhaq* (Lev 13:39) because it presents whiteness without another symptom.

Real power lies in completely different quarters. This feature anticipates 6:17, where Elisha asks for his servant to be allowed to get a glimpse of the divine force supporting the holy man. Even Elisha's presence is immaterial in a sense. In sharp relief from the previous story (4:29-31), but similar to 4:1-7, what matters is not Elisha's presence or ritual acts but Naaman's obedience to his instructions.[57] Naaman's character is remarkable, especially for an enemy army commander. He is renowned for his religious perceptiveness. While his healing demonstrates that there is a prophet in Israel (v. 8), Naaman perceives that the ultimate responsibility lies with YHWH, the only true god in all the earth (v. 15). He immediately "converts" to the exclusive worship of YHWH. Even more sophisticated is his recognition that his compulsory prostration in the temple of Hadad is meaningless because its namesake is but a figment (v. 18). A less obvious positive trait is Naaman's attentiveness to his subordinates. Listening to his Israelite slave girl sets him on the track to healing in the first place. Then when ego and national chauvinism threaten to derail him he quickly rights himself, thanks to his servants and to his own willingness to pay them heed.

The importance of the "minor" characters

The significance of the minor characters in the story is well articulated by Römer, whose observations are worth quoting at length:

> Such a discovery emancipates the reader from the injustices of the narrative caste system (major vs. minor characters). It encourages us to engender alternative reading practices that might result in a more equitable and just assessment of all the characters present. This in turn cultivates a new sensitivity toward our own context and a more equitable and justice-based assessment of those residing among us. How we read important texts like the bible impacts how we read and interpret the "text" of our world.[i] A reading practice that privileges the supporting cast not only unearths the greatness of servants in this story but also cultivates a praxis of justice. Ironically, such a practice also resoundingly echoes the message and priorities of a well-known teacher from years ago who himself was a servant and likely studied these texts: "And Jesus said to them, ... whoever wishes to become great among you must be your servant" (Mark 10. 43).[58]

The glaring exception to the positive subordinate characters is the only one who is named: Gehazi, whose actions threaten to undermine the lesson that YHWH was responsible for Naaman's healing.[59] Gehazi does not grasp all the implications of there being a prophet in Israel. He tries to take advantage of Elisha's divine gift of prophecy for personal gain. However, Gehazi is not Elisha's foil but Naaman's. The Aramaean comes to believe—with sophisticated theological insight—in YHWH as the only true god, while Gehazi the Israelite now acquires Naaman's skin disease and becomes an outsider.

---

57 Accounts of healings from a distance of a person the healer has never met are attested in Mesopotamia. See Zucconi, "Aramean Skin Care," 171–73.

58 Römer, "II Kings 5:1-14." The reference in footnote i is to L. Hutchinson, *The Poetics of Postmodernism* (New York: Routledge Press, 1988), 160. See also Brueggemann ("A Brief Moment") on the Israelite servant girl.

59 *Pace* Rehm, *Zweite Könige*, 66.

The Floating Axe Head (2 Kings 6:1-7)

Text

[Prophetic legenda]
1 The members of the prophetic guild said to Elisha, “The place where we are sit-
ting before you is too cramped for us. 2 Let us go to the Jordan and each of us
bring a beam from there so that we can make a place to sit.” [Elisha] said, “Go.”
3 One of them said, “Please come with your servants.” He replied, “I will go.”
4 So he went with them. They arrived at the Jordan and began cutting the trees.
5 As one of them was felling the beam, the axe head fell into the water, and he
cried out, “Alas, my lord, it was borrowed.” 6 The man of god asked, “Where did
it fall?” When [the prophet] showed him the spot, [Elisha] cut off a stick and
threw it there, making the axe head float. 7 He said, “Pick it up,” and [the
prophet] reached out and took it.

Textual Notes

1 **where we are sitting before you**: See 4:38 where the same expression, ישב לפני, occurs. Here, as there, it is ambiguous and may refer to the site where the prophets lived under Elisha’s direction or to the place where they would gather with Elisha for instruction.

2 **each of us**: So MT (איש). G^{BL}: ἀνὴρ εἷς = איש אחד under the influence of קורה אחת.[1]

beam: The word קורה occurs elsewhere in Gen 19:8; Song 1:17; 2 Chr 3:7, and perhaps, by reconstruction, in 1 Kgs 6:15; 7:7, referring to rafters or beams. In v. 6 it is used for the tree that one of the men fells (מפיל), suggesting that such a beam was rough-hewn.

so that we can make: So G^{L}. MT, G^{B} + *there*, which occurs later in the verse.

a place to sit: So MT (מקום לשבת שם) and perhaps G^{L} (σκέπην τοῦ οἰκεῖν ἐκεῖ), though the antecedent of σκέπην (*shelter*) is uncertain. G^{B} (τοῦ οἰκεῖν ἐκεῖ) lacks a noun, but one seems required for sense.

3 **One**: Lit. *the one*. The word is definite because he is the one who speaks.

Please: Lit. *consent, acquiesce* (*Hip'îl* imperative of √יאל), a polite way of requesting agreement. The word furnishes a link with ch. 5 (v. 23).

He replied, “I will go”: So MT, G^{B}. G^{L}: *Elisha replied, I will go with you.*

4 **cutting**: Possibly a Northernism (גזר), but this is questionable in view of other occurrences of the verb (e.g., Isa 9:19).[2]

5 **As one of them was felling the beam**: So MT (ויהי האחד מפיל הקורה). G^{BL} agree, though G^{B} reflects והנה for ויהי. Klostermann, followed by a number of scholars, proposed reading הקרדם (adze) instead of הקורה (thus: *as one was lowering the adze*), arguing that

---

1 Burney, *Notes*, 284.
2 Cogan and Tadmor, *II Kings*, 69. See the discussion of Schniedewind and Sivan, “Test Case,” 330–31.

"beam" must be incorrect because one fells a tree but not a "beam."[3] But the conjecture is unnecessary if one understands the reference to the finished product as proleptic.[4]

the axe head fell: MT has ואת־הברזל נפל. At least four explanations have been offered for the את: (1) an error;[5] (2) a construct noun usually rendered "ploughshare" but referring to an undefined cutting tool;[6] (3) an indication that the verb √נפל should be *Hip'îl* rather than *qal*;[7] (4) an acceptable use of את to mark a subject especially of an intransitive verb.[8] Although (2) is ingenious, there is no textual support for it. Despite the adduced precedents (4) seems to be special pleading. Both (1) and (3) require textual emendation; taking את as an error influenced by the foregoing מפיל is the simplest solution, especially in view of v. 6 where Elisha repeats נפל. G^{L}: *the blade fell off the handle* (καὶ ἐξέπεσεν στελεοῦ τὸ σιδήριον) is expansive.

he cried out: So G^{B}. MT (he cried out and said) and G^{L} (the man cried out and said).

7 **Pick it up**: So MT, G^{B}. G^{L}: *pick it up and take it*, in anticipation of ויקחהו.

Synchronic Analysis

A pattern of varying story lengths

The brief story in vv. 1-7 follows the much longer and more complex one about Naaman in chapter 5, just as the two tales in 4:38-41, 42-44 follow that of Elisha's revival of the Shunammite's son in 4:8-37, as 4:1-7 follows the story in chapter 3, and as the stories in 2:19-22, 23-25 follow that of Elijah's ascension in 2:1-18. The precise reason for this pattern of varying long and short stories is not clear but it may be at least in part for aesthetic reasons and to hold the interest of readers. The present anecdote shares with the Naaman story the motif of immersion in the Jordan.

6:1: The ambiguity of the place

The anecdote is another concerning the "sons of the prophets," like those in 2 Kings 2 and 4. Other details of the setting are uncertain because of the ambiguity of ישב לפני in v. 1. As pointed out in the Note, the prophets may be claiming that the village or even the quarters in which they live under Elisha's charge is/are too small or that the location where they sit before him as his pupils is too confined. The first possibility would indicate that Elisha lives among the members of the prophetic guild while the latter would mean that he is an occasional visitor. The term "place" (מקום) contributes to the ambiguity, since it can refer to an abode—be it village or dormitory—to a sanctuary, or to a meeting place. One need not try to remove the ambiguity, especially since it is not crucial to the point of

---

3 Klostermann, *Könige*, 480.
4 Stade, *Kings*, 204.
5 Montgomery, *Kings*, 382.
6 Klostermann, *Könige*, 480.
7 GKC 117mN.
8 WO, 182. For more detailed discussions relating to this option see J. Blau, "Zum angeblichen Gebrauch von את vor dem Nominativ," *VT* 4 (1954): 7–19; J. MacDonald, "The Particle את in Classical Hebrew: Some New Data on Its Use with the Nominative," *VT* 14 (1964): 264–75; and P. P. Saydon, "Meanings and Uses of the Particle את," *VT* 14 (1964): 192–210.

the anecdote. More important is the link the expression provides between the present tale and the two at the end of ch. 4.

6:2-3: Elisha with the prophets by the Jordan

The background continues in v. 2, where the prophets beg leave of Elisha to go to the vicinity of the Jordan to gather wood and build a "place" there for living or meeting. Various small trees, including willow, tamarisk, acacia, and plane, were available in the immediate vicinity of the Jordan, but the main reason for seeking materials on the shore of the Jordan is that the river provides the water required for the anecdote.[9] The special invitation to Elisha to come along (v. 3) may suggest that he is not normally one of their guild. It also serves several literary functions. Most obviously it places Elisha at the riverside where he can perform the miracle that is the focus, and it prolongs the story and introduces suspense as the reader is anxious to find out what wonder he will perform this time.

6:4-5: A crisis

In the course of cutting wood one of the prophets loses the head (lit. "the iron") of the axe he is wielding (vv. 4-5). It falls into the river, presumably in a place where it is too deep to be reached. The man cries out (ויצעק) that the tool was borrowed (*shā'ûl*, lit. "requested"), implicitly soliciting Elisha's help. As frequently observed, iron implements were probably quite expensive. The fact that this one was borrowed added the embarrassment of having lost it to the cost of replacement. Depending on the value of the tool and hence the amount of the debt incurred, the man who lost it could be in danger of debt slavery for himself and/or members of his family. This suggests the extreme poverty of the man involved and probably of the entire guild of prophets. The loss, therefore, truly is a crisis. Hence this story fits the pattern of others in which the victim of a crisis situation cries out for help to the man of god, who in turn works a miracle resolving it. The title אדני that the prophet uses for Elisha recalls that the sons of the prophets sat or lived under Elisha's supervision.

6:6-7: A summative resolution

Elisha's question in v. 6 ties the details of the anecdote together. His *where* (אנה) resonates with the man's outcry (אהה) at the loss of the axe. The use of *the place* returns the reader to vv. 1-2, where the limited size of the place where the prophets sat/lived launched the search for a new place. The term *wood* occurred in v. 4 in the description of the collection of building materials. This climax of the story presents a good deal of irony. The prophets left their place that was too small and went to gather wood for a new place. Wood is all that the man with the borrowed axe is left with after the axe head falls off. Elisha restores the fallen head, using more wood cast upon the water where it submerged. The recovered axe head, replaced on its wood, can once more aid in the collection of wood for building.

Diachronic Analysis

A basic *legenda* intact

The story in 6:1-7 is a basic *legenda*. The first four verses set up the circumstances of the *legenda* proper—the expedition to the Jordan and the reason for it, the cutting of wood and hence the involvement of an axe, and the presence of Elisha.

9 Nelson, *Kings*, 185.

Verse 5 recounts the crisis and the appeal to the man of god in the form of the prophetic disciple's outcry. Then, in vv. 6-7, Elisha resolves the crisis by means of sympathetic magic. The *legenda* has not been editorially retouched; the magic act is the man of god's own doing. Nor is there any other evidence of literary revision: the passage is a unit.

6:1: The setting near the Jordan

Affinities between the present *legenda* and the two at the end of chapter 4 suggest that they may once have gone together. Those two tales are set in Gilgal (4:38), and the proximity to the Jordan assumed in 6:1-7 indicates that it is also set either in Gilgal or in Jericho. The situation of sitting/dwelling before Elisha is the same as in 4:38, and the reference to the prophetic guild having outgrown its location for "sitting" comports with the reference in 4:43 to one hundred men. The separation and rearrangement of these *legenda* is editorial; the purpose is to achieve alternation of long tales with one or two short ones as described above. The long tales also have to do with military and/or political affairs, except for the Shunammite story.

6:2-4: Gathering wood by the Jordan

Since the second שם in v. 2 is erroneous (see the Note), the actual building site is not next to the Jordan. Heat, humidity, frequent flooding, poor soil, and the presence of disease (malaria) make a location so close to the Jordan impractical as a living or meeting place. The vicinity of the Jordan is simply the location for gathering building materials. The structure was probably a light shelter from sun and rain rather than an actual building.

6:5-7: An act of symbolic magic

The potentially dire nature of the consequences for losing the axe outlined in the Synchronic Analysis poses a crisis as severe as that of the prophetic widow in 4:1. The man's outcry (ויצעק) parallels hers and signals the impending miraculous intervention that is the nature of such a *legenda*. Elisha's response (v. 6) is an act of sympathetic magic much like those described in 2:19-22 and 4:38-41. Taking a piece of wood—probably a stick—he casts it into the water at the spot where the blade sank. The verse uses a causative form of the verb (*he made the iron float*), explicitly establishing a cause-effect relationship between Elisha's act and what happens to the axe head. The stick may represent a new handle, so that the axe head is understood as being attracted to it.[10] The magic act therefore reverses the natures of the two parts of the implement: the iron floats and the wood acts like magnetized iron.[11]

Rationalistic interpretations

A number of interpreters have tried to rationalize the miracle or explain the origin of the *legenda* by positing that Elijah used a long stick to pick up the iron head through the hole where its handle had been inserted or to move it to shallow water where the man who had lost it could recover it.[12] Such explanations misconstrue the genre of the story as *legenda* and miss its point about the nature of the holy man.[13]

---

10 Qimḥi (Rosenberg, *Kings II*, 279).

11 Nelson, *1 Kings*, 185.

12 See Gray, *Kings*, 511; Jones, *Kings*, 421; Rehm, *Das zweite Buch der Könige*, 58; Thenius, *Könige*, 292. Šanda (*Könige* II, 49) suggests that the stick cast in the water caused a wave that carried the axe head to shore.

13 The following reactions are apropos: "'Wonders' are not to be explained; they are to be wondered at" (Brueggemann, *Kings*, 342). "It is our age rather than Elisha's which seeks always to find justification for stories of the miraculous" (Robinson, *First Kings*, 58).

Synthesis

A typical prophetic *legenda*

Like the other prophetic *legenda*, this one illustrates the power and authority of the man of god. He acts of his own volition to perform a miracle without any explicit recourse to YHWH. At the same time, in the larger setting of the *legenda* in a collection put together by PN that repeatedly makes a point of giving YHWH the ultimate credit for the wonders performed by Elisha, the power of YHWH is assumed. As in other *legenda* the holy man's motive is appealing. He acts to resolve a crisis that has arisen for one of the members of the prophetic guild and may be moved by concern and compassion for the man. The story seems to assume that the members of this guild live in community and at a bare subsistence level. Implicit in such a portrait is the devotion of the members of the community to their calling, their mentor, and their god. They endure a difficult life of impoverishment and seek to learn from figures like Elisha, whom they regard as a model, because they feel called to be YHWH's messengers. The *legenda* about Elisha probably had their beginnings in such communities.

Elisha Defeats the Aramaeans (2 Kings 6:8-23)

Text

[Prophetic legenda; *PN]*
[8] When the king of Aram was at war with Israel he took counsel with his ser-
vants, saying, "At such and such a place hide yourselves (in ambush)." [9] Then
the man of god sent to the king of Israel, "Be careful to avoid this place because
the Aramaeans are hiding there." [10] The king of Israel sent to the place the man
of god had mentioned and he was on guard there. *This happened more than
once or twice.* [11] The king of Aram became enraged because of this thing, and
summoning his servants he said to them, "Won't you tell me who is betraying
me to the king of Israel?" [12] One of his servants answered, "No, my lord king.
Rather, Elisha the prophet who is in Israel tells the king of Israel the words you
speak in your bedroom." [13] [The king of Aram] said, "Go and see where he is so
that I can send and capture him." He was told, "He is in Dothan," [14] *so he sent
there horses and chariotry and a powerful force. They arrived at night and sur-
rounded the city.* [15] *When the man of god got up early the next morning and
went outside, there was the army around the city with horses and chariotry. His
servant said to him, "Alas, my lord, what shall we do?"* [16] *[Elisha] replied, "Don't
be afraid, for those who are with us are more than those who are with them."*
[17] *Elisha prayed and said, "YHWH, open his eyes so that he may see." YHWH opened
the servant's eyes and he saw that the hill(s) was/were filled with horses and fiery
chariots all around Elisha.* [18] When [the Aramaeans] came down to him, [Elisha]
prayed to YHWH and said, "Strike this people with blindness." So [YHWH] struck
them with blindness *according to Elisha's word.* [19] Elisha said to them, "This is
not the way, and this is not the city. Follow me, and I will lead you to the man
whom you seek." So he led them to Samaria. [20] When they arrived at Samaria,
[Elisha] *said, "YHWH, open their eyes so that they may see." So [YHWH]* opened
their eyes, and they saw they were in the middle of Samaria. [21] When the king
of Israel saw them, he said, "Should I indeed kill them, my father?" [22] [Elisha]
said, "You shall not kill them. Are you going to kill those you have not taken
captive with your own sword and bow? Set food and water before them so that
they may eat and drink and go to their master." [23] So he prepared a great feast
for them. After they ate and drank, he sent them to their master. Aramaean raid-
ing parties did not again enter the land of Israel.

Textual Notes

8 **hide yourselves**: Reading תֵּחָבְאוּ (*Nip'al* imperfect, 2nd plural of √חבא), following the common emendation.[1] MT's תחנתי *[will be] my encampment*, followed by G^B ("I will camp," παρεμβαλῶ), is a *hapax legomenon*. The *Vorlage* of G^L (*let us set an ambush, and they set it*, ποιήσωμεν ἔνεδρον καὶ ἐποίησαν) is uncertain but it shares the sense of hiding and ambush. Another possibility is to read a form of the verb נחת, *go down*, which may have connotations of military attack (Jer 21:13; Joel 4:11).[2] The matter also concerns the last word in v. 9, all the more since v. 12 suggests that the verbs in vv. 8 and 9 should come from the same root. The witnesses may reflect different understandings of the verse relating to ambush vs. planned attack at a specific location.

9 **the man of god**: So MT, G^L. G^B: *Elisha*. See the note on 4:16.

because the Aramaeans are hiding there: So G^B (ὅτι ἐκεῖ Συρία κέκρυπται = כי־שם ארם נחבים) with v. 8. Similarly, G^L (ὅτι ἐκεῖ Συροι ἐνεδρεύουσιν), *for there the Aramaeans are laying an ambush*. MT: כי־שם ארם נחתים *for the Aramaeans are descending there.*

10 **the man of god had mentioned**: So G^L. MT, G^B + *to him*. G^B also replaces *man of god* with Elisha's name. See 4:16.

and he was on guard there: So G^{BL}. MT precedes with *he had warned him* (והזהירה, *Qere'*: והזהירו), a gloss.

11 **betraying me**: So G^{BL} (προδίδωσίν με = מגלני, *Pi'ēl* participle √גלה).[3] MT: משלנו, *from among us.*

12 **the words you speak**: So MT. G^L *all that you speak* has an equal claim. G^B (πάντας τοὺς λόγους οὓς ἐὰν λαλήσῃς) conflates the two.

13 **[The king of Aram] said**: So MT, G^B (lit., *he said*). G^L: *The king said.*

where: אֵיכֹה is unique and may be an Aramaism or a variant of אֵיכָה (Cant 1:7) with the vocalization of אֵיפֹה.[4]

he was told: So MT. G^{BL} (*they told him*) is equally possible.

Dothan: Tel Dotan, ca. ten miles north of Samaria.[5] It commanded the pass on the southern end of the Carmel range separating it from the Ephraimite highlands. It was near modern Jenin, where the Dothan Valley opens into the Jezreel Valley. The tell of Dothan was isolated in a fertile "bay" off the southeastern edge of the Dothan Valley, with hills and mountains marking the perimeter of the bay.[6]

14 **horses and chariotry**: So G^B with singulars used as collectives, as in v. 15. G^L has plurals in both instances. MT mixes plural and singular/collective (סוסים ורכב).

15 **When the man of god got up early the next morning**: Reading וישכם ממחרת for MT's וישכם משרת, *when the assistant arose early in the morning.*[7] This explains the different term for the servant (נער) later in the verse. On the use of לקום with √שכם see Ps 127:2.

---

1 Cf. BHS; Thenius, *Könige*, 292; Klostermann, *Könige*, 408–409; Kittel, *Könige*, 210–11.

2 See Cogan and Tadmor, *II Kings*, 72 and works cited by them.

3 So Klostermann, *Könige*, 409. Kittel's suggestion that מגלני originally followed משלנו and was lost by haplography is also possible. The relative שׁ is either Northern (Judg 5:7; 6:17; 7:12; 8:26) or colloquial. Schniedewind and Sivan, "Test Case," 329–30 argue for the former; WO (328n) propose the latter.

4 Schniedewind and Sivan, "Test Case," 324.

5 For a summary of occupational periods see W. G. Dever, "Dothan," *ABD* 2:226–27.

6 J. M. Monson, "Regional Settlement: Dothan in the Northern Arena," *Dothan I: Remains from the Tell (1953–1964)* (ed. D. M. Master *et al.*; Winona Lake, IN: Eisenbrauns, 2005): 7–14.

7 Cf. Klostermann, *Könige*, 409.

horses and chariotry: So MT, G^B with singulars as in v. 14. G^L has plurals. Both readings are possible.

16 **with them**: Reading אִתָּם in place of MT's אוֹתָם on the basis of sense.

17 **his eyes ... the servant's eyes**: So MT. G^B: *the eyes of the servant ... his eyes.* G^L: *his eyes ... his eyes.*

the hill: So MT, G^B. G^L: *the entire hill.*

18 **came down to him**: So MT, G^B. G^L: *came down to them* under the influence of the plural later in the verse.

to YHWH: So MT, G^B. G^L has *to god*. Either reading is possible.

blindness: סנורים occurs elsewhere only in Gen 19:11. It is probably a loan word from Akkadian *shunwurum*, "to make radiant" (*CAD* N 1.217) for a sudden, dazzling flash of light that does not permanently blind but temporarily disables.[8]

19 **and this is not the city**: So MT, G^L. G^B has the reverse order of *city* and *way*; it also does not repeat the negative. Either order is possible; the absence of the second negative is idiomatic: *this is not the city or the way.* The demonstrative זֹה occurs elsewhere in Judg 18:4; 2 Sam 11:25; 1 Kgs 14:5; Ezek 40:45; Qoh 2:2, 24; 5:15, 18; 7:23; 9:13. It may be a Northernism or an Aramaism befitting Elisha's address to the Aramaean army.[9]

20 **their eyes (1)**: So G^{BL}. MT has את-עיני-אלה, *the eyes of these*, which appears corrupt.

they were in the middle of Samaria: MT lacks the suffix on הנה, but its presence is indicated by G^B (καὶ ἰδοὺ ἦσαν ἐν μέσῳ Σαμαρείας) and G^L (καὶ ἰδοὺ αὐτοὶ ἐν μέσῳ Σαμαρείας).

21 **he said**: So G^{BL}. MT + *to Elisha.*

Should I indeed kill them: Reading אַכֶּה הַהַכֵּה (interrogative particle on *Hip'il* inf. abs. + 1st pers. singular) as indicated by G^B (εἰ πατάξας πατάξω).

22 **you have not taken captive**: So G^L (οὓς οὐκ ᾐχμαλώτευσας ἐν ῥομφαίᾳ σου καὶ τόξῳ σου σὺ τύπτεις). G^B, though more idiomatic, also seems to reflect the negative: εἰ μὴ οὓς ᾐχμαλώτευσας ἐν ῥομφαίᾳ σου καὶ τόξῳ σου σὺ τύπτεις = *unless you would kill those you have captured with your own sword and bow.*[10] MT lacks the negative, but it is hard to make sense of it (but see the Diachronic Analysis).

Set food and water before them: G^L lacks *before them*, which was probably omitted after a dittography with לחם resulted in reading להם.

23 **he prepared a great feast for them**: The meaning of the root כרה is derived from the context. It has been viewed as cognate to Akkadian *qerû*, "to invite," and the corresponding noun *qerītu*, but the differences in initial consonant and meaning make this derivation suspect.[11]

he sent them to their master: So G^B. MT, G^L: *he sent them and they went to their master.*

Synchronic Analysis

Context and structure

The subject-first construction of v. 8 marks the beginning of a new story. Its background is the state of war between Israel and Aram. Strikingly, it is the king

8 E. A. Speiser, *Genesis* (AB; Garden City, NY: Doubleday, 1964), 139–40.
9 Schniedewind and Sivan, "Test Case," 327.
10 So also Kittel, *Könige*, 212.
11 See Cogan and Tadmor, *II Kings*, 74 and the objections of W. von Soden, "Zum hebräischen Wörterbuch," *UF* 13 (1981), 162.

of Aram rather than the king of Israel who is mentioned first. The entire story with its focus on Aram and especially the use of raiding parties (v. 23) is reminiscent of 5:2 and connects with the Naaman story. The term "place" (*māqôm*), used three times in vv. 8-10, also connects this story with vv. 1-7 (esp. vv. 1, 6). The reader may assume that the tensions between Aram and Israel that were latent in the Naaman story erupted again. The story unfolds in three scenes: the strategy in the Aramaean court (vv. 11-13), the appearance of the Aramaean army at Dothan (vv. 14-18), and Elisha's delivery of the Aramaean army to the king of Israel in Samaria (vv. 19-22). The anecdote in vv. 8-10 and the banquet in v. 23 serve as prologue and epilogue respectively

6:8-9: Subverting Aramaean strategy

The opening scene is in the Aramaean court, where the king of Aram with his advisors is planning his strategy against Israel (v. 8). How the Israelite narrator has come into possession of the details of the deliberations of the Aramaean court is not explained. Perhaps they are surmised from the larger circumstances of the story. The words תחנתי and נחתים at the end of vv. 8 and 9, respectively, are difficult. Following the usual understanding the Aramaean king plans to move his camps, i.e., his army, to a certain unnamed place as part of his military strategy. Elisha, with his second sight, discerns the move and cautions the king of Israel against venturing to the location to which the Aramaeans are descending to attack (v. 9). This understanding may not be correct. Since Elisha is able to tell the king of Israel the very words that the king of Aram speaks in his bedroom according to v. 12, one expects that the words in vv. 8 and 9 would be similar if not identical. It is also possible, though, that the servant's statement in v. 12 is hyperbole. Even if the two words in question are from different roots, they pun on one another because of the consonants and vowels they share, so that they display the artistry of this text, all the more since each is followed by the verb וישלח.[12] The king of Israel takes Elisha's warning to heart and sends word to the place (v. 10a). Exactly how the king of Israel uses this information is unclear. He may alert the Israelites who live or are stationed at the place so that they can leave in advance of the Aramaean assault. Alternatively he may inform his soldiers who would otherwise be going to or passing through the place to avoid it. What is important is the ongoing intelligence that Elisha provides, protecting the king of Israel and frustrating the plan of the Aramaean king. This is the point of v. 10b with its statement that this warning happened repeatedly (*not once or twice*) and its use of perfect verb forms emphasizing continuous or repeated action in the past. There is a slight issue with the verb והזהירה (Qere': והזהירו). Its suffix is masculine and refers to the king of Israel, not to *the place* as the recipient of the warning.[13] This in turn means that the source of the warning is Elisha rather than the king of Israel as in certain English translations. Further indication of this is that the next verb, נשמר, is also masculine, so that it is the king of Israel as a synecdoche for the

12 R. LaBarbera, "The Man of War and the Man of God: Social Satire in 2 Kings 6:8–7:20," *CBQ* 46 (1984), 639.

13 The *ketiv* evinces the older *mater lectionis* with *heh*, which has been "corrected" with the *qere'*: והזהירו. The NRSV and Tanak versions construe the *ketiv* suffix as feminine: "he warned/alerted such a place." However, in Codex Leningradensis the vocalization on the *ketiv* is that of the masculine suffix.

nation of Israel who is on guard *there*, at the place where the Aramaeans were planning to attack.

6:11-13: Elisha's second sight

The incident in vv. 9-10 is the latest of several occasions when the king of Israel is forewarned and prepared for the Aramaeans' military move. In v. 11 the Aramaean king reaches peak frustration (lit. "his heart was stormy") and demands to know who is responsible for the leak in his court. A servant informs him that the leak is not internal but is because of *Elisha the prophet* in Israel (v. 12). It is striking that the Aramaeans knew Elisha by name and reputation. This contrasts with 5:3 where the Israelite girl did not know the prophet's name, although her ignorance may be attributable to her youth. The Aramaeans' awareness of his whereabouts (v. 13) also contrasts with 3:11 where the king of Israel does not know that Elisha is present with the army. The preceding story of Naaman shows how this could happen; Elisha's fame has been spread by the man he healed. The courtier's way of describing the extent of Elisha's familiarity with his master's plans is artfully salacious: He knows the words the king speaks in his bedroom—in his most intimate moments. This motif of Elisha's insight recalls 5:26, where Gahazi tried unsuccessfully to hide his deceitful acquisition of Naaman's present from his master and was accompanied by Elisha's *heart.* It contrasts with 4:27, where YHWH hid the reason for the Shunammite's distress from the prophet. This information bodes quite ill for the Aramaeans' future success. Clearly they will be unable to strategize effectively until Elisha is neutralized. But whatever plan they concoct to counter Elisha can be perceived by him and thwarted. The king sends his servants to ascertain his whereabouts (*go and* see, v. 13). The mandate is ironic in view of Elisha's second sight and of the soldiers' subsequent loss of sight. Why the king decides on capture rather than assassination is unclear; perhaps the prophet is too valuable a resource to kill, and the king hopes to turn him to his own service. Verse 13 might imply that Elisha's whereabouts are not immediately known and that some research is required to discover them. How long this takes is not divulged and is unimportant to the main point of the story. This in turn suggests that Elisha was in Dothan only temporarily, a possibility buttressed by the absence of any other connection between Elisha and Dothan. Meanwhile the discerning reader suspects that Elisha is aware of the king's inquiries and well prepared for what comes next.

6:13-17: The Aramaean incursion

The king of Aram sends a large force—apparently his entire army—to capture Elisha (v. 13). He is deluded in thinking that size and force can overcome divine insight. The scene is comical and reminiscent of the story of Elijah in 1:7-16. The army comes overnight and surrounds the city of Dothan (v. 14). When Elisha's servant sees them the next morning he despairs, asking his master what they can do (v. 15). His lament (אהה אדני) is the same as in v. 5 and connects the two episodes. Elisha's response of reassurance, אל־תירא (v. 16) is identical, *mutatis mutandis,* to that of Elijah to the widow in 1 Kgs 17:13. His continuation, *Those who are with us are more than those who are with them* (v. 16), appears nonsensical. But what the servant cannot see at first is YHWH's heavenly army that surrounds Elisha (v. 17). Thus the verb *fear* in אל־תירא puns with the verb *see* (ראה) to make clear that the remedy for fearing is perceiving the reality of the divine army. The servant's eyes are opened in answer to Elisha's prayer and he is given second sight like his master—at least temporarily. This army, with chariots and horses of fire—like the one that separated Elisha from Elijah when the latter was taken to heaven (2 Kgs 2)—fills *the hill(s)* round about Elisha. The word may also mean *mountain* and can be taken as singular or as a collective. In v. 18 the Aramaeans are said to come down to Elisha so that the story apparently envisions the Aramaeans in the hills on the edge of the bay in which the city was located (see the Note). The heavenly army then could be located behind them higher up on the mountains. A better alternative, however, may be to envision the heavenly army occupying the tell itself. The point seems to be made with contrasting descriptions in vv. 15 and 17:[14]

v. 15: והנה־חיל סובב את־העיר וסוס ורכב
v. 17: והנה ההר מלא סוסים ורכב אש סביבת אלישע

The correspondences are obvious: והנה־חיל = והנה ההר; סובב = סביבת; העיר = אלישע; וסוס ורכב = סוסים ורכב אש. The Aramaeans have come to capture Elisha; they surround the city where he is. But the divine army, which they cannot see, provides a ring of protection around him on the *hill* of the city between him and the Aramaean army.

6:18: The Aramaeans blinded

In v. 18 Elisha prays a second time. Before, he prayed for vision for his servant (v. 17); now he requests blindness for the Aramaeans. The sight/blindness is of two different kinds—spiritual perception in v. 17 versus actual sight in v. 18. The prayer is answered as the Aramaean army are stricken with temporary blindness. It disables them and places them at Elisha's mercy, which sets up the next scene.

6:19-22: The Aramaeans blinded and captured

Verse 19 gives a curtailed report of a conversation between Elisha and the blinded Aramaeans. The latter are silent as befits their powerlessness. They are helpless because of their blindness and, though they are not aware of it yet, they are prisoners.[15] We are not told how Elisha approached, nor do we know what they told him about their mission. Since Elisha tells them that they have taken the wrong way and come to the wrong city we must infer that they have told him they are trying to reach Dothan. We must also infer that they mention Elisha by name since he promises to lead them to the man they seek. They are foolish to trust him.[16] But what choice do they have? Ironically, Elisha fulfills his word since he is in fact that man. Moreover, he delivers them to the king of Israel who is in a sense their ultimate target. When they reach Samaria (v. 20) Elisha prays a third time, again for sight for someone else—this time the Aramaeans. He thus aids them to fulfill their mandate to "go and see" (v. 13).[17] They realize that they are trapped in Samaria (בתוך שמרון). The city's name puns with Elisha's injunction to guard (השמר) the site of prospective attack in v. 9. Each word defines the confinement of the Aramaeans and the two words together form a frame that contains the narrative of their limitation and capture.[18] The king of Israel is dumbfounded to have the enemy army delivered to him (v. 21); he does not know what to do

---

14 Cf. LaBarbera ("Man of War and Man of God," 641), who errs in equating Elisha with the army (חיל). Elisha corresponds to the city; both of them are surrounded. Still, to the extent that Elisha calls forth the "chariotry of Israel and its horsemen," after which he is titled, he is worth an army to Israel.

15 Hens-Piazza, Kings, 269.

16 Cf. Hobbs, *2 Kings*, 78.

17 Nelson, *Kings*, 187.

18 Cf. LaBarbera, "Man of War and Man of God," 644.

with them. Deferring to Elisha, whom he respectfully calls *my father* as in 2:12 and 13:14 (cf. also 8:9), he falteringly asks whether he should kill them, repeating the verb. This might be rendered in translation as a stutter: “Should I k-k-kill them?” The effect is to portray him as perplexed and indecisive if not weak-willed. Elisha responds in the negative, indicating with his rhetorical question that the king would not kill those he had captured on his own. The response recalls 1 Kgs 20:32-35. In that story the king of Israel was denounced for releasing the king of Aram whom YHWH had devoted to *ḥerem*. In the present story YHWH has not ordained the destruction of the Aramaean army. The resulting impression is that YHWH can be arbitrary about what to humans are life-and-death matters.[19]

6:23: A banquet for the captives

The king of Israel follows Elisha's command but takes it to an extreme, as he does not just feed the Aramaeans but prepares a lavish feast for them. Is he again weak-willed and foolish? Or is his hospitality a clever way of dissuading the Aramaeans from future attacks (v. 23b). The latter seems unlikely given the propensity of these stories to praise the prophet and belittle the king. The Aramaeans are probably deterred from future raids because of the presence of the man of god and the power of YHWH on Israel's side. The next verse, which describes a siege of Samaria by the Aramaeans, is jarring in the wake of the statement that the Aramaeans stopped making raids. The narrator evidently makes a distinction between raiding parties (גדודים) and a full-scale invasion.

Diachronic Analysis

The elaborated *legenda*

The basis of the present story was an elaborated *legenda* about the prescience of Elisha and a failed attempt by the Aramaeans to capture him that is preserved in vv. 8-13*, 18aα (וירדו אליו) bα (ויכם בסנורים), 19, 20aα (ויהי כבאם שמרון) b (minus יהוה), 21-23.[20] It recounted an occasion when Elisha captured an entire Aramaean raiding band. The band's mission was to capture him because of the intelligence he provided for the king of Israel. The story was probably about Elisha from the beginning, and there is no reason to assume a separate “man of god” level.[21]

6:8-13: Background information

Verses 8-13 were background. Israel and Aram were at war (v. 8), so that the setting of the *legenda* was the same as that of 1 Kgs 20; 22; 2 Kgs 13:14-25. Neither the king of Aram nor the king of Israel was named, nor were many details forthcoming, as is typical of *legenda*. It is not clear whether it was an ambush or an impending attack about which Elisha warned the king of Israel, nor was the loca-

19 The impression is deepened by the absence of instructions about *ḥerem* to the king of Israel in 1 Kgs 20.

20 The foundations for compositional reconstruction of this passage have been well laid by Schmitt (*Elischa*, 91–93), Würthwein (*1. Könige 17–2. Könige 25*, 304–307), and Sauerwein (*Elischa*, 66–71). My own reconstruction agrees with theirs in general contours but with adjustments that make it different from each of theirs.

21 *Pace* Schmitt. Incidentally, Schweizer (*Elischa in den Kriegen*, 221–22) argued the opposite—that the original tale was about Elisha and the title “man of god” was original only to v. 15a, which is part of the interpolation in vv. 15-17. Elsewhere (vv. 9a, 10a) the title was an accommodation of the interpolation to the older Elisha story.

tion of the assault named. The focus was on the prophet and his ability to undermine the Aramaean military strategy with his prescience (v. 9). The notice in v. 10a may mean that the king sent a warning to the residents of the place about the impending assault or ambush or that he sent to notify his troops in the area to be on guard for such. The Israelites obviously anticipated the ambush/attack and were prepared for it because that was what frustrated the Aramaean king and led him to accuse his servants of aiding the enemy (v. 11). Verse 10b is probably an addition,[22] but its point that Elisha was able to warn the king of Israel in this way more than once or twice was implied already in vv. 11-12: The king of Aram's reaction in v. 11 that someone in his court *is betraying* (see the Note) and the response in v. 12 that Elisha hears his most intimate words assume continued activity. Verse 12 especially makes clear that Elisha's knowledge of the Aramaean king's most intimate conversations—military and otherwise—was not isolated but ongoing. Besides, it is unlikely that the Aramaean king would become so angry and frustrated at a singular event that could have various explanations. The use of the verb *wayyuggad* to relate how the king was told of Elisha's location in Dothan (v. 13) resonates with the *gĕdûd* that was envisioned in the *legenda* as coming to capture Elisha. It shows that the *gĕdûdîm* in v. 23 were part of the *legenda*.

Why Dothan?

The significance of Dothan is uncertain. It is mentioned only once more in the HB (Gen 37:17), though it occurs several times in Judith (3:9; 4:6; 7:3, 18; 8:3). Schmitt argued that it pointed to a local tradition about a nameless man of god from Dothan who subsequently came to be identified with Elisha.[23] He distinguishes this tradition from his later *Gottesmannbearbeitung* but the explanation still reflects his tendency to see the title *man of god* as a marker of redactional levels.[24] It could be that Dothan was chosen because of its relative proximity to Samaria (v. 19). It was between Carmel and Samaria and might be seen as a convenient stopover for an itinerant prophet.[25] The site was destroyed in the Assyrian period of the late eighth century and not resettled until Hellenistic times,[26] suggesting that the *legenda* may have originated in ninth-eighth century Israel.

6:14-17: PN's interruption

At this point (v. 14) the *legenda* is interrupted. The *powerful force* (חיל כבד) complete with horses and chariots and large enough to surround the tell of Dothan (v. 14) differs from the raiding party the king of Aram sends to capture Elisha and that he leads into Samaria (vv. 13, 19, 23). An army so deep in Israelite territory could hardly be ignored by the king of Israel and would call forth some response from him even if the story assumes a period of extreme weakness as in

---

22 *Pace* Würthwein (*1. Könige 17–2. Könige 25*, 306) and Sauerwein (*Elischa*, 67).

23 Schmitt, *Elisa*, 155–56.

24 More problematic is Gray's explanation (*Kings*, 513–16), which argues that Dothan's strategic location allowed Elisha to manage "an efficient intelligence service" of informants that kept him aware of Aram's military plans and of the king's bedroom conversations. This explanation is typical of a rationalistic approach to the prophetic stories that overlooks the nature of the genre (ironically because of the assumption that it is based in historical fact) and misses its point concerning the extraordinary and entertaining abilities of the man of god.

25 Sauerwein, *Elischa*, 67.

26 D. Ussishkin, "Dothan,"*NEAEHL* 1:372–73.

13:7. The horses and chariotry introduced in v. 14 form a motif that continues in vv. 15 and 17 where the heavenly horses and chariotry contrast with and outnumber those of the Aramaeans.[27] Furthermore, the addition in vv. 14-17 introduces Elisha's servant (נער), whose presence and question *What shall we do?* (v. 15) provide the occasion for a demonstration of Yhwh's power. The addition therefore has a theological agenda distinct from the *legenda* in that it is concerned to show that the divine army is more numerous and powerful than any human foe and can only be perceived by special spiritual sight into the heavenly realm. This second sight is a motif borrowed from 2 Kings 2 and represents a different phenomenon from Elisha's *prescience* in the *legenda*. This second sight is a gift from Yhwh. It is awarded to the servant in response to Elisha's prayer (v. 17). Outside of this passage Elisha prays to Yhwh only one other time, in 4:33b, a PN addition. Here he will do so three times (vv. 17, 18, 20).

6:18-20: Legenda and PN revision

The *legenda* resurfaces in v. 18 with the descent of the raiding party and Elisha's blinding them. The singular suffix "they came down *to him*" at the beginning of the verse indicates Elisha alone without the added servant. As typically in *legenda*, the man of god performed the wonder himself (v. 18). The blindness is caused by a dazzling flash of light. This does not mean, as some commentators aver, that the soldiers' malady is disorientation or confusion rather than loss of sight.[28] That explanation is based on English or German (*Blendung*) meanings of "dazzle" rather than Hebrew. It is also driven by the effort to explain an inconcinnity in the present story of blind soldiers following Elisha on the four- or five-hour journey from Dothan to Samaria (v. 19). This "problem" is negligible because it results from the nature of the *legenda* and its focus on the wonder; the walk to Samaria might even be considered part of the wonder. Elisha's prayer and the attribution of the blinding to Yhwh are editorial and what we have come to expect of PN. They continue the theme of second sight from vv. 14-17, playing on the notions of true vision and blindness, a theme that is perhaps developed from 2 Kings 2. In a sense for PN the Aramaeans cannot tolerate the glimpse of the divine force that Elisha and his servant have enjoyed. The blindness ended for the Aramaean soldiers in the *legenda* when they reached Samaria and Elisha opened their eyes (v. 20*). PN revises this with a third prayer and restoration of vision for the Aramaeans attributed to Yhwh.

6:21-23: The end of the *legenda*

The remainder of the story (vv. 21-23) was in the *legenda*. The king of Israel was unsure what to do with his new captives. His first thought was to kill them (v. 21), but Elisha demurred. *My father* was a term of respect and honor as in its use for Naaman in 5:13 (cf. 8:9). It is used for Elisha in 2:12; 13:14. The reason behind the man of god's demurral in v. 22 is obscured by the uncertain reading.

---

27 Schmitt initially focused on the reference to the fiery chariotry in v. 17 as added material. Würthwein noted that it was horses and chariotry in general as part of a "great army" that varied from the older story, which presupposed a much smaller band of Aramaeans. This means that the addition included all of v. 14 following the first two words וישלח־שמה, *he sent there*. It also suggests that the raiding bands in v. 23b were part of the original story (so Sauerwein) rather than an addition (*pace* Schmitt, Würthwein).

28 *Pace* LaBarbera ("Man of God and Man of War," 643) citing A. Jirku ("Materialen zur Volksreligion Israels," in *Von Jerusalem nach Ugarit: Gesammelte Schriften* [Graz: Akademischer Verlag, 1966]: 233–46.

If one accepts the MT reading the man of god was apparently arguing on the basis of customary practice, i.e., that the king would not customarily execute prisoners. But execution was sometimes expected, especially when *ḥerem* was in effect (e.g., 1 Samuel 15). Witness 1 Kgs 20:35-43 where the king of Israel is denounced for releasing his prisoner. Cogan and Tadmor argue that the Assyrians released captives to sing their praises and that this is the prophet's objective here.[29] Still the most efficient solution is to follow G^{BL} in reading the negative, "those you have *not* taken captive." Then the point is that the prisoners belonged to YHWH, who effected their capture, and not to the king. The *legenda* ended with the king of Israel preparing a feast of some sort—the exact meaning of כרה is unknown, but it was a *great* (גדולה) occasion—and letting the Aramaeans return home (v. 23a). Their return served as a warning of the futility of raiding parties against Israel, as suggested by the following notice that this episode stopped the incursion of such parties (v. 23b). The tension with the next verse, which began an account about invasion of the Aramaean army, is left over from the independence of the older stories behind 6:8-23 and 6:24–7:20. Nevertheless, the two might be seen as complementary: the ineffectiveness of raiding parties became the impetus for large-scale invasion on the part of the Aramaeans. Similarly, Elisha and YHWH first put an end to the incursions of the raiding parties (6:23b) and then decisively defeated the entire Aramaean army, which was on the verge of victory after an extended siege of Samaria (6:24–7:20).

Synthesis

A comical *legenda*

The elaborated *legenda* upon which the present narrative is founded was light and comical in orientation. It demeaned the Aramaeans and also poked fun at the king of Israel while venerating Elisha for the ease and grace with which he handled the Aramaean party sent to arrest him. He knew the intimate secrets of the king of Aram, even those spoken in his bedroom (v. 12). Elisha made quick work of the Aramaeans, blinding them and leading them to Samaria (vv. 18*-19). The king of Israel was surprised to have his enemies delivered to him and did not know what to do with them; he first proposed killing them but then treated them to a banquet before releasing them (vv. 21-23a). In this way Elisha single-handedly halted the incursion of Aramaean raiding parties into Israel (v. 23b).

The need for a prophet

In PN's hands the comical *legenda* becomes a more serious and theologically driven story about YHWH's power and protection. Elisha is not just prescient but is able to see into the heavenly realm (vv. 15-16). He prays for the same perception for his servant (v. 17) but is unable to bestow it himself. With this perception come important theological ramifications. The heavenly realm influences and controls what takes place on the earth and can intervene in human affairs. YHWH is in charge of both realms. While the events in the narrative take place in Israel, Elisha's god-given ability to know what the Aramaean king is planning in his own capital implies that YHWH is superior to the gods of other nations, if they even

29 Cogan and Tadmor, *II Kings*, 75.

exist. YHWH is Israel's god. He favors and saves Israel but also punishes them through other nations when they sin. The man of god no longer performs miracles on his own but by praying to YHWH. The story exhibits YHWH's attentiveness to Elisha's requests. Elisha is in tune with YHWH and the heavenly realm. The importance of such a figure is evident in vv. 20-21 especially in comparison with 1 Kgs 20:35-43. YHWH's insistence that the Aramaean king in the latter should have been devoted to destruction while in the present passage Aramaeans are to be released hints at capriciousness on his part or, positively phrased, inscrutability. A prophet like Elisha is needed to communicate what the divine will is in a given situation.

A non-violence reading

Further consideration by a modern reader, though, suggests that YHWH's will is not as capricious or inscrutable as indicated at first glance. There is a difference between the execution of a single king who is guilty of invading YHWH's land and attacking his people and the wholesale slaughter of an entire army of soldiers who are following their marching orders according to the duty of their station. The holy man's presence in Israel proves to be a deterrent to Aramaean incursion that saves many lives and much bloodshed. If the feast given by the Israelite king also plays a role in this process the story can be taken to show that kindness is a much more effective (and less costly!) way of dealing with one's enemies than violence.

The Siege of Samaria (2 Kings 6:24–7:20)

Text

[Prophetic legenda (normal, *italic* = different sources); *PN; Additions and glosses*
to PN]
6:24 *Afterwards* Ben-Hadad king of Aram gathered all his force and went up and
laid siege to Samaria. 25 There was a severe famine in Samaria while they
pressed the siege against it to the point that a donkey's head sold for eighty
shekels of silver and a fourth of a kab of doves' dung for five shekels of silver.
26 When the king of Israel was passing in review on the city wall *a woman cried*
out to him, "Help, oh my lord king!" 27 *He answered, "If YHWH will not help you,*
from where can I find help for you? From the threshing floor or the wine vat?
28 *The king said to her, "What is your problem?" She replied, "This woman told me,*
'Give up your son for us to eat today, and we will eat my son tomorrow.' 29 *So we boiled*
my son and ate him. But the next day when I said, 'Give up your son so we can eat
him,' she did not give him up for us to eat but hid her son." 30 *When the king heard*
the woman's words he tore his clothes and, since he was passing in review on the city
wall, the people saw that there was sackcloth on his skin beneath. 31 *He said, "So*
will god do to me and so will he add if the head of Elisha son of Shaphat stays
on him today. 32 Now Elisha was sitting in his house, and the elders were sitting
with him. *[The king] sent a man ahead of him. Before the messenger came to*
him [Elisha] had told the elders, "Have you seen how this murderer has sent to re-
move my head? Watch. When the messenger arrives, close the door and hold him
back with the door; the sound of his master's feet is right behind him, isn't it?
33 He was still speaking with them when the king came down to him *and said,*
"The present disaster is from YHWH; how can I have hope in YHWH any longer?"
7:1 Elisha said, *"Hear YHWH's word: Thus says YHWH,* 'At this time tomorrow, a seah
of flour will sell for a shekel and two seahs of barley for a shekel in Samaria's
gateway." 2 *The adjutant on whose arm the king leaned responded, "Even if YHWH*
opened the windows in heaven, such a thing could not happen, could it?" [Elisha]
replied, "Your eyes will see it but you will not eat any of it." 3 There were four
men with skin disease at the opening of the gateway who said to one another,
"Why should we keep sitting here until we die? 4 If we decided to go into the
city, the famine is in the city and we would die, and if we stay here we will die.
So now let's defect to the Aramaean camp. If they let us live we'll be alive, but
if they kill us we'll die." 5 *So they arose at twilight to go to the Aramaean camp.*
When they arrived at the edge of the camp of Aram no one was there. 6 *YHWH*
had made the Aramaean camp hear the sound of chariots, horses, and a large
army. They said to each other, "Look, the king of Israel has hired the kings of the
Hittites and the kings of Egypt to come against us." 7 So they got up and fled at

twilight, abandoning their tents, horses, and donkeys in the camp as it was, fleeing for their lives. 8 *So when these men with skin diseases came to the edge of the camp* they entered a tent where they ate, drank, and took silver, gold, and clothing and then left and hid it. Then they returned and entered another tent, taking their plunder and going to hide it. 9 Then they began saying to each other, "What we are doing is not right. This day is a day of good news, yet we are keeping silent. If we wait until morning, guilt will find us. Come on now, let's go back and tell the king's house." 10 So they returned and called to the city gatekeepers and told them, "We went into the Aramaean camp and no one was there, nor human sound, but the horses and donkeys were tied up and their tents were as they were." 11 So the gatekeepers called and announced the news to the king's house. 12 The king arose and said to his servants, "Let me tell you what the Aramaeans have done to us; they knew that we are starving, so they went out from the camp and hid in the field thinking, "When [the Israelites] come out from the city, we will take them alive and enter the city." 13 One of his servants responded, "Let them take five of the horses that are left so that we can send and find out" 14 So they took two mounted riders, and the king sent them after the Aramaeans, saying "Go and find out." 15 They followed [the Aramaeans] as far as the Jordan, and the whole way was filled with clothing and weapons that the Aramaeans had cast off in their haste. Then the messengers returned and told the king. 16 The people went out and plundered the Aramaean camp, and a seah of flour sold for a shekel and two seahs of barley for a shekel according to the word *of YHWH* which Elisha had spoken. 17 *The king appointed the adjutant on whose arm he leaned over the gateway, and the people trampled him to death as the man of god had foretold as he had spoken* when the king came down to him. 18 *It happened as the man of god had said to the king, "A seah of flour will sell for a shekel and two seahs of barley for a shekel; it will happen at this time tomorrow in the gateway of Samaria."* 19 *The adjutant answered the man of god, "Even if YHWH opened the windows of heaven, such a thing could not happen, could it?" [The man of god] said, "You will see it with your eyes, but you won't eat any of it."* 20 *So it happened: The people trampled him to death in the gateway.*

Textual Notes

6:24 Afterwards: So MT (ויהי אחרי־כן). G^{BL}: *after these things.*

Ben-Hadad king of Aram: This is Ben-Hadad III, who ruled Damascus in the early eighth century. See the Diachronic Analysis.

25 while they pressed the siege against it: So MT (והנה צרים עליה), G^{B}. The construction may be idiomatic in omitting the pronoun with הנה where the subject is clear from the context.[1] On the other hand, G^{L} does not reflect הנה but seems to read והם instead.

---

1 Burney (*Notes*, 288) citing Driver (*Tenses*, 135.6).

eighty shekels of silver: So MT. G^{BL}: *fifty shekels of silver* under the influence of *five* later in the verse. On the amount of silver in a shekel see the Note on 5:5.

kab: A *hapax legomenon* in the HB, this is obviously a measure of capacity but its amount is uncertain. Modern equivalents vary among commentators but are in the range of one to two liters or a pint to a quart, so that one-fourth of that amount would be between a one-half cup and a cup.[2]

doves' dung: So MT *ketiv* (חרייונים), understood as two words, חרי (construct of *חראים), *dung*, and יונים *doves*. Similar compounds occur in בליעל "worthlessness" and צלמות "death shadow." The rarity of the construction makes חרייונים all the more suspect, but a clearly superior alternative reading has yet to emerge. The *qere'* דביונים entered the text after חרי came to be considered obscene. However, the precise etymology and meaning of דב remain unknown.

26 **Passing in review**: עבר has the sense of moving past another (typically stationary) object. Hence the king is not simply walking or strolling on the wall but surveying the condition of the city. The verb may even have a ceremonial nuance.[3] The same expression occurs again in v. 30a.

Help: So MT, G^{B}. G^{L} *help me*.

27 **He answered**: So MT (ויאמר). G^{BL} + *her* (αὐτῇ = אליה). I adopt the *lectio brevior*, though haplography is possible.

If Yhwh will not help you: On the use of the jussive in the protasis (here negative) of a conditional sentence see Driver, Tenses §152(3); GKC §109h.

28 **and we will eat my son tomorrow**: So MT, G^{L}. G^{B} (καὶ τὸν υἱόν μου καὶ φαγόμεθα αὐτὸν αὔριον) was probably influenced by the previous occurrence of ונאכלנו.

29 **the next day**: So MT, G^{L}. G^{B}: *on the second day*.

she did not give him up for us to eat: Based on G^{L}, which reads this sentence (καὶ οὐκ ἔδωκεν αὐτὸν ἵνα φάγωμεν αὐτὸν) after *she hid her son*. The reading proposed here assumes that the two sentences were reversed in MT, G^{B} leading to loss by haplography of the sentence preserved in G^{L}.

30 **passing in review**: So MT, G^{B}. G^{L}: *he was standing* (reflecting עמד instead of עבר). The *Wiederaufnahme* from v. 26 supports MT's reading.

that there was sackcloth: So MT, G^{L} (והנה השק); G^{B}, Syr, Vulg reflect a less colorful את־השק.

on his skin: So MT, G^{B}. G^{L}: *upon his loins, upon his flesh*, a double reading.

31 **So will god do to me and so will he add**: On this oath formula see the note on 1 Kgs 19:2.

Elisha son of Shaphat: So MT, G^{L}. G^{B}: *Elisha*.

32[4] **the elders** (1): So MT, G^{B}. G^{L}: *all the elders*.

[The king] sent a man ahead of him: So MT, G^{B}. G^{L} supplies *the king* and reads an indirect object *to him* at the end of the clause.

33 **the king**: The major witnesses all read *the messenger*, although G^{L} (*the messenger who was from the king*) may reflect the variant *king/messenger*. The former is required by 7:2 where the king is present, and is assumed in 7:18. The change to *messenger* occurred after the addition in v. 32.

---

2 M. A. Powell ("Weights and Measures," *ABD* 6:904–905) considers the measurements reflected here an adaptation of the Late Babylonian system in which a *kab* was 1/6 of a *seah*, which was 1/3 of an ephah.

3 I owe these observations to members of the Biblical Colloquium (Baltimore, Nov. 4, 2013), especially Jodi Magness, Ron Tappy, and David Vanderhooft.

4 The two Qumran fragments of this verse agree with MT. Ulrich, *Biblical Qumran Scrolls*, 328.

the present disaster: There is precedent for the (rare) adjectival use of the demonstrative before the noun it modifies (Joüon §143i). However, it is probably best understood as emphatic (WO, 313).

how can I have hope in Yhwh: So MT (מה־אוחיל ליהוה). √יחל + ל expresses hope in divine help (Pss 42:6, 12; 43:5; 130:5; Lam 3:21, 24).[5] G^L: *how will I entreat god* presupposes אחל (*Pi'el* of √חלה).

7:1 **Hear**: So G^{BL} reading the singular. MT has the plural. The addressee is the king. The change to plural may have come as a result of the insertion in 6:32.

and two seahs of barley for a shekel: So MT, G^L. The phrase is missing from G^B due to haplography occasioned by the two occurrences of *shekel*.

2 **the adjutant on whose arm the king leaned**: So G^B (ὁ τριστάτης ἐφ' ὃν ὁ βασιλεὺς ἐπανεπαύετο ἐπὶ τὴν χεῖρα αὐτοῦ = השליש אשר־המלך נשען על־ידו). MT is identical except for reading למלך instead of המלך. G^L: ὁ τριστάτης ὁ ἀπεσταλμένος ἐφ' ὃν ἐπανεπαύετο ὁ βασιλεὺς ἐπὶ τὴν χεῖρα αὐτοῦ = השליש השלוח אשר נשען המלך על־ידו. The passive participle השלוח is an expansion or a corrupt dittography of השליש.

responded: So Syr. MT, G^L + *to the man of god*. G^B + *to Elisha*.

Even if Yhwh opened: Reading ואם יהוה עשה as reflected in G^L, Syr, Tar, and Vulg. MT, G^B have הנה for ואם under the influence of the particle's occurrence later in this verse as well as in 6:33; 7:6.

[Elisha] replied: So MT (ויאמר). G^B: *Elisha said*. G^L: *Elisha said to him*.

3 **Why**: On this use of מה see WO, 323.

4 **we would die**: So G^L. MT, G^B + *there*.

let's defect: This sense of נפל + אל/על is attested in 1 Sam 29:3; 2 Kgs 25:11; Jer 21:9; 37:14; 38:19; 2 Chr 15:9.[6]

If they let us live we'll be alive, but if they kill us we'll die: Reading אם־יחינו נחיה ואם־ימיתנו ומתנו. The leading witnesses have the conjunction either before *we'll be alive* (G^L) or before *we'll die* (MT) or both (G^B). The various placements suggest that it is secondary. In both instances it might easily arise from dittography of the plural ending.

5 **at twilight**: So MT, G^B. G^L + ἤδη διαυγάζοντος, *at daybreak*, an attempt to adjust the timeframe of the story from evening to morning.[7]

at the edge: So MT (עד־קצה), G^L (εἰς μέρος). G^B's εἰς μέρον *to the middle* is an inner-Greek corruption.

6 **Yhwh**: As in many Hebrew manuscripts and probably reflected in G^B's κύριος. G^L has *god*. It is not clear why the usual *qere'* ואדני came to be the *ketiv* here.

the sound of chariots, horses, and a large army: The major witnesses disagree about the placement of conjunctions. G^L has plurals of *chariot* and *horse*, while MT and G^B read singulars (collectives).

They said: MT has the plural, G^{BL} the singular. There is no clear way of deciding between them.

to each other: Lit. *to his brother*; so MT, G^B. G^L: *to his fellow* (πρὸς τὸν πλησίον αὐτοῦ = אל־רעהו under the influence of this reading in v. 3.

Look: So MT and G^L (הנה = ἰδού). G^B: νῦν = עתה.

7 **at twilight**: So MT, G^B. G^L: ἤδη διαφώσκοντος. See on 7:5.

in the camp: So G^{BL}. MT reads *the camp* in apposition.

as it was: Although מחנה *camp* is generally masculine it is sometimes construed as feminine (Gen 32:9; Ps 27:3; 1 Chr 11:15) as it is here with the pronoun היא.

---

5 Cogan and Tadmor, *II Kings*, 81.

6 Cogan and Tadmor, *II Kings*, 82.

7 For an explanation of possible reasons for this change see S. W. Holloway, "Antiochian Temporal Interpolations in 2 Kgs 6,24–7,20," *Bib* 78 (1997), 543–47.

8 **to the edge of the camp**: So MT, G^{B}. G^{L}: *to the tents at the camp's edge*, an expansion indicated by comparison to v. 5, which the present verse repeats.

and then left and hid it. Then they returned and entered: So MT (וילכו ויטמנו וישבו ויבאו). G^{L} expands by supplying *the lepers* as the subject. G^{B} attests only three verbs: καὶ ἐπορεύθησαν καὶ ἐπέστρεψαν ἐκεῖθεν καὶ εἰσῆλθον apparently having lost ויטמנו by haplography. ἐκεῖθεν is an expansion and is absent from many Greek witnesses. The verb ויטמנו, though ostensibly *Hip'îl*, may preserve an older *i*-imperfect since the root appears elsewhere only in *Qal* and *Nip'al* (once).[8]

their plunder: Lit. "their burden" as in G^{L} (ἄρσιν αὐτῶν), 6QpapKgs10-14 (משואם). MT has משם, *from there*, a corruption.

9 **What we are doing is not right**: G^{L} + *today*, a dittography.

This day: So MT, G^{B}. G^{L} precedes with "and."

guilt will find us: So MT. G^{BL}: *we will find punishment* (reading 3ms + suffix as opposed to 1cs).

Come on: So 6QpapKgs, MT, G^{B}: לכו. G^{L}: לכן.

10 **and called to the city gatekeepers**: Reading the construct plural (שערי) in accord with the following phrase ("told *them*") and with v. 11. MT has the singular (see on v. 11). G^{B} reads *gate*. G^{L} attests a double reading: καὶ ἐβόησαν πρὸς τὴν πύλην τῆς πόλεως καὶ ἐκάλεσαν τοὺς στρατηγοὺς τῆς πόλεως.

but the horses and donkeys were tied up: G^{B} does not reflect the second occurrence of אסור as the result of haplography occasioned by the repetition of the sequence ור.

their tents: So G^{BL}, with the suffix, for sense. MT has simply *tents* without suffix or article.

11 **called**: Reading the plural verb as required by the subject and with G^{BL}. MT's singular here and in the previous verse may preserve a double reading.[9]

to the king's house: MT, G^{B} + *inside* (פנימה).

12 **The king arose**: So G^{L}. MT, G^{B} + *at night*.

in the field: So MT *qere'* בשדה instead of the *ketiv* בהשדה.[10]

thinking: G^{B} + ὅτι = כי, which is unnecessary.

13 **five of the horses that are left**: Reading חמשה מן־הסוסים הנשארים. The repetition of אשר נשארו־בה הנם ככל־המון ישראל is a dittography and is absent from some Hebrew mss and the versions (G, Syr, Vulg). It also seems to be a gloss on הנשארים explaining that the horses left in Samaria are the only ones remaining in all Israel. אשר־תמו is an expansion on that gloss.

14 **mounted riders**: So G^{BL} (ἐπιβάτας ἵππων = רֹכְבֵי סוּסִים). MT has רֶכֶב סוּסִים, perhaps under the influence of רֶכֶב in v. 6.

the king: So MT. G^{BL}: + *of Israel*.

the Aramaeans: So G^{L} (lit. *Aram*). MT: *the camp of Aram*; G^{B}: *the king of Aram*. The variants suggest that the shorter reading of Aram alone is primitive.

15 **in their haste**: So MT *ketiv* (בהחפזם). The *Nip'al* is attested with this meaning elsewhere (1 Sam 23:26; Ps 48:6; 104:7), so that there is no need to replace it with the *Qal* form (בחפזם) as in the *qere'*.

16 **The people went out**: So MT, G^{B}. G^{L} + *from the city*.

and two seahs of barley for a shekel according to the word of Yhwh: So MT, G^{L}. G^{B}: *according to Yhwh's word—and two seahs of barley for a shekel*. The reference to

8 GKC §47i and J. Barth, "Das *i*-Imperfekt im Nordsemitischen," *ZDMG* 43 (1889): 177–91.

9 Wevers, "Double Readings in the Books of Kings," 309–10.

10 On the unsyncopated article see GKC §35n. Cf. also Schniedewind and Sivan, "Test Case," 317–18.

barley was lost by haplography or was omitted to accord with v. 1 and then subsequently added.

which Elisha had spoken: At the end of v. 16 G^L^ has the plus ὃς ἐλάλησεν ἐλισσαιε = אשר דבר אלישע, which appears initially to be an expansion. However, its resumption in v. 17bβ (אשר דבר ברדת המלך אליו) where the אשר דבר is not a dittography as is often assumed, points to the *Wiederaufnahme* in v. 17abα.[11]

17 **trampled him**: So G^L, which lacks *in the gate* found in MT, G^B and indicates that this is an expansion influenced by the mention of the gate earlier in the verse.

when the king came down: So MT. G^{BL}: *messenger* because of the interpolation in 6:32.

18 **the man of god**: So MT. G^{BL}: *Elisha*. This may be due to systematic change in G, as Barthélemy contended (see on 4:16).

a seah of flour will sell for a shekel and two seahs of barley for a shekel: Following the order of vv. 1, 16. MT, G^B attest the reverse order (i.e., barley before flour). G^L follows the order of vv. 1, 16 but also reads *a seah of barley* instead of *two* for reasons that are not clear.

19 **the man of god**: So MT, G^L. G^B has Elisha's name. See on v. 18.

such a thing could not happen, could it: So G^{BL} as in v. 2. MT has כדבר for הדבר.

20 **So it happened** ויהי כן as indicated by G^{BL} (καὶ ἐγένετο οὕτως). MT + *to him*.

The people trampled him to death in the gateway: 6QpapKgs15 + *according to the word of the man of god* (כדבר איש האלהים). While only the *mem* is visible on the papyrus, the reading is widely accepted.[12]

Synchronic Analysis

Ben-Hadad's new strategy

The phrase *afterwards* (ויהי אחרי־כן) with which the present story begins signals a new episode. The king of Aram, identified as the infamous Ben-Hadad, gathers his entire "camp" and lays siege to Samaria (v. 24). The use of "his camp" (מחנהו) recalls "my camp" (תחנתי) at the beginning of the previous story (v. 8). In that story, the Aramaean "camp," though a "heavy force" (v. 14) turned out to be a raiding band that was frustrated, like others before it, by Elisha's prescience and warning (v. 10b). Because of those experiences Ben-Hadad has given up his use of mere raiding bands (v. 23b). He now pulls out all the stops and assembles his entire "camp," i.e., his whole army. His strategy is different. No more ambushes or assaults on fringe targets. Now he will attack Samaria directly.

6:24-25: Siege and famine

Verse 24 shares several features with 1 Kgs 20:1, including the name of Ben-Hadad, his title (*king of Aram*), the verb *gather* (קבץ), and the statement that he went up and besieged Samaria. The trouble caused by the present siege therefore, is the result of the king of Israel releasing Ben-Hadad in 20:31-43. The initial impression of v. 25 is that the siege has caused a famine but, as with the transition from v. 23 to v. 24, things are more complicated. The beginning clause of v. 25 (ויהי רעב גדול בשמרון) can be interpreted to mean that the famine occurred before

11 Trebolle, "Le texte de 2 Rois 7,20–8,5 à la lumière des découvertes de Qumrân," *RQ* 13 (1988), 561–65; *Centena*, 173–74.

12 See Ulrich, *Biblical Qumran Scrolls*, 329.

the siege of the city.[13] This would explain why the famine becomes so severe so quickly. Such an interpretation receives further support from the adjutant's statement in 7:2 that Elisha's prophecy of abundant food could not come true even if YHWH were to open the *windows of heaven*, which suggests that the initial cause of the famine was drought. The famine might be the one Elisha is said to have predicted in 8:1-6. Nevertheless, the mention of the famine following the notice of the siege indicates that the siege at least worsened the famine.

Donkey heads and doves' dung

The scarcity of food in the city in v. 25 illustrates the law of supply and demand: the less available an item is, the more expensive it becomes.[14] In this case the desired item is food. It becomes so scarce that it is nonexistent, and even barely edible items are costly. There are two indicators of the desperateness of the famine: what people are willing to eat and the price those who can afford it must pay for something that is barely edible. The verse gives market prices for two items: a donkey's head and 1/4 *kab* of dove's dung. The most natural reading in the context is that both were eaten during the desperate conditions of the siege but that neither was a normal part of the diet. Donkeys were considered unclean and would not normally have been eaten (Lev 11:3; Deut 14:6). It goes without saying that the same was true of dove droppings. As for price, eighty shekels—the cost of the donkey's head—was about two pounds of silver. A more meaningful comparison is Exod 21:32, which gives the price of a slave as thirty shekels, so that the cost of a donkey's head was approaching that of three slaves! As for doves' dung, paying any amount for it as a comestible seems excessive and vividly illustrates the dire circumstances. (For other interpretations see the Diachronic Analysis).

6:26-27: A cry for help

The notice of the siege and of the famine's seriousness is followed by the anecdote in vv. 26-30 that further illustrates the desperate circumstances of both people and king. The king is walking on the city wall. He is to be identified as J(eh)oram, within whose regnal formulae the story occurs. But his nameless status suggests that he is something of a placeholder for any king of Israel. He is reviewing the city's defenses and how its citizens are coping with the starvation conditions when a woman—also nameless—cries out to him for help. Her cry is a formal appeal for legal judgment, as both the further context and the parallel with 2 Sam 14:4 make clear. As in this latter verse the word *Help!* literally means "save" (הושיעה). The verb puns on Elisha's name ("YHWH saves") and anticipates his involvement. King Joram is so focused on the siege and famine that he does not initially recognize the woman's cry for justice but assumes it has to do with food. His response (v. 27) is probably the protasis of a conditional sentence (see the Note) that is a rhetorical question: "If YHWH does not help you, how can I help you?" Alternatively the first part is a refusal and disclaimer of responsibility: "No, (but) let YHWH help you." Either way Joram blames YHWH for not saving the city and expresses frustration at his own impotence. The reference to the threshing

---

13 Cf. Burney, *Notes*, 288.

14 See J. C. Greenfield ("Doves' Dung and the Price of Food: The Topoi of II Kings 6:24–7:2," in S. M. Paul, M. E. Stone, and A. Pinnick [eds], *'Al Kanfei Yonah: Collected Studies of Jonas C. Greenfield on Semitic Philology* [Leiden: Brill, 2001], 815–19) for a nice overview of this *topos*. Also R. S. Nam, *Portrayals of Economic Exchange in the Book of Kings* (BIS 112; Leiden: Brill, 2012), 167–70.

floor and wine vat in the second half of the verse is obscure and has given rise to at least three interpretations.[15] First, and probably most common, is the recognition that these are sources of produce, so that Joram may be saying there is nothing left to feed the people. Second, Joram may be using prophetic imagery of the threshing floor as a place of judgment (Hos 13:3; Mic 4:12; Jer 51:33). Third, *between the threshing floor and the wine vat* could be an idiom for hopelessness comparable to the English phrase "between hell and high water." The third option is speculative, without any supporting evidence. The second is rendered unlikely by the fact that kings are typically clueless about the prophetic calling and show no familiarity with prophetic imagery. This option also leaves the *wine vat* portion of the saying unexplained. The first possibility, therefore, seems the most likely. Joram's mention of sources of food here seems to be sarcastic—accusing the woman of failing to understand that the usual sources of food are empty, so that an order from the king would be ineffective for increasing production or distribution.

6:28-29: Cannibal mothers

To his credit Joram inquires as to the exact nature of the woman's problem (v. 28a). His question is identical to 4:13 and thus provides a link between the two stories or, better, a contrast, for Joram will not be able to help this woman as Elisha helped the Shunammite. The anecdote related by the woman (vv. 28b-29) makes use of the *topos* of cannibalism in time of siege, which is paralleled in a number of biblical and ancient Near Eastern documents, not least Deut 28:52-57.[16] The woman's openness at bringing her petition to the king and her lack of emotion at the loss of her son highlight the utter horror of the situation. Perhaps most horrible is her apparent expectation that the king will side with her and order the other woman to comply with the original agreement. This reading, though, assumes that the boy was alive and the woman was guilty of murder. The text does not state this, and it is possible that both boys, especially if they were infants, had died in the famine. The king's lack of judgment in the matter might support this possibility and diminish the harshness of the assessment of the two women.[17]

Comparison with 1 Kgs 3:16-27

The parallel case of the two prostitutes in 1 Kgs 3:16-27 is instructive.[18] Solomon exhibited decisiveness and great wisdom but Joram abdicates decision, tearing his clothes in grief and threatening Elisha (v. 29). The contrast might point to the decline of the kingdom since Solomon. At the same time the two stories function differently in their contexts. Solomon's celebrated case demonstrated his divinely endowed wisdom (1 Kgs 3:38), while the present one shows the horror of the siege. Solomon's judgment was based on the real mother's affection for her child while the plaintiff in

15 Following the list of Hobbs, *2 Kings*, 79–80. The third proposal is Hobbs's own.

16 See Greenfield, "Doves' Dung and the Price of Food," 819. Also Cogan and Tadmor, *II Kings*, 80 and Long, *2 Kings*, 92.

17 I am grateful to my wife, Aimee McCarley, for this observation. For a postmodern literary analysis of this story that exposes the tendency of the Bible and its interpreters to marginalize women and downplay societal violence, see G. Hens-Piazza, *Nameless, Blameless, and Without Shame: Two Cannibal Mothers Before a King* (Collegeville, MN: Liturgical, 2003).

18 As shown by LaBarbera, "Man of God and Man of War" and S. Lasine, "Jehoram and the Cannibal Mothers," *JSOT* 50 (1991): 27–53.

the present case had lost her motherly affection to hunger. Joram certainly could not uphold her complaint, but to condemn her when she was already starving would be pointless.[19] What could he do but despair?

6:30-31: Joram despairs and blames Elisha

When Joram tears his clothes in grief over the desperate straits of his city and his people he reveals the sackcloth he is wearing underneath (v. 30) and the people know that he, too, is repentant. This implies that he is fasting as well, albeit presumably out of sympathy with his people rather than out of necessity. The portrait of him, therefore, is a sympathetic one, so that his threat against Elisha (v. 31) is unexpected. Despite his empathy—or perhaps because of it—he is driven to despair. It is not that he failed to turn to YHWH for help; his words to the woman in v. 27 suggest that he solicited YHWH but YHWH did not respond. Hence Joram has given up on YHWH. In fact, he is angry with YHWH and that is why he threatens YHWH's representative. Joram's animosity toward Elisha, furthermore, makes sense in view of the story in 6:8-23; he blames Elisha for Samaria's current plight because he (Elisha) released the Aramaean army that he (Joram) was ready to slaughter.

6:32–7:1: The king's attempt on Elisha's life and Elisha's prediction

The scene that plays out in 6:32–7:2 is high drama. Elisha is at home in consultation with the city elders, which bespeaks his status. Because of his prescience Elisha is aware of King Joram's plans against him even before the king's messenger, who is apparently serving as executioner, arrives. He announces the king's intent to murder him to the elders and solicits their help in resisting him. He tells them to hold the door fast and prevent the messenger from entering. His rhetorical question, "Have you seen?" (הראיתם) possesses an exclamatory element of disbelief akin to "Can you believe this guy?"[20] Understandably, Elisha does not take such a sympathetic view of the king, disparaging him as *the son of a murderer.* While the phrase is idiomatic in referring to a group or class rather than the father, in this instance it may well be *double entendre*, denouncing not only Joram but his father Ahab and thereby recalling the Naboth story. Elisha also foresees that the king is not far behind his messenger, and indeed the two arrive so close together that the text records no separate notice of the king's arrival as for the messenger's arrival in 6:33a. Yet in 7:1 (note the plural *hear*) and certainly in 7:2, where the adjutant on whose arm the king leans is mentioned, the king is there. The identity of the speaker in 6:33b is not specified. The nearest antecedent is the messenger, and the words spoken—blaming YHWH for this evil (זאת הרעה)—accord with the anger and despair previously expressed by Joram. It is also possible, though, to take Elisha as the speaker. In this understanding the prophet would be anticipating his death at the hands of the messenger, resigning himself to the fate determined for him by YHWH. Still, the lack of any further mention of an attempt on Elisha's life favors the former possibility. The messenger, speaking for King Joram, states that he has given up hope in YHWH; he may as well execute Elisha.

7:2: The incredulity of the king's adjutant

The explicit naming of Elisha in 7:1 also favors the likelihood of a change in speaker. He delivers an oracle that is couched in terms of the prices for produce and as such provides a counterpart to 6:25. One is forced to imagine that he speaks

19 For a reader-response treatment of this passage and the danger of revictimizing the woman in the story see L. Lanner, "Cannibal Mothers and Me: A Mother's Reading of 2 Kings 6.24–7.20," *The Feminist Companion to the Bible (Second Series)* 7 (ed. A. Brenner; Sheffield: Sheffield Academic Press, 2000): 129–37.

20 Joüon §161b.

through the closed door the elders are blocking. He begins with a summons to hear Yhwh's word, which is characteristic of prophetic collections (Jer 2:4; 10:1; 11:2; 17:20; 19:3; 21:11; Mic 1:2; 3:1, 9; 6:1; Amos 7:16). The oracle itself is alliterative: סאה־סלת בשקל וסאתים שערים בשקל בשער שמרון.[21] It predicts a radical turnaround of current circumstances such that regular foodstuffs will be readily available at reasonable prices. The king's adjutant (שליש) is incredulous. The reader can almost hear him scoffing that even direct divine intervention could not resolve the crisis with the immediacy Elisha predicts. Elisha's response that he would see with his own eyes but would not taste any of the newly available food piques the reader's curiosity as to exactly how this will transpire. The reference to the adjutant as the officer *on whose arm the king leaned* presupposes Joram's presence, yet he does not speak and his actual arrival is not recounted. The narrative therefore downplays his significance in favor of Elisha's. This impression is further conveyed by the fact that the king comes to Elisha's house rather than summoning or bringing Elisha to the palace. The king is inferior to the prophet. Elisha's oracle is evidently what persuades Joram to belay the order of execution, since there is no further mention of it. Joram and his advisor will wait to see whether Elisha's prophecy comes true.

7:3: A new anecdote

With 7:3 the narrative transitions to the account of how Elisha's oracle is fulfilled. The new episode is signaled by the subject-first sentence structure. The tone of the episode is light and comic, in marked contrast to the grim tone of 6:26-30. It begins with puns: *four* (ארבעה) resembling *windows* (ארבות) in 7:2 and *skin diseased* (מצרעים) resembling *Egypt* (מצרים) in 7:6. The skin disease from which the four men suffer links this story to that of Naaman.[22] There are other similarities as well. The men represent the lowest stratum of Israelite society yet, as in the Naaman tale, the socially disadvantaged take the initiative and play a major role in saving Israel. In contrast to the Naaman story the limitations posed by the men's disease are clearer, suggesting that Aram and Israel may have regarded skin disease differently.[23] It accounts for the men's location outside the city (Lev 13:46; Num 5:2; 12:15; 2 Kgs 15:5) and thus for their discovery of the empty Aramaean camp. The men propose entering the city (7:4), but the proposal is hypothetical and designed to show that the city was an unrealistic option.

7:4: The options of the skin-diseased men

The real options boil down to a choice between certain death and possible life. Entering the city means death by starvation if not execution; staying put means death when the city is attacked. The only course that offers any hope of survival is to surrender to the Aramaeans. If that strategy fails they will be no worse off than if they had gone into the city or stayed put. So they reason. The time frame is not entirely clear, since בנשף in v. 5 may refer to early morning (1 Sam 30:17; Jer 13:16; Ps 119:147; Job 3:9; 7:4) or late evening (Isa 5:11; 21:4; Prov 7:9). Their conversation suggests that it is the latter, since otherwise they would have to get up quite early in the morning to hold it. They may be using the darkness to facilitate their departure from the city and to hide their disease and thereby improve their chances for survival among the Aramaeans.[24]

---

21 LaBarbera, "Man of God and Man of War," 647.

22 Rabbinic interpretation (*Sotah* 47a) even identified the men as Gehazi's sons.

23 As argued by Zucconi, "Aramean Skin Care."

24 Kittel *Könige*, 217; Klostermann, *Könige*, 412.

7:5-7: The panic and flight of the Aramaeans

Venturing to the edge of the Aramaean camp, they are surprised to find it deserted (v. 5b). The explanation is provided in a flashback (vv. 6-7) that fills in the circumstances of the Aramaeans' departure, known to the narrator but not to the four men.[25] The result is a recounting of the event from the successive perspectives of the narrator, the Aramaeans, and the four men with skin disease, then later of the king of Israel, the Israelite scouts, and ultimately the people of Samaria.[26] The Aramaeans panic because of what YHWH causes them to hear. They fear the attack of the united forces of two of the ancient Near East's greatest empires, against which they do not stand a chance. The idea that the Hittites and Egyptians would come to the assistance of Israel is irrational. It indicates the divine origin of their panic and fits the comedic nature of the tale. What they hear may indeed be a great army, but it is the heavenly chariotry and cavalry, which are ineffably connected with Elisha and supply another link between this story and the one in 6:8-23. In their panic the Aramaeans have abandoned their camp with the animals and all the gear. The mention of horses among the items left behind is surprising, as horses would provide a more rapid escape than by foot. Since chariots are not mentioned as items left in the camp the abandoned horses were apparently either replacement chariot horses or horses for riding. If the latter they would presumably have been abandoned because the panicking Aramaeans felt they could not take the time to bridle them and otherwise prepare them for mounting.

7:8-11: The men take the good news to the city

Following the flashback the narrator resumes the main tale by reiterating the men's arrival at the edge of the Aramaean camp (v. 8aα). The verb בוא is used twice in v. 5 and three times in v. 8, driving home the idea that the men penetrated the enemy camp. Furthermore, v. 8 reports the activities of the four with a series of "piled up consecutive verbs" that "create the effect of a flurry of looting."[27] As individuals ostracized from a city in the throes of famine their first instinct is to eat and drink. The notice that they do the same at a second tent prolongs the tension of the narrative, for it is at this point in their frenzy of scavenging that they begin to question what they are doing. Fearing guilt or reprisal (עוון) for keeping good news to themselves, they decide to inform the palace (v. 9). They return and announce their discovery to the city gatekeepers (v. 10), who in turn tell it to the palace (v. 11). The verb נגד (*Hip'îl*) occurs once in each of these verses, mirroring this chain of announcements.

7:12: Joram suspects a trick

The verb *tell* occurs yet again in v. 12, but with a slightly different nuance. Joram is not simply passing on what he has heard but is declaring to his servants his opinion about what he sees as the snare laid by the Aramaeans. The verb *arise* (קום) also occurs in this verse for the third time, again in a different sense than in its previous two occurrences (vv. 5, 7). In both of those instances the verb has the sense of "proceed." Thus the four skin-diseased men, after discussing their options, proceeded to make their way to the Aramaean camp (v. 5). The Aramaean army, terrified by the sound of an approaching host, proceeded immediately to flee (v. 7). Each of these events occurred at twilight. In v. 12, however, King Joram is in bed in the middle of the night. The text does not say that he is roused by

---

25 Cohn, *2 Kings*, 52.
26 Cohn, *2 Kings*, 53.
27 Nelson, *Kings*, 190.

someone else. While the four men were looting the Aramaean tents Joram had been trying to sleep, but to no avail because of his worry about the siege and the famine. Now he receives the news about the empty Aramaean camp with suspicion, convinced that it is a ruse perpetrated by the Aramaeans to draw out the residents of Samaria and hasten its capture. Perhaps he harbors this suspicion because it is a strategy used by the Israelites themselves in past battles (Josh 8:14-23; Judg 20:29-48). The narrative is sophisticated and multilayered, reporting what the king thinks the Aramaeans are plotting. Joram does not even consider the possibility that this is Elisha's prediction starting to play out.

7:13-14: A reconnaissance party

As in the Naaman story it is one of the servants who is the voice of reason (v. 13). The servant speaks with trepidation, perceiving his king's agitation at the predicament of the city and his suspicion about the Aramaeans' tactic. His nervousness is perceptible in his confused and repetitive speech. Still the gist is clear. He proposes sending men with five of the remaining horses as scouts to determine whether the king's suspicions are valid. The reason for the horses is to allow for a quick escape if the men discover a trap. It is unclear why the servant sets "five" as the number of horses, especially since it is not the number eventually sent (v. 14). It may be that five is a round number for "a few," i.e., "a handful." How many more horses remain is unknown, but they are not many. Israel's chariot force is practically nonexistent. Joram accepts his servant's proposal and orders the party to be sent. They take with them two *chariots of horses* (understanding רֶכֶב as a collective), which may mean two teams or four horses total. His command to them, *go and find out* (לכו וראו), complies with the servant's proposal at the end of v. 13: *let us send and find out* (ונשלחה ונראה).

7:15-16: Report confirmed, Aramaean camp plundered

The party arrives at the Aramaean camp and finds it deserted, as the four men reported. The party then follows the trail of the fleeing Aramaeans all the way to the Jordan River, finding it littered with clothing and various implements discarded in flight. With this vivid description the narrative shows that the report of the initial discoverers was correct. The camp was empty; the Aramaeans had fled. What has happened is unknown to any of the Israelites witnessing the aftermath; only the narrator and the reading audience understand it. While the reconnaissance party, now called *messengers* (v. 15b), report to King Joram it is impossible to keep the news quiet in the besieged and starving city. In short order its citizens pour out to despoil the uninhabited camp (v. 16). Foodstuffs are replenished and prices return to more reasonable if not normal levels. A *seah* of flour and two *seahs* of barley each sell for a shekel, exactly as Elisha predicted (7:1). Verse 16 adds the new but not novel datum that the prediction did not originate with Elisha but was given to him by YHWH.

17:17-20: Elisha's prophecy fulfilled

Having revealed the story's primary outcome, the narrative backtracks in vv. 17-20 to tie up a final loose thread of Elisha's prophecy—the fulfillment of the prediction about the king's adjutant. King Joram had appointed him *over the gateway*, perhaps to monitor the numbers of people trying to exit the city for the Aramaean camp, or perhaps as the administrator for the distribution of food and other booty from the camp. Either way he is trampled to death as a direct result of the sudden abundance of food, which he had derided as impossible. Verses 18-20 go into greater detail, rehearsing nearly verbatim Elisha's oracle about food (v. 1), the adjutant's dubious response, and Elisha's prediction that he would see it but not taste it (v. 2). The only real difference between the two is the order of the flour and barley from v. 1. This slight change produces a chiastic *inclusio* around the account of the fulfillment of Elisha's prognostication and reaffirms the artfulness of the narrative.

Diachronic Analysis

A new *legenda*

A new story is introduced in v. 24. It is once again a prophetic *legenda* that has been edited by PN. It is linked loosely with the previous one by the adverbial phrase *afterwards* (ויהי אחרי־כן). However, the rather jarring contrast between vv. 23-24 vis-à-vis Aramaean incursions into Israel shows the original independence of the two stories. The story is self-contained. The famine in 6:25 is a result of the siege in v. 24. The idea mentioned in the Synchronic Analysis that the famine came from a drought that preceded the siege hinges principally on the adjutant's statement that the abundance of food predicted by Elisha was impossible even if YHWH were to open the *windows of heaven* (7:2). However, this verse is part of a PN addition.

Similarities with 1 Kings 20

The similarities with 1 Kings 20 mentioned in the Synchronic Analysis suggest that the two passages are related. The same name—Ben-Hadad—occurs in both for the Aramaean king. Israel is depicted in both of them as extremely weak militarily and essentially at the mercy of the Aramaeans, who have penetrated all the way to Samaria and now besiege it. Israel has only a few remaining horses (7:13) and therefore no chariotry to speak of. As with 1 Kings 20, this situation does not fit well in the Omrid dynasty and is a remnant of the story's setting during the reign of one of the kings of the Jehu dynasty (compare 2 Kgs 13:7).[28] The Ben-Hadad of 6:24 should be identified as the son of Hazael (2 Kgs 13:24), as explained in the following excursus. The story in 6:24–7:20, like the one in 1 Kings 20, is out of place and the king of Israel, who is unnamed, was not Joram, as the story's current placement indicates, but one of the grandsons of Jehu. This also explains the tension between the present story about Samaria being under siege and the subsequent description of Joram defending Ramoth-Gilead against Aramaean threat (2 Kgs 8:28-29; 9:14).

Excursus: The Identity of Ben-Hadad in 2 Kgs 6:24

The identification of Ben-Hadad in 2 Kgs 6:24 has been closely tied with the reference to Bir-Hadad in the Aramaic Melqart stela discovered near Aleppo. From its initial publication in 1939 the stela was associated with a king of the city-state of Damascus, though because of the poor condition of the patronymic there was disagreement about which Bir(Ben-) Hadad was the one named on the stela.[29] There were essentially three options: Ben-Hadad I, Ben-Hadad II, and Ben-Hadad III.

---

28 Cogan and Tadmor (*II Kings*, 84): "The siege of Samaria of the proportions described, in which Israel could hardly muster a few horses for a scouting party, is hard to imagine before the reign of Jehu."

29 For the history of readings and interpretation of the stela see Pitard, *Ancient Damascus*, 138–41, and "Identity of the Bir-Hadad," 4 n. 2.

Three years after the initial publication of the stela's inscription, Albright identified the Aramaean king on the inscription and in 2 Kgs 6:24 as Ben-Hadad I, son of Tabrimmon son of Hezion, who was hired by Asa of Judah to intervene in a border dispute with Baasha of Israel (1 Kgs 15:16-22//2 Chr 16:1-6).[30] Albright recognized that this identification required Ben-Hadad to have reigned fifty years or more according to Kings' chronology. He appealed to 2 Chr 16:1, which dates the border dispute between Asa and Baasha to Asa's thirty-sixth year (1 Kgs 16:8 has Elah succeeding Baasha in Asa's twenty-sixth year), thereby lowering the required length of Ben-Hadad's reign to around forty years—still long, but more feasible than fifty. However, Chronicles' chronology is theologically motivated: Asa's appeal to Ben-Hadad and his subsequent mistreatment of the prophet Hanani account for the disease of the feet from which he dies. Hence the fifty-year reign disqualifies Ben-Hadad (I) of 1 Kings 15 as the Ben-Hadad of 2 Kgs 6:24.

The identification of this king with Ben-Hadad II is just as tenuous. In fact, the very existence of Ben-Hadad II is questionable. According to 2 Kgs 8:7-15 he would be the immediate predecessor and apparent victim of Hazael of Damascus. But there is no mention outside of this story of an immediate predecessor of Hazael named Ben-Hadad. Rather, an inscription of Shalmaneser III mentions the death of Hadadezer and then states that Hazael, "the son of nobody" (*mār [DUMU] la mamana*) took the throne (*ANET* 280b; *COS* 2.113G). This has generally been understood to confirm the biblical portrait of Hazael as a usurper, albeit of Hadadezer rather than Ben-Hadad. The discrepancy is sometimes solved by taking Ben-Hadad as a throne name or alternate name for Hadadezer.[31] Pitard revived a proposal of Jepsen, pointing out the telescopic nature of the Shalmaneser inscription and its focusing on events of importance to the Assyrians while excluding others.[32] Hence the death of Hadadezer and the rise of Hazael are mentioned by Shalmaneser, but other persons and events that were not important to him and to the objectives of the inscription may have been omitted. In other words, it is possible that Hadadezer was succeeded by a king named Ben-Hadad whose name was not included in Shalmaneser's inscription because the two did not confront one another.[33] While this proposal cannot be definitively excluded, features of the story in 2 Kgs 8:7-15 raise doubts about its historical validity. For instance, it is odd that the Israelite prophet visits Damascus and even stranger that his fame precedes him, such that the Aramaean king eschews his own gods in favor of inquiring of Yhwh. Also, the gift he sends to Elisha in payment, forty camel loads of all the goods of Damascus, stretches the imagination. These features resemble elements of stories like those in 2 Kings 1 and 5 and betray literary imagination rather than historical detail. Although the biblical story

30 W. F. Albright, "A Votive Stele Erected by Ben-Hadad I of Damascus to the God Melcarth," *BASOR* 87 (1942): 23–29.

31 Wiseman (*Kings*, 226) takes it as a throne name. He also (p. 227) takes the reference to Hazael as "the son of nobody" to mean he was a commoner but not necessarily a usurper. The distinction is not clear to me; as a commoner Hazael had no hereditary right to the throne. The Tel Dan inscription also raises questions about the interpretation of Hazael as a usurper, though it provides no certain evidence against it. The stela is commonly attributed to Hazael, yet it refers to the author's father as a king. It may be that this is a propagandistic tactic to lend Hazael legitimacy, or the author may not be Hazael after all (*pace* Sauerwein, *Elischa*, 84).

32 Pitard, *Ancient Damascus*, 132–28; Jepsen, "Israel und Damaskus," 158–59.

33 This would be Ben-Hadad II, not Ben-Hadad I, son of Tabrimmon, who reigned earlier in the ninth century and is mentioned in 1 Kgs 15:18-20. It is also not Ben-Hadad (III), son of Hazael, who is to be identified as the Aramaean king in the misplaced narratives of 1 Kgs 20 and 22 and who reigned during the Jehu dynasty in Israel.

may preserve the memory of Hazael as a usurper, it is risky to reconstruct an otherwise unknown Ben-Hadad (II) based on this story alone. The name "Ben-Hadad" was most likely used in 2 Kgs 8:7-15 under the influence of the other references to this king in 1–2 Kings, especially 2 Kgs 6:24–7:20.

Except for the initial publication, all the readings of the stela except one made use of photographs rather than personal examination.[34] In 1985, though, Pitard reexamined the stela and published a new reading with photographs of the patronymic: Bir-Hadad son of Attarhamek, whom he identified as an otherwise unknown king of a northern Aramaean city-state rather than Damascus.[35] Building on Pitard's reading, Puech proposed that *ʿtrhmk* (Attarhamek) should be read as *ʿtrsmk* (Attarsumki).[36] Puech's proposal is attractive because Attarsumki was a known king of Arpad, although it has yet to be verified paleographically and linguistically. Nevertheless, it is clear that there is no longer any reason to identify Ben-Hadad in 1 Kings 20 or 2 Kgs 6:24 with the Bir-Hadad of the Melqart inscription. The identification of the figure in the biblical texts must be made on other considerations. The likely identification of the king of Israel as one of the Jehuides (Jehoahaz or Joash) places the story in the early eighth century rather than the mid-ninth century. The Ben-Hadad in the story is Ben-Hadad (III), the son of Hazael.

Interpretations of donkey's head and doves' dung

There has been a great deal of discussion about what is meant by the *donkey's head and one-fourth kab of dove's dung* that illustrate the severity of the famine in v. 25. Scholars have typically taken *donkey's head* at face value, an interpretation supported by Plutarch's reference to the Persian army being compelled by the scarcity of food to eat their beasts of burden, such that a donkey's head cost sixty drachmas or more.[37] There is much less agreement about *doves' dung*. The literal meaning of the word and the quantity of a *kab* are discussed in the Notes. Certainly the prospect of consuming excrement would illustrate the desperation of the famine. But the idea is distasteful and has led scholars to propose other possibilities. The proposals fall into three categories: textual emendation, something other than food *per se*, and an idiom for a food item.

Emendation

There are various proposals for emendation. Winckler prefers חרי "white meal" for חרייונים, regarding the remainder of the word in MT as a dittography of שמנים.[38] Klostermann suggests חַרְצַנִּים "sour wine."[39] De Vaux vocalizes *ḥarṣōnîm*, which he takes as a reference to the "star of Bethlehem," a bulbous lily (*ornithogalum*) or "wild onion," as he renders it, the tuber of which might have been eaten by the poor.[40] Cheyne reads חֲרוּבִים "carob pods."[41]

A non-food item

In the second category Josephus (*Ant* 9.62) posits that dove excrement served as a substitute for salt. Similarly, Qimḥi (RaDaK) suggested that it served as fuel for fire.[42]

---

34 The exception was P. Bordreuil and J. Teixidor, "Nouvel examen de l'inscription de Bar-Hadad," *Aula Orientalis* 1 (1983): 271–76.

35 Pitard, "Identity of the Bir-Hadad."

36 Émile Puech,"La stele de Bar-Hadad à Melqart et le rois d'Arpad," *RB* 99 (1992): 311–34.

37 *Life of Artaxerxes* 24.2. In a similar vein Pliny the Elder, *The Natural History* viii.82 (57) refers to a siege by Hannibal during which the price of a mouse rose to 200 denarii. Winckler's proposal to read חמר תירוש, "a homer of new wine," instead of ראש־חמור, is often noted but rarely adopted, though Šanda, (*Könige* II, 54) accepts it.

38 Cited by Šanda, (*Könige* II, 54).

39 Klostermann, *Könige*, 410.

40 De Vaux, *Rois*, 145. So also A. Vaccari, "Scrittura fenicia-samaritana nella Bibbia ebraica," *Bib* 19 (1938), 198–99.

41 T. K. Cheyne, "Something Better than Husks," *Expositor* 10 (1899): 32–35.

42 Rosenberg, *Kings II*, 284.

Apart from the context, which is focused on food because of the famine, these proposals face other problems. Buying salt in the middle of a famine when food was in such short supply would be of minimal interest, so that it is an unrealistic illustration of the severity of the famine. A fire with one-half to one cup of dry doves' dung would be quite small and short-lived, and the problem was not a lack of things to burn in Samaria but a lack of things to cook.

An idiom

The third kind of interpretation takes *doves' dung* as a popular name for a common food item such as chick peas. This idea goes back to Samuel Bochart's *Hierozoicon* of 1663 (par. 2. l. 1. c. 7. col. 44). Bochart cited the Arabic name *ḥarwu 'al 'aṣāfir* "sparrows' dung," used for the herb *kali* as an analogy. Other scholars mention that in Arabic "doves' dung" (*ḥara' 'al ḥamām*) is used as a popular name for a plant.[43] Cogan and Tadmor cite an Akkadian lexical text of plants in which *ḫalla/zē summāti*, "dove's dung," is defined as *zēr ašāgi* = *ḫarūbu*, "the seed of the (false) carob," and understand *doves' dung* to be the popular name for (usually) inedible husks. Like the literal interpretation of the expression, this one nicely parallels *donkey's head* in describing an exorbitant price for a typically inedible item now being sold as food. It thus has the advantages of Cheyne's proposal without resorting to emendation, since the context and the parallel with the donkey's head indicate that doves' dung referred to some item not usually eaten but being consumed under the duress of the siege.

The interpolation in 6:26b-30

The anecdote about the woman in 6:26b-30a is an interpolation by *Wiederaufnahme* (ויהי מלך ישראל עבר על־החמה ... והוא עבר על־החמה).[44] This is evident in v. 30, where the statement that the people noticed the king's sackcloth does not follow directly after the statement about him tearing his clothes, as one would expect, but after the resumption that he was passing in review on the wall. Initially the people noticed the king's sackcloth because he was walking on the wall rather than because he tore his outer garments. The king's encounter with this woman impels him to go to Elisha's house to seek his counsel. The cannibalism vividly illustrated by the story is a *topos* (Deut 28:52-57), but it may also have been a very real part of siege warfare. The story recalls the anecdote about the two prostitutes meant to illustrate Solomon's wisdom (1 Kgs 3:16-28) and is possibly an adaptation of it. In each case there are two women and their two small sons, one of whom has died; the complainant is the one without the child who alleges that the living child in some sense belongs to her and that her peer has him as the result of deception. Nevertheless, the differences are telling. Although the language of appeal (*Help, oh my lord king!*) and the airing and hearing of the complaint reflect a legal process, the setting of the anecdote in the present passage, unlike the Solomon story, is not a legal one. The form has been removed from its proper *Sitz im Leben* for a narrative purpose. The lack of detail in the present story over against the other one is also striking. In the Solomon version the two women are both present along with the living son. Both are identified as prostitutes who share a house. The specifics are helpful for understanding the circumstances that lead to the complaint. Here, by contrast, it is not clear whether the accused is present, or how the two women know each other, or how they came to their bargain. The reader must assume the setting of the Solomon story or something like it to make sense of this story. Above all, the king in 2 Kings 6 renders no judgment. The story thus does not illustrate the king's wisdom or sense of justice as it does for Solomon, but rather his

43 Gray, *Kings*, 518n.

44 This interpolation is overlooked by the redaction-critical treatments of Schmitt (Elisa, 37–41), Würthwein, *1. Könige 17–2. Könige 25*, 307–16, and Sauerwein, *Elischa*, 72–79.

impotence and the desperation of his people, which in turn move him to consult Elisha. In the present story the king's penitence as exhibited by his sackcloth plays no role. In the older *legenda*, though, his contrition was both a sign of the desperate nature of the city's predicament (even the king was affected) and a factor in his favor that evoked Elisha's positive oracle.[45]

PN's addition in v. 27

Within the interpolation in 6:26b-30a, v. 27 signals itself as an addition by the repetition of ויאמר in v. 28 without a change in speaker.[46] Also, the proper response to the woman's cry for justice in v. 26 is the king's inquiry as to the nature of her problem (מה־לך) in v. 28 rather than the king's expression of impotence and frustration with YHWH in v. 27. This inquiry then introduces the case she brings before him in vv. 28-29. The addition plays on ישע, which is the verb in the woman's outcry. It is used to request legal help (cf. 2 Sam 14:4) but is more common in the HB (e.g., Judges) as a cry for military salvation or victory over an enemy. Either sense (or both) is appropriate here. The king's response has been rendered in four ways: (1) Taking אל־יושעך יהוה as the protasis of a conditional sentence (see the Note); (2) emending אל to אם לא to produce the protasis of a conditional sentence; (3) as a straightforward refusal followed by a dismissive wish for YHWH's salvation: "No! Let YHWH save you"; (4) as a curse or an oath ("May YHWH not save you") spoken by the angry king.[47] The fourth option reads into the text and is unlikely. For the meaning proposed in (3), one would normally expect the negative לא rather than אל; it also requires a change in the Masoretic vocalization.[48] In any case, with the following question, "How can I save you?" its sense is not much different from the first two possibilities, which are identical in meaning. The king's blaming of YHWH contrasts with the view of the king in v. 20b as penitently wearing sackcloth. The tension is even sharper between vv. 30 and 31, where the king blames Elisha and swears to kill him, suggesting that vv. 27 and 31 come from the same writer.[49] His oath to have Elisha beheaded (6:31) resembles Jezebel's oath to kill Elijah in 1 Kgs 19:2. Both use the same oath formula and both swear to kill the prophet within a day (Jezebel: *by this time tomorrow*; here: *today*). The messenger sent by the king and anticipated by Elisha in 6:32 is like the messenger sent by Jezebel to Elijah in 1 Kgs 19:2; in both cases the messenger plays no further role.

6:32a–7:1: The continuation of the *legenda* and PN's additions

The *legenda* continued from v. 30b to v. 32a and the scene switches to Elisha's house, where he is meeting with the city elders. They are still conversing when the king, moved by what he saw in his review of the city, comes to him (v. 33a). The use of the pronominal phrase *with them* in v. 33a attests proximity to 6:32a. Then in 7:1 Elisha delivers his prophecy about the reversal of food prices (and availability). The scene at this level is one of respect for Elisha. Both the king and

---

45 Cf. Schmitt, *Elias*, 39.

46 See Trebolle, *Centena*, 171–72.

47 de Vaux, *Rois*, 145–46.

48 A *Rebîa'* should appear over אל as in 2 Kgs 3:13.

49 The reason for the king's animosity toward Elisha is unspecified (see Schmitt, *Elisa*, 39n). The proposal that Elisha was calling for resistance finds no support in the text. Neither does the notion that Elisha had called for the drought. Schmitt concludes that the writer simply blames the king for not trusting god. Seow (*Kings*, 204) asserts the similar idea that the king wants to make Elisha the scapegoat. If the story in 6:8-23, where Elisha released the Aramaean army, is assumed (see Synchronic Analysis), the king's animosity would presuppose the joining of 6:8-23 with 6:24–7:20*.

the elders go to him rather than the reverse, and both consult him as a resource for how to deal with the siege and the famine. The supplements in 6:32b, 33b reflect an entirely different attitude. In 6:32b the king follows up on his oath in 6:31 by sending someone to behead Elisha. Elisha calls the king a *murderer*, using the same verb employed by Elijah in his accusation of Ahab in 1 Kgs 21:19. The verse is confusing not only because of the different perspective on the king but also because of the change in terms within it from *man* to *messenger* and because of the similarity of מלאך to מלך. In addition, the messenger turns out to be only a transition to the king's arrival, so that Elisha's concern to keep him out is not pursued beyond this point. The confusion is further exacerbated by the king's complaint in 6:33b,[50] which makes essentially the same point as v. 27 but in starker terms—the king no longer has hope in YHWH (see the Note). His reproaches of YHWH remind one of the desperation and complaint of the king of Israel in 3:10.

7:1: The references to YHWH and the prices

The fact that the references to YHWH elsewhere in this passage are secondary (6:27, 33b; 7:2, 6, 16, 19) is reason to take them as secondary in Elisha's prediction in 7:1. This fits with the other prophetic *legenda* we have treated in which the integration of YHWH is typically PN's supplement. As in other *legenda*, the prediction comes from Elisha as the holy man. His prophecy is couched in economic terms. The phrase *in the gate of Samaria* refers to market price based on the practice of vending at or near the city gate.[51] Unfortunately, it is not known how the prices here compare with those before the siege. They may still have been higher than normal.[52] The city was barely out from under the siege and the entire region around it would have been plundered by the invading army, so a higher price would be reasonable. Then again, higher-than-usual prices would mean that only the matter of food scarcity mentioned in 6:25 was addressed but not that of elevated prices. The radical change presumed by Elisha's prophecy would seem to indicate that the new prices were equal to or lower than before.

7:2: The *šālîš* and his doubt

The demurral of the adjutant (שליש) in 7:2 is an addition. He is a new character,[53] presented with the title "the one on whose arm the king leaned," as though his presence with the king were assumed. The derivation and exact role of the *šālîš* remain elusive despite a number of proposals; a reasonable hypothesis is that the title referred to an officer "of the third rank," i.e., below the king and senior officers, who was attached to the king's person but whose official duties remain obscure.[54] He is evidently a high court official, the king's "right-hand man" or chief advisor. The adjutant expresses his disbelief with a rhetorical question: "Even if YHWH opened the windows in heaven, could such a thing happen?" The image alluded to is *not* that of god

---

50 Hobbs (*2 Kings*, 81–82) even takes the complaint as Elisha's.

51 Cogan and Tadmor, *II Kings*, 81.

52 Šanda (*Könige* II, 59–60) points to the Mishnah (*Eruvin* 8.2) as putting the price of barley at a shekel for four *seahs* or half the price named here. Cogan and Tadmor (*II Kings*, 81) suggest on the basis of Babylonian evidence that the normal price may have been many times less.

53 *Pace* Sauerwein (Elischa, 75), who considers him the same as the *man* and the *messenger*.

54 This is the conclusion of Mastin, "Was the *ŠĀLÎŠ* the Third Man in the Chariot?"), who provides a useful overview of the term and critique of the older theory that the title referred to the third man in a chariot. Contrast C. Rabin ("Hittite Words in Hebrew," *Or* 32 [1963], 133), who argues that the *šālîš* was a fairly low official.

handing down bounty from heavenly storehouses, which ignores the mythological background of the allusion.[55] It is, rather, to YHWH opening the sluices of heaven that hold back the cosmic waters above the earth, as in Gen 7:11; 8:2; Mal 3:10. The image has been taken as indicating that the source of the famine in 6:25 was originally drought rather than siege, but since 7:2 is secondary this interpretation is unfeasible. The skeptical question implies that even with abundant rainfall the famine could not be reversed within a day as Elisha forecast. It reflects animosity toward Elisha and vice-versa, as is clear from Elisha's response in v. 2b, which bodes ill for the adjutant, whose death is recounted in an interpolation in v. 17.

7:3-5: The decision of the skin-diseased men

The deliverance of the city *per se* in 7:3-16a* goes back to the *legenda*. The *skin disease* of the four men was not leprosy (v. 3), as explained in ch. 5, but some unknown malady perhaps closer to psoriasis, eczema, or a fungus infection. The portrait of the men is more consistent with the perspectives on skin disease in other biblical texts than was the case in the Naaman story. The men live outside of the city, away from social intercourse with most of their fellow Israelites. This makes them the perfect candidates for discovering that the Aramaeans have fled. They go to the camp as a last resort before starvation, figuring that at worst a quick death at Aramaean hands would be better than a slow one by starvation (v. 4).

7:6-8a: The deserted Aramaean camp

The explanation for the deserted camp in vv. 6-8a is another addition.[56] As Trebolle observes, v. 5a with its reference to twilight is part of the addition. In the *legenda* the empty Aramaean camp was unexplained except as the means to fulfilling Elisha's prophecy in v. 1.[57] The addition explains that YHWH induced a panic in the Aramaeans from noises they identified as the combined army of the *kings of the Hittites and the kings of the Egyptians*. The reference to these two great second millennium empires is ill suited to the ninth-century setting of this story. It has been explained by positing that *Hittites* refers not to the twelfth-century Neo-Hittite Anatolian power but to small Aramaean states that retained the name,[58] or by echoing Winckler's proposal that *Miṣrayim* (*Egypt*) be read or understood as referring to the northern Anatolian kingdom of Musri.[59] However, as early as 1961 Tadmor argued forcefully that evidence for the existence of Musri as a kingdom is wanting.[60] The reference

55 Pace Provan, *Kings*, 203.

56 Würthwein (*1. Könige 17–2. Könige 25*, 308, 315–16), Sauerwein (*Elischa*, 75), Trebolle (*Centena*, 172–73).

57 Würthwein, *1. Könige 17–2. Könige 25*, 314): "Die alte Komposition nennt weder einen Grund für die Belagerung noch einen Grund für die Befreiung." (The old composition does not give a reason for the siege or a reason for the liberation.)

58 Buis, *Rois*, 207.

59 Winckler, *Alttestamentliche Untersuchungen*, 170–72.

60 H. Tadmor, "Que and Muṣri," *IEJ* 11 (1961): 143–50. N. Na'aman ("Looking for KTK," *WdO* 9 [1978], 225) put it more starkly, calling the Anatolian Musri "nothing but a scholarly fiction, entirely baseless." See also the more cautious discussion of P. Garelli ("Nouveau coup d'oeil sur Muṣur," in *Hommages a André Dupont-Sommer* [ed. A. Caquot and M. Philonenco; Paris: Librairie Adrien Maisonneuve, 1971]: 37–48) who also ultimately acquiesces to Tadmor's conclusion that "every reference in the Assyrian records to a foreign country *Muṣri/Muṣur* from the tenth century B.C. onwards should be taken as referring exclusively to Egypt." The existence of such a Musri seems to have been perpetuated mostly by biblical scholars trying to explain this passage and 1 Kgs 10:29.

to Hittites and Egyptians is rather "an old literary image, of little value for historical purposes."[61]

These verses continue the *legenda* that PN interrupted with v. 5a, 6-8a. The four men enjoy their discovery—eating, drinking, taking plunder to hide and then moving to another tent—before they begin to fear that keeping the secret much longer will bring *guilt* upon them (7:9). The *guilt* they fear is more than an abstract value; it is something approximating a tangible entity that attaches to a person and can only be expiated by the person's death.[62] They decide, therefore, to return to the city and make their discovery known. This they do, and the word reaches the king, who arises in the middle of the night to deal with the matter (7:10-12aα). The king suspects a ruse on the part of the Aramaeans. His advisors come up with a plan to test the veracity of the report; they propose sending out five of the remaining horses. As suggested in the Synchronic Analysis, this may be a round number for a small quantity ("a handful"). Following the Greek reading in v. 14, only two mounted riders are sent. This makes more sense from a practical point of view than the MT reading *chariots*, since individual horses would be quicker and easier to maneuver than chariots and thus better suited to the purposes of scouts.[63] The two riders follow the Aramaeans' trail all the way to the Jordan, noting that it is littered with items, including weapons discarded in their haste to flee (v. 15).

7:8b-15: The deserted Aramaean camp

The report of the starving residents of Samaria rushing out of the city to plunder the Aramaean camp as soon as they receive the news (v. 16*) fulfilled Elisha's prophecy in the *legenda*. It was, however, revised in two particulars. First, YHWH's name has been added, in accord with the editing of v. 1 that turned Elisha's prophecy into an oracle from YHWH. This revision has been obscured in MT by the loss of the last three words of the verse (אשר דבר אלישע), which are preserved in G^L (see the Notes). MT's loss may have been occasioned by the second revision, which was the interpolation of v. 17abα. Thus the fulfilment notice of the *legenda* in v. 16 told of the new prices for flour and barley *according to the word which [Elisha] had spoken when the king came down to him* (v. 17bβ), corresponding to the setting described in 6:32a of Elisha sitting with the elders in his house. The abundance of grain found in the Aramaean camp shows that the cause of the famine in Samaria in the *legenda* was siege rather than drought.

7:16: The plundering of the Aramaean camp as prophesied

Verse 17abα fulfills Elisha's secondary prophecy about the skeptical adjutant in v. 2b. Verses 18-20 are supplementary.[64] The sudden surplus of food triggers a

7:17-20: The end of the story and a reiteration of it

61 H. Gunkel, *Geschichten von Elisa* (Meisterwerke hebräischer Erzählungskunst 1; Berlin: Karl Curtius, 1924), 59.

62 K. Koch, "עוון," *TDOT* 10:550–51.

63 This assumes that the scouts would be adept at riding horseback. See Cantrell (*Horsemen of Israel*), who argues that the transition from chariot to mounted combat took place in Israel from the 9th–7th centuries (p. 139). However, this does not preclude all horseback riding in the 9th century, especially since there is contemporary evidence of mounted warriors from other parts of the ANE. What is more, horseback riders were more common by the time of the Jehu dynasty, when this level of the story probably originated.

64 There is no evidence for Šanda's creative surmise (*Könige* II, 62) that the people in effect lynch the adjutant in order to provide a fulfillment to Elisha's oracle because the prophet is the hero of the day.

riot, and the adjutant, whom the king had appointed to control the gate and probably its traffic, is trampled to death. His trampling in a sense plays out in reverse the king's attempt to behead Elisha. The entire episode involving the adjutant—both the prediction against him and its fulfillment—are rehearsed in vv. 18-20. They are pedantic and probably derive from a marginal gloss.

Synthesis

The *legenda* about Elisha's salvation of Samaria

The story in 2 Kgs 6:24–7:20 began as a prophetic *legenda* about Elisha in which he effectively delivered Samaria from an Aramaean siege and the near starvation it caused. The portrait of the king of Israel and the identification of the Aramaean king as Ben-Hadad son of Hazael locate the *legenda* in the Jehuid dynasty during the early eighth century. Typically, Elisha acts unilaterally without any explicit mention of YHWH.

PN's revision

PN supplemented the *legenda*, interpolating a separate anecdote about the women cannibals (6:26b-30a*) and an explanation for the empty Aramaean camp (7:6-7). Above all, he brought YHWH into the story, crediting him with the rout of the Aramaeans and the series of prophecies and fulfillments. PN identified the king as the Omrid Joram and presented him in negative terms as faithless and a murderer. PN's changes turned Elisha into a judgment prophet rather than a wonder worker. The miraculous defeat of the Aramaeans was accomplished by YHWH's word, for which Elisha was only the spokesman.

Two Stories about Elisha (2 Kings 8:1-15)

Text

[Prophetic legenda; *PN]*
1 Elisha had spoken to the woman *whose son he restored to life,* "Get up and
leave, you and your household, and sojourn wherever you can, because *Yhwh*
has called for famine *that* is coming on the land for seven years." 2 So the
woman arose and went according to the word of the man of god to the land of
the Philistines for seven years. 3 At the end of seven years when the woman re-
turned from the land of the Philistines, she went to appeal to the king for her
house and her land. 4 *The king had been speaking to Gehazi the servant of the*
man of god, saying "Tell me all the great things that Elisha has done." 5 *And as*
[Gehazi] was recounting for the king how [Elisha] had restored the dead boy to
life, the woman whose son he had revived came appealing to the king for her
house and her land. Gehazi said, "My lord king, this is the woman and this is her
son whom Elisha restored to life!" 6 When the king asked her, she recounted the
story. Then the king assigned an official to her, instructing him, "Restore all that
belongs to her, *and the revenue of the land from the day she left the land until*
now."
7 When Elisha came to Damascus, Ben-Hadad king of Aram, who was sick, was
told, "The man of god has come here." 8 The king said to Hazael, "Take a gift
with you and go meet the man of god to make inquiry of YHWH from him
whether I will recover from this illness of mine." 9 So Hazael went to meet him,
taking a gift with him—*40 camels loaded with all the goods of Damascus.* Arriv-
ing, he stood before him and said, "Your son Ben-Hadad, king of Damascus, has
sent me to you to ask, "Will I recover from this illness?" 10 Elisha said to him,
"Go tell him, 'You will indeed recover,' *although Yhwh has shown me that he*
will in fact die." 11 *[Hazael] stood in front of him and set gifts before him until he*
was ashamed. When the man of god wept, 12 *Hazael said, "Why is my lord weep-*
ing?" He said, "Because I know what you will do to the Israelites: Their fortifica-
tions you will set on fire; their young men you will kill by the sword; their children
you will dash in pieces, and their pregnant women you will rip open." 13 *Hazael re-*
plied, "What is your servant, the dog, that he should do such a thing?" Elisha an-
swered, "Yhwh has shown me that you will reign over Aram." 14 When he left Eli-
sha he came to his master, who asked him, "What did Elisha say to you?" He
answered, "You will certainly live." 15 But the next day, he took the coverlet
and, dipping it in water, he spread it over [Ben-Hadad's] face until he died. Then
Hazael reigned in his place.

Textual Notes

1 **you**: Reading the *ketiv.* (אתי), a genuine or affected Northern form as in ch. 4.
and your household: So MT, G^{B}, 6QpapKgs15 (spatial considerations). G^{L}: *your son and your household* (= ובנך וביתך) as in v. 2.
wherever you can: So MT (באשר תגורי), G^{B} (οὗ ἐὰν παροικήσῃς). G^{L}: οὗ ἐὰν εὕρῃς ἐκεῖ = באשר תמצאי שם is also possible. The *idem per idem* construction gives a nuance of indeterminateness to the prophet's order.[1] The verb גור means to live abroad as a resident alien, i.e., without citizen's rights, with the intent of returning home.
famine: So MT (לרעב), 6QpapKgs15. G^{BL} + *on the land.* The use of ל for the direct object occurs mostly in late texts (Isa 53:11; 61:1; Jer 40:2; Pss 69:6[ET 5]; 86:9; Job 19:28). It may be an Aramaism (GKC 117n) or dialectal.
on the land: So 6QpapKgs15, G^{BL} (ἐπὶ τὴν γῆν). MT: אל־הארץ.

2 **So the woman arose and went according to the word of the man of god to the land of the Philistines for seven years**: So 6QpapKgs15, which attests a more succinct reading than MT, G^{BL}.[2]

3 **At the end of seven years**: So MT, G^{B}. Lacking in 6QpapKgs15 (reconstructed) as the result of haplography after *seven years* at the end of v. 2. G^{L} + *of the famine.*
Philistines: So MT, G^{L}. G^{B} + *to the city.*
she went to appeal: So G^{L}: καὶ ἦλθεν βοῆσαι = ותבא לצעק. MT, G^{B}: ותצא לצעק. 6QpapKgs15: ותבא אל העיר The witnesses attest two sets of variants: ותצא/ותבא and לצעק/אל העיר.
for her house and her land: So G^{BL} (περὶ τοῦ οἴκου ἑαυτῆς καὶ περὶ τῶν ἀγρῶν ἑαυτῆς) reflecting the preposition על twice where MT and 6QpapKgs15 have אל.

4 **the man of god**: So MT. 6QpapKgs15: *Elisha.* G^{BL} conflate the two. Syr has the prophet's name under obelus, indicating that it was absent from the OG.
Tell me: So MT. 6QpapKgs15 has the shorter form of the imperative: ספר.

5 **the dead boy**: So MT: lit., *him that was dead* (את־המת), which effectively requires a noun in English. Similarly, G^{B} (υἱὸν τεθνηκότα) and G^{L} (τὸν υἱὸν αὐτῆς τὸν τεθνηκότα) supply one.
for her house and her land: As in v. 4, MT twice uses the preposition אל where G^{BL} reflect על.

6 **When the king asked her**: So G^{L}. MT, G^{B}: *when the king asked the woman.*
she recounted the story: Lit. *she recounted to him.* So MT, G^{B}. G^{L}: *the woman told the king everything.*
an official: See the Note on 1 Kgs 22:9. Since the Shunammite is unaccompanied by a man, this official may have been a eunuch.
the revenue: So G^{B}. MT, G^{L} have *all the revenue.*
of the land: So MT, G^{B}. G^{L}: *of her lands.*
she left: Construing עזבה as an infinitive construct with feminine suffix (ה-) rather than a third person feminine perfect, since *day* is indefinite (מיום).

8 **from this illness of mine**: So G^{BL}. See the Note on 1:2.

9 **40 camels loaded with all the goods of Damascus**: So MT (וכל־טוב דמשק משא ארבעים גמל). G^{B} (καὶ πάντα τὰ ἀγαθὰ Δαμασκοῦ ἄρσιν τεσσαράκοντα καμήλων δῶρα) essentially agrees except for *a gift* at the end. G^{L} is only slightly different: *from all the good things of Damascus a load of 40 camels.* The *waw* before כל is explicative, i.e., *consisting of.*

10 **tell him**: The *ketiv* reads לא instead of לו, yielding *you will not recover* instead of *you will indeed recover,* which may reflect an early effort to keep Elisha from engineering a lie.

---

1 Joüon 158o; cf. S. R. Driver, *Tenses*, 38B.
2 Ulrich, *Biblical Qumran Scrolls*, 329.

although YHWH has shown me that he will in fact die: So MT and G^B. G^L: *although he will in fact die as YHWH has shown me.*

11 **[Hazael] stood in front of him and set gifts before him**: So G^L: καὶ ἔστr Αζαηλ κατὰ πρόσωπον αὐτοῦ καὶ παρέθηκεν ἐνώπιον αὐτοῦ τὰ δῶρα. This reading explains the verb וישם, which is problematic in MT because it lacks an object. It also explains the reason for Elisha's shame—i.e., the embarrassment of riches being set before him.

12 **what you will do to the Israelites**: So G^L, which reads the pronoun you (אתה) where MT and G^B have *evil* (רעה). Joüon (127b) refers to the construction in MT as an "attributive accusative of limitation," i.e., "what you will do to the Israelites in regard to evil/destruction." But the placement is awkward, and reading with G^L avoids it.

fortifications: So MT, G^B. G^L: *fortified cities.*

13 **What is your servant**: So G^{BL}. MT precedes with כי, probably in anticipation of the particle later in the verse. But see Joüon 157c; WO, 172.

the dog: So MT. G^{BL}: *the dead dog.*

that he should do: So MT, G^B. G^L has the first person. Either is possible.

such a thing: Lit: *this thing.* So G^B. MT, G^L: *this great thing.*

that you will reign over Aram: Vocalizing מלך as a participle with G^{BL}. MT has the noun *king*: perhaps *YHWH has shown me you (as) king over Aram.* See Joüon 126c.

14 **You will certainly live**: The preceding clause, *he told me*, is marked in Syr as hexaplaric.

15 **in his place**: So MT, G^B. G^L + *over Aram.*

Synchronic Analysis

These verses contain two stories (vv. 1-6, 7-15) that have little in common apart from the character of Elisha, who is not even physically present in the first story. One may surmise that Elisha is absent from vv. 1-6 because he is on his way to Damascus, where the story in vv. 7-15 takes place. There is no notice of his departure in v. 1, only of his arrival in Damascus in v. 7. Like his mentor, Elijah, Elisha has a tendency to disappear unpredictably.

Two stories connected by Elisha

The new story is introduced in v. 1 with a subject-first construction, ואלישע דבר. The verb is pluperfect, referring to a conversation seven years earlier in which Elisha had advised the woman to leave her home in advance of an impending famine. The verb בא in the last clause of the verse is ambiguous. It may be taken as a participle with the sense that the famine is about to begin on the land or as a perfect meaning that it has begun and will last for seven years. If the latter it could be understood as the same famine mentioned in 4:38 that may have been a contributing factor to the starvation of Samaria in 6:24–7:20. The famine seems to be restricted to *the land* of Israel, since Elisha encourages the woman to *sojourn* where she can, a word referring to status as a resident alien, and she ends up in the *land of the Philistines* on the southern coastal plain. The duration of the famine—seven years—may be literal or symbolic of an extended time period. The lengthy time accounts for the loss of property the woman suffers in her absence. She is identified as the Shunammite from 4:8-37 by the notice that Elisha had restored her son to life (8:1). *Her household* (8:2) evidently refers to her husband and son, since 4:8-37 does not mention any other children or family members. It is striking that she is depicted as the leader of her family; as in ch. 4, her husband is passive—so much so that he is not explicitly mentioned here.

8:1-2: Sequel to 4:8-37

8:3-6: The woman's case preempted

Verse 3 jumps to the end of the famine, the present time from the standpoint of the narrative. The woman complied with the prophet's instructions and has returned home. There is no reference to her household this time; v. 5 mentions only her son. Her husband probably died in the intervening seven years, not surprising since he was already old in ch. 4. This makes the story reminiscent of the book of Ruth and the Shunammite like Naomi. The husband's absence makes no difference in the story since he was barely present anyway. She was always the one who took the initiative. Her property has been confiscated or seized, but no details are forthcoming. If it was relatives who seized the land, the ties with her clan or her husband's whose stability she affirmed in 4:13-14 may now be the source of her problems. The narrative is unconcerned with the legalities behind the loss. Its interest is in Elisha's role in getting it back. In so doing it shortchanges the woman. She is quite capable and independent. She does not appeal to Elisha to intercede for her, though he made the offer to do so in 4:13. Instead, she goes straight to the king. Her chance of success does not appear good; she has been gone a long time and is now alone. Why should the king heed the case of one nameless petitioner (no doubt among many)? But she does not get a chance to prove herself because the men preempt her. Gehazi happens to be there filling the king in on the *great things* that Elisha has done (v. 4). Just as he is telling about Elisha's bringing her son back to life, the very woman and her son show up (v. 5). As the narrative presents it, this is a serendipity. The participles in vv. 4-5 emphasize the simultaneity of the action: as Gehazi is relating (מספר) Elisha's greatest miracle, the woman raises her petition (צעקת). The change to direct speech with Gehazi as the speaker in v. 5b signals the good timing. The implication is that this is YHWH's doing. Perhaps so. But it also means that the woman has no chance to plead her case or to receive justice on its merits. The king's question in v. 6 is not about her case but about Elisha's miracle with her son. The decision is rendered on the basis of an ancient "good-old boys" network. To be sure, the decision works to the Shunammite's benefit. Not only does she receive her property back but also the income from it for the entire period she was away. Still, this is all because of Elisha, not because of her. There is even condescension in the king's implementation of the decision. He hands it off to an official, a eunuch, whose liminal sexual status makes him more suitable than a "real" man for seeing to the needs of the woman, whose name we still do not learn.

8:7-8: An inquiry from Ben-Hadad

The second story combines two motifs or genres around the matter of Ben-Hadad's death: the consultation of a prophet about illness (vv. 7-10) and the investiture of a king by a prophet (vv. 11-15).[3] Elisha appears not as a miracle worker but as a seer who foresees the future and also is able to look into the thoughts and intentions of other people. The story begins with the notice of Elisha's arrival in Damascus at a time when Ben-Hadad the king of Aram was ill (v. 7). No explicit connection is drawn between the two, but coincidence does not exist where YHWH is in meticulous control. Informed of the man of god's presence, Ben-Hadad dispatches Hazael with a gift to inquire of YHWH whether he will recover (v. 8). Elisha's reputation thus precedes him, evidently because of previous encounters with Aramaeans in chs. 5 and 6:8-23. Ben-Hadad's question to Elisha (8:8) is essen-

---

3 Buis, *Rois,* 208.

tially the same as that of Ahaziah in 1:2. Both use the verb *dāraš* in the sense of making inquiry of a deity. Both kings want to know whether they will recover from their respective infirmities. Ironically, the king of Aram turns to YHWH through the Israelite man of god, while the Israelite king sends to the Philistine Baal Zebul.

8:9: Hazael brings gifts

There is no introduction of Hazael. He is obviously a close and trusted personal attendant to the king. Although the title is not used for him he seems comparable to the official on whose arm the king leans (5:18; 7:2, 17). Hazael appears to discharge his duty faithfully. A gift for the prophet is customary, as we have seen, but forty camel loads of Damascus's finest is extravagant (v. 9). The enormous quantity may be intended to influence the outcome of the inquiry (compare Mic 3:5), or it may reflect great esteem for Elisha. It may even be that the gift is Hazael's rather than Ben-Hadad's, because he is already planning to overthrow his master and seeks Elisha's help.[4] Ben-Hadad refers to himself as Elisha's son, at once elevating Elisha's status to that of royalty and articulating his own subservience.

8:10: Elisha's ambiguous response

As is typical of oracles, Elisha's response (v. 10) is ambiguous. As written (*ketiv*) it tells Hazael to assure Ben-Hadad that he will live, even though YHWH has shown Elisha that Ben-Hadad will die. Does this mean that the disease will prove fatal after all, despite the message to Ben-Hadad that he will "surely live?" If so, then Elisha is directing Hazael to lie. He is also giving Hazael advance warning to prepare to usurp power. Alternatively, Elisha may be saying that Ben-Hadad will survive the illness only to die from another cause. In this case Elisha is either predicting that Hazael will assassinate his lord or moving him to do so. Then there is the question of YHWH's involvement. Elisha reports what YHWH has shown him. This may mean that Elisha, as a seer, has seen a vision. On the other hand, the verb "see" may have the sense of "know," such that YHWH has led Elisha to understand or realize that Ben-Hadad will die. Either way, this brings another element of ambiguity into the mix. Is Hazael's accession ordained by YHWH, as 10:32; 13:2 imply, or is it Hazael's own doing, though with YHWH's and Elisha's foreknowledge?

8:11-12: Elisha's glimpse of Hazael's future

With these words Elisha fixes his look in a stare at Hazael. This is, at any rate, the apparent meaning of v. 11a. The first clause (ויעמד את־פניו) *he fixed* [*Hip'îl*] *his face* is clear enough. The sense of וישם (*he set, placed*) without an object is less evident but is usually understood to refer to setting the eyes in a stare. The subject of both verbs is probably the same, and it is probably Elisha. He delivers his oracle, including the revelation that Ben-Hadad will die, and then peers intently at Hazael, as YHWH reveals to him the true nature of the man before him (v. 13b). There is also ambiguity in the next clause, עד־בש, about who is ashamed. If the two previous verbs are attributed to Elisha, then Hazael is probably the one who withers in shame at Elisha's penetrating stare. What Elisha perceives about Hazael leads him to weep (v. 11b). When Hazael asks him why, he replies with a litany of war-related atrocities (v. 12) that he knows Hazael will perpetrate against Israel. His knowledge is presumably by virtue of his ability as a man of god to foresee the future, and it can easily be perceived as a mandate to seize the throne.

---

4 Cohn (*2 Kings*, 60). Cohn does not actually explain what he thinks is Hazael's motive for the gift.

8:13: You will be king of Aram

Hazael is incredulous, assuming his response in v. 13 is sincere. He is portrayed as naïve and ambitionless as concerns his future kingship. He does not hide his hatred for Israel, referring to the atrocities Elisha has just mentioned as a *great thing.* In quoting him the text does not hide its contempt for him and its view of him as morally bankrupt in that he would laud such activities as dashing suckling infants to pieces and cutting open pregnant women. The *great thing* contrasts with and balances the *great things* (הגדלות) done by Elisha (v. 4).[5] Elisha's deeds are salvific and beneficial for the most part; Hazael's idea of great deeds is genocide. Hazael describes himself as powerless—as powerless as a lowly *dog.* But the savvy reader suspects disingenuousness—a false modesty masking a *dog* that lacks human empathy and is capable of savagery. Elisha cuts through Hazael's surprise—whether feigned or genuine—and announces plainly that he is to be king of Aram (v. 13b).

8:14-15: Hazael ascends to the throne of Aram

Hazael's report to his master and the aftermath in vv. 14-15 correspond to vv. 9-13:[6]

So Hazael went to meet him (v. 9)	[Hazael] went from (וילך מאת) Elisha (v. 14)
He came and stood before him [Elisha] (v. 9)	he came to his master (v. 14)
He said, "Your son Ben-Hadad, king of Damascus, has sent me to you to ask, "Will I recover from this illness?" (v. 9)	who asked him, "What did Elisha say to you?" (v. 14)
Elisha said, "Go tell him, 'You will indeed recover," (v. 10)	He answered, "You will certainly live." (v. 14)
although_YHWH has shown me that he will in fact die." (v. 10)	But the next day, he took the coverlet and dipping it in water, he spread it over [Ben-Hadad's] face until he died. (v. 15)
Elisha answered, "YHWH has shown me that you will reign over Aram" (v. 13).	Then Hazael reigned in his place (v. 15).

Hazael follows Elisha's instructions, telling Ben-Hadad that he will live. The course of the narrative that follows in v. 15 is unclear on several counts. There are three verbs in quick succession: *he took, he dipped*, and *he spread.* The three almost certainly have the same subject, but that subject is unspecified. It is usually understood to be Hazael, but the subject may be impersonal, referring to an unnamed person or even Ben-Hadad himself. This relates to the intent behind dampening the coverlet and placing it over the king's face, and more important, to the connection between this act and Ben-Hadad's death. Again the most common interpretation, and one that goes back at least to Josephus (*Ant* 9.92), is that the coverlet was used as a murder weapon and dampened to facilitate the king's suffocation. However, it may have been a means of relieving the king's fever[7] or used as a

5 Long, *1 & 2 Kings*, 348.

6 Hobbs, *2 Kings*, 98–99.

7 Šanda, *Könige* II, 70.

bed screen or mosquito netting that also served for air conditioning.[8] In this interpretation a servant came to refresh the netting by wetting it and replacing it and in so doing discovered the king dead. Since the exact nature of the מכבר, a *hapax legomenon*, is unknown, it does not help with the interpretational quandary; it could refer to either a coverlet or a net.[9] However, the murder interpretation can be defended on two grounds. The first is narrative coherence. If Ben-Hadad's death was due to illness there is no reason for the ruse in v. 10 or the detailed description in v. 15. The reader is led to seek some cause-effect relationship between Elisha's instructions to Hazael to lie to his master and the cause of the master's death, especially when Hazael had so much to gain and the circumstances surrounding Ben-Hadad's death raise the specter of foul play. The second factor favoring this interpretation is 1 Kgs 19:15, where Elijah is commissioned to anoint Hazael king of Aram. Elijah does not personally anoint Hazael—or Jehu, for that matter. But he does designate Elisha as his successor (19:16, 19), who commissions Jehu's anointing (2 Kgs 9:1-10). Elisha impels Hazael to murder and replace his lord in much the same way that he impels Jehu to assassinate and overthrow his.

Diachronic Analysis

The *legenda* behind vv. 1-6

Previous analyses of vv. 1-6 have isolated two levels.[10] Verses 1*-3, 6abα are a *legenda* about a certain prosperous but nameless woman whom Elisha warned about an impending famine.[11] The *famine* may be the same as that mentioned in 4:38, though this is not certain. It is not the same as the one in 6:25, which was the result of siege. Nevertheless, the references to famine explain the editorial linking of the three texts. The famine is a long one, whether *seven years* is taken literally or as a round number. The reference to Yhwh calling the famine is PN's addition, as is the word גם. The original text would have been כי בא רעב or the like. The motif of a seven-year famine is found elsewhere in the Bible in the Joseph story in Genesis 41, where the length of the famine shows its severity. Elisha advised the woman to take her family (*household*) and leave. The notice that *she did according to the word of the man of god* is absent from 6QpapKgs15 and is unnecessary. Her compliance is registered by the same verbs in v. 2 as in v. 1: *she arose ... she went ... she sojourned.* To *sojourn* is to live as a resident alien and shows that she went to another country—*the land of the Philistines.* This region on the

---

8 Gray, *Kings*, 528, 532.

9 The similar word כביר in 1 Sam 19:13, 16 refers to some kind of netted or woven cloth (cf. also כברה, "sieve" in Amos 9:9 and מכבר, "grating, lattice-work" in Exod 27:4; 35:16; 38:4, 5, 30; 39:39).

10 Würthwein, *1. Könige 17–2. Könige 25*, 317, followed by Hentschel, *2 Könige*, 34–35 and Fritz, *Kings*, 272.

11 On this rendering of the definite article see on 1 Kgs 19:9. This use of the definite article undermines Sauerwein's objection (Elischa, 80) against seeing the phrase that follows as secondary.

southern coastal plain of Palestine is not removed from Israel by any natural boundaries, suggesting that the famine is a literary *topos* (cf. Gen 26:1).

The woman's return

After seven years the woman returns to find that her property has been taken over by someone else. There is no mention of a husband or other family members; such details were irrelevant to the initial *legenda*. Nor is there any explanation of what happened to her property, and this has given rise to a good deal of speculation. Some commentators cite the laws about the sabbatical year (Exod 21:2-3; 23:10-11; Lev 25:1-7, 23-28; Deut 15:1-6), presuming that the seventh year, when the woman returned, was the year of release.[12] But the seven years in the story are the length of the famine; its duration rather than the time required for redemption is what determines the period of the woman's absence. There is also no mention in the story of the possibility of redemption. To complicate matters further, it is unclear why she had to appeal to the king. Various explanations have been posed: (1) The land was confiscated by the king, since he is the one to whom the woman appealed and who ultimately returned it to her;[13] (2) the king had granted the land as a fief to a servant as a reward for loyal service;[14] (3) the land was taken by member(s) of the woman's husband's family or clan;[15] (4) the land was being worked by sharecroppers who refused to surrender it upon her return.[16] None of these explanations is conclusive, especially if the woman in the *legenda* was not the Shunammite. The *legenda* is uninterested in the fate of the land during the seven years because its focus is on its restoration to the woman afterward and especially Elisha's role in that restoration. For the same reason the woman in the *legenda* did not appeal on the grounds of legalities but because she did what Elisha told her to do. That was enough for the king, who ordered that her property be restored to her and assigned an official to see to it personally (v. 6abα). The *legenda* illustrated Elisha's ability to see the future and his reputation before the king.[17]

PN's revisions

The woman was secondarily identified with the Shunammite with the addition of vv. 4-5 and the phrase אשר־החיה את־בנה in v. 1a. The use of the term *household* in v. 1 is already a hint that the identification with the Shunammite was secondary,

12 E.g., Gray, *Kings*, 527.

13 A. Alt, "Der Anteil des Königtum an der sozialen Entwicklung in den Reichen Israel und Juda," *Kleine Schriften 3*, 364; Gray, *Kings*, 527; G. C. Macholz, "Die Stellung des Königs in der israelitischen Gerichtsverfassung," *ZAW* 84 (1972), 174–75; de Vaux, *Ancient Israel*, 124–25. Ahab's possession of Naboth's vineyard is often cited as comparable, though it is unclear by what right Ahab claimed the vineyard. Indeed, the king's return of the property in the present story contrasts with Ahab's seizure of Naboth's (Hobbs, *2 Kings*, 101).

14 K. H. Henrey, "Land Tenure in the Old Testament," *PEQ* 86 (1954), 12.

15 Rehm (*Das zweite Buch der Könige*, 82) argues that confiscation by the crown would be contradictory to Israelite law, which also prohibited the transfer of ownership of property between clans. The Shunammite's refusal of Elisha's offer to intercede with the king in 4:13 shows that she was from a powerful clan, so that it was probably a member of her clan who took the property, especially since her husband had evidently died.

16 E.g., Šanda, *Könige* II, 66.

17 Hentschel (*2 Könige*, 34–35) thinks this story once formed the conclusion of a short collection of wonder tales about Elisha (4:1-44; 6:1-7), though it was not the original continuation of 4:8-37.

since in ch. 4 her family consisted only of her husband and her son. In vv. 4-5 the focus changes from the woman's property to Elisha's great deeds.[18] The verb חיה occurs in the added phrase in v. 1 and then three more times in v. 5, but not at all in vv. 1*-3, 6. Also, the king's inquiry in vv. 4-5, where he simply wants to know about Elisha's deeds, is different from that of v. 6, where he asks about the woman's property. The last phrase of v. 6 (ואת כל־תבואת השדה מיום עזבה את־הארץ ועד־עתה) is in tension with the foregoing *legenda* since there would be no produce to speak of during a famine. It was added as part of the revision.[19]

The revised story suggests that the Shunammite's husband died while they were away. It is not so much that she takes the lead and is the one who deals with Elisha; that was the case in 4:8-37, but the husband was already old in 4:14 and the glimpse of him in 4:18-23 indicated that his work on the land was his primary interest and preoccupation, so that one would expect him to be engaged in the effort to appeal for the return of the land or not to have left it in the first place. Yet he is not mentioned at all in 8:1-6.[20] The other main issue raised by the identification of the woman as the Shunammite is whether Elisha was also understood to have died during the famine. This question has important ramifications for the nature and purpose of the revised story. Under the assumption that the story presumes Elisha's death, it has been taken as the conclusion to a collection of miracle stories about Elisha including the Shunammite tales in 2 Kgs 4:8-37.[21] The arguments favoring this view are circumstantial: (1) the Shunammite's recourse to the king rather than Elisha begs the question as to his whereabouts; (2) Gehazi's reminiscing about *the great things that Elisha did* (v. 4) suggests reflection on the past long gone, now that Elisha is no longer active. Neither argument is compelling. The *legenda* gives no reason to think that Elisha is dead. The woman whom Elisha warns about the famine goes to petition the king upon her return according to normal practice, particularly for a person of status. At the secondary level Elisha's absence is not due to his death but to his separation from Gehazi because of his disloyalty and contraction of skin disease, as recounted at the end of ch. 5. The reviser's familiarity with Gehazi from 4:8-37 and ch. 5 identify him as PN. As in those previous stories, PN once more made use of Gehazi as a utility character in order to identify the woman in the older *legenda* as the Shunammite. The notion of a skin-diseased peasant having a conversation with the king is ridiculous on the face of it, but Gehazi's affiliation with Elisha as witness to the prophet's deeds interests the king and gives Gehazi access. For that reason, his skin disease does not limit his social interaction any more than Naaman's did in ch. 5.[22] PN further enhanced the tale with the

---

18 Hentschel, *2 Könige*, 34–35. Hentschel notes the use of צעק על in v. 5 in contrast to צעק אל in v. 3. However, the frequency of interchange of אל and על throughout the HB casts doubt on the value of this argument as an indicator of different hands.

19 Cf. Würthwein, *1. Könige 17–2. Könige 25*, 319.

20 Cogan and Tadmor (*II Kings*, 88), posit that the land belonged to the woman by inheritance or from a previous marriage, so that she had to be the appellant and her husband was not necessarily dead.

21 E.g., Kittel, *Könige*, 203, 220; Šanda, *Könige* II, 65; Thenius, *Könige*, 300–301.

22 Similarly, Longman (*Kings*, 843) and Rehm (*Das zweite Buch der Könige*, 82). Longman even suggests that Gehazi might have been cured. Kissling (*Reliable Characters*, 187–88) finds Gehazi's presence here indicative of the unreliable nature of Elisha's prediction about him.

addition of v. 6bβ so that the woman received not only her land but also its revenue from the intervening years (of famine!).

The *legenda* behind 8:7-15

The second episode was originally a *legenda* about the consultation of Elisha by the king of Aram. It began with Elisha's journey to Damascus (v. 7). No reason is given; in terms of plot it was obviously to facilitate the encounter with Hazael. There is no mention of Elijah's commission in 1 Kgs 19:15-17 to anoint Hazael, indicating that the present passage was not written as a fulfillment of that commission. Rather, 1 Kgs 19:15-17 reflects an acquaintance with the edited form of 2 Kgs 8:7-15. Historically, Elisha's journey and the encounter are highly improbable, and it is no accident that the "omniscient narrator" reports more than one private meeting to which there were no witnesses. Elisha's fame precedes him and is such that Ben-Hadad learns of the visit and sends to inquire whether he will recover from the illness he is currently suffering. Royal inquiry regarding illness or injury is a genre or motif encountered with some frequency in previous prophetic stories (1 Kgs 14:1-18; 2 Kgs 1:2-17; 5:1-19a). Ben-Hadad's solicitation of Elisha assumes a different relationship between the two men than the one reflected in 2 Kings 7.

The historical Hazael

The identification of Ben-Hadad was discussed in the previous chapter, where it was determined that it was probably secondary, based on the name Ben-Hadad elsewhere in the Elisha stories for the Aramaean king. As for Hazael, the name means "El sees." It occurs in two forms in the HB: *plene* as חזהאל in 8:8, 13, 15, 28, 29, and 2 Chr 22:6, and defectively as חזאל elsewhere (1 Kgs 19:15, 17; 2 Kgs 8:9, 12; 9:14, 15; 10:32; 12:17, 18; 13:3, 22, 24, 25; 2 Chr 22:5; Am 1:4). He is depicted as a king whose reign had devastating consequences for Israel (2 Kgs 10:32; 13:3, 22) and to a lesser extent for Judah as well (2 Kgs 12:17-18). Recently uncovered evidence of his destruction of ancient Gath (Tell eṣ-Ṣafi) confirms that he was a powerful king.[23] Nothing is known of him before he became king except for his designation as a "son of nobody," presumably a usurper.[24]

The secondary nature of the gift

The Aramaean king sent Hazael with a gift (מנחה) as was customary in payment for the inquiry about his health (vv. 8, 9aαb). The nature of the gift was not specified in the initial *legenda*. The description of it in v. 9aβ as *40 camels loaded with all the goods of Damascus* is the first of a series of additions that make the encounter between Elisha and Hazael instrumental to the latter's accession to the throne. It prepares for v. 11a, where Hazael sets the gifts before Elisha (following G^L).[25] Damascus was renowned as a center of trade, so that its wealth would be considerable. The enormous size of the gift and the syntactic ill fit of the phrase signals its secondary status.[26]

---

23 See Maier, "Historical Background and Dating of Amos VI 2."

24 *ANET* 280b; *COS* 2.113G. But see the discussion in the previous chapter.

25 Würthwein (*1. Könige 17–2. Könige 25*, 318n) takes it as a gloss intended to glorify Elisha as if he were a king.

26 So also Hentschel, *2 Könige*, 36; Jones, *Kings*, 441–42; Schmitt, *Elisa*, 83; Würthwein, *1. Könige 17–2. Könige 25*, 320. Schmitt points to the similar addition in 5:5b, though this verse also serves the purpose of preparing for 5:22.

Overview of the *legenda* and PN

Elisha's response in v. 10 is a long-standing *crux interpretum*.[27] The problem is resolved with the recognition that vv. 10b-13 are an addition.[28] Initially Elisha's message for Ben-Hadad was positive: he would live (v. 10a). The older story then moved to vv. 14-15: Hazael conveyed the good news to his master (v. 14) but then took things into his own hands the next day, suffocating his king in order to replace him. The initial story affirmed Elisha's ability as a seer able to divine through inquiry whether a sick person would recover, and it also painted Hazael, Israel's hated enemy, as a murderer and usurper. The addition led to the *qere'* לא for the לו (*ketiv*) in v. 10a in order to make the two half-verses consistent.[29] Verse 10b continued the change to a negative response by making clear that Ben-Hadad would die. Thus Elisha's foreknowledge was complete and perfect.[30] If Hazael did not already have the idea of assassination in mind, Elisha has just given it to him. Such is the interpretation of 1 Kgs 19:15.[31] In that case v. 10b shows that Elisha was aware of what Hazael would do before Hazael himself did.

8:11-12: Elisha's vision of the future in PN

The difficulties of v. 11a are obviated by reading with G^L. This reading does away with the unique expression ויעמד את־פניו, whose meaning is uncertain (*he set his face?*), by replacing the *Hip'îl* of עמד with the Qal (*he stood before him*), and it furnishes an object for וישם.[32] The subject of both verbs is Hazael, since he is the one bringing gifts to Elisha. It is also likely that Hazael is the one who is ashamed at trying to ply Elisha with gifts; we know from ch. 5 that Elisha is unmoved by

27 As Würthwein (*1. Könige 17–2. Könige 25*, 319) put it: "Wer diese Verse liest, ist irritiert."

28 Schmitt's reason (*Elisa*, 82) for limiting the addition to vv. 11b-13a was his isolation of a *Gottesmannbearbeitung*. But the designation of Elisha by name rather than title varies in the textual witnesses and is too inconsistent to bear the weight of a reconstructed "man of god" literary stratum, as Trebolle (*Centena*, 174) has shown.

29 Another reason for reading the *ketiv* is that syntactically the negative should stand between the infinitive absolute היה and the finite verb (GKC 113v).

30 Würthwein (*1. Könige 17–2. Könige 25*, 319–21) perceives two stages, with vv. 10b-11a, 13b being added first to show Elisha's foreknowledge of Hazael's assassination of his predecessor and usurpation of the throne, then vv. 11b-13a being inserted, expounding on the devastation Hazael would wreak. Hentschel (*2 Könige*, 35–36) also perceives two levels: vv. 11-13a were the first insertion, showing Elisha's awareness of the harm to be brought by Hazael, and then vv. 10b and 13b were added to make clear that Elisha was aware of the king's impending death. He suggests that vv. 10b, 13b were modeled on Amos. Both theories depend on acceptance of the MT in v. 11a and construal of it as referring to Elisha staring at Hazael; they will not work with the G^L reading.

31 The idea that Elisha is telling Hazael that Ben-Hadad will not die unless he is killed is also the view of a number of interpreters going back to Qimḥi (RaDaK), Rosenberg, *Kings II*, 295. Cf. Fricke, *Das zweite Buch von den Königen*, 105; Long, *2 Kings*, 104. Other interpretations include: (1) Elisha's initial opinion (*you shall indeed live*) is followed by a more considered reply drawn from his gift of second sight (Montgomery, *Kings*, 392). (2) The negative *lō'* in v. 10a should be read as *lu'*, understood as a greeting, "May you live" (Gray, *Kings*, 530). (3) Similarly, *you shall live* is like the coronation wish *long live the king*, but it is directed to Hazael, while *he shall die* refers to Ben-Hadad (C. J. Labuschagne, "Did Elisha Deliberately Lie? – A Note on ii Kings 8 10," *ZAW* 77 [1965]: 327–28).

32 Because of its lack of an object, וישם is often derived not from √שים but from √שמם, yielding *he shuddered, was appalled*. Despite its appeal for meaning, the idea has no textual support and still leaves ויעמד את־פניו unexplained.

such gifts. It is possible, though, that there is a change of subject, as with the identical expression in 2 Kgs 2:17, and that Elisha is embarrassed by the riches being laid before him. Either way, Elisha's reaction is not what Hazael expected—he breaks into tears (v. 11b). The list of horrors of war that Elisha foresees (v. 12) makes use of literary *topoi* found especially in prophetic texts (Isa 13:16; Hos 14:1; Am 1:13; Ps 137:9; 2 Kgs 15:16). It also accords with the memory reflected elsewhere in Kings (2 Kgs 10:32; 13:3, 22) of Hazael's reign as devastating for Israel.

8:13: The characterization of Hazael

Much has been made of Hazael's reference in v. 13 to the devastation of Israel as a *great thing*. As an Aramaean, Hazael may well have considered such tactics appropriate against an enemy, or at least the Israelite writer may portray him this way. However, the expression is not a moral judgment. It is, rather, part of Hazael's expression of incredulity that he would possess the political and military authority necessary to carry out such deeds. Moreover, the better reading here may be without the word *great* (so G^{B}), which would make the matter a non-issue. In that case *great* would be a scribal expansion, perhaps motivated in part by an interest in portraying Hazael as villainous. Hazael's reference to himself as *the dog* is quite the opposite of greatness. Dogs in the ancient Near East were undomesticated, opportunistic scavengers that were widely disparaged in the Bible and other texts.[33] On the face of it the image accords with Shalmaneser's designation of Hazael as a "son of nobody" who lacks the authority to carry out the attacks on Israel that Elisha envisions. As the story unfolds it becomes clear that Hazael's modesty is false or grossly understated. It is difficult to accept any interpretation of vv. 10b-11a that sees Hazael as conscience-stricken or embarrassed at the revelation that he will seize and exercise such power.

Synthesis

Using the legenda to paint Elisha as judgment prophet

The *legenda* behind the two stories in these verses were originally independent. They have been juxtaposed and linked as illustrations of Elisha's reputation and power. He deals with kings both at home and abroad. They have such esteem for him that they accede to his authority even when he is not present and consult him rather than their own prophets on matters of extreme importance. Both stories link with previous ones in the Elijah-Elisha material. PN's identification of the woman in vv. 1-6 as the Shunammite demonstrated YHWH's continued protection over her and her son in Elisha's absence as is suggested by the "providential" timing of the encounter, such that Gehazi is in the middle of telling the king the story of the boy's revival when he and his mother appear to petition for their land. The second story (vv. 7-15) was used to show Elisha's ability not only to foresee the future but to determine it as well, to the extent that he directed

33 1 Sam 17:43; 24:14; 2 Sam 9:8; 16:9; 1 Kgs 16:4; 21:24; 2 Kgs 9:36; Pss 22:17; 59:7, 15-16; Jer 15:3. See also Lachish letters 2:3-4; 5:3-4; 6:3, all cited in *ANET* 322. For other references from Amarna, Mari, and Assyrian texts see D. W. Thomas, "*Kelebh* 'Dog': Its Origin and Some Usages of it in the Old Testament," *VT* 10 (1960): 410–27, and *CAD* K 72 [*kalbu*]). G^{BL} here read *dead dog*, probably influenced by 1 Sam 24:14; 2 Sam 9:8; 16:9.

Hazael to usurp Aram's throne. Through his prophets YHWH is in charge of affairs in nations beyond Israel. The disasters Hazael is foreseen to bring upon Israel indicate that YHWH uses other nations to punish his people. This is one of the main things judgment prophets do—they announce the use of foreign rulers and nations as tools to carry out YHWH's will. As the book of Kings now stands, Hazael's rise to power is the second of the three steps in the process of judgment envisioned by PN in 1 Kgs 19:15-17. Elisha has been "anointed" as Elijah's successor. Hazael is now "anointed" king of Aram. There remains only Jehu to be anointed king over Israel. All three are YHWH's agents to execute judgment on the house of Ahab in the fight against Baal. According to the order of 19:17 Hazael's sword is the first step. Elisha, the son of "Judgment" (Shaphat), as the successor to Elijah is the one who fulfills his commissions to anoint Hazael and Jehu. He is also the one who carries out the final judgment against any who may have escaped the swords of Hazael or Jehu. In broader perspective Elijah and Elisha are the forerunners of the judgment prophets of the eighth century who warned Israel, and later Judah, that YHWH would use foreign powers to destroy them as nations if they did not turn from their evil paths.[34] Their stories constitute an introduction to judgment prophecy that supplements those of Samuel and Nathan and extensively develops the portrait of what such prophets looked like and what they did.

34 Cf. E. Ruprecht, "Enstehung und Zeitgeschichtlicher Bezug der Erzählung von der Designation Hasaels durch Elisa," *VT* 28 (1978): 73–82.

Joram of Judah
(2 Kings 8:16-24)

Text

[DtrH's sources; DtrH, Additions to DtrH]
16 In the fifth year of Joram son of Ahab king of Israel, Jehoram
son of Jehoshaphat began to reign over Judah. 17 He was thirty-
two years old when he began to reign and he reigned eight years
in Jerusalem. 18 He walked in the way of the kings of Israel as the house of
Ahab had done because Ahab's daughter was his wife. He did what YHWH consid-
ered evil. 19 But YHWH did not want to destroy Judah on account of David his ser-
vant, as he had promised to give him a fiefdom before him forever. 20 In his days
Edom revolted against Judah's dominion and crowned a king over themselves.
21 So Joram crossed over to Zair and all his chariotry. But Edom
arose by night and, surrounding him, defeated him and his chari-
otry commanders, so that the army fled to their homes. 22 So Edom
has remained in revolt against Judah's dominion to this day.
Then Libnah revolted at that same time. 23 The rest of Joram's acts and all that he
did are written on the scroll of the chronicles of the kings of Judah, aren't they?
24 Joram lay down with his forebears and was buried with them in the city of Da-
vid, and Ahaziah his son reigned in his place.

Textual Notes

16 **In the fifth year of Joram**: So MT (minus *and* at the beginning), G^{BL}. The OG chronology is not extant, but based on foregoing figures would have had Jehoram of Judah taking the throne in the second year of Ahaziah of Israel and reigning eleven years.[1] As explained in the Introduction, the placement of Joram's reign in the OG assumes the MT chronology and thus shows the latter's primacy.

king of Israel: MT, G^{BL} + *and of Jehoshaphat king of Judah*. The plus is absent from a number of witnesses, including most Greek miniscules, the OL, and Syr.[2] Syntactically it is intrusive, disrupting the transition between the introductory subordinate clause of v. 16a and the main clause of v. 16b. It is also patently absurd in content, since Joram could not have become sole ruler until his father had died.[3] It is a misplaced dittography of the name and title of Jehoshaphat from the end of the verse.[4]

Jehoram: See the Note on 1 Kgs 22:51.

---

1 Such is Shenkel's reconstruction (*Chronology*, 37–38, 68–82).

2 For a full list see Stade, *Kings*, 217.

3 Shenkel, *Chronology*, 81.

4 Burney, *Notes*, 294; Stade, *Kings*, 217. Even Thiele (*Mysterious Numbers*, 100), who advocates a coregency of Jehoshaphat with Jehoram on other grounds, does not accept the originality of this plus.

over Judah: Reading על יהודה instead of MT's מלך יהודה, which is awkward in view of the occurrence of מלך earlier in the verse. Stade and Šanda point out that על ישראל is used everywhere in the formulae except 1 Kgs 14:23, and על יהודה is used in all passages about kings of Judah before 8:16 (1 Kgs 15:1, 9; 22:41), as well as in 9:29, which is a repetition of 8:25.[5] However, after 8:16 מלך ישראל is used (8:25; 14:1; 15:1, 32; 16:1; 18:1). These data suggest that על יהודה was the original idiom in the regnal formula but that it was replaced from 2 Kgs 8:16 on for unknown reasons.

17 **eight**: So MT and most other witnesses, including Josephus (*Ant.* 9.102) and 2 Chr 21:5. G^{AB} have *forty*, which does not fit with any chronological system and must be erroneous, perhaps the result of adding thirty-two (Jehoram's age) and eight.[6] The main Lucianic witnesses are divided, b (= *b* and *b'*) reading *eight* with MT and oc_2e_2 reading *ten*. Shenkel reconstructs *eleven* to fit with the OG chronology.[7]

years (2): So MT *qere'* and 2 Chr 21:5 (שנים), following the rule that numbers from two to ten take a plural object. However, there are a few exceptions (22:1; Exod 16:22; Ezek 45:1; see GKC §134e).

18 **had done**: So MT with the plural (עשו), also Syr, Tar, 2 Chr 21:6. G^{BL} read the singular in accord with Greek style.

daughter: The witnesses are nearly unanimous in the reading. However, Syr reads *sister* both here and in 2 Chr 21:6, probably in an effort to harmonize with 2 Kgs 8:26// 2 Chr 22:2.

wife: So MT (לאשה), G^{BL} (εἰς γυναῖκα). 2 Chr 21:6: אשה.

19 **before him**: MT, followed by G^{N} and many other Greek miniscules as well as the Eth and Syr (under asterisk), have "for his sons." But, as Burney observes, the sons are the *nîr*, so the *nîr* cannot be for them.[8] Other witnesses reflect efforts to resolve the problem. G^{B} omits *for his sons*. G^{LA} and other witnesses, including the parallel in 2 Chr 21:7, attest the same reading preceded by *waw*, i.e., *and to his sons*, which is syntactically awkward since it separates the two indirect objects with the direct object. The emendation to לפניו follows Kittel and Burney, among others, and is in line with 1 Kgs 11:36.[9]

21 **crossed over**: So MT (ויעבר), 2 Chr 21:9. G^{BL}: καὶ ἀνέβη = ויעל in accord with the idiom for going to war in Kings (1 Kgs 15:17; 20:1, 26; 22:20, 29; 2 Kgs 6:24; 14:11; 15:14; 16:9; 17:5). Either is possible.

and all his chariotry: So G^{L}. MT, 2 Chr 21:9; G^{B}: *and all the chariotry/chariots with him.*

But Edom arose by night and surrounding him, defeated him and his chariotry commanders: This is Stade's conjectural reconstruction (ויקם אדום לילה ויסב אליו ויך אתו ואת שרי הרכב).[10] MT is corrupt, and other witnesses do not help. There are several peculiar features of MT's reading: ויהי־הוא קם לילה is awkward and not elegant Hebrew; one expects ויך as the converted form rather than ויכה; one also expects the chariotry commanders to be Judah's rather than Edom's since Judah's chariotry is mentioned earlier in the verse; in light of v. 22, which notes Edom's continued independence, the army that fled home at the end of v. 21b must be Judah's rather than

5 Stade, *Kings*, 217; Šanda, *Kings* II, 71.

6 Montgomery, *Kings*, 398; Hobbs, *2 Kings*, 96.

7 Shenkel, *Chronology*, esp. 81–82. Shenkel suggests that the other Lucianic mss follow the lead of c_2 in the reading *ten*. Hendel ("Two Editions," 109) explains it as relating to the OG chronological deficiency for the length of Joram's reign that exists without Shenkel's reconstruction.

8 Burney, *Notes*, 295.

9 Kittel, *Könige*, 223.

10 Stade, *Kings*, 218.

Edom's. The actual reading is probably beyond restoration, but Stade's conjecture gives an idea of its probable content.

22 **against Judah's dominion**: So MT (מתחת יד־יהודה) = G^B (ὑποκάτωθεν χειρὸς Ιουδα). G^L has τοῦ μὴ δοῦναι χεῖρα Ιουδα = מתת ידי יהודה, reflecting loss of the ח from מתחת and the plural *hands*, the usual Greek rendering.

Libnah: So MT, G^L. G^B inexplicably has Σεννὰ. Libnah was a city conquered by Joshua (Josh 10:29-39; 12:15), allotted to Judah (Josh 15:42), and given to the Levites (Josh 21:13; 1 Chr 6:42 [ET 57]). It lay somewhere in the Shephelah in the vicinity of Lachish. It has been identified with Tell eṣ-Ṣafi (now generally agreed to be Gath), Tell Burna, Tell Judeideh (traditionally thought to be Moreshet-Gath), and Tell Zayit.[11] To judge from 2 Kgs 19:8//Isa 37:8, where it is reported that Sennacherib fought against it, the city was of strategic importance, perhaps as a guardian of Judah's western border.

24 **David**: So MT, G^L. G^B + *his father.*

Synchronic Analysis

Content and structure The account of Jehoram's reign is preoccupied with regnal formulae—opening (vv. 16-18) and closing (vv. 23-24). The intervening verses are dominated by the successful revolt of Edom (vv. 20-22), with v. 19 explaining why Judah was not destroyed despite Jehoram's wickedness. This account, therefore, has two emphases: Jehoram's link with the house of Ahab, which led him to do evil and would have imperiled Judah's very existence had it not been for YHWH's loyalty to David (vv. 18-19), and the loss of Edom, which was punishment for Jehoram's offenses (vv. 20-22). The first emphasis is bolstered by the sameness of the names Jehoram and Joram and their interchangeability. A similar point holds for the name Ahaziah, which is shared by kings of Israel and Judah. The names illustrate the entanglement of the two kingdoms during the reigns of these kings as a result of Omrid (or Ahabid) influence on Judah.

8:18: Ahabid influence on Jehoram This depth of influence is explained in the DtrH evaluation of Jehoram in v. 18, which draws Jehoram by stages ever closer to the house of Ahab. First he is said to have walked in the ways of the kings of Israel, the only king of Judah so accused. Next his behavior is likened to that of the house of Ahab. Finally, v. 18 explains that Jehoram became a member of Ahab's house by marrying his daughter. She was the explicit cause (כי) that Jehoram followed the ways of the kings of Israel and did evil. The implication is that she was like her mother Jezebel and abetted Jehoram's apostasy much as Jezebel had Ahab's. The accusation is reminiscent of that leveled against Solomon for allowing his foreign wives to lead him astray (1 Kgs 11:1-10).

8:19: Reminder of the Davidic promise The explanation in v. 19 that YHWH did not destroy Judah despite Jehoram's sin is the second such statement for a king of Judah. The first was for Abijam (1 Kgs 15:4-5), who was the last king of Judah judged evil. The reigns of such kings call for the reminder that Judah endured because of YHWH's promise to David. Cohn perceives a "not yet" sense to the verse that forebodes the exile to come,

---

11 J. L. Peterson, "Libnah," *ABD* 4:322–23; R. K. Hawkins, "Libnah," *NIDB* 3:645.

all the more since this is the last mention of the promise to David in Kings: "Why raise the specter of the destruction of Judah unless events are leading inevitably in that direction?"[12] The reaffirmation of the promise immediately before the account of Jehu's revolt also highlights the contrast between Israel's royal houses and Judah's single Davidic dynasty. Above all it underscores divine control of events. But if destruction is a possibility—perhaps even an inevitability— what is meant by *forever*? The tension between possible destruction and an eternal *nîr*, whatever the meaning of the term, creates suspense and induces the reader's interest in the rest of the story.

8:20-22: Judah loses Edom and Libnah

The notice about Edom's revolt, (v. 20) following the negative evaluation of Jehoram and the reminder of the Davidic promise, implies that the revolt was punishment. The details are sketchy (v. 21), due in part to the ambiguity of the verb נכה, which can mean "attack" or "defeat." It is uncertain whose chariot captains were defeated and whose troops fled, but it looks as if Jehoram crossed the Jordan intending to reconquer Edom, found himself surrounded, and was barely able to break through and escape. In any case the outcome was that Edom gained independence (v. 22a). Whatever Jehoram's success, it was too close a call for him to continue to hold Edom in submission. And Edom was not alone. Libnah also revolted, evidently with success (v. 22b). Thus in addition to being apostate—or because of it—Jehoram was weak. Under his rule Judah lost ground and prestige, again because of Israel's influence. Judah's pairing with Israel would soon prove disastrous.

Diachronic Analysis

A DtrH unit

As it stands this is a DtrH unit with the opening and closing formulae for Jehoram (vv. 16-19, 23-24) enclosing the notices of Edom's and Libnah's revolts (vv. 19-22). The greatest difficulty the unit presents relates to MT's numbers for Jehoram. In v. 16 MT has Jehoram accede to the throne of Judah in Joram of Israel's fifth year. Not only is this before Jehoshaphat's death according to 1 Kgs 22:42 but it contradicts both 2 Kgs 1:17b, where MT contains a fragment of the OG chronology, and, more seriously, 3:1, which dates Joram of Israel's accession to the eighteenth year of Jehoshaphat's twenty-five-year reign. A popular way of dealing with the discrepancy has been to posit a coregency between Jehoshaphat and Jehoram. This theory is identified especially with E. R. Thiele, who initially postulated coregency based in part on the reference to Jehoshaphat in v. 16.[13]

8:16: The chronological problem

Shenkel's theory of the priority of the OG chronology seemed to solve this and other chronological problems in the MT, at least in the period of the Omrid dynasty, by showing that the MT's numbers were a systematic revision of the

---

12 Cohn, *2 Kings*, 63.

13 Thiele, *Mysterious Numbers* (Chicago: University of Chicago Press, 1951), 35–36. Thiele later reversed himself as far as the mention of Jehoshaphat is concerned, recognizing that it is erroneous, but not regarding the coregency. See *Mysterious Numbers*, rev. ed. (1983), 100.

primitive and more consistent chronology preserved in the OG.[14] However, Hendel has undermined Shenkel's work by showing that it is the OG that revised the MT chronology rather than the other way around. I have found further support for Hendel's thesis in 1 Kings 22, 2 Kings 3, and in the present passage (see the Introduction). Unfortunately, this means that the discrepancy between 2 Kgs 3:1 and 8:16 remains unresolved. A number of other scholars have continued to postulate coregency for Jehoshaphat and Jehoram based on 2 Kgs 8:16 in MT.[15] The problem with the theory is that it is unprovable and a little too convenient. It seems more likely that the numbers in one instance or the other (or possibly both) are wrong. But without further evidence it is impossible to know which ones are wrong or how they came about.[16]

Excursus: A Single J(eh)oram over Israel and Judah?

The fact that two kings with the same name are said to reign over Israel and Judah at the same time has been seen by some scholars as more than a coincidence. The case for their identity has been made by Strange and Miller and Hayes, who identify a single J(eh)oram as the king of Judah.[17] Strange builds his case on the observation that the typical reference to the ספר דברי הימים למלכי ישראל/יהודה is absent for Joram of Israel and Ahaziah of Judah, suggesting that there was no record of these two kings in the annals of their respective countries. He reconstructs a chronology for this period that includes coregencies for Jehoram of Judah both at the beginning of his reign (with Jehoshaphat) and at the end (with Ahaziah). Strange then lists eleven peculiarities of the accounts in Kings and Chronicles that are explained by the postulation of a single J(eh)oram: (1) kings of Israel and Judah with the same name at the same time; (2) 2 Kgs 1:17, which reports that Joram succeeded Ahaziah of Israel but was not his son; (3) Jehoram's assassination of Israelite officials when he seized the throne of Judah (2 Chr 21:4) is odd for a king of Judah but makes sense if he also sat on the throne of Israel; (4) the revolts of Mesha (2 Kgs 1:1; 3:4-27) and Edom (8:20-22), which have often been linked by scholars on economic grounds, make even better sense as a joint effort of the two kingdoms against a single overlord; (5) Ahaziah's visit to Joram (2 Kgs 8:29) is best explained as a son and coregent visiting his father;[18] (6) connections with the South would account for the involvement of the Rechabites (2 Kgs 10:15-16), the slaughter of Ahaziah's brothers (2 Kgs 10:12-14), and Athaliah's violent reaction (2 Kgs 11:1); (7) the lack of mention of the two J(eh)orams together outside of the DtrH framework; (8) Joram's removal of the Baal stela (2 Kgs 3:2) makes more sense if he was from Judah; (9) Ahaziah's absence from the annals of Judah is understandable if he was never sole ruler; (10) Joram may have brought the practice of antedating from Israel to Judah; (11) if Jehoram of Judah usurped the throne from the seventy sons of Ahab (2 Kgs 10:1), it would explain the involvement of princes of Israel in his accession (#3 in the list above). Strange concludes by suggesting that DtrH invented the "ghost"

---

14 Shenkel, *Chronology.*

15 Buis, *Rois*, 211; Fricke, *Das zweite Buch von den Königen,* 107n; Gray, *Kings*, 532; Nelson, *Kings*, 198.

16 See Galil (*Chronology*, 39–43), who reconstructs a coregency on the basis of the chronological data but not because of the mention of Jehoshaphat in 8:16, which he recognizes as problematic.

17 J. Strange, "Joram, King of Israel and Judah," *VT* 25 (1975): 191–201; Miller and Hayes, *History*, 320–23.

18 Strange suggests that the account of Jehoram's illness in 2 Chr 21:18-19a is a reflection of Joram of Israel's convalescence from wounds.

Joram of Israel out of misinterpretation of his sources and/or to avoid the involvement of any Davidid in ruling apostate Israel.

Miller and Hayes add the following considerations to Strange's case: (1) based on 2 Kgs 1:17 J(eh)oram seems to have been Ahaziah of Israel's brother-in-law and the husband of Athaliah; (2) the chronology preserved in the Lucianic witnesses lacks synchronisms for Jehoram and Ahaziah of Judah since the synchronisms present in these witnesses are the result of secondary recension; (3) a series of events (reconstructed) seems to have compelled Jehoram to be preoccupied with a new threat from Hazael of Damascus and caused him not to renew his kingship over Judah after the beginning of his eighth year as per 2 Kgs 8:17 MT.

This theory of a single J(eh)oram has a good deal to recommend it, not least the name shared by the two kings whose reigns are essentially simultaneous. The preceding list of items helps to refine the case. The reference to Joram as Ahaziah's brother in 2 Kgs 1:17 is a late, interpretive addition and is therefore irrelevant to the issue. There are, however, reasons for thinking that the single J(eh)oram was from Israel rather than Judah. For one thing, it is more likely that the dominant Omrid would have usurped the throne of Judah rather than the weak Davidid assuming power in Israel.[19] Furthermore, the name of the king's mother, a regular portion of the introductory formula for kings of Judah,[20] is lacking for Jehoram. The lack of reference to the ספר דברי הימים for Joram of Israel and Ahaziah of Judah can be accounted for literarily as the result of intrusion of the story of Jehu's revolt and the resulting loss or dispersal of elements of the regnal formulae. But the absence of the queen mother's name is not so easily explained.

Some of the peculiarities noted by Strange are explained as well or better by positing that Joram was from Israel, especially the involvement of Northerners in Judah's politics (#3, 11) and the revolts of Moab and Edom (#4). A Northern origin of Joram also explains the reference to Jezebel as his mother (2 Kgs 9:22), with which Strange struggles Joram may have deposed Jehoshaphat and then assassinated his sons in accord with Northern protocol (cf. 2 Chr 21:4). If Jehoshaphat submitted to Ahab, as 1 Kgs 22:44 suggests, Joram may have been taking control of what he considered to be part of his domain. Ahaziah of Judah is not a literary construct, as the reference to him in the Tel Dan stela shows. However, the relationship between him, Joram, and Athaliah is open to question. Athaliah is clearly described as Ahaziah's mother (2 Kgs 8:26; 11:1). She is also usually understood as Jehoram of Judah's wife based on 8:18. This notice is part of the DtrH evaluation of Jehoram and may not be historically reliable. Ahaziah may have been Joram's cousin, following 8:26, rather than his son. His father is unknown but may have been another of Jehoshaphat's sons. Ahaziah may have been acting in some official capacity as his uncle's representative in Judah. He went to visit his wounded cousin in Jezreel when the revolt occurred, and the two of them were killed. The fact that he was a direct descendant of Omri/Ahab helps to explain why Jehu targeted him along with Joram for assassination. There was no need for Jehu to do so if he was a Davidid. An ideological reason for the invention of Jehoram of Judah to match Joram of Israel is the promise of a continuing Davidic dynasty, which may be part of the reason for the unusual reiteration of that promise in 2 Kgs 8:19.

---

19 Also J. W. Rogerson and P. Davies, *The Old Testament World* (Englewood Cliffs, NJ: Prentice-Hall, 1989), 146.

20 It occurs for all the kings of Judah (albeit in Rehoboam's closing formula, 1 Kgs 14:31, rather than his opening formula) except Jehoram and Ahaz. Its regular occurrence makes it unlikely that it is missing for Jehoram because his mother died before he took the throne (*pace* Šanda, *Könige* II, 71 and Jones, *Kings*, 446).

8:16-18: Jehoram's opening regnal formulae

The information in vv. 16-17 derives from official sources, although the figures may have evolved subsequently. DtrH assesses Jehoram as evil (v. 18), blaming his affiliation with the "house of Ahab."[21] While the dynasty is known in Assyrian annals as the "house of Omri," the Bible typically refers to it by Ahab's name. Amos's similar designation of the Jehu dynasty as "Jeroboam's house" (Amos 7:9) suggests that a dynasty could be called after its reigning member or perhaps, in the present case and the references in 2 Kings, after the latest member to have established a succession. As the book of Kings developed and more evildoing was attributed to Ahab, especially because of Jezebel, the designation of the dynasty as Ahab's came to take on more theological tones, signaling Ahab's family as the nadir of Israel's history.[22]

A treaty between Israel and Judah

Jehoram's marriage to Ahab's daughter would have sealed a political pact between Israel and Judah. The historical situation may have been more complicated, as suggested in the excursus. While the reader assumes that the daughter in question is Athaliah, she is not named. She is also referred to elsewhere as Omri's daughter (8:24; 2 Chr 22:2), and there are reasons to consider this parentage more historical.[23] Jehoram's marriage to Ahab's daughter could have been part of the development or invention of a separate king of the same name in Judah.

8:19: DtrH's use of the Davidic promise

The negative evaluation of Jehoram leads to the statement in v. 19 about YHWH refusing to destroy Judah for David's sake. The verse is a theological assertion on DtrH's part of the validity of the Davidic promise in face of the indications of his sources that Judah experienced Omrid rule for a time (in addition to Athaliah, whom he did not consider legitimate). The word ניר has the metaphorical sense of "dominion, fiefdom" here rather than the more common translation, "lamp."[24] The term *forever*, literally "all the days," does not mean eternity or endless time but rather a long period of time, a person's lifetime or the foreseeable future.[25]

8:20-22a: Edom's independence

The notice about Edom's revolt (vv. 20-22a) was probably also borrowed by DtrH from source materials and incorporated at this point as punishment for

---

21 The evaluation and account in 2 Chr 21 is much more negative: Jehoram not only kills his brothers in order to assure his hold on the throne (21:4), but he also builds *bamot* on the mountains and leads Jerusalem and Judah into apostasy (21:11). His behavior evokes a letter of condemnation from Elijah (21:12-15) announcing disaster, which is fulfilled in the form of invasion and an agonizing death (21:16-20).

22 T. Ishida, "House of Ahab." Micah 6:16, which parallels the *statutes of Omri* with the *works of the house of Ahab* is also instructive in this regard.

23 Katzenstein, "Who Were the Parents of Athaliah?"

24 This is the conclusion reached by both P. D. Hanson ("The Song of Heshbon and David's *Nir*," *HTR* 61 [1968]: 297–320) and E. Ben Zvi ("Once the Lamp Has Been Kindled ... A Reconsideration of the Meaning of the MT *Nîr* in 1 Kgs 11:36; 15:4; 2 Kgs 8:19 and 2 Chr 21:7," *ABR* 39 [1991]: 19–30), albeit through different means. Hanson argues from cognate evidence, especially Aramaic and Akkadian, that the original meaning of נר/ניר was "yoke," which taken metaphorically means "dominion." Ben Zvi contends that נר and ניר are distinct words, the latter having the basic sense of "field" as in Jer 4:3; Hos 10:12; and Prov 13:23. Again, though, it has the metaphorical sense of "dominion," i.e., "territorial domain."

25 Compare the discussion of עולם, "forever, for a long time" by H. D. Preuss in *TDOT* 10:530–45.

Jehoram's sinfulness.[26] Historically the revolt would have been motivated largely by economic concerns, including not only control of the overland trade routes from Arabia but also of sea trade coming through the Gulf of Aqaba and from points west. The seriousness of the economic consequences is suggested by Jehoram's personal leadership of the campaign to regain Edom.[27] Edom's act of rebellion was also impelled by Moab's success (3:4-27) and may have been part of the same revolt (see the excursus). The move to institute autonomous kingship in Edom accords with 1 Kgs 22:46-47 but contradicts 2 Kgs 3:9 and is another indication that the latter is post-DtrH.

The identification of Zair

The account of the encounter between Judah and Edom in v. 21 presents the problem of the identification of Zair, which is otherwise unknown and for which there are four proposals. (1) Zair may be another name for Zoar (Gen 13:10; 14:2, 8; 19:22, 23, 30; Deut 34:3; Isa 15:5; Jer 48:34). Both names mean "small." Assuming that Zoar was southeast of the Dead Sea, which is not certain,[28] this identification would fit with the implication that Jehoram *crossed over* (ויעבר) into Edomite territory. The identification of Zair and Zoar is sometimes rejected because of their different Greek renderings: Σ(ε)ιωρ and Σηγωρ, respectively. But it is difficult to see the force of this argument since the names are different in Hebrew. (2) Another possibility is Zior near Hebron (Josh 15:54). However, this would fail to account for the use of the verb עבר and would indicate that Edom invaded Judah, which does not fit the story. (3) Seir, the name of the mountain country in Edom, is a third candidate. The difficulty here is that the reference to Seir is vague and unexpected—unexpected in that elsewhere the name used is Edom, and vague in that it is not the name of a specific place as the narrative leads one to expect. Furthermore, if Seir refers to the mountains of Edom it would be very odd for Joram to deploy his chariotry in such a terrain. (4) Zair may refer to a site in Edom that remains unknown. Thus options 1 and 4 seem most likely and it is difficult to choose between the two of them.

Edom victorious

To this day in v. 22 is the alteration of an etiological formula to mean *as is the case presently*, equivalent to כיום הזה. The formula is used twice more in texts relating to Edom in 2 Kings (14:7; 16:6), and in all cases describes circumstances that continue at the time of the author.[29] This makes clear that in the present verse Edom rather than Judah was victorious in the foregoing battle and gained independence. This outcome was obscured by the corruption of the text in v. 21b (see the Note). The expression *fled to their tents* may have a nomadic origin. In any

26 Würthwein (*1. Könige 17–2. Könige 25*, 323) contends that the notice about Edom in vv. 21-22a has been interpolated by *Wiederaufnahme*. The resumption is imprecise; vv. 20 and 22 contain different forms of פשע and v. 22a concludes with *to this day* rather than *in his days* (בימיו) as in v. 20. The repetition could also have been used by DtrH to include the anecdote. The loss of Edom illustrates the consequences of Jehoram's apostasy, which fits DtrH's interest (Seow, *Kings*, 214).

27 Fricke, *Das zweite Buch von den Königen*, 108.

28 B. C. Jones, "Zoar," *NIDB* 5:990–91.

29 Childs, "A Study of the Formula, 'Until This Day.'" J. C. Geoghegan (*The Time, Place, and Purpose of the Deuteronomistic History: The Evidence of "Until This Day,"* [BJS 347; Providence, RI: Brown University Press, 2006]) builds a case for the formula in Kings belonging to a pre-exilic DtrH.

case it is idiomatic for "fled home" and indicates a battle has concluded in defeat. It was therefore Judah's chariotry that was defeated and whose army fled home rather than the Edomites. The later references to kings of Judah defeating Edom (14:7, 22; 16:6) do not contradict the *to this day* statement in 8:22, because Edom retained its independence from Judah even through those defeats.

8:22b: The addition about Libnah

The reference to Libnah in v. 22b is probably an addition,[30] although its revolt may well have occurred in conjunction with Edom's.[31] Libnah's proximity to the Philistines suggests that it may have been they who came to control the city and foment its revolt. Again, the motive was probably economic and linked with Edom's revolt as part of the trade network from the Mediterranean across the Negeb to the Gulf of Aqaba and Arabia.[32] בעת ההיא at the end of v. 22 is further clarification of the link between Libnah's revolt and Edom's and not necessarily the beginning of a new sentence that has been lost.[33]

8:23-24: Jehoram's closing formulae

There is nothing remarkable about the closing formulae for Jehoram in 8:23-24 apart from the absence of the queen mother's name, as discussed in the excursus. The much more detailed and gruesome account of his death in 2 Chr 21:18-20 is tendentious and interpretive but it highlights the view of Jehoram found in Kings as the worst king of Judah to this point because of his close affiliation with the house of Ahab.

Synthesis

Yhwh's faithfulness to David despite Jehoram's betrayal

DtrH's account of Jehoram's reign continues the contrast between Israel and Judah. The latest king of Judah is a far cry from his righteous father. Nevertheless, Yhwh holds fast to his promise to David of an enduring dynasty over a lasting domain. Still, the ties with wicked Israel and its worst ruling family have an effect on Judah. Kings ascribes those ties to Jehoshaphat's treaty with Ahab, sealed by the marriage of their children. Critical analysis suggests that the historical situation may have been more complex; there may have been only one J(eh)oram—Ahab's son—who ruled both Israel and Judah. In any case the writer of Kings depicts Jehoram as acting corruptly, more like Ahab than like Jehoshaphat. His wrongdoing is not enough to move Yhwh to destroy Judah but it is enough to cause Yhwh (and the narrator) to imagine the possibility. Jehoram does not get off free, either. He and his kingdom suffer consequences for his sinfulness. The

---

30 Würthwein, *1. Könige 17–2. Könige 25*, 323.

31 The particle אז, which often signals an addition, is used with the imperfect to express contemporary action in the past, indicating that Libnah's rebellion took place at about the same time as Edom's. Rabinowitz, "'*ĀZ* Followed by Imperfect," esp. 57. Cf. 1 Kgs 16:21.

32 2 Chr 21:16-17, either because of its other sources or by inference from Kings, mentions an attack of the Philistines and Arabs that devastated Jehoram's household. Libnah later returned to Judah or at least had ties with Judah if the origin of Hamutal, Josiah's wife and the mother of Jehoahaz and Zedekiah, is any indication (2 Kgs 23:31; 24:18).

33 Rabinowitz, "'*ĀZ* Followed by Imperfect," 57. Pace Klostermann, *Könige*, 418; Kittel, *Könige*, 225; Šanda, *Könige* II, 74; Stade, *Kings*, 219; de Vaux, *Rois*, 153.

link with Ahab's house will soon be Jehoram's demise. More immediately Jehoram loses his domain over Edom and Libnah, both of which were important for Judah's economic well-being. His attempt to restore Edom fails. His reign, all told, is more like that of a king of Israel when viewed theologically, and it ends with a net loss for the kingdom of Judah in terms both of extent of domain and of its stock in divine favor that restrains final judgment.

Ahaziah of Judah and Jehu's Revolt (2 Kings 8:25–9:37)

Text

[DtrH's sources; DtrH; Additions to DtrH; *PN*; *Additions to PN*]
8:25 In the twelfth year of Joram son of Ahab king of Israel Ahaz-
iah became king. 26 Ahaziah was twenty-two years old when he be-
came king, and he reigned one year in Jerusalem. His mother's
name was Athaliah, daughter of Omri, the king of Israel. 27 He
went in the way of Ahab's house and did what YHWH considered evil, like Ahab's
house, because he was related by marriage to Ahab's house. 28 Joram son of Ahab
went to war against Hazael king of Aram in Ramah of Gilead, where the archers
wounded Joram. 29 After King Joram returned to recuperate in Jezreel from the
wounds which the archers inflicted on him in Ramah when he went to war with
Hazael king of Aram, Ahaziah son of Jehoram king of Judah went down to see Jo-
ram *son of Ahab in Jezreel since he was injured.* 9:1 *Elisha the prophet summoned a*
member of the prophetic guild and said to him, "Gird your loins, take this juglet of oil
with you, and go to Ramah of Gilead. 2 *When you arrive look for Jehu son of Jehosha-*
phat son of Nimshi; make him get up from his comrades and bring him into an inner
chamber. 3 *Then take the juglet of oil, pour it on his head, and say, 'Thus says YHWH, "I*
anoint you king over Israel."' Then open the door and flee without delay." 4 *So the*
prophet went to Ramah of Gilead 5 *and entering where the army commanders were*
sitting he said, "I have a message for you, commander." Jehu responded, "For which of
us?" He replied, "For you, commander." 6 *So [Jehu] arose and went inside. Then [the*
prophet] poured oil on his head, saying to him, "Thus says YHWH the god of Israel, 'I
anoint you king over YHWH's people Israel.' 7 *You shall cut off the house of Ahab your*
master from before you and avenge the blood of my servants the prophets and the
blood of all of YHWH's servants from Jezebel 8 *and from all of Ahab's house. You shall*
cut off every high class royal member of Ahab's in Israel. 9 *I will make Ahab's house like*
the house of Jeroboam son of Nebat and like the house of Baasha son of Ahijah.
10 *The dogs will eat Jezebel within the rampart of Jezreel with no one to bury [her]."*
Then he opened the door and fled. 11 *When Jehu went out to the servants of his mas-*
ter, they said to him, "Is everything all right?" He told them, "It's fine." They asked, "Why
did this madman come to you?" He responded to them, "You know the man and his
prattle." 12 *They said, "Not so. Tell us!" So he said, "Such and such he told me, saying,*
'Thus says YHWH, "I have anointed you king over Israel."'" 13 *As soon as they heard,*
each of them hastily took his robe and placed it under him on the bare steps. They
blew the trumpet, saying, "Jehu is king." 14 *So Jehu son of Nimshi conspired against Jo-*
ram. (Joram had been guarding Ramah of Gilead—he and all Israel—from Hazael
king of Aram. 15 *Jehoram the king returned to recuperate in Jezreel from the wounds*
which the archers inflicted on him when he went to war with Hazael king of Aram.)

Jehu said, "If this is what you want, let no one escape from the city to go tell [the news]
in Jezreel." 16 Jehu mounted [a chariot] and rode toward Jezreel because Joram the
king of Israel was recuperating in Jezreel from the wounds that the archers had in-
flicted on him in Ramah (of Gilead) when he fought with Hazael king of Aram, and
Ahaziah king of Judah had gone down to see Joram. 17 The watchman was stand-
ing on the tower in Jezreel and saw Jehu's company as it ap-
proached. He said, "I see a company." Jehoram responded, "Take
a horseman and send to meet them to ask if everything is peace-
ful." 18 So the horseman rode to meet them, and he said, "Thus
says the king, 'Is everything peaceful?'" Jehu replied, "What
do you have to do with peace? Turn around behind me." The watch-
man announced, "The messenger reached them but did not return."
19 He sent a second horseman who came to them and said, "Thus says
the king, 'Is everything peaceful?'" Jehu replied, "What do you
have to do with peace? Turn around behind me." 20 The watchman an-
nounced, "He came to them but did not return. The driving is the
driving of Jehu son of Nimshi, for he drives madly." 21 Jehoram
commanded, "Harness [my chariot]." So they harnessed his char-
iot. Then Jehoram king of Israel and Ahaziah king of Judah rode out
each in his chariot to meet Jehu, and they found him in the plot of Naboth the
Jezreelite. 22 When Jehoram saw Jehu he asked, "Is everything peace-
ful, Jehu?" He answered, "What do you have to do with peace *during*
the harlotries of Jezebel your mother and her many sorceries?"
23 Jehoram turned and fled, saying to Ahaziah, "Treachery, Ahaziah!" 24 But
Jehu had taken a bow in his hand, and he shot Jehoram between the
shoulder blades. The arrow went out through his heart, and he
slumped down on his knees. 25 He said to Bidqar his adjutant, "Take [him] and
throw him on the plot of land of Naboth the Jezreelite. For I remember when you
and I were riding as a team behind his father Ahab and YHWH raised against him
this oracle, 26 'I will surely avenge the blood of Naboth and the blood of his sons
that I saw last night,' says YHWH, 'and I will repay you on this plot of land,' says YHWH.
Now take [him] and throw him on the plot of land according to YHWH's word."
27 When Ahaziah saw, he fled in the direction of Beth Haggan.
Jehu pursued after him and said, "Shoot him also." So they shot him on
the ascent to Gur, which is beside Ibleam. He fled to Megiddo and
died there. 28 His servants brought him by chariot to Jerusalem where they buried
him in his tomb in the city of David. 29 In the eleventh year of Joram son of Ahab,
Ahaziah began to reign over Judah. 30 *When Jehu came to Jezreel, Jezebel having*
heard, decorated her eyes with kohl, arranged her hair, and looked out of the window.
31 When Jehu came in the gate, she said, "Is everything all right, Zimri, killer of your
master? 32 Looking up at the window, he said, "Who are you that you would contend
with me?" When two eunuchs looked down at him, 33 he said, "Throw her down." So
they threw her down. Her blood spattered on the wall and on the horses, which tram-
pled her. 34 After he had eaten and drunk inside, he said, "See to this cursed woman

and bury her, since she was a king's daughter." 35 When they went to bury her they did not find any of her except her skull, feet, and the palms of her hands. 36 When they returned and told him he said, "This is Yhwh*'s word which he spoke through Elijah the Tishbite, saying, 'Within the rampart of Jezreel the dogs will eat Jezebel,' 37 and the ruin of Jezebel's corpse became like dung on the surface of the field so that they cannot say, 'This is Jezebel.'"*

Textual Notes

25 **in the twelfth year**: Omitting שנה, which is in MT but lacking in the Greek witnesses and some Hebrew mss, and unnecessary after בשנת.[1] MT, G^{B} read *twelfth*, while G^{L}, Syr, 2 Kgs 9:29 MT have *eleventh*. The reason for the doublet in the MT is not clear,[2] but the OG (= G^{L}) may be harmonistic.[3]

Ahaziah: So G^{L}. MT, 2 Chr 22:1: *Ahaziah son of Jehoram king of Judah*; G^{B}: *Ahaziah son of Jehoram*.

26 **Ahaziah**: So MT, G^{B}. G^{L} + *son of Joram* (but lacking in 10:36+).

twenty-two years old: 2 Chr 22:2 has *forty-two years old*, the result of inner-Chronicles corruption.[4]

in Jerusalem: So MT, G^{L}. G^{B}: *in Israel*.

Omri: So MT, G^{B}. G^{L} here and in 10:36+ has *Ahab*, a harmonization with 8:18.

27 **because he was related by marriage to Ahab's house**: So MT, G^{L}. Absent from G^{B} due to haplography occasioned by the repetition of *Ahab's house*.

28 **Joram son of Ahab went**: The reading that Ahaziah went to war with Joram results from the erroneous addition of the preposition את making Ahaziah the subject instead of Joram.[5] There is otherwise no reference to any involvement of Ahaziah or Judah at Ramah, and the verb ירד in v. 29 indicates that Ahaziah went from Jerusalem to visit Joram.

against Hazael: So G^{L} (ἐπὶ Ἁζαὴλ), 2 Chr 22:5. MT, G^{B} have *with Hazael* (עם־חזהאל = μετὰ Ἁζαὴλ).

king of Aram: G^{B} has ἀλλοφύλων, typically used in G to translate *Philistines*. See the Note on 13:22.

at Ramah of Gilead: See the Note on 1 Kgs 22:3.

the archers: Reading המורים based on 2 Chr 22:5, G^{BL}.[6] The error caused the repetitive references to the Aramaeans/Aram and the absence of the article on ארמים.

29 **in Jezreel**: So MT, G^{L}. G^{B} typically renders *Jezreel* as "Israel."[7]

the archers: See the Note on 8:28.

son of Jehoram: So G^{B}. MT, G^{L} + *the king of Judah*.

son of Ahab: So MT, G^{B}. G^{L}: *son of Ahab king of Israel*.

---

1 WO (286) appeal to Gen 7:11 as evidence of a framing construction in the repetition of *year*. But this is the only occurrence of such a construction in the regnal formulae.

2 Thiele (*Mysterious Numbers*, 101) attributes it to a change in Judah in the method of reckoning regnal years, Provan (*Kings*, 213) to an effort to harmonize 3:1 and 8:25.

3 See the discussion of Hendel, "Two Editions," 109.

4 Klein, *2 Chronicles*, 311.

5 So Klostermann (*Könige*, 418) and Würthwein (*1. Könige 17–2. Könige 25*, 324, 328) among others.

6 Burney, *Notes*, 296; Gray, *Kings*, 533; Klostermann, *Könige*, 418. Cf. Ps 78:9; Jer 4:29.

7 Cf. Hugo, *Les deux visages*, 285–86.

9:1 **Ramah of Gilead**: See the Note on 1 Kgs 22:3.

2 **When you arrive**: So G^L without the שמה in MT and G^B. Its occurrence so close to שם suggests that it is secondary.

Jehu son of Jehoshaphat son of Nimshi: So MT and 6QpapKgs,[8] since Jehu is elsewhere called *the son of Nimshi* (1 Kgs 19:16; 2 Kgs 9:20), perhaps to distinguish his father from Jehoshaphat king of Judah. G^B: *the son of Jehoshaphat, Jehu, son of Nimshi*; G^L: *Jehu, son of Nimshi, son of Jehoshaphat*. The reason for the different order of G^L is unclear.

make him get up: So G^L; preceded in MT, G^B with ובאת.

comrades: Lit. *brothers.*

an inner chamber: So MT, G^B (חדר בחדר = ταμίειον ἐν τῷ ταμιείῳ). G^L: ταμίειον ἐκ ταμιείου due to confusion of ἐκ for ἐν.

3 **over Israel**: So G^{BL} (ἐπὶ Ισραηλ) and some Hebrew mss. MT: אל־ישראל.

4 **the prophet**: So G^B. Most witnesses reflect הנער, *the young man*, either before or after *the prophet*. MT has a dittography: הנער הנער הנביא. The different positions suggest that הנער is expansive, perhaps added to avoid confusion between the prophet and his mentor Elisha.

5 **I have a message**: So MT, G^B. G^L: *I have a secret message*, probably influenced by Judg 3:19.

6 **over**: So G^{BL}. MT: *to* (אל) in both instances of the preposition.

7 **cut off**: As presupposed by G^{BL} (καὶ ἐξολεθρεύσεις) = והכרתה as in the other anti-dynastic oracles (1 Kgs 14:10; 21:21; cf. 2 Chr 22:7) in place of MT's והכיתה.[9]

from before you: So G^{BL} (ἐκ προσώπου μου = מפניך), lost by haplography from MT.

and avenge: So G^{BL} with the second person. MT has the first person (ונקמתי), *and I will avenge*, which introduces a theological rationalization that Yhwh himself is effecting vengeance.

8 **and from all of Ahab's house**: So G^{BL} (καὶ ἐκ χειρὸς ὅλου τοῦ οἴκου Ἀχααβ). MT has *all of Ahab's house will perish* (ואבד כל־בית אחאב), i.e., אבד instead of מיד, which is redundant following the order to annihilate Ahab's house.

You shall cut off: Reading the second person as in v. 7 with G^{BL} where MT has first person.

high class royal member: See the Introduction.

of Ahab's: So MT, G^L. G^B's *of Ahab's house.*

10 **within the rampart of Jezreel**: As explained in the Note on 1 Kgs 21:23, the reading here and in v. 36 is based on two considerations. First, these three verses contain the same elements and hence must refer to the same oracle; they must have originally been in agreement except perhaps for word order.[10]

הכלבים יאכלו את־איזבל בחל יזרעאל (1 Kgs 21:23)
ואת־איזבל יאכלו הכלבים בחלק יזרעאל (2 Kgs 9:10)
בחלק יזרעאל יאכלו הכלבים את־בשר[11] איזבל (2 Kgs 9:36).

Second, it is difficult to account for the loss of the *qoph* in 1 Kgs 21:23. The change from חל to חלק in 2 Kgs 9:10, 36, on the other hand, may be the result of confusion caused by the curse that Jezebel's corpse would become dung throughout the territory (חלק) of Jezreel (9:37) and by the references to Naboth's חלקה in 9:21, 25 reinforcing a measure-for-measure reprisal.

---

8 Ulrich, *Biblical Qumran Scrolls*, 329.

9 Trebolle, *Centena*, 174–76.

10 Eissfeldt ("Die Komposition von I Reg 16,29–II Reg 13,25," 57) sensed the same thing in his attempt to equate חל and חלק, although his solution was harmonistic.

11 On the word "flesh" here, see the textual note.

11 **they said**: So G^{BL}. MT has the singular, *one said*, but the antecedent is plural (*servants*), and Jehu's response is directed *to them.*

He told them, "It's fine." They asked: So G^{L}. Lost by haplography from MT, G^{B}.

12 **They said**: So MT. G^{L} + *to him.* G^{B}: *he said.*

So he said: So MT. G^{B}: *So Jehu said to them.* G^{L}: *So he said to them.*

saying: So MT, G^{L}. G^{B}: λέγων καὶ εἶπεν, a double reading.

over Israel: So G^{B}. MT: *to Israel* (אל for על). G^{L}: *over my people Israel.*

13 **As soon as they heard**: So G^{BL}, reflecting וישמעו. Lost by haplography from MT.

on the bare steps: So MT (אל־גרם המעלות), though אל is an error or substitute for על. גרם ("bone, self") is evidently synonymous with עצם ("bone") and refers to the substance of the stairs.[12]

14 **Jehu son of Nimshi**: See the Note on 9:2. G^{L} again reflects a different order.

against Joram: So G^{L} (ἐπὶ Ἰωρὰμ = על יורם). MT, G^{B}: אל־יורם = πρὸς Ἰωρὰμ.

15 **the archers**: See the Note on 8:28.

to tell: So MT *qere'* (להגיד) in preference to the *ketiv* (לגיד). G^{BL} precede with the conjunction.

16 **Jehu mounted [a chariot] and rode to Jezreel**: So MT, G^{L}. G^{B} attests a third verb: ... *rode and went down* ... On the meaning of the verb רכב, see the Note on 1 Kgs 18:45.

because Joram the king of Israel was recuperating in Jezreel from the wounds that the archers had inflicted on him in Ramah (of Gilead) when he fought with Hazael king of Aram, and Ahaziah king of Judah had gone down to see Joram: So G^{L}, based on 8:29, which it rehearses following the interpolation of 9:1-13 (see Diachronic Analysis). For the reading *archers* (המורים) for *Aramaeans* see on 8:28. Between *Hazael king of Aram* and *Ahaziah king of Judah* G^{B} has the plus *for he was a warrior and a powerful man.* This is a misplaced gloss intended to add to the description in v. 14.[13]

17 **was standing**: So MT, G^{L}. G^{B}: *went up.*

on the tower in Jezreel: So MT, G^{L}. G^{B}: *on the tower of Israel.*

Jehu's company: So MT, G^{B}. G^{L}: τὸν κονιορτὸν τοῦ ὄχλου Ιου, a double reading.

I see a company: Reading שפעה in place of MT's construct form שפעת.

Take a horseman and send: So MT (קח רכב ושלח), G^{B} (λαβὲ ἐπιβάτην καὶ ἀπόστειλον). G^{L} (λάβετε ἐπιβάτην ἵππου καὶ ἀποστείλατε) has plurals and also reflects רכב סוס.

18 **to meet them**: So G^{L}. MT, G^{B}: *to meet him*, but Jehu's identity is not determined yet.

What do you have to do with peace?: See the note on 1 Kgs 17:18.

reached them: That is, עדיהם (בא) instead of MT's anomalous עד־הם. Compare עדיכם in Job 32:12.[14]

19 **to them**: So MT (אלהם). G^{B}: *to him.* (πρὸς αὐτὸν). G^{L}: ἕως αὐτῶν = עדיהם.

---

12 Gray (*Kings*, 542–43) mentions two other possible solutions: (1) Take גרם as a rare architectural term cognate to Arabic *jarama* "cut off" that referred to a landing at the top of the staircase leading into the building from which Jehu emerged (cf. Šanda, *Könige* II, 96). (2) Read מרום "height, elevation" for גרם, thus yielding "the top of the stairs." Gray ascribes the second of these interpretations to Grätz but does not include a citation of the work.

13 Šanda, *Könige* II, 96.

14 This form is also anomalous in its vocalization. One expects עֲדֵיכֶם instead of עָדֵיכֶם. GKC §32n, 103o; Joüon [Muraoka] §103mN.

Is everything peaceful: I.e., השלום with the interrogative particle as in v. 18 and reflected here in G^{BL}.[15]

What do you have to do with peace?: See the Note on 1 Kgs 17:18.

20 **He came**: So MT, G^{B}. G^{L}: + καὶ οὗτος = גם הוא.

to them: Reading עדיהם as in v. 18. MT's עד־אליהם conflates עדיהם and אליהם.[16]

the driving is the driving of Jehu: So G^{BL}. MT: *the driving is like the driving of Jehu.*

21 **Harness [my chariot]. So they harnessed his chariot**: Reading plural verbs with G^{L} where MT, G^{B} have singulars.[17]

to meet Jehu: So G^{L}, which lacks the verb immediately before לקראת.

22 **What do you have to do with peace**: So G^{L} (τί σοι καὶ εἰρήνῃ) reflecting the same idiom found earlier (vv. 18-19). MT, G^{B}: *what is (the) peace.*

during: So MT (עד), construed in G^{B} (ἔτι) as עוד. For the meaning *during* see Judg 3:26; Jon 4:2 (WO, 215). G^{L} lacks the particle.

23 **and fled**: So MT, G^{B}. G^{L}: *to flee.* Either reading is possible.

24 **had taken a bow in his hand**: Lit. *filled his hand with the bow.* G^{L} reads *hands.*

the arrow: So MT, G^{L}. G^{B}: *his arrow.* The word חצי for *arrow* (vs. חץ) occurs also in 1 Sam 20:36-38.

on his knees: So G^{BL} (ἐπὶ τὰ γόνατα αὐτοῦ = על ברכיו). MT *in his chariot* (ברכבו) has been influenced by the other references in the context to the chariot and perhaps by 1 Kgs 22:35.

25 **he said**: So MT, G^{B}. G^{L}: *Jehu said.*

Bidqar: The origin and meaning of the name are uncertain. It is often seen as equivalent to בן־דקר (1 Kgs 4:9), but this remains uncertain.[18]

his adjutant: So MT *qere'* (שלשו) in place of the *ketiv* שלשה "three."[19]

take [him]: So MT, G^{L}, also in v. 26. Absent from G^{AB}, Syr.

for I remember when you and I: So G^{L} (διότι μέμνημαι ἐγὼ ὅτε ἐγὼ καὶ σὺ = כי־זכר אני כי אני ואתה. MT lost כי אני by haplography, after which the participle was read as an imperative. Cf. BHS.

were riding: Reading רכבים without the preceding את of MT, which is a partial dittography of אתה.

as a team: So G^{B} (ἐπὶ ζεύγη).[20] צמד means *pair* and is used in the plural elsewhere only in 1 Kgs 19:19, where it refers to Elisha's twelve pairs of oxen. It does not make sense in the present verse to say that Jehu and Bidqar rode in separate pairs; rather, they were partners on a chariot team. The plural has probably come in under the influence of the preceding רכבים.

26 **I will surely avenge the blood of Naboth and the blood of his sons that I saw last night**: So G^{L}: (εἰ μὴν τὰ αἵματα Ναβcυθαι καὶ τὰ αἵματα τῶν υἱῶν αὐτοῦ εκδικήσω ἃ εἶδον ἐχθές = אם־לא את־דמי נבות ואת־דמי בניו אקם אשר ראיתי אמש (cf. Josh 14:9; 1 Kgs 20:23; Isa 5:9; 14:24; Jer 15:11; Job 1:11; 22:20; Ps 131:2).

---

15 H. G. Mitchell ("The Omission of the Interrogative Particle," in *Old Testament and Semitic Studies in Memory of William Rainey Harper,* vol. 1 [ed. R. F. Harper, F. Brown, and G. F. Moore; Chicago: University of Chicago Press, 1907]: 115–29) suggested that the interrogative particle could be omitted in questions prompted by strong emotions, including uncertainty, as is the case here.

16 Stade, *Kings*, 223.

17 Buis (*Rois*, 214) suggests reading אסר as an infinitive absolute used as a surrogate for an imperative. While possible, this would not explain the following singular ויאסר.

18 Noth, *Personennamen*, 149.

19 See the commentary on 7:2 and Mastin, "Was the *ŠĀLÎŠ* the Third Man in the Chariot?"

20 Kittel, *Könige*, 232.

repay you: So MT, G^{L}. G^{B}: *repay him*

Now take [him] and throw him: So MT, G^{B}, v. 25. G^{L} has plurals, but the addressee is still Bidqar.

on the plot of land: So MT, G^{B}. G^{L} + *of Naboth* in accord with v. 25.

27 **Beth Haggan**: Also called En-Haggan (Josh 19:21; 21:29), is identified as present-day Jenin ca. 7 mi/11 km south of Jezreel. Jenin preserves the ancient name, and Iron Age remains have been found there.[21]

Shoot him also. So they shot him: So Syr גם־אתו הכהו ויכהו. MT has Jehu's order without the note of compliance. G^{BL}: *him also. So he/one shot him.* Separate haplographies account for the reading in each case. My reading also deletes the phrase *on the chariot* as a misplaced gloss intended for v. 28.[22] While מרכבה is used here, רכב occurs elsewhere in this context for *chariot*.[23]

on the ascent to Gur, which is beside Ibleam: Ibleam is modern Khirbet Bel'ame ca. two kilometers south of Jenin. The ascent of Gur is unknown but may have been the eastern pass near Ibleam controlled by Khirbet en-Najjar, which preserves the name of ancient Gur.[24]

28 **his servants brought him by chariot to Jerusalem**: MT has the verb וירכבו, while G^{L} reflects ויביאו. GB conflates the two.

in his tomb: So G^{BL}. MT, G^{A}, Syr + *with his forebears*.

29 **son of Ahab**: So MT. G^{BL}: *king of Israel.* These are variants identifying Joram as Northern.

over Judah: G^{L} continues with *and he reigned one year in Jerusalem*, a harmonization of the datum here with that of v. 25.

30 **to Jezreel**: So MT, G^{L}. G^{B} (ἐπὶ Ισραηλ) reflects על/אל confusion/variation.

decorated her eyes with kohl: ותשם בפוך עיניה. The *bet* is instrumental. פוך was black eye paint, perhaps consisting of antimony trisulphide mixed with olive oil to facilitate application. Its purpose was to darken the area around the eyes to give the appearance of enlargement.[25]

31 **in the gate**: So MT. G^{BL}: *in the city*, an inner-Greek error (πύλῃ for πόλει).

she said: So MT, G^{B}. G^{L} precedes with *to him.*

32 **Looking up at**: So MT, G^{B}, lit. *he raised his face.* G^{L} has *Jehu raised his eyes. Eyes* and *face* are variants. Either is possible.

he said: Preceded in G^{BL} with *and he saw her.* G^{L} also has the object *to her* after *he said.*

Who are you that you would contend with me?: I tentatively adopt an old suggestion of Klostermann's based on G^{BL} (τίς εἶ σύ κατάβηθι πρὸς μέ/μετ' ἐμοῦ = מי את[י] תרדי אלי/אתי).[26] MT's repetition of *who* is corrupt, and the longer Greek reading suggests that something is missing. But it makes no sense for Jehu to question Jezebel's identity or to order her to come down to him right before having her thrown down.

two: So G^{BL}. MT: *two or three. Two* can also stand for a few (1 Kgs 17:12).

33 **Throw her down**: So MT *qere'*; the *ketiv* has the masculine suffix.

her blood: So G^{L}. MT, G^{B}: *some of her blood.*

trampled: Reading the plural with G^{BL}, as appropriate for the subject, *horses.* MT has a singular verb.

---

21 A. Zertal, "Beth-Haggan," *ABD* 1:687.
22 Montgomery, *Kings*, 402.
23 Stade, *Kings*, 225.
24 A. Zertal, "Gur," *ABD* 2:1099.
25 W. Sommer, "The Meaning of פוך in the Old Testament," *JBL* 42 (1943): 33–35.
26 Klostermann (*Könige*, 422) proposed עם as the preposition, but את is attested with the appropriate meaning.

35 **any of her**: So MT. On this partitive use of ב see GKC §119m.
36 **through Elijah**: So G^B. MT, G^L: *through his servant Elijah.*

within the rampart: See the Notes on 1 Kgs 21:23 and 2 Kgs 9:10.

Jezebel: The witnesses agree in reading *the flesh of Jezebel.* But the other two occurrences of this oracle lack the word *flesh*, suggesting that it is an addition. It may have come in due to the content of the story in which only non-meaty parts of Jezebel are left.

37 **ruin**: So MT *ketiv* (והית), rendered as the construct of a noun for "destruction, ruin" (Job 6:2), following a proposal by Walsh.[27]

like dung: So MT, G^B. Preceded in G^L with *like Naboth's corpse*: a gloss tightening the prophecy-fulfillment connection with 1 King 21 and enhancing the sense of justice in Jezebel's death as retribution for Naboth's.

field: So G^L. MT, G^B + *in the territory of Jezreel.* Another gloss stressing Jezebel's death as retribution in kind for Naboth's on his own land.

so that they cannot say, 'This is Jezebel': G^L + *and there will be no one saying, "Alas"* (καὶ οὐκ ἔσται ὁ λέγων οἴμμοι = ואין אמר אהה). Absent any evidence for haplography in MT, this is probably best considered a gloss adding to the disparagement of Jezebel as not mourned in Israel. The plural is impersonal and has the sense "so no one can say."

Synchronic Analysis

8:25-29: Opening Ahaziah's dossier

This passage opens the file on Ahaziah of Judah in (8:25-27), which remains open as the account moves into chapter 9 where the reigns of Ahaziah and Joram are treated together.[28] This is a change from the usual practice of treating the reigns of overlapping kings as discrete units. The change is due to the nature of the account. The report of Jehu's revolt in ch. 9 will close the dossiers of both kings at once, albeit without the usual closing formulae. In Ahaziah's case the lack of closing formulae stresses the nature of his brief reign (one year) as a bridge connecting the Omri dynasty and Israel to Judah and opening onto Athaliah's reign. Otherwise Ahaziah is insignificant. He is an evildoer who is consistently in someone else's shadow—his father's, Joram of Israel's, Athaliah's. He boasts no independent accomplishments. The note about his visit to the wounded Joram following their mutual venture to Ramoth-Gilead in 8:28-29 sets the stage for the account of Jehu's revolt and how it impacted Judah as well as Israel. The mentions of Ramoth-Gilead and Jezreel recall Naboth's death (1 Kgs 21) and Ahab's (1 Kgs 22) and suggest that the demise of Ahab's house is at hand, especially with the mention of Hazael in 8:28. Elisha has succeeded Elijah; Hazael is king of Aram; can Jehu's overthrow of Ahab's house (1 Kgs 19:15-17) be far behind?[29]

---

27 J. T. Walsh, "On היה in 2 Kgs 9:37," *VT* 60 (2010): 152–53. The proposal obviates the need for emendation and aligns Jehu's citation more closely with Elijah's oracle. Others (Burney, *Kings*, 301; Stade, *Kings*, 226) identify היה as a form of the 3fs that occurs with other third weak verbs (Lev 25:21; 26:34; Ezek 24:12; Jer 13:19).

28 The file metaphor is borrowed from Nelson, *Kings*, 197.

29 Cohn, *II Kings*, 64.

9:1: Mission to Ramoth-Gilead

The subject-first sentence in 9:1 marks a new episode as Elisha instructs one of the prophetic guild to take oil and go to Ramoth-Gilead.[30] His order to *gird your loins* may imply urgency, as occasioned by the window of opportunity that Joram's absence from Ramoth affords for revolution. The involvement of a prophet as well as Jehu's name show that this is more than a political overthrow. The name means "YHWH is he," i.e., "YHWH is the one" or "YHWH is god." It therefore has the same sense as Elijah's name and is appropriate for the man who will purge Baal worshipers from Israel along with the house of Ahab. It is for that dual purpose that Jehu is anointed.

9:2-3: A secret anointing

Elisha himself does not go, perhaps because he is already suffering from the illness that will claim his life (13:14). Another possibility, though, is suggested by the mention of an interior room. The expression referred previously (1 Kgs 20:30; 22:25) to a hiding place and therefore implies strict secrecy and privacy. Perhaps Elisha wished to avoid the attention his presence would attract and so sends a surrogate. The secrecy of the anointing also fits well with the nature of Elisha's activities in the stories about him (4:33; 5:9-10; 6:12, 32).[31] The reference to the inner room is a reminder that if Ahab had killed the king of Aram when he had the chance (1 Kgs 20:30) and had trusted in YHWH's true prophets (1 Kgs 22:25) Israel would not be in its present predicament.[32]

9:4-5: Distringuishing Jehu

The prophet is young (v. 4) and eager to please. He leaves immediately and journeys to Ramoth-Gilead where he finds army commanders sitting together, probably in conference (v. 5). They are apparently outside, since Jehu and the prophet enter a house (v. 6). This would mean that in v. 5 the young prophet enters the city of Ramoth. The setting is imprecise; the focus is on the dialogues, which attenuate the narrative and create suspense. The fact that the prophet can approach the commanders and announce that he has a message for one of them suggests that his clothing or some other feature (hairstyle, tattoo) gives away his vocation. Or they may know him as a disciple of Elisha's. He either recognizes Jehu or his initial vagueness is a ploy to get Jehu to speak out and distinguish himself as the leader among the officers.[33] The language is egalitarian in v. 2 ("brothers"),[34] but Jehu's response and the enthusiastic support of his comrades (v. 13) point to him as the leader among equals.

9:6-10: The anointing and an extension

The young prophet's words in v. 6 match those given him by Elisha (v. 3), with two additions: to *thus says YHWH* he adds *the god of Israel*, and he expands *king over Israel* to *king over YHWH's people, over Israel.* The additions are all the more pronounced in view of Jehu's rehearsal in v. 12, which matches the wording in v. 3. They emphasize the drama of the moment and YHWH's claim on Israel and control of its history through its regnal transitions, despite the apostasy of its kings.[35] According to Elisha's instructions the young prophet is supposed to flee (v. 3) at

---

30 Jewish tradition identifies this prophetic disciple as Jonah. See H. W. Guggenheimer, *Seder Olam: The Rabbinic View of Biblical Chronology* (Northvale, NJ/Jerusalem: Jason Aronson, 1998), 160–62.

31 Leithart, *Kings*, 220.

32 Sweeney, *Kings*, 333.

33 Cohn, *II Kings*, 66.

34 Long, *2 Kings*, 118.

35 Cohn, *II Kings*, 66.

this point. He does not, though, launching instead into an oracle commissioning Jehu to annihilate the house of Ahab (9:7-10a). He prefaces his words with *thus says* YHWH (v. 6) and he speaks in the first person, for YHWH (vv. 6, 9). Nor is this the first prediction of the annihilation of Ahab's house (1 Kgs 21:21-24). Still, the violation of Elisha's order raises doubts about the extent of the genuine oracle from YHWH to Jehu. It is possible that the young prophet received additional revelation unbeknownst to Elisha or that YHWH and Elisha are not on the same page. It is perhaps more likely that the supplemental oracle reflects the exuberance of the implied author for the violence that will be carried out by Jehu. The mention of vengeance for the prophets and servants of YHWH in v. 7 especially feels that way. The young prophet's supplement raises the possibility that Jehu's extreme violence and slaughter beyond the bounds of Ahab's house and the celebration of that violence exceeded YHWH's will.

9:11: The absence of *shalom*?

The subject-first sentence in v. 11 signals a new episode as Jehu emerges from the house to rejoin *the servants of his master.* This designation of his fellow officers is ironic in view of the revolt that is about to begin. They ask him if everything is all right (השלום). This is a *leitmotif*, occurring eight more times in the chapter and playing on different nuances of the root שלם. The term functions as a greeting and reply but also expresses a state of balance and proper relationship with YHWH.[36] The expected response is שלום, "everything is fine" (Gen 29:6; 43:27-28; 2 Kgs 4:26; 5:21-22), and the absence of the response can be ominous (2 Sam 18:32; 20:9-10). Jehu tries to dismiss the question, but the absence of שלום in his reply shows that things are not as they should be. Later on (vv. 18-19) Jehu will explain that שלום is impossible so long as Jezebel lives and the apostasies introduced by her continue (v. 22), thus activating yet another nuance of the root—payback.

9:12: Madman's deed

The השלום of Jehu's peers implicitly inquires about the reason for the visit of the prophet, whom they refer to as a *madman*. Prophets are called mad elsewhere in the HB (Hos 9:7; Jer 29:26), and behind this designation may lie the idea that the insane or mentally unstable were seen in antiquity as divinely "touched" and therefore sacrosanct (1 Sam 21:12-15). But there is also something contemptuous and dismissive in the soldiers' reference to the prophet as crazy. This may reflect how those in the military generally view prophets.[37] Still, the designation again implies that they recognize him as a member of the prophetic guild, and they take his message seriously by making Jehu king. Jehu tries to dismiss *the man and his prattle.* The word שיח is relatively common in Psalms and Wisdom literature and refers to musing or a complaint (1 Kgs 18:27). Here it has the sense of "idle talk" or *prattle*, although "complaint" might also fit for a prophet. Jehu tries to get his comrades to ignore it, but this proves impossible with oil dripping off his brow. They call "lie" (v. 12) and demand to know what the prophet said and did. Jehu summarizes the young man's oracle, repeating the essential part from v. 3 verbatim: *Thus says* YHWH, *"I anoint you king over Israel."*

9:13-15: Instant support

The speed and enthusiasm with which the other commanders react attest Jehu's popularity among them or their disgust with Joram and the Omrids, or

36 S. M. Olyan, "*Hăšālôm*: Some Literary Considerations of 2 Kings 9," *CBQ* 46 (1984): 652–68. See also Pruin, *Geschichten und Geschichte,* 179–85, who discusses the different nuances of the term at different levels of this narrative.

37 Wilson, *Prophecy and Society,* 204–205.

both. In a gesture of allegiance and submission in which each man's garment evidently represents him they remove their outer cloaks and lay them at Jehu's feet (v. 13; cf. Matt 21:8; Mark 11:8; Luke 19:36). They also sound the *shofar* or ram's horn and proclaim Jehu king. With these acts the revolt is in full swing (v. 14a). As the narrative moves with Jehu to Jezreel the reader is reminded of the positions of the players, particularly King Joram, the target of the revolt (vv. 14b-15a). Jehu's words to his peers (אם־יש נפשכם) are not a request for permission, which, as Würthwein observes, Jehu hardly requires.[38] Nor is it an oath as Würthwein translates it. Rather, it is an expression of modesty (*if you want*) that places at least partial responsibility on his companions by ordering their collusion to prevent anyone from Ramoth from going to Jezreel to publish the news of the unfolding revolt (v. 15b). The order emphasizes that Jehu launches his revolt from the place where Ahab was fatally wounded (1 Kgs 22). Jehu gets into his chariot and heads immediately toward Jezreel (v. 16). The occurrence of his name alone, without mention of his comrades, shows the solidarity of their support. Skipping the details about the journey, the narrative leaves the impression that Jehu traveled at a feverish pace, especially with the watchman's subsequent reports of a dusty company led by a mad driver.

9:16-17: Jezreel unawares

In Jezreel, King Joram is lying (שכב), completely unaware and unprepared for the approaching revolt (v. 16). Ahaziah is also there. The pace of the narrative slows with the approach of the chariots. Verses 17-29 describe the dispatch of messengers from the city to the advancing force from different perspectives, drawing in the reader.[39] The time frame is attenuated and unrealistic with its two separate emissaries followed by Joram himself all riding out in sequence as the company draws ever closer. Its threefold cycle with the climax and confrontation in the third installment has appeared previously in 2 Kgs 1:9-15; 2:1-7; 4:29-36.[40] The word *company* or "multitude" applied to Jehu and his troops in v. 17 is used only here for people. Elsewhere it refers to groups of horses (Ezek 26:10), camels (Isa 60:6), and an abundance of water (Job 22:11; 38:34), suggesting the amorphous configuration the watchman perceives. The approach of the group from the direction of Ramoth-Gilead probably leads Joram to think they are bringing news about the standoff there. The question he sends by rider, "Is everything all right?" (השלום), betrays his naïveté. It is the same as what Jehu's comrades asked him after his encounter with the prophet in Ramoth. It was also posed in 4:26 to the woman by Elisha, who was unaware that her son had died, and by Naaman to Gehazi in 5:21. It is a clue that things are not well.[41]

9:18-19: Nothing to do with *shalom*

The emissary's messenger formula, *thus says the king* (v. 18), contrasts with the *thus says* Yhwh of Jehu's commission (vv. 3, 6, 12) and sets Joram in opposition

38 Würthwein, *1. Könige 17–2. Könige 25*, 331n.

39 Long, *1 & 2 Kings*, 365.

40 Hens-Piazza, *Kings*, 290; Hobbs, *2 Kings*, 113.

41 Wiseman's (*Kings*, 319–20) interpretation of השלום as an invitation to negotiate does not work here. Joram does not know who the approaching party is or what they want, though he evidently assumes that they come from Ramoth-Gilead. He therefore seeks information, not negotiation. Requesting negotiation after he learns Jehu's identity would indicate that he was aware of Jehu's real purpose, but that is not the case; he is caught off guard.

to YHWH.[42] Joram's question is concerned with the situation in Ramoth; Jehu's response is a rhetorical question that puns on the different meanings of שלום and carries ominous overtones. Everything is fine in Ramoth, and everything is fine for those with Jehu. Joram's messenger, however, has nothing in common with שלום and may even be in opposition to it. This is because שלום is more than the absence of conflict. Jehu and his followers come bringing conflict. They also come to restore שלום. The source of the problem, he avers, is in Jezreel. The emissary is on the wrong side for שלום, so Jehu orders him to join his company.[43] The emissary complies. The narrative reports this scene through the eyes of the watchman, thereby returning the perspective to that of the people in Jezreel, to whom the emissary's actions must have been puzzling, yet they rouse no suspicions on the part of Joram, who sends out a second rider (v. 19). This rider is breathless from the excitement and omits the interrogative particle, but it is still Joram's question that he repeats, "Is everything all right?," as is clear from the repetition of the previous response, "What do you have to do with peace?" Again Jehu orders the emissary to ride behind him, and again the narrative uses the watchman to report his compliance.

9:20-21: Riding to their doom

In the meantime the company draws close enough for the watchman to recognize the driving style of the lead chariot (v. 20). It looks like that of Jehu, who drives "with madness" (בשגעון), that is, "recklessly, with abandon." The root is the same as that used to designate the prophet in v. 11 as a *madman* and thus identifies Jehu with the prophets. The defection of the second emissary impels Joram to ride out himself (v. 21), blithely unaware of Jehu's real intent. He may even have found the report that Jehu was in the lead to be reassuring. The entire threefold cycle is testimony to the effectiveness of Jehu's strategy of secrecy in not allowing anyone from Ramoth to give warning in Jezreel. It also presents Joram as a fool. The fact that he is well enough to ride suggests that his departure from Ramoth was an error in judgment—for which he is about to pay dearly.[44] Ahaziah of Judah is also foolish. He follows Joram in his own chariot. Both kings are now fully exposed. Not by accident, the moment of their assassination occurs when they are on property that belonged to Naboth (1 Kgs 21).

9:22-23: The impediment to *shalom*

Coming upon Jehu, Joram asks the same question as his emissaries: "Is everything all right?" (השלום). Jehu's response differs this time, though it is still a rhetorical question. "What is peace, as long as the harlotries and many sorceries of Jezebel your mother persist?" Jehu does not invite him to fall in, as he did with the emissaries. "Harlotries" is commonly used in the HB for the worship of other gods (Exod 34:16; Lev 17:7; Deut 31:16; Judg 2:17; 8:33; Jer 2:1-13; Hos 1–3). Similarly, "sorcery" can be a catch-all for non-Yahwistic practices (Isa 47:9, 12; Mic 5:11-13; Nah 3:4; Mal 3:5).[45] Together the two terms represent Jezebel as foreign, idolatrous, and leading Israel astray. She is an impediment to *shalom*, which can

42 Olyan, "*Hăšālôm*," 664.

43 Barnes, *Kings*, 258.

44 Sweeney, *Kings*, 334.

45 On both terms see Pruin, *Geschichten und Geschichte*, 152–56. G. Brewer-Boydston (*Good Queen Mothers, Bad Queen Mothers*, 109) points out that either Jehu is calling Jezebel a whore and a witch, for which there is no other evidence, or the expression is metaphorical.

only exist in proper relationship to YHWH through adherence to his regulations for Israel.[46] These two verses, then, pinpoint Israel's problem as the lack of right relationship with YHWH, the source of this problem as Jezebel, and her crimes as abuse of power and worship of other gods. Finally realizing his general's real intent, Joram turns his chariot to flee. He warns Ahaziah that *treachery* (מרמה) is afoot. It is the opposite of שלום.[47] For Joram, Jehu's actions represent treason and threaten the peace of the kingdom; for Jehu, the Ahabids are the source of *treachery,* and Jehu is restoring *shalom.*

9:24-26: Assassination and the question of motive

Jehu takes his bow and shoots the fleeing Joram in the back, killing him in his chariot (v. 24). His death resembles that of his father Ahab (1 Kgs 22:34-35). Both were shot by arrows that killed them; both chariots were turned around in efforts to avoid death; both died in their chariots. Joram's death partially fulfills the oracle against Ahab and his house in 1 Kgs 21:19-24.[48] Jehu, indeed, is reminded of an oracle. His citation (vv. 25-26), though, differs from the earlier one: (1) Jehu was accompanying Ahab when the oracle he cites is given, while in 1 Kings 21 Ahab is alone. (2) Jehu does not mention Elijah, the bearer of the earlier oracle. (3) The oracle Jehu cites mentions Naboth's sons. (4) The oracle Jehu cites dates the crime against Naboth to "last night." (5) Jehu cites a promise to repay Ahab on Naboth's plot of land, which is not the same as the place where the dogs lick Naboth's and Ahab's blood (1 Kgs 21:19; 22:38), nor is it Naboth's vineyard. Jehu's citation identifies the place where Naboth was killed as his own property. It may be that Jehu is citing a different oracle, one not preserved in the HB. On the other hand, it fits his character in chs. 9–10 to paraphrase and loosely interpret the oracle in 1 Kings 21 in order to justify the bloodshed he perpetrates. The oracle he cites envisions retribution for the crime against Naboth falling upon Ahab, as does 1 Kgs 21:19, yet Jehu takes it to extend to future generations in line with 1 Kgs 21:20-24. He portrays himself as authorized by prophetic commission to fulfill the prophecy by exterminating Ahab's line and supporters. His words are directed as much to the reader as to Bidqar. His use of שלמתי suggests that in his view the slaughter he carries out is necessary to reestablish *shalom* between YHWH and Israel. But the citation in vv. 25-26 begs the question as to how much of his purge is fulfillment of prophecy and how much the manipulation of it for military, political, and even religious legitimation.

9:27-29: A second assassination and more questions

The point is illustrated by the next three verses (vv. 27-29) detailing Ahaziah's assassination. The narrative does not justify Jehu's order to kill Ahaziah, though one assumes it is because of Ahaziah's kinship to Ahab. If this is the reason, his corpse should be left for the dogs and birds, yet Ahaziah is buried (v. 28). A subject-first construction sets vv. 27-29 apart as a side note that leaves Ahaziah's assassination without a clear rationale. Ahaziah's burial with his forebears in Jerusalem affords him a measure of dignity. But there are no concluding formulae for him. Verse 29 reiterates his opening formula, leaving the account of his reign astonishingly open-ended. The evil that Ahaziah represented in the link with the house of Ahab continues with Athaliah, so that Jehu's murder of Ahaziah did nothing to eradicate the Omrid problem from Judah.

---

46 Olyan, "*Hăšālôm.*"

47 As shown by Olyan, "*Hăšālôm,*" 667, citing Ps 35:20; Prov 11:1; Jer 9:7.

48 Long, *1 & 2 Kings*, 366.

9:30: Jezebel's preparation

With Jehu's entry into Jezreel (v. 30) the narrative becomes darker and more carnivalesque in its humor and graphic depiction of violence, and it will continue in this vein into ch. 10.[49] Jezebel has somehow heard about Jehu's approach and his assassination of the two kings and has prepared for him. She has put on eye makeup and arranged or adorned her hair (lit. "her head") and is gazing out the window, waiting for him. Her toilette is rich with ambiguous imagery. Cosmetics are a luxury item emphasizing her high social status.[50] For some she is the queen mother, attended by royal officials (v. 32) and presenting herself at the audience window of the palace,[51] either anticipating reception of the reins of power[52] or at least prepared to depart life as a proud and strong woman with the dignity and style fitting her station.[53] The flaunting of her status recalls her treatment of Naboth to the extent that it evokes passages like Amos 6:6 that condemn the upper class for their abuse of and callous attitude toward the poor. What is more, some biblical texts associate the use of makeup with seduction and sexual looseness (Jer 4:30; Ezek 23:40-45). There are inescapable sexual overtones in the passage, to the point that Jezebel has been interpreted as trying to seduce Jehu.[54] Makeup and hair adornment are the property of women. The officials are probably eunuchs who administer the harem, which may be the building where Jezebel appears. The hints at sexual promiscuity bring to mind the *harlotries and sorceries* Jehu accuses her of perpetrating (v. 22), even if these are metaphors.

9:31: Jezebel's greeting

Jezebel calls Jehu *zimri* (v. 31). She may want him to think she is flirting, since the name/word can mean "strong one, hero."[55] If so, it is an illustration of her cleverness and duplicity, for the allusion to Zimri in 1 Kgs 16:9-20, who led a revolt and assassinated his master as Jehu has just done, is unmistakable. Zimri, like Jehu, was a military commander—also of chariotry. Both kill the sitting king and overthrow the ruling dynasty to seat themselves as kings. Zimri's reign lasted only seven days before he was overthrown by Omri, Jezebel's father-in-law. By calling Jehu "Zimri," Jezebel implies that his reign will likewise be short and unsuccessful. Her greeting in the first part of the verse is similarly deceitful. On the surface solicitous, it barely masks sarcasm and contempt. The answer to her question *Is everything all right?* which has been asked repeatedly in the chapter, is decidedly

---

49 García-Treto, "Fall of the House."

50 Amos 6:6; Qoh 7:1; cf. V. H. Matthews, "Cosmetics," NIDB 1:754–55.

51 Fretheim, *Kings*, 170; Landersdorfer, *Könige*, 172. Pruin (*Geschichten und Geschichte*, 188, 318–21) problematizes this idea by contending that the queen mother in ancient Israel and Judah had no official role but only ruled temporarily when her son was a minor.

52 So Fricke, *Das zweite Buch von den Königen*, 126; Steck, *Überlieferung und Zeitgeschichte*, 57–58. García-Treto ("Fall of the House," 58) suggests that Jezebel's hairdo symbolizes crowning.

53 Cohn, *II Kings*, 70; Hens-Piazza, *Kings*, 292. Hobbs, *2 Kings*, 118.

54 See S. B. Parker, "Jezebel's Reception of Jehu," *Maarav.* 1 (1978): 67–78. Brewer-Boydston (*Good Queen Mothers, Bad Queen Mothers*, 110–11) stresses the distinction between sexual overtones and seduction and observes that a man who adorned himself with royal robes would not be seen as preparing for seduction.

55 So Parker, "Jezebel's Reception of Jehu." See also the Note on 1 Kgs 16:9. Olyan ("2 Kings 9:21—Jehu as Zimri") refutes Parker's theory and suggests that Zimri's name puns on an alternative √*zmr*, meaning "prune a vineyard," thus recalling the story in 1 Kgs 21 and depicting Zimri as the "pruner" of the Omrid "vineyard."

"No." From her standpoint things are not all right and there is no peace: Jehu is leading a revolt and has killed her son; she is in imminent peril. From Jehu's perspective as well things are not all right, and Jezebel is the main cause (v. 22). Her death is a major step on the way to *shalom*.

9:32-33: Jezebel's death

Raising his view to the upper-story window where she is, Jehu addresses others in the building, asking who is on his side (v. 32). He has changed from unassuming to authoritative.[56] When two or three officials/eunuchs look out at him he tells them to pick Jezebel up and throw her down (v. 33). They comply. (They dare not refuse!) Her blood spattering on the wall reminds one of the prophecy against the Omrid males (*everyone who urinates on the wall*). The implicit comparison of her blood to urine fits with that of her body as dung in vv. 35-36. Whether the fall kills her or the horses trample her to death is not clear.

9:34-37: Jezebel's end

Jehu enters the palace to eat and drink (v. 34). After the ride from Ramah and the series of assassinations, he and his men are no doubt hungry. Still, their actions betray callousness, given the gore they have just witnessed. The meal serves the narrative function of postponing the order to bury Jezebel in order to give dogs the chance to fulfill prophecy. When Jehu issues the burial order only her skull, feet, and palms can be found uneaten (v. 35)—presumably because they are inedible or have little meat on them. When Jehu receives this news he again cites prophecy, once more imperfectly (vv. 36-37). Verse 36 has changes in both wording and order vis-à-vis 1 Kgs 21:23 and 2 Kgs 9:10. Jehu refers to the *flesh of Jezebel* that is to be eaten by dogs rather than to Jezebel. More important, he agrees with 9:10 against 1 Kgs 21:23 in mentioning the *territory* of Jezreel rather than the *rampart*. This change accommodates the continuation in v. 37 according to which Jezebel's remains end up as dog dung in the field. Jehu cites this element of the prophecy (*in the territory of Jezreel*) first, over against the other two versions, as a way of emphasizing the fulfillment location. The agreement of 9:10, 37 in reading *territory*, as opposed to *rampart* as in Elijah's original oracle, shows Jehu's willingness to bend prophecy to his own purposes.

Diachronic Analysis

8:25-27: DtrH's regnal formulae for Ahaziah

The introductory formulae for Ahaziah in 8:25-27 are DtrH's composition. The data in vv. 25-26 probably stem from sources available to DtrH, while the evaluation in v. 27 is his. Ahaziah's one-year reign (v. 26) may have been only a few months, depending on the system of reckoning used.[57] The theory explained in the previous chapter, that the reign of Jehoram of Judah may have been a fiction, in turn

56 García-Treto, "*Fall of the House*," 57.

57 For instance, by antedating, the period of time between his date of accession and the New Year would be reckoned as his single year of reign. Theoretically this could be as brief as a day. However, since special note is taken of Zimri's seven-day reign (1 Kgs 16:15) and of Shallum's one-month reign (2 Kgs 15:13), it would appear that a one-year reign was at least a few months long but somehow shorter than the two years attributed to the other Ahaziah (1 Kgs 22:52).

raises questions as to whether Ahaziah was ever actually king of Judah. That his historical existence and kingship are not fictional is assured from the reference to him in the Tel Dan inscription.[58] At the same time that inscription raises doubts about other details in the Bible's account, since the Aramaean author of the inscription takes credit, in place of Jehu, for the assassinations of Joram and Ahaziah.[59] Moreover, if the theory of a single Northern Joram is correct, the details of how Ahaziah came to the throne of Judah are obscure because they are misrepresented in the DtrH framework texts. He would not have been Joram's son but rather his cousin, the son of Athaliah (see on 8:26).[60] He may have been a regent in charge of Judah under Joram, or Joram could have given up the throne of Judah
because of other preoccupations.[61] Verse 26 (//2 Chr 22:2) names Athaliah as 8:26
Omri's daughter and therefore Ahab's sister rather than his daughter as implied in v. 18 (//2 Chr 21:6). *Daughter* may be used idiomatically to mean "descendant" and apply to a granddaughter. However, 8:18 (//2 Chr 21:6) does not mention Athaliah by name, and the relevant figures make it likely that she was born during Omri's reign and thus was quite possibly his daughter rather than Ahab's.[62] The noun חתן has the sense of being related by marriage and does not necessarily
mean that Ahaziah was Ahab's son-in-law, though this is a possibility.[63] Ahaziah's 8:27
evaluation (8:27) is much like Jehoram's. Ahaziah also was guilty of walking in the way of "the house of Ahab." Like Jehoram, he was corrupted by his in-law relationship with the house of Ahab. By not repeating the mention of the direct relationship through Athaliah the statement focuses on Ahaziah's Davidic lineage through Jehoshaphat and in turn implies that it was less his blood relationship with Ahab that was the source of influence than the political alliance forged by marriage.

Verses 28-29bα (through לראות את־יורם) also belong to DtrH. They set the stage for the story of Jehu's revolt and explain how he came to assassinate the kings of both Israel and Judah. Joram's war with Aram was initially a solo venture; Ahaziah's accompaniment resulted from a scribal error (see the Note), no doubt abetted by scribal acquaintance with 1 Kings 22 and 2 Kings 3. The Israelite army occupies Ramah of Gilead, where it periodically battles with the Aramaeans. In one such encounter King Joram is wounded, and he withdraws to Jezreel to convalesce. His absence affords a

8:28-29: DtrH's account of Joram's wounding and Ahaziah's visit

58 A. Biran and J. Naveh, "The Tel Dan Inscription: A New Fragment," *IEJ* 45 (1995): 1–18 is the *editio princeps* of the complete (reconstructed) inscription. Frevel (*Geschichte Israels*, 207) takes the Tel Dan reference to Ahaziah as king of the house of David to refer to kingship not descent, so that it does not disprove his Omrid origin.

59 The discrepancy might support the proposal that Jehu was in league with the Aramaean king, probably Hazael. See W. M. Schniedewind, "The Tel Dan Stela: New Light on Aramaic and Jehu's Revolt," *BASOR* 302 (1996): 75–90. Also I. Epha'l-Jaruzelska, *Prophecy, Royal Legitimacy and War*, 48–49, who points out the agendas of both the biblical and Aramaean accounts and the difficulty of deciding between them.

60 2 Chr 22:1 states that Ahaziah was Jehoram's youngest son. But this is probably due to the Chronicler's tendentious portrayal of the loss of the rest of Jehoram's family because of sin in 21:16-17.

61 As suggested by Miller and Hayes, *History*, 321.

62 Katzenstein, "Who Were the Parents of Athaliah?"

63 T. C. Mitchell, "The Meaning of the Noun *ḤTN* in the Old Testament," *VT* 19 (1969): 93–112, esp. 97–98.

perfect opportunity to mount a military *coup d'état*. Ahaziah's presence there, on a visit from Jerusalem, makes it easy to be rid of both Omrid heads of state. The relationship of 8:28-29 and 9:14-16 has long been a source of controversy. It is also crucial for understanding the role of 9:1-13. Würthwein takes 9:14a as the continuation of 8:29 and sees the repeated elements of 8:28-29 in 9:14b-15a, 16aβb as "a kind of *Wiederaufnahme*" indicating that 9:1-13 is an interpolation.[64] The two ideas are in conflict; the perception of an interpolation can be reinforced, but 9:14a is not the continuation of 8:29. As is often recognized, 9:14a-15a are an intrusion, interrupting the continuity between the proclamation of Jehu as king by his men in v. 13 and his agreement and stipulation to them about how to proceed in v. 15b (note the plural suffix on נפשכם).[65] Once they are bracketed from consideration it is relatively easy to see the *Wiederaufnahme* in the references to Joram's convalescence and Ahaziah's descent from Jerusalem in 8:29 and 9:16 (G^L). Hence 9:1-13 are a prophetic interpolation, for which we immediately suspect PN.

Relationship to 9:14-16

9:1-13: The young prophet's mission

In 9:1-13 Jehu's revolt is presented as the response to prophetic commissioning; he is doing YHWH's will by seizing power. Elisha is the instigator. He orders one of the "sons of the prophets," who are apparently at his disposal, to go to Ramah and anoint Jehu. The expression *gird your loins* (9:1) arose from the practice of cinching an outer garment around one's waist in order to free the legs for running or other vigorous physical activity. It is often used idiomatically, as here, meaning "prepare, get ready." In 1 Kgs 18:46 (with a different verb) and 2 Kgs 4:29 it refers specifically to preparation for a journey, though it may have the added nuance in 4:29 and here of urgency. The word *juglet* or flask (*pak*) occurs outside this context only in 1 Sam 10:1. It is onomatopoetic (HALOT), derived from the sound of liquid being poured from a small opening. It was a clay vessel, small enough to be held in the hand and therefore easily concealable. No one would know what the prophet was up to until he got there. The olive oil it contained was probably of the finest quality, to judge from its purpose, and probably a special mixture with spices and fragrances.[66] It would have been costly and not normally in the possession of the poor prophet, so Elisha gives it to him. He is told whom to anoint. Whether Jehu's name, meaning "YHWH is he," i.e., "YHWH is god," signals anything about his family background or personal piety, as often presumed, is debatable. However, the name is certainly appropriate to the role he plays in purging Israel of Baal in chs 9–10. His patronym is typically Nimshi (1 Kgs 19:16; 2 Kgs 9:20; 2 Chr 22:7), though here and in v. 14 he is the son of

64 Würthwein, *1. Könige 17–2. Könige 25*, 328, 330. Trebolle (*Jehú y Joás*, esp. 118–25, and "Textual Criticism and the Literary Structure and Composition of 1-2 Kings / 3-4 Reigns. The Different Sequence of Literary Units in MT and LXX," in *Die Septuaginta: Entstehung, Sprache, Geschichte*. 3. Internationale Fachtagung veranstaltet von Septuaginta Deutsch [LXX.D]. Wuppertal 22.-25. Juli 2010 [ed. S. Kreuzer, M. Meiser, and M. Sigismund; WUNT 286; Tübingen: Mohr Siebeck, 2012], 55–78) argues that 8:28-29 and 9:14b-15a are compilations based on 9:16 G^L (= OG), which preserves the original location and content of the material, and drawing from Ahaziah's regnal notice in 10:36+ (OG). In the next chapter the case will be argued that 10:36+ is a secondary compilation rather than the original version of Ahaziah's formulae.

65 Barré, *Rhetoric*, 13; Jones, *Kings*, 458; Schmitt, *Elisa*, 23–24; White, *Elijah Legends*, 50.

66 See the Note on 1 Kgs 19:15.

Jehoshaphat son of Nimshi. Nimshi may have been Jehu's grandfather, prominent ancestor, or clan.[67] Judging from its Arabic cognate, it means "weasel" or "mongoose" and may have been a nickname.[68]

Anointing

Anointing—pouring or smearing oil on someone's head—signified divine election (Ps 133). It was a sacramental act to the extent that it was understood to mark the transfer of holiness from YHWH to the designee.[69] Jehu's anointing places him in the select company of Saul (1 Sam 10:1), David (1 Sam 16:13; 2 Sam 2:4; 5:3), Absalom (2 Sam 19:10), Solomon (1 Kgs 1:39), Joash (2 Kgs 11:12), and Jehoahaz (2 Kgs 23:30) as the only kings for whom anointing is mentioned. Jehu is the only king of the Northern kingdom who is anointed in Kings. His anointing shares the motif of secrecy with those of Saul and David (1 Sam 16:13) and to lesser extent with those of Absalom, Solomon, and Joash. Since all these figures except Saul and Jehoahaz were anointed while someone else was king it may be a way of making explicit the claim of divine election. This claim is stressed in the David story, where the theme of "YHWH's anointed" is key, especially in the story of David's rise. So too Jehu's anointing legitimizes not only his reign but also the bloody revolt that seated him on the throne.

The PN's fashioning of the prophet's oracle

The prophet is to flee immediately upon completing his task (9:3b). It is, after all, an act of treason against a sitting king. At first he follows instructions (9:4-6), but instead of fleeing he extends his oracle. This is one of the features of vv. 7-10a that make them stand out. PN has extended the form of the anointing story he used here in order to incorporate these verses. They rehearse the anti-dynastic oracle in 1 Kgs 14:10-11; 16:2-4; and 21:21-24*. In fact, vv. 8b-9 are identical to the portion of Elijah's oracle against Ahab's house in 1 Kgs 21:21b-22a except for the shift of *your house* to *house of Ahab* occasioned by the change from direct address:

1 Kgs 21:21b-22a: והכרתי לאחאב משתין בקיר ועצור ועזוב בישראל
ונתתי את־ביתך כבית ירבעם בן־נבט וכבית בעשא בן־אחיה
2 Kgs 9:8b-9: והכרתי לאחאב משתין בקיר ועצור ועזוב בישראל
ונתתי את־בית אחאב כבית ירבעם בן־נבט וכבית בעשא בן־אחיה

---

67 It is attested in the Samaria ostraca. See F. W. Dobbs-Allsopp, *et al.*, *Hebrew Inscriptions: Texts from the Biblical Period of the Monarchy with Concordance* (New Haven/London: Yale, 2005), 475. T. J. Schneider ("Israel in the Eyes of Others," *Truth: Interdisciplinary Dialogues in a Pluralist Age* [ed. by C. Helmer and K. De Troyer; Leuven: Peeters, 2003]: 119–27) argued partly on the basis of the patronymic that Jehu was Omri's descendant. Her argument, though accepted by D. T. Lamb (*Righteous Jehu and His Evil Heirs: The Deuteronomist's Perspective on Dynastic Succession* [Oxford: Oxford University Press, 2007], 27–28), is largely obviated by Na'aman's recognition of "son of Omri" for Jehu in the inscriptions of Shalmaneser III as legitimation in acknowledgment of his new pro-Assyrian policy. See N. Na'aman, "Jehu son of Omri: Legitimizing a Loyal Vassal by his Overlord," *IEJ* 48 (1998): 236–38.

68 Noth, *Personennamen*, 230; Jerome T. Walsh, "Nimshi," *ABD* 4:1118

69 The rite of anointing has been much discussed. For a brief sketch of its sacral significance see McCarter, *I Samuel*, 178. Hatti (M. Noth, "Office and Vocation in the Old Testament," *The Laws in the Pentateuch and Other Studies* [trans. D. R. Ap-Thomas; Edinburgh/London: Oliver & Boyd, 1966], 237–39) and Egypt (de Vaux, *Ancient Israel*, 103-107) have been proposed as its place of origin. Mettinger (*King and Messiah*, 185–232) thinks it was indigenous to Israel and was a contractual symbol. See also Halpern, *Constitution*, 13–19.

However, there are differences with DtrH's oracles. This one in vv. 7-10a has been curtailed so that the focus is on the destruction of Ahab's house, with no mention of non-burial except for Jezebel (v. 10a). Verses 7-8a are concerned with avenging the blood of the prophets and servants of YHWH on Jezebel, a concern not in the other anti-dynastic oracles. Above all, this oracle has a different function from that of its precursors. It is not directed at the king who heads the ruling house; it commissions the usurper who effects the prophesied annihilation. The text-critical evidence, moreover, indicates two stages of development within vv. 7-10a. $G^{BL'}$'s translation καὶ ἐξολεθρεύσεις in v. 7 points to a *Vorlage* והכרתה, *you shall cut off*, rather than MT's והכיתה, *you shall strike down*.[70] The former is used elsewhere in the oracles against the Northern dynasties (1 Kgs 14:10; 21:21) as well as in the report in 2 Chr 22:7. This in turn suggests that vv. 7-8a were interpolated by *Wiederaufnahme* (the repetition of *you shall cut off*) into the DtrH formula about cutting off all the males of Ahab's house.[71] The expression *my servants the prophets* (v. 7b) occurs especially in Kings (1 Kgs 15:29; 2 Kgs 17:13, 23; 21:10; 24:2) but also in Jeremiah (7:25; 25:4; 26:5; 29:19; 35:15; 44:4) and in other prophetic texts (Am 3:7; Zech 1:6; Ezek 38:17).[72] In this context it especially recalls Jezebel's slaughter of YHWH's prophets in 1 Kings 18–19. The extension referring to *all of YHWH's servants* was designed to include Naboth among those to be avenged.[73] The threat against Jezebel in v. 10a recalls 1 Kgs 21:23 and signals it as the inspiration for vv. 7-10a. It applies the curse of non-burial particularly to her in anticipation of her death in 9:30-37. Thus PN borrowed the DtrH oracle in 1 Kgs 21:21-24, including the addition against Jezebel in 21:23, and inserted vv. 7-8a into it. He used the anti-dynastic oracle to commission Jehu as a tool of measure-for-measure vengeance against Ahab's house, especially Jezebel, for their slaughter of prophets and other loyal Yahwists like Naboth.

9:11-13: Proclaiming Jehu king

Now the prophet flees, and Jehu emerges to the questioning of his comrades.[74] His statement *you know the man and his prattle* (v. 11) suggests that they are acquainted with this prophet and his past messages. More important, it portrays Jehu as hesitant to accept the prophet's commission, showing that he is not driven by personal ambition.[75] Only when pressed does he admit that the prophet anointed him as king (v. 12). The historical Jehu was no doubt ambitious for power, but his revolt must have been fueled by other factors such as discontent at high taxes imposed by the Omrids to support their military and construction projects and Joram's failure to quell the Aramaean threat. When the truth comes out, Jehu's colleagues become his first supporters, spreading their garments on the ground in obeisance before him, blowing the *shofar* and proclaiming him king (v. 13). The last two activities are mentioned in connection with the anointings of

---

70 Trebolle, *Centena*, 174–76.

71 On the formula משתין בקיר ועצור ועזוב בישראל see the Introduction and 1 Kgs 21:21, as well as Talmon and Fields, "Collocation."

72 See Schmitt, *Elisa*, 20n.

73 An observation that goes back at least as far as Klostermann (*Könige*, 419).

74 It is sometimes argued that their reference to the prophet as a *madman* (משגע) in v. 11 disqualifies 9:1-13 as a prophetic story. The logic is hardly compelling, since the term also occurs for prophets in both Hosea (9:7) and Jeremiah (29:26).

75 Sweeney, *Kings*, 333.

Solomon (1 Kgs 1:34, 39) and of Joash (2 Kgs 11:14), although the proclamation for them is "long live the king" (יחי המלך) rather than "X is king (*mālak*)." The form of proclamation here also occurs for Absalom (2 Sam 15:10). Jehu's proclamation, like Absalom's, was not a full-fledged coronation ceremony but an affirmation of the revolt and a call to arms (in the sounding of the *shofar*).[76] He is proclaimed king by his immediate circle; the next step is to seize power.

9:14-15a: An intrusion

As noted above, vv. 14-15a are intrusive; they separate Jehu's response to his peers in v. 15b from their proclamation of him as king. The intrusion may have originated as a marginal gloss or variant to v. 16, perhaps motivated by the desire for a conspiracy notice ahead of the story in vv. 17-37. While conspiracy notices are common in Kings, the one in v. 14a is secondary.[77] It is the only instance of one with the *Hitpa'el* of קשר rather than the *Qal* (1 Kgs 15:27; 16:9, 16; 2 Kgs 10:9; 12:21; 14:19; 15:10, 25, 30; 21:23, 24). The *Hitpa'el* occurs only twice more in the HB (2 Chr 24:25-26). The account in vv. 17-28* that was incorporated by DtrH was self-contained, making clear Jehu's identity, both personal and as a chariot commander (v. 20), and his intentions, so that a conspiracy notice was not necessary. If there was one, it has been displaced by the addition in vv. 1-13, 15b-16a. That Joram had been guarding (שמר) Ramah in v. 14b can be inferred from 8:28–9:13. Verse 15a effectively repeats 8:29a.

9:15b-16: Jehu acts on his proclamation as king

In v. 15b Jehu responds to his comrades' proclamation (v. 13). The expression, אם־יש נפשכם, occurs only once more in the HB (Gen 23:8) and seems to be an acknowledgment of purpose or intent. As noted in the Synchronic Analysis, it serves rhetorically to place responsibility for the *coup* on Jehu's peers. Jehu's first order as king-in-waiting is to maintain confidentiality about the *coup* by preventing anyone from taking a warning to Jezreel. How his companions follow up is not spelled out. The point of the order is to explain how the revolt catches Joram and Jezreel by surprise. There is no attention given to the ride to Jezreel (v. 16a), which would take several hours by chariot (ca. 40 miles, 65 km), because of the jump to the episode in vv. 17-28 where DtrH made use of an older account of Jehu's revolt proper.

9:17-28: DtrH's use of an account of Jehu's revolt

The tower from which the watchman of Jezreel saw Jehu's approach must have faced east (v. 17), the direction of Ramah. It was probably built into the city wall, and towers have been discovered at the northeast and southeast corners of the Iron Age wall.[78] Joram orders a rider to be sent to find out if everything is all right.[79] The order is pointless from a practical standpoint. The rider cannot return to the city far enough ahead of the company to provide any effective warning or useful information. Its point is literary—to draw attention to the theme of *shalōm*

---

76 Halpern (*Constitution*, 125–48) views both cries as separate steps in the coronation ritual. This is doubtful, for reasons expressed by Mettinger, *King and Messiah*, 131–37. Halpern (pp. 136–38) does agree that in its mythic origins *X mālak* was an expression of loyalty for a *coup*. Long (*2 Kings*, 120) and Wiseman (*Kings*, 234) suggest that the proclamation for Jehu mimics the officially sanctioned rite participated in by the full public.

77 White, *Elijah Legends*, 47–51.

78 N. Franklin, "Jezreel," *OEBA* 37–42.

79 Although the verb רכב can refer to riding and mounting a chariot, here it most likely refers to a single rider, given the urgency of the situation.

that plays out in the following verses. The first rider joins the company (v. 18), as does a second one (v. 19) before the company draws close enough for the watchman to recognize the erratic driving of Jehu (v. 20).[80]

Joram and Ahaziah ride out

Upon the news that his general is approaching, Joram himself rides out in his chariot (v. 21a). It is highly unrealistic to think that the king would do such a thing unaccompanied. Even more incredibly, Ahaziah joins him, albeit as an afterthought in the narrative. The scene is ludicrous: two kings, both unaccompanied, riding out unprotected into the open country to meet a charging company whose intent is unknown. The point is literary—to set up the assassinations and at the same time to ridicule the two kings for such a foolish move. Ahaziah's presence is DtrH's addition (ואחזיהו מלך־יהודה איש ברכבו) to the revolt story, as is apparent from the fact that Joram gives orders to prepare his chariot but there is no order for Ahaziah's chariot. Also, the verb *rode out* is singular, referring to Joram alone. The final clause of v. 21 (וימצאהו בחלקת נבות היזרעאלי), which locates the encounter of the kings with Jehu on Naboth's property, is also DtrH's addition, anticipating vv. 25-26 (see below).[81]

9:22bβ: Targeting Jezebel in PN

Joram addresses the same question to Jehu as had the emissaries (v. 22): *Is everything peaceful?* (השלום). Jehu's response is also the same at first (following G^L): *What do you have to do with peace?* However, it takes on a different nuance when addressed to Joram. As king, he is the cause of the disorder. The response has also been expanded by a PN addition. There can be no peace as long as the many *harlotries and sorceries* of Jezebel persist. These are metaphors for religious apostasy that caricature Jezebel as idolatrous, harking back to 1 Kgs 16:31. As in 1 Kings 18, PN blames her for the apostasy of the Ahabids as well as the persecution of YHWH's servants (v. 7). The question designates Jezebel rather than Joram as the main target of the revolt.

9:23-24: The assassination of Joram

With a warning shout to Ahaziah, Joram turns his chariot to flee (v. 23). The warning (v. 23b) comes from DtrH. Joram does not get far. Jehu is prepared, bow in hand. The expression מלא ידו בקשת is sometimes taken to refer to nocking a bow (*HALOT* 584) on the basis of קשת מלאתי אפרים in Zech 9:13 or of the Akkadian expression *qašta mullû* (*CAD* 10:185). However, in Zech 9:13 as in the Akkadian expression, the "bow" (Judah) is the direct object with which the arrow (Ephraim) is filled. In 2 Kgs 9:24, in contrast, the direct object is *hand*, and the *bow* is the implement with which it is filled. Thus Jehu filled his hand, i.e., grasped or armed himself with the bow (BDB 570). The writer next reports that he shot Joram, the intermediate steps of nocking and drawing the bow being self-evident. Joram is unprepared, not wearing armor. Jehu shoots him in the back as he rides away. The arrow penetrates Joram's back *between his arms* or shoulder blades and exits through his heart so that he is killed immediately.

9:25-26: An older version of the Naboth story

Verses 25-26 interrupt the continuity between the assassination of Joram (v. 24) and Ahaziah's flight upon witnessing it (v. 27). At the same time they presuppose a

80 As is often noted, the Targum, followed by Josephus (*Ant.* 9.117) leaves precisely the opposite impression, reporting that he drives calmly (בניח). The reason for the discrepancy is unexplained. The preoccupation with his driving style suggests that Jehu was the commander of Israel's chariotry (Šanda, *Könige* II, 97).

81 Hentshel, *Könige 2*, 43; Schmitt, *Elisa*, 27; Würthwein, *1. Könige 17–2. Könige 25*, 332.

different, and older, version of the Naboth story than 1 Kgs 21:1-16.[82] In addition to indicating that Naboth's property is a field outside the city rather than a vineyard next to the palace, 9:26 mentions the blood of Naboth's children or sons, who are not in 1 Kings 21.[83] The name Bidqar, which occurs only here in the HB, does not seem made up and may also originate from the older account of Jehu's revolt with the datum that he was Jehu's *shalish* and one-time riding partner. Above all, the oracle cited here is addressed to Ahab (*you*) and does not implicate Jezebel. Thus vv. 25-26a are DtrH's addition to the story of Jehu's revolt based on an older version of the Naboth story before it was replaced by 1 Kgs 21:1-16. The dumping of Joram's corpse is retribution for the murders of Naboth and his sons and fulfills DtrH's anti-dynastic oracle's prediction of non-burial.[84] PN added v. 26b (signaled as an addition by ועתה) further emphasizing Jehu's actions as the fulfillment of Yhwh's word.[85]

9:27-29: The assassination of Ahaziah

Ahaziah flees not when he hears Joram's warning (v. 23b), which is a DtrH addition, but when he witnesses Joram's murder (v. 27a). Jehu's order to shoot Ahaziah in v. 27b is also DtrH. In the older revolt narrative Ahaziah remained in Jezreel rather than riding out with Joram and then fled south toward Judah and home on the main road to Beth-Haggan when he saw Joram killed. He was able to get close to Ibleam, some seven kilometers from Jezreel, before Jehu's men caught up to him and shot him according to Jehu's order. It is not hard to understand why Jehu orders Ahaziah's execution in DtrH. The Judahite king was also an Omrid, either a son or a nephew of Ahab and probably an underling and appointee of Joram. He might have sought revenge for Jehu's *coup*. From DtrH's perspective he was a participant in Ahab's sins (8:27). As the story now has it, the wounded Ahaziah does not continue toward Judah but turns sharply to the northwest to go to Megiddo (9:28), where he dies. This could have been because Megiddo was fortified and defended by forces loyal to Joram, but the same was probably true of Taanach, which was closer. The transport of his body to Jerusalem (v. 28) resembles the account of Josiah's burial in 2 Kgs 23:29-30 after he was killed in Megiddo, and this was probably the model for the report about Ahaziah.[86]

---

82 Miller, "Fall of the House of Ahab."

83 The dating of the murder of Naboth to *last night*, אמש (9:26), is also cited as a difference from the Naboth story, but it is probably used in the general sense of "previously." Jehu obviously dates the crime against Naboth to the reign of Ahab (v. 25); the point is that the oracle occurred subsequent to that crime.

84 Würthwein (*1.Könige 17–2. Könige 25*, 332–33) explains these features as stemming from the talionic function of the story. Naboth's property becomes the plot of land where Joram is slain in order to emphasize the *quid pro quo* nature of the assassination, and the crime against Naboth involves not just Joram but his sons, because it is the heirs of Ahab who are being slaughtered. This explanation may have validity for describing some of DtrH's *modus operandi*, but it does not account for all of the contrasts (e.g., Bidqar's name and position) between the recollection here and 1 Kgs 21:1-16.

85 Pace Trebolle (*Jehú y Joás*, 163), who sees the bulk of vv. 25-26 as an insertion by *Wiederaufnahme*. PN may have substituted Yhwh's name in v. 25 for that of Elijah, who otherwise is not mentioned. The repetition of נאם־יהוה in v. 26, despite its attestation in the leading textual witnesses, is unnecessary and is probably a gloss if not a dittography.

86 The account of Ahaziah's assassination in 2 Chr 22:8-9 is entirely different. Ahaziah is captured in Samaria where he was hiding and is executed and then buried, presumably in Jerusalem.

At this point we expect to find the closing regnal formulae for Ahaziah. There are none for him or for Joram. The chronological note in v. 29 is out of place since it belongs to the beginning formulae, not the concluding ones. It is a secondary correction of 3:1 and 8:25 (MT) based on a recalculation according to antedating in order to make clear that Joram and Ahaziah died at the same time. If DtrH's account did include closing formulae for Ahaziah they have been displaced by the account of Jezebel's death in vv. 30-37.

9:30-37: PN's addition of Jezebel's death

The story of Jezebel's assassination in vv. 30-37 presupposes what precedes, but it is not the original continuation. This is apparent from v. 30, where Jezebel had already heard of the *putsch* and the assassination of Joram before Jehu's arrival and had prepared herself. It is in tension with Jehu's prohibition against anyone leaving Ramah to warn of the revolt in v. 15b. Also, Jezebel's assassination interrupts Jehu's extermination of the males in the line of Omri/Ahab, which is DtrH's main concern. Chapter 10, which continues the account of that extermination, attests awareness of the assassinations of Joram and Ahaziah but does not mention Jezebel. Since v. 36 interprets her death as the fulfillment of the prophecies in 1 Kgs 21:23 and 2 Kgs 9:10b, both PN additions, all of 9:30-37 should be assigned to PN, like all of the other references to Jezebel in Kings.

Jezebel in the window

The various interpretations of Jezebel's toilette (v. 30) are also discussed in the Synchronic Analysis. Another dimension of this portrait is the motif of the woman looking out of a window (Judg 5:28; 2 Sam 6:16; Prov 7:6 [G]; Song 2:9), which corresponds to an artistic motif in ivory plaques found at Samaria and various other ancient Near Eastern cities.[87] Both in its origins with the Babylonian goddess Kililu and in its literary form in the Hebrew Bible this motif has two sides—awaiting the return of a warrior (Judg 5:28; 2 Sam 6:16) and seduction (Prov 7:6 [G]; Song 2:9).[88] The *double entendre* is also at work in the case of Jezebel, with the added components of her royal status and her impending death. It is a scene rich in meaning and innuendo. The *double entendre* may continue in v. 31 in Jezebel's reference to Jehu as Zimri (v. 31), as also discussed in the Synchronic Analysis.

9:32-33: Eunuch assassins

The reading adopted in v. 32 for Jehu's question is conjectural for reasons explained in the Notes. It appears to be either a challenge to Jezebel or an effort to call supporters. The term סריס could be used generally for a court official; this was because so many such officials were eunuchs, following a long-standing practice in the ancient Near East for forestalling loyalties to other than the royal house. The likelihood that these figures were eunuchs does not necessarily mean that the building they were in was the harem, since eunuchs were ubiquitous in palaces. However, the mention of eunuchs in the immediate context of Jezebel's toilette does favor the possibility that it is the harem quarters from which the eunuchs throw their mistress (v. 33). It was probably a second-story window—not a great distance, but then Jezebel is old, and the pavement on which she lands is hard and spatters her blood. If that did not kill her, trampling by horses did. This was not an accidental stampede. Horses were trained and employed in the ancient Near East as weapons in their own right, and such is the use made of them here.[89]

---

87 King and Stager, *Life in Biblical Israel*, 31.

88 McCarter, *II Samuel*, 172.

89 Cantrell, *Horsemen of Israel*, esp. 27–31.

9:34-35: Jezebel's remains

Although v. 34 does not specify the reason for it, the meal taken by Jehu at this point may have had political significance as an occasion to garner support from local nobles and officials in exchange for pledges of protection, beneficence, and the like.[90] Jehu shows an intent to bury Jezebel because of her royal status, but the detail he sends finds only her skull, feet, and palms. The rest of her has been consumed and carried off by dogs. Interpretations as to why those particular body parts were not eaten include the paucity of meat on them, the presence of cosmetics that made them repulsive to dogs either in reality or in legend[91] and the inversion or parody of Phoenician/Canaanite ritual and religion or its texts that describe Anat as a warrior wearing a belt with human heads and hands on it.[92] Jezebel's non-burial and consumption by dogs constitutes the application of the anti-dynastic oracle against the house of Ahab to her as was predicted in the additions in 1 Kgs 21:23; 2 Kgs 9:10a. If we read חל, *rampart*, in all three verses (see the Note on 1 Kgs 21:23) they agree rather than indicating separate levels of composition.[93] All three are PN additions. Jezebel is killed, as predicted, between the outer and inner defensive walls of the city, with the palace being built into the latter.[94] Verse 37 adds to the ignominy of her death by tracing her remains to the ultimate degrading conclusion, through the digestive tract of dogs, to dung on open ground in the district of Jezreel.[95] While the same or similar expression is attested in Jeremiah (Jer 8:2; 9:21; 16:4; 25:33) and Ps 83:11 for unburied corpses, it is applied only here, to Jezebel, in Kings.

---

90 Gray, *Kings*, 551. Compare Fritz, *Kings*, 127.

91 L. J. A. Loewenthal, "The Palms of Jezebel," *Folklore* 83 (1972): 20–40.

92 J. L. Koosed, "Death of Jezebel," www.bibleodyssey.org/en/people/related-articles/death-of-jezebel (May 19, 2016). Compare D. A. Appler ("From Queen to Cuisine: Food Imagery in the Jezebel Narrative," *Semeia* 86 (1999): 55–71; "Jezebel," *NIDB* 3:313–14), who suggests that the description parodies the idea of dogs as healers and guides to the afterlife in Canaanite mythology and that the head and appendages were symbols of power paralleling items worn by the goddess Anat. Similarly, C. E. Walsh, "Why Remember Jezebel," in *Remembering Biblical Figures in the Late Persian and Early Hellenistic Periods: Social Memory and Imagination* [ed. D. V. Edelman and Ehud Ben-Zvi; New York: Oxford University Press, 2013] esp. 323–27) suggests that the dogs that consumed Jezebel were "healers" of Israel. The theory of a healing cult involving dogs is L. Stager's, based on his excavation of dog burials at Ashkelon. See his *Ashkelon Discovered* (Washington, DC: BAS, 1991), 25. Appler cites D. N. Fewell and D. M. Gunn (*Gender Power, and Promise: The Subject of the Bible's First Story* [Nashville: Abingdon, 1993], 169) as arguing that the hands and feet are phallic euphemisms symbolizing male power.

93 *Pace* Schmitt, *Elisa*, 21–22. The further supposition by Schmitt and Steck (*Überlieferung und Zeitgeschichte*, 36–37) that vv. 36-37 presuppose a different cause of death than the foregoing story (eaten by dogs vs. trampled by horses) is also groundless. The dogs do not kill Jezebel but scavenge on her corpse and prevent its burial. The בחלק in v. 37 influenced the change of original בחל in v. 36.

94 Cronauer, *Stories about Naboth*, 81n.

95 So also Barré, *Rhetoric*, 16.

Synthesis

DtrH and PN

In this passage DtrH retouched an older account of Jehu's revolt (vv. 17-28*), adding the references that placed Ahaziah alongside Joram in their fatal encounter with Jehu and interpreting both as the working out of Elijah's prophecy against Ahab. He prefaced it with his usual opening regnal formulae for Ahaziah in 8:25-27 and set the stage for the double assassination with the notices of Joram's wounding at Ramah and Ahaziah's visit to him in Jezreel, where he was recuperating (8:28-29*). His account did not include the prophetic commission in 9:1-13 or Jezebel's death in 9:30-37, both of which were added by PN. His additions represent a kind of crescendo in his tracing of judgment prophecy, as they attest prophecy in control of monarchy and judgment coming to graphic fruition as prophesied.

The quest for *shalom*

The narrative is a sophisticated one that slows the plot with detours, description, and dialogue to create and prolong suspense. It also describes deeds of characters in order to give insight into their motives and personalities, and it uses repetition to drive home major themes, the main one being right order (*shalōm*) that can only come with the restoration of the proper relationship of Israel with YHWH. After all, the land and people of Israel belong to him. Those who have given primacy to other gods in YHWH's land must be destroyed for their offense. *Shalōm* is the ultimate goal of judgment prophecy.

Historical factors behind the revolt

Historically the factors that sparked Jehu's revolt and its success were probably the ambitious and costly building projects of Omri and Ahab, which would have meant higher taxes and Joram's loss of Moab (2 Kgs 3) and perhaps other vassals, which not only did away with offsets to increased taxes but also meant a wounding of national pride. As is often suggested, oppression and the appropriation of family lands as illustrated by the Naboth story was likely to have been another such factor, even though the original version of this story is no longer extant due to its replacement in 1 Kgs 21:1-16 by PN.

Ahaziah and the Ahabids

The regnal formulae in 8:25-27, specifically the reference to Athaliah, Ahaziah's mother, as Omri's daughter rather than Ahab's and the statement that Ahaziah was related by marriage to Ahab's household, raise questions about Ahaziah's relationship with Ahab's family. This furthers suspicion, or at least does not quell it, that Joram son of Ahab reigned alone over Israel and Judah for a period and that his kinsman Ahaziah came to power in Judah for a brief time only toward the end of Joram's reign.

Threshold to Athaliah

The absence of the usual closing formulae for Joram and Ahaziah leaves the account ominously open-ended. The assassination of Joram (and of Jezebel in PN) is the beginning of the fulfillment of the anti-dynastic oracle against the house of Ahab. The extermination of the rest of the royal house will take place in the next chapter. Even then Judah will not experience the decisive conclusion of the royal house in Israel. Its influence will live on in Athaliah, whatever her exact position within the house of Omri/Ahab her account will follow.

Jehu's Revolt and Reign (2 Kings 10)

Text

[DtrH's sources; DtrH; Additions to DtrH; *PN*; *Additions to PN*]
1 Ahab had seventy sons in Samaria. Jehu wrote a letter and sent it to Sa-
maria, to the leaders of the city, to the elders, and to the
guardians, saying, 2 "Now when this letter comes to you, since
your master's sons are with you and you have chariots and
horses, fortified cities, and weapons, 3 choose the best and
most fitting one from among your master's sons and set him on his
father's throne so you can fight for your master's house."
4 They were terrified and thought, "Two kings could not stand be-
fore him; how will we stand?" 5 So the chief steward, the city
mayor, the elders, and the guardians sent to Jehu saying "We are
your servants who will do whatever you tell us. We won't crown
anyone king. We will do as you see fit." 6 [Jehu] wrote them a sec-
ond letter in which he said, "If you are on my side and you will
do what I tell you, let each of you take the head of his master's
son and bring them to me at Jezreel at this time tomorrow." The
sons of the king were seventy men whom the city leaders were raising. 7 When
the letter reached them, they took the king's sons and slaugh-
tered all seventy of them, placed their heads in baskets, and
sent them to [Jehu] at Jezreel. 8 Someone came and announced,
"They delivered the heads of the king's sons." [Jehu] said,
"Put them in two piles at the city gate until morning." 9 In the
morning when he came out and stood he said to all the people,
"You are innocent. It was I who conspired against my master and
killed him. But who killed all these? 10 Know then that none of the
word of YHWH which he spoke concerning the house of Ahab will fail; YHWH has
done what he said through his servant Elijah." 11 Jehu killed all those who were left
to the house of Ahab in Jezreel—all of his kinsmen, his close friends, and his
priests—until he left him no survivor. 12 Then he got up and went to Samaria.
When he was at the shepherds' binding house on the way 13 he came upon the
brothers of Ahaziah king of Judah. "Who are you?" he asked. They answered, "We
are Ahaziah's brothers. We have come down to avenge the sons of the king and the
sons of the queen mother." 14 [Jehu] ordered, "Seize them alive." They seized them
alive and slaughtered them at the pit of the binding house—forty-two men. He did
not leave any of them alive. 15 *Going on from there, he came upon Jehonadab son of*
Rechab on the way to meet him. He greeted him and said to him, "Is your heart
aligned with my heart as my heart is with yours?" Jehonadab answered, "It is." [Jehu]

replied, "If so, give me your hand." When he did so, Jehu brought him up to him into the chariot. [16] *[Jehu] said, "Come with me and witness my zeal for* Yhwh*." So [Jehu] drove him in his chariot.* [17] When he came to Samaria, he killed all those remaining to Ahab in Samaria until he had exterminated him according to Yhwh's word, which he spoke to Elijah. [18] *Then Jehu gathered all the people and said to them, "Ahab served Baal a little; Jehu will serve him a lot."* [19] *Now all his worshipers, all his priests, and all his prophets—let none of them be absent—for I am making a great sacrifice to Baal. Whoever is absent will not live." (But Jehu was acting deceitfully in order to destroy the worshipers of Baal.)* [20] *…* [21] *… So all the worshipers of Baal attended; no one was left who did not attend. They entered the temple of Baal till it was filled to capacity.* [22] *[Jehu] said to the keeper of the wardrobe, "Bring out clothing for all the worshipers of Baal." So he brought out the clothes for them.* [24b] *Jehu had appointed eighty of his men outside, and he told them, "The man who allows any of the people whom I have delivered to you to escape will pay with his life.* [23] *Jehu and Jehonadab son of Rechab entered the temple of Baal and [Jehu] said to the worshipers of Baal, "Look around and make sure there are no worshipers of* Yhwh *with you. Send out all the worshipers of* Yhwh *who are found there. So it was according to Jehu's order that no worshipers of* Yhwh *were there but only worshipers of Baal.* [24a] *When they entered to offer the sacrifices and whole burnt offerings,* [25a] *Jehu said to the runners and the adjutants, "Enter. Kill them. Don't let anyone escape." So they killed them with the sword.* [25b-27bα] *Then he tore down the temple of Baal: He took the pillar of Baal and smashed it to pieces, throwing it to the left of the temple,* [27bβ] *and turned it into a latrine until today.* [28] *Thus Jehu destroyed the temple of Baal from Israel.* [29] Only from the sin of Jeroboam the son of Nebat who made Israel sin Jehu did not turn away—the golden calves that were in Bethel and Dan. [30] Yhwh said to Jehu, "Because you have done well to carry out what I considered just/you have done according to all my intention to the house of Ahab, your descendants to the fourth generation will sit on the throne of Israel. [31] But Jehu did not keep walking in the way of Yhwh god of Israel with all his heart. [Jehu] did not turn from the sin of Jeroboam who led Israel to sin. [32] In those days Yhwh began to cut off parts of Israel. Hazael defeated them throughout Israel's territory: [33] from the Jordan east, all the land of Gilead, of the Gadites, Reubenites, and Manassites, from Aroer which is on the edge of Wadi Arnon, both Gilead and Bashan. [34] The rest of the affairs of Jehu, all that he did, and all his power are written in the scroll of the chronicles of the kings of Israel, aren't they? [35] When Jehu lay down with his forebears, they buried him in Samaria, and Jehoahaz his son reigned in his place. [36] The length of time that Jehu reigned over Israel in Samaria was 28 years.

Textual Notes

1 **a letter**: So G^{BL}. MT: *letters.*

to the leaders of the city to the elders: So G^{L}. G^{B}: *to the leaders of Samaria.* MT: (אל־שרי יזרעאל) is nonsensical since Jehu is already in Jezreel; יזרעאל is a corruption of העיר ואל.

and to the guardians: MT, G^{B} (ואל־האמנים אחאב). The use of the absolute אמנים suggests that Ahab's name was added secondarily. G^{L}: *and to the guardians of the sons of Ahab.*

2 **Now when**: MT, G^{B} (lit. *and now*), following typical Hebrew letter form. G^{L}: *When.*

since your master's sons are with you: So MT, G^{B}. Preceded in G^{L} by *and behold.*

fortified cities: So G^{BL} and some Hebrew mss: πόλεις ὀχυραὶ = וערי מבצר. MT has the singular, *a fortified city*, the result of metathesis of ר and י.

3 **your master's sons**: So MT, G^{B}. G^{L}: *the sons of the king your master.*

4 **They were terrified**: So G^{BL}. MT repeats מאד, a dittography.

5 **chief steward**: Lit. "the one who was over the house." See the Note on 1 Kgs 16:9.

city mayor: Lit. "the one over the city" (אשר על־העיר). The title is unique but perhaps identical in meaning to שר־העיר in 1 Kgs 22:26; 2 Kgs 23:8.

We are your servants: So MT, G^{B}. G^{L} precedes with *behold.*

We will do as you see fit: So G^{BL} in line with the preceding declarations of fealty. MT: *Do as you see fit.*

6 **a second letter**: Reading ספר שני for MT's שנית ספר.

let each of you take the head of his master's son: So G^{L} (λαβέτω ἕκαστος τὴν κεφαλὴν τοῦ υἱοῦ τοῦ κυρίου αὐτοῦ = קחו איש את־ראש בן אדניו). Cf OL: *accipiat unusquisq' nutritorum caput eius que nutriuit ex filis regis.* MT: קחו את־ראשי אנשי בני־אדניכם = G^{B}: λάβετε τὴν κεφαλὴν ἀνδρῶν τῶν υἱῶν τοῦ κυρίου ὑμῶν.

and bring them: So G^{BL}; MT: *and come.*

whom the city leaders were raising: Reading אשר for MT's את with G^{L}, yielding אשר־גדלי העיר מגדלים אותם.

7 **baskets**: דוד, an earthenware vessel in 1 Sam 2:14; 2 Chr 35:13; Job 41:12. But Jer 24:1-2 indicates that it may also refer to a basket of some kind (see also Ps 81:7), which fits here.

8 **someone came and announced**: Reading ויבא ויגד לאמר as impersonals. The witnesses reflect different ways of making the impersonal more specific: MT, G^{B} with *the messenger* as subject (MT + *to him*); G^{L} has plural verbs.

at the city gate: So GL (παρὰ τὴν πύλην τῆς πόλεως) = שער העיר. MT has a double reading: פתח השער. GB is conflate: τὴν θύραν τῆς πύλης πόλεως.

9 **and stood**: So MT, G^{B}. G^{L} + *in the city gate.*

10 **none of the word**: So MT, G^{B}. G^{L} has the plural, *words.* Either reading is possible.

which he spoke: So G^{L}. MT, G^{B} supply Yhwh's name as subject.

11 **kinsmen**: So G^{L} (τοὺς ἀρχιστεύοντας αὐτοῦ = גאליו); corrupted in MT, G^{B} to גדליו partly on the basis of the latter's occurrence in v. 6. גדליו was then added to G^{L} as the last item in the list.

his close friends: So MT, G^{B}. G^{L}: *all his close friends.*

until he left him no survivor: Reading the infinitive construct (השאיר) as indicated by the negative בלתי and the infinitives in G^{BL}. The supposed *hiqṭîl* form of the infinitive found here in MT is suspect.[1]

12 **Then he got up and went**: So G^{B}. וילך and ויבא are variants in MT.

When he was at the shepherds' binding house: Preceded in G^{L} by *and. Binding house* is usually rendered as a proper name: Beth-eqed, but the qualifier "of the shepherds" suggests that it might refer to a functional structure or installation.

---

1 Joüon §54c and 54cN.

13 **he came upon**: So G^{L} (καὶ εὗρε = וימצא). MT, G^{B} have ויהוא מצא. Driver's *Tenses* (§169, Obs. 2) proposes והוא מצא, but the consecutive preterit is syntactically preferable.[2]

to avenge: Reading לְשַׁלֵּם (*Piel* infinitive construct) for לְשָׁלוֹם ("for peace"). לשאל לשלום "to inquire about the welfare of," is also possible but lends less clarity to the passage.[3]

14 **They seized them**: So G^{L}. MT repeats *alive*. G^{B} has lost the clause by haplography.

at the pit: So MT. *Pit* is lacking in G^{BL} due to haplography.

15 **he came upon**: So MT (וימצא), G^{L}. G^{B}: *he took* (καὶ ἔλαβεν), an inner-Greek error for εὗρεν.

on the way: So G^{L}. Lacking in MT, G^{B} but required for sense.

Is your heart aligned with my heart: So G^{BL} = היש לבבך עם לבבי ישר. MT (היש את־לבבך ישר) lacks balance with the second part of the question and makes less sense.

[Jehu] replied: So G^{B}. G^{L} + *to him*. Lacking in MT, which reads יש ויש as a repetition apparently for emphasis: *it is and it is* = *it certainly is*.[4] But the expression is unique in the HB, and the change of speaker reflected in the G witnesses seems required.

If so: The vocalization וָיֵשׁ instead of וְיֵשׁ is unique.[5]

16 **[Jehu] drove him**: So G^{BL} (καὶ ἐπεκάθισεν αὐτὸν). MT has the plural verb.[6]

17 **according to Yhwh's word**: So MT, G^{B}. G^{L} + *the god of Israel*.

to Elijah: So MT, G^{B}. G^{L}: *by the hand of Elijah*. Either is possible.

18 **Then Jehu gathered**: So MT (ויקבץ יהוא), G^{L}. G^{B}: καὶ ἐζήλωσεν (ויקנא) Εἰοὺ: *Jehu was zealous*.

all the people: So MT, G^{B}. G^{L} + *in Samaria*.

Jehu will serve: So MT, G^{B}. G^{L}: *but I will serve*. Either reading is possible.

19-21a **Now all his worshipers ... who did not attend**: The reading follows Trebolle's reconstruction based on the OG:[7] the OG reading for v. 19a is preserved in G^{L} and in the G^{B} pluses in v. 21: [λέγων] καὶ νῦν πάντες οἱ δοῦλοι αὐτοῦ καὶ πάντες οἱ ἱερεῖς αὐτοῦ καὶ πάντες οἱ προφῆται αὐτοῦ μηδεὶς ἀπολειπέσθω ὅτι θυσίαν μεγάλην ποιῶ ὃς ἂν ἀπολειφθῇ οὐ ζήσεται = לאמר ועתה כל־עבדיו וכל־כהניו וכל־נביאיו איש אל־ישאר כי זבח גדול עשה לבעל כל אשר־ישאר לא יחיה. Verses 20-21aα introduce confusion into the narrative by referring to multiple assemblies—one that is sanctified (קדשו) and called (ויקראו) in v. 20 and another in v. 21aα that involves gathering Baal worshipers from *all Israel*. The reference to Jehu calling an assembly in v. 19 (קראו אלי) is similarly additional. G^{L} (v. 21) is similar to the OG reading but shows some corruption from other witnesses (καλέσατε πρός με = קראו אלי) and some independent expansion (ἐξ αὐτῶν following ἀπολειπέσθω). After the sentence *so that all the worshipers of Baal attended* G^{B} attests another plus: καὶ ἦλθον πάντες οἱ δοῦλοι τοῦ Βάαλ καὶ πάντες οἱ ἱερεῖς αὐτοῦ καὶ πάντες οἱ προφῆται αὐτοῦ. This is another listing of the Baal adherents that belongs in v. 19.

21b **till it was filled**: So G^{L} (καὶ ἐπλήσθη ὁ οἶκος). MT, G^{B}: *the temple of Baal was filled*.

---

2 So also Kittel, *Könige*, 238.

3 Burney, *Notes*, 304.

4 Sweeney, *Kings*, 328

5 Because it serves as a protasis, according to Joüon (§105dN).

6 Klostermann's (*Könige*, 425) וירכב אתו, *he rode with him*, lacks textual support. Kittel's (*Könige*, 240) וירכבו אתו, *he had him ride with him*, is unnecessarily complex.

7 Trebolle, *Jehú y Joás*, 157–62.

to capacity. Lit: mouth to mouth (פה לפה), as in 21:16. The vowel under the ל is an instance of "strong" vocalization occasioned by the repetition of the monosyllabic noun פה (Joüon §103c; GKC §102h).

22 **to the keeper of the wardrobe**: So G^{BL} (τῷ ἐπὶ τοῦ οἴκου μεσθααλ). מלתחה is a hapax. Its meaning is presumed from the context.[8] 2 Kgs 22:14 mentions a similar functionary in the Jerusalem temple, and Gen 35:2; Exod 19:10 reflect the practice of changing clothes for cultic activity.

the clothes: So MT (המלבוש). G^{BL}: ὁ στολιστής = המלבישה, yielding *the keeper of the sacred robes brought (them) out.*

24b The placement follows OL = OG, which makes better sense than MT: Jehu has the garments for Baal worshipers distributed to facilitate the identification of Yhwh worshipers left among them. Then he orders the Yhwh worshipers to be removed (v. 23).[9]

eighty: So MT, G^{B}. G^{L} has *3000*, an exaggerated figure. Syr has 380, a sort of conflation.

outside: So MT, G^{B} (בחוץ). G^{L} has *in secret* (ἐν τῷ κρυπτῷ = בסתר), an equally possible variant.

allows ... to escape: Reading ימלט as *Pi'el*, as required by sense, in place of MT's *Nip'al.*

23 **no worshipers of Yhwh with you**: So G^{BL}. MT + *here.*

Send out all the worshipers of Yhwh who are found there. So it was according to Jehu's order that no worshipers of Yhwh were there: So OL.[10] Lost from MT, G^{B} by haplography but partially preserved in G^{L} here and in v. 25.

25a **Jehu said**: So OL. MT precedes with *when he finished making the sacrifice*, added to accommodate the misplacement of v. 24b and subsequently introduced into G^{BL} in the *kaige* recension.[11] The other G^{L} plus in this verse (καὶ οὐκ ἦν ἐκεῖ τῶν δούλων κυρίου καθὼς ἐλάλησεν Εἰου ὅτι ἀλλ' ἢ οἱ δοῦλοι τοῦ Βαάλ μονώτατοι) is a misplaced preservation of the primitive reading from v. 23.

escape: So G^{L} (= ימלט) as in v. 23. MT, G^{B}: *go out.*

So they killed them with the sword: So MT, G^{BL}. OL has the singular verb, which Trebolle considers primitive here in line with the OL reading to be discussed next. But the plural fits the scheme of order-execution, since the runners and adjutants carry out Jehu's command.

25b-27bα **Then he tore down the temple of Baal**: So G^{L}, OL, with this general statement of destruction of Baal's temple before the specific measures that follow. In MT it is a doublet to the tearing down of the מצבה in v. 27 and interrupts the pattern for the profanation of a pagan temple (see next Note).

He took the pillar of Baal and smashed it to pieces, throwing it to the left of the temple: Based on G^{L} (καὶ ἔλαβεν Εἰοὺ τὴν στήλην τοῦ Βαάλ καὶ συνέτριψεν αὐτήν καὶ ἔρριψεν αὐτήν ἐξ ἀριστερῶν Βααλειμ) and OL (*et accepit idolū bahal et contriuit eum et proiecit eum ad sinistrā templi*) = ויקח את מצבת בעל וישברה וישלכה משמאל לבית. Following Trebolle, who shows that OL and G^{L} conflate readings of the OG and proto-MT and argues that the OG reading is more primitive because it follows a pattern also attested elsewhere (2 Kgs 23:6-12) for the

8 See the discussion of Cogan and Tadmor, *II Kings*, 115.

9 Cf. J. Trebolle, "From the 'Old Latin' through the 'Old Greek' to the 'Old Hebrew' (2 Kings 10:23-25)," *Textus* 11 (1984): 17–36, esp. 30–32; *Jehú y Joás*, 153–54.

10 B. Fischer, E. Ulrich, and J. Sanderson, "Palimpsestus Vindobonensis: A Revised Edition of L 115 for Samuel – Kings," *BIOSCS* 16 (1983): 13–87.

11 Trebolle, "From the 'Old Latin,' 34; *Jehú y Joás*, 154.

description of profanation of a foreign cult, which involves bringing out cult objects, smashing or burning them, and throwing the remains into an impure or shameful place.[12] The superiority of the OG reading avoids the difficulties in the MT such as the multiple references to pillar(s) of Baal and whether they are burned or smashed and the repetition of the verb נתץ.

27 **latrine**: So MT *ketiv* (מחראות), a *hapax legomenon* from √חרא or √חרי, "dung" (see on 6:25). The *qere'* מוצאות is euphemistic.

28 **Baal**: So MT, G^{B}. G^{L} + *and his house.*

30 **you have done well to carry out was I considered just/you have done according to all my intention to the house of Ahab**: A double reading.

fourth generation: Reading רִבֵּעִים as in Exod 20:5; 34:7; Num 14:18; Deut 5:9 instead of MT's רְבִעִים.

Between vv. 30 and 31 OL attests the two Elisha stories in 13:14-21 MT and identifies the king of Israel in the first of those stories as Jehu. The reasons for following MT are explained in the treatment of ch. 13.

31 **in the way of Yhwh**: So OL. MT, G^{BL}: *in the law of Yhwh*, reflecting a concern for *Torah.*

Jeroboam: So MT, G^{B}. G^{L} + *the son of Nebat.*

32 **Yhwh began to cut off parts of Israel**: The reading is suspect because of its unique use of ב to mark the object. (The *Qal* typically takes את.) Emendation to לקצוף has been proposed:[13] "Yhwh began to be angry with Israel." But the object of √קצף is elsewhere marked with על. Another proposal is to read לקוץ, "Yhwh began to loathe Israel."[14] But the context speaks of Israel losing territory rather than total destruction. The *Pi'ēl* may help to account for the ב, though the only other use of this *binyan* in the HB (Prov 26:6) has its object unmarked.

33 **all the land of Gilead**: So MT, G^{BL}. OL lacks "Gilead," due to haplography (הגלעד הגדי).

the edge of Wadi Arnon: So G^{BL} as in Deut 2:36; 3:12; 4:48; Josh 12:2; 13:9, 16. MT has lost the word *edge* (שפת).

Gilead and Bashan: So MT, G^{B}. G^{L}: *Gilead, the Jabbok, and Bashan.*

34 **and all his power**: So MT. G^{BL} + *and the conspiracy he made* (= וקשרו אשר קשר). While appropriate for Jehu, it is hard to see how this phrase would have been lost from MT. Hence it is best considered a gloss drawn from 1 Kgs 16:20; 2 Kgs 15:15.

35 **they buried him**: So MT, G^{B}. G^{L} *he was buried.*

Excursus: The G^{L} Plus in 10:36

After v. 36, G^{L} offers the following substantial plus, which is also reflected in the OL.[15]
[36a] ἐν ἔτει δευτέρῳ τῆς Γοθολίας βασιλεύει Κύριος τὸν Ἰοὺ υἱὸν Ναμεσσεί. [36b] καὶ Ὀχοζείας υἱὸς ἦν εἴκοσι καὶ δύο ἐτῶν ἐν τῷ βασιλεύειν αὐτὸν, καὶ ἐνιαυτὸν ἕνα ἐβασίλευσεν ἐν Ἰερουσαλήμ. [36c] καὶ ὄνομα τῆς μητρὸς αὐτοῦ Γοθολία θυγάτηρ Ἀχαὰβ βασιλέως Ἰσραήλ. [36d] καὶ ἐπορεύθη ἐν ὁδῷ οἴκου Αχαὰβ, καὶ ἐποίησε τὸ πονηρὸν ἐνώπιον Κυρίου ὡς ὁ οἶκος Ἀχαὰβ. [36e] καὶ ἐπορεύθη Ὀχοζείας ἐπὶ Ἀζαὴλ βασιλέα Συρίας εἰς πόλεμον. [36f] τότε συνῆψεν Ἰοὺ υἱὸς Ναμεσσεὶ ἐπὶ Ἰωρὰμ υἱὸν Ἀχαὰβ βασιλέα Ἰσραήλ, καὶ ἐπάταξεν αὐτὸν ἐν Ἰεζραήλ, καὶ ἀπέθανεν. [36g] καὶ ἐτόξευσεν Ἰοὺ καὶ Ὀχοζείας βασιλέα

---

12 Trebolle, *Jehú y Joás*, 126–38.

13 Benzinger, *Könige*, 155.

14 Kittel, *Könige*, 243.

15 The text of the plus is reproduced from Fernández and Busto, *El texto antioqueno*, 114–15. However, in lieu of its versification (vv. 36-42) I have followed the convention used for other G pluses (36a-h).

Ἰούδα ἐπὶ τὸ ἅρμα καὶ ἀπέθανεν. [36h] καὶ ἀνεβίβασαν αὐτὸν οἱ παῖδες αὐτοῦ ἐν Ἰερουσαλὴμ καὶ θάπτουσιν αὐτὸν μετὰ τῶν πατέρων αὐτοῦ ἐν πόλει Δαυιδ.

[36a] In the second year of Athaliah YHWH made Jehu son of Nimshi king. [36b] Ahaziah was twenty-two years old when he began to reign, and he reigned one year in Jerusalem. [36c] His mother's name was Athaliah the daughter of Ahab king of Israel. [36d] He went in the way of Ahab's house and did evil in YHWH's eyes like the house of Ahab. [36e] Ahaziah went to war against Hazael king of Aram. [36f] Then Jehu son of Nimshi conspired against Joram son of Ahab king of Israel and struck him down in Jezreel so that he died. [36g] Jehu also shot Ahaziah king of Judah with the bow upon his chariot so that he died. [36h] His servants carried him to Jerusalem and buried him with his forebears in the city of David.

Trebolle argues that the plus constitutes an original conspiracy notice from Judah whose constituent elements were separated and distributed in the Northern story of Jehu's revolt in 8:28a; 9:14a, 27bβ (וימת שם), 28.[16] He contends that in form these elements constitute a notice of conspiracy and overthrow. The conspiracy notice (vv. 36e-h) aptly follows directly after the introductory formulae for Ahaziah (vv. 36b-d) and leads into the account of Athaliah and then the reign of Joash in chapter 11.

There are problems with this proposal, especially when the entire plus is considered rather than just the latter half (vv. 36e-h) that is Trebolle's focus. First, the plus places the opening of the account of Ahaziah's reign after that of Jehu. Since Ahaziah begins his reign before Jehu and then dies at the very beginning of Jehu's reign (at his hand), the appropriate placement of his opening regnal formulae would be before the story of Jehu's revolt as the MT has it (8:25-27). More serious, the details of the plus cannot stand on their own but require the story in 8:28–9:37 in order to make sense: The plus states that Ahaziah went to war against Hazael but does not say that he accompanied Joram. Then it has them both being assassinated in Jezreel without explaining why Ahaziah was there. The statement in v. 36e that Ahaziah went to war against Hazael is dependent on the erroneous reading of 8:28 MT. The use of the *hithpael* of קשר in 9:14a also suggests that it is late and not derived from annals (cf. 2 Chr 24:26). The statement in v. 36f that Joram was killed *in Jezreel* is an interpretation of 9:26, where Joram is killed *in the territory of Jezreel*. The mention of Ahaziah's assassination on his chariot in v. 36g also indicates dependence on the MT of 9:27, where the reference to the chariot is a misplaced gloss from 9:28.[17] The notice of Ahaziah's transfer and burial in 10:36g-h does not mention his attempted flight or death in Megiddo and appears to be an abbreviated summary of 9:27-28 rather than their source. The reason for the plus is unknown. Like the other OG "supplements," this is a *précis* or condensed synthesis of the (proto-)MT account.

Synchronic Analysis

Having taken Jezreel, Jehu turns his attention to Samaria (10:1). The notice that Ahab had seventy sons there is ominous in view of Jehu's charge to destroy Ahab's house and cut off every male in it (9:7-8). It is odd, therefore, that he writes letters to the leaders of Jezreel. The statement recalls the Naboth story in 1 Kings 21 in its linking of Samaria and Jezreel as well as the use of letters to plot a death. The

10:1-3: Jehu's letters to the leaders of Jezreel

16 Trebolle (*Jehú y Joás*, 110–25, 184–89).

17 As argued in the previous chapter.

implicit comparison with Jezebel raises doubts about the legitimacy of Jehu's bloody rampage, despite his commission. The letters are a challenge to the city leaders to choose a champion to fight him (Jehu) for the kingship of Israel. The repeated reference to *your master* (3x in vv. 2-3) is a constant reminder of where their allegiance is placed and an implicit invitation to them to change that allegiance. *Your master* refers to Ahab, as in v. 1a, rather than Joram, so that the focus in the narrative remains on the ruling house, which Jehu has been commissioned to annihilate. The term *house* is a *Leitmotif* and is used in a variety of ways to refer to family, dynasty, and the community of Baal worshipers and his temple in Samaria; it emphasizes the contrast between the house of Ahab and the house of David.[18]

10:4-7: The leaders submit to Jehu

The leaders are terrified because of the two dead kings Jehu has left in his wake (v. 4). Jezebel is not mentioned—as if she never existed. The leaders of the city are specifically identified in v. 5 as *the chief steward* (אשר־על־הבית) and *the city mayor* (אשר על־העיר). The isolation of the chief steward, as a royal official, highlights the royal house as Jehu's target. The recipients respond to Jehu perhaps by letter or, more probably, by messenger. They declare themselves his servants, thereby abandoning their former *master.* They continue with a series of statements of submission: *We will do whatever you tell us; We won't crown anyone king; Do as you see fit* (v. 5). After receiving their acquiescence, Jehu writes another letter, again a signal of impending death (v. 6). He orders them to come to him at Jezreel with *the heads of the men of your master's sons.* The order is strategically phrased. The word *men* initially seems superfluous. It does not refer to the servants of the king's sons but to the sons themselves. It confirms their male identities, recalling the dynastic oracle against every Ahabid *who urinates on a wall.* The mention of *heads* is ambiguous as either a metaphor for leaders among the king's sons or to their actual body parts. The city leaders must interpret Jehu's words, allowing him room to claim ignorance of their act (v. 9). They decide to deliver the severed heads of the king's heirs. This is certainly the course of least personal risk,[19] since Jehu's order is a test of their professed loyalty, as is clear from his continued reference to the sons of their *master.* His specification of the time of delivery (*at this time tomorrow*) recalls Jezebel's threat against Elijah in 1 Kgs 19:2 and shows that the tables have turned. A fervent Yahwist is now in power. In the ultimate act of betrayal of their former master, it is the *guardians* or caretakers of the princes who execute them. Contrary to Jehu's order, they do not travel to Jezreel, but send the heads in baskets (v. 7), hoping to appease Jehu while minimizing their own involvement and risk.

10:8-11: Ridding Jezreel of Ahabids

Jehu is not surprised at the delivery of the heads (v. 8). He orders them placed in two piles at the city gate, probably on either side of the gate, where everyone who enters or exits will see them. His speech the next morning acknowledges responsibility for the revolt but feigns ignorance about the slaughter of the princes (v. 9). His declaration צדקים אתם is typically understood either as an exoneration (*you are innocent*)[20] disclaiming their complicity in the assassination of Joram

---

18 García-Treto, Fall of the House," 60–61.

19 Fricke, *Das zweite Buch von den Königen*, 131.

20 Sweeney (*Kings*, 337) draws on H. J. Boecker (*Redeformen des Rechtslebens im Alten Testament* [WMANT 14; Neukirchen-Vluyn, 1970], 122–43) and sees this as a judicial formula for the pronouncement of innocence.

or as an appeal for fair judgment (*you are impartial*) that will lay the blame for the princes' deaths on the leaders and people of Samaria.[21] There is no need to choose between these two options, as the statement may be ambivalent. Jehu is saying that they are both innocent of the conspiracy against Joram and fair-minded, so as to recognize that he did not kill the princes. His question, *who killed all these?* is open-ended and part of a ploy to garner support. It is designed to show that Jehu is not alone but is part of a larger movement to overthrow the king and the ruling house. Jehu then cites the heads as fulfillment of prophecy (v. 10b) and as evidence that all prophecies against Ahab's house would be fulfilled (v. 10a). The implication, therefore, is that the severed heads were YHWH's own doing, either directly or through unknown allies of Jehu's. In either case resistance is futile. Jehu uses the heads, then, not to conclude his revolt as the city leaders, elders, and guardians may have hoped, but to bolster it and to claim that he is doing YHWH's bidding.[22] Energized by the prophetic fulfillment, Jehu continues by killing all those left to Ahab's house in Jezreel, not just heirs but other notables (גדליו), friends and acquaintances (מידעיו), even his priests (כהניו). Verse 11 introduces the theme of שאר, which recurs in vv. 14, 17, and 21, as Jehu leaves no survivors of the houses of Ahab and Baal.

10:12-14: The slaughter of Ahaziah's kin at Beth-Eqed

On his way to Samaria, Jehu encounters relatives of Ahaziah of Judah (vv. 12-14) on their way to visit their Omrid kin in Jezreel, blissfully unaware of the purge Jehu has just carried out there. Jehu orders them seized and slaughtered at a place called Beth-Eqed or "house of binding." The word "house" as part of the name or designation of the installation participates in the "house" theme in this chapter and echoes the nearby references to the "house of Ahab."[23] Jehu's order is also reminiscent of Elijah's disposal of the prophets of Baal in 1 Kgs 18:40.[24] The total of those killed is forty-two, a conventional number for death and ill fortune. There were also forty-two children mauled by bears following Elisha's curse in 2 Kgs 2:24 (cf. Rev. 11:2; 13:5). The anecdote concludes with the statement that Jehu left no survivor (*Hip'îl* of שאר), which is very similar to the end of v. 11. Jehu's purge is thorough.

---

21 Two other proposals are less feasible. The JPS *Tanakh* (1985) renders צדקים אתם as a rhetorical question, "Are you blameless?" thus implicating the people of Jezreel. This interpretation, however, creates tension with the rest of the verse. Jehu admits conspiring against Joram, so he cannot be insinuating their complicity. But blaming them for the deaths of the princes would undermine his question about who was responsible. Gray (*Kings*, 555) renders צדקים אתם as "you are loyal to the right" and then understands the מי-clause as an aside: "whoever killed these, know that there shall not fall ..." Gray's construal of מי as a relative rather than interrogative is problematic.

22 Compare Cohn, *2 Kings*, 72.

23 Cohn, *2 Kings*, 73.

24 Fricke, *Das zweite Buch von den Königen*, 133.

10:15-17: Jehonadab and the purge of Samaria

Another encounter takes place in vv. 15-16, this one with Jehonadab son of Rechab.[25] Jehonadab is the ancestor and leader of the Rechabites, who, according to Jer 35:6-7, lived in tents, abstained from wine, and did not practice agriculture. The name Rechab puns on the root for *chariot* and *ride* in vv. 15-16 (and repeated elsewhere in the story), as well as on the root √ברך, "bless."[26] The name *Jehonadab* means "YHWH is generous/noble" and casts Jehonadab as a willing servant of YHWH. The word ישר in Jehu's question, *Is your heart aligned with my heart?* is used in v. 3, where Jehu invites the leaders of Samaria to choose the most *fitting* among Joram's sons to lead them in battle. More significant, it is used in v. 30 where YHWH commends Jehu for having done what is *right* in annihilating Ahab's house. It thus constitutes a significant motif in this chapter. Jehonadab's clasping of Jehu's hand may be more than an assist into the chariot. Elsewhere (1 Chr 29:24; 2 Chr 30:8; Ezra 10:19; Ezek 17:18) offering the hand constitutes a pledge of political or religious allegiance, and that is apropos here.[27] As such, Jehonadab's *willing* expression of fealty both recalls and contrasts with the pledges of loyalty of the leaders of Samaria in v. 5, which are given under some compulsion. Jehu's zeal for YHWH recalls Elijah's professions of zealousness in 1 Kgs 19:10, 14. Entering Samaria, Jehu exterminates the remaining Ahabids (v. 17). This time it is the narrator rather than Jehu who cites prophetic warrant and fulfillment, drawing again on Elijah's anti-dynastic oracle in 1 Kgs 21:20-24. Jehu interpreted the warrant liberally, slaughtering not only the male heirs of Ahab who might have succeeded Joram but also the king(s) (in ch. 9), the queen mother, the king's kin, friends, and supporters, and priests of Ahab's house.

10:18-28: Removing the cult of Baal

In vv. 18-28 Jehu extends his killing spree in a new direction—Baal worshipers. This is the seventh and last of the killing sprees that comprise his revolt in chapters 9–10.[28] He begins his reign, like Solomon (1 Kgs 3:4), with what is ostensibly a cultic celebration, albeit to Baal rather than to YHWH. He announces that in contrast to Ahab, who worshiped Baal a little, he will worship Baal a lot (v. 18). His point is one of contrast for the purpose of deceit (v. 19b). This parenthesis puns on Jehu's statement in v. 18: Jehu pretends to worship (עבד) Baal in order to destroy (אבד) Baal's worshipers. The same word, זבח, means both sacrifice and slaughter. His order to prospective attendees (v. 19) is laden with irony:[29] Baal

---

25 The structural function of these verses is debated. Cohn (*2 Kings*, 74) sees 10:15-16 as structurally parallel to the scene with Bidqar in 9:25-26. This is part of his view (pp. 65–76) that the structure of ch. 10 mirrors or balances that of ch. 9. But the elements do not exactly mirror or balance each other in his ordering: ABCDB'C'D'A'. Long (*2 Kings*, 134) calls 10:15-17 "a kind of motival hinge" within the chapter, since it completes a series of episodes of annihilation and anticipates Jehu's destruction of Baalism. But the supposed hinge occurs before the completion of the annihilation of the Ahabids in v. 17.

26 Cohn, *2 Kings*, 73.

27 Barnes, *Kings*, 264; Greenberg, *Ezekiel*, 315. See also D. Oates, "The Excavations at Nimrud (Kalḫu), 1962," *Iraq* 25 (1963), esp. the panel from the throne dais of Shalmaneser III (plate VIIc), in which he extends his hand to Marduk-zakir-shumi.

28 Joram (9:24), Ahaziah (9:27), Jezebel (9:33), Joram's sons (10:6-7), Ahaziah's relatives (10:14), the rest of Ahab's house in Samaria (10:17), and the worshipers of Baal (10:24-25). Cf. Nelson, *Kings*, 200.

29 Cohn, *2 Kings*, 74.

worshipers are required to attend on pain of death. However, those who do show up will (unbeknownst to them) be part of the sacrifice, so that the absentees will actually be the only survivors. Because of the threat to kill non-attendees, all of the Baal worshipers come; no one is left (נשאר) who does not attend (v. 21). The word נשאר here refers to non-attendees who would be survivors (vv. 11, 14, 17) if they did not come. But they do come, because Jehu is thorough. His thoroughness is exhibited narratively by his repeated calling of assemblies (v. 18, ויקבץ; v. 19, קראו; v. 20, קדשו עצרה). The temple of Baal is filled to capacity (v. 21). Jehu is equally cautious to ensure that no worshiper of YHWH will be unintentionally included in the sacrifice. He orders the distribution of cultic vestments to the worshipers of Baal as a way of signaling their Baalist identity (v. 22)[30] and then orders them to send out any adherents of YHWH (v. 23).

The action, which has been outside the Baal temple till now, moves inside in vv. 23-25a.[31] Jehu enters, accompanied by Jehonadab, to witness the gore that will display his zeal for YHWH (v. 16). When the sacrifice commences he gives the order to kill. He has previously stationed eighty men outside with the order on pain of death not to allow any of the Baalists to escape (v. 24b). He now tells the runners and adjutants—members of the royal bodyguard and thus professional soldiers—to slaughter everyone inside (v. 25a). The text recoils from the horror by relating their compliance in the sparest of terms: *they killed them with the sword* (ויכום לפי־חרב). It is not clear whether the next clause (וישלכו הרצים והשלשים) explains the disposal of bodies (NRSV: "threw them out") or continues the description of the killing ("attacked them with the edge of the sword and left them lying where they were," cf. Tanak). MT's placement of the *athnach* favors the former. The narrative turns quickly from the scene to the bloodless destruction of buildings and cult objects. It is also not clear exactly what is meant by the *city of the temple of Baal* (עד־עיר בית־הבעל) to which the runners and adjutants proceed, but it is evidently the whole or part of Baal's temple complex. Verses 26-27 mention two sets of pillars, some that are burned and thus perhaps made of wood and one that is smashed, and so probably of stone. The entire temple area is then defiled in the basest of ways by being turned into a latrine. The scatological image corresponds to the one at the end of the previous chapter in reference to Jezebel and to the antidynastic curse against those who "piss against the wall." The colophon in v. 28 shows that Jehu took the purge of the house of Ahab and extended it to the house of Baal. He not only destroyed the temple building but also all those who were members of the "family" of Baal adherents.

10:29-36: Jehu's failures

Despite his righteous indignation and zeal for YHWH against the Omrids, Jehu falls short by retaining the shrines at Bethel and Dan (v. 29). He is still a Northern king. He is different from the others, and this may account for the reversal of the usual formula "Dan and Bethel." He is perhaps the best of the lot; he is rewarded for his faithful execution of YHWH's sentence against the Ahabids (v. 30)—four generations beyond himself, a record for a Northern house. Though similar in expression to the Davidic promise, the contrast between four generations and

30 Cohn (*2 Kings*, 74) finds a structural parallel here (v. 22) to Jezebel's dressing up in order to meet Jehu (9:30), although the latter verse contains no mention of clothing.

31 Cohn, *2 Kings*, 74.

"forever" is striking. Hobbs even characterizes it as promise turned to parody.[32] Jehu is no David. The distinction is substantiated by another slight difference in expression. Jehu did all that YHWH wanted (lit. "all that was in my heart"). This is quite similar to what is said about David (1 Kgs 14:8; 15:3) except David did so "with all his heart." Jehu ultimately does not measure up to David's heart for *torah*. The gradual loss of territory beginning in Jehu's reign (vv. 32-33) is the result of this failure. It is a down payment on the full loss that is to come. But there is no other recourse if the best has failed. The closing formulae for Jehu are essentially the same as for any other king of Israel (10:34-36); ultimately he is not very exceptional.

Diachronic Analysis

10:1: From Joram's sons to the ruling house

The older account of Jehu's revolt continues from ch. 9. The note about Ahab's seventy sons in Samaria that begins the chapter (v. 1a) is generally recognized as a later addition. It is best assigned to DtrH, since it focuses on Ahab's sons whom Jehu will slaughter in fulfillment of Elijah's oracle in 1 Kings 21. Ahab's name at the end of the verse is also probably secondary (see the Note), so that vv. 1-7 were initially concerned with Joram's sons. The additions move the focus from Joram's immediate family to the ruling house of which he was a part. Jehu's slaughter of them, therefore, becomes not just a political act to consolidate power but the fulfillment of prophecy against the *house of Ahab*.

10:2-3: The body of Jehu's letter

Jehu's letter addresses three groups of officials in Samaria: city leaders, elders, and guardians. The first group (שרים) consists of political and perhaps military officials and is at least partly defined in v. 5 as the chief steward of the palace and the *mayor*. The elders were the local administrators of justice who derived their authority from the people (see on 1 Kgs 21:8). The guardians (אמנים) were in charge of the royal heirs, as caretakers for the younger ones (2 Sam 4:4; Ruth 4:16) and educators for the older ones (Est 2:7; Prov 8:30 [reading אֹמֵן?]). *Now* (ועתה) in v. 2 marks the formal transition to the letter's core (cf. 5:6). The letter is a challenge to war. The list of assets available to the leaders of Samaria for waging war shows that not all the army had been under Jehu's command at Ramah of Gilead; a force of some strength remained in Samaria and other locations. *Your master* refers to Joram who had young sons in need of guardians. Jehu's proposal that they choose a leader and successor to Joram suggests that primogeniture was not absolute as the determiner of royal succession but only one consideration.[33]

10:4-5: Professions of vassalage

The letter terrifies the officials, who acknowledge that there is no one among themselves or Joram's sons capable to *stand before* (עמד לפני) Jehu's onslaught. Würthwein overreaches in concluding that the expression connotes armed resistance on the part of the *two kings* (v. 4) and thus assumes a different story of Jehu's

32 Hobbs, *2 Kings*, 126.

33 So I. Eph'al-Jaruzelska, *Prophets, Royal Legitimacy and War in Ancient Israel* (Warsaw: Warsaw University Press, 2009), 29. A. Knapp reached the same conclusion in a paper at the 2016 IOSOT conference in Stellenbosch, South Africa.

revolt than that in ch. 9.[34] The exact expression occurs only once elsewhere in the HB (Judg 2:14), where it might simply mean "endure, remain in place before."[35] There is no reason to believe that it excludes defeat by surprise attack, the way Joram and Ahaziah fell in ch. 9. Besides, the officials are afraid and may be making excuses to avoid war at all costs. Their response makes use of declarations of vassalage drawn from treaty language.[36] The promise not to crown a king, for instance, borrows from an oath guaranteeing the vassal king that his heir would succeed him. The officials are simultaneously disavowing their fealty to Ahab's house and professing subjection and loyalty to Jehu as their new master.

10:6-7: Slaughter of the king's sons

Jehu orders each of the leaders to bring the head of a king's son (v. 6 G^L).[37] The distributive *each* is important for involving all the city leaders, making them all complicit in the assassinations of the royals. It also suggests a correspondence between guardians and the king's sons, such that each of the guardians brings the head of the king's son who is under his charge. Verse 6b is widely acknowledged as a gloss that interrupts the narrative and anticipates the reference to seventy heirs in v. 7.[38] Thus v. 7 connects directly with v. 6a, reporting the reception of the letter and the compliance of the city leaders. "Seventy" is a round number attested elsewhere in the Bible (Gen 46:27; Judg 8:30; 9:2, 5; 12:13-14) and in the Panamuwa inscription from Zincirli (ancient Sam'al) (KAI 215.3; COS 2.36). It may be intended to include sons of different wives and concubines and maybe even grandsons and less direct relatives.

10:8-9: Jehu's claim of widespread support

Jehu has the heads piled in two heaps at the city gate (v. 8). The public display is clearly for reasons of intimidation and warning, as practiced by other ancient Near Eastern kings (*ANET* 277b, *ANEP* 236).[39] It is not clear how much the people of Jezreel know. They may be aware that the heads were sent from Samaria and therefore implicate the leaders of Samaria in the *coup*.[40] They may even know or suspect that Jehu ordered the slayings. If so, then Jehu's question at the end of v. 9 raises the issue of who bears greater responsibility, one who issues an order or

---

34 Würthwein, *1. Könige 17–2. Könige 25*, 336.

35 Jos 10:8; 21:44; 23:9; the verb is used with בפני instead of לפני with what appears to be the same meaning. The verb by itself has a similar nuance in Amos 2:15; Mal 3:1.

36 Kalluveettil (*Declaration and Covenant*, 139–65) and Long (*2 Kings*, 135) identify the following elements and biblical parallels as covenant formulae attested here. "We are your servants" (declaration of vassalage: Josh 9:8 [cf. v. 6]; 1 Kgs 20:31-34; 2 Kgs 16:7); "All you say we will do" (address to a superior: Exod 19:8; 24:3, 7; Neh 5:12); "Do whatever is good in your eyes" (expression of a loyal attitude on the part of a vassal); "We will not make anyone else king" (guarantee that king's son will succeed to throne). Kalluveettil (pp. 160–61) regards Jehu's words in v. 6 not as conditional ("if") but as a command ("since"), given that he is the superior party in the new treaty.

37 On the question of whether *sons of the king* was a title for an administrative office or an indication of royal descent see 1 Kgs 22:26 and Fox, *In the Service of the King*, 43–53.

38 E.g., Hentschel, *2 Könige*, 46; Šanda, *Könige* II, 106; Thenius, *Könige*, 316; De Vaux, *Rois*, 160; Würthwein, *1. Könige 17–2. Könige 25*, 336.

39 Severed heads also become a literary motif in the inscriptions of Ashurnasirpal II (RIMA 2, 201:117; 203:19; 210:108; 220:107–108) and in the Kurkh monolith by Shalmaneser III (RIMA 3, 15:35, 16:48). See Eph'al-Jaruzelska, *Prophecy, Royal Legitimacy and War*, 49–50. Cf. also 1 Sam 17:51; 31:9; 2 Sam 4:8.

40 Barré, *Rhetoric*, 83.

those who carry it out.[41] The point of the question is the implication that the slaughter of Joram's sons has widespread support. It is with this question and its implication that the older narrative ended.

10:10-14: DtrH's focus on the end of the Ahabids

DtrH's interest in the fulfillment of the dynastic oracle against the house of Ahab surfaces again in vv. 10-11. Verse 10 cites Elijah's oracle in 1 Kgs 21:20-24* and interprets Jehu's revolt as its fulfillment. The verse thus changes the focus from Joram and his sons to the house of Ahab, in agreement with v. 1a. It also alters the question in v. 9 from an open-ended one about responsibility to a rhetorical one by stating that YHWH was ultimately behind the slaughter of Joram's (now Ahab's) sons and that fulfillment of his word against Ahab's house is inevitable.[42] It casts Jehu as YHWH's instrument, justifying not only his bloody accession to power but his wholesale slaughter of the royal house and its supporters (v. 11). The theme of leaving no survivor in v. 11 is part of DtrH's fashioning of this story into a fulfillment of the oracle against the house of Ahab.[43] This theme also occurs at the end of v. 14, signaling vv. 12b-14 as DtrH's work as well. Jehu moves to Samaria to continue his purge there (vv. 12a, 17). On the way he encounters a party of *brothers* or *relatives* of Ahaziah. Several details of the encounter are curious. It takes place at בית־עקד הרעים, which is usually taken as a proper name, Beth-eqed, and construed either as an installation for the "binding" of sheep for shearing[44] or as a meeting place (binding together) of shepherds, perhaps a market center.[45] The account is peculiar because of the Judahites' seeming lack of awareness of recent events in Jezreel and Samaria. It is also strange that the party is so large (42) for a mere visit. These issues and more may be resolved by reading *to avenge* in v. 13.[46] The travelers from Judah were aware of Jehu's revolt and had come to seek revenge not only for Ahaziah but also for their northern kinsmen and treaty partners, the *sons of the king*, apparently Joram's sons from Samaria, and the *sons of the queen mother*, which would have included both Joram and Ahaziah. Their mission was clandestine, which explains their travel off the beaten path. Jehu kills them not because he is interested in Judah's politics but because they are Ahab's blood kin and are seeking revenge for him.[47]

A vengeful party from Judah

10:15-16:PN's insertion of the encounter with Jehonadab

The anecdote about Jehu's encounter with Jehonadab in vv. 15-16 is a post-DtrH addition. The reference to Jehu's *zeal for* YHWH (v. 15) alludes to and prepares

41 Würthwein, *1. Könige 17–2. Könige 25*, 337.

42 Verse 10b is sometimes taken as a dtr gloss (e.g., Benzinger, *Könige*, 153), though one of the main reasons for this judgment—its subject-first construction—may simply be a display of reverence for the deity.

43 Schmitt, *Elisa*, 23 and Würthwein, *1. Könige 17–2. Könige 25*, 337.

44 Slotki, *Kings*, 225; Sweeney, *Kings*, 328.

45 Gray, *Kings*, 556; Jones, *Kings*, 467. The name is preserved in Beit Qad (ca. 3 mi./5km E/NE of Jenin), but its distance from the ancient road led to the proposal of Kafr Raʿi ("village of the shepherds") as an alternative (M. Hunt, "Beth-Eked," *ABD* 1:685). Nelson (*Kings*, 204) accepts the identification with Beit Qad and suggests that the Judahites may have been traveling to Jezreel via the "back door" of the Jordan Valley and Beth-Shan, which would have kept them out of touch with current events.

46 Hobbs, *2 Kings*, 128.

47 Several scholars (Benzinger, *Könige*, 149; Buis, *Rois*, 219; Gray, *Kings*, 556; de Vaux, *Rois*, 161) propose that this anecdote is out of place, but its original location is not evident.

for his destruction of the Baalists in vv. 18-28.[48] It is reminiscent of Elijah's zeal for Yhwh in 1 Kgs 19:10, 14 and is, therefore, the work of PN. The mention of Jehonadab the Rechabite leader is borrowed from Jeremiah 35. It interrupts DtrH's account of Jehu's extermination of the house of Ahab, which concludes in v. 17 with the notice of Jehu's arrival in Samaria followed by the annihilation of all those left (הנשארים) in Ahab's house in fulfillment of Elijah's oracle in 1 Kings 21. Just as Jehu killed all those remaining to Ahab's house in Jezreel (v. 11) and among the Judahite royals (v. 14), so now he kills all those remaining to that house in Samaria, thus bringing complete fulfillment to Elijah's oracle.

Interpreting the Rechabites

There are essentially two interpretations of Jehonadab's significance in the present anecdote. The first sees him as the founder of a conservative and somewhat ascetic religious sect consisting mainly of the members of his clan, the Rechabites (Jer 35, esp. vv. 6-7).[49] The point of the excerpt and of the alliance according to this interpretation was to make clear that Jehu's revolt was motivated by religious concerns and was not merely a grasp for personal power. The other interpretation is social-scientific in orientation and sees the Rechabites not as a clan but, consonant with their name ("chariot, rider"), as a guild of wainwrights or chariot builders.[50] Their non-sedentary lifestyle was a feature of their craft of repairing chariots and wagons in different places. Their aversion to wine was a strategy for guarding the secrets of that craft. Jehu, the charioteer, was interested in Jehonadab because of the latter's access to and repair of chariots. This interpretation further allows for the presence of Jehonadab with Jehu in v. 23; while a conservative Yahwist would surely rouse the suspicions of Baal worshipers, a wainwright would not. While commendable for its innovation, the latter interpretation fails to explain why vv. 15-16 would have been added to this passage. What interest would an editor have in Jehonadab as a wainwright and why would Jehu invite him to witness his *zeal for Yhwh*? The addition is more understandable if Jehonadab represents a group of religious conservatives, especially since it depicts Jehonadab as sympathetic with Jehu's revolt for reasons of piety. Hence, whatever the historical origin of the Rechabites—and it is possible that they began as a guild—the reason for the introduction of their leader into this narrative is religious: namely, to illustrate Jehu's Yahwistic motive and agenda in anticipation of his pending destruction of Baalism.

10:17: DtrH's report of the slaughter of the royals in Samaria

Verse 17 picks up the DtrH narrative thread and interest in the slaughter of the Ahabids from v. 14. It reports Jehu's annihilation of those pertaining to Ahab in Samaria and notes the fulfillment of Elijah's oracle from 1 Kgs 21:20-24*. It is a fitting conclusion to DtrH's account of Jehu's revolt, which next moves to the synthesis of his reign and his concluding formulae in vv. 31b-36*. The intervening material is preoccupied with a different concern—that of the annihilation of Baal in Samaria.

---

48 Würthwein (*1. Könige 17–2. Könige 25*, 339) takes וראה בקנאתי ליהוה as a gloss pointing to what he considers the DtrH text in vv. 18-27.

49 H. B. Huffmon, "Rechab, Rechabites," *NIDB* 4:744–45. Montgomery (*Kings*, 410) cites several instances in antiquity of ascetic religious groups comparable to this understanding of the Rechabites. Hobbs (*2 Kings*, 128) states that characters bearing the name Nadab are persons of high social status, suggesting that Jehonadab was a nobleman (Exod 6:23; 1 Kgs 14:20; 1 Chr 2:28; 9:36).

50 F. S. Frick, "The Rechabites Reconsidered," *JBL* 90 (1971): 279–87; "Rechab," *ABD* 5:630–32.

10:18-28: PN's focus on the Baal purge

The unit in vv. 18-28* is quite different from the preceding narrative.[51] Jehu acts essentially alone here, without the army, and his target is not the royal house but Baal worshipers and their temple. There is no mention of destroying Baal from Israel in Elijah's oracle or in the commendation of Jehu's deeds in 10:30, but only of what he did *to the house of Ahab.* These verses are similar in interest to 1 Kings 18, which also shares references to the prophets of Baal and the slaughter of Baal worshipers. The beginning of the episode is confused and repetitive in MT, where Jehu calls multiple assemblies (vv. 18-20). The assemblies undercut his objectives and run counter to the rapid pace of the narrative.[52] The longer Jehu delays and the more people he involves, the greater the chance that his ruse will be suspected and thwarted. The confusion has led to the theory that the references to the servants or worshipers (עבדים) are secondary and part of a redaction (DtrN) of an older description (DtrP) of the destruction only of the Baalist priests and prophets.[53] Text-critical analysis obviates such redaction-critical proposals (see the Notes). It indicates that the substantial augmentation especially in vv. 20-21 MT was not the result of redaction but of expansion in the proto-MT textual tradition. Jehu's characterization of Ahab as a minimal worshiper of Baal (v. 18) is historically realistic in view of the fact that his sons bear Yahwistic names and that he maintains the royal shrines to YHWH in Dan and Bethel. The extent of his worship of Baal may have been limited to providing for Jezebel's cultic activities. This in turn suggests that the historicity of the present episode with its sharp distinction between the worshipers of YHWH and those of Baal is doubtful.[54]

10:21-25a: The slaughter of the adherents of Baal

Jehu meticulously assembles all the Baal worshipers in Israel and distinguishes them from Yahwists (vv. 21-23). The use of distinct garments for worship, especially by cultic personnel, is well attested elsewhere in the Bible (Gen 35:2; Exod 19:10; 28; Lev 16:4; Ezek 42:14; 44:19) and outside of it (Lucian, *De Dea Syria* 42), including the white clothing worn by Muslims encircling the Kaaba. Jehu's intent becomes clear with v. 24b, whose proper place before v. 23 is indicated by the OL.[55] He has stationed eighty men outside the temple and now instructs them on pain of death not to allow any of their prey to escape. Jehu enters the temple (v. 23).[56] He tells those inside to

---

51 Cf. McKenzie, *Trouble with Kings*, 78; Y. Minokami, *Die Revolution des Jehu* (Göttinger Theologische Arbeiten; Vandenhoeck & Ruprecht, 1989), 96–97; Würthwein, *1. Könige 17–2. Könige 25*, 342.

52 Trebolle, *Jehú y Joás*, 157–58.

53 Cf. Kittel (*Könige*, 240) following Klostermann (*Könige*, 425); Würthwein, *1. Könige 17–2. Könige 25*, 341–42.

54 Verse 19b has often been seen as secondary (Schmitt, *Elisa*, 24–25). While it is rather pedantic and could be a gloss, it is just as likely PN making Jehu's duplicity explicit.

55 MT's confusion in vv. 23-24 is apparent in the use of both singular and plural verbs (ויבא and ויבאו) for Jehu. Following the OL does away with this problem and also obviates the difficulty in MT (v. 25aα) of Jehu offering sacrifices to Baal. See the Notes and Trebolle, *Jehú y Joás*, 153–54.

56 Most commentators see the reference to Jehonadab in v. 23 as a gloss based on vv. 15-16 because the presence of such a prominent Yahwist would undermine Jehu's ruse. He also plays no role in the rest of the story and is not mentioned again. This does not necessarily assume a historical orientation to the story or that PN was using an older document; Jehonadab has served his narrative purpose of highlighting Jehu's zeal.

look around for adherents of Yhwh and to send them out from their midst. When it is determined that there are no Yahwists present but only worshipers of Baal,[57] these proceed to the offering of sacrifices (v. 24a), at which point Jehu gives the order to the men he has stationed outside to enter the temple and kill them all (v. 25a). The order is directed to the *runners and adjutants*, who appear to be members of an elite royal bodyguard and in any case part of the royal entourage. The change in terminology may be a way of indicating that this royal institution now supports the rebel, Jehu, or that the rebel has become the establishment.[58]

10:25b-27: Destroying the temple of Baal

Once again in vv. 25b-27, MT is repetitive and confusing on several points, including the reference to the *city* of Baal's temple (v. 25), the mentions of both pillars and the pillar of Baal (vv. 26-27), and the question of how the stone pillars could be burned (v. 26). These problems also are obviated by following the OL reading, which is shorter, follows a logical sequence, and is not redundant. Having killed all the worshipers of Baal, Jehu turns his attention to the temple itself. His measures follow a pattern found elsewhere (23:4, 6) for destroying foreign temples. He takes the pillar and smashes it to pieces, casting it to the left side and then turning the site into a latrine or dung heap, which ensures that it will never be used again as a sanctuary. The reference to the *left* is probably scatological and denigrating, alluding to the typical use in the Middle East of the left hand for self-cleaning after defecation, which would befit the other scatological references in this context.[59]

10:29-31: Jehu's reward and shortcomings

Verses 29-31 are overfull and repetitive. The theme of Jeroboam's sin appears twice (vv. 29a, 31b), in what Trebolle argues is a *Wiederaufnahme*.[60] But, as he points out, the repetition is imprecise because the elements in v. 29a are reversed (*from the sins of Jeroboam … Jehu did not turn*) vis-à-vis the usual formula. Also, the standard and presumably older version is in v. 31b, the opposite of the way interpolation by *Wiederaufnahme* functions. The רק that begins v. 29 suggests that it is the start of an addition, and the definition of the sin of Jeroboam in v. 29b is already generally considered a gloss because it reverses the usual order of sites to "Bethel and Dan." The etiology for the length of Jehu's dynasty in v. 30 fits with DtrH's sketch of the main difference between the monarchies of Israel and Judah. It explains Israel's endurance through the next four kings as an act of loyalty on Yhwh's part.[61] It rewards Jehu for his dispatch of the house of Ahab but says nothing about his acts against Baalism in vv. 18-28. Verse v. 31a faults Jehu for failing to follow the *way of Yhwh* (OL), an expression attested in a broad range of passages (Gen 18:19; Judg 2:22; 2 Kgs 21:22; Prov 10:29; Isa 40:3; Jer 5:4,

57 Jehu's order and its execution have been lost by haplography from MT but are preserved in OL. See the Note.

58 Runners were part of the royal entourage and thus symbols of kingship (2 Sam 15:1; 1 Kgs 1:5) who also had guard duties (1 Sam 22:17; 1 Kgs 14:27-28; 2 Kgs 11:4, 6). See the discussion of שליש relating to 7:2.

59 The term could be directional, referring to the north, assuming an eastern orientation of the temple of Baal. It might also be ambivalent. A similarly denigrating use of "left" may occur in 2 Kgs 23:8 in reference to *bamot* being to the left of a particular gate of Jerusalem.

60 Trebolle, *Centena*, 178–79.

61 Mullen, "Royal Dynastic Grant."

5; Ezek 18:25, 29; 33:17, 20) that is not associated with any one school of thought or writing style.[62] The verbal construction *keep walking* (שמר ללכת) is also unique in the HB and seems unnecessarily extended. The precise origin and purpose of the additions in vv. 29, 31a remain obscure. However, they reflect the perception of vv. 30, 31b as an important moment in DtrH, one that all but completes the theme of the sin of Jeroboam by showing that five generations was a record among the Northern royal houses; there was no single dynasty there like David's.[63] The final cap to the theme will come with Israel's fall in 2 Kings 17.

10:32-33: DtrH's punishment of Jehu

The remainder of the chapter is DtrH except for a couple of glosses. DtrH notes in v. 31b that Jehu succumbed to the sin of Jeroboam despite his righteous implementation of the prophetic curse against the house of Ahab. As a Northern king and a faithful Yahwist, he maintained the royal shrines. The implication is that the loss of the Israelite territory to Hazael was a consequence of this shortcoming (vv. 32-33*). Verse 33 is again repetitive and overfull, this time with geographical designations; the cause is an interpolation by *Wiederaufnahme* in the repetition of *Gilead.*[64] The remaining reference to Gilead and Bashan is compatible with the information in the Mesha stela and 2 Kings 3, according to which Israel had already lost the Madaba plateau to Moab. Jehu submitted to Assyria early in his reign, as indicated by the Black Obelisk (ca. 841 BCE), and he enjoyed rest from Hazael during the next few years while Shalmaneser III harassed Hazael. He may have turned to Assyria in the first place for help against Hazael. After 838, though, Assyrian pressure on Damascus eased and Hazael began his campaigns against Israel. The loss of the northern Transjordan to Aram may not have taken place entirely during Jehu's reign, since Yhwh *began to cut off* territory (v. 32). Much of the loss may have occurred during the reign of Jehoahaz, when Israel reached its military nadir (13:7). The losses, even if spread over several decades, would have had a serious impact on Israel, economically and in terms of security.

10:34-36: DtrH's concluding formulae for Jehu

The next two verses (vv. 34-35) contain DtrH's closing formulae for Jehu, complete with notices of his death and burial and his successor. It is not clear what the evidence of Jehu's *power* (v. 34) may have been other than his revolt. The total

---

62 The MT reading *law of Yhwh* occurs in a variety of texts referring mostly to the Priestly law code (Exod 13:9; 1 Chr 22:12; 2 Chr 12:1; 17:9; 34:14; Ezra 7:10; Neh 9:3; Ps 19:8; Isa 5:24; 30:9; Amos 2:4).

63 D. T. Lamb ("The Non-Eternal Dynastic Promises of Jehu of Israel and Esarhaddon of Assyria," *VT* 60 [2010]: 337–44) argues that the promise to Jehu originated in Jehu's reign and served as a propagandistic tool for stabilizing his reign at a time of political upheaval. See also his *Righteous Jehu and His Evil Heirs.* He does not take note of the peculiarities of vv. 29-31a or give serious consideration to the arguments of other scholars for literary unevenness in chs. 9–10. In addition to other authors cited in this chapter and the previous one see M. Mulzer, *Jehu Schlägt Joram. Text-, literar- und strukturkritische Untersuchung zu 2 Kön 8,25-10,36* (ATSAT 37; St. Ottilien: EOS, 1992).

64 A. Lemaire, "Hazaël de Damas, roi de Aram," in *Marchands, diplomates et empereurs: études sur la civilisation mésopotamienne offertes à Paul Garelli* (ed. D. Charpin et F. Joannes; Paris: Éditions Recherche sur la civilisations, 1991), 101–102, 105 ; Richelle, *Le testament d'Élisée*, 100. Aroer was a fortress about 3 miles southeast of Dibon on the northern rim of the Wadi Arnon (modern Mujib). It is identified with the tell beside the present-day village of 'Ara'ir. See, G. L. Mattingly, "Aroer," *ABD* 1:399–400. Cf. Deut 2:36; 3:12, 16; 4:48; Josh 12:2; 13:9, 16.

of Jehu's years of reign that follows (v. 36) is unusual, as such totals typically occur with the introductory regnal formulae. It may be that the circumstances of Jehu's reign—the absence of a synchronism because of essentially simultaneous assassinations of Joram and Ahaziah and the resulting lack of a set of opening formulae for Jehu—induced DtrH to move the total to this point. The aberration may have been a motivating factor for the OG plus preserved by the Lucianic witnesses in v. 36.[65]

Synthesis

Textual matters

Textually, three matters from this chapter should be highlighted.

1. First, many of the most complicated interpretational problems of this chapter are resolved or obviated by appeal to the Old Latin. This is especially so in the account of Jehu's destruction of the temple of Baal in vv. 18-28.
2. The OL attests the presence of the stories about Elisha found at 13:14-21 in MT between 10:30 and 10:31 and identifies the king of Israel in those stories as Jehu. This matter will be taken up in detail in the discussion of ch. 13.
3. There is a lengthy plus in the Antiochene text at 10:36+, which some scholars see as original. In my view it is, rather, a secondary agglomeration of items culled from the OG concerning the reign of Ahaziah of Judah and Jehu's revolt.

History of composition

Compositionally 2 Kings 10, like its predecessor, is a composite of smaller units. The overall structure that can be discerned, for instance, in the series of assassinations across the two chapters[66] was imposed in the process of bringing together original independent units and later additions. Thus vv. 15-16 and 18-28 were not part of the story of Jehu's revolt initially but were added to it. The chapter evinces a history of composition in stages.

1. Verses 1b-9* constitute the original version of the story of Jehu's annihilation of Joram's sons in Samaria.
2. To these DtrH added vv. 1a, 10-14, 17, 31b-36*, changing the focus from the annihilation of the sons of Joram to that of the house of Ahab. Verses 11, 14, and 17 share the theme that no survivor was left in fulfillment of prophecy.
3. PN contributed the account of Jehu's destruction of the temple of Baal in vv. 18-28* and that of the encounter with Jehonadab that prepares for it (vv. 15-16).
4. There were minor glosses in vv. 6b, 23a (reference to Jehonadab), and 33b (the list of sites supplementing Gilead and Bashan). Verses 29, 31a contain a secondary etiology for the length of the Jehu dynasty that is neither DtrH nor PN. However, they highlight the moment of the Jehu dynasty as the last serious royal house in Israel, verifying the DtrH theme of the sin of Jeroboam.

---

65 *In Samaria* in v. 36 is a misplaced dittography of the same phrase in the previous verse. So also Benzinger, *Könige*, 155; Cogan and Tadmor, *II Kings*, 117; Kittel, *Könige*, 243; Stade, *Kings*, 234.

66 Nelson, *Kings*, 200.

Historical reconstruction

Historically, complex international events lay behind Jehu's revolt and accession. The beginning of the reign of Hazael of Damascus, ca. 843, marked the end of the alliance, of which Israel had been a part, that resisted Shalmaneser III. Hazael sought to carve out his own empire in Syria-Palestine. His aggression and Joram's lack of success against it were likely factors motivating Jehu to seize power. Shalmaneser entered Syria-Palestine in his eighteenth year (ca. 841), and Hazael retreated. Jehu acted, either to take advantage of Hazael's retreat or by prearrangement with Shalmaneser, to take the throne of Israel.[67] His thoroughness in purging the royal house—reflected in 2 Kings 9–10 and Hos 1:4—may have had the political objective of distancing him from Ahab, who had been an important member of the anti-Assyrian coalition in 853 BCE. Jehu capitulated to Shalmaneser III in 841 shortly after taking the throne, as depicted on the Black Obelisk. His designation as "the son of Omri" is probably an attempt to legitimize him and may reflect Assyrian understanding of Omri as Israel's founder. Jehu's strategy against Aram worked for a few years as the Assyrians harassed Hazael and Damascus. After ca. 838, however, Assyrian pressure let up because of domestic issues and Hazael resumed his assaults on Israel, gradually taking control of Israelite holdings east of the Jordan, controlling the trade routes in Syria-Palestine, and even encroaching into Israel proper on the west side of the Jordan.[68] The stories of the Israelite-Aramaean wars in 2 Kings had their origin in this period during the Jehu dynasty.

Theology

Theologically, 2 Kings 9–10 present an ambivalent portrait of Jehu. He is lauded and rewarded for wiping out the wicked house of Ahab in fulfillment of prophecy. PN added to the praise, paralleling the slaughter of the Baalists in vv. 18-28 to the assassination of Jezebel in ch. 9 and heartily approving of both as Jehu's *zeal for* YHWH. DtrH's ambivalence comes from Jehu's perpetuation of *the sin of Jeroboam* by virtue of being a Northern king who maintained the royal shrines built by the founder (vv. 30, 31b) and was expanded by a later writer to general disobedience of the law (vv. 29, 31a). Readers may query Jehu's extreme violence. His slaughter of the worshipers of Baal goes beyond the commission he received against the house of Ahab, and his citation of prophecy often comes across as a veneer of self-justification for his personal ambition and quest for power. These suspicions are not just modern "political correctness," since Hos 1:4 already describes Jehu's bloodshed as excessive.

---

67 See Na'aman, "Forced Participation," esp. 83; also Miller and Hayes (*History*, 329–38), who argue that Jehu plied Shalmaneser with gifts.

68 See Miller and Hayes, *History*, 338–40.

The Rule of Athaliah and Restoration of the Davidic Monarchy (2 Kings 11)

Text

[DtrH's sources; DtrH; Additions to DtrH; *PN]*
1 When Athaliah, Ahaziah's mother, saw that her son was dead, she
arose and destroyed all the royal descendants. 2 But Jehosheba
the king's daughter took Joash, her brother's son, and stole him
away from the sons of the king who were about to be executed, him
and his nurse, and hid him in a particular bedroom from Athaliah
so that he was not killed. 3 He remained hidden with her in YHWH's
temple for six years while Athaliah ruled over the land. 4 In the
seventh year Jehoiada the priest sent and took the centurions of
the Carites and the runners and brought them to him at YHWH's tem-
ple where he made a covenant with them and made them swear alle-
giance before YHWH before he showed them the king's son. 5 He com-
manded them, "This is what you must do: one third of you coming on
duty for the Sabbath should be in charge of guarding the royal pal-
ace; 6 another third will be at the Gate of Secret Council; the
last third will be at the gate behind the runners. You shall all
have the responsibility of guarding the palace. 7 The two divi-
sions of all of you who go off duty on the Sabbath will have charge
of guarding YHWH's temple for the king. 8 You shall surround the king,
each man with his weapons in his hand. Whoever enters the rows is
to be killed. Accompany the king when he comes out and when he
goes in." 9 The centurions did as Jehoiada the priest commanded;
each of them brought his men—the ones coming on duty on the Sabbath along
with those going off duty on the Sabbath—and they came to Jehoiada the priest.
10 The priest gave to the centurions the spears and bow cases that had belonged to
King David that were in YHWH's temple. So the centurions and the runners did accord-
ing to all that Jehoiada the priest commanded them. 11 The runners took
their posts, each with his weapon in his hand, from the south side
of the temple to the north side of the temple, around the altar
and the temple all around the king. Jehoiada the priest assembled all
the people of the land to the temple of YHWH. 12 He brought out the
king's son and placed the diadem upon him and gave him the brace-
lets. When he anointed him and made him king the people clapped
their hands and said, "Long live the king." 13 When Athaliah
heard the sound of the runners and the people, she came out to the
people in YHWH's temple. 14 When she saw that the king was standing

beside the column according to the custom and the officers and the runners beside the king and all the people rejoicing and blowing trumpets, she tore her clothes and shouted, "Conspiracy, conspiracy." [15] Jehoiada the priest commanded the centurions, telling them, "Bring her through the rows. Take her behind the officers' barracks, and execute her with the sword. Do not execute her in YHWH's temple. Kill anyone who follows her in." [16] They laid hands on her and brought her via the horses' entrance into the royal palace where they put her to death. [17] Jehoiada made a covenant between *YHWH and* the king and the people *to be YHWH's people.* [18] *All the people of the land came to the temple of Baal and tore it down. Its altars and its images they smashed to bits and they killed Mattan, the priest of Baal, before the altar. The priest then set guards over YHWH's temple.* [19] He took the centurions, the Carites, the runners, and all the people of the land and they brought the king down from YHWH's temple. They brought him into the royal palace via the Runners' Gate and sat him on the throne of the kingdom. [20] Then all the people of the land rejoiced and the city was quiet; <u>they had put Athaliah to the sword in the royal palace.</u>

Textual Notes

1 **Athaliah**: The root and meaning are unclear. The most common suggestion is that it is derived from a cognate of Akkadian *etellu*, "prince, lord" meaning "to be or become great or exalted." Hence the name would mean something like "YHWH has manifested his glory" or "YHWH has shown himself ruler."[1] It occurs in both long (עתליהו, vv. 2, 20) and short (עתליה, vv. 1, 3, 13, 14) forms.

saw: So *qere'*. The conjunction on the *ketiv* is a dittography of the final *waw* of Ahaziah's name.

she arose and destroyed: So MT, G^L. G^B lacks *she arose*, probably because of haplography.

the royal descendants: זרע הממלכה is unique in the HB to this verse and the parallel in 2 Chr 22:10. More common is זרע המלוכה (25:25; Jer 41:1; Ezek 17:13; Dan 1:3). Both refer to males, i.e., the male heirs of the Davidic line. 2 Chr 22:10 + *of the house of Judah.*

2 **Jehosheba**: "YHWH is perfection, happiness."[2] It appears in Chronicles as Jehoshabeath, perhaps for assonance with Jehoshaphat.

the king's daughter: So 2 Chr 22:11 in preference to the longer *the daughter of King Joram (and) the sister of Ahaziah* (MT).

Joash: "YHWH has given."[3] The name occurs in long (Jehoash, 12:1, 3, 5, 7, 8, 19; 14:13) and short (Joash, 11:2; 12:20; 13:1, 10; 14:1, 3, 17, 23) forms. The latter is probably older and predominated in the monarchical period; the long form became prominent in the post-

---

1 See Noth, *Personennamen*, 191; Fritz, *Kings*, 297. Other proposals derive the verb from a root cognate to Arabic *'adala*: "YHWH is upright" (H. Bauer, "Die hebräischen Eigennamen als sprachliche Erkenntnisquelle," *ZAW* 48 [1930], 78) or from *'aṯala* "to be abundant, bulky," referring perhaps to a large child (Gray, *Kings*, 536).

2 Noth, *Personennamen*, 146–47.

3 Noth, *Personennamen*, 171.

exilic period because of its more sacral or official sound,[4] although Chronicles uses only the short form. In order to avoid confusion with the Israelite king of the same name (2 Kgs 13:9-13) "Joash" will be used for the king of Judah and "Jehoash" for the king of Israel except in the translations, which will reflect the form used in the Hebrew.

her brother's son: So G^B υἱὸν ἀδελφοῦ αὐτῆς. MT: *the son of Ahaziah* (בן־אחזיה). The previous two occurrences of Ahaziah's name are the long form אחזיהו, suggesting that the short form in this instance in MT is an error for אחיה. G^L *the son of Ahaziah her brother* is probably conflate, though haplography in the other witnesses is possible.

who were about to be executed: So MT *qere'* (המומתים), the *Hop'al* participle.

him and his nurse, and hid him in a particular bedroom from Athaliah: So G^L. MT, G^B (*him and his nurse in a particular bedroom and hid him from Athaliah*) lack a verb for the object phrase *him and his nurse*. 2 Chr 22:11 supplies the verb ותתן, *she put*, but its reading is probably corrective.

3 **in Yhwh's temple**: So MT, G^L. G^B omits the divine name, apparently locating the hiding place within the palace, perhaps to avoid perceived profanation of the temple.

4 **the priest**: So G^L. The title is missing from MT, G^B but occurs every other time in this chapter and the next where Jehoiada's name appears except in 11:17. It is expected here with his first appearance.

centurions of the Carites and the runners: There are several minor issues here: (1) G^B construes the three items as a list rather than the *commanders of 100s* as officers over the Cherethites and runners; (2) G^L attests a double rendering of *runners*; (3) The *ketiv* form הַמֵּאיוֹת, *hundreds*, occurs only in this chapter (vv. 4, 9, 10, 15);[5] (4) The ל on לכרי and לרצים expresses a genitival relationship with a double *nomen rectum* (cf. GKC §129b, Joüon § 130c).

a covenant: So MT, G^L. G^B: + κυρίου.

before Yhwh: So G^L. MT (*in Yhwh's temple*) is repetitive. Absent from G^B.

5 **coming on duty**: Reading the participle with MT, G^L. G^B reflects the imperative.

should be in charge: So G^{BL}, which reflect a volative (jussive or imperative). MT has the participle.

the royal palace: So MT, G^L. G^B: + *in the gate.*

6 **Gate of Secret Council**: So Jepsen (BHS) based on Syr and following Brockelman.[6] MT has סור, "gate of turning(?)" and is defended by scholars who point to the Talmudic reference to the Sur Gate as the eastern gate of the temple court, which was called "depart" because unclean persons and animals were forbidden from entering it.[7] But this reflects Jerusalem at a much later period, and the gate in our passage is to the palace grounds, not the temple. G^{BL} have "gate of the roads." A common emendation is סוס, "horse gate," which could be equated with the "horses' entrance" in v. 16, but it is hard to see how this could have led to so much confusion among the witnesses. The proposed reading finds support in 2 Chr 23:5, "gate of the foundation (היסוד)."

At the end of the verse MT has מסח = G^L μεσσαε; lacking in G^B This is a hapax that has been derived from √נסח, "to tear away," such that the meaning "repulse, defense" is hazarded. Another proposal draws on this same root but understands the word to mean "replaced" or "alternating" and cites Arabic *nasaḫa*.[8]

---

4 Norin, "Jô-Namen und J^ehô-Namen."

5 Muraoka (Joüon 100kN) posits מְאָיוֹת or מָאיוֹת. Burney (*Notes*, 309), citing König, suggests that the *yod* is euphonic due to Aramaic influence, but this does not explain its uniqueness in the present passage.

6 C. Brockelman, *Lexicon Syriacum*² (Halle: Max Niemeyer, 1928), 698.

7 *Erub* 22c (Venice edition). Cf. Longman (*Kings*, 864); Slotki (*Kings*, 231).

8 G. R. Driver, "Studies in the Vocabulary of the Old Testament VI," *JTS* 34 (1933), 376; *HALOT* p. 605; Montgomery, *Kings*, 424; Stade, *Kings*, 235.

Neither of these explanations is entirely satisfying; the word is best deleted as a copyist's error.[9]

7 **all of you who go off**: So MT, G^B. G^L: *all of you who go in*, under the influence of v. 5.

8 **the rows**: השדרות occurs outside of v. 15 // 2 Chr 23:14 only in 1 Kgs 6:9. It is usually taken as a reference to the ranks of soldiers, but it may be an architectural term as in 1 Kgs 6:9 referring to some kind of enclosure or wall—a line or row of columns or the like delimiting the temple precinct.[10]

9 **the priest**: So MT. G^B: ὁ συνετός = המבין, *wise, intelligent*. G^L ὁ συνετός ἱερεύς conflates.

commanded: So MT, G^B. G^L + *they accompanied the king when he went in*, an extension of the compliance notice at the end of v. 8 that also expands the interpolation in this and the next verse (see the Note on v. 10).

brought: So MT, G^L with the plural; G^B reflects the singular.

the ones coming on duty on the Sabbath along with those going off duty on the Sabbath: G^B has suffered haplography occasioned by the repetition of *Sabbath*. G^L (*... along with those coming on and those going off on the Sabbath*) reflects the intrusion of באי from earlier in the verse.

and they came: So MT, G^L. G^B has the singular again.

10 **to the centurions**: So MT, G^B, 2 Chr 23:9. G^L precedes with *to them*.

the spears: Reading the plural as reflected in the versions. Both masculine and feminine plurals are attested for חנית. 2 Chr 23:9 has החניתים, but a feminine ending could more easily have been lost by haplography (writing a single ת instead of two).

bow cases: This meaning for שלט is based on Akkadian *šalṭu* and the captioned relief from Naqsh-e Rustam of the Persian official Aspathines carrying the bow case of King Darius.[11]

So the centurions and the runners did according to all that Jehoiada the priest commanded them: So G^L: καὶ ἐποίησαν οἱ ἑκατόνταρχοι καὶ οἱ παρατρέχοντες κατὰ πάντα ἃ ἐνετείλατο αὐτοῖς Ιωδαε ὁ ἱερεύς. G^L precedes with καὶ ἦσαν ἐν ταῖς χερσίν αὐτῶν = בידיהם, continuing the foregoing endowment with the weapons. The rest repeats v. 9aα and signals an interpolation by *Wiederaufnahme* in vv. 9aβ-10.[12]

11 **weapon**: So G^B. MT, G^L have the plural. The consonantal Hebrew form is identical for both, and the singular makes better sense.

Jehoiada the priest assembled all the people of the land to the temple of Yhwh: So G^L (= OG), attested also by G^{inuxy} and Syr at the end of v. 10. Its placement at the end of v. 11 is indicated also by MT's use of a singular verb at the beginning of v. 12.[13]

12 **bracelets**: Following Wellhausen's proposal to read הצעדות as royal insignia, as in 2 Sam 1:10.[14] MT's העדות, "the testimony," is interpreted in the light of the "law of the king" in Deut 17:18-20 or of 2 Sam 7:14-16 as a document relating to the king's obligation to

---

9 Cogan and Tadmor, *II Kings*, 127.

10 Šanda, *Könige* II, 129; Trebolle, *Jehú y Joás*, 179.

11 R. Borger, "Die Waffenträger des Königs Darius. Ein Beitrag zur alttestamentlichen Exegese und zur semitischen Lexikographie," *VT* 22 (1972): 385–98. The interpretation is supported by the G^L rendering τὰς φαρέτρας, "the quivers."

12 Trebolle, *Jehú y Joás*, 177.

13 The references to the temple (of Yhwh) at the end of v. 11 MT and of the plus suggest that the latter was lost by haplography from the proto-MT.

14 J. Wellhausen, *Composition des Hexateuchs und der Historischen Bücher des Alten Testaments* (Berlin: Georg Reimer, 1899), 292n. Z. W. Falk ("Forms of Testimony," *VT* 11 [1961]: 88–91) hazards the same meaning without Wellhausen's emendation. Another possibility that goes back to Qimḥi (Rosenberg, *Kings II*, 323) and is mentioned by Klostermann (*Könige*, 430) is to read עדיות, "ornaments."

keep the law or to the promises of the Davidic covenant.[15] But there is no reference to the king taking up such a document at his coronation. Moreover, עדות is a late, usually Priestly, term.[16] Also, the context here indicates some article of apparel coordinating with the diadem.

he anointed him and made him king: So G^L^. MT has plural verbs in reverse order: *they made him king and anointed him.* G^B^ has singular verbs but agrees with MT's order. The G^L^ order is logical, as anointing marks the endowment of kingship.

14 **the officers:** So MT. The celebratory scene here evoked the reading *singers* (*haššārîm*) in G^BL^ (οἱ ᾠδοὶ) and 2 Chr 23:13. However, MT's *haśśārîm, the commanders, officers,* is more appropriate, given the military setting and the concern to protect the king. See the next Note.

and the runners: MT (והחצצרות), G^B^ (καὶ αἱ σάλπιγγες) "and the trumpets." G^L^: + καὶ οἱ στρατηγοὶ = *wěhaśśārîm*, a double reading with *haššārîm* earlier. The reference to instruments where one expects another group of people is problematic, and efforts to make "trumpets" mean "trumpeters" lack grammatical support. "Trumpeters" would also then appear without introduction or precedent in the narrative. I follow Klostermann, therefore, in supposing that והחצצרות is a corruption of הרצים that took place after *śārîm* "officers" was read as *šārîm* "singers."[17]

beside the king: So G^L^ (περὶ), 2 Chr 23:13 (על). MT, G^B^: אל.

all the people: So G^L^. MT, G^B^: *all the people of the land.*

she tore her clothes: MT and G^B^ supply Athaliah's name after the verb *tore*, while G^L^ places it after *her clothes.* The different placements suggest that the name is secondary.

15 **the centurions:** Followed by פקדי החיל, which should be read as פְּקֻדֵי החיל "officers of the army," spelled defectively. One of the two titles is probably superfluous, and scholars usually regard *centurions* as secondary, seeing it as an effort to harmonize the account in vv. 13-18a with vv. 4-12. This assumes, however, that vv. 13-18a are an interpolation from a separate source, an assumption that is questionable on other grounds. If the chapter is essentially a unit, פקידי החיל is intrusive, perhaps a marginal gloss that found its way into the text.

through the rows: The phrase אל־מבית לשדרת. (G^L^: ἔσωθεν τῶν σαδηρωθ.) is unique in the HB. The compound preposition apparently has the meaning "inside," comparable to למבית (Num 18:7). However, that meaning is awkward in view of v. 15b, where the queen is to be taken outside the temple precincts for execution. "The queen is to be taken *outside* the Temple, and therefore not *inside* the ranks which, according to v. 8, surround the king within the Temple."[18] A number of scholars regard the phrase as a gloss. If retained it is probably to be understood as "between" or "through" the border constituted by the שדרת. Stade proposes אל מחוץ לחצרות, "outside of the courts,"[19] which is attractive for its meaning and has the support of G^B^ (ἔσωθεν τῶν ἀσηδρῶθ) and the Vulgate (*extra consepta templi*).

Take her behind the officers' barracks, and execute her with the sword. Do not execute her in Yhwh's temple. Kill anyone who follows her in: So G^L^. MT lacks any explicit order to execute Athaliah and does not specify the place of her execution. This makes the order to kill anyone who follows Athaliah interrupt the continuity between the order to take her outside and the order not to let her die in the temple.

---

15 Cf. Barnes, *Kings*, 274; Hens-Piazza, *Kings*, 308; Fretheim, *Kings*, 178.
16 Burney (*Notes*, 311).
17 Klostermann, *Kings*, 431.
18 Burney, *Notes*, 312.
19 Stade, *Kings*, 237.

The clause כי אמר הכהן is intrusive and repetitive. MT lost the order to take Athaliah behind the barracks but retained the phrase *by the sword*, which was applied to anyone who followed her.

16 **laid hands**: שים ידים is unique and its exact sense unknown. It was taken by medieval exegetes and older commentators to mean "make room," based on the use of ידים for "space" (Gen 34:21; Josh 8:20; Ps 104:25).[20] Cogan and Tadmor propose "take by force," based on the use of *yād* with other verbs to denote hostile action (Exod 7:4; 22:7; 1 Sam 24:10; 26:11; Ps 55:21).[21] The translation adopted here implies hostility while retaining ambiguity.

and brought her: So G^{L} in compliance with Jehoiada's order. MT, G^{B}: *she came* (ותבוא).

they put her to death: So G^{L} again as per Jehoiada's order. MT: *she was put to death* (ותומת); G^{B}: *she died.*

17 **Jehoiada**: So MT, G^{B}. G^{L} + *the priest.*

between Yhwh and the people and the king to be Yhwh's people: So G^{L}. MT, G^{B} + *and between the king and the people* (ובין המלך ובין העם) is repetitive and seems to be a dittography. 2 Chr 23:16: *between himself and all the people and the king to be Yhwh's people.*

18 **came**: MT has the plural, while G^{BL} reflect the singular; either is possible.

and tore it down: So MT, G^{L}, 2 Chr 23:17, reading the plural verb. G^{B} has the singular. Some manuscripts, as well as the Syr and Vulgate, lack the suffix, taking "its altars" as the direct object.

Its altars: Preceded by *and* in G^{BL} and 2 Chr 23:16 but lacking in MT.

before the altar: Reading the singular for sense. The major witnesses have the plural, but the singular fits better as a reference to the temple's main altar, especially in view of the destruction of the other altars noted earlier in the verse.

19 **He took**: So MT, G^{B}. G^{L} + *Jehoiada the priest.*

They brought him: So G^{L}. MT: *they came*; G^{B}: *he came.*

and sat him: So G^{B}; 2 Chr 23:20 (ויושיבו את־המלך). MT: *and he sat.*

throne of the kingdom: Reading כסא המלוכה as in 1 Kgs 1:46 instead of כסא המלכים *the kings' throne*. The proposal accounts for both the peculiar MT reading and that of 2 Chr 23:20 (כסא הממלכה).[22]

20 **in the royal palace**: So *qere'* (בית המלך); *ketiv*: בית מלך.

Synchronic Analysis

11:1: Athaliah's purge

With its subject-first sentence v. 1 marks a new beginning. It returns to some point after 9:27 when Athaliah learned of Ahaziah's death. Her reaction is unexpected. There is no mention of grief or anger at Jehu. Instead, she destroys the *royal heirs*, i.e., the males in the line of David, and seizes power herself (v. 3b). The move reflects encroachment of the customary practice in Israel. Athaliah behaves like Jehu. It is also impossible not to associate her act with Jezebel. Since those slaughtered were close relatives of hers—sons, grandsons, and nephews—the act raises questions about her character. Did her son's assassina-

---

20 E.g., Thenius, *Könige*, 327.

21 Cogan and Tadmor, *2 Kings*,130.

22 Stade, *Kings*, 238.

tion make her irrational, or was this a calculated act by a power-hungry woman? But would such questions be raised about a man who behaved this way? Besides, Athaliah obviously did not act alone; she had supporters in the court about whom the text is silent. Were they also seduced by their own self-interests, or did they further enable her by cowering and refusing to "speak truth to power?"

Athaliah's purge is a crisis for the Davidic promise; the line cannot continue if all its heirs are dead. The text hastens to assure readers that one heir is rescued (v. 2). The blanket statement in v. 1 turns out to be hyperbole, but only slightly so. It is rhetorically effective in highlighting the crisis. It is also effective for masking a "dirty little secret" of the story: the surviving Davidid, Joash, is a member of the house of Ahab as well because Athaliah is his grandmother. Joash's rescuer is also apparently an Ahabid, the sister of Ahaziah of Judah (v. 2). She, along with the priest, Jehoiada, are the heroes of this story. Her name, Jehosheba, recalls Jehoshaphat, Judah's last righteous king. Like him she is involved with the family of Ahab but chooses to do right. She can rescue only one of the doomed sons, but she does that much. The narrative is tantalizing for what it leaves out. How does she choose which boy to save? Perhaps he is the youngest? How does she gain access to the condemned heirs? How does she hide him? Why does Athaliah not know one is missing? Where is Joash's mother? The narrative addresses none of these questions but provides only the barest specifics. What is clear is that Jehosheba's gender is crucial. As a female, she was not one of the *royal seed* under attack. Her life was not in danger from Athaliah but she risks it to save her nephew. The rescue of a baby boy by a woman recalls the Moses story and enhances Joash's reputation as well as Jehosheba's.[23] 11:2: The rescue of Joash

Jehosheba's heroism includes not only "stealing" the boy (v. 2) but hiding him for six years (v. 3). The participial clauses in v. 3 parallel the period of Joash's hiding (מתחבא) with that of Athaliah's ruling (מלכת). She rules only so long as he remains hidden. The parallel also sets up a public/private opposition that contrasts falsity with genuineness.[24] The boy's presence in the temple brings Yhwh into that dynamic. Athaliah's public rule is a façade because the real king is closeted. The Davidic dynasty is intimately connected with the temple and both are under Yhwh's protection; Yhwh and his priests are against Athaliah. She is a pretender whose rule does not count. No regnal formulae are supplied for her. Her rule is not a reign. It is a parenthesis that does not merit inclusion in the list of kings of Judah. There is little actual information about it. She merely occupies the time until the real king can be enthroned, so the account moves from her seizure of power to her replacement, with nothing specific about the interval. This is the first of many references to the temple; its interplay with the palace is a significant motif in this and the next chapter. 11:3: Six years of Athaliah's rule

The seventh year (v. 4) may symbolize the end of a lengthy period, when things were ripe for change. Joash is a child whose ascent to the throne must be orchestrated. The character responsible is Jehoiada, who is presented the first time without title or introduction. We learn in v. 9 that he is *the priest*, presumably the high 11:4: A secret pact

---

23 Cohn, *II Kings*, 78; Hens-Piazza, *Kings*, 307; Long, *1 & 2 Kings*, 388; Longman, *Kings*, 862.
24 Cohn, *II Kings,* 78.

priest, but in any case a person of status and authority. Meanwhile, the uncertainty about his identity creates suspense and allows the narrator to paint his character through words and deeds.[25] He convenes *the centurions of the Carites and runners*. The *runners* were charged with guarding the entrance to the king's house (1 Kgs 14:27) as a kind of palace guard. The identity of the Carites is less clear though they were also a military group, perhaps an elite or specialized one. His pact with these two military contingents shrewdly transfers Athaliah's protection to Joash and gives him (Jehoiada) the freedom to carry out the enthronement ceremony. He adjures the troops by YHWH to silence, attesting their loyalty to the national god. The word used for his adjuration (*wayyašba'*) uses the root present in Jehosheba's name and brings her brave deed to mind. Then, having extracted their oaths of loyalty and silence, he shows them the boy king. The reader can imagine the amazement and joy of the two groups of soldiers upon learning that the Davidic line is not defunct as they had believed.

11:5-8: The priest's conspiracy

In vv. 5-8 Jehoiada lays out his plan. While the details are obscured by our unfamiliarity with the groups and locations mentioned, several important features are discernible. First is the meticulousness of the plan's construction. Jehoiada knows exactly what he is doing and leaves nothing to chance. Years of planning have gone into it. Jehoiada takes on the role of commander and assigns the troops positions that will restrict access to the venue and afford maximum protection for the young king while allowing Athaliah no escape. Readers are co-conspirators who are brought into the group of those privy to details Athaliah does not know.[26] The story of a conspiracy led by a priest to place an heir on the throne recalls Solomon's enthronement in 1 Kings 1 and highlights the theme of dynastic continuity.[27]

Protecting the king

Part of the genius of Jehoiada's plan is that it launches on the Sabbath, when the insurgents take advantage of the customary rotation of the guard so that the large number of active soldiers—double or even triple the average number—does not appear unusual. The prime directive for both groups of guards is the protection of the king. They are armed and surround the king constantly during these procedures (v. 8aα). The procession moves from the palace to the temple for the coronation and then back to the palace for the king to be seated on the throne. The different divisions of guards are charged with protecting the king in both buildings and along the route, especially the gateways, between them. They prevent anyone else, on pain of death, from entering the precincts formed by the "rows"—be this an architectural feature of the temple or the formation of the soldiers—during the ceremonies (v. 8aβ).

11:9-10 Symbols of continuity of the Davidic line

The centurions follow Jehoiada's orders closely and completely (v. 9aα). The narrative then turns to another important aspect of the proceedings: the symbolic and ritual (v. 10). Jehoiada lends two weapons or sets of weapons to the troops for the occasion: *the spear and the bow cases* (see the Note) that had belonged to David. It is common among commentators to emend *spear* to a plural. In addition to the parallel with the plural *bow cases*, the plural number of recipients—the

25 Dutcher-Walls, *Narrative Art*, 33.
26 Dutcher-Walls, *Narrative Art*, 34.
27 Dutcher-Walls, *Narrative Art*, 79–82.

centurions—makes such a move attractive. Still, *spear* can be interpreted as a collective. Alternatively, the reference is to a specific spear that may or may not have been used by David. This possibility seems unlikely, though, since the spear was Saul's weapon, not David's (1 Sam 18:10-11; 19:9-10; 20:33; 22:6; 26:7, 8, 11, 12, 16, 22), and there is no story about David wielding a particular spear of renown. The closest thing to it is Goliath's spear (1 Sam 17:7, 45, 47), but there is no explanation of what happened to it or reference to David using it himself. The *bow cases* were taken by David from Hadadezer (2 Sam 8:7). Their composition of gold makes them impractical as weapons and ceremonial in function.[28] They are important symbols of the continuity of the Davidic house and serve as legitimation for the king in the Davidic line who is about to be installed.

11:11: Setting the guard

Having received their instructions and their implements, the soldiers now take up their appointed posts (v. 11). *Runners* here seems to be used generically for the entire guard including the Carites. The guard forms a semicircle, running south to north in front of the eastern-oriented entrance to the temple, that will protect the king inside the temple and block Athaliah's access to it.[29] The last phrase of the verse, *all around the king*, is anticipatory, since the king has not yet appeared. The phrase and the verse as a whole elevate the reader's anticipation of the impending advent of the king and the associated events: his coronation and the unseating of Athaliah.

11:12: Long live the king

Verse 12 is the chapter's keystone, as it succinctly describes the moment of transition. Jehoiada brings Joash out. Actually, Jehoiada is not named. The subject of the verb *brought out* is anonymous and might be rendered as an impersonal or passive; the focus is on the king. He is not yet called king; rather, he is *the king's son*. The epithet denotes him as the Davidic heir and king designate. It is only at the end of the verse that he is hailed as *the king*; he will not be called *the king's son* again. The transformation is at once entirely ceremonial and yet profound. It is effected by endowment with the insignias of kingship: the crown or diadem and the *ēdût* (*testimonies*?) and by anointing and perhaps proclamation. These simple acts immediately alter Joash's status and power. They produce excitement and joy in the assembly, as indicated by its applause and shouts of *long live the king*. There is a sense of restoration of security: a Davidid is back on the throne; the kingdom again has YHWH's support.

11:13-16: The last of Athaliah

In vv. 13-16 the narrative turns from Joash's coronation to Athaliah's reaction. She must be removed before he can be enthroned in the palace. The drama is enhanced by the description through her senses.[30] She hears the clapping and shouts of *long live the king* without grasping their significance (v. 13). Only when she views the scene before the temple does she comprehend (v. 14). There is the new king standing beside the column. It is *according to the custom*, so that she knows even without the royal insignia and the proclamations that a new king has been anointed in her stead. Her lack of awareness of the movement to that point

---

28 Wiseman (*Kings*, 246) misses the ceremonial point in his claim that the soldiers were not allowed to bring weapons into the temple but had to use David's weapons that were already inside.

29 On the term *shoulder* (כתף) used here for the two ends see R. D. Haak, "The 'Shoulder' of the Temple," *VT* 33 (1983): 271–78.

30 Cohn, *II Kings*, 79.

is testimony to the care and effectiveness of Jehoiada's planning. The commanders and trumpets mean that the opposition has the support of the military and that there is celebration going on. It marks the end not only of her rule but of her life. The narrative captures her mortification and cry of distress with a pun: ותקרע ... ותקרא, *she tore [her clothes] and she cried out.* Her exclamation, *conspiracy, conspiracy,* is ironic. For Joash's supporters *conspiracy* was Athaliah's seizure of the throne and six-year rule; their act is a restoration of right order in the Davidic dynasty. Athaliah's cry combines Joram's מרמה in 9:23 with Jehu's confession of conspiracy (קשרתי) in 10:9. It signals that her end is at hand. It contrasts with the jubilant noise being generated by the people. But hear her they do, and the celebration, or at least the report of it, pauses long enough for Jehoiada to give instructions concerning the dethroned woman and to detail their implementation. He orders the centurions to take her outside the temple precincts for execution (v. 15). The *rows*—whether the column of soldiers or a colonnade—constitute the border between the temple and palace precincts. Jehoiada's concern is that she not be executed within the temple grounds so as to avoid ritual pollution. He further orders the executioners to kill anyone who follows, not distinguishing between adherents and gawkers. In compliance, she is led off to a part of the palace compound via the horses' entrance, presumably the way to the stables. The mention of horses echoes Jezebel's death in 9:30-37.

11:17-18: Covenant renewed, Baal's temple destroyed

Athaliah's death does not affect the chronological progression of the narrative since the people can continue to celebrate while she is taken away. In contrast, the covenant renewal and demolition of the temple of Baal in vv. 17-18 would delay the king's enthronement. Hence the narrative logic is thematic rather than chronological. Athaliah's rule has interrupted the sequence of Davidic kings, requiring a reaffirmation and renewal of the covenant, yet the covenant renewed here seems to be the one at Horeb rather than the Davidic one. The specifics of this covenant are not laid out because it is a renewal, but the concern is for the people to belong to YHWH. The king is part of the people and is included in the covenant. He is mentioned separately because he is the representative of the people. The people are not a party to the Davidic covenant. Besides, the entire story about Athaliah already illustrates YHWH's faithfulness to the Davidic covenant. Verse 18 clarifies further. It was not the Davidic covenant that required renewal because of Athaliah but the Horeb covenant because she led the people into the worship of Baal. The people's pledge of loyalty to the covenant with YHWH impels them to move against the Baal temple. This is the only mention in the HB of a temple of Baal in Jerusalem. The implication is that Athaliah was responsible for it. Athaliah is Judah's version of Jezebel, the foreign woman who led the country astray.

11:19: The king installed

Verse 19 describes the enthronement. The singular verb *he took* that opens the verse refers to *the priest* at the end of v. 18. Since this is the epithet of Jehoiada elsewhere in the context it is he who once again orchestrates the enthronement. He leads the military groups as well as the people of the land. But the verbs then change to plurals as the entire convocation now moves with the king from the temple to the palace. The mention of *the house of YHWH* and *the house of the king* in close proximity to one another recalls 2 Samuel 7 and the promise to David occasioned by his offer to build the temple as well as Solomon's construction of palace and temple in 1 Kings 6–8. Joash's anointing shows that the promise remains in effect. The procession goes through the Runners' Gate, the most direct access between the two precincts. Jehoiada and the crowd around him then install the king on his throne in the palace. The assembly witnesses this. In a sense it is they who seat him; he represents them.

11:20: Rest

The statement in v. 20 that the city was quiet or at rest (שקטה) evokes the refrain in Joshua (11:23; 14:15) and Judges (3:11, 30; 5:31; 8:28) that the "land had rest" from war after the victory and installation of a new judge. It is noteworthy, though, that v. 20 connects the joy and tranquility not with the beginning of the new king's reign but with Athaliah's execution. Her rule is considered a time of chaos. The nature of the chaos is not delineated. It may refer to lingering feelings of unease in the wake of her slaughter of the Davidids. The comment draws yet another parallel between Athaliah and Jezebel and the absence of YHWH's *shalom* in the account of the latter's reign in 2 Kings 9. With this comment Athaliah's tale ends.[31] There is no death or burial notice, no closing formulae at all, in accord with the dismissal of Athaliah's rule as an illegitimate interruption of the history of Judah's Davidic dynasty.

Diachronic Analysis

A basic unit

Kritiker haben hier das Gras wachsen hören ("Critics have heard the grass growing here") was Hölscher's colorful assessment of critical analyses of this chapter, particularly the influential theory by Stade (see below on vv. 13-18a). Hölscher's assessment is confirmed by text-critical work showing that observations of disturbance in the narrative must be balanced by consideration of the textual evidence, and this has typically not been the case. Except for a few glosses and additions, the chapter is a unit.[32] Its origin is uncertain. The language and ideology are not characteristic of DtrH; there is, for instance, only a single mention of David in the (DtrH) interpolation in vv. 9aβ-10. Attempts to prove that the account derives from an apologetic or propagandistic document have not proven persuasive.[33] More likely is the possibility that it stems from an official source, perhaps from the integrated king list.[34]

Causes of revolt

The rebellion against Athaliah was probably an extension of the movement that fueled Jehu's revolt. Additionally, in Judah there was probably discontent over its domination by the Omrids even to the point of losing its independent monarchy, especially if the theory of a single J(eh)oram from Israel is correct. Gender

31 G^B and versions based on it have a different versification, reading MT's 12:1 as 11:21. The versification followed here is MT's.

32 On the basic unity of the chapter see J. Trebolle, "La coronación de Joás (2 Re 11). Texto, narración e historia," *EstBib* 41 (1983): 5–16.

33 M. Liverani ("L'histoire de Joas," *VT* 24 [1974]: 438–53) compares chs. 11–12 to the inscription of Idri-mi of Alalakh, which he defines as propaganda. But see the critique by Hobbs, *2 Kings*, 156–58. Barré (*Rhetoric*, esp. 1–55) sees chs. 9–11 as a "political novella" of propaganda for Joash's newly inaugurated reign.

34 Levin (*Sturz*, 81–82) points out the detailed nature of the account and contends that it is an excerpt from the "book of the days of the kings of Judah."

was also a factor; Athaliah—an Omrid of partly Phoenician descent, and a woman to boot—was the last straw. The rebellion was less about restoring the Davidic dynasty *per se* than about restoring Judah's independence. It would make sense for the temple, as Judah's royal shrine, to be the fount of the rebellion.

11:1: Athaliah's purge and Jehu's revolt

Verse 1 connects Athaliah's slaughter of the royal heirs with the death of her son, King Ahaziah, without explaining exactly what it was about Ahaziah's death that provoked such a murderous act. A common explanation is that in the absence of her son as king her position as queen mother, with whatever power and prestige accompanied it, was in jeopardy. While a fair inference, this explanation remains uncertain because of the paucity of information regarding the queen mother.[35] Athaliah's actions do have a narrative function in the larger historical scheme of Kings. The background to this chapter, with the intermarriage of Joram and Athaliah (8:26), meant that the Davidic king from that point on would also be a descendant of Omri and Ahab. Athaliah's attempt to murder the Davidic heirs creates separation between the two royal houses and effectively undoes the bond between them.

11:2-3: Bare details

The details of Athaliah's purge are not supplied. Jehu's slaughter of the Judahite princes in 10:12-14 suggests that there were not many of the royal seed left for Athaliah to kill, unless the two accounts reflect different sources. One scholar has argued that it was Jehu rather than Athaliah who was responsible historically for nearly annihilating Judah's royal seed.[36] If those killed by Athaliah were few, it sharpens the question whether Athaliah was aware of Joash's rescue (vv. 2-3); did she search for him? Nor are there many details about the rescue. There is little about Jehosheba and her motive. She may have been Athaliah's own daughter or the daughter of a different wife, i.e., Athaliah's step-daughter. Verse 2 with its reference to Jehosheba as Ahaziah's sister hints that she was moved by loyalty and love for her brother and perhaps for the royal line. Second Chronicles 22:11 adds to this motive by identifying her as the wife of Jehoiada the priest. It implies that *the bedroom* was in the temple and that it remained the hiding place for six years.[37] If so, he could have been hidden "in plain sight," as the son of one of the priests, so that it was his identity rather than his actual person that was hidden. Still, the Kings account remains vague and sparse in details. The verb *steal* implies an act of secrecy and daring, one that required great courage and commitment, not just in taking the child but in hiding him for six years. The phrase *him and his nurse* is sometimes seen as an intrusion from 2 Chr 22:11 because

---

35 For instance, Z. Ben-Barak ("The Status and Right of the *Gĕbîrâ*," *JBL* 110 [1991]: 23–34) argues that the queen mother had no official political status in Judah and that (p. 27) Athaliah's slaughter of the Davidids was an act of desperation and self-preservation to which she was driven by the purge of Omrids in the North. Hens-Piazza (*Kings*, 306–307) describes Athaliah's deed as the result of "grief-filled insanity" by a person who seeks the death of all presumptive heirs to the throne because her son was killed.

36 C. Levin, *Sturz*, 85–87.

37 Provan (*Kings*, 221) suggests that the bedroom was the place from which Joash and his nurse were rescued, though it is difficult to construe the ב in בחדר as meaning "from." Sweeney (*Kings*, 345) claims that the temple was chosen as the hiding place because Athaliah as a foreigner could not enter it. But it is doubtful that Athaliah, whose name was Yahwistic and who was born and raised in Israel, was considered a foreigner. Even if she were a foreigner and Baal worshiper she could have the temple searched by Judahite citizens.

the nurse is not mentioned again and plays no role in the story. However מֵינֶקֶת refers to a wet-nurse and thus signals that Joash was a baby.[38] Nor are we told what happened to Joash's mother, Zibiah (12:2). Perhaps she was also killed by Athaliah[39] or maybe she was already dead (in childbirth). Obviously the narrative supplies the bare details of the setting before moving to the plot against Athaliah.

11:4: The Carites and runners

In Joash's seventh year of hiding, the priest Jehoiada takes action (v. 4). *Seventh* is a common motif in and outside the Bible for a complete period of time. It signals, in essence, that the time was ripe. It is not clear whether Jehoiada was the high priest, but he certainly had a leadership role among both temple and military personnel in Jerusalem (cf. 12:8).[40] The main problem in the verse is the identity of the "Carites." Since Ewald in 1871 this group has commonly been identified with the Carians (οἱ Κᾶρες) mentioned by Herodotus (*Histories* 2:152-54) as mercenaries from southwest Anatolia hired by Psammeticus I (ca. 664–610 BCE).[41] Aside from the chronological difference—Athaliah and Joash being about 200 years earlier—there is also a linguistic discrepancy between the Hebrew כרי and the transcription of the name "Carian" elsewhere in ancient Near Eastern documents as *krs* or *krk*.[42] Another possibility is suggested by the occurrence of כרי in 2 Sam 20:23 *ketiv*, where it is an error for "Cherethites" (כרתי). As a group of mercenaries originally from Crete who served as David's bodyguard (2 Sam 8:18; 15:18; 20:7; 1 Kgs 1:38, 44), the Cherethites and Carites had the same function and may have been the same group, a sort of "Swiss Guard" for the king of Judah.[43] Such was more clearly the function of the *runners* (1 Kgs 14:27). Hence what Jehoiada does as a preliminary step to revolt is to swear the *commander of 100s* or centurions of the royal guard[44] to fealty to YHWH and to the protection of the royal heir. The language of v. 4 suggests that he reminded them of the basic duty to the king that was their *raison d'etre*, and, having secured their agreement in principle, he revealed the surviving heir.

---

38 P. Dutcher-Walls, *Narrative Art*, 31.

39 Suggested by Rehm, *Das zweite Buch der Könige*, 115; Sweeney, *Kings*, 344.

40 De Vaux (*Rois*, 165) thinks the title *the priest* here is the high priest. Jehoiada's name does not occur in the list of 1 Chr 5:27-41 (Rehm, *Das zweite Buch der Könige*, 115). But it is not certain that 1 Chr 5:27-41 is the high priestly list, and if it is, it is probably incomplete. See Cross, Canaanite Myth, 211–12; Knoppers, *1 Chronicles 1-9*, 408–13.

41 H. Ewald, *The History of Israel* (vol. 4; ed. J. Estlin Carpenter; London: Longmans, Green, and Co., 1871), 135.

42 Cogan and Tadmor, *II Kings*, 126.

43 See McCarter, *II Samuel*, 256. Sweeney's (*Kings*, 345) proposal that "Carite" derives from כר "ram" and refers to a military rank between officers and foot soldiers has no supporting evidence. Würthwein (*1. Könige 17-2. Könige 25*, 347) argues that as foreigners the Carites could not have been involved in the coronation or partners in the covenant renewal, nor would they have been guardians of the temple. They are, with the runners, a secondary addition influenced by additions in vv. 5b, 7, 9 that reflect the postexilic practice of the weekly change of the temple guard. In Chronicles the priests and Levites replace the Carites and runners and the temple guard.

44 Würthwein (*1. Könige 17-2. Könige* 25, 349) connects the *centurions* with the *people of the land*, since he regards the *Carites* and *runners* as secondary. He argues that the verbs for the summoning and dismissal of the centurions assume that they lived outside of Jerusalem and served as the military for the landowners in Judah.

11:5-10: The rotations of the guards

Verses 5-7 and 9-10 have been the source of much confusion because of the references to three divisions in vv. 5-6 and to two divisions in v. 7. Wellhausen regarded v. 6 as an addition because of its contradictions with v. 9 and assumed that the two-thirds in v. 7 complemented the one-third in v. 5.[45] His reconstruction has been highly influential and adopted by probably the majority of critical commentators.[46] However, this reconstruction ignores the OL, which suggests that most of v. 9 and all of v. 10 are an interpolation (see below).[47] The contradictions between vv. 6 and 9 result from this interpolation; Wellhausen had it backward: v. 6 is an integral part of the narrative and vv. 9aβ-10 are the addition. Thus Jehoiada's instructions concern not one large guard divided into thirds, as often supposed, but two guards: those who are rotating on duty for the Sabbath, subdivided into thirds (vv. 5-6), and those who are rotating off duty for the Sabbath, subdivided into halves (v. 7).[48] Jehoiada places the guard that is rotating on in charge of the palace (vv. 5-6) and the guard that is rotating off in charge of the temple (v. 7). Those rotating on are posted at three locations: the palace (presumably at its entrance) and two inner gates that grant access to the palace precincts, the Council Gate and the gate behind the runners. The latter might be the same as the Runners' Gate referred to in v. 19. If so, it would communicate between the southern side of the temple grounds and the palace precincts, and this would make sense as a location to be guarded. The name "Council" Gate is conjectural (see the Note) and its location uncertain. If the MT (סור) is emended to סוס, "horse gate," it might be identified with the "horses' entrance" mentioned in v. 16, which evidently led to the stables outside the palace grounds. This would also make sense as a place to post guards, but the uncertainty of the text and of the layout of the palace area leave the details unclear. Obviously, though, Jehoiada limits access to the palace and its grounds both to protect Joash and to confine Athaliah.[49] He posts the two divisions of the guard going off duty for the Sabbath at the temple (v. 7).[50]

Protecting the king

The prime directive for both guards is the protection of the king. They are armed and surround the king constantly during these proceedings (v. 8aα). *Rows* probably refers to a colonnade or the like enclosing the temple grounds rather

---

45 Wellhausen, *Composition des Hexateuchs*, 292n.

46 See the list provided by Barré (*Rhetoric of Persuasion*, 23n), who also follows Wellhausen. Important recent dissenters include Levin (*Sturz*) and Fritz (*Kings*, 296), who follows his *Schichtenaufteilung.* See also G. Robinson, "Is 2 Kings XI 6 a Gloss?" *VT* 27 (1977): 56–61.

47 Trebolle, *Jehú y Joás*, 171–77; "Glosas en 2 Re 11,6-10. De la crítica textual a la crítica literaria e histórica," *EstBib* 41 (1983), 375–80.

48 Cf. Hobbs, *2 Kings*, 140.

49 Provan (*Kings*, 222) uniquely interprets the *house* at the end of v. 6 as the temple of Baal, arguing that מסח at the end of the verse means "tearing down, destruction" and is an allusion to the temple of Baal that is about to be destroyed. Jehoiada sends the guard there to keep the Baal worshipers from interfering in the change of monarchs and to arrest the priest of Baal, Mattan. The obscurity of מסח makes this interpretation quite tenuous.

50 The phrase *for the king* (אל־המלך) at the end of v. 7 is probably a gloss. The phrase is awkward there; the verse reads better without it and it seems to be a misplaced dittography from the similar על־המלך in v. 8.

than to the guards (see Note). For the king's protection no one is allowed to enter the temple precincts from the outside during these ceremonies (v. 8aβ). The coronation takes place in the temple and then the king will move to the palace to be seated on the throne. The guard remains with the king when he enters the temple and when he exits it to go to the palace (v. 8b).

With v. 8 Jehoiada's verbal instructions to the two bodies of guards come to an 11:9aβ-10: An
end. Verse 9 begins, as might be expected, with a statement of compliance: that the interpolation
centurions did as Jehoiada had commanded (v. 9aα). However, the rest of the verse, along with v. 10, is an interpolation introduced by *Wiederaufnahme* as preserved in the OL reading. The interpolator misunderstood Jehoiada's instructions in vv. 5-7. The word *each* in v. 9 seems to indicate that each centurion commanded both men who were rotating on and men who were rotating off. As a result, v. 10 blurs the distinction between the two bodies of guards in vv. 5-7 and thus has contributed to the confusion about their meaning. The reason for the interpolation was to introduce the reference to David's weapons in v. 10. These are ceremonial (2 Sam 8:7) and symbolize the continuity of the Davidic house and the legitimation of the sitting king.[51] This concern hints at DtrH as the interpolator.

Verse 11 describes the positioning of the *runners* in preparation for the emer- 11:11
gence of the king-designate from the temple. The last three words of the verse in MT, *around the king* (על־המלך סביב), are problematic since the king has not yet appeared. For this reason they are considered secondary by many commentators. The G^L plus to the verse preserves an original reading. Its mention of the people of the land is assumed in the narrative that follows. They are key to the process of making Joash king. It is only when they are assembled that he brings out the king designate. There may be a kind of blending of traditions here: kingship defined in Israelite terms by popular approval but granted by divine right to David's heirs in Judah.[52] Athaliah as a non-Davidid who seized power of her own initiative was illegitimate on both counts.

Excursus: The People of the Land (עם הארץ)

The expression "people of the land" has elicited a great deal of scholarly discussion. At issue is whether it is a technical term, and if so for what group of people.[53] The different proposals vary widely and include but are not limited to: a representative assembly, poor citizens, upper-class citizens, landowners, provincial dwellers (as opposed to the citizens of Jerusalem), faithful Yahwists, a constituency of the Deuteronomic movement, and a generic term. A crucial moment in the history of the discussion was Würthwein's 1936 monograph, which contended that the people of the land were the enfranchised citizenry of Judah who constituted a social class with economic, judicial, and military power and who were therefore an important force in the appointment of kings (2 Kgs 14:21; 21:24).[54] Subsequent scholars have basically responded to

51 They are apparently meant to be distinguished from Solomon's golden shields (מגנים) that were seized by Shishak/Sheshonq (1 Kgs 14:26).

52 Provan, *Kings*, 220.

53 For surveys of the literature see J. P. Healey, "Am Ha'aretz," *ABD* 1:168–69; L. E. Ijezie, *The Interpretation of the Hebrew Word* עם *(People) in Samuel-Kings* (European University Studies; Bern: Peter Lang, 2007), 210–14; Jones, *Kings*, 483–84.

54 E. Würthwein, *Der 'amm ha'arez im Alten Testament* (BWANT 17; Stuttgart: Kohlhammer, 1936).

Würthwein's proposal, either adjusting it or refuting it. Thus Alt contrasted the people of the land with the people of Jerusalem, arguing that the former were the population of the provincial towns who championed the Davidic line and intervened on its behalf when it was threatened by the city-dwellers.[55] De Vaux and Halpern stressed the tie with the land as characterizing YHWH's people.[56] Soggin broke with the consensus in defining the people of the land in religious rather than socio-economic terms as those faithful to YHWH.[57] A more serious break was that of Nicholson, whose examination of the expression in books other than Kings and Chronicles led him to conclude that it is ambiguous if not generic.[58]

The present chapter has always been an important text for the topic, and careful reconsideration of it in light of the text-critical evidence, which has generally been ignored in the discussion, raises questions about the topic as *ein exegetisches Phantom.*[59] In trying to establish the unity of this chapter against Stade's two-source theory Rudolph contended that all the references to *the people of the land* (vv. 14, 18, 19), except the final one in v. 20 were secondary.[60] This was because the earlier references presumed that this group had an active role in deposing Athaliah and installing Joash, as opposed to their joyful acceptance of the *fait accompli* in v. 20. Redaction-critical arguments are adduced as support, but what they amount to is that the people of the land appear suddenly in the narrative and then are out of place beside the centurions and

55 A. Alt, "The Monarchy in the Kingdoms of Israel and Judah," in *Essays on Old Testament History and Religion* (trans. R. A. Wilson; Oxford: Blackwell, 1966), esp. 251–55. Original German publication 1951.

56 R. De Vaux, "Le sens de l'expression 'Peuple du pays' dans l'Ancien Testament et le rôle politique du peuple en Israël," *RA* 58 (1964): 167–72; Halpern, *Constitution*, 191–98. Halpern's remarks on p. 196 are especially helpful: the construction refers to people who are bound together by what they have in common, in this case the land, so that they are "the people belonging to the land" (land ownership as a subjective genitive).

57 J. A. Soggin, "Der judäische ʿam-ha'areṣ und das Königtum in Juda. Ein Beitrag zum Studium der Deuteronomistischen Geschichtsschreibung," *VT* 13 (1963): 187–95.

58 E. W. Nicholson, "The Meaning of the Expression עם הארץ in the Old Testament," JSS 10 (1965): 59–66.

59 The phrase belongs to Levin (*Sturz*, 69) who uses it specifically for the narrow definition of the *people of the land* as excluding Jerusalemites. In part because of his views about the people of the land, Würthwein adopts a rather convoluted reconstruction of the chapter (*1. Könige 17-2. Könige 25,* 344–51). He regards vv. 1-11* + 17*, 18b-20* as an old and basically historical account that was not included in DtrH but inserted later. It was also revised by a series of later additions involving the temple guard and the royal insignia that were borrowed from the ordination of the high priest. Among these revisions was the identification of the centurions as Carites and runners. Würthwein is compelled to identify the *centurions* as the military branch of *the people of the land* because otherwise this group would have no part in the ceremony, and he thinks that the oldest ritual of king-making in Israel involved acclamation by them. He also thinks that the old ritual resurfaced at times when the dynasty was threatened, as in vv. 9-12, though these verses in MT contain no reference to *the people of the land.* He considers the account of Athaliah's assassination (vv. 13-16) a later addition, but because these verses refer to *the people of the land* he must also assert that they preserve the memory of the group's participation.

60 Rudolph, "Die Einheitlichkeit," 476–78. Barré (*Rhetoric*, 28–29) agrees but includes the reference in v. 20 as secondary to the original narrative. For Barré the secondary hand in these cases, as well as for v. 18a, is DtrH.

guards with whom Jehoiada planned the event.[61] Textual criticism is crucial in two respects. First, following G^L, *the people of the land* do not appear in v. 14 but only *all the people*. More important, the G^L plus in v. 11, which is probably original, includes *the people of the land*. The mention is important not only because it is the first reference to them in this context but also because it states that Jehoiada assembled them for participation in what follows. This means that they do not appear out of nowhere in the narrative and that the subsequent mentions of them as participants are fitting.[62] The mention of *the people of the land* in v. 11 thus signals the overall unity of the narrative and shows them playing a significant role in the process rather than being brought in secondarily from a separate source. They can safely be distinguished from the priests, court officials, and military, who are all mentioned separately. They support the Davidic king and have an important role in his acclamation, but there is no indication that they are a representative body or have military or judicial authority. They seem to be simply a popular assembly, in accord with their designation elsewhere in the chapter as *the people* (vv. 13, 14 [G^L], 17). Verse 20 is often cited as indicating a contrast between *the people of the land* and the residents of Jerusalem (*all the people of the land rejoiced but the city was quiet*). But a better interpretation of the verse is that the statements about the people of the land and the city are complementary: *all the people of land rejoiced and the city was quiet*, the point being that there was no uprising or turmoil in the wake of Athaliah's removal and assassination. In this interpretation the residents of Jerusalem are not necessarily distinct from *the people of the land*. In terms of the sense of the story, *the people of the land* represent the citizenry of Judah, including those in Jerusalem. The expression is at once hyperbolic, since not every citizen of the country was present, and realistic, since there would not be time for Jehoiada to summon even a representative sample of the group if it did not include Jerusalemites. "Citizenry" was, in a word, *Gesamtheit*, the free population of Judah, consisting of different socio-economic groups.[63]

11:12: The *nēzer* and the *'ēdût*

The preparations having all been made, Jehoiada brings out Joash. He places two items on him according to MT: the *nēzer* and the *'ēdût*. The exact nature of both is uncertain. The *nēzer* is a symbol of kingship and is typically translated "crown," or better, "diadem" (2 Sam 1:10; Jer 13:18; Ezek 21:31 [Eng. v. 26]; Ps 89:40 [Eng. v. 39]; 132:18). The word derives from the root for "dedicate, consecrate," from which the word נזיר "dedicated one, Nazirite" comes, and has been compared to the priestly turban with a golden plate (Exod 28:36-37; 29:6; 39:30; Lev 8:9).[64] The other term,*'ēdût*, is more difficult. The word is used in P for the tablets of the law stored in the ark (Exod 25:16, 21, 22; 26:33, 34; 30:6, 26; 39:35; 40:3, 5, 20, 21; Num 4:5, 7:89) and elsewhere in Kings for the law in general (1 Kgs 2:3; 2 Kgs 23:3). It may be compared with Akkadian *adê* and Hebrew עדת and refer to the testimonies or stipulations for keeping the covenant with god. From there it derives the sense of "covenant." It is difficult to imagine something as extensive as the Priestly or

61 It is worth noting that if one reads "singers and trumpeters" in v. 14 they also appear suddenly in the story.

62 Rudolph ("Einheitlichkeit," 476–77) takes note of the G^L plus but dismisses it as secondary and out of place because the people of the land would not have remained silent and uninvolved till this late point. Thus his dismissal is based not on text-critical grounds but on his assumption of the identity of this group.

63 Most likely excluded were women and slaves, who were owned by others, as well as foreigners and resident aliens, who were non-natives. Cf. Levin, *Sturz*, 66–68.

64 Mettinger, *King and Messiah*, 287–88.

Deuteronomic law being placed upon the king and worn as a regular part of his regalia. It is not unusual, though, to find scholars who take the *ʿēdût* here as a reference to a written document relating to the "law of the king" (Deut 17:18) or to a royal protocol relating YHWH's promises to David (Ps 2:7-9) or the king's covenant obligations (Ps 132:12).[65] Mettinger recognizes the problem and suggests that the *ʿēdût* was a (brief) inscription articulating the covenant relationship between the king and YHWH on the metal plate of the *nēzer.*[66] Despite the viability of this suggestion, the simpler solution of Wellhausen is preferable.[67] He reads הצעדות "bracelets, armbands" for העדות. The bracelets are attested as royal insignia along with the *nēzer* in 2 Sam 1:10.[68] The scribal error resulting in *ʿēdût* fits with the nature of the coronation as a sacral ceremony and with DtrH's view of kingship as entailing the king's keeping of the law as well as YHWH's promises to David. Hence the error produced a rich source for the reconstruction of royal ritual and theological symbolism.

Joash anointed and acclaimed king

Joash is now anointed by Jehoiada and thereby made king (G^L). The two verbs together form a hendiadys expressing a single idea. It is striking that a priest rather than a prophet anoints the new king. However, there is precedent. Not only was Samuel both priest and prophet when he anointed David (1 Sam 16:13), but Zadok the priest anointed Solomon (1 Kgs 1:39). Also, the people are said to have anointed David in 2 Sam 2:4 and the elders in 2 Sam 5:3. They also anoint Jehoahaz in 2 Kgs 23:30. The people participate in Joash's anointing. The acclamation, *Long live the king* is confirmation of the king's anointing (1 Sam 10:24; 2 Sam 16:16; 1 Kgs 1:25, 39) and offer an expression of popular support, but it is not clear that it was a formal part of the coronation process as is sometimes claimed.

Continuity in vv. 13-18a

Verses 13-18a have commonly been viewed since Stade in 1885 as a separate, religiously-oriented account contrasting with the primarily political one in vv. 1-12 + 18b-20.[69] However, Stade's arguments are not convincing.[70] First, the two notices of Athaliah's death in vv. 16 and 20 are not a doublet, as he claims, but v. 20 is part of a summary of the foregoing story. Second, the covenants in vv. 4 and 17 are not at odds; they are of two different sorts and serve different functions in the narrative. In v. 4 the covenant is a secret pact between the conspirators, while in v. 17 it is a public agreement of a political and religious nature. Third,

---

65 E.g., Fricke, *Das zweite Buch von den Königen*, 150–51; Gray, *Kings*, 573. For a nice, albeit dated, overview of these different understandings of *ʿēdût* with references to both primary and secondary sources see Rehm, *Das zweite Buch der Könige*, 117–18.

66 Mettinger, *King and* Messiah, 288. Cf. also Falk ("Forms of Testimony," 88–91), who sees the *ēdût* as an inscribed article worn by the king. He stresses its function as a witness.

67 Wellhausen, *Composition des Hexateuchs*, 292n. See the Note. This emendation obviates the attempt to see the reference to the *nēzer* and the *ʿēdût* as later additions (Fritz, *Kings*, 299; Würthwein, *1. Könige 17-2. Könige 25*, 348).

68 2 Sam 1:10 actually reads אצעדה; the emendation is unquestionable. The noun is attested elsewhere in Isa 3:20.

69 Stade, "Miscellen 10," *ZAW* 5 (1885), 284–87. For a list of scholars who accept this theory up to 1988 see Barré, *Rhetoric*, 25n. In addition to Levin and Fritz, Hoffmann (*Reform und Reformen*, 106–108) dissents, though in a different way, arguing that the account is the unified product of a single author.

70 Cf. Barré, *Rhetoric of Persuasion*, 25–26; Hoffmann, *Reform und Reformen*, 106–108.

there are no literary seams distinguishing vv. 13-18a from its surroundings. The noise heard by Athaliah in v. 13 presupposes the previous verse.[71] Stade recognized this and argued that vv. 13-18a had been isolated from their original beginning in order to be inserted into the primary story after v. 12. The posting of the guard in v. 18b fits well as a security measure to prevent acts of revenge on the part of Baal worshipers following the purge in v. 18a. Hence there is continuity rather than a break between vv. 18a and 18b. Finally, inconsistencies in terminology do not support Stade's division. For instance, both short (vv. 1, 3) and long (vv. 2, 20) forms of Athaliah's name occur in vv. 1-12, 18b-20, suggesting that the usage of the short form only in vv. 13-18a (vv. 13, 14) is inconsequential. Other differences in wording relating to the title *the priest* and to *the people of the land* have been dealt with already.

11:13-14: What Athaliah saw

Alerted by the sound of the clapping and popular acclamation, Athaliah emerges from the palace to see what is going on in the temple precincts. The introduction of the people in vv. 11 and 12 G^L means that the reference to them here in v. 13 is not sudden or novel but in continuity with the narrative that has preceded. The references to the sound of the people and the location in the temple presuppose the account in vv. 4-12, so that v. 13 could not have stood on its own as the beginning of an independent anecdote. As Athaliah proceeds into the temple area (v. 14), the scene before her involves the same persons as in vv. 4-12. The boy king stands beside *the column*; the commanders and runners are next to him, and the people are celebrating with shouts of joy and trumpet blasts. The word עמוד refers elsewhere to a pillar or column in the tabernacle (Exod 27:10, 11, 17; 36:38; Num 3:37), in Solomon's temple (1 Kgs 7:2, 3, 6, 15, 16), in Dagon's temple (Judg 16:25, 26, 29), in a Persian palace (Esth 1:6), in a metaphoric description of a body (Song 5:15), in descriptions of columns of cloud or smoke (Exod 13:21-22; 14:24; Num 14:14; Judg 20:40; Neh 9:12, 19; Ps 99:7), and as columns on which the earth or heavens stand (Job 26:11; Ps 75:4). The preposition על is well attested in the sense of "beside, next to." Hence the king stands next to a specific column in the temple rather than on a stage or dais. Since the king's location is according to custom (כמשפט, 2 Kgs 23:3) *the column* is probably one of the two in the center of the temple, whose names form a sentence: "YHWH establishes (Jachin) with strength (Boaz)." In taking his stand near one of these columns the king lays claim to the promise of YHWH's support that they represent and to the continuity of the Judahite monarchy and perhaps the Davidic line.

11:15: The G^L reading

When Jehoiada hears Athaliah's cry of *conspiracy* he gives orders that she be taken behind the officers' quarters for execution (v. 15). Killing her in the temple would ritually contaminate it. Both Levin and Barré, following him, have argued that v. 15b is secondary based on its attachment with *kî*, the reference to *the priest* (also in vv. 19, 18b, which are secondary), and the nature of the verse as an interpretation rather than a part of the course of the narrative.[72] However, the superior G^L reading does away with all three of these problems. Neither the particle *kî* nor the title *the priest*

71 The absence of the conjunction and the Aramaic plural signal *the runners* in MT as a gloss, especially since they hold weapons and would not be able to clap. Cf. Cogan and Tadmor, *II Kings*, 129.

72 Levin, *Sturz*, 23; Barré, *Rhetoric*, 26–27.

occurs in G^L, so that v. 15b gives the rationale for taking Athaliah away as a continuation of Jehoiada's speech from the first part of the verse and therefore as a part of the narrative account rather than an interpretation of it.

11:16: Taking Athaliah to her death

The language of v. 16 suggests that the executioners adopted a circuitous route in carrying out Jehoiada's instructions, perhaps in order to avoid having Athaliah torn apart by the crowd. Rather than taking the runners' gate, to be used by the king (v. 19), they lead her out of the temple precincts and into the palace via the horses' entrance. If the latter is the same as the Horses' Gate it was on the eastern side of the city (Jer 31:40; Neh 3:28; cf. 2 Kgs 23:11), in contrast to the Runners' Gate on the southern side of the temple grounds. Hence they exited the temple area on the east and reentered the palace from the east. Assuming that the Horses' Gate led to the stables, these were likely to have been at the rear of the palace, and certainly outside the temple enclosure.

11:17: The pact between king and people

Verse 17 is overfull, and several critics conclude that *between YHWH and the king and the people to be YHWH's people* is an addition, so that the original statement was that Jehoiada made a covenant between the king and the people.[73] G^L's lack of *between the king and the people* (ובין המלך ובין העם), suggests that these words are a dittography (see the Note). Even with their omission, though, the remaining three-way covenant (YHWH, the king, and the people) is unprecedented. The concern for the people to belong to YHWH could be DtrH's addition (Deut 4:20; 7:6; 14:2; 26:18; 27:9; Jer 7:23; 11:4; etc.), but it is not articulated elsewhere in the chapter. These mentions of YHWH anticipate v. 18 and are part of the same addition.

11:18: PN's addition

The covenant between the king and the people was the final act in the ceremony before processing to the palace for the king's enthronement (v. 19) as presupposed in vv. 5-8. Verse 18 is an interruption. It leaves Joash and Jehoiada standing alone in the temple as the people head to the temple of Baal.[74] The mention of a temple of Baal in Jerusalem is new and unique to the story. It resembles 10:18-28 with its sudden focus away from the destruction of the house of Ahab and to the house of Baal. It also resembles that passage and the story in 1 Kings 18 in its account of the violent response to Baal, in this instance killing Mattan, the priest of Baal. Furthermore, the verse uses the title *the priest* without Jehoiada's name, as was the case in the interpolation in v. 10 and in the corrupt MT reading in v. 15b. We have already seen that v. 18b fits well as a response to v. 18a and is not the resumption of the story from v. 12.[75] The similarities to 1 Kings 18 and 2 Kings 10 suggest that v. 18 and the revisions to v. 17 came from

---

73 Barré (*Rhetoric*, 27), Spieckermann (*Juda unter Assur*, 177–79), and Würthwein (*1. Könige 17–2. Könige 25*, 350) assign it to DtrG or a later dtr redactor. Levin (*Sturz*, 19, 59–61) attributes it to a *bundestheologische Bearbeitung.*

74 Dutcher-Walls (*Narrative Art*, 83) makes the point about Joash, but Jehoiada is also not mentioned in v. 18.

75 To refine that point somewhat, Jehoiada is not posting a guard over the temple for the first time in v. 18b, since v. 7 already mentioned a guard force there. Nor does v. 18b state that he reset the guard or posted it again. There is really only one way to understand v. 18b, and that is as a response to anticipated retribution on the part of Baal worshipers after their temple has been destroyed (v. 18a). It is not a resumption from v. 12, but there is also no reason to see it as later than v. 18a (*pace* Barré); both are parts of the same addition.

PN as a final installment of the purge of Baal and the Ahabids in their incarnation in Judah.

The supposed cult of Baal in Jerusalem

The existence of a temple of Baal in Jerusalem in this period is questionable, as is the notion that Athaliah was a Baal worshiper. The latter claim is not explicit here, but it is implied by the fact that the account of the destruction of the temple of Baal immediately follows that of Athaliah's execution. Still, there is ambiguity about the source of the Baal worship in Judah that comes across in the name of the priest of Baal. *Mattan*, meaning "gift," is attested as a personal name in a handful of Phoenician and Punic inscriptions.[76] On the other hand, the name could also be Yahwistic, an abbreviation of Mattaniah (2 Kgs 24:17; 1 Chr 9:15; 20:14; Ezra 10:26, 27, 30, 37; Neh 11:17, 22; 12:8, 35; 13:13) or Mattanyahu (1 Chr 25:4, 16). The short form occurs in the parallel in 2 Chr 23:17 and in Jer 38:1, as well as on stamps and seals from Lachish.[77] Thus there is no way to determine Mattan's ethnicity, leaving open the question whether the supposed presence of Baal worship in Judah was envisioned as the result of importation from Phoenicia because of Athaliah's ethnic heritage through her mother or apostasy on the part of Judahites—or both, the result of deliberate ambiguity.

11:18-19: Tranquility

The ceremony closes with the king's installation on the throne in v. 19 There is a brief recap in v. 20. The first half of the verse has been important for the discussion of *the people of the land*. It can be read in two different ways, either complementary (*all the people of the land rejoiced and the city was quiet*) or contrastive (*all the people of the land rejoiced but the city was quiet*). The latter interpretation contrasts the reactions of two populations such that *the people of the land* are seen as rural as opposed to the urban dwellers in Jerusalem. *The people of the land* are imagined to have received Joash with enthusiasm and thus have been more loyal to the Davidic line, while Jerusalemites were supportive of Athaliah and hence muted about the new king. The contrast can then be used to explain features of the story such as Jehoiada's posting of guards before (vv. 5-7) and after (v. 18b) the event (to fend off the pro-Athaliah factions in Jerusalem) and the focus on urbanites in the planning of the event (v. 4), since they are the ones who need to be convinced rather than the pro-Davidic rural population. The problem with this interpretation is that the verb שקט does not mean to be silent or stifled but to be tranquil, at ease or rest, as in the formula in Joshua and Judges that the land had rest (Josh 11:23; 14:15; Judg 3:11, 30; 5:31; 8:28). But the contrast interpretation would mean that the silence in the city following Joash's enthronement was uneasy, muzzling the discontent just below the surface. The other interpretation fits better. The city was quiet in exactly the sense of being at ease now that Athaliah was gone. There was no uprising as a result of her removal, no effort to take revenge. This understanding accords well with the presentation of Athaliah as a hated interloper who seized power through genocide and whose rule was an interruption of the proper state of dynastic continuity. The statement does not mean that the Jerusalemites were not included in *the people of the land* or that there was no rejoicing there at Athaliah's deposition. To the contrary, the tranquility that settled in after her demise

76 *KAI* 18.2; 65.6; 160.5.

77 J. A. Thompson, "On Some Stamped Seals from Lachish," *BASOR* 86 (1942), 24–25; A. E. Cowley, *Aramaic Papyri of the Fifth Century B. C.* (Oxford: Clarendon, 1923), 22, ll 62, 76, 77 (pp. 68–69); 23, l. 11 (p. 77).

in the very place where she made her home showed that people were content at her replacement. The statement in v. 20b that Athaliah was killed in the palace is repetitive and superfluous, especially after the fitting conclusion in v. 20a. It therefore seems likely to be a gloss stressing the point that Athaliah was executed in the palace precincts and not on temple grounds, which might have been of special concern to certain readers and scribes.[78]

Synthesis

DtrH: Downplaying the threat to the Davidic promise

This chapter constitutes an interlude historically and narratively in the larger account of Judah's history. The chapter is not really about Athaliah *per se* but about the threat she poses to the Davidic dynasty. It is the story of promise (to David) endangered.[79] DtrH dealt with that threat by downplaying it. The account of Joash's revolt that he borrowed from official sources did not mention David. DtrH followed suit, adding David's name only in his interpolation in v. 10 in reference to the golden bow cases that alluded to the continuity of the Davidic line represented by Joash.[80] He did not directly refer to Athaliah's threat to the line. Rather, he made it clear that she did not "count" by not supplying her with any regnal formulae. Her "seven years" of rule did not constitute a reign. The new king, Joash, is called "king" before he is anointed and crowned. Thus Athaliah's rule occurs outside time and outside of the regnal sequence.[81] She is a liminal character. The subject-first word order of v. 1 doubles back to describe activity concurrent with Jehu's revolt. The verb could be translated as a pluperfect: *When Athaliah had seen that her son was dead ...* In this sense the chapter begins with Ahaziah's death in 9:27. Athaliah is also effectively a silent character. Apart from her cry of *conspiracy!* in v. 14 we hear nothing of her voice or thoughts.[82] DtrH let the earlier account speak for itself. The Davidic line survived, if only barely. Its narrow escape from obliteration demonstrated YHWH's faithfulness and watchfulness over his promise.

The question of history

The older document and DtrH's use of it naturally press the question of historical veracity. Was Athaliah actually successful in ending the Davidic line, so that Joash was a substitute put in by priests as a legitimate heir and the story was then furthered by DtrH to perpetuate the Davidic myth?[83] The question is impossible to answer, but it is a reminder of the ideological nature of the history presented in Kings.

---

78 So also Barré, *Rhetoric*, 28; Levin, *Der Sturz*, 23–24; Spieckermann, *Juda unter Assur*, 178n, 414.

79 Fretheim, *Kings*, 176.

80 Nelson, *Kings*, 207.

81 Brueggemann, *Kings*, 407.

82 Cohn, *II Kings*, 77.

83 See Miller and Hayes (*History*, 349–50), who point out the similar close call related in 2 Chr 21:16-17 where only Jehoahaz is left after an invasion by Philistines and Arabs. See also the provocative and insightful piece by L. K. Handy, "Speaking of Babies in the Temple," in *Proceedings*, Eastern Great Lakes and Midwest Biblical Societies 8 (1988): 155–65. Again Levin (*Sturz*, 85–87) thinks it was really Jehu, not Athaliah, who killed the Davidids, based on 10:12-14.

For PN Athaliah was "Jezebel south." The two women were related, if only by marriage (8:26). Athaliah's story and character are inevitably shaped for the reader by Jezebel's shadow. Thus the presence of a temple to Baal in Jerusalem (v. 18) is assumed to be her doing in the tradition of Jezebel. Both were "other"—foreign and female. Athaliah had to be destroyed in order to restore right order with YHWH in Jerusalem and Judah just as Jezebel had to be destroyed to restore *shalōm* in Jezreel and Israel. Jezebel south

Joash of Judah (2 Kings 12)

Text[1]

[DtrH's sources; DtrH; Additions to DtrH]
[1] In the seventh year of Jehu son of Nimshi Jehoash son of Ahaziah began to reign. Jehoash was seven years old when he began to reign, [2] and he reigned forty years in Jerusalem. His mother's name was Zibiah, from Beersheba. [3] Jehoash did what YHWH considered right all his life as Jehoiada the priest instructed him, [4] except that the cultic installations were not removed; the people continued slaughtering animals and burning food offerings on them. [5] Jehoash told the priests, "All the money from sacred offerings that is brought into YHWH's temple—the money from personal valuations and all the money that is brought voluntarily to YHWH's temple— [6] let the priests receive it each from his assessor, and they will repair all of the fissures found in the temple. [7] By the twenty-third year of King Jehoash, though, the priests not having made any repairs to the temple, [8] King Jehoash summoned Jehoiada the priest and the (other) priests and said to them, "Why are you not effecting repairs to the temple? Now you are to receive no more money from your assessors but you shall donate it for the repair of the temple."
[9] The priests agreed not to take money from the people and not to effect repairs on the temple. [10] Jehoiada the priest took a chest and bored a hole in its door; he placed it to the right of the altar as one entered YHWH's temple, and the priests who guarded the threshold would deposit there whatever money was brought into YHWH's temple. [11] Whenever they saw that there was a large quantity of money in the chest, the king's scribe and the high priest would come up and cast the money that was found in YHWH's temple into ingots and count it. [12] They would give the money that had been certified to the laborers who were overseeing YHWH's temple. Then they would pay it to the carpenters and builders who were doing the work on YHWH's temple, [13] as well as to the woodcutters and stonecutters to buy wood and hewn stones for repairing the fissures in YHWH's temple and for any other repair expenses. [14] However, no silver thresholds, snuffers, basins, or trumpets or any utensil of gold or silver were made from the money that was brought into YHWH's temple, [15] because they would pay it to the laborers who would repair YHWH's temple with it. [16] They did not demand an account of the men to whom they gave the money to pay the laborers, because they dealt honestly. [17] The money from the guilt offerings and sin offerings was not brought into YHWH's temple; it was for the priests. [18] At that time Hazael king of Aram

---

1 G^{B} and most English versions have a different versification, reading MT's 12:1 as the final verse of chapter 11, so that MT's 12:2 becomes 12:1 and so on throughout the chapter. The versification followed here is MT's.

came up and fought against Gath and captured it, after which he set his face to come up against Jerusalem. [19] Joash took all the sacred items that his forebears, the kings of Judah, Jehoshaphat, Joram, and Ahaziah, had consecrated and his own sacred items, and all the gold that was found in the treasuries of YHWH's temple and of the palace, and he sent this to Hazael king of Aram, who lifted the siege against Jerusalem. [20] The rest of Joash's activities and all that he did are written in the scroll of the chronicles of the kings of Judah, aren't they? [21] His servants proceeded to form a conspiracy, and they attacked Joash in the Millo palace/when he went down to the Millo. [22] Jozakar son of Jemuath and Jehozabad son of Shomer, his servants, assassinated him. After he died they buried him with his forebears in the city of David, and Amaziah his son reigned in his place.

Textual Notes

1-2 So G^{L}, which preserves the typical order of elements in the regnal formulae as well as the patronymics. MT, G^{B} reverse that order and lack the patronymics.[2]

Jehoash: See 11:2.

Zibiah, from Beersheba: *Zibiah* means "gazelle."[3] It is rendered 'Aβια by G^{BL}, perhaps by confusion of ע and צ or by inner-Greek error for Σαβια (2 Chr 24:1).[4] G^{B} also has *from the land of Beersheba* (ἐκ γῆς Βηρσάβεε), the result of confusing γ for τ.

3 **as Jehoiada the priest instructed him**: On אשר having an antecedent that does not immediately precede it see Joüon §158t. Its antecedent here is *what YHWH considered right* (הישר בעיני יהוה).

4 **the people continued**: So MT, G^{L}. Preceded in G^{B} with *and there.*

slaughtering animals and burning food offerings: See the Note on 1 Kgs 22:44.

5 **all the money from sacred offerings**: Lit. "all the money of the holy things" (כל כסף הקדשים). Money is used in the broad sense of a medium of exchange, lit. *silver.* It does not refer to coins, which did not become current in Palestine until the Persian period. These donations were items of silver that could be melted down into ingots.

the money from personal valuations: Reading כסף ערך איש as indicated by G^{L} (ἀργύριον συντιμήσεως ἀνδρός). In MT ערך has become corrupted to עובר. G^{B} (ἀργύριον συντιμήσεως ἀνὴρ) reflects a similar reading, except that it construes ἀνὴρ (nominative) with the clause that follows.

and all the money: The conjunction was lost following ערכו.

6 **his assessor**: The root and meaning of the word מכרו are long standing uncertainties. It has typically been derived from √נכר, "to recognize, be acquainted with," and has been taken to mean "friend, acquaintance" (BDB 648). But this meaning makes little sense in the present context since contributors were not friends of the priests.[5] G^{BL}

---

2 See Trebolle ("Division Markers," 209) who observes that the enclosure of v. 1 between *setumah* and *petuhah* in MT marks it as being out of place.

3 Noth, *Personennamen*, 230.

4 Stade, *Kings*, 238.

5 Würthwein's (*1. Könige 17–2. Könige 25*, 354) translation "client," is more appropriate than "friend" but does not capture the sense of the post as a temple official.

(τῆς πράσεως αὐτοῦ/αὐτῶν) construe the word from √מכר and the *qaṭṭāl* form, which typically designates a profession,[6] also fits √מכר better than √נכר. Hence the meaning would have to be *his merchant*. Ugaritic lists of temple personnel (*KTU* 4.36; 4.38; 4.68 [l.75]) include *mkrm*, which may refer to officials who helped priests to fix market values for offerings.[7]

the temple: So MT, G^B. G^L + *of* Yhwh.

7 On the syntax of this verse as a circumstantial clause ahead of the main sentence in the next verse see Driver, *Tenses*, §165.

8 **your assessors**: See the Note on v. 6.

9 **to take**: The infinitive קְחַת is vocalized, anomalously, as though it were a segholate noun (GKC §93h). It should probably be altered to קַחַת.

and not to effect repairs: So MT, G^B. G^L lacks the negative for Greek style. G^B inexplicably has βδέλυγμα *abomination* for the transliteration βεδεκ.

the temple: So MT, G^B (lit. *the house*). G^L + *of* Yhwh (κυρίου).

10 **a chest**: אחד functions as an indefinite article (Joüon §138u).

and bored a hole in its door: So MT (ויקב חר בדלתו). G^B (καὶ ἔτρησεν τρώγλην ἐν τῇ τρώγλῃ αὐτῆς) has an inner-Greek dittography. G^L: *and made a hole in it* (καὶ ἐποίησεν ἐν αὐτῇ ὀπὴν μίαν).

to the right of the altar: So MT *qere'*: אצל המזבח מימין (*ketiv* has בימין), G^L (παρὰ τὸ θυσιαστήριον ἐν δεξιᾷ). G^B has παρὰ ιαμιβιν, a transliteration of מימין without reference to the altar. בימין occurs only one other time in the HB, in Isa 41:10, where the preposition expresses agency. מימין, on the other hand, is relatively common and expresses direction ("on the right/south of," Gen 13:9; 1 Sam 23:19; 1 Kgs 7:39, 49; 2 Kgs 23:13; 2 Chr 3:17; 4:6-8; Ezek 10:3; Zech 4:3). Stade contended that the reading המזבח could not be correct because the altar stood in the middle of the court rather than near its entrance. He proposed המצבה, "the pillar," instead.[8] For similar reasons Klostermann proposed "the doorpost" (המזוזה) on the basis of 2 Chr 24:8.[9] See the Diachronic Analysis.[10]

as one entered Yhwh's temple: G^B (ἐν τῷ οἴκῳ ἀνδρὸς οἴκῳ κυρίου) reflects an error of בבית for בבוא.

would deposit: The use of the perfect ונתנו here is durative, expressing repeated action in the past. This durative sense continues through v. 17.[11]

---

6 L. S. Wright ("*MKR* in 2 Kings XII 5-17 and Deuteronomy XVIII 8," *VT* 39 [1989]: 438–48) argues that *qaṭṭāl* can be used for the act inherent in a verb and that the word here means "selling." He does not explain why such a form was adopted in preference to one of the better-attested nouns from מכר. He is also unique to my knowledge in distinguishing the proceeds of these sales from the sources of revenue mentioned in v. 5.

7 Gray, *Kings*, 586.

8 Stade, "Miscellen 10," 289–90; *Kings*, 239. Šanda (*Könige* II, 141–42) accepted the emendation. Stade pointed to the transliterations of some Greek witnesses (αμμαζεειβη, αμαζειβι, αμμαζιβι) for support. This evidence is not strong, especially since Greek *zeta* typically corresponds to Hebrew *zayin* rather than to *ṣade* (Barthélemy, *Critique textuelle*, 399; W. McKane, "A Note on 2 Kings 12 10 [Evv. 12 9]," *ZAW* 71 [1959]: 260–65).

9 Klostermann, *Könige*, 434.

10 Cogan and Tadmor (*Kings*, 138) accept the *altar* reading, contending that the guardians of the threshold deposited money (v. 10b) because the people were not allowed to approach the main altar. But this does not solve the problem of whether the chest was near the main entrance or the altar.

11 Burney, *Notes*, 315; Driver, *Tenses*, §113.4β; 120; Joosten, *Verbal System*, 177–78, 285–87, 307; Joüon §119v.

there: So MT, G^L. Not reflected in G^B, but crucial for the point of the verse, since it was precisely in the chest prepared by Jehoiada that the money was deposited.

was brought: So MT (המובא), G^L (τὸ εἰσφερόμενον). G^B (τὸ εὑρεθὲν) reads a passive of √מצא, probably הנמצא, which occurs in the next verse.

11 **they saw**: So MT, G^L. G^B: *he saw.*

the high priest: On the title הכהן הגדול as a late scribal modification see the discussion in the Diachronic Analysis.

and cast the money that was found in Yhwh's temple into ingots and count it: MT, G^B: *they would tie up* (ויצרו) is usually interpreted to mean that the silver was tied up in bags, but then the verbs would be out of order, since counting would precede bagging.[12] An improvement in the understanding of this verb was adduced by Eissfeldt based on Torrey's identification of the role played by temples in the economy of the ancient Near East by virtue of their containing foundries.[13] This verb should either be revocalized as *wayyiṣĕrû* (<√יצר) or left as is and taken from a root √צור that is a biform of √יצר. Its meaning in either case is "cast" or "smelt" metal. 2 Chr 24:11 reads ויערו (< √ערה *Pi'el*), *they emptied*.[14]

12 **They would give**: So MT, G^L. G^B again has the singular.

the money that had been certified: So MT, G^B. G^L has simply αὐτό, "it." The word מתכן, evidently a *Pu'al* participle, seems to be a technical term for a quantity or weight of metal that has been officially smelted and measured.[15]

to the laborers: So MT *ketiv* (על־יד עשי המלאכה); the *qere'* and G^{BL} have the plural ידי.

who were overseeing: So MT *qere'* (המפקדים), a *Hop'al* participle; the *ketiv* is a *Qal* passive participle. The *Qal* passive has the sense of being mustered or appointed, while the *Hop'al* entails a supervisory role.

13 **woodcutters**: Reading ולגזרים for MT's ולגדרים as proposed by Ehrlich.[16] The reference to woodcutters not only pairs nicely with *stonecutters*, it also corresponds well to the following reference to buying wood. "Masons" (גזרים) does not share these correspondences and is repetitive following the mention of builders.

and stonecutters: So MT, G^B. G^L has a double reading: καὶ τοῖς οἰκοδόμοις τῶν λίθων καὶ τοῖς ξύσταις τῶν λίθων.

to buy: So G^{BL} without the conjunction that precedes the infinitive in MT.

wood and hewn stones: So MT, G^B. G^L has the reverse order—*hewn stones and wood.*

and for any other repair expenses: So MT (ולכל אשר־יצא על־הבית לחזקה), except that the *Qal* infinitive is to be read as *Pi'el* (as earlier in the verse) with a resumptive suffix: לחזקו.[17]

---

12 Provan (*Kings*, 225–26) suggests that the silver was tied in bundles to facilitate calculating a total. But if the silver was in the form of jewelry and other items rather than ingots, what kind of count could be done?

13 O. Eissfeldt, "Eine Einschmelzstelle am Tempel zu Jerusalem," *Forschung und Fortschritte* 13 (1937), 163–64; C. C. Torrey, "The Foundry of the Second Temple at Jerusalem," *JBL* 55 (1936): 247–60. See also his "The Evolution of a Financier in the Ancient Near East," *JNES* 2 (1943): 295–301.

14 Preferred by Cogan and Tadmor (*II Kings*, 139), Gray (*Kings*, 584), and Klostermann (*Könige*, 434). This verb takes as its object the thing that is emptied rather than its contents, as is the case in 2 Kgs 12:11.

15 Cf. O. Eissfeldt, "Die Menetekel-Inschrift und ihre Deutung," *ZAW* 63 (1951), 109 n. 8.

16 Ehrlich, *Randglossen* 307–308.

17 Burney (*Notes*, 315) and Klostermann (*Kings*, 435) take the final ה in the MT as a *mater lectionis* for the suffix. But cf. GKC §45d.

14 G^{L} has the reverse order of clauses: *However, from the money that was brought in to Yhwh's temple there were no silver thresholds, nails, bowls, trumpets, or utensils of gold or silver* (πλὴν ἐκ τοῦ ἀργυρίου τοῦ εἰσενεχθέντος εἰς οἶκον κυρίου οὐκ ἐγένετο πρόθυρα ἀργυρᾶ ἧλοι φιάλαι σάλπιγγες πᾶν σκεῦος χρυσοῦν ἢ ἀργυροῦν). The difference may be stylistic. More important, G^{L} indicates that the first reference to Yhwh's temple, which appears superfluous in the MT, is a gloss.[18]

thresholds: This meaning for סף was demonstrated by Honeyman.[19]

snuffers: The exact nature of this item is uncertain. *HALOT* suggests "shears" or a "knife" for trimming wicks. Again, the context refers to a utensil of some sort rather than "nails" as in G^{BL}.

were made: So MT (יעשה), G^{B} (ποιηθήσεται), in preference to G^{L}'s ἐγένετο.

17 **The money from the guilt offerings and sin offerings**: Reading כֶּסֶף אָשָׁם וְכֶסֶף חַטָּאת with the singular for *sin* (with G^{BL}) where MT has the plural. Both are collectives. The Greek witnesses attest the reverse order of *sin offering* and *guilt offering*.

was not brought: So MT, G^{L}. G^{B} lacks the negative and instead reflects the relative (ὅ τι = אשר?).

it was for the priests: Reading לכהנים היה as indicated by G^{BL} (τοῖς ἱερεῦσιν ἐγένετο). MT has the imperfect plural יהיו, which does not fit the context. G^{L} precedes this sentence with the particle ὅτι.

19 **his forebears, the kings of Judah**: So MT, G^{L}. G^{B}: *his forebears and the kings of Judah*, reflecting dittography of the final *waw* of אבתיו.

had consecrated: So MT (הקדישו) in agreement with the plural subject (Jehoshaphat, Joram, and Ahaziah). G^{BL} have the singular.

21 **His servants**: So MT, G^{B}. G^{L}: *the servants of Joash.*

form a conspiracy: So MT (ויקשרו־קשר). G^{B}: καὶ ἔδησαν πάντα δεσμόν. G^{L} attests a double reading: καὶ ἐποίησαν σύνδεσμον καὶ συνῆψαν ἐπ' αὐτὸν.

they attacked Joash: So MT, G^{B}. G^{L}: *they attacked him.*

in the Millo palace: The text is corrupt. MT reads בֵּית מִלֹּא הַיֹּרֵד סִלָּא . G^{B}: ἐν οἴκῳ Μαλλὼ τῷ ἐν Γααλλά. G^{L}: ἐν οἴκῳ Μααλλὼν τῷ ἐν τῇ καταβάσει Ἀλάμ. While Beth-Millo is a site near Shechem (Josh 9:6, 20), this is probably a reference to the Millo of Jerusalem (2 Sam 5:9; 1 Kgs 9:15, 24; 11:27; 1 Chr 11:8; 2 Chr 32:5). "Silla" is probably a corruption of Millo resulting from the miswriting of ס for מ, such that בית מלא and היורד סלא are variants.[20]

22 **Jozakar son of Jemuath**: So G^{B} (Ἰεζειχὰρ υἱὸς Ιεμουὰθ), G^{L} (Ἰωζαχὰρ υἱὸς Ἰεμουὰθ). MT contains a double reading; that is, *Jozakar son of Shimeath* and *Jehozabad son of Shomer* are variants of the same name and patronymic. The G readings indicate *Jozakar* as the name of the first conspirator; the retroversion of his patronymic is uncertain.

---

18 Gray (*Kings*, 585) retains the phrase, suggesting that it forbids the manufacture of such items from being done within the temple precincts. This is unlikely in view of the verb for smelting in v. 11.

19 A. M. Honeyman, "Hebrew סף, Basin, Goblet,'" *JTS* 37 (1936): 56–59.

20 Kittel (*Könige*, 256) follows the Syriac in combining the two to read היורד בית מלא, "when he went down to the Millo palace." Two other readings have been offered for Silla: (1) A ramp, street, or commercial district below Beth Millo (e.g., Barnes, *Kings*, 281). This compels the emendation of היורד to במורד, "on the descent to" (Klostermann, *Könige*, 436), although Barnes does not say so since the notion of Beth Millo descending makes no sense. Barnes also suggests that Silla might be Sela in Edom (2 Kgs 14:7). But Silla ends in *'aleph* while Sela ends in *'ayin*; (2) an error for מסלה, "road" (Gray, *Kings*, 590; Thenius, *Könige*, 333). Again this requires a change of היורד. Gray, for instance, proposes והוא יורד מסלה "as he was going down the ramp."

his servants: So MT, G[B]. G[L]: *the servants of Joash.*

Amaziah: The name means "YHWH is strong, mighty." It is the same name as "Amoz" (אמוץ) the father of Isaiah (Isa 1:1), but not the same as the prophet Amos (עמוס).

Synchronic Analysis

Structure and content

The account of Joash's reign is comprised of his introductory (vv. 1-3) and concluding (vv. 20-22) formulae, enclosing two anecdotes relating to economic matters—the fundraising procedure he instituted for temple repair (vv. 5-17) and his bribe of Hazael to keep the Aramaeans from attacking Jerusalem (vv. 18-19). Despite the narrative length of the first one, the two anecdotes are paltry remembrance of a forty-year reign, especially of a king assessed as among Judah's best.

12:1-4: Joash's opening regnal formulae

The notice of Joash's accession in Jehu's seventh year (v. 1) highlights his youth (11:1-4) and links him to Josiah (22:1). There is a sense of energy and high hopes for the child-king under the aegis of the priest Jehoiada. There is also plenty of time for the hopes placed in him to be realized, since he reigns forty years (v. 2). The figure places Joash in the august company of David and Solomon and invites comparison with them in other ways. Like them, Joash is said to have done right where YHWH was concerned, although there is ambiguity in Joash's case (v. 3b). Did he do right all his life because of Jehoiada's instruction or only so long as the priest was around? There is also a reservation (v. 4); it is because of the people's cultic activity rather than Joash's, but its mention here makes Joash responsible. Did the people begin these activities after Jehoiada's death?

12:5-7: A rift starts between Joash and the priests

The temple is the focus of vv. 5-17; *house of YHWH* occurs in every one of vv. 10-17 except v. 16. It is fitting that Joash, who was raised in the temple, should take an interest in its upkeep. At some point, perhaps early in his reign, he devises a plan whereby the priests will devote the income from personal assessments[21] and volunteer donations to the repair of the temple structure. Just how the building fell into disrepair is not explained, but it is natural to blame Athaliah and her sons (cf. 2 Chr 24:7). In contrast to the previous chapter where Joash did not speak, here he takes center stage, issuing commands and replacing Jehoiada as the figure in charge. He presents a plan to the priests (vv. 5-6). They ignore it (v. 7), perhaps because of his youth or the fact that he was raised among them ("familiarity breeds contempt"), or both. Ultimately they show a lack of respect

---

21 כסף עובר איש has been taken as a reference to currency, based on Gen 23:16. Thus Šanda (*Könige* II, 139) argues that it refers to ingots that had been officially weighed and stamped, although he queries why unstamped silver would have been unacceptable. Likewise, V. Hurowitz ("Another Fiscal Practice in the Ancient Near East: 2 Kings 12:5-17 and a Letter to Esarhaddon [LAS 277]," *JNES* 45 [1986], 290n) translates כסף עובר as "silver that travels," i.e., silver of a standard recognized quality. But again, why would silver items of lesser quality be excluded as donations? It is more commonly understood as a registration tax (½ shekel according to Exod 30:13-14) for everyone who is entered ("crosses over," עבר) into the records. Buis (*Rois*, 229), Slotki (*Kings*, 235), and Wiseman (*Kings*, 251), among many others, adopt this view.

for him. It is not until his twenty-third year that he discovers their lack of compliance, suggesting that his visits to the temple have become sporadic. The anecdote reveals a growing rift between Joash and the priests who had raised him, including Jehoiada.

12:8-17: A new means for collecting donations

The rift widens in the rest of the story as Joash imposes measures to stop the priests from taking any more of the donations and then to alter the process of collection and disbursement so that the repair work will be completed. He makes no allegation of wrongdoing—no accusation of embezzlement or corruption—perhaps because Jehoiada is among the addressees (v. 8). But the policy changes that follow reveal a suspicion that the priests are untrustworthy if not dishonest. As a whole the anecdote undercuts the heroic stature of the priests in the previous chapter. They agree not to take any more of the money and not to be involved in the repairs (v. 9). Still, Joash or Jehoiada or both are evidently skeptical. Either of his own volition or by commission from the king, Jehoiada builds a chest to hold donations (v. 10). Hence he is not cut out of the process entirely. Neither are the priests who guard the threshold, since they are charged with taking the funds from entering worshipers and depositing them in the chest. But the chest is in a public location where the worshipers and others can watch to make sure the priests make the deposits. Furthermore, the chest is locked, since the king's scribe must come to retrieve and count the money along with the high priest (v. 11). The task of collection or at least supervision of it has been taken away from the priests and assumed by the court. The royal scribe and the high priest then give the money to the supervisors who, in turn, use it to pay the various artisans working on the temple—carpenters, builders, masons, and stonecutters—and to buy the necessary building materials (vv. 12-13). None of it was used to make any of the vessels or implements for the temple service but only for labor and materials (vv. 14-15). The list of laborers in vv. 12-13 recalls those who worked on Solomon's temple (1 Kgs 5:29-32), and most of the utensils in vv. 14-15 are found in 1 Kgs 7:50. Like his forty-year reign, they show Joash to be a reflection of Solomon.[22] On the other end Joash's repairs are a model for Josiah's work on the temple in 22:3-10. The utensils also occur in the list of things taken by Nebuchadrezzar (25:14-15). These similarities stress Joash's role as a key link in the dynastic chain from David to the exile. The royal scribe and high priest trust the supervisors and do not demand an itemized account of their expenditures because they are honest (v. 16). It is hard to avoid seeing this last remark as a contrast with the priests, since the next verse returns to the priests and the money that properly accrued to them from guilt and sin offerings.

12:18-22: Joash's bribe of Hazael and his assassination

The second, much briefer anecdote describes an invasion by Hazael of Aram and the bribe paid by Joash to keep him from attacking Jerusalem (vv. 18-19). Along with Joash's assassination (v. 21) this is retribution for his cultic failure (v. 4), as shown by comparison with the other kings of Judah who have similar failings and suffer similar tragedies.[23] Joash's failure in dealing with Hazael could be read

---

22 Nelson, *Kings*, 212; Olley, *Kings*, 278.

23 Mullen, "Crime and Punishment," 234–35. The only king in the list who might be questionable is Jehoshaphat, though his alliance with Ahab is probably one in which he is a vassal, as Mullen implies (see on 1 Kgs 22:45).

as what precipitated the conspiracy against him detailed in his closing formulae, especially as it follows immediately (vv. 20-22). The anecdote and the closing formulae leave a hollow impression about Joash's reign as a whole. He is judged to be a good king but there are few details to support this assessment. His refusal to confront Hazael may show a lack of faith, and his payment of a bribe nullifies his major accomplishment, at least financially. His forty years as king seems to be a zero-sum except for the legacy of his plan for financing the temple, which informs and shapes Josiah's reform (2 Kgs 22–23).

Diachronic Analysis

12:1: The sources for DtrH's opening formulae of Joash

The major critical issue of this chapter is the existence and nature of DtrH's sources. This issue surfaces first with regard to the opening formulae for Joash (vv. 1-2). The reference to Joash's mother probably derives from an official source but the other data are more suspect. Galil's contention that Athaliah's seven years were reckoned as the first seven of Joash's reign makes sense considering the treatment of her rule as illegitimate.[24] The figure of forty years for the length of Joash's reign (v. 2) is not unreasonable considering his young age of accession. At the same time it is historically suspect because it is so commonly a round number. As suggested in the previous chapter, DtrH threads the needle. Rather than expunging Athaliah he includes her rule, presenting it as an illegitimate "interlude" that did not derail the continuity of the Davidic line. The datum about Joash's age at accession in v. 1 is out of place in MT. The king's age occurs as the first element of the regnal formulae for kings of Judah after the fall of Israel (21:1, 19; 22:1; 23:31, 36; 24:8, 18). Before that point the accession notice typically follows the synchronism as G^L has it here. The atypical order is indirectly responsible for the different versification in this chapter; the synchronism was reckoned, consistently with previous examples, as the first element of the opening regnal formula, so that the king's age at accession was considered the last verse of the previous chapter in some translations. Zibiah, Joash's mother, has a fitting name ("gazelle") for someone from the steppe region around Beersheba. Her marriage to Ahaziah may indicate his effort to consolidate rule over all parts of the country, especially in the south following the loss of Edom as a vassal (8:20, 22).[25] This means that Joash probably had family ties with upper-class families in the Negev.

12:2-4: DtrH's evaluation

Joash's evaluation by DtrH is positive. The clause אשר הורהו יהוידע הכהן is interpreted in 2 Chr 24:2 to mean that Joash did right only so long as Jehoiada was alive, although there is nothing in Kings to indicate that such was the case. To the contrary, Joash is more faithful than Jehoiada, at least in carrying out the temple repairs. Hence אשר here might better be taken to mean "which" or "as;" Joash did right during his lifetime as Jehoiada had taught him. Its awkwardness following *all his days* has prompted the suggestion that it is a gloss

24 Galil, *Chronology*, 47–48.
25 Sweeney, *Kings*, 350.

based on Chronicles.[26] But such "back glosses" are dubious: there is not a single uncontested instance of an addition in Kings that originates with Chronicles. It is more likely that the Chronicles interpretation results from its author's *Tendenz* in favor of the priests. In addition, for the Chronicler, Joash's assassination demanded theological justification in the form of some transgression or shortcoming on the king's part. That said, v. 3 does indicate that Jehoiada continued, after placing the boy king on the throne, as his mentor and perhaps even as regent. Joash's only failing—signaled as such by the word רק, *only, except*—is that he tolerated the *bamot* (v. 4). Often translated *high places*, these were shrines to YHWH outside Jerusalem (v. 3) that were built and maintained at state expense like the sanctuaries of Dan and Bethel in the North.[27] The charge is anachronistic because the principle of cultic centralization did not exist until Deuteronomy was written, some 200 years after Joash. Joash is not the only king of Judah against whom this complaint is registered (1 Kgs 3:2-3; 22:44; 2 Kgs 14:4; 15:4, 35).

The source behind vv. 5-17

The question of sources resurfaces with the anecdote in vv. 5-17. Theories about the nature of the source behind this anecdote have varied widely. Wellhausen's postulation of a temple history from which the account was drawn continues to influence scholars who regard it as a priestly composition, albeit pre-DtrH in origin.[28] The priestly terminology, though, and the practice of fundraising for the temple that is depicted here have led others to regard this anecdote as an etiology for Second Temple cultic practice and thus a post-DtrH addition.[29] Such views focus too narrowly on language. There are, to be sure, several terms that reflect acquaintance with the vocabulary of priests, but the perspective on priests as a whole in this passage is negative.[30] They are not only inefficient and apathetic about maintaining the temple's physical plant; the narrative falls just short of accusing them of outright theft (v. 17). The point of the system set up in vv. 11-17 is to prevent them from keeping the money that is donated. This negative outlook would seem to preclude priestly authorship. In addition, not all of the "priestly" terminology is necessarily late, and the items that are may be glosses. What these terms indicate, therefore, is the author's familiarity with some of the professional language of the priesthood.[31]

The practice of collection and use of cash boxes

As for the process of funding the temple repairs, what Joash was apparently doing was changing from a system of royal patronage to one of self-support (vv. 5-6). It is unclear what motivated this change, though some have connected it with Hazael's incursion (see on vv. 18-19). It is also unclear how radical a change this would have been and the extent to which the account is anachronistic. Heretofore in Kings temple maintenance has been the king's responsibility, as with the Northern sanctuaries at Dan and Bethel. Still, Joash's decrees continue to assume the

26 Burney, *Notes*, 313; Würthwein, *1. Könige 17–2. Könige 25*, 352.

27 Barrick, "The Word BMH in the Old Testament," and "What Do We Really Know about 'High Places?'"

28 Wellhausen, *Composition des Hexateuchs*, 293–97; Gray, *Kings*, 582–83. For a sketch of other sources that have been proposed see Rehm, *Das zweite Buch der Könige*, 122.

29 Würthwein, *1. Könige 17–2. Könige 25*, 354–57, and Fritz, *Kings*, 303–304.

30 So also Šanda, *Könige* II, 148–49; Hobbs, *2 Kings*, 148.

31 Na'aman, "Royal Inscriptions and the Histories of Jehoash and Ahaz," 349.

principle of the king's jurisdiction over temple operations.[32] More to the point, the presence of a cash box near the entrance was a regular feature of Neo-Babylonian temples, which boasted a system for collecting taxes, donations, and the like and melting down the metal into ingots.[33] That the same kind of system was older is shown by a letter to Esarhaddon (680–669 BCE) that presents gold stores in the temple of Uruk as a matter for the jurisdiction of both royal and temple personnel.[34] Joash's plan in the last quarter of the ninth century would be the earliest attested instance of this kind of system. It may be anachronistic,[35] but it is not impossible that the practice was already known in his day. In any case it was known in DtrH's day, so there is no compelling reason to push this anecdote to the Second Temple era or to deny it to DtrH. The anecdote is not concerned with the temple repairs *per se* but with setting in place the process for financing them in order to prepare for Josiah's finding of the law in 22:3-10. Hence DtrH's source need not be a document but merely temple practice at the time of Josiah or of DtrH.[36]

The *money* (or "silver") *from the sacred offerings* (v. 5) was made up of articles of silver that could be melted to form ingots of standard weight (shekels). The nature of these offerings is further specified as individual valuations and voluntary donations.[37] *Money from a person's valuation* (כסף ערך איש, G^L^) refers to the practice of making a vow concerning another person (Lev 27:2-8). In lieu of human sacrifice a monetary valuation (ערך) was accepted. The next phrase in MT, כסף נפשות ערכו, is generally recognized as an interpretive gloss alluding to Lev 27:2.[38] The suffix on ערכו refers to the priest and thus changes the subject from the previous sentence, another sign of secondary status. 12:5: Valuation

---

32 The principle is illustrated by two Assyrian inscriptions published by A. K. Grayson, *Assyrian Royal Inscriptions* 2 (Wiesbaden: Harrassowitz, 1976). The first is from Adad-nirari III (paragraph 437 on p. 92), the second from Ashur-nasir-apli II (para. 480, p. 105). The rationale is explained in another inscription of Ashur-nasir-apli II (para 666, p. 170), i.e., temple maintenance, including preserving older kings' memorials before the gods in order to assure military and social success for the king who carries out the maintenance.

33 Torrey, "Foundry of the Second Temple" and "Evolution of a Financier"; Eissfeldt, "Einschmelzstelle"; A. L. Oppenheim, "A Fiscal Practice of the Ancient Near East," *JNES* 6 (1947): 116–20; Cogan and Tadmor *II Kings*, 138.

34 Hurowitz, "Another Fiscal Practice."

35 So Fritz, *Kings*, 304; Würthwein, *1. Könige 17-2. Könige 25*, 355–56.

36 O. Lipschits, "On Cash-Boxes and Finding or Not Finding Books: Jehoash's and Josiah's Decisions to Repair the Temple," in *Essays on Ancient Israel in Its Near Eastern Context: A Tribute to Nadav Na'aman* (ed. Y. Amit, E. Ben-Zvi, I. Finkelstein, and O. Lipschits; Winona Lake, IN: Eisenbrauns, 2006), 239–54.

37 Wiseman (*Kings*, 251) considers the *sacred offerings* to be the first in a series of four (following MT) sources of revenue rather than the general source to which the others are in apposition. He refers to הקדשים as *daily sacred dues* without supporting evidence or further indication of what he imagines them to have been. Hoffmann (*Reform und Reformen*, 123) and Würthwein (*1. Könige 17-2. Könige 25*, 354) point out that קדשים is used in this sense of consecrated gifts in Deuteronomistic and younger literature, especially P. Again, though, the concept is older.

38 Benzinger, *Könige*, 159–60; Burney, *Notes*, 313–14; Kittel, *Könige*, 253; Stade "Miscellen 10," 288–89; *Kings*, 238.

12:6: Assessors and repairs

Joash's initial plan entails the assessment of donations by a temple official called a *mkr* ("assessor," see the Note), who might even have been in charge of selling some items and delivering the funds to the priests for temple repairs (v. 6).[39] The *mkrym* are not mentioned in the revised plan (vv. 10-17), which may have required the people to make exchanges on their own and bring only silver or articles made of silver for donation. The expression חזק בדק (*repair*) is a technical term for patching cracks and holes in buildings (vv. 6, 7, 8, 9, 13; 22:5) due to settling, though it can be used in the extended sense of effecting repairs in general and perhaps even, like its Akkadian cognate, with the meaning "inspection, maintenance."[40] It is also used in Ezek 27:9, 27 to refer to patching the hulls of ships.[41]

12:7-9: The non-compliance of the priests

Joash's plan does not work because the priests do not comply (v. 7). Exactly how long the first plan was in effect is unclear because Joash's first order in vv. 5-6 is undated. The revised plan comes in the twenty-third year of his reign. The specific date is unusual and may indicate an official source behind this account, or more likely behind that of Hazael's incursion in vv. 18-19, which occurred at about the same time (see on v. 18). Joash confronts the priests, Jehoiada included (v. 8). Since Jehoiada is listed first and titled *the priest* he seems still to be their leader and thus the one most responsible for not executing Joash's order. The reason for the non-compliance is not spelled out. Was it simply inertia? Lack of central oversight due to Jehoiada's weakness in dotage? Or were there deeper disagreements about the authority over temple matters or the source of financing its upkeep? The report here does not reflect favorably on the priests, since they have been accepting the donations evidently for personal use. Joash's confrontation secures their consent to stop taking donations for themselves and relieves them of the charge to carry out the repairs (v. 9).

12:10: The collection box and the threshold guards

It is somewhat surprising to find Jehoiada fabricating the chest for the donations (v. 10) after the last verse. Evidently the priests were not excluded from any role in the collection of funds, just from keeping them. Jehoiada's assembly of the chest may be an act of contrition for his failure to carry out the first order, and it is probably at the king's behest. The chest is installed beside the altar near the temple entrance. Assuming that *altar* is the correct reading (see the Note), it is probably a threshold altar rather than the main temple altar, which stood in the middle of the court.[42] The mention of *the priests who guarded the threshold* is another surprise if the priests were no longer to be involved in collecting funds.

---

39 Provan (*Kings*, 225) and Rehm (*Das zweite Buch der Könige*, 124) take *mkrw* to refer to the actual donor rather than to an intermediary. But the restricted use of the term (only in vv. 6, 8) and its *qaṭṭāl* form, indicating a vocation, suggest that it refers to an official.

40 B. Levine, *IDBS* "Priests," 689.

41 Na'aman ("Royal Inscriptions and the Histories of Jehoash and Ahaz") argues that such technical language suggests a dedicatory inscription as the source or inspiration for the present account. But see P. Bordreuil and D. Pardee, "King's Command and Widow's Plea: Two New Hebrew Ostraca of the Biblical Period," *NEA* 61 (1998): 2–13. The first ostracon in the article, from the 7th century, mentions the king's order to donate silver to the temple. It is not a dedicatory inscription but it shows that informal documents could have served as sources for the account.

42 So McKane, "A Note on 2 Kings 12 10."

These guardians were an important class of temple officials. There were three of them for the three entrances to the temple, and they are mentioned elsewhere just after the high priest and second priest(s) (2 Kgs 23:4; 25:18; Jer 52:24). They lived in the temple (Jer 35:4). Their function was probably to assure the ritual cleanness of entering worshipers and perhaps to oversee the preparation of sacrifices at the threshold altars.[43] Their new duty of receiving and depositing donations into the collection chest again indicates that the priests were not completely excluded from the process but only from keeping the funds.[44] The full view of incoming worshipers would serve as a safeguard against pilfering. It remains unclear why the people give their gifts to *the guardians of the threshold* instead of making the deposits themselves.[45] The process seems cumbersome. Perhaps the point was to retain some role for the priests in the collection process.

12:11: The high priest

When the threshold guardians notice that the chest is becoming full—perhaps by looking through the bored hole or by the sound of a new contribution—they are to advise the court, which will send the king's scribe to gather the silver and count it (v. 11). Stade argued long ago, on the basis of three considerations, that the mention of *the high priest* was an addition drawn from 22:4.[46] These are (1) the presence of the singular verb (ויעל); (2) the fact that the priest lives in the temple and would not *go up* to it; (3) the lateness of the title הכהן הגדול. The first two considerations are not strong. The use of a singular *wayyiqtol* followed by a compound subject is relatively common in biblical Hebrew, and the verbs that follow in this case are plurals (ויצרו וימנו). Also, since the sanctuary is the site of the divine presence everyone ascends to it, even if the priest is housed elsewhere in the complex. In addition it would be strange for the priests to be completely excluded from this part of the collection process—all the more in view of priestly involvement in chapter 22. One expects representation of both the crown and the temple.[47] As for the third consideration, it is important to distinguish between the office of a head priest and the title הכהן הגדול. The office was quite ancient; the Ugaritic texts attest a *rb khnm, head of the priests* (*KTU* 2.4.1; 6.6-10). But the title הכהן הגדול is post-exilic and in this passage is probably a scribal modification.[48] In view of the reference to Jehoiada previously as הכהן I tentatively adopt it here, taking הגדול as an anachronistic gloss.

---

43 McKane, "A Note on 2 Kings 12 10."

44 Chronicles identifies them as Levites (2 Chr 34:9) and commonly uses the title "gatekeepers" (שערים) for them (Cogan and Tadmor, *II Kings*, 138).

45 2 Chr 24:10 has the people making their own deposits. But this is a democratization of the Kings account emphasizing the full and joyful participation of the people (Klein, *2 Chronicles*, 341–42). For the explanation of Cogan and Tadmor see the Note on v. 10. Hentschel (*2 Könige*, 55–56) offers a redactional explanation.

46 Stade, "Miscellen 10," 290–91; *Kings*, 239. If so, the next two verbs, *cast* and *count*, should also be read as singulars.

47 The letter to Esarhaddon (LAS 277) treated by Hurowitz ("Another Fiscal Practice") mandates the presence of a priest when the king's delegate came to check on the funds available for repair of the temple of Uruk.

48 So de Vaux (*Ancient Israel*, 378, 397–98) some time ago. Hoffmann (*Reform und Reformen*, 122–23) contended that this title proves the late postexilic composition of the passage because there is no good explanation for it.

Smelting the silver

Translators and commentators have struggled to make sense of the verb ויצרו, *they bound, tied*, often assuming an implicit reference to bags and that it describes the emptying of the collection chest. Another possibility follows Chronicles ויערו, *they emptied*, except that the verb has *the silver* as its object rather than "the chest." As explained in the Note, this verb is better derived from √יצר or a biform and refers to smelting or casting metal. It assumes the presence of a foundry in or connected with the temple, as was common in the ancient Near East, where temples served something of the role of banks, storing donated funds and maintaining standards of weight and purity. The silver placed into the chest was melted down into ingots of common weight to be tallied and stored or disbursed to workers.

12:12-13: Paying the workers

The first half of v. 12 identifies the workers (עשי המלאכה) as supervisors (המפקדים *qere'*) who serve as middlemen in the distribution of funds. There appears to be tension between the mention of supervisors here and vv. 15-16 where the workers are the ones carrying out the various repairs and are the payees. The tension is clarified by 22:5, which also refers to the workers both as supervisors and as payees. This suggests that there were two classes of workers, one of which handled pay distribution as well as performing some of the work.[49] They dispersed funds to the other workers, that is, the carpenters, builders, and other craftsmen who were effecting repairs.[50] The money was also used to acquire raw materials of wood and stone (v. 13). The list of specialists and materials suggests that the needed repairs were extensive and may have essentially called for renovation of the building.

12:14-16: Items not made with the silver

The list of items not produced from donations in v. 14 allows for a charitable interpretation of the priests' former inaction: perhaps they had been using the income from donations to manufacture vessels for the temple.[51] There is nothing else in the passage that suggests this, however.[52] The four items in the list are as follows.

- סף was a bowl or goblet used for holding the blood of the Passover lamb (Exod 12:22) but also for drinking (2 Sam 17:28; Zech 2:12).
- מזמרת is disputed and depends on the זמר root from which one derives it; it refers either to a musical instrument (so especially medieval commentators)

---

49 This understanding obviates the need for Stade's proposal ("Miscellen 10," 291–95; *Kings*, 241) that v. 12a and *to pay the workers* in v. 16 are glosses.

50 They were the intermediate recipients of the funds, as indicated by the phrase על־יד. See the comments by Pardee and Bordreuil ("King's Command," 4) on ביד. Also, the use of יצא in *Hip'îl* to mean *pay* seems to be a technical term further indicating the affinity of this chapter with ch. 22. See Cogan and Tadmor, *II Kings*, 139; Lipschits, "On Cash-Boxes," 249.

51 Fricke, *Zweite Königen*, 162; Jones, *Kings*, 493.

52 Würthwein (*1. Könige 17–2. Könige 25*, 354), following Rendtorff (*Studien zur Geschichte des Opfers*, 54) and Klostermann (*Könige*, 435), renders the verbs in vv. 14-17 not as iteratives but as jussives and thus regards them as distinct from the foregoing verses (5-13) and a separate post-DtrH addition. However, vv. 14-17 are clearly dependent on vv. 5-13 and address the situation they describe. They are hardly principles to be followed perpetually (cf. v. 16). If the verbs were jussives one would expect אין as the negative rather than לא as in vv. 16-17. Verses 14-17, then, continue the iterative sense of vv. 11-13 (Joosten, *Verbal System*, 287, 307) and are of a piece with them.

or a tool for trimming the wicks of lamps (hence "snuffers"). It occurs elsewhere in the HB only in 1 Kgs 7:50 and 2 Kgs 25:14 and parallels (2 Chr 4:22; Jer 52:18), where the latter meaning is more apropos.

- מזרק was a large bowl or basin for cultic purposes (Num 7; Zech 14:20). Its use in Amos 6:6 is sarcastic, accusing elite Samarians of drinking copious amounts of wine from large basins intended for sacred use.
- חצצרה was a clarion or trumpet of metal (as opposed to the ram's horn, שופר). It is unique in the list unless the מזמרת is also a musical instrument. However, its presence suggests the representative nature of the items in the list as samples of the implements used in the temple.

12:15-16: Reliable payment for workers

Instead of being used for utensils, the funds for repair go to the workers (v. 15).[53] Those who disburse the money to the workers in v. 16 are the supervising workers of v. 12, who are trustworthy.

12:17: A priestly interpolation

The statement that silver from sin and guilt offerings remained with the priests (v. 17) is an affirmation that the priests' regular income was not taken from them. The verse is probably a priestly interpolation based on the procedures for sin and guilt offerings in Leviticus 4–5.[54] This conclusion is driven more by the verse's priestly interest and its intrusiveness than by its terminology, which seems to be known in the pre-exilic period (Mic 6:7). The difference between the sin offering and guilt offerings is hard to discern. Both appear to be for unintentional ritual offenses. The *sin offering* was basically for ritual purification and in some cases for the forgiveness of sin. It involved animal sacrifice, and in the case of an individual's offering the meat was eaten by the priests as their perquisite. The *guilt offering* was for reparation of an offense involving the misappropriation or profanation of sacred items. Restitution rather than punition was its primary concern. Hence, unlike other offerings, it could simply be paid.[55] As the current verse attests, that payment went to the priests.

12:18: Hazael's invasion

The second anecdote from Joash's reign begins with the particle אז plus the imperfect, which signals a separate narrative unit set in the same time frame as the foregoing episode (v. 18). This means that Hazael's invasion takes place around the time of Joash's efforts to fund and repair the temple and may be the reason for the insufficiency of funds to begin with.[56] If the invasion happened first it would also explain why v. 19 says nothing about Joash emptying the chest for donations to pay Hazael.[57]

---

53 2 Chr 24:14 directly contradicts this verse by stating that the surplus silver was used for making utensils.

54 *Pace* Hentschel, *2 Könige*, 156.

55 These descriptions and distinctions are based on J. Milgrom (*Cult and Conscience: The* Asham *and the Priestly Doctrine of Repentance* [SJLA 18; Leiden: Brill, 1976]), which remains the fundamental study of these two kinds of offerings. See also G. A. Anderson, "Sacrifice and Sacrificial Offerings," *ABD* 5:879–81, and F. H. Gorman, "Sacrifices and Offerings," *NIDB* 5:25–27.

56 Rabinowitz, "'ĀZ Followed by Imperfect," esp. 61–62.

57 Alternatively, Lipschits ("On Cash-Boxes," 250–51) suggests that the payment to Hazael subverted the repair project, so that the collection system was put in place under Joash but no repairs were undertaken until Josiah, when the lawbook was found.

The capture of Gath

Hazael's capture of the Philistine city of Gath has recently been confirmed by excavations at Tell es-Safi.[58] Since Gath was only about 30 kilometers west and south of Jerusalem this was cause for alarm on Joash's part. Despite the implication that Hazael was intent on attacking Jerusalem,[59] however, it does not seem to have been his real interest. The payment from Joash was a bonus. Hazael's main interest was probably the trade route along the coastal plain. The fact that he was able to penetrate so far into Judah shows how weak it was at the time. Hazael may have launched the campaign shortly after Jehoahaz's accession to the throne of Israel in Joash's twenty-third year, since his forays against Jehu seem to have been mostly in the Transjordan (10:32-33), and Jehoahaz's reign represented Israel's military nadir (13:3-7). It was most probably before Assyria resumed its western campaigns under Adad-Nirari III (810–783).

12:19: Bribing Hazael

The source of Joash's bribe for Hazael is the קדשים, that is, sacred gifts or offerings to the temple by his predecessors Jehoshaphat, Joram, Ahaziah, and by himself (v. 19). These are the kings of Judah since Asa, who last emptied the treasuries of the temple and palace to ward off a king of Damascus (1 Kgs 15:18). Hezekiah will later follow suit, buying off Sennacherib (2 Kgs 18:15). The inclusion of Joram and Ahaziah in this list is significant. Royal dedications were conventional signs of piety on the part of the king toward the national deity (1 Kgs 7:51), yet Joram and Ahaziah were both condemned for walking in the way of the Ahabids and doing what YHWH considered evil (8:18, 27). They may have opened themselves to reproach by DtrH for allowing the worship of other gods to take place in Jerusalem, perhaps as a courtesy to non-Israelites in the royal house. Their blood ties to the Omrids did not win them any points in DtrH's mind either.[60]

12:20-22: Joash's closing formulae

The closing formulae for Joash stand out because of his assassination. The details of the conspiracy in vv. 21-22 are obscured by text-critical problems. The two locations in v. 21, Beth Millo and Silla, are variously interpreted. It is unlikely that Joash would have been in the Beth Millo of Judg 9:6, 20, which was near Shechem in the Northern kingdom. A better candidate is Millo as a reference to some architectural feature of Jerusalem (2 Sam 5:9; 1 Kgs 9:15, 24; 11:27). The name may derive from √מלא "to be full" and refer to a stone filling of the saddle between the Temple Mount and the City of David. The Beth Millo or Millo palace might then have been some structure on top of this fill or perhaps the section of

---

58 Maier, "Historical Background and Dating of Amos VI 2." The finds disprove Fritz's (*Kings*, 305) contention that vv. 18-19 were contrived by DtrH from the account of Sennacherib's invasion in 18:13-15 and are historically inaccurate in their report of Aram's penetration so deep into Judah's territory.

59 The expression *śîm pānîm* expresses intention, especially of a hostile nature (Gen 31:21; Jer 42:15, 17; Ezek 6:2; Dan 11:17).

60 Würthwein (*1. Könige 17–2. Könige 25*, 358) considers the reference to the kings' dedications to be an addition by *ein aufmerksamer Ergänzer* who remembered Asa's having emptied the treasuries in 1 Kgs 15:18. He offers no source-critical arguments for this conclusion and his idea of this "attentive reviser" is peculiar: He took the trouble to add the reference to the dedications of these kings but ignored the fact that two of them were identified previously as worshipers of other gods. This tension is more likely to be a sign of DtrH's use of source material.

the city on top of the fill.[61] Silla (סלא) is probably a miswriting of Millo (מלא), so that *the Millo palace* and *when he went down to the Millo* are variants. The assassin may have been an individual, since Jozakar (so G^B) and Jehozabad are similar and probably variants. Joash is buried with full honors in the City of David in accord with his recognition as a righteous king as per his evaluation in v. 2.[62]

Synthesis

The characteristic Judahite king

Joash is an in-betweener. He is between the start of the monarchy with David and Solomon and Josiah and the exile at its end. Perhaps better than any other king of Judah he embodies his country's kingship. His reign is the essence of the continuity of the Davidic monarchy. It participates in the dynasty's strengths; Joash does what YHWH considered right, like others of Judah's best kings. He does so because of Jehoiada's mentoring. But he falls short by retaining the cultic sites outside Jerusalem, again like many of his peers. He has good intentions but is incapable of following them through. He tries to effect repairs on the temple, but the priests who put him in place do not carry out his orders. The procedure he then devises to reduce priestly involvement and exercise more direct control is promising but is short-circuited by Hazael's invasion. Historically this appears to have been a move to make the temple self-funding in response to the drain on the royal treasury caused by the payoff to Hazael. The resulting overall impression is that Joash's reign is a disappointment, especially after the anticipation raised by his installation. The behavior of the priests is a disappointment as well, again all the more following their initiative in ch. 11 to place Joash on the throne. One is left to wonder how much of the responsibility for the disappointment of Joash's reign falls to Jehoiada and the priests—maybe for not properly instructing him about the error of the cultic installations outside Jerusalem and certainly for the failure to carry out his instructions to see to the temple repairs.

61 Cf. E. Mazar, *The Palace of King David: Excavations at the Summit of the City of David. Preliminary Report of Seasons 2005–2007* (Jerusalem/New York: Shoham, 2009). Fritz (*Kings*, 306) understands Beth Millo as a quarter of the city.

62 2 Chr 24:25 paints a very different portrait: Joash's assassination (in bed) and denial of burial in the royal tomb are judgments against him for his mistreatment of Jehoiada's son. The Chronicler's theology required a theological explanation for the foreign invasion and assassination at the end of his reign. Frevel (*Geschichte Israels*, 223) sees Joash of Judah and Joash of Israel as one and the same and argues that the assassination of the former was really his transfer to Samaria. This would give Joash of Judah a rather long reign—forty years in Judah and another ten or so in Israel. However, the forty years could well be a round number, as mentioned.

Jehoahaz and Jehoash of Israel; Elisha's Last Acts (2 Kings 13)

Text

[DtrH's sources; DtrH; Prophetic story; Additions to DtrH; *PN*]

1 In the twenty-third year of Joash son of Ahaziah king of Judah, Jehoahaz son of Jehu became king over Israel in Samaria, reigning seventeen years. 2 He did what YHWH considered evil, following the sin of Jeroboam son of Nebat who made Israel sin; he did not turn from it. 3 So YHWH became angry with Israel and turned them over to the domination of Hazael king of Aram and of Ben-Hadad son of Hazael during [Jehoahaz's] entire reign 7 until he left Jehoahaz no army except fifty horsemen, ten chariots, and two thousand cavalry, for the king of Aram threshed them until they were pulverized like dust. 8 The rest of Jehoahaz's deeds—both all he did and his strength—are of course written on the scroll of the chronicles of Israel's kings. 9 Jehoahaz lay down with his forebears and they buried him in Samaria, and Joash his son reigned in his place. 10 In the thirty-seventh year of Joash king of Judah, Jehoash son of Jehoahaz became king over Israel, reigning sixteen years. 11 He did what was displeasing to YHWH, not turning from the sin of Jeroboam who made Israel sin; he walked in it. 4 [Jehoash] entreated YHWH, and YHWH listened to him because he saw the oppression of Israel because the king of Aram oppressed them. 5 YHWH gave Israel victory and brought them out from under Aram's domination. He restored Israel's border to them so that the Israelites lived tranquilly in their homes as previously. 6 Still, they did not turn from the sin of Jeroboam who made Israel sin; they walked in it. *Also, the asherah remained in Samaria.* 14 Elisha became ill with the illness from which he would die. When the king of Israel came down to him, he wept over him and said, "My father, my father, Israel's charioteer and horseman!" 15 Elisha told him, "Get a bow and arrows." So he got a bow and arrows. 16 [Elisha] said to the king, "String the bow." As he strung [the bow], Elisha placed his hands on the king's hands. 17 [Elisha] said, "Open the window to the east." When he opened it, [Elisha] said, "Shoot," and when he shot, Elisha said, "It is *the arrow of YHWH's victory and* the arrow of victory in Israel. You will defeat Aram in Hazeroth, which is opposite Samaria, completely." 18 *[Elisha] said, "Take the arrows." So he took them. He told the king of Israel, "Strike the ground." When [the king] struck it three times and stopped,* 19 *the man of god became angry with him and said, "You should have struck five or six times. Then you would have defeated Aram until you finished them completely. But now you will only defeat Aram three times."* 20 After Elisha died and they had buried him, Moabite raiding bands began coming into the land. 21 While a man

was being buried, a raiding band approached them, so they threw the man into Elisha's tomb and fled. When he touched Elisha's bones he came to life and stood on his feet. 22 Hazael had oppressed Israel the whole reign of Jehoahaz. Hazael the Aramaean took from [Jehoahaz's] dominion from the sea of the Arabah as far as Aphek. 23 YHWH was gracious and merciful to them for the sake of his covenant with Abraham, Isaac, and Jacob. He did not wish to destroy them and did not cast them from his presence. 24 When Hazael king of Aram died, Ben-Hadad his son reigned in his place. 25 Jehoash son of Jehoahaz retook from the dominion of Ben-Hadad son of Hazael the cities that he had taken from Jehoahaz his father in war. *Three times Jehoash defeated him and recovered the cities of Israel.*

Textual Notes

1 **Jehoahaz:** "YHWH grasps (in protection)."[1] This is a variant of the name Ahaz, Ahaziah. It has been found on a seal from the late seventh century.[2]

over Israel: So MT, G^L. G^B lacks the phrase here but has it in v. 10. It is a regular part of the formula elsewhere.[3]

2 **the sin of Jeroboam:** Reading the singular as indicated later by *from it*.

3 **with Israel:** So MT, G^B. G^L: *against Israel*. Either reading is possible.

to the domination of: Lit.: *into the hand of*. So MT, G^B. G^L: *into the hands of*.

during [Jehoahaz's] entire reign: Lit. *all the days*. Sometimes translated "for a long time" to avoid tension with vv. 4-5. It is used several times in preference to the suffixed form (כל־ימיו) but with the same meaning (1 Kgs 12:17; 14:30; Gen 43:9; 44:32; 2 Sam 13:37). Cf. v. 22.

4-6 See below after v. 11.

7 **until:** So G^L (ἕως ὅτου = עד אשר in preference to MT and G^B, which have כי.

he left: So MT (השאיר). G^{BL} have a passive, reflecting a change that was made after the insertion of vv. 4-6a, which separated the verb from its original subject, Hazael, in v. 3.

army: A common meaning of the noun עם, *people*, as determined by context.[4]

two thousand cavalry: Conjectural.[5] The figure of 10,000 is inordinately high. עשרת probably arose from dittography of עשרה two words before. Then אלפים is read as a dual.

threshed them until they were pulverized like dust: So G^L. The metaphor in MT is unclear: *he set them like dust for threshing*.

G^L places v. 23 between vv. 7 and 8. See v. 23.

10 **thirty-seventh:** So MT, G^{BL}. Most Greek witnesses have thirty-ninth, a correction based on 13:1.

---

1 Noth, *Personennamen*, 179.

2 Avigad and Sass, *Stamp Seals*, 54, #13. The seal is unprovenanced and has been suspected of being a forgery.

3 Stade (*Kings*, 242) observes that it occurs in every introductory formula for kings of Israel except 1 Kgs 16:15.

4 Gray (*Kings*, 596) proposes emending to עצם, *strength*, but this is unnecessary and is generally rejected.

5 Šanda (*Könige* II, 152) and Cogan and Tadmor (*II Kings*, 143).

11 **He did**: Reading ויעש instead of MT's long form ויעשה, which is probably a dittography of the ה in הרע.[6] G^L provides Joash's name as subject.

the sin of Jeroboam: So MT, G^B. G^L: *sins of Jeroboam*, which led to the addition of *all*. The singular is supported by בה later in the verse.

in it: So MT, G^B. G^L: *in them*.

4-6 These verses are widely considered secondary because of the tension they create with vv. 3 and 7. As the text stands, Jehoahaz entreats Yhwh, who hears the prayer (v. 4), and then Jehoahaz continues to grow weaker (v. 7). The tension is also strong between vv. 5 and 7, such that the Aramaean oppression continues until virtually nothing is left of Israel's army (v. 7), but this is *after* Yhwh has given Israel victory and security (v. 5). There is text-critical confirmation of this deduction in the G^L reading (*until*) in v. 7, which makes its continuity with v. 3 clear. The language and ideology of these verses, however, appear to be DtrH,[7] so that I would propose that they are not an addition but a misplacement. They probably originally referred to Jehoash and followed his regnal formulae in vv. 10-11.[8] They would have been lost by haplography due to the reference to Jeroboam's sin in vv. 6a and 11 and then restored in the wrong place.[9]

4 **Jehoash**: Contingent on the theory of the original placement of vv. 4-6a as just explained.

entreated Yhwh: את פני (*pi'el*) חלה has the literal meaning "make (someone's) face sweet/pleasant" and is used in the sense of appeasing or even flattering someone to gain their favor.[10] In the HB it is used for entreating other people (Ps 45:13; Job 11:19; Prov 19:6) but especially for seeking Yhwh's favor by such means as prayer (Exod 32:11; 1 Kgs 13:6 [its only other occurrence in 1–2 Kings]; Jer 26:19; Ps 119:58; 2 Chr 33:12), sacrifice (1 Sam 13:12; Zech 7:2; 8:21-22; Mal 1:9), and/or repentance (Dan 9:13).

5 **victory**: So G^{BL}: σωτηρίαν = תשועה as in v. 17. MT's מושיע is unique to Kings and has engendered widespread speculation about the identity of the *savior*. The connection with v. 17 suggests that the abstract is the better reading.

and brought them out: So G^L. MT, G^B: *they/he went out* reflects the loss of the suffix by haplography.

He restored Israel's border to them: So G^L. Lost from MT, G^B by haplography (וישבו ... וישב).

6 **the sin of Jeroboam**: The singular *sin* is indicated by the subsequent בה, *in it*. The word *house* before Jeroboam's name is omitted with a few Hebrew manuscripts and the Syriac (cf. BHS) in line with the theme of the *sin of Jeroboam* elsewhere in Kings.

who made Israel sin: Reading the *qere'* החטיא in preference to the *ketiv* החטי, which reflects the loss of the final א by haplography.

they walked in it: Reading הלכו בה. The singular suffix on the preposition accords with MT, G^B against the majority Greek tradition. The latter reflect harmonization with the plural "sins" earlier in the verse. The plural verb follows the majority Greek and other versions against MT, G^B but in agreement with סרו. G^L reflects a haplography from אשר to האשרה.

the asherah: See on 1 Kgs 16:33.

---

6 Joosten (*Verbal System*, 14n) attributes it to a lack of scribal expertise.

7 Cf. D. J. McCarthy, "2 Kings 13,4-6," *Bib* 54 (1973), 409–10.

8 Cf. Jepsen ("Israel und Damaskus," 159) and Gray (*Kings*, 594), who suggested that confusion of Jehoahaz's name for Jehoash's in v. 4 led to the misplacement of vv. 4-6.

9 Verse 6b is a later gloss, as indicated by its beginning with וגם and its change of subject.

10 Burney, *Notes*, 181.

12-13 This is the first of three locations for the closing regnal formulae of Jehoash in the witnesses. The others are 13:25+ (G^L) and 14:15-16 (G^L has only 14:16). That it is secondary here is indicated by (1) its absence from G^L; (2) the fact that it immediately follows his opening formulae (vv. 10-11) without any other information about his reign in between; and (3) the intrusive reference to Jeroboam sitting on the throne in v. 13.[11] Despite its intrusiveness this reference helps to explain the occurrence of the formulae here. It recalls YHWH's promise that Jehu's descendants would sit on the throne for four generations (10:30), which is appropriate since Jeroboam II was the next-to-last (his son Zechariah would reign only six months) and most powerful of the Jehu line.[12]

14-21 OL places the two stories in these verses between 10:30 and 31 and identifies the king as Jehu. As a PN addition they are secondary in either location: in MT Elisha reappears after a long absence of between 45 and 61 years[13] and thus lives into his 90s—an exceptional, though not impossible lifespan, especially for a man of god.[14] In OL his age at death is a more reasonable 65–70. Also, the king in the first story is respectful of Elisha, who is in turn favorably inclined toward him, which fits well with Jehu whom Elisha had helped to place on the throne (9:1-10) but less so with Jehoahaz. The OL placement between 10:30 and 31 suggests a reason for Jehu's failure to follow YHWH's law completely despite the promise he received in 10:30—namely, that Elisha died in the meantime. These features might suggest the originality of the OL placement except that it is clearly secondary as well, interrupting the continuity between the promise to Jehu (10:30) and the report of his less-than-faithful behavior (10:31a). MT is the more difficult location, given the considerations about Elisha's long absence and lifespan. OL's placement is probably part of the systematic chronological adjustment that took place in the OG *Vorlage*.

14 **the king of Israel came down to him**: So OL (*et descendit at eum rex israel*). MT, G^{BL} identify the king as Joash.

Israel's charioteer and horseman: See on 2:12.

16 **[Elisha] said to the king**: So G^B. MT + *of Israel*. G^L also has Elisha's name as subject. OL identifies the king of Israel as Jehu.

---

11 This reference does not belong in the regnal formulae at all. It expresses a claim to power and is especially common in the Solomon narrative (1 Kgs 1:13, 17, 20, 24, 27, 30 35, 46, 48; 2:12, 19, 24; 3:6; 8:20, 25; also 22:10; 2 Kgs 10:30; 11:19). Montgomery, *Kings*, 434. Hobbs (*2 Kings*, 168–69) objects that the expression is well attested in Kings. But this misses the point that it is anomalous among the regnal formulae and interrupts Jehoash's death and burial notices.

12 Hobbs (*2 Kings*, 185), following Thiele, suggests that the notice that Jeroboam sat on the throne indicates a coregency with Jehoash. But as Long (*1 & 2 Kings*, 405) points out, this does not take into consideration the use of the expression elsewhere, especially in the Solomon story, or in 2 Kgs 10:30. It is also odd that the writer would choose to allude to a co-regency so obliquely.

13 The reigns of Jehu (28 years) and Jehoahaz (17 years) and part of Jehoash's (16 years).

14 In MT Elisha's career begins during Ahab's reign (1 Kgs 19:19-21) and spans the rest of his 22 regnal years plus those of Ahaziah (2), Joram (12), Jehu (28), Jehoahaz (17), and part of Jehoash's (16). Assuming an initial age of 20 and overlap of a year each with Ahab and Jehoash, his minimum age at death is 81; his maximum (allowing all but a year overlap each with Ahab and Jehoash) is 115.

String the bow: Lit. *ride your hand on the bow.* If the meaning were "draw the bow" (NRSV)[15] it would be impossible for the king to open the window (v. 17). The translation and interpretation adopted here follows the proposal by Barrick.[16]

As he strung [the bow]: G^B supplies Joash's name as subject. OL supplies Jehu's name.

17 **Elisha said, "Shoot," and when he shot**: Lost from G^B by haplography. The form ויור (as well as the long version יורה) is *Qal*, as shown by the preceding imperative (ירה), but has been considered *Hipʿîl* because of its resemblance to that *binyan* (GKC §69r; Joüon §75fN).

in Israel: So G^L, OL. MT, G^B have בארם, which must be construed as [*victory*] *over/against Aram.* Since it is the same *arrow of victory*, the reading *in Israel* makes more sense, especially in view of the geographical setting (see the next Note).

in Hazerot, which is opposite Samaria: So OL, *in aseroth in quae est contra faciem samariae*, in contrast to MT and G^{BL}, which read *in Aphek.*[17] Hazeroth (meaning "enclosures, settlements") is mentioned in the eighth-century Samaria ostraca (15, 18, 22-26) and was located ca. eight km east-southeast of Samaria. It was not the Hazeroth of the wilderness journey (Num 11:35; 12:1, 16; 33:17-18; Deut 1:1).

completely: עד־כלה makes use of an infinitive[18] in an adverbial construction. It occurs outside of vv. 17 and 19 only in Ezra 9:14 but has the same sense as עד־כלתם in 1 Kgs 22:11. Following this the OL attests the plus: *Then opening a second window, he said, "Shoot," and he shot the arrow of* Yhwh*'s victory and the arrow of victory in Israel. Elisha said, "You will defeat Aram completely."* This is probably a double reading designed to incorporate features of the MT variant of the previous order and bow shot, as it is superfluous to the tale and somewhat confusing.[19]

18 **[Elisha] said**: So MT. G^B + *to him.* G^L: *Elisha said to Joash.* OL: *et iterum dixit.*

Take the arrows: So MT. G^B: *take a bow.* OL lacks this command and its execution due to haplography. G^L has *five arrows*, derived from the total of arrows shot previously (2) plus the number of times the king strikes the ground (3) or from the number *five* in the next verse.

He told the king of Israel: So MT, G^B. G^L supplies Elisha's name. OL also gives Elisha's name and then reads *to King Jehu.*

You should have struck: Lit. [*It was*] *to strike.*[20]

---

15 Cf. KB 891; Thenius, *Könige*, 337; de Vaux, *Rois*, 173.

16 W. B. Barrick, "Elisha and the Magic Bow: A Note on 2 Kings XIII 15-17," *VT* 35 (1985): 355–63.

17 A detailed case for the reading is presented by M. Richelle, "Revisiting 2 Kings 13:14-21 (MT and LXX)," in *Making the Biblical Text: Textual Studies in the Hebrew and the Greek Bible* (ed. I. Himbaza; OBO 275; Fribourg/Göttingen, Academic Press/Vandenhoeck und Ruprecht, 2015), 67–70. See also his *Le testament d'Élisée*, 58–61.

18 There is some question about whether it is infinitive construct or absolute. The form is that of the latter (Joüon 123c), but its use with a preposition indicates the former (Joüon 79pN).

19 Richelle (*Le testament d'Élisée*, 33–35) defends the plus, arguing that it was lost from (proto-)MT by haplography with the subsequent revision of the G witnesses to conform. He points out that the plus is not identical to the MT reading. While true, neither does it add anything, and the differences account for its addition. Richelle also contends that the plus contributes to the chiastic structure of the passage, but this is so only insofar as it doubles the execution of the order that is already the crux of the structure.

20 Šanda (*Könige* II, 156) raises the possibility of reading לו הכית, "would that you had struck," though he rejects this possibility in favor of MT's "pregnant" construction.

20 **began coming into the land**: So OL. MT, G[BL] + *coming every year* (בא שנה) or *when the new year came* (ἐλθόντος τοῦ ἐνιαυτοῦ).[21]

21 **While a man was being buried**: Lit. *While they were burying a man.*

a raiding band approached them: So G[L] (καὶ ἤγγισε τὸ πειρατήριον αὐτοῖς = ויקרב להם הגדוד). The OL (*cum sepellirent pirate hominem unum accesserunt ad monumentum*) attests a similar reading. MT, G[B]: *they saw the raiding band*, which does not convey the direct nature of the threat.

and fled (וילכו): So OL, G[L]. Preserved in MT, G[B] (and as a double reading in G[L]) as a singular that is construed, according to the Masoretic accentuation (preceded by *athnach*), as referring to the dead man.

When he touched: So G[B]. MT, OL supply *the man.* G[L] + *the one being buried.*

22 **Hazael**: So G[B]. MT, G[L] + *king of Aram.*

Hazael the Aramaean took from [Jehoahaz's] dominion from the sea of the Arabah as far as Aphek: So G[L]. The fact that the information in this verse is alluded to in v. 25 proves it to be original. That said, the sentence presents several difficulties. First, countering previous efforts to identify this expression as a reference to the "Western Sea" or Mediterranean,[22] Richelle shows that the expression θαλάσσης τῆς καθ' ἑσπέραν designates the Dead Sea.[23] Hence there is no reason to identify Aphek as a site on the coastal plain. It is rather somewhere near the Sea of Galilee, most likely En-Gev on the eastern shore.[24] The reference to Hazael as the ἀλλόφυλος is curious, since this is the term generally used elsewhere to translate "Philistine." However, there is precedent in 2 Kgs 8:28, where Hazael is called *king of Aram*, for which one finds βασιλέως ἀλλοφύλων in G[B].[25]

23 G[L] places this verse between vv. 7 and 8. The different locations highlight the nature of the verse as a gloss. While it interrupts the continuity of vv. 22 and 24, dealing

---

21 Burney, *Notes*, 317; Cogan and Tadmor, *II Kings*, 148.

22 Especially A. Rahlfs (*Septuaginta Studien* 3, *Lucians Rezension der Königsbücher* [Göttingen: Vandenhoeck & Ruprecht, 1911], 289), who thought it reflected the translator's misunderstanding and argued that it did not go back to a Hebrew original. More recently Schenker (*Älteste Textgeschichte*, 113–14) also found it to be a reference to the Mediterranean and identifies Aphek as Antipatris (Ras el-Ain) about 20 km east of Joppa.

23 Richelle, *Le testament d'Élisée*, 95–98.

24 On the various candidates for Aphek see the discussion of 1 Kgs 20:26. The site posited by Miller and Hayes (*History*, 346) in the Jezreel Valley near Mount Gilboa is also possible; while not in the Arabah, it would illustrate Hazael's encroachment into Israelilte territory.

25 Other proposed solutions include: (1) correcting ἀλλόφυλον to γαλαάδ (Gilead) (Klostermann, *Könige*, 439), though it is unclear how the corruption could have occurred; (2) perceiving ἀλλόφυλον as a translation of הגוי, itself a corruption of הגל־ל, "Galilee" (Gray, *Kings*, 601); but Galilee cannot be the original reading since the description includes all of the Arabah; (3) seeing ἀλλόφυλον = פלשתים as a replacement for הערלים, "the uncircumcised," which was a corruption of הערים, "the cities" (S. Hasegawa, "The Conquest of Hazael in 2 Kings 13:22 in the Antiochian Text," *JBL* 133 [2014], 64–68); though uncertain, the reconstruction of "cities" is attractive for its match with v. 25. This is one feature of a more extensive reconstruction by Hasegawa that results in quite a different reading from G[L]. It includes mention of Kinneret in place of Aphek and a reversal of order so that the territory is traced from north to south (Kinneret to the Dead Sea) rather than the reverse as in G[L]. Hasegawa ("Conquest," 64–65) and Richelle (*Le testament d'Élisée*, 100) also discuss the unusual accusative form (ἀλλόφυλον).

with Hazael's oppression and his successor, there is a certain logic to this location, explaining Hazael's death and succession by his weaker son as the working out of YHWH's mercy toward Israel. Between vv. 7-8 it relates that YHWH did not allow Israel to fall despite its military nadir under Jehoahaz, but without any account of what happened politically or militarily to avert the fall.

YHWH was gracious and merciful to them: So G^{L}. MT, G^{B} continue with *and turned toward them*, influenced by other passages where the two expressions occur together.[26]

Isaac: So MT. G^{BL} reflect the conjunction before the name.

from his presence: So G^{B}. MT and G^{L} + *until now*.

25 **Jehoash (1)**: So MT, G^{B}. G^{L} precedes with *after Hazael died*, which appears expansive after v. 24.

Three times Jehoash defeated him: So MT, G^{B}. G^{L} is again expansive: *Jehoash defeated Ben-Hadad son of Hazael three times in battle in Aphek according to YHWH's word.*

and recovered the cities of Israel: So MT, G^{B}. G^{L} + *and the things he had taken.*

25+ G^{L}, OL have the concluding regnal formulae for Jehoash here rather than in 13:12-13 or 14:15-16, where MT has them (the latter is partially represented in OL 14:16). Some scholars believe that, as the most appropriate of the three, this is the original location of the formulae.[27] There are, however, reasons to think that this is another instance of hypercorrection in the OG *Vorlage*. See on 14:15-16.

Synchronic Analysis

Two kings, a prophet, and YHWH

The present chapter is built around three characters—two kings of Israel, Jehoahaz and Jehoash, and a prophet, Elisha. In the background but closely related to their activities are the kings of Aram, Hazael and Ben-Hadad. Each of the three main characters receives the focus in turn: Jehoahaz (vv. 1-9, Jehoash (vv. 10-13), and Elisha (vv. 14-25). The lives of all three are determined by another character—YHWH—and their activities are occupied with trying to influence or determine what YHWH does (vv. 4, 14-19).

13:1-4: Jehoahaz's entreaty

The first two verses with the opening regnal formulae of Jehoahaz are standard. He reigns seventeen years, a respectable tenure, and does what YHWH considers evil. The statement in v. 3 that YHWH became angry with Israel is unusual in Samuel and Kings, though it is common in Judges (Judg 2:14, 20; 3:8; 10:7; cf. Num 25:3; Deut 29:26).[28] A similar sentiment is found in 2 Kgs 23:26 near the end of Judah's history. It might be construed as alluding to a "sin of accumulation," since there is no other clear reason why Jehoahaz's offense should be considered worse than his predecessors'. Perhaps this is YHWH's frustration and disappointment that matters did not improve with Jehu. The consequence is military defeat and oppression—what the text terms delivery *into the hand of* a foreign ruler, in this case Hazael and Ben-Hadad of Aram. Israel's plight moves Jehoahaz to entreat

---

26 Trebolle, *Centena*, 180n. Richelle (*Le testament d'Élisée*, 90) reports that G^{L} lacks the phrase *for the sake of his covenant with Abraham, Isaac, and Jacob*. See Fernández and Busto, *El texto antioqueño*, 122.

27 Würthwein, *1. Könige 17–2. Könige 25*, 363, 369.

28 Olley, *Kings*, 279; also his "2 Kings 13: A Cluster of Hope in God," *JSOT* 36 (2011), 202.

YHWH for relief (v. 4). The entreaty places him in the company of Moses (Exod 3:9) and Hezekiah (as reported by Jer 26:19), among others. This is the way punishment is supposed to work as an incentive for repentance, and we are told that YHWH reacts immediately, though he is evidently less motivated by Jehoahaz's entreaty than by Israel's suffering. Jehoahaz, after all, is no Moses or Hezekiah.

13:5-9: The bleakness of Jehoahaz's reign

YHWH sends a *savior* or *deliverer* (מושיע, v. 5). Exactly who this is remains undisclosed; there is no shortage of candidates—Elisha, Jehoahaz himself or his son Jehoash, the Assyrian king Adad-Nirari (who might have drawn Hazael s attention away from Israel). Given the prominence of the term *salvation* or *deliverance* (תשועה) in the story in vv. 14-19, Elisha probably has the best claim to the title because his name means "my god is salvation." The name suggests another candidate—YHWH himself. The anonymity of the *savior* shows that what is important is that the people of Israel come to live in tranquility as *previously*. The word *savior* resonates with the book of Judges, especially after a mention of entreaty. On closer inspection, however, there are clear differences from Judges. YHWH does not *raise up* but *gives* the savior. There is also no mention of military action. Rather, Israel *goes out* from under the hand of the oppressor so as to settle tranquilly *in their homes*. The word *homes* is literally *tents*, so that the image is that of living undisturbed on open land without the protection of a fortified city; it is a metaphor for security.[29] Verses 4-5, in other words, are less about the judges than about the exodus and settlement in Canaan. This is what is meant by *as previously* (כתמול שלשום). YHWH's salvation is restorative. But it does not last. It is as though v. 5 and its last two words especially express a furtive longing on YHWH's part for an ideal time that never was. Israel will not depart from the sins of Jeroboam (v. 6). YHWH reacts with anger and hurt; the punishment is severe, as Israel's army is reduced to virtually nothing—like dust that is threshed or trampled, although the exact nuance of the metaphor is elusive (v. 7). With such a legacy the reference to Jehoahaz's *strength* (גבורתו) in his closing formulae (vv. 8-9) can only be read as sarcasm or as a faint memory of the past long gone.

13:10-17 The opening of Jehoash's reign and the first anecdote from it

Jehoash (vv. 10-13) is a virtual copy of his father. His sixteen-year reign is comparable to his father's seventeen years. Like his father and every other king of Israel he does what YHWH considers evil by continuing in the sin of Jeroboam (v. 11). What distinguishes him, curiously, is the absence of a story or other detail between his opening and closing formulae. There is another set of closing formulae for him (14:15-16), which adds to his distinction. It is as though he is given a second chance, as if his reign was initially dismissed too quickly as just a duplicate of his father's. The stories about him in 13:14-21 and 14:8-14 expand and explore his character in more detail. What emerges is a character of some depth. In 13:14-21 he has an amicable relationship with Elisha. He goes to the prophet when he learns of his illness. He is aware that the illness is serious, and he is genuinely distressed both personally (*my father, my father*) and for the fate of Israel (*Israel's charioteer and horseman*). Elisha tries to assuage Jehoash's anxieties with the symbolic act in vv. 15-17. Elisha issues a series of imperatives (*get ... string ... open ... shoot*), each followed immediately by a notice of the king's compliance. The only

29 Gray's (*Kings*, 594) proposal that this refers to pilgrimage to a central sanctuary for covenant renewal obscures the sense of the metaphor.

interruption is for Elisha's laying-on of hands (v. 16b) in a gesture of unity and support that may also impart a blessing or transfer of power.[30] All of this is a sign act interpreted in v. 17 as *the arrow of* Yhwh's *victory and the arrow of victory in Israel*, with a promise: *You will defeat Aram in Aphek until they are finished.*

13:18-19: Jehoash's chance to destroy Aram

The last phrase in Hebrew (עד־כלה) together with the sign act evokes Zedekiah's oracle in 1 Kgs 22:11. Jehoash was there (22:26). Elisha was not, but he has evidently learned of it from fellow prophets. He speaks with sarcasm or a wink and a nod, reminiscing, as if to say, "Remember when Zedekiah predicted Aram's complete destruction? Now's your chance." It is a warning that the next set of instructions is a test or a trick. Even so, there is nothing in the story in 1 Kings 22 to tell Jehoash how best to respond. He complies immediately with Elisha's order to strike the ground with the arrows, doing so three times (v. 18). Why he stops at three is unclear. Elisha is angry with him for not continuing to five or six times (v. 19) since that would have meant finishing Aram off completely (עד־כלה) (again channeling Zedekiah). The anger may be primarily frustration at a lost opportunity and the damage that will result to Israel.[31] This seems unfair to Jehoash, who does not know in advance what striking the ground means or how many times he should do it. There is no account of his reaction. The narrative places all the focus on Elisha, giving him the power and control. Jehoash must be happy with the three victories he gets.

13:20-21: Elisha's post-mortem power

The next anecdote (vv. 20-21) relates Elisha's power even after death. It is set at least a year after his passing, based on the deterioration of the flesh from his bones (v. 21). Another man is about to be buried when those carrying his corpse are frightened by a band of Moabite raiders operating in the area. They hurriedly dispose of the body in the closest tomb, which happens to be Elisha's. Inertia carries the corpse in the tomb until it comes in contact with the bones of Elisha (וילך ויגע), at which point the dead man revives and stands up. The divine power lodged in Elisha's very bones was evidently so great that it either took a long time to dissipate completely or never did so; it seems that his bones would be capable of such wonders today if one could find them and touch them.

13:22-25: Oppression and recovery

While there is little new activity described in the last segment of the chapter (vv. 22-25), these four verses are quite busy in what they contribute to the account of Jehoash's reign. They sum up Israel's changing political and military relationship with Aram, offer a theological explanation for these changes and for Israel's survival, and provide a fulfillment notice for Elisha's promise to Jehoash of victories over Aram. The resumptive function of v. 22 is conveyed by the pluperfect sense of the verb in its subject-first sentence. It ignores the brief respite that came to Israel as a result of Jehoahaz's entreaty (vv. 4-5) and characterizes his reign as one of oppression at the hands of Hazael. The recovery comes after Hazael's death during the tenure of his successor, Ben-Hadad, when Jehoash is able to restore lost territory. Verse 25 correlates the recovery with the three

---

30 Hens-Piazza, *Kings*, 322; Wiseman, *Kings*, 257.

31 G lends itself to this interpretation by having Elisha become grieved (ἐλυπήθη) rather than angry, which balances Jehoash's weeping in v. 14. See Richelle, *Le testament d'Élisée*, 18, 47, 63. Note, though, that this rendering of √קצף also occurs in 1 Sam 29:4; Isa 57:17; Est 1:12; 2:21, where anger seems to be indicated.

victories promised by Elisha as a benefit from Jehoash's visit to the dying prophet in vv. 14-19.

13:23: Yhwh's covenant love for Israel

Lest anyone give Jehoash credit for the recovery or misunderstand it as the product of Elisha's bellomancy, v. 23 explains the real theological cause. Israel's survival was because of YHWH's mercy and loyalty to Abraham, Isaac, and Jacob. The covenant with the patriarchs thus has the same effect for Israel as the covenant with David for Judah.[32] Like the Davidic covenant, the patriarchal promise may be interpreted as a ground for hope beyond Israel's end as a kingdom or as an explanation for why Israel lasted as long as it did but was ultimately destroyed when YHWH's patience finally gave out,[33] or perhaps both. The verse is unique in the book of Kings and completely unexpected. It is a surprise, given the disapproval of the Northern Kingdom in Kings, to find such a verse at all—one that expresses YHWH's love and mercy toward Israel. The reference to YHWH as gracious and merciful is not common in Kings. It is used in a range of other settings, especially liturgical ones (Exod 33:19; 34:6; 2 Chr 30:9; Neh 9:17; Ps 86:15; 103:8; 111:4; 112:4; 145:8; Joel 2:13; Jon 4:2). There is only one other reference in all of Kings to the three patriarchs (1 Kgs 18:36), and it has nothing like the theological elaboration found in the present verse. The final phrase of the verse, *until now*, is open to the same ambiguity of interpretation as is the verse as a whole. It may represent a glance ahead to 2 Kgs 17:20 and to 2 Kings 25 in acknowledgment that YHWH's grace and love would soon and ultimately give way to judgment for Israel and Judah, or it may be intended to offer hope for future restoration of Israel or its remnant based on YHWH's continued love and covenant faithfulness.

Diachronic Analysis

13:1: The synchronism for Jehoahaz

The chapter begins with the opening regnal formulae for Jehoahaz (v. 1), which are regular in form. As previously, it is reasonable to assume that DtrH had official sources of some kind for the synchronism and length of reign. The synchronism ascribes Jehoahaz's accession to the twenty-third year of Joash of Judah (who reigned forty years according to 12:2). Jehoahaz's predecessor, Jehu, reigned twenty-eight years according to 10:36 (MT). Since Joash replaced Athaliah in her seventh year, Jehoahaz should have acceded to the throne of Israel in Joash's twenty-first year (28-7 = 21).[34] The discrepancy is usually explained as reflecting either a coregency or Israel's adoption of antedating for reckoning Jehoahaz's reign. While both options are theoretically possible, there is no compelling support for either. There is no hint in the biblical text of any coregency at either end of Jehoahaz's reign. The appeal to antedating becomes arbitrary when one assumes that the same kingdom alternated between methods as a means of explain-

32 Provan, *Kings*, 229–30.

33 Nelson, *Kings*, 217–18.

34 Josephus's (*Ant.* 9.173) dating to Joash's 21st year is probably a correction based on this calculation.

ing otherwise unruly figures.[35] Another possibility is that the figure of Joash's twenty-third year is an error. This was the same year that Joash instituted his program of financing for the temple (12:6). The text makes no connection between the two events, leaving the impression that the common figure is coincidental. However, given the chronological problems in 13:1, one wonders whether it was influenced by 12:6.[36] In a second, related chronological problem 13:1 ascribes seventeen years to Jehoahaz, while v. 10 (MT) assumes a fourteen-year reign, since he is succeeded in Joash's thirty-seventh year after taking the throne in his twenty-third year. If twenty-third is an error for twenty-first, the two regnal lengths are close but still not identical, so the problem remains unresolved.[37]

13:2-3: DtrH's evaluation of Jehoahaz

The indictment of Jehoahaz for persisting in the sin of Jeroboam (v. 2) continues DtrH's etiological theme for Northern kings. Jehu's heirs are not accused of worshiping Baal as were the Ahabids. DtrH also uses the sin of Jeroboam to account theologically for Israel's complete subjugation to Aram by Hazael (v. 3). This is a fulfillment of the disaster foreseen by Elisha (8:12). The expression כל־הימים contrasts Jehoahaz's reign, dominated by Hazael, with that of Jehoash, when Yhwh gives Israel victory. This is in agreement with vv. 22, 25, though its historical accuracy is questionable. The details are discussed in the context of those verses. Suffice it to say here that Hazael seems to have died at least three or four years before Jehoahaz, making the latter the king responsible for Israel's early success against Aram.[38] If so, the account here exemplifies DtrH's scheme of periodization whereby the period of oppression was the reigns of Hazael and Jehoahaz while liberation was realized under Ben-Hadad and Jehoash. Such a periodization illustrated the value of entreaty.[39]

13:7: The continuation of v. 3

That v. 7 is the continuation of v. 3 is clear in G^L, which begins with the adverb "until," though it is apparent as well in MT, which starts with כי. In both cases the subject of the verb השאיר is Yhwh. The exceedingly small numbers of military personnel and equipment, which may derive from DtrH's sources, illustrate Israel's defenselessness. By contrast, Ahab contributed 2000 chariots and 10,000 foot soldiers to the battle at Qarqar (*ANET* 279). MT attributes the same number of infantry (10,000) to Jehoahaz in the present verse, but the figure seems large for Jehoahaz's diminished army and it may be a mistake, as argued in the Notes. If not, it may indicate that Aram had focused, successfully, on reducing Israel's chariotry.[40] The metaphor of military defeat as threshing is found in Isa 41:15; Amos 1:3; Micah 4:13; Hab 3:12, as well as in Tiglath-Pileser III's inscrip-

---

35 Thiele's (*Mysterious Numbers,* 105) treatment of Jehoahaz illustrates the arbitrariness of this kind of appeal. Gray (*Kings,* 593) suggests that the Judahite writer assumed that antedating, used in Judah, was also in effect in Israel.

36 Jehoahaz's accession in Joash's 23rd year agrees with the OG chronology in 10:36+ where Jehu acceded in Athaliah's second year, but this is due to OG's chronological adjustment, which is part of the reason for the plus.

37 Cogan and Tadmor (*II Kings,* 142–43) posit a coregency in order to harmonize the 14- and 17-year figures.

38 See Miller and Hayes (*History,* 336–47), who think Jehoahaz is the "savior" in v. 5. But this does not account for the literary tensions between vv. 3 and 7 and vv. 4-6.

39 See Na'aman, "Forced Participation," 87.

40 Gray, *Kings,* 596.

tions.[41] It may have been suggested here by Josiah's handling of non-Yahwistic cultic items in 2 Kgs 23:6, 15. The people who worship images are treated the way the images themselves should be treated—by being pulverized to *dust* (G^L). Hazael thus objectifies the Israelites and perhaps treats them as religiously illegitimate. Such treatment is considered criminal by Amos (1:3).

13:8-11: Regnal formulae for Jehoahaz and Jehoash

The next four verses (8-11) consist of the closing formulae for Jehoahaz and opening formulae for Jehoash. Jehoahaz's closing formulae (vv. 8-9) curiously contain a reference to his strength (גבורתו). This element may be formulaic and without historical value.[42] It occurs for every king of Israel from Omri to Jeroboam except Ahaziah and Joram. Alternatively, it might support the view that DtrH's presentation of Jehoahaz as extremely weak is theological periodization, and Jehoahaz did have success against Aram toward the end of his reign. With Jehoash's succession (vv. 10-11) Israel and Judah have kings with the same name for the second time in their shared history. Here, though, there is no question of their being the same individual as was the case with J[eh]oram. Their overlap will be brief, since Joash of Judah is near the end of his forty-year tenure while Jehoash of Israel is at the beginning of his sixteen years.

12:4-6a in their initial location

In the reconstruction proposed here vv. 4-6a come next. They initially concerned Jehoash, but his name was replaced with that of Jehoahaz after they were moved to their present location in MT. They interrupt the continuity between vv. 3 and 7 and contradict them in implying that Yhwh gave Israel victory during Jehoahaz's reign. The proposed reconstruction portrays that reign as Israel's military nadir, with limited victories under Jehoash and then full restoration under Jeroboam (14:26-27). This is not a historical claim; it reflects DtrH's periodization.[43] The depiction of the king as pious, entreating Yhwh in time of crisis (v. 4), might seem surprising initially, since the *sin of Jeroboam* brands him as rebellious and apostate. However, his maintenance of the shrines founded by Jeroboam was a service of piety and is therefore perfectly complemented by his entreaty to Yhwh.

13:5: Israel's "savior"

The identity of the "savior" or "deliverer" (v. 5) has occasioned a great deal of discussion. At least seven candidates have been put forward. The first is Jehoash, whose strongest support is in Elisha's promise of threefold *victory* (the same root as *deliverer*) in 13:17, 19 and the fulfillment notice in v. 25b.[44] Second is Jehoahaz, assuming that the success against Aram and Ben-Hadad began during his reign.[45] Jeroboam II is third, based especially on the statement in 14:27 that Yhwh *saved them* through the agency of Jeroboam.[46] A fourth candidate is Elisha,

---

41 See the *CAD* entry on *dajaštu* (D, 33b).

42 Benzinger, *Könige*, 162; Würthwein, *1. Könige 17–2. Könige 25*, 160.

43 T. Mullen ("Royal Dynastic Grant") takes Israel's survival as a benefit of the promise to Jehu in 10:30, which he (Mullen) stylizes as a royal grant according to DtrH ideology. His article highlights the surprising absence of any reference to the promise to Jehu, supporting the attribution of 10:30 to a post-DtrH hand.

44 So Qimḥi (Rosenberg, *Kings II*, 336); Benzinger, *Könige*, 162; A. Cody, "A New Inscription from Tell al-Rimāḥ and Jehoash of Israel," *CBQ* 32 (1970), 336–37; Sweeney, *Kings*, 357.

45 Miller and Hayes, *History*, 336–47.

46 Kittel, *Könige*, 257; Montgomery, *Kings*, 433; Šanda, *Könige* II, 153; Skinner, *Kings*, 348; Stade, "Miscellen 10," 296; Thenius, *Könige*, 336.

whose name incorporates the ישע root and who endows Jehoash with victories.[47] Still a fifth proposal is the Assyrian Adad-Nirari III because the Assyrian assaults on Damascus occupied Hazael's attention and distracted him from his oppression of Israel, thereby relieving the pressure on them.[48] Sixth, Zakkur of Hamath has been nominated because he resisted a coalition of kings led by Ben-Hadad and in so doing probably relieved Aramaean pressure on Israel at least temporarily.[49] Finally, the anonymity of the *deliverer* has drawn the attention of some scholars away from any specific human individual and highlighted YHWH's role as Israel's deliverer.[50] The difficulty of identifying a specific deliverer in preference to the other possibilities is a point in favor of adopting the G^{BL} reading *victory, deliverance, salvation.* This reading obviates speculation about the identity of the figure here and supports the understanding of YHWH as the source of Israel's victories. It also accords well with the use of the root ישע in association with various candidates. As already observed (Synchronic Analysis) the language and imagery here are not focused on the judges, as might appear at first glance, but rehearse the exodus and settlement.

13:6: DtrH's sin of Jeroboam with a PN addition

Verse 6a reiterates the accusation about the sin of Jeroboam from v. 11 but democratizes it, applying it to the people of Israel. This could be taken as an indication that vv. 4-6a are post-DtrH except that one of the ways DtrH has of expressing the motif is that Jeroboam made Israel sin (החטיא, e.g., 13:11). Also, the subject of the verb *turn* is the *children of Israel* in v. 5. These are reminders that the sin of Jeroboam is committed not just by Israel's kings but by the people as well. The repetition of the theme was what led to the loss of vv. 4-6a from their initial location after v. 11, after which they were mistakenly reinserted between vv. 3 and 7. Verse 6b is secondary. It is introduced with וגם, a common marker of additions, and abruptly changes the subject from the sin of Jeroboam. The asherah mentioned in v. 6b is apparently the one installed by Ahab in 1 Kgs 16:33, an indication that v. 6b comes from PN.[51]

The absence of 13:12-13

The instance of Jehoash's closing regnal formulae in vv. 12-13 MT is not included in this passage because this is probably not their original location, as explained in the Note. Their original location is 14:15-16 where they are discussed in more detail.

---

47 Gray, *Kings*, 595; Hobbs, *Kings*, 168.

48 W. W. Hallo, "From Qarqar to Carchemish: Assyria and Israel in the Light of New Discoveries," *BA* 23 (1960), 42; M. Haran, "The Rise and Decline of the Empire of Jeroboam Ben Joash," *VT* 17 (1967), 267–68; Hentschel, *2 Könige*, 59; B. Mazar, "The Aramean Empire and Its Relations with Israel," *BA* 25 (1962), 115; Wiseman, *Kings*, 255. Landersdorfer (*Könige*, 184) takes the reference to "savior" as a pun on Adad-Nirari, "Adad is my savior."

49 S. A. Cook, *CAH* 3 (1925), 376.

50 Hens-Piazza, *Kings*, 320; Olley, *Kings*, 280 and "2 Kings 13," 203–204; Würthwein, *1. Könige 17–2. Könige 25*, 362.

51 Some have suggested that this was a replacement for Ahab's asherah (Kittel, *Könige*, 257; Landersdorfer (*Könige*, 185); Provan, *Kings*, 231), but there is no intervening notice about its demolition or reconstruction. On the nature of the asherah see on 1 Kgs 16:33. If the notice has historical validity in that the asherah was indeed a part of the worship of YHWH, this would explain why it was not removed by Jehu (2 Kgs 10:26-27).

13:14-21: PN's interpolation of Elisha *legenda*

The two *legenda* about Elisha in vv. 14-21 were interpolated by PN into DtrH's account. The choice of the present (MT) location for them may have been influenced by the reference in v. 5 to YHWH bringing deliverance (or a deliverer, MT) from Aram. The deliverance was wrought by Jehoash in DtrH's account (v. 25), but vv. 14-19 credit it to Elisha. The *legenda* respectively anticipate and assume his death, but they were independent of one another. Still, the notice in v. 14 that Elisha had become fatally ill sets the stage for both stories. The verse begins with a subject-first sentence, an indication of the independence of the episode it recounts. The king is identified by name as an accommodation to the context but is otherwise anonymous and designated by title, *the king of Israel*. He comes to visit the ailing prophet and weeps over him (על־פניו; cf. Gen 50:1). The location of the visit is unclear. The most prominent suggestions are Samaria, Gilgal, Jericho, and Abel-Meholah (Elisha's hometown). The last three are in the Jordan Valley and would suit the reference to the king going down to visit. However, the verb may indicate Elisha's abode in a lower part of Samaria than the palace (cf. 3:12; 6:33; 7:17) or perhaps is used because Elisha is sick in bed, so that its occurrence here is not decisive for determining the story's location.[52] All the places named were (south)west of Aram and of the probable location of Aphek, so the reference to shooting the arrow eastward in v. 17 does not narrow the list. However, if the OL reading, Hazeroth, is correct, the location of the story is most likely in Samaria.

13:15-17: Elisha's sign act

Jehu's weeping is not occasioned by sorrow at Elisha's impending death but by trepidation at what his death will mean for Israel, especially its military security. Such is the sense behind his outcry in v. 14bβ. The same title occurs in 2:12 in the context of Elijah's transition to heaven and is informed by the scene in 6:15-17. *Father* is a title of respect especially for an older man. The remainder of the title alludes to Elisha's command of heavenly chariotry, illustrated in 6:15-17. As a man of god who has the heavenly army at his disposal Elisha is more valuable in war than Israel's entire chariot force. Elisha seeks to allay the king's fears with the sign in vv. 15-17. He tells the king to string a bow and shoot an arrow eastward out of the window. As the king strings the bow Elisha places his hands on those of the king.[53] This is not a blessing but the imparting of the power to defeat Aram. The shooting of the arrow functions as a sign act to illustrate and ensure victory.[54] The phrase translated *completely* (עד־כלה), is similar to that used by Zedekiah in 1 Kgs 22:11 (עד־כלתם); he also used a symbolic act to predict Aram's complete destruction. The similarity of terminology, sign, and message between the two passages is striking and yet one more connection between the present story and the three battles in 1 Kings 20; 22.

PN's additions in vv. 17, 18-19

The mention of YHWH's arrow of victory in v. 17 is added by PN in order to make the victory YHWH's doing rather than Elisha's. PN also supplemented the

52 Schmitt (*Elisa*, 174–75) argues that ירד in these passages does not mean "go down" but only "come" or "go" and does not indicate that Elisha lived in a lower part of the city. He thinks that ירד in 13:14 favors a site in the Jordan Valley rather than Samaria. He argues for Gilgal based on vv. 20-21, but they were initially independent.

53 The meaning of this symbolic act is paralleled by an Egyptian relief in which Seth supports Thutmoses III with a drawn bow. See Keel, *Wirkmächtige Siegeszeichen*, image 56 and the discussion of the magic act on pp. 113–21.

54 On the location of Aphek, if one follows the MT reading, see on 1 Kgs 20:26, 30. Some have argued that *in Aphek* is a gloss. Cf. Šanda *Könige* II, 156; Hentschel, *2 Könige*, 61.

legenda with the act of bellomancy in vv. 18-19. As often noted, these verses contain several significant changes vis-à-vis vv. 14-17. The arrows function differently; they are no longer part of a symbolic act but now serve an act of sympathetic magic since the number of times the king strikes the ground with them determines the number of victories he will have. The relationship between Elisha and the king is also different. The *man of god* (v. 19) becomes angry with the king for striking the ground only three times, although he gives no directions beforehand about either the number or purpose of the strikes. Efforts on the part of commentators to find fault with the king for vacillating, thinking small, or acting without enthusiasm or conviction are not supported by the text and are not convincing.[55] Rather, vv. 18-19 are to be explained as an addition correcting the promise of complete victory over Aram and limiting the number of victories won by Israel to three, probably to connect to the three battle accounts now in 1 Kings 20; 22.[56]

13:20-21: The *legenda* about the power in Elisha's bones

The tale in vv. 20-21 has no connection to a king or warfare. It is a basic *legenda* illustrating Elisha's continuing power even in the grave. It was originally independent of vv. 14-19 and was joined to it because of references in both to Elisha's death. Its geographical setting is not specified but is probably Gilgal or Jericho in view of the incursion of raiders from Moab. Verse 20 sets the scene by explaining that Elisha had died and been buried. His burial was not "six feet under" in a grave but in a rock-cut tomb where his corpse would have been laid out on a shelf so that his flesh decomposed over time, leaving only his bones. The verse also explains that Moabite raiding groups had begun coming into Israel. MT offers an obscure temporal note (בא שנה) indicating that this occurred annually or at the beginning of the year. However, the phrase is textually dubious (see the Note) and the raids could be understood as occurring more frequently and sporadically. In the *legenda* itself (v. 21) a raiding band approaches as a man is being buried. Fearing for their lives, the burial party cut their task short by depositing (lit. *throwing*) the dead man into Elisha's tomb. The story thus assumes that Elisha's tomb, probably one of a complex, is nearby and readily accessible, that is, easily opened. They act in haste, carelessly tossing the dead man's corpse very close to Elisha's bones, perhaps even on top of them. Upon making contact, the dead man revives and stands up. What happened next—how long the man lived after his reanimation, whether he and the burial party escaped the raiders, etc.—is not recounted. The focus is on the power latent in the dead prophet's bones even after his decomposition. The story recalls Elisha's previous revival of a dead person in 2 Kings 4, though the present tale is more impressive for its lack of reference to any kind of symbolic magic or ritual. Neither is there a reference to Yhwh. The power is in the man of god's bones.

13:22: Hazael's oppression

Verses 22-25 give a kind of summary of the reigns of Jehoahaz and Jehoash vis-à-vis Aram. They are similar in this respect and complementary to vv. 3-7, offering a theological (entreaty) and a historical (change of regime) explanation

55 Seow (*Kings*, 238) proposes that the king shows disregard for holy war as in 1 Kgs 20:25. The possible connection is intriguing, but there is no indication in 2 Kgs 13:18-19 that holy war is at issue.

56 Hentschel, *2 Könige*, 60–61; Jones, *Kings*, 498; Rehm, *Das zweite Buch der Könige*, 132; Würthwein *1. Könige 17–2. Könige 25*, 365. Schmitt (*Elisa*, 80–81) assigns vv. 18-19 to his "man of god" redaction because of the use of the title in v. 19.

for Israel's resurgence, much like the double explanation for the division of the kingdom in 1 Kings 11–12 (Solomon's sin vs. Solomon's oppressive labor force). Verse 22a presents or illustrates the major chronological problem of this chapter and may stem from source material available to DtrH. Assyria's preoccupation with internal problems, beginning about 838 BCE, drew its attention away from Damascus and freed Hazael to expand his holdings at Israel's expense already during Jehu's reign.[57] The subjugation of Israel continued throughout Hazael's reign. He appears to have died some time shortly before 806/5 BCE.[58] Jehoahaz's death has typically been dated around or shortly after the turn of the century, ca. 799–797 BCE[59] but may have occurred as early as 802.[60] In either case the references in vv. 5, 22 to Hazael oppressing Israel during Jehoahaz's entire lifetime are somewhat hyperbolic and are best viewed as periodization, as explained above at v. 4: Jehoahaz's reign was the time of oppression and Jehoash's the time of recovery resulting from his turning to Yhwh for help. The continuation preserved in the G^L plus in v. 22b details the territory taken by Hazael from Jehoahaz, i.e., the Arabah, the Jordan Valley, from the Dead Sea to the Sea of Galilee. The information complements that in 10:32-33, where Hazael took Israelite territory east of the Jordan in Gilead and Bashan from Jehu. Under Jehoahaz he moved farther west, wresting the Arabah from Israel.

13:23: A theological addition with a priestly perspective

Verse 23 interrupts the historical summary to address the question of Israel's continued existence, given its low state. The mention of Yhwh's covenant with the patriarchs is unusual; references to the patriarchs are rare in the Former Prophets and in preexilic literature in general in the HB. This verse is influenced by Priestly ideology (Exod 2:24[61]; 6:3-4; Lev 26:42; Ps 105:8-10). Its final phrase,

---

57 An additional factor may have been Israel's loss of its alliance with Phoenicia following the assassination of Jezebel, as Robinson (*Second Kings*, 121) suggests.

58 This conclusion is based on the assumption that Mari' in the Saba'a inscription, which is dated to Adad-Nirari's fifth year (806/5 BCE), is a title (Cody, "New Inscription," 327) or hypocoristic (W. F. Albright, "A Votive Stele Erected by Ben-Hadad I of Damascus to the God Melcarth," *BASOR* 87 [1942], 28n; F. M. Cross, "The Stele Dedicated to Melcarth by Ben-Hadad of Damascus," *BASOR* 205 [1972]: 36–42) for Bar-Hadad, Hazael's son. The Zakkur inscription names Bar-Hadad as the leader of the coalition attacking Zakkur, presumably with the intent of forcing him to join them against Assyria. While the Zakkur inscription is undated and its date as well as the date of the event it describes are disputed, Na'aman ("Forced Participation," 85–86) has made the case for dating the event to 804.

59 E.g., Gray, *Kings*, 601; Jones *Kings*, 505.

60 So A. Jepsen ("Ein neuer Fixpunkt für die Chronologie der israelitischen Könige?" *VT* 20 [1970]: 359–61) based on correlation of the campaign mentioned in the Rimaḥ inscription with that of the Assyrian eponym list. Also J. A. Soggin, "Ein ausserbiblisches Zeugnis für die Chronologie des Jᵉhô'āš/Jô'āš, König von Israel," *VT* 20 (1970): 366–68. The inscription mentions both Mari' and Adad-nirari III's receipt of tribute from Jehoash "of the land of the Samarians." See S. Page, "A Stela of Adad-Nirari III and Nergal-Ereš from Tell al Rimah," *Iraq* 30 (1968): 139–53 and "Joash and Samaria in a New Stela Excavated at Tell Rimah, Iraq," *VT* 19 (1969): 483–84.

61 Exod 2:24 says that Yhwh remembered his covenant with the patriarchs when he heard the groaning of the Israelites in Egypt. Hence the reference to the patriarchal covenant in 2 Kgs 13:23 also participates in the exodus motif that is more pronounced in 13:4-5.

until now (עד־עתה) may be even later. It is suspect textually (absent from G^B) and literarily.[62]

13:24-25a: Some restoration under Jehoash

The implication of vv. 24-25a that the regnal transitions in Aram and Israel took place at the same time is due to telescoping and periodization. Their placement here also serves the ideological purpose of illustrating Yhwh's delivery of his people in fulfillment of prophecy. These factors caution against the assumption that the verses were drawn directly from an official source. They are DtrH's handiwork. The oppression that Israel suffered at the hands of Aram probably did begin to change after Hazael's death and replacement by his son Ben-Hadad. This may have had less to do with a difference between the Aramaean kings than with Assyria's renewed aggression toward Aram under Adad-Nirari III. This forced Aram to turn its efforts toward defending itself and away from trying to dominate Israel. If Hazael died several years before Jehoahaz, then Jehoahaz rather than Jehoash may have been the king who recovered the cities mentioned in v. 25. Under DtrH's periodization scheme the cities recovered by Jehoash would be west of the Jordan, since Jehu had lost those on the east while Jehoahaz lost the Arabah (v. 22 G^L) and cities presumably on the west.[63]

13:25b: Three victories over Aram

The reference to three victories in v. 25b is PN's addition, fulfilling Elisha's prophecy of three in vv. 18-19 and entered with the addition of 13:14-21. The similarity to 1 Kgs 20:34 once again highlights the connection between the battle stories in 1 Kings 20; 22 and the Elisha legends in 13:14-21.[64]

Synthesis

Disobedience and entreaty in DtrH

The constituent elements and layers of this chapter deal with the theological key to matters of military success, national security, and ultimately national survival for Israel. DtrH synthesized an era of complex international politics into two periods, disobedience and entreaty. Unrelenting perpetuation of the sin of Jeroboam led to severe military decline and extensive loss of national territory under Jehoa-

---

62 Richelle (*Le testament d'Élisée*, 91–92) suggests that it is *une imitation maladroit* of the more common עד־היום. *Pace* Sweeney (*Kings*, 361), who ascribes these words to an eighth-century writer who has yet to experience Israel's fall. Cf. also J. Van Seters, "Confessional Reformulation in the Exilic Period," *VT* 22 (1972), esp. 453–54.

63 Barnes, *Kings*, 288; Cogan and Tadmor, *II Kings*, 149; Wiseman, *Kings*, 258. If this recovery is linked with the battles in 1 Kgs 20; 22, however, the distinction between east and west will not hold, since Ramat-Gilead is east of the Jordan.

64 Assuming the connection between these two passages, Miller and Hayes (*History*, 343–45; also Miller, "Elisha Cycle," 442–43) give two additional arguments for Jehoahaz rather than Jehoash as the victorious Israelite king: the identity of the king's son in 1 Kgs 22:26 as Joash and the death of the king in the story in 1 Kings 22, which suggests that the victories took place at the end rather than the beginning of the king's reign. Other scholars who accept the connection of 1 Kgs 20; 22 as displaced fulfillments of Elisha's prediction of victory continue to maintain Jehoash as the successful king in line with DtrH's presentation. See Pitard (*Ancient Damascus*, 122–24), who follows Jepsen (*Israel und Damaskus*, 157) and Whitley ("Deuteronomic Presentation," 144–45).

haz. Jehoash's pious entreaty of YHWH stirred him to grant Israel victory over its oppressors and recovery of its lands. But entreaty alone would not be enough without real repentance and adherence to the exclusive worship of YHWH in Jerusalem. Jehoash's failure to stop the sin of Jeroboam bodes particularly ill for Israel.

PN's revision with prophetic *legenda*

The prophetic tales in vv. 14-21 see the key as one of personnel, specifically prophets. In the first *legenda* behind vv. 14-17 Elisha on his own prophesies the impending victory and gives a sign, with the announcement to guarantee it. PN's revision of the story explicitly attributed the victory to YHWH, but it also produced a picture of Elisha as rather capricious. It is good to have a prophet on your side, but prophets can be unpredictable and uncontrollable.

Israel's survival through Yhwh's mercy

The gloss in v. 23 stressed YHWH's mercy and compassion, and his loyalty to the covenant with the patriarchs ensuring his care for their descendants. The verse is reassuring: Israel's survival does not depend on humans, who are rebellious and disobedient, but on YHWH who is faithful and loving. But the reassurance is arrested by the final words of the verse (MT), *until now* or, as we might say, *yet.* It undercuts the message of the verse by implying that YHWH's mercy and patience and thus Israel's survival are not infinite. Either they are stretching thin or the hand that penned these words is aware that they reached a point of exhaustion.

The Reigns of Amaziah of Judah and Jeroboam II of Israel (2 Kings 14)

Text

[DtrH's sources; DtrH; Additions to DtrH]
1 In the second year of Joash son of Joahaz king of Israel, Amaz-
iah son of Joash began to reign over Judah. 2 He was twenty-five
years old when he became king, and he reigned twenty-nine years
in Jerusalem. His mother's name was Jehoaddan from Jerusalem.
3 He did what YHWH considered right—only not like David his ancestor—according
to all that Joash his father had done. 4 Only the cultic installations were not re-
moved; the people continued slaughtering and sacrificing at the cultic installations.
5 When the kingdom was firmly in his grasp he executed his servants who had as-
sassinated his father. 6 He did not have their children executed, as it is written in the
scroll of the law of Moses which YHWH commanded: "The parents shall not be exe-
cuted for the children, nor shall the children be executed for the parents. Rather,
each person will die for his sin." 22 He it was who rebuilt Elath and re-
stored it to Judah after the king lay with his forebears. 7 He it was who de-
feated 10,000 Edomites in Salt Valley and captured the Crag in
the battle, naming it Joktheel, which remains its name till to-
day. 8 Then Amaziah sent messengers to Jehoash son of Jehoahaz son of Jehu
king of Israel to say, "Come, let's look one another in the face." 9 Jehoash king of Is-
rael sent to Amaziah king of Judah, "The thornbush that was in Lebanon sent
to the cedar tree that was in Lebanon saying, 'Give your daugh-
ter to my son as a wife.' But when the wild animals that were in Leba-
non passed by, they trampled the thornbush. 10 You did indeed defeat
Edom and your pride has swelled you to boastfulness. Now stay home. Why should
you stir up trouble for yourself and fall—you and Judah with you? 11 But Amaziah
would not listen. So Jehoash king of Israel went up, and he and Amaz-
iah king of Judah faced each other in Bethshemesh, which be-
longed to Judah. 12 Judah was defeated before Israel so that they
all fled home. 13 Having captured Amaziah in Bethshemesh, Je-
hoash king of Israel brought him to Jerusalem where he tore down
the wall of Jerusalem for 400 cubits from the Ephraim Gate to the
Corner Gate. 14 Taking the gold and silver that were found in
YHWH's temple and in the treasuries of the king's palace, as well
as hostages, he returned to Samaria. 15 The rest of the affairs of Jehoash,
including all that he accomplished—his strength and how he fought with Amaziah
king of Judah—are of course written on the scroll of the chronicles of the kings of Is-
rael. 16 Joash lay down with his forebears and was buried in Samaria with the kings

of Israel. Jeroboam his son reigned in his place. 17 Amaziah son of Joash king of Israel lived fifteen years after the death of Jehoash son of Jehoahaz king of Israel. 18 The rest of Amaziah's affairs, including all that he accomplished, are of course written on the scroll of the chronicles of the kings of Judah. 19 When a conspiracy arose against him in Jerusalem he fled to Lachish. But they sent to Lachish after him and killed him there. 20 Then they brought him up on horses so that he was buried in Jerusalem with his forebears in the city of David. 21 All the people of Judah took Azariah, who was sixteen years old, and made him king in place of his father Amaziah. 23 In the fifteenth year of Amaziah son of Joash king of Judah, Jeroboam son of Joash began to reign over Israel in Samaria forty-one years. 24 He did what YHWH considered evil, not turning from the sin of Jeroboam the son of Nebat who made Israel sin. 25 He it was who restored the border of Israel from the entrance of Hamath to the Sea of the Arabah according to the word of YHWH the god of Israel who spoke through the agency of Jonah son of Amittai the prophet who was from Gath Hepher. 26 For YHWH had seen the very bitter affliction of Israel; for it was pulverized; there was no ruler-deliverer left and no one helping Israel. 27 YHWH had not wanted to wipe out Israel's name from under the heavens so he saved them through the agency of Jeroboam son of Joash. 28 The rest of the affairs of Jeroboam, all that he did, and his strength with which he fought [...] are of course written on the scroll of the chronicles of the kings of Israel. 29 When Jeroboam lay with his forebears and was buried in Samaria with the kings of Israel, Zechariah his son reigned in his place.

Textual Notes

1 **Amaziah**: See on 12:22.
over Judah: See on 8:16.

2 **Jehoaddan**: So MT *qere'*, 2 Chr 25:1: יהועדן. MT *ketiv*: יהועדין. It means "YHWH is bliss."[1]

3 **had done**: Deleting the final עשה of the verse as a dittography.

4 **were not removed**: A regular variant between MT and G^{BL}. MT has לא־סרו in other instances of the formula in 1 Kgs 15:14; 22:44; 2 Kgs 12:4; 15:4, 35 but הוא הסיר־ (*he removed*) in 2 Kgs 18:4; cf. 18:22; 23:19. G^{BL} have *he did not remove* in all these instances except for 2 Kgs 12:4.

5 **in his grasp**: Lit. *in his hand*. So MT, G^{B}. G^{L}: *in the hand of Amaziah*.
his father: So G^{BL}. MT: *the king his father*.

6 **their children**: So G^{L}, 2 Chr 25:4. MT, G^{B}: *the children of the assassins* (בני המכים).
as it is written: Preceded by כי in 2 Chr 25:4, resulting from dittography of the *kaph* in ככתוב.
law of Moses: So MT, G^{L}. G^{B}: *laws of Moses*.
be executed (2): So MT, G^{BL}. 2 Chr 25:4 has the active form (לא־ימותו) *they will not die*.
Rather: So MT (כי אם), G^{BL} (ἀλλ' ἤ). 2 Chr 25:4 has כי.

1 Noth, *Personennamen*, 166.

will die: So MT *ketiv* (ימות), G^{BL} (ἀποθανεῖται). MT *qere'*: *will be killed* (יומת). 2 Chr 25:2 has the *Qal* plural, "they will die" (ימותו), while Deut 24:16 has the *Hop'al* plural (יומתו).

for his sin: So MT, G^{L}, 2 Chr 25:4. G^{B}: *for his sins.*

22 In its present location this verse is appended to Amaziah's closing formulae and the account of his assassination and burial (compare v. 25). It is not clear whether it refers to Amaziah or to Azariah. Some scholars propose moving it to chapter 15.[2] Others point out its affinity with 14:7 in that access to the port at Elath with its lucrative trade would be a logical reason for war with Edom. It begins, as does 14:7, with הוא followed by a perfect, and this would provide a trigger for haplography if it preceded v. 7 as proposed here. The second half of the verse (*after the king lay with his forebears*) would have been added after the displacement to make clear that it referred to Azariah and not to his father Amaziah.[3]

7 **in Salt Valley**: So MT *ketiv*, 2 Chr 25:11; cf. 1 Chr 18:12. The *qere'* lacks the definite article on *salt*; cf. 2 Sam 8:13; Ps 60:2. G^{B}: Ῥεμέλε is a corrupt transliteration. G^{L} + *in battle.*

and captured: Reading ויתפש for MT's ותפש.[4]

Joktheel: So MT (יקתאל). G^{BL}: Καθοήλ. The meaning of the name is uncertain.

8 **Then Amaziah sent**: So MT, G^{B}: אז שלח. G^{L} = וישלח. Cf. v. 9.

9 **the wild animals**: Taking חית השדה as a collective as suggested by the G rendering as plural.

10 **and your pride has swelled you to boastfulness. Now stay home**: Reading ונשאך לבך להכבד עתה שבה בביתך based on 2 Chr 25:19, but changing its *Hip'îl* infinite to a *Nip'al* for sense.[5]

Why: So G^{BL} and 2 Hebrew mss + 2 Chr 25:19. MT precedes with *and.*

should you stir up trouble for yourself: The *Hitpa'ēl* of גרה means to rouse oneself for battle, wage war (Deut 2:5, 19). Its object is marked with ב. Amaziah is warned against initiating conflict with evil (רעה) by going ahead with his plans to fight Jehoash.

11 **Jehoash**: Lacking in G^{B}.

which belonged to Judah: So MT (אשר ליהודה), G^{L} (τῆς Ἰουδαΐος). G^{B} (*in the land of Judah*, τῇ τοῦ Ἰουδα) reflects the erroneous writing of γῇ for τῇ.

12 **Judah**: So MT, G^{B}. G^{L}: *the people of Judah.*

fled: Reading the plural with MT, G^{L}, and 2 Chr 25:22. G^{B} has the singular.

home: Lit. *to his tents.* So *qere'*, 2 Chr 25:22. *Ketiv*, G: *to his tent.* Cf. 1 Sam 4:10; 13:2; 2 Sam 18:17 (*qere'*); 19:9; 20:1.

13 **Amaziah**: MT, 2 Chr 25:23: "Amaziah king of Judah, son of Jehoash, son of Ahaziah." G^{B}: "Amaziah son of Joash, son of Joahaz." G^{L}: "Amaziah son of Joash king of Judah." The different versions and locations of the title and patronymic suggest that they are secondary.[6]

brought him: So G^{L}, 2 Chr 25:23. MT, G^{B} have *Qal* forms, singular (*ketiv*, G^{B}) or plural (*qere'*).

the wall of Jerusalem: So MT, G^{B}, 2 Chr 25:23. G^{L}: "*the walls of Jerusalem.*"

from the Ephraim Gate: So G^{L}, 2 Chr 25:23. MT, G^{B}: *in the Ephraim Gate.*

---

2 E.g., Šanda, *Könige* II, 170, who places it after 15:4.

3 Würthwein, *1. Könige 17–2. Könige 25*, 374. Stade (*Kings*, 249) suggests that 14:22b was the direct sequel to 14:21, but this makes v. 22b repetitive.

4 Gray, *Kings*, 604.

5 Klostermann, *Könige*, 441.

6 Stade, *Kings*, 248.

14 **Taking**: MT's ולקח is either an error for ויקח or has been misplaced from its original position immediately preceding וישב at the end of the verse.[7]

the gold and silver: So G^L. G^B + *and all the utensils.* MT, 2 Chr 25:24: *all the gold and silver and all the utensils.*

hostages: So MT, G^B (בני התערבות). G^L (καὶ τοὺς υἱοὺς τῶν συμμίξεων τῶν βδελυγμάτων =בני התערבות התועבת) reflects a corrupt dittography.

14:15-16 The formulae in these verses have parallels in 13:12-13 (MT, G^B) and 13:25+ (G^L). G^L lacks 14:15. On the question of which location is original see the Diachronic Analysis below.

15 **all that he accomplished**: So G^B; MT, G^B (13:12); G^L (13:25+). MT lacks *all.*

are of course written: So MT, G^B. G^L (13:25+) = הלא הנם כתובים. A perpetual variant between MT and the OG.

18 **and all that he accomplished**: So G^{BL}; lacking in MT but a regular part of the regnal formulae.

are of course written: So MT, G^B: הלא־הם כתובים. G^L, 2 Chr 25:26: הלא הנם כתובים, a perpetual variant.

19 **they sent ... and killed**: So MT, G^L. G^B reflects singular verbs (impersonals).

20 **they brought him up**: So MT: וישאו אתו. 2 Chr 25:28: וישאהו. Either reading is possible. The verb is used here in the sense of "transport" as in Gen 46:5 rather than "lift up."[8]

21 **took**: So MT, 2 Chr 26:1 with the plural. G^{BL} have the singular, but most witnesses agree in reading the next verb as a plural.

Azariah: So MT, G^B. G^L + *his son.* Syr and 2 Chr 26:1 have *Uzziah*, another name for the same king. The two names do not have the same meaning: Azariah = YHWH has helped, Uzziah = YHWH is my strength. The relationship between the names and why the same king bears both are not certain.

in place of his father Amaziah: G^L + *and he stayed in Judah*, probably a misplaced dittography of וישבה ליהודה in v. 22.[9]

23 **over Israel**: So G^B (cf. 1 Kgs 15:25, 33; 16:8, 23; 2 Kgs 3:1; 13:1, 10; 15:8, 17, 23, 27; 17:1). MT has *king of Israel*, referring to Joash of Israel. G^L (*king of Israel in Samaria over Israel*) conflates.

forty-one years: So MT, G^B. G^L: *and forty-one years he reigned in Samaria.*

24 **from the sin of Jeroboam**: Reading the singular based on the theme that runs through the book of Kings[10] and deleting the *all* before it with G^L.

26 **bitter**: Reading המר in place of MT's מרה, "rebellious," which is inappropriate.[11] G's πικρὰν indicates מרה "bitter," which is feminine while עני is masculine. The transposition of ה to produce המר "is speculative," as Hobbs observes, "but does offer a readable text."[12]

for it was pulverized: So G^L (διότι ἐλεπτύνθη), though its antecedent is unclear (כי הודקו?).

ruler-deliverer: On the collocation עצור ועזוב see the Introduction.

27 **had not wanted**: So G^L based on sense (√אבה). MT, G^B: *had not spoken.*

name: So MT, G^L. G^B: *seed.* Cf. Deut 25:6; 29:19; Ps 109:13.

28 **his strength**: So MT. G^{BL} attest the plural, *feats.*

---

7 Klostermann, *Könige*, 443; so also Benzinger, *Könige*, 164; Stade, *Kings*, 248.
8 Ehrlich, *Randglossen*, 310
9 Stade, *Kings*, 249.
10 Stade, *Kings*, 143.
11 So Burney, *Notes on Kings*, 320; Gray, *Kings*, 616.
12 Hobbs, *2 Kings*, 176.

with which he fought: So MT, G^{B}. G^{L} precedes with *and* = *and how he fought.*

[...]: The reading shared by MT and G^{BL}, *and how he restored Damascus and Hamath to Judah in Israel,* is obviously corrupt. The Syriac, which has *to Israel* with no reference to Judah, is sometimes adopted (cf. BHS). But it has not previously been claimed that Jeroboam conquered either Damascus or Hamath. Besides, such a conquest would hardly constitute restoration, since Damascus and Hamath were never considered part of Israel. For further discussion see the Diachronic Analysis.

are of course written: MT, G^{B}: הלא־הם כתובים. G^{L} reflects הלא־הנם כתובים, a perpetual variation.

29 **and was buried in Samaria**: So G^{L}. The unusual apposition of *with his forebears* and *with the kings of Israel* in MT and G^{B} suggests that something is missing.

Zechariah his son reigned in his place: So MT, G^{L}. G^{B}: *Azariah son of Amaziah reigned in place of his father,* a misplaced dittography from 15:1.

Synchronic Analysis

Layout of the chapter

The chapter has three uneven parts. The reigns of Jehoash of Israel and Amaziah of Judah overlap in vv. 1-16. Then, after Jehoash's death, the rest of Amaziah's reign is recounted (vv. 17-22) followed by that of Jeroboam (vv. 23-29). The chapter thus nicely illustrates the narrative technique of alternating between the two kingdoms as the chronology allows.

Amaziah of Judah

The chapter begins by introducing Amaziah of Judah, who succeeds to the throne early (the second year) in the reign of Jehoash (of Israel). Amaziah's opening formulae (vv. 1-4) portray him as a king very much like his father (v. 3). He is basically good; the reference to him having the kingdom in his grasp (v. 5) even recalls Solomon (1 Kgs 2:46). As a further illustration of his righteousness we read that he justly executed those who had assassinated his father (v. 5), adhering to the Mosaic principle of not punishing the children for their forebears' crimes (v. 6). His success against the Edomites here (v. 7) and in an appendix to his reign (v. 22) rewards his faithfulness. But Amaziah does not meet the David standard (v. 4). As in his father's case, the stumbling block is the *bāmôt*. The mention of them and Amaziah's failure to remove them leads one to expect an anecdote about some defeat or tragedy suffered by him as implicit punishment.[13] Sure enough, vv. 8-14 recount a devastating defeat suffered by Amaziah at the hands of his Northern counterpart, Jehoash. The defeat is even more humiliating because Amaziah brought it on himself by challenging Jehoash (v. 8) and then not backing down when he had the chance (vv. 10-11). Amaziah was confident about his challenge because Israel's army was the same size as Edom's (v. 7 MT), which he had already defeated.

Jehoash's fable

An important part of the story is Jehoash's "fable" in v. 9. Such, at least, is the usual genre designation of this anecdote, and it seems appropriate in that its characters are non-humans and it is intended to make a point relating to the situation in which it is told. In Hebrew it would be called a *māshāl*, though that term is not used here. What is more important than genre designation is how the anecdote functions. It does not, in and of itself, have a moral in the sense of calling for a response from

---

13 Mullen, "Crime and Punishment."

Amaziah. There is nothing the thorn bush could have done differently to avoid being trampled by the wild animal. It is possible that Jehoash's version of it is an excerpt, just enough to make the comparison or to prod Amaziah to recall the story in full. On the other hand, as it is, the fable adequately makes the point about the difference in size and strength between the thorn bush and the cedar, even though both are plants. The wild animal illustrates this point by trampling the thorn bush—something it could never do to the cedar.[14] The marriage proposal shows that the thorn bush does not appreciate the contrast between it and the cedar, just as Amaziah's challenge assumes that he is the equal or superior of Jehoash.[15] The response is especially fitting for the wording of the challenge in v. 8: *let's look each other in the face*. That assumes equality; Jehoash regards this premise as false, as he explains in v. 10. Amaziah's success against Edom has gone to his head, or rather his *heart*, which has "lifted" him up. Jehoash's advice is: "honor yourself" (הכבד), both by being content with self-congratulation and by keeping yourself safe at home, the alternative to war (Judg 8:29; Isa 37:37; 2 Chr 19:4).[16] The advice comes with a warning: if Amaziah goes to war he will *fall*, the natural consequence of being *lifted up*.[17]

Jehoash as bully

Amaziah ignores Jehoash's advice and warning and as a result is defeated (vv. 11-12). The consequent embarrassment and despoliation he and his people suffer (vv. 13-14) are, therefore, his fault. However, certain details hint that there may be more to the story than a surface reading allows. It is Jehoash who *went up* (v. 11). He is the one who seized the initiative and evidently mounted the attack. The battle, moreover, takes place in Beth-Shemesh, *which belonged to Judah*. In other words Judah is in the defensive posture; Israel is on the offensive. The passive verb at the beginning of v. 12 conveys the same impression. Judah *is smitten* or *stricken* because it is on the defense *before Israel*, the aggressor. Jehoash does not stop at Beth-Shemesh as a king repelling an attacker might but proceeds with a captured Amaziah to Jerusalem (v. 13), where he breaks down a length of the city wall and takes gold, silver, valuables, and hostages from the temple and the palace. Clearly Jehoash is the stronger of the two kings. But the years of submission to Aram in his father's regime (13:3-7) and the taste of victory thanks to Elisha and Yhwh (13:25) have turned him into a bully who hazes weaker kings with the same oppression he experienced. His destruction of the city wall, leaving Jerusalem vulnerable, if not just meanness betrays a self-loathing that attributes the vengefulness he feels to Amaziah. His plundering of the temple and palace were meant to recoup his losses to Aram by taking from another, weaker country. Judah was too weak and poor to yield as much wealth as Jehoash desired so he sought to make up the difference by taking hostages who served as collateral for future payments. The timing of his aggression was no accident: he wanted to take advantage of

---

14 *Pace* Olley (*Kings*, 289) the חיה does not represent a third party (Aram) from whom Israel protects Judah. I also see no reason to identify the wild animal as Jehoash or Assyria/Babylonia, *pace* A. M. Vater Solomon, "Jehoash's Fable of the Thistle and the Cedar (2 Kings 14.8-14 and 2 Chronicles 25.17-24)," *Sage, Legend, Tale, Novella, Fable: Narrative Forms in Old Testament Literature* (ed. G. W. Coats; JSOTSup 35; Sheffield: JSOT, 1985), 130.

15 Again, the marriage proposal in the fable does not imply that Amaziah has proposed a marriage alliance with Jehoash (*pace* Fricke, *Das zweite Buch von den Königen*, 185).

16 Ehrlich, *Randglossen*, 310.

17 Cohn, *II Kings*, 101.

Amaziah's recent defeat and plundering of Edom (vv. 7, 10). It was a dog-eat-dog world, and Jehoash was the biggest dog on the block at the moment. Adding to the suspicions about Jehoash being the aggressor are the mention in his closing regnal formulae of *his strength* and how he fought with Amaziah (v. 15), neither of which is paralleled in Amaziah's formulae (vv. 17-21).

Effects of the defeat on Judah

The defeat permanently scars Amaziah's reign. The conspiracy that resulted in his assassination (v. 19) was a delayed reaction to the defeat and to the intervening fifteen years of vassalhood to Israel (v. 17), and further punishment for his retention of the *bāmôt*. The text implies this by juxtaposing the accounts of the two events and by the use of the verb *lifted up* (*they lifted him up on horses*) in v. 20, which links to Jehoash's accusation of pride in v. 10, each signaling Amaziah's downfall.[18] The connection between Amaziah's defeat and his assassination is further indicated by the mention of the restoration of Elath in v. 22. The verse stands out because of its location outside the closing formulae for Amaziah but before those for Azariah (15:1-4). This positioning suggests that the restoration of Elath (and the valuable trade income accruing from it) was properly the accomplishment of Amaziah, who paved the way for it by his defeat of Edom but was unable or unwilling to follow up because of the servitude of Israel that he was forced to endure in the intervening years.

Jeroboam II

Before moving on to Azariah's reign the narrative turns to that of Jeroboam II (vv. 23-29), whose reign represents a key structural moment in the history of the Northern kingdom: Jeroboam I + 6 kings = Ahab + 6 kings = Jeroboam II + 6 kings > the end.[19] The reign of Jeroboam II constitutes a kind of new beginning. Verse 25 presents his leading accomplishment with a subject-first clause, *he it was*, as in vv. 7, 22. This was the restoration of Israel's borders back to those of the David-Solomon era, *from the entrance of Hamath to the Sea of the Arabah* (v. 25; cf. 1 Kgs 8:65), including even Damascus and Hamath (v. 29). It is a fresh start after the low point described in vv. 26-27, which allude to the oppression suffered at the hands of Hazael especially under Jehoahaz (13:7, 23). At that point there was absolutely no one to sustain Israel. The state of absolute powerlessness evokes Deut 32:36.[20] In such a circumstance YHWH is moved to compassion and intervenes, as at the exodus (Exod 3:7; Deut 26:7) and as in the book of Jonah so that people—here Israel—are not obliterated (v. 27).[21] It is through Jeroboam II that YHWH saves his people and starts over with them, and this according to Jonah's unrecorded prophecy (v. 25).

---

18 Cohn, *II Kings*, 101. The mention of horses may be a synecdoche for the horse-drawn vehicle (wagon, etc.) on which he was transported (Šanda, *Könige* II, 170).

19 Leithart, *Kings*, 245.

20 Following Talmon and Fields ("The Collocation," 85–92) the expression עצור עזוב is a nominal hendiadys referring to a ruler, such that in 2 Kgs 14:26 as in Deut 32:36 (ואפס עצור עזוב) Israel is leaderless. This may be hyperbole, but it expresses the sense of desperation and aloneness of a people severely oppressed.

21 The verb מחה has the sense of "wipe or blot out." Cogan and Tadmor (*II Kings*, 161) suggest that it is based on the practice of wiping a piece of papyrus clean. A similar image is found in 2 Kgs 21:13—that of wiping a dish clean on both sides. To wipe out the name is to obliterate not only the existence of a person or group of people but the very memory of them.

The new beginning of Jeroboam II, however, is the beginning of the end. The optimism of a new start is immediately dampened by his evaluation in v. 24. The same old problem persists; he follows the sin of the original Jeroboam and does what YHWH considers evil. The impact of Jeroboam's account is a mixed one that we have seen before. It is a tension between divine mercy and human trespass that is embodied in miniature in the wording of v. 26. The word modifying *affliction* can be viewed as a sort of *double entendre*. It is usually translated *bitter*, and this meaning fits the context, especially since the word resembles the root for *bitter* (מרר). However, as the word appears it actually means "rebelling," suggesting that Israel's bitter affliction is the result of its rebelliousness. Israel is saved again because of YHWH's mercy, but the unshakable sin of Jeroboam points inevitably toward judgment and once more presses the question as to how long Israel can rely on YHWH's mercy and whether there is still hope for divine mercy on the other side of destruction.

The unshakable sin of Jeroboam

Diachronic Analysis

The chapter as it stands is a DtrH unit based on earlier sources. The regnal data in vv. 1-2 probably stem from an integrated king list. The figure of a twenty-nine-year reign is in conflict with 15:1, which dates the beginning of the reign of Amaziah's successor Azariah to Jeroboam II's twenty-seventh year instead of the expected fourteenth or fifteenth year of his reign (13:10). The chronological problems involved in correlating these two verses as well as 14:17 are formidable. Scholarly solutions diverge considerably, and the problems have yet to find a resolution.[22]

A basic DtrH unit forged from sources

Amaziah is the second in a series of four kings of Judah (Joash, Amaziah, Azariah, Jotham) who are judged basically righteous with two reservations signaled by רק (*only, except*). The double occurrence of this word in such close proximity suggests that one of the reservations is secondary, and it is probably the first one, *only not like David his ancestor* in v. 3aβ. The second one about the *cultic installations* (*bāmôt*) in v. 4 is more common in DtrH's regnal formulae (2 Kgs 12:4; 15:4, 35; cf. 1 Kgs 22:44);[23] while v. 3aβ is unique (1 Kgs 15:11; 2 Kgs 16:2 are similar) it is also unnecessary. The point is that Amaziah did what was right just as his father had done except that (as was the case with his father) the *bāmôt* were not removed. The comparison to David is intrusive. The similarity of the reference to the kingdom being firmly in his grasp (v. 5) to what is said about Solomon after his purge of Adonijah and supporters (1 Kgs 2:46) suggests that there was a struggle of some kind for the throne following Joash's death and perhaps related to his assassination (12:22). The frequent claim that Amaziah's

14:1-6: The opening of Amaziah's reign

22 For overviews see Galil (*Chronology*, 57–61), esp. nn. 42 and 47. Galil's own proposal holds to the reliability of 14:1, 17 and considers 15:1 as erroneous. He also posits a brief co-regency of Amaziah with his father, Joash, and an extensive one (12 years) with his son, Uzziah.

23 See 22:44 and the works of Barrick and Vaughn cited there.

refusal to execute the children of the assassins represented a radical departure from typical practice is misleading.[24] The typical punishment for treason appears to have been execution and the confiscation of the traitor's property; it could occasionally include execution of the family according to the discretion of the king or the judges, depending on the circumstances of the case.[25] For reasons that are unexplained Amaziah did not have the children of the assassins executed,[26] or at least no record of their executions was found. The explicit mention of his clemency or the silence of the sources on the matter led to DtrH's editorial comment in v. 6, as the quotation from Deut 24:16 supports the evaluation that Amaziah did what YHWH considered right.[27]

14:22, 7: Amaziah and Edom

The similar beginning of vv. 22a and 7 occasioned the loss of the former from its original location. Both concern the same conflict with Edom. Verse 22b (*after the king lay with his forebears*) was added after the replacement of v. 22a in its current location.[28] The addition clarified exactly who *he it was* referred to, applying it to Azariah. Amaziah's seizure of Elath (v. 22a) led to war with Edom. Elath (or Aqaba), on the tip of the Gulf of Aqaba, would have been the real reason for the conflict because of the trade advantages its port afforded (cf. 1 Kgs 22:48). Beyond control of the trade route Amaziah had no interest in the rest of Edom. Judah's control of Elath and the trade route stemming from it would last through the rest of his reign and those of Azariah and Jotham, eventually reverting to Edom during the reign of Ahaz of Judah (16:6). The number ten thousand is symbolic, representing a large force.[29] The Valley of Salt where the Edomites were defeated (cf. 2 Sam 8:13) was probably the wide valley south of the Dead Sea (the Arabah) that formed a buffer between Judah and Edom. Amaziah would have been defending his seizure of Elath. As for Sela, here translated "*the Crag*," it is not clear whether it is to be understood as a proper name for a settled location or as a common noun. The later understanding as a certain rock or cliff from which the Edomite captives were hurled to their deaths is in 2 Chr 25:12. The identification of Sela with Petra may go back to the Septuagint, where הסלע is translated τὴν πέτραν.[30] Perhaps under the influence of G, Eusebius (*Onomasticon* 142:7-8; 144:7-9)

24 E.g., Kittel, *Könige*, 260.

25 R. Westbrook, ("The Character of Ancient Near Eastern Law," in *A History of Ancient Near Eastern Law* [ed. R. Westbrook; HO 72/1; Leiden: Brill, 2003], 76) cites the case of the priests of Nob (1 Sam 22) and that of Naboth's sons (2 Kgs 9:26). But see the reservations expressed in this commentary on 2 Kgs 5. Z. Ben-Barak ("Trials for Treason against the King in Israel and the Near East," *RIDA* 28 [1991]: 11–19) collects other examples from the HB and the ancient Near East that corroborate Westbrook's synthesis.

26 Landersdorfer (*Könige*, 188) suggests that not killing the assassins' children was a demonstration of restraint that aided Amaziah in his struggle to retain power.

27 The differences are minor and possibly due to textual variants rather than free citation.

28 On the expression *lie with one's forebears* see 1 Kgs 22:40. It is not used exclusively for kings who die peacefully, as was once thought, but represents uninterrupted dynastic succession (Suriano, *Politics of Dead Kings*). Its use here, therefore, does not preclude Amaziah as the king who restored Elath to Judah.

29 Cogan and Tadmor, *II Kings*, 155. This is why it is erroneous in 13:7 where it is meant to represent a small force.

30 A. Rainey, "Sela (of Edom)," *IDBSup*, 800.

furthered this identification, which was widely accepted until fairly recently.[31] But the lack of evidence for occupation of Petra before the seventh century BCE renders it improbable as the site taken by Amaziah in 2 Kgs 14:7. More likely is the site of *es-Selaʿ*, 2.5 miles northwest of Buseira (biblical Bozrah), where there is evidence of an eighth-century fortified town. This fits the time period required for Amaziah. It also fits the description in v. 7 that it was captured, as is more fitting for a settlement or fortification than a cliff. Furthermore, es-Selaʿ commanded the major north-south trade route in the Transjordan, which could account for Amaziah's interest in it.[32] Amaziah gives the place a new name: Joktheel, which is used in Josh 15:38 for another city in the Shephelah of Judah near Lachish.

14:8-14: Northern origin

Verses 8-14 are based on an independent anecdote of Northern origin that served in DtrH's account as punishment for Amaziah's failure to remove the cultic installations outside of Jerusalem (*bāmôt*).[33] Indications of Northern perspective include the presentation of Amaziah as the aggressor who proposes the confrontation and foolishly fails to heed the warning he receives and the reference to Beth-shemesh, *which belonged to Judah* (v. 11), as well as the detail about Jehoash's approach via Bethshemesh (v. 13). What may remain from an official source is limited to vv. 11aβ-14. The setup in vv. 8-11aα is DtrH's doing, except possibly for the fable in v. 9, which may have a separate origin in Wisdom for its moral not to overreach one's situation.[34] DtrH used these materials for his own purposes in line with his scheme of "crime and punishment" as the price paid by Amaziah for his failure to remove the *bāmôt*.[35]

14:9: Jehoash's fable

With the lifting of Aramaean oppression Jehoash was free to turn his attention elsewhere, and Judah's new-found income from Elath could have attracted his attention. Still, it was Amaziah according to DtrH in v. 8 who was the *provocateur.* The expression *look each other in the face* refers to military confrontation, as v. 11 makes clear. The fable in v. 9, however, interprets Amaziah's move in social or political terms. Amaziah's challenge, if historical, would have been an assertion of parity that sought to terminate a relationship of vassalhood, probably experienced by Judah vis-à-vis Israel since the Omrid dynasty, and defied Jehoash to take military action to restore it. This would explain why Jehoash is the one who initiates the conflict (v. 11). This is one of only two fables (with Judg 9:8-15) in the HB in the sense of being a brief story with anthropomorphized plants and animals that

---

31 The specific feature within Petra that invites this identification is Umm el-Biyara, the crag that rises ca. 1000 feet above the floor of Wadi Musa and comports well with the Chronicler's portrait of the event. Würthwein (*1. Könige 17–2. Könige 25*, 371) sees v. 7aβb as a late addition, so that the absence of evidence for 8th-century occupation is irrelevant and Sela would probably be understood by the author of the addition as Petra.

32 Wiseman, *Kings*, 260.

33 This widely-held view goes back to Klostermann (*Könige*, 437–38), who thought that it was transposed from the account of Jehoash's reign in ch. 13, complete with his closing formulae in vv. 15-16.

34 Cf. E. Jenni, "Distel und Zeder. Hermeneutische Überlegungen zu 2 Kö 14:8-14," in *Studia Biblica et Semitica* (Fs. T. C. Vriezen; Wageningen: Veenman & Zonen, 1966), 165–66.

35 Mullen, "Crime and Punishment."

is told by a character with the intent of making a point or teaching a lesson.[36] It may have had an independent origin, warning against self-delusion from conceit. Otherwise the marriage proposal that is part of the fable is curious, although it fits if Amaziah is eschewing vassal status.[37] Jehoash's stinging rejoinder is that the change in political status that Amaziah desires requires social equality, but the two of them are not equals; Israel and Judah are not in the same league. He continues by acknowledging Amaziah's success against Edom but then warns him not to let it go to his head and cause him to "bite off more than he can chew," which will result in disaster for him and his country (v. 10).[38] Exactly how it was that Amaziah *would not listen* (v. 11) is not divulged, but again, if he rebelled against Jehoash's suzerainty he would have withheld his annual payment of tribute, and that would have impelled Jehoash to take the offensive.

14:11: Jehoash's approach

Jehoash's route via Bethshemesh is revealing. Located 24 km west of Jerusalem in the Shephelah (modern Tell el-Rumeileh), it guarded the Sorek pass and the ascent to Jerusalem from the coastal plain. Jehoash could have attacked Jerusalem from the north, departing from Bethel. Instead he went out of his way to approach from the west. This is similar to what Hazael did (12:18-19), and it indicates that Jehoash had another agenda. He may, like Hazael, have sought to gain control of the trade route from Elath to the Mediterranean.[39] The notice that Bethshemesh belonged to Judah may have been intended to distinguish it from two other sites of the same name—one in Naphtali (Josh 19:38; Judg 1:33) and another (Ain es-Samsiyeh) south of Bethshan. It may also hint that by the end of the conflict Bethshemesh and the route from Jerusalem to the coast were in Israel's control.

14:12-14: Amaziah's humiliation

As anticipated by Jehoash, Judah is routed (v. 12). The statement that each man fled home (lit. *to his tents*) is an expression denoting defeat of an army (1 Sam 4:10; 13:2; 2 Sam 18:17; 2 Kgs 8:21). Amaziah is captured at Bethshemesh. Jehoash humiliates him by conducting him back to Jerusalem, thus making his defeat and his vassalhood

---

36 Vater Solomon ("Jehoash's Fable," 130) asserts that Jehoash uses the fable to warn Amaziah against going to war for political gain. But this can hardly be its point if it was once independent. J. M. Bidmead, "Fable," *NIDB* 2:407 mentions the Adam and Eve story and Balaam's donkey, which are parts of narratives rather than related by a character. The genre is represented elsewhere in ANE literature (*ANET* 592–93; *COS* 1.178). Plants and animals are used widely in the Bible and the ANE in metaphors and similitudes, especially in Wisdom (cf. also Isa 10:15; Ezek 17:3-8; 19:1-9).

37 The phrase *that was/were in Lebanon* appears three times in v. 9 in reference to the thorn bush, cedar tree, and wild beasts respectively. It is appropriate only for the cedar, for which Lebanese origin was a mark of distinction (Judg 9:15; 1 Kgs 5:13; 7:2; 10:17, 21; Ezra 3:7; Ps 29:5; 37:35; 92:13; 103:16; etc.). It is a gloss in the other two instances; there was nothing distinctive about thorn bushes or wild animals in Lebanon.

38 See the Note. The MT has Jehoash tell Amaziah to "honor himself" or "be honored," an inferior reading.

39 Gray, *Kings*, 608. Gray also suggests, based on the mention in 2 Chr 25:13 of *cities of Judah from Samaria to Beth-horon*, that Judah had taken advantage of Israel's extreme weakness under Jehoahaz to push its border northward and that Jehoash sought to recover lost territory. But it is unlikely that Judah would still hold that territory, given Israel's superiority. This part of the Chronicles account has an obvious theological agenda that renders it problematic for historical reconstruction.

obvious (v. 13). Its king captured and its army routed, the city is an easy target. Jehoash inflicts further damage by destroying a 200-meter (400 cubit) section of its wall from the Ephraim Gate to the Corner Gate. The wall line for this period is unknown, so it is uncertain where these gates stood. Judging from its name, the Ephraim Gate faced north and probably stood directly west of the temple in the middle of the northern wall of the city, which probably ran along the Transversal Valley following the line of Hezekiah's wall built a few decades later (cf. 2 Chr 25:23; Neh 8:16; 12:39).[40] The Corner Gate, mentioned in Jer 31:38; 2 Chr 25:23; 26:9, and probably Zech 14:10, was at the western end of this wall line at the point where it turned south and served as the entrance into the city from the Western hill.[41] This northwest approach to Jerusalem was the city's most vulnerable point because of the absence of ravines, which protect it on other sides. For this reason King Uzziah later fortified it with towers (2 Chr 26:9). Jehoash's demolition of the wall here left the city especially vulnerable to attack. Jehoash also plundered the palace and temple treasuries (v. 14). This was not likely to have been very profitable so soon after Joash of Judah's payment to Hazael (12:18-19). The plundering probably did not include the temple vessels mentioned in MT. These are absent from G^L and likely were added to enhance the anticipation of the sacking of the temple by the Babylonians in 2 Kings 25.[42] Jehoash also takes hostages (בני התערבות). The word is a *hapax legomenon* deriving from the root ערב II meaning "take, give in pledge." The reason for the hostages is not explained but it may be that they were held for ransom to make up for the shortage of gold and silver in Judah's treasuries and/or to ensure Amaziah's good behavior, especially if they were members of the royal family.[43]

14:15-17: Jehoash's closing formulae

Verses 15-16 are the third and probably the original occurrence in the witnesses of the closing regnal formulae for Jehoash (13:12-13 MT; 13:25+ OL). Because he made use of a Northern source, DtrH postponed the concluding formulae for Jehoash until vv. 15-16. This led to the somewhat unusual situation of having two closing regnal formulae more or less on top of one another (vv. 15-16, 18-22), though it was still in keeping with DtrH's "rule" of recounting stories about a king's reign within the formulae for that king. This unusual situation and the fact that the story in 14:8-14 was now applied to Amaziah and set within his formulae induced the scribe who was adjusting the chronology of the OG *Vorlage* to move the closing formulae for Jehoash to 13:25+ where the OL retains them. DtrH added v. 17 as a "cushion" to avoid the anomalous situation of having two sets of regnal formulae one right after the other. The figure of fifteen years for the remainder of Amaziah's reign is a calculation based on the numbers in 13:10; 14:2, 23: Amaziah's accession in the second year of Jehoash's sixteen-year reign means that Amaziah

---

40 D. Liid, "Ephraim Gate," *ABD* 2:556.

41 D. Liid, "Corner Gate," *ABD* 1:1156.

42 Würthwein (*1. Könige 17–2. Könige 25*, 371) considers v. 14a, with the possible exception of the reference to the hostages, as a later addition based on his perception of the verse's more formal style.

43 Cogan and Tadmor, *II Kings*, 156; Gray, *Kings*, 611. Galil (*Chronology*, 58) argues that the reference to hostages undermines Thiele's (*Mysterious Numbers*, 115) theory that Jehoash installed Uzziah as Amaziah's co-regent at this point. Galil thinks the co-regency began a few years later.

was in his fourteenth year when Jehoash died; since Amaziah reigned a total of twenty-nine years, he reigned fifteen years beyond Jehoash.

14:18-20: Amaziah's assassination

The details about Amaziah's assassination are between the source notice (v. 18) and the burial notice (v. 20) as expected (compare 12:19-21). Only v. 22 is out of place. The conspiracy drives Amaziah to flee to Lachish, where he is pursued and assassinated. Once thought to be Tell el-Hesi, Lachish has been widely identified since its excavation in 1973–1994 as Tell ed-Duweir, about 55 kilometers southwest of Jerusalem in the western Shephelah.[44] Close to a main route from the coastal plain to the Judean hills, it defended Jerusalem on the west and facilitated Judah's control of its western border and the Mediterranean coast. During the period of the Divided Monarchy (Levels IV–III) it was heavily fortified and became the second most important city in Judah behind Jerusalem as well as a probable royal residence. Amaziah's flight there indicates the site's importance. He evidently hoped to take advantage of its fortification and its residence in order to escape the conspiracy. However, either the conspirators followed him from Jerusalem or the conspiracy had spread to Lachish. The statement *they sent after him* could mean that conspirators followed him or that they sent a message to comrades in the city. In either case the conspiracy appears to have been widespread and strong within the army. There is no indication of any retribution against those who plotted or carried out the assassination.[45] Despite his assassination Amaziah is afforded full honors, with transport to Jerusalem for burial in the royal tombs (v. 20).

14:21: Azariah's installation

Azariah is installed as king by *all the people of Judah*. The expression is ambiguous. It could refer to the citizenry of Judah or to the army. The latter possibility is supported by the fact that the army seems to have been responsible for Amaziah's assassination, since it took place in the fortified city of Lachish. Azariah's young age (16) suggests that he was not the oldest son. Amaziah would have been thirty-eight when Azariah was born. His older brothers may have died (in defense of or opposition to their father?) or been deemed unacceptable as successors, perhaps out of a concern that they would follow his policies too closely. Many scholars see Azariah's youth as evidence for co-regency, especially in view of the overall length assigned to his reign (52 years, 15:2). The content and placement of v. 21 after the notice of Amaziah's death, though, do not support the theory of co-regency.[46]

---

44 For summary articles and bibliography see D. Ussishkin, "Lachish," *ADB* 114–26; "Lachish," *NIDB* 3:555–62; "Lachish," *NEAEHL* 3:897–911; and H. G. M. Williamson, "Lachish," *DOTHB*, 635–38.

45 Sweeney (*Kings*, 363) followed by Barnes (*Kings*, 295) sees Amaziah's assassination as another fulfillment of the anti-dynastic oracle against the Omrid dynasty (1 Kgs 21:20-24), considering all the kings of Judah from Ahaziah on as heirs of Ahab through his daughter Athaliah. While technically true, this is not the way the book of Kings presents things, since not every king of Judah from Ahaziah on is assassinated.

46 תחת is regularly used in the formulae for replacement. Thiele (*Mysterious Numbers*, 110, 119, 199, etc.) argues that v. 21 is misplaced from immediately after 14:14, coordinating the start of the co-regency with Jehoash's plunder of Jerusalem. Galil (*Chronology*, 58) highlights Azariah's installation by the people as evidence of popular opposition to Amaziah stemming from Jehoash's invasion though not simultaneous with it. He deduces evidence for co-regency in the regnal figures without consideration of the implication and location of v. 21.

14:23-29: Jeroboam II's reign

The remainder of the chapter (vv. 23-29) is devoted to the reign of Jeroboam II. The chronological data for him agree with those of 14:1 but are at odds with those of 15:1, 8. His success and the length of his reign pose a problem for DtrH because he is judged to have done evil by retaining the *sin of Jeroboam*. DtrH deals with this problem in three ways. First he downplays Jeroboam's significance by devoting a minimum of space to him—seven verses (vv. 23-29) with very little detail about his reign. As with Omri we must rely on sources outside of Kings to get a sense of the prosperity and strength of Jeroboam's reign. We have such information in the books of Amos and Hosea and in the eighth-century Samaria ostraca. Amos especially condemns the upper class of Samaria during Jeroboam's reign for their luxurious lifestyle at the expense of the poor and needy. He goes into detail about the excesses of those he criticizes, thereby giving important glimpses into the opulence of the elite under Jeroboam. DtrH says nothing about Israel's prosperity under him.

Fulfillment of prophecy

The second way of dealing with Jeroboam's success was to describe it as the fulfillment of prophecy. What Jeroboam's restoration of Israel's borders (v. 25) shows, therefore, is YHWH's faithfulness to the prophetic word. The Sea of the Arabah here is the Dead Sea, the northern shore of which represented Israel's southern border. The *entrance of Hamath* (Lebo-Hamath) probably referred to the northern Beqaʿa valley and perhaps specifically the site of the modern village of Lebweh at the head of the Orontes. This is expansion beyond the restoration of cities between the Dead Sea and the Galilee described in ch. 13. Jeroboam was apparently renowned for this accomplishment in his own day, as Amos 6:14 uses these same dimensions to threaten Israel's impending oppression.[47] From a historical perspective this success in expanding Israel's borders was due largely to the Assyrian defeat of Damascus in 773–772 BCE and then Assyria's own preoccupation during the reign of Ashur-dan III (772–755) with Urartu.[48] This left Israel free to reclaim territory that had belonged to Aram. From DtrH's perspective the success was YHWH's doing and had been predicted by the prophet Jonah, whose identity was borrowed for the short story preserved in the book that bears his name. That short story, though, is a later development that is independent of the role of the prophet in Kings. Gath-hepher was on the eastern border of the tribal territory of Zebulon (Josh 19:13).[49]

Jeroboam II as Israel's rescuer

Third, in vv. 26-27 Jeroboam is cast as YHWH's instrument of salvation, in response to Israel's distress, to keep the country and people from extinction. Verse 26 alludes to 13:7 and the desperate circumstances during Joahaz's reign (note the pluperfect *had seen*). Despite Israel's severe oppression and the devastation result-

47 Amos 6:13 further alludes to Israel's success in *Lo-debar* (probably Lidebir) and *Karnaim* (= Ashteroth-Karnaim), both sites in Bashan just north of the Yarmuk in Transjordan, which had previously been under Aramaean aegis. See M. C. Astour, "Ashteroth-Karnaim," *ADB* 1:491; D. V. Edelman, "Lo-Debar," *ADB* 4:345–46.

48 Miller and Hayes, *History*, 353–54.

49 Identified both with el-Meshed ca. 3 mi. N of Nazareth where there is a tomb attributed to Jonah and with the nearby Khirbet ez-Zurraʿa. R. Greenberg, "Gath-Hepher," *ADB* 2:909–10; E. R. Cheney, "Gath-Hepher," *NIDB* 2:525.

ing from it, YHWH did not intend to destroy Israel at that time.[50] YHWH in his mercy provided Jeroboam, who rescued Israel from the abyss by restoring its greater proportions and its prosperity.

The corrupt reading of v. 28aβ has occasioned numerous reconstructions (see the Note).[51] A couple of these deserve comment because of the adherents they have attracted. One is based on Winckler's proposal to identify "Iaudi" in Assyrian inscriptions with Y'DY, Sam'al = Zinjirli.[52] This led the NEB to render "in Jaudi for Israel." In addition to the undefended transposition of prepositions, though, Winckler's proposal has been shown to be untenable: "All references in Akkadian to *Iaudi* refer to biblical Judah and the kings of Y'DY are always termed the kings of Sam'al."[53] A second popular suggestion has been Burney's emendation of the text to read "how he fought with Damascus and how he turned away the wrath of Yahweh from Israel" (אשר־נלחם את־דמשק ואשר השיב את חמת יהוה מישראל).[54] The proposal is ingenious, but it stands in tension with v. 27 where YHWH saves Israel through Jeroboam out of mercy for his people. Na'aman has proposed "and how he restored Damascus, and the wars of Judah against Israel" (ואשר השיב את דמשקו ומלחמות יהודה בישראל).[55] In addition to the questionable claim that Jeroboam *restored Damascus*, which Na'aman does not explain in detail, the grammar of the verse, as he admits, is unusual. Absent textual evidence for a viable alternative reading or a convincing emendation the best course of action is to recognize this portion of the verse as corrupt and to leave it unreconstructed. With the accession of Zechariah the prediction of 10:30 that the fourth generation of Jehu's sons would occupy Israel's throne has come to fulfillment (v. 29).

---

50 MT has the verb דבר: YHWH had not *said* he would destroy Israel. This verb implies delivery of a prophetic oracle, and F. Crüseman ("Kritik an Amos im deuteronomistische Geschichtswerk. Erwägungen zu 2. Könige 14.27," in *Probleme biblischer Theologie. Gerhard von Rad zum 70. Geburtstag* (ed. H. W. Wolff; Munich: Kaiser, 1971): 57–63 and Dietrich (*Prophetie und Geschichte*, 35n) find in it a critique of Amos's threats of the impending end. Würthwein (*1. Könige 17–2. Könige 25*, 376) disagrees and takes the statement to mean that YHWH had not *decided* to bring the end at this point. He sees this not as a critique of Amos but as an explanation for why Israel's demise as a nation did not come during Jehoahaz's reign. If G presupposes אבה instead of דבר, it indicates an interpretation more along the lines advocated by Würthwein.

51 See those listed by N. Na'aman, "Azariah of Judah and Jeroboam II of Israel," *VT* 43 (1993), 231 n. 9.

52 H. Winckler, "Das syrische Land Jaudi und der angebliche Azarja von Juda," *AF* 1 (1893): 1–23.

53 Cogan and Tadmor, *II Kings*, 162. It was already called into question by D. D. Luckenbill, "Azariah of Judah," *AJSL* 41 (1925): 217–32. See also H. Tadmor, "Azriyau of Yaudi," *Scripta Hierosolymitana* 8 (1961): 232–71.

54 Burney, *Notes on Kings*, 320.

55 Na'aman, "Azariah of Judah and Jeroboam II of Israel," 230–31.

Synthesis

The issue of divine fairness

The accounts of the two kings in this chapter—Amaziah of Judah and Jeroboam II of Israel—are both concerned with the issue of divine justice. Each reign on its own presents a challenge to the doctrine of god's fairness. Amaziah is a basically righteous king who follows in his father's footsteps. His only fault is his failure, like that of his father, to remove the cultic installations outside Jerusalem (v. 4). His scrupulous adherence to Deuteronomic law (v. 6) indicates that he was a pious and upright king otherwise. Yet, despite some military success against Edom (v. 7), he is badly defeated by Jehoash of Israel, resulting in Jerusalem being rendered defenseless and its treasuries plundered (vv. 8-14). The invasion takes place sometime before the mid-point of his reign (v. 17), overshadowing it and eventually culminating disastrously in conspiracy and assassination (v. 19). By contrast, Jeroboam II is a wicked king of the North who enjoys an unusually long and prosperous reign, expanding Israel's territorial holdings to a point equivalent to the "glory days" under David and Solomon.

DtrH's explanation: A critique

DtrH offers different explanations for these two reigns, each meant to safeguard the notion of god's justice. For Amaziah it is the scheme of "crime and punishment."[56] Amaziah's failure to remove the *bāmôt* is a crime in YHWH's eyes that occasions the punishments of defeat and assassination. Jeroboam's success, in contrast, is because of the mercy of YHWH who does not want Israel to perish, at least not yet. Considered separately each explanation makes sense, particularly within the history of its respective kingdom as traced by DtrH. For instance, readers know that Israel's destruction as a kingdom is looming. Hence one can take the long view with regard to Israel and recognize that YHWH's mercy in Jeroboam's case is only a pause in the working out of divine justice. When the two accounts are read together, however, as they are juxtaposed in this chapter, the tension between them is stark and almost unbearable and raises a host of questions about DtrH's scheme of crime and punishment. Above all, if YHWH can show mercy to a wicked king like Jeroboam and make his reign prosperous and successful, why must he follow rules prescribing devastating punishments for a king like Amaziah who is basically righteous? DtrH might respond that the scheme is not rigid and YHWH is not subject to it; his judgments are beyond human ken. But then how can one rely on YHWH's mercy if it is so fickle? And how can one rely on divine justice and be assured of being rewarded for right behavior? These two accounts back to back leave both YHWH's justice and YHWH's mercy in doubt as qualities upon which nations and persons can depend. The failure of the righteous and success of the wicked are themes in tune with Wisdom, but they seem to undermine a main point of the Deuteronomistic History and the book of Kings.

56 Mullen, "Crime and Punishment."

Azariah and Jotham of Judah; Zechariah, Shallum, Menahem, Pekahiah, and Pekah of Israel (2 Kings 15)

Text

[DtrH's sources; DtrH; Additions to DtrH; Glosses and corruptions to the
additions; *Additions to PN*]
1 In the twenty-seventh year of Jeroboam king of Israel Aza-
riah son of Amaziah became king over Judah. 2 He was sixteen
years old when he became king, and he reigned fifty-two years
in Jerusalem; his mother's name was Jekoliah from Jerusalem.
3 He did what YHWH considered right just like all that Amaziah had done, 4 ex-
cept the cultic installations were not removed; the people continued slaughter-
ing animals and burning food offerings on the cultic installations. 5 YHWH struck
the king so that he became skin diseased until he died, living in
a quarantined residence. Jotham, the king's son, was over the
house, governing the people of the land. 6 The rest of Azariah's af-
fairs including all that he accomplished are of course written on the scroll of
the chronicles of the kings of Judah. 7 Azariah lay down with his forebears and
was buried with his forebears in the city of David. Jotham his son reigned in
his place. 8 In the thirty-eighth year of Azariah king of Judah,
Zechariah son of Jeroboam became king over Israel in Samaria
for six months. 9 He did what YHWH considered evil just as all his forebears
had done; he did not turn from the sin of Jeroboam son of Nebat who made Is-
rael sin. 10 Shallum son of Jabesh conspired against him and at-
tacked him in Ibleam and killed him, taking his place as king.
11 The rest of Zechariah's affairs are written on the scroll of the chronicles of
the kings of Israel. *12 This was the word of YHWH that he spoke to Jehu, "Your de-
scendants to the fourth generation will sit on the throne of Israel." So it happened.*
13 Shallum son of Jabesh became king in the thirty-ninth year
of Uzziah king of Judah, reigning one month in Samaria. 14 Me-
nahem son of Gadi came up from Tirzah, entered Samaria, and at-
tacked Shallum son of Jabesh, killing him, and becoming king
in his place. 15 The rest of the affairs of Shallum including the conspiracy
he engineered are written on the scroll of the chronicles of the kings of Israel.
16 Then Menahem destroyed Tappuah and all who were in it and its borders
from Tirzah because they did not open, and the pregnant women in it he cut
open. 17 In the thiry-ninth year of Azariah king of Judah, Mena-
hem son of Gadi became king over Israel in Samaria for ten

years. 18 He did what YHWH considered evil, not turning from the sin of Jero-
boam son of Nebat who made Israel sin. In his days 19 Pul king of As-
syria came up against the land, and Menahem gave to Pul 1000
talents of silver to ensure his support to secure his hold on
the kingdom. 20 Menahem exacted the money to give to the king
of Assyria from all the wealthy of Israel: fifty shekels from
each man. Then the king of Assyria returned and did not stay any longer in
the land. 21 The rest of Menahem's affairs including all that he accomplished
are of course written on the scroll of the chronicles of the kings of Israel. 22 Me-
nahem lay down with his forebears, and Pekahiah his son became king in his
place. 23 In the fiftieth year of Azariah king of Judah, Peka-
hiah son of Menahem became king over Israel in Samaria for two
years. 24 He did what YHWH considered evil, not turning from the sin of Jero-
boam son of Nebat who made Israel sin. 25 Pekah son of Remaliah, his
adjutant, conspired against him and attacked him in Samaria
in the citadel of the king's house with fifty men from the Gil-
eadites, killing him and reigning in his place. 26 The rest of Pe-
kahiah's affairs, including all that he accomplished, are written on the scroll of
the chronicles of the kings of Israel. 27 In the fifty-second year of Aza-
riah king of Judah Pekah son of Remaliah became king over Is-
rael in Samaria for twenty years. 28 He did what YHWH considered
evil, not turning from the sin of Jeroboam son of Nebat who made Israel sin.
29 During Pekah's reign Tiglath-Pileser the king of Assyria
came up and captured Ijon, Abel Beth-Maacah, Janoah, Qadesh,
Hazor, Gilead, and Galilee—all the land of Naphtali—and took them
into exile to Assyria. 30 Hoshea son of Elah engineered a con-
spiracy against Pekah son of Remaliah and attacked him and
killed him, reigning in his place in the twentieth year of Jotham son
of Uzziah. 31 The rest of the affairs of Pekah, including all that he accomplished,
are written on the scroll of the chronicles of the kings of Israel. 32 In the sec-
ond year of Pekah son of Remaliah king of Israel, Jotham son
of Uzziah became king over Judah. 33 He was twenty-five years
old when he became king, and he reigned sixteen years in Jeru-
salem; his mother's name was Yerushah daughter of Zadok. 34 He
did what YHWH considered right according to all that Uzziah his father had
done, 35 except that the cultic installations were not removed; the people con-
tinued slaughtering animals and burning food offerings on the cultic installa-
tions. He it was who built the upper gate of YHWH's temple. 36 The
rest of Jotham's affairs, including all that he accomplished, are of course writ-
ten on the scroll of the chronicles of the kings of Judah. 37 At that time YHWH
began to send Razon king of Aram and Pekah son of Remaliah into Judah.
38 Jotham lay down with his forebears and was buried in the city of David. His
son Ahaz reigned in his place.

Textual Notes

1 **twenty-seventh**: The figure contradicts those given elsewhere: Amaziah reigned twenty-nine years (14:2), fifteen of which followed the death of Joash of Israel (14:17). Thus Azariah would have acceded in Jeroboam's fifteenth year.[1]

Azariah: The short form of the name (עזריה) occurs in 14:21; 15:1, 7, 17, 23, 27, the long form (עזריהו) in 15:6, 8. He is also known as Uzziah (עזיה in 15:13, 30; עזיהו in 15:32, 34). In v. 13 G^{BL}, Vulgate, and Targum have Azariah in place of MT's Uzziah, and in v. 32 G^{B} reflects Azariah instead of Uzziah. Chronicles consistently reads עזיהו (double ו) except for 1 Chr 3:12, which has עזריה. Isaiah 1:1; 6:1; 7:1 employ עזיהו while Hos 1:1; Amos 1:1; Zech 14:5 have עזיה. The name Azariah for this king is therefore unique to Kings and 1 Chr 3:12. The reason for the two names is unknown. It is often suggested that Azariah was the king's personal name and Uzziah his throne name, based on the fact that the prophets use the latter exclusively.[2] However, there is no unambiguous evidence for distinct throne names in Israel, so that the two names are more likely variants. They differ in Hebrew by only one consonant, and the two roots on which they are based are similar semantically, with meanings of "YHWH has helped" (Azariah) and "YHWH is my strength" (Uzziah). The Azriau mentioned in the annals of Tiglath-Pileser III is not to be identified with Azariah of Judah.[3] Uzziah's name occurs on two unprovenanced seals referring to two different servants of his who are not mentioned in the Bible.[4]

over Judah: See on 8:16.

2 **his mother's name was Jekoliah from Jerusalem**: The witnesses reflect two different vocalizations stemming from different names. MT *Jekoliah* from √יכל means "YHWH has shown himself capable, powerful."[5] *Jekiliah* reflected in G^{L} (Ιεχελια) in agreement with the *ketiv* of 2 Chr 26:3 (יכיליה) is from √כול, meaning "YHWH sustains." G^{B} (Χαλειὰ) reflects the loss of the initial *yod* due to haplography.

4 **cultic installations**: See on 1 Kgs 22:44.

were not removed: See on 14:4.

continued slaughtering animals and burning food offerings: See on 1 Kgs 22:44.

5 **struck**: נגע (*to touch*) is used in certain contexts for divine affliction (1 Sam 6:9; Job 1:11; 2:5; 19:21), and this is the exclusive sense of the three instances of the *Pi'el* in the HB (15:5//2 Chr 26:20; Gen 12:17). The noun often refers to a divinely sent plague (Gen 12:17; Exod 11:1; 1 Kgs 8:27//2 Chr 6:28; Pss 38:12; 39:11. In Leviticus 13 it is used repeatedly to refer to skin disease.

living: So MT, G^{L}. G^{B}: *reigning.*

---

1 The figure of 27 years may have been miscalculation by subtracting the 15th year of Amaziah's reign when Jeroboam acceded (14:23) from his regnal total of 29 years (14:2) and then the 14-year remainder from Jeroboam's 41-year total (14:23).

2 E.g., Seow, *Kings,* 245. Stade (*Kings*, 569n) proposed that the name Uzza' (עזא, 21:18) was an abbreviation for Azariah that subsequently was transformed into Uzziah.

3 N. Na'aman ("Sennacherib's 'Letter to God' on His Campaign to Judah," *BASOR* 214 [1974]: 25–39) showed that a fragment formerly identified as part of these annals and containing the names [...]*yau* and *Iaudi* (formerly read as "Judah") is from a later inscription of Sennacherib and refers to a ruler of northern Aram. The identity of Azriau is unknown. The name appears to be Yahwistic and suggests the presence of Israelites or Judahites in northern Aram, the area dealt with in Tiglath-Pileser III's annals, but how they got there is unclear. See also the earlier discussion on 14:28aβ.

4 Avigad and Sass, *Stamp Seals*, 50–51 (#3 and 4).

5 Noth, *Personennamen*, 190.

a quarantined residence: The exact sense of בבית החפשית is elusive. חפשית occurs only here and in the parallel in 2 Chr 26:21 (*qere'*), whose *ketiv*, חפשות, may be the better spelling. חפשי is used for a person who is freed from slavery (Exod 21:2, 5, 26, 27; Deut 15:12, 13, 18; Jer 34:9-11, 14, 16; Isa 58:6; Job 3:19) or exempt from taxes and conscription (1 Sam 17:25). This meaning has been applied to the present passage, so that Azariah/Uzziah is understood to be exempted from his kingly duties.[6] In Ps 88:6 the psalmist describes himself as "free" among the dead, having been abandoned by YHWH. Similarly, the Baal cycle (*KTU* 1.4 8.7-9) contains the expression *btḫpṯt* as a single word, probably a euphemism, referring to the underworld:[7]

wrd. btḫpṯt.'arṣ Go down to the *btḫpṯt*, the underworld;
tspr.byrdm.'arṣ Be counted among those who descend to the underworld.

By extension a euphemism for the underworld might be used for some kind of sanatorium.[8] The rendering here borrows Rudolph's conclusion that "house of freedom" is a euphemism actually meaning "house of no freedom" i.e., a place of isolation or quarantine.[9]

Jotham: So MT, G^L^ (Ιωαθαμ). G^B^, OL: *Jonathan*. Meaning: "YHWH has shown himself righteous."[10]

over the house: The phrase is used elsewhere in Kings as a title for the royal steward (1 Kgs 16:9; 18:3; 2 Kgs 10:5; 18:18, 37; 19:2), and that may be its sense here as well—that Jotham served as royal steward while his father was alive but in quarantine.[11]

governing: Judging legal matters was a significant function of the king (2 Sam 15:2-4). Nonetheless, the point of the present verse is not that Jotham took over only the judgeship function of his father's kingship but that he assumed his governing role as a whole. The verb שפט is usually translated "judge" but also contains more general connotations of ruling and leading in battle, as in the book of Judges. The verbs *ṯpṭ* (= Hebrew *špṭ*) and *mlk* are used as synonyms in Ugaritic (*KTU* 1.4 4.43-44). Still, the HB retains a clear distinction between the roles of judge and king, as is clear from the books devoted to each, and the absence of the title "king" and of the verb מלך from the present verse cautions against too readily assuming that Jotham was officially considered to have been king before his father's death,[12] all the more if Jotham's post was that of royal steward.

---

6 Cogan and Tadmor, *II Kings*, 166 (citing Qimḥi [Rosenberg, *Kings II*, 350]); Montgomery, *Kings*, 448. Klostermann (*Könige*, 444), followed by Gray (*Kings*, 618n, 620), emends to בביתה חפשית, "in his house released (from royal obligations)."

7 M. S. Smith and W. T. Pitard, *The Ugaritic Baal Cycle* Vol. II (VTSup 114; Leiden: Brill, 2009), 714–16, render *btḫpṯt* as "House of Servitude."

8 M. D. Coogan (*Stories from Ancient Canaan*, 106) translates "sanatorium." In the 2nd edition (Coogan and M. S. Smith [2012], 138) the translation is "isolation ward.". Cf. Würthwein, *1. Könige 17–2. Könige 25*, 376n.

9 W. Rudolph, "Ussias 'Haus der Freiheit,'" *ZAW* 89 (1977): 418–20. He does not consider the Ugaritic evidence.

10 Noth, *Personennamen*, 189–90. The name *ytm* attested on a seal found near Elath and previously taken as a reference to King Jotham or a Judahite official is actually Edomite and refers to a name (Yatom) meaning "orphan." See J. Naveh and S. Shaked, "A Recently Published Aramaic Papyrus," *JAOS* 91 (1971), 381.

11 Alternatively, "over the house" is not a title but contrasts the palace where Jotham rules with the בית החפשית where Azariah is housed. So Hentschel *Könige 2*, 68; Šanda, *Könige* II, 179.

12 Similarly Hobbs, *2 Kings*, 195.

7 **and was buried**: So G^L. MT, G^B: *and they buried him*. The passive occurs in nearby instances of the formula (14:16, 20; 15:38). The second instance of the phrase *with his forebears* is redundant despite its attestation in the major witnesses (MT, G^{BL}, and 2 Chr 26:23).

8 **over Israel in Samaria**: So MT, G^B following the order predominating elsewhere (1 Kgs 16:8, 29; 22:52; 2 Kgs 3:1; 13:1, 10; 15:23, 27). G^L: *in Samaria over Israel* as in 17:1 (MT).

9 **just as all his forebears had done**: So G^L. MT, G^B lack *all*. Its inclusion in identical and similar expressions in 14:3; 15:3, 34; 23:32, 37 (MT) suggests that it should be included here as well.

the sin of Jeroboam: Reading the singular as in previous instances of this theme.

10 **Shallum**: This may be an independent name or an abbreviation of a longer name (HALOT 1511). Its meaning could be active ("replacement")[13] or passive ("replaced," HALOT). In the latter case a better sense might be "compensated for," i.e., "one for whom compensation has been paid," suggesting that his birth was viewed as the response of the deity to a vow made and subsequently paid by his parents.

conspired: So MT, G^L. G^B has the plural verb even though its subject, Shallum, is singular. The plural results from the interpretation of קבל־עם as the name of Shallum's co-conspirator. See next Note.

in Ibleam: So G^L. MT, G^B read קבל־עם, a *hapax legomenon* that is nonsensical. It is sometimes explained as two words: Aramaic *qᵒbol* taken to mean "before" and *'am*, "people," although the latter would require the definite article. This is the place in a conspiracy notice where one expects a place name, and Ibleam is associated elsewhere (2 Kgs 9:27) with royal assassination.

and killed him: So MT, G^B. Lost from G^L by haplography (וימיתהו ... וימלך).

taking his place as king: So MT, G^B. G^L expands with Shallum's name at the end of the verse.

11 **Zechariah's affairs**: So MT, G^B. G^L + *including all that he accomplished* (= וכל־אשר עשה) as per the usual formula. In view of the brevity of Shallum's reign and the absence of any mechanism for haplography, the plus is probably an expansion.[14]

are written: Here and in three other instances of the formula in this chapter (vv. 15, 26, 31) MT and G^B have an irregular version—הנם כתובים instead of הלא־הם כתובים—without the interrogative or negative particle. G^L reflects the same variant to MT as elsewhere.

12 **This was the word of Yhwh**: So MT, G^L. G^B lacks the demonstrative pronoun.

to Jehu: So MT, G^B. G^L + *son of Nimshi*.

13 **Shallum son of Jabesh became king in the thirty-ninth year of Azariah king of Judah, reigning one month in Samaria**: Based on MT. G^{BL} have only minor variants. This instance of the opening regnal formula is different from the others in ch. 15 (vv. 8, 17, 23, 27) and is reconstructed by Stade to resemble them.[15] However, the formula here resembles those in 1 Kgs 15:25; 16:29; 22:52; 2 Kgs 3:1, and is retained for that reason.

14 **Menahem**: The name means "comforter." It may have been given because of the loss of a previous child or with a view to the parents' old age.

Jabesh: G^L + *in Samaria.*

and becoming king in his place: So MT, G^L. Lost from G^B by haplography (αὐτόν ... αὐτοῦ).

15 **he engineered**: Lit. "which he conspired." So MT, G^B. G^L + *against Zechariah.*

---

13 Noth, *Personennamen*, 174.
14 Stade, *Kings*, 252.
15 Stade, *Kings*, 252.

are written: See on v. 11.

16 **destroyed**: On the use of the preterit *yiqtol* with *'az* see Joüon 113i. ויך is a misplaced dittography of יכה.[16] In MT it conflicts with בקע. It is absent from G^{L}. G^{B} (καὶ ἐπάταξεν αὐτὴν) corrects by supplying an object.

Tappuah: So G^{L}. G^{B}: (Tirzah) is influenced by Tirzah's occurrence later in the verse. MT reads *Tipsah*. Meaning "ford," this city, later known as Thapsacus, was on the bend of the upper Euphrates and marked the northern and eastern extent of Solomon's empire according to 1 Kgs 5:4 (EV 4:24). The distance from Israel makes it unlikely that this was the site of Menahem's brutal act. The point is not so much whether anything would have prevented him from traveling such a distance but that there was no real motive for him to do so.[17] The reason for his brutality is to be sought in his struggle for the throne and hence close to home. Moreover, Thapsacus is not attested in ancient sources before Xenophon's *Anabasis* (I.4 11, 18), 1 Kgs 5:4 probably being a gloss.[18] The exact location of Tappuah ("quince" or "apple") is uncertain, though a good candidate is Tell Sheikh Abu Zarad, some 10 km (6 mi) southwest of Shechem (Nablus). The city was on the border of Ephraim and Manasseh (Josh 16:8; 17:7-8).

they did not open: So G^{B}. MT's masculine singular is impossible.[19]

the pregnant women in it: MT's ההרותיה is a double reading with both suffix and definite article.[20]

17 **in Samaria for ten years**: So G^{L} following the usual order. See on v. 8.

18 **from the sin of Jeroboam**: MT's מעל is a mistake for מכל.[21] But G^{L}, which lacks *all*, is preferable. Again the singular *sin* accords with the theme in the book of Kings.

In his days: So G^{B}. Similarly G^{L}: "In the days of Menahem." MT's כל־ימיו is a corruption that occurred after the phrase was construed with v. 18.

19 **Pul**: A nickname of Tiglath-Pileser III (745–727) from the Assyrian word *pūlu*, "limestone block," though it appears in the Neobabylonian period.[22]

came up: So G^{BL} (ἀνέβη) reflecting עלה, the verb typically used in Kings for the invasion of a foreign king (1 Kgs 9:16; 14:25; 2 Kgs 16:7; 17:3; 18:9, 13, 25; 23:29; 24:1, 10). MT has בא.

Pul (2): So MT, G^{B}. G^{L} + *the king of Assyria*.

1000 talents of silver: See on 5:5. A talent was a unit of weight roughly equal to 75.4 lbs. Hence 1000 talents would be more than 37 tons.

to secure his hold on the kingdom: So MT, G^{L}. Lost by haplography from G^{B}.

---

16 Cf. S. Talmon, "Double Readings in the Massoretic Text," *Textus* 1 (1960), 177.

17 Jones, *Kings*, 523. P. Dubovský ("Menahem's Reign before the Assyrian Invasion [2 Kgs 15:14-16]," in *Literature as Politics, Politics as Literature: Essays on the Ancient Near East in Honor of Peter Machinist* [Winona Lake, IN: Eisenbrauns, 2013], 29–45) accepts the *Tipsah* reading, taking it as ideological hyperbole. But the accuracy he finds in other details of vv. 14-16 suggests that he is trying to have it both ways.

18 Cogan and Tadmor, *II Kings*, 171.

19 Provan (*Kings*, 243) retains the MT, taking it to mean that Menahem could not persuade the city to open to him. But this meaning is unattested and would probably require the *Hip'îl*. Dubovský ("Menahem's Reign," 40–41) also keeps the MT, citing an Akkadian parallel for פתח as "to breach."

20 Talmon, "Double Readings," 177.

21 Benzinger (*Könige*, 168), Burney (*Notes*, 322), Gray (*Kings*, 623), *et al.*

22 O. Loretz and W. Mayer, "Pūlu-Tiglatpileser III. und Menahem von Israel nach assyrischen Quellen und 2 Kön 15,19-20," *UF* 22 (1990), esp. 228–29.

20 **exacted**: יצא (*Hip'îl*) in the sense of exacting a payment or levying a tax is unparalleled, though Akkadian *šūṣû* can mean "deliver payment" and the *Hip'îl* of יצא in post-biblical Hebrew can mean "carry away."[23] The use of על suggests that the verb has the sense of imposing a tax upon.[24]

of Israel: So MT, G^{B}. G^{L}: *of all Israel* (ἐπὶ πάντα Ισραηλ).

fifty shekels: So G^{BL}. MT + *of silver.*

any longer: So G^{L}. MT, G^{B}: שם, which is unnecessary preceding *in the land.*

21 **are of course written**: So MT. G^{BL}: οὐκ ἰδοὺ ταῦτα γεγραμμένα [B]/γέγραπται [L], a constant variant between MT and G^{L} in Kings. G^{B} agrees with G^{L} against MT.

22 **Pekahiah**: The name means "Yhwh has opened (the eyes/womb)."[25] It occurs on an unprovenanced seal from the eighth–seventh century.[26]

23 **for two years**: So MT, G^{B}. G^{L}: *for ten years.*

24 **from the sin of Jeroboam**: As elsewhere and in accord with the theme of the sin (singular) of Jeroboam in the book of Kings. Here MT and G^{B} have the plural *sins* while G^{L} has *all the sins.*

25 **Pekah**: The name is the same as Pekahiah without the theophoric element. It occurs on an unprovenanced seal and on a jar handle from Hazor.[27]

in the citadel of the king's house: So MT. G^{L} lacks *in the citadel*, the result of haplography.

with fifty men: Deleting MT's את־ארגב ואת־האריה as a misplaced gloss to *Gilead* in v. 29.[28] The misplacement occurred because of the reference to Gilead here in v. 25. Stade reconstructed the gloss as referring to Argob and Havvoth-Jair in the region of Bashan and northern Gilead (1 Kgs 4:13).[29]

from the Gileadites: So G^{L}. MT has the same reading without the article.[30] G^{B}: *from the 400.*

26 **are written**: See on vv. 11, 15.

28 **the sin of Jeroboam**: Reading the singular *sin* in accord with the theme in the book of Kings. The witnesses read the plural. G^{BL}: *all the sins of Jeroboam.*

29 **During Pekah's reign**: Lit. *In the days of Pekah.* So G^{L}. MT, G^{B} + *king of Israel.*

Tiglath-Pileser: Previously called Pul (v. 19), Tiglath-Pileser (*Tukulti apil Esharra*) means "my help is the son of Esharra" ("house of the universe," the temple of Ashur in the city of Ashur.[31]

---

23 Stade (*Kings*, 253) cites similar phenomena with Arabic and Aramaic verbs.

24 Klostermann (*Könige*, 446) proposed ויצו ("he commanded") by analogy with Ezra 8:17, and is followed by Benzinger (*Könige*, 168), Burney (*Notes*, 322–23), and Kittel (*Könige*, 265), among others. But the emendation requires further changes—the deletion of הכסף, the substitution of כל for על (1), and the deletion of על (2). In view of the structure of the sentence and the possibilities for יצא it is best to retain MT (so Stade, *Kings*, 253).

25 So Fowler, *Theophoric Personal Names*, 94. Noth (*Personennamen*, 186) suggests "Yhwh is open-eyed, alert."

26 Avigad and Sass, *Stamp Seals*, #1123, p. 426.

27 Avigad and Sass, *Stamp Seals*, #1170, pp. 443, 526–27. Y. Yadin, et al., *Hazor II* (Jerusalem: Magnes, 1960) plates 170–71.

28 Stade, *Kings*, 253–54.

29 Other proposals include "the eagle and the lion," a circumlocution for sphinx statues positioned as guardians of the palace in Samaria where Pekahiah was murdered (M. J. Geller, "A New Translation for 2 Kings XV 25," *VT* 26 [1976]: 374–77) and "Argob and Aryeh" referring to units of guards (Wiseman, *Kings*, 271).

30 MT may reflect a double reading, conflating מבני גלעד and מהגלעדים (Benzinger, *Könige*, 168).

31 A. R. Millard, "Assyrian Royal Names in Biblical Hebrew," *JSS* 21 (1976), 7.

came up: So G^L (ἀνέβη =עלה) in preference to MT, G^B. See on v. 19.

Qadesh: So MT. G^{BL}: τὴν Κενεζ.

Galilee: The final syllable (unstressed *-ah*) on *Galil* is dubious (Joüon 93k) and perhaps a sign of the name's secondary status.[32]

all the land of Naphtali: So MT, G^B. G^L: *and all the land of Naphtali.* The reading has possible implications for the composition and geography of the passage. See the Diachronic Analysis.

30 **Hoshea**: So MT (הושע). An abbreviated form of הושעיה meaning "Yhwh has saved."[33] The same in Hebrew as the prophet Hosea. Found also in Elephantine (*COS* 3.49, 67, 87A; *ANET* 492).

and killed him: So MT, G^L. G^B lacks the object pronoun *him*, which is syntactically necessary.

in the twentieth year of Jotham son of Uzziah: So MT. Absent from G^L. G^B uniquely reads *Ahaz* for *Uzziah*. The sentence is chronologically problematic since Jotham reigned only sixteen years (16:2).

31 **are written**: See on v. 11.

32 **Uzziah**: So MT, G^L, OL. G^B: "Azariah."

over Judah: See on 8:16.

33 **Yerushah**: So 2 Chr 27:1 and certain mss of Kings (ירושה). MT has ירושא. The name, meaning "taken into possession," is one of a class of names that describe particular circumstances experienced by the bearer in childhood.[34]

34 **had done**: So G^{BL}. The second עשה at the end of the verse in MT is a misplaced dittography.

35 **were not removed**: So MT. G^{BL}: *he did not remove*. The predominant formula elsewhere in Kings uses the *Qal* (1 Kgs 15:14; 22:44; 2 Kgs 12:4; 13:6; 14:4; 15:35; 17:22).

the people continued slaughtering animals and burning food offerings: See on 1 Kgs 22:44.

36 **including all that he accomplished**: So G^{BL}. MT lacks *all*, which nonetheless predominates in this formula (1 Kgs 11:41; 14:29; 15:3, 7, 23, 31; 16:14; 19:1; 22:39; 2 Kgs 10:34; 12:20; 13:8, 12; 14:28; 15:6, 21, 26, 31; 23:12, 28; 24:5).

are of course written: So MT, G^B. G^L as usual has οὐκ ἰδοὺ ταῦτα γέγραπται.

37 **Razon**: The Greek Ραασσων together with the Akkadian transcriptions *ᵐRa-ḫi-a-nu*, *ᵐRa-qi-a-nu* < **Raṣyan* indicate that this is the correct vocalization of the second syllable.[35] The name was originally *Raḏyān*, from the Proto-Semitic root **rḏy* "to be pleased with." The *yod* was part of the root but was taken as a *mater lectionis*.[36]

into Judah: So MT, G^L; absent from G^B.

38 **Jotham**: So MT, G^{BL}. OL: Jonathan.

and was buried: MT, G^B repeat *with his forebears*. G^L has the phrase after *in the city of David*, suggesting that it is secondary.[37]

David: So G^L, OL. MT, G^B + *his ancestor.*

---

32 Cogan and Tadmor (*II Kings*, 174) call it a late, Aramaized form.

33 Noth, *Personennamen*, 22, 32, 176.

34 Noth, *Personennamen*, 231–32.

35 Cogan and Tadmor, *II Kings*, 182.

36 Pitard, *Ancient Damascus*, 181–82.

37 Stade, *Kings*, 142–43, 255.

Synchronic Analysis

Five kings of Israel between two kings of Judah

The chapter begins and ends with kings of Judah: Azariah and Jotham. Sandwiched between them are the reigns of five kings of Israel—Zechariah, Shallum, Menahem, Pekahiah, and Pekah. The difference in the number of kings covered for each kingdom in roughly the same period of time is indicative of the instability of the North. The brevity of most of their reigns suggests a precipitous decline toward a disastrous end for the nation. It is the sin of Jeroboam, which all its kings commit, that propels Israel inevitably toward that end—the end suggested by the "not yets" of the previous two chapters, which explain how YHWH's mercy in the reigns of Jehoahaz, Jehoash, and Jeroboam held off Israel's destruction.

15:1-7: Azariah/ Uzziah of Judah

Azariah/Uzziah (vv. 1-7) reigns second longest (after Manasseh, 21:1) of any king of Israel or Judah, yet the account of his reign is minimal. He is basically righteous, although the statement that he did right as his father had done (v. 3) is a two-edged sword. The standard of judgment is his father Amaziah rather than David. Amaziah did as his father Joash had done, neither of them measuring up to David (14:3). The reason for the reservation is the cultic installations (*bāmôt*) that continued in existence under Azariah's reign as they did under Joash and Amaziah. According to the scheme of "crime and punishment" that has been unfolding in Kings we expect the report of some disaster to follow that of his retention of the *bāmôt*, and as with Amaziah we do not have to wait long. The text is explicit in v. 5: YHWH struck Azariah with skin disease, making his name in both forms ("YHWH has helped" and "YHWH is my strength") ironic. The only reason for the disease that is hinted at in the narrative is Azariah's non-removal of the *bāmôt*. The notice helps to explain why the account of Azariah's reign is so short. His long-standing disease prevented him from undertaking many of the duties and responsibilities of the king; these fell to his son Jotham instead. Hence there was little to report about his actual time on the throne. By the time Jotham becomes king in his own right (v. 7) he has had years of experience in the exercise of the office.

15:8-12: Zechariah of Israel

Despite his brief reign (6 months), Zechariah receives a full account, complete with regnal formulae (vv. 8-12), including his evaluation. Like all of his peers in Israel he subscribes to the sin of Jeroboam. Although his reign is shorter than most, he is just as guilty of this sin. His closing formulae do not include the clause "including all that he did," perhaps because he was not in power long enough to accomplish much. His assassination by Shallum brings an end to his reign and to the Jehu dynasty. The notice in v. 12, by its position outside the regnal formulae, draws attention to the fulfillment of the oracle in 10:30 about the duration of the Jehu dynasty. Zechariah occupies the throne just long enough, it appears, to fulfill that prophecy. Verse 12b, ויהי־כן, brings to mind the creation in Genesis 1 (vv. 7, 9, 11, 24, 30) as a reminder that the god who created the world is the one who oversees Israel's history.

15:13-16: Shallum of Israel

The reign of the assassin, Shallum, is even shorter than Zechariah's (vv. 13-16). It stands out for its less common, though not unique, beginning with Shallum's name and patronymic preceding the dating formula. This beginning ensures that Shallum will not be completely ignored by readers despite the brevity of his reign.[38] The narrative illustrates this potential danger by its lack of the standard evaluation for Shallum. There is no mention of the sin of Jeroboam, yet there is no reason to believe that Shallum was innocent of it or that YHWH did not consider him evil like all the other kings of Israel. Shallum's reign is the definition of *quid pro quo*; he is assassinated after barely having had a chance to be seated on the throne. His assassin is Menahem. In brutal contrast to the meaning of his name, Menahem brings grief rather than comfort. The level of violence illustrated by the anecdote in v. 16—again highlighted because of its location outside the regnal formulae—is unprecedented in Israel's regnal history. Jehu's purge of the Omrids and Athaliah's slaughter of the royal heirs at least had political agendas. The language (אז + imperfect) connects Menahem's deed with his assassination of Shallum and his assumption of power. But the act itself appears gratuitous. The reason given for it—*one did not open* (לא פתח)—is obscure. Who did not open what, and why was this significant? It explains nothing and is more in the way of a grotesque play on ideas. Someone did not open something that Menahem wanted opened, so he responded by opening all the pregnant women of Tipsah. The point lies in what the anecdote reveals about the character of Menahem and of the monarchy of Israel at this (as it turns out) late date in the nation's existence.

15:17-22: Menahem of Israel

Menahem is not explicitly condemned for his extreme violence. The only condemnation he receives is the usual—that he committed the sin of Jeroboam (v. 18). The narrative again slants toward cultic issues rather than concerns about violence. The single episode from Menahem's reign is the incursion of the Assyrian king, Tiglath-Pileser III (vv. 19-20). It is peculiar in that Menahem pays off the invading Assyrian not so that he would call off the invasion but to ensure his support (lit. *so that his hands would be with him*) in order to strengthen his own hold on the kingdom. The statement implies that there were rivals within Israel for Menahem's throne. These might be supporters of Shallum, whom Menahem assassinated, and might include Pekah, who would assassinate and replace Menahem's son and successor, Pekahiah. Menahem's cleverness at manipulating the situation to his advantage is impressive. He uses the invasion of a much stronger foreign power—a potentially devastating turn of events—to his own political advantage. In addition, he finances the payoff with a special levy on the wealthy (v. 20). The stratagem worked at least in the short run since Menahem lived out his life as king and passed the throne to his son (vv. 21-22). Still, the move probably infuriated the upper class and exacerbated the subsurface discontent that Menahem held at bay but that would overthrow his son. In sum, it is only seven months since Jeroboam II when Menahem becomes king. Menahem restores stability for a time, but there are hints that the turmoil that burst forth at the end of the Jehu dynasty is just being held in check by Menahem's ruthless and clever machinations. Uncertainty and discontent are palpable.

15:23-26: Pekahiah of Israel

Pekahiah's reign (vv. 23-26) is little more than a residual of his father's reign and lasts as long as it does (two years) because of Menaham's force of character and the policies he put in place. The only portion of the account of Pekahiah's reign that is not an element of the standard regnal formulae is the report of his assassination (v. 25). Even here the report closely follows the standard form for a conspiracy with its sequence of verbs: *conspired* (ויקשר) ... *attacked* (ויכהו) ... *killed*

38 Cf. Cohn, *II Kings*, 107; Wray Beal, *Kings*, 428.

(וימיתה) ... *replaced* (וימלך תחתיו). The neatness of the account belies the turmoil of the moment. The leader and instigator of the conspiracy as well as the assassin who replaces Pekahiah is his adjutant, Pekah. The title "adjutant" (שליש) indicates that the two men had a close personal relationship, one suggested also by the sameness of their names. The mention of the citadel alludes to Zimri's assassination/suicide (1 Kgs 16:18) and hints that Pekahiah, like Zimri, had taken himself there for protection. Only a trusted servant like Pekah would have been able to gain access. The fifty men with him could have posed as a special body guard. Their designation as Gileadites may identify them as relatives of Shallum, whose patronymic was Jabesh (v. 13), the name of the prominent city Jabesh-Gilead. Revenge was thus a likely ingredient of the motive. The fifty may have been necessary to counter the two figures Argob and Aryeh. Their mention here is difficult; the text is ambiguous, but they are apparently victims of assassination along with Pekahiah. Argob is used elsewhere as a place name for a region north of Gilead in Bashan. Aryeh means "lion" and hints at the ferocity of the bearer.

15:27-31: Pekah of Israel

The length of Pekah's reign (vv. 27-31)—twenty years—doubles Menahem's, yet he seems less important because less is reported about him and because he is a passive rather than an active participant. His name resembles his predecessor's and suggests that he is little more than a carbon copy.[39] Again most of Pekah's account consists of regnal formulae (vv. 27-28, 31). Encased within them are accounts of Tiglath-Pileser III's invasion (v. 29) and Pekah's assassination (v. 30). The former lists five cities in the tribal territory of Naphtali followed by the names of three regions, one of which is Naphtali. The cities are not necessarily places the Assyrians besieged and captured. Both lists serve to give a configuration of the area captured and from which people were deported to Assyria. The episode forebodes the greater deportation associated with the destruction of Samaria and the end of the kingdom of Israel a decade or so later (2 Kgs 17). For the regions mentioned, though, that end has already arrived. What remains of Israel is a rump state. The most natural reading of v. 30 in its location immediately after v. 29 is that Hoshea's conspiracy and the assassination of Pekah were the direct result of the Assyrian invasion. That is, because of the invasion and loss of territory Pekah was deemed unfit to continue ruling and was killed.

15:32-38: Jotham of Judah

After the litany of Northern kings the narrative turns back to Judah and the reign of Jotham (vv. 32-38). As with his Israelite counterparts, his regnal account is mostly formulaic. Like his father, grandfather, and great-grandfather he is basically righteous. But also like them he does not remove the cultic installations (v. 35a). The account of disaster that we have come to expect following this reservation is in the non-formulaic part of his account (v. 37). An earlier non-formulaic notice (v. 35b) mentions that Jotham built the upper gate of the temple. This notice suggests Jotham's concern for the temple and helps to explain why the disaster he faced in punishment for the crime of not removing the *bāmôt* is less severe than those suffered by his forebears. It is not a devastating skin disease or assassination, but only the beginning encroachments of Pekah and Rezin king of Aram (v. 37). The location of this verse outside of Jotham's regnal formulae calls attention to it. He is not let off completely free for failing to remove the *bāmôt*; the narrative stresses that Pekah and Rezin came at

---

39 Cohn, *2 Kings*, 108.

YHWH's behest (החל יהוה להשליח). But the bulk of the ill effects of Pekah's and Rezin's incursions comes in the reign of Jotham's son and successor, Ahaz, as the next chapter and its companion piece, Isaiah 7, show.

Diachronic Analysis

DtrH regnal accounts with chronological problems

This chapter contains seven brief regnal accounts, all consisting predominantly of DtrH formulae with source materials mixed in. A few later additions are discernible mainly because they lie outside the DtrH formulae. The issues of chronology presented by the chapter are daunting, and there are many of them. The disagreement of the textual witnesses is not really an issue here because the OG chronology is no longer extant.[40] However, the figures within a given witness are also inconsistent. Thus the reference in 15:1 MT to Azariah taking the throne of Judah in the twenty-seventh year of Jeroboam of Israel disagrees with the chronological references in 14:2, 17, 23, which indicate the fifteenth year of Jeroboam as that of Azariah's accession. Likewise, 15:8, 13, 17 agree with each other in dating Zechariah's accession to Azariah's thirty-eighth year, but they are at odds with 14:17, 23, which indicate that Zechariah acceded in Azariah's twenty-sixth year (since Azariah acceded in the fifteenth of Jeroboam's forty-one years). These major disagreements transcend the minor disparities of a year or two that also exist but might be explained by differences in record-keeping or the use of different calendars.

Jepsen's theory of co-regency with Azariah

Another illustration of the chronological problems is the totals for the kings of Israel and kings of Judah, which are very far apart for the period from the beginning of Azariah's reign to the fall of Samaria:

Judah	**Israel**
Azariah/Uzziah - 52	Jeroboam - 26[41]
Jotham - 16	Zechariah - 6 months
Ahaz - 16	Shallum - 1 month

40 Shenkel, *Chronology*, 26. MT and G^{BL} agree on the chronological data in the synchronisms everywhere except at v. 23, and this one variant reading does not represent an independent chronology. G^{L} also lacks the reference in v. 30 to Jotham's 20th year, which is incompatible with MT's chronology elsewhere. The Lucianic witness c_2 attests a unique chronological system that is late and artificial and not OG (Shenkel, *Chronology*, 28–31). C. M. Tetley (*The Reconstructed Chronology of the Divided Kingdom* [Winona Lake, IN: Eisenbrauns, 2005], esp. 54–63) dismisses Shenkel's arguments and relies heavily on c_2 for her chronological reconstruction. The result is an impossibly high chronology in which Pekahiah is given 12 years instead of 2, and Pekah is given 30 years instead of 20. The resulting figure raises Menahem's dates to 780–769, forcing Tetley (pp. 176–78) to identify Pul, to whom Menahem paid tribute, as Shalmaneser IV.

41 Numbered from the year of Azariah's accession as calculated from 14:17, 23.

Judah	Israel
Hezekiah – 6[42]	Menahem – 10
	Pekahiah – 2
	Pekah – 20
	Hoshea – 9
TOTAL: 90 years	TOTAL: 67 years, 7 months

Azariah's long reign and the administration of part of it by Jotham because of his father's skin disease (v. 5) are unusual features that have suggested a partial solution to the problem of totals. In a widely accepted proposal Jepsen suggested that all of Jotham's reign and part of Ahaz's as well were included within Azariah's.[43] Jepsen pointed out the consistency in the ages of the kings of Judah at the births of their oldest sons as determined from the ages given for their successors when they ascended to the throne. The average age for this milestone is twenty.[44] Jotham is reported to have been twenty-five years old when he became king (15:33). Assuming that his father Azariah was about twenty when Jotham was born, he would have been forty-five at Jotham's accession. Since Azariah became king at age sixteen, Jotham's accession would have taken place in Azariah's twenty-ninth regnal year. This would have been the year that Azariah became afflicted with skin disease and was removed to his quarantined residence (v. 5). The remaining twenty-three years attributed to his reign, then, would have included all of Jotham's sixteen years plus the first seven years of Ahaz's reign.

Caveats

Jepsen's theory is attractive for its reduction of the total regnal years of the kings of Judah for the period from Azariah to the fall of Samaria from ninety to sixty-seven years, which is very close to the total (68) for Israelite kings during the same period. However, there are caveats. It may not be accurate to cast Jotham's *governing* (שפט) as "co-regency" since the text does not state that he was made king at this time and seems to avoid the root מלך, placing him in the role of the royal steward. This situation was also clearly atypical and not a license for postulating coregencies throughout the history of the monarchy. Moreover, however the overlap between Azariah and Jotham was understood by contemporaries, v. 7 indicates that DtrH construed their "reigns" as sequential; he employs the regular succession formula and indicates thereby that Jotham had an independent reign that began with the death of his father (v. 7).

42 The 84 years assigned to the reigns of Azariah, Jotham, and Ahaz are too long for the allotted period, which covers between 61 and 73 years. Figuring the start of Azariah's reign ca. 788 and the start of Hezekiah's reign in 727 = 61 years. If the beginning of Hezekiah's reign is dated to 715 the difference is 73 years. 2 Kings 18:10 dates the fall of Samaria to Hezekiah's sixth year (721 + 6 = 727). However, 18:13 dates the invasion of Sennacherib (701 BCE) to Hezekiah's 14th year, marking 715 as the start of his reign.

43 A. Jepsen, "Zur Chronologie der Könige von Israel und Juda: Eine Überprüfung," in *Untersuchungen zur israelitisch-jüdischen Chronologie* (ed. A. Jepsen and R. Hanhart; BZAW 88; Berlin: de Gruyter, 1964), 1–48.

44 The exceptions are readily explained (Jepsen, "Zur Chronologie," 43).

Apart from matters of chronology it is striking how little information is narrated about Azariah's reign, especially given its length. Perhaps DtrH felt there was little to say because Azariah's skin disease prevented him from accomplishing much. But other biblical writers (Amos 1:1; cf. 8:8; 9:1; Zech 14:5) mention a major earthquake during his reign, and it was a relatively prosperous time for Judah, thanks mainly to Israel's prosperity under Jeroboam II. The turmoil in Israel after Jeroboam's death and the Jehu dynasty left Judah alone to pursue its own interests.

Characterizing Azariah's reign

Azariah's skin disease is attributed to YHWH. The only reason that suggests itself for YHWH to afflict Azariah is the *bāmôt* (v. 4).[45] The exact nature of the disease is unclear (cf. 5:1). Azariah, unlike Naaman, apparently lives in isolation, his *house of freedom* being a euphemistic reference to quarantine (see the Note). While Azariah's life does not appear to be in immediate danger, fear of the disease impedes his ability to rule, so that his son Jotham takes care of the affairs of government. Kings says nothing about the disease affecting Azariah's burial, as found in other sources.[46]

Azariah's disease

The brief reign of Zechariah concludes the Jehu dynasty. The notice that he became king in Azariah's thirty-eighth year is in disagreement with 15:1 and the chronological notices in 14:17, 23 (see above). The reason is unclear. The major witnesses (MT, G^{BL}) all attest "thirty-eighth;" others that read "twenty-eighth" in agreement with 15:1 result from correction. As an Israelite king and true to his Yahwistic name ("YHWH has remembered") Zechariah maintained the shrines at Dan and Bethel, for which DtrH judged him guilty of the *sin of Jeroboam* (v. 9). Verse 10 has the usual elements of a conspiracy notice: (1) statement of conspiracy with the naming of the conspirator(s), statements that the king was (2) struck down and (3) killed, and (4) the notice of the king's replacement (1 Kgs 15:27-28; 16:9-10; 2 Kgs 12:21-22; 15:25, 30; cf. 2 Kgs 14:19-21). As with other notices, the conspirator, Shallum, bears a patronymic, *Jabesh*, which is also the name of a city and perhaps a clan in Gilead, suggesting that Shallum may have come from there. Unlike other notices, there is no information about Shallum's position or affiliation with Zechariah. This has suggested to some that Shallum was not officially

15:8-12: Zechariah and the end of the Jehu dynasty

45 Mullen, "Crime and Punishment." This explanation is insufficient for the Chronicler. After describing Uzziah's military successes, building projects, and agricultural endeavors (2 Chr 26:1-15), he states that Uzziah became proud in his strength and took upon himself prerogatives limited to the priests (26:16-21). He became angry with the priest (Azariah), who rebuked him, and he received the skin disease as punishment. In this way the Chronicler periodizes Uzziah's reign and refers in the regnal formulae to the "first and last [parts]" (2 Chr 26:22).

46 2 Chr 26:23 notes that Uzziah is buried in a field belonging to the kings of Judah but not in the royal tomb (*with his fathers* is probably a gloss). Josephus (*Ant.* 9.227) has Uzziah buried in his garden, probably an interpretation of the information in 2 Kgs 21:18, 26 that Manasseh and Amon were buried in the garden of Uzzah (C. Begg, "Josephus' Story of the Later Monarchy (AJ 9,1–10,185)," *BETL* 145 [2000], 284n). The plaque discovered in the Russian Orthodox Church on the Mount of Olives referring to "the bones of Uzziah, king of Judah" (E. Sukenik, "The Funerary Tablet of Uzziah," *PEQ* 2 [1931]: 217–21) is of unknown provenance and its historical value negligible. See W. F. Albright, "The Discovery of an Aramaic Inscription Relating to King Uzziah," *BASOR* 44 (1931), 10; P. K. McCarter, *Ancient Inscriptions: Voices from the Biblical World* (Washington, DC: Biblical Archaeology Society, 1996), 132–33.

tied with the army or the court but led a force of landowners from Transjordan.[47] Comparison with the other notices also confirms the reading Ibleam instead of MT's קבל־עם, since this phrase occurs where the other notices detail the place of assassination. Ibleam was where Jehu assassinated Ahaziah of Judah (9:27), so that its recurrence in 15:10 provides a full-circle end to the Jehu dynasty.[48]

The Jehuids' pro-Assyrian policy

The reason for Shallum's conspiracy is undisclosed, but the brevity of Zechariah's reign suggests that it may have been due to dissatisfaction with his father's policies, which he had continued. Scholars frequently surmise that the pro-Assyrian stance of the dynasty dating back to Jehu himself was unpopular. This is combined with the suggestion that Shallum was from Gilead and therefore represented Transjordanian opposition to Assyria and the Jehuids, perhaps even with the support of Damascus. The evidence is largely circumstantial,[49] though the theory does fit with clues about the origins and shifting policies vis-à-vis Assyria that can be discerned for the usurpers described in this chapter. If the theory is correct, Shallum's overthrow of Zechariah was intended to bring an end to Israel's affiliation with Assyria that had been forged and maintained by the house of Jehu.

Jeroboam II as the last real Jehuid king

There is no burial formula for Zechariah (v. 11) or any other king of Israel in this chapter, and only for Menahem (15:22) does one find the statement that he lay with his forebears. Zechariah is the last king of the last real dynasty of Israel. Given the brevity of his reign, he may never have consolidated his hold on power. Shallum may have launched his revolt at Jeroboam's death, especially if his target was the dynasty, and Zechariah's "reign" may have been spent trying to fend off the rebels, a battle he eventually lost. It is clear in any event that Jeroboam II was the last truly powerful and independent king of Israel's dynastic history; Zechariah's short stint as king marks the beginning of Israel's slide to its end.[50]

The fulfillment notice in 15:12

Verse 12 is obviously a fulfillment notice for 10:30 and could be DtrH. However, it stands between the closing formula for Zechariah (v. 11) and the opening of the account for Shallum (v. 13), i.e., outside DtrH's structural framework in Kings. It also uses the expression ויהי־כן, which is P and limited to Genesis 1 except for Judg 6:38; 2 Kgs 7:20 (ויהי־לו כן), and the present verse, which is, therefore, probably a pedantic fulfillment notice much like 7:20.

Shallum's reign

The opening for Shallum (v. 13) does not follow the format of the other regnal formulae in this chapter (vv. 8, 17, 23, 27), though it resembles a less common type of opening formula elsewhere in Kings (1 Kgs 15:25; 16:29; 22:52; 2 Kgs 3:1). Shallum's name comes first rather than the date formula. The reason for the choice of this type for Shallum may relate to the instability of his "reign." It may also have something to do with the absence of an evaluation of Shallum. It cannot be due to the brevity of Shallum's reign, since 1 Kgs 16:19 includes an evaluation for Zimri, whose reign was even shorter. The figure of Azariah's thirty-ninth year as the year of Shallum's accession is consistent with 15:8 by rounding up Zechariah's six-month reign to a year, but it disagrees with the figures in 14:17, 23; 15:1. Shallum's one month on the throne

---

47 Fricke, *Das zweite Buch von den Königen*, 196.

48 Hobbs (*2 Kings*, 196) is sensitive to the need for a place name here but argues that MT is to be preferred as the more difficult reading. He therefore reads MT's קבל־עם as an otherwise unknown place name.

49 See T. Ishida, *Royal Dynasties*, 175–76.

50 Barnes, *Kings*, 302.

is reminiscent of 1 Kings 16 in which there was an interregnum as different factions vied for control of the kingship. The month attributed to Shallum probably does not adequately represent the length of this contentious period, which probably began with Jeroboam's death. Zechariah and Shallum were temporary pretenders. This also explains why there is no conspiracy notice for Menahem; his assassination and replacement of Shallum (v. 14) was more a victory over a rival military faction than the overthrow of a sitting king.[51] In some respects DtrH treats Shallum's month in power as a discrete reign and in other respects sees it as an interregnum. The concluding formulae for Shallum (v. 15) are standard and resemble those for Zimri in 1 Kgs 16:20. The conventional nature of the formulae is evident from these two examples, since a king could not accomplish much in a week or a month.

Verse 16 is between the source notice that closes Shallum's account (v. 15) and 15:16
the opening formulae for Menahem (v. 17) and is outside of the DtrH structure. It begins with the particle אז, and it is enclosed by *setumah* and *petuhah*.[52] These features mark the verse as an addition. As it stands, the אז clause indicates that the event described here took place in conjunction with Menahem's seizure of power in v. 14.[53] He attacks the city of Tappuah (so G^L) on the Ephraim-Manasseh border, killing its citizens and ripping open its pregnant women. The reason for the attack is that the city's residents did not *open*, i.e., refused to surrender or submit to him (Deut 20:11).[54] His vicious reprisal was intended to make an example of Tappuah in order to forestall defiance by others.[55] The deed portends the brutality of Menahem's reign, though no other details to this effect are forthcoming. On the other hand, it may help to account for Menahem's relative longevity as king compared to his immediate predecessors.

Menahem is called the son of Gadi, a short form of Gadiel or Gadiyahu ("god/ 15:17: Menahem's opening formulae
YHWH is my fortune").[56] It does not identify Menahem as a member of the tribe of Gad; he comes from Tirzah in Manasseh (v. 14), the pre-Omri capital of the Northern Kingdom (1 Kgs 15:33). Menahem did not share Shallum's transjordanian roots; he probably appealed for a return to Israel's older monarchic traditions as he wrested the kingdom back from the transjordanian pretender. The date for the beginning of Menahem's reign in Azariah's thirty-ninth year is in accord with Shallum's one-month reign in that year (15:13). However, the ten years attributed to his reign in v. 17 vary from the eleven years expected with Pekahiah's accession in Azariah's fiftieth year according to v. 23. The discrepancy is minor but may be

---

51 Dubovský ("Menahem's Reign," 33–35) makes a similar point from the verbs ויעל ... ויבא in v. 14 instead of ויקשר.

52 Cf. Trebolle, "Division Markers," 210.

53 Joosten, *Verbal System*, 108–11; Rabinowitz, "'ĀZ Followed by Imperfect."

54 This interpretation takes ויך as a variant of אז יכה and accepts Trebolle's argument (*Centena*, 183–86) that ואת־כל־אשר־בה is a corruption of ואת כל־הרותיה בקע (the original reading preserved in G^L), which occurred as a consequence of the interpolation of ואת־גבוליה מתרצה כי לא פתח. Trebolle does not adopt the reading *Tappuah*.

55 Gray (*Kings*, 623), followed by Fricke (*Das zweite Buch von den Königen*, 207), argued that Menahem's motive was to annihilate the line of Shallum, whose hometown of Yasib was near Tappuah according to Josh 17:7 G.

56 Attested in the Samaria ostraca. See McCarter, *Ancient Inscriptions*, 103–104.

key for indicating a change in the method of record-keeping. Galil has suggested that the one-year difference reflects a change from ante- to postdating in Israel under the influence of Assyrian practice, which distinguished the accession year from the first regnal year, which began with the New Year.[57] The suggestion is intriguing and potentially very significant, but too many gaps and variables remain in the extant evidence to afford certainty.

15:18-19: The invasion of Tiglath-Pileser III

The evaluation of Menahem (v. 18) is standard and expected for a northern king. Like his peers, Menahem is guilty of the sin of Jeroboam. Verse 19 has its beginning at the end of v. 18 with the word בימיו (reconstructed), *in his days*. "Pul" = Tiglath-Pileser III (reigned 745–727 BCE) was the founder of the Neo-Assyrian empire and one of the greatest kings of the ancient Near East. In his second through fifth years (743–739) he campaigned in northern Aram against Arpad (north of Hamath), seeking to eliminate the influence of Urartu (Arpad's ally) and secure Assyrian control over the trade routes to/from the Mediterranean.[58] A number of fragmentary annalistic inscriptions from Tiglath-Pileser's capital in Kalḫu (Nimrud) as well as an inscribed stela from western Iran mention Menahem's payment of tribute and indicate that he was on the throne in 738, fixing an important chronological anchor for this period.[59]

---

57 Galil, *Chronology*, 62. Galil argues that the change began with Joash of Israel. Weingart ("2Ki 15–18") strengthens Galil's suggestion by placing the change in Menahem's reign and contending that the regnal formulae of kings before Menahem reflect antedating, while those after him reflect postdating. But the records for many kings before him are incomplete, so the practice of antedating is largely supposition. Also, Menahem was not the first Israelite king to be an Assyrian vassal, so it is not clear why a change in reckoning should have begun with him.

58 Miller and Hayes, *History*, 363–66. For an overview of Tiglath-Pileser's rise and its implications for the ancient Near East and Israel in particular see also Cogan and Tadmor, *II Kings*, 176–79.

59 H. Tadmor and S. Yamada (*The Royal Inscriptions of Tiglath-Pileser III [744-727 BC], and Shalmaneser V [726-722 BC], Kings of Assyria* [RINAP 1; Winona Lake, IN: Eisenbrauns, 2011], nos. 14, 27, 32 and 35) see the lists in the annals (14, 27, 32) as variants of the same record and date them to 738, Tiglath-Pileser's 8th regnal year (*palû*), based on the reference to his 9th *palû* in the section of annals that follows. The inscription from Iran (text 35) is undated, but its list of tribute payers is earlier since it has Tubail (Itto-Baal) as king of Tyre instead of his successor, Hiram, who is mentioned in the annals (text 32 and reconstructed by Tadmor and Yamada in texts 14, 27). W. H. Shea ("Menahem and Tiglath-pileser III," *JNES* 37 [1978]: 43–49, and N. Na'aman ("Historical and Chronological Notes on the Kingdoms of Israel and Judah in the Eighth Century B.C.," *VT* 36 [1986], 81) date the Iran inscription to 740 and correlate it with the notice of Menahem's payment in 2 Kgs 15:19. Na'aman (p. 82) argues further that Menahem made a second payment in 738 and that this is the one recorded in the annals. Shea (p. 49) denies that a second payment was necessary and thinks Menahem's name was simply listed again as part of a general summary. But his argument does not adequately consider the difference in genre between the annals and the non-annalistic text. The change in the name of the Tyrian king indicates the different settings of the two documents and nullifies Thiele's (*Mysterious Numbers*, 125–28) attempt to date Menahem's payment to 743.

Menahem's submission and payment

There were different levels of domination by Assyria that ranged from voluntary submission to conquest and population displacement.[60] Israel would experience different ones, including its ultimate demise as an independent kingdom and conversion into an Assyrian province complete with the deportation of its upper class and the transplantation of a non-native population from elsewhere in the empire. Menahem's overture initiated this process. His voluntary submission to Tiglath-Pileser indicated his pro-Assyrian policy. The exact reason for his appeal to Assyria is suggested by the statement *to ensure his support to strengthen the kingdom in his hand*;[61] he was seeking support against an internal rival—evidently Pekah, who favored an anti-Assyrian, pro-Damascus policy. The amount of Menahem's payment, 1000 talents (ca. 34 tons) of silver,[62] seems extraordinary but is in line with amounts mentioned elsewhere, whether they are realistic or not.[63] The source of Menahem's payment may be understood in two ways, depending on the interpretation of the phrase גבורי החיל, which might refer to men of strength (soldiers) or to men of wealth and social standing (cf. Ruth 3:11). Thus the fifty shekels could be the amount paid to each Assyrian soldier or that extracted from each wealthy man of Israel.[64] The different interpretations have different implications. The figure of fifty shekels from each wealthy man would suggest that there were some 60,000 prominent citizens in Israel at the time.[65] The allotment to each Assyrian soldier might have been set based on the standard price for a slave in Assyria.[66] In either case the levy on Israel, especially if it occurred toward the end of Menahem's reign, may have galvanized the opposition to Assyria and contributed to the brevity of Pekahiah's reign and his overthrow. The notice of Pul's departure (v. 20b) betrays the parochial nature of the account. It leaves the impression that the Assyrians departed from the region because they had received Menahem's

60 Miller and Hayes, *History*, 367–69.

61 On the meaning of the expression *for his hand to be with him* compare 2 Sam 14:19; Jer 26:24; 1 Chr 4:10.

62 A talent was either 3000 or 3600 shekels, with a shekel being about 11.4 grams (.4 oz). Hence a talent was minimally about 75 lbs.

63 Sennacherib claims to have received 800 talents of silver and 30 of gold from Hezekiah (*ANET* 288; *COS* 2:303); 2 Kgs 18:14 gives the amounts as 300 talents of silver and 50 of gold. Adad-nirari III got 2300 talents of silver and 20 of gold from Mari' of Damascus (*ANET* 281–82; COS 2:276). Tiglath-Pileser III imposed 1000 talents of silver and 10 of gold on Hulli of Tabal and 2000 of silver and 150 of gold on Metenna of Tyre (ITP 47:rev. 14'-17'). The latter two cases are especially apt because they, much like Menahem, seem to be usurpers who are buying Assyrian support (Wray Beal, *Kings*, 429).

64 Hobbs (*2 Kings*, 198–99) and Miller and Hayes (*History*, 377) prefer the former. The major drawback is that it requires taking the preposition *ʿal* in two different ways. On the other hand, if the גבורי החיל are the wealthy rather than soldiers one might expect מאיש אחד, *<u>from</u> each man* later in the verse rather than לאיש אחד, *<u>to</u> each man.*

65 E.g., Buis, *Rois*, 243. The figure rises to 72,000 if a talent is calculated to be 3600 shekels. This conclusion cannot be pressed, though, since there are numerous possibilities about how the money could have been paid. For instance, it could have been extended over time, allowing assessment of more individuals, or the royal treasury could have furnished a percentage of the total, in which case the number of individuals actually assessed would be unknown (Cogan and Tadmor, *II Kings*, 172).

66 Wiseman, *Kings*, 271.

payment. In fact the Assyrian army withdrew after having put down revolts and organized provinces in northern Aram as well as gaining control of the trade routes. The statement also ignores Tiglath-Pileser's return to the region in 734–731 to suppress a rebellion led by Damascus. Menahem is alone among the kings of Israel in this chapter in having the statement that he lay with his forebears as part of his closing formulae (vv. 21-22) because he alone succeeds in placing an heir on the throne after him.[67]

15:23: Pekahiah's two years

MT and G^B ascribe two years to Pekahiah's reign, while G^L reads *ten* (v. 23). The numbers in vv. 27 and 32 accord with the two-year figure but 17:1 (MT) agrees with the ascription of ten years to Pekahiah. Ten years is impossible. Tiglath-Pileser III's annals place Menahem on the throne in 738. They and other inscriptions also note the installation of Hoshea as king of Israel in 731/30 after the Assyrian campaigns against Pekah and Razon and the conquest of Damascus.[68] This leaves no more than nine years (738–730 inclusive) for the reigns of both Pekahiah and Pekah, whereas MT assigns twenty-two years, two for Pekiahiah and twenty for Pekah. The main problem is the twenty-year reign ascribed to Pekah (discussed below). The two-year reign of Pekahiah resembles the situations of Nadab (1 Kgs 15:15) and Elah (1 Kgs 16:8); this may be due to literary patterning or reflect a period just long enough to ascertain the new king's policies but preclude his gaining a firm grasp on power.[69] Like his predecessors, Pekahiah is overthrown by a military officer early in his reign before he could establish firm leadership over the military. The transition to a new king was an opportune moment for someone who wished to change the policies of the royal house to strike, as appears to be the case with Pekah.

The distinctiveness of Pekahiah and Pekah

Pekahiah's name is Yahwistic, indicating that his father Menahem was an adherent of YHWH. As a devotee himself Pekahiah maintains the royal shrines, for which he receives DtrH's censure for continuing the *sin of Jeroboam* (v. 24) The name of the usurper, Pekah, is the same as that of his master (v. 25), raising the possibility that the two were identical.[70] This possibility would reduce the number of kings of Israel for this period and might help with the chronological problems by reducing the total number of regnal years required for Pekahiah and Pekah. Nevertheless, there are cogent reasons for distinguishing them. First, the formula Menahem *lay with his forebears* indicates that he was succeeded by his son Pekahiah, while Pekah has a distinct patronymic, Remaliah.[71] Then there is the radical difference between the two kings embodied in the account of a *coup d'état* and assassination as well as the change of policy toward Assyria. Pekahiah might have altered his father's pro-Assyrian stance but

---

67 Suriano, *Politics of Dead* Kings, 71–97.

68 See esp. Na'aman, "Historical and Chronological Notes," 71–74.

69 Cf. Ishida, *Royal Dynasties*, 173–74.

70 F. Hommel ("Assyria," in *A Dictionary of the Bible* [ed. J. Hastings; vol. 1 [Edinburgh: T & T Clark, 1898], 186) argues that Pekahiah and Pekah were the same king who reigned only two years. D. Olson ("Pekah," *ADB* 5:214–15) posits that "Pekah" adopted his predecessor's name as a way of claiming legitimacy and suggests that this is the reason why Isaiah 7 uses Pekah's patronymic, "son of Remaliah," but not his name.

71 The meaning of the name Remaliah is unknown because of the lack of an attested verb רמל. Šanda (*Könige* II, 187) proposes *rām lî yahu* "YHWH is lofty, sublime to me" on analogy with טבליהו in 1 Chr 26:11.

there would be no need to hide this by inventing another king with the same name and an overthrow. Finally, v. 25 raises the possibility that Pekah was from Gilead in Transjordan and hence had an entirely different origin from Pekahiah. Apparently, therefore, the similarity of the names is coincidental.

15:25: Pekah's revolt

The details of Pekah's revolt are obscure, but some specifics lend themselves to reconstruction. Pekahiah was evidently holed up in the citadel (cf. 1 Kgs 16:18), suggesting that he was aware of the threat against him. Pekah's access was probably a function of his position as the king's adjutant,[72] either because he was trusted or because he knew the structure and grounds. He brings a contingent of fifty men—a military unit (2 Kgs 1:9-13)—comprised of Gileadites. This designation harks back to Shallum and suggests that their agenda was the one that motivated Shallum in the first place, namely, the wish to change the pro-Assyrian policy of Menahem in favor of an anti-Assyrian, pro-Damascus policy, probably under the aegis of Razon of Damascus.[73] If Pekah himself was not from Gilead, his choice of Gileadites to accompany him must have been deliberate. Perhaps as a military man he believed the time was ripe for Israel to throw off the Assyrian burden. Under Pekah, Israel would become part of a coalition with Razon and Damascus allied against Assyria. Pekahiah's failure to place his heir on the throne upon his assassination is reflected in the absence of a notice in his concluding formulae (v. 26) that he lay with his forebears.

15:27: The length of Pekah's reign

The synchronism for Pekah in v. 27 accords with v. 23 (MT), where Pekahiah is assigned a two-year reign beginning in Azariah's fiftieth year. However, the figure of twenty years for Pekah's reign is problematic. As noted in the discussion of vv. 19-20, the annals and other inscriptions of Tiglath-Pileser III indicate that the reigns of Pekahiah and Pekah must both fit in the period between 738 and 730 BCE. Obviously the twenty years for Pekah are too long. This discrepancy has not yet been satisfactorily explained, although several possibilities have been put forward. The simplest of these is that the number *twenty* is a scribal error.[74] This suggestion cannot be dismissed as easily as Na'aman wishes in view of the evidence for textual and chronological variation in Kings and especially in the present chapter.[75] Still, a clear understanding of how *twenty* came to replace the original number is necessary before this proposal can be fully convincing.[76] Another widely accepted explanation that assumes the genuineness of the twenty-year reading posits that it includes years spent by Pekah as the ruler of a rival kingdom in Transjordan beginning with the accession of Menahem, if not the

---

72 On the meaning of שליש see the discussion of 7:2.

73 Cf. Miller and Hayes, *History*, 371–74.

74 W. F. Albright, "The Chronology of the Divided Monarchy of Israel," *BASOR* 100 (1945), 21–22; Barnes, *Kings*, 157. For additional scholars who adopt this position see Na'aman, "Historical and Chronological Notes," 75, n. 9.

75 Na'aman, "Historical and Chronological Notes," 75.

76 The reading of *ten* (עשר) instead of *twenty* (עשרים) proposed by Gray (*Kings*, 64–65) and Rehm (*Das zweite Buch der Könige*, 150) is still more than the time allotted by the Assyrian evidence. Hentschel (*2 Könige*, 71) suggests that 16 years were added to Pekah's 4-year reign in an effort to accommodate the 16 years attributed to Jotham of Judah after it was forgotten that Jotham's years were incorporated within his father's (following Jepsen's theory).

end of Jeroboam II's reign.[77] Scholars who favor this view find allusions to the division in Kings and the Prophets.[78] But there is no clear reference in Kings to this division as there was for the factions of Zimri, Tibni, and Omri (1 Kings 16). Another problem is the reference to Pekah as Pekahiah's *šālîš* (v. 25). It is hard to believe that Pekah, as head of a rival kingdom from the time of Menahem, would have been appointed to such a position.[79] Two other proposals are similar to the rival kingdom theory and to each other.[80] One holds that Pekah considered himself the legitimate heir of the Jehu dynasty and therefore counted his regnal years from the end of Zechariah's or even Jeroboam II's reign, ignoring the reigns of Menahem and Pekahiah.[81] Alternatively, an early chronographer who considered Menahem and Pekahiah usurpers counted back from the beginning of Pekah's reign to the end of the Jehu dynasty and attributed the intervening years to Pekah. Na'aman finds support for these theories in the supposition that both Jehu and Pekah, along with Elijah and Elisha, were from Gilead and that they all reflect a Gileadite strain of opposition to the Omrids and then to Menahem and Pekahiah as interlopers. The theory may be on to something in its perception of Gileadite roots behind these characters. Nevertheless, it remains speculative. Elijah and Elisha are not always portrayed as opponents of the king. There is also no indication in Kings that Pekah was related to the Jehuids or had any grounds for being considered the legitimate heir of that dynasty. In short, the reason for the attribution of twenty years to Pekah's reign remains obscure. Fortunately, it does not seriously affect the overall chronology, since it is clear from external evidence that Pekah's reign in Samaria was limited to the period from 738 to 731/30.

---

77 As conceived by C. Lederer (*Die biblische Zeitrechnung vom Auszuge aus Ägypten bis zum Beginne der babylonischen Gefangenschaft* [Erlangen: Kleeberger, 1888], 135–38) and developed especially by H. J. Cook, "Pekah," *VT* 14 (1964): 121–35, and followed by E. R. Thiele ("Pekah to Hezekiah," *VT* 66 [1966], 89–91), Miller and Hayes (*History*, 370–72), and Wiseman (*Kings*, 31, 273), among others.

78 Miller and Hayes (*History*, 371–72) appeal to the statement in 15:37 that Pekah, with Razon, had begun harassing Judah already in the reign of Jotham. But the timeframe of this verse is very vague (*in those days*), and it is a post-DtrH addition. Buis (*Rois*, 44) finds an allusion to the divided North in the reference to Manasseh devouring Ephraim and vice-versa in Isa 9:19-20. It is not clear, though, that the intertribal strife alluded to in this passage entails a separate Transjordan kingdom. B. Oded ("The Historical Background of the Syro-Ephraimitic War," *CBQ* 34 [1972], 162–63) and K. L Younger ("The Deportations of the Israelites," *JBL* 117 [1998], 202) hold that Pekah ruled Gilead as a vassal of Razon of Damascus, who helped him overthrow Pekahiah.

79 Galil (*Chronology*, 65–66) rejects the theory of a Transjordan kingdom for Pekah because of his designation as Pekahiah's adjutant. He surmises that Pekah was an official appointed by Jeroboam II over Gilead and that the 20 years of his reign are calculated from that appointment. Likewise, Patterson (*1, 2 Kings*, 887) suggests that Pekahiah tried to solve the problem of Pekah's rivalry by giving him a prominent position—the rulership of Gilead.

80 Na'aman, "Historical and Chronological Notes," 76–80.

81 W. J. Chapman, "The Problem of Inconsequent Post-Dating in II Kings XV. 13, 17, and 23," *HUCA* 2 (1925), 59.

Like his predecessors and in accord with his responsibilities as king of Israel, Pekah maintains the royal shrines to YHWH at Dan and Bethel and so, also like his predecessors, is judged guilty of the sin of Jeroboam according to DtrH's usual regnal formula (v. 28). This is the last instance of such a formula in Kings, but not yet the end of that theme, which will find its climax in 2 Kings 17.

15:28: Pekah commits the sin of Jeroboam

The single verse in the account of Pekah's reign that is not formulaic (v. 29) synthesizes the results of Tiglath-Pileser III's three campaigns in the southern Levant in 733–731. In those years, according to the eponym list, the Assyrian king first moved down the coast against the Philistines and then set his sights on Damascus.[82] It is unclear whether the list of names in this verse originates from one of these campaigns (and if so, which one?) or is cumulative.[83] The north-south orientation of the list favors the first possibility. However, this is complicated by the fact that the location of Janoah at the center of the list is uncertain. The other four are clearly identified and form a more-or-less straight line from north to south in the upper Galilee and Jordan Valley.[84] Janoah has been variously identified with Giv'at ha-Shoqet in the upper Huleh,[85] Yunuḥ, 18 km northeast of Acco,[86] and Lebanese Yunuḥ, 10 km east of Tyre.[87] It cannot be the site of the same name mentioned in Josh 16:6-7, which is in Ephraim and thus too far south for the present context. The order of the sites may reflect the route of the Assyrian army (Rainey).[88] In its present setting, however, the list illustrates the point that the Assyrians conquered all the land of Naphtali.[89] It does not fill out the further details surrounding this event, such as the multiple Assyrian campaigns, Pekah's alliance with Damascus, and the destruction of Damascus. It thus leaves the impression that the "Syro-Ephraimitic crisis" described in ch. 16 was a distinct event. This is partly because the present passage describes the Northern perspective while ch. 16 focuses on Judah. It was probably at this time that Tiglath-Pileser divided the conquered territory into provinces—Megiddo (Galilee and the northern

15:29: Assyrian conquest of Naphtali

82 A. Millard, *The Eponyms of the Assyrian Empire 910–612 BC* (SAAS 2; Helsinki, 1994), 44–45, 59.

83 Šanda, *Könige* II, 188.

84 Ijon is Tell ed-Dibin, modern Marj-ʿAyun in the western foothills of Mount Hermon. Abel Beth-Maacah is Abil el-Qamḥ south of Ijon in Upper Galilee. Ijon and Abel Beth-Maacah are both mentioned in 1 Kgs 15:20 in a list of places attacked by Ben-Hadad of Damascus. Qadesh is Tell Qadis northwest of the Huleh basin. Hazor is Tell Qadaḥ. See Cogan and Tadmor, *II Kings*, 174; A. Curtis, *Oxford Bible Atlas* (Oxford: Oxford University Press, 2007), 72; and R. Frankel, "Janoah," *ABD* 3:640–41.

85 J. Kaplan, "The Identification of Abel-Beth-Maacah and Janoah," *IEJ* 28 (1978): 157–66.

86 Aharoni, *Land of the* Bible, 371–74, 437.

87 A. Rainey, "Toponymic Problems (cont.)," *TA* 8 (1981): 146–51.

88 Wiseman (*Kings*, 273) contends that Qadesh was Abu Qedeš near Megiddo rather than the Qadeš northwest of the Huleh basin. He thus traces the Assyrian advance west to Qadesh and then to Janoah northeast of Akko, thereby cutting off northern Israel from Aramaean aid.

89 An older suggestion reconstructing the name of Naphtali in Tiglath-Pileser's annals (F. Hommel, *Geschichte Babyloniens und Assyriens* [Berlin: G. Grote, 1884–88], 665) was perpetuated in scholarly literature until the publication of other annals fragments that compelled correction to *Bīt-Ḫazaili* (*ITP* 42m l. 7', p. 105). Cf. Cogan and Tadmor, *II Kings*, 174.

plains), Dor (the Sharon coastal plain), and Gilead (Transjordan).[90] He did so after having deported the population, as our verse reports, 13,250 of them according to Tiglath-Pileser III's annals.[91] The mention of Gilead and Galilee (and in G^L Gad)—probably in reference to these provinces—is intrusive and secondary. This is clear from consideration of the geography presupposed in the verse: the five cities named are in the tribal territory of Naphtali so that *all the land of Naphtali* is a recapitulation. *Gilead and Galilee* do not fit.

15:30-31: The end of Pekah's account

The annexation of this region and deportation of its population were a punishment for Pekah's rebellion. They may also have been a warning against further resistance.[92] But it was probably Hoshea's overthrow of Pekah (v. 30) that saved Israel from suffering the fate of Damascus at this moment. The conspiracy notice credits Hoshea with Pekah's assassination. The Assyrian annals are more ambiguous as to whether Pekah's own people or the Assyrian king was responsible.[93] The text of the annals is clearer in its claim that Tiglath-Pileser III installed Hoshea,[94] but the two claims are not mutually exclusive. The internal *coup d'état* may have saved Tiglath-Pileser the trouble of conquest and prolonged Israel's payment of tribute. Hoshea's leadership of the revolt made him the natural candidate to succeed Pekah so long as he swore loyalty to Assyria and made his tribute payments. Verse 30b is a later addition. Besides being absent from G^L, it is not a regular feature of the conspiracy notice represented in v. 30a. The chronological datum in v. 30b is a secondary calculation based on vv. 27, 32, where Pekah becomes king in the same year as Jotham, though slightly before him. It also obviously contradicts v. 33, where Jotham reigns sixteen years. The source formula that closes Pekah's account (v. 31) is standard. There is no reference to him *lying with his forebears*, as there was for Menahem, since Pekah was deposed and did not succeed in placing an heir on the throne.

Jotham's reign and the chronology for Judah

Despite the chronological assistance rendered by Jepsen's theory, sixty-seven years is still too large a total for the period since the twenty years ascribed to Pekah must be reduced to six or seven, yielding a total of fifty-four or fifty-five regnal years for Israel in this period. The total for Judah's kings must be further reduced by a dozen years to correspond. This need for further reduction is the impetus behind appeals to additional co-regencies, though other evidence for them is lacking. It seems more likely that one of the recorded numbers is erroneous. The suggestion to read *six* instead of *sixteen* in v. 33 for the length of Jotham's reign may have merit.[95] While there is no textual evidence for the emendation, there is precedent for scribal error where numbers are concerned, especially in this chapter, and it is suspicious that both Jotham and Ahaz are credited with sixteen-year reigns. If so, following Jepsen's theory, Uzziah's fifty-two years would have coincided with the reigns of Jotham and Ahaz and the first year of Hezekiah,

---

90 Cf. Younger, "The Deportations of the Israelites," 202–204.

91 *ITP* 21:1-9. This text is dated by Tadmor to 733.

92 Wiseman, *Kings*, 273.

93 *ITP* 42, l. 17'b (p. 106). A lacuna in the text allows for either a first-person or a third-person plural reading. See also 44, l. 18' (p. 112), where the verb is missing.

94 *ITP* 42, l. 17'b. Cf. also 45, rev. 10 (p. 132), where the verb is again missing.

95 Gray, *Kings*, 628–29; also Jones, *Kings*, 531. Alternatively, the *sixteen* years for Ahaz in 16:1 should be changed to *six*. See on that verse.

yielding a total of fifty-seven years for the period. If we grant the possibility that Uzziah may have been eighteen when Jotham was born, this total is reduced to fifty-five, matching Israel's total. This is all speculative, though, and ultimately the chronological problem may be beyond resolution.

15:32-38: Jotham's reign

The other information in the regnal formulae for Jotham (vv. 32-35a) includes the name of the queen mother (Yerushah) in v. 33b. Her designation as the daughter of Zadok suggests that she was from a priestly family, which might account for the memory of Jotham's building (or rebuilding) of the upper gate of the temple (v. 35b), much as Joash, who was raised by priests, was remembered for his repair of the temple. This is the only portion of the account of Jotham's reign, except for v. 37, that is not formulaic. The gate in question is probably the upper Benjaminite gate (Jer 20:2) communicating between temple and palace on the north side of the temple precinct (Ezek 9:2). The evaluation of Jotham is mixed. The statement that he did right is mitigated by the comparison with Azariah rather than with David and more importantly by the notice—the last one in Kings—that the *bāmôt* were not removed but continued to be used by the people (v. 35). As expected, v. 37 supplies DtrH's "punishment" for the "crime" of retaining the *bāmôt*.[96] The language of "sending against" (השליח ב) is used elsewhere to describe YHWH's levying of punishment (Exod 8:17; Lev 26:22; Ezek 14:13; Amos 8:11; cf. 2 Kgs 24:2). The verse draws on 16:5, 7-9 for its allusion to the "Syro-Ephraimitic crisis."

Synthesis

Israel and Judah contrasted

The sandwich arrangement of the seven regnal accounts in this chapter contrasts kings of Israel and Judah in several respects. The kings of Judah are both judged righteous while the kings of Israel are all wicked. Although Shallum is not explicitly accused of the offense, the kings of Israel are all guilty of the sin of Jeroboam, with the result that they lose individuality and appear to be copies of one another or models cast in the same mold. Hoshea, Israel's final king, will be evil, though not as bad as his predecessors, nor is he specifically blamed for the sin of Jeroboam (17:2), though it is a primary reason for Israel's fall (17:21-23). Thus the theme of Jeroboam's sin, which has been so prominent in Kings, is coming to its conclusion in the destruction of Israel as a kingdom. The rapid succession of Northern monarchs corresponding to just two kings of Judah illustrates the instability of Israel. Four of the five are assassinated by usurpers. The country is unraveling.[97] Its story sounds a warning to Judah. The two kings of Judah—Uzziah and Jotham—get passing marks but not ringing endorsements. Each does right as his father had done, but neither is compared to David. Both fail to remove the cultic

---

96 Mullen, "Crime and Punishment," 234, 241–42. Precedent for this insertion of an extra notice into a king's concluding formulae is found in 1 Kgs 14:30; 15:23b; 2 Kgs 14:19-21. See Grabbe, *1 & 2 Kings*, 26.

97 See P. D Dubovský, "Why Did the Northern Kingdom Fall According to 2 Kings 15?" *Bib* 95 (2014): 321–346 on this point and the other factors he deduces.

installations (*bāmôt*). Azariah/Uzziah is a particularly ambiguous figure, one who presented a theological challenge for DtrH that continues to challenge readers. He has a very long reign and is evaluated positively, yet YHWH strikes him with skin disease, forcing him to relinquish control over his kingdom prematurely. DtrH's scheme of crime and punishment offers only a tepid explanation since other kings who retain the *bamot* do not suffer skin disease. The encroachments of Pekah and Razon (v. 37) may be seen as punishment for the same shortcoming on Jotham's part, though it is much less personal than skin disease.

Compositional levels The accounts of the seven kings in this chapter consist mostly of DtrH formulae, though these formulae make use of older sources. The opening and closing formulae for each king take two to four verses. Between them one finds a single notice for each king about a single event—perhaps the defining event—of his reign. For Uzziah it is his skin disease (v. 5). For Zechariah and Shallum it is conspiracies that unseated them (vv. 10, 14). Menahem's reign is marked by the invasion of Tiglath-Pileser III and payment of tribute to him (vv. 19-20). As with Zechariah and Shallum, the toppling of Pekahiah is the non-formulaic portion of his regnal account (v. 25). Pekah's overthrow is supplemented by the notice of the Assyrian conquest of Galilee (vv. 29-30). In Jotham's case a single sentence notes his (re)building of an entry gate into the temple (v. 35b). The incursion of Pekah and Razon (v. 37) constitutes a second piece of information for Jotham, albeit one incorporated into his closing formulae. Additional notices about the prophesied end of the Jehu dynasty (v. 12) and Menahem's brutal treatment of Tappuah and its pregnant women (v. 16) are just that—later additions that are indicated as such by their location outside of DtrH's structure furnished by the regnal formulae. **Chronology** The greatest interpretive problem of this chapter—that of chronology—may be attributable in part to DtrH's misunderstanding of his sources. Scholars are nearly unanimous in recognizing that the fifty-two-year reign assigned to Azariah/Uzziah is too long if it is sequential to those before and after him. The fact that his son takes over at least some of the royal duties because of his illness, which also forces him to live apart (v. 5), has led to the widespread suspicion that a significant portion of the fifty-two years was concurrent with the reign of his successor or successors. The twenty years ascribed to Pekah may be a similar case in which the figure results from a rival kingship or the claim to legitimacy as the heir of the Jehu dynasty. Here, though, there is a need for caution, as there is sometimes a tendency for the cart of theory to lead the horse of evidence. There is no unambiguous evidence for a rival kingdom or for a claim to be Jehu's rightful heir. For that matter there is no real evidence for the frequent postulation of coregencies beyond that of Uzziah. Even with Uzziah and Jotham it is not clear that they were considered real co-regents, i.e., two kings at once, at least in DtrH's account. It is possible that the twenty years ascribed to Pekah are simply an error. In the chapter as a whole the figures for synchronisms and royal tenures are problematic and difficult if not impossible to coordinate perfectly.

Ahaz of Judah (2 Kings 16)

Text

[DtrH's sources; DtrH; Additions to DtrH; Additions to the additions]
1 In the seventeenth year of Pekah son of Remaliah king of Is-
rael, Ahaz son of Jotham became king over Judah. 2 Ahaz was
twenty years old when he became king, and he reigned sixteen
years in Jerusalem. He did not do what YHWH considered right as had Da-
vid his ancestor. 3 He followed the way of the kings of Israel, even passing his
son through the fire according to the abominations of the nations whom YHWH
had dispossessed from before the Israelites. 4 He slaughtered and offered food
offerings at the cultic installations and on the hills and under every flourishing
tree. 5 Then Razon king of Aram with Pekah son of Remaliah king
of Israel came up to Jerusalem for war but was not able to
fight against it. 6 At that time the king of Edom restored Elath to Edom
and cleared away the Judahites from Elath, and Edomites came to Elath and
settled there to this day. 7 Ahaz sent messengers to Tiglath-Pileser king of As-
syria to say, "I am your servant and your son. Come up, rescue me from the
domination of the king of Aram and of the king of Israel who have risen
against me. 8 Ahaz took the silver and the gold that were found in the treasur-
ies of YHWH's temple and of the king's palace and sent a bribe to the king of
Assyria. 9 The king of Assyria paid attention to Ahaz and came up to Damascus
and captured it; he deported the population and executed Razon. 10 When
King Ahaz went to meet Tiglath Pileser king of Assyria in Da-
mascus he noticed the altar that was in Damascus, and King
Ahaz sent the altar's measurements and its design in all its de-
tails to Uriah the priest. 11 Then Uriah built the altar. Ac-
cording to all that King Ahaz sent, so Uriah the priest did,
until the king returned from Damascus. 12 When the king returned from Damas-
cus and inspected the altar, he approached the altar and offered sacrifices
upon it, 13 burning his whole offering and grain offering, pouring out his liba-
tion, and sprinkling the blood of his peace offerings upon the altar. 14 As for
the bronze altar that had been before YHWH, he had moved it from in front of
the temple, [between the altar and YHWH's temple,] and placed it on the north
side of the altar. 15 [King Ahaz] commanded him, "Go up on the great altar and
on it burn the morning offering and the grain offering of the evening as well
as the king's whole burnt offerings, his grain offering, and the whole burnt of-
fering of all the people and their grain offering [and their libations]. Also sprin-
kle all the blood of the whole burnt offering and all the blood of the sacrifice
upon it. The bronze altar will be for me to inquire. 16 Uriah the priest did ac-

cording to all that Ahaz commanded him. 17 King Ahaz cut off the panels of the stands and removed the basins from them. He took down the sea from the bronze oxen that were under it and placed it on the stone pavement. 18 The dais of the throne, which he built in YHWH's temple, and the king's outer entryway he removed from YHWH's temple on account of the king of Assyria. 19 The rest of Ahaz's affairs, including all that he accomplished, are of course written on the scroll of the chronicles of the kings of Judah. 20 Ahaz lay down with his forebears and was buried in the City of David. Hezekiah his son reigned in his place.

Textual Notes

1 **Ahaz**: A short form of J(eh)oahaz and Ahaziah, attested in Assyrian inscriptions as *Iauḫazi*,[1] meaning "YHWH grasps (in protection)."[2] It is also attested in the Samaria papyri and on two seals.[3]

king of Israel: So Syr. Restored by Stade on the grounds that it is lacking elsewhere only in 1 Kgs 15:1.[4]

over Judah: See the Note on 8:16.

2 **Yhwh**: So 2 Chr 28:2. MT, G^{L}: + *his god*. G^{B}: κυρίου θεοῦ πιστῶς.[5]

3 **kings of Israel**: So MT, G^{L}. G^{B}: *king of Israel*, an allusion to Jeroboam I, named in G^{ANrell}.

even passing his son through the fire: So MT, G^{B}. G^{L} and 2 Chr 28:3 have the plural *sons* or *children*, thus further disparaging Ahaz. See the Diachronic Analysis.

according to: So MT, G^{L} (κατὰ), 2 Chr 28:3. G^{B}: καί.

the nations: So MT, G^{B}, 2 Chr 28:3. G^{L}: the gods of the nations.

4 **He slaughtered and offered food offerings on the cultic installations**: See the notes on 12:4.

5 **Razon**: See on 15:37.

for war but was not able to fight against it: Reading למלחמה ולא יכל להלחם עליה, based on Isa 7:1, for the reasons laid out by Trebolle.[6]

6 **king of Edom restored Elath to Edom**: As Klostermann and a host of scholars since have argued, we should read here a reference to Edom rather than Aram and should delete Razon's name as an intrusion from v. 5.[7] The reasons are many: *Edom* and *Aram* are similar in Hebrew (אדם and ארם) and are easily confused. It makes sense that the king of Edom takes advantage of Judah's preoccupation with the assault of Aram and Israel to reclaim the port of Elath, which had belonged to Judah since the reign of

---

1 *ANET* 282; *ITP* 2011:122–23 (text 46, rev. 11).

2 Noth, *Personennamen*, 179.

3 Diringer, *Le iscrizioni*, 23, 202; C. C. Torrey, "A Hebrew Seal from the Reign of Ahaz," *BASOR* 79 (1940): 27–28.

4 Stade, *Kings*, 255; cf. Šanda, *Könige* II, 195. It is also lacking in 2 Kgs 9:29; 12:1, although G^{BL} attest the former, where they also lack the patronymic, "son of Ahab." 12:1 is a shortened version.

5 Klostermann (*Könige*, 448) suggests that πιστῶς arose from אמנים as a variant to אלהיו.

6 Trebolle, *Centena*, 186–87.

7 Klostermann, *Könige*, 449. Sweeney (*Kings*, 383) is virtually unique among modern critical scholars in retaining the reference to Rezin.

Amaziah (14:22). Later in the verse (see below) it states that the Edomites (*qere'*)[8] resettled Elath. Since the Edomites occupied Elath it was they and not the Aramaeans who conquered it (cf. 14:25). It is hard to believe that Razon would send troops to rescue Elath for Edom while he was threatened by Assyria.

Judahites: Or "Jews." Elsewhere in Kings only 2 Kgs 25:25; it is more prominent in Jeremiah (32:12; 38:19; 40:11-12; 41:3, 9; 44:1; 52:28, 30) and then in Ezra–Nehemiah and Esther. It seems to come into use no earlier than the end of the seventh century and then to become common in the Persian period.

from Elath: Reading מֵאֵילַת as indicated by G^{BL} (ἐξ Αἰλάθ) and as earlier in the verse in preference to MT's מאילות.

Edomites: So MT *qere'*, G^{BL}: (οἱ) Ἰδουμαῖοι. MT *ketiv*: *Aramaeans.*

7 **who have risen against me**: Reading הקמים עלי as reflected in G^{B} (τῶν ἐπανισταμένων ἐπ' ἐμέ). MT הקומים is probably an error, though GKC 72p cite it as an alternative form by analogy with middle weak verbs like בוש. G^{L}: ὅτι ἐπανέστησαν μοι = כי קמו עלי.

8 **in the treasuries of Yhwh's temple and of the king's palace**: So G^{BL}: εν θησαυροῖς οἴκου κυρίου καὶ οἴκου τοῦ βασιλέως (cf. 12:19). MT: בית יהוה ובאצרות בית המלך, *in Yhwh's temple and in the treasuries of the king's palace*, where *in the treasuries* is misplaced.[9]

of Assyria: So MT, G^{L}. Lacking in G^{B}.

9 **he deported the population**: So G^{L}: καὶ ἀπῴκισε τὴν πόλιν = ויגל את־העיר. MT: ויגלה קירה, *he deported it to Kir*, which is mentioned in Amos 1:5; 9:7 as the original home of the Aramaeans to which Yhwh will send them (back) into exile. It is also found in association with Elam in Isa 22:6. However, no place called Kir in Mesopotamia is mentioned for certain in ancient records outside of the Bible. Hence its location and even its existence are uncertain.[10] Many scholars regard the reference to Kir here as an addition providing a fulfillment of Amos 1:5. MT's corrupt reading may be influenced by the Amos passages. *The city* in G^{L} refers to Damascus or more specifically to its population. G^{B} (καὶ ἀπῴκισεν αὐτὴν) lacks *Kir*, perhaps reflecting haplography caused by the final *heh* in ויגלה and קירה.

10 **to meet**: So MT, G^{L}. G^{B}: εἰς ἀπαντὴν αὐτοῦ but then follows with Tiglath-Pileser's name, so that the pronominal object is superfluous.

Damascus (1): Reading דמשק according to the usual spelling in preference to MT's anomalous דומשק.

measurements: Reading מדות as reflected in G^{L} (τὸ μέτρον αὐτοῦ).[11] The reference to the altar as *great* (v. 15) suggests that its measurements were extraordinary, further indicating the correctness of this reading.

in all its details: Lit. *to all its workmanship* (לכל־מעשהו).

11 **Uriah** (1): So G^{L}. MT, G^{B} + *the priest*. The name means "Yhwh is my light" (2 Sam 11:3-4; 23:39; Ezra 8:33, Neh 3:4, 3:21, 8:4).

sent: G^{L} + *to him*; MT, G^{B} + *from Damascus.*

the king: So G^{L}. MT: *King Ahaz.*

12 **When the king returned from Damascus**: So MT. G^{L}: *King Ahaz.* G^{B} is missing this clause, the result of haplography with *from Damascus* in v. 11.

---

8 Even Sweeney agrees in reading "Edomites" here.

9 Hobbs (*2 Kings*, 214) states that the expression "in the temple and in the palace treasury" occurs elsewhere, but the list of passages he provides does not support this contention.

10 Gray (*Kings*, 633), for instance, takes *qir* as a common noun, "wall, fortress," hence *city*, referring to Nineveh and unconnected to the Amos passages. See H. Park, "Kir," *EBR* 15:340–41.

11 Proposed by Klostermann (*Könige*, 450) and widely adopted since.

he approached the altar: So G^L (καὶ προσῆλθε πρὸς τὸ θυσιαστήριον ὁ βασιλεὺς). MT (ויקרב המלך על־המזבח) is similar, but על is a mistake for אל, as reflected in G^L.[12]

13 **his whole offering**: So MT, G^B. G^L lacks *his* because of the conjunction that follows.

pouring out his libation: So MT: ויסך את־נסכו. G^B lacks the verb, which is required for sense. G^L + ἐπ' αὐτὸ *upon it.*

and sprinkling: So MT (ויזרק), G^B (καὶ προσέχεεν). G^L: + *upon it.*

14 **the bronze altar**: MT's reading, המזבח הנחשת, reflected also in G^L (τὸ χαλκοῦν θυσιαστήριον), is technically ungrammatical. It may be that the article on *altar* should be deleted. However, in view of the same construction in v. 17 it is probably best to explain it, with several grammarians, as apposition or a "noun of material."[13] There is no need to delete *bronze* as a gloss from v. 15.[14] G^B has suffered haplography triggered by the repetition of "altar" construing the bronze altar as the one mentioned at the end of v. 13 upon which the king sprinkled blood.

he had moved it: So G^L (προσήγαγεν = הקריב). MT, G^B: ויקרב = καὶ προσήγαγεν.

in front of the temple: So MT, G^L. G^B + *of* Yhwh.

and placed it: So MT, G^L. G^B has καὶ ἔδειξεν, an inner-Greek corruption (ἔδειξεν for ἔδωκεν).

of the altar: So MT, G^B. G^L: + *which he had made.*

15 **[King Ahaz] commanded him**: Reading the *ketiv* ויצוהו in preference to the *qere'* (ויצוה).

Go up: So G^L: ἀνάβηθι = עלה. Lost from MT, G^B because of its similarity to the preposition על.

and on it: So G^L (καὶ ἐπ' αὐτὸ = (ועליו). Dropped from MT, G^B after the loss of עלה.

the morning offering: So MT, G^B. G^L: τὴν ὁλοκαύτωσιν τῶν εἰρηνικῶν, *the peace offering*, which does not balance with the evening offering mentioned next.

and the grain offering of the evening: So MT, G^B (καὶ τὴν θυσίαν τὴν ἑσπερινὴν). G^L: καὶ τὴν ἑσπερινὴν, the result of an inner-Greek haplography.

the king's whole burnt offerings: So G^L. MT, G^B: *the king's whole burnt offering.*

his grain offering: So MT, G^B. G^L: *his grain offerings.*

of all the people: So G^{BL}. MT + *of the land.*

and their grain offering: So MT, G^B. G^L again has the plural *offerings.*

16 **Ahaz**: MT, G^B have the title *the king* before Ahaz's name; G^L has the title after the name. The different locations suggest that it is secondary.

commanded him: So G^{BL}. MT lacks the suffix.

17 **King Ahaz**: So MT, G^L. G^B lacks Ahaz's name.

the panels of the stands: המסגרות המכנות is ungrammatical. The simplest solution is to remove the article from מסגרות and take it as a construct form (BHS). While המסגרות is sometimes taken as a gloss intended to mitigate the contradiction with 25:13,

---

12 J. Milgrom, *Studies in Levitical Terminology 1: The Encroacher and the Levite: The Term 'Aboda* (Near Eastern Studies 14; Berkeley: University of California Press, 1970), 37n. M. Cogan (*Imperialism and Religion: Assyria, Judah, and Israel in the Eighth and Seventh Centuries B.C.E.* [Missoula, MT: Society of Biblical Literature/Scholars Press, 1974], 74n) misconstrues Milgrom (pp. 5–56) as arguing for a meaning of "encroach" here. Milgrom argued that the verb has the sense of "encroach" in prohibitions and that elsewhere its meaning goes beyond physical proximity to express legitimate access or admission to cultic phenomena. Klostermann (*Könige*, 450); Ehrlich (*Randglossen*, 312) and Gray (*Kings*, 634) propose reading the *Hip'îl*. But Milgrom (n. 37n) points out that הקריב על does not mean "sacrifice" on an altar. Even if it did, it would be repetitive of the next clause, ויעל עליו, where the verb is *Hip'îl.*

13 Cogan and Tadmor, *II Kings*, 189; GKC 127h; Joüon, 131d.

14 *Pace* Stade, *Kings*, 257; Würthwein, *1. Könige 17–2. Könige 25*, 386.

16, where the stands appear to be still intact,[15] this may be unnecessary. According to the description in 1 Kgs 7:27-37 the frames of the stands had decorated panels or insets (מסגרות) between their rungs. It was these panels that Ahaz removed along with the bronze basins (הכיר, a collective). The stands remained intact until they were dismantled by the Babylonians (25:13, 16).

the basins: Reading with the MT *qere'* (without *and*) and understanding כיר as a collective.

bronze oxen: הבקר הנחשת is an apposition or noun of material (see on v. 15; Driver, *Tenses*, 249; WO, 228, 231). הבקר is a collective as indicated by the Greek plural.

18 **The dais of the throne**: MT *qere'* (ואת־מוסך השבת) and G^{B} (καὶ τὸν θεμέλιον τῆς καθέδρας = ואת־מוסד השבת) have different readings that are conflated in G^{L} (καὶ τὸν θεμέλιον τῆς καθέδρας τῶν σαββάτων). It is uncertain, therefore, whether this item is a throne platform (G^{B}) or some kind of covering (MT), perhaps an awning,[16] used on the Sabbath. In either case it is a luxury item provided for the king.[17] G^{BL} continue with the verb ᾠκοδόμησεν = בנה. However, the object-first order of the sentence lends preference to MT's relative clause אשר־בנו, whether one reads the singular or plural verb. This item, therefore, whatever its nature, is under the domain of the main verb in the sentence (הסיר in my reading; see below) and was removed by Ahaz.

outer: Reading החיצון instead of MT's החיצונה, which reflects dittography of the *heh* of הסב.

he removed from Yhwh's temple: The verb הסב, which is reflected also in G^{BL} (ἐπέστρεψεν), may have the sense of "move, remove" (2 Sam 20:12; 1 Sam 5:8-9; HALOT 740), which fits here. However, the preposition מן is also required, as in 2 Sam 20:12. Alternatively one may emend to הסיר מבית יהוה.[18]

on account of the king of Assyria: A number of scholars have followed Šanda in moving this phrase (v. 18b) to the end of v. 17.[19] This suggestion depends on the interpretation of v. 17 as relating Ahaz's measures to collect bronze for tribute. See the Diachronic Analysis.

19 **including all that he accomplished**: So G^{L} as per the usual formula. MT, G^{B}: *which he did.*

are of course written: MT, G^{B}: הלא־הם כתובים. G^{L} reflects הלא־הנם כתובים, a perpetual variation. 2 Chr 28:26 agrees with G^{L} but without the negative particle: הנם כתובים.

20 **and was buried**: So G^{BL}. MT: + *with his forebears.*[20] 2 Chr 28:27: *and they buried him.*

Synchronic Analysis

The longer and more detailed account of Ahaz's reign in comparison to those of Azariah (15:1-7) and Jotham (15:32-38) slows the narrative of Judah's history and Structure

15 Šanda (*Könige* II, 204), *et al.*

16 Cogan and Tadmor, *II Kings*, 189.

17 Na'aman ("Royal Inscriptions and the Histories of Jehoash and Ahaz," 346–48) suggests that it was a hall where guards could rest. But he has trouble making this fit the context: *because of the king of Assyria.*

18 Gray, *Kings*, 635.

19 Šanda (*Könige* II, 204). Hentschel (*2 Könige*, 77) argues along similar lines that v. 18a is an interpolation interrupting the original continuity between vv. 17 and 18b.

20 Cf. Stade, *Kings*, 142–43.

fosters reflection about its decline and submission to a Mesopotamian power in the shadow of what is about to happen to Israel (ch. 17). The elements of the account are arranged chiastically:[21]

A Opening regnal formulae and other introductory remarks (vv. 1-4)
- B Ahaz sends tribute to Tiglath-Pileser III (vv. 5-9)
  - C Ahaz has an altar built after the design of one in Damascus (vv. 10-11)
    - X Ahaz worships at the new altar and moves the old one (vv. 12-14)
  - C′ Ahaz commands daily sacrifices to be offered on the altar he had built (vv. 15-16)
- B′ Ahaz raids the temple because of the king of Assyria (vv. 17-18)

A′ Closing regnal formulae (vv. 19-20)

The outline shows how the account focuses on Ahaz's cultic activity on the new altar. Given his negative evaluation, the activity must be considered sinful despite the absence of a specific condemnation of it.

Evaluation of Ahaz

The evaluation accuses Ahaz of behaving like an Israelite king (v. 3a), and the account presents him as such. Thus his regnal formulae lack mention of the queen mother. The only other king of Judah for whom this datum is missing is Jehoram (2 Kgs 8:16-17), so that its absence effectively places Ahaz in association with the kings of Israel. The comparison with the Northern kings is shared only by Jehoram (8:18) among the kings of Judah, and he at least had the "excuse" of belonging to Ahab's family.[22] Since the Northern Kingdom is in its final days (2 Kgs 17), this assessment bodes ill for Judah. Verse 2b stated that Ahaz did not do right as David had done. This part of the evaluation is unusual in two respects. First, rather than saying that he did evil the text uniquely states that he did not do right. Second, while the comparison to David is not unique, it is not used for every king of Judah (1 Kgs 11:4-6; 15:3, 11; 2 Kgs 14:3; 18:3; 22:2). Ahaz's evaluation converts the positive comparison with David found for some kings of Judah (1 Kgs 15:11; 2 Kgs 18:3; 22:2) into a negative one.[23] The result is an understatement: Ahaz did not do right as David had done, not even close. He is the worst king of Judah to this point and will be surpassed only by Manasseh. The evaluation also distinguishes Ahaz clearly from his predecessors like Joash and Amaziah (and to some extent Azariah), who did right at first and then changed; Ahaz never did right.

16:3b-4: Ahaz's apostasies

The way of the kings of Israel is shorthand for idolatry, since it does not describe Ahaz actually traveling to Dan or Bethel. In addition (וגם), Ahaz is accused of child sacrifice (v. 3b) according to the custom of the Canaanite predecessors in the land and sacrificing and burning incense "on the hills and under every green tree" (v. 4). Saying that he burned his son as a sacrifice in the worship of other gods ascribes to Ahaz one of the worst sins of fallen Israel (17:17) and of Manasseh (21:6), the worst king of Judah and the one ultimately responsible for its demise (21:11-15). The expression about

---

21 Based on Cohn, *2 Kings*, 111. However, Cohn identifies element A as vv. 1-6 and B as vv. 7-9. His arrangement fails to note the proper extent of the opening formulae through v. 4 and to account for the cause-effect relationship of the invasion of Aram and Israel in v. 5 and Ahaz's appeal to Tiglath-Pileser in v. 7

22 Ahaziah (8:27) is said to have walked in way of Ahab.

23 Nelson, *Kings*, 223.

sacrificing on the hills and under the trees is used in other contexts referring to the worship of other gods (1 Kgs 14:23-24; 2 Kgs 17:7-12; Jer 3:6-13), and that is the case here. Ahaz is guilty of religious apostasy.

The first episode narrated for Ahaz's reign proper is the "Syro-Ephramitic crisis" in which the kings of Aram and Israel besieged Jerusalem with the goal of replacing Ahaz with a puppet king who would join with them in opposing Assyria, something Ahaz had evidently refused to do. These details can be filled in from Isaiah 7. On the other hand, v. 5 resolves the dilemma of Ahaz in Isaiah 7 when it states that the two invaders were unable to do battle against Jerusalem. Exactly what this means is uncertain, but it is clear that the siege was unsuccessful. The statement suggests that Jerusalem's fortifications precluded open warfare or even combat to enter the city and thus protected its inhabitants. It may also imply that Assyria's response to Ahaz's petition did not allow sufficient time for an effective siege of Jerusalem.

16:5: Introduction of the Syro-Ephraimitic crisis

The narrative pauses at this point for the aside in v. 6. It is perhaps better termed a "tangent," since it is related to the story. The relationship is indicated by the temporal expression *at that time* (בעת ההיא), which introduces an activity that is in conjunction with and often follows from that to which it is attached (e.g., Deut 1:16, 18; 2:34; 3:4; Judg 3:29; 21:14; 1 Kgs 8:65; 24:10; 1 Chr 21:28). Rezin's seizure of Elath and expulsion of the Judahites from there is retribution for his inability to take Jerusalem.

16:6: Rezin's recovery of Elath

The thread from v. 5 is resumed in v. 7. Ahaz solves the crisis facing him by resorting to Tiglath-Pileser III and the Assyrian army. He refers to himself from the beginning of his message as Tiglath-Pileser's servant and son, that is, his subject, and on those grounds seeks his aid. As incentive he sends a bribe of gold and silver (v. 8). Other kings, such as Menahem (15:19-20) and Hezekiah (18:15-16), employ the same strategy. Intertextual appeal to Isaiah 7 shows that Ahaz's act emanates from a lack of trust in Yhwh. Moreover, the word שחד may have negative connotations. It is not tribute (מנחה), but inducement,[24] and bribes are condemned in legal (Exod 23:8; Deut 16:19), prophetic (Isa 1:23; 5:23; Ezek 22:12; 23:8), and wisdom texts (Prov 17:23).[25] To make matters worse, Ahaz empties the treasuries of the temple as well as the palace to raise the funds (v. 8). The Assyrian king responds to Ahaz's petition, marching against Damascus, capturing it, exiling its population, and killing its king (v. 9). Strikingly, there is no mention of Israel's fate. Nonetheless, the exile of Damascus's population to Kir fulfills Amos's prediction (Amos 1:5) and calls to mind his oracles against Israel. The narrative of Kings in connection with Amos anticipates the same fate for Israel as for Damascus; the time of reckoning has arrived (ch. 17).

16:5-9: Ahaz's bribe of Tiglath-Pileser III

The next section of the chapter concerns the altar Ahaz commissioned for the Jerusalem temple. It is modeled on one he saw in Damascus when he went to render obeisance to Tiglath-Pileser. The meeting was probably at the Assyrian's insistence and adds to the parallel between Ahaz and Manasseh in the canon at large (2 Chr 33:10-13). The deity for whom the altar was used in Damascus is not

16:10-16: Ahaz copies the altar in Damascus

24 Kalluveettil, *Declaration and Covenant*, 127–29.

25 M. Cogan and H. Tadmor, "Ahaz and Tiglath-Pileser in the Book of Kings: Historiographic Considerations," *Bib* 60 (1979), 499–500, and *II Kings*, 188.

identified, but it would have been an Aramaean deity, not YHWH. The parallel account of Ahaz's reign in 2 Chronicles 28 states that he turned away from YHWH to worship the Aramaean gods (v. 23). He must have entered the temple of the god in Damascus in order to see the altar and may have worshiped at it. The larger context of the chapter, especially the negative evaluation in 16:2b-4, places a shadow of suspicion over the altar account. When considered with the condemnation that he *walked in the way of the kings of Israel* (v. 3a) Ahaz's new altar is much like the cultic innovations that formed *the sins of Jeroboam* (1 Kgs 12:25–13:6).[26] The initiative for the innovation is all Ahaz's, just as the shrines at Dan and Bethel were Jeroboam's invention (1 Kgs 12:26). King Ahaz is the subject of all the verbs in v. 10: *he went ... he saw ... he sent*; Uriah the priest simply follows his king's instructions.[27] Ahaz ascends to the altar to dedicate it (v. 12) as Jeroboam did the shrine at Bethel (1 Kgs 12:33). The suspicion is deepened in view of vv. 3b-4, which portray Ahaz as apostate—guilty not just of following the ways of the kings of Israel but of yielding to the seductive influence of foreign cults. The fivefold repetition of the name Damascus in vv. 9-11 emphasizes the foreign origin of Ahaz's altar and implies that it represented yet another instance of this king's proclivity for the *abominations of the nations* (v. 3). The reference to the altar's design or pattern (תבנית), a term used for the design of the tabernacle (Exod 25:9, 40) and the temple (1 Chr 28:11-19) and their contents, suggests that Ahaz's replacement of the original was presumptive: he removed the altar that was *before YHWH* and of divine design, replacing it with a foreign model. The inappropriateness of this act is reinforced by Josh 22:28-29 where the Transjordanian Israelites who built a copy (תבנית) of the sacrificial altar before the Tabernacle for memorial purposes affirm that it would be sinful to use any other than the Tabernacle altar for sacrifice.[28] How much more sinful must be Ahaz's replacement of the temple altar with one of non-Israelite design?

16:17-18: Ahaz's removal of items from temple and palace

The final segment of the account of Ahaz's reign before his closing formulae details his removal of several items from the temple and palace (vv. 17-18). The two verses raise a number of questions about the nature of the items removed and the reason(s) for their removal. The two most common understandings are (1) that these measures were imposed by Assyria in order to diminish the splendor of the temple, downgrade YHWH to a minor deity, and remove royal privilege for Ahaz, and (2) that they were luxury items sent as gifts and tribute to the king of Assyria. The chiastic structure of the passage, paralleling these two verses with vv. 5-9 favors the latter possibility, as does the similarity with 18:14-16. The compound preposition מפני ("ahead of," "because of") in v. 18 is of no help because it does not specify a cause. What it does is make clear the pervasive impact of Tiglath-Pileser and the Assyrians on Ahaz's reign. It thereby hints at the devastating impact that Judah's vassalhood with Assyria will have on its economic and political future, an impact that Kings and Isaiah blame on Ahaz.

---

26 K. A. D. Smelik, "The New Altar of King Ahaz (2 Kings 16): Deuteronomistic Re-Interpretation of a Cult Reform," in *Deuteronomy and Deuteronomic Literature* (FS C.H.W. Brekelmans; ed. M. Vervenne; Leuven: Peeters, 1997), 263–78.

27 Cohn (*2 Kings*, 113) sees the proper names and titles in these verses as highlighting the official nature of Ahaz's mission.

28 Wray Beal, *Kings*, 442–43.

Diachronic Analysis

The five parts of the chapter

After the cursory treatments of Azariah (15:1-7) and Jotham (15:32-38), the present chapter devoted entirely to Ahaz provides a striking contrast. The difference in length and detail is attributable to the well-remembered Syro-Ephraimitic crisis and the link that Ahaz forged with Assyria and perhaps also to the replacement altar he installed in the temple. The account consists of five parts.[29] Between the opening (vv. 1-4) and closing (vv. 19-20) regnal formulae for Ahaz are the accounts of the assault by Aram and Israel against Jerusalem and Ahaz's appeal to Tiglath-Pileser III (vv. 5-9), of Ahaz's construction of an altar modeled on the one he saw in Damascus (vv. 10-16), and of other changes made by Ahaz in and around the temple (vv. 17-18).

16:1-2a: The length of Ahaz's reign

The formulae that begin Ahaz's reign are regular except for the absence of the queen mother's name, which may be part of a strategy to cast him as Northern, as suggested in the Synchronic Analysis. The reference to Pekah's seventeenth year accords with the figure of twenty years ascribed to Pekah's reign in 15:27, although this figure is historically impossible, as we saw in the previous chapter. There is a further complication. Ahaz is purportedly twenty years old and reigns for sixteen years. According to 18:2//2 Chr 29:1 Hezekiah was twenty-five years old when he became king. This would mean that Ahaz was eleven years old when he fathered Hezekiah. Though theoretically possible, this is highly unlikely. Proposed solutions often posit a co-regency between Ahaz and Jotham, suggesting that his sixteen years are counted from the beginning of his sole reign, so that he was older when Hezekiah was born.[30] However, there is no direct support for the existence of such a co-regency in the biblical account. It seems more likely that at least one of the numbers is erroneous; there is a good possibility, for instance, that Ahaz's reign should be six rather than six*teen* years.[31]

16:2b-3a, 4: DtrH's evaluation

Ahaz differs from his predecessors going back to Joash in that he did not do what was right even for part of his reign (v. 2b). The portrait of Ahaz in vv. 1-3a, 4 is quite different from that of Isaiah, where no mention is made of cultic violations.[32] The particle וגם signals v. 3b as an addition (see below). DtrH's evaluation in v. 4 explains how Ahaz followed the ways of the kings of Israel by sacrificing at the cultic installations outside Jerusalem on the hills and under every green tree (v. 4; cf. 1 Kgs 12:31-32). The *bāmôt* have been mentioned several times (1 Kgs 22:44; 2 Kgs 12:4; 14:4; 15:4, 35) but always with the people worshiping at them,

---

29 Smelik, *Converting the Past*, 275.

30 Hobbs, *2 Kings*, 212. Inrig (*Kings*, 307) and Wray Beal (*Kings*, 437) posit a three-year co-regency. Gray (*Kings*, 631) suggests that Ahaz's reign was calculated from his recognition by the king of Assyria in 730.

31 So Weingart ("2Ki 15–18"), following C. Schedl ("Textkritische Bemerkungen zu den Synchronismen der Könige von Israel und Juda," *VT* 12 [1962], 90–93). Cogan and Tadmor (*II Kings*, 186) adopt the reading of certain G mss in 2 Chr 28:1 that Ahaz was 25 rather than 20 years old when he became king. This may reflect a different reading than that preserved in MT of Kings (Klein, *2 Chronicles*, 390).

32 Hentschel, *2 Könige*, 74.

not the king.[33] The expression "on the hills and under every flourishing tree" (v. 4) is Deuteronomistic, though it is found somewhat more broadly in prophetic literature to refer to the worship of other gods.[34]

16:3b: Child sacrifice

The accusation of child sacrifice as an example of walking in the way of the kings of Israel is odd, since no king of Israel is accused of this crime,[35] and it confirms the secondary status of v. 3b. The expression את־בנו העביר באש literally means to pass one's son through fire. Some scholars have argued on the basis of the command in Exod 13:12-13 to devote (*Hip'îl* of עבר) every firstborn to YHWH that the reference in 2 Kgs 16:4 and elsewhere is to a ceremonial act of consecration rather than to actual sacrifice.[36] But the use of *in the fire* (באש) and 2 Chr 28:3's more explicit *burned* (*Hip'îl* of בער) *with fire* indicate that actual sacrifice is envisioned. The practice is explicitly condemned in Lev 18:21; 20:2-3; Deut 12:31 (where the verb שרף "to burn" is used); in 18:10 it is described as a Canaanite practice the Israelites are not to emulate; and it is denounced in Jer 7:31; 19:5; 32:35; Ezek 16:21 as one they have adopted and that Josiah halted (2 Kgs 23:10). Some of these passages link the practice with the cult of Molech.[37] There is debate about whether Molech refers to a deity or a type of sacrifice.[38] Child sacrifice was practiced elsewhere in the ancient world, especially at Carthage and in

33 2 Kgs 23:12 mentions altars made by the kings of Judah on the upper room of Ahaz but does not use the word *bāmôt*. It is also not clear whether the upper room was built by Ahaz as a cultic installation or was just used as such by later kings, though the occurrence of his name in the same context as Manasseh's is noteworthy.

34 M. Weinfeld, *Deuteronomy and the Deuteronomic School* (Oxford: Clarendon Press, 1972), 322. In 1 Kgs 14:23 it appears to be part of an addition that changes the focus from Rehoboam (14:21) to Judah (14:22-24), and in 2 Kgs 17:10 it is part of an addition in 17:7-20 (McKenzie, *Trouble with Kings*, 140–42). In the Latter Prophets it is found in Jer 2:20; 3:6, 13; 17:2; Isa 57:5; Ezek 6:13. W. L. Holladay ("On Every High Hill and Under Every Green Tree." *VT* 11 [1961]: 170–76) believes that the expression originates with Hos 4:13 and that 2 Kgs 16:4 is dependent on Deut 12:2, while the other instances in Kings depend on Jer 2:20. Holladay does not discuss the uniqueness of the portrait of an individual king following these practices in 2 Kgs 16:4.

35 Hobbs, *2 Kings*, 213. Again the accusation in 2 Kgs 17:17 that the Israelite kings as a whole practiced child sacrifice is probably part of an addition.

36 E.g., Buis, *Rois*, 246; Cogan and Tadmor, *II Kings*, 186, both following M. Weinfeld, "The Worship of Molech and of the Queen of Heaven and Its Background," *UF* 4 (1972): 133–54.

37 Not to be confused with the Ammonite god Milcom; Molech in 1 Kgs 11:7 is an error for Milcom.

38 The identification of Molech as a deity was generally accepted until the study of O. Eissfeldt (*Molk als Opferbegriff im Punischen und Hebräischen und das Ende des Gottes Moloch* [Beiträge zur Religionsgeschichte des Altertums 3; Halle, 1935]), who argued that *molek* (<*mulk*) described a type of sacrifice rather than a deity. This theory gained wide acceptance and was reasserted by P. G. Mosca ("Child Sacrifice in Canaanite and Israelite Religion: A Study in *Mulk* and *mlk*," PhD dissertation, Harvard University, 1975). Since then, however, it has been called into question by G. C. Heider (*The Cult of Molek: A Reassessment* [JSOTSup 43; Sheffield: Sheffield Academic Press, 1992]; "Molech," *ABD* 4:895–98) and J. Day (*Molech: A God of Human Sacrifice in the Old Testament* [University of Cambridge Oriental Publications 41; Cambridge: Cambridge University Press, 1989]; "Molech, Moloch," *NIDB* 4:129–30), who contend that Molech was an underworld deity whose rites included child immolation, perhaps as part of an ancestor cult.

other Punic colonies. It seems to have become more common in Judah in the seventh and early sixth centuries, perhaps because of political distress. The other instance of it that we have seen—Mesha's sacrifice of his son on the city wall of Qir Haresheth in 2 Kings 3—suggests that it may have been a measure for desperate situations. This has led to the suggestion that Ahaz engaged in the practice under the pressure of the "Syro-Ephraimitic crisis."[39] However, the evidence for the secondary nature of v. 3b suggests that the reference to child sacrifice is more an effort to add to Ahaz's condemnation than a historical reality. The G^L and 2 Chr 28:3 reading *sons* presents an even darker picture of repeated child sacrifice rather than a one-time event.

16:5-9: The Syro-Ephraimitic crisis

The second segment of the chapter (vv. 5-9) deals with the "Syro-Ephramitic war or crisis."[40] The episode begins with Razon and his siege of Jerusalem and ends with Razon and his execution by Tiglath-Pileser III.[41] Begrich first drew the connection between the invasion described here and the anti-Assyrian coalition headed by Razon of Damascus. The coalition included Moab, Ashkelon, Edom, and Gaza, in addition to Aram, Damascus, and Israel (*ITP* 122–23). Whether these other city-states were involved in the siege of Jerusalem is unknown. This event was Judah's first direct dealing with Assyria, because Israel had effectively buffered Judah from the rising empire during the period of the reigns of Jeroboam II and Azariah. Ahaz's appeal would create a tie with Assyria and would prove a long-term burden for Judah. The beginning of the account of the Syro-Ephraimitic crisis in v. 5 is strikingly similar to Isa 7:1 and is probably derived from it or from a common source that is better preserved in Isaiah.[42] As it now stands v. 5 introduces the report in vv. 7-9. This report follows a pattern found elsewhere (1 Kgs 15:16-20; 2 Kgs 18:13-16; cf. 12:18-19) relating the payoff of a foreign king for assistance or to abort an attack.[43] It seems likely, therefore, that vv. 7-9 are a synthesis by DtrH of source material.

16:6: An interruption

Verse 6 is intrusive; it interrupts the report on the Syro-Ephraimitic crisis in vv. 5 + 7-9 with a note about Edom's recovery of the port at Elath.[44] The secondary nature of the verse is suggested as well by its beginning (*at that time*) and ending (*to this day*),[45] and by the term *Judahites* or *Jews* (היהודים) (see the Note) and the use of נשל in the *Pi*ʿ*el*.[46] Nonetheless, v. 6 may have historical validity, as it would make sense for the Edomites to strike in the south while Judah was preoccupied with the northern force of Aram

39 E.g., Jones, *Kings*, 534; Rehm, *Das zweite Buch der Könige*, 159, who lists others.

40 The term was coined by J. Begrich, "Der syrisch-ephraimitische Krieg und seine weltpolitischen Zusammenhänge," *ZDMG* 83 (1929): 213–37, reprinted in Begrich, Gesammelte Studien zum Alten Testament, ed. Walther Zimmerli (TB 21; Munich: Kaiser, 1964): 99–120.

41 Würthwein, *1. Könige 17–2. Könige 25*, 388.

42 See the Note and Trebolle, *Centena*, 186–87.

43 Kalluveetil (*Declaration and Covenant*, 122–39), and Long (*2 Kings*, 176)

44 On the reading of *Edom* (אדם) for *Aram* (ארם) see the Note.

45 While neither expression necessarily signals interpolation in and of itself, *at that time* (בעת ההיא) highlights a chronological aside; it does not *per se* indicate a quotation from archival sources (*pace* Cogan and Tadmor, *II Kings*, 186). *To this day* (1 Kgs 8:8; 9:13, 21; 10:12; 12:19; 2 Kgs 2:22; 8:22; 14:7; 17:23, 34, 41; 20:17) is a quasi-etiological formula that may or may not derive from a second hand (Childs, "A Study of the Formula 'Until This Day.'").

46 Cogan and Tadmor (*II Kings*, 493) assert that the use of נשל in the *Pi*ʿ*el* instead of *Qal* is late Hebrew; it occurs only here in the HB.

and Israel. Judah could have been assailed from both ends essentially at the same time.[47] The verse is the last in a series of texts in Kings dealing with Judah's relationship to Edom focused especially on Elath (1 Kgs 9:26; 22:47-48; 2 Kgs 3; 8:20-22; 14:7, 10, 22), and it ends with Edom's independence and control over the port, which would have had an economic impact on Judah.

Coloring a neutral act

Seeking help from another king was a reasonable strategy employed by other kings (Menahem, 15:19-20 and Hezekiah, 18:15-16). Here it is used effectively by Ahaz to save Jerusalem. The report in vv. 5, 7-9, in other words, may have been originally neutral or positively oriented toward Ahaz, illustrating his military and political astuteness.[48] It took on negative tones as a result of the evaluation of Ahaz and the perspective of Isaiah 7, which portrayed this as a faithless act. This negative orientation may also be present in the use of the term *bribe* in v. 8. Payment of a שחד is condemned in several other texts in the HB (see the Synchronic Analysis), but in 1 Kgs 15:19, the only other place it is used in Kings and the closest parallel to 2 Kgs 16:8, it is more ambiguous. King Asa of Judah, who pays the bribe, is not explicitly condemned for it, and he is judged a righteous king.

16:7-8: Ahaz's appeal

The expression *your servant and your son* in v. 7 is unique in the HB in this precise form. There are analogous expressions relating especially to David's and the psalmist's relationship to YHWH (Pss 89:21, 27; 116:16). In 1 Sam 25:8 David refers to himself as Nabal's servant and son. The two terms also occur together in the Amarna correspondence (*ANET* 488–89), which shows them to be language of submission that a vassal uses toward his suzerain. Ahaz "made use of a double title to reinforce and highlight his subservience, as well as to make his appeal for help more effective."[49] Cogan and Tadmor raise doubts about the historicity of the title *son* in this context, suggesting that Ahaz would not have dared to use it for himself in addressing the Assyrian king because of its designation of a familial relationship that could be interpreted as presumptive.[50] Thus the precise form of the title found here may be an invention in imitation of formal address, but the point remains that it is intended to portray Ahaz's submission.

Ahaz's vassal status

This raises the question of timing. Was Ahaz already an Assyrian vassal when he made his appeal or did the appeal initiate the relationship? The question is impossible to answer with certainty.[51] Judah is listed without distinction in Tiglath-Pileser's annals as one among several countries and city-states (Moab, Ashkelon, Edom, Gaza) that paid tribute, but the list is summative and does not contain the details of each capitulation. The perspective of the biblical writers, though, is fairly clear. In Isaiah the prophet pleads for Ahaz to maintain Judah's independence by doing nothing—neither giving in to Razon and Pekah nor sending to Assyria for aid. In Kings, Ahaz's decision to turn to Tiglath-Pileser marks a decisive and disastrous moment for Judah. Both see Ahaz's move as the initiation of Judah's vassalhood to Assyria. This is also the perspective of 2 Chr 28:20-21, which is unambiguous in portraying the appeal to As-

---

47 2 Chr 28:18-18 concurs, though its reference to the attacks of Edom and the Philistines also fits the Chronicler's theological agenda of immediate retribution.

48 So Würthwein, *1. Könige 17–2. Könige 25*, 388, and Nelson, *Kings*, 224–25.

49 Kalluveettil, *Declaration and Covenant*, 134.

50 Cogan and Tadmor, "Ahaz and Tiglath-Pileser," 504; *II Kings*, 187.

51 Sweeney (Kings, 380) argues that because of its subordinate relationship with Israel Judah was an Assyrian vassal from the time of the Jehu dynasty.

syria as leading to oppression rather than salvation. The narrative in Kings is certainly Judah-centric in its presentation of Ahaz's appeal as the reason for Assyria's conquest of Damascus: *the king of Assyria listened to Ahaz* (v. 9).[52] The situation was more complicated historically. Assyrian sources indicate that Damascus had long been a thorn in Assyria's side, and Tiglath-Pileser had his own reasons for moving against Damascus that were entirely separate from Judah. Still, the biblical account may be right in its depiction of Judah's subordination to Assyria beginning with Ahaz. It is often noted that Kings does not link Ahaz's appeal to the destruction of Israel in the same way as it does to that of Damascus. While this is somewhat curious, an easy explanation lies at hand: the primary reason for Israel's fall given in 2 Kings 17 was its history of sin against Yhwh. Since this was the main theological point of ch. 17, and indeed of the story of Israel leading up to that event, the role of Ahaz's appeal was inconsequential.

16:9: The capture of Damascus

The Assyrian attack on Damascus took place in 734/3 BCE, two years before the destruction of Samaria.[53] Verse 9 mentions the exiling of the population of Damascus and the execution of Razon. MT states that the people (lit. *it*, referring to the city) were deported to Kir, the location and even the existence of which are uncertain. As indicated in the Note, this reading is also uncertain. The mention of Kir is often taken as an insertion providing a fulfillment of Amos 1:5, threatening exile of the Aramaeans to Kir. G^L, which is followed here, simply relates that *the city*, i.e., Damascus, referring to its population, was exiled by Tiglath-Pileser without naming a destination. Its king, Razon, was executed.[54]

16:10-16: The source behind DtrH's altar report

The next segment of the chapter (vv. 10-16) reports the erection and use of a new, large altar ordered by Ahaz on the model of one he saw in Damascus when he went there to meet Tiglath-Pileser III. There is a general consensus among commentators that these verses were drawn from a distinct source because of their use of titles (King Ahaz, Uriah the priest) in contrast to the preceding verses.[55] The nature of this putative source is debated, but it is often associated with a temple or priestly archive. The appeal to a source, however, needs be modified by two considerations. First, text-critical analysis shows that the use of

---

52 J. McKay (*Religion in Judah under the Assyrians, 732–609 BC* [SBT^2 26; Naperville, IL: A. R. Allenson, 1973], 6) points out that 2 Chr 28:20-21 places the initiative with Tiglath-Pileser rather than Ahaz.

53 Cogan, *Imperialism and Religion*, 65–66; Cogan and Tadmor, "Ahaz and Tiglath-Pileser," 491–92; Miller and Hayes, *History*, 370.

54 The execution of Razon was reportedly confirmed in an Assyrian fragment that has subsequently been lost. G. Smith, "The Annals of Tiglath Pileser II," *ZÄS* 7 (1869): 9–17.

55 Contrast C. Levin ("Die neue Altar unter Ahas von Juda," in *Ein Herz so weit wie der Sand am Ufer des Meeres* [Fs. G. Hentschel; ed. S. Gillmayr-Bucher, A. Giercke, and C. Nießen; Würzburg: Echter Verlag, 2006], 57–60), who regards the notice that Ahaz went to Damascus to meet Tiglath-Pileser in v. 10a as the only historical part of these verses, the rest derived from biblical texts. Still, his interpretation of vv. 17-18 as detailing measures undertaken by Ahaz to safeguard bronze as a precaution against Assyrian conquest seems historically based, though Levin sees them as a contrast to Hezekiah's payment of tribute (pp. 66–68). His argument that vv. 10aβ-12a were inserted by *Wiederaufnahme* is not acceptable. The repetition is inexact and leaves אשר בדמשק hanging without explanation. It is hard to believe that Ahaz's ascent to an altar in Damascus was seen in the older level only as a violation of the law of centralization.

titles for Ahaz and Uriah is not as consistent in these verses as has been asserted. Verses 10-11bα use *King Ahaz* three times and *Uriah the priest* twice. But then each title is only used once more in vv. 11bβ-16. This accords with the other consideration—that vv. 11bβ-16 are an interpolation marked by a loose *Wiederaufnahme:* ככל אשר־שלח המלך אחז מדמשק כן עשה אוריה in v. 11 to ויעש אוריה הכהן ככל אשר־צוה המלך אחז in v. 16. The interpolation incorporated the details about sacrifices offered by Ahaz in v. 13 and ordered by him in v. 15 and explained what happened to the previous bronze altar.

The nature of the source

DtrH's source, then, seems to have been limited to the material in vv. 10-11bα, the notice that Ahaz commissioned and Uriah built an altar on the pattern of the one the former saw in Damascus. It is possible, perhaps even likely, that this information came from a priestly or temple source, but the removal of the cultic material in vv. 13 and 15 from consideration renders the priestly nature of the presumed source less pronounced.[56] Ahaz's meeting with Tiglath-Pileser III in Damascus is apparently understood as subsequent to his appeal for aid. It is probably to be seen as a meeting required by the Assyrian king to affirm Ahaz's vassal status and perhaps for paying further tribute. There is no mention in extant Assyrian records of Ahaz's journey to Damascus, though the practice is known for other kings. In the Kings narrative the point of the meeting is to provide an occasion for Ahaz to see the altar.

The affiliation of the altar

Verse 10 does not state the affiliation of the altar viewed by Ahaz, a fact that has occasioned a long-running debate among scholars and is central to the interpretation of vv. 10-18.[57] Österreicher's thesis that the altar was Assyrian in style and represented the empire's imposition of its cult on Judah was generally accepted until the studies by Cogan and McKay.[58] Cogan argued that the evidence from the Assyrian side indicated that it imposed its religion on provinces but not on vassals. In addition, Assyrians did not typically practice holocaust sacrifices as did Israel, so that a large altar of the kind described here was inappropriate for Assyrian ritual.[59] It is more likely that

---

56 The priestly tone is further reduced if the reference to the תבנית of the altar is a gloss, as Würthwein (*1. Könige 17–2. Könige 25*, 386) supposes. It was probably intended to darken the suspicion about Ahaz's deed that is cast by DtrH's evaluation of him.

57 See Smelik ("The New Altar") for a concise summary and critique of the history of this debate.

58 T. Österreicher, *Das deuteronomistische Grundgesetz* (BFCT 27.4; Gütersloh, 1923), esp. p. 38. Cogan, *Imperialism and Religion*; McKay, *Religion in Judah under the Assyrians.* H. Spieckermann (*Juda unter Assur in der Sargonidenzeit* [FRLANT 129; Göttingen: Vandenhoeck & Ruprecht, 1982]) returned to the older view. In response, Cogan ("Judah under Assyrian Hegemony: A Reexamination of *Imperialism and Religion*," *JBL* 112 [1993]: 403–14) pleaded for a more nuanced view while reaffirming, against Spieckermann, that the altar in 2 Kgs 16 was not an Assyrian cultic imposition. As if in response to this plea, S. W. Holloway (*Aššur is King! Aššur is King! Religion in the Exercise of Power in the Neo-Assyrian Empire* [CHANE 10; Leiden: Brill, 2002] has provided the definitive analysis of the question to date. On p. 107n he states: "For those readers interested in the 150-years-old debate concerning the construction of an Assyrian-style altar by Ahaz of Judah during the reign of Tiglath-Pileser III (2 Kgs 16), there is not the slightest evidence that the historical Assyrians forcibly exported liturgical architecture anywhere."

59 See K. Galling, *Der Altar in den Kulturen des alten Orient: Eine archäologische Studie* (Berlin: Curtius, 1925) 43–44, 54–57, and H. L. Oppenheim, *Ancient Mesopotamia: Portrait of a Dead*

the altar in Damascus was part of the temple and cult of Hadad, the perspective reflected in 2 Chr 28:23. This does not mean that Ahaz was trying to import the cult of Hadad into Judah. There are indications that the new altar was used for the worship of YHWH and was considered religiously legitimate in the original source and perhaps by DtrH as well. The narrative does not explicitly condemn Ahaz's act. The altar was placed directly in front of the main entrance to the temple of YHWH. Surely such an act would have been condemned by DtrH if it were understood as an act of apostasy. Also, it is unlikely that Uriah the priest, who is described in Isa 8:2 as a "reliable witness," would have so readily built the altar according to Ahaz's instructions had the altar introduced the worship of another god into YHWH's temple.[60] Indeed, an altar to a new god would have required a new priest,[61] so that Uriah's continued presence indicates continuity of worship of YHWH. Also, Hezekiah's and Josiah's reported use of the altar draws no disparaging comment.[62] Some scholars contend that Ahaz's motives were practical and even pious as well as aesthetic.[63] The bronze altar Ahaz replaced was too small for the large quantities of sacrifices demanded by certain occasions (1 Kgs 8:64). The new, larger altar could accommodate such quantities that its size and décor might have been seen as enhancing the temple's grandeur. This is suggested as well by Ahaz's dedication of the altar in vv. 12-13, which recalls Solomon's dedication in 1 Kgs 8:62-64.[64]

Civilization (Chicago: University of Chicago, 1964), 191–92. This is not to say that Assyrians never offered holocausts, but they were not a typical part of the Assyrian cult. For a detailed comparison of the Mesopotamian and Israelite sacrificial systems see J. A. Scurlock, "Animal Sacrifice in Ancient Mesopotamian Religion," in *A History of the Animal World in the Ancient Near East* (ed. B. J. Collins; Leiden: Brill, 2002): 389–403, and "The Techniques of the Sacrifice of Animals in Ancient Israel and Ancient Mesopotamia: New Insights through Comparison, Part 1," *AUSS* 44 (2006): 13–49.

60 M. E. W. Thompson, *Situation and Theology* (Sheffield: Almond, 1982), 84. Uriah seems to have been high priest, though his name is not in the list of Zadokite priests in 1 Chr 5:27-41, which may be faulty (Cross, *Canaanite Myth*, 211–12; Knoppers, *1 Chronicles 1-9*, 408–13). See Cogan and Tadmor, *II Kings*, 189.

61 McKay, *Religion in Judah*, 7.

62 Another observation in favor of the altar's legitimacy that is often put forward is the sacrificial terminology in vv. 13 and 15, which is characteristic for Israel. This observation is muted if vv. 13 and 15 are part of an interpolation. Still, they show that early interpretation of the passage had Ahaz making legitimate sacrifices on the altar.

63 E.g., Nelson, *Kings*, 225–27.

64 The last argument is undermined if vv. 12-13 are part of an interpolation. McKay (*Religion in Judah*, 7–8) contends that Ahaz's erection of the new altar must illustrate DtrH's negative assessment of the king in some way. He raises two possibilities. The first is Saggs's view (H. W. F. Saggs, *Assyriology and the Study of the Old Testament* [Cardiff: University of Wales, 1969], 19–22) that the altar was Phoenician and represented Ahaz's attempt to strengthen Judah's trade links with Phoenicia. This idea was countered by Cogan (*Imperialism and Religion*, 76), who noted that this proposal was contrary to the story, which sets the altar in Damascus, and that Tyre was a member of the anti-Assyrian coalition with Aram and Israel and hence was Judah's enemy. McKay's second possibility is that Ahaz's altar was a copy of the one on which he had affirmed his treaty with Tiglath-Pileser, an altar that symbolized Assyria's supremacy rather than YHWH's. However, the narrative does not state this and it is hard to believe that the altar would not have come in for some criticism were this known.

16:11bβ-16: An interpolation

The clause *until the king returned from Damascus* in v. 11bβ is awkward. It serves as an anticipatory bridge to the mention of Ahaz's return in v. 12 and marks the beginning of the interpolation in vv. 11bβ-16.[65] These verses use the title "the king" rather than "King Ahaz" as in vv. 10-11bα, and this is a sign of a change of hands. First vv. 15-16 were interpolated by *Wiederaufnahme* as described. Then vv. 11bβ-14 were added. The two-stage process is indicated by the *ketiv* ויצוהו in v. 15. The suffix on this verb refers to Uriah, who was last mentioned in v. 11abα. The insertion of vv. 12-14 effects considerable distance between the last reference to Uriah and the suffix in v. 15, so much so that it was felt necessary after their insertion to specify Uriah as the object.[66] Rendtorff points out the differences in terminology and order of the sacrifices between vv. 13 and 15 that suggest composition by different hands. Specifically, v. 13 reports Ahaz's own activities while v. 15 gives instructions for the priest. Then, while v. 13 has Ahaz offering the four types of sacrifices more or less at once, v. 15 makes distinctions between the עלה, to be offered in the morning, and the מנחה, offered in the evening. It also distinguishes between the king's עלה and מנחה and those of the people. Furthermore, while v. 13 refers to the blood of the שלמים, v. 15 mentions the blood of the עלה and the זבח. The purpose of the first interpolation in vv. 15-16 was evidently to give prescriptions for the sacrifices to be offered on the altar according to Priestly tradition. The second in vv. 12-14 sought to explain what happened to the previous bronze altar (v. 14), especially in face of the mention of it in Ezek 9:2 as still standing in the temple, and to update the list of sacrifices drawing on Num 29:39. While the terms and order are different in vv. 11bβ-13, they anticipate v. 15 in providing a list of sacrifices offered on the new altar. All these features are indications that vv. 11bβ-14 are secondary not only to vv. 10-11bα but also to vv. 15-16.

16:12-13: Ahaz's offerings

The notice that the king saw the altar (v. 12) when he returned from Damascus is best translated *inspected*. It is parallel to the same statement in v. 10 (וירא את־המזבח), where the king initially noticed the altar. Having inspected the altar and found it to meet with his approval, the king moves to dedicate it. This he does with the series of offerings listed in v. 13. Like David (2 Sam 6:17-18) and Solomon (1 Kgs 8:62-64), but also like Jeroboam (1 Kgs 12:32-33), Ahaz personally presides over the dedication.[67] He is the subject of all the verbs in these two verses. The order of his offerings (עלה, מנחה, נסך, שלמים) is identical to that of Num 29:39 (P).[68] This points to a late date for v. 13,

---

65 Similarly Würthwein, *1. Könige 17–2. Könige 25*, 385.

66 Cf. Rendtorff (*Studien zur Geschichte des Opfers*, 46–47; Stade, *Kings*, 257. The subject *King Ahaz* was also part of this work. Before the addition of vv. 12-14 Ahaz did not need to be identified as the subject. Würthwein (*1. Könige 17–2. Könige 25*, 389) argued that vv. 12-13 are secondary because the transfer of the bronze altar reported in v. 14 would have to be completed before the new altar could be built, much less dedicated. But Uriah's building of the altar is already reported in v. 11a, so that excising vv. 12-13 does not solve the problem. It is, however, mitigated by reading the first verb as a perfect (הקריב) with pluperfect sense.

67 Cohn (*2 Kings*, 114) highlights the picture of the king sacrificing, thereby suggesting dramatic enhancement as the motive behind vv. 12-13, which, given his synchronic treatment, he does not view as an addition.

68 The parallel undermines Šanda's (*Könige* II, 201) contention that the reference to the libation in v. 13 is an addition.

consistent with its nature as a post-DtrH addition.[69] Priestly details about how to make these offerings are found in Leviticus 1 (עלה), 2 (מנחה), and 3 (שלמים), with instructions for the נסך in Numbers 15. The מנחה is here distinguished as an offering on its own, a grain offering, rather than in a more general sense for any offering (BDB 585; *HALOT* 601). This is also Priestly terminology. The use of קטר (*Hip'îl*) for offering sacrifices is typically P. While the sprinkling of blood on the altar was a common part of the "peace offerings" (שלמים), it may serve the additional function in this context of marking the consecration of the new altar.

16:14: Situating the altar

The phrase *before* YHWH in v. 14 may allude to 1 Kgs 8:64 in situating the altar before the temple. The older altar evidently stood directly in front of the entrance to the sanctuary, probably on the east.[70] Ahaz set it to one side, the northern or right side facing the sanctuary. The phrase *between the altar and* YHWH*'s temple* is hard to make sense of in its present location. It would fit better following the statement that the bronze altar was moved to the northern side of the new altar. It may, therefore, be a gloss attempting to clarify the placement of the altar.[71] The use of the verb קרב (*Hip'îl*), though somewhat unusual, apparently has the sense, with מן, of moving or removing an object from one location to another (*HALOT* 1134); there is no need to emend it to ויסר as is sometimes proposed.

16:15: Dating the morning burnt offering and evening grain offering

The reference in v. 15 to the morning burnt offering (עלת־הבקר) and the evening grain offering (מנחת הערב) is revealing for dating purposes. Rendtorff and Levine have demonstrated that the practice of making a burnt animal sacrifice (עלה) twice a day, morning and evening, as a regular, daily offering or *tāmîd* was a late, Priestly one as reflected in Exod 29:38-42; Num 28:2-8.[72] It does not follow, however, that the present passage must be pre-exilic because Ahaz mandates only one burnt offering in the morning and a grain offering (מנחה) in the evening. Rendtorff shows that there are traces in P (Lev 9:17; Num 28:3) of the earlier practice of a single, morning *tāmîd*, and both he and Levine point to Ezek 46:13-15—an exilic text—as also presupposing a single burnt offering in the morning. Levine observes that "as of the destruction of the First Temple of Jerusalem we have no evidence of a two-phased *tāmîd*" and that "it is in overtly postexilic literature that we find references to the two-phased *tāmîd*" (e.g., 1 Chr 16). Exactly when the change from one to two daily burnt offerings occurred is uncertain, but 2 Kgs 16:15, as part of a post-DtrH interpolation, appears to come from the transitional period when the single morning עלה and the evening מנחה had yet to transition to a twice daily עלה.

Secondary libations

Rendtorff's assumption about the pre-exilic date of v. 15 compels him to argue that the words ונסכיהם וכל־דם עלה וכל־דם־זבח עליו תזרק are secondary Priestly retouchings. Once one perceives this verse as part of a post-DtrH interpolation, though, there is no need to deny its P language. The purpose of the interpolation in vv. 15-16 was to specify the offerings to be made on the new altar, a Priestly concern. Only in the case of the mention of libations (ונסכיהם) are there other considerations besides P terminology to suggest that it may be secondary. It is

69 Rendtorff, *Geschichte des Opfers*, 128; Würthwein, *1. Könige 17–2. Könige 25*, 389–90.
70 Gray, *Kings*, 636.
71 Würthwein (*1. Könige 17–2. Könige 25*, 386).
72 Rendtorff, *Studien zur Geschichte des Opfers*, 74–76, 196, and Levine (*Numbers 21–36*, 48).

part of a stereotypical expression ומנחתם ונסכיהם (e.g., Lev 23:18; Num 29:18, 21, 24), so that the presence of ומנחתם alone might lead to its addition. Also, the libation is mentioned as a part of the people's offerings but has no correspondence among the king's offerings. Finally, the verb presently governing ונסכיהם is הקטר, which is inappropriate for libations.[73]

The king's inquiry

The other major issue in v. 15 is the meaning of Ahaz's statement in v. 15b about the bronze altar. The root בקר has the general sense of "seek, inquire, discern," but its precise nuance here is uncertain. It is used in Rabbinic Hebrew for examining sacrificial animals for quality control and has been construed with that meaning here,[74] but this hardly seems a proper function for a king. Ehrlich took it to mean "show the difference" between the two altars, but his proposal has not won wide acceptance.[75] A more common view is that Ahaz reserved the altar for extispicy, the examination of animal entrails to obtain an omen. It is not clear, though, why one would need an altar for this, and besides, one would expect a word of condemnation for such an activity, given the attitude toward divination elsewhere in the Bible.[76] A general reference to cultic acts for the purpose of obtaining an oracle from Yhwh (acceptable divination) seems more appropriate.[77] An even more general sense of "reflect" has been proposed on the basis of Ps 27:4.[78] Again, though, it is unclear why the altar would be needed for reflection or prayer, so that this more abstract interpretation is dubious. The notice in v. 16 that Uriah did as Ahaz instructed him (v. 16) offers a consideration for the meaning of לבקר, as it is difficult to believe that a "reliable priest" of Yhwh (Isa 8:2) would accede to the king's order to bring the Assyrian divinatory cult into the temple of Yhwh or that he would be described as doing so without condemnation from the writer.

16:17-18: Source material

The last segment of DtrH's account before the concluding regnal formulae (i.e., vv. 17-18) describes measures taken by Ahaz in the temple in order to send a gift or tribute to Tiglath Pileser III. The detail in these descriptions as well as the ambiguity of the phrase *on account of the king of Assyria* suggest that we are dealing with source material. These verses are not a continuation of vv. 10-16, as is sometimes alleged. The concerns of the two texts are different. In vv. 17-18 the

---

73 Rendtorff, *Studien zur Geschichte des Opfers*, 47.

74 Buis, *Rois*, 248; Skinner, *Kings*, 371.

75 Ehrlich, *Randglossen*, 12.

76 Spieckermann (*Juda unter Assur*, 362–69, esp. 368) argued that Ahaz used the old bronze altar for divination according to Assyrian practice as a way of demonstrating his loyalty to his overlord. At the same time he continued to observe the cult of Yhwh, which entailed animal sacrifice, using the new and larger stone altar. The strategy was politically astute or even a political necessity as he sought to appease both the people and the religious leadership of Judah as well as his Assyrian suzerain. This clever explanation is rendered doubtful by the uncertainty of the meaning of לבקר and by the secondary nature of this addition, as well as by the arguments adduced by Cogan and McKay that Assyria did not impose its religion on vassals.

77 So A. T. Olmstead (*History of Palestine and Syria to the Macedonian Conquest* [New York: 1931], 452), who otherwise argues for Assyrian imposition of religion on Judah. Cf. Jones, *Kings*, 540; McKay, *Religion in Judah,* 8.

78 Benzinger, *Könige*, 171; Kittel, *Könige*, 271. Similarly, Cogan and Tadmor (*Kings*, 189) take it to mean "to frequent," i.e., for private use; Hobbs (*2 Kings*, 217) and Olley (*Kings*, 301) favor "pray" or "worship."

concern is no longer the new altar but the measures undertaken by Ahaz *on account of the king of Assyria.* Also, while Ahaz removes the bronze from other items in vv. 17-18, the bronze altar remains untouched (v. 15).[79]

Removal of luxury items

The major interpretational question of these verses is the reason for the measures described in them. Hand in hand with Österreicher's theory that Assyria imposed its cult on Judah went Olmstead's interpretation of vv. 17-18, which saw the measures undertaken by Ahaz as imposed by Assyria to denigrate both the deity and the king of Judah. Thus the bronze panels and oxen, which suggested YHWH's might, were removed, and a throne for the god Ashur along with a stela of the king of Assyria were set up in the temple.[80] However, this interpretation has been called into question by Cogan's assertion that Assyrians would not have taken offense at the continued display of royal prerogatives such as those described in v. 18 and by McKay's that there is no evidence that the Assyrians had statues installed in non-Assyrian temples.[81] A different understanding was offered by Winckler, whose comparison of 16:7-9 + 17-18 with 18:13-16 led him to conclude that 16:17-18 describe luxury items removed by Ahaz and sent as gifts or tribute to Tiglath-Pileser III.[82] This makes good sense for the items mentioned in v. 17—the decorated panels and basins from the mobile laver stands, and the oxen from beneath the sea—all of which were made of bronze. There is precedent for Assyrian kings receiving such articles.[83] The items in v. 18 are more difficult, in part because the reading of the verse is uncertain. Nevertheless, it is still relatively easy to conceive of the items in v. 18 as luxury goods that were removed and sent as gifts to the king of Assyria.[84] Following G, "the dais of the throne" must have been a raised platform for the king to sit enthroned during cultic celebrations. If one subscribes to the MT (*qere'*), the מוסך השבת would be an awning or canopy of some sort—quite possibly metal—presumably used by the king on Sabbath.[85] *The king's outer*

---

79 Hentschel, *2 Könige*, 73.

80 "A throne for the divine king was built in the temple and the outer royal entry was turned to the house of Yahweh from before the face of the king of Assyria, presumably represented in stele form" – Olmstead, *History of Palestine*, 452. The "throne for the divine king" was based on the G reading in v. 18. "From before the face of the king of Assyria," i.e., of the king's statue, was Olmstead's understanding of the phrase מפני מלך אשור.

81 Cogan, *Imperialism and Religion*, 74n; McKay, *Religion in Judah*, 9. Some scholars do not think the Assyrians imposed their religion but still contend that these items of royal privilege were removed to emphasize Ahaz's vassal status (Fritz, *Kings*, 345; Gray, *Kings*, 638; Sweeney, *Kings*, 385).

82 Winckler, *Alttestamentliche Untersuchungen*, 48–49; cf. Kittel, *Könige*, 271; Šanda, *Könige* II, 203–204; Thenius, *Könige*, 364.

83 Cogan, *Imperialism and Religion*, 74n.

84 Another way of dealing with the difference between vv. 17 and 18 is to regard מפני מלך אשור at the end of v. 18 as misplaced from the end of v. 17 (Šanda, *Könige* II, 204; Jones, *Kings*, 541). Then v. 17 is seen as referring to tribute while v. 18 refers to other changes carried out by Ahaz for unspecified reasons. Hentschel (*2 Könige*, 77) makes a similar move when he argues that v. 18a is an addition that breaks the continuity between v. 17 and v. 18b.

85 Cf. M. J. Mulder, "Was war die am Tempel gebaute 'Sabbathalle' in II Kön. 16,18?" in *Von Kanaan bis Kerala* (Fs. J. P. M. Van der Ploeg; ed. W. C. Delman, *et al.*; AOAT 211; Neukirchen-Vluyn: Neukirchener Verlag, 1982), 161–72.

entryway probably referred not to a gate but to a covered passageway, again probably metal, at least in part.

Occasioned by the king of Assyria

These items were removed מפני מלך אשור. The exact nuance of the preposition מפני here is uncertain, as is evident from the variety of translations of it: "before," "because of," "on account of," "in deference to," even "to satisfy" (NEB). However one renders it, the phrase makes clear that the Assyrian king was the reason for the preceding measures. They were either ordered by him or were undertaken in order to elicit a positive response from him. Since the Assyrians do not appear to have squelched royal privilege for local kings, the removal of these items is best understood as voluntary for the purpose either of fulfilling the quota of tribute demanded or as gifts in hopes of currying the Assyrian king's favor.[86]

16:19-20: Ahaz's closing formulae

The closing regnal formulae for Ahaz (v. 19-20) are standard. His burial with his royal forebears in the city of David suggests that he may not have been judged as harshly by his contemporaries as he was by DtrH. The Chronicler, though, has the judgment of Ahaz reflected in his burial, 2 Chr 28:27 declaring that he was buried in Jerusalem but not with the kings of Israel,[87] that is, not in the royal tombs.

Synthesis

DtrH's negative view of Ahaz

The evaluation of Ahaz in vv. 2b-3a makes it clear that DtrH and did not look positively upon him, but the reasons for the negative assessment are not clear. Ahaz is not blamed for a failure to trust in Yhwh, as one might expect if his account were narrated through the lens of Isaiah 7. The reason DtrH gives is that Ahaz followed the way of the Israelite kings by using the *bāmôt*, which he identifies at least in this case with the worship of other gods.[88] What remains obscure is how DtrH relates the anecdotes he cites from Ahaz's reign to his assessment. Was Ahaz's bribe of Tiglath-Pileser and his use of temple treasures to do so (vv. 5, 7-9) an act of faithlessness and an encroachment on the cult or an astute political move that saved Jerusalem and Judah from Aram and Israel? Was his copying of the Damascus altar (vv. 10-11bα) a damnable apostasy or an enhancement of the temple facilities that enlarged the capacity for sacrifice? Assuming that his removal of bronze and objects from the temple was some sort of gift or tribute and not the imposition of Assyrian cult, should it be understood as punishment — Ahaz's just desserts for apostasy and lack of trust in Yhwh—or is it simply related as a further "cost of doing business" with Assyria? The absence of any overt condemnation of Ahaz for these deeds makes these questions difficult to answer.

---

86 Wray Beal (*Kings*, 441) advances a third possibility, that these measures were uncoerced acts of deference that reflected acculturation to the environment of the time represented in the Damascus-style altar.

87 On the use of "Israel" for "Judah" after the demise of the former, see Klein, *2 Chronicles*, 407.

88 Thompson, *Situation and Theology*, 88.

The additions to DtrH

The additions to the chapter in vv. 3b and 11bβ-16 do not make it any easier. The accusation of child sacrifice in v. 3b darkens Ahaz's reputation and makes him guilty of reverting to Canaanite practice. One can then read his construction of the new altar as a cultic innovation with overtones of turning to other gods. Such an act resembles the innovations of Jeroboam I and further illustrates Ahaz's subscription to the ways of Israelite kings. The additions in vv. 11bβ-16 turn the altar episode into the focal point of the chapter, but they complicate the question of Ahaz's evaluation by legitimating the new altar with their prescriptions about the sacrifices to be offered upon it.

Bibliography

Abbreviations

*	an earlier, unspecified version of the designated passage
√	Hebrew root or stem
AB	Anchor Bible
ABD	*Anchor Bible Dictionary*
ABR	*Australian Biblical Review*
AF	*Altorientalische Forschungen*
AHw	Wolfram von Soden, *Akkadisches Handwörterbuch: unter Benutzung des lexikalischen Nachlaßes von Bruno Meissner (1868–1947).* Wiesbaden: Harrassowitz, 1965–1981.
ANEP	*Ancient Near Eastern Texts in Pictures Relating to the Old Testament.* Edited by J. B. Pritchard. 3d ed. Princeton, NJ: Princeton University Press, 1969.
ANET	*Ancient Near Eastern Texts Relating to the Old Testament.* Edited by J. B. Pritchard. 3d ed. Princeton, NJ: Princeton University Press, 1969.
AO	*Archiv für Orientforschung*
AOAT	Alter Orient und Altes Testament
AOS	American Oriental Series
AOTC	Abingdon Old Testament Commentary
ASORDS	American Schools of Oriental Research Dissertation Series
ATANT	Abhandlungen zur Theologie des Alten und Neuen Testaments
ATD	Das Alte Testament Deutsch
ATSAT	Arbeiten zu Text und Sprache im Alten Testament
BAR	*Biblical Archaeology Review*
BASOR	*Bulletin of the American Schools of Oriental Research*
BASORSup	*BASOR* Supplementary Studies
BDB	Francis Brown, Samuel R. Driver, and Charles A. Briggs, *A Hebrew and English Lexicon of the Old Testament.* Oxford: Clarendon Press, 1907
BE	Biblical Encyclopedia/Biblische Enzyklopädie
BEATAJ	Beiträge zur Erforschung des Alten Testaments und des Antiken Judentums
BFCT	Beiträge zur Förderung christlicher Theologie
BI	*Biblical Interpretation*
Bib	*Biblica*
BibOr	Biblica et orientalia
BIOSCS	*Bulletin of the International Organization of Septuagint and Cognate Studies*

BIS	Biblical Interpretation Series
BHS	*Biblia Hebraica Stuttgartensia*
BJS	Brown Judaic Studies
BKAT	Biblischer Kommentar, Altes Testament. Edited by Martin Noth and Hans Walter Wolff
BRL	*Biblisches Reallexicon.* Edited by Kurt Galling. HAT 1/1. 2d ed. 1977. Tübingen: Mohr Siebeck.
BTB	*Biblical Theology Bulletin*
BWANT	Beiträge zur Wissenschaft vom Alten und Neuen Testament
BZ	*Biblische Zeitschriften*
BZAW	Beihefte zur *ZAW*
CAD	*The Assyrian Dictionary of the Oriental Institute of the University of Chicago.*
CAH	*Cambridge Ancient History*
CahRB	Cahiers de la *Revue Biblique*
CBA	Catholic Biblical Association of America
CBC	Cambridge Bible Commentary
CBQ	*Catholic Biblical Quarterly*
CBQMS	*Catholic Biblical Quarterly* Monograph Series
CHANE	Culture and History of the Ancient Near East
ConBOT	Coniectanea Biblica, Old Testament Series
COS	*The Context of Scripture.* Edited by William W. Hallo and K. Lawson Younger. 3 volumes. Leiden: Brill, 1997–2002.
DDD	*Dictionary of Deities and Demons in the Bible.* Second edition. Edited by Karel van der Toorn, Bob Becking, and Pieter W. van der Horst. Leiden: Brill; Grand Rapids: Eerdmans, 1999.
DJD	*Discoveries in the Judaean Desert of Jordan*
DOTHB	*Dictionary of the Old Testament: Historical Books.* Edited by Bill T. Arnold and H. G. M. Williamson. Downers Grove, IL: InterVarsity, 2005.
DSI	De Septuaginta Investigationes
DZGW	*Deutsche Zeitschrift für Geschichtswissenschaft*
EBR	*The Encyclopedia of the Bible and its Reception.* Berlin: De Gruyter, 2009–
EI	*Eretz Israel*
EncJud	*Encyclopedia Judaica*
EstBib	*Estudios Bíblicos*
ETL	*Ephemerides Theologicae Lovanienses*
EvTh	*Evangelische Theologie*
ExpT	*Expository Times*
FAT	Forschungen zum Alten Testament
FB	Forschung zur Bibel

GELS	Takamitsu Muraoka, *A Greek-English Lexicon of the Septuagint.* Louvain: Peeters, 2009.
GKC	*Gesenius' Hebrew Grammar.* Edited by Emil Kautzsch and revised by A. E. Cowley. Oxford: Clarendon Press, 1910.
HALOT	Ludwig Koehler, Walter Baumgartner, and Johann Jakob Stamm, *The Hebrew and Aramaic Lexicon of the Old Testament.* Translated and edited under the supervision of M. E. J. Richardson. 4 vols. Leiden: Brill, 1994–1999.
HAT	Handbuch zum Alten Testament
HBAI	*Hebrew Bible and Ancient Israel*
HSM	Harvard Semitic Monographs
HSS	Harvard Semitic Studies
HTR	*Harvard Theological Review*
HUCA	*Hebrew Union College Annual*
ICC	International Critical Commentary
IDBS	*Interpreter's Dictionary of the Bible, Supplementary Volume.*
IEJ	*Israel Exploration Journal*
JANES	*Journal of Ancient Near Eastern Studies*
JAOS	*Journal of the American Oriental Society*
JBL	*Journal of Biblical Literature*
JBS	Jerusalem Biblical Studies
JETS	*Journal of the Evangelical Theological Society*
JJS	*Journal of Jewish Studies*
JNES	*Journal of Near Eastern Studies*
JNSL	*Journal of Northwest Semitic Languages*
Joüon	Paul Joüon, S. J., *Grammar of Biblical Hebrew.* Translated and revised by Takamitsu Muraoka. 2 vols. Subsidia biblica 14/1-2. Rome: Biblical Institute Press, 1991–1993.
JPOS	*Journal of the Palestinian Oriental Society*
JQR	*Jewish Quarterly Review*
JSOT	*Journal for the Study of the Old Testament*
JSQ	*Jewish Studies Quarterly*
JTS	*Journal of Theological Studies*
KAI	Herbert Donner and Wolfgang Röllig, *Kanaanäische und Aramäische Inschriften.* 3 vols. Wiesbaden: Harrassowitz, 1964.
KEHAT	Kurzgefasstes exegetisches Handbuch zum Alten Testament
KHAT	Kurzer Hand-Commentar zum Alten Testament
KTU	Manfred Dietrich, Oswald Loretz, and Joaquín Sanmartín, *Die keilalphabetischen Texte aus Ugarit, Ras Ibn Hani und anderen Orten/The Cuneiform*

	Alphabetic Texts from Ugarit, Ras Ibn Hani and Other Places. AOAT 360/1. 3rd ed. Münster: Ugarit Verlag, 2013.
KUSATU	Kleine Untersuchungen zur Sprache des Alten Testaments und seiner Umwelt
LHBOTS	Library of Hebrew Bible/Old Testament Studies
LSJ	Henry G. Liddell and Robert Scott, *A Greek-English Lexicon.* Edited and revised by Henry Stuart Jones. Oxford: Clarendon Press, 1930.
MHUC	Monographs of the Hebrew Union College
NAC	New American Commentary
NEAEHL	*The New Encyclopedia of Archaeological Excavations in the Holy Land.* Edited by Ephraim Stern. Jerusalem: Carta, 1993.
NCB	New Century Bible
NIB	*The New Interpreter's Bible*
NIBC	New International Biblical Commentary
NIDB	*New Interpreter's Dictionary of the Bible*
OBO	Orbis biblicus et orientalis
OEBA	*The Oxford Encyclopedia of the Bible and Archaeology.* Edited by Daniel M. Master. New York: Oxford University Press, 2013.
OLZ	*Orientalische Literaturzeitung*
OTL	Old Testament Library
OTS	*Oudtestamentische Studien* (journal)
OTS	Oudtestamentische Studiën (series)
PJ	*Palästina-Jahrbuch*
PEQ	*Palestine Exploration Quarterly*
RA	*Revue d'Assyriologie*
RB	*Revue biblique*
RHR	*Revue de l'histoire des religions*
RIDA	*Revue Internationale des Droits de l'Antiquité*
RINAP	The Royal Inscriptions of the Assyrian Period
RQ	*Revue de Qumran*
RSOu	Ras Shamra—Ougarit. Publications de la Mission archéologique française de Ras Shamra–Ougarit
SAIS	Studies in the Aramaic Interpretation of Scripture
SANER	Studies in Ancient Near Eastern Records
SANT	Studien zum Alten und Neuen Testament
SBLAIL	Society of Biblical Literature. Ancient Israel and Its Literature
SBLDS	Society of Biblical Literature Dissertation Series
SBLMS	Society of Biblical Literature Monograph Series
SBLWAW	Society of Biblical Literature. Writings from the Ancient World

SBS	Stuttgarter Bibelstudien
SBT	Studies in Biblical Theology
SCJ	*Stone-Campbell Journal*
SEÅ	*Svensk Exegetisk Årsbok*
SHCANE	Studies in the History and Culture of the Ancient Near East
SJLA	Studies in Judaism in Late Antiquity
SJOT	*Scandinavian Journal of the Old Testament*
TA	*Tel Aviv*
TDOT	*Theological Dictionary of the Old Testament*. Translation of *Theologisches Wörterbuch zum Alten Testament.* Edited by G. Johannes Botterweck and Helmer Ringgren.
TLOT	*Theological Lexicon of the Old Testament.*
TOTC	Tyndale Old Testament Commentaries
TRE	*Theologische Realenzyklopädie*
TZ	*Theologische Zeitschrift*
UF	*Ugarit Forschungen*
VT	*Vetus Testamentum*
VTSup	Supplements to *Vetus Testamentum*
WBC	Word Biblical Commentary
WMANT	Wissenschaftliche Monographien zum Alten und Neuen Testament.
WO	Bruce K. Waltke and Michael Patrick O'Connor, *An Introduction to Biblical Hebrew Syntax.* Winona Lake, IN: Eisenbrauns, 1990.
WuD	*Wort und Dienst*
ZA	*Zeitschrift für Althebraistik*
ZÄS	*Zeitschrift für ägyptische Sprache und Alterthumskunde*
ZAW	*Zeitschrift für die alttestamentliche Wissenschaft*
ZDPV	*Zeitschrift des Deutschen Palästina-Vereins*
ZTK	*Zeitschrift für Theologie und Kirche*

Literature

Aharoni, Yohanan. *The Land of the Bible: A Historical Geography.* Rev. ed. Trans. A. F. Rainey. Philadelphia: Westminster, 1979.

Avigad, Nahman, and Benjamin Sass. *Corpus of West Semitic Stamp Seals.* Jerusalem: Israel Academy of Sciences and Humanities/IES/Institute of Archaeology, Hebrew University, 1997.

Barnes, William Hamilton. *1–2 Kings.* Cornerstone Biblical Commentary. Carol Stream, IL: Tyndale House, 2012.

Barré, Lloyd M. *The Rhetoric of Political Persuasion.* CBQMS 20. Washington, DC: CBA, 1988.

Barrick, W. Boyd. "What Do We Really Know about 'High Places?'" *SEÅ* 45 (1980): 50–57.

____. "The Word BMH in the Old Testament." Unpublished dissertation. University of Chicago, 1975.

Barthélemy, Dominique. *Critique textuelle de l'Ancien Testament. 1. Josué, Juges, Ruth, Samuel, Rois, Chronique, Esdras, Néhémie, Esther.* OBO 50/1. Fribourg/Göttingen: Éditions Universitaires/Vandenhoeck & Ruprecht, 1982.

Benzinger, Immanuel. *Die Bücher der Könige.* KHAT 9. Freiburg: Mohr, 1899.

Blum, Erhard. "Die Nabotüberlieferungen und die Kompositionsgeschichte der Vorderen Propheten." Pp. 111–29 in *Schriftauslegung in der Schrift. Festschrift für Odil Hannes Steck zu seinem 65. Geburtstag.* Edited by Reinhard Gregor Kratz, Thomas Krüger and Konrad Schmid. BZAW 300. Berlin: de Gruyter, 2000.

____. "Der Prophet und das Verderben Israels: Eine ganzheitliche, historisch-kritische Lektüre von 1 Regum XVII–XIX." *VT* 47 (1997): 277–92.

Brewer-Boydston, Ginny. *Good Queen Mothers, Bad Queen Mothers: The Theological Presentation of the Queen Mother in 1 and 2 Kings.* CBQMS 54. Washington, DC: CBA, 2015.

Brueggemann, Walter. *1 & 2 Kings.* Smyth & Helwys Bible Commentary. Macon, GA: Smyth & Helwys, 2000.

Buis, Pierre. *Le Livre des Rois.* Sources Bibliques. Paris: Librairie Lecoffre, 1997.

Burney, C. F. *Notes on the Hebrew Text of the Books of Kings.* Oxford: Clarendon Press, 1903.

Cantrell, Deborah O'Daniel. *The Horsemen of Israel: Horses and Chariotry in Monarchic Israel (Ninth–Eighth Centuries B.C.E.).* Winona Lake, IN: Eisenbrauns, 2011.

Chavel, Simeon. "The Face of God and the Etiquette of Eye Contact: Visitation, Pilgrimage, and Prophetic Vision in Ancient Israel and Early Jewish Imagination." *JSQ* 19 (2012): 1–55.

Cogan, Mordechai (Morton). *I Kings.* AB 10. New York: Doubleday, 2001.

Cogan, Mordechai, and Hayim Tadmor. *II Kings.* AB 11. New York: Doubleday, 1988.

Cohn, Robert L. *2 Kings.* Berit Olam: Studies in Hebrew Narrative & Poetry. Collegeville, MN: Liturgical Press, 2000.

Cranz, Isabel. "Naaman's Healing and Gehazi's Affliction: The Magical Backgrounds of 2 Kgs 5." *VT.* Forthcoming

Cronauer, Patrick T. *The Stories about Naboth the Jezreelite: A Source, Composition and Redactional Investigation of 1 Kings 21 and Passages in 2 Kings 9.* LHBOTS 424. London/New York: T & T Clark, 2005.

Cross, Frank Moore, Jr. *Canaanite Myth and Hebrew Epic: Essays in the History of the Religion of Israel.* Cambridge, MA: Harvard University Press, 1973.

DeVries, Simon J. *1 Kings.* 2nd ed. WBC. Waco, TX: Word Books, 2003.

Dietrich, Walter. *Prophetie und Geschichte. Eine redaktionsgeschichtliche Untersuchung zum deuteronomistischen Geschichtswerk.* Göttingen: Vandenhoeck & Ruprecht, 1972.

Diringer, David. *Le iscrizioni antico-ebraiche palestinesi raccolte e illustrate.* Florence: Felice Le Monnier, 1934.

Dray, Carol A. *Translation and Interpretation in the Targum to the Books of Kings.* SAIS 5. Leiden: Brill, 2006.

Driver, Samuel Rolles. *A Treatise on the Use of the Tenses in Hebrew.* Oxford: Clarendon Press, 1892.

Dutcher-Walls, Patricia. *Narrative Art, Political Rhetoric: The Case of Athaliah and Joash.* JSOTSup 209. Sheffield: Sheffield Academic Press, 1996.

Ehrlich, Arnold B. *Randglossen zur hebräischen Bibel. Textkritisches, sprachliches und sachliches.* Vol 7. Leipzig: Hinrichs, 1914.

Eissfeldt, Otto. "Die Komposition von I Reg 16,29–II Reg 13,25." Pages 49–58 in *Das ferne und nahe Wort. Festschrift Leonhard Rost.* Edited by Fritz Maass. BZAW 105. Berlin: Töpelmann, 1967.

Eph'al-Jaruzelska, Izabela. "Officialdom and Society in the Book of Kings: The Social Relevance of the State." Pages 467–500 in *The Books of Kings: Sources, Composition, Historiog-*

raphy, and Reception. Edited by André Lemaire and Baruch Halpern. VTSup 129. Leiden: Brill, 2010.

____. *Prophets, Legitimacy and War in Ancient Israel.* Warsaw: Warsaw University Press, 2009.

Fernández Marcos, Natalio, and José Ramón Busto Saiz. *El texto antioqueno de la Biblia Griega. II. 1–2 Reyes.* Madrid: Instituto de Filología des CSIC. Departamento de Filología Bíblica y de Oriente Antiguo, 1992.

Fischer, Bonifatius, Eugene Ulrich, and Judith Sanderson. "Palimpsestus Vindobonensis: A Revised Edition of L 115 for Samuel–Kings." *BIOSCS* 16 (1983): 1387.

Fohrer, Georg. *Elia.*2nd ed. ATANT 53. Zürich: Zwingli, 1968.

Fowler, Jeaneane D. *Theophoric Personal Names in Ancient Hebrew: A Comparative Study.* JSOTSup 49. Sheffield: Sheffield Academic Press, 1988.

Fox, Nili Sacher. *In the Service of the King: Officialdom in Ancient Israel and Judah.* MHUC 23. Cincinnati: HUC, 2000.

Fretheim, Terence E. *First and Second Kings.* Westminster Bible Companion. Louisville, KY: Westminster John Knox, 1999.

Frevel, Christian. *Aschera und der Ausschließlichkeitsanspruch YHWHs. Beiträge zur literarischen, religionsgeschichtlichen und ikonographischen Aspekten der Ascheradiskussion.* 2 vols. Weinheim: Belz Athenäum, 1995.

____. *Geschichte Israels.* Stuttgart: Kohlhammer, 2016.

Fricke, Klaus Dietrich. *Das erste Buch von den Königen.* Die Botschaft des Alten Testaments. Stuttgart: Calwer, 1964.

____. *Das zweite Buch von den Königen.* Die Botschaft des Alten Testaments. Stuttgart: Calwer, 1972.

Fritz, Volkmar. *1 & 2 Kings.* A Continental Commentary. Trans. Anselm Hagedorn. Minneapolis: Fortress Press, 2003.

Galil, Gershon. *The Chronology of the Kings of Israel and Judah.* Leiden: Brill, 1996.

García-Treto, Francisco O. "The Fall of the House: A Carnivalesque Reading of 2 Kings 9 and 10." *JSOT* 46 (1990): 47–65.

Gray, John. *I & II Kings: A Commentary.* Rev. ed. OTL. Philadelphia: Westminster, 1970.

Green, Alberto R. W. *The Role of Human Sacrifice in the Ancient Near East.* ASORDS 1. Missoula, MT: Scholars Press, 1975.

Greenberg, Moshe. *Ezekiel 1–20.* AB 22A. Garden City, NY: Doubleday, 1983.

Halpern, Baruch. *The Constitution of the Monarchy.* HSM 25. Chico, CA: Scholars Press, 1981.

Harris, Zelig S. *A Grammar of the Phoenician Language.* AOS 8. New Haven, CT: American Oriental Society, 1936.

Hauser, Alan J., and Russell Gregory. *From Carmel to Horeb: Elijah in Crisis.* JSOTSup 85. Sheffield: Almond Press, 1990.

Hens-Piazza, Gina. *1–2 Kings.* AOTC. Nashville: Abingdon, 2006.

Hendel, Ronald S. "The Two Editions of the Royal Chronology in Kings." Pages 99–114 in *Textual Criticism and Dead Sea Scrolls Studies in Honour of Julio Trebolle Barrera.* Edited by Andrés Piquer Otero and Pablo A. Torijano Morales. Leiden: Brill, 2012.

Hentschel, Georg. *1 Könige.* NEB 10. Würzberg: Echter Verlag, 1984.

____. *2 Könige.* NEB 10. Würzberg: Echter Verlag, 1985.

Hobbs, T. R. *2 Kings.* WBC 13. Waco, TX: Word, 1985.

Hoffmann, Hans-Detlef. *Reform und Reformen. Untersuchungen zu einem Grundthema der deuteronomistischen Geschichtsschreibung.* ATANT 66. Zürich: Theologischer Verlag, 1980.

Hölscher, Gustav. "Das Buch der Könige, seine Quellen und seine Redaktion." Pages 158–213 in *Eucharisterion: Studien zur Religion und Literatur des Alten und Neuen Testaments.*Teil 1: *Zur Religion und Literatur des Alten Testaments.* Fs. Hermann Gunkel. Edited by Hans Schmidt. Göttingen: Vandenhoeck & Ruprecht, 1923.

House, Paul R. *1, 2 Kings.* NAC. Nashville: Broadman & Holman, 1995.

Hugo, Philippe. *Les deux visages d'Élie: Texte massorétique et Septante dans l'histoire la plus ancienne du texte de 1 Rois 17–18.* OBO 217. Fribourg/Göttingen: Academic Press/Vandenhoeck & Ruprecht, 2006.

Hurowitz, Victor. "Another Fiscal Practice in the Ancient Near East: 2 Kings 12:5-17 and a Letter to Esarhaddon (LAS 277)." *JNES* 45 (1986): 289–94.

Inrig, Gary. *I & II Kings.* Holman Old Testament Commentary. Nashville: Holman, 2003.

Ishida, Tomoo. "The House of Ahab." *IEJ* 25 (1975): 135–37.

____. *The Royal Dynasties in Ancient Israel.* BZAW 142. Berlin: de Gruyter, 1977.

Jepsen, Alfred. "Elia und das Gottesurteil." Pages 291–306 *Near Eastern Studies in Honor of William Foxwell Albright.* Edited by Hans Goedicke. Baltimore: Johns Hopkins University Press, 1971.

____. "Israel und Damaskus." *AO* 14 (1942): 153–72.

Jones, Gwilym H. *1 and 2 Kings.* Vol. 1. *1 Kings 1–16:34.* Vol. 2 *1 Kings 17:1–2 Kings 25:30.* NCB. Grand Rapids: Eerdmans, 1984.

Joosten, Jan. *The Verbal System of Biblical Hebrew: A New Synthesis Elaborated on the Basis of Classical Prose.* JBS 10. Jerusalem: Simor, 2012.

Kalluveettil, Paul. *Declaration and Covenant: A Comprehensive Review of Covenant Formulae from the Old Testament and the Ancient Near East.* AnBib 88. Rome: Biblical Institute Press, 1982.

Katzenstein, H. Jacob. "Who Were the Parents of Athaliah?" *IEJ* 5 (1955): 193–97.

Keel, Othmar. *Wirkmächtige Siegeszeichen im Alten Testament. Ikonographische Studien zu Jos 8, 18-26; Ex 17, 8-13; 2 Kön 13, 14-19 und 1 Kön 22, 11.* OBO 5. Fribourg/Göttingen: Universitätsverlag/ Vandenhoeck & Ruprecht, 1974.

Keinänen, Jyrki. *Traditions in Collision: A Literary and Redaction-Critical Study on the Elijah Narratives in 1 Kings 17–19.* Helsinki/Göttingen: Finnish Exegetical Society/Vandenhoeck & Ruprecht, 2001.

Kilian, R. "Die Totenerweckung Elias und Elisas—eine Motivwanderung?" *BZ* 10 (1966): 44–56.

King, Philip J., and Lawrence E. Stager. *Life in Biblical Israel.* Louisville, KY: Westminster John Knox, 2001.

Kissling, Paul J. *Reliable Characters in the Primary History: Profiles of Moses, Joshua, Elijah, and Elisha.* JSOTSup 224. Sheffield: Sheffield Academic Press, 1996.

Kittel, Rudolf. *Die Bücher der Könige.* HAT. Göttingen: Vandenhoeck & Ruprecht, 1900.

Klein, Ralph W. *1 Chronicles: A Commentary.* Hermeneia. Minneapolis: Fortress Press, 2006.

____. *2 Chronicles: A Commentary.* Hermeneia. Minneapolis: Fortress Press, 2012.

Klostermann, August. *Die Bücher Samuelis und der Könige.* Nördlingen: C. H. Beck, 1887.

Knoppers, Gary N. *I Chronicles 1–9.* AB 12. New York: Doubleday, 2003.

Laffey, Alice L. *First and Second Kings.* New Collegeville Bible Commentary 9. Collegeville, MN: Liturgical Press, 2012.

Landersdorfer, Simon. *Die Bücher der Könige.* Bonn: Peter Hanstein, 1927.

Law, Timothy Michael. *Origenes Orientalis: The Preservation of Origen's Hexapla in the Syrohexapla of 3 Kingdoms.* DSI 2. Göttingen: Vandenhoeck & Ruprecht, 2011.

Leithart, Peter. *1 & 2 Kings.* Brazos Theological Commentary on the Bible. Grand Rapids: Brazos Press, 2006.

Leuchter, Mark. "The Sociolinguistic and Rhetorical Implications of the Source Citations in Kings. Pages 119–34 in *Soundings in Kings: Perspectives and Methods in Contemporary Scholarship.* Edited by Mark Leuchter and Klaus-Peter Adam. Minneapolis: Fortress Press, 2010.

Levin, Christoph. *Der Sturz der Königin Atalya. Ein Kapitel zur Geschichte Judas im 9. Jh. v. Chr.* SBS 105. Stuttgart: Katholisches Bibelwerk, 1982.

Levine, Baruch A. *Numbers 21–36.* AB 4A. New York: Doubleday, 2000.

Long, Burke O. *1 Kings with an Introduction to Historical Literature.* FOTL 9. Grand Rapids: Eerdmans, 1984.
____. *2 Kings.* FOTL 10. Grand Rapids: Eerdmans, 1991.
Long, Jesse C., Jr. *1 & 2 Kings.* College Press NIV Commentary. Joplin, MO: College Press, 2002.
Longman, Tremper III. *1 Samuel–2 Kings.* The Expositor's Bible Commentary. Revised ed. Grand Rapids: Zondervan, 2009.
Maier, Aren M. "The Historical Background and Dating of Amos VI 2: An Archaeological Perspective from Tell eṣ-Ṣâfî/Gath." *VT* 54 (2004): 319–34.
Mastin, B. A. "Was the *ŠĀLÎŠ* the Third Man in the Chariot?" Pp. 125–54 in *Studies in the Historical Books of the Old Testament.* Edited by John A. Emerton. VTSup 30. Leiden: Brill, 1979.
McCarter, P. Kyle, Jr. *I Samuel.* AB 8. Garden City, NY: Doubleday, 1980.
____. *II Samuel.* AB 9. Garden City, NY: Doubleday, 1984.
McKenzie, Steven L. *The Trouble with Kings: The Composition of the Book of Kings in the Deuteronomistic History.* VTSup 42. Leiden: Brill, 1991.
Mettinger, Tryggve. *King and Messiah: The Civil and Sacral Legitimation of the Israelite Kings.* Lund: Gleerup, 1976.
Miller, J. Maxwell. "Another Look at the Chronology of the Early Divided Monarchy." *JBL* 86 (1967): 276–88.
____. "The Elisha Cycle and the Accounts of the Omride Wars." *JBL* 85 (1967): 441–54.
____. "The Fall of the House of Ahab." *VT* 17 (1967): 307–324.
____. "The Moabite Stone as a Memorial Stela." *PEQ* 106 (1974): 9–18.
Miller, J. Maxwell, and John H. Hayes. *A History of Ancient Israel and Judah.* 2nd ed. Louisville/London: Westminster John Knox, 2006.
Montgomery, James A. *A Critical and Exegetical Commentary on the Books of Kings.* ICC. Edinburgh: T & T Clark, 1951.
Mullen, E. Theodore. "Crime and Punishment: The Sins of the King and the Despoliation of the Treasuries." *CBQ* 54 (1992): 231–48.
____. "The Royal Dynastic Grant to Jehu and the Structure of the Book of Kings." *JBL* 107 (1988): 193–206.
Na'aman, Nadav. "Forced Participation in Alliances in the Course of the Assyrian Campaigns to the West." Pages 80–98 in *Ah Assyria ... Studies in Assyrian History and Ancient Near Eastern Historiography Presented to Hayim Tadmor.* Edited by Mordechai Cogan and Israel Eph'al. Scripta Hierosolymitana 33. Jerusalem: Magnes, 1991.
Nelson, Richard D. *First and Second Kings.* Interpretation. Atlanta: John Knox, 1987.
Noort, Edward. "Child Sacrifice in Ancient Israel: The Status Quaestionis." Pages 103–25 in *The Strange World of Human Sacrifice.* Edited by Jan N. Bremmer. Leuven: Peeters, 2007.
Noth, Martin. *Die israelitischen Personennamen im Rahmen der gemeinsemitischen Namengebung.* Stuttgart: Kohlhammer, 1928.
____. *Könige I. I Könige 1-16.* BKAT 9/1. 2nd ed. Neukirchen-Vluyn: Neukirchener Verlag, 1983.
____. *Überlieferungsgeschichtliche Studien: Die sammelnden und bearbeitenden Geschichtswerke im Alten Testament.* Tübingen: Niemeyer, 1957.
Olley, John W. *The Message of Kings.* The Bible Speaks Today. Downers Grove, IL: Inter-Varsity, 2011.
Olyan, Saul M. *Asherah and the Cult of Yahweh in Israel.* SBLMS 34. Atlanta: Scholars Press, 1988.
____. "2 Kings 9:21—Jehu as Zimri." *HTR* 78 (1985): 203–207.
Otto, Susanne. *Jehu, Elia und Elisa: Die Erzählung von der Jehu-Revolution und die Komposition der Elia-Elisa-Erzählungen.* BWANT 152. Stuttgart: Kohlhammer, 2001.

Patterson, Richard D., and Hermann J. Austel. *1, 2 Kings*. The Expositor's Bible Commentary, Revised Edition. Vol. 3. Grand Rapids: Zondervan, 2005.
Pitard, Wayne T. *Ancient Damascus: A Historical Study of the Syrian City-State from Earliest Times until its Fall to the Assyrians in 732 B.C.E.* Winona Lake, IN: Eisenbrauns, 1987.
____. "The Identity of the Bir-Hadad of the Melqart Stele." *BASOR* 272 (1988): 3–21.
Provan, Iain W. *1 and 2 Kings*. NIBC 7. Peabody, MA: Hendrickson, 1995.
____. *Hezekiah and the Books of Kings: A Contribution to the Debate about the Composition of the Deuteronomistic History.* Berlin/New York: de Gruyter, 1988.
Pruin, Dagmar. *Geschichten und Geschichte. Isebel als literarische und historische Gestalt.* OBO 222. Fribourg/Göttingen: Academic Press/Vandenhoeck & Ruprecht, 2006
Rabinowitz, Isaac. "'ĀZ Followed by Imperfect Verb-Form in Preterite Contexts: A Redactional Device in Biblical Hebrew." *VT* 34 (1984): 53–62.
Rehm, Martin. *Das erste Buch der Könige. Ein Kommentar.* Würzburg: Echter Verlag, 1979.
____. *Das zweite Buch der Könige. Ein Kommentar.* Würzburg: Echter Verlag, 1982.
Rendsburg, Gary A. *Israelian Hebrew in the Book of Kings.* Occasional Publications of the Department of Near Eastern Studies and the Program of Jewish Studies, Cornell University, 5. Bethesda, MD: CDL, 2002.
Rendtorff, Rolf. *Studien zur Geschichte des Opfers im Alten Israel.* WMANT 24. Neukirchen-Vluyn: Neukirchener Verlag, 1967.
Richelle, Matthieu. "Revisiting 2 Kings 13:14-21 (MT and LXX)." Pages 62–81 in *Making the Biblical Text: Textual Studies in the Hebrew and the Greek Bible.* Edited by Innocent Himbaza and Mary-Gabrielle Roth-Mouthon. OBO 275. Fribourg/Göttingen, Academic Press/Vandenhoeck & Ruprecht, 2015.
____. *Le testament d'Élisée. Texte masorétique et Septante en 2 Rois 13.10–14.16.* CahRB 76. Pendé: Gabalde, 2010.
Robinson, Joseph. *The First Book of Kings.* Cambridge Bible Commentary. Cambridge: Cambridge University Press, 1972.
____. *The Second Book of Kings.* Cambridge Bible Commentary. Cambridge: Cambridge University Press, 1976.
Robker, Jonathan M. *The Jehu Revolution: A Royal Tradition of the Northern Kingdom and Its Ramifications.* BZAW 435. Berlin: de Gruyter, 2012.
Rofé, Alexander. *The Prophetical Stories: The Narratives about the Prophets in the Hebrew Bible. Their Literary Types and History.* Jerusalem: Magnes, 1988.
____. "The Vineyard of Naboth: The Origin and Message of the Story." *VT* 38 (1988): 89–104.
Römer, Thomas. *The So-Called Deuteronomistic History: A Sociological, Historical, and Literary Introduction.* London: T & T Clark, 2005.
Rosenberg, A. J. *Kings II.* Mikraoth Gedoloth. New York: Judaica, 1980.
Rosenberg, A. J., and Reuven Hochberg. *Kings I.* Mikraoth Gedoloth. New York: Judaica, 1980.
Saint-Laurent, George E. "Light from Ras Shamra on Elijah's Ordeal upon Mount Carmel." Pages 123–39 in *Scripture in Context: Essays on the Comparative Method.* Edited by C. D. Evans, W. W. Hallo, and J. B. White. Pittsburgh, PA: Pickwick, 1980.
Šanda, Albert. *Die Bücher der Könige* I. Münster: Aschendorf, 1911.
____. *Die Bücher der Könige* II. Münster: Aschendorf, 1912.
Sauerwein, Ruth. *Elischa. Eine redaktions- und religionsgeschichtliche Studie.* BZAW 465. Berlin: de Gruyter, 2014.
Schenker, Adrian. *Älteste Textgeschichte der Königsbücher. Die hebräische Vorlage der ursprünglichen Septuaginta als älteste Textform der Königsbücher.* OBO 199. Fribourg/Göttingen: Academic Press/Vandenhoeck & Ruprecht, 2004.
Schmitt, H.-C. *Elisa. Traditionsgeschichtliche Untersuchungen zur vorklassischen nordisraelitischen Prophetie.* Gütersloh: Gerd Mohn, 1972.

Schniedewind, William, and Daniel Sivan, "The Elijah-Elisha Narratives: A Test Case for the Northern Dialect of Hebrew," *JQR* 87 (1997): 303–37.

Schweizer, Harald. *Elischa in den Kriegen: Literaturwissenschaftliche Untersuchung von 2. Kön 3; 6, 8–23; 6, 24–7, 20.* SANT 37. Munich: Kösel, 1974.

Seebass, Horst. "Tradition und Interpretation bei Jehu ben Chenani und Ahia von Silo." *VT* 25 (1975): 175–90.

Seow, Choon-Leong. "The First and Second Books of Kings." *NIB*, Vol. 3. Nashville: Abingdon, 1999.

Shenkel, James Donald. *Chronology and Recensional Development in the Greek Text of Kings.* HSM 1. Cambridge, MA: Harvard University Press, 1968.

Skinner, John. *Kings.* The Century Bible. Edinburgh: T & T Clark, 1904.

Slotki, Israel W. *Kings.* Soncino Books of the Bible. London: Soncino, 1950.

Smelik, Klaas A. D. *Converting the Past: Studies in Ancient Israelite and Moabite Historiography.* OTS 28. Leiden: Brill, 1992.

Stade, Bernhard. *The Books of Kings: Critical Edition of the Hebrew Text.* Assisted by Friedrich Schwally. Leipzig: J. C. Hinrichs, 1904.

____. "Miscellen 10. Anmerkungen zu 2 Kö. 10–14." *ZAW* 5 (1885): 275–97.

Steck, Odil Hannes. *Überlieferung und Zeitgeschichte in den Elia-Erzählungen.* WMANT 26. Neukirchen-Vluyn: Neukirchener Verlag, 1968.

Stipp, Hermann-Josef. *Elischa - Propheten - Gottesmänner.* ATSAT 24. St. Ottilien: EOS Verlag, 1987.

Suriano, Matthew J. *The Politics of Dead Kings.* FAT 48. Tübingen: Mohr Siebeck, 2010.

Sweeney, Marvin A. *I & II Kings: A Commentary.* OTL. Louisville/London: Westminster John Knox, 2007.

Talmon, Shemaryahu, and Weston W. Fields. "The Collocation משתין בקיר ועצור ועזוב and its Meaning." *ZAW* 101 (1989): 85–112.

Thenius, Otto. *Die Bücher der Könige.* KEHAT 9. Leipzig: Weidmann, 1849.

Thiel, Winfried. *Könige.* BKAT IX/2. Neukirchen-Vluyn: Neukirchener Verlag, 2002–2009.

Thiele, Edwin R. *The Mysterious Numbers of the Hebrew Kings.* Rev. ed. Grand Rapids: Kregel 1983.

Timm, Stefan. *Die Dynastie Omri: Quellen und Untersuchungen zur Geschichte Israels im 9. Jahrhundert vor Christus.* Göttingen: Vandenhoeck & Ruprecht, 1982.

Trebolle Barrera, Julio. *Centena in libros Samuelis et Regum: Variantes textuales y composición literaria en los libros de Samuel y Reyes.* Madrid: Consejo superior de investigaciones científicas, Instituto de filología. Departamento de Filología Bíblica y de Oriente Antiguo, 1989.

____. "Division Markers as Empirical Evidence for the Editorial Growth of Biblical Books." Pages 165–215 in *Empirical Models Challenging Biblical Criticism.* Edited by Raymond F. Person and Robert Rezetko. Atlanta: SBL, 2016.

____. *Jehú y Joás: Texto y composición literaria de 2 Reyes 9–11.* Valencia: Institución San Jerónimo, 1984.

____. "The Practice of Textual Criticism after Qumran." Forthcoming.

____. *Salomón y Jeroboán. Historia de la recensón y redacción de 1 Reyes 2–12; 14.* Bibliotheca Salmanticensis 3. Madrid: Universidad Pontificia, 1980.

____. The Textcritical Value of the Old Latin in PostQumranic Textual Criticism (1 Kgs 18:26-29, 36-37). Pages 313–31 in *From 4QMMT to Resurrection: Mélanges qumraniens en hommage à Émile Puech.* Edited by Florentino García Martínez, Annette Steudel, and Eibert Tigchelaar. Leiden/Boston: Brill, 2006.

Turkanik, Andrzej S. *Of Kings and Reigns: A Study of Translation Technique in the Gamma/Gamma Section of 3 Kings (1 Kings).* FAT 2.30. Tübingen: Mohr Siebeck, 2008.

Ulrich, Eugene. *The Biblical Qumran Scrolls: Transcriptions and Textual Variants.* VTSup 134. Leiden: Brill, 2010.

Vaughn, P. H. *The Meaning of "bama"in the Old Testament.* Society for Old Testament Study Monograph Series 3. London: Cambridge University Press, 1974.
de Vaux, Roland. *Ancient Israel: Its Life and Institutions.* London: Darton, Longman & Todd, 1961.
____. *Les livres de Rois.* La Sainte Bible. Paris: Les éditions du Cerf, 1949.
Walsh, Jerome T. *Ahab: The Construction of a King.* Interfaces. Collegeville, MN: Liturgical Press, 2006.
____. *1 Kings.* Berit Olam. Collegeville, MN: Liturgical Press, 1996.
Weingart, Kristin. "2Ki 15–18—A Chronological Conundrum." In *The Last Days of the Kingdom of Israel.* Edited by Shuichi Hasegawa. Berlin: De Gruyter. Forthcoming.
Westbrook, Raymond. "Law in Kings." Pages 445–66 in *The Books of Kings: Sources, Composition, Historiography, and Reception.* Edited by André Lemaire and Baruch Halpern. VTSup 129. Leiden: Brill, 2010.
Wevers, John W. "Double Readings in the Books of Kings." *JBL* 65 (1946): 307–10.
White, Marsha C. *The Elijah Legends and Jehu's Coup.* BJS 311. Atlanta: Scholars Press, 1997.
Whitley, C. F. "The Deuteronomic Presentation of the House of Omri." *VT* 2 (1952): 137–52.
Wilson, Robert R. *Prophecy and Society in Ancient Israel.* Philadelphia: Fortress Press, 1980.
Winckler, Hugo. *Alttestamentliche Untersuchungen.* Leipzig: Eduard Pfeiffer, 1892.
Wiseman, Donald J. *1 and 2 Kings.* TOTC. Downers Grove, IL: InterVarsity, 1993.
Wray Beal, Lissa M. *1 & 2 Kings.* Apollos Old Testament Commentary. Nottingham/Downers Grove, IL: Apollos/InterVarsity, 2014.
Würthwein, Ernst. *Die Bücher der Könige. 1.Könige 1-16.* ATD 11,1. Göttingen/Zürich: Vandenhoeck & Ruprecht, 1985.
____. *Die Bücher der Könige. 1.Kön. 17-2.Kön. 25.* ATD 11,2. Göttingen/Zürich: Vandenhoeck & Ruprecht, 1984.
Zucconi, Laura M. "Aramean Skin Care: A New Perspective on Naaman's Leprosy." Pages 169–77 in *Sacred History, Sacred Literature: Essays on Ancient Israel, the Bible, and Religion in Honor of R. E. Friedman on His Sixtieth Birthday.* Edited by Shawna Dolansky. Winona Lake, IN: Eisenbrauns, 2008.

Indexes

Index of Hebrew Words

Index of Key Words

Index of Biblical Citations

Index of Other Ancient Literature

Plan of volumes

Genesis
I (1–11): David Carr
II–III (12–50): Konrad Schmid

Exodus
I–II: Helmut Utzschneider / Wolfgang Oswald

Leviticus
Baruch Schwartz / Naphtali Meshel

Numbers
I–II: NN

Deuteronomy
I–II: Jeffrey Stackert / Joel S. Baden

Joshua
I–II: Michaël N. van der Meer / Cor de Vos

Judges
Andreas Scherer

Ruth
Shimon Gesundheit

1./2. Samuel
I (1. Sam 1–15): Regine Hunziker-Rodewald
II (1. Sam 16–2. Sam 5): Johannes Klein
III (2. Sam 6–24): Thomas Naumann

1./2. Kings
I (1 Kgs 1–15): NN
II (1 Kgs 16 – 2 Kgs 16): Steven L. McKenzie
III (2 Kgs 17–25): Shūichi Hasegawa

1./2. Chronicles
I–II: Ehud Ben Zvi

Ezra / Nehemia
I–II: Richard J. Bautch

Tobit
Beate Ego

Judith
Barbara Schmitz

Esther
Jean-Daniel Macchi

Job
Melanie Köhlmoos

Psalms
I–III: NN

Proverbs
I–II: Jutta Krispenz

Ecclesiastes
Katharine Dell / Tova Forti

Song of Songs
Martien A. Halvorson-Taylor

Wisdom
Luca Mazzinghi

Sirach
Frank Ueberschaer

Isaiah
I–III: NN

Jeremiah
I (1–25): Christl M. Maier
II (26–52): Carolyn J. Sharp

Baruch
Maria Häusl

Lamentations
Andreas Michel

Ezekiel
Michael Konkel